International Directory of

COMPANY
HISTORIES

International Directory of

COMPANY

HISTORIES

VOLUME 78

Editor

Tina Grant

ST. JAMES PRESS

An imprint of Thomson Gale, a part of The Thomson Corporation

THOMSON

GALE

Detroit • New York • San Francisco • New Haven, Conn. • Waterville, Maine • London • Munich

International Directory of Company Histories, Volume 78

Tina Grant, Editor

Project Editor
Miranda H. Ferrara

Editorial
Virgil Burton, Donna Craft, Louise Gagné,
Peggy Geeseman, Julie Gough, Linda Hall,
Sonya Hill, Keith Jones, Lynn Pearce, Holly
Selden, Justine Ventimiglia

Editorial Systems Implementation Specialist
Mike Weaver

Imaging and Multimedia
Leslie Light, Michael Logusz

Composition and Electronic Prepress
Gary Leach, Evi Seoud

Manufacturing
Rhonda Dover

Product Manager
Jennifer Bernardelli

LIBRARY OF CONGRESS CATALOG NUMBER 89-190943

ISBN 1-55862-582-8

This title is also available as an e-book
ISBN 1-55862-626-3

BRITISH LIBRARY CATALOGUING IN PUBLICATION DATA

International directory of company histories, Vol. 78
I. Tina Grant
33.87409

Printed in the United States of America
10 9 8 7 6 5 4 3 2 1

Contents

Preface

The St. James Press series *The International Directory of Company Histories* (*IDCH*) is intended for reference use by students, business people, librarians, historians, economists, investors, job candidates, and others who seek to learn more about the historical development of the world's most important companies. To date, *IDCH* has covered over 7,800 companies in 78 volumes.

INCLUSION CRITERIA

Most companies chosen for inclusion in *IDCH* have achieved a minimum of US$25 million in annual sales and are leading influences in their industries or geographical locations. Companies may be publicly held, private, or nonprofit. State-owned companies that are important in their industries and that may operate much like public or private companies also are included. Wholly owned subsidiaries and divisions are profiled if they meet the requirements for inclusion. Entries on companies that have had major changes since they were last profiled may be selected for updating.

The *IDCH* series highlights 10% private and nonprofit companies, and features updated entries on approximately 50 companies per volume.

ENTRY FORMAT

Each entry begins with the company's legal name; the address of its headquarters; its telephone, toll-free, and fax numbers; and its web site. A statement of public, private, state, or parent ownership follows. A company with a legal name in both English and the language of its headquarters country is listed by the English name, with the native-language name in parentheses.

The company's founding or earliest incorporation date, the number of employees, and the most recent available sales figures follow. Sales figures are given in local currencies with equivalents in U.S. dollars. For some private companies, sales figures are estimates and indicated by the abbreviation *est.* The entry lists the exchanges on which the company's stock is traded and its ticker symbol, as well as the company's NAIC codes.

Entries generally contain a *Company Perspectives* box which provides a short summary of the company's mission, goals, and ideals; a *Key Dates* box highlighting milestones in the company's history; lists of *Principal Subsidiaries, Principal Divisions, Principal Operating Units, Principal Competitors*; and articles for *Further Reading*.

American spelling is used throughout *IDCH*, and the word "billion" is used in its U.S. sense of one thousand million.

Users of the *IDCH* series will notice some changes to the look of the series starting with Volume 77. The pages have been redesigned for better clarity and ease of use; the standards for entry content, however, have not changed.

SOURCES

Entries have been compiled from publicly accessible sources both in print and on the Internet such as general and academic periodicals, books, and annual reports, as well as material supplied by the companies themselves.

CUMULATIVE INDEXES

IDCH contains three indexes: the **Index to Companies**, which provides an alphabetical index to companies discussed in the text as well as to companies profiled, the **Index to Industries**, which allows researchers to locate companies by their principal industry, and the **Geographic Index**, which lists companies alphabetically by the country of their headquarters. The indexes are cumulative and specific instructions for using them are found immediately preceding each index.

SUGGESTIONS WELCOME

Comments and suggestions from users of *IDCH* on any aspect of the product as well as suggestions for companies to be included or updated are cordially invited. Please write:

The Editor
International Directory of Company Histories
St. James Press
27500 Drake Rd.
Farmington Hills, Michigan 48331-3535

St. James Press does not endorse any of the companies or products mentioned in this series. Companies appearing in the *International Directory of Company Histories* were selected without reference to their wishes and have in no way endorsed their entries.

Notes on Contributors

Gerald E. Brennan
Writer based in Germany.

M. L. Cohen
Novelist and researcher living in Paris.

Ed Dinger
Writer and editor based in Bronx, New York.

Paul R. Greenland
Illinois-based writer and researcher; author of two books and former senior editor of a national business magazine; contributor to *The Encyclopedia of Chicago History*, *The Encyclopedia of Religion*, and the *Encyclopedia of American Industries*.

Robert Halasz
Former editor in chief of *World Progress* and *Funk & Wagnalls*

New Encyclopedia Yearbook; author, *The U.S. Marines* (Millbrook Press, 1993).

Evelyn Hauser
Researcher, writer and marketing specialist based in Germany.

Frederick C. Ingram
Utah-based business writer who has contributed to *GSA Business*, *Appalachian Trailway News*, the *Encyclopedia of Business*, the *Encyclopedia of Global Industries*, the *Encyclopedia of Consumer Brands*, and other regional and trade publications.

Bruce Montgomery
Curator and director of historical collection, University of Colorado at Boulder.

Carrie Rothburd
Writer and editor specializing in corporate profiles, academic texts, and academic journal articles.

Christina M. Stansell
Writer and editor based in Louisville, Kentucky.

Frank Uhle
Ann Arbor-based writer; movie projectionist, disc jockey, and staff member of *Psychotronic Video* magazine.

A. Woodward
Wisconsin-based writer.

List of Abbreviations

¥ Japanese yen
£ United Kingdom pound
$ United States dollar
A.E. Anonimos Eteria (Greece)
A.O. Anonim Ortaklari/Ortakligi (Turkey)
A.S. Anonim Sirketi (Turkey)
A/S Aksjeselskap (Norway)
A/S Aktieselskab (Denmark, Sweden)
AB Aktiebolag (Finland, Sweden)
AB Oy Aktiebolag Osakeyhtiot (Finland)
AED Emirati dirham
AG Aktiengesellschaft (Austria, Germany, Switzerland, Liechtenstein)
ARS Argentine peso
ATS Austrian shilling
AUD Australian dollar
ApS Amparteselskap (Denmark)
Ay Avoinyhtio (Finland)
B.A. Buttengewone Aansprakeiijkheid (The Netherlands)
B.V. Besloten Vennootschap (Belgium, The Netherlands)
BEF Belgian franc
BHD Bahraini dinar
BRL Brazilian real
Bhd. Berhad (Malaysia, Brunei)
C. de R.L. Compania de Responsabilidad Limitada (Spain)
C.A. Compania Anonima (Ecuador, Venezuela)

C.V. Commanditaire Vennootschap (The Netherlands, Belgium)
CAD Canadian dollar
CEO Chief Executive Officer
CFO Chief Financial Officer
CHF Swiss franc
CIO Chief Information Officer
CLP Chilean peso
CNY Chinese yuan
COO Chief Operating Officer
COP Colombian peso
CRL Companhia a Responsabilidao Limitida (Portugal, Spain)
CZK Czech koruna
Co. Company
Corp. Corporation
D&B Dunn & Bradstreet
DEM German deutsche mark
DKK Danish krone
DZD Algerian dinar
EEK Estonian Kroon
EGP Egyptian pound
ESOP Employee Stock Options and Ownership
ESP Spanish peseta
EUR euro
FIM Finnish markka
FRF French franc
G.I.E. Groupement d'Interet Economique (France)
GRD Greek drachma
GmbH Gesellschaft mit beschraenk-

ter Haftung (Austria, Germany, Switzerland)
HKD Hong Kong dollar
HUF Hungarian forint
I/S Interesentselskap (Norway)
I/S Interessentselskab (Denmark)
IDR Indonesian rupiah
IEP Irish pound
ILS new Israeli shekel
INR Indian rupee
IPO Initial Public Offering
ISK Icelandic krona
ITL Italian lira
Inc. Incorporated (United States, Canada)
JMD Jamaican dollar
K/S Kommanditselskab (Denmark)
K/S Kommandittselskap (Norway)
KG Kommanditgesellschaft (Austria, Germany, Switzerland)
KGaA Kommanditgesellschaft auf Aktien (Austria, Germany, Switzerland)
KK Kabushiki Kaisha (Japan)
KPW North Korean won
KRW South Korean won
KWD Kuwaiti dinar
LBO Leveraged Buyout
Lda. Limitada (Spain)
L.L.C. Limited Liability Company (United States)
Ltd. Limited (Various)
Ltda. Limitada (Brazil, Portugal)

Ltee. Limitee (Canada, France)
LUF Luxembourg franc
mbH mit beschraenkter Haftung (Austria, Germany)
MUR Mauritian rupee
MXN Mexican peso
MYR Malaysian ringgit
N.V. Naamloze Vennootschap (Belgium, The Netherlands)
NGN Nigerian naira
NLG Netherlands guilder
NOK Norwegian krone
NZD New Zealand dollar
OAO Otkrytoe Aktsionernoe Obshchestve (Russia)
OMR Omani rial
OOO Obschestvo s Ogranichennoi Otvetstvennostiu (Russia)
Oy Osakeyhtiö (Finland)
PHP Philippine peso
PKR Pakistani rupee
PLC Public Limited Co. (United Kingdom, Ireland)
PLN Polish zloty
PTE Portuguese escudo
Pty. Proprietary (Australia, South Africa, United Kingdom)

REIT Real Estate Investment Trust
RMB Chinese renminbi
RUB Russian ruble
S.A. Société Anonyme (Belgium, France, Greece, Luxembourg, Switzerland, Arab speaking countries)
S.A. Sociedad Anónima (Latin America, Spain, Mexico)
S.A. Sociedades Anônimas (Brazil, Portugal)
S.A.R.L. Sociedade Anonima de Responsabilidade Limitada (Brazil, Portugal)
S.A.R.L. Société à Responsabilité Limitée (France, Belgium, Luxembourg)
S.A.S. Societá in Accomandita Semplice (Italy)
S.A.S. Societe Anonyme Syrienne (Arab speaking countries)
S.R.L. Sociedad de Responsabilidad Limitada (Spain, Mexico, Latin America)
S.R.L. Società a Responsabilitá Limitata (Italy)
S.R.O. Spolecnost s Rucenim

Omezenym (Czechoslovakia
S.p.A. Società per Azioni (Italy)
SAA Societe Anonyme Arabienne
SAR Saudi riyal
SEK Swedish krona
SGD Singapore dollar
Sdn. Bhd. Sendirian Berhad (Malaysia)
Sp. z.o.o. Spólka z ograniczona odpowiedzialnoscia (Poland)
Ste. Societe (France, Belgium, Luxembourg, Switzerland)
THB Thai baht
TND Tunisian dinar
TRL Turkish lira
TWD new Taiwan dollar
VAG Verein der Arbeitgeber (Austria, Germany)
VEB Venezuelan bolivar
VND Vietnamese dong
YK Yugen Kaisha (Japan)
ZAO Zakrytoe Aktsionernoe Obshchestve (Russia)
ZAR South African rand
ZMK Zambian kwacha

Amcor Ltd.

679 Victoria Street
Abbotsford, Victoria 3067
Australia
Telephone: (61) 3 9226-9000
Fax: (61) 3 9226-9050
Web site: www.amcor.com

Public Company
Incorporated: 1926 as Australian Paper Manufacturers Ltd.
Employees: 29,063
Sales: AUD 11.1 billion ($8.43 billion) (2005)
Stock Exchanges: Australia NASDAQ
Ticker Symbol: AMCR, AMC
NAIC: 322212 Folding Paperboard Box Manufacturing; 332431 Metal Can Manufacturing; 326160 Plastics Bottle Manufacturing

■ ■ ■

Headquartered in Australia, Amcor Ltd. operates as an international packaging company. It has manufacturing facilities in 39 countries across the globe that produce corrugated boxes, cartons, aluminum and steel cans, flexible plastic packaging, polyethylene terraphthallate (PET) plastic bottles and jars, closures, and multi-wall sacks. As part of a reorganization plan, the company sold off noncore and unprofitable assets—including its paper business—during the late 1990s and into the new millennium. Amcor acquired the PET and Closures business of Schmalbach-Lubeca AG in 2002. The deal positioned Amcor as the third largest packaging concern in the world.

THE EARLY YEARS

Amcor began as a paper making business called the Australian Paper Manufacturers Ltd. (APM). The origins of APM (although it was not incorporated under this name until 1926) can be traced back to the 1860s and to some of the earliest Australian ventures in paper making. The 1860s were years of rapid industrial growth in Australia's New South Wales and neighboring Victoria. The gold rushes initiated not only rising prosperity, but also an explosion in the area's population and available labor force. Furthermore, the introduction of a governmental protection policy for manufacturers in Victoria created a climate in which factories exploded in number. The paper making industry was no exception to this trend.

In 1864, the Collingwood Mill at Liverpool, New South Wales, was constructed for the Australian Paper Company. Four years later in Melbourne, Samuel Ramsden built his own mill and began production with the Number One Paper Machine. In 1871, William Fieldhouse erected Melbourne Number Two Paper Machine adjacent to Ramsden's mill; this operation was subsequently purchased by Ramsden. By the time a new entity—the Australian Paper Mills Company—was formed and registered in 1895, mills had been combined in Melbourne, Broadford, and Geelong. The company's capital was AUD 214,000 and its output was approximately 730 tons per year. The following year, it became the Australian Paper Mills Company Ltd.

Meanwhile, in the New South Wales capital of Sydney, John Thomson Brown had started a business of his own, trading in meat, grain, and farming and household goods. In 1885 David Henry Dureau became Brown's Melbourne partner. Their company would later play an important role in APM/Amcor's future. Brown and Dureau's company thrived, and was incorporated as Brown & Dureau, Ltd. in 1910. Over the years, as general commission agents, Brown and Dureau handled a wide range of goods.

In the first two decades of the 1900s, the Australian Paper Mills Company Ltd. entered a period of expansion as Australia's overseas trade doubled from the start of the century. In 1920, the Australian Paper Mills Company Ltd. combined forces with Sydney Paper Mills Ltd. to form the Australian Paper and Pulp Company Ltd. This entity then merged with the Cumberland Paper Board Mills Ltd. in 1926, and the operating company of APM was finally formed. This company would continue to function under that name for years to come, and into the 1990s as the pulp and paper making arm of Amcor.

THE WAR YEARS

In 1936, an agreement was signed between APM and the Victorian Forest Commission covering the procurement of wood pulp. Later that year, the 1936 Wood Pulp Agreement Act was passed by the Victorian parliament and led to the establishment of the Maryvale pulp mill. This pilot mill began semi-commercial production of eucalyptus kraft pulp in March 1938, and the main mill started commercial production the following year.

The year 1939 saw the outbreak of World War II and the worst bush fires in Victoria's history. APM's mill buildings survived, but the majority of its prime pulp wood source was destroyed. The company found, however, that fire-killed timber could still be used for pulping. This was fortunate, as the advent of the war brought about drastic changes in APM's operations:

Imports ceased abruptly, price controls were imposed by the federal government, a wartime profits tax was imposed, and Australian industries were required to provide military equipment to meet defense needs. Within two years, 70 percent of APM's total production was directed toward the manufacture of ammunitions and war equipment. During this period, the company demonstrated its strength as an innovator, supplying purified cellulose for the manufacture of smokeless cordite and other propellants for the Allied forces. APM also developed special papers and boards to resist moisture penetration for the troops fighting in tropical regions.

Wartime conditions also prompted APM to increase its self-sufficiency. For example, before the war began, 80 percent of APM's total pulp requirements was imported, compared with times during and after the war, when 80 percent of its necessary raw materials was derived from local sources. In addition, the war demanded self-sufficiency in fuel; in 1946, the company acquired a controlling interest in Maddingley Brown Coal Pty. Ltd. This acquisition, combined with the purchase of further coal-bearing land, soon produced 10,000 tons of coal per week and supplied all of the Victorian mills as well as other commercial and public enterprises.

Although APM was designated a "protected" industry by the Australian federal government during the war, the company nevertheless saw 25 percent of its workforce enlist. Therefore, it recruited women to work in the mills. The company still operated with a decreased staff, but despite this and other hardships—such as a coal strike in New South Wales and further bush fires in 1944—the company managed to continue the expansion of its mills. Production grew dramatically from 92,000 tons in 1938, to 131,000 tons in 1942.

Toward the end of the war, APM's managing director, Sir Herbert Gepp, set up a Post-war Planning Committee to win back freedom from government control and the wartime profit tax and to prepare a case for reasonable tariff protection against the inevitable resurgence of competitive imports. The committee also discussed APM's future strategy, which was to include the extension of operations in wrapping paper and board; expansion into converting operations, such as the manufacturing of cartons and containers from APM's paper and board; and the manufacture of allied products such as cellophane and tissues.

POSTWAR DIVERSIFICATION EFFORTS

War time had resulted in major reorganizations, both financial and administrative. The development of public

KEY DATES

1864: Collingwood Mill at Liverpool, New South Wales, is constructed for the Australian Paper Company.

1868: Samuel Ramsden builds his own mill and begins production with the Number One Paper Machine.

1871: William Fieldhouse erects Melbourne Number Two Paper Machine adjacent to Ramsden's mill; this operation is subsequently purchased by Ramsden.

1895: Australian Paper Mills Company is formed and registered.

1910: Brown & Dureau, Ltd. is incorporated.

1920: The Australian Paper Mills Company Ltd. combines forces with Sydney Paper Mills Ltd. to form the Australian Paper and Pulp Company Ltd.

1926: Australian Paper and Pulp merges with Cumberland Paper Board Mills Ltd. to form Australian Paper Manufacturers Ltd. (APM).

1978: APM sets plans in motion to purchase Brown & Dureau.

1986: The company adopts the Amcor Limited moniker.

2000: The company spins off its Amcor Printing Papers Group.

2002: The PET and Closures business of Schmalbach-Lubeca AG is acquired.

established the jointly owned Kimberly-Clark Australia Ltd., in partnership with the Kimberly-Clark Corporation of the United States. The subsidiary produced all kinds of tissue products.

It was in the 1970s that Brown & Dureau, Ltd. took on a significant role in the history of APM/Amcor. Brown & Dureau acquired the Eastern Tool Company, Lukey Mufflers, and Angus Hill Holdings, which would later form the nucleus of Amcor's automotive division. In 1975 Stan Wallis became the deputy managing director of APM, which marked the beginning of many years of strong leadership for the company. Under Wallis, APM began a process of diversification in the late 1970s. One of the most important acquisitions was that of Brown & Dureau in the financial year 1978-79. This purchase brought APM substantial interests in the fields of international trading, automotive, retailing, and aviation.

ACQUISITIONS: 1980 TO 1990

In the following decade, more major acquisitions for APM included the Ingram Corporation Ltd. and Edwards Dunlop & Co. Ltd., a paper merchant and stationery manufacturer, respectively. From these acquisitions grew the merchanting, stationery, and designer products divisions. During the same period, APM acquired 40 percent of James Hardie Containers, manufacturers of corrugated fiber boxes for packaging food and drink.

In 1982, APM acquired Containers Packaging, the fourth major wholly owned subsidiary. That same year, New Zealand Forest Products (NZFP)—that country's leading forestry group—formed a joint venture company with APM, allocating 50 percent of the shares to each corporation, and called it Anfor. This was set up to develop a corrugated box plant in Hong Kong, with NZFP supplying liner board and APM supplying the corrugating medium to make boxes to be sold to Chinese, South Korean, and Japanese customers.

In 1986, APM bought the balance of James Hardie Containers and an era of rationalization began. During this time period, plants were acquired from Reed Corrugated Containers, J. Fielding & Co., Tasman U.E.B., United Packages, Corrugated Paper, Fibreboard Containers, Fibre Containers, J. Gadsden Paper Products, Tasmanian Fibre Containers, and Cardboard Containers. Also in 1986, the company adopted the name of Amcor Ltd., in order to better reflect the company's emerging diversity in its holdings.

Near the middle to end of the decade, Stan Wallis embarked on an ambitious program of capital investment in import-substituting plants, and in reopening

relations at APM was changed, and a new emphasis on industrial relations was adopted. The company still possessed a monopoly on the country's wrapping paper and board markets, and was firmly established in mainland Australia as the country's largest paper and pulp company. In the 1950s, APM initiated a foray into the corrugated packaging industry in which it was later to make significant acquisitions. Before 1940, there were four Australian companies operating in the corrugated packaging field; J. Fielding & Co. was the earliest, installing the first corrugator in 1914 at Buckingham Street in Sydney to produce the corrugating medium for packaging. In 1950, APM bought the first 96-inch corrugator, with plans to install it on the Springvale wastepaper recycling site, but instead sold it to Fielding.

The 1960s saw APM extend its interests to the production of other paper products. In 1963, it existing plants to supply growing export markets. But not all of Stan Wallis's plans were successful. In April 1987, a possible merger between NZFP and Amcor was announced. The proposed merger would have covered only the pulp and paper production and marketing of the two companies, thus stopping short of a full merger of operations. But in August 1987, Amcor received the New Zealand Commerce Commission's decision: The merger would not go ahead.

The principal reason for the commission's rejection was that the proposed new entity would have a virtual monopoly of the manufacture and import of kraft paper and paperboard in New Zealand. The same obstacle did not impede Fletcher Challenge, Amcor's main domestic rival. Amcor promptly sold its 11 percent stake in NZFP to the Rada Corporation, which some thought was a defense against a Fletcher Challenge takeover. In 1986-87 Kiwi Packaging of New Zealand also became a wholly owned subsidiary of Amcor, running five corrugating plants and two sheet plants.

Amcor then turned to offshore investment opportunities. In 1988, the year following the failed merger with NZFP, the group announced that it was concentrating on overseas business expansion; as evidence, it switched Don B. Macfarlane to the newly created post of general manager of international business development. According to Amcor, the creation of Macfarlane's new post signified its commitment to a structured and systematic approach to expansion outside Australia.

Throughout the decade, Amcor's packaging division established two plants: one at Smithfield, New South Wales; and another at Scoresby, Victoria. In the financial year 1988-89 it bought 46 percent of Sydney's Universal Containers. During the 1980s Amcor's key objectives were to broaden its range of activities, particularly into packaging; to restructure its core pulp and paper businesses and integrate forward into paper converting in Australia; and to commence major overseas expansion. In June 1989, Amcor bought Twinpak, the largest plastics containers producer in Canada with 13 plants spread across the country. The acquisition accounted for a significant proportion of the 32 percent increase in containers packaging sales in the financial year 1989-90.

In 1989 Amcor appointed a new chairman, Sir Brian Inglis. He replaced Alan Skurrie, who had held the office for five years and had an association of more than 55 years with Amcor. Amcor's 1989-90 annual report recorded expenditures during the five years through June 1990 of AUD 2 billion on capital equipment and acquisitions. The company's commitment to growth was clear. Yet for all the ambition of the program, funding for Amcor's investments came principally from internal cash flow, as well as from the sale of assets and some borrowing. The program was financially conservative.

It was at that time that Sunclipse Incorporated was acquired, which was a California-based corrugated box manufacturer and distributor of packaging products. Amcor Packaging (Europe) Ltd. was another development, constituting Amcor's first direct investment in the United Kingdom—a corrugated box plant on a greenfield site in Cambridgeshire. A 49 percent share in SACOC, a French corrugated box manufacturer, also was acquired near the turn of the decade.

1990 TO 2000: CONTINUED DIVERSIFICATION

After setting out to diversify in the 1980s, paper accounted for only 19 percent of Amcor's 1990 sales, compared with 57 percent a decade earlier. Much of this diversification was achieved through acquisitions, which typified almost all of the company's activity in the 1980s and 1990s. In June 1990 Amcor Fibre Packaging was formed to manage the group's international corrugated box manufacturing and related activities. It included APM Packaging, Kiwi Packaging, Sunclipse, Amcor Packaging (Europe), SACOC, and Anfor. At that time, in total, it had the capacity to manufacture almost one million tons per year of corrugated products, accounting for more than half of the capacity of others outside Australia.

The following year, Amcor's Containers Packaging subsidiary added New Zealand Can Ltd. to its holdings for AUD 45 million. Amcor also purchased an eventual 42 percent stake in Spicers Paper Ltd., an Australian stationery producer, and a 49 percent portion of Willander Holdings, another corrugated box manufacturer that was stationed in the United Kingdom.

In 1993 Amcor moved to consolidate its rapidly expanding holdings into three main divisions. Its Containers Packaging division was mainly responsible for the production of plastic and metal containers for food packaging; Amcor Fibre Packaging dealt with the company's corrugated cardboard products; and the Amcor Paper Group division was responsible for the manufacture of paper, stationery, paperboard, and coated paper products. In the wake of numerous acquisitions that year, Amcor also began to sell off operations that either deviated from the above categories, or that were generally unprofitable. Divestitures included the company's games division (including Amcor's rights to "Scrabble"), Amidale Industries Ltd./Croxley Collins Olympic N.Z., and Petersen Contact Stationers. Amcor also purchased almost 20 new holdings in 1993 and 1994.

In 1994, Amcor also began operations at a new paper mill in Prewitt, New Mexico in the United States. This mill, dubbed the McKinley Paper Company, was constructed to be a cost-effective operation and was positioned strategically to service the market in southern California and surrounding areas. The McKinley location immediately received high accolades from Amcor's top Australian-based executives due to its high-quality production and efficient operations, as well as to its intelligent geographic placement and ability to serve the surrounding market.

Internationally, Amcor continued its expansion-through-acquisitions plan, making 12 substantial purchases and selling four of its holdings in 1995. The company increased its revenue that year by more than AUD 1 billion from its 1994 figures. Activity in 1996 followed suit, as the company again consolidated its holdings with new purchases and the divestiture of inconsistent and unprofitable operations.

INTO THE 21ST CENTURY

Entering the end of the 20th century, Amcor positioned itself for continued future success. Major challenges facing the company were the ability to adapt to vastly increasing public awareness of environmental issues, and also the ability to continue its trend of becoming even more competitive at the international level. Amcor's focus on the second goal was obvious, however, after the company had spent almost the entire span of the 1990s acquiring holdings on a global level that would help position it for growth. In 1997, the company formed subsidiary Amcor Europe.

During this time period, Amcor found it necessary to restructure its holdings and sell off noncore assets as part of its plan to become a global force in the packaging industry. It sold the Brown and Dureau Building Materials business, its rigid plastics division, and Amcor Fibre Packaging Europe. Overall, Amcor divested approximately $300 million in assets during the late 1990s.

The company entered the new millennium focused on its global strategy. In 2000, Amcor decided to spin off Amcor Printing Papers Group—the paper business with roots dating back more than 100 years. The group was spun off as PaperlinX Limited in April of that year. This step in Amcor's reorganization strategy allowed it to focus on its international packaging operations, which it bolstered over the next several years through a series of acquisitions.

In 2001, the company acquired CNC Containers, a U.S.-based PET bottle manufacturer. It also merged its Amcor Flexibles Europe subsidiary with Danisco Flexible and Akerlund & Rausing. Perhaps its boldest move

to date came in 2002, when it made a play for the PET and Closures business of Germany-based Schmalbach-Lubeca AG. The $1.6 billion deal positioned Amcor as the largest PET packaging manufacturer in the world and the third largest packaging company overall.

With the Schmalbach-Lubeca purchase under its belt, Amcor added Tobepal S.A., Rexam plc's healthcare flexibles business, and Alcoa's Latin American PET business to its growing arsenal. In 2003, Amcor bought the PET injection and blow molding assets of Mexico's Embotelladoras Arca S.A. de C.V.

During 2004 Amcor found itself at the center of an investigation by the Australian Competition and Consumer Commission (ACCC) and the New Zealand Commerce Commission (NZCC) for cartel, or price-fixing, activity. As part of an internal investigation of four senior executives in its corrugated box division, Amcor had uncovered illegal activity. Amcor notified the ACCC and NZCC of the potential breach of anti-competition laws and agreed to cooperate fully in their investigations. Meanwhile, Amcor's managing director, Russell Jones, and managing director of Amcor Australasia, Peter Sutton, stepped down. In July 2005, Ken MacKenzie was named managing director. In December, Amcor was granted immunity by the ACCC as a result of its cooperation while competitor Visy Industries Pty. came under attack for its involvement in cartel activities.

By this time, slowing global economies and rising raw material costs were eating into Amcor's bottom line. With MacKenzie at the helm, the company embarked on a mission to review the operations at its 240 manufacturing facilities in an attempt to shore up profits. According to an August 2005 *Wall Street Journal* article, MacKenzie promised to "fix, sell or close" unprofitable plants. While Amcor had successfully transformed itself into one of the largest packaging companies in the world, its future hinged on its ability to control costs, streamline operations, and secure solid profits.

Mary Scott
Updated, Laura E. Whiteley, Christina M. Stansell

PRINCIPAL SUBSIDIARIES

Amcor Investments Pty. Ltd.; Amcor Packaging (New Zealand) Ltd.; Amcor Packaging (United States), Inc.; Amcor Sunclipse – North America, Inc.; Amcor Europe (United Kingdom); Amcor Packaging Asia Pty. Ltd.; Amcor Packaging (Australia) Pty. Ltd.; Amcor European Holdings Pty. Ltd.; Amcor European Consolidated Holdings Ltd.; Amcor Holding (United Kingdom); Amcor Flexibles A/S (Denmark).

Amcor Ltd.

PRINCIPAL DIVISIONS

Amcor PET Packaging; Amcor Australasia; Amcor Flexibles; Amcor Sunclipse; Amcor Rentsch and Amcor Closures; Amcor Asia.

PRINCIPAL COMPETITORS

Georgia-Pacific Corporation; Smurfit-Stone Container Corporation; Svenska Cellulosa AB SCA.

FURTHER READING

"Amcor Ltd.: New Packaging Company CEO Plans 'Fix, Sell or Close' Review," *Wall Street Journal*, August 25, 2005.

Askew, Kate, "Crumpled But Intact, Former Amcor Executives Escape from Dispute," *The Age*, December 18, 2004.

"Australia's Amcor Granted Immunity in Cartel Case," *Dow Jones International News*, December 21, 2005.

Braude, Jonathan, "Amcor Buys Packaging Business," *Daily Deal*, May 9, 2002.

"Cardboard Is Gold in McKinley County," *New Mexico Business Journal*, October 1994, p. 66.

Hughes, Anthony, "Amcor Finds Itself Boxed In," *Australian Financial Review*, January 23, 2006.

"McKinley Paper Co.: New Mexico's First Mill Will Tap the Lucrative L.A. Market," *Pulp & Paper*, September 1993, p. 72.

Potter, Joanne, "Amcor Comes In for an Overhaul," *PPI*, June 1999, pp. 69-71.

Sinclair, E. K., *The Spreading Tree: A History of APM and AMCOR 1844-1989*, Sydney: Allen & Unwin, 1991.

American Seating
Company

---

401 American Seating Center
Grand Rapids, Michigan 49504-4499
U.S.A.
Telephone: (616) 732-6600
Toll Free: (800) 748-0268
Fax: (616) 732-6502
Web site: http://www.americanseating.com

Private Company
Incorporated: 1887 as Grand Rapids School Furniture
    Company
Employees: 895
Sales: $93.2 million
NAIC: 337214 Nonwood Office Furniture Manufactur-
    ing; 337127 Institutional Furniture Manufacturing;
    337211 Wood Office Furniture Manufacturing

■ ■ ■

American Seating Company is a private company based in Grand Rapids, Michigan, that has been involved in the seating business since the 1880s. Markets include education, sports and entertainment, transportation, commercial business, government, and renovation. The company's original focus, the education division, offers a wide variety of seating products, desks, and tables for classrooms, lecture halls, and common areas. American Seating is also well known for its sports and entertainment work, its chairs installed in such venerable institutions as Boston's Fenway Park, Chicago's Wrigley Field, and New York City's Radio City Music Hall. For more than half a century, American Seating has also been involved in the transportation industry, providing seats for buses and rail travel. Since the 1970s American Seating has provided contract office furniture products for both the commercial and government markets. Finally, American Seating offers refurbishing services to restore its older seating products.

ORIGINS

According to company lore, American Seating was conceived during a long Grand Rapids school board meeting in 1886. For two hours board President Gaius W. Perkins gained firsthand knowledge of the uncomfortable chairs and desks students had to endure several hours a day during the school year. He also had plenty of time to calculate the total hours many would have to suffer before completing their schooling. He told fellow board members Seymour W. Peregrine and William T. Hess that from kindergarten through college children sat for more than 15,000 hours. "The desks that these children sit in are shaping their bodies," he added. To address this problem, the three men formed Grand Rapids School Furniture Company, forging a partnership in 1886 and establishing a factory on the corner of Prescott and Ionia streets in Grand Rapids. In May 1887 they incorporated the business with a capital stock of $100,000, and used the money to build a new factory, which opened in August 1888. The company quickly introduced a major innovation in classroom furniture, the combination desk, which fixed a desktop to the back of a chair for the use of the child sitting in the rear. The chairs also encouraged good posture. This combination of efficiency and comfort would become the hallmark of the company. Grand Rapids School Furniture soon ventured beyond the classroom; in 1889 it provided the seats for the Tabor Opera House in Leadville, Colorado. This contract led to more work in the entertainment arena, fueled in large part by another innovation, the 1893 introduction of the tilt-back opera chair. By now Grand Rapids School Furniture had emerged as the leading seating manufacturer in the world.

While success came quickly, the company's independence was also fleeting. In 1899, Grand Rapids School Furniture and 18 other furniture manufacturers merged to create American Furniture Company, the headquarters of which resided in New York City. Although the products were now made under the American Seating banner, the innovative spirit of Grand Rapids School Furniture remained intact. For the school market, the company in 1901 introduced the Model 101, a tubular steel standard desk. It then developed the Friction Side, an adjustable chair and independent desk. This led to the Universal Desk in 1921, which joined the adjustment chair and desk. The company also did considerable business in the entertainment field with the introduction of the squeak-free theatre folding chair. It also took advantage of a wave of baseball parks that were built in the early years of the 1900s, as old wooden ballparks, prone to fire, were replaced by concrete and steel edifices. In 1912 American Seating installed the seats in Boston's Fenway Park, followed later by Wrigley Field, Comiskey Park, and other ballparks. In the 1930s it began producing seats for buses, as well as church pews and related furniture.

The company regained its independence in 1927 as publicly traded America Seating Company, and then moved its headquarters back to Grand Rapids in 1932. Like many companies during the Great Depression of the 1930s, American Seating endured difficult times. It suspended the payment of dividends in 1930, then lost money for three straight years before posting a profit of $134,075 in 1934 and $330,262 in 1935. The company had turned the corner, but it would not fully regain momentum until the economy revived the business of its customers. It would require a world war to make that

happen. During the war years of 1942 to 1945, American Seating devoted much of its energies to supporting the military effort. Not only did it produce tables and chairs for Navy war rooms and other military uses, it also made spar caps for the Douglas A-26 dive bomber, wooden training models of antiaircraft guns, seats for tanks and ejector seats for airplanes, airplane and glider wings, and ammunition boxes. The company produced five million folding chairs alone during the war years, on average 10,000 per day.

POSTWAR POPULATION BOOM SPURS BUSINESS

After the war and a brief recession, the U.S. economy roared to life and American Seating took full advantage. It closed the decade with sales in the neighborhood of $25 million. For many years the company continued to serve the military, producing aluminum airframe components and inertia safety reels for airplane pilots. But military sales accounted for a modest part of American Seating's revenues, which were more impacted by the rapid growth of the school market, a function of the country's rising population. From 1941 to 1950 the U.S. population increased by 19.3 million to more than 151 million. Moreover, from 1950 to 1954 another 10 million people were added. As servicemen returned home from World War II, married, and began raising the baby boom generation, they moved to the suburbs, where schools had to be built and furnished. Aside from providing chairs and desks, American Seating would also distribute a wide variety of school supplies manufactured by other companies, including chalkboards, paper, and pencils. By 1954 the company's annual revenues topped $35 million, of which 60 percent were school related. In 1956 sales exceeded $40 million. According to a *Barron's National Business and Financial Weekly* article, "Since 1939 its sales have increased 30% faster than the Gross National Product. Perhaps more impressively, the past nine years have seen American Seating boost its volume at a rate nearly comparable to that of hard-driving General Motors, and faster than either Standard Oil of New Jersey or du Pont."

Aside from new schools, the baby boom meant expanded or new churches, and American Seating thrived during the 1950s on the increased sale of pews and folding chairs to the religious market. With more people to transport, the United States also needed more buses and trains, and American Seating stepped up its efforts in this area as well. In 1951 it acquired the bus seat division of S. Karpen Co. American's product development efforts helped to serve this sector as well as the company's other markets. It developed a fiberglass-reinforced plastic

KEY DATES

1887: Grand Rapids School Furniture Company is incorporated.
1899: Company becomes part of American Furniture Company located in New York City.
1927: Company becomes independent as American Seating Company.
1932: Headquarters returns to Grand Rapids.
1951: Bus seat division of S. Karpen Company is acquired.
1983: Company is acquired by Fuqua Industries Inc.
1987: Management takes over ownership of company.
1992: New Transportation Seating factory opens.
2003: Transportation Seating Inc. is acquired.

seat for the New York Transit Authority, considered radical at the time. It also used the material to make classroom chairs. In addition, American Seating introduced the cantilevered bus seat in the 1950s, a development that lead to the company's emergence as the industry leader in the heavy-duty bus seating market, a position it would maintain into the next century.

Business leveled off in the late 1950s and early 1960s as the school building boom curtailed. By the mid-1960s classroom furniture sales would account for just one-third of all sales, as the company faced increased competition in this and its other markets, resulting in depressed profits. Despite the cost, American Seating took steps to adjust its business mix, achieved through acquisitions as well as startups. In 1960 it bought the Pacific Northwest School Supply Company to expand its school supplies operation. American Seating also looked to the hospital market, establishing a hospital furniture unit in Grand Rapids in the early 1960s. Aside from hospital room side chairs and waiting room lounge chairs, the unit's products included bedside cabinets, over-bed tables, and electrically and manually operated adjustable beds. In 1963, in another effort to diversify, American Seating paid $3.5 million for E.H. Shelton Company, maker of laboratory furniture used mostly in high schools and colleges. By 1965 laboratory sales contributed from 15 to 20 percent of American Seating's $53.8 million in revenues. According to *Barron's*, "Amusement, transportation, church, and hospital furniture contribute the rest, roughly in that order."

Sales jumped to $60.9 million in 1966, spurred in large measure to a surge in theater and architectural seating sales. The company installed seats for the New York World's Fair, the Los Angeles Coliseum, and a host of new ballparks, stadiums, arenas, performing arts centers, and convention halls that sprouted up around the country during this period. Once again proving to be an industry innovator, American Seating produced the first molded plastic seats for sports stadiums, in part a response to Dutch elm disease. Stadium seats had previously relied on steam-bent elm.

Through its subsidiary, Universal Bleacher, the company also produced outdoor grandstands, folding gymnasium bleachers, as well as basketball backboards and the football training device, still on the market, called "Smitty's Blaster," which helps teach players to hold onto the ball. In the 1970s American Seating became involved in the contract furniture business, competing with the likes of another Grand Rapids company, Steelcase, Inc., in the sale of office systems to corporations. While Steelcase gave cubicles to the world, American Seating offered the Acton Stacker chair and the Framework family of chairs, table, cabinets, and panels for office and laboratory use. As a result of this new revenue stream, American Seating reached $100 million in annual sales during the 1970s, but would stall at this level.

NEW OWNERSHIP IN 1986

The early 1980s was a period of transition for American Seating, which found itself in a poor competitive position. As the era of new school construction came to a close, the company temporarily exited the classroom furniture business in 1982, selling off the equipment used to manufacture the line. It now depended on the office furniture business to supply the bulk of sales, with auditorium and stadium seating, and mass transportation seating providing the rest. Also in 1982 the company endured a bitter ten-week strike with workers represented by the United Auto Workers Union after the company proposed a two-year freeze on wages. American Seating also went on the block and in 1983 the company was sold to Fuqua Industries Inc., an Atlanta, Georgia-based conglomerate, which in 1982 had acquired a 40-percent stake in the company and gained three seats on the American Seating board of directors.

In its first year under new ownership, American Seating fared well, but over the next three years the company struggled. In 1985 and 1986 the company lost money, the first time in its history that American Seating experienced consecutive losing years. Fuqua was known to quickly jettison money-losing operations and

American Seating proved to be no exception. The parent company also followed a policy of first offering management a chance to buy the company. Hence, Chief Executive Officer Edward Clark was asked if he was interested. "It took me about two nanoseconds to say yes," Clark told the *Grand Rapids Business Journal* in a 1989 profile. "The opportunity doesn't come around too often to buy a $100 million company." Clark had only been with American Seating since being installed as CEO in February 1986. An Ohio State University graduate, Clark had worked for Ford Motor Company before taking a position in 1976 with Haworth Inc., one of the top office furniture manufacturers in the United States. Then, in 1982, he assumed the top job at Hardwood House, a Rochester, New York, woodworking company.

Clark and his managers completed a leveraged-buyout of American Seating in 1987. He soon launched an effort to cut costs and invested about $10 million in a plant modernization program. He also smoothed over differences with the union and negotiated a new three-year contract in the summer of 1988. Business quickly improved, with sales totaling about $140 million by the end of the decade.

Another wave of stadium and arena building provided a steady source of income for American Seating in the 1990s. The company installed seats in Denver's Mile High Stadium as well as Oriole Park at Camden Yard in Baltimore, a baseball park that harkened back to an earlier era and led to a number of similar baseball-only facilities. Football-only stadiums were also built across the country in the 1990s and early 2000s, replacing the multipurpose stadiums of the 1960s. As a result, American Seating had twice as many seating contracts to bid on, and in some cases even if it lost out on a job it could get a second bite at the apple. The New Comiskey Park, which opened in 1991 and was later renamed U.S. Cellular Field, hired American Seating in 2005 to replace the seats installed by a competitor. Other ballparks also hired American Seating to replace their seating, a decision made easier because fans were willing to buy the old seats as souvenirs at a price much higher than the new seats. This period also saw a rash of new arenas being built as team owners and communities wanted facilities that offered tiers of revenue-enhancing luxury suites. And as the boom in professional sports facilities began to wane, business picked up with colleges, which built new facilities and upgraded old ones in order to remain competitive in recruiting athletes for their lucrative football and basketball programs. Moreover, the alumni who gave major contributions to the universities wanted to sit in comfortable luxury suites and not benches from the 1920s. Never at a loss for product development, during this period American Seating also introduced the first heated outdoor stadium seat (employing thin electric heaters in the backs and bottoms), installed in a limited number in Orchard Park, New York, where the National Football League's Buffalo Bills played.

With much of its facilities a century old, American Seating was in dire need of an upgrade. Although a number of sunbelt communities courted the company, offering to build a new plant if it would relocate, Clark turned them down, electing to remain in Grand Rapids. "I couldn't see taking a company founded in the same spot in the 1800s and covering the factory windows with a bunch of plywood," Clark told the *Grand Rapids Press* in 2004. "Too many people worked hard to build this company. This is our home, and we're staying." As an expression of that commitment to the community—which had experienced a significant erosion in manufacturing jobs—and the community's commitment to the company, a new Transportation Seating factory was built in 1992 with government assistance. In the early 2000s American Seating made a further commitment to Grand Rapids, teaming up with investors and real estate investors to create American Seating Park, a $30-million project intended to revitalize a major portion of Grand Rapids, turning shuttered factories into apartments and offices. Part of the project included a refurbished headquarters for American Seating.

American Seating had found a flexible business mix by the start of the new century. Office furniture sales crumbled following the meltdown of the technology sector in the early 2000s. A number of companies went out of business and the market was flooded with used office furniture and equipment. But American Seating was able to make up the difference in transportation and architectural seating sales. The company bolstered the former with the 2003 purchase of Georgia competitor Transportation Seating Inc., a small company, but one that rivals also wanted. In addition, it also held a patent on a product American Seating did not have, a fiberglass shell-style seat used on military and prison buses. The sports business also continued to offer opportunities. A new potential source for contracts was with NASCAR, the popular stock car racing circuit. Many of its 32 tracks were massive, with seating capacities as high as 200,000. They also featured grandstands of steel benches, made all the more uncomfortable by the length of NASCAR races. Just as it had done more than a century before when it offered theater goers the tilt-back opera chair, American Seating developed a product to appeal to the race fan: a seat with a cup holder and closed-circuit radio/scanner holder to accommodate the scanners fans used to monitor radio communications between drivers and their pit crews.

Ed Dinger

PRINCIPAL COMPETITORS

American Stadium Seating Company; Steelcase Inc.; HNI Corporation.

FURTHER READING

"American Seating Slated for Smart Profits Gain," *Barron's National Business and Financial Weekly,* October 30, 1967, p. 47.

Fast, Doug, "Clark in the Head Seat," *Grand Rapids Business Journal,* May 19, 1986, p. 7.

Kirkbride, Rob, "Seating the American Pastime," *The Grand Rapids Press,* July 31, 2005, p. I1.

———, "True to Its Roots," *The Grand Rapid Press,* February 29, 2004, p. B1.

"New Marketing Program Spurs American Seating," *Barron's National Business and Financial Weekly,* May 19, 1958, p. 38.

Radigan, Mary, "American Seating Staging Strong Comeback," *The Grand Rapids Press,* July 8, 1990, p. D1.

Rivers, Anne, "American Seating: The First Century," *Grand Rapids Business Journal,* September 8, 1986, p. 7.

Turner, Mike, "Amesco Turns Corner on Profits," *Grand Rapids Business Journal,* May 18, 1987, p. O-10.

———, "Change Is in the Works at American Seating Co.," *Grand Rapids Business Journal,* August 14, 1989, p. 3.

AOK-Bundesverband
(Federation of the AOK)

Kortrijker Strasse 1 53177
Bonn,
Germany
Telephone: (49) (228) 843-0
Fax: (49) (228) 843-502
Web site: www.aok.de

Private Institution
Founded: 1895
Employees: 64,260
NAIC: 524113 Direct Life Insurance Carriers; 524114 Direct Health and Medical Insurance Carriers.

■ ■ ■

The AOK-Bundesverbund (Federation of the AOK) is Germany's largest health insurance provider. AOK is one of a handful of public Krankenkassen, literally "sickness funds," that Germans whose annual earnings fall below a certain income ceiling are required by law to join. In 2004 AOK and its national network of over 1,700 offices in 17 autonomous regions throughout Germany insured more than 18.55 million people, nearly one-third of the nation's total population. Although based in statute and regulated by the German federal government, AOK is a self-administered entity. It is managed by a board consisting of individuals directly elected by members and their employers. Members are insured by local AOK member funds—the Ortskrankenkassen—located in the geographical region in which they live and work. Premiums are paid in equal amounts by the insured and their employers and are calculated according to the so-called solidarity principle. Rather than risk factors such as marital status, family size, age, or health, the premiums are based solely on a member's wages up to a specific statutorily determined ceiling. The amount of an individual's premium payment varies according to which local fund provides coverage, from as low as 12 percent of income in Saxony to as high as 14.6 percent in Berlin. Hospital treatment comprised AOK's largest outlay in 2004 at approximately EUR 19 billion. Medication for members was in second place at EUR 9 billion. In addition to providing a forum for communication of its various member Krankenkassen, AOK also represents their interests before the German parliament and the professional associations of physicians and other healthcare providers.

THE INVENTION OF GERMAN STATUTORY HEALTHCARE IN THE 19TH CENTURY

AOK's history goes hand in hand with the history of Germany's long and sometimes rocky experience with statutory healthcare. Organized health insurance was available to Germans decades before the introduction of government-mandated Krankenkassen by many years. In the Middle Ages, guilds set up funds to help members in time of hardship. By the early 1800s many German communities were empowered to organize and regulate Krankenkassen, as well as to require local citizens to join them and employers to contribute a percentage of premiums. These local public healthcare funds were the first significant predecessors to AOK. However, the local organization of such healthcare was as chaotic as Germany's preunification political organization; in 1870 it consisted of four kingdoms, five grand duchies, 13 duchies and principalities, and three free cities, each of them fully independent. There was little intercommunication between the local Krankenkassen. There was no standardization of coverage and next to no national commercial organization. By 1880 these local providers had been joined by various private commercial insurance companies. A long wave of industrialization followed the founding of the German Empire in 1871 and with it an explosive growth of the working class and poor, which quickly outstripped the resources of existing private and public healthcare funds. A period of social tensions ensued. Workers' political parties, especially the Socialist Party, seemed to pose a mortal danger to the status quo. In an adept move to head off the threat, the German government led by Chancellor Otto von Bismarck proposed a wide-ranging series of social welfare laws designed to appease the workers and ease their lot. In November 1881, a message from German Kaiser Wilhelm I to the Reichstag called for "cooperative societies under state protection and with state support" that would provide universal healthcare for Germans. The resulting bill, the Krankenversicherungsgesetz (KVG) or Health Insurance Law, became law in late 1884.

Termed "a revolutionary turning point in social policy" by Franz Knieps in his history of AOK, the KVG authorized communities to form local insurance funds, so-called Ortskrankenkassen, to provide insurance coverage for their residents. The coverage was based on a series of basic principles: Healthcare was provided according to need, not the ability to pay; premiums were based solely on income, not risk or actuarial calculations—the so-called "solidarity principle"; and the funds would be administered directly by the insured and their employers, not by the government. These principles remained in force at the AOK in the 21st century. Ortskrankenkassen were originally set up not only for local residents, but also for workers in different trades or industries. One reason for this was that members of the same profession shared many of the same health risks,

evening out the per capita expenses. In addition it was felt that members would be less likely to file fraudulent claims against monies of friends and co-workers. Self-administration was also considered a means of combating insurance fraud by members.

Few new Ortskrankenkassen were founded as a result of the KVG. Most were older local funds that had been reorganized under the law. Older Krankenkassen won an important advantage from the KVG. Previously the funds were run at the community's own expense. Under the KVG, however, additional funds were allocated for administrative costs. In Berlin, for example, one year after the law went into effect only seven of 68 Ortskrankenkassen were new. In all, the Berlin Ortskrankenkass had about 160,000 members.

The largest of these, with some 52,000 members, was the Allgemeine Ortskrankenkasse, or "General Local Health Fund." This was an organizational forerunner to the current AOK. At the time the premiums its members paid were among the lowest of any local fund Germany (about 0.77 Marks) and the AOK's administration was considered one of the best in the country. As a result, Berlin's public officials came to see larger Ortskrankenkassen as preferable to smaller ones; they provided better service, while operating more efficiently and at a lower cost to members. A central Ortskrankenkasse for all Berlin was recommended. Nonetheless, the resulting Allgemeine Ortskrankenkasse was not a true "general" health fund in the later sense but rather an Ortskrankenkassen only for commercial workers. When general local funds were introduced in the early 20th century, they were still limited to a specific geographical area but were required to accept workers from all trades and industries.

DEVELOPMENT OF THE ORTSK-RANKENKASSEN BETWEEN 1890 AND WORLD WAR I

Membership in the Ortskrankenkassen grew rapidly, from 1.7 million members in 1886, to 2.68 million in 1891, to 4.22 million in 1900, when they accounted for over 46 percent of total health fund membership. In 1894 a national association of local funds was established in Frankfurt am Main, the Centralverband von Ortskrankenkassen im Deutschen Reich (Central Association of Local Health Funds in the German Empire). The Centralverband was founded to represent the interests of individual Ortskrankenkassen before lawmakers, other insurance groups, and physicians and other medical service providers, as well as to be an advisor and information clearing house for member funds.

KEY DATES

1881: Chancellor Otto von Bismarck reads the Kaiser's Message to the Reichstag calling for a system of public health insurance.

1883: Health Insurance Law goes into effect.

1894: The national association of insurance funds, Centralverband, is founded in Frankfurt am Main.

1911: Centralverband is renamed Hauptverband deutscher Orts-Krankenkassen.

1934: The National Socialist government does away with self-administration of Ortskrankenkassen.

1935: The Hauptverband is absorbed by the Nazi-controlled Reichsverband der Ortskrankenkassen.

1945: Reichsverband is banned by Allied occupation government.

1948: Its successor, the Vereinigung der Ortskrankenkassenverbände e.V. (VOV), is established.

1955: Self-administration of the Krankenkassen is reinstated by Bundestag.

1955: VOV is renamed Bundesverband der Ortskrankenkassen (BdO).

1977: The Health Insurance Cost Containment Act is passed.

1987: BdO is renamed AOK-Bundesverband.

1988: Healthcare Reform Act is passed.

1990: The Federal Republic of Germany and the German Democratic Republic are united; AOK gains millions of new members.

The founding of the Centralverband came at the beginning of a decade of heated discussion on the future of the Ortskrankenkassen in Germany. Physicians were increasingly unhappy with the payment schedule built into the participating provider system, a system which required Ortskrankenkassen members to use doctors approved by their fund. Physicians formed their own association in 1900 and on various occasions before 1913 went on strike for improved contracts with the Ortskrankenkassen. At the same time employers were growing dissatisfied with what they perceived as the socialist control of the Centralverband. In the 1900s they organized their own association to lobby parliament in healthcare matters. In 1910, in response to the calls for change, the Reichstag opened debate on a compre-

hensive new system of national health insurance regulations, the Reichsversicherungsordnung (RVO). Its two sections were passed in 1911 and 1914, respectively. The RVO specified Ortskrankenkassen as the country's fundamental health insurance providers. It was the RVO that introduced the concept of the allgemeine Ortskrankenkasse—under its provisions local funds were no longer required to restrict their membership to particular professional groups. It was the beginning of the age of the general local fund. The RVO capped a period of intense growth in the local funds. Transportation and office workers were first given coverage in 1901, agricultural, forestry, and domestic workers in 1911, and civil servants in 1914. By 1913 Ortskrankenkassen had 7.74 million members, 57 percent of the total for all German insurance providers. After 1914, however, the number of Ortskrankenkassen declined as local funds consolidated their operations and membership.

ECONOMIC UPHEAVAL BETWEEN THE WORLD WARS

The start of World War I in autumn 1914 launched a long period of political and economic difficulty in Germany. The changeover to a war economy led to disruption in employment. At the same time large numbers of working-age men left the economy altogether to enter the military. Rather than relieving these problems, the armistice in 1919 only made matters worse. With millions of Marks in reparations imposed by the Allies, the shattered country soon found itself in a far more serious unemployment crisis as millions of former soldiers and refugees from eastern territories lost to Poland, precisely at the moment that Krankenkasse coverage had been extended to the unemployed.

By 1923 Germany entered a desperate period of runaway inflation. Because of their premium structure, the Ortskrankenkassen were hit by the inflation particularly hard. During this time, wages were rising by the *millions* every working day, far outstripping the statutory ceilings above which premiums were not calculated. With no legal means of keeping up with inflation, the Ortskrankenkassen were financially crippled. Eventually assistance came when legislators authorized the local funds to raise premiums to as high as 8 percent of wages, with an additional 2 percent "emergency fee", and by the end of 1923 the currency had restabilized. The government, by contrast, remained debt-ridden. Politicians in the Weimar Republic were the first to juggle public health funds, in this case from the Ortskrankenkassen, to pay for other government expenses.

If the Ortskrankenkassen experienced relief from their financial woes in the mid-1920s it was only short-lived. During the Great Depression, the local health funds had nearly 13 million members—many unemployed—and were under tremendous pressure to cut costs. To avoid premium hikes, the local funds started limiting service to the most urgent cases and introduced general service cuts as well as procedures designed to make filing claims more difficult. In the early 1930s the Ortskrankenkassen were targeted by the Nazi Party as a sort of Communist elite that should be abolished. After Hitler came to power in 1933, virtually every employee of the Hauptverband deutschen Krankenkassen, as the Centralverband had been renamed, lost his job. In 1935 the Hauptverband itself disappeared when it was merged into a Nazi-controlled national health insurance association, the Reichsverband der Ortskrankenkassen.

POSTWAR REORGANIZATION

After the defeat of the Third Reich in spring 1945, the Allies dissolved the Reichsverband. For the next three years, the individual regional associations of the allgemeine Ortskrankenkassen took over its functions. It was not until after the founding of the Federal Republic of Germany—sometimes known as West Germany—in 1948 and the adoption of the country's constitution which gave the federal government exclusive authority in public health insurance affairs that a successor organization to the old Hauptverband could be formed. It was the Vereinigung der Ortskrankenkassenverbände e.V. (VOV) (the Union of Local Health Insurance Fund Associations). The regional associations and the VOV play different roles on behalf of the Ortskrankenkassen. The VOV acted on behalf of the entire system of local funds, liaised with the German federal government, interacted with the national associations of physicians and other healthcare providers, and acted as the Ortskrankenkassen's public spokesman. The regional associations provided a forum for the exchange of ideas, regulated Ortskrankenkasse relations, and offered advice to member funds.

In 1951 self-administration of Ortskrankenkassen was reestablished for the first time since the mid-1930s. In 1955 the VOV was renamed Bundesverband der Ortskrankenkassen (BdO) (Federal Association of Local Health Insurance Funds). In the 1960 and 1970s coverage was extended to additional segments of the economy. Salespeople came under the plan in 1966, self-employed agricultural workers in 1972, and students and the disabled in 1975. The consolidation of various towns and communities in the 1970s resulted in a concurrent consolidation in Ortskrankenkassen, and their number fell.

CUTTING COSTS AND EXPANDING: 1980 TO THE PRESENT

During the 1970s, the healthcare community in Germany took the first steps to brake costs which were threatening to spin out of control. The year 1977 witnessed the passage of the Health Insurance Containment Act, which established a board comprised of representatives from the most important groups in German healthcare, including the Ortskrankenkassen, charged with developing non-binding guidelines for healthcare costs. The act was followed up five years later with the Hospital Cost Containment Act and Cost Containment Act Amendment, which required AOK members to make low co-payments for medication, hospitalization, dental treatment, and other treatment. By 1983 the number of Ortskrankenkassen in Germany had consolidated to 270. The number of insured had risen to 16.3 million, or about 45.5 percent of the total membership of German public healthcare plans. In 1987 the BdO changed its name to the AOK-Bundesverband, the Federal Association of Local Health Insurance Funds. Additional reforms, which placed further monetary burdens on the insured, were introduced in 1989.

The 1990s were the most ground-shaking decade in a century for the AOK. On October 3, 1990, less than a year after the fall of the Berlin Wall, the German Democratic Republic, also known as East Germany, ceased to exist. Its states and citizens were absorbed into the Federal Republic. With a stroke of the pen millions of East Germans lost their state-paid health insurance and had to be integrated into West Germany's system. For the lion's share, that meant integration into the AOK. As a result, the association not only had to process millions of new members, it also had to organize an infrastructure from the ground up in eastern Germany.

Despite more than a decade of reforms, by the mid-1990s, Germany's statutory healthcare system, represented by the AOK, was wide-reaching. It offered care by physicians of choice, hospital care, extensive dental and optical coverage, liberal maternity leave payments, physical therapy, and prescription costs. Nonetheless the 1990s were also a decade of new legislation and cost-cutting efforts. Between 1993 and 2005 no fewer than eleven major healthcare laws were passed by the German parliament, aimed primarily at cost reduction. Cuts were effected by various means: service cuts and requiring the insured to pay an increasing percentage of the cost of treatment; exerting greater oversight over the payment of physicians; renegotiating the cost of treatment by physicians and hospitals; and, raising the premium rates charged. Relief was often of short duration. The 1993 reforms brought the AOK a budget surplus of DM 2.7 billion. Unfortunately the group still had deficits of DM 4 million from 1992 on the books, and in 1995 it would suffer new shortfalls.

In 1994 a complicated risk structure compensation scheme was introduced. It was designed to minimize the financial inequalities between various Krankenkassen resulting from premiums based on the solidarity principle rather than risk. As a consequence, beginning in the mid-1990s Germans were given the freedom to join any public health fund, including national health plans organized for specific professions, the so-called Ersatzkassen or "substitute funds." Another reform established a common "risk fund" in 2002 which was contributed to and used by all public Krankenkassen, including the AOK. This fund covered a percentage of Krankenkassen costs for prescriptions, sick pay, hospital stays, and dialysis. The risk structure compensation scheme is to be extended to the entire healthcare system by 2007.

In 2003 the German parliament introduced a "capitation fee" under which members of AOK and other Krankenkassen were required to pay an extra one-time fee for every quarter in which they received medical treatment. The Health Modernization Law of 2004 introduced further cost reforms, such as patient co-payments of 10 percent up to 2 percent of the annual net income. The entire reform package was intended to save some EUR 10 billion. At the same time average AOK premiums dropped by one-tenth of a percent.

Gerald E. Brennan

PRINCIPAL COMPETITORS

DAK Deutsche Angestellten-Krankenkasse; Techniker Krankenkasse; Barmer Ersatzkasse; DKV Deutsche Krankenversicherung AG; Debeka-Gruppe.

PRINCIPAL SUBSIDIARIES

AOK-Consult; Wissenschaftlichen Instituts der AOK.

FURTHER READING

"Analysis: Better Get Sick in Germany," *UPI,* May 10, 2002.

Banze, Sonja, "Kranke Kasse," *Welt am Sonntag,* June 16, 2002, p. 4.

Kirk, Don Lewis, "Germans Disagree on Effect on Rates if Health Reform Fails," *Business Insurance,* October 25, 1999.

Knieps, Franz. "Die GKV im Spannumgfeld von Kontinuität und Wandel." In: *Hundert Jahre AOK-Bundesverband,* AOK, 1994, pp. 772-75.

Pittman, Patricia M., "Care Management in Germany and the U.S.: An Expanded Laboratory," *Health Care Financing Review,* September 22, 2005.

Töns, Hans, *Hundert Jahre gesetzliche Krankenversicherung im Blick der Ortskrankenlassen,* Bonn, Germany: Verlag der Ortskrankenkassen Bonn, 1983.

Arch Chemicals, Inc.

501 Merritt 7
Norwalk, Connecticut 06851
U.S.A.
Telephone: (203) 229-2900
Fax: (203) 229-3652
Web site: http://www.archchemicals.com

Public Company
Incorporated: 1998
Employees: 2,675
Sales: $1.12 billion (2004)
Stock Exchanges: New York
Ticker Symbol: ARJ
NAIC: 325998 All Other Miscellaneous Chemical Product and Preparation Manufacturing

■ ■ ■

Arch Chemicals, Inc., is a global specialty chemical company based in Norwalk, Connecticut, involved in two main business segments: treatment products and performance products. Treatment products include chemicals to sanitize drinking water and swimming pools; industrial biocides, used to inhibit the growth of microorganisms in metal working fluids, paint, and other coatings; industrial wood preservatives and fire retardants; stains and lacquers to coat wood; and active ingredients and preservatives used in shampoos, cosmetics, and other personal care products. Arch's performance products include polyols used to make adhesives, sealants, and coatings; glycols for making antifreeze, cleaning products, and consumer goods; and hydrazine hydrate, used to make drugs, treat water, and blowing agents that strengthen plastics and rubbers by expanding them. In 2004 Arch sold off most of its microelectronic materials business segment, which provided slurry used by semiconductor manufacturers to remove and polish surfaces. In addition to 16 U.S. locations, Arch maintains operations in 20 other countries around the world. A spinoff of the Olin Corporation in 1999, Arch is a public company listed on the New York Stock Exchange.

HERITAGE DATING TO THE 19TH CENTURY

Arch Chemicals' lineage is linked to two companies, both of which were founded in 1892: Olin Industries and Mathieson Chemical Corporation. Olin was founded by Franklin Walter Olin, a Cornell-trained engineer and part-time major league baseball player, as Equitable Powder Company in East Alton, Illinois, a company that made blasting powder for coal mining. After adding small arms ammunition to the product mix, it became known as Western Cartridge Company in 1898. The move into ammunition put the company in the brass business, which would become a mainstay. The company added to its holdings in 1931 by acquiring famous Winchester Repeating Arms Company, the Connecticut maker of one of the most popular rifles of all time, the lever-action, repeating rifle, model 1873 Winchester. In 1944 Olin retired, well into his 80s, and consolidated his different businesses under Olin Industries, Inc., keeping most of the stock but distributing the rest to his sons, Spencer and John, who by this time were in their 60s. Olin died in 1951 at the age of 91. His sons, along with executive Bill Hanes, who was of similar age, took over the running of the company in the mid-1940s. Over the next several years the company expanded beyond metals and ammunition and became involved in cellophane, lumber, paper production, and petrochemicals.

With Olin's management team aging and no successor available, company president John Olin turned to a 44-year-old friend named Tom Nichols, who had proven to be an extremely effective president of Mathieson Chemical Company. Mathieson had been founded in Saltville, Virginia, in 1892 by a group of investors who acquired the U.S. rights to an alkali process developed by English chemical manufacturer Neil Mathieson. At the outset the company sold soda ash to the glass, textile, and paper industries, but just a year later began selling the United States' first commercial bleaching powder, made from chlorine. Chlor-alkali products would become a core business for the company. Mathieson developed swimming pool and spa sanitizers, and during World War II served the war effort by producing chemicals to purify water and sanitize field medical equipment. In 1944 Nichols took over and Mathieson began to expand into industrial and agricultural chemicals, involved in products such as sulfuric acid, pesticides, and fertilizers. In 1952 it acquired pharmaceutical E.R Squibb & Sons, deemed a good fit because chlorine served as an important precursor chemical in about 85 percent of all pharmaceutical products.

In 1952 Nichols and John Olin talked about the possibility of merging their companies, which at the time were both generating sales in the neighborhood of $250 million. The two companies had already demonstrated they could work well together in a successful rocket fuel venture, but neither Nichols nor Olin wanted to be subordinate to the other and talk of a merger was dropped. It was during a hunting trip in 1953 that Olin convinced Nichols to allow Hanes to formulate an equitable power-sharing arrangement that would allow for the merger. Under Hanes's subsequent plan, Olin would serve as chairman, Nichols as president would run the company, and Hanes would head finances. Nichols agreed and in August 1954 the merger took place, resulting in the Olin Mathieson Chemical Corporation.

While both Olin and Mathieson had been involved in basic chemicals, Nichols was not content just to focus on its core chemicals, metals, and ammunition products. Through acquisitions the company became involved in industrial phosphates, paper bags and corrugated containers, and aluminum production, which led to the purchase of an African bauxite mine to provide a primary raw ingredient of aluminum. In the 1960s the company tried its hand at home construction, and leisure products, selling camping equipment under the Winchester name as well as skis. It ended the 1960s by shortening its name to Olin Corporation.

Olin's assets proved to be an unwieldy mix and in the 1970s the company took steps to concentrate its resources on core businesses. It sold off its aluminum assets and spun off its forest products subsidiary, and then in 1981 sold the arms portion of Winchester while holding onto the sporting ammunition plant in East Alton, Illinois. With some of the money it received through divestitures, Olin invested in key businesses. It became involved in the electronic chemicals industry through the 1984 acquisition of the Phillip A. Hunt Chemical Corporation, forming one of the components of Arch Chemicals.

The recession of the early 1990s forced Olin to once again pare down its diverse mix of businesses. By the end of 1995 Olin sold or simply closed 18 businesses and product lines in order to focus on three core businesses: chemicals, defense, and metals. But management was still not satisfied with the return it was receiving from its assets and further fine-tuning became the order of the day. The Ordnance and Aerospace divisions were combined to create Primex Technologies, Inc., which was then spun off to shareholders. In addition, Olin's isocyanates business was sold to Arco Chemical for $565 million. Olin was now left with two noncomplementary businesses: specialty chemicals and basic materials. Management decided that they would be better off operating independently, and by being split would enhance shareholder value. Hence, in mid-1998 it was announced that the specialty chemical businesses would be spun off as a separate publicly traded company. Olin would retain three divisions: brass, chlor-alkali, and Winchester ammunition.

OLIN'S SPINOFF OF SPECIALTY CHEMICALS BEGINS IN 1999

The name Arch Chemicals, Inc. was selected and in August 1998 the new entity was incorporated in Virginia, although its headquarters would be established in Norwalk, Connecticut. To head the new company, Olin pulled from its executive ranks. To serve as chairman and chief executive officer, Olin executive vice-president

---

KEY DATES

1892: Olin Corporation is founded.
1954: Olin and Mathieson Chemical Corporation merge.
1998: Olin incorporates Arch Chemicals.
1999: Olin spins off specialty chemical assets as Arch Chemicals.
2000: Hickson International PLC is acquired.
2004: Avecia biocides business is acquired.

Michael E. Campbell was selected. Leon B. Anziao, who previously served as president of Olin's specialty chemicals operation, was named president and chief operating officer. In addition, the general manager of Olin's Conductive Materials division, James LaCasse, was named vice-president and general manager of Arch's semiconductor division. They would head a company with three business segments: microelectronic chemicals, performance chemicals, and water chemicals, which combined for $863 million in sales in 1998. Performance chemicals contributed 40 percent of that amount, some $345 million, followed by water chemicals with 34 percent or $290 million, and microelectronic chemicals with 26 percent or $228 million. It also would inherit $75 million in debt from Olin, which arranged a $250 million credit line in Arch's name. The spinoff was completed in February 1999, with Olin shareholders receiving one share of Arch for every two shares of Olin they held. Wall Street, however, was not especially excited by the presence of Arch on the New York Stock Exchange, as its shares' opening price of $20 quickly slipped to $18.

Campbell and his team developed a three-prong growth strategy: adding to existing product lines, launching internally developed products, and making selective acquisitions. The company also hoped to improve on operational efficiencies and significantly trim overhead costs. In September 1999, Arch completed its first acquisition, adding the HQEE-hydroquinone di (beta-hydroxyethyl) Ether business of Eastman Chemical Company. Arch had manufactured HQEE for Eastman at its Brandenburg, Kentucky plant. The addition of Eastman's business gave Arch 80 percent of the HQEE market in the United States and a strong presence in Europe. When 1999 came to a close, Arch, in its first year of independence, increased sales 2 percent to $880 million, while earnings per share improved 17 percent to $1.82, due in some measure to the company reducing costs by $5 million.

Arch continued to reshape its business portfolio in 2000. It sold subsidiary Superior Pool Products, Inc., not deemed a strategic asset, receiving $21 million. The company also restructured its microelectronic materials unit, devoting resources to higher-margin formulated products rather than wet process chemicals, which were more akin to price-sensitive commodities and offered meager returns. Arch also completed a pair of acquisitions in 2000. In August it paid $140.4 million for United Kingdom-based Hickson International, a move that strengthened Arch's global position in high-growth biocides and performance urethanes. Subsequently, Arch began looking to cast off Hickson's organics division, which was not a good fit for the company. Arch also added to its roster of personal care intermediates with the November 2000, $38 million cash purchase of New Jersey-based Brooks Industries. Brooks mostly served global cosmetics and toiletries companies, offering specialty products like biopolymers, proteins, botanicals, and liposomes; and standard products, including lanolin, lanolin derivatives, emulsifiers, and protein products. In keeping with its growth strategy Arch also introduced several new products in 2000, such as Poly-G 30-400T, a polyol used primarily in elastomer, coating, and adhesive applications; and Zinc Omadine, a fungicide-algicide for masonry paint. For the year, Arch grew revenues to $941 million, to go with earnings per share of $1.66.

POOR BUSINESS CONDITIONS EARLY IN THE 21ST CENTURY

With the U.S. economy slipping in 2001 and the manufacturing sector struggling, especially the semiconductor industry, Arch experienced a drop in sales to $921 million and an earnings plunge to just 15 cents per share. Nevertheless, the company succeeded in integrating Hickson and Brooks into its operations. It also completed three minor acquisitions in 2001, adding Walker Brothers, a Canadian maker of anti-sapstain products used by sawmills. Later in the year Arch acquired United Kingdom-based Butler Mabbutt & Wrightto, producer of wood, leather, and plastic products finishes; and the International Division of Humbrol Limited, which manufactured varnishes, textured finishes, and other industrial coatings. Arch also supported its coating business in the Far East in 2001 by opening a sales support and technical support operation in Suzhou, China. In the pool chemical category, Arch introduced 17 new products in its retail pool chemical line.

The manufacturing sector did not pick up in 2002, forcing Arch to trim its workforce. The company was able to sell the Hickson DanChem unit, realizing $25

---

million that was used to pay down debt. In 2003 it was able to finally sell off Hickson's organics division for $18 million, as well as Peak Sulphur Inc., which brought in another $25 million. As a result, Arch was able to further trim its debt and put itself in a strong position to benefit from a rebound in the economy, as revenues topped the $1 billion mark in 2003.

The year 2004 was marked by a pair of major transactions. In March the company paid $210 million in cash and stock to acquire the biocides business of Avecia Group plc, enhancing Arch's U.S. position in pool chemicals by adding nonchlorine products to supplement Arch's chlorine-based sanitizers. Whereas Arch was aggressive in building on its expertise in treatment products, it shied away from microelectronic materials, which were cyclic in nature and also required a dedicated research and development effort. In December 2004, Arch sold virtually all of the operations to Fuji Photo Film Company Ltd. for approximately $160 million in cash. In 2005 Arch sold its 50 percent stake in another slurry operation, a joint venture called Planar Solutions, to Fuji for another $17 million. As a result treatment products now accounted for 85 percent of the company's revenues, which increased to $1.1 billion in 2004 and a projected $1.3 billion in 2005. Going forward, Arch planned to focus even more attention on its treatment business.

Ed Dinger

PRINCIPAL SUBSIDIARIES

Arch Chemicals Canada, Inc.; Arch Chemicals GmbH; Arch Chemicals Suzhoy Co., Ltd.; Arch Chemi-cals UK Holdings Limited; Arch Person Care Products, L.P.; Arch Treatment Technologies, Inc.; Arch Woods Protection, Inc.

PRINCIPAL COMPETITORS

Cytec Industries Inc.; The Dow Chemical Company; Nalco Holding Company.

FURTHER READING

Brown, Robert, "Arch Chemicals Buys Eastman's Specialties Business in HQEE," *Chemical Market Reporter*, October 4, 1999, p. 3.

Chang, Joseph, "Arch Chemicals Spinoff Sets Its Sights on Costs and Growth," *Chemical Market Reporter*, February 15, 1999, p. 1.

D'Amico, Esther, "Arch to Buy Avecia's Biocides Business," *Chemical Week*, March 10, 2004, p. 6.

Dawkins, Pam, "Downturn Forces Norwalk, Conn.-Based Arch Chemicals to Reorganize," *Connecticut Post*, March 6, 2002.

"Executive Insights: Arch Chemicals: CEO Discusses Goals for Arch and ACC," *Chemical Market Reporter*, February 21, 2005, p. 17.

Haberlin, Steven Ray, "Connecticut-Based Chemical Company's Spinoff Gets Profitable Head Start," *Providence Journal-Bulletin*, August 9, 1999.

Hunter, David, "Arch Chemicals Gets New Respect," *Chemical Week*, May 8, 2002, p. 41.

Westervelt, Robert, "Arch Chemicals Makes a Quiet Public Debut," *Chemical Week*, February 17, 1999, p. 12.

The Auchter Company

———————— ■ ————————

4804 South Kernan Boulevard South
Jacksonville, Florida 32224
U.S.A.
Telephone: (904) 355-3536
Fax: (904) 353-0234
Web site: http://www.auchter.com

Private Company
Founded: 1929 as George D. Auchter Company
Employees: 150 (est.)
Sales: $300 million (2004 est.)
NAIC: 236220 Commercial and Institutional Building
Construction.

■ ■ ■

The Auchter Company is Jacksonville, Florida's oldest
general construction contractor, responsible for building
most of the city's premiere structures: Jacksonville City
Hall, the Modis Building, The Jacksonville Landing,
Humana Building, Riverplace Tower, BellSouth Tower,
and the SunTrust Building. Auchter has also completed
projects from the Bahamas to Washington, D.C. The
firm offers a full array of preconstruction and construction services, including design, engineering, scheduling,
and project managing. Auchter boasts a wide ranging
portfolio of projects, having been involved in the
construction of office buildings, warehouses, factories,
power generating stations, resort and residential projects,
hospitals and other healthcare projects, churches,
museums, theaters, retail establishments, entertainment
complexes, academic and institutional buildings, over-

passes, bridges, parking garages, and condominiums.
The firm has also built numerous government projects,
including jails, military bases, courthouses, and the
Jacksonville International Airport. Although Dave
Auchter, a grandson of the firm's founder is an executive, Auchter is a private company owned by the Glass
family.

ORIGINS IN 1929

The Auchter Company was founded as the George D.
Auchter Co. in 1929 by George David Auchter.
Originally from Red Bank, New Jersey, Auchter was an
engineer who originally came to Jacksonville in the 1920s
to work on a bridge project for a New Jersey employer.
At the time there were few engineers in Florida, but the
state was at the start of a building boom and Auchter
decided to settle in Jacksonville. It was a fast-growing
city and he believed it was becoming the center of
Florida's expanding economy. In 1922 he received his
license as a Florida engineer, his number 375 an indication of the state's shortage of engineers. Jacksonville,
known as the "The River City" was also an attractive
location because bridges were Auchter's area of expertise.
At first, Auchter concentrated on bridge construction
and overpasses, as well as the building of pulpwood
barges and concrete ships. The firm soon moved beyond
the immediate Jacksonville area and began taking on
projects along Florida's "First Coast," the northeast
Florida section centered on St. Augustine. Noteworthy
bridge and overpass projects of the early years included
Jacksonville's Hendricks Avenue Overpass and Haines
Street Expressway, the Beach Boulevard Intercostal
Waterway Bridge in Jacksonville Beach, Amelia Island

River Bridge in Fernandina, and the Vilano Bridge in St. Augustine.

Despite the Depression of the 1930s, Auchter's company expanded its capabilities beyond roads and bridges and developed into a general contractor. Two important projects in this diversification were the construction of the Crane Building and the Western Union Building in Jacksonville. Greater opportunities would be available in the early 1940s as the United State made preparations and eventually became involved in World War II. Jacksonville's coastal location made it an important site for the military, and consequently much of Auchter's work during this period became defense related. It received a large share of the $75 million contract to build the Jacksonville Naval Air Station, which opened in 1940. Two years later the Mayport Naval Air Station opened in Jacksonville and once again Auchter played a significant role in the project. The firm also helped in the war effort by building dry docks, which were then used around the world.

The experience gained from wartime projects paid further benefits in the postwar economic boom that ensued after a brief recession. Jacksonville's population was growing rapidly, opening up further opportunities for the firm. Auchter was involved in the construction of several major factories in the area, including the St. Regis Paper Company factory, the Maxwell House Coffee Plant, and the Anheuser Busch Yeast Plant. The firm was also the general contractor for the Jacksonville Port Authority Wharf and built three power generating stations for the Jacksonville Electric Authority. Auchter became a major contractor in the health care field as well. In the 1940s it did major work at Jacksonville's St. Vincent's Medical Center, which led to further work at the complex over the decades and other major health care projects in the First Coast area. Auchter landed institutional work, including the construction of the University of Florida's landmark Century Tower, which was built in 1953 to commemorate the school's 100th

anniversary. Auchter would later build a women's dormitory on the campus and a gymnasium. Auchter also provided construction services for a number of public projects in the decades following World War II, such as the City Hall Annex, the Duval County Courthouse, the Jacksonville International Airport, and the Civic Auditorium.

HIGH-RISE PROJECTS AND DIVERSIFICATION

In the 1960s Auchter began to take on high-rise construction projects, becoming involved in many of the buildings that would define Jacksonville's skyline. The City Hall Annex, completed in 1960, was a 15-story building. The 28-story Gulf Life Tower (renamed the Riverplace Tower) was added in 1967, followed in 1974 by the 37-story Independent Life Building (renamed the Modis Building). Also in 1974, Auchter built the Sun Trust Bank Building, an 18-story structure. From the early 1960s, Auchter was also involved in the construction of high-rise residential projects, including the 14-story Broadview Terrace and 16-story Commander Apartments in 1961. Auchter was also involved in the long-term Cathedral Residences project. It completed the 17-story Cathedral Towers in 1968, 18-story Cathedral Townhouse two years later, and the 21-story Cathedral Terrace in 1974. Other projects of note during the 1970s were Jacksonville's Baptist Hospital Complex and the city's First Baptist Church.

Nearly a decade would pass before Auchter resumed its work on high-rise buildings. In the meantime it underwent a change in ownership. With George Auchter having grown elderly, his family decided to sell the company to a group of executives and outside investors, including William H. Glass Jr., whose father had been the firm's president for 14 years. The younger Glass held a degree in civil engineering. After serving in the U.S. Army, he joined Auchter in 1957 as a field engineer. He later became a project manager and in 1979 was named a vice president. In 1993 he was finally able to realize a long-held dream and buy out the firm's other stockholders. The well-respected company name was retained.

During the dozen years that passed between the time the Auchter family sold the firm and the Glass family bought it, the firm continued to enjoy success, becoming involved in projects in a wide range of fields. In the 1980s, there was another phase of high-rise building projects in Jacksonville. Auchter built the 32-story BellSouth Tower in 1983, followed by the 21-story Two Prudential Plaza in 1985, and the 24-story Jacksonville Center in 1989. Furthermore, during the 1980s Auchter built the Jacksonville Landing, a waterfront shopping,

```
┌─────────────────────────────────────────────┐
│                                               │
│              KEY DATES                        │
│  ───────────────────●───────────────────      │
│                                               │
│  1929:  George D. Auchter founds the company. │
│  1981:  The Auchter family sells the firm to  │
│         group of employees and investors.     │
│  1993:  William H. Glass buys out his partners.│
│  2000:  Dave Auchter, the founder's grandson, │
│         joins the company.                    │
│  2002:  Brad Glass succeeds his father as     │
│         president.                            │
│                                               │
└─────────────────────────────────────────────┘
```

dining, and entertainment complex on the St. John's River. The firm also participated in the construction of new hospitals, such as the St. Luke's Hospital Complex.

Auchter could not, however, depend on office towers and hospital work, projects that were cyclical in nature. As a result the firm placed an increasing emphasis on resort and residential buildings, such as the Ponte Vedra Surf Club and a variety of projects on the 1,300-acre Amelia Island Plantation complex, which included the Amelia Inn and Beach Club, the Osprey Village assisted living facility, the Ocean Club Villas luxury ocean front condominiums, and golf courses. Auchter also took on suburban office park projects and built Gate Petroleum Convenience Stores and three big box Target stores in the North Florida area.

Auchter enjoyed especially strong growth in the second half of the 1990s, when Jacksonville grew rapidly. One of the firm's greatest challenges became the recruitment of qualified construction workers and design engineers. In the second half of the 1990s, to keep pace with the building boom, Auchter increased its employment by more than 25 percent. The contract base, in the meantime, grew from $48 million in 1995 to about $150 million in 2000. The firm also outgrew its headquarters, and in 1999 bought 3.36 acres in the First Coast Technology Park located on the campus of the University of North Florida. Furthermore, Auchter established a relationship with the school, taking on students as interns. There was already a connection between the company and the university, since William Glass's son, Brad, earned a degree in business administration from the university a decade earlier, and then joined the family business in 1995.

NEW CENTURY BRINGS FRESH FACES

Both Brad Glass and his brother, Jeff Glass, worked for Auchter by the mid-1990s. Their father soon began taking steps to turn over day-to-day control to his sons, whom he brought in as partners. Ultimately Brad Glass bought out his brother's interest in the family business. In 2000 Auchter brought in new talent and experience by adding five project managers, four superintendents, a finance director, and a director of corporate marketing. During the same period, Dave Auchter, the grandson of the firm's founder, became the new director of corporate development and the only family member to be employed by the firm that bore the Auchter name. Previously Auchter had been the media director for World Golf Village and the National Football League's Jacksonville Jaguars. The average age of these new employees was 35. "The recent hirings are really directly related to our increased work," Brad Glass told the *Jacksonville Business Journal* in July 2000. "But," he continued, "they also represent an opportunity to mix some of the younger talent in with our veterans. It's a mentoring type of environment we're going after."

Brad Glass's situation was a case in point, as he was being groomed by his father to lead the firm. In 2002, 35-year-old Brad Glass was named Auchter's president. While his father, at the age of 67, retained the title of chief executive officer, he was clearly backing away and would soon turn over the CEO role to his son as well. Nevertheless, the elder Glass retained the chairmanship and would remain very much involved in the business. In fact, Brad Glass told the *Jacksonville Business Journal*, "No matter what Dad says about stepping down, you can bet I'm not going to let him go too far." He added, "I told him the other day even if he goes fishing he'd better take his cell phone with him in case I have questions." But his father was just as adamant about his son being ready for the added responsibility, saying Brad had "clearly earned the responsibility to guide Auchter into this new era for our company." However, he did maintain, "We will continue to work together as I did with my father more than 40 years ago." To add to the sense of transition, Auchter was also in the midst of moving into its new 25,000-square-foot office building, which the firm, not surprisingly, built itself.

A diversified mix of construction projects continued for Auchter in the early years of the new century. They included a new downtown Public Library, a building for the Jacksonville Airport Authority, and a number of luxury condominium projects, including the Landmark Condominium project at Jacksonville Beach, the Water-Mark condominiums, Ortega River Club Condominiums, Villa Riva Condominiums, and Costa Verano. Other projects included the Strand and Peninsula residential towers on Jacksonville's Southbank, and the Fidelity National Financial expansion in Riverside. Auchter had developed a reputation as the premiere contractor in Jacksonville and the First Coast, and with the transition to a new generation of leadership all but complete, the firm was well positioned to maintain that designation for many years to come.

Ed Dinger

PRINCIPAL COMPETITORS

Elkins Constructors Inc.; The Haskell Company; The Turner Corporation.

FURTHER READING

"Amid Changes, Auchter Co. on Ground Floor of City's Rise," *Jacksonville Business Journal,* October 17, 2005.

Daniels, Earl, "Auchter Co. is Building its Jacksonville Legacy," *The Florida Times Union,* March 15, 2002, p. C1.

Mathis, Karen Brune, "Auchter Wants to Build Company Headquarters at Tech Park," *The Florida Times Union,* July 29, 1999, p. E1.

"Sky's Not The Limit," *Jacksonville Business Journal,* July 24, 2000.

"Third Generation Takes Helm of The Auchter Co.," *Jacksonville Business Journal,* March 13, 2002.

Ball

Ball Corporation

10 Longs Peak Drive
Broomfield,, Colorado 80021
U.S.A.
Telephone: (303) 469-3131
Fax: (303) 460-2127
Web site: http://www.ball.com

Public Company
Incorporated: 1922
Employees: 13,500
Sales: $5.75 billion (2005)
Stock Exchanges: New York
Ticker Symbol: BLL
NAIC: 326160 Plastics Bottle Manufacturing; 332431 Metal Can Manufacturing; 332116 Metal Stamping; 334511 Search, Detection, Navigation, Guidance, Aeronautical, and Nautical System and Instrument Manufacturing; 336419 Other Guided Missile and Space Vehicle Parts and Auxiliary Equipment Manufacturing

∎ ∎ ∎

Once identified with its glass home canning jars, Ball Corporation has traded its glass packaging activities for plastic and metal, while maintaining a thriving aerospace business since the 1950s. After spinning off its home canning line and other consumer-oriented business in Alltrista in 1993, the company quickly became a global leader in advanced plastic and metal food and beverage containers, with strong positions in China, Europe and the United States. The company has also acquired aerosol can operations in the United States and Argentina. Altogether, Ball has operations in a dozen countries, and has about 30 joint ventures or licensee plants.

19TH CENTURY ORIGINS

The Ball Corporation began in 1880 when the Ball brothers (Edmund, Frank, George, Lucius, and William) went into the business of making tin-jacketed glass containers for kerosene lamps. From this type of operation it was an easy shift to the manufacture of canning jars and lids. Moreover, it was wise business strategy: Thomas Edison's recent invention of the incandescent light bulb had antiquated the kerosene lamp. The glass jar, on the other hand, had a great future. (After moving the business to Muncie, Indiana, in 1887, the brothers also launched what would become Ball State University.)

Until the end of World War II, Ball was primarily a jar and bottle manufacturer with few other interests. In the late 1940s, however, a problem had to be confronted—nearly 70 percent of the company's glass production facilities were in need of modernization. Ball had either to diversify and grow in order to underwrite necessary modernization costs or liquidate the company. The family decided to diversify the company because a 1947 antitrust ruling prohibited Ball from purchasing more glass subsidiaries. Under president Edmund F. Ball, they made a number of key acquisitions outside the glass container field. Before the company ventured too far afield, Ball hired a New York management consulting team to help establish a long-range program. In the words of Edmund Ball's successor, John Fisher, "We wanted to plan for growth, not just hope for it."

SPACE AGE OPPORTUNITIES

The significant changes at Ball, those which have molded the company's future, took place in the late 1950s and early 1960s. The launching of Sputnik by the Soviets in 1958 ushered in the Space Age and created many new opportunities in the field of aerospace. Ball had already decided to take advantage of the situation, establishing Ball Brothers Research Corporation in 1956. "We got into the space field because it was the beginning of the biggest scientific effort in our nation's history," said Fisher, adding "We knew it could be profitable for us, and that we could get commercial 'fall-out' from it."

The Ball management proved itself correct on both counts. A substantial portion of the company's business would come from the sale of computer components, pointing controls for NASA satellites, electronic data display devices, and many related items such as Sound-Guard, a preservative for phonograph records that was a derivative of a lubricant developed for spacecraft. The company also built the cameras for the Viking I and II spacecraft that were used to determine the landing site on Mars; the Space Shuttle tether system, which allows small payloads to trail up to 65 miles away from the parent ship; and the telescope on the Infrared Astronomical Satellite launched in 1983 that helped scientists to determine more precisely the size of the Milky Way galaxy. Ball procured $180 million in defense contracts alone by 1987. Chief Executive Officer Richard Ringoen hoped the company's "strong position in infrared and ultraviolet instrumentation [would] continue to allow it to compete favorably with larger aerospace firms like General Dynamics."

Ironically, Ball had entered the high-tech market almost by mistake. In the 1950s, the company hired a small engineering firm in Boulder, Colorado, to develop a device that would more accurately weigh glass batch materials. The original device was never developed, but Ball was impressed enough by the technical skill of the small operation to purchase it. From this small start Ball

invested heavily in research and development and made this sector a vital part of the company's overall business.

POSTWAR CONTAINER BOOM

The 1960s were years of unparalleled growth in the container industry, especially in the consumer beverage area. Americans began drinking more beer and soft drinks than ever before, and innovations such as the pop-top can and the non-returnable bottle helped container companies make large profits. While not being a large-volume can manufacturer on the order of American Can or Continental, Ball was nonetheless extremely successful in this competitive market. Cans soon made up two-thirds of the company's packaging sales, supplanting jars and bottles as the company's primary container product.

Ball's success in this area can be traced back to 1968 when the firm made an early switch to two-piece cans. The two-piece can, which was lighter, less expensive, and faster to make, was by the early 1990s used to package 70 percent of all soft drinks and 94 percent of all beer. Since Ball was already in the container industry, it was able to win manufacturing contracts from such important customers as PepsiCo, Inc., The Coca-Cola Co., and Anheuser-Busch Co. In fact, Anheuser-Busch and Ball constructed a $32 million plant in New England to manufacture two-piece aluminum cans for the brewer on an exclusive basis. While Ball controlled less than one percent of the total can market in the 1980s, it had 7 to 8 percent of the two-piece can market.

GREATER DIVERSIFICATION: 1970-1990

Ball's diversification efforts during the 1950s and 1960s were bold in concept but fairly modest in scope. The man responsible for creating the widely diversified company that the Ball Corporation would become, John W. Fisher, was chosen president and chief executive officer in 1971. Fisher directed Ball into such fields as petroleum engineering equipment, photo-engraving, and plastics, and established the company as a leading manufacturer of computer components and high-tech hardware for defense and space.

Fisher, the last company president to be a member of the Ball family (his wife was the daughter of one of the five founding Ball brothers), resisted the traditionalists within his firm and pushed Ball into new markets all over the world. In 1972, Fisher acquired a Singapore-based petroleum equipment company that built and

KEY DATES

1880: Ball brothers form the Wooden Jacket Can Company in Buffalo, New York.
1884: The renamed Ball Brothers Glass Manufacturing Company begins making home canning jars.
1887: Business moved to Muncie, Indiana to benefit from abundant natural gas.
1947: Company begins diversification push.
1956: Ball Brothers Research Corporation (later Ball Aerospace) formed.
1969: Ball Brothers Corporation renamed Ball Corporation, buys Denver's Jeffco Manufacturing Company.
1972: Ball Corporation goes public.
1973: Ball-Bartoe Aircraft Corporation established in Boulder, Colorado.
1974: Ball acquires small California computer company.
1986: Packaging joint venture established in China.
1992: Kerr Group's commercial glass assets acquired.
1993: Ball exits home canning with spinoff of Alltrista; Heekin Can acquired in stock swap.
1994: Ball launches plastic container business.
1995: Ball Aerospace joint venture, Ball-Foster Glass Container, is formed.
1996: Ball sells its interest in Ball-Foster to Group Saint Gobain, exiting glass business.
1997: Purchase of M.C. Packaging makes Ball China's largest supplier of cans.
1998: Ball buys Reynolds Metals' metal beverage container business, relocates headquarters to Colorado.
2002: Germany's Schmalbach-Lubeca AG acquired; Ball Packaging Europe formed.
2006: Ball acquires U.S. and Argentina operations of aerosol can leader U.S. Can Corporation.

sold production gear and provided engineering expertise to oil firms in the Pacific. This purchase gave Ball subsidiary operations in Singapore, Malaysia, Indonesia, Panama, and Japan. The following year the Ball-Bartoe Aircraft Corporation was established in Boulder, Colorado. It was involved in the development of an experimental STOL (short take-off and landing) military jet in the 1980s.

The company then acquired agricultural systems and prefabricated housing. Fisher established a Ball Corporation division in Boulder devoted solely to the production and sale of "turnkey" irrigation packages for agricultural development in arid but arable areas of Libya and other nations in the Middle East. Ball also designed a modular home that could be erected on-site in a little more than six hours. In desert nations where building materials are scarce and therefore expensive, Ball has succeeded in selling a large number of these "kit" houses. Then, in 1974, Fisher acquired a small California computer company. This concern was expanded into Ball Computer Products Division based in Sunnyvale, California, in the heart of Silicon Valley.

Following Ball's success in the foreign petroleum engineering equipment business, Fisher established similar operations in the United States. However, stiff competition, higher technological standards, and prohibitive start-up costs thwarted this venture from the start. Fisher wasted no time in selling it in 1976 for 40 cents per share. In the mid 1970s, Ball also developed and introduced Freshware food containers. Made of plastic with tight-fitting lids, these were designed to compete with Tupperware. The product was never actually marketed and Ball had to write it off as a loss, phasing out the project in a matter of months. But these were relatively small setbacks. Fisher's management strategy was long-term and he was willing to bear the burden of brief, small-scale problems. The two large obstacles he never surmounted, however, were the company's image and the stock market's ambivalent opinion of it. Despite its interesting acquisitions, the American public still associated Ball almost exclusively with its glass jars.

Ball Corporation became a public company on July 13, 1972. There were two reasons for going public. The company management wanted to establish accurately the market value of the Ball family holdings, and they intended to raise equity money to finance the company's diversification efforts. But despite its impressive history, Ball's stock price did not significantly increase. Fisher's efforts to give Ball a more technological image, his trips across the United States to speak with investors, and his dedication to growth did not change the minds of many people. The executive could not understand why a profitable company would not be an attractive stock purchase. He remarked, "We live in a world where products must be packaged, in good times or bad. This is all a bit mystifying to me." Originally traded over the counter, shares were admitted to the New York Stock Exchange on December 17, 1973.

When Fisher retired in 1981 he was replaced by Richard Ringoen. Ringoen concentrated on two areas, technology and packaging. Many of the other sectors, while being neither divested nor disregarded, had been left to operate on their own. From 1988 to 1992, Ball's annual sales increased dramatically, from $86 million to $2.177 billion, on the force of acquisitions. Net income only increased slightly, however, from $50.5 million to $69.1 million during the same period.

In the late 1980s, Ball began to focus on international packaging markets where growth far outpaced that of the United States. In 1986, Ball entered into a joint venture with Guangzhou M. C. Packaging in China. By 1993, that business ranked as one of that country's most successful foreign joint ventures, and Ball had established five beverage can manufacturing plants in China, one in Taiwan, and one in Hong Kong.

CONSOLIDATION: 1990-2000

Ringoen served Ball for a decade, and was succeeded by Delmont A. Davis in 1991. Davis led Ball's early 1990s consolidation and rationalization. In 1992, the company acquired Kerr Group Inc.'s commercial glass assets for $68.4 million, which helped boost Ball's share of that market. Heekin Can, Inc., one of the Midwest's largest food can manufacturers, was purchased in 1993 through a tax-free exchange of stock. The integration of Heekin and Ball's existing Canadian can operations made Ball the third largest supplier to the combined U.S.-Canadian food can market. At the same time, Ball spun off its Alltrista Corporation subsidiary, which was comprised of Ball's consumer products, zinc products, metal decorating and services, industrial systems, and plastics businesses, to shareholders.

Ball's aerospace business also faced challenges in the late 1980s and early 1990s, as the end of the Cold War and the shifting governmental priorities that resulted helped reduce the federal defense budget and intensify competition for contracts. Still, in 1993, Ball was proud to have played a major role in the well-publicized repair of the Hubble Space Telescope. The Ball-built COSTAR optics system helped correct the telescope's notoriously blurry vision.

The net result of these reorganizational activities was that Ball's sales more than doubled from $1.12 billion in 1990 to $2.44 billion in 1993, while the corporation's staff was reduced by over ten percent. Ball was compelled to take a $95 million pre-tax restructuring provision, half of which was used for plant shutdowns and consolidations. Although CEO Davis rightly called Ball's $65.1 million loss for the year "simply not acceptable," he also expressed confidence that the company's "unparalleled restructuring" would bring new opportunities for profitability in the last half of the decade.

Ball had shed its home canning line with the Alltrista spinoff, and would soon leave the glass business altogether. The company launched its first plastic container development in 1994, originally basing this operation in Smyrna, Georgia. A PET plant was soon opened in California.

In September 1995, the Ball-Foster Glass Container joint venture was formed by combining Ball's last remaining glass operations with Compagnie de Saint-Gobain's recently acquired Foster-Forbes. Saint-Gobain bought out Ball's 42 percent interest the next year. These changes were overseen by George Sissel, a longtime company veteran who had become CEO in 1994 after Davis left. Also in 1995, Ball grouped its aerospace business into the subsidiary Ball Aerospace & Technologies Corporation.

The 1997 purchase of M.C. Packaging Ltd. made Ball China's largest supplier of cans. Ball bought Reynolds Metals' metal beverage container business for $746 million in 1998. This made Ball the North American market leader (it also brought its total debt up to $1.6 billion). Ball was among manufacturers developing new contours for the ubiquitous aluminum can. It was taking advantages of new printing processes to offer customers cans with photo quality graphics. The company was also working on metal beverage cans with plastic liners.

Another major change in 1998 was the relocation of the headquarters to Broomfield, Colorado, from Muncie, Indiana, which had been its home for more than 100 years. By this time, noted Knight Ridder, divestments had reduced the company's employment in Indiana from 1,300 to just 180 administrative staff within a few years. Though Colorado housed Ball Aerospace and 3,000 workers, most of the company's 13,000 employees were at other sites around the world.

MORE ACQUISITIONS IN 2000 AND BEYOND

Ball's total sales were $3.7 billion by the end of the decade. In 2000, Ball joined ConAgra in a metal food container joint venture, Ball Western Can Company LLC, which was based in Oakdale, California. Ball would buy out ConAgra's interest in the plant in March 2004. Ball got a new CEO, David Hoover, in early 2001. Hoover had been with the company for 30 years. By this time, divestments had reduced the global work force to about 10,000 employees.

Germany's Schmalbach-Lubeca AG, a $1 billion metal beverage canning company, was acquired in 2002 in a deal worth about $855 million (EUR 900 million). Ball Packaging Europe was created around this acquisition. In 2004, the company began building an $80 million aluminum can plant near Belgrade to serve the Eastern European market.

The company's packaging technology development operations were consolidated at a site in Westminster, Colorado in 2004. Ball also had an R&D Center in Bonn, Germany. Sales reached $5.75 billion in 2005. The largest segment was North American Packaging, with revenues of $3.7 billion. International Packaging accounted for $1.4 billion, while Aerospace and Technologies reported record sales of about $695 million. The unit was enjoying the success of America's Mars rovers, for which it supplied electronics and antennas. It was also participating in the Deep Impact comet exploration project.

Ball began 2006 by announcing two major acquisitions. First was that of the U.S. and Argentinean operations of U.S. Can Corporation, the leading producer of aerosol cans in the United States. Second, Ball acquired the North American plastic bottle container assets of Alcan, providing Ball with new manufacturing facilities, greater technologies, and a broader range of customers.

Updated, April Dougal Gasbarre, Frederick C. Ingram

PRINCIPAL SUBSIDIARIES

Ball Aerospace & Technologies Corporation; Ball North America Corporation; Ball Packaging Corporation.: Ball Aerospace & Technologies Corporation; Ball Packaging Europe GmbH (Germany).

PRINCIPAL COMPETITORS

Alcan Inc.; Alcoa Inc.; Crown Holdings Inc.; Rexam plc; U.S. Can Corporation.

FURTHER READING

"Ball Corp. Focuses on Core Business; Ball Jars, Penny Blanks Find New Home in Spin-Off Alltrista," *Indianapolis Business Journal,* April 12, 1993, p. 1A.

Ball, Edmund F., "From Fruit Jars to Satellites: The Story of Ball Brothers Company, Incorporated," Newcomen Society in North America, 1960.

Birmingham, Frederic Alexander, *Ball Corporation: The First Century,* Indianapolis: Curtis Publishing Co., 1980.

Blodgett, Richard, *Ball Corporation at 125,* Old Saybrook, Connecticut: Greenwich Pub. Group, 2005.

"The History of Ball: From Wood-Jacketed Tins to Aerospace," Broomfield, Colorado: Ball Corporation, 2006.

Hudson, Kris, "Packaging Giant Ball Corp. Moves to Broomfield, Colo.," *Knight Ridder/Tribune Business News,* August 21, 1998.

"In a Native Tongue, Ball Says 'Can' Do with Commitment to Eastern Europe," *Packaging Strategies,* January 31, 2003, p. 1.

Koenig, Bill, "Ball Corp. of Muncie, Ind., Selling Stake in Ball-Foster Glass," *Knight Ridder/Tribune Business News,* September 17, 1996.

Marcus, Alfred A., *Big Winners and Big Losers: The 4 Secrets of Long-Term Business Success and Failure,* Upper Saddle River, NJ: Pearson Education, Inc., 2006.

Sfiligoj, Eric, "The Shape of Cans to Come," *Beverage World,* June 1996, p. 52.

Ball Horticultural Company

———————— ■ ————————

622 Town Road
West Chicago, Illinois 60185
U.S.A.
Telephone: (630) 231-3600
Fax: (630) 231-1383
Web site: http://www.ballhort.com

Private Company
Incorporated: 1905 as George J. Ball Inc.
Employees: 3,000
Sales: $90 million (2004 est.)
NAIC: 111422 Floriculture Production

■ ■ ■

Ball Horticultural Company is the leading North American producer and distributor of ornamental plants and their seeds. The company operates through an array of subsidiaries throughout the world, breeding and producing most of the plants sold through nurseries and garden centers in the United States. Its two main U.S. subsidiaries are Ball FloraPlant and PanAmerican Seed Company. Ball produces seeds and seedlings for worldwide distribution at huge plantations in Costa Rica, Guatemala, and Chile. It also produces ornamental plants at facilities in California for the North American market, supplies the Japanese market through several plant farms in that country, and serves the European market from a growing facility in Portugal. Ball also operates plant and seed distribution companies. Ball Seed, Ball Superior, and ColorLink serve the North American market. Ball products reach some 8,000 U.S.

wholesale greenhouse growers every year, and are then sold to approximately 17,000 garden centers, from small family-owned operations to big chain stores such as Home Depot and Wal-Mart. Ball operates several distribution companies in the United Kingdom and others in France, Germany, Holland, Italy, and in South Africa. Ball also operates six distribution subsidiaries in South America. Other subsidiaries serve the Asian market, with Ball outposts in Japan, Korea and China. Overall, the company has huge worldwide reach. Ball also operates a demonstration garden, several horticultural research firms, and a publishing arm, which produces several magazines for gardening hobbyists. The company has been in the Ball family since its inception in 1905, and is now headed by the founder's granddaughter, Anna Caroline Ball.

EARLY YEARS

The company that became Ball Horticultural was founded by a hardworking Ohio native, George Jacob Ball. Ball was born in 1874 in Milford, Ohio. He left school at 13 and began working at a greenhouse near Cincinnati. Ball remained committed to the greenhouse business, working for several different companies in the area until he was in his mid-twenties. Ball's career as a flower grower was interrupted by his service to his country in the Spanish-American war of 1898. After this brief military action, Ball resettled in the Chicago area. He began growing flowers in suburban Glen Ellyn, and brought them to markets in the city by train. By 1905, Ball was known for his improved sweet peas. He founded George J. Ball Inc., and built greenhouses in Glen Ellyn. There he grew not only new strains of sweet peas, but

COMPANY PERSPECTIVES

■

Ball Horticultural Company's mission is to be the world leader in the research, breeding, production and marketing of ornamental crops.

also improved asters and calendulas. He sold these as cut flowers or potted plants to Chicago-area florists.

Ball became financially viable as a seed-producer in 1915 with a lucky crop of so-called "Orange King" calendulas. He sent the "Orange King" seeds to a California grower, where they did very well. By 1918, George J. Ball Inc. was selling mail-order seeds to customers around the country. The company did well through the 1920s, a time of buoyant growth in many American industries, and by 1927, the company had outgrown its Glen Ellyn location. That year, the company moved to a 50-acre plot in another Chicago suburb, West Chicago, where the company headquarters are still located. The company opened a trial garden in West Chicago in 1933. Despite the horrendous economic conditions that gripped most industries during the years of the Great Depression, George J. Ball Inc. apparently continued to do well. Its staple product was still cut flowers, which were in constant demand for occasions like weddings and funerals. Because flowers were tied to social rituals that continued in good times or bad, Ball's industry was relatively recession-proof. So Ball continued to introduce new products in the 1930s. In 1937, the company launched an influential horticulture magazine, *Grower Talks*. George Ball became president of the Society of American Florists in 1938. Ball died in 1949, while travelling to Japan. After his death, his four sons each took a turn running the company.

DIVERSIFICATION AFTER WORLD WAR II

After World War II, many American gardeners became increasingly interested in growing their own vegetables, and Ball branched out into supplying vegetable seeds. Ball bought one wholesale vegetable seed firm in the 1960s, and the company also became increasingly entwined with another American seed producer, W. Atlee Burpee & Co. Burpee was a storied company that had been selling mail-order seeds since the 1880s. Whereas many seeds used by American growers had been imported from Europe, early on, Burpee began hybridizing garden plants that were adapted to North American growing conditions. The company originated many well-

known flower and vegetable varieties, and its catalogs were such a staple of American life that farm children often used them to learn to read. Burpee and Ball did not formally merge until 1991, and then they separated again in the mid-1990s. However, the two companies had close ties from the 1960s onward. Ball was the less visible company, supplying seed and new hybrids, while Burpee was a prominent brand name in American gardening.

Ball also began supplying plants and seeds for the food processing industry after World War II. The company developed types of tomatoes that were ideally suited for making into tomato paste and tomato catsup. The three elder Ball sons, George K., Victor, and Robert, each took an approximately ten-year stint running the company from 1949 until 1970. That year the presidency passed to the youngest of the Ball brothers, G. Carl Ball. While his three brothers had passed the baton among them relatively quickly, G. Carl Ball stayed at the head of Ball Inc. until 1995, when his daughter Anna Caroline Ball took over.

NEW PRODUCTS AND MARKETS: 1970-89

G. Carl Ball was born in 1921. After graduating from high school in Glen Ellyn, he returned to his father's home state, Ohio, and attended Kenyon College until he joined the Air Force in World War II. He had learned to fly planes while still in high school, and in the war he served as a DC-3 pilot. After the war, he became a commercial airline pilot, but he soon gave it up to work for Ball Inc. By 1947, G. Carl Ball had earned a business degree from the University of Illinois, and he joined the family firm, where he eventually became Ball's national sales manager. He was very interested in management techniques, and became a friend and devotee of the management expert Peter Drucker. Drucker authored almost 40 books on management, and in many ways set the agenda for the science of management in the U.S. from the 1970s until the 2000s. Perhaps it was Drucker's influence that led G. Carl Ball to expand the family company into new products and into European markets.

Through 1970, cut flowers, or the seeds and hybrids of cut flowers, were Ball's mainstay. This market, which thrived even during the Depression, had picked up nationwide in the postwar years. Yet G. Carl Ball drove his company in a new direction, believing that bedding plants would be the new trend. Bedding plants are typically annual flowers, that is, cold-sensitive plants that North American gardeners need to plant anew each year. These plants are such staples of American gardens today that it is difficult to imagine they were once only a small

```
┌─────────────────────────────────────────────┐
│                                               │
│              KEY DATES                        │
│                  ■                            │
│                                               │
│  1905:  The company is incorporated as George J. │
│         Ball Inc.                             │
│  1927:  The company moves to new headquarters in │
│         West Chicago.                         │
│  1949:  Founder George Ball dies.             │
│  1970:  G. Carl Ball becomes president.       │
│  1991:  Ball acquires Burpee.                 │
│  1995:  Anna Caroline Ball becomes president, │
│         Burpee is spun off, and the company's │
│         name changes to Ball Horticultural.   │
│  2001:  Ball Horticultural buys the English   │
│         consortium Colegrave Group.           │
│                                               │
└─────────────────────────────────────────────┘
```

piece of the flower market. G. Carl Ball set his company's horticulturists to work hybridizing impatiens, a low-growing, typically red, pink, or white shade-tolerant flower. Ball Inc. developed the first hybrid impatiens seed, and fueled a boom in this plant that began in the mid-1960s and continued in the 2000s. Similarly, Ball Inc. researched new hybrid petunias and brought many varieties to market. Ball remained a behind-the-scenes player, however, and plants that it developed were branded and marketed by other companies, including W. Atlee Burpee.

G. Carl Ball pushed his company to make acquisitions and expand into new markets worldwide. During G. Carl Ball's tenure, the company purchased Petoseed Company, a prominent California firm known especially for its tomato and pepper varieties. Petoseed also marketed its products to home growers through Burpee, while other varieties were geared towards commercial markets. Petoseed expanded into Mexico and was dominant in Western U.S. markets. By 1995, when it combined with several competitors to become Seminis Inc., it had its own European vegetable seed subsidiaries. Ball moved into marketing and distribution in Europe through the 1970s and 1980s. Beginning in the 1980s, the company also began penetrating Asian markets.

REORGANIZATION: 1990-2000

In 1991, Ball Inc. acquired its long-time collaborator, W. Atlee Burpee & Co. The new president of Burpee was G. Carl Ball's son, George Ball Jr., who had previously been head of research and development for Ball Inc. Four years after this merger, Ball Inc. went through some significant transitions. G. Carl Ball retired in 1995 at the age of 74, and was succeeded by his daughter,

Anna Caroline Ball. Anna Ball made swift changes that aimed to narrow the company's commercial focus. Ball wanted to jettison the company's vegetable businesses in order to focus on ornamental plants. Ball Inc. had been spread out, leading the North American market in bedding plants and also selling many new vegetable varieties through Burpee and through its Petoseed subsidiary, which had grown to have international subsidiaries of its own. Anna Ball sold off Burpee, which again became a freestanding entity. Her brother George Ball Jr. remained as head of Burpee. Petoseed was also spun off and combined with several other companies in its industry, becoming Seminis Inc. Ball Inc. then changed its name to Ball Horticultural Company. Anna Ball brought in an outside board for consultation, though she was firmly committed to keeping the company private and under family control.

Anna Ball seemed to have a keen sense of the competitiveness of the current ornamental plant industry. A *Washington Post* profile of Ball in October 2005 compared her to fashion designers like Calvin Klein and Donna Karan, in the sense that she was a visionary trendsetter in a fickle, worldwide market. Ball claimed she was not worried about competition from other horticultural companies as much as she was concerned about other consumer amusements: "What worries me is competing with video phones," she said, continuing, " … we have to keep the eye candy coming. We have to keep producing plants that are unavoidably attractive." To do that, the company emphasized research and development. In 1998, Ball formed a subsidiary called Ball Helix, which developed new techniques in plant breeding and genetics. Ball Helix worked with other Ball subsidiaries around the globe on advanced methods of plant propagation, including tissue culture. And Ball Horticultural already had plant breeding and distribution companies across the planet. With this cutting edge technology, when Ball horticulturalists or even amateur gardeners discovered an interesting new plant, the company was able to rapidly develop it. "We can take something that someone has found in a garden in Hoboken [New Jersey] and sell it in South Africa. We can really give it the light of day," explained a Ball scientist to the Vancouver *Columbian* in June 2005. As an example of how rapidly Ball could bring a fashionable plant forward, in 2003, Ball brought out a new ornamental plant, "Purple Majesty" millet. Only a year later, "Purple Majesty" had found its way into gardens in 24 different countries. Nearly a century after the company's founding, Ball had put together a powerful combination of advanced propagation techniques and widespread distribution to give it truly global influence.

Ball strengthened its ties to European markets by purchasing the British company Colegrave Group in 2001. Colegrave included 11 seed and research companies doing business in England, France, Holland, and Australia. By the mid-2000s, Ball Horticultural claimed 3,000 employees across the globe. With subsidiaries in South America, Korea, Japan, and Australia, its new European group of subsidiaries, and businesses in North America, the company performed such diverse tasks as publishing, biomedical research, marketing, and plant production. In 2005, the company celebrated its first 100 years. Still family-owned, Ball Horticultural was nevertheless a large, complex, and modern company. Its combination of technological savvy, huge distribution reach, and long-standing and thorough knowledge of the ornamental plant market seemed to justify its prominent position in world horticulture.

A. Woodward

PRINCIPAL SUBSIDIARIES

Ball FloraPlant; PanAmerican Seed Co.; Ball Chile; Ball Colombia, Ltda.; Ball Costa Rica S.R.L.; Ball Ecuador Cia, Ltda.; Ball Helix; Ball Publishing; Ball/SB; Ball Seed Co.; Ball Superior; Ball Tagawa Growers; Ball Uruguay; Ball Van Zanten, Ltda. (Brazil); Chrysantis, Inc.; ColorLink; Floricultura & CIA, Ltda. (Guatemala); Linda Vista, S.A. (Costa Rica); Seed Technology Services; Semillas PanAmerican Chile, Ltda.; V+B FloraPlant S.A. de C.V. (Mexico); Ball Australia Pty., Ltd.; Korea-America Plug Co., Ltd.; M&B Flora Co. Ltd. (Japan); T.M. Ball Laboratory Co., Ltd. (Japan); Ball Colegrave, Ltd. (United Kingdom); Ball Ducrettet, S.A.S. (France); Ball Dummen GmbH (Germany); Ball Holland B.V.; Ball Straathof Pty., Ltd. (South Africa); BiGi Seeds SLR (Italy); KinderGarden Plants Ltd. (United Kingdom); Novo Sol Plantas, Ltda. (Portugal); PanAmerican Seed Europe B.V. (Holland).

PRINCIPAL COMPETITORS

Syngenta AG.; Hines Horticulture, Inc.; Vilmarin Clause & Cie.

FURTHER READING

Carlson, Will, "The Guru of Floriculture," *Greenhouse Grower*, November 2004.

Fosdick, Dean, "Gardeners' Creations Take Seed," *Columbian* (Vancouver, B.C.), June 15, 2005, p. D4.

Higgins, Adrian, "Seeds of Doubt," *Washington Post*, October 16, 2005, p. F01.

Kukec, Anna Marie, "Ball Flower Business Grows with West Chicago, Suburbs," *Daily Herald* (Arlington Heights, Ill.), July 23, 2003, p. 18.

Mack, Patricia, "Reaping What He Sowed," *Record* (Bergen County, N.J.), September 26, 2001, p. F01.

"The Passing of a Visionary: G. Carl Ball, 1921-2004," *Ball Foundation Review*, Fall 2004, Volume 4, No. 3, pp. 1-2.

Wisby, Gary, "G. Carl Ball, 83; Headed Innovative Horticultural Firm," *Sun Times* (Chicago), September 22, 2004, p. 93.

Blackwell Publishing
(Holdings) Ltd.

9600 Garsington Road
Oxford,
United Kingdom
Telephone: (44) 01865 776868
Fax: (44) 01865 714591
Web site: http://www.blackwellpublishing.com

Private Company
Founded: 1897 as BH Blackwell
Employees: 923
Sales: £191 million ($367 million) (2004)
NAIC: 511120 Periodical Publishers

■ ■ ■

Blackwell Publishing (Holdings) Ltd. is the world's lead-ing independent and privately owned publisher of scholarly journals and books. The Oxford, England based company publishes more than 800 journals spanning the medical, academic, scientific, and professional fields. Nearly half of the company's journal list is published in partnership with more than 650 academic and profes-sional societies around the world. The company also owns its own list of journals, and continues to acquire new titles from other commercial publishers and from small presses. In addition to journal publishing, Black-well publishes more than 600 new books per year, and maintains a back list of some 4,500 books. Blackwell began as one of Oxford's most renowned bookstores. Throughout the 20th century, Blackwell continued to operate a chain of largely university and academic-oriented bookstores in the United Kingdom. In the mid-

2000s the company adopted a new strategy focusing on its publishing wing; it began selling off its retail opera-tions in 2005. The company continues to expand its reach, however, through the development of Blackwell Synergy, which provides online, full-text access to the company's journal list. The company also operates a number of research portal web sites, focusing on such specialties as literature, history, linguistics and gastroenterology. Blackwell maintains a global presence, with subsidiaries and offices in the United States, Australia, Germany, Denmark, Japan, China, and, since October 2005, in Singapore. Blackwell is a privately owned company; nearly all of the company's shares are held by the founding Blackwell family.

FAMED BOOKSTORE IN THE 19TH CENTURY

The Blackwell family's involvement in England's book selling and publishing trades began in the mid-19th century, when Benjamin Harris Blackwell first began selling books in Oxford in 1846. Blackwell's son, Benjamin Henry Blackwell, later established his own bookshop in Oxford in 1879. That store soon became an Oxford landmark, and gained a global reputation as being one of the world's finest bookstores. B.H. Black-well *Booksellers*, as the store became known, entered the publishing side before the end of the century with the production of *Mensae Secundae*, written by H.C. Beech-ing and published in 1897.

Blackwell continued to add new titles into the new century. While Benjamin Blackwell focused on operating the book store, he turned to son Basil H. Blackwell to develop the family's publishing operation. The younger Blackwell accordingly started his career at the Oxford University Press, based in London. By 1913, however, Basil Blackwell had gained sufficient experience to return to Oxford and take over the family's publishing business. Exempted from military service during World War I because of poor eyesight, Basil Blackwell focused his efforts on publishing, while his father took care of the family's thriving book selling business.

Blackwell's publishing interests led him to form a partnership in 1920 with Bernard Newdigate and others in order to take over the Shakespeare Head Press in Stratford-upon-Avon, founded in 1904. Newdigate had already established a reputation as one of England's most distinguished printers and typesetters, a position he confirmed at the Shakespeare Head Press. The collaboration between Blackwell and Newdigate continued for more than two decades. In the meantime, Blackwell launched another publishing business, forming a partnership with Adrian Mott in 1922. Blackwell & Mott Limited, as the new company was called, formed one of the cornerstones of the later Blackwell Publishing Limited. Through the 1920s, Blackwell & Mott established itself as a prominent literary house, publishing such authors as W. H. Auden, J. R. R. Tolkien, and Graham Greene.

The death of Benjamin Blackwell in 1924 forced Basil Blackwell to place his publishing interests on the back burner as he took over the leadership of the family bookselling operation. Blackwell nonetheless remained active in publishing, and in 1929 moved the Shakespeare Head Press to Oxford. That house remained in operation until 1942. By then, Blackwell had already expanded into what later became the group's main business focus, the publication of scientific and scholarly works.

In 1939, Blackwell founded Blackwell Scientific Publications (BSP). That business initially focused on publishing books for the medical market. By the early 1950s, BSP had expanded its range to include the distribution of medical textbooks brought in from the United States and Canada. Within a few years, BSP had established itself as a small but respected medical publisher, with sales of £23,000 per year.

SCHOLARLY PUBLISHING: 1950-60

The arrival of Richard Blackwell, son of Basil Blackwell, into the company in the early 1950s marked the beginning of a new era for Blackwell. The younger Blackwell was credited with transforming the company from a small family business into one of the world's pre-eminent academic publishers. Another major figure in the company's success was Denmark native Per Saugman, who was appointed the managing director of BSP in 1954. Saugman led Blackwell's foray into the publishing of scholarly journals, with the launch of the *British Journal of Haematology*. The Blackwell family also confirmed its position as a publisher of scholarly works when, in 1953, Basil Blackwell reached an agreement to publish the entire body of work by analytic philosopher Ludwig Wittgenstein.

Blackwell expanded strongly through the 1960s. The BSP wing of the family's operations established an office in Edinburgh, Scotland. Initially meant to provide support to the company's book publishing operations, the Edinburgh office soon focused on publishing journals, and helped lead Blackwell's extension into biology. By the end of the decade, BSP was already a well-respected journal publisher in the international market. Blackwell itself had developed an international component, acquiring Denmark's Munksgaard, based in Copenhagen. That purchase enabled Blackwell to extend its publication reach into the fields of dermatology, immunology and dentistry, among others. By 1970, Saugman had succeeded in expanding BSP's annual revenues to more than £1 million.

Blackwell's expansion continued through the 1970s. The company entered Australia, establishing a joint venture through BSP in Melbourne in 1971. The company took full control of its Australian operations in 1984, and used its Melbourne base to expand into Japan, and later into other Asian markets. Blackwell also moved into the North American market, notably through the acquisition of Richard Abel, an important supplier to the library market that had gone bankrupt. That purchase led to the formation of Blackwell North America in 1982. Back at home, Blackwell's book publishing business acquired Martin Robertson. The purchase brought in David Martin as Basil Blackwell Ltd's managing director. Under Martin, that company, which would become Blackwell Publishers in 1991, shifted its primary focus to the academic book market,

KEY DATES

1846: Benjamin Harris Blackwell begins selling books in Oxford, England.

1879: Blackwell's son, Benjamin Henry Blackwell, opens his own store, B.H. Blackwell *Booksellers*, in Oxford, and is later joined by his son, Basil Blackwell.

1920: Basil Blackwell forms a partnership with Bernard Newdigate and others in order to take over the Shakespeare Head Press in Stratford-upon-Avon.

1922: Basil Blackwell and Adrian Mott form a new publishing company called Blackwell & Mott.

1929: The Shakespeare Head Press moves to Oxford.

1939: Blackwell Scientific Publishers (BSP) is launched.

1954: BSP publishes its first scholarly journal, The British Journal of Haematology.

1963: Blackwell acquires Munksgaard, in Copenhagen, Denmark.

1971: Through BSP, Blackwell forms a joint venture in Melbourne, entering the Australian market.

1982: The company acquires bankrupt library supplier Richard Abel, which leads to the formation of Blackwell North America.

1987: Blackwell purchases Collins Professional & Technical, forming the basis of BSP's Professional Division.

1988: Blackwell enters the French and German markets through acquisitions.

1993: BSP becomes Blackwell Science, and the company enters the Japanese market as Blackwell Scientific Publications Asia.

1999: Blackwell acquires the Iowa State Press.

2001: Blackwell Publishers and Blackwell Science merge to form Blackwell Publishing Ltd.

2004: Blackwell opens an office in Shanghai, China.

2005: The company launches a subsidiary in Singapore.

helping to establish the company as a world leader. In another expansion effort, the company founded University Bookshops, a joint venture with Oxford University, in order to supply academic books to the growing number of new universities in the United Kingdom.

By then, Blackwell's had undergone a changing of the guard, following Richard Blackwell's death in 1980, and Basil Blackwell's death in 1984. The company remained firmly in the Blackwell family's hands, and members of the family remained active in the company's direction as well. Through the end of the decade, the group's expansion continued, particularly through acquisitions, which permitted the company to enter the French and German markets. Acquisition also allowed Blackwell to broaden its range, as with the purchase of Collins Professional & Technical in 1987, which formed the foundation of BSP's Professional Division.

BSP's entry into the Japanese market came in 1993, with the formation of Blackwell Scientific Publications Asia. In that year, BSP changed its name to Blackwell Science. The company also developed a new subsidiary operation, Blackwell Healthare Communication, which partnered with and targeted the pharmaceutical industry. Blackwell Publishers, in the meantime, had begun increasingly to target the North American market, in an effort to establish itself as a world leader in a number of publishing segments. As a result, the company captured the world lead in the social sciences and humanities segments by the middle of the 1990s. In 1999, Blackwell boosted its North American presence through the purchase of Iowa State Press. This purchase helped shift the group's focus, with more than half of its revenues coming from North America by the early 2000s.

INTERNATIONAL LEADER IN THE NEW CENTURY

Blackwell had in the meantime begun to explore new horizons, and especially the growing Internet market. In 1999, the company launched its own online effort, Blackwell Synergy, providing online access to the full text of its journals. Throughout the 1990s and into the 2000s, Blackwell also moved to increase its portfolio of titles; by the middle of the 2000s, the company more than doubled its title list, topping 800 in 2006. A major part of this effort came through partnerships with small university presses or private publishers which turned over the publication of their journals to Blackwell. At the same time, Blackwell continued to acquire other publishers, including Futura Publishing Company and its 42 journals, purchased in 2002.

Until the early 2000s, Blackwell Publishers and Blackwell Science had operated as separate companies under the Blackwell family's control. In 2001, however, the two companies were merged under a single holding company, Blackwell Publishing Ltd. The move seemed to spark a family feud, as members of the Blackwell family began to disagree about the company's direction and even found themselves faced with a hostile takeover offer. The company remained in the Blackwell family's control, however, and remained committed to its status as a private company.

Into the mid-2000s, Blackwell adapted its strategy to the shifting global market. The company announced its decision to sell off many of its retail holdings, which by then numbered some 50 stores. The first store sell off was completed in the first half of 2005.

Blackwell set its sights on expanding its publishing presence in the booming Asian market. The company opened a new office in Shanghai, China, in 2004. The October of the following year, Blackwell expanded its regional presence with the opening of a new subsidiary in Singapore. These efforts quickly paid off, and by the beginning of 2006, Blackwell could already boast a portfolio of more than 100 journal titles in the Asian market. In early 2006 the company announced it expected to add as many as 60 new titles in the year to come, boosting its total to more than 800. From a small bookstore in Oxford, the Blackwell name had grown into the world's leading international society journal publisher.

M.L. Cohen

PRINCIPAL SUBSIDIARIES

Blackwell Asia (Japan); Blackwell Futura (United States); Blackwell Munksgaard (Denmark); Blackwell Publishing Asia (Australia); Blackwell Publishing Inc. (United States); Blackwell Publishing Ltd.; Blackwell Publishing Professional (United States); Blackwell Publishing Services Singapore PTE Ltd.; Blackwell Publishing Shanghai (PRC); Blackwell Verlag (Germany).

PRINCIPAL COMPETITORS

ABC Inc.; Bertelsmann AG; Bio-It World Inc.; VNU Business Media Europe Ltd.; Reed Elsevier N.V.; Quebecor Inc.; Recruit Company Ltd.; R.R. Donnelley and Sons Co.; Wolters Kluwer N.V.

FURTHER READING

"After 125 Years of Building a Diverse Retail Portfolio," *Bookseller*, November 26, 2004, p. 7.

Aronovich, Hanna, "Making an Imprint: Through Unified Operations and Strategic Acquisitions, Blackwell Publishing Says It Is Leading the Academic Market," *U.S. Business Review*, April 2005, p. 99.

"Blackwell Boosts Professional Society Publishing in Asia," *Access*, June 2005.

"Blackwell Profits from Journal Expansion," *Information World Review*, July 25, 2005, p. 3.

Bury, Liz, "Blackwell Publishing Builds on Merger," *Bookseller*, June 11, 2004, p. 8.

——, "China Base for Blackwell," *Bookseller*, September 3, 2004, p. 9.

Cave, Andrew, "Blackwell Investors to Press for Sale," *Daily Telegraph*, January 25, 2002.

Dean, Jonathan, "Blackwell Bulks Up Journals List," *Bookseller*, October 22, 2004, p. 10.

"Four New Journals from Blackwell Publishing," *Business Publisher*, May 16, 2005, p. 4.

Fraser, Fiona, "Blackwell's Sells Off First Store," *Bookseller*, April 22, 2005, p. 8.

——, "Blackwell's Rebels Fight Back," *Bookseller*, December 3, 2004, p. 7.

Rushton, Katherine, "Blackwell Grows Sales by 10%," *Bookseller*, June 25, 2005, p. 8.

Strydom, Martin, "New Chapter in Blackwell Flight," *Daily Telegraph*, January 14, 2002, p. 35.

Blizzard Entertainment

———————— ■ ————————

P.O. Box 18979
Irvine, California 92623
U.S.A.
Telephone: (949) 955-1380
Toll Free: (800) 953-7669
Fax: (949) 737-2000
Web site: http://www.blizzard.com

Division of Vivendi Universal S.A.
Incorporated: 1991 as Silicone & Synapse
Employees: 750
Sales: $750 million (2005 est.)
NAIC: 511210 Software Publishers

■ ■ ■

Blizzard Entertainment makes the world's most popular online computer game, World of Warcraft. The company was an early leader in the field of so-called massively multiplayer online games with a string of hits including Diablo, Warcraft, and Starcraft. These are essentially role-playing games, similar to the long-popular Dungeons and Dragons, in that players create characters that acquire powers, carry out quests, and kill enemies while interacting with other player-created characters. Blizzard Entertainment brings in revenue both by selling the game software and by collecting monthly user fees. World of Warcraft has as many as 5 million subscribers worldwide, with over 1 million in North America and another 1.5 million in China. Other subscribers are in Europe, Australia, New Zealand, and South Korea. Blizzard thus dominates the industry, as the games of its

next nearest competitor claim only 1.8 million subscribers. Blizzard was founded by three avid gamers in 1991, and has gone through a series of owners. The company is now a part of the French conglomerate Vivendi S.A. and its Vivendi Universal Games division.

AT THE DAWN OF THE INDUSTRY: 1990

Blizzard Entertainment began as a game software developer called Silicone & Synapse. Three friends, Allen Adham, Michael Morhaime, and Frank Pearce, started the firm in Irvine, California, in 1991. For the company's first three years, Silicone & Synapse was a third-party developer, working on software to support games created by other companies. This was evidently a successful niche, and Silicone & Synapse worked on games for Sega Genesis, Super Nintendo, and DOS- and Mac-compatible games for personal computers. Some games Silicone & Synapse worked on included popular titles such as The Lost Vikings, The Death and Return of Superman, Rock 'n Roll Racing, and Blackthorne.

In 1994, Silicone & Synapse changed its name to Blizzard Entertainment and released the first of its own game titles. This was the first edition of Warcraft, called Warcraft: Orcs and Humans, which won accolades as one of the best strategy games of the year. The game featured a blighted landscape, ruined by a long-running war between humans and orcs. The game's kingdom of Azeroth had a quasi-medieval feel, long a popular formula among game makers, and players chose characters and developed strategies to allow survival in this perilous place.

In 1994, multiplayer computer games were still relatively new. The ancestor of multiuser online games like Warcraft and World of Warcraft grew out of the role-play board game Dungeons and Dragons. The first multiplayer computer version of Dungeons and Dragons debuted in 1978 as MUD1. According to Steven L. Kent's history of multiplayer online games in a September 2003 article in *Gamespy*, "All the elements of MMOGs (massively multiplayer online games) existed by the late eighties, but they did not exist in a single product." Some early games were text based, with words scrolling across a static graphic background. In the mid-1980s, a few games existed that could link as many as 16 people playing at once through a single server. Other games had developed a so-called "persistent world," where the game landscape did not start over from the beginning every time a player logged on. Most multiplayer games required players to log on to a proprietary network set up by the game maker, or to a service such as CompuServe or America Online, and pay by the hour or the minute. Some games thus brought in a lot of revenue, as dedicated gamers played for hours every week. According to a history of the gaming industry from *Computer Graphic World* in March 2002, the first multiplayer game to break out of the hardcore gaming niche and do well at a retail level was Meridian 59, which came out in 1996, two years after Warcraft.

So while Blizzard's Warcraft was a highly touted game, it was not as popular as console games like Nintendo products, or single-player computer games, which dominated the game market in the early 1990s. Warcraft's early buyers would have been aficionados who had the time, money, and technical know-how to access and play the game. A July 1997 profile of the gaming industry published in the *New York Times* described typical players as "hundreds of thousands of well educated, technically savvy, bewilderingly intense men (mostly) who spend hour upon week locked in various sorts of virtual combat." When Warcraft was first introduced, it was not mainstream entertainment, but a product that appealed to a niche of dedicated fantasy game enthusiasts.

UNDER VARIOUS OWNERS IN THE LATER PART OF THE DECADE

In 1994, the same year that the first Warcraft game came out, Blizzard's founders sold the company to a Los Angeles firm called Davidson & Associates for $7 million. Davidson & Associates was run by a couple, Jan and Bob Davidson, who had developed and marketed an extremely successful educational computer game for children called Math Blaster. The Davidsons "never told us what to do," claimed Blizzard founder Morhaime in an interview with the *Los Angeles Times* in September 2003. But Blizzard passed through several more owners who were not always so hands-off.

In 1995, Blizzard introduced a new version of Warcraft, called Warcraft II: Tides of Darkness. The next year, Blizzard acquired another California gaming company, Condor Inc., and renamed it Blizzard North. Blizzard North's programmers were principally responsible for Blizzard's next hit, Diablo. The company launched a free online service called Battlenet in 1996 so that more people could play Diablo simultaneously. Diablo itself was not launched until almost two months later, behind schedule. Though it came out just after the Christmas buying season, on December 30, 1996, Diablo went on to be the best-selling game of 1997. By that time, massively multiplayer online games were edging into the mainstream. Diablo and competitors' games such as Everquest and Ultima Online all attracted much bigger markets in the late 1990s than their predecessors had a few years earlier. By that time, too, the industry's revenue model had changed, and players could pay a subscription fee for unlimited play within a certain time period, rather than pay a private network by the minute. This seemed to make the games more accessible. Blizzard came out with another number one game in 1998, Starcraft.

Blizzard had been a subsidiary of Davidson & Associates since 1994. In 1996, Davidson & Associates was bought in a stock swap valued at approximately $1 billion by a company called CUC International Inc. CUC International's principal business was running shopping clubs, which offered members discounts on all sorts of products through catalog sales and telemarketing. CUC's founder, Walter Forbes, had been interested in something like Internet shopping in the early 1970s, before there was an Internet. An earlier incarnation of his company had failed, but by 1997, the company had

KEY DATES

■

1991: Company is founded as Silicone & Synapse.
1994: Name is changed to Blizzard Entertainment; company releases first game title, Warcraft, and is acquired by Davidson & Associates.
1996: Davidson is acquired by CUC International; Blizzard releases Diablo.
1998: Blizzard becomes a part of Vivendi Universal Games division.
2000: Diablo II sells a million copies in its first month.
2004: Company releases World of Warcraft.

revenue of some $2 billion, generated through 73 million memberships in its 20 different clubs.

Davidson & Associates actually seemed something of an odd fit for CUC. But soon after acquiring Davidson, CUC bought two other West Coast computer game companies, Sierra Online Inc. and Knowledge Adventure Inc. These companies were then put together as an operating unit called CUC Software, though they retained their separate names and management. Jan and Bob Davidson remained with their company for only a short time after they sold it to CUC. Then in late 1997, CUC announced that it was merging with a huge hotel franchise company called HFS, owner of well-known brands such as Howard Johnson, Days Inn, and Ramada Inn. HFS also owned the Avis car rental firm and three leading real estate agencies, Coldwell Banker, Century 21, and ERA. The combination of HFS and CUC International led to a new company called Cendant Corporation with revenues in the neighborhood of $5 billion.

Blizzard Entertainment became part of a unit within a much larger company whose principal businesses were in unrelated industries: hotels, realty, and shopping clubs. Working under this management umbrella apparently caused friction at Blizzard. A team of 11 software developers left Blizzard in 1998 to start their own company, citing a lack of creative freedom as their reason for leaving. The seceding designers also hinted at problems with Blizzard's parent. These sentiments were echoed a few years later when the founders of Blizzard North left the company. Yet despite some apparent chafing in its role as a small cog in a big conglomerate, Blizzard continued to turn out best-selling products which became increasingly profitable.

In late 1998, Blizzard's parent Cendant announced that it was selling its software division, comprising Knowledge Adventure, Blizzard, Davidson & Associates, and Sierra Online, to a French company called Havas SA for $800 million. Cendant explained the sale by saying it wanted to shed its noncore businesses. Havas was a division of the French conglomerate Vivendi S.A., and Blizzard soon became a subsidiary of Vivendi grouped into its Vivendi Universal Games division. Vivendi had a leading share in the telecommunications market in France, and also ran Universal Music Group, a global music company comprised of several well-known labels.

MOVING INTO THE MAINSTREAM IN 2000 AND BEYOND

Blizzard was yet again a small part of a large conglomerate with several other principal businesses when it joined Vivendi in 1998. It may, however, have been a good thing to get out from under Cendant, which soon began to unravel under charges of accounting fraud. Cendant's chief financial officer pleaded guilty to several criminal charges in 2000 and testified against his boss, company founder Walter Forbes, and Cendant's vice-chairman E. Kirk Shelton. Trials relating to Cendant were still ongoing in 2005, but the amount of fraud, which apparently originated in CUC International's shopping clubs, was said to reach $14 billion.

Meanwhile Blizzard continued to do what it did best. The company released a sequel to its 1997 hit Diablo in 2000, called Diablo II. Diablo was so popular that Blizzard needed to do next-to-no marketing in order to promote the sequel, which sold more than a million copies in its first month of sales. This was astonishing, given that the entire computer game market was estimated at 170 million units sold annually. The computer game market had grown tremendously by 2000, with the number of games sold tripling between 1993 and 1999. The market continued double-digit growth in 2000, at a time when other media such as books, movies, and recorded music, showed flat or declining sales. An article about Diablo II in the *New York Times* in August 2000 compared the game's success to the tremendous selling power of J.K. Rowling's Harry Potter children's book series. While the Potter books were an obvious juggernaut, Diablo II had a comparable though lower-profile following, and revenue was also similar. Diablo II retailed for over $50 in the United States, while the fourth volume of the Potter series, released at almost the same time, sold for less than $30 and was often deeply discounted. Diablo II brought in something in the neighborhood of $50 million in the first month of its release. Then in 2001, Blizzard came out with an expansion set for Diablo II called Diablo II: Lord of Destruction, and this too sold more than a million copies in its first month.

By the early 2000s, massively multiplayer online games had reached new popularity. Blizzard had many competitors, including Verant/Sony Interactive Studios, which put out Everquest, Origin Systems, with Ultima Online, and NCsoft, which dominated South Korea's passionate online gaming market. The games were getting better in terms of graphics and support, and subscribers paid substantially less in user fees in the 2000s than they had in the early 1990s, when an hour of play might cost from $20 to $30. Blizzard's third version of Warcraft, Warcraft III: Reign of Chaos, came out in 2002, and according to company documents, it was the "fastest selling PC game ever." Blizzard released an expansion, Warcraft III: The Frozen Throne, in 2003.

Blizzard had revenue of approximately $750 million in 2002, which represented more than 10 percent of parent Vivendi's total revenue. Warcraft III: The Frozen Throne alone made up 25 percent of Vivendi's games unit's revenue. Yet despite the evident success of the subsidiary, Vivendi announced that it wanted to shed its entire games unit, along with its Universal movie studio, Universal Music, and Universal theme parks, in order to raise cash to pay off debts. Friction between Blizzard and Vivendi caused four top game developers to leave Blizzard in 2003. Vivendi had hoped for $2 billion for its games division, and then reportedly was considering a lower price of $800 million. Uncertainty about the sale evidently made things difficult at Blizzard, and more key designers left the company over the next two years, including Blizzard cofounder Allen Adham.

In 2004, Blizzard released its most successful game by far, World of Warcraft. The game broke all previous sales records for a PC-based computer game. It promptly collected 1.5 million subscribers in North America, and then took off across Europe and Asia. It sold more than 280,000 copies on the first day it was available in Europe. Though only games with an Asian flavor were said to do well in China, World of Warcraft became one of the top games in that country as soon as it was released there, and Chinese players eventually outnumbered North Americans. World of Warcraft was indeed something of a category-killer, vastly outselling its competitors. The Korean company NCsoft had subscriber bases of some 1.8 million players for its top two games, but World of Warcraft had reached 5 million subscribers by mid-2005. Competitors could not equal World of Warcraft even if they could reproduce the polished graphics and exciting storylines. According to the *New York Times* in September 2005, a Sony multiplayer online game based on the hit movie series *The Matrix* had to axe six of its virtual worlds, leaving only three for its 50,000 subscribers, because "users were having a hard time finding one another in the game's vast digital ghost town."

Since players paid a monthly subscription fee and spent hours online, gamers were unlikely to pay for more than perhaps two games at once. So World of Warcraft effectively dominated the online gaming world, where at peak times roughly 250,000 people might be simultaneously playing it. Blizzard was a bit unprepared for the enthusiastic response to World of Warcraft. One Blizzard principal detailed to the *New York Times* in February 2005 how he had left a little early for a World of Warcraft promotion event that the company expected would draw maybe 2,500 people. More than twice that many people showed up, and the Blizzard executive was barely able to make it through the crowd to the store where the game was being sold.

Users apparently loved the new game for its many complex worlds. Because people played against other people online instead of against computer-created characters, World of Warcraft took on a social dimension often thought missing from single-player computer games. The game's virtual world also began to leak in odd ways into the real world. Players could earn virtual gold in the game, but Blizzard experienced terrific problems when some players turned thief and stole World of Warcraft money, then sold it for real money on eBay. Blizzard closed the accounts of over 1,000 players in 2005, suspecting them of being "gold farmers." Players also sometimes paid other players to operate their characters for them, because they didn't want to wade through the early levels of the game. In late 2005, some World of Warcraft characters became infected with a fantasy disease called Corrupted Blood, which then spread throughout several areas of the game like a real-world medical epidemic. This virtual plague attracted the interest of genuine epidemiologists, who were interested in the social aspects of the disease's spread. With millions of players, World of Warcraft found a mainstream status other online games had not reached. By the end of 2005, Blizzard was reportedly at work on a new version of Starcraft, and there was no mention of Vivendi's plan to sell the company.

A. Woodward

PRINCIPAL COMPETITORS

Ncsoft Corporation; Warner Brothers Interactive Entertainment; Origin Software Systems.

FURTHER READING

Berenson, Alex, "Watch Your Back, Harry Potter," *New York Times,* August 3, 2000, p. C1.

"Blizzard under a Cloud," *Orange County Business Journal,* September 28, 1998, p. 3.

Chuang, Tamara, "Key Departures Foul Weather at Blizzard," *Orange County Register,* July 2, 2003, p. OC.

Goodfellow, Kris, "Playing for Profits," *New York Times,* July 7, 1997, p. D4.

Kent, Steven L., "Alternate Reality," *Gamespy,* September 23, 2003, p. NA.

Moltenbrey, Karen, "Gaming for the Masses," *Computer Graphics World,* March 2002, p. 12.

Nuttall, Chris, "Virtual War Game that Has Delivered Pots of Real Gold," *Financial Times,* May 23, 2005, p. 18.

O'Sullivan, Kate, "Jail Time for Cosmo?" *CFO,* February 2005, p. 72.

Pham, Alex, "Vivendi Leaving Blizzard in Cloud of Uncertainty," *Los Angeles Times,* September 1, 2003, p. C1.

Scheisel, Seth, "Conqueror in a War of Virtual Worlds," *New York Times,* September 6, 2005, p. E1.

———, "Die, Vile Orc! Never, Puny Human!" *New York Times,* July 7, 1997, pp. D1, D4.

———, "The Game Is a Hit, But the Work Isn't Done," *New York Times,* February 10, 2005, p. G1.

Turner, Dan, "East Coast Firm Takes Over Two of L.A.'s Hottest Software Outfits," *Los Angeles Business Journal,* February 17, 1997, p. 8.

Walt, Vivienne, "Birth of an Internet Salesman," *U.S. News & World Report,* December 22, 1997, p. 33.

BOC Group plc

Chertsey Road
Windlesham, GU20 6HJ
United Kingdom
Telephone: (44) 1276 477 222
Fax: (44) 1276 471 333
Web site: http://www.boc.com

Public Company
Incorporated: 1886 as Brin's Oxygen Co., Ltd.
Employees: 30,000
Sales: £4.61 billion ($7.9 billion) (2005)
Stock Exchanges: London New York
Ticker Symbol: BOC.L BOX
NAIC: 325120 Industrial Gas Manufacturing; 325412 Pharmaceutical Preparation Manufacturing; 339112 Surgical and Medical Instrument Manufacturing; 541611 Administrative Management and General Management Consulting Services

■ ■ ■

BOC Group plc is one of the world's largest producers of the industrial gases essential to almost every manufacturing process. It supplies the petroleum, electronic, steel manufacturing, metal producing and fabricating, construction, ceramic, and food and beverage industries. Industrial gases make up more than 80 percent of revenues. The company also provides vacuum technology through BOC Edwards and distribution services through its Gist unit. Its principal related companies operate in about 50 countries across the globe.

COMPANY ORIGINS

Although oxygen had been used in an extremely limited capacity since the late 18th century as a respiratory agent, the development of chemically produced oxygen was hampered by costly methods, yielding only small amounts of relatively impure gases. Commercially produced oxygen was largely confined to "limelight," used to illuminate the stages of theaters and music halls, and that popular means of entertainment and enlightenment, the lantern lecture.

In 1885 two French brothers and chemists, Arthur and Leon Quentin Brin, traveled to the Inventions Exhibition in South Kensington, London, and erected a demonstration of their recently patented method of making oxygen by heating barium oxide, with a view to attracting financial support. They found it in Henry Sharp, an English stoneware manufacturer. In January of 1886 the brothers established Brin's Oxygen Company Ltd.

In the spring of 1886 the fledgling company hired its first foreman, a young Scotsman by the name of Kenneth Sutherland Murray. A man of remarkable mechanical ingenuity, Murray redesigned the plant in his first year on the job. In 1888 the new plant went into operation and production increased from nearly 145,000 to 690,000 cubic feet of oxygen. One year later the plant installed an automatic gear, invented by Murray, and improved Brin's production to nearly a million cubic feet of oxygen a year.

From the beginning, however, limelight was a limited market, and so the company board members searched for new ideas to develop oxygen sales. They

COMPANY PERSPECTIVES

The BOC Group is built around its customers. Whatever the industry or interest, our goal is to respond to their needs as quickly and effectively as possible. Their ever-changing requirements are the driving force behind the development of all our products, technologies and support services. We recognize that BOC people are our most important asset, and through them we ensure that we play a full and active role in communities around the world and are committed to the highest standards of safety and environmental practice. At the same time, we believe that the best way we can assist any of the communities in which we operate is to build a successful business. That's why, as the BOC Group continues to expand and develop, one thing will never change. We will always remain built around our customers.

promoted the use of oxygen in preserving milk, bleaching sugar, manufacturing saccharine, vinegar and linoleum, maturing whisky, and in the production of iron and steel. They hired a horse and carriage for the express purpose of "pushing business." As a result, sales of oxygenated water in any form, flavored or not, increased dramatically. Moreover, the beverage found favor among temperance groups. The company published signed physicians' testimonials extolling the virtues of this new "health" drink, prescribing it as a sort of universal remedy.

The company then turned its attention to the means of gas containment and distribution. The early method of storing and distributing gas, the gas bag, was an inefficient method which resulted in a significant loss of both gas and profit, and was soon replaced by the sturdier iron cylinder. However, even with this vast improvement over the gas bag, the new method of containment was cumbersome and costly. The cylinder itself weighed and cost more than the gas it held, making the product economically impractical to distribute over a large geographical area. Consequently, in 1887, under the guiding hand of Henry Sharp, Brin's began granting licenses to a handful of independent companies throughout Great Britain to produce oxygen under the patented Brin process. In 1890 Brin's introduced another improvement in containment, a steel cylinder, which soon became the standard of gas containment worldwide, and expanded its production to related products, such as valves and fittings.

At the same time, in a move that marked the beginning of the company's international growth, Brin's began exporting oxygen in cylinders to Australia for medical use, and developed plants in France, Germany and the United States, granting them sole rights to operate under the Brin process.

In the decade that followed, Brin's did little more than consolidate its operations and improve its market share. The company took over two of the British companies which had been granted licenses earlier to produce its product. The company also elected its second chairman, Edward Badouin Ellice-Clark. After several years into his chairmanship, Ellice-Clark expressed some regret that the industry had produced no advances in the application of industrial oxygen.

By 1900, however, a new method of producing oxygen by converting air to liquid had been devised independently in Britain, the United States and Germany. The German scientist reached a patent office first, and the patent went to Dr. Carl von Linde. Brin's almost immediately negotiated an agreement to use the Linde patents and within several years abandoned both its now dated barium oxide method of oxygen production and the company name. In 1906 Brin's Oxygen Company Ltd. became the British Oxygen Company Ltd., or BOC.

EARLY 20TH CENTURY EXPANSION

There followed steady expansion spurred by development of new technologies using oxygen in metal cutting and welding. In 1914 Britain declared war on Germany, and business increased significantly. No previous war had equaled the output of munitions, and the essential element of oxygen was apparent in almost every aspect of munitions production. Every means of transport, including ships, tanks and trucks, involved either metal cutting or welding, usually both.

BOC continued to grow in the immediate post-World War I years through acquisitions and through development in the commercial use of products such as acetylene and the rare gases. These various gases, with their exotic sounding names of argon, krypton, helium, neon and xenon, were developed and marketed for use in such products as the neon light, fog lamps, miner's lamps, respiratory gas in obstetric analgesia, and as protection for divers against the "bends."

In 1920 BOC acquired a London company called Sparklets Ltd. A major producer of small arms munitions during World War I, Sparklets had originally formed for the purpose of manufacturing small bulbs of carbon dioxide for carbonated drinks. Ten years later,

KEY DATES

1886: Brin's Oxygen Co., Ltd., established in London by two French chemists, mainly supplying oxygen gas for theatrical limelight.

1887: Company begins licensing its manufacturing process.

1890: Brin's exports oxygen in newly invented steel cylinders as far as Australia.

1906: Brin's is renamed British Oxygen Company Ltd. after licensing new German method of producing liquid oxygen.

1914: Wartime welding boosts oxygen demand; new gases are developed for commercial use.

1935: Etonox anesthetic gas is introduced.

1968: Company embarks on new ventures in liquid nitrogen and refrigeration.

1970: Diversification campaign is launched.

1978: U.S. industrial gases giant Airco is acquired after 11 years of antitrust litigation.

1982: United States-based Glasrock Home Health Care is acquired.

1985: BOC enters the Chinese market.

1993: Healthcare businesses are combined into Ohmeda unit.

1990: BOC begins an international buying spree and expands into distribution business.

1998: The Ohmeda healthcare businesses are divested.

2000: Federal Trade Commission blocks takeover of BOC by Air Liquide and Air Products.

2005: BOC agrees to be acquired by Germany's Linde AG.

BOC merged with Allen-Liversidge Ltd., a South African company with whom BOC had collaborated throughout the 1920s in further developing the acetylene welding process. In 1925 Kenneth Sutherland Murray, the company's first foreman, was appointed chairman.

TECHNOLOGICAL ADVANCES IN THE WAR YEARS

As an adjunct to its admittedly limited production of medical oxygen, and in response to a request by the National Birthday Trust Fund, BOC designed a machine for use by midwives in 1935 called the "Queen Charlotte's Gas-Air Analgesia Apparatus." Soon afterwards, BOC introduced an improved anesthetic gas, called "Entonox," used extensively to ease pain in child-birth and which was available in ambulances for use during emergencies.

That same year, in a pioneering accomplishment, the company set up a separate medical division equipped to install oxygen which would be available "on tap" by means of an extensive circuit of copper pipes connecting hospital wards and operating theaters to a battery of cylinders usually located in the basement of a hospital. Four years later, the company developed a machine which was the forerunner of surgical anesthetic equipment in use today. In an effort to further increase its welding interests, during 1936 BOC acquired the Quasi-Arc Company, a British company which had a refined welding electrode instrument that improved the process of arc welding.

With the onset of World War II, BOC produced gases for munitions and for medical needs. The Air Ministry enlisted the assistance of the company to produce oxygen and equipment designed to withstand high pressures for the Royal and allied Air Forces. Sparklets again began producing a variety of its unique bulbs, including bulbs used to inflate lifejackets; bulbs filled with insecticide, used to protect soldiers against malaria; bulbs used to lower landing gear in emergencies; and larger bulbs filled with ether, enabling engines to quick-start in the below-freezing Russian temperatures.

By 1950 BOC had formed subsidiary companies in over 20 countries. It was a decade that brought with it a revolution in the manufacture of steel as an increased demand for automobiles also led to increased productivity in both the steel and the gases industries. The common method of tanking liquid oxygen to various industries to be evaporated, pressurized and then fed to furnaces proved inadequate to the new demands of steel-making. The search for a new method gave rise to the production of "tonnage" oxygen.

A variation of medical oxygen on tap, tonnage oxygen is, as the name suggests, the production of oxygen by the ton. Rather than tank in the oxygen, and then have it converted, tonnage plants were built on or near the customer site to pump in the already converted oxygen by pipeline. Toward the end of the 1950s BOC was supplying tonnage oxygen to Wimpey for use in rocket motor testing and liquid oxygen for the launching sites of the Thor and Blue Streak missiles. For use in manufacturing semiconductor devices, BOC began supplying argon to Texas Instruments.

In 1957 the British Monopolies and Restrictive Practices Commission published a report stating that the company's prices for oxygen and dissolved acetylene were "unjustifiably high" and operated "against the public interest." According to the report, BOC had deliberately set out to build a monopoly. Successfully so, it would seem, as by this time the company had managed to secure 98 percent of the British market. The commission disclosed BOC's practice of providing plant equipment under highly restrictive conditions, and stated that BOC had concealed ownership of several of its subsidiaries while at the same time pretending to be in competition with them in a deliberate effort to drive up prices.

The report was the most scathing ever produced by the commission, according to one reporter. However, at the same time, the commission admitted there was nothing to suggest that BOC was operating under substandard levels of efficiency in any area, as might otherwise be expected in a company of similar standing and resources. The commission also noted that not one of the company's customers had actually complained about the high prices.

BOC drew criticism again in 1962 when the Board of Trade released the company from some of its obligations to the Monopolies and Restrictive Practices Commission. In response to the board's action, and immediately following a recent 6 percent price raise, the British division of Air Products of America noted that BOC still controlled 95 percent of the British market and argued that the action would restore the company to a monopoly.

DIVERSIFICATION: 1960-1979

New applications for liquid nitrogen prompted the company to develop new markets in refrigeration, food preservation and packaging, preserving medical tissues, and storing and transporting bull semen for artificial insemination. Along these lines, BOC set up BOC-Linde Refrigeration Ltd., with Linde A.G. of Germany in 1968, acquired Ace Refrigeration Ltd., and J. Muirhead Ltd., quick frozen food suppliers, in 1969, and held Batchelors Ltd., Ireland, a food processor, from 1969 to 1973.

The 1960s and 1970s were marked by an accelerated program of diversification at BOC. Under Chairman Leslie Smith, the company began planning for the 1980s, particularly with an eye to expansion in the Far East, by setting up British Oxygen (Far East) Ltd., in Tokyo. Diversification took BOC even farther afield into such areas as fatty acids, resins, and additives produced for paints, inks, and adhesives. In 1970 the company began producing cutting and welding machines which incorporated sophisticated techniques using lasers and electron beams.

The company also began developmental work on underwater welding techniques, producing DriWeld, a system that made structural welds possible at depths of 600 feet. Factories, joint ventures and new holdings were established in Jamaica, Holland, South Africa, Sweden and Spain for a variety of products, including transformers, magnetizing equipment, frozen foods, stable isotopes and radioactively labeled compounds and cryogenic systems. Furthermore, in 1971 the company installed the largest mainframe computer in Britain, linking a network of computers throughout the country. In a move characteristic of BOC, the company sold computer time to outside customers and, as a result, BOC found itself suddenly in the computer business.

In the wake of the 1973-74 oil crisis, BOC reassessed its portfolio and decided to divest itself of its more peripheral interests in order to concentrate on its primary business, especially the gases and health care markets. This was done with the intention of expanding production in these areas, particularly in Europe, the Americas and the Far East.

Perhaps the most important and far-reaching move in the history of BOC involved the acquisition of one of America's major industrial corporations, Airco, a company whose history, in terms of products and growth, nearly mirrored that of BOC. It was an acquisition that came after 11 years of litigation in which the U.S. Federal Trade Commission instigated antitrust proceedings against BOC in order to force the company to divest itself of all Airco stock. The decision was appealed and then delayed, but in 1978 Airco became a wholly owned subsidiary of BOC. This doubled the size of the company, and consequently the British oxygen company changed its name to the BOC Group.

1980: EXPANSION INTO HOME HEALTH CARE

Although secondary to its gas production, BOC's health care division was a world leader in the 1980s in researching and manufacturing completely integrated anesthesia systems, including the Modulus II Anesthesia System, one of the most technologically sophisticated anesthesia devices ever produced. Indeed, the bulk of the group's health care effort was concentrated in its anesthetic pharmaceuticals and equipment and in critical care and patient monitoring. The group's health care market was largely concentrated in the United States. Encouraged by the U.S. government's determination to contain hospital costs, the company was aggressively promoting home health care services.

In 1982 BOC acquired a U.S. company called Glasrock Home Health Care, which provided oxygen therapy and medical equipment to chronically ill and elderly patients at home. In 1986 Glasrock became the exclusive national distributor of the first portable defibrillator designed for home use and of the Alexis computer-controlled, omnidirectional wheelchair. And the company anticipated a growing need for long-range in-home care for AIDS patients, whom hospitals were often not equipped to handle.

BOC's chairman and chief executive officer, Richard Giordano, who came to the Group along with the acquisition of Airco, noted in 1987 that the likely future markets for further development in health care services would be in wealthier countries, such as the United States and Germany, followed by Sweden and Switzerland. In the United Kingdom, he stated, home health care was "in the hands of the politicians," and he complained that "the health service is absolutely Neanderthal." Japan was an additional possibility for the expansion in health care services, according to Giordano, since it was a country burdened with an aging population.

The group's third important area of business in the 1980s, the graphite division, which principally made graphite electrodes for furnaces, was described as a "slow leak in BOC's earnings performance." This was a business that, like Giordano, came to BOC along with the Airco acquisition. During 1980, in an act that was described as a fit of misguided loyalty, Giordano invested in two new U.S. graphite plants; in 1985 the group experienced a loss of six million British pounds.

Under the leadership of Giordano, the BOC Group streamlined its portfolio through divestments and liquidations, concentrating on its two strongest businesses of gases and health care. Thirty of the companies acquired during the 1960s and 1970s diversification program had been sold by the late 1980s, and the work force trimmed by about 20,000.

1990: FURTHER GROWTH

Having divested numerous unrelated subsidiaries in the 1980s, BOC resumed its expansion efforts, this time focusing on adding to its principal business units. Although this new direction was initiated under the leadership of Giordano, it was primarily executed by Patrick Rich, who became chief executive officer in 1991 and chairman in 1992.

In particular, the company invested in the first half of the 1990s in numerous gas companies. In 1990 BOC purchased the remaining shares of Commonwealth Industrial Gases in Australia, and the following year doubled its investment in the Nigerian company Industrial Gases Lagos, bringing its stake to 60 percent. In 1992 BOC formed a gases joint venture with Hua Bei Oxygen in northern China and in 1993 purchased

Huls A.G., a German hydrogen business, as well as a 70 percent stake in one sector of Poland's state industrial gases business. The company spent $50 million in 1995 to purchase a 41 percent stake in Chile's leading industrial gases company, Indura SA Industria Y Commercio.

BOC made similar investments in its health care unit in the early 1990s. The company initiated a medical equipment joint venture with Japan's NEC San-ei and purchased the home medical businesses of Healthdyne Inc., both in 1990. The following year, BOC purchased Delta Biotechnology Ltd. for $23 million. In 1993 BOC combined its health care businesses, giving them the name Ohmeda. Acquisitions continued in 1994 with the purchase of the Calumatic Group, a Dutch manufacturer of filling, sterilizing, and packaging equipment for injectable pharmaceuticals.

BOC also expanded into the distribution business in the 1990s, becoming one of Britain's largest logistics operations. In 1990 the company purchased the U.K. distribution facilities of SmithKline Beecham consumer brands, and in 1993 acquired the Dutch distribution company Kroeze and the distribution operations of Gaymer Group. The following year BOC purchased the French distribution company TLO and the London Cargo Group, an airside cargo-handling specialist based in Heathrow.

BOC's finances in 1996 seemed strong, despite a slide in the performance of its health care business Ohmeda. Overall, the company reported record profits, up 11 percent from the previous year to $745 million. Sales had also risen, up 7 percent to $2.5 billion. In 1997, Ohmeda revenues were again down, this time by 6 percent. Profits declined even further, to 16 percent below 1996 levels. Overall, BOC revenues increased somewhat, to £4 billion from £3.75 billion in 1996. Profits also rose slightly, to £288 million.

In the late 1990s BOC increased its focus on its core gas business, both by expanding investment in that area and divesting other areas of the company. The first business to go was the underperforming health care subsidiary Ohmeda. In January 1998 the company announced it had reached an agreement to sell Ohmeda to a group of companies that comprised the Finnish business Instrumentarium Corporation and the U.S. businesses Becton, Dickinson & Company and Baxter International Inc. In mid-1998 BOC announced its intention to exit the carbide industry by selling Odda Smelteverk A/S. The company was to be sold to Philipp Brothers Chemicals, Inc., for £11.5 million cash.

BOC's core gas business was performing strongly in the late 1990s, with growth in each major region of the world. The company commissioned ten new plants in the United States in 1997 to meet its long-term contracts and began construction on several large plants in Europe in 1998. In a joint venture with Foster Wheeler, BOC built the largest hydrogen plant in South America, which began operation in late 1997. Several other new plants were either under construction or began operations in the late 1990s in Africa and the Asia-Pacific region; both regions saw double digit rates of growth in their profits in 1997.

LOCAL CONSOLIDATION AFTER 2000

The global industrial gases market was going through a period of consolidation around the turn of the Millennium. However, an $11 billion (£7 billion) takeover bid by France's Air Liquide SA and Air Products & Chemicals Inc. failed to satisfy U.S. antitrust regulators, even though the purchasers intended to divide BOC's assets between them. BOC Group would remain independent for at least another few years.

BOC's products were used to produce or package an enormous range of goods, from computer chips to potato chips; steel and energy companies were large users of oxygen and nitrogen. The slowing global economy affected these lines of business for the entire industrial gases industry. As a result, in 2001 BOC announced it was cutting 1,500 jobs.

In late 2002, the company merged its Japanese industrial and medical gas businesses with those of Air Liquide to form Japan Air Gases. It had annual revenues of $1 billion and expected to realize about ¥5 billion ($43 million) a year in efficiencies. Local consolidation such as this was seen as an alternative to megamergers thwarted by regulators, reported *Reuters*. BOC was also acquiring Praxair Inc.'s Polish operation.

The group built new facilities as the recession eased. In 2005, BOC began building a $50 million hydrogen plant near Salt Lake City, Utah to supply oil refineries there. The U.S. Environmental Protection Agency was requiring oil producers to reduce the levels of sulfur and nitrogen in fuels. Hydrotreating was one process for doing this. BOC had another half-dozen U.S. plants at the time. It had 30,000 employees in 50 countries, serving two million customers around the world. BOC was expecting the most growth from Asia.

According to *Chemical Week*, BOC was poised to benefit from its position in China, which had one of the largest and fastest growing economies in the world. BOC had been active in the People's Republic since 1985 and claimed to be its leading supplier of industrial gases. The BOC Edwards unit was due to profit from the shift of semiconductor manufacturing from other Asian

countries. However, according to *Chemical Week*, BOC and the other global suppliers had failed to penetrate much of the tonnage and local cylinder market. Four local joint ventures accounted for 80 percent of BOC's sales in China.

LINDE TAKEOVER IN 2005

BOC Group's total revenues, including its share of joint ventures and associates, were £4.6 billion in 2005, with adjusted profit before tax of £506 million. Both figures were up very slightly from 2004. Industrial gases made up more than 80 percent of sales. The group was getting nearly one-third of its revenues from Asia and the Pacific; Europe accounted for 28 percent and the Americas, 27 percent.

BOC Group was then the second largest industrial gas supplier in the world. After several years of intermittent courtship, the company's board accepted a £8.5 billion ($15 billion or EUR 12.4 billion) takeover offer from Linde AG, the fifth largest gases business, in March 2006; it was expected to close in the third quarter. The combination of two complementary product lines would give each business's customers a larger selection while overtaking Air Liquide in the role of global market leader.

Updated, Susan Windisch Brown, Frederick C. Ingram

PRINCIPAL SUBSIDIARIES

BOC Gases Australia Ltd.; BOC Cylinder Gas NV (Belgium); BOC Canada Ltd.; BOC Distribution Services Ltd.; BOC Ltd.; BOC Overseas Finance Ltd.; BOC Technologies Ltd.; Edwards High Vacuum International Ltd.; BOC Gaz SA (France); BOC Group Ltd. (Hong Kong); BOC Gases Ireland Ltd.; BOC AG (Switzerland); The BOC Group, Inc.; Japan Air Gases (55%).

PRINCIPAL DIVISIONS

Process Gas Solutions; Industrial and Special Products; BOC Edwards; Gist.

PRINCIPAL COMPETITORS

L'Air Liquide SA; Air Products & Chemicals Inc.; Praxair Inc.

FURTHER READING

"BOC, Air Liquide Combine Japanese Interests," *Reuters News*, September 4, 2002.

"BOC Megadeal Fizzles," *The Oil and Gas Journal,* May 22, 2000, p. 32.

"BOC's Record Profits Dispel Gloom," Reuter Business Report, November 29, 1996.

Chang, Joseph, "BOC Accepts $11.2 Bn Offer from Air Liquide & Air Products," *Chemical Market Reporter,* July 19, 1999, p. 1.

Davis, Brian, "BOC in China," *Chemical Week,* August 28, 2002, pp. S20f.

"Foster Wheeler/BOC Gases Will Celebrate Start-Up of the Largest Hydrogen Plant in South America," *Business Wire,* October 6, 1997.

Demoss, Jeff, "New Salt Lake City Plant Will Generate Cleaner-Burning Fuel," *Standard-Examiner* (Ogden, Utah), June 24, 2005.

Dowsett, Sonya, "BOC Chip Unit Sees Little Recovery Hope," *Reuters News,* November 12, 2002.

——, "BOC FD Remains Cautious on Chip Outlook," *Reuters News,* September 4, 2002.

Hunter, David, "Industrial Gases: Getting a Lift from the Recovery," *Chemical Week,* February 18, 2004, pp. 15ff.

Moore, Matt, "Linde: BOC Group Accepts Takeover Offer," *BusinessWeek online,* March 7, 2006.

Newman, Judy, "Ohmeda Foresees a Painless Transition," *Wisconsin State Journal,* February 8, 1998.

Oliver, Judith, "Patrick Rich," *Management Today,* August 1993, pp. 32-35.

Van Arnum, Patricia, "The Dust Settles After the Industrial Gases Storm," *Chemical Market Reporter,* December 11, 2000.

Brady Corporation

6555 West Good Hope Road
Milwaukee, Wisconsin 53223
U.S.A.
Telephone: (414) 358-6600
Fax: (414) 358-6798
Web site: http://www.bradycorp.com

Public Company
Incorporated: 1914 W. H. Brady Company
Employees: 3,900
Sales: $816.4 million (2005)
Stock Exchanges: New York
Ticker Symbol: BRC
NAIC: 32552 Adhesive Manufacturing; 322222 Coated and Laminated Paper Manufacturing; 339999 All Other Miscellaneous Manufacturing

■ ■ ■

Brady Corporation, formerly known as W. H. Brady Company, is an international manufacturer of high performance labels and signs, printing systems and software, label application and data collection systems, safety devices, and precision die-cut materials. Brady serves over 300,000 customers in a wide variety of industries including general manufacturing, maintenance and safety, construction, electrical, telecommunications, electronics, laboratory/healthcare, airline/transportation, security/brand education, governmental, and public utility industries. Its more prominent customers have included NASA, Boeing, Hollywood's film industry, IBM, PepsiCo, General Electric, and the Alaskan oil

pipeline. The company manufactures over 50,000 products, which are distributed in more than 100 countries across the globe.

1914 ORIGINS

W. H. Brady traces its origins to founder W. H. (Will) Brady's early career as a salesman for an Ohio remembrance advertising firm that manufactured calendars, yardsticks, and other promotional items on which advertising messages were printed. After turning down a promotion to the company's New York office, in 1914 Brady founded the W. H. Brady Company in Eau Claire, Wisconsin, Brady's hometown. His first product was promotional photographic calendars sold to offices and stores, but he soon followed with elaborate color displays for ice cream parlors, printed glass beer signs, point-of-purchase displays, and pre-billboard roadside advertising.

After a decade and a half of growth, the stock market crash of 1929 and the depression that followed drove many of Brady's customers out of business, forcing him to sell his home and, with his parents' support, enroll in college. In the midst of this crisis, an unusual promotional gimmick saved the firm. Candy-maker Webster's Famous Fudge included in its fudge packages a small, paperboard card that contained rows of perforated circles, each of which concealed a prize number. When customers exposed a winning number by pushing out one of the circles on the card, they won four free candy bars. The product fit neatly into Brady's printing, die-cutting, and laminating capabilities, and, aided by the cross-country marketing efforts of Will

COMPANY PERSPECTIVES

At Brady, our mission is to provide innovative identification solutions which improve safety, security, productivity and performance for customers worldwide.

Brady's oldest son Fred, Brady-manufactured push (or punch) cards, as they were called, were soon being used to sell everything from cigars and cigarettes to beer and turkeys. Throughout the 1930s and 1940s, Brady manufactured millions of push cards, becoming their largest producer in the United States. By the late 1930s, the company had declared that its new purpose was to carry on the business of printers, publishers, and painters of advertising matter and, in general, to engage in advertising businesses of all kinds.

POSTWAR NEW PRODUCT LINES

As World War II erupted, Will Brady yielded leadership to his two sons, Fred and Bill Jr., who from 1942 to 1955 shared direction of the company. The war brought shortages in the paperboard Brady used to make push cards, which was only partially offset by stopgap contracts such as printing morale booklets for the Red Cross. In 1944, however, while working at Milwaukee electrical control manufacturer Cutler-Hammer, Bill Jr. discovered the wire marker card—an adhesive card from which numbered cloth strips could be pulled and wrapped around electrical wires for identification purposes. The self-adhesive (or "pressure-sensitive") tape technology on which the wire marker card was based was still relatively new, but there was an urgent need for a clear and easy way to identify the ever-more dense masses of wiring being installed in ships, planes, and other military equipment. Moreover, the printing, die-cutting, and laminating processes for the paperboard backings on which the wire markers were placed were the same ones Brady used to make push cards. The new Brady markers were quickly embraced by the war industries; among their uses was the identification of wiring for the Manhattan Project construction work.

Sensing an untapped market, Brady began sending its four-page sales brochure to electrical manufacturers around the country and was quickly bombarded by inquiries. It began improving its markers' flexibility and applications by adapting them to customers needs: it made wire markers easier to remove from their backing, for example, and improved the type of material used for the backing itself. After the war's end, wire markers continued to eclipse push cards as Brady's main product, and Brady began performing the typesetting for the marker's label, offered new marker sizes and numbering systems, and introduced new marker types—from circular labels and Underwriters Laboratories seals of approval to small safety signs, pipe and conduit markers, and foil-, epoxy-, and vinyl-based markers that could resist oil, acid, and temperature extremes. Brady's first Caution and Danger safety signs appeared in 1949, and Brady's fallout shelter and radiation hazard signs enjoyed brisk sales during the 1950s and 1960s when the threat of nuclear weapons and radiation was at a peak.

At the same time, Brady was developing proprietary machines that could laminate, die cut, print, and cut to length in a single operation, boosting production volumes and cutting unit production costs. Because it was inexpensive for Brady simply to mail potential customers samples of its markers, it was not until after 1950 that it developed a national sales force. By the late 1940s Brady nevertheless claimed distributors in over 125 cities, most of which were local outlets of national electrical firms. By 1967 the 200 distributors Brady claimed in the early 1950s had grown to more than 1,000.

NATIONAL PRESENCE: 1950-60

By the early 1950s, Brady had become a national presence and chose "identification specialists" as the way to describe its specialized product niche to the increasingly interested industrial consumer. In desperate need of more production space, it moved permanently from Chippewa Falls, Wisconsin, to a new facility in Milwaukee in late 1952. The move hastened the pace of new product development, which averaged one new product every one to two months. The thirteen products listed on the company's letterhead in 1954, for example, had grown to twenty-one by 1956, and between 1944 and 1969 alone Brady introduced more than eighty new products in a variety of materials, sizes, and colors. By the late 1960s, Brady was offering 10,000 stock items in 35 distinct product groups.

Brady's 1953 introduction of Blue Streak Release —an adhesive so effective that labels and markers could be dramatically increased in size without loss of adhesion—was another major step forward in Brady's labeling capability. It also led Brady into a new product group—coatings—that would eventually form a crucial component of its product line and signaled Brady's desire to control as many stages of the label production process as it could. To manufacture its coatings, Brady engineers designed and built proprietary machinery that was used to produce a vinyl tape product suitable for making

KEY DATES

1914: Will Brady establishes the W. H. Brady Company in Eau Claire, Wisconsin.

1944: Brady's son, Bill Jr., discovers the wire marker card—an adhesive card from which numbered cloth strips can be pulled and wrapped around electrical wires for identification purposes.

1949: Brady's first Caution and Danger safety signs appear.

1955: Profits surpass the $1 million mark for the first time.

1966: Brady opens Brady Europa, a warehouse/factory in Belgium.

1971: Brady experiences a decline in sales for the first time since the wartime years.

1984: The company goes public.

1994: Katherine M. Hudson becomes the first non-family member to run the company.

1998: The company changes its name to Brady Corporation.

2004: EMED Company is acquired for $190 million.

warning stripes for factory floors. Brady could now free itself of its traditional dependency on 3M, its major tape supplier, and by supplying its own tape could now determine the characteristics, price, and quality of the materials it used in production.

In 1955 profits surpassed the $1 million mark for the first time, and two years later Brady—with Bill Jr. now alone at the helm—expanded into another new product line: nameplates. Thousands of consumer products, from power tools to washing machines, required plates that identified the manufacturer or displayed ratings or instructions. The sale of its aluminum and polyester nameplates (Quik-Plates and Poly-Plates, respectively) gave Brady a new niche in another lucrative market.

The same year, yet another innovation, the Markermatic automatic wire marker application system, solidified Brady's position in the expanding identification products industry. When loaded with a wire marker card, Markermatic automatically peeled back the card's adhesive starter strip, picked off an individual marker, wrapped it around the wire, and returned for the next pass—at a rate of one thousand markers an hour. The machine proved to be a substantial source of lease income

for Brady while simultaneously promoting the adoption of its wire marker brands. As Bill Jr. later remarked, "Markermatic made us king of the hill in our industry. Customers perceived us as the leader." Quickly capitalizing on the product's success, Brady followed with Printermatic (an automatic label printer), Wrapmatic (a device for wrapping tape around cylindrical objects), and Aisle Markermatic (a machine, resembling a floor polisher, for the precision-marking of factory lanes).

OVERSEAS EXPANSION: 1960-70

With the establishment of Brady Canada on the outskirts of Toronto in 1958, Brady moved into the international marketplace, which within 40 years would generate nearly half its annual sales. In the following years Brady added a nameplate manufacturing operation in Mexico (Uquillas-Brady) and a marketing/distribution operation in England (Simpson-Brady), which by 1962 had evolved into Brady England, Brady's first overseas facility. Although Brady claimed to have no strategic plan for its foreign expansion, a pattern nevertheless emerged. It first established a sales presence in the new foreign market, followed it by building a warehouse to maintain stock for the market, graduated to a leased manufacturing plant managed by local staff, and finally moved on to a new factory owned by a full-fledged subsidiary.

In 1966 Brady opened Brady Europa, a warehouse/factory in Belgium, and in the early 1970s, it bought out its ailing Australian distributorship to form Brady Australia. A formal international division was established in 1972 when Brady Sweden and Brady Germany joined the fold. Discovering that its foreign operations tended to thrive only when it established a subsidiary, rather than merely a distributorship, Brady opened a combined sales/warehouse/factory as Brady France in 1980. By the end of the year, Brady's international subsidiaries were accounting for 20 percent of the company's annual sales—the level at which they stayed for years, despite the addition of Brady Japan in 1987.

The 1960s and 1970s were a time of both continued growth and difficult transitions. Brady's new microscopic, fireproof component markers were being launched into orbit on Gemini space missions, and Brady had presciently seen the potential of the computer market as early as 1962 when it began selling computer-printable wire markers.

Before the end of the decade Brady was manufacturing labels, markers, drafting aids, and keypunch-hole correction seals specifically for the still-infant computer industry. Annual sales broke the $10 million mark in 1968, driven by a robust annual growth rate of

18 percent between 1953 and 1969, and Brady's policy of plowing profits back into new product development continued to reap benefits. By the 1990s, Brady was investing roughly four percent of annual revenue into new product R & D, and its expectations for such innovations were high. In 1989, for example, Bill Brady Jr. announced that he expected new products to account for 25 percent of Brady sales every year.

CORPORATE REORGANIZATION: 1970-80

Brady's hierarchic management structure was meanwhile showing signs of obsolescence, and its sales force, overwhelmed by the sheer number of products Brady now offered, could only show a limited part of the company's product line to each customer. Partly as a result of these problems, in 1971 Brady experienced a decline in sales for the first time since the wartime years of push cards and morale booklets.

Brady's answer to its troubled business structure was to scrap it in favor of a group of individual divisions, each focusing on a specific product line and market: the Nameplate Division, the Data Processing Division, and the Industrial Products Division, each with its own sales, marketing, and manufacturing units. Rather than conform to a top-down corporate plan, each division manager established his or her own pace for the division, which operated virtually as an independent company.

As the company adjusted to its new structure in the 1970s, product innovation forged ahead. Circuit tracers, hot stampers, nameplates made of specialized materials, and portable wire marker books were added to the Brady catalog in the 1970s. More importantly, typewriter lift-off correction tape and BOT/EOT markers for detecting the beginning and end of recorded data on computer tapes provided Brady with two lucrative new markets to pursue, and it was soon a major player in both. In 1977 Brady unveiled its LiteTouch membrane switches, in which electricity-conducting inks and adhesives enabled consumers to turn on microwave ovens, dishwashers, and sewing machines with a touch of the finger. Ironically, given Bill Brady Jr.'s disdain for government intervention, major federal legislation in the 1970s helped to further boost demand for Brady products. The Occupational Safety and Health Act of 1970 imposed a series of regulations regarding signage, safety warnings, and hazard identification in the workplace, and a related law in 1977 required all trucks carrying hazardous materials to sport high-visibility warning signs. By 1980, Brady had climbed past the $50 million sales plateau.

Not all of Brady's new product gambles bore fruit.

In 1969 it introduced Phodar, a method for manufacturing printed circuit boards using dry resist techniques rather than the traditional liquid resist method. It had to abandon the product in 1972, however, when DuPont's competing brand won the battle for market share and Brady's engineers were unable to overcome Phodar's poor shelf life limitations. The same year Brady unveiled Kalograph, an instant, one-step label maker that promised to enable customers to create their own custom industrial labels. The product's high cost, however, combined with its inability to create black lettering and its labels' tendency to fade in sunlight, undermined Kalograph's early promise, and in 1979 Bill Jr. finally pulled it from the marketplace, making it the most expensive failure in Brady's history.

GROWTH: 1980-90

After the lull in acquisitions of the 1970s, Brady began shopping for potential targets again in the 1980s. Small- to mid-sized, privately owned businesses with stock product lines and technologies similar to Brady's were scrutinized, and between 1981 and 1987 Brady acquired the Weckesser Corporation, a manufacturer of plastic wiring accessories (later sold); the M. C. Davis Company, a maker of miniature and subminiature coils; the MPV Company, a manufacturer of hard protective coatings; Browncor International, a distributor of shipping and packaging supplies; Revere Products, a direct marketer of maintenance products; and, most importantly, the Seton Name Plate Corporation, a manufacturer of nameplates and a business-to-business direct marketer, established in 1956. The Seton acquisition allowed Brady to supplement its traditional niche-focused sales and distribution network with blanket mail order sales through Seton's industrial catalog, which in 1988 alone reached eight million potential customers. Brady soon was establishing Seton subsidiaries in England (1985), Canada (1986), and Germany (1988).

Now operating six domestic divisions and eight international subsidiaries, Brady's annual sales grew 350 percent through the 1980s to $175 million, and profits soared past the $10 million mark. In 1984 Brady became a private/public hybrid when it sold 500,000 shares of nonvoting stock to avoid the estate taxes due when Bill Brady Jr.'s heirs inherited his stake in the company. That moment came in 1988 when Bill Jr., the Brady Company's second founder, died, and a longtime Brady insider, Paul Gengler, took over direction of the company. Brady retired its family-run reputation permanently in 1994 by hiring Katherine M. Hudson, a vice-president at Eastman Kodak, to lead it into the 21st century. An aggressive, hands-on executive with a ready sense of humor, Hudson announced her intention to quadruple annual sales to $1 billion, improve earnings, and exploit new opportunities for joint ventures, acquisitions, and geographic expansion, particularly in such new markets as Italy, Brazil, and the Far East.

A year into her tenure, Hudson announced that Brady's far-flung operations would be reorganized into three international divisions: the Identification Systems and Specialty Tapes Group, the Signmark Group (renamed Graphics Group in 1996), and the Seton Group. A year later Brady acquired Varitronic Systems, a U.S. manufacturer of high-tech printing systems, and two British firms: TechPrint Systems Ltd., a printer producer, and the Hirol Company, a manufacturer of printing systems and die-cut parts for electronics, telecommunications, and medical testing markets. Brady also sold off its nameplate and medical wound care operations to concentrate on its core businesses and entered into a joint venture with a South Korean marker equipment firm. It was also continuing to push the technological envelope of labeling and coating product design. Between 1980 and 1996 it introduced bar code software; a fully automated labeling machine for circuit boards and electrical components; and the Bradywriter printer, which allowed customers to print their own marker legends in house. It also began offering an express custom sign-making service; computer systems to exactly match customers color samples; installation, training, and contract services for Brady products; and integrated product groups that widened the number of labels and markers customers could choose from.

1998 AND BEYOND

As Brady prepared to enter the new millennium, the company opted to change its name to Brady Corporation. Hudson gave reasoning for the change in a July 1998 company press release stating, "As a company that's operating on a global stage to provide high-performance products and services, Brady needs a strong identity which communicates the quality, innovation and global reach we represent." She continued, "W.H. Brady Co. was named after the company founder, William H. Brady. While the name has served us well through the years, the name Brady Corporation reflects our growth from a private, small company founded in 1914 to a publicly traded, international business."

Exposure to international markets however, proved costly as the Asian financial crisis cut into the company's bottom line. Sales in Asia faltered and the company was forced to trim costs and cut 200 jobs. Nevertheless, Brady was determined to continue its growth strategy and take advantage of burgeoning new markets. In August 1998, it purchased Brazilian label manufacturer VEB Sistemas de Etiquetas Ltda.

Movement into foreign countries continued in 2000 and 2001 as Brady purchased companies in Australia and Germany. A new manufacturing facility was established in Penang, Malaysia, in 2002, while a second facility went online in China the following year. Overall, the company made four acquisitions in 2003 including TISCOR Inc., which was based in San Diego, California; Etimark GmbH of Germany; and two Brady distributors based in the United Kingdom.

Hudson stepped down in 2003, leaving Frank M. Jaehnert at the helm. Growth continued under his leadership. In fact, Brady made its largest acquisition to date in 2004 when it purchased EMED Co., a New York-based sign manufacturer with sales of $55 million. Shortly thereafter, Brady added Singapore-based ID Technologies Ltd., New York's Electromark, U.K.-based Signs & Labels Ltd., and Technology Print Supplies of Thailand to its arsenal. The company also expanded its operations in Wuxi, China; Sydney, Australia; and Manaus, Brazil. Sales in fiscal 2005 increased by 21.6 percent to $816.4 million while net income jumped to $81.9 million—an increase of 61.1 percent over the previous year. Approximately half of Brady's sales stemmed from its operations in the Americas while Europe accounted for 34 percent. Sales in the Asia Pacific region accounted for 15 percent of total revenues.

Along with its growth-through-acquisition plan, the company also eyed product development as crucial to its future success. Some of its new products included the LabXpert laboratory labeling and printing system that offered more than 140 laboratory-specific symbols and label templates for vials and test tubes. It also introduced BradyGlo photoluminescent products and the AquAlert labels that changed color when they came into contact with water or water-based liquids. The company's strong product lineup left it well positioned for future growth. Indeed, with record sales and profits in its coffers, Brady appeared to be on track for success in the years to come.

Paul S. Bodine
Updated, Christina M. Stansell

PRINCIPAL SUBSIDIARIES

Tricor Direct Inc.; Worldmark of Wisconsin Inc.; Brady Investment Company; Brady International Sales, Inc.; Brady International Company; Brady Worldwide, Inc.; Brady Australia Pty. Ltd.; Visi Sign Pty. Ltd.; Seton Australia Pty. Ltd.; W.H. Brady, N.V.; W.H.B. do Brasil Ltda.; W.H.B. Identification Solutions, Inc.; BRC Financial; EMED Co., Inc.; Stopware, Inc.; Permar Systems, Inc.; Henryc, Inc. (United States); Oliver of New York (United States)

PRINCIPAL COMPETITORS

3M Company; Avery Dennison Corporation; Integrated Security Systems Inc.

FURTHER READING

Barrett, Rick, "Brady Corp.'s Profits Double on Strength of Acquisitions," *Milwaukee Journal Sentinel*, February 17, 2005.

———, "Milwaukee-based Brady Corp. to buy Singapore Disk-Drive Supplier," *Milwaukee Journal Sentinel*, August 10, 2004.

"CEO Interview—Katherine M. Hudson, W. H. Brady Co.," *Wall Street Transcript Digest*, May 8, 1995.

Grube, Lorri, "Katherine M. Hudson, Chief Executive," *Chief Executive*, January/February 1995, p. 29.

Gurda, John, *Sticking to It: A History of the W. H. Brady Co., 1914-1989*, Milwaukee: W. H. Brady Co., 1989.

Hawkins Jr., Lee, "W.H. Brady Trims Costs," *Milwaukee Journal Sentinel*, August 12, 1998.

Holley, Paul, "Global Spending Slows Earnings at W. H. Brady," *Business Journal Serving Greater Milwaukee*, May 18, 1996, p. 7.

Joshi, Pradnya, "W. H. Brady Labels Its Fiscal Year Exceptional," *Milwaukee Journal Sentinel*, September 14, 1995, p. 1.

———, "W. H. Brady Wants Growth to Continue," *Milwaukee Journal Sentinel*, August 14, 1995, p. 3.

Kirchen, Rich, "With New Owner, Former Brady Unit Sticks to Growth Track," *Business Journal Serving Greater Milwaukee*, April 8, 1995, p. 7.

Romell, Rick, "Brady Announces its Largest Acquisition Ever," *Milwaukee Journal Sentinel*, April 6, 2004.

Shapiro, Joshua, "An Unusual Climb at Kodak Wins Her a Place at the Top," *New York Times*, January 30, 1991, p. 8.

"W.H. Brady Co. to Change Its Name to Brady Corporation," *PR Newswire*, July 28, 1998.

Bunge Brasil S.A.

Av. Maria Coelho de Aguiar 215
São Paulo, São Paulo 05804-900
Brazil
Telephone: (55) (11) 3741-3575
Fax: (55) (11) 3741-7292
Web site: http://www.bunge.com.br

Wholly Owned Subsidiary of Bunge Ltd.
Incorporated: 1905 as S.A. Moinho Santista Indústrias
    Gerais
Employees: 10,578
Sales: BRL 23.2 billion ($7.92 billion) (2004)
NAIC: 212312 Crushed and Broken Limestone Mining
    and Quarrying; 212392 Phosphate Rock Mining;
    212393 Other Chemical and Fertilizer Mineral
    Mining; 311119 Other Animal Food Manufactur-
    ing; 311211 Flour Milling; 311221 Wet Corn Mill-
    ing; 311222 Soybean Processing; 311223 Other
    Oilseed Processing; 311225 Fats and Oils Refining
    and Blending; 311941 Mayonnaise, Dressing, and
    Other Prepared Sauce Manufacturing; 551112 Of-
    fices of Other Holding Companies

■ ■ ■

Bunge Brasil S.A. is the holding company for Bunge
Alimentos S.A. and Bunge Fertilizantes S.A., vertically
integrated subsidiaries that, in combination, form the
biggest food company in Brazil, in terms of annual
revenue. The latter entity produces and sells fertilizer for
the crops that form the basis for the animal and human
foods produced and sold by the former. Bunge Brasil's
more than 300 installations in 16 states include factories,
ports, distribution centers, and silos. Bunge brands such
as Serrana, Manish, Iap, Ouro Verde, Salada, Soya, Delicia, and Primor have a presence that continues to
resonate in contemporary Brazil. The company is a
wholly owned subsidiary of the New York-based
multinational corporation Bunge Ltd. Its assets come to
about half that of Bunge Ltd., and its sales comprise
about one-third of the parent company's sales.

POWERFUL BRAZILIAN
CONGLOMERATE: 1908-90

The Bunge enterprise dates from 1818, when Johann-
peter G. Bunge founded, in Amsterdam, Koninklijke
Bunge (Bunge & Co.), to sell imported products from
Dutch colonies abroad, including grains. Some years
later, the company moved its headquarters to Rotterdam
and opened subsidiaries in other European countries. In
1859, at the invitation of the king of Belgium, Bunge
relocated its headquarters to Antwerp. Ernest Bunge, a
grandson of the founder, moved in 1884 to Argentina,
where, with partners, including his brother-in-law, Jorge
Born, he established Casa Bunge y Born, with the object
of participating in the export of the country's bountiful
grain crops. Bunge y Born entered Brazil in 1908, when
it became a minority shareholder in S.A. Moinho Santista Indústrias Gerais, a company engaged in the trading and milling of wheat.

This was the beginning of a rapid expansion in
Brazil, with Bunge y Born acquiring a number of
companies, mostly in the fields of food, agribusiness,
chemicals, and textiles. The acquisition of Cavalcanti e

COMPANY PERSPECTIVES

Bunge is committed to furthering the well-being of its clients, employees, shareholders, and the communities where it is present.

Cia., for example, in 1923, led to the establishment in 1926 of Sociedad Algodonora del Nordeste Brasileno, or Sanbra S.A., an enterprise that first financed cotton growers, and then, the following year, began to produce and refine cottonseed oil. In 1929 Bunge y Born founded S.A. Moinhos Rio Grandenses (Samrig) from two companies previously acquired, and then built a big factory for extracting plant-based oils in Porto Alegre, Rio Grande do Sul. This product was widely used in cattle feed. Bunge y Born's first textile company in Brazil, acquired about 1930, was Fábrica de Tecidos Tatuapé S.A. Its participation in cement and fertilizers began in 1938, and soon after Serrana S.A. de Mineração was established for the exploitation of a limestone deposit. Tintas Coral S.A. put Bunge into the paints-and-dyes business in the mid-1950s.

Soybeans were just beginning to be an important crop in 1954, when Samrig began to buy them from Rio Grande do Sul farmers in exchange for fertilizer and pesticides (made by Bunge y Born enterprises in Brazil), seeds, and technical support. In 1969 Samrig opened the first factory in Latin America to extract soy proteins. Sanbra, two years earlier, had begun similar activities in the states of São Paulo and Paraná. Both companies—fierce competitors—made and marketed an array of products from vegetable fats and oils, particularly margarine.

Bunge y Born, at the beginning of the 1970s, expanded into the Brazilian financial sector, purchasing a bank, a brokerage house, and an insurance agency. It entered real estate by constructing a corporate park and the information sector with Proceda Serviços Administrativos S.A. The following year the brothers Jorge Born III and Juan Born, sons of the chief executive, Jorge Born, Jr., were taken prisoner by leftist guerrillas in Argentina; the former was not released until nine months later, after the company had paid a ransom of $60 million. Bunge y Born headquarters then were moved from Buenos Aires to São Paulo, where the Borns took up residence. Gross sales in Brazil rose from 5.95 billion cruzeiros (about $850 million) in 1974 to 158.6 billion cruzeiros (about $1.5 billion) in 1981, when employment reached 26,395, and agroindustry and foods ac-

counted for slightly more than half, chemicals for almost one-fourth, and textiles 14 percent, of sales.

In Brazil, as in Argentina, Bunge y Born was known for the secrecy in which it operated. Neither Jorge Born III, who became president in 1987, nor his successor in 1991, Octavio Caraballo, gave interviews; not a single photo of Caraballo, who, like Born, belonged to one of the shareholding families, was available. Company executives even habitually denied that the Bunge group existed in Brazil. The organizational structure of the group was also obscure. Bunge y Born's holdings in Brazil reached a peak of at least $3 billion in annual revenue during the 1980s, and one of its subsidiaries, Santista Indústrias Têxtil do Nordeste S.A., was designated by the Brazilian business magazine *Exame* as its company of the year for 1988.

SLIMMING DOWN: 1990-2000

By 1990, according to *Exame,* Bunge y Born was a worldwide group with $15 billion in annual sales and operations in nine countries. Its Brazilian holdings consisted of some 170 enterprises employing about 30,000 employees and yielding an estimated $2.3 billion to $2.9 billion in annual revenue. A chart in *Exame* showed a complex web of 20 companies tied to four larger ones: S.A. Moinho Santista Indústrias Gerais, Moinho Fluminense S.A. Indústrias Gerais, Moinho Recife S.A. Empreedimentos e Participações, and Sanbra. The first three were public and sold shares, while the last was private. Each was a holding company that also exercised operational functions, and each held shares in the others. A company executive later compared the organizational structure to a computer chip with both vertical and horizontal lines of connection.

The Brazilian recession that began in 1989 took its toll on such Bunge y Born companies as Sanbra, Moinho Santista, Quimbrasil S.A. (or Química Industrial Brasileira Ltda.), Santista Têxtil do Nordeste, and Tintas Coral, all of which lost money—reportedly for the first time—in 1990. In all, Bunge y Born was said to have lost as much as $150 million in Brazil. The losses extended into 1991, resulting, near the end of the year, in a managerial purge that shook the traditionally paternalistic enterprise to its foundations. Brazil was now entering an era of free trade in which powerful corporate lobbies like that of Bunge y Born could no longer protect their products from foreign competition. With support from other shareholders, Caraballo ousted Jorge Born as chief executive but returned to Buenos Aires after appointing a German executive resident in Brazil, Ludwig Schmitt-Rhaden, to direct Brazilian operations. The sizable debt of $472 million was refinanced so that payments could be stretched over a

KEY DATES

1908: Argentina-based Bunge y Born enters Brazil by taking shares in a wheat miller and trader.

1926: Sanbra is founded, and soon begins producing cottonseed oil.

1929: Samrig, which, like Sanbra, begins producing fats and oils, is founded.

1938: Bunge y Born begins participating in Brazilian cement and fertilizer production.

1954: Samrig starts buying soybeans from farmers in exchange for fertilizer and pesticides.

1969: Sanbra and Samrig are both heavily engaged in soybean processing, a major industry.

1974: Bunge y Born moves its headquarters from Argentina to Brazil.

1981: The company's gross sales in Brazil have reached $1.5 billion.

1990: Bunge y Born's holdings in Brazil consist of 170 companies employing 30,000 people.

1993: After losing $176 million in three years, Bunge y Born has cut back its Brazilian operations.

1997: The company's Santista Alimentos S.A. has become Brazil's largest food producer.

1999: Now called Bunge International, the company moves its headquarters to the United States.

2000: Bunge has become the largest and only vertically integrated fertilizer producer in Brazil.

2002: Bunge consolidates its Brazilian operations in publicly traded Bunge Brasil S.A.

2004: Now totally owned by Bunge Ltd., Bunge Brasil remains the nation's top food company.

longer period of time. The number of companies was reduced to 75.

One result of the restructuring was greater transparency. In December 1993, for the first time in the conglomerate's history, its executives presented themselves formally to an audience of journalists. They were told that the enterprise would henceforth be known in Brazil as Bunge Brasil, with the Bunge y Born name retained only in Argentina. This was followed by a two-hour presentation in which company executives explained that the enterprise was being divided into five areas: wheat, soybeans, textiles, paints, and cement, each with a president reporting to Schmitt-Rhaden. Restructuring had been completed with the whittling of companies to 30 and of employees to 20,000, including

the dismissal of 400 managers and the reduction of levels among personnel from nine to five. The enterprise, it was announced, would earn an operational profit for the year, ending a three-year period in which it lost $176 million. Even slimmed down, the enterprise was a considerable one, with about $2 billion in annual revenue. It ranked third in Brazil in the food sector, third in textiles, and second in paints and dyes. (The enterprise was not officially named Bunge Brasil until years later. Most of the businesses not engaged in consumer foods were placed in 1995 under a holding company named Serrana S.A.; the rest became part of Santista Alimentos S.A.)

Bunge International Ltd. was created in 1994 as the main holding company in which the Bunge y Born shareholding families held stock, and Schmitt-Rhaden became its president. The structure of the Brazilian operation was simplified further. By 1995, Santista Alimentos was responsible for all foods, Moinho Santista for both cement and textiles, and Tintas Coral for paints. By late 1995, Coral had been combined with Bunge's similar holdings in Argentina (Alba) and Uruguay (Inca) to form Bunge Paints, which now had eight factories and was the leader in its field in Latin America. But Schmitt-Rhaden had decided to exit sectors that it considered outside Bunge's core businesses. The following year he sold Bunge Paints for $390 million, and in early 1997 he sold Serrana's cement business for $430 million. Schmitt-Rhaden also sold Proceda, Banco Santista S.A., and Vera Cruz Seguradora S.A., an insurance company. Bunge diluted its textile segment—now called Empresas Têxteis Santista—in 1994, maintaining only a minority holding in a joint venture with São Paulo Alpargatas S.A.

Meanwhile, in 1995-96, Santista Alimentos added $1 billion in annual revenues by purchasing 13 companies. Among them were three soybean-processing factories, five wheat mills, a bread producer, and a margarine manufacturer. And, in 1997, parent Bunge swallowed a giant in the Brazilian food sector: Ceval Alimentos S.A., a company with sales of $2.7 billion in the previous year and the leader in the processing of soybeans and production of soy meal and oils in Brazil. Purchased for about $700 million from Companhia Hering, the acquisition turned Santista Alimentos into the largest food producer in Brazil, with 48 industrial units turning out an array of goods from margarine, frozen meat, and bread. It was also the world's fifth largest processor of soybeans into meal and the national leader in vegetable oils and pasta as well as margarine. Ceval's third-place position in frozen meat filled a gap in Bunge's food holdings. At the same time, Bunge was investing heavily in fertilizer. Between 1996 and 2000 the company acquired eight Brazilian fertilizer companies to become the largest and only vertically integrated fertilizer company in Brazil, with holdings that included two phosphate-rock mines.

Oscar Bernardes, a protege of Schmitt-Rhaden, succeeded him as president of Bunge International in 1997. One of his first acts was to transfer Santista Alimentos' activities in soybean processing to Ceval, so that the former would be free to concentrate on consumer products, including Ceval's margarine and vegetable-oil brands. Ceval's meat division became an independent company called Seara Alimentos. Many analysts expected these actions to be a prelude to another sale that would put Bunge International out of consumer products entirely, and the company itself announced this intention in 1998. Bunge International was not interested in any offer made for Santista Alimentos, however, which was losing money, despite annual sales of BRL 2.2 billion (about $2 billion).

FOCUS ON AGRIBUSINESS AND FERTILIZERS: 2000-05

In 1999 Bunge International moved its headquarters from São Paulo to White Plains, New York. The following year Santista Alimentos and Ceval became parts of a new entity, Bunge Alimentos S.A. Fertilizantes Serrana S.A., Ouro Verde Ltda., and the recently purchased companies IAP S.A. and Manah S.A. were among the units placed in newly formed Bunge Fertilizantes S.A.

By this time Bernardes had been succeeded as president by Alberto Weisser. Twice a month Weisser flew to São Paulo from New York, since Bunge's Brasil operations accounted for half the group's $10 billion in annual revenues. Santista, with its more than 100 food brands and 20 factories, was still part of Brazil operations and still considered a headache. This division had lost BRL 104 million ($57 million) in 2000, and in any case group headquarters wanted to integrate its holdings internationally, an endeavor impossible for consumer products, because each country had its separate brands. When a buyer could not be found, Weisser looked to eliminate the most poorly performing brands. Others, it was thought, could be directed to institutional clients, such as bakeries, not only in Brazil but in the United States.

Bunge International became Bunge Ltd. in August 2001 and began selling shares on the New York Stock Exchange. In Brazil, all Bunge Fertilizantes and Bunge Alimentos shares were exchanged for shares of Serrana, which, in 2002, was renamed Bunge Brasil S.A. (and was 83 percent owned by Bunge Ltd.). This reduced the number of Bunge Ltd.'s publicly traded subsidiaries in Brazil from four to two: Bunge Brasil and Fosfertil S.A.,

a leader in raw materials for fertilizers that soon came to be controlled by Bunge Brasil. Bunge Brasil retained its position as the leading Brazilian agribusiness company. With ten million metric tons of soybeans and two million tons of wheat sold in 2002, it was the nation's fourth largest exporter and also the principal producer of fertilizers, comestible oils, wheat flour, margarine, and vegetable fats in Brazil. It was the leading company in Latin America in the processing and exportation of soybeans and wheat. The company had 79 units, ports, and distribution centers and 185 silos in 14 states.

Bunge Alimentos, in 2003 and 2004, resumed its effort to concentrate on agribusiness rather than food production and consumer food sales. Seara, its frozen-meat unit, was sold. Bunge Alimentos transferred to J. Macêdo S.A. its consumer flour, pasta, and cake-mix brands and operations. In return, it assumed flour and cake-mix brands for industrial-size bakeries. It took a minority share in the establishment of Solae do Brasil Indústria e Comércio de Alimentos Ltda., which was founded in 2003 with Du Pont do Brasil Ltda. to furnish ingredients for producers of soy-based drinks and yogurt. In August 2004, Bunge Ltd. decided to take Bunge Brasil private, buying all the outstanding shares. When this was accomplished, Bunge Brasil was delisted from the São Paulo Stock Exchange.

In 2005, Bunge Alimentos was buying soybeans from 30,000 growers. It was also buying and processing wheat, corn, and cottonseed. For commercial clients, it was producing flour, premixes, margarine, and fats under the Bunge Pró brand; mayonnaise and margarine under the Soyua and Primor brands; and texturized soy protein under the Maxten brand. For retail consumers, it was producing margarine under the Cyclus, Delicis, Mila, Primor, and Soya labels; oils under the Soya, Primor, and Salada labels; and mayonnaise under the Delicia, Primor, and Soya labels. All Day and Cyclus were the names of its beverages. Bunge Fertilizantes was a vertical enterprise engaged in all steps of producing and selling fertilizers and mineral supplements for animal feed. It also was selling nutrients such as bicalcic phosphate, extracted from its own phosphate mines, for use in animal feed. A number of brands were being produced and sold to more than 60,000 customers by the four units of this company: IAP, Manah, Ouro Verde, and Serrana.

Robert Halasz

PRINCIPAL SUBSIDIARIES

Bunge Alimentos S.A.; Bunge Fertilizantes S.A.

PRINCIPAL COMPETITORS

Archer Daniels Midland Co.; Cargill Agrícola S.A.

FURTHER READING

Caetano, José Roberto, "Mexeu, mexeu e voltou ao ponto de partida," *Exame,* July 1, 1998, pp. 56-61.

Caplen, Brian, "Decline of an Argentine Dynasty," *Euromoney,* January 1999, pp. 51-52, 54-56.

Green, Raúl, and Catherine Laurent, *El poder de Bunge & Born,* Buenos Aires: Editorial Legasa, 1988.

Majul, Luis, *Los dueños de la Argentina,* Buenos Aires: Editorial Sudamericana, Vol. 1, 1992, pp. 249-303.

Mano, Cristiane, "Não sei," *Exame,* March 7, 2001, pp. 74-76, 78.

Netz, Clayton, "O mistério começa a ser desvendado," *Exame,* December 22, 1993, pp. 20, 22-26.

"O outro plano da Bunge y Born," *Exame,* July 10, 1991, pp. 96-98.

Paduan, Roberta, "O poder do Bunge," *Exame,* September 29, 2004, pp. 68-70.

"Sunset Over the River Plate," *Economist,* June 6, 1998, p. 63.

"Um império está no olho do furacáo," *Exame,* May 13, 1992, pp. 42-44.

Vassallo, Cláudia, "Por que o Bunge quer a Ceval," *Exame,* September 10, 1997, pp. 48-50.

The Campina Group

Hogeweg 9 NL-5301
LB Zaltbommel,
Netherlands
Telephone: (31) 418 571-300
Fax: (31) 418 571-582
Web site: http://www.campina.com

Cooperative
Incorporated: 1989 as Campina Melkunie; 2001 as Campina
Employees: 7,099
Sales: EUR 3.56 billion ($5 billion) (2004)
NAIC: 311513 Cheese Manufacturing; 311511 Fluid Milk Manufacturing; 311512 Creamery Butter Manufacturing; 311514 Dry, Condensed, and Evaporated Dairy Product Manufacturing; 311520 Ice Cream and Frozen Dessert Manufacturing

■ ■ ■

The Campina Group is one of Europe's leading producers of fresh milk and dairy products, including dairy drinks, cheeses, yogurts, quark (a type of farmer's cheese), vla (custard) desserts, and snacks and butter products. The Group is comprised of Zuivelcooperatie Campina u.a., an umbrella company, and Campina B.V., a farmer's cooperative with nearly 9,000 member-farmers, is the leading dairy group in the Netherlands and also one of the largest in the world. Campina operates in more than 100 countries worldwide, and holds significant positions in many foreign markets—such as the number three spot in Germany, the largest single European market, a strong position in Russia and Poland, and fast growing sales in Asia, and especially in Thailand and Vietnam. Germany is the company's largest market, followed closely by the Netherlands, with each accounting for approximately one-third of sales. Campina's operations are structured into five primary divisions: Campina Netherlands, Campina Germany, Campina International, Cheese and Butter, and Industrial Products. Campina's range of consumer brands includes Mona, Campina, Puddis, Landliebe, Smakija, Joyvalle, and organic dairy brands De Groene Koe and Zuiver Zuivel, among others. The Industrial Products division includes butter and other food ingredients for the industrial food industry, dairy derivatives (notably lactoferrin, protein hydrolysates, and lactose) produced by the company's DMV International operation for the pharmaceutical and health industries. The company's Polderland Dairy supplies the catering and trade professional market in the Netherlands. Campina also produces Valess, a dairy-based meat substitute. In 2004, Campina posted revenues of more than EUR 3.5 billion ($5 billion).

ORIGINS AND CONSOLIDATING THE DUTCH DAIRY INDUSTRY

The Dutch dairy industry remained at a local, artisan level until well into the second half of the 19th century. Dairy products were typically prepared on the farm, by the farmers themselves, using milk from their own herds. Farms at the time were almost wholly of the mixed usage variety, meaning that production levels at individual farms remained highly limited. The region's industrial development, the growing population, and the accompanying development of urban markets stimulated demand for larger quantities of dairy products. The first dairy factories in the Netherlands appeared only in the 1870s. Over the next decade, the number of butter and cheese factories grew rapidly. By the outbreak of World War I, the Netherlands boasted more than 1,200 dairy factories.

From the start, the Dutch dairy products industry was marked by the cooperative movement, which had swept across Europe during the 19th century. While the operation of cooperatives and mutual aid societies had become commonplace in a number of industries-such as the banking sector, in the form of British building societies, for example-the agricultural sector formed the true center of the cooperative movement. This was especially true in the Netherlands, and particularly in the country's dairy industry, where farmers' cooperatives remained the dominant force into the 21st century.

For most of the 20th century, these farmer cooperatives remained quite small, locally or at best regionally focused. The consolidation of the Dutch dairy sector began in earnest in the years following World War II, however. That period saw a Dutch population explosion, which in turn boosted demand for dairy products. Other innovations, such as new self-service supermarket formats and new refrigeration and packaging techniques, also stimulated demand for a wider variety of products. Meanwhile, the developing transportation and logistics industries made it possible to expand more brand names, and especially perishable dairy brands, to a national scale. At the same time, the industry saw the development of increasingly sophisticated production equipment, coupled with rising demands for greater hygiene and food security in the food production process. These factors combined to place demands for increasingly larger investments on the part of farmers and the farmer cooperatives.

The consolidation of the dairy industry began in earnest in the 1960s, and saw the creation of most of the major names in the Dutch dairy industry. Among these were Campina, formed as part of a large-scale merger among several cooperatives in the southern Netherlands region. Campina, named for the De Kempen region near Eindhoven, stemmed from that region's first cooperative, created in Tunglelroy in 1892. The merger of several cooperatives produced the De Kempen Cooperatives Dairy Association, based in Eindhoven, in 1947. That cooperative began marketing its dairy products under the Campina brand name.

Campina carried out a new large-scale merger in 1976, emerging as the dominant cooperative in its region. By the end of the decade, the cooperative had joined with another major dairy group, De Meijerij, based in Veghen, in the southeast of the Netherlands. That cooperative had been founded in 1926 by six farmer-members under the name Cooperatieve Centrale Melkproductenfabriek-De Meijerij. Over the next decades, and a number of mergers, the Meijerij group became its regions' major dairy cooperative, changing its name to De Melkindustrie Veghel (or DMV). Following the merger with Campina in 1979, the combined group became DMV Campina. While Campina gradually became the cooperative's flagship consumer brand, the DMV name became associated with the group's actively developing industrial ingredients operations. These included the production of butter and other dairy products for the professional catering and food processing industries, as well as such products as lactose (milk sugar) and protein hydrolysates, bioactive peptides, and lactoferrin.

The consolidation of the Dutch dairy sector was largely completed by the end of the 1980s, which saw the creation of two national-and international-giants, Friesland Coberco (later Friesland Foods), in the north, and Campina Melkunie, created through the 1989 merger of Campina with Melkunie Holland, in the west and south. Melkunie stemmed from one of the first Dutch dairy cooperatives, founded in 1872. Melkunie became a leading force in the consolidation of its region, becoming CMC/Melkunie by the end of the 1960s, and finally established as Melkunie Holland in 1979. By then, the cooperative had established itself on a national level, in large part through its highly popular Mona dessert brand, launched in 1970. By the end of the 1970s, Mona had become the largest dairy dessert brand in the Netherlands. By the mid-1980s, the company produced more than 100 million Mona-branded dairy items annually.

INTERNATIONAL DAIRY LEADER IN THE NEW CENTURY

With further growth limited in the Netherlands, Campina Melkunie turned to the international. The European market was then beginning its own consolidation, marked by a series of cross-border mergers and the appearance of a smaller number of large-scale,

KEY DATES

1872: Creation of a dairy cooperative that is a forerunner to Melkunie.

1892: Creation of first dairy cooperative in southern region, a forerunner to Campina.

1926: Creation of farmers' cooperative in Meijerij region, which later becomes De Melkindustrie Veghel (DMV).

1947: Mergers form De Kempen Cooperatives Dairy Association, which launches Campina brand, in Eindhoven.

1964: Campina formally established through new large-scale merger.

1970: CMC/Melkunie launches Mona dairy dessert brand.

1979: Merger of Campina and DMV forms DMV Campina.

1980: New merger establishes Melkunie Holland.

1989: DMV Campina and Melkunie Holland merge and form Campina Melkunie.

1991: Company acquires Comelco in Belgium as part of international expansion effort.

1993: Company enters German market through purchase of majority control of Sudmilch in Stuttgart.

1997: The Polish market is penetrated with the acquisition of Bacha and Tojo.

1998: An organic dairy operation, De Vereeniging, in the Netherlands is acquired.

2000: Campina opens yogurt plant in Russia.

2001: Corporate restructuring.

2004: Company enters Thailand and Vietnam.

internationally operating dairy concerns. Germany and Belgium became natural markets for Campina Melkunie's expansion, especially given the central role of dairy cooperatives in these markets as well. The company's first acquisition came in 1991, with the purchase of Comelco, in Belgium. This acquisition was followed two years later by the purchase of Sudmilch AG, based in Stuttgart, Germany. In 1997, the company expanded its presence in Germany, forming Tuffi Campina, a joint venture with Miclhwerke Koln/Wuppertal. Germany quickly grew into Campina Melkunie's largest market, outstripping even its sales at home in the Netherlands. At the same time, the cooperative eyed further expansion, now beyond Western Europe, buying up two dairy concerns, Bacha and Tojo, in Poland in 1997.

Back at home, Campina Melkunie boosted its presence on the liquid milk market with the acquisition of those operations from the Dutch company Menken van Grieken in 1997. The cooperative later took over two more parts of Menken, Menken Dairy Food and Menken Polderland, both in 1998. In that same year, the company also added an organic dairy products component in the Netherlands through the acquisition of De Vereeniging. Campina Melkunie returned to Germany that year, adding Kutel, based in Essen. The following year, the company's Tuffi Campina joint venture expanded as well, merging with Berlin's Emzett.

During this period, the group's industrial ingredients operations, grouped under DMV International since 1992, had expanded strongly as well. The company entered the United States, buying up Deltown Chumurgic, in 1991, in order to develop and produce protein hydrolysates and bioactive peptides. DMV turned to Germany in 1998, buying up ingredients specialist Nupron. Into the 2000s, DMV added a new lactoferrin joint venture in the United States, in partnership with Farmland National Beef Packing.

Campina Melkunie's expansion returned to Eastern Europe in 2000, as the company traveled to Russia to open a yogurt factory there. Closer to home, the cooperative was joined by two new cooperative members, Milchwerke Koln /Wupertal, in Germany, and Belgium's Milchwerke Koln/Wuppertal. That merger also gave the cooperative full control of the Tuffi Campina joint venture.

Faced with shrinking profits and a dwindling membership base at the end of the 1990s, the cooperative, then the ninth-largest dairy concern in the world, underwent a thorough restructuring. Completed in 2001, the exercise involved a streamlining of the group's brand portfolio, and a new name for the cooperative itself, which became simply Campina. The following year, Campina merged its German holdings into a single entity as well, Campina GmbH. That subsidiary expanded again in 2003, acquiring German desserts brand Mokerei H. Strothmann, based in Gutersloh.

Into the mid-2000s, Campina continued to explore new markets. The company entered the Asian market, buying up the Thai operations of failed Italian dairy group Parmalat in 2004, and opening a sales office in Vietnam that year as well. Also in 2004, Campina directly entered Greece, where it bought up its distribution partner there, Quality Brands International.

Campina also targeted a more significant horizon in 2004 when it announced that it had entered merger talks with Nordic dairy giant Arla Foods. The merger between the two cooperatives proposed to create the leading European dairy group and one of the top three dairy groups worldwide. By 2005, however, the two companies had failed to agree to terms of a merger and instead agreed to call off the talks.

Forced to go it alone, Campina sought new expansion through international opportunities. In 2005, the company acquired Aveve Zuivel, based in Belgium, which specialized in milk fat production. Campina also boosted its presence in its Asian markets. By the end of 2005, the company had formed a production joint venture with Vinamilk, the largest dairy group in Vietnam. In January 2006, Campina turned to Thailand, where it formed another joint venture, now with Thai Dairy Industries. Already a major force on the global dairy market, Campina had not ruled out a future merger with Arla; both sides acknowledged an interest in resuming merger talks as early as in 2007.

M.L. Cohen

PRINCIPAL SUBSIDIARIES

Campina BV; Zuivelcoperatie Campina u.a.

PRINCIPAL DIVISIONS

Campina Netherlands; Campina Germany; Consumer Products Europe; Cheese & Butter; Industrial Products.

PRINCIPAL COMPETITORS

Nestle SA; Danone SA; Arla Foods amba; Lactalis; Unilever; Royal Friesland Foods NV; Bongrain SA; Humana Milchunion eG; NORDMILCH eG; Koninklijke Wessanen NV; Glanbia PLC.

FURTHER READING

"Campina and Arla Scrap Merger," *Dairy Industries International*, May 2005, p. 6.

"Campina Announces New Organisational Structure," *just-food.com*, July 7, 2005.

"Campina Buys Up Parmalat Thailand," *Dairy Industries International*, May 2004, p. 6.

"Campina Moves into Russia," *Dairy Industries International*, September 2000, p. 9.

"Campina Opens Facility in Belgium," *Dairy Industries International*, November 2005, p. 7.

"Campina Set for Further Growth in Russia," *just-food.com*, November 2, 2005.

"Campina to Scrap Melkunie Brand," *Dairy Markets Weekly*, January 4, 2001, p. 8.

Clarke, Richard, "Milking the World," *Grocer*, September 10, 2005, p. S20.

"DMV Plans Huge Plant," *Dairy Industries International*, March 2005, p. 11.

Druenen, Peter van, *Een begeerlijk produkt. De geschiedenis van Melkunie Holland en haar voorgangers 1872-1989*, Melkunie Holland: Woerden, 1989.

"Dutch-German Dairy Merger Agreed," *Agra Europe*, December 8, 2000.

McRitchie, Sarah, "Planning for the Future," *Dairy Industries International*, March 1992, p. 31.

Rubio, Ruby Anne M., "Dutch Dairy Firm Campina Buys into Alaska," *BusinessWorld*, January 3, 2006.

Van Roost, Michelle, "The Making of a Meat Replacer from Milk," *Food Engineering & Ingredients*, June 2005, p. 26.

Vickers, Alan, "Bouncing Back," *Dairy Industries International*, July 2001, p. 20.

Walkland, Chris, "How the Proposed Marriage of Two Dairy Giants Collapsed," *Grocer*, April 30, 2005, p. 55.

❒ Carnival®

Carnival Corporation

———— ∎ ————

3655 N.W. 87th Avenue
Miami, Florida 33178-2428
U.S.A.
Telephone: (305) 599-2600
Fax: (305) 406-4700
Web site: http://www.carnivalcorp.com

Public Company
Incorporated: 1972
Employees: 71,200
Sales: $8.7 billion (2005)
Stock Exchanges: New York London
Ticker Symbol: CCL
NAIC: 483112 Deep Sea Passenger Transportation; 487210 Scenic and Sightseeing Transportation, Water

∎ ∎ ∎

Begun with one ship that ran aground on its maiden voyage, Carnival Corporation has since grown into the most successful and prominent American cruise line. Carnival is the largest cruise company in the world with 12 brands in its arsenal, including Carnival Cruise Lines, Princess Cruises, Holland America Line, Seabourn Cruise Line, Windstar Cruises, Costa Cruises, P&O Cruises, Cunard White Star Line, Swan Hellenic, Ocean Village, Aida, and P&O Cruises Australia. Carnival has combined these cruise lines into an operating fleet of 79 state-of-the-art ships that sail the seven seas. Through innovative vacation packaging and extensive advertising campaigns, the family-operated company has changed the face of the cruise industry by coaxing thousands of middle-class customers aboard its floating resorts. After its purchase of P&O Princess Cruises plc in 2003, Carnival Corporation became a dual-listed company with U.K.-based Carnival plc.

EARLY HISTORY

Carnival was founded in 1972 by Ted Arison, an Israeli immigrant. After serving in World War II with the British Army and in Israel's War of Independence, in the late 1940s Arison founded a cargo line running between Israel and New York, but was put out of business by competition from the Israeli state-run shipping line. In 1954 he moved to the United States, where he took a position as cargo manager for El Al, Israel's national airline. He eventually founded his own air freight company, Trans Air System, which went public in the late 1960s.

In 1968, at the age of 42, Arison moved to Miami to operate a small Israeli-owned cruise ship running between Florida and the Caribbean. When the Israeli government impounded the boat to collect the owners' debt, Arison quickly filled a Norwegian Caribbean Line ship with the customers he had lined up. Convinced that he should own boats rather than operate them for others, in 1972 he entered into a partnership with former schoolmate Meshulam Riklis, who then owned the travel conglomerate American International Travel Service (AITS). They formed Carnival Cruise as a subsidiary of AITS, and for $6.5 million they purchased the ship *Empress of Canada,* which they renamed the *Mardi Gras.*

The ship's first voyage was less than spectacular: The *Mardi Gras* ran aground off the Florida coast with several hundred travel agents on board. Future voyages went more smoothly, however, and in 1974 Arison bought Riklis's share of Carnival for $1, also assuming the company's debt of more than $5 million. To cut costs, Arison sought to reduce fuel consumption by reducing the speed of the *Mardi Gras* and the number of stops it made. This simple economizing measure was to revolutionize the entire cruise industry. Since passengers would have to spend more time at sea between Caribbean ports of call, Arison added more on-board entertainment features, including a disco, casino, movie theater, and nightclubs. Carnival's marketing staff quickly dubbed the *Mardi Gras* the "Fun Ship," and other cruise lines soon followed Arison's lead.

GROWTH AND EXPANSION: 1970-80

In the 1970s the hit television series *The Love Boat* helped revitalize the cruise industry, bringing people on board ships in larger numbers than ever before: Between 1970 and 1986 the number of people taking cruises soared from 500,000 to 2.1 million. By 1978 Arison had three ships running seven-day cruises from Florida to the Caribbean and in the Caribbean itself: the *Mardi Gras*; the *Carnivale*, which he bought in 1975; and the *Festivale*, which he bought in 1977. Despite a bad economy and high fuel prices, in 1978 Arison also contracted for a fourth ship, the *Tropicale*, which was completed in 1982. In 1979 Arison's 30-year-old son, Micky Arison, was named president and chief executive of the company.

The 1980s brought the cruise industry massive expansion: Between 1981 and 1991 the number of berths on North American cruise ships grew from 41,000 to 84,000. Carnival was the chief exponent and beneficiary of the boom. In 1982 Carnival's four boats carried some 200,000 passengers, with the firm earning $40 million on revenues of about $200 million. During the next decade the number of passengers carried per year nearly quintupled. Beginning in 1980, Carnival's revenues grew 30 percent annually, three times faster than the average for the cruise business as a whole. During the recession of the early 1980s, Carnival ordered three more ships, the first from the Danish Aalborg shipyard at a cost of $180 million and two additional ships from the Swedish state shipbuilding company, Svenska Varv, for a total of $262 million. With the completion of these three "superliners"—*Holiday, Jubilee,* and *Celebration*—Carnival had the world's largest cruise line fleet, with seven ships.

1980-90: AN INNOVATIVE MARKETING CAMPAIGN

To help fill these ships, Carnival adopted aggressive marketing and advertising strategies. In 1984 Carnival initiated the memorable "Fun Ship" advertising campaign, which featured talk show host Kathie Lee Gifford partaking of shipboard amenities and singing "We've Got the Fun." In 1984, for what was then the largest network television advertising campaign in the cruise industry, Carnival spent $10 million to advertise during *The Love Boat* and network news shows.

To gain support from travel agents, Carnival routinely sent representatives to travel agencies to inquire about vacation options. If the agent recommended a cruise as a first option, the representative would give the agent $10. If the agent's first recommendation was a Carnival cruise, he or she would get $1,000. By the end of 1989 Carnival had given away more than $500,000 with this program.

In an attempt to attract younger, more middle-class customers to cruises, which had traditionally been the preserve of older, upper-class travelers, Carnival offered cheaper, shorter trips—in 1988 the company's low-priced air and sea packages were approximately 20 percent below industry averages. Advertising efforts targeted toward the younger market included a 1988 Fourth of July party on a Carnival ship that was broadcast on MTV. These strategies paid off: In 1989 the annual household income of passengers was between $25,000 and $50,000, and 30 percent of the passengers in the early 1990s were between the ages of 25 and 39. In addition, Carnival's ships were consistently running at full capacity.

STRATEGIC ACQUISITIONS

In 1987 Ted Arison sold 18 percent of the shares of his private empire, raising nearly $400 million for the company, and Carnival went on a spending spree. The company entered into a contract for the *Ecstasy*, sister ship to the *Fantasy*, which had been ordered earlier in

KEY DATES

1972: Ted Arison and Meshulam Riklis establish Carnival as a subsidiary of American International Travel Service (AITS).
1974: Arison buys Riklis's stake in Carnival.
1984: Carnival initiates its "Fun Ship" advertising campaign, which features talk show host Kathie Lee Gifford.
1987: Carnival goes public.
1988: The company purchases the Holland America Line for $625 million.
1992: Carnival agrees to acquire a percentage of Seabourn Cruise Lines.
1997: The company buys a 50 percent interest in Costa Cruise Lines.
1998: Carnival gains a controlling interest in the Cunard White Star Line.
2003: P&O Princess Cruises plc is acquired; its name is changed to Carnival plc.

passengers, generating $600 million in revenues and earning profits of $196 million.

In 1989 Carnival completed the Crystal Palace Resort & Casino, a lavish 150-acre resort in the Bahamas, which cost Carnival $250 million to develop. The 1,550-room hotel had many extravagant features, including a $25,000-per-night suite that included a robot that brought bath towels and an aquarium with a stingray. With its 13 restaurants, golf course, tennis courts, and other recreational facilities, the Crystal Palace was the biggest resort in the region. Carnival's 1989 revenues surpassed $1 billion, and the firm earned profits of $193 million while carrying 783,485 passengers.

CHANGE AND GROWTH: 1990-2000

The following year Ted Arison, at the age of 66, stepped down as chairperson of Carnival and was succeeded by his son Micky. Shortly thereafter, the industry's boom of the previous decade began to taper off. The war in the Persian Gulf brought higher fuel and airline costs and deterred tourists. The effects were reflected in Carnival's stock price, which slid from 25 points in June 1990 to 13 points late in the year. At the same time, it became apparent that the Crystal Palace would be an unprofitable venture. At the end of fiscal year 1990, Carnival incurred a $25.5 million loss from the resort and casino operation and not long after began attempting to sell the Crystal Palace. In 1991, with no prospective buyers, Carnival agreed to turn over a large portion of the resort to the Bahamian government, in exchange for cancellation of some of the debt incurred during construction. Carnival took a $135 million write-down on the Crystal Palace for that year.

Still, in 1991 Carnival enjoyed a 26 percent share of the passengers in the $5 billion cruise ship market, with revenues of $1.4 billion. Its average occupancy level stood at 103 percent, well above the industry's average of 90 percent. In April 1991 Carnival signed a $300 million contract for a ship, the *Sensation*, to be delivered in 1993. In September of the same year the *Fascination*, to be ready in late 1994, was ordered at a cost of $315 million. In an effort to gain more working capital, Carnival offered 7.85 million Class A common shares for sale in 1991.

The company also entered into an agreement in 1991 to acquire Premier Cruise Lines for $372 million. Though smaller than Carnival, Premier had a lucrative contract with Walt Disney Co. to be the official cruise line for Walt Disney World in Orlando, Florida. The deal fell through, however, when a final agreement could not be reached on the price.

the year. In addition, Carnival attempted to buy the cruise ship business of Gotaas-Larsen Shipping Corporation, which owned part of Royal Caribbean and a majority of Admiral Cruise Lines, but the sale did not go through.

In 1988 Carnival purchased the Holland America Line for $625 million. A longstanding company with four cruise ships and about 4,500 berths, Holland America sailed to the Alaska coast in the summer and the eastern Caribbean in the winter. Holland's trips were aimed at higher-income travelers—its Caribbean cruises cost 27 percent more than a Carnival cruise of the same length. In addition, as part of the package, Carnival acquired two other companies that Holland America owned: Windstar Sail Cruises and Holland America Westours, which included Westmark Hotels.

The acquisition greatly expanded the company's operations. Windstar Sail Cruises, whose three large passenger sailing ships operated in the South Pacific, Mediterranean, and Caribbean, served the luxury market. Westours operated Westmark's 18 hotels in addition to five dayboats, 240 motor coaches, and eight glass-domed railcars in Alaska and the Canadian Northwest. Already the world's largest cruise operator based on passengers carried, with this single purchase Carnival boosted its number of berths by more than 50 percent. During the year following the acquisition, Carnival carried 579,000

In 1992 Carnival agreed to acquire a percentage of Seabourn Cruise Lines. Seabourn, operated in partnership with Atle Byrnestad, served the ultra-luxury market, running tours to locations such as South America, the Baltics, the Mediterranean, and Southeast Asia. The company also signed a contract for a $330 million ship, the *Imagination,* to be delivered in the fall of 1995. Perhaps the most impressive ship introduced in the modern era was the *Carnival Destiny,* the largest passenger ship afloat at 101,000 tons and room for 2,640 people. Its maiden voyage was in 1996.

In 1997 Carnival purchased a 50 percent interest in Costa Cruise Lines, in partnership with Airtours, a travel company. These acquisitions strengthened the company's presence around the world, but especially in the Caribbean. Yet the company's most important acquisition came in 1998 when it purchased a controlling interest in the Cunard White Star Line. Cunard's five ships, including the *QE2,* the *Vistafjord,* the *Royal Viking Sun,* and *Sea Goddess I* and *II* catapulted Carnival into the super-luxury cruise line business.

By 1998 the company had changed its legal name to Carnival Corporation, to emphasize the growing diversity within its cruise lines. Yet when every indicator seemed to point the way toward uninterrupted and uneventful prosperity for the company, disaster struck. In July 1998, the cruise ship *Ecstasy* caught fire after leaving the port in Miami, Florida bound for Newport News with 2,575 passengers on board. Although no one was injured during the fire and evacuation, the ship suffered extensive damage to more than 100 cabins, while heat and smoke damaged adjacent sections of the ship. The precise cause of the fire remained unknown, but the *Ecstasy* was examined meticulously and refitted in drydock; it re-entered cruising service not long afterward.

Carnival did not suffer financially or from a public relations standpoint because of the fire on the *Ecstasy,* and it continued to look forward to further growth, building on its name recognition, which was the highest in the industry. Since studies showed that only 5 percent of the 70 million Americans who could afford cruises chose that type of vacation, Carnival seemed to have plenty of room for expansion.

SAILING INTO THE NEW MILLENNIUM

While Carnival dealt with challenges in the early years of the new millennium, it managed to make its largest purchase to date in 2003. Before that, however, the company and its peers found themselves exposed to a slowdown in the travel industry brought on by the ter-

rorist attacks in 2001, the ensuing war in Iraq, and the outbreak of illnesses, including severe acute respiratory syndrome (SARS). At the same time, Carnival's deal to purchase timeshare company Fairfield Communities Inc. fell through as its share price fell and profits waned. The company's venture with Star Cruises to acquire NCL Holding, the parent of the Norwegian cruise line, also was canceled.

To make matters worse, Carnival came under fire for covering up illegal dumping practices. During this time period, the cruise industry as a whole felt pressure from environmental groups to clean up their act. According to these groups, sewage from cruise ships contributed to a host of problems, including contamination of the world's oceans. In April 2002, Carnival pled guilty to dumping pollutants into the ocean. It paid an $18 million fine and faced five years of probation.

Meanwhile, the company was preparing to significantly bolster its holdings. In 2001, Carnival set its sights on P&O Princess Cruises plc. P&O, formed by the demerger of The Peninsular and Oriental Steam Navigation Company in October 2000, had more than 150 years of experience in passenger cruising and had become a leader in the United Kingdom and Australian cruise markets. A bidding war with competitor Royal Caribbean Cruises Ltd. began in 2002. In the end, P&O shareholders accepted Carnival's $5.67 billion bid.

Upon completion of the deal in 2003, Carnival controlled more than 43 percent of the $11 billion cruise market. It had far surpassed Royal Caribbean, which held a 24 percent share of the market. Carnival Corporation became a dual-listed company with U.K.-based Carnival plc; P&O adopted the Carnival name after the deal. Both companies shared the same executive team, with Micky Arison as chairman and CEO.

Carnival's union with Princess showed early signs of paying off. In 2004, the company achieved record financial results with revenues of $7.68 billion and net income of $1.46 billion. The company launched eight new ships that year including the *Queen Mary 2,* the world's largest cruise ship; *Costa Magica;* Carnival's *Miracle* and *Valor;* Princess Cruises' *Diamond, Sapphire,* and *Caribbean Princesses;* and Holland America Line's *Westerdam.* The company planned to have an additional 12 ships in operation by 2009.

Revenue and profits climbed even higher in 2005, reaching $8.7 billion and $1.78 billion, respectively. The company claimed that with 123,000 berths and almost 55,000 crewmembers, there were roughly 175,000 people at sea with Carnival at any given time. Indeed, travel enthusiasts would no doubt be sailing with Carnival, the world's largest cruise operator, for years to come.

Daniel Gross
Updated, Thomas Derdak, Christina M. Stansell

PRINCIPAL SUBSIDIARIES

Costa Crociere, S.p.A. (Italy); HAL Antillen N.V. (Netherlands Antilles); Holland America Line N.V. (Netherlands Antilles); Princess Bermuda Holdings Ltd.; Princess Cruise Lines Ltd. (Bermuda); Sitmar International S.R.L. (Panama); Sunshine Shipping Corporation (Bermuda).

PRINCIPAL COMPETITORS

Royal Caribbean Cruises Ltd.; Star Cruises Ltd.; TUI AG.

FURTHER READING

Adams, Marilyn, "Cruise-Ship Dumping Poisons Seas, Frustrates U.S. Enforcers," *USA Today,* November 8, 2002, p. A1.

Barker, Robert, "Is This a Dream Cruise for Investors?," *BusinessWeek,* November 25, 2002.

Blum, Ernest, "Carnival Is Expected to Postpone Re-Entry of Ecstasy Beyond July 31," *Travel Weekly,* July 27, 1998, pp. 1, 45.

Brown, Jerry, "Carnival Corporation Set to Buy Cunard," *Travel Weekly,* April 9, 1998, pp. 1, 4.

"Carnival Inks Deal with Shipyard to Build Queen Mary 2," *Wall Street Journal,* November 7, 2000, p. B8.

Fins, Antonio N., "Batten Down the Hatches and Rev Up the Jacuzzis," *Business Week,* August 19, 1991.

———, "Carnival Tries Sailing Upstream," *Business Week,* September 25, 1989.

Golden, Fran, "New Deals," *Travel Weekly,* June 4, 1998.

———, "Ted Arison Turns Hardship into 'Fun Ship'," *Travel Weekly,* March 30, 1998, p. 44.

Harris, Nicole, "At Carnival, Cruise Prices Stay Low," *Wall Street Journal,* June 26, 2003, p. D3.

"Pacesetter for Cruise Industry," *New York Times,* July 25, 1987.

Perez, Evan, "Carnival, Winning Princess Bid, Is Poised to Expand Dominance," *Wall Street Journal,* October 28, 2002, p. A3.

Peterson, Iver, "Leading Passengers to Water," *New York Times,* September 28, 2003.

Rice, Faye, "How Carnival Stacks the Decks," *Fortune,* January 16, 1989.

20 Years of Fun: A History of Carnival Cruise Lines, Miami: Carnival Cruise Lines, 1992.

Tagliabue, John, "Amid a Glut, the Biggest Ship Ever Rises," *New York Times,* June 27, 2003.

Wayne, Leslie, "Carnival Cruise's Spending Spree," *New York Times,* August 28, 1988.

Cinemeccanica S.p.A.

Viale Campania, 23 20133
Milano,
Italy
Telephone: (39) 02 74 81 151
Fax: (39) 02 70 100 470
Web site: http://www.cinemeccanica.it

Private Company
Incorporated: 1920
Employees: 130
Sales: $40 million (2005 est.)
NAIC: 333315 Photographic and Photocopying Equipment Manufacturing

■ ■ ■

Cinemeccanica S.p.A. is a leading manufacturer of motion picture projection equipment. Its products include 35mm and 70mm film projectors; lamphouses; theater automation systems; film handling equipment; screens; and a digital cinema projector made in partnership with Belgian imaging technology firm Barco. The company also distributes sound equipment and provides installation of full "turnkey" projection systems. Cinemeccanica's products are sold around the world by a network of more than 90 dealers and used in major theater chains like AMC, Warner Brothers, Gaumont, and Rank, as well as at studios and other production facilities.

EARLY YEARS

Founded in 1920 in Milan, Italy on the site of the former R. Bossi factory, Cinemeccanica started out making a number of different products, including motorcycle engines and various items of cast metal, as well as motion picture equipment. Its first film projector, the Victoria I model, was unveiled at the Milan Trade fair that same year, and in 1924 the company was reorganized to concentrate exclusively on film equipment under chairman Professor Francesco Mauro and managing director Dr. Umberto Cecchi.

In 1926 Cinemeccanica opened a new manufacturing plant to make lightweight magnesium 35mm cameras for use in aerial cinematography, and in 1929 the introduction of talking pictures led the firm to develop its first sound movie projector, the Victoria 2. The new technology necessitated the company's expansion into electrical engineering, as the machine required electronic systems in addition to mechanical ones.

After Italy's defeat in World War II Cinemeccanica began seeking to export its products, initially targeting France to the north. Foreign sales grew during the 1950s, and in 1959 the company signed an agreement with the Rank Organisation of England in which the latter firm agreed to install Cinemeccanica equipment in its theater chain and market it in 33 countries, while ending production of its own Gaumont Kalee line. The agreement would bring the name Cinemeccanica to a new level of international recognition.

COMPANY PERSPECTIVES

■

Since it was founded in 1920, Cinemeccanica has been known for the quality and reliability of its products and for the high level of service to customers. Today, Cinemeccanica, with headquarters in Milan, Italy, and more than ninety sales points all over the world, is one of the top theater-equipment manufacturers with a large international installed base. Cinemeccanica, combining tradition and experience with innovation, is more than ever committed to satisfying today's and tomorrow's needs of worldwide customers.

INTRODUCING THE VICTORIA 8 IN 1961

In 1961 the company introduced a projector called the Victoria 8, which was capable of showing both the longtime theatrical standard of 35mm and the new 70mm gauge. The latter offered much higher resolution images as well as multichannel sound via magnetic stripes laid on the film, though it added significantly to the cost of production and was used only for epics like *Ben-Hur* and *The Sound of Music*. The technically advanced machine helped solidify the firm's status as one of the premier manufacturers of projection equipment in the world. Unlike some of its competitors, Cinemeccanica had never made gear for nontheatrical film gauges like 16mm and 8mm.

The company's equipment reached the United States in 1962 when the Hornstein family of New York began marketing its products. Two years later American distribution was picked up by Carbons, Inc. (later known as Xetron).

In 1966 Cinemeccanica was chosen to outfit the first four-screen cinema in the world, the Metro Plaza in Kansas City, Missouri, which was run by Stan Durwood's American Multi-Cinema (AMC). The installation utilized the Victoria 8 model. The multiscreen concept proved highly successful due to the savings realized from using a small lobby staff to service new audiences every few minutes. Other theater owners soon took the same approach, and equipment firms like Cinemeccanica benefited as the number of screens began to grow exponentially.

In 1968 the industry began to adopt the platter system, which allowed a film to be shown continuously from beginning to end without reel changes. Prior to its development theaters had used two projectors for each screen, with the movie shipped on reels of ten- to 20-minute duration that were either changed one after the other or spliced onto larger reels about one hour long for a single change mid-feature. Over the next few years Cinemeccanica would begin producing both platters and automation systems that could trigger changes in lighting and volume level (between previews and feature), and shut off the projector at the end. The platter system would help make the multiplex even more economically efficient, as one projectionist could oversee multiple screenings at the same time, further reducing overhead costs.

DEBUT OF THE VICTORIA 5 IN 1975

In 1975 Cinemeccanica introduced the Victoria 5 projector. Developed as a lower-cost 35mm machine for use in multiplexes, it would become the firm's most-installed unit worldwide, eventually accounting for 95 percent of sales. Two years later the company also developed a fully automated system that used a pair of projectors to eliminate rethreading the film between showings (as was necessary with even the platter system). This concept was especially popular in Korea and Japan, where the firm's equipment had first been distributed in 1970. Other Pacific Rim nations like Singapore, Thailand, and Australia were beginning to adopt the firm's equipment during this period as well.

The Victoria 5 also resulted in increased sales to the United States, as Cinemeccanica projectors were installed throughout the rapidly growing AMC chain. General Cinema and Loews (both of which would much later be absorbed by AMC) would begin using the firm's equipment in their theaters, too, with some 1,300 machines installed by General Cinema alone over the next few years.

In 1978 Vittore Nicelli was named managing director of the company, while long-term leader and owner Dr. Umberto Cecchi retired. Nicelli had begun working for Cinemeccanica in 1964 as an electronics engineer to design transistorized sound systems, before working his way into management.

In 1985 Cinemeccanica formed an American subsidiary in Clearwater, Florida, as distribution through Xetron had ended four years earlier. The firm's agreement with Britain's Rank also had ended in 1984 when that firm gave up all of its theaters save those in the United Kingdom.

The company's technical innovation continued in 1992 with the introduction of a new "basement" sound reader that had been developed in conjunction with Dolby Labs, which could read that firm's new SRD

KEY DATES

●

1920: Cinemeccanica is founded in Milan; the Victoria I film projector is introduced.

1924: The company begins producing movie equipment exclusively.

1926: A second factory is opened to make a lightweight magnesium-bodied camera.

1945: Expansion to France starts the firm's international expansion.

1959: An agreement is signed to put Cinemeccanica equipment in Rank theaters.

1961: The Victoria 8 dual 35mm/70mm projector is introduced.

1962: Sales to the United States begin through the Hornstein family of New York.

1966: The firm's equipment is installed in the world's first four-screen theater in Kansas City.

1975: The Victoria 5 multiplex-ready projector is introduced; it becomes the firm's top seller.

1978: Vittorio Nicelli is named managing director.

1985: An American subsidiary is formed in Clearwater, Florida.

1992: The company develops a new digital sound reader in partnership with Dolby Labs.

1995: A French subsidiary is formed.

2005: DLP digital cinema projector manufacturing begins in partnership with Barco.

---

digital audio format while also yielding improved results from the older SV-A analog soundtrack.

The year 1995 saw the creation of a French subsidiary, Cinemeccanica France S.A., in Paris. In addition to selling through its two subsidiaries, the firm utilized numerous professional cinema equipment dealers around the world to sell and service its products, with repair work performed by technicians trained by Cinemeccanica. Some installations were performed by the company's own staff, such as those done in Persian Gulf countries like Dubai.

In 1996 Cinemeccanica lost a suit filed by Leonard Studio Equipment, which had alleged patent infringement in the firm's manufacture of Dario and Super Dario camera dollies. They were subsequently discontinued.

By the start of the 21st century the company had become the dominant supplier of professional projection equipment to much of Europe and in many other countries of the world. An estimated 80 to 85 percent of installations in Italy, Spain, and the Middle East utilized Cinemeccanica projectors, while South America and South Africa also were supplied in large part by the firm, and theaters in Asia and those of several major U.S. chains used significant numbers as well. The firm's products had gained a reputation for reliability and long-term service support, with some machines from as far back as the 1940s and 1950s still in operation, and production of the classic Victoria 8 from 1961 ongoing. The firm machined parts and assembled projectors at its factory in Milan, with production averaging about 1,500 units per year.

DIGITAL ERA BEGINNING IN 2004

In 2004 Cinemeccanica signed an agreement to partner with Belgian imaging technology firm Barco to produce a digital video projector. The company had recently performed an installation of digital projection equipment in Bratislava, Slovakia, and was seeing increasing demand for such equipment. Barco's 2K technology was based on Texas Instruments' DLP Cinema, which was the first digital video format approved by Hollywood studios for use in theaters. Barco also would work with several other projector makers, including Cinemeccanica rival Strong, to produce digital projection equipment.

DLP had been developed to respond to the specific requirements of projecting large high-definition film-like images from digital media in darkened theaters, with the minimum goal being an improvement over the visual quality of 35mm film. It offered a number of advantages including scratch-, flicker-, and jitter-free images, with minimal cost for producing and shipping prints as compared with the significant expense of manufacturing and distributing the 35mm format. Replacement of damaged prints would be as simple as creating another digital copy of a master, and piracy concerns were alleviated somewhat by the noncompatibility of digital theater formats with home video. The latter was recorded at 25 or 30 images per second, in contrast with the worldwide film standard of 24, which DLP would continue to use. DLP theoretically offered a contrast ratio of 1,000:1 and could reproduce 4.4 trillion different shades of color, some 40 percent more than high-definition television. It was expected eventually to replace film in first-run theaters, though as with earlier innovations like 3-D and 70mm, theater owners balked at the initial cost of installing the equipment. In contrast with those specialized formats, however, digital cinema was clearly on its way to becoming the industry standard, though the exact timeline for adoption was still unclear.

In 2005 the new D-CineStar DP60 digital projector was introduced. The liquid-cooled machine, which was co-branded with Barco, utilized a modified Cinemeccanica 35mm projector lamphouse and offered the option of a switcher that could accept a variety of formats from different sources to show advertising or other content before films. In addition to saving costs on the production end, the new development was expected to be a boon for the projection equipment industry, which soon would have many thousands of screens to re-equip worldwide.

After more than 85 years Cinemeccanica S.p.A. had established itself as a leader in the motion picture projection equipment industry. The firm's long-term management continuity, as well as its partnerships with developers of cutting-edge technology like Dolby and Barco, put it in a strong position for future success.

Frank Uhle

PRINCIPAL SUBSIDIARIES

Cinemeccanica France S.A.; Cinemeccanica U.S., Inc.

PRINCIPAL COMPETITORS

Ballantyne of Omaha, Inc.; Christie Digital Systems, Inc.; Kinoton GmbH.

FURTHER READING

"Barco, Cinemeccanica to Develop Digital Cinema Products," *AFX European Focus,* October 25, 2004.

Johnston, Sheila, "High Tech in Short Supply; Equipment Manufacturers 'Swamped,'" *Variety,* June 23, 1997, p. 35.

Kelleher, Ed, "Cinemeccanica Celebrates 75 Years of Service," *Film Journal,* July, 1995, p. 74.

Lally, Kevin, "Buon Compleanno," *Film Journal International,* July 1, 2005.

"Milan's Cinemeccanica Supplies Projection Gear Around the World," *Variety,* October 22, 1986, p. 342.

Sandler, Adam, "Leonard Wins Dolly Patent Fight," *Daily Variety,* May 2, 1996, p. 6.

Columbia Forest Products Inc.

222 S.W. Columbia Street, Suite 1575
Portland, Oregon 97201
U.S.A.
Telephone: (503) 224-5300
Toll Free: (800) 547-4261
Fax: (503) 224-5294
Web site: http://www.columbiaforestproducts.com

Private Company
Incorporated: 1957
Employees: 4,000
Sales: $1 billion (2005 est.)
NAIC: 321210 Veneer, Plywood, and Engineered Wood Product Manufacturing; 321211 Hardwood Veneer and Plywood Manufacturing; 321213 Engineered Wood Member (Except Truss) Manufacturing; 321910 Millwork; 423310 Lumber, Plywood, Millwork, and Wood Panel Merchant Wholsesalers

■ ■ ■

Columbia Forest Products Inc. is among North America's largest manufacturers of hardwood plywood and hardwood veneer. Through its subsidiary, Columbia Flooring, it is also a leading marketer of hardwood and laminate flooring. The 100 percent employee-owned company makes products used in flooring, cabinets, architectural millwork, and commercial fixtures. The company has 20 plants throughout the United States and Canada and sells its products through a network of distributors, mass merchandisers, cabinet makers and furniture manufacturers, and independent dealers across the continent. Its products can be milled upon request to bear the FSC ecolabel.

ORIGINS

In 1957, A. J. Honzel and a small group of businessmen purchased a defunct mill south of Klamath Falls, Oregon. They opened Klamath Hardwoods, which produced hardwood plywood. The mill was initially a cooperative, financed in part by its 43 employees.

Honzel remained president of Klamath Hardwoods until 1962. He died in 1993. In 1963, Columbia Plywood Corporation, a holding company, was formed to purchase Klamath Hardwoods. Operations continued as usual until 1966, when the company purchased a company called Indian Head and acquired hardwood veneer operations in Presque Isle, Maine, and Newport, Vermont. Then, in 1976, employees purchased the company from Columbia Plywood Corporation and reorganized the company as an Employee Stock Ownership Plan. They changed its name to Columbia Forest Products Inc.

Columbia underwent a significant growth spurt throughout the 1980s, building and acquiring new facilities across the United States. In 1982, the company built a hardwood plywood manufacturing plant in Old Fort, North Carolina. In 1986, it acquired two hardwood plywood plants in Chatham, Virginia, and Trumann, Arkansas. Three years later, in 1989, it bought a hardwood veneer manufacturing mill in Rutherglen, Ontario, Canada, and a half-round slicing operation in New Freedom, Pennsylvania. It also established its Laminated Products Division in Thomasville, North

Carolina, where it produced laminated panel products and, later, from 1996 until 2001, when the company sold it, laminated flooring.

1990: CONSOLIDATING A NORTH AMERICAN PRESENCE

The 1990s were another decade of strong growth and nationwide expansion for Columbia. In 1990, it built a poplar core veneer plant in Craigsville, West Virginia. In 1995, the International Division began exporting hardwood plywood. In 1996, the company purchased Levesque Plywood in Hearst, Ontario, giving the company a larger presence in the Canadian marketplace. The Levesque division of Columbia Forest Products consisted of four separate operations: a plywood mill, a particle board plant, a melamine overlay mill, and a hardwood plywood mill. Columbia also acquired two other hardwood plywood plants in Danville, Virginia, and DeQueen, Arkansas in 1996. That year, too, the Laminated Product Division became Columbia Flooring, a subsidiary of the company.

Harry Demorest left his position as managing partner at Arthur Anderson and Co. and became chief executive officer of Columbia in 1996, having joined the company in 1991, and serving as its president from 1994 to 1996. Under Demorest, Columbia continued its focus on expansion through acquisition; it acquired a hardwood plant in Cuthbert, Georgia, in 1997 and also purchased a veneer raised panel and door insert plant in Corpus Christi, Texas. The company's Columbia Flooring subsidiary acquired an equity position in Arkansas-based Century Flooring in 1999. However, Columbia also engaged in some plant closings: In 1998, it closed the DeQueen, Arkansas, hardwood plywood plant, and, in 1999, it closed the New Freedom, Pennsylvania, slicing plant, laying off 210 workers.

2000: A FOCUS ON GREEN CERTIFICATION

In the late 1990s, so-called green certification became a hot topic in the lumber products industry as European wood buyers, Home Depot, Nike, and a number of other large American companies declared a preference for buying certified wood. The FSC, an internationally recognized organization, promoted sustainable, environmentally sound forest management. Its oversight ensured consistent reforestation, more selective harvesting, enhanced biodiversity, better road construction, special site protection, and forester and contractor training. As of late 1999, there were about 45 million forested acres under FSC certification, including 6.4 million acres in the United States. Logs from these forests were followed under chain-of-custody procedures so that customers could be sure that the products they bought were "green." In 1999, Columbia joined the FSC, and its Klamath Falls plant began producing plywood using logs harvested from FSC certified lands. It was also named Home Depot's Environmental Leader of the Year award.

From 1999 on, Columbia introduced a certified and/or environmentally progressive product each year. In 2000, it won certification of its plywood from Smart-Wood, a program of the Rainforest Alliance accredited by the FSC and began offering a line of environmentally certified hardwood plywood and particle board. By the middle of the next decade, the company's mills in Arkansas, Maine, North Carolina, Virginia, Ontario, and Quebec produced certified products as well. With certified core material making up 92 percent of finished panel volume, most of the company's hardwood veneers met FSC labeling requirements.

Additional acquisitions in 2000 broadened Columbia's presence in the hardwood veneer market. The company purchased two hardwood veneer manufacturing mills in Mellen, Wisconsin, from Louisiana-Pacific Corp., its thirteenth and fourteenth acquisitions in 15 years. One mill dated back to the 1920s, the other had opened in 1982. It also increased capacity by expanding its plants in Trumann, Arkansas; Craigsville, West Virginia; Klamath Falls, Oregon; and Hearst, Ontario, Canada. Two years later, it purchased Weyerhauser's Multiply plywood factory on the shores of Lake Superior in Nipigon, Ontario, and began marketing Multiply, a branded, three-ply quarter-inch plywood used as underlayment for flooring. And in 2001, it sold the Thomasville, North Carolina, laminate flooring plant and the Corpus Christi, Texas, veneer raised panel and door insert plant. It also partnered with West Virginia-based International Industries in constructing a solid-strip hardwood flooring plant in Holden, West Virginia.

Several unfortunate events drew media attention to Columbia in the early years of the next decade. In 2000, the Occupational Safety and Health Administration investigated a July 1999 accident that had crushed an employee to death at the Indian Head division and

```
┌─────────────────────────────────────────────┐
│                                               │
│              KEY DATES                        │
│                    ■                          │
│  ───────────────────────────────────────      │
│                                               │
│  1957:  Klamath Hardwoods' hardwood plywood   │
│         mill begins operation.                │
│  1963:  The Columbia Plywood Corporation is   │
│         formed as a holding company to        │
│         purchase Klamath Hardwoods.           │
│  1966:  Columbia purchases Indian Head        │
│         hardwood veneer operations in         │
│         Presque Isle, Maine and Newport,      │
│         Vermont.                              │
│  1976:  Columbia reorganizes as an Employee   │
│         Stock Ownership Plan (ESOP) and       │
│         changes its name to Columbia Forest   │
│         Products.                             │
│  1989:  Columbia establishes its Laminated    │
│         Products Division in Thomasville,     │
│         North Carolina.                       │
│  1996:  The Laminated Product Division        │
│         becomes Columbia Flooring.            │
│  2003:  Columbia acquires Millwood Specialty  │
│         Flooring in Ellijay, Georgia, and     │
│         completes the equity buyout of        │
│         Century Flooring in Melbourne,        │
│         Arkansas.                             │
│  2004:  Columbia acquires McMinnville         │
│         Manufacturing Company of              │
│         McMinnville, Tennessee; completes     │
│         the equity buyout of Appalachian      │
│         Precision Hardwood Flooring and       │
│         Appalachian Custom Dry Kilns,         │
│         Holden, West Virginia.                │
│  2005:  Columbia acquires Malaysia Wood       │
│         Industries in Sungai Petani,          │
│         Malaysia.                             │
│                                               │
└─────────────────────────────────────────────┘
```

issued citations to Columbia totaling $235,000. In 2004, a second employee was crushed by a particleboard press, leading company and union officials to work together to identify safer solo work conditions. Workers pushed for a buddy system as an alternative to working alone.

And in 2003, Robert Washburn, a former Columbia worker, who had been fired from his job operating heavy equipment in 2001 after he tested positive for marijuana use, sued the company for violating the state Disabilities Act, saying that he had procured and smoked the marijuana through Oregon's medical marijuana program. The Multnomah County judge ruled against Washburn, saying state law didn't require a company to make accommodations for workers with marijuana in their system, but Washburn appealed and won his case, which then went to the Oregon Supreme Court for review. As of early 2006, the court's decision was still pending.

However, the company remained strong and consolidated its position as a green manufacturer. In 2003, it struck an agreement with Dow BioProducts to become the only hardwood plywood manufacturer to use Dow's Woodstalk Fiberboard made from formaldehyde-free and renewable wheat straw fiber. It also introduced EcoColors, a line of environmentally certified decorative particleboard. In 2005, it launched Pure-Bond, a cost-neutral formaldehyde-free plywood panel and began converting all of its plywood mills to formaldehyde-free manufacturing processes.

Columbia also entered into a project partnership with Clark County Forestry and Parks Department and the Wisconsin Department of Natural Resources to plant and oversee a 12-acre naturally regenerating hardwood site. When BuildingGreen Inc. announced its selections for the 2005 Top 10 Green Building products in early 2006, it chose Columbia's hardwood plywood and agrifiber-core panels.

Throughout the early years of the new decade, the company also continued to grow in the flooring market. In 2003, it acquired Millwood Specialty Flooring in Ellijay, Georgia, manufacturer of unfinished solid strip hardwood flooring, and completed the equity buyout of Century Flooring of Melbourne, Arkansas, which made pre-finished solid hardwood flooring.

In 2004, it purchased McMinnville Manufacturing Company of McMinnville, Tennessee, which also manufactured unfinished, solid strip, hardwood flooring, and completed the equity buyout of Appalachian Precision Hardwood Flooring and Appalachian Custom Dry Kilns of Holden, West Virginia, maker of prefinished solid hardwood flooring. In 2005, Columbia Flooring acquired Malaysia Wood Industries in Sungai Petani, Malaysia, the manufacturer's first large-scale investment in offshore manufacturing facilities. There was also a partnership between Columbia Flooring and Laura Ashley Inc. to manufacture a line of hardwood and laminate flooring under the Laura Ashley brand name.

The 2006 closing of its particleboard plant in Ontario was, according to the company, the result of escalating energy costs, low product prices, the rising Canadian dollar, and global competition. It indicated that Columbia, despite its strengths, had to deal with the ongoing struggles in the wood products industry. However, throughout the years, Columbia had managed to insulate itself from most of the ups and downs of the wood products industry, and in fact, it had turned a profit every year since its inception.

Carrie Rothburd

PRINCIPAL DIVISIONS

Hardwood Plywood; Hardwood Veneer; Columbia Flooring.

PRINCIPAL COMPETITORS

Roseburg Forest Products Company; SierraPine Ltd.; Georgia-Pacific Corporation.

FURTHER READING

"Columbia Forest Products to Produce Formaldehyde-Free Panels," *Wood & Wood Products*, June 2005, p. 24.

"Growth Marks First 40 for Hardwood Plymaker," *Wood Technology*, October 1997, p. 8.

Kryzanowski, Tony, "Buyout of Independent Plymill Speeds Modernization, Growth," *Wood Technology*, May 1999, p. 38.

Dale Carnegie & Associates Inc.

290 Motor Parkway
Hauppauge, New York 11788
U.S.A.
Telephone: (631) 415-9300
Fax: (631) 415-9390
Web site: http://www.dalecarnegie.com

Private Company
Incorporated: 1945 as Dale Carnegie & Associates Inc.
Employees: 300
Sales: $50 million (1997 est.)
NAIC: 61141 Business & Secretarial Schools

■ ■ ■

Based on Dale Carnegie's classic self-help book, *How to Win Friends and Influence People*, family-owned Dale Carnegie & Associates, Inc. offers a path to successful living, with a heavy emphasis on success in business. In the early years of the new millennium there were over 2,700 Dale Carnegie instructors offering training in more than 70 countries and in 25 languages, making it one of the world's largest adult-education operations. Among its seven million graduates were such noted entrepreneurs and business leaders as Tom Monaghan (Domino's Pizza), Mary Kay Ash (Mary Kay Cosmetics), Frank Perdue (Perdue Farms), and Lee Iacocca (Ford Motor Company and Chrysler Corporation).

THE CARNEGIE COURSE: 1912-44

The son of a hardscrabble Missouri farm couple, Dale Carnegie found, while attending college, that training in public speaking enabled him to overcome shyness and raise his level of self-confidence and self-esteem. After a brief stint as a salesman, Carnegie moved to New York City to become an actor. He soon became discouraged, left show business, and returned to sales but did not find his niche until, in 1912, he offered to teach an evening course in public speaking at a Manhattan YMCA. Refused a $2-per-session salary, he negotiated payment on a commission basis instead and soon was earning $30 to $40 a night, teaching at YMCA locations in Philadelphia, Baltimore, and Wilmington, Delaware, as well as in New York City.

As Carnegie's course evolved, it broadened from public speaking to confidence building and increased personal effectiveness. By 1914 he was making $500 a week and hiring assistants to help him teach what he came to call the Dale Carnegie Course in Public Speaking and Human Relations. At first Carnegie simply posted rules or points for the 16-session course on a series of postcards he distributed to instructors. The postcards evolved into a series of booklets given both to instructors and to students taking the course. But despite Carnegie's hiring of instructors, his course remained essentially a one-man operation for many years, with average enrollment of fewer than 1,000 students a year. In 1935 he named his enterprise The Carnegie Institute for Effective Speaking and Human Relations.

Following the publication of Carnegie's 1936 book, *How to Win Friends and Influence People*, which more than 60 years later was still in print, the public flocked to his banner. A 1937 *New York Times* advertisement offering a free demonstration by Carnegie at the Hotel Astor promised 15 benefits in taking the course, among in 168 cities in the United States, Canada, and Norway.

COMPANY PERSPECTIVES

Founded in 1912, Dale Carnegie Training has evolved from one man's belief in the power of self-improvement to a performance-based training company with offices worldwide. We focus on giving people in business the opportunity to sharpen their skills and improve their performance in order to build positive, steady, and profitable results.

them the ability to think on one's feet, increase income, win more friends, improve one's personality, develop latent powers, and get to know intimately 40 ambitious men and women. It drew 2,500 people. According to a 1937 Saturday Evening Post article, the course consisted of 40 sessions over 16 weeks and cost $75. Classes were given such names as The Magic Formula Session, The Crashing-Through Session, The Heckling Session, and The Making-Your-Body-Talk Session. They were presided over by professional instructors who were paid $25 a night.

Other articles, written at various times, described the course in somewhat different ways. In order to master his techniques, Carnegie first required each student to seek a new approach to achieving his or her goals and then to share the results with the other students. In keeping with his maxim that "a man's name is to him the sweetest sound in any language," much of the first session was given to learning how to remember the names of the other participants. The fourth was a kind of show-and-tell session in which each class member was to bring "an exhibit that represents an achievement." The fifth, or "breakthrough" session was devoted to "coming out of your shell." In the seventh, the participants divided into smaller groups. The eleventh, like the fifth, was given to breaking down inhibitions, through role-playing exercises. Each student was expected to give at least a one two-minute talk per session.

TRAINING FOR CORPORATE
MANAGERS: 1945-90

In 1944 Carnegie began licensing certain territories to sponsors who agreed to pay a percentage of revenues to the home office and follow its instructional guidelines. Privately held Dale Carnegie & Associates, Inc. was established in 1945, with Carnegie as president and his wife Dorothy as vice-president. By 1949 the Dale Carnegie Course (now 14 rather than 16 sessions) was being offered annually to 15,000 students attending 300 classes

The annual number of Carnegie students had reached 60,000 by 1957, in 14 countries. License holders generally held classes in office buildings or hotels, but in some cases conducted sessions in conjunction with business or commercial colleges that they also operated. Nearly 900 teachers were trained by a supervisory staff of 20 instructors from national headquarters. The course continued for 14 weeks, with one four-hour session each week, generally from 6:30 to 10:30 p.m. Tuition, including all books and materials, usually cost between $125 and $150. Subjects covered included developing poise, relaxation techniques, overcoming shyness, and displaying enthusiasm.

Although Carnegie's students sought personal growth and happiness, they commonly had more tangible goals, notably increasing their earning power. Business, in turn, was seeking enthusiastic, motivated, self-starting employees and middle managers who could motivate the people working for them. The Carnegie course instilled practical leadership skills based on cooperation rather than confrontation. General Motors Corporation began sending employees to Dale Carnegie & Associates in 1949, paying half the tuition. By 1959, 67 companies were sending staffers to Dale Carnegie, and some, such as The Coca-Cola Company, were paying the entire cost.

Dale Carnegie died in 1955 and was succeeded by his widow as head of Dale Carnegie & Associates. She was credited by Joseph Kahn of the New York Times with transforming the enterprise from "'a Mom-and-Pop store' into a carefully managed commercial operation." She continued the policy of seeking enrollment from the ranks of corporate America and started a workshop for women that did not, however, prove financially successful. Although she remained the major stockholder of the closely held family corporation and had the title of chairwoman, her son-in-law, J. Oliver Crom, became president and chief executive officer of the enterprise in 1978.

Executives of Dale Carnegie & Associates said in 1983 that enrollment was at a record high and that they expected before the end of the year to graduate their three millionth student. The company now had its own "institutes" in 13 cities and 135 licensed sponsors in about 60 countries. There were Carnegie courses covering sales, customer relations, professional development, and executive presentations, as well as the original course on public speaking and human relations—testimony to the growing interest in business training.

Dale Carnegie & Associates also continued, however, to stress the founder's commonsense principles on how to win friends and influence people: smile, listen to oth-

```
┌─────────────────────────────────────────┐
│                                         │
│            KEY DATES                    │
│               ◆                         │
│  ───────────────────────────────────    │
│  1912:  Dale Carnegie offers to teach an evening
│         course in public speaking at a Manhattan
│         YMCA.
│  1914:  Carnegie hires assistants to help him teach
│         what he came to call the Dale Carnegie
│         Course in Public Speaking and Human
│         Relations.
│  1935:  Carnegie names his enterprise The Carnegie
│         Institute for Effective Speaking and Human
│         Relations.
│  1936:  How to Win Friends and Influence People is
│         published.
│  1945:  Privately held Dale Carnegie & Associates,
│         Inc. is established in 1945.
│  1957:  The annual number of Carnegie students
│         reaches 60,000.
│  1987:  Dale Carnegie & Associates celebrates the
│         75th anniversary of the original Dale Carn-
│         egie course.
│  1990:  The company has worldwide annual enroll-
│         ment of more than 170,000.
│  2003:  Dale Carnegie teams up with Walchand
│         Capital to launch Dale Carnegie Training
│         classes in India.
└─────────────────────────────────────────┘
```

ers, make them feel important, encourage and praise good work, call attention to mistakes without violating Carnegie's first principle, "don't criticize, condemn or complain." Required reading, in addition to *How to Win Friends and Influence People*, included two more of Carnegie's books: one on public speaking, first published in 1926, and *How to Stop Worrying and Start Living* (1948).

The Dale Carnegie enterprise of the 1980s received renewed attention partly due to the efforts of Lee Iacocca, who, after reviving the fortunes of Chrysler Corporation credited, in his 1984 autobiography, the Carnegie course with transforming him from a "shrinking violet." By 1987 more than 400 of the nation's 500 largest companies had sent employees to take a Carnegie course at one time or another, and more than 75 percent of the 157,000 students enrolled annually were under corporate sponsorship. Licensed instructors were required to pay $750 and spend two years in part-time training. The basic course cost $700 to $1,000. Dale Carnegie & Associates celebrated the 75th anniversary of the original Dale Carnegie course in 1987 with a four-day convention in St. Louis.

The public-speaking course, based on Dale Carnegie's original seminar, remained by far the most popular of the eight different courses being given in 1989. This course was offered one night a week for 12 to 14 weeks. (The others focused individually on sales, management, professional development, strategic presentations, customer relations, employee development, and executive image.)

1990-2000

By 1990 Dale Carnegie & Associates had worldwide annual enrollment of more than 170,000—an increase of 60 percent since 1983—and 4,500 instructors. In that recession year, however, the enterprise suffered its first drop in enrollment since 1980 (during another recession). Even Chrysler eliminated its policy of paying the tuition (now $895 for the basic 14-session course) for any employee who wanted to take a course. Crom said in 1991 that the company was still profitable. However, it cut its courses from 14 to 12 weeks, updated the basic course, and added new business-related "modules."

There was no change nor need of change in Dale Carnegie's orientation. A *Los Angeles Times* reporter who attended a class in 1991 wrote, "Most enrolled because they want to do better on the job, though a few say they need help in family and personal relationships." In 1994 there were 4,000 Dale Carnegie instructors and 142 licensed sponsors in over 70 countries on every continent except Antarctica. The eight courses were being offered in 20 languages.

Stuart Levine succeeded Crom as chief executive officer in 1992, although he still reported to Crom, who remained president. Interviewed for *Newsday* in 1995, Levine told Drew Fetherston, "I have to tell you, this business was going south. ... When income starts to drop, you take it personally." The problem, he felt, was that the company's offerings were out of date, with just one training course added in 15 years and a host of aggressive competitors nipping at the enterprise's heels. Levin continued, "We took a year and spent a large proportion of our advertising dollars on research." The result, according to Levine, was a greater emphasis on international sales—now responsible for 41 percent of revenue—new courses, and training companies to use workplace teams. The company also adopted the Dale Carnegie Training brand moniker and developed a new logo and mission statement.

One result of the research effort was the creation of a short leadership program for middle- and upper-management people, titled "The Leader in You." Another was a book cowritten by Levine: *The Leader in You: How to Win Friends, Influence People and Succeed in a Changing World.* A quarterly newsletter, "The Leader," was introduced in 1995. Levine, in October 1995, said the company's market share had increased eight to nine percent in the last year, on top of a three percent increase the year before, thereby reversing a three-year decline.

The flagship Dale Carnegie Course also underwent a revision during this period. It now began by asking participants to write a vision of how they would like to see themselves in the future. This vision became the anchor for the individual's course experience and was examined through what the company called "the five drivers of success," namely, self-confidence, human relations, communications, leadership, and controlling stress. These areas provided the framework of the course, leading to a four-phase continuous-improvement cycle, consisting of attitude change, knowledge, practice, and skill development.

The revised 12-session program covered the following dozen subjects: laying the foundation for success, remembering names, building self-confidence, setting breakthrough goals, using the power of enthusiasm, crashing through barriers, strengthening relationships, using the power of recognition, becoming flexible, stating opinions, inspiring others, and identifying breakthrough results. Firms could also request a course tailored to their particular needs or problems.

By mid-1998 Crom was again chief executive officer, and Levine had departed. Crom indicated that the company, in which family members held all the stock, would remain private. "For us, the benefit of being private is more stability in terms of the people we have," he told James T. Madore of *Newsday*, continuing, "This is a very secure business. ... We have certain strengths that we believe would be lost as part of a larger corporation." Dale Carnegie Training had offices in 70 countries and five million graduates in 1998. Annual revenues, including that of the licensees, came to $187 million in fiscal 1996 (the year ended August 31, 1996). The company reserved for itself operations in ten or more cities, including New York and Washington.

In addition to the basic Dale Carnegie Course, Dale Carnegie Training was, in early 1999, offering six other courses: sales advantage, leadership training for managers, high-impact presentations, leadership advantage, customer relations/employee development, and professional development.

MODERNIZING IN THE NEW MILLENNIUM

Dale Carnegie entered the new millennium under the leadership of Peter Handal, the second non-family CEO in Dale Carnegie history. Handal immediately set out to modernize the company. "Mr. Carnegie's principles are still good," he told the *New York Times*, continuing, "What's changed is the world around us." As part of Handal's strategy, he moved company headquarters to the training center in Hauppauge, New York and renegotiated the contract with its franchisee, or sponsor, association. The company created new curriculum, adding courses including Negotiation, High Impact Presentations, Public Speaking Mastery, and Creating an Executive Image to its arsenal. It also began promoting its Youth Training Course, which was designed to foster teamwork and confidence among high school students. Overall, the company nearly tripled its course offerings between 2000 and 2001.

Dale Carnegie also made its first move to embrace the Internet and began developing Web-based classes, which was a marked departure from the company's emphasis on face-to-face communication. In addition, the company began to restructure some of its class formats, offering more two and three-day seminars instead of the 12-week courses. A direct sales program was also launched to increase sales.

A slowing economy in 2001 threatened Dale Carnegie's bottom line. "It's tough out there," Handal told a gathering at the Little Rock Regional Chamber of Commerce. He continued, "But sometimes that means there are things you can seize upon, pieces of business that you can go after that you might not otherwise been able to do." For Dale Carnegie, that meant taking advantage of new opportunities including adding new business from smaller training companies that had been forced to declare bankruptcy, like Fred Pryor Seminars. Dale Carnegie and its sponsors were approved to offer products and services to federal government agencies in 2001. At the same time, the company looked to international markets to fuel growth. In 2003, Dale Carnegie teamed up with Walchand Capital to launch Dale Carnegie Training classes in India.

After more than 90 years, Dale Carnegie stood as a leader in the training industry in 2006. Its impressive and wide-ranging client list included the likes of Harvard University, Time Warner Cable, American Express, Ford, Coca-Cola, and Wal-Mart Stores. With more than seven million graduates annually and operations in over 70 countries, Dale Carnegie was positioned to continue sharpening the skills of business people for years to come.

Robert Halasz
Updated, Christina M. Stansell

PRINCIPAL COMPETITORS

Franklin Covey Co.; Nightingale-Conant Corporation; SkillSoft PLC.

FURTHER READING

Abrams, Garry, "All Smiles," *Los Angeles Times*, June 14, 1991, pp. E1, E16-E17.

Barron, James, "Old Ways Pay Off for Dale Carnegie," *New York Times*, August 8, 1983, pp. D1, D8.

Berry, Joe, "Dale Carnegie's Blues," *Adweek's Marketing Week*, February 17, 1992, p. 16.

Conniff, Richard, "The So-So Salesman Who Told Millions How to Make It Big," *Smithsonian*, October 1987, pp. 82-86, 88, 90, 92-93.

"Dale Carnegie Launches India Operations," *Businessline*, November 14, 2003.

Fetherston, Drew, "Winning Friends, Influencing People," *Newsday*, October 9, 1995, pp. C1+.

Furio, Joanne, "His Own Success Story: He Knows How to Win in Business," *New York Times*, October 15, 1995, Sec. 13, p. 2.

Harriman, Margaret Case, "He Sells Hope," *Saturday Evening Post*, August 14, 1937, pp. 13-14, 30, 33-34.

Hatch, Addy, "A New Dale," *Journal of Business*, August 30, 2001, p. A17.

Johnson, Dirk, "At 75, Carnegie's Message Lives On," *New York Times*, December 13, 1987, p. A28.

Kahn, Joseph, "Dorothy Carnegie Rivkin, 85, Ex-Dale Carnegie Chief, Dies," *New York Times*, August 8, 1998, p. A13.

Kelley, Bill, "How to Make Friends and Sell to People," *Sales & Marketing Management*, August 1989, pp. 40-42.

Kemp, Giles, and Claflin, Edward, *Dale Carnegie: The Man Who Influenced Millions*, New York: St. Martin's Press, 1989.

Lovell, Michael, "Training at Dale Carnegie," *Des Moines Business Record*, June 23, 2003, p. 3.

Madore, James T., "All in the Family for Most Privates," *Newsday*, June 8, 1998, p. C21.

Marshall, Jeannie, "Still a Man of Charm and Influence," *National Post*, February 15, 2002, p. B7.

Nelton, Sharon, "How to Win Friends—for Half a Century," *Nation's Business*, December 1986, pp. 40-41.

"Perk Up Your Personality," *Changing Times*, February 1957, pp. 15-17.

Smith, David, "'Tough out There,' Carnegie CEO Tells LR Chamber," *Arkansas Democrat Gazette*, January 14, 2003.

Strugatch, Warren, "At Dale Carnegie, Looking to a New Generation," *New York Times*, November 5, 2000.

❦ **Dewberry**

Dewberry

────── ■ ──────

8401 Arlington Boulevard
Fairfax, Virginia 22031-4666
U.S.A.
Telephone: (703) 849-0100
Fax: (703) 849-0118
Web site: http://www.dewberry.com

Private Company
Founded: 1956 as Greenhorne, O'Mara, Dewberry &
    Nealon
Employees: 1,840
Sales: $562 (2005 est.)
NAIC: 541310 Architectural Services; 541330 Engineer-
    ing Services

■ ■ ■

Dewberry is a professional services firm involved in such areas as architecture, building engineering, design and build, emergency management, environmental, land development, municipal infrastructure, telecommunications, transportation, water resources, and survey and mapping. The private company employs more than 1,800 people and operates 30 offices in 14 states, including Pennsylvania, New York, Illinois, and California. Dewberry maintains its headquarters in Fairfax, Virginia, where it employs 800 people at a 200,000-square-foot complex. Dewberry does a great deal of public sector work, its federal clients including the Federal Emergency Management Agency, the Department of Defense, Department of Labor, the US Postal Service, US Veterans Affairs, Federal Highway Admini-

stration, and National Park Service. Local and regional government and public authorities that employ Dewberry include the Virginia Department of Transportation, the Virginia Department of Transportation, various units of New York City's Metropolitan Transit Authority, and the cities of Norfolk, Virginia; Tulsa, Oklahoma; Rochester, New York; and Greensboro and Raleigh, North Carolina. Dewberry is the third largest engineering firm in the Washington, D.C., area, and according to *Engineering News-Record* is one of America's "Top 50" design firms and among the top 25 in several market categories.

1956 ORIGINS

Dewberry was co-founded in 1956 by its longtime chairman Sydney Oliver Dewberry, a civil engineer trained at George Washington University. It was originally known as Greenhorne, O'Mara, Dewberry & Nealon. The six-person firm initially set up shop in Arlington, Virginia, to offer engineering and surveying services. Another key employee, Richard N. Davis, joined the firm in 1958 and soon made partner. In the early years the firm concentrated on projects in Northern Virginia and Washington, D.C. A notable contract during this time was the design of the Southeast Relief Water Main in the Capital.

The 1960s was a period of growth on a number of fronts for the firm. It enjoyed considerable success building up its residential land development portfolio during this time. In the mid-1960s it was involved in the construction of Fairfax County's King Park development. Other major Virginia projects included the Skyline Center in Alexandria, a 100-acre mixed-used development, and Lake Braddock in Fairfax County. In addition, the firm opened an office in Maryland in the 1960s to become involved in the building of Montgomery Village, one of America's first upscale planned communities. It was during this period that the firm became involved in the transportation area, winning contracts at Washington National Airport for runway and support system design. In 1964 computers were used by Dewberry engineers for the first time. A year later the firm, now more than 50 employees in size, moved its headquarters to Fairfax, Virginia. It also underwent a name change becoming Dewberry, Nealon, and Davis in 1968.

Dewberry diversified further in the 1970s and opened regional offices throughout Virginia and Maryland, as well as expanding into North Carolina. Maintaining these branches were more than 500 employees. The firm became especially well known for its mapmaking services, design expertise and architecture, and urban planning services. In 1974 Dewberry became involved in the emergency management field when it received a contract related to the National Flood Insurance Project of the federal Office of Preparedness, which in 1979 became part of the newly formed Federal Emergency Management Agency. Dewberry's relationship with FEMA would continue over the next quarter-century. It was also during the 1970s that Dewberry began to make its mark in environmental services, advising a number of communities as well as offering other municipal services. In addition Dewberry expanded its landscape architecture and program management services. Some of the firm's major projects during this time included Pentagon City, a planned "urban village" located in Arlington, Virginia, in the shadow of the military's Pentagon headquarters; another planned community, Lake Ridge, located in Prince William County, Virginia; and Fairfax County's upscale Fair Oaks Shopping Center. The firm also received a major University contract: the Biological Sciences building on the University of Maryland's Baltimore campus.

GROWTH AND DIVERSIFICATION: 1980-90

Dewberry reached its 25th anniversary in 1981 and with the departure of Nealon shortened its name to Dewberry & Davis. The firm also moved its headquarters to a new six-story building in Fairfax, designed and engineered by its own personnel. In that same year, Dewberry expanded by way of acquisition, picking up TOLK, Inc., a mechanical, electrical, plumbing, and fire protection, engineering consulting firm. Dewberry would also end the decade with an acquisition, adding Goodkind & O'Dea in 1989. Founded in 1952, Goodkind & O'Dea provided services in engineering, design and consulting; construction engineering and inspection; land and engineering survey; and land use planning. The firm specialized in the transportation field, which accounted for about 70 percent of its revenues. Dewberry, on the other hand, generated just 10 percent of its business from transportation. Moreover, Goodkind & O'Dea expanded Dewberry's geographic reach, adding offices in Rutherford, New Jersey; New York City; and Hamden, Connecticut. Dewberry also began working throughout the United States in the 1980s, as its consulting services to FEMA were enlarged to include aiding regions declared by the President to be disaster areas. Dewberry expanded in other ways during the decade. It was quick to adopt state-of-the-art computer-aided design (CAD) and drafting technology. It also established the Dewberry & Davis Institute in 1984, a professional development program that helped to teach CAD and other subjects to Dewberry personnel.

In addition to disaster response work throughout the United States, projects with the U.S. military took Dewberry to other parts of the country as well as to Europe in the 1980s. The firm was also involved in a number of non-military government contracts during this time. In the transportation field, the firm fulfilled contracts with the Washington Metropolitan Area Transit Authority and worked on the Fairfax County Parkway. Additional public contracts included surveying and mapping services to the White House and national monument grounds. Major private contracts included the championship-caliber TPC Avenel golf course and upscale residential community in Potomac, Maryland, and Tysons II, a mixed-use development that included high-rise office buildings, a luxury hotel, condominiums, and a major shopping mall.

Dewberry continued to diversify in the 1990s, through start-ups but growth was especially achieved through acquisitions. In 1991 the firm launched Dewberry Project Managements Inc. to provide consulting services to real estate developers. A year later Dewberry opened a Boston office. In 1993 the firm

KEY DATES

1956: Firm founded as Greenhorne, O'Mara, Dewberry & Nealon.

1958: Richard Davis joins the firm.

1968: Firm's name is changed to Dewberry, Nealon, and Davis.

1981: Name is shortened to Dewberry & Davis.

1989: Goodkind & O'Dea is acquired.

1991: Dewberry Project Managements Inc. is formed.

1993: Architectural/engineering firm HTB, Inc. is acquired.

2004: PSA, an Illinois-based design firm, is acquired.

completed a pair of acquisitions. First it added Dillsburg, Pennsylvania-based Capitol Engineering Corporation, which was tucked into Goodkind & O'Dea, followed by another architectural/engineering firm, HTB, Inc., a national leader in institutional and healthcare design based in Oklahoma City. In 1995 Dewberry acquired Philip A. Genovese & Associates, Inc., a Connecticut firm. Two years later Dewberry established a Baltimore office by acquiring Beavin Company Consulting Engineers, which provided water/waste water, transportation, telecommunications, surveying and mapping, and other engineering services throughout Maryland. Finally, in 1999, Dewberry acquired Anderson-Nichols & Company to expand its Boston office. The acquisitions completed in the 1990s allowed Dewberry to expand its environmental services to include water resources, coastal engineering, and hazardous materials management.

One of the most significant projects undertaken by Dewberry in the 1990s was the design of the 14-mile Dulles Toll Road extension, a limited access freeway which ran from Leesburg, Virginia, to Dulles National Airport. The first privately owned toll road to be built in the United States in more than 30 years, it was a high-profile project and something of a national experiment. There was concern in many quarters about the crumbling infrastructure of the United States, and some saw "privatization" projects such as this as a way to fix the problem. In charge was the Virginia Toll Road Corporation, headed by a former Regan Administration official. The company originally hired Parsons, Brinckerhoff, Quade and Douglas, one of the most respected engineering firms in the country, to design the extension. But the two parties had a falling out, the cause of which

was uncertain. Nevertheless in August 1990, Parsons, Brinckerhoff was replaced by Dewberry. All told, the firm provided engineering for 36 bridges along the 14-mile freeway, the longest of which was 660 feet, spanning the Goose Creek Reservoir.

Other prominent contracts in the 1990s included the repair of the Riverside Drive Viaduct in New York City, which had opened to traffic in 1928. Also in the city, Dewberry was involved in some pier restoration work. The firm won a number of contracts related to new educational facilities, including the George Mason University's Prince William Institute. During the 1990s Dewberry also added to its work with FEMA, which during the 1990s received a greater commitment from President Clinton. Dewberry increased its disaster response, emergency management, and mapping services to the agency. On the private sector side of the ledger, a major contract for Dewberry during this period was the Lansdowne Executive Conference Center in Virginia's Loudoun County. The firm was also engaged in a number of industrial projects in southeastern states over the course of the decade.

CO-FOUNDER STEPS DOWN AS CEO IN 1998

The 1990s also witnessed the rise of Barry K. Dewberry to prominence in the firm. After joining the business in the 1970s, he became a general partner in 1988 and was named chief operating officer in 1991 and replaced his father as chief executive officer in 1998. He would only hold the post for three years. In 2001, John P. Fowler took over as CEO, while the elder Dewberry assumed the chairmanship and his son became vice-chairman. Fowler, an engineering graduate from the University of Kansas, had been with the firm since 1983 and had played an instrumental role in Dewberry's rise to the top ranks of U.S. engineering firms. He would soon begin grooming his replacement. In 2002 Ronald L. Ewing, an engineer with more than 30 years of experience, was recruited to serve as chief operating officer. He replaced Fowler as CEO in April 2005.

The firm also underwent a branding initiative with the new century, as its name was shortened to Dewberry and all subsidiaries assumed the Dewberry brand. The firm continued to add to its holdings in the 2000s. It opened an office in Winchester, Virginia, in 2003 as well as an office in Culpepper, Virginia, in 2004. In that same year, Dewberry completed a pair of acquisitions. It expanded its presence in West Virginia by adding Ranson, West Virginia-based Appalachian Surveys, a 25-year-old firm that provided surveying, land planning, and civil engineering services to clients in West Virginia as well as the Eastern Panhandle and western parts of

Maryland. In November 2004, Dewberry acquired Peoria, Illinois-based PSA, a design firm two years older than Dewberry. It was founded above a Peoria Drug store in 1954 by Forest A. Phillips and Eugene C. Swager to provided architectural, engineering, and planning services. In 1983 the two firms first began working together on criminal justice projects. While Dewberry was adding offices in the Mid Atlantic area and taking on national work through FEMA, PSA was expanding into Chicago and Naperville, Illinois; Dallas; and in 1996 entered Dewberry's home territory by opening an office in McLean, Virginia. The two firms proved to be a good fit, leading to the 2004 acquisition. Dewberry merged its building services practice with PSA to form PSA-Dewberry.

In the aftermath of Hurricane Katrina, which devastated New Orleans and the Gulf Coast, Dewberry established a project office in Baton Rouge, Louisiana, in September 2005 to coordinate its work with FEMA in its response to the disaster. Given the extent of the damage, Dewberry was likely to maintain a presence in the area for an extended period of time.

In another significant step, Dewberry decided to merge its design group into PSA-Dewberry. As a result PSA-Dewberry became the architectural and building services unit of the Dewberry conglomerate, generating about $37 million of the parent company's estimated annual revenues of more than $500 million. The union took effect on January 1, 2006, as Dewberry began its 50th anniversary year.

Ed Dinger

PRINCIPAL SUBSIDIARIES

Dewberry Project Managements Inc.; PSA-Dewberry.

PRINCIPAL COMPETITORS

CH2M HILL Companies, Ltd.; The McClier Corporation; Tetra Tech, Inc.

FURTHER READING

"Dewing a Deal," *North Valley Business Journal,* March 1, 2004.

Isaac, Daniel, "Dulles Toll Road Designer Fired by Developer," *Washington Business Journal,* August 27, 1990, p. 7.

Merle, Renae, "Fairfax Engineering Company Assesses Gulf Coast Damage," *Washington Post,* September 12, 2005, p. D1.

"News Design Firm Moves North by Acquisition," *Engineering News-Record,* April 13, 1989, p. 14.

Dictaphone®

Dictaphone Healthcare Solutions

—■—

3191 Broadbridge Avenue
Stratford, Connecticut 06614-2559
U.S.A.
Telephone: (203) 381-7000
Fax: (203) 386-8566
Web site: http://www.dictaphone.com

Division of Nuance Communications Inc.
Incorporated: 1923
Employees: 1,650
Sales: $153 million (2005 est.)
NAIC: 333313 Office Machinery Manufacturing; 334119 Other Computer Peripheral Equipment Manufacturing; 334210 Telephone Apparatus Manufacturing; 334290 Other Communications Equipment Manufacturing; 334310 Audio and Video Equipment Manufacturing; 334515 Instrument Manufacturing for Measuring and Testing Electricity and Electrical Signals; 334613 Magnetic and Optical Recording Media Manufacturing; 511210 Software Publishers

■ ■ ■

Based in Stratford, Connecticut, Dictaphone Healthcare Solutions is a leading developer of dictation, voice processing, and voice management systems. The company markets both hardware and software related to these three areas. Dictaphone is especially focused on the healthcare industry, and its systems are found in more than half of all U.S. hospitals. In addition, the company also serves clients in other "report intensive" fields such as insurance, legal, and public safety. In addition to its Connecticut headquarters, Dictaphone has offices devoted to marketing, sales, support, and service in locations, throughout the United States, Canada, Europe, and the United Kingdom. In 2006 Dictaphone was acquired by Massachusetts-based Nuance Communications and became Nuance's new Dictaphone Healthcare Division. Nuance retained Dictaphone's management team to head up the operations.

PIONEERING DICTATION TECHNOLOGY

Dictaphone's roots stretch back to early experiments in human voice recordings at the Volta Laboratory in Washington, D.C., run by Alexander Graham Bell, the famous inventor who developed the microphone and the telephone. These experiments were carried out during the late 1870s by Bell, his cousin Chichester Bell, and scientist/instrument maker Charles Sumner Tainter.

In 1881 these pioneers, who sought to develop a practical means of recording telephone sounds, produced the Dictaphone and placed the new invention in the Smithsonian Institution. According to the company, this breakthrough recording device "used a rotating cylinder on whose wax coating a steel stylus would cut up-and-down grooves." The Dictaphone included a mouthpiece that was somewhat similar to Bell's telephone.

According to the May 1979 issue of *Modern Office Procedures*, Tainter "gave the new invention its initial test" by reciting a passage from Act 1, Scene V of *Hamlet* into the Dictaphone's mouthpiece. "As he spoke," the article noted, "he hand-cranked the machine, turning the drum at a speed calculated to properly 'cut' this historic record."

In 1888 Alexander Graham Bell and Tainter established the Volta Graphophone Company. Based in the Connecticut city of Bridgeport, the new business venture was formed to market their invention to businesses. The Dictaphone was trademarked by Columbia after the American Graphophone Company, which ultimately became the Columbia Graphophone Company, bought the patent for the recording machine in 1907.

In the December 1990 issue of *The Office*, Darryl C. Rehr explained that initial market acceptance of the new devices was slow: "The steep, $150 price tag and difficulty in using the machines—the wax-coated cardboard cylinders had to be changed every four minutes—militated against the Graphophone's quick acceptance. Sales took off only when the phonographs entered the home-entertainment market. Businessmen, familiar with home versions of the machines, began buying them for office work, and by World War I they were in popular use."

For 27 years Dictaphone operated as a division of Columbia Graphophone, which was more focused on producing sound recordings for entertainment purposes than on developing the business dictation market. Financial conditions forced Columbia to sell Dictaphone in 1923, leading to the formation of Dictaphone Corporation.

During the 1920s Dictaphone found success with the introduction of its Telecord system, which combined the telephone with a recording machine that amplified the speaker's voice and captured it for dictation purposes. Dictaphone unveiled the first electronic desk model recording devices in 1939.

ESTABLISHING INDUSTRY LEADERSHIP: 1940-70

Similar to many other U.S. companies, the onset of World War II resulted in wartime production for Dictaphone. In 1942 the company was asked to develop technology that could be used to record enemy communications and help the military with its code-breaking efforts. According to the company this initiative resulted in the development of "voice logging" equipment (used for recording telephone calls and radio transmissions), which was put to commercial and public safety use in 1947.

Following the war, Dictaphone contacted leading plastics companies about the development of a plastic recording belt. When the company was told that such a product would be impossible to develop, Dictaphone's engineers went to work and made it themselves, producing an affordable, lightweight plastic media that could record 15 minutes of sound. Called the DictaBelt, the new recording media was used with Dictaphone's new Time-Master dictation machine, which used the plastic records instead of wax cylinders. This development, followed by the use of transistors shortly thereafter, enabled the company to produce dictation machines that were much smaller than previous models.

In 1953 Lloyd Maledon Powell was named president of Dictaphone. Powell had joined the company in the early 1920s, shortly after graduating from Purdue University with a civil engineering degree. After working as a contracting engineer and salesman at Dictaphone he became general sales manager and then vice-president in 1951. Powell served as Dictaphone's president until 1966, at which time he was named company chairman. Powell retired in 1969, but remained a company director until 1977. In addition to shaping the company throughout his long career, Powell served as an advisor to President Eisenhower in the Office of Economic Opportunity. He also was a consultant to President Johnson, via the National Economic Stabilization Board, during the Vietnam War.

Throughout the 1950s Dictaphone continued to introduce new products. During this time period a variety of professionals, namely physicians and attorneys, accepted dictation as a better and faster method than handwriting and stenography. The company played a large role in promoting the use of dictation systems. This was evident by its sponsorship of the first National Secretaries Week in June 1952. Dictaphone introduced the Dictet in 1957. Weighing only two pounds, it used a magnetic cassette to record sound and was the first portable dictation machine.

Dictaphone continued on a path of steady progress during the 1960s. The company ended the decade by acquiring Vista-Costa Mesa Furniture in January 1969. By mid-year Dictaphone had opened a manufacturing complex in Killwangen, Switzerland, in order to capture some of the European business equipment market, which was expected to reach $7 billion by the mid-1970s.

MERGER MANIA: 1970-80

Dictaphone continued to introduce new products during the 1970s. A portable battery-powered calculator, priced at $495, was unveiled in 1970. On the dictation front, the company's Thought Tank recorder was introduced in 1972. The device, which included an endless loop of magnetic tape, was unique in that it consolidated both the transcription and dictation functions into one unit. The following year Dictaphone unveiled a minicassette dictation recorder called the Model 1111, as well as its first standard cassette unit, which was named the Model 241.

In 1978 Dictaphone introduced a microcassette dictation/transcription system called Microdictation that employed microprocessor technology, as well as a dozen different units for voice processing. The company also introduced several word management computer systems. In addition, by the late 1970s Dictaphone had established a strong foothold in the automatic telephone answering systems market through its Ansafone product line.

A number of leadership changes took place during the 1970s. In August 1971, E. Lawrence Tabat was named as Dictaphone's president and CEO, succeeding Walter W. Finke. While Finke remained with the organization as a director and consultant, he passed away in February 1972, at the age of 64. In mid-1977 Tabat was succeeded as president by Hobart C. Kreitler, who had been serving as president of Dictaphone's products and systems group. Tabat remained Dictaphone's chairman and CEO until retiring in 1982.

The decade of the 1970s was marked by a flutter of merger activity at Dictaphone. The company avoided several attempted mergers during the first half of the decade. These included proposed takeovers by Gould Inc. in 1971 and Northern Electric Co. in 1974, as well as a failed merger with Sterndent Corporation in 1975.

Merger activity continued during the second half of the decade, beginning with Dictaphone's $21.9 million acquisition of Data Documents Company, an Omaha, Nebraska-based supplier of computer forms and data processing supplies, in 1976. Finally, the decade concluded with Stamford, Connecticut-based Pitney Bowes purchasing Dictaphone for $131 million in cash and stock. Following the acquisition, Dictaphone continued to operate as an autonomous, wholly owned subsidiary of Pitney Bowes.

As Dictaphone headed into the late 1970s, the company was doing quite well financially. Its annual sales, which totaled $132.26 million in 1976, increased to $211.59 million the following year. Net income also increased, from $4.17 million to $5.53 million. In 1977 Dictaphone announced that it would relocate its manufacturing operations from Bridgeport, Connecticut, to Melbourne, Florida, where it planned to invest $2.2 million in the construction of a new facility. Dictaphone's sales increased again in 1978, to $243.83 million, and the company's net income shot up considerably, reaching $11.60 million.

PRODUCT EVOLUTION: 1980-90

The 1980s were characterized by a variety of new product rollouts at Dictaphone. Many of the company's new offerings were capable of handling more than one function. For example, in 1980 the company introduced the Dictamation product line. Dictamation units combined dictation-transcription machines with telephone answering machines capable of recording messages up to 30 minutes long.

Dictaphone continued to pursue the emerging electronic word processing market and introduced its Dictaphone Integrated Office System, which included the System 6000 word processor with data retrieval capabilities. The company's Omninet was a local area network that linked the System 6000 to other like terminals, as well as to personal computers. In addition, System 6000 gave users the ability to send e-mail messages to one another.

By 1983 Dictaphone was marketing a tape-based telephone answering system that bank customers could use to request money transfers after hours. The following year the company began offering a variety of digital recording products. By 1986 Dictaphone had developed a desktop system called Connexions that combined IBM-compatible computers with telephony, voice/text messaging, transcription, and dictation. By the decade's end, the company offered products like the Digital Express 7000 System, which allowed up to 22,000 users to access, store, and record hundreds of reports and voice messages at the same time.

1990-2000: TURBULENT TIMES

The 1990s proved to be a pivotal time period for Dictaphone. Early in the decade the company acquired California-based Elite Communications Systems, a sales and service organization that had focused on Sony dictation products until Sony decided to exit the digital dictation products market.

In 1995 Pitney Bowes decided to sell Dictaphone to Stonington Partners, an investment fund, for $462 million in cash. The sale was part of the parent company's strategy of focusing on its paper communications business. An interim company called Dictaphone Acquisition Inc. was formed to facilitate the sale. John H. Duerden—a former Xerox executive who most recently had been serving as Reebok International's president; chief operating officer; and executive vice-president of sales, finance, operations, and production—was named Dictaphone Acquisition's president, chairman, and CEO. He carried those titles over to Dictaphone Corporation when the acquisition was officially completed in August.

In the October 30, 1995, issue of the *Fairfield County Business Journal*, Duerden remarked: "Our task, now that we're out from under the umbrella of Pitney Bowes, is to chart our own destiny. We're talking about taking a mature company, one that's maybe a little tired, and turning it into something exciting."

Around this time, Dictaphone had annual sales of about $355 million and 3,500 employees. A number of the company's products cost more than $1 million. Duerden sought to cash in on the development of voice-related systems that functioned at the point where fax, voicemail, computers, and other devices were converging.

By 1997 Dictaphone had embarked upon the path

that Duerden had previously charted, focusing on systems that recorded digital and verbal images simultaneously. The company was moving away from a hardware focus, and began concentrating more on software.

As part of its strategy, Dictaphone began concentrating more on research and development and forming strategic alliances with other firms to develop new products. In the January 13, 1997, issue of the *Fairfield County Business Journal*, Don Dzikowski wrote: "One of the first things Duerden said he did was double the company's research and development budget to more than $20 million a year. Next, he began to form a string of strategic alliances with national, smaller companies on top of the desired technology in integrated voice and data management systems. In return, Dictaphone offered its extensive national distribution network."

In 1996 Dictaphone introduced its Enterprise Express digital dictation solution in hospitals throughout the United States. That year, sales totaled $350 million, where they had been for the previous two years, and employees totaled 3,320. By 1997 digital systems accounted for more than 75 percent of Dictaphone's sales. The following year its field sales and service force had grown to more than 1,700 representatives worldwide.

By 1999 Dictaphone had attempted to introduce new products related to voice mail and court reporting, but the efforts were unsuccessful. However, the company was making progress with an Internet-based medical transcription product, as well as its Windows-based Da Vinci monitoring and recording system for large call centers. While Dictaphone's new products offered hope on the financial front, the company remained saddled with $345 million in debt.

The early 2000s arguably were the most turbulent times in Dictaphone's long history. The turbulence began in March of 2000 when Belgium's Lernout & Hauspie (L&H) announced that it planned to acquire Dictaphone from Stonington Partners for $935 million, including approximately $425 million in debt.

The acquisition was completed in May, and by November both Dictaphone Corporation and L&H had filed for Chapter 11 bankruptcy. After L&H acknowledged irregularities and errors in past financial statements, related to one of its divisions in Korea, investigations were launched by Belgian authorities and the U.S. Securities and Exchange Commission. Stonington Partners attempted to sue L&H and sought to rescind the merger, claiming that L&H engaged in fraud by using misleading financial information during the deal. However, the litigation was frozen due to the bankruptcy proceedings.

In June 2001 Rob Schwager, a 23-year Dictaphone

employee who also was president of Dictaphone Health-care Solutions Group—a combined business unit of Dictaphone and L&H—was named president and chief operating officer of Dictaphone Corporation. At this time, L&H President and CEO Philippe Bodson served as Dictaphone's CEO.

By 2001 L&H was quickly selling off business units to raise cash. That August, L&H's creditors agreed in principal to a "debt-for-equity trade." Dictaphone would become an independent company, with the majority of its shares divided amongst various secured creditors and bondholders, and a small number of shares going to unsecured creditors and L&H.

NEW BEGINNINGS: 2002 AND BEYOND

In March 2002 Dictaphone emerged from Chapter 11 as a privately held organization when its reorganization plan was approved by the U.S. Bankruptcy Court for the District of Delaware. According to the company, at the time Dictaphone was "one of the five oldest surviving U.S. Brands." The company emerged with 1,500 employees, down from 2,100 in late 2000. While it had lost $27 million in 2000, Dictaphone generated revenues of $15 million in 2001 and lowered its debt to $50 million.

While Dictaphone got a second chance and a fresh start, by mid-2003 the Delaware Chancery Court had ordered L&H founders Jo Lernout and Pol Hauspie to pay $539 million to Stonington Partners, which charged L&H for acquiring Dictaphone under fraudulent terms.

By the mid-2000s Dictaphone had embarked upon a strategy to focus mainly on the market for healthcare information technology, which it expected would exceed $25 million by 2010. As part of this strategy, the company began selling off some of its business units.

In April 2005 Dictaphone sold its Communications Recording Systems unit, which provided recording systems to call centers, financial companies, and 911 centers, to Israel's NICE Systems for $38.5 million. In January 2006 Dictaphone sold its Florida-based Electronic Manufacturing Systems division, which produced circuit boards, to Pennsylvania-based Bulova Technologies LLC.

A major development took place in February 2006 when Burlington, Massachusetts-based Nuance Communications announced that it would acquire Dictaphone in a cash deal worth $357 million. In a news release Nuance Chairman and CEO Paul Ricci commented on the acquisition, which was completed by the end of March, stating: "The combined resources, experi-ence and talents of Nuance and Dictaphone will help accelerate the adoption of speech recognition to eliminate most manual transcription for healthcare in North America this decade, delivering over $5 billion in sav-ings to care facilities and transcription service organi-zations." Under new parentage, Dictaphone was named a division of Nuance—the Dictaphone Healthcare Solu-tions division—and Schwager was named its president.

Paul R. Greenland

PRINCIPAL COMPETITORS

Sony Corporation; Harris Corporation

FURTHER READING

"Bank and Trust Services Customer Accounts with Answering Machine," *Communications News*, December 1983.

Dennis, Sylvia, "L&H Snaps Up Dictaphone to Enter Healthcare Mkt," *Newsbytes*, March 8, 2000.

Deutsch, Claudia H., "Take a Memo: Dictaphone Is Still in Business; Nowadays, Voice Is Just Another Form of Data," *New York Times*, December 27, 1999.

"Dictaphone Acquires Elite Communications," *PR Newswire*, March 18, 1991.

"Dictaphone Acquisition Completed for $450 Million," *Canada Newswire*, August 11, 1995.

"Dictaphone Acquisition Inc. Hires John Duerden, Former President and COO of Reebok International, to Head New Company," *PR Newswire*, June 14, 1995.

"Dictaphone Emerges from Bankruptcy, Free of L&H," *The Daily Deal*, April 2, 2002.

"Dictaphone Sells Unit to Bulova," *Connecticut Post*, January 4, 2006.

"Dictaphone to Be an Independent Company," *The New York Times*, August 11, 2001.

"Dictaphone to Sell Communication Recording Systems to NICE," *Customer Interaction Solutions*, May 2005.

"Dictaphone Unit for Phone Messages," *The New York Times*, September 4, 1980.

"Dictaphone Unveils Word Processor with Data Retrieval," *Computerworld*, November 8, 1982.

Dzikowski, Don, "Dictaphone Speaks to Future with High-Tech Applications," *Fairfield County Business Journal*, January 13, 1997.

"E. Lawrence Tabat; Executive, 88," *The New York Times*, July 31, 2001.

Fleischer, Jo, "Dictaphone's New CEO Ready to Give Company a Wake-up Call," *Fairfield County Business Journal*, October 30, 1995.

"Former President and Chief Executive of Dictaphone Corporation, WW Finke, Is Dead at 64," *The New York Times*, February 10, 1972.

"Founders of Bankrupt Company Told to Pay Investor $539M," *Miami Daily Business Review*, July 15, 2003.

Gitlin, Bob, "New Image for Dictaphone," *Communications News*, August 1989.

Kerber, Ross, "Burlington, Mass.-Based Voice Technology Firm to Buy Dictaphone Corp.," *The Boston Globe*, March 8, 2000.

"L & H Files Plan to Give Dictaphone to Creditors," *Client Server News*, September 3, 2001.

"Lernout & Hauspie Completes Acquisition of Dictaphone Corporation," *EDGE: Work-Group Computing Report*, May 15, 2000.

"Lernout & Hauspie Speech Products NV—Appointment of Rob Schwager as President and COO of Dictaphone Corporation," *Market News Publishing*, June 1, 2001.

"L.M. Powell, Ex-Chief of Dictaphone, Is Dead," *The New York Times*, March 2, 1982.

"NICE Systems Acquires Call Recording Business from Dictaphone," *CommWeb*, April 11, 2005.

"Nuance to Acquire Dictaphone, Accelerating Strategy to Eliminate Manual Transcription in Healthcare," Stratford, CT: Dictaphone Corp., February 8, 2006, Available from http://www.dictaphone.com.

"Pitney Bowes to Sell Dictaphone for Cash," *The New York Times*, April 27, 1995.

"Plans to Sell Dictaphone Corp. Subsidiary to Private Investors," *S&P Daily News*, April 26, 1995.

Rehr, Darryl C., "Dictation Machines: A Long, Colorful History," *The Office*, December 1990.

Spiro, Leah Nathans, "New Life for a Household Name," *The New York Times*, April 7, 2002.

Strempel, Dan, "Dictaphone Files Chapter 11 Bankruptcy," *Fairfield County Business Journal*, December 18, 2000.

"The Pioneer in Voice Processing," *Modern Office Procedures*, May 1979.

"Voice Processing System Out; Dictaphone Desktop Mixes Dictation, Messaging on PC," *Computerworld*, September 15, 1986.

editis

Editis S.A.

———————————■———————————

31 rue du Colisee
Paris,
France
Telephone: (33) 01 53 53 30 00
Fax: (33) 01 53 53 37 37
Web site: http://www.editis.com

Wholly Owned Subsidiary of Wendel Investissement
Incorporated: 2004
Employees: 2,300
Sales: EUR 717.4 million ($907.30 million) (2004)
NAIC: 511130 Book Publishers

■ ■ ■

Editis S.A. is France's second largest publishing group (following Lagardère), operating in four primary publishing areas: Education, including textbooks for primary and secondary schools, as well as educational aids, software, and games; Literature; Reference; and Services, including marketing and distribution services for third-party publishers. Editis was formed from the breakup of the former Vivendi Universal Publishing empire, acquired by Lagardère in 2002, and includes parts of historic publishing groups Havas, CEP Communications, and Les Presses de la Cité. The company has been 100 percent owned by Wendel Investissement since 2004.

Editis's Literature holdings include noted subsidiaries such as Plon, La Découverte, Editions First, Perrin, Hemma, Julliard, Seghers, Robert Laffont, Pocket, and 10/18, among others. Under Education, the company includes Bordas, CLE International, Nathan, and Retz. The company's Reference division consists of Bordas References Culturelles and the Le Robert series of dictionaries, among others. Editis's Services division includes the Interforum distribution unit, which handles the marketing and distribution for Editis's own operations, as well as for unaffiliated publishers such as Panini, Scali, Mango, and others. Editis has adopted a firmly francophone strategy, focusing its publishing empire on the French-speaking world. In addition to acquisitions, such as the July 2005 purchase of Le cherche midi éditeur, Editis has begun launching new publishing imprints, including Fitway Publishing in 2004, and Kurokawa, a publisher of French-language mangas, in 2005. The company, led by Chairman Alain Kouck, posted sales of EUR 717 million ($907 million) in 2004.

1980-90: FRENCH PUBLISHING CONSOLIDATION

Formed in 2004, Editis represented the latest chapter in the long-running consolidation of the French publishing industry. Controlled by Havas into the mid-1990s, then reformed as Vivendi Universal Publishing by the end of that decade, Editis stemmed primarily from two major French publishing groups, Les Presses de la Cité and Havas-dominated CEP Communications.

Havas's own origins lay in the early 19th century, when Charles Havas founded one of the world's first news agencies. Over the next century, Havas developed a number of other interests, including newspaper and book publishing, advertising (including billboard

COMPANY PERSPECTIVES

Our Group, a wholly-owned subsidiary of Wendel Investissement, is the second-largest publishing group in France. It operates mainly in the French-speaking world, playing a major role in Europe (France, Belgium and Switzerland), Canada and Africa. Our objective is to develop Editis's business in all of its publishing activities, either by extension of our current commercial offerings or by acquisition. We are particularly concerned to maintain a business offering with a coherent range of products and efficient services while remaining faithful to its culture: broadening access to education and culture for all.

advertising), and travel and tourism operations, among others. These activities became the group's central focus after the news agency business was taken over by the French government in the 1930s; that business later became known as Agence France Presse.

Following World War II, and tainted by its collaboration with the German occupier, Havas was nationalized by the French government. Through the 1950s and 1960s, the company's tourism and advertising businesses became the major parts of its operations. Nonetheless, by the 1970s, Havas also had begun to redevelop an interest in publishing. In 1971, for example, the company launched operations publishing free, advertising-supported newspapers.

Havas's true entry into publishing came in 1975, when it took part in the creation of a new magazine publishing group, La Compagnie Européenne de Publication (CEP). Havas's stake in the company reached nearly 75 percent into the mid-1990s; in 1997, Havas took full control of CEP. By then, CEP had established itself as one of France's publishing powerhouses.

CEP's first title, the business-oriented *L'Usine Nouvelle*, appeared in 1976. The following year, the company took a major step forward, acquiring Compagnie Française d'Edition, a major publisher of professional and technical trade journals. That company was also a leading organizer of conferences and trade fairs in France, an activity CEP maintained into the 1990s.

CEP continued to grow into the 1980s, notably through a series of acquisitions. In 1979, for example, the company acquired Librarie Nathan, a publisher of reference books and textbooks, marking Havas's entry into book publishing. These operations were expanded

further by the acquisition of Sofilsa in 1983, and by the well-known Librairie Larousse operations in 1984. Also that year, the company acquired Groupe Tests, specialized in computer-oriented publishing, as well as a stake in Robert, a publisher of dictionaries and related reference works. In 1986, CEP changed its name to CEP Communications and listed its stock on the Paris Stock Exchange. Havas nonetheless retained majority control of the company. The following year, CEP agreed to merge with Générale Occidentale, which had recently taken over rival publishing group Les Presse de la Cité. That merger produced France's newest publishing giant, Groupe de la Cité, controlled by Havas. By then, Havas—which had recently added a television broadcasting component—had itself been privatized, with a listing on the Paris Stock Exchange.

CEP remained a separate entity in Groupe de la Cité into the mid-1990s, representing primarily its magazine publishing and trade show units. Its counterpart, Les Presses de la Cité, in the meantime, continued to build an impressive collection of some of France's most important publishing houses.

That company was founded in 1944 by Sven Nielsen, a Danish native who had emigrated to France in 1924. Both Nielsen's father and grandfather had been booksellers, and Nielsen himself had started out as an exporter of French books to the international market. Nielsen's contacts with the international publishing industry encouraged him to move into publishing. At first, Nielsen focused on introducing Anglo-Saxon authors to France, and published his first book in 1944. The company was incorporated in 1947 as Les Presses de la Cité (LPC). Following World War II, Nielsen convinced Georges Simenon, under contract at another house, to publish a memoir with him—that book, *Je me souviens*, appeared in 1946 and marked the beginning of a long relationship with the internationally best-selling author. Over the next decades, LPC published some 140 books by Simenon.

Nielsen quickly established himself as a major presence in the French publishing world, specializing in the popular American fiction, and then expanding into major genres such as crime fiction, science fiction and fantasy, among others. One of Nielsen's major achievements was the creation of the Larousse publishing imprint, which, through a series of international partnerships, became one of the world's best-known French imprints. The company's success allowed it to make a series of acquisitions through the 1950s and into the 1960s. In 1958, for example, LPC acquired Amiot-Dumont, which published popular novels as well as travel books. This was followed by the 1959 purchase of Perrin, a publisher of historical works, essays, and reference books, founded

KEY DATES

1835: Charles Havas founds the Agence Havas news agency.

1947: Sven Nielsen incorporates his publishing business, launched in 1944, as Les Presses de la Cité (LPC) and becomes Simenon's publisher.

1975: Havas becomes a founding shareholder in a new magazine publishing group, Compagnie Européenne de Publication (CEP).

1986: CEP changes its name to C.E.P. Communication.

1987: Générale Occidentale acquires LPC.

1988: LPC merges with CEP's publishing wing, becoming Groupe de la Cité (GDC).

1995: CEP acquires 98 percent of GDC; Havas acquires majority control of CEP.

1997: Havas takes full control of CEP and changes its name to Havas Publications Edition.

1998: Vivendi takes control of Havas and sells off its tourism and advertising operations.

2000: Havas's publishing business is renamed as Vivendi Universal Publishing (VUP).

2001: VUP acquires Houghton Mifflin.

2002: VUP is sold to Lagardère.

2004: Lagardère agrees to sell 60 percent of VUP, which is renamed as Editis, to Wendel Investissement.

2005: Editis refocuses as a French-language specialist and acquires Le Cherche Midi Editeur and Editions First; a distribution agreement with Quebecor is reached.

2006: Editis acquires full control of Editions XO.

in 1884. LPC added a youth wing with the purchase of Editions GP in 1961, which was followed by the purchase of children's book publisher Solar. The following year, LPC launched a new imprint, Presses-Pocket.

Other major acquisitions of the 1960s and 1970s included the 1963 merger with Editions Fleuve Noir, which had achieved fame as a genre (crime, science fiction, adventure, erotic) publisher since its founding in 1949. In 1966, the company acquired Editions Plon, founded in 1845, and one of the country's leading nonfiction publishers. The Plon acquisition included the company's 10/18 imprint, targeting the youth market and formed in 1962. In 1970, LPC added a mail-order unit, France-Loisirs, in partnership with Germany's Bertelsmann. Also during the 1970s, LPC developed its

own distribution operation, Messageries du Livre.

LPC continued acquiring scale into the 1980s; in 1985 alone the company acquired several publishers, including the publishing houses Bordas, Dunod, Gauthier, and Villars. In this respect, LPC fit in with the desire of the French government, which had been encouraging consolidation within the French publishing industry in order to create a French-language counterpart to the fast-growing international publishing empires, as exemplified by Reed-Elsevier and Bertelsmann.

LPC itself was acquired by Générale Occidentale, a subsidiary of Alcatel Alsthom, in 1987. That company quickly turned around the purchase, completing the merger of LPC and CEP's publishing business. The merged entity then became known as Groupe de la Cité (GDC), and featured Havas as a major shareholder. The company was then listed on the Paris Stock Exchange in 1989.

1990-2000: MEDIA EMPIRE COMPONENT

GDC grew steadily into the mid-1990s. The company expanded into the international publishing market, starting with the purchase of Grieswood & Dempsey, in England, in 1998. That company published under the Kingfisher imprint. In 1989, GDC acquired Dalloz, a French specialist in legal text publishing. That same year, GDC launched a new publishing company, The Millbrook Press, in the United States. Returning to France in 1990, GDC added that country's well-known Robert Laffont, a highly regarded publisher of literature founded in 1941. That purchase also brought Laffont's distribution business, Interforum.

Spain became an important market for the group, with the acquisitions of Boixareu and Marcombo in 1990, and then the launch of the joint venture Larousse Planeta in 1991. In that year also GDC merged its distribution operations into a single unit, Interforum. The company also acquired a majority of Spain's Espasa Calpe that year, before taking full control in 1992. Also in 1992, GDC bought up the editorial business of Harraps, the U.K.-based producer of bilingual dictionaries. The following year, GDC launched a reorganization of its structures, which included regrouping its British publishing operations (excepting Harraps) under a single entity, Larousse PLC. Other acquisitions included the purchase of Groupe Masson, then the leading publisher of medical and scientific information in southern Europe.

In 1995, Générale Occidentale agreed to transfer its own press holdings, which included the magazines *L'Express, Le Point,* and *Courrier International,* among others, to CEP Communications. At the same time,

CEP raised its share of GDC to more than 98 percent. These moves preceded the transfer of Générale Occidentale's holding in CEP Communications to Havas. In exchange, Alcatel Alsthom gained control of more than 21 percent of Havas.

Havas completed its takeover of CEP Communications in 1997, gaining control of France's second largest publishing empire. CEP's name was then changed to Havas Publications Edition. Yet Havas itself quickly became the target of another fast-growing group. In the mid-1990s, Jean-Marie Messier, then the head of Compagnie Générale des Eaux (CGE), had become determined to redevelop the former French utilities and construction giant into a global media powerhouse. In 1997, CGE acquired 30 percent of Havas, and began refocusing the group onto CGE's primary interest, telecommunications and electronic media. Soon after, CGE changed its name to Vivendi.

Under Vivendi, Havas began selling off much of its newly noncore operations, including its advertising and tourism businesses, as well as much of the former CEP's magazine titles. Meanwhile, Havas's book publishing side grew strongly, through acquisitions such as those of Quotidien Santé, the largest medical publisher in France, and its Spanish counterpart, Ediciones Doyma, and leading Spanish textbook and reference publisher Group Anaya, all in 1998. In 1999, Havas entered Latin America, acquiring Argentina's Aique, then forming a joint venture to acquire Brazilian textbook publishers Atica and Scipione.

FRENCH-LANGUAGE SPECIALIST FOR THE NEW CENTURY

The creation of Vivendi Universal (VU), the world's second largest media and communications empire, in 2000 launched a new phase in development of the future Editis. Following the creation of VU, Havas was renamed as Vivendi Universal Publishing (VUP). The company's operations by then included five major divisions: Literature, News, Games, Education, and Health.

VUP became the world's third largest publishing group in 2001 when VU's ambitious expansion program led to the purchase of the United States' Houghton Mifflin. To finance that purchase, VUP sold off its Health and News divisions for EUR 1.2 billion in 2002. Soon after the company sold a number of magazine interests, including *Courrier International* and *Newbiz*.

The landmark merger between VU and AOL-Time Warner, however, suddenly changed that group's focus. At the same time, VU's intense acquisition drive had saddled it with recordbreaking debt levels. This led the company to begin a selloff of large chunks of its hold-

ings, including its publishing interests. By December of that year, Vivendi had reached agreement to sell VUP's European publishing holdings to the Lagardère Groupe—already France's leading publisher through its Hachette holding.

The acquisition met with opposition from the European mergers and monopolies commission. As part of a compromise, Lagardère agreed to keep just 40 percent of VUP, including Larousse, Dalloz, Dunod, Nathan, Anaya, and Sedea. The remaining 60 percent was renamed as Editis and put up for sale. Under intense pressure from the French government to find a French buyer for what was to become the country's second largest publishing group, Lagardère reached an agreement to sell Editis to Wendel Investissement in September 2004. Wendel had been formed by the merger of Marine-Wendel and CGP in 2002, although both had been financial vehicles controlled by the Wendel family since the early 19th century.

Under Wendel, Editis has adopted a new strategy of redefining itself as a French-language specialist, with an interest in developing its publishing operations throughout French-speaking Europe (Belgium, France, and Switzerland) and elsewhere, including Quebec and parts of Africa. The company made a first step in July 2005 with the acquisition of France's Le Cherche Midi Editeur. That purchase was followed in December of that year by the purchase of Editions First, a publisher of reference works and other materials for the young reader market. By then, Editis had reached a long-term distribution agreement with Quebecor Media, the leading publisher and distributor for the Quebec market.

In another international step, Editis acquired full control of Editions XO in January (as VUP, the company had been involved in the creation of Editions XO in 1999). That company specialized in introducing and placing French authors onto international bestseller lists. With sales of more than EUR 700 million ($900 million) in 2004, Editis planned to build on its status as France's second largest book publisher to become the leading French-language specialist worldwide.

M. L. Cohen

PRINCIPAL SUBSIDIARIES

10/18; Belfond; Fitway Publishing; Fleuve Noir; Hemma-Lipokili-Langue au Chat; Kurokawa; La Découverte; Langues Pour Tous; Le cherche midi éditeur; Les Presses de la Cité; Perrin; Plon Editions; Pocket; Presses de la Renaissance; Robert Laffont-Nil-Julliard-Seghers; Solar.

PRINCIPAL COMPETITORS

Lagardère Groupe SCA; Hachette Livre S.A.; Editions Nathan; Altavia S.A.; Societe du Figaro S.A.; Bayard Presse S.A.; Eppe S.A.; Editions Gallimard; Imprimerie Nationale; Groupe La Martiniere-Le Seuil; Lamy S.A.; Eurodis; Editions ENI.

FURTHER READING

Casassus, Barbara, "Editis Hits 10% Sales Growth," *Bookseller,* December 16, 2005.

——, "Editis Snaps Up Cherche Midi," *Bookseller,* May 6, 2005, p. 9.

——, "Editis to Publish Lonely Planet in France," *Bookseller,* September 24, 2004, p. 10.

——, Wendel Wins Takeover Race for Editis," *Bookseller,* June 4, 2004, p. 11.

"Editis and Quebecor Establish Ties in Canada," *Canadian Corporate News,* October 12, 2005.

"Editis va racheter les Editions XO," *Nouvelobs.com,* January 12, 2006.

Johnson, Jo, "Lagardère Sells Editis Arms to Seillière Family," *Financial Times,* May 29, 2004.

Tran, Pierre, "French Publishing Baron Lagardère Closes Book on Vivendi Unit's Buyout," *Sunday Business,* December 14, 2003.

Evans & Sutherland
Computer Corporation

600 Komas Drive
Salt Lake City, Utah 84108
U.S.A.
Telephone: (801) 588-1000
Fax: (801) 588-4500
Web site: http://www.es.com

Public Company
Incorporated: 1968
Employees: 340
Sales: $69.2 million (2004)
Stock Exchanges: NASDAQ
Ticker Symbol: ESCC
NAIC: 334111 Electronic Computer Manufacturing;
334119 Other Computer Peripheral Equipment
Manufacturing; 335999 All Other Miscellaneous
Electrical Equipment and Component Manu-
facturing

■ ■ ■

Evans & Sutherland Computer Corporation (E&S) creates technology and products for the visual simulation,
visualization, and digital theater industries. The
company's products include visual simulation software,
image generators, databases, and display systems used by
commercial airline pilots, military pilots, tank com-
manders, motor vehicle operators, and ship operators.
E&S products also are used in military training,
homeland security applications, engineering design, and
domed theaters. Its digital theater products are found in
planetariums and science centers across the globe. During the early years of the new millennium, sales and
profits fell due to cuts in commercial airline and military
spending. As a result, E&S was forced to significantly
reduce its work force.

FOUNDERS AND COMPANY ORIGINS

E&S began with the collaboration of two men, David
C. Evans and Ivan E. Sutherland. Evans was born in
1924 in Salt Lake City, where in 1953 he received his
Ph.D. in physics from the University of Utah. From
1953 to 1962, Evans was director of engineering in
Bendix Corporation's computer division. In 1962 he
started a visiting professorship at the University of
California at Berkeley. In those early years Evans became
more and more interested in using computers for more
than just number crunching. Since humans use sight as
a primary means of interacting with the world, Evans
became focused on using computers to produce visual
images for a wide range of applications. When in 1966
he returned to Salt Lake City to start the University of
Utah's computer science department, he continued his
interest in computer graphics and was on the lookout
for others with similar interests.

Ivan Sutherland at the same time was working in
the field of computer graphics. In 1960, as part of his
Ph.D. dissertation at the Massachusetts Institute of
Technology, he produced a movie called *Sketchpad: A
Man-Machine Graphical Communication System,* which
for the first time portrayed three-dimensional objects on
a two-dimensional computer screen.

COMPANY PERSPECTIVES

Evans & Sutherland has consistently played a leading role in the development of computer graphics over the past 37 years. With one of the longest histories of any technology company today, E&S has maintained its leadership position by providing innovative products and technologies for visual simulation, visualization, and digital theaters.

In 1967 Sutherland and Evans talked about collaborating in the relatively new field of computer graphics. Sutherland, then a Harvard professor, told Evans he could get him a position at Harvard, while Evans made a similar proposal for Sutherland to come to the University of Utah. In the end, Evans decided he definitely could not leave Utah, partly because of his devout faith as a member of the Latter Day Saint church headquartered in Salt Lake City. So Sutherland decided to join Evans at the University of Utah.

About the same time, the University of Utah computer science department began receiving $5 million from the Defense Department's ARPA (Advanced Research Projects Agency) to develop a flight simulator. Both Evans and Sutherland felt, however, that their common goals concerning the development of graphics as a means to create computer simulations would require the creation of a private company.

In 1968 the two founders created Evans & Sutherland on a financial shoestring. They and some employees and family friends contributed what they could. Venrock, a group of investors associated with the famous Rockefeller family, also provided crucial funds for the firm incorporated on May 10, 1968, in Utah.

At its base in an old Army barracks at the University of Utah, E&S produced in 1969 its first product, LDS (Line Drawing System) 1. Although E&S sold only three or four of this new and expensive technology, the firm later used LDS 1 in its first simulator.

By 1972 the firm had developed LDS 2 and other new products but had not generated any profits. At the same time it recruited three key engineers from General Electric (GE). Rod Rougelot, Bob Schumacker, and Ed Wild had approached GE about using computers for pilot training, but GE was not interested at the time. GE's loss eventually proved to be a huge gain for E&S.

Writing in the firm's 1990 newsletter, secretary/treasurer Dick Leahy described what had happened as

Christmas approached in 1972: "The company had around $700 left in the bank, had used up its lines of credit, and was running on personal loans taken out on the founders' homes." Just in time, an overseas investment firm sent a check for $500,000 to save the struggling company.

1970-809: EXPANSION

With the aid of the three former GE engineers, Evans & Sutherland entered what would become one of its key markets. In 1973 the company began a joint project with RSL (Rediffusion Simulation Limited) of Great Britain, in which E&S would make NOVOVIEW visual simulators for commercial airlines, and RSL would market those items. The Dutch airline KLM bought the first NOVOVIEW system.

NOVOVIEW products brought E&S its first profits in 1974 and continued success as the decade progressed. The flight simulator business boomed following the Arab oil embargo of 1974, which made fuel and thus live pilot training much more expensive. By 1977, the SP1, NOVOVIEW's successor, was certified by the Federal Aviation Administration and brought in more sales to E&S than all its other simulators combined. In 1978 the SP2 became a full color product and in 1980 the FAA certified the SP3 for meeting its requirements for a daylight training system.

At the same time, E&S was developing its CT (continuous tone) line of high-performance image generators. In 1972 the company sold a CT1 system to Case Western Reserve University, and in 1975, a CT2 was shipped to CAORF, a maritime facility for training and research. E&S also contracted with NASA in 1976 for a CT3 and with Lufthansa for a CT4 in 1977.

The CT systems to that point were specialized products for single customers and, therefore, not very marketable. But then engineer Bob Schumacker designed the CT5, which increased the system's capability about 1,000 percent. That gained the firm a contract with the Naval Training Equipment Center. Delivered in 1981, the CT5 was so powerful it could serve many customers without individual changes.

In the 1970s David Evans led the E&S effort to produce graphics systems for the CAD/CAM (computer-aided design/computer-aided manufacturing) market. The company created the picture system family, starting with PS1 in 1973 and culminating in the PS 300 in 1981. One key advantage of the more advanced PS systems was decreasing reliance on one host computer; for the first time several designers could work simultaneously.

With this variety of products, E&S expanded its workforce in the 1970s and early 1980s. The firm

```
┌─────────────────────────────────────────────┐
│                                             │
│              KEY DATES                      │
│                 ▪                           │
├─────────────────────────────────────────────┤
│  1968: David C. Evans and Ivan E. Sutherland│
│        incorporate E&S.                     │
│  1973: The company begins a joint project   │
│        with RSL of Great Britain to make    │
│        NOVOVIEW visual simulators for       │
│        commercial airlines.                 │
│  1978: E&S goes public.                     │
│  1986: Three formal divisions are formed    │
│        including the Simulation Division,    │
│        the Interactive Systems Division, and │
│        the Computer Division.               │
│  1996: By now, almost half of E&S's annual  │
│        revenues are from international sales.│
│  1998: AccelGraphics Inc. is acquired.      │
│  2003: The company posts a $36 million loss.│
└─────────────────────────────────────────────┘
```

employed 88 persons in 1973 and 144 in 1975. During the company's early years as a private firm, it was backed by eastern companies, including Venrock, the Venture Capital Investment Company of the Rockefeller family, GCA Corporation, the Endowment Management and Research Corporation, and Hambrecht & Quist investment bankers. E&S continued to grow after it became a public firm in 1978. By 1983, 779 individuals worked for E&S.

Realizing they could not run such a growing firm and fulfill their faculty responsibilities, both Evans and Sutherland had resigned from the University of Utah by 1974. And in 1974, Sutherland decided to resign as the vice-president and chief scientist of the firm he helped start. He continued his role as a company director, however, into the 1990s.

1980-90: BOOM TIMES

Although E&S had started creating products for military flight simulators in the mid-1970s, that aspect of its business rapidly expanded in the 1980s, in part because of the growth of the military under President Ronald Reagan.

In his firm's 1990 newsletter, founder David Evans pointed out key challenges in approaching military markets: "There's a lot of ritual, a lot of regulation, a lot of standards that are required of military contractors in terms of documentation, the security of ... information, and the nature of contracts. The typical military contractor is not a risk taker. Your typical military contractor does research and development paid for by

the government and produces intellectual property they don't own. E&S has always developed products at its own expense and offered those products for sale. That's part of our ... culture."

Military requirements, tremendous growth, and more competitors influenced E&S to become more structured in the 1980s. By 1986 E&S employed 1,072 persons. More firms entered the simulator market after the 1986 federal deregulation of civilian airlines. So E&S in June 1986 created three formal company divisions.

The Simulation Division was headed by Rod Rougelot, and Gary Meredith led the Interactive Systems Division. Previously both divisions had operated as informal working groups. E&S also created the Computer Division from a new group of European employees. Unlike the other two divisions based in Salt Lake City, the Computer Division was based in Mountain View, California.

Shortly after this reorganization, E&S also renegotiated its contract with RSL regarding marketing tactics. E&S now began its own marketing efforts to the U.S. military, which RSL had been cautious about approaching. Since E&S products had been marketed under the name RSL, many in the military were not aware of E&S's contributions until the late 1980s.

At the same time, E&S improved its product lines for both the military and civilian markets. It began creating simulators to train entire crews, not just the pilot or main operator. In 1988 E&S also renamed the CT and SP product lines to use the ESIG (Evans & Sutherland Image Generator) prefix.

In the 1980s Evans & Sutherland entered into several joint agreements to share technology and in some cases acquired related firms. For example, it invested in VLSI Technology Inc. in 1980 to gain access to that company's computer modeling tools, which enabled E&S to develop its Shadowfax circuit chips. Shadowfax enabled E&S to display nonvertical and nonhorizontal lines in a smooth and continuous manner, instead of the jagged stair-step lines previously used.

In 1987 the firm acquired Tripos Associates, a St. Louis-based firm which in 1979 had pioneered the field of Molecular Information Analysis Systems. That important new technology for the scientific community enabled researchers to see and manipulate either two- or three-dimensional images of simple or complex molecules.

In 1988 E&S and Digital Equipment Corporation (DEC) announced the availability of the VAXstation 8000, a color workstation featuring DEC's VAX computer and a very fast graphics system produced by

E&S. Both corporations marketed the jointly produced item.

E&S also diversified in the 1980s by beginning to use its technology for entertainment and education. For example, the 1982 movie *Tron,* a science fiction tale of human entities living inside a computer at the microchip level, employed some E&S products to create its special effects.

In the 1980s the company cooperated with Salt Lake City's Hansen Planetarium to create Digistar, a computerized projection system that could do much more than the old mechanically based methods of projecting stars onto the dome of a planetarium. E&S sold a couple Digistar systems in the 1980s, but the market for this technology was quite limited.

To finance such expanding operations, E&S in 1987 offered investors convertible debentures worth $56 million. Then it started constructing its new Building 600 at the University of Utah Research Park and planning for another building to house the Simulation Division's dome projection system.

Not all E&S ventures succeeded in the 1980s. One dead end was its supercomputer project. In April 1988 the firm announced it would develop and market the world's first general supercomputer and in 1989 it introduced the ES-1 supercomputer. About 70 other firms, however, also were exploring new technology sponsored by the Department of Defense's ARPA and based at Carnegie-Mellon University. By 1989 commercial versions were available from not only E&S, but also three other companies. All these supercomputer projects featured parallel processing, in which several microchips were linked together for advanced computing power. Due to technical problems and severe competition, in late 1989 Evans & Sutherland decided to end its supercomputer project and use its funds for other purposes.

In 1989, after being diagnosed with a neurological condition, David Evans retired from his position as president and CEO, while remaining company chairman. The offices of president and CEO were turned over to Rodney Rougelot, who would then work with Stewart Carrell, who became chairman of the board in 1991.

1990-2000: CHALLENGES

With the end of the Cold War and the dissolution of the Soviet Union, the U.S. military closed many bases and in other ways decreased its forces. At the same time, total U.S. aerospace sales dropped dramatically from almost $140 billion in 1991 to about $108 billion in 1995.

Like other military contractors, Evans & Sutherland during this period significantly reduced its workforce. In 1991, 50 employees lost their jobs. In January 1994 E&S announced that 170 workers would lose their positions, and the following January the firm reduced its numbers by another 200. By 1997 it had downsized to only about 800 employees, several hundred less than the boom times of the 1980s.

At the same time, E&S experienced declining finances. Compared with 1988 and 1989 when the company had net earnings of $1.88 million and $1 million, in 1994 it had a net loss of $3.7 million. Due to Evans & Sutherland's declining revenues and profits and several other difficulties, Moody's Investors Service in March 1994 reduced the Utah firm's convertible subordinated debentures rating from B1 to B2.

Evans & Sutherland made several positive moves, however, in the midst of these trying times. In November 1993, E&S and Iwerks Entertainment introduced their jointly produced "Virtual Adventure," a location-based system used at theme parks. Whether traveling through space or through an underwater scene, individuals enjoyed themselves without the risk of real dangers. By 1997, E&S had sold 22 of its Virtual Glider systems to customers in several American cities, London, Hong Kong, and Canada. These products represented the company's diversification into the rapidly growing consumer market for entertainment and education, a small but expanding part of the firm's business in the 1990s.

International sales also increased significantly for Evans & Sutherland in the 1990s. For example, in April 1991 E&S sold a newly introduced ESIG-2000 image generator to Germany's Krupp Atlas Elektronik. By 1993 Krupp was using that E&S technology in simulators to train operators of Britain's main Challenger battle tank. In 1994, E&S opened an office in Beijing.

To expand into such foreign markets, E&S took advantage of the language abilities and cultural sensitivities learned by employees who had served foreign missions for the LDS church. The bottom line: By 1996 almost half of Evans & Sutherland's annual revenues were from international sales.

Since 1973, E&S and Rediffusion jointly had sold more than 400 simulator systems to civil airlines worldwide. But since Rediffusion, renamed Thomson Training and Simulation, began offering its own image generators, E&S in 1994 ended their contract and began marketing its own systems directly to civil aviation customers.

The company in 1994 also spun off its Tripos, Inc. subsidiary to become an independent public company.

E&S shareholders each received one share of Tripos common stock for every three shares of E&S common stock they owned.

The following year, 1995, the corporation sold two of its CAD/CAM products called CDRS (Conceptual Design and Rendering System) and 3D Paint. Those systems had been developed in the late 1980s and early 1990s to help designers of automobiles and other products become more efficient. Evans & Sutherland had contracted with Ford, Chrysler, Fiat, Hyundai, and other companies for these products.

In December 1994, upon the retirement of Rougelot, James R. Oyler became the company's new president and CEO. There were some indications by the mid-1990s that managerial and technological changes at E&S were good for the company. After a 14-month study of the American aerospace industry, Aviation Week & Space Technology, in its June 3, 1996 issue, ranked E&S second in the total company index of competitiveness and first in the total multi-industry company index of competitiveness. The magazine cited Evans & Sutherland as a good example of smaller firms that generally had done better than those with more than $500 million in annual sales. The company attributed its success to significantly slashing operating expenses and increasing research and development spending.

In the E&S 1996 annual report, Oyler noted that other signs were very positive. For example, in August 1996 the firm announced that the U.S. Air Force had awarded it a contract to provide upgrades on training systems for KC-135 and KC-10 pilots. The firm estimated that this contract, the largest in its history, could generate about $70 million in revenues over the next five years. Moreover, Oyler stated that E&S would be the "only company in the world supplying a complete range of graphics systems priced from $2,000 to $2 million." To implement that goal, in late 1996 the company initiated a new strategy called Universal 3D to make its graphics technology available to customers using widely available Windows NT workstations and personal computers.

In 1996, E&S sold a subsidiary called Portable Graphics Inc., an Austin, Texas-based firm acquired just two years earlier. It also completed its purchase of Terabit Computer Specialty Company, Inc., a firm that provided cockpit instruments and other displays for airplane simulators. E&S organized its new Display Systems division using these new resources.

To market its trademarked REALimage technology, which produced 3D graphics for personal computers, Evans & Sutherland organized in 1996 its new Desktop Graphics division or business unit. E&S and Mitsubishi had formed a nonexclusive partnership to create REALimage.

Also that year, David Evans and Ivan Sutherland received a major honor for their contributions to the computer industry. They won the Price Waterhouse Information Technology Leadership Award for Lifetime Achievement at the annual Computer World Smithsonian Awards ceremony. That recognition for past work and the fact that for two years (1995 and 1996) the firm had continual growth in operating profits and annual revenues proved to the company's leadership that it had completed its turnaround from the struggles of the early 1990s and had created a strong basis for future growth.

In cooperation with Salt Lake City's Bonneville International, E&S in January 1997 formed Digital Studios to produce real-time virtual sets for television, film, and video producers. That year, Evans & Sutherland's leadership seemed quite upbeat about the firm's future prospects in the rapidly changing high-tech field. President/CEO Oyler said in the February 2, 1997 issue of Salt Lake City's *Deseret News*: "What excites me is the chance to develop at the high end and migrate down to the desktop. There really is no other company in the world doing that. Our belief is that we're only at the beginning of this. We're at the edge of doing things that have been too expensive [for the consumer or small firm] to do in the past."

CONTINUING PROBLEMS: 1998 AND BEYOND

During 1998, E&S acquired AccelGraphics Inc. along with Silicon Reality Inc. At the same time, Intel Corporation purchased an 8.2 percent stake in E&S. These strategic moves were part of the company's strategy to adapt to the Window NT operating system platform and to utilize microprocessors made by Intel. Overall, the strategy proved costly. During 1998, the company posted a net loss of $16 million due mainly to integration costs related to the AccelGraphics purchase. Losses continued the following year, climbing to $23.5 million.

E&S entered the new millennium on shaky ground. By this time, the simulation industry was undergoing major change brought on by cuts in military and commercial airline spending on simulation and training equipment. These changes were exacerbated by the terrorist attacks of September 11, 2001. By 2004, the market for simulation visual systems was just one-third the size it had been five years previously. In response, E&S implemented a major cost reduction program. The company cut its staff from 1,000 employees to just fewer than 300, and sold more than half of company-owned buildings.

On a brighter note, the market for planetariums was experiencing growth. As such, E&S continued to focus on its digital theater products. During 1999 the company landed a multimillion contract to construct a 360-degree dome theater for the Madame Tussaud's New York City attraction. The company also launched its Digistar 3 product, which was used by digital theater and planetarium customers.

By this time, E&S realized that new product development was crucial to its survival. The company met this challenge head on and developed lower-cost hardware and software that could be used with personal computers. It also developed a laser projector display device that provided high-quality images using lasers as light sources. Sales and profits continued to fall despite the company's attempts to strengthen its product line. In 2001, Intel cut its stake in the company to 3.73 percent. During 2003, E&S was forced to make its sixth round of job cuts in two years. The company also ran into trouble when it discovered bookkeeping errors from its U.K. operations that overstated revenue and earnings. In the end, the errors forced the company to restate its unaudited results for most of 2003 with a reduction of $8.9 million in revenue and $5.7 million in earnings. Overall, the company posted a $35 million loss for the year.

President and CEO Oyler commented on the rough year in a March 2004 *Knight Ridder Tribune Business News* article. Recognizing that the company's key markets had changed dramatically, he claimed, "We have been expecting for some time that 2003 would be a transition year for the company, leading to a return to profitability."

Profits, however, continued to elude the company in 2004. Nevertheless, management was confident that its strategy would lead to future success. With a focus on visual systems for training simulation, strategic visualization, and digital theaters, E&S was determined to overcome the challenges brought on by changes in market demand.

David M. Walden
Updated, Christina M. Stansell

PRINCIPAL SUBSIDIARIES

Evans & Sutherland Graphics Corporation; Evans & Sutherland Computer Limited (U.K.); Xionix Simulation, Inc.; REALimage, Inc.

PRINCIPAL COMPETITORS

CAE Inc.; Lockheed Martin Corporation; Quantum 3D Inc.

FURTHER READING

Boulton, Guy, "Evans & Sutherland Shakes Off Losses, Looks Forward," *Salt Lake Tribune*, October 23, 1999.

———, "'Tough Year' Doesn't Dim Hopes for Evans & Sutherland," *Salt Lake Tribune*, February 17, 2000.

Brennan, Laura, "Color Workstation Offers High Speed, Exceptional Clarity," *PC Week*, February 9, 1988, p. 23.

Carricaburu, Lisa, "A Whole New Mind-Set," *Deseret News*, January 21, 1997, p. D1.

Cortez, Marjorie, "Evans & Sutherland Lays Off 170 Workers in Restructuring Move," *Deseret News*, January 13, 1994.

Davidson, Lee, "Evans, Sutherland Win Life Achievement Awards," *Deseret News*, June 3, 1996.

"E&S Buys Accelgraphics," *Computer Aided Design Report*, June 1, 1998.

"E&S Continues Acquisition Spree, Buys Silicon Reality," *Electronic News*, July 13, 1998.

"Evans & Sutherland Gets $3.4 Million in [CDRS] Contracts," *Deseret News*, January 17, 1991.

"Evans & Sutherland Lays Off 50 Workers," *Deseret News*, May 8, 1991.

"Index of Competitiveness," *Aviation Week & Space Technology*, June 3, 1996, pp. 42-49.

Knudson, Max B., "Evans & Sutherland Branching into the Entertainment Business," *Deseret News*, September 22, 1993.

———, "E&S Cuts 200 from Work Force," *Deseret News* (Web Edition), January 13, 1995.

McGrath, Dylan, "E&S Justifies Intel Confidence," *Electronic News*, August 10, 1998.

McWilliams, Gary, "Parallel Processing Finds a Champion in Carnegie Project," *Datamation*, February 15, 1988, p. 19.

Mims, Bob, "Salt Lake City-Based Evans & Sutherland to Lay Off More Computer Workers," *Knight Ridder Tribune Business News*, September 13, 2003.

———, "2003 Losses Mount, Sales Plunge for Utah-Based Computer Graphics Firm," *Knight Ridder Tribune Business News*, March 19, 2004, p. 1.

Rapaport, Richard, "Mormon Conquest," *Forbes ASAP*, December 7, 1992, pp. 76-81, 84-88, 91.

Rashid, Richard, "A Catalyst for Open Systems," *Datamation*, May 15, 1989, pp. 32.

Rivlin, Robert, "Filming By Computer," *Technology Illustrated*, February 1983, pp. 26, 28-30.

Siegel, Lee, "The Reality Factory," *Salt Lake Tribune*, April 17, 1994, pp. A1, A3.

"A Virtual Vision: Evans & Sutherland Using Its Technology to Conquer New Worlds," *Deseret News*, February 2, 1997.

Wysocki, Bernard, Jr., "Global View Part of Faith and Business," *Deseret News*, March 29, 1996.

Expeditors
You'd be surprised how far we'll go for you.

Expeditors International
of Washington Inc.

1015 Third Avenue, 12th Floor
Seattle, Washington 98104
U.S.A.
Telephone: (206) 674-3400
Fax: (206) 682-9777
Web site: http://www.expeditors.com

Public Company
Incorporated: 1979
Employees: 9,400
Sales: $3.9 billion (2005)
Stock Exchanges: NASDAQ
Ticker Symbol: EXPD
NAIC: 488510 Freight Transportation Arrangement

■ ■ ■

A fast-growing global logistics company, Expeditors International of Washington Inc. provides international air and ocean freight-forwarding and customs-clearance services to large, globally-oriented corporations through a vast network of sales offices in over 50 countries. Expeditors robust pace of financial growth began during the early 1980s when the company started providing both freight-forwarding and customs-brokerage services, a novel concept at the time for companies involved in coordinating international cargo transportation. Propped up by its ability to orchestrate the transportation of cargo and clear such cargo through customs, Expeditors recorded animated growth throughout the 1990s as customers increasingly sought the aid of full-service shippers. The company's success continued into the new millennium and in 2005, sales surpassed $3.9 billion.

ORIGINS OF A UNIQUE SHIPPING SERVICES COMPANY

Expeditors' history was shaped not by the company's founders but through the vision of Peter J. Rose. Rose, a Canadian-born son of a National Express employee who spent his life in the shipping business, and four of his colleagues, Kevin Walsh, Glenn Alger, Robert Chiarito, and James Wang, each of whom shared experience in the business of shipping freight, changed the business focus of Expeditors. From the group, Rose emerged as the prominent, guiding personality. More than a decade after the incorporation of Expeditors, one industry observer noted that the company mirrored the personality of the person chiefly responsible for its enviable record of financial growth, Peter Rose.

Rose was born in Montreal, Quebec, and, as the story went, entered the vocation that would occupy his professional career at the age of five when he donned his father's cap and delivered packages door-to-door. As a young adult, Rose attended Sir George Williams University, then after shelving dreams of becoming a professional hockey player, embarked on his career when he went to work for Canadian Pacific. Rose's entry into the transportation field would define his working life in the decades to follow, but his greatest success would be achieved in the United States where Rose accumulated the experience that eventually predicated Expeditors' existence. Rose arrived in the United States in 1965 and immediately began working as the Inward Traffic Manager for Compass Agencies, a steamship agent. From there, Rose went on to work for other companies involved in the transportation business, serving short stints at Harper and Circle Airfreight. Rose finished his long-served apprenticeship in the freight-forward business by the late 1970s, and from the 1980s Rose orchestrated the growth of a unique shipping services company.

After joining Circle Airfreight in 1975, Rose returned to Harper, where he and several other Harper executives discussed the possibilities of creating a superior and unique type of shipping service for the corporate world. The business approach discussed by these Harper executives was simple yet novel. They resolved to fuse the functions of a freight-forwarding company and a custom-house broker at a time when other shipping services companies either shipped cargo or facilitated the clearance of cargo through customs, but rarely offered both services. By offering both services, Rose and his other Harper executives could offer the full gamut of services sought by international, blue-chip corporations. "We wanted to take big freight," Rose later explained in a hypothetical example, "and be able to move it from the door in Hong Kong to the door in Minneapolis," which the company did, but without its own transportation equipment. Instead, the handful of Harper executives planned to move cargo via other companies' transportation equipment, ensuring that the cargo moved through customs speedily and reached its ultimate destination.

Once the plans for this door-to-door, customs-clearance, and freight-forwarding company were finalized by Rose and his associates, during a late-night drinking session on the island of Lantau, the course was set for a new force in the shipping services industry. That night, on the island near Hong Kong, the talks transformed into action. In 1981, the group joined Expeditors, a company with an office in Seattle that had been founded two years earlier. Rose was immediately named Executive Vice President of Expeditors, and before the year was through sales offices were established in San Francisco, Chicago, Hong Kong, Taipei, and Singapore.

Despite its far-ranging sales offices, the company was a contrastingly modest enterprise during the early days following the arrival of Rose and the other Harper executives. As Rose would later reflect, Expeditors was a modestly-sized enterprise during the early 1980s, "almost that proverbial phone booth and a note pad," he later remembered. Though the company grew quickly and swiftly became the leading U.S.-based airfreight importer from the Far East, it did not lose the lean and focused quality to its operations that described Expeditors during the early years of the decade. Operating without ownership of any transportation equipment or any of the attendant responsibilities of owning capital equipment, Expeditors focused on service, service that attracted the business of the nation's largest corporations who appreciated the benefits a genuine full-service shipper could provide. The business strategy formulated by Rose and his colleagues worked, and worked unexpectedly well, prompting Rose, more than a decade after he joined Expeditors, to confide, "I wouldn't have believed we could've done this ... we created this monster; it has to be fed."

ROBUST GROWTH BEGINS IN 1982

Rose fed the "monster" by entering the export market in 1982 and the ocean freight market in 1985. Sandwiched in between these two diversifying moves was Expeditors' initial public offering in 1984, which was completed in September and yielded the company the financial resources to expand its operations on a worldwide basis. Though the trappings at Expeditors' headquarters near Seattle-Tacoma International Airport (Sea-Tac) remained unassuming throughout its explosive rise in the shipping industry, the company's network of international sales offices grew increasingly formidable. In the wake of the 1984 conversion to public ownership, Expeditors grew vigorously, adding sales offices in the Far East, where the company first had distinguished itself, and by branching out into other overseas markets. The company entered the expansive European market in 1986, with an office in London, and continued to flesh out its network of foreign offices as the decade progressed.

As Expeditors recorded exponential financial growth during the latter half of the 1980s, the company began to attract the attention of industry observers and the mainstream business press. *Inc.* magazine ranked Expeditors as one of the 100 fastest growing companies in the United States in 1987 and other testaments to the company's prolific growth were soon to follow. By 1988, sales had been increasing at a rate of more than 50 percent during the previous five years, fueled by the business garnered from clients such as Apple Computer,

KEY DATES

1979: Expeditors is established.
1981: Peter Rose joins Expeditors and is named executive vice-president.
1982: Expeditors enters the export market.
1984: The company goes public.
1985: The company enters the ocean freight market.
1986: Offices are established in Europe.
1992: Fourteen new sales offices are opened; the company posts $333.2 million in sales and $11.3 million in earnings.
1998: Sales surpass $1 billion.
2004: Expeditors celebrates its 25th anniversary; sales climb to $3 billion.

IBM, Nike, and Motorola who helped Expeditors generate nearly $150 million that year. By the end of the following year, when the company's number of sales offices had increased to 22, annual sales neared $200 million, a volume derived from 42 countries.

1990-2000

Entering the 1990s, Expeditors' global reach was extensive, extending across the world and enabling the company to meet the variegated shipping needs of large, international companies. Though much had been achieved during the 1980s, the company's growth during the 1990s would overshadow the accomplishments of Expeditors' inaugural decade of business as a freight-forwarder and customs-house broker. As if anticipating the rapid growth to come during the 1990s, the company expanded its headquarters near Sea-Tac during the early months of 1990, increasing the square footage at its executive offices from 13,000 to 26,000, then set about expanding its network of sales offices as well. In 1991, the company opened an office in Kuwait and placed representatives in offices in Istanbul, Cairo, Athens, and Dubai. Expeditors also opened an office in Antwerp, Belgium, two offices in Portugal, and four offices in Germany. On the domestic front, the company expanded as well, establishing new offices in Louisville, Kentucky, and Phoenix, Arizona. The spate of new office additions enabled Expeditors to generate a record $254 million in revenue in 1991 and an unprecedented $10.2 million in earnings, the bulk of which was earmarked for financing further expansion, as were the profits from earlier years.

Focused on growth and service, Expeditors grew rapidly during the early 1990s, winning customers from its competitors with its capacity as a dual shipping service provider and earning praise from the business press. The company was selected as one of Forbes' 200 best small companies in the United States in 1990 and again in 1992. Not lost on the industry pundits who lauded Expeditors' innovative business strategy and its financial vitality was the company's performance during the economically recessive early 1990s, a time when the Sea-Tac-based shipper was growing by leaps and bounds. As many businesses reeled from the stifling affects of waning consumer confidence and bleak economic forecasts, Expeditors surged ahead and opened 14 new sales offices in 1992, helping the company post $333.2 million in sales and $11.3 million in earnings.

Financial growth continued unabated in 1993, when Expeditors generated $361.4 million in sales and more than $10 million in earnings, although the company's physical pace of growth slowed in comparison to 1992. After establishing 14 new sales offices in 1992—most of which were located in Europe and Asia—the company opened only four new offices in 1993, but its coveted ability to coordinate cargo movement and consolidate shipments to win low rates pushed revenues upward, nonetheless. As 1994 began, Expeditors moved resolutely forward with its expansion program, opening two new sales offices each in Sweden, Spain, and South Africa early in the year. An office in New Delhi was opened in March, with an office in Bombay slated to open by the end of the year.

In addition to the company's expansion of its sales office network, Expeditors was also diversifying the value-added services it provided to its customers by signing long-term contracts for customs brokerage and by making its foray into distribution. The company's first customer in the distribution business was Koss Corporation, for whom Expeditors agreed to distribute imported headphones throughout the United States. Expeditors' customs-brokerage operations, meanwhile, received a substantial boost in business when the company signed a contract with retailer Montgomery Ward in early 1994. Under the terms of the contract, Expeditors was expected to clear imported merchandise through customs for Montgomery Ward's 360 retail stores, with the bulk of the activity to take place in the Los Angeles area—Ward's eventually went out of business in late 2000. Growing and diversifying on all fronts, Expeditors entered the mid-1990s with sanguine hopes, an optimism that prevailed not only at the company's headquarters but outside the company as well. Noting Expeditors' strategic expansion and its evolution as a freight forwarder and customs broker, one industry analyst remarked to a reporter for the *Puget Sound Business Journal,* "It's becoming a global company. They're diversifying well geographically and I think they're doing a good job of diversifying away from import air freight. I think they're in a good position to benefit from worldwide economic recovery."

Twelve new sales office were opened in 1994, with another six slated to open in 1995, as Expeditors continued to broaden its presence overseas. China was considered as one of the important markets for the company as it prepared for the late 1990s and looked to sustain its consistent, record-setting pace of financial growth, with markets in South America and India offering strong opportunities for future growth as well. Annual sales, which in 1995 totaled $584.6 million, had been increasing 25 percent to 30 percent annually during the 1990s, setting the stage for commensurate growth during the latter half of the decade.

INTO THE NEW MILLENNIUM

As the company headed toward the late 1990s, with 25 percent to 30 percent annual increases in sales projected through the year 2000, Rose was confident that Expeditors' future would be as profitable as its past, prompting him to promise that he and the company's more than 2,400 employees would "continue on in our boringly consistent manner." Whether or not the company's financial growth would continue to be "boringly consistent" in the future remained to seen, but considering Expeditors' record of physical expansion during its first decade-and-a-half of business, progress appeared to be inevitable as Rose and other executives set their sights on new and potentially lucrative markets. With sales operations on six continents and more than 100 offices worldwide during the mid-1990s, the company still had room to grow as it embarked on its future course, intent on securing its position as one of America's leading shipping services companies. Indeed, Expeditors' growth remained steady and strong in the late 1990s. In fact, sales surpassed $1 billion in 1998. The company celebrated its 20th anniversary the following year by opening additional offices in Turkey, Greece, Lebanon, and the United Kingdom and adding over 1,000 employees. By now, there were 149 offices spanning the globe and 12 international service centers. Expeditors' global logistics services included air and ocean freight forwarding, vendor consolidation, customers clearance, marine insurance, distribution, and various other related services.

Expeditors entered the new millennium on solid ground under the continued leadership of chairman and CEO Peter Rose. The company received many accolades and awards each year, proof that its strategy of internal growth and focus on customer service had paid off. In 2000, the company was rated One of the Best Places to Work in Washington by *Washington CEO Magazine*, the

Leader in International Trade by the *Journal of Commerce*, and the Best International Logistics Company of the Year by *International Freighting Weekly*. In 2001, *Forbes* magazine placed Expeditors among the top 400 companies in America while *Fortune* ranked the company third on its America's Most Admired Companies in the Freight Delivery Industry list.

In 2002, sales climbed past the $2 billion mark. That year, earnings rose to over $100 million for the first time. Throughout its history, Expeditors preferred organic growth over mergers and acquisitions. As such, the company strategically opened new offices to bolster profits and revenues. Locations were opened in Costa Rica, Florida, and Texas in 2003. The company also focused on strengthening its foothold in China, a region experiencing significant growth. While many of its peers were faltering due to the sluggish domestic economy, Expeditors remained a step ahead of its competition thanks in part to its dedication to long-term profits. Employees were given much incentive to perform; each office kept 20 percent of its pretax income, which was then distributed each month among the employees.

During the company's 25th year of operation, revenues reached $3 billion. By 2005, sales were just under $4 billion and net profit was $218.6 million, up 40 percent over the previous year. The company appeared to be on track for additional success in the years to come. Known for his blunt comments, Rose denied reports that the company would seek out additional growth through acquisitions or merge with another company. When asked in the company's 2004 annual report if Expeditors had a poison pill in place to prevent a hostile takeover, Rose replied, "What hostile takeover? We would be about as easy for an outsider to digest as a porcupine."

Jeffrey L. Covell
Updated, Christina M. Stansell

PRINCIPAL COMPETITORS

DHL Worldwide Network S.A./N.V.; EGL Inc.; UPS Supply Chain Solutions.

FURTHER READING

Armbruster, William, "Expeditors' Next Stop: India and the Middle East," *Journal of Commerce and Commercial*, September 14, 1994, p. 3B.

———, "Profiting from Chaos," *Journal of Commerce and Commercial*, November 27, 2000.

"Expeditors Hits Record," *Traffic World*, February 20, 2006.

Fagerstrom, Scott, "Expeditors International to Relocate from SeaTac Airport to Seattle," *Knight-Ridder/Tribune Business News*, May 9, 1996, p. 50.

"Freight Forwarder's Unique Idea Brings Growth, Honors," *Puget Sound Business Journal*, May 14, 1990, p. S15.

Gordon, Joanne, "Expeditors Take No Prisoners," *Forbes*, January 10, 2000.

Knee, Richard, "Expeditors Contracts with Hanjin, OOCL," *American Shipper*, October 1991, p. 74.

Levere, Jane L., "Movers and Shippers," *Journal of Commerce and Commercial*, February 27, 1995, p. S17.

Robertshaw, Nicky, "Expeditors, Memphis Newcomer," *Memphis Business Journal*, June 3, 1996, p. 16.

Smith, Sarah, "Expeditors International of Washington Inc.," *Fortune*, June 6, 1988, p. 152.

Wilhelm, Steve, "Airborne, Expeditors Ride Outsourcing Boom," *Puget Sound Business Journal*, August 19, 1994, p. 1.

————, "Executive of the Year: Peter Rose, the Protector, Rose: Relentless Guardian of Profits, People," *Puget Sound Business Journal*, December 24, 2004, p. 8.

————, "Expeditors International Hits Fast-Forward Mode," *Puget Sound Business Journal*, March 11, 1994, p. 3.

————, "Globe-Trotting Peter Rose Mirrors Reality of Expeditors International," *Puget Sound Business Journal*, September 11, 1992, p. 1.

————, "Personal Service Packs a Payoff for Expeditors," *Puget Sound Business Journal*, January 22, 1990, p. 10.

Wolcott, John, "Expeditors Continues its 'Organic' Growth," *Puget Sound Business Journal*, February 20, 1998.

Farmer Jack Supermarkets

18718 Borman Avenue
Detroit, Michigan 48228
U.S.A.
Telephone: (313) 270-1000
Toll Free: (877) 327-5225
Fax: (313) 270-1333
Web site: http://www.farmerjack.com

*Wholly Owned Subsidiary of The Great Atlantic & Pacific
   Tea Company, Inc.*
Incorporated: 1955 as Borman Food Stores, Inc.
Employees: 6,000
Sales: $1.1 billion (2005 est.)
NAIC: 445110 Supermarkets and Other Grocery (Except
   Convenience) Stores

■ ■ ■

Farmer Jack Supermarkets operates one of the leading
grocery store chains in the Detroit, Michigan area, with
nearly 70 outlets that emphasize low prices and fresh
food products. The company is a unit of The Great
Atlantic & Pacific Tea Company, Inc. (A&P), which has
struggled to operate it profitably in a highly-competitive
marketplace.

BEGINNINGS

The origins of Farmer Jack date to 1924, when a Russian Jewish immigrant named Tom Borman opened a
small grocery store called Tom's Quality Meats in
Detroit, Michigan. Three years later his brother Abraham "Al" Borman opened a similar store on the east side

of the city, and they subsequently formed a business
partnership which lasted until 1945, when Tom founded
a chain of markets called Lucky Stores and Al started
another called Food Fair.

In 1955 the brothers once again combined operations, creating a single entity called Borman Food Stores,
Inc. Their outlets were consolidated into the 33-store
Food Fair grocery chain, all located in the Detroit
metropolitan area.

In early 1959 the company went public with the
sale of 404,900 shares of stock for $6.8 million. The
funds were used to buy several smaller area chains
including State Super Markets, American Stores, and
Lipson-Gourwitz Co., which boosted the Bormans' total
holdings to 56 stores by mid-1960. For the fiscal year
ended in June, the company reported sales of $98.4 mil-
lion and net earnings of $1.75 million.

Growth continued over the next several years as
more stores were opened in the Detroit area and in
outlying cities like Ann Arbor and Jackson. For 1962
sales grew to $134.2 million, with net earnings of $4.3
million. In 1963 the company began operating a number
of groceries inside or near Kmart stores in Michigan,
Indiana, and Illinois, which helped boost the total
number of outlets to 77.

In early 1965 Borman Food Stores paid more than
$2 million to buy Arnold Drugs, Inc., which operated
13 Arnold and Pay Less discount drug stores in the
Detroit area. The company also named Abraham Borman's 32-year old son Paul to succeed his uncle Tom
Borman as president, with the latter moving into the
role of chairman.

COMPANY PERSPECTIVES

Farmer Jack's mission is to be the "Supermarket of Choice" … the place where people choose to shop, choose to work, and choose to invest. We will provide goods and services to our targeted customers through the concerted efforts of motivated and dedicated employees. As a result of our sustained effort to successfully achieve our mission, we will become the "supermarket of choice" for our customers to shop, for our employees to work, for our suppliers to partner with, and for our communities to be served.

Not long afterward the firm acquired Yankee Distributors, Inc. in a stock swap worth $5.8 million. Yankee operated a discount department store chain in the Detroit area which had annual sales of approximately $30 million. By early 1966 the Bormans' company had 81 supermarkets, 16 drug stores, 18 Yankee discount stores, and a dairy plant, the Detroit Pure Milk Co.

CONVERSION TO FARMER JACK IN 1967

In 1967 the firm rebranded its Food Fair stores as Farmer Jack supermarkets, with a logo that featured a cartoon farmer character. The Bormans also secured new financing during the year to fund expansion, and opened two large shopping centers which combined Farmer Jack, Yankee, and Arnold Drug stores under one roof. Meanwhile, Tom Borman sold his stake in the firm to brother Abraham and turned over the chairmanship to Joseph Kron.

In 1968 Borman Food Stores raised nearly $5 million to fund expansion by issuing an additional 200,000 shares of stock, and the following year the company shortened its name to Borman's, Inc. and became a Delaware-registered corporation. For 1970 the firm reported sales of $412 million and earnings of $4.6 million.

Sales at Yankee stores had been declining for several years, and after first announcing that they would be closed, Borman's found buyers in Hartfield-Zodys, Inc. and Mangel Stores Corp. The grocery industry was now facing hard times as well, and the decision by segment leader A&P to offer deep discounts on food prices via the new "Where Economy Originates" campaign had an immediate impact on the company, with Paul Borman telling shareholders in the summer of 1972 that A&P's strategy had "pretty much destroyed the supermarket industry."

By 1973 the Farmer Jack chain had shrunk from more than 90 outlets to 88, and it recorded a loss of $603,000 for the year. In 1975 the firm was unexpectedly forced to take on an additional financial burden when the owners of its former Yankee stores both filed for bankruptcy, leaving it liable for payments on property they had sub-leased. As a result the company posted a net loss of $3.8 million on the year's sales of $499 million.

The late 1970s saw renewed expansion, and in 1979 revenues hit $789 million and the firm earned a profit of $5.8 million. In 1981 Borman's sold 10 unprofitable Arnold's drug stores to Revco Discount Drug Centers, Inc.

The company continued to open additional Farmer Jack stores, and by 1984 revenues had grown to $996 million. A&P, now with 55 stores in the area, was aggressively seeking to unseat Farmer Jack from its position as market leader with a massive ad campaign touting "warehouse prices." The company slashed its own prices in order to keep up, resulting in a loss of $10.9 million during the year. Farmer Jack now had an estimated 20 percent share of the Detroit-area grocery market and A&P 12 percent.

In 1985 the company sold its dairy subsidiary, and sales topped $1 billion for the first time, with an improved loss of $1.1 million recorded. The following year Borman's acquired five Detroit-area Chatham stores and converted them to Farmer Jacks, while also shutting down five of its smaller outlets. Competition remained intense, with area supermarket chains now giving customers double the face value of manufacturers' coupons, which wreaked further havoc on the firm's bottom line. By year's end the Farmer Jack chain had shrunk to 83 stores.

In early 1987 the company paid $75 million to buy 61 Safeway Stores in five western states, after which it converted them to Farmer Jacks and sold an affiliated dairy operation to Borden, Inc. In August 5,400 members of the United Food and Commercial Worker's Union went on strike. The company later agreed to buy out 800 employees' contracts for $12.9 million, and at the start of 1988 Borman's sold its newly-acquired Safeway stores, citing the difficulty of running them from a long distance and their unexpectedly high operating costs.

SALE TO A&P IN 1988

Stung by all of these developments, in December 1988 Borman's sold the Farmer Jack chain to Montvale,

1924: Tom and Abraham Borman begin opening food stores in Detroit.

1945: The Borman brothers separately found Lucky and Food Fair grocery stores.

1955: The Bormans combine operations into a single Food Fair chain.

1959: Food Fair makes a public stock offering and begins acquiring more area groceries.

1965: The Bormans buy the Arnold Drug and Yankee Discount chains.

1967: Food Fair stores begin conversion to the new Farmer Jack name; Tom Borman leaves the company.

1981: Unprofitable Arnold's drug stores are sold.

1987: An August strike ends with a $12.9 million worker buyout; 61 Safeway stores are acquired.

1988: The Safeway stores are sold early in the year, and in December the Farmer Jack chain is sold to A&P for $76 million.

1996: The 100th Farmer Jack store is opened.

2000: The company expands into Ohio with the purchase of three Churchill's Super Markets in Toledo.

2003: More than a dozen Farmer Jack stores in Michigan and Ohio are shuttered or slated to close.

2004: Parent company A&P reopens 13 former Farmer Jack locations as Food Basics outlets.

2005: Numerous Farmer Jack and Food Basics stores are closed; A&P puts chain up for sale.

New Jersey-based A&P for $76 million and the assumption of $105 million in debt. Afterwards the stores would continue to bear the Farmer Jack name, and Paul Borman would become chairman of A&P's Midwest division, which also oversaw the Kohl's supermarket chain in Wisconsin. After making the acquisition, A&P sold four Farmer Jack stores and three of its own markets to Meadowdale Foods, Inc.

Though A&P had initially planned to convert its 40 remaining area stores into Farmer Jacks, sales dropped at the first ones completed, and the process was quickly halted. The firms' distribution operations had also been combined to cut costs, but the two corporate cultures were dissimilar and problems with product flow soon

appeared. In the months after the purchase combined market share of the two chains fell from 34 to 30 percent, and in October 1989 Paul Borman was reinstated as head of Farmer Jack to try to get it back on track. He quickly restored the more aggressive advertising that had been successfully used in the past, and in 1990 A&P replaced many of the unit's executives with ones imported from corporate headquarters in New Jersey. The early 1990s saw Farmer Jack begin accepting credit and debit cards, and in 1992 the company became the first Michigan grocer to offer an automated self-checkout lane. Six were installed in the firm's newly-renovated West Bloomfield store, which had been expanded from 35,000 to 60,000 square feet with the addition of a flower shop, pharmacy, kosher food department, and bakery. By this time Paul Borman had been replaced by Craig Sturken as company president.

In 1993 A&P shut down five underperforming Farmer Jacks and three A&Ps in an effort to boost profits, causing the loss of 500 jobs. The combined market share of the two chains had now fallen to 28 percent, with slices going to arch-rival Kroger and growing regional chain Meijer, whose massive outlets combined food and department stores under a single roof. As the A&P name continued to lose its luster, the parent company decided to convert many of its Detroit area locations to Farmer Jacks and close the remainder, leaving a total of 93 Farmer Jack stores by the fall of 1994. The firm was now rolling out a frequent shopper program called the Farmer Jack Bonus Savings Club, in which patrons received discounts after buying a certain amount of goods.

In 1995 A&P announced that Farmer Jack was now its most profitable division, giving credit to a $130 million campaign to improve stores and upgrade warehousing facilities throughout the state. Like competing Meijer stores, some Farmer Jacks were now open 24 hours per day, and this policy was later adopted chain-wide.

In 1996 the 100th Farmer Jack store opened in Chesterfield Township, Michigan. The firm's newest outlets were larger, ranging from 45,000 to 73,000 square feet. Advertisements now bore the tagline, "It's Savings Time at Farmer Jack," emphasizing the chain's low prices.

In 1998 the company unveiled the new Farmer Jack Food Emporium on the site of an older store in the affluent Detroit suburb of Grosse Pointe Woods. The upscale market featured a sushi bar, a selection of organic vegetables, and a wine steward. Similar outlets were opened in other well-to-do suburbs over the next several years.

The year 1999 saw Farmer Jack begin to offer its customers one Northwest Airlines WorldPerks Bonus

Mile for each dollar spent, and in late fall the firm opened six new stores in six weeks, bringing it up to a total of 105 outlets. In 2000 the company also bought three Felice Food Markets and three Churchill's Super Markets. The latter were located in Toledo, Ohio, and marked Farmer Jack's first venture into that state. The firm spent some $75 million to open a total of eight new stores during the year, which also included the first in Michigan's state capital of Lansing.

In 2001 Farmer Jack built a new store in downtown Toledo, as well as a new $43 million distribution center in the Detroit suburb of Livonia, which employed 300. The company now had a 27.2 percent share of the Detroit grocery market, followed closely by Kroger at 22.7 per cent and Meijer with 10.7 percent, according to industry publication Market Scope.

MANAGEMENT CHANGES IN 2002

As A&P was struggling with losses in all of its divisions in 2002, accounting problems were discovered in the Detroit area which required it to restate earnings for the three previous fiscal years. In July 2002 Midwest division head Dennis Eidson and several other top Farmer Jack executives resigned, and the CEO job was taken over by Michael Carter, who had run A&P's Super Fresh chain. Farmer Jack was doing especially poorly as competition intensified and unemployment in the auto industry-dominated area began to climb, which helped push parent A&P's losses to $193 million for the year. There were now 110 Farmer Jacks among A&P's shrinking national total of just over 700 stores.

In early 2003 more executives departed and the company announced it was closing four stores and buying out 400 workers, while also preparing to open or upgrade five groceries at a cost of $20 million. A recent attempt to shift away from the chain's long-time emphasis on low prices had failed miserably, and in June the company closed its stores for 37 hours to prepare them for a new focus on daily low prices and fresher meats and produce. The "We're Thinking Fresh" campaign also offered free samples of produce on demand, and later added a guarantee of a free fresh item if an outdated one was found in the store. The firm's customers also would no longer need their Farmer Jack Bonus Savings Club card to get lower advertised prices.

A week later the company opened a new 64,000 square foot outlet on Detroit's east side, the city's largest to date. Farmer Jack continued to struggle, however, and in October construction of a new store in Dearborn Heights was halted, and not long afterward a third of its stores reduced their operating hours. The firm was now reportedly losing $1 million per week.

In December 2003 Farmer Jack renegotiated its contract with the United Food and Commercial Workers' union to cut wages by 5 percent in a bid to stem losses and save jobs. Shortly afterward the company announced it was closing its two Lansing stores and 16 others in the Detroit metro area and Toledo. In the spring parent A&P reopened 13 of them as Food Basics outlets, which had found some success in the East and in Canada. The deep-discount concept was similar to a warehouse club (though no membership fee was charged). Food Basics stores offered only the best-selling products at very low prices, with no fresh meat department, bakery, or deli, and limited service including no bagging assistance.

In April 2004 the first new Farmer Jack in almost a year opened in the Detroit suburb of Waterford Township, and in November the firm launched a program called Wine and Dine, in which wines were relocated next to produce and information was added to the firm's Web site offering advice on pairing wine and food.

In late April 2005 A&P closed 12 of its 13 Food Basics stores in Detroit and Toledo as well as two Detroit-area Farmer Jacks. Several weeks later the company announced plans to sell the rest, and over the next month nearly 20 stores were closed or sold to independent grocers. In the fall, as a sale of the remaining 70 to Michigan-based Spartan Stores neared completion, Farmer Jack renegotiated its union workers' contract to win a 10 percent pay cut for the prospective new owner. Talks broke off shortly afterward, however, and company president Mike Carter quickly resigned.

In October, after realizing $919 million from the sale of its Canadian operations, A&P announced that it was reconsidering selling Farmer Jack, which had now slimmed down to 67 stores and was starting to break even. The company's union workers subsequently agreed to take the pay cuts they had earlier ratified for the prospective Spartan sale, and the chain ended its free replacement guarantee for outdated items to save additional money.

More than 80 years after Tom Borman entered the grocery business, Farmer Jack Supermarkets had undergone much growth and change. Long the market leader in the Detroit area, the firm was struggling to become profitable under the ownership of A&P, and its future prospects were growing increasingly cloudy.

Frank Uhle

PRINCIPAL SUBSIDIARIES

Bev Ltd.; Detroit Pure Milk Co.; Farmer Jack Pharmacies, Inc.; Farmer Jack's of Ohio, Inc.; Seg Stores, Inc.; Wesley's Quaker Maid, Inc.

PRINCIPAL COMPETITORS

Kroger Company; Meijer, Inc.; Wal-Mart Stores, Inc.; Costco Wholesale Corporation; Aldi, Inc.

FURTHER READING

"Borman's Had Big Loss in Fourth Quarter Due to $4.9 Million Charge," *Wall Street Journal*, March 31, 1975, p. 8.

Bott, Jennifer, "Detroit-Based Supermarket Chain Replaces Top Management," *Detroit Free Press*, July 11, 2002.

Dixon, Jennifer, "A&P Seeks to Contain Spiraling Losses at Detroit-Based Farmer Jack Subsidiary," *Detroit Free Press*, February 13, 2003.

Gallagher, John, "New President of A&P's Midwestern Region Takes on Tough Challenge," *Detroit Free Press*, July 20, 2002.

Guest, Greta, "Thirteen Farmer Jack Groceries Will Close in Detroit, 10 Will Reopen," *Detroit Free Press*, January 13, 2004.

Lane-Wilke, Katie, "A&P Takes Aim at Farmer Jack," *Crain's Detroit Business*, May 12, 1986, p. 1.

Mathews, Ryan, "Going Against the Grain," *Grocery Headquarters*, February 1, 2004, p. 10.

Mercer, Tenisha and Dybis, Karen, "Farmer Jack for Sale," *Detroit News*, May 11, 2005.

Mossa, Lara, "More Farmer Jacks May Close," *Oakland Press*, November 4, 2005.

Narang, Pamela, "Farmer Jack Stores Going Super," *Oakland Press*, June 5, 1993.

Radigan, Mary, "A Fresh Acquisition: Spartan Stores May Acquire Floundering Grocery," *Grand Rapids Press*, September 10, 2005, p. B1.

Snavely, Brent, "Exec Departures a Symptom of Farmer Jack Difficulties," *Crain's Detroit Business*, July 22, 2002, p. 18.

———, "Food Fight: Top Execs at Farmer Jack, Kroger Plot Similar Course," *Crain's Detroit Business*, May 21, 2001, p. 1.

Springer, Jon, "Resignation, End of Talks Cloud Farmer Jack Sale," *Supermarket News*, October 10, 2005, p. 1.

Stopa, Marsha, "$60M, 2,000 New Jobs: Farmer Jack Plans Major Expansion Program," *Crain's Detroit Business*, November 20, 1995, p. 1.

Weigant, Elizabeth, "Farmer Jack Plans to Add Up to 17 Stores," *Crain's Detroit Business*, December 11, 2000, p. 25.

Wilson, Melinda, "Togetherness Flops: A&P, Farmer Jack Seek Separate Identities," *Crain's Detroit Business*, March 19, 1990, p. 1.

Zwiebach, Elliot, "A&P, Borman's to Sell Some Detroit Stores," *Supermarket News*, January 23, 1989, p. 1.

Farouk Systems, Inc.

250 Pennbright
Houston, Texas 77090
U.S.A.
Telephone: (281) 876-2000
Toll Free: (800) 237-9175
Fax: (281) 876-1700
Web site: http://www.farouk.com

Private Company
Incorporated: 1986
Employees: 150
Sales: $56.7 million (2004)
NAIC: 325620 Toilet Preparation Manufacturing

■ ■ ■

Farouk Systems, Inc., is a private, Houston-based company that produces hair care and spa products for the professional market. Owned and operated by more than 1,500 professional hairdressers located in more than 60 countries, Farouk is headed by its founder, Palestinian immigrant Farouk Shami, who serves as the chairman of the board. His son, Rami Shami, is the company's chief executive officer. Major products include the Sunglitz line of ammonia-free, hair-color lighteners; the BioSilk line of ammonia-free hair dyes that provide grey coverage; and a wide variety of hair styling equipment and accessories sold under the Chi brand. The most popular of the Chi products is a ceramic straightening iron, but the label also is to be found on professional dryers, clippers, curling irons, brushes, and combs, as well as hair care products, including dyes, hair thickeners, and "transformation" systems for use with the ceramic straightening iron. Farouk also offers services to hair salons, including styling education and merchandising programs. In addition, the company operates an upscale spa in Houston's Galleria Mall.

FOUNDER'S EMIGRATION TO THE UNITED STATES IN 1965

Farouk Shami grew up in Ramallah, Palestine, a suburb of Jerusalem. Here he watched his mother make tapestries, rugs, and blankets. She also made her own dyes, relying on readily available vegetables and plants, and taught her son the secrets of coloring, passed down from one generation to the next, while also fueling a passion in him to become a commercial artist. As a youngster Shami also was influenced by a Palestinian pharmacist who lent him books about the production of hair care products. Like his mother he developed dye and pigments from plants and tree bark and began to experiment, making his own hair dyes, shampoos, and conditioners. In addition, Shami grew up fascinated with the United States, heavily influenced by Westerns in the movie theaters as well as his education in American schools. Determined to sample the personal freedom the United States had to offer, he emigrated to the United States in 1965 and enrolled at the University of Arkansas, which had awarded him a scholarship. His plan was to earn a degree in commercial art and become a teacher, but he continued to dabble in hair care products and also became interested in hairdressing, a form of art in his opinion. He began to attend cosmetology school and college simultaneously, and he grew to love hairdressing so much that he decided to make it his career. His

COMPANY PERSPECTIVES

I began Farouk Systems based on a mission and a dream. My mission and dream was to provide my fellow hair artists with a safer workplace environment - free of harsh chemicals, advanced knowledge through education and new professional only systems that could not be duplicated at home. This is why Farouk Systems' mission statement has always been and still is: Environment, Education, & Ethics.—Farouk Shami.

conservative father, however, was less than pleased with his choice and wrote to him asking Shami to forget his plans and to return home. Instead, Shami defied his father and stayed in the United States to pursue a hairdressing career, resulting in an estrangement between father and son. Many years would pass before they reconciled.

Shami learned the art of hairdressing, working at a variety of salons before settling in Lafayette, Louisiana, where in 1972 he opened his first shop. In 1978 he moved to Houston. He continued to work behind the chair and develop his own hair care products, in particular dyes, but his career reached a crossroads in 1981 when he began to experience an adverse reaction to dyes and other harsh chemicals, experiencing difficulty breathing and skin irritation. He went to a doctor and learned that he was allergic to ammonia. It amounted, in effect, to a career death sentence for Shami. "I was told it is impossible to do color without [ammonia] and the doctor said I had to quit pursuing my passion," Shami recalled in a 2002 interview with *Houston Business Journal*. "But there was no way I was going to do that. I had to come up with another route."

Shami recalled the lessons learned from his mother about formulating dyes and pigments from natural sources. In addition, according to the *Houston Business Journal*, "Shami committed himself to studying chemistry, ophthalmology and the physics of color to examine how humans see and perceive color. That led him to approach hair color from the standpoint of physics rather than chemical formulation." Drawing $1,000 from his savings as seed money, Shami bought chemicals and began to develop his own non-ammonia-based products. He spent his days cutting hair at Salon Farouk and at night worked in his garage on product development, often customizing products to suit the individual needs of his clients. After years of experimentation Shami

developed a non-ammonia hair lightening system that was so unique in the marketplace that Shami became the first hairdresser to receive a patent on a hair care product. In 1986 he formed Farouk Systems, Inc. to market his new products, which he called Sunglitz, unveiled in October 1986.

MAJOR BREAK IN 1986

At first Shami sold Sunglitz to Houston-area salons, but soon began to branch out across the country. His major break came in 1986 when Austin, Texas-based Armstrong McCall, a U.S. distributor of hair care products and salon equipment, took on the marketing of Sunglitz. One of the principals of the firm, John McCall, had learned about the product from one of the company's franchise stores, and then invited Shami to make a demonstration. McCall told *Houston Business Chronicle*, "My mother, who had been in the business all her life, said it was the most innovative product she'd ever seen." McCall was impressed enough that he signed a 20-year agreement to carry Farouk products. Moreover, McCall would take a minority ownership stake in Farouk Systems.

With the success of Sunglitz, Shami began to add products. About a year after the launch of SunGlitz, he developed the BioSilk product line. Using silk in hair care products was not new, but Farouk Systems took the process of liquefying the silk of butterfly cocoons much further than competitors, making the molecules extremely small. Thus, instead of coating the hair with a silk formula, BioSilk's product was small enough to enter the hair shafts, where it could mend damaged hair, add shine, and eliminate frizzies. An increasing amount of Shami's time was taken up by the hair care products business, so that by the early 1990s he decided it was time to ease out of the salon business in order to become a full-time supplier to the beauty industry. Over the course of the decade, Shami built an 80,000-square-foot manufacturing plant in Houston and a pair of area warehouses, one 75,000 square feet in size and another 150,000 square feet. The company turned out a bevy of new ammonia-free professional hair care products.

During the 1990s Shami was joined by his son Rami, who would become CEO of Farouk Systems. Another son, Basim, also went to work for his father, but he drifted away from hair care products for humans, becoming more interested in fur-care products for dogs and cats. In 1995, when he was in his mid-20s, he learned through salon channels that some champion show dog owners had begun to use Farouk's BioSilk products to soften dog fur and give it a sheen and were now asking if the company could offer a product that was specifically formulated for animal use. Basim Shami adjusted the amino acid content of BioSilk, and then conducted field testing at a local veterinary clinic to produce a product that gave a clean feel and clean scent, important for show dogs because they could be disqualified if a judge detected anything foreign on the skin. The new grooming product, called Pet Silk, was launched in 1995. It became the flagship product for a new company, Shami's Pet Silk Inc., which Basim Shami would head.

1995-2000: PERIOD OF STRONG GROWTH

Starting in the late 1990s, Farouk Systems began enjoying a period of especially strong growth. Much of that could be attributed to new packaging, changes in the sales and marketing departments, and the phasing out of product duplication. At the same time, the company unveiled a host of new products and formulations. For example, in 2000 Farouk Systems came out with Power Plus, a hair loss prevention system; the SunGlitz Color Maintenance System; Color Vision Highlighting System; BioSilk Dandruff Shampoo & Conditioner; Root Booster Power Spray; Silk Therapy Hair Care System; Silk Therapy Thickening Line; Chromatic Colors; and SunGlitz Spray Gel. As a result of these changes and product launches, Farouk Systems grew sales 50 percent each year from 1999 to 2001. In 2003 sales grew by 55 percent, and internationally the company did even better, doubling sales. Part of its success was attributable to the products capturing the attention of celebrities who became devoted users and significantly raised the company's profile. They included the likes of Madonna, Britney Spears, Gloria Estefan, Uma Thurman, Renee Zellweger, Gwyneth Paltrow, Courtney Cox, and Demi Moore. It was no surprise that the Farouk products also found their way onto the sets of television shows and movies. They were used on television shows such as *Sex in the City*, *General Hospital*, *ER*, and *America Dreams*, as well as the Miss USA, Miss Universe, and Miss Teen USA beauty pageants. Films included *Miss Congeniality*, *Beauty Shop*, the Austin Powers movies, *Crouching Tiger, Hidden Dragon*, and *The Muhammad Ali Story*.

It was also in the early 2000s that Farouk Systems would venture beyond hair care products by opening the BioSilk Spa in Houston's Galleria Mall. It was the first in what the company hoped would be a worldwide chain of tony spas. The company gained even wider appeal in the 2000s with the introduction of the Chi straightening iron, which led to the introduction of hair dressing equipment and accessories. Farouk Systems took advantage of its proximity to the National Aeronautics and Space Administration (NASA) in Houston, inviting NASA scientists to help it in developing ceramic technology. As a result of these brainstorming sessions, the company was able to develop an iron that used plates that were made from pure ceramics, rather than coated with ceramics, to save on cost. By employing pure ceramics, the Chi heated quicker, kept a more consistent temperature, and produced straightened hair that was better able to ward off humidity and retain its shape longer. The difference in performance was noticeable, and soon hair stylists were using the Chi on the hair of the stars. Farouk Systems then made the product more widely available and found that young women, who had been spending $20 on drugstore flatirons or rolling their hair on orange-juice cans to straighten it, were more than willing to pay as much as $150 for the Chi. It was so popular that Chi became Farouk Systems' most important brand, and the company considered launching new spas under the Chi name rather than BioSilk.

While the Chi flatiron was bringing the Farouk name to a wider audience, the company's founder was also achieving personal acclaim for his charitable activities. He had long been involved with Houston-area charities and national organizations like the Juvenile Diabetes Research Foundation and City of Hope, and he had joined in celebrity causes as well, such as Britney Spears's "Make a Wish Foundation" Tour and NSYNC's Challenge for the Children. But being a successful businessman of Palestinian birth, Shami was especially well positioned to make an appeal for peace in the Middle East. He sought out influential Arabs and Israelis, urging them to find common ground. He opened a branch of Farouk Systems in the Middle East, a place where he hoped Arabs and Israelis could work together. Shami also teamed up with a longtime Texas friend, Richard "Kinky" Friedman, who had fronted the popular 1970s band, The Texas Jewboys, and later became a bestselling author of detective novels. Friedman was also a former member of the Peace Corps and like Shami was eager to broker peace in the Middle East. Together Shami and Friedman created and promoted a product called Olive Oil from the Holy Land, a beauty product that could be applied to hair, soften lips, and added to a bath to produce softer skin. The proceeds of the product were earmarked for the Neve Shalom/Wahat Al-Salom (Oasis of Peace), the only community in Israel where Jews and Arabs sought to educate and raise their families together. Farouk Systems remained an innovative company in the early years of the 2000s. In 2004 it began publishing *Chi Magazine,* which was distributed to salons for patrons to read. Nor was technology neglected. The company developed nano silver technology, which it wanted to incorporate in all of its hair tools. The microscopic particles served as an antiseptic, eliminating the need for chemicals to clean the tools. In effect, the tools would be as good as brand new each time they were used. To make sure it was on the cutting-edge of technology, Farouk Systems hired one of NASA's top scientists, Dr. Dennis Morrison, as soon as he retired, to serve as a consultant.

Ed Dinger

PRINCIPAL COMPETITORS

Conair Corporation; Goody Hair Brushes; Helen of Troy Ltd.

FURTHER READING

Barr, Greg, "Reigning Cats and Dogs," *Houston Business Journal,* May 3, 2004.

"Farouk Scores Record Profits," *SalonNews,* December 2000, p. S2.

Finan, Kristin, "Wave Goodbye To Those Curls," *Houston Chronicle,* April 11, 2005, p. 1.

Tawasha, Mary Ann, "Color of Success," *Houston Business Journal,* May 3, 2002.

"Vision for Growth," *Global Cosmetic Industry,* May 2004, p. 6.

Focus Features

—■—

65 Bleecker Street, 2nd Floor
New York, New York 10012
U.S.A.
Telephone: (212) 539-4000
Fax: (212) 539-4099
Web site: http://www.focusfeatures.com

Wholly Owned Subsidiary of NBC Universal, Inc.
Incorporated: 2002
Employees: 100
Sales: $250 million (2006 est.)
NAIC: 512110 Motion Picture and Video Production

■ ■ ■

Focus Features produces and distributes specialty films for Universal Pictures, a unit of NBC Universal, Inc. The firm has achieved success with titles like *Brokeback Mountain, Lost in Translation, Eternal Sunshine of the Spotless Mind,* and *Pride and Prejudice.* Focus also markets films abroad via Focus International, and operates a sister unit called Rogue Pictures to release genre movies like *Shaun of the Dead* and *Assault on Precinct 13.* The company was created in 2002 by the merger of USA Films and Good Machine and is headed by key executives from the latter firm, including Co-president James Schamus, a longtime collaborator of *Brokeback Mountain* director Ang Lee.

BEGINNINGS

Focus Features was founded in 2002, but its origins can be traced to 1991, when James Schamus and Ted Hope formed an independent film production company in New York called Good Machine. Their purpose was to make interesting films on topics that were not commercially viable for the major studios, which had become increasingly addicted to big-budget blockbusters. Schamus was an assistant professor at Columbia University, where he taught classes in film theory, history, and "no-budget" production techniques, while Hope had worked on a number of independent films, including several with director Hal Hartley. The pair had become acquainted when Schamus taught at Yale in the 1980s.

Their first project together was a film entitled *Pushing Hands (Tui Shou),* which was directed by Taiwanese filmmaker Ang Lee and financed by a $400,000 grant he had won through a national screenwriting contest in his home country. With help from Schamus and Hope, the film was produced and released to a few specialty "art house" theaters in the United States, where it grossed $150,000 at the box office.

At first Good Machine was run almost as a hobby by its founders, releasing films the company had produced (features as well as shorts), and a few others it arranged to distribute in the United States like *The Hours and Times,* a drama about an alleged homosexual affair between Beatle John Lennon and the group's manager Brian Epstein. The company typically sought outside investors for each project, and most made their money back, an unusual result for films of this type. While some titles were distributed by the company itself, others were passed off to larger firms, as Good Machine had no serious distribution apparatus in place.

COMPANY PERSPECTIVES

Focus Features is a motion picture production, financing, and worldwide distribution company committed to bringing moviegoers the most original stories from the world's most innovative filmmakers.

The company's Rogue Pictures label is devoted to producing and distributing high-quality suspense, action, thriller, comedy, and urban entertainment with mainstream appeal and franchise potential.

Schamus and Hope enjoyed cultivating relationships with artists they respected, in particular Ang Lee, and over the years Good Machine would produce all of his films. Schamus also co-wrote the scripts for many, including the second, 1993's *The Wedding Banquet,* which earned $28 million at the box office after it was sold to the Samuel Goldwyn Company. It also was nominated for the best foreign-language film Oscar. Another successful release of this period, *The Brothers McMullen,* was picked up after director Edward Burns had failed to sell it and Hope helped him edit it into a more coherent form. The company was involved with as many as a half-dozen films per year, including titles like Todd Haynes's *Safe* and Nicole Holofcener's *Walking and Talking.*

THE FOUNDING OF AN INTERNATIONAL SALES UNIT IN 1997

In 1997 Good Machine and another independent producer/distributor, October Films, formed a joint venture to sell overseas rights to films the two companies owned. Good Machine International would be headed by Hope and Schamus's new partner David Linde, who had previously done similar work for Fox/Lorber and Miramax.

Good Machine was part of a new wave of independent production companies, and as their brand of offbeat, sometimes edgy films increasingly turned a profit and even began to reach mainstream audiences (via hits like *Pulp Fiction*), the dynamic of the marketplace began to change. More aggressive firms such as Miramax began to heat up the competition for new titles at festivals like Sundance, while theater owners raised their expectations for ticket sales and asked for greater advertising support from distributors. Meanwhile, the major studios had begun noticing the independents' growing profits as well as their ability to win prestigious

Academy Awards, and were swooping down to cut deals with or buy them.

In early 2000 Good Machine broadened its scope to television by initiating projects with both HBO and the Sci-Fi Channel, while also announcing plans to produce family films and what it called "uncensored cinema." The latter category was expected to yield two to five films per year with budgets of less than $5 million on sexually explicit themes. The first, Alfonso Cuaron's *Y Tu Mama Tambien,* proved an art-house hit.

December 2000 saw the U.S. release of *Crouching Tiger, Hidden Dragon,* a philosophical martial arts movie directed by Ang Lee and co-scripted by Schamus, which had cost $12 million to make in China. It was co-produced by Good Machine International and several other firms, with Linde and Schamus acting as executive producers. U.S. distribution rights were sold to Sony Pictures Classics and worldwide distribution was handled by Columbia and other firms. The subtitled film proved a sensation, earning more than $125 million in the United States and winning Oscars for best foreign-language film, cinematography, music score, and art direction. In 2001 Good Machine cut a deal with Miramax (which had just picked up the company's critically acclaimed *In the Bedroom*) that gave the latter firm exclusive "first-look" access to future titles in exchange for $1 million per year. The company also began work on its largest production to date, Lee's filmization of the Marvel Comics classic *Hulk,* again co-scripted by Schamus. The $120 million film would be released by its financial backer, Universal Pictures.

GOOD MACHINE'S ACQUISITION IN 2002 AND THE CREATION OF FOCUS FEATURES

In May 2002 Good Machine was purchased by Universal for an undisclosed sum and merged with USA Films, an independent production/distribution company that Universal had acquired in December 2001 as part of the $7 billion purchase of USA Networks, Inc. The combined enterprises were renamed Focus Features, with Good Machine co-presidents Schamus and Linde put in charge and partner Ted Hope producing pictures for the firm via his own This Is That unit. In addition to helping run the studio and writing scripts for Lee, Schamus would continue to teach classes at Columbia as well as working to complete a book on Danish film director Carl Theodor Dreyer.

The firm that was now allied with Good Machine, USA Films, had been formed in the spring of 1999 when Barry Diller's USA Networks, Inc. had acquired October Films and parts of Universal Studios division PolyGram Filmed Entertainment. October had been

KEY DATES

1991: Good Machine is founded by James Schamus and Ted Hope; October Films is founded.
1992: Gramercy Pictures is founded.
1997: Good Machine International is created for foreign sales under David Linde.
1999: USA Films is formed from October, Gramercy, and other PolyGram units.
2002: Good Machine and USA merge to create Focus, headed by Schamus and Linde.
2004: Rogue Pictures is formed to release action, sci-fi, and urban features.
2005: Ang Lee's Brokeback Mountain is released to strong critical and audience response.

founded in 1991 and released and/or produced such independent hits as *The War Room, Breaking the Waves,* and *Secrets and Lies.* Universal had bought a stake in 1997, but sold it to USA Networks two years later.

USA Films also incorporated Gramercy Pictures and subunits Propaganda Films and Interscope Communications. Gramercy had been founded in 1992 as a co-venture between PolyGram and Universal, and had released hits such as *Four Weddings and a Funeral, Dead Man Walking, The Usual Suspects,* and *Fargo.* USA Films' own successes had included Spike Jonze's *Being John Malkovich* (1999) and Steven Soderbergh's *Traffic* (2000), and it also had distributed Ang Lee's money-losing $35 million Civil War film of 1999, *Ride with the Devil.* It had 100 employees and 2001 sales estimated at $167 million.

After the merger USA Films' production, marketing, and distribution operations would remain in place, as would Good Machine's international sales unit, now known as Focus International. The latter would represent third-party producers as well as Focus and Universal for foreign sales, and would continue to be run by Linde. Focus would operate as a completely independent unit of Universal, with Schamus and Linde reporting directly to Universal Chairman Stacey Snider. The Focus name had previously been used for Universal's own inhouse specialty film unit, which had been shut down just a month earlier. Focus Features reportedly operated with a $30 million budget limit, with Universal given final say on whether projects were undertaken. The company, which would aim for ten to 12 releases per year, would be headquartered in USA's former offices in New York's Greenwich Village.

In the spring of 2002 Focus acquired U.S. and some foreign rights to Roman Polanski's Cannes Film Festival award-winner *The Pianist,* and in July bought *21 Grams,* a drama about drug use starring Naomi Watts and Sean Penn. A new film from Todd Haynes, *Far From Heaven,* was released in the fall, as was *The Pianist.* Both were art-house hits and were nominated for Academy Awards the following spring, with the latter winning in three categories.

In 2003 Focus released Sofia Coppola's critically acclaimed $4 million *Lost in Translation,* while parent Universal put out the $120 million *Hulk.* The latter received mixed reviews and did a relatively disappointing $132 million in wide release in the United States, while the former was a critical and financial smash on the art-house circuit, pulling in $44 million and winning an Oscar for Coppola's script (one of four nominations it received). *Lost* and several other successes like French mystery *Swimming Pool* (which grossed $10 million) contributed to the firm's total box office of $101 million for the year. Not every film was a profit-maker, however, with a British Sylvia Plath biopic that starred Gwyneth Paltrow doing just $1 million domestically and Australian import *Ned Kelly* pulling in a mere $85,000 in ticket sales.

FOUNDING ROGUE PICTURES IN 2004

In March 2004 Focus launched a new imprint called Rogue Pictures, which would specialize in suspense, action, thriller, and urban genre films for a more mainstream audience. Its first releases included action remake *Assault on Precinct 13* and a sequel to the successful horror film franchise about a killer doll, *Seed of Chucky,* as well as British import *Shaun of the Dead.*

Focus had another respectable art-house hit with the March release *Eternal Sunshine of the Spotless Mind,* starring Jim Carrey and Kate Winslet, and also did well with Che Guevara biopic *The Motorcycle Diaries,* taking in $16.7 million for the subtitled release. One of 2004's major disappointments was the $23 million Reese Witherspoon period piece *Vanity Fair,* which earned just $16 million in the United States.

In the fall of 2004 the company signed first-look agreements with Priority Pictures, Deacon Entertainment, and Completion Films, whose output Focus would have first pass on in exchange for annual fees. The firm also was seeking to improve sales of its DVDs by working with retailers like Virgin, which highlighted Focus titles in a special rotating rack. Some films that had underperformed in theaters proved more popular on home video, including Rogue's *Assault on Precinct 13,* which sold more than two million copies in its first week of its release through Universal Studios Home Entertainment.

In May 2005 Focus announced that it was expanding Rogue Pictures to a new level of activity, with ten releases per year planned. In addition to theatrical films, it would also begin releasing some titles directly to DVD. Rogue would become a sister to Focus within the Universal family, with David Linde continuing to oversee the unit's activities and former head of Miramax genre unit Dimension Films Andrew Rona later added as head of production. Rogue's most recent release, an action picture called *Unleashed* that starred Jet Li and Morgan Freeman, had debuted at number three on the U.S. box office rankings with a $10.9 million gross its first weekend.

Fall of 2005 saw an agreement signed with Random House to co-produce and co-finance films via a new venture known as Random House Films, whose offerings would be based on titles from the latter company's extensive book catalog. Random House was the largest publisher in the world, and incorporated some 100 imprints that together were responsible for approximately one-fourth of all U.S. consumer book sales, with titles including bestsellers from authors like John Grisham and Toni Morrison. Film projects would be jointly owned by Random House and Focus, with the latter controlling worldwide sales and distribution and the publisher releasing books based on films or original Focus screenplays. Random House vice-president and editor-at-large Peter Gethers, himself an author and screenwriter, would head the unit.

During 2005 Focus had success with Jim Jarmusch's Cannes Film Festival Grand Prix winner *Broken Flowers* (starring *Lost in Translation*'s Bill Murray), *The Constant Gardener* with Ralph Fiennes and Rachel Weisz, and *Pride and Prejudice,* with Keira Knightly. December saw the release of Ang Lee's *Brokeback Mountain,* a drama based on an Annie Proulx short story about two cowboys who carry on a decades-long gay love affair despite their outwardly straight lifestyles. The $14 million film won numerous awards on the film festival circuit and became a surprise crossover hit, earning more than $60 million in a carefully platformed release that hit 2,000 screens by February 2006. Though marketed in a low-key way as a simple love story, the subject matter sparked controversy in some quarters, with the U.S. Conference of Catholic Bishops rating the film "Morally Offensive" and a multiplex in Utah refusing to show it due to the theme alone (no explicit sex was shown). In March the Academy of Motion Picture Arts and Sciences, which had nominated it for eight Oscars, awarded the film three, for best director, adapted screenplay, and score. Focus also had been nominated for four awards apiece

for *The Constant Gardener* and *Pride and Prejudice,* making it the most-nominated studio of the year.

In just four years Focus Features had become one of the top names in the specialty film business. Its leaders, including the multitasking co-president, James Schamus, had established relationships with key directors, including Ang Lee, and with the powerful backing of NBC Universal the firm's continuing success appeared likely.

Frank Uhle

PRINCIPAL SUBSIDIARIES

Rogue Pictures; Focus International, Inc.

PRINCIPAL COMPETITORS

Miramax Film Corporation; Sony Pictures Classics; Paramount Classics; Fox Searchlight Pictures; Warner Independent Pictures; United Artists Corporation; Lions Gate Entertainment Corporation; Picturehouse.

FURTHER READING

Dunkley, Cathy, "Good Machine Revs Expansion," *Hollywood Reporter,* May 18, 2000, p. 1.

Hernandez, Greg, "Bucking the Trend—Gay Film a Test for Industry," *Los Angeles Daily News,* December 7, 2005, p. B1.

Hornaday, Ann, "A Film Scholar Conjures Up a Hit Machine," *New York Times,* February 20, 1994, p. 21.

Kaplan, Fred, "Producing the Tiger, Neglecting His Dissertation," *Boston Globe,* March 25, 2001.

Kaufman, Anthony, "Range Rovers: Subversive Western Poses Special Challenge for Ang Lee and Focus," *Daily Variety,* October 27, 2005, p. A2.

Kilday, Greg, "Uni to Buy Good Machine," *Hollywood Reporter,* May 3, 2002, p. 1.

Lyons, Charles, "New Machine Comes into Focus," *Variety,* May 13, 2002, p. 9.

Mohr, Ian, "Focus Unleashes Rogue," *Variety,* May 9, 2005, p. 7.

"'Roller-Coaster' Ride for USA As It Unites," *Hollywood Reporter,* January 6, 2000, p. 38.

Rooney, David, "Focus Takes Rogue Turn with Launch of Genre Arm," *Daily Variety,* March 25, 2004, p. 1.

———, "Niche Biz Comes into Focus," *Daily Variety,* August 1, 2004.

Schamus, James, "The Pursuit of Happiness: Making an Art of Marketing an Explosive Film," *The Nation,* April 5, 1999.

Souccar, Miriam Kreinin, "Focus Features Translates Buzz into Oscar Edge," *Crain's New York Business,* February 23, 2004, p. 4.

Traister, Rebecca, "Crouching Budget, Hidden Profits: James Schamus, Columbia Professor, Bets $137 Million on Ang Lee Epic," *New York Observer,* June 23, 2003.

"USA Films in High Gear," *Hollywood Reporter,* January 4, 2002, p. 15.

Walch, Tad, "Distributor Says Film Is Still a Hit in S.L. Area," *Deseret Morning News,* January 12, 2006, p. B1.

Zeitchik, Steven, "Random Harvest: Book Giant, Focus Open Page to Pic Partnership Via Lit Adaptations," *Daily Variety,* November 2, 2005.

GLEN DIMPLEX GROUP

Glen Dimplex

—————————•—————————

Ardee Road
Dunleer, County Louth
Ireland
Telephone: (353) 041 685
Fax: (353) 041 685
Web site: http://www.glendimplex.com

Private Company
Incorporated: 1977 as Glen Dimplex
Employees: 8,500
Sales: EUR 1.5 billion $1.9 billion (2004)
NAIC: 335221 Household Cooking Appliance Manufacturing; 335211 Electric Houseware and Fan Manufacturing; 335222 Household Refrigerator and Home and Farm Freezer Manufacturing; 335224 Household Laundry Equipment Manufacturing; 335228 Other Household Appliance Manufacturing

■ ■ ■

Glen Dimplex is the world's leading manufacturer of electrical heating products and also produces a wide range of other appliances. Based in Ireland, Glen Dimplex has built up a collection of prominent appliance brands, including Dimplex, Stoves, New World, Belling, Galaxy Showers, Burco, AquaVac, Faber, Glen, Gobline, Roberts Radio, and others since its founding in 1973. The company's products include a full range of domestic and commercial heaters, boilers, stoves, gas and woodburnng decorative fireplaces, radios, vacuum cleaners, among other products. Glen Dimplex has established a global presence, with manufacturing and sales subsidiaries in the United Kingdom, Germany, Norway, Canada and China and sales offices in France, the Netherlands, Belgium, Italy, Japan, and Poland. The company also owns two distribution subsidiaries in Ireland, and maintains a 20 percent stake in NACCO Industries subsidiary Hamilton Beach/Proctor-Silex in the United States. Together, these operations combine to produce sales estimated at more than EUR 1.5 billion ($1.9 billion) into the mid-2000s. Glen Dimplex is a private company owned and led by founder and chairman Martin Naughton.

FOUNDING AN APPLIANCE GIANT IN 1973

Martin Naughton held a degree in engineering and worked at a number of jobs through the 1960s before becoming production manager at AET, a prominent Irish appliance company, based in Dunleer. AET slipped into losses at the beginning of the 1970s, and by 1973 had been taken over by the Irish government's bailout arm, Foir Teo. At that time, Naughton offered to buy out AET. When his bid was rejected, Naughton led a number of other AET employees in setting up a new business, in the town of Newry, in Northern Ireland. Naughton named the company Glen Electric, and launched operations with just ten employees. The company then began producing its own electric radiators. Naughton's original goal was modest, hoping to build the company to an employee base of 100 people and sales equivalent of EUR 1.5 million per year.

Naughton's timing was inauspicious, to say the least. The oil crisis, coupled with a long miners' strike, had sent the country into a long recession, and had also sent electricity rates spiraling upward. By the mid-1970s the government had raised electricity rates, and especially the off-peak rates, by some 70 percent. The British government had also begun promoting a scheme encouraging people to switch off their electricity during parts of the day in order to save energy.

Yet Naughton later viewed the challenges of the period as part of the company's later success. As he told the *Sunday Business Post*: "It was probably no bad thing to start at a difficult time. If you start at an easy time, you get soft. I think we learned from it. We run a very big organisation now, but we have the discipline and attitude of a small company. Every big company was once a small company. Every company has a style and it is trying to keep those attitudes—running it the same way—that has proven to be successful."

By 1975, Glen Electric had indeed succeeded in growing despite the worst of the recession, and in that year the company launched a new subsidiary in Newry. The company leased a factory building and began producing an expanded range of electric home appliances, including electric kettles and percolators.

Glen Electric's big break came in 1977, when Dimplex, then the United Kingdom's leading heating appliances brand, went into receivership. Originally founded as Habin Limited, an operator of garages and service stations in the Southampton region, that company had acquired the rights to the "Dimplex" electric radiator design in 1949. By the following year, the company had focused its operations on heating appliances, and changed its name to Dimplex Plc. The company grew strongly through the 1950s. In 1954, for example, the company launched construction of two new factories in Southampton. Before construction had even been

completed, demand for the Dimplex heater proved so strong that the company was forced to double the size of its factories.

Dimplex went public in 1959 and continued to build on its success over the next decade, expanding its range of heaters, and developing a strong export business. By the end of the 1960s, the company was not only the U.K.'s leading electric heater brand, but was also a prominent name in markets including Canada, Australia, South Africa, New Zealand, Belgium, the Netherlands, Italy, Portugal and Japan. At the beginning of the 1970s, Dimplex also entered the United States.

The 1970s spelled disaster for Dimplex, however, as electricity prices soared, and the extended recession crippled its sales. Dimplex began posting losses as early as 1973, and by 1976 its losses had continued to top £600,000 per year. Despite its efforts to rebuild its profitability, Dimplex was forced to throw in the towel in 1977, entering receivership.

In that year, Naughton arranged a meeting with the company's receiver, claiming an interest in acquiring the far-larger Dimplex. Naughton later admitted to the *Irish Examiner* that his real interest in the meeting was in order to engage in a bit of "industrial espionage." Yet Naughton, joined by financial advisor and future business partner Lochlan Quinn, quickly became captivated by the idea of taking over Dimplex itself. By the end of that year, Glen Electric had completed the Dimplex acquisition, becoming Glen Dimplex. Naughton took 74 percent of the newly enlarged company, with Quinn holding the remainder.

EXPANSION: 1970-89

Naughton quickly turned the Dimplex operations around, and by the following year, Glen Dimplex was prepared for more expansion. In 1978, Naughton came full circle, as it were, when Glen Dimplex agreed to acquire AET, which had continued to struggle against losses through the 1970s. The new subsidiary was then relaunched as Bitech Engineering.

In 1981, Glen Dimplex expanded again, this time boosting its commercial operations through the creation of a joint-venture with Burco Dean. Founded in the late 19th century, Burco Dean's greatest success had come through the lauch of its "Baby Burco" Washboiler in the 1950s. Over the next decades, the Burco name became one of the most well-known in the catering sector in the U.K. By the mid-1980s, however, expansion of the joint venture required too steep an investment for Burco Dean, and in 1985, the company agreed to sell the Burco appliance business to Glen Dimplex.

The mid-1980s marked a period of significant expansion for Glen Dimplex. By the end of 1985, the

KEY DATES

1946: Habin Ltd. is incorporated.

1949: Habin acquires the rights to Dimplex electric heaters and the company name is changed to Dimplex.

1959: Dimplex goes public.

1973: Martin Naughton, formerly production manager at appliance company AET, founds Glen Electric.

1975: Glen Electric builds a new factory in Newry, Northern Ireland.

1977: Glen Electric acquires Dimplex and becomes Glen Dimplex.

1978: The company acquires the AET factory in Dunleer, which is relaunched as Bitech Engineering.

1981: Glen Dimplex forms a joint venture with Burco Dean.

1985: The company takes over the Burco Appliances joint venture and acquires Morphy Richards and Blanella in the United Kingdom.

1986: Glen Dimplex acquires the Hamilton Beach company in the United States.

1990: Hamilton Beach merges into Nacco's Procter Silex and Glen Dimplex acquires control of Siemen's KKW in Germany.

1991: The company enters the Canadian market through the purchases of Westcan and Chromalox.

2000: Glen Dimplex acquires Faber in the Netherlands.

2002: The company establishes a night-storage heater joint venture in China and enters the Scandinavian market with the acquisition of Norway's Nobo.

2003: Glen Dimplex acquires Norway's Siemens Electrical Heating.

2004: The Glen Dimplex Japan joint venture is established.

company had acquired two more leading British appliance brands, Morphy Richards, a specialist in small home appliances, and Blanella, which produced electric blankets. The following year, Glen Dimplex expanded into the international appliance market, acquiring Hamilton Beach in the United States, paying $105 million. For Naughton, the Hamilton Beach acquisition

not only gave the company a foothold in the North American market, but also allowed the company to expand its product technology. As Naughton told *HFD* at the time: "We see the companies as a lovely fit. We make heat-driven appliances; Hamilton Beach makes motor-driven appliances. We plan to market Hamilton Beach products under the Morphy Richards name in Europe and Morphy Richards products under the Hamilton Beach name in the United States."

At the beginning of the 1990s, however, Glen Dimplex appeared to take a step back from its international operations. In 1990, the company agreed to sell most of Hamilton Beach to NACCO Industries, which had just recently acquired the Procter-Silex brand group. NACCO then combined Hamilton Beach and Procter-Silex into a single subsidiary. Glen Dimplex's share of the new company initially stood at 35 percent, but was later reduced to just 20 percent.

INTERNATIONAL LEADER IN THE NEW CENTURY

Although it was refocused more closely on its core electric heating appliance operations, Glen Dimplex had not abandoned its interest in overseas operations. By the end of 1990, the company had completed the acquisition of KKW, the Siemens electric heating division, taking the company into the German market and giving it a strong position throughout the European market.

The following year, Glen Dimplex turned to Canada, where it acquired Chromalox, that market's leading electrical heater producer, and another Siemens' subsidiary, Westcan. In 1992, Glen Dimplex expanded its product range, buying up troubled stove British manufacturer Belling.

Through the mid-1990s, the company continued to combine geographic expansion with extensions of its product range. In 1995, for example, the company bought EIO, a manufacturer of floor care appliances and products based in Germany. The same year the company bought British electrical heating appliance producer Seagoe Technologies. These purchases followed the acquisition of Roberts Radio, a producer of high-end radios and audio equipment, in 1994.

Into the mid-1990s, Glen Dimplex's revenues had topped the EUR 600 million mark. The company showed no sign of slowing its growth. By the end of the decade, the company had nearly doubled its revenues. Part of this growth came from its entry into France, where it acquired that market's electric heating appliance leader Mullen in 1996. The company also added a new range of floor care products through its purchase of AquaVac in 1997, and established the leading position in the German portable electric heater segment through the purchases of that company's AKO and WET in 1998.

By the end of the decade, Glen Dimplex had also established its first offices in Asia, setting up procurement operations in Hong Kong and China. These were followed by the creation of a manufacturing joint venture, Shenyang Dimplex Electronics, which began producing night-storage heaters for the vast Chinese market. The move was seen as an important investment, especially as the Chinese government introduced new low-priced nighttime electricity rates, encouraging the adoption and use of night-storage heaters. The joint-venture, with the Chinese government and a electricity producer, called for the production of one million heaters.

By then, Glen Dimplex had also added a new subsidiary and product category, by acquiring the Netherlands-based Faber, a leading European name in the production of gas and log-burning decorative fires, in 2000. The company also added two new leading British cooker brands, Stoves and New World, in 2001; these were then combined with its Belling subsidiary.

Glen Dimplex entered the Scandinavian market in 2002, buying up Nobo, based in Stjoerdal, near Trondheim, Norway. This purchase was soon followed by the 2003 acquisition of Siemens Electrical Heating, also based in Trondheim, and the last of Siemens' electric heating appliance operations.

Glen Dimplex continued to grow into the mid-2000s, adding two new subsidiaries in 2004. The first, Halstead Boilers Ltd., strenghtened the company's range of home central heating boilers in the U.K. The second, Glen Dimplex Japan, was a joint venture with Globally Incorporated, part of the Matsumoto Kenko construction group, which established Glen Dimplex in Japan for the first time.

By then Glen Dimplex had considered, but rejected, the idea of going public, in part to allow Quinn to cash in on his 26 percent holding in the company. But, as Naughton told the *Sunday Business Post*: "We did look at it. We had a beauty show of various commercial banks. Basically, I didn't think I would enjoy running a public company. I value my privacy too much. And we are able to grow from our resources and will continue to grow. A lot of people are driven by quarterly figures and they look at their profits, and other people are doing things to please the analysts, but not because it is the right thing to do strategically. All our decisions now are strategic."

Instead, Naughton agreed to buy out Quinn's stake, reportedly for some EUR 200 million in 2004, giving

him 100 percent control of the firm. The possibility of a future public offering appeared limited, particularly as Naughton had by then been joined by his son, Niall, in the company.

In 2005, Glen Dimplex went from hot to cold, when it acquired LEC Refrigeration Plc, based in the United Kingdom. Founded in the 1940s, that company produced and distributed refrigerators for both the domestic and commercial markets. Glen Dimplex promptly shifted LEC's production and headquarters to Merseyside, in a move completed in January 2006, ahead of the launch of a new LEC product line slated for April of that year. Martin Naughton had built Glen Dimplex from a humble startup in the 1970s to a world appliance leader in the 2000s.

M. L. Cohen

PRINCIPAL SUBSIDIARIES

Bitech Engineering; Burco Appliances Ltd.; Dimpco Ltd.; Dimplex AS (Norway); Dimplex Cleaning Systems; Dimplex North America Ltd. (Canada); Faber International BV (Netherlands); Galaxy Showers; Glen Dimplex Benelux BV (Netherlands); Glen Dimplex Design; Glen Dimplex Deutschland GmbH (Germany); Glen Dimplex Espana Spain; Glen Dimplex Exports Ltd.; Glen Dimplex France France; Glen Dimplex Home Appliances; Glen Dimplex Hong Kong; Glen Dimplex Italia (Italy); Glen Dimplex Japan; Glen Dimplex N.I. Ltd.; Glen Dimplex Polska (Poland); Glen Dimplex U.K. Ltd.; Glen Electric Northern; Halstead Boilers; KKW Kulmbacher Klimageräte-Werk GmbH (Germany); Lec Refrigeration plc; Morphy Richards Ltd.; Muller France; Nobo Electro AS (Norway); NOBO Heating UK Ltd.; Roberts Radio Ltd.; Seagoe Technologies Limited Northern; Shenyang Dimplex Electronics (Glen Dimplex China)

PRINCIPAL COMPETITORS

Siemens AG; Samsung Electronics Company Ltd; Sanyo Electric Company Ltd; Aisin Seiki Company Ltd; Electrolux AB; Whirlpool Corp; BSH Bosch und Siemens Hausgeraete GmbH; LG Electronics Inc; GE Appliances; Liebherr-International AG; Maytag Corporation.

FURTHER READING
Bacher, Mary Ann, "Glen Dimplex's Naughton," *HFD-The Weekly Home Furnishings Newspaper*, December 22, 1986, p. 47.

Carswell, Simon, "The Quiet Man," *Sunday Business Post*, September 15, 2002.

"Glen Dimplex Buys Siemens Heating Arm," *ERT Weekly*, October 2, 2003, p. 12.

Hardiman, Cyril, "How EUR 1.5bn Business Created One of the Great Irish Partnerships," *Irish Independent*, September 15, 2004.

Hurley, Sandra, "Glen Dimplex Goes Nordic," *Irish Examiner*, September 24, 2003.

"Lec Settling In after Its Relocation," *ERT Weekly*, January 12, 2006, p. 6.

Micheau, Ed, "Quinn's Exit Puts Naughton in Billionaire Club," *Sunday Business Post*, September 19, 2004

Power, Edward, "Glen Dimplex Moves into Scandinavian Market with NOBO," *The Irish Times*, November 6, 2002, p. 21.

Roe, David, "Glen Dimplex Expands into Asian Markets," *ERT Weekly*, June 13, 2002, p. 10.

Groupe Lactalis

10-20, rue Alolph Beck
53089 Laval Cedex 09,
France
Telephone: (33) 2 43 59 42 59
Fax: (33) 2 43 59 42 63
Web site: http://www.lactalis.fr

Private Company
Incorporated: 1933
Employees: 15,700
Sales: EUR 5.5 billion ($6.5 billion) (2005)
NAIC: 311511 Fluid Milk Manufacturing; 311512 Creamery Butter Manufacturing; 311513 Cheese Manufacturing; 422430 Dairy Product (Except Dried or Canned) Wholesalers

∎ ∎ ∎

Groupe Lactalis, formerly known as Besnier S.A., is France's largest dairy products producer and the second largest producer of cheese in the world. Its products are sold under the company's renowned President label, but also under brand names such as Bridel, Lactel, Sorrento, Rondele, and Locatelli. The company also owns approximately two-thirds of famed Société des Caves et des Producteurs Reunis de Roquefort, the world's leading producer of Roquefort cheese. Best known for its brie and Camembert, Groupe Lactalis produces a wide variety of cheese, butter, and milk products. Its products reach 143 countries; the company operates 65 plants in France and 13 in foreign countries. A private company, Groupe Lactalis is owned 100 percent by the Besnier family. Emmanuel Besnier, grandson of the company's founder, continues to lead the family business.

A SMALL FAMILY BUSINESS FOUNDED IN 1955

Besnier was founded as a single plant in Laval, in the Loire Valley region of France, by Andre Besnier, a former cooper by trade. In 1955, Andre's son, Michel, who had started with the family business as a delivery boy, took over the dairy company's operations. Besnier remained a small, single-plant operation until well into the 1960s. But after a flood destroyed the factory's entire dairy production in 1966, Michel Besnier became determined to protect the company from such calamities in the future by expanding its operations to multiple plants and diversifying the company's dairy products. As a first step, in 1968, Besnier created its own brand, the President label, which, in many parts of the world, would become synonymous with French cheese. The following year, the company opened a second plant, in Mayenne, adding to its cheese production capacity. By then, however, Michel Besnier was already preparing to take a new direction in an ambitious plan to build the family's business. In 1969, Besnier made the first of a long string of acquisitions, buying the cheese maker Bourdon, based in the Normandy region.

That first acquisition made Besnier hungry for more. In 1973, the company acquired a cheese making plant in Charchigné from Preval and followed that acquisition with the purchase of the Buquet cheese dairies. The following year, Besnier solidified its position in the Normandy region, the traditional center of Camembert

KEY DATES

1933: Andre Besnier establishes a cheese making business.
1968: Besnier creates the President brand.
1969: Cheese maker Bourdon is purchased.
1974: Besnier forms the Société Laiterière de Normandie with rival Bridel.
1990: Besnier acquires competitor Bridel.
1992: The company secures a 57 percent interest in Caves de Roquefort.
1996: Marcillat is acquired.
1999: The company changes its name to Groupe Lactalis.
2004: Groupe Lactalis enters the Indian market.

cheese production, by forming the Société Laiterière de Normandie with rival Bridel. At the same time, the company expanded its own Camembert production with the acquisitions of Groupement Laitier du Perche and of Laiteries Prairies de l'Orne. One year later, Besnier expanded again, adding brie to its product line with the purchase of cheese producer Renault of Doué la Fontaine. Another takeover followed in 1976, when Besnier acquired Stenval Sud.

By 1978, Besnier was thriving; in that year, the company built a new, state-of-the-art production facility in Donfront. The capacity of the new plant, located on 18 acres in the heart of Normandy, was reported to be three times larger than that of the company's principal competitors of the time. With production levels reaching up to 400,000 units of Camembert per day, the Donfront factory was among the largest soft-cheese plants in the world. Meanwhile, the company's line was augmented with the Lepetit brand name. Then, in 1979, Besnier expanded its butter production unit, building a butter plant in Isigny le Buat.

Besnier started the next decade strongly. In 1980, the company acquired the cheese making group Atlalait and that group's six plants in the Loire and Deux-Sévres, building on the company's position in western France. In that year, Besnier also moved into eastern France, with the takeover of the Jean Lincet cheese dairy. By then, foreign demand was building for Camembert and other French soft cheeses. In response, Besnier established a small plant in the United States, in Belmont, Wisconsin in 1981, which focused on supplying soft cheeses to the U.S. market. The company also began industrial production in Villalba, Spain in 1983.

By then, Besnier's sales had swelled to more than FRF 5 billion per year. The company's takeover drive continued, with the acquisition of Martin Collet in 1982, and the acquisition, between 1982 and 1985, of six cheeses from Claudel Roustand Galac. To fuel further expansion, however, Besnier set its sights on acquiring a larger cheese operation. When the Société de Collecte des Prodicteirs de Preval (SCPP) went bankrupt in 1982, Besnier purchased that group's 34 percent stake in the FRF 3 billion-per-year Preval dairy operation. Besnier claimed that its purchase also gave it the right to exercise an option to buy an additional 24 percent of Preval from majority stakeholder Union Laitière Normande (ULN). More than twice Besnier's size at the time, with annual turnover of some FRF 10 billion, the ULN denied Besnier's action to exercise the option. Despite threatening legal action, Besnier lost that takeover bid.

The Preval setback proved to be a rarity in Besnier's aggressive expansion. The company completed its acquisition of Claudel Roustand Galac in 1985. That group had been a subsidiary of Nestlé, of Switzerland; its acquisition by Besnier had given Nestlé a 20 percent share of Besnier. In 1987, however, Nestlé agreed to sell its stake back to Michel Besnier, once again giving him complete control over the family business. With the 1985 acquisition of the Picault dairy operations, based in Normandy, and the cheese dairy plant of Moreau, based in the Ardennes region, the Besnier family business was worth some FRF 8.8 billion by 1987. Profits also were soaring, jumping from FRF 60 million in 1986 to FRF 194 million in 1987. Exports had grown to represent more than 25 percent of the company's sales, with approximately 60 percent of export sales going to neighboring European countries. Besnier also boosted its U.S. presence in 1987 with the opening of a larger plant in Turlock, California, which enabled the company to add fresh milk products, including cream and yogurt, to the U.S. market.

EYEING THE EUROPEAN UNION: 1990-99

By the late 1980s, Besnier had built the family business into a dairy empire of some 36 plants, processing more than two billion liters of milk per year into more than 400 products under the President, Lepetit, Claudel, Lactel, and other branded and private label names. Sales in 1988 had risen to FRF 9.7 billion, and profits had nearly doubled to FRF 378 million. Besnier's growth during the previous two decades had been impressive, but it proved to be just the beginning. By the early years of the 1990s, Besnier would more than double its sales.

With the creation of the European common market looming in 1992, Besnier moved to consolidate its position in France while simultaneously stepping up its expansion into foreign countries, the better to compete with the European dairy giants. The next phase of the company's expansion began in 1989. In that year Besnier made a number of smaller acquisitions, including that of Hugerot, of the Aube region of France, and the acquisition of the milk production operations of Valmont, a subsidiary of the Perrier group. The Valmont acquisition also helped confirm Michel Besnier's reputation for transforming the failing operations of some of its acquisitions into profitable additions to the Besnier group. Also in 1989, the company expanded into the Los Angeles market, with the acquisition of the small fresh dairy operation, Atlantis, while the company deepened its European presence with the purchase of Laiterie Ekabe, of Luxembourg, and the formation of a partnership to bring the company into the Catalonia region of Spain. Another partnership, with a Belgian dairy cooperative, led to the formation of SA Laiterie Walhorn Molkerel.

Besnier, however, reserved its biggest move for 1990. In that year, the company outmaneuvered its larger competitors, including Sodiaal, ULN, and Bongrain, as well as a number of foreign competitors, to purchase the Bridel dairy company, another family business described as the patriarch of the French Camembert industry and Besnier's fiercest competitor. The purchase, for an estimated FRF 2 billion, catapulted Besnier to the top of the French dairy industry, giving the company total annual revenues of more than FRF 17 billion. The combined operations gave Besnier a large share of the French dairy market, with 16 percent of cheese products, 24 percent of milk, and 24 percent of the country's butter production. In January 1991, Besnier reinforced its position with the acquisition of another family-controlled cheese producer, Girod, based in Saint-Julien-en-Genevois, adding that company's FRF 240 million in sales. Three months later, Besnier outmaneuvered its competitors again, acquiring the Jean-Jacques fresh dairy operations and the rest of the Valmont dairy operations from the troubled Perrier group, which had been forced to recall all of its bottled water after the water had been found to contain traces of benzene. These purchases helped raise Besnier's sales to some FRF 22 billion by the end of that year.

By October 1992, Besnier caused a new stir in the French dairy industry. After Nestlé's takeover of Perrier in the beginning of 1992, the Swiss company announced its intentions of selling off another Perrier subsidiary, the renowned Caves de Roquefort, the leading maker (with 80 percent of world production) of the famous French blue cheese. Again, Besnier outran its competitors, pay-ing Nestlé FRF 863 million for 57 percent of Caves de Roquefort. The remaining shares of the Roquefort operation continued to be controlled by French bank Crédit Agricole. To finance the Roquefort acquisition, Besnier set up a subsidiary unit, Société pour le Financement de l'Industrie Laitière (SOFIL), which increased its participation in Roquefort to 69.5 percent in 1993. Besnier's acquisition spree in the 1990s, however, had brought the company heavily into debt, with FRF 2.5 billion owed even before the Roquefort acquisition. To finance its debt without going public, Besnier sold 40 percent of SOFIL to three French banks—Crédit Lyonnais, Banque Nationale de Paris, and Société Generale—raising as much as FRF 800 million in capital.

After the Roquefort acquisition, Besnier slowed the pace of its purchases. Turning to consolidating the company's operations and improving the profitability of its recent operations, Besnier considered selling off the Roquefort subsidiary, Sorrento, based in Buffalo, New York, to Kraft Foods. The lull did not last long, however. By the end of 1993, Besnier had made several new investments, including the acquisition of small (FRF 60 million) cheese producer Rousel, based in Puy-de-Dome, near Chamalieres, and a 51 percent controlling interest in Alsace Lorraine-based Unicoolait (Union des Cooperatives Laitières), a group of 820 cheese producers in the region with FRF 550 million in sales. Besnier also was maneuvering toward another major purchase. In January 1993, he stepped up his stake in Fromageries Bel, the maker of the worldwide top-selling processed cheese product La Vache Qui Rit (Laughing Cow) with FRF 6.8 billion in 1991 sales. Besnier's share increased to 8 percent, giving him slightly more than 5 percent of the voting rights in the company. By the beginning of 1994, however, Besnier had extended his share of Bel's voting rights to 20.57 percent. Bel's main shareholder and chairman, Robert Fievet, was then 84 years old; at the same time, succession issues were beginning to present themselves to the Bel founding family and controllers of the majority of that company's voting rights. Besnier adopted a wait-and-see attitude, making no secret of its interest in eventually adding Bel to the Besnier fold.

With FRF 24 billion in annual sales in 1993, Besnier was not only France's largest dairy products group, it also had become one of the largest in Europe, behind industry leader Nestlé. As the French dairy industry moved closer to consolidation, Besnier began focusing on new product development, introducing, among others, its own emmental cheese. In 1995, the company expanded its U.S. operation, building a 60,000-square-foot facility in Belmont, Wisconsin. The following year, the company made its first move to expand into the reviving Eastern European market. In April 1996, Besnier created a joint venture in the Ukraine with Nikolaiev. Four months later, Besnier entered Poland with the 83 percent purchase of that country's Polser dairy. In 1997, the company set up a Russian subsidiary, Besnier Vostok. Meanwhile, questions about the possible successor to Michel Besnier, who turned 67 in 1996, were answered as Besnier began grooming son Emmanuel, 26, to take over the company's operations. When Michel died in 2000, Emmanuel assumed control of the company.

A NEW NAME FOR THE NEW MILLENNIUM

Besnier continued its growth through acquisition strategy into the late 1990s. During 1998, the company added Italy-based Locatelli to its arsenal. Besnier bolstered its U.S. holdings in 1999 with the purchases of Concord Marketing and Simplot Dairy Group Inc. By this time, the United States was the company's second largest market behind France. The addition of Concord and Simplot nearly doubled Besnier's U.S. sales.

As part of its policy to focus on international markets, Besnier announced it would adopt the Groupe Lactalis corporate moniker in early 1999. The company stressed that the new name was easy to pronounce in all languages and reflected its dedication to milk and dairy products.

As the largest privately held dairy in Europe, Groupe Lactalis entered the new millennium on solid ground. In 2002, it purchased the remaining shares of the Bel group of soft cheeses. The following year, it added Kraft Foods Inc.'s Invernizzi cheese operations in Italy to its holdings. During the latter half of 2004, Groupe Lactalis purchased a total of six companies in the Ukraine, Moldavia, Kazakhstan, Spain, Italy, the United Kingdom, the United States, and Poland. Included in these deals was the McLelland Group, the third largest cheese company based in the United Kingdom, and U.S.-based Rondele gourmet cheese. Italy's Edigio Galbani S.p.A. was purchased in early 2006.

While it continued to make strategic purchases, the company also eyed entering new markets as crucial to its future success. In early 2004, Groupe Lactalis began importing and distributing its President and Bridel brands throughout India, including Delhi, Mumbai, Chennai, Bangalore, Kolkata, Goa, and Pondicherry. It also entered the Japanese consumer market in 2005 by selling its President brand in department stores and upscale supermarkets. In 2006 the company announced a partnership with Nestlé to manufacture and market a line of yogurts and chilled desserts in Europe.

Groupe Lactalis's actions over the past several years left it in an enviable position among its competitors. Indeed, the company claimed that every second, seven President brand products were sold somewhere in the world. By this time, Groupe Lactalis's annual cows' milk collection was more than 6.9 billion liters, including 2.2 billion liters processed outside of France. The company also processed 160 million liters of sheeps' milk and 55 million liters of goats' milk. From this, Groupe Lactalis produced 275 million gallons of fluid milk, 310 million pounds of butter, 1.25 million pounds of cheese (including 190,000 tons outside of France), and 627 million pounds of fresh dairy products, including cream and yogurt. With sales of Euro 5.5 billion, Groupe Lactalis appeared to be on track for success in the years to come.

M. L. Cohen
Updated, Christina M. Stansell

PRINCIPAL SUBSIDIARIES

Lactalis United Kingdom; Lactalis Europe du Nord; Lactalis Deutschland; Lactalis Iberia; Lactalis Locatelli; Lactalis Luxembourg; Lactalis Portugal; Lactalis Polska; Lactalis Ukraine; Lactalis Vostok; Lactalis USA; Sorrento Lactalis.

PRINCIPAL COMPETITORS

Arla Foods amba; Bongrain S.A.; Groupe Danone.

FURTHER READING

"Besnier Changes Name to Groupe Lactalis, Expands in US," *Les Echos,* January 12, 1999.

Dawkins, William, "Roquefort Returns to the French Cheeseboard," *Financial Times,* October 3, 1992, p. 12.

"French Cheese Maker Lactalis Aims to Expand Sales in Japan," *Asia Pulse,* March 14, 2005.

"French Cheese Move in Poland," *East European Markets,* August 30, 1996.

"French Dairy Major Lactalis Enters Indian Cheese Market," *Indian Business Insight,* January 9, 2004.

"Groupe Lactalis," *Wall Street Journal,* January 16, 2006, p. A12.

"Groupe Lactalis Acquires the McLelland Group," *Gourmet Retailer,* January 27, 2005.

Herzog, Karen, "French Connection: Wisconsin Village Says 'Oui' to Cheese," *Milwaukee Journal Sentinel,* September 8, 1996, Food Sec., p. 1.

"How a French Connection Found a Taste for the UK," *Grocer,* January 15, 1994.

Mans, Jack, "C'est le Brie," *Dairy Foods,* January 1996, p. 49.

McRitchie, Sarah, "Very Private, Increasingly Global: Name Change, International Acquisitions Position French Company for the Millennium," *Dairy Foods,* April 1, 1999.

"Nestlé, Lactalis Making Deals," *Dairy Foods,* January 1, 2006.

Gulf Agency Company Ltd.

Corporate Head Office
Jebel Ali Free Zone
P.O. Box 18006
Dubai,
United Arab Emirates
Telephone: (971) 4 881 1
Fax: (971) 4 881 1
Web site: http://www.gacworld.com

Private Company
Incorporated: 1956
Employees: 6,000
Sales: $1.2 billion (2005 est.)
NAIC: 484110 General Freight Trucking, Local; 484121 General Freight Trucking, Long-Distance, Truckload; 484122 General Freight Trucking, Long-Distance, Less Than Truckload; 484220 Specialized Freight (Except Used Goods) Trucking, Local; 484230 Specialized Freight (Except Used Goods) Trucking, Long-Distance; 488320 Marine Cargo Handling; 488330 Navigational Services to Shipping; 488390 Other Support Activities for Water Transportation; 488490 Other Support Activities for Road Transportation; 488510 Freight Transportation Arrangement; 541614 Process, Physical Distribution, and Logistics Consulting Services

■ ■ ■

Gulf Agency Company Ltd., which trades as GAC, is a leading global provider of shipping, logistics, and marine services. Its 200 offices span five continents and are staffed with knowledgeable locals. It handles logistics for a slew of multinational corporations. As part of its marine services, a fleet of crew supply vessels brings food and fresh water to oil platforms and passing freighters. Originally formed in Kuwait in the mid-1950s by Swedish shipping interests, the company is the largest shipping agent in the Middle East and operates at more than 1,000 locations around the world. Its international reach has been enhanced through acquisitions such as that of Benair Freight in 2005. GAC has a number of regional affiliates with local partners as majority shareholders. It also maintains a number of marketing alliances for regions of the world it does not cover on its own.

ORIGINS

Gulf Agency Company (GAC) was originally set up as a Kuwait joint venture in 1956 by a top Swedish shipping agency, Nyman & Schultz, looking to expedite things at the country's busy seaport at the dawn of the containerized shipping age. Nyman & Schultz dated back to Carl Oscar Strindberg's shipping agency, which had been formed in Stockholm in 1861 and acquired by the Lindberg family in the 1920s.

Offices were soon established in nearby Saudi Arabia and throughout the Arab world. Branches in Lebanon, Syria, Egypt, and Libya would eventually be closed, however, due to the outbreak of war or nationalization. Egypt closed the Suez Canal for eight years following the Six Day War with Israel in 1967. After it was reopened, GAC handled traffic to the Suez Canal from its Athens office. GAC also had opened an office at the Jebel Ali Free Zone in Dubai.

COMPANY PERSPECTIVES

For nearly half a century, seafarers have been cabling, phoning and, more recently, e-mailing GAC, confident of a professional and courteous reception when they reached port. And it's precisely that peace of mind that has come to be associated with every aspect of GAC's operations today. From its start as a regional player, GAC has grown to become the largest independent shipping and transport services provider in the world. Its hallmark: providing clients with the highest standards in shipping, logistics and marine services. GAC has evolved into a modern, sophisticated enterprise while retaining some reassuringly traditional values. Belief in the importance of face-to-face contact keeps it an unusually personal kind of company in an otherwise technological age. Awareness that other suppliers can offer similar services has only reinforced an abiding determination to do things well. And lessons learned in locations far off the beaten path serve as a reminder that the world is still a big, and sometimes formidable, place.

GAC entered the Nigerian market in the 1970s, first overseeing ships to haul cement to the country's construction boom. Oil development later brought more business.

GAC opened an office in Jordan in 1985. Within about ten years, reported *Lloyd's List*, it was the country's leading shipping agent. The shipping business in the Persian Gulf was going through an unprofitable couple of years, exacerbated by the war between Iran and Iraq. In January 1985 GAC began operating a less-than-container-load (LCL) freight forwarding service in the Persian Gulf through its Cargo Gulf unit, which grew quickly following the end of hostilities in the region.

NEW FRONTIERS IN 1990

The fall of the Soviet Empire opened new opportunities for GAC. It became the first international shipping agent in Poland in November 1989. GAC introduced a cargo service for the former Soviet republics several years later, in 1997, attracted in part by Azerbaijani oil developments. At the same time, GAC was expanding its reach to the east, working in partnership with a local carrier in Indonesia to begin operations there. A Singapore unit had opened a few years earlier.

GAC staff had to be evacuated from Kuwait during its invasion by Iraq and the subsequent Operation Desert Storm. Growth soon resumed following this turbulence. A new door-to-door air freight unit, Air Gulf Express, was launched in May 1991. It began with connections from the Middle East to Europe and the United States. (Oil industry forwarder specialist Danaher America Inc. was its U.S. freight forwarding partner.)

In 1993, GAC spent $3 million to open a large, technologically advanced freight center in the emerging trade center of Dubai. It had a capacity exceeding 3,000 containers a year, according to *Lloyd's List*, and was operated by GAC's freight forwarding division, Gulf Express Freight. A portion of the facility was temperature-controlled.

GAC's Dubai distribution facility was instantly successful with multinational corporations, and underwent a $10 million upgrade within a couple of years. The shipping agent business was becoming more competitive, an official told *Lloyd's List*. The Dubai center offered co-packing and online services in addition to warehousing.

Besides distribution and shipping agency, GAC's third main line of business was shipping support services. This included representation for property and indemnity clubs (a kind of marine insurance), repair facilities, and the ability to ferry cargo, supplies, or crew to or from passing ships that did not want to spare the time or expense of docking at port. The company was expanding the scope of its services, transporting heavy equipment such as construction cranes.

In the mid-1990s, GAC began coordinating its European ports through a common hub office. The center of GAC's trade, the distribution facility in Dubai's Jebel Ali Free Zone, was expanded yet again in the late 1990s, bringing its total capacity to 75,000 cubic meters. It also began building a 10,000-square-meter facility in Bahrain in 1999.

GAC benefited from the privatization of the agency business at the Suez Canal in 1998. The company subsequently formed GAC Egypt. The company was also active at the other end of the continent. Due to interest from its existing multinational clients in Nigeria, GAC launched operations in Angola. The company reported that within a few months, it had a 50 percent share of the tanker market there, which was booming following recent deepwater finds. GAC also was beginning to operate in South Africa.

By 2000, GAC had about 4,000 employees and 160 offices in 60 countries around the world. It had amassed one of the largest truck fleets in the Middle East, noted *Traffic World*. As oil development intensified

KEY DATES

1956: Swedish shipping interests set up Gulf Agency Company (GAC) in Kuwait.
1958: GAC Saudi Arabia is formed.
1967: Operations in Bahrain begin.
1983: GAC enters East Asia with the opening of a Hong Kong office; the first office in India is opened.
1984: GAC Singapore begins operations.
1985: The Jordan office opens; the CargoGulf less-than-container-load freight forwarding service is launched.
1987: Headquarters are established in Athens.
1990: GAC begins operations in Indonesia.
1991: Air Gulf Express is launched.
1993: A new distribution center opens in Dubai.
1997: Cargo service to former Soviet republics is launched.
1998: GAC begins operations in Angola and South Africa.
2002: Headquarters are relocated from Athens to Dubai.
2003: GAC Marine Logistics is launched.
2005: Benair Freight is acquired.

in the Caucasus, GAC opened an office in the Black Sea port of Novorossiysk in May 2001.

NEW HEADQUARTERS IN 2002

Headquarters were relocated from Athens to Dubai, the center of the company's trade, in January 2002. The new offices cost $4 million. The company continued to expand in Europe, adding offices in Denmark and Sweden.

GAC's freight forwarding unit, GAC Cargo Systems, was growing rapidly through alliances and acquisitions. In 2001 it began a marketing agreement with Benair Freight International Limited, a U.K. freight forwarder focused on the Asian market. GAC bought Benair's Malaysian subsidiary within a year. It also acquired the Singapore shipping agency operations of Shell International Eastern Trading Company.

GAC began a marketing agreement with Emirates SkyCargo in November 2001. The deal allowed Emirates to offer its customers door-to-door service, while providing preferential rates and treatment for GAC's air freight.

GAC was restructured in 2002 into four geographic areas and three business units. GAC Marine Logistics, a marine parts supply business, was launched in 2003. The company was expanding its operations in India and West Africa. At the same time, GAC was undergoing an initiative to reduce costs and increase productivity in a competitive market. According to *Lloyd's List,* GAC was seeing a dramatic increase in project cargo at its Abu Dhabi base related to construction of the $3.5 billion Dolphin gas pipeline and a desalination plant.

GAC teamed up with Australia's Adstream Agency in 2002. The alliance allowed each to expand its geographical reach by sharing marketing and IT information. Other alliances were unveiled in the next two years, with U.S.-based Rice Unruh Reynolds, South Korea's Unipros, Malaysia's Kudrat Maritime, Panama's Wilford & McKay, and the Ultramar Group of South America.

In 2003, the company revamped its corporate identity and logo. The initials "GAC" became the global brand rather than the traditional "Gulf Agency Company." The company adopted a new catchphrase, "wherever you go." One service offering GAC was growing was its door-to-door deliveries.

GAC won a huge contract to handle United Nations food shipments to Iraq following the U.S. invasion to ouster Saddam Hussein. The war devastated Dubai's leisure cruise industry, however, for which GAC was the leading agent. The company's affiliate in Saudi Arabia was seeing more cruise business due to the opening of that market to nonreligious tourists.

A company official told *Lloyd's List* that while the freight forwarding business was extremely competitive, GAC felt it had a distinct advantage in operating in emerging markets. It was planning further expansion in Southeast Asia, Africa, and Latin America.

The company's reach from Europe to the Far East was strengthened by the 2005 purchase of Benair Freight International Ltd. and Benair Freight Pte from the United Kingdom's Dart Group plc for $9 million. Benair, which had been in business since the mid-1970s, offered GAC more truck and train capacity.

Frederick C. Ingram

PRINCIPAL DIVISIONS

Shipping Services; Logistics Services; Marine Services.

PRINCIPAL COMPETITORS

Barwil Agencies A.S.; Globalink Transportation & Logistics Worldwide LLP; Hull Blyth & Co.; Inchcape Shipping Services; The Kanoo Group.

FURTHER READING

"Adstream Agency in Alliance with Gulf Agency Company," *Lloyd's List Daily Commercial News,* October 8, 2002, p. 1.

Bangsberg, P. T., "Gulf Agency Acquires Asia Forwarder," *Journal of Commerce—JoC Online,* January 9, 2002.

"Blow to Tourism Has No Impact on Other Sectors," *Lloyd's List International,* February 25, 2002.

"Building Boosts Project Cargo Volume," *Lloyd's List International,* April 17, 2002.

"CargoGulf Starting Weekly Service to Middle East Ports," *Business Times Singapore,* June 15, 1989, p. 1.

"A Continuing Decline in Freight Rates...," *Middle East Economic Digest,* January 31, 1987, p. 27.

"Dart Group Agrees £5.1M Disposal," *Dow Jones International News,* August 31, 2005.

Everden, Kathi, "Special Report on Dubai: GAC Opens Freight Centre," *Lloyd's List,* May 28, 1992, p. 17.

"Foresight Pays Off As GAC Spreads Its Net to Over 40 Countries," *Lloyd's List,* April 29, 2005, p. 19.

Fromme, Herbert, "Special Report on Dubai: Freight '94—Gulf Agency Expands Warehouse Facility," *Lloyd's List,* November 3, 1994, p. 13.

"GAC and Emirates SkyCargo Sign First Global Agreement," *Middle East Company News,* November 18, 2001.

"GAC Base at Jebel Ali," *Lloyd's List International,* April 3, 2002.

"GAC Buys Freight Forwarder," *Traffic World,* September 12, 2005.

"GAC Drives Its Logistics Business," *Lloyd's List International,* November 18, 2002.

"GAC Launches New Inbound Service," *International Freighting Weekly,* May 20, 1991, p. 21.

"GAC Markets Mina Sulmanone Stop Cargo Centre," *Lloyd's List International,* June 22, 2001.

"GAC to Invest $10M in New Jebel Ali Facilities," *Lloyd's List International,* July 2, 1993.

"GAC to Use Dubai to Tap the African Markets," *Khaleej Times,* January 30, 2003.

"GAC—RUR to Boost Global Port Agency Services," *Middle East Company News,* August 30, 2003.

"GAC, Wilford & McKay Sign Global Network Agreement," *Kuwaiti News Digest,* January 20, 2004.

"Gulf Agency—GAC's Historic Roots Shape Its Cruise Agency Style," *Dream World Cruise Destinations,* February 2002, p. 98.

"Gulf Agency Company (corporate restructuring)," *Air Cargo World,* November 2002, p. 71.

"Gulf Agency Company Gears Up for Expansion As Project Cargo Grows," *Lloyd's List,* February 13, 2002, p. 17.

"Gulf Agency Company (GAC) Is to Further Expand Its Ship Supply Operations in the United Arab Emirates with the Introduction of a New 110 Ft Steel Crew/Supply Launch," *Lloyd's List International,* February 3, 1987, p. 2.

Hastings, Philip, "Demand Brings a Break with Tradition," *Middle East Economic Digest,* September 13, 1993.

Kennedy, Frank, "Sea Views: GAC Sets Challenging Global Goals for 2004," *Gulfnews.com,* February 16, 2004.

Lewis, Ian, "GAC to Increase Staff in China," *Lloyd's List International,* January 28, 1991, p. 2.

Lin, Tham Choy, "GAC Group Buys Benair Freight Malaysia," *Bernama Daily Malaysian News,* January 8, 2002.

Nadkarni, Shirish, "Special Report on Sri Lanka: GAC Shipping Seeks Growth," *Lloyd's List,* April 16, 1999, p. 9.

"Name Change Underpins GAC's Global Ambitions," *Lloyd's List,* October 1, 2003.

"National Shipping Remains One of the Largest Agents," *Lloyd's List International,* October 11, 1994.

Osler, David, "Special Report on Jordan: GAC Jordan Now a Major Ship Agency," *Lloyd's List,* September 30, 1996, p. 7.

Parker, John, "Middle East Consumer Market: Dubai Is the Region's Commercial Capital and the Gulf Agency Is Its Largest Shipping Agent," *Traffic World,* November 20, 2000, p. 28.

Rissik, Dee, "Old Rivals and Newcomers Fight for Angola Oil Supremacy," *Lloyd's List,* February 27, 1999, p. 3.

"Ship Agent GAC Is Here to Stay in Both Shipping and Logistics," *Lloyd's List,* April 27, 2004, p. 12.

"Shippers Wait for the Boom," *Middle East Economic Digest,* October 21, 1988, p. 11.

Tan Hua Joo, "Joint Effort to Transport Heavy Machinery," *Business Times Singapore,* April 16, 1992.

Taylor, Alan, "Gulf Express Demand High," *International Freighting Weekly,* November 11, 1991, p. 24.

Thomas, Karen, "New GAC Run Targets Angola Offshore Sector," *Lloyd's List International,* September 8, 1998.

———, "Special Report on Qatar: Gulf Agency Takes on Second Club," *Lloyd's List,* April 7, 2000, p. 11.

Urquhart, Donald, "Gulf Agency Gets Massive UN Food Aid Contract; ME Shipping Firm to Handle UN Chartered Vessels Moving Aid to Iraq," *Business Times Singapore,* April 4, 2003.

"Versatile GAC [Saudi Arabia] Handles 2,000 Ships Per Year," *Lloyd's List,* June 27, 2002, p. 15.

Haggar Corporation

Two Colinas Crossing
11511 Luna Road
Dallas, Texas 75234
U.S.A.
Telephone: (214) 352-8481
Fax: (214) 956-4502
Web site: http://www.haggar.com

Private Company
Incorporated: 1926
Employees: 3,300
Sales: $487.9 million (2004)
NAIC: 315224 Men's and Boys' Cut and Sew Trouser, Slack, and Jean Manufacturing; 315222 Men's and Boys' Cut and Sew Suit, Coat, and Overcoat Manufacturing; 315223 Men's and Boys' Cut and Sew Shirt (except Work Shirt) Manufacturing

■ ■ ■

Haggar Corporation and its subsidiaries are leading designers, manufacturers, importers, and marketers of men's apparel. Established in 1926, Haggar has played an important role in the fashion industry. "Slacks" did not exist until Haggar introduced them in the 1940s. Since that time, Haggar has expanded its line to include men's shorts, wrinkle-free cotton shirts, suits, and pants, including occasional forays into women's clothing. The company's goods are sold through about 10,000 department stores, specialty stores, and mass market retailers in the United States, the United Kingdom, Canada, Indonesia, and Mexico. Haggar also sells its clothing in 70 company-operated retail outlets. Haggar markets its products under its namesake, and under the licensed brands of Claiborne, Kenneth Cole, and Kenneth Cole Reaction. A private equity group led by Infinity Associates LLC acquired Haggar in 2005.

J.M. Haggar, a 34-year-old Lebanese immigrant, started Haggar in 1926. Born in 1892, Haggar sailed from his homeland to Mexico at the age of 13. He moved to the United States a few years later, settling first in Texas, moving on to New Orleans, and finally reaching St. Louis, Missouri. His first jobs were menial ones, such as dishwasher and window washer, but over the years his skill with people landed him inevitably in sales. After stints in the oil and cotton businesses, where his prowess as a salesman became legendary, by 1921 Haggar found himself selling overalls in Texas, Louisiana, and New Mexico for a company based in Missouri. While working at that job, Haggar concluded that selling many items at a single, stable price would bring more profit than selling a lot of different grades of merchandise each of which yielded a different and constantly shifting profit margin.

NO DEPRESSION AT HAGGAR

By 1926, Haggar had saved enough money to launch his own enterprise. He set up shop in Dallas and began to make and sell high-quality, low-cost pants for working men. Within three years, his Dallas Pant Manufacturing Company had 250 employees and occupied 6,000 square feet of space on two floors of the Santa Fe Building in Dallas. The company managed not only to survive, but to thrive during the Great

Depression. In 1933 Haggar staged a "Prosperity Picnic/Parade" in downtown Dallas to demonstrate that his company was still hiring, and that good times were bound to return. By 1936 the company had opened a facility in Greenville, Texas, its first outside of Dallas.

Haggar's son, E.R. (Ed) Haggar, joined the company in the 1930s. Until the late 1930s, Haggar products were sold to chain stores and other accounts with no brand name attached to them. Under E.R. Haggar's direction, the company introduced brand names. In 1938, Haggar began its first national advertising campaign and began the creation of a national sales organization in order to raise customer awareness of the Haggar name, as well as its trademark Mustang brand. Haggar's second son, J.M. (Joe Jr.) Haggar, Jr., began to play a major role in company operations in the 1940s. During that decade, Haggar, with the assistance of the Tracey Locke Advertising Agency (a forerunner of advertising giant DDB Needham), coined the term "slacks." The idea behind slacks was that they were to be worn during the slack time away from work. Slacks quickly became an accepted part of the American male wardrobe vocabulary.

Around the same time, the Haggar name was becoming increasingly familiar across America through relentless advertising. The company became the first pants manufacturer to advertise in the trade journals, beginning with *Daily News Record* and *Men's Wear Daily*. With the success of those early ads, the company gradually expanded its advertising budget. Its ads soon appeared in such big-name magazines as *Life, Collier's,* and *Esquire*. Haggar's *Life* ad featured a gimmick called the "Haggar Harmony Chart." The chart showed men how to "mix and match" in order to triple their wardrobe with the purchase of a few pairs of Haggar slacks. The charts were also made available through retailers and by mail order from the company. The chart eventually disappeared, but by that time the idea of mixing and matching had sunk into the heads of previously fashion-shy American men. Several other now-common merchandising tactics can be credited to Haggar during this period, including two-pairs-at-a-reduced-price offers and prepackaged, precuffed, ready-to-wear slacks.

Haggar regularly placed ads in at least a dozen major magazines by 1950, and its distribution system grew accordingly. By 1954 there were 32 Haggar sales representatives roaming the country, more than double the number during World War II. As the "slacks" concept continued to gain momentum, Haggar latched onto the idea of well-known sports figures as the ideal pitchmen for their products. Advertising heavily in such publications as *Sport* and *Sports Illustrated,* the company began to associate its name with dashing sports heroes like Mickey Mantle, Bobby Lane, and Arnold Palmer.

THE TELEVISION AGE

One of Haggar's product innovations of the 1950s was "forever-prest," one of the first lines of pants made from wrinkle-resistant material. Meanwhile, television was emerging as an important new way to advertise, and Haggar became one of the first clothing manufacturers to take advantage of this new medium. One of Haggar's early television spots showed a pair of Haggar "forever-prest" slacks being crumpled up and run over by a steamroller. They were then picked up, shaken out, and shown to be wrinkle free. The ad was so successful that the Gimbels department store in New York sold out of the slacks less than 24 hours after its initial airing in that city. As with its early magazine ads, the success of Haggar's first television commercials led to a full-blown commitment to television advertising. The company became a sponsor of such shows as *Sugarfoot, Bronco, Twelve O'Clock High,* and *Naked City.*

As television expanded its coverage of sports in the 1960s, Haggar found a new male-dominated outlet for its advertising. The company became a sponsor of ABC's *Wide World of Sports* in 1963, and a few years later it became a major advertiser during NFL football game broadcasts. Haggar also advertised during other televised sporting events, including baseball, basketball, hockey, and tennis, as their television coverage grew.

In addition to advertising, Haggar meanwhile continued to innovate in other areas as well. New products such as the "Imperials" line of dress slacks created new market niches in the gaps between "casual"

KEY DATES

1926: J.M. Haggar establishes a pant manufacturing company in Dallas.
1938: The company launches a national advertising campaign.
1963: Haggar becomes a sponsor of ABC's Wide World of Sports.
1983: The Reed St. James discount brand is launched.
1992: Haggar unveils a new line of wrinkle-free cotton pants; the company goes public.
1998: Jerell Inc. is acquired.
2005: Private equity firms Infinity Associates LLC, Perseus LLC, and Symphony Holdings Ltd. purchase Haggar in a $212 million deal.

and "dress" clothing. Haggar also introduced the "Haggar hanger," a special hanger that streamlined the distribution process by allowing the company to ship pants already on hangers, ready to be put on racks by retailers. Among other innovations were Haggar's pre-cuffed pants that didn't need to be tailored.

In the late 1960s, Haggar popularized polyester-and-wool permanent press pants. By the beginning of the 1970s, Haggar controlled the biggest chunk of the men's dress slacks market, with a 20 percent share, and the Haggar brand name was the one recognized most for dress pants among American men. So omnipresent was the Haggar label in American retail outlets that the company's unofficial slogan was "We cover the asses of the masses."

In the 1970s, Haggar introduced leisure tops to go with its slacks. By the company's 50th birthday in 1976, it increased its sales of slacks during a year in which sales for the industry had experienced substantial drop off. As in previous decades, new styles and products were added on a regular basis. A line of slacks called 640 was introduced in 1972, and in 1976, a contemporary line of slacks and tops called the Gallery, featuring a trimmer, updated fit and made of slick 1970s fabrics, was launched. A young men's line called Body Work was also added. The 1970s also brought the addition of Haggar sport coats and vests, and by the middle of the decade a customer fond of Haggar merchandise could pretty much clothe himself entirely in Haggar goods regardless of the occasion. By the end of the 1970s, the aging J.M. Haggar, while still retaining a powerful voice in company affairs, had handed over most of the duties

of operating the company to sons Ed, who served as president, and Joe Jr., executive vice-president. By this time there were 16 plants manufacturing Haggar clothing, located across Texas and Oklahoma.

In 1983, Haggar launched the Reed St. James brand, a clothing line specifically conceived to be sold through discount retailers. The development of the Reed St. James brand solved the problem of how to tap into the lucrative discount store market without cannibalizing the company's department store sales. By creating a quality brand that could compete favorably with cheap imports, Haggar was able to gain a strong foothold in discount stores. The idea was so good that within a few years Haggar was licensing the Reed St. James name to several other menswear manufacturers, including Levi Strauss and Jockey. By 1986 the line was generating sales of $50 million for Haggar. Other 1980s breakthroughs for Haggar included the first use of both bar codes and Quick Response electronic data interchange technology among apparel manufacturers.

In 1986 competitor Levi Strauss caught Haggar off guard when it introduced its Dockers line of all-cotton pants. Dockers did what Haggar had made its reputation by doing; it found a space between casual and dressy that was not yet occupied. Since the tastes of American men had taken a turn toward the casual, Dockers took a sizable bite out of the market for Haggar's slightly dressier slacks. Haggar responded with its own line of all-cotton pants, but the company did not initially focus its marketing attention on this line. In 1990, Haggar's sales dropped 6 percent to $292 million, its first backslide in many years.

COTTON IS KING: 1990-2000

In 1990 Joseph Haggar III—known inside the company as Joe Three—took over company leadership from his father Joe Jr. Under Joe Three, Haggar unveiled a new line of wrinkle-free cotton pants, and spent $20 million advertising it. In 1992, after operating as a family business for its first 65 years of existence, Haggar went public, offering its stock on the NASDAQ exchange. By 1993, Haggar's wrinkle-free line had seized the momentum from Dockers in the race for king of the all-cotton's, and the company's position as a prime mover in casual pants—tough competition from Levi Strauss notwithstanding—was once again secure. Led by this new line, Haggar's sales rebounded to $380 million.

In 1994 Haggar introduced shirts made out of its fabulously successful wrinkle-free cotton material. The company also launched a line of casual/office clothing called the City Casuals Collection. Revenue reached $491 million that year. Disaster struck in 1995, however, as the roof on the company's main distribution center collapsed, interfering with Haggar's ability to keep stores supplied with its merchandise. As the company recovered from this mishap and worked out the bugs at its new Customer Service Center, Haggar recorded a net loss, the third in its history, in 1996.

In 1997 Haggar invented Cotton Flex, an all-cotton fabric with advanced stretch and memory capabilities, to compete against Levi Strauss. Officials at Haggar expected the company's new line of pants using Cotton Flex—dubbed the Black Label collection—to become dominant as everyday pants, taking over the wardrobe spot occupied by basic cotton twills.

2000 AND BEYOND

The company acquired Jerell Inc., a manufacturer of women's sportswear, in 1998. At the time of the deal, Jerell sold its products in major department stores and retail outlets including Dillard's, J.C. Penney, Coldwater Creek, Sears, Federated Stores, Foley's, and Nordstrom. After the Jerell purchase, the company established subsidiary Haggar Canada to oversee its womenswear businesses. By now, Haggar had also formed subsidiaries in the United Kingdom, South Africa, and Japan.

Haggar adopted a new marketing and branding strategy as it entered the new millennium. In an attempt to make the Haggar brand more casual, the company's new logo included a lowercase h. With the tagline "American Generations," the brand campaign divided the company's offerings into six major lines: haggar generations; haggar collections; haggar black label; haggar city casuals; haggar golf; and haggar heritage. Competition was fierce and despite the new brand campaign, sales remained lackluster.

During this time period, the company attempted to expand its business by forming key partnerships. In 2000, Haggar inked a deal with Donna Karan International to manufacturer its DKNY brand of men's pants. One year later, it teamed up with Liz Claiborne to manufacture its line of men's pants and shorts. In 2002, the company launched a line of pants that featured a hidden expandable waistband. It introduced its stain-resistant and liquid-repellant Freedom line the following year. In 2004, the fade and wear-resistant line, Forever-New, hit stores shelves. Company sales grew slightly, from $481.8 million in 2002 to $487.9 million in 2004.

In 2005, the company announced plans to shutter its facilities in Mexico and the Dominican Republic. Later that year, a group of private equity firms including Infinity Associates LLC, Perseus LLC, and Symphony Holdings Ltd. made a $212 million play for Haggar. Joseph Haggar III and his management team believed

the deal would allow Haggar to grow and succeed in the global marketplace. Shareholders agreed, and the purchase was complete on November 1, 2005. The next day, Haggar III, President Frank Bracken, and Executive Vice-President and Chief Marketing Officer Alan Burks were ousted from the company.

Haggar's new owners appointed Jim Lewis—an industry veteran who had previously worked for Haggar, Liz Claiborne, and Levi Strauss & Co.—president and CEO. The private equity group believed Lewis would breathe new life into the Haggar brand. "Over the years that Haggar was publicly traded, sales were basically flat or down," claimed Lewis in a November 2005 *DNR* article. He added, "With the resources of [Infinity Associates] I feel that we can truly grow this business." While Lewis was optimistic, only time would tell if that growth would materialize. The new CEO and his management team were confident, however, that Haggar's brand strategy and its return to private ownership left the company well positioned for future growth.

Robert R. Jacobson
Updated, Christina M. Stansell

PRINCIPAL SUBSIDIARIES

Haggar Clothing Company; Haggar Canada, Inc.; Haggar Canada Company; Haggar Direct, Inc.; Jerell Clothing Management, Inc.; Haggar Women's Wear, Ltd.; San Gabriel Enterprises, Inc.; Multiples USA, Inc.; Haggar Apparel Ltd. (United Kingdom); Dallas Pant Manufacturing Company; McKinney Pant Manufacturing Company; Waxahachie Garment Company; La Romana Manufacturing Corporation; Bowie Manufacturing Company; Weslaco Cutting, Inc.; Weslaco Sewing, Inc.; Olney Manufacturing Company; Duncan Manufacturing Company; Haggar Japan Co., Ltd.; Haggar Services, Inc.; Edinburg Direct Garment Company, Inc.; Corsicana Company; Haggar Mex Manufacturing, S.A. (Mexico); Greenville Pant Manufacturing Co.; Weslaco Direct Cutting Company, Inc.; Haggar.Com, Inc.; HJMex S. de R.L. de C.V. (Mexico).

PRINCIPAL COMPETITORS

Levi Strauss & Co.; Phillips-Van Heusen Corporation; VF Corporation.

FURTHER READING

Bailey, Lee, and Stan Gellers, "Haggar Shakeup: Jim Lewis In, Key Execs Out," *DNR*, November 7, 2005.

Choi, Amy S., "Haggar Corp. Sold for $212M," *DNR*, September 2, 2005, p. 14.

Dodd, Annmarie, "Haggar Acquisition Takes Pants Maker, Brand into Women's Wear," *DNR,* December 18, 1998.

Forest, Stephanie Anderson, "Pumping No-Iron Slacks," *Business Week,* February 7, 1994, pp. 30-31.

"Haggar Clothing Co. Continues International Expansion with Canadian Subsidiary," *Canada Newswire,* August 17, 1999.

Haggar, Joe M., Jr., "Our Game Plan to Beat the Competition," *Venture,* October 1987, p. 126.

J.M. & Haggar Company: The First Fifty Years, Dallas: Haggar Company, 1976.

Karr, Arnold J., "Haggar Shuts Last Plants; Q2 Profits Up," *DNR,* May 9, 2005.

"A New Generation for Haggar," *PR Newswire,* March 29, 1999.

Palmer, Christopher, "Joe Three Fights Back," *Forbes,* November 22, 1993, pp. 46-47.

Richardson, Lynne, "New Slacks Line Adds to Haggar Loss," *DNR,* February 14, 2005.

Romero, Elena, "Haggar Ups Ante in Wrinkle-Resistant Game," *Daily News Record,* May 30, 1997.

Sloan, Pat, "Haggar Targets Women; Dumps TV, Men's Titles," *Advertising Age,* January 27, 1997, p. 3.

Spiegel, Joy G., "J.M. and His Haggar Slacks," *Dallas Magazine,* November 1975.

———, *That Haggar Man,* New York: Random House, 1978.

Stern, Aimee, "Success Has Seventeen Fathers," *Dun's Business Month,* August 1986, pp. 54-55.

Verespej, Michael A., "Creativity and Technology," *Industry Week,* April 6, 1987, pp. 55-56.

HARRIS

Harris Corporation

———————•———————

1025 West NASA Boulevard
Melbourne, Florida 32919-0001
U.S.A.
Telephone: (321) 727-9100
Fax: (321) 727-9646
Web site: http://www.harris.com

Public Company
Incorporated: 1926 as Harris-Seybold-Potter Company
Employees: 10,900
Sales: $3 billion (2005)
Stock Exchanges: New York
Ticker Symbol: HRS
NAIC: 334511 Search, Detection, Navigation, Guidance, Aeronautical, and Nautical System and Instrument Manufacturing; 334290 Other Communications Equipment Manufacturing

■ ■ ■

Harris Corporation, whose roots date back to a printing company established in 1895, operates as a leading international communications and information technology company. Harris began as a minor manufacturer of printing press machinery and evolved during the 20th century into an important developer of cutting-edge electronics technology. In fact, the firm's role in the American electronics industry is so important that in 1987 the Pentagon stepped in to prevent its acquisition by a foreign company. Harris sold its semiconductor business and spun off its office equipment division during a major restructuring effort in the late 1990s. The

company emerged as a major player in the communications equipment industry with an impressive client list that includes many civil and military federal government agencies as well as commercial customers in more than 150 countries across the globe.

E PLURIBUS UNUM: 1895-1950

In 1895 the Harris Automatic Press Company was founded in Cleveland, Ohio. This company manufactured the large multicolor presses that are used to print books and newspapers. In the early decades of the 20th century, the Harris Automatic Press acquired the properties of two other companies involved in the printing business—Seybold Machine Company of Dayton, Ohio, and Premier & Potter Printing Press Company, Inc. of New York. The name of the company was then changed to Harris-Seybold-Potter Company. In June 1957 the company merged with the Intertype Corporation of Brooklyn, New York, and its name was again changed, this time to Harris-Intertype Corporation. Intertype was a manufacturer of hot metal typesetting machines and operated a plant in England in addition to the plant in New York.

Throughout these acquisitions the company's business remained essentially unchanged: It built and marketed printing and broadcasting machinery. Such machinery included offset lithographic presses, envelope presses, paper cutting machines, and bindery equipment, and at Intertype, hot metal typesetting machines. Later acquisitions, in particular the Gates Radio Company, gave the company the capacity to manufacture broadcasting transmitters and microwave equipment.

COMPANY PERSPECTIVES

Harris Corporation will be the best-in-class global provider of mission-critical assured communications systems and services to both government and commercial customers, combining advanced technology and application knowledge to offer a superior value proposition.

RADIATION, INC.: 1950-67

The boom in the aerospace industry that began in the 1950s gave rise to many companies that produced components for government projects. One of the earliest of these businesses was Radiation, Inc., established in 1950 by Homer Denius and George Shaw, both of whom were electronics engineers. At first Radiation employed a staff of only 12 and was housed in space rented from the Naval Air Station in Melbourne, Florida. The site was convenient because it was located only a few miles south of the Cape Canaveral (now Kennedy) Space Center. From the start, the company produced miniaturized electronics, tracking, and pulse-code-modulation technologies, all of which are crucial to aerospace programs. Radiation's involvement with the aerospace program included equipment for the Telstar and Courier communication satellites and the Nimbus and Tiros weather satellites. Military systems that relied upon Radiation equipment included the Atlas, Polaris, and Minuteman missiles.

Radiation's initial success was due in part to the high quality of its staff. Many of the highest-level managers held advanced degrees in engineering. John Hartley, the CEO of the firm until 1995, joined Radiation after serving on the faculty of Auburn University. Hartley joined the firm in 1956, the same year that Radiation stock was first sold to the public. Another person who left academia to join the staff at Radiation was Joseph Boyd. In the late 1950s and early 1960s Boyd taught electrical engineering at the University of Michigan. At the same time he was also director of the Willow Laboratories, a prestigious science and technology research institute with a staff of more than 1,000 scientists and engineers. Boyd joined Radiation in 1962 and within a year was made president of the firm. His first significant action as president was to set up a microelectronics plant to develop and produce integrated circuits. The following year, Hartley was named as director of this division of Radiation.

During the early 1960s, Radiation devoted itself to improving its market position in the interconnected fields of digital communication, space communication, data management, and computer-based control systems. The company was also successful with satellite tracking systems and alphanumeric data processing. By 1967 the company was one of Florida's largest employers (at 3,000 employees) and sales passed $50 million a year. The company was well-established as a government contractor for both military and nonmilitary projects. But Radiation's management wanted to expand the company's business activity in the commercial sector. To do this, they decided to merge with a commercial company. At roughly the same time, the Harris-Intertype Corporation was seeking to expand its operations into the electronics field.

George Dively, the chairman of Harris-Intertype, had succeeded in building up the company's business from $10 million in annual sales to almost $200 million. But Harris-Intertype's printing machines were still mechanical, and Dively realized that future technological developments would require electronics. Radiation seemed a perfect candidate for acquisition. Dively and Harris-Intertype's president, Richard Tullis, paid $56 million for Radiation. The purchase price was considered quite steep—Harris shares were traded for Radiation's in a ratio that valued Radiation's earnings at twice those of Harris. Harris's management wanted Radiation's electronics talent, however, not just its earning power. The two companies merged in 1967 under the Harris-Intertype name. Dively remained chairman of the company; Homer Denius, one of the founders of Radiation, became vice-chairman; and Boyd became an executive vice-president for electronics. After the merger, annual sales surpassed the $250 million mark and the combined number of employees exceeded 12,000.

GROWTH THROUGH ACQUISITIONS: 1968-79

The Harris-Radiation hybrid proved to be a success and innovations began to flow from the company almost immediately. Electronic newsroom technology, for example, was the direct result of a study made by Radiation of how to update Harris's mechanical presses. Most important, however, the merger gave birth to an essential management strategy known as "technology transfer"—developing commercial applications of technology originally developed for the government.

Two years later, RF Communications, Inc. of Rochester, New York, was purchased through an exchange of shares. By the time of its purchase, RF was well established as a manufacturer of point-to-point radio equipment. Even after this rapid expansion, the

KEY DATES

1895: Harris Automatic Press Company is established in Cleveland, Ohio.

1950: Homer Denius and George Shaw create Radiation Inc.

1957: Harris Automatic Press merges with Intertype Corp. and changes its name to Harris-Intertype Corp.

1967: Radiation and Harris-Intertype merge; the Harris-Intertype moniker remains intact.

1972: General Electric's product line of TV broadcasting cameras, transmitters, studio equipment, and antennas is purchased.

1974: The company changes it name to Harris Corp.

1980: Harris acquires Farinon Corporation.

1983: Harris sells its printing business to concentrate exclusively on electronics.

1987: The Pentagon stops a takeover of Harris by the British communications company Plessey.

1999: Harris sells its semiconductor business; its Lanier Worldwide subsidiary is spun off.

2005: Leitch Technology Corp. is acquired.

company's electronics business remained primarily with the government, especially in the aerospace field. Harris-Intertype was responsible for the production and development of the data-handling systems for the preflight check of the Apollo spacecraft and for the digital command-and-control computer of the Gemini spacecraft.

At the beginning of the 1970s, the company made several other major acquisitions. In 1972, Harris-Intertype purchased General Electric's product line of TV broadcasting cameras, transmitters, studio equipment, and antennas for $5.5 million in cash, adding greatly to its original broadcasting product line. In addition, UCC-Communications Systems, Inc. of Dallas, Texas, was purchased from the University Computing Company for $20 million in cash. This company was a leading producer of computer terminals and communications subsystems for the data processing industry in general. Two years later, in 1974, Harris-Intertype acquired Datacraft Corporation and also divested itself of its corrugated paper machinery business. Datacraft was a producer of superminicomputers. During the same year the company changed its name to the Harris Corporation.

These acquisitions, made under the leadership of Richard Tullis, were integral to Harris's evolution from a company that was 84 percent mechanical into a company that was 70 percent electronic. The integration of the purchases and the continual introduction of new product lines, however, took its toll on the company's earnings. From the late 1960s to the late 1970s earnings growth was not outstanding and investors, in large part, ignored the company. But by 1976 things began to change for Harris; over the following three years its stock rose more than 100 percent. Meanwhile, the acquisitions campaign did not slow down even during the fallow period.

Subsequent acquisitions were all in the field of data processing and handling. Purchases were made every year throughout the remainder of the decade and well into the 1980s. By 1977 Harris's sales were more than $646 million and earnings were greater than $40 million. Boyd was appointed chairman and CEO two years later, in 1979.

That year Harris reached a significant agreement with Matra, a French state-owned electronics company. Under this agreement, which was to provide the French with a factory to manufacture integrated circuits, all of the $40 million funding was supplied by Matra and the French government; Harris provided only technology and management. The French retained 51 percent of the company, leaving Harris with the remaining 49 percent.

TECHNOLOGY TRANSFER: 1980-89

Since Harris had begun to deal predominantly in electronics, the company found itself in a market with extremely powerful competition. By this time the concept of technology transfer was the central element of the company's management policies. Although defense contracts accounted for only around 20 percent of Harris's business, military projects were its most advanced production efforts. In general, government contracts are for custom products instead of standard items, which helps to push the state of a technological art to its limit. In addition, these projects tend to be motivated more by technology than by cost considerations.

Harris's challenge was to translate work on customized, ultra-high technology products into profitable commercial projects. Among the problems Harris faced in doing this was military secrecy—an obstacle that would eventually stymie attempts to take over Harris. To overcome problems such as these, Harris instituted managerial policies that made promotion and demotion dependent upon the successful development of commercial products from defense projects. Harris also adopted a more general strategy of competing for government work only in those areas in which the company anticipated the ready development of commercial products. The development of a video terminal for electronic newsrooms, derived from the company's Vietnam-era work on an Army battlefield message sender, was a successful example of this technology-transfer policy.

Throughout Harris's history its acquisitions program has been well planned. In 1980 Harris made another important purchase, of the Farinon Corporation, a manufacturer of microwave transmitters, electronic switchboards, and other sophisticated telephone products. At the time of its purchase, Farinon was a small company, with sales of only $100 million. Outside observers believed that the purchase price of four million Harris shares, worth around $125 million, was much too high. Management at Harris justified the price, however, on the grounds that it had to beat out other bids (GTE, RCA, Siemens, and Loral Corporation had all expressed interest in Farinon) and that Harris was buying technology and market position, not earnings or revenues.

Harris passed the billion-dollar mark in annual revenues in 1981, and went on to weather the recession of the early 1980s quite well; earnings per share grew roughly 15 percent a year during this period. New plants were in operation 30 miles south of the Kennedy Space Center in Florida and the company had become the largest industrial employer in Florida. In 1983 Harris marked another turning point in its history. Harris had risen from the sixth largest supplier of printing machines to the number one position in the country, but in the spring of that year, Harris sold its printing business to concentrate exclusively on electronics. In the autumn of that year, Lanier Business Products, Inc. was merged into Harris on a $276 million stock purchase. Lanier was involved primarily in office automation and was noted for its business computers, dictating systems, copying machines, and word processing systems. Lanier brought Harris greater strength in the commercial sector since it boasted 350 sales offices throughout the United States and a sales force of more than 2,000 people, 700 of them marketing Lanier's copying machines (which were manufactured by the 3M Corporation). Later in the year the Federal Communications Commission (FCC) ordered Harris to stop production and marketing of a system that allowed AM radio stations to broadcast in stereo. The FCC also ordered the stations that had already purchased the units to cease broadcasting using the units. According to the FCC, the unit actually marketed by Harris differed significantly from one that the agency had approved the preceding year. Management at Harris claimed that the order had little effect on the company's overall business performance since Harris

had a backlog of only $2 million for the system, out of a total of $430 million for the communications sector that year.

But massive layoffs and a major reorganization began in the same year and continued for about three years. The company's government communications systems group was dissolved and employees from that group were reassigned to other divisions in the government systems sector. As other divisions also were consolidated, the workforce at Harris was reduced by several thousand employees. At the end of this period of adjustment, Harris and 3M entered into a joint venture to market and service copiers and facsimile machines as a result of their earlier connection through Lanier. The new company, named Harris/3M Document Products, Inc., was headquartered in Atlanta, Georgia, and owned equally by 3M and Harris.

Harris had a spate of problems with government contracts. In June 1987 the company agreed to settle out of court, for $1.3 million, a claim that Harris had overcharged NASA to upgrade the security system for a ground tracking station. Later in the year the company pleaded guilty to making false claims relating to a contract with the U.S. Army. The settlement in this case came to more than $2 million refunded as excess profits and another $2 million in penalties.

That same year the Pentagon stopped a takeover of Harris by the British communications company Plessey. Plessey, roughly the same size as Harris and one of Britain's largest electronics manufacturers, was itself acquired by Britain's General Electric Co. PLC and Germany's Siemens in 1989. The takeover was apparently blocked because of the security-sensitive nature of much of Harris's activities. For instance, the company is the major supplier of electrical components that are hardened against damage from the electromagnetic pulse generated by nuclear weapons. It is reported that Harris also manufactures top-secret equipment for the National Security Agency, which operates the government's spy satellites and communication-interception equipment.

In addition to being well protected against takeover, Harris is well established in custom electronic systems, office automation, communications, and microelectronic products. Company revenues more than doubled in the 1980s, from $850 million to more than $2 billion. The largest growth in both sales and profits came in the semiconductor and government systems sectors. By 1989 Harris had become the largest U.S. supplier of radio and television broadcasting equipment and dictating equipment and the largest producer of low- and medium-capacity microwave radio equipment. It was the largest supplier of integrated circuits to the U.S. government and the sixth largest producer of integrated circuits in the country. It was also the largest producer of satellite communications earth stations, a major supplier to NATO armed forces, and sold commercial products in more than 100 countries.

CENTENNIAL DECADE: 1990-97

By the early 1990s the future of the Harris Corporation seemed difficult to assess. Competition with the Japanese continued to be fierce, growth was slowing in the communications industry, and office automation had been a more competitive field than Harris anticipated. But cutbacks in personnel and the major reorganization of divisions at Harris streamlined the company. In late 1988 Harris bought GE Solid State, General Electric's semiconductor company, for more than $200 million, and in 1989 Harris purchased 3M's 50 percent interest in Harris/3M and renamed the company Lanier Worldwide, Inc. after adding Lanier Voice Products to that business.

Harris's corporate strategy in the 1990s was marked by four emphases: It would continue to transfer the technology expertise of its Electronic Systems Sector to nondefense markets; it would build on the growth of Harris Semiconductor following the purchase of GE Solid State; its Communications Sector would lead the company into international markets; and it would continue to promote the products, services, and globalization of Lanier Worldwide. In January 1991 Harris learned that it had won a $1.7 billion Federal Aviation Administration contract to develop the voice switching and control system of the nation's air traffic control (ATC) communications systems. The contract—the largest in the company's history—demonstrated that Harris's strategy of diversification into nondefense work was bearing fruit and led to other major ATC projects in Alaska, the airports of Washington, D.C., and in Malaysia.

Harris's push into another nondefense high-tech sector—advanced energy management systems for electric utilities—was strengthened in 1992 when Harris acquired Westronic Inc. of Canada. A year later Harris won a major contract to upgrade the FBI's National Crime Information Center database records using its specialized information processing technology. By the mid-1990s Harris added two new nondefense markets to its technology transfer strategy: healthcare and railroads. Harris developed information processing and communication technologies to improve diagnostic capabilities and cost efficiencies in the healthcare field, and in a joint venture with General Electric, Harris designed and manufactured an advanced electronic system for managing railroad traffic. Although the U.S.

defense budget was reduced by two-thirds between 1984 and 1995, Harris continued to pursue—and win—major defense projects, primarily in defense communications and aerospace, most notably the Air Force's F-22 Advanced Tactical Fighter and the Army's Comanche helicopter.

Because of unexpected problems integrating Harris Semiconductor with General Electric's much larger semiconductor business following the merger in 1988 as well as a downturn in the semiconductor market in the late 1980s, Hartley reassigned Electronic Systems director Phil Farmer to Harris's semiconductor operations in 1991. Farmer immediately began flattening the unit's management structure, reducing costs and expenses, and rationalizing its plant capacity. By the end of 1992 Harris Semiconductor was profitable again and by 1995 it was introducing more than 200 new products a year, particularly for the automotive, communication, and power-control circuits industries.

Harris's Communications Sector meanwhile established itself as one of the company's fastest-growing businesses by moving aggressively to fill the communication infrastructure needs of the world's developing countries. Between 1990 and 1994, international sales in its communications division grew from one-third to one-half of its total business. It upgraded television stations in Mexico, sold digital microwave radio systems to emerging countries, and supplied telephone equipment to remote regions of China and India. It also moved quickly into the promising new markets of high-definition television and cell phone-based personal communications services (PCS).

Harris's 1989 formation of Lanier Worldwide also was paying off. By 1995 Lanier's global sales had climbed to $1 billion and with 1,600 international sales and service centers it had become the largest independent office equipment distributor in the world. Lanier enjoyed two important firsts in 1994: It introduced a line of multifunctional printer/fax/copy machines and began offering facilities management services to major corporations, in which Lanier not only provided clients with all of the office machines and supplies they needed but brought in Lanier employees to perform the copying. In 1995, Phil Farmer, a 13-year veteran with Harris, succeeded Hartley as Harris's chairman and CEO.

In 1996 Harris acquired the wireless products business of NovAtel Communications, formed a joint venture to provide telecommunications and broadcast equipment to China, demonstrated the first HDTV transmitter, announced the construction of a semiconductor plant in China and a new U.S. facility to make power metal oxide semiconductors, and won a $73 million contract from the FAA for weather and radar processor systems.

In 1997, Harris announced the construction of a $5 million new space antenna facility, a $10 million digital television center in Cincinnati, a joint venture with GE to develop a new generation of digital information management systems for electric utilities in developing countries, and the acquisition of Northeast Broadcast Lab, a maker of radio broadcast equipment. It also strengthened Lanier's corporate office services business by acquiring American Legal Copy Services, a copying service for the legal profession; Quorum Group, an information services business for lawyers; Trans-Comp, a provider of medical transcription services; and Agfa-Gevaert, the photocopier business of Bayer.

CHANGES IN 1999 AND BEYOND

As Harris prepared to enter the new millennium, the company faced challenges brought on by a severe downturn in the semiconductor market. At the same time, weak conditions in Asian economies wreaked havoc on the company's bottom line. As such, Harris launched a restructuring effort that dramatically reshaped the company. In early 1999, Harris put its semiconductor business up for sale in order to focus on its core communications equipment operations. Intersil Corp., which was created by investment firm Sterling Holding Co., bought the group in a deal worth approximately $700 million. Harris then spun off its Lanier Worldwide subsidiary. The company planned to use the proceeds from the spinoff to fund its acquisition strategy.

When the dust settled, Harris stood as a leaner, more focused entity. During the early years of the new millennium, the company operated with four main divisions that served the government, RF, microwave, and broadcast communications markets. To strengthen these divisions, the company formed strategic partnerships and made key purchases. Shortly after it sold its semiconductor unit, Harris formed an alliance with Wavtrace Inc. to distribute and manufacture technology related to wireless broadband products that would be marketed to service providers. It also added Exigent International, a satellite command and control software manufacturer, to its fold in 2001.

Harris continued its growth-through-acquisition policy over the next several years. The Orkand Corporation was purchased in 2004 in a deal that added new customers to Harris's lineup, including the U.S. Postal Service, and the U.S. Departments of State, Energy, Health and Human Services. Encoda Systems became part of Harris's Broadcast Communications division that

same year. Encoda's operations included automation, media asset management, traffic, and billing software.

In 2005, Harris took its Broadcast Communications expansion one step further with the $450 million acquisition of Leitch Technology Corporation. Harris Chairman, President, and CEO Howard Lance commented on the purchase in an October 2005 *Sound & Video Contractor* article stating, "The addition of Leitch's talented workforce, complementary product portfolio and customer base helps establish Harris as the partner of choice for broadcasters upgrading their equipment and software systems to operate in a digital environment." He went on to claim, "This acquisition enables Harris to further expand into larger, faster-growing broadcast markets." Indeed, Harris's share of the global broadcast/video production market grew to 20 percent after the deal.

With both sales and profits on the rise, Harris's transformation appeared to have paid off. The company enjoyed record results in 2005 as revenue increased by 19 percent over the previous year, reaching $3 billion. Harris's net income also experienced hefty gains as it rose 52 percent to $202 million. The company's strategy in the years to come included new product development—the company's dedication to research and development was evident as it spent $870 million in 2005 alone. At the same time, Harris continued to position itself as the provider of choice to its customers. Its most recent contracts included a $1 billion, ten-year technical services program for the National Reconnaissance Office; a $350 million, ten-year program to provide tactical common data links for U.S. Navy helicopters; a $275 million contract to provide mission support services to the Federal Aviation Administration; and a $175 million contract to provide maintenance and engineering services for the Defense Information Systems Agency's Crisis Management System.

Updated, Paul S. Bodine, Christina M. Stansell

PRINCIPAL SUBSIDIARIES

Harris Asia Pacific Sdn. Bhd. (Malaysia); Harris Australia Pty. Limited; Harris Canada, Inc.; Harris Cayman, Ltd.; Harris Communication Argentina S.A.; Harris Communication (Netherlands) B.V.; Harris Communication France S.A.S.; Harris Communications Systems Nigeria Limited; Harris Communications GmbH (Germany); Harris Communications Austria GmbH; Harris Communications Honduras, S.A. de C.V.; Harris Communications International, Inc.; Harris Communications Ltd. (Hong Kong); Harris Communications (Shenzhen) Ltd. (China); Harris Controls Australia Limited; Harris Denmark ApS; Harris Denmark Holding ApS; Harris do Brasil Limitada; Harris-Exigent, Inc.; Harris Foreign Sales Corporation, Inc.; Harris Orkand Information Services Corporation; Harris Pension Management Limited (England); Harris S.A. (Belgium); Harris S.A. de C.V. (Mexico); Harris Semiconductor GmbH (Germany); Harris Semiconductor Design & Sales Pte. Ltd. (Singapore); Harris Semiconductor Patents, Inc.; Harris Semiconductor Pte. Ltd. (Singapore); Harris Semiconductor (Suzhou) Co., Ltd. (China); Harris Solid-State (Malaysia) Sdn. Bhd.; Harris Systems Ltd. (United Kingdom); Harris Systems L.L.C.; Harris Technical Services Corporation; Harris Two Thousand Limited; American Coastal Insurance Ltd.; Anshan Harris Broadcast Equipment Company Limited (China; 51%); BG-COM Information and Communication Limited Partnership (Hungary); BWA Technology, Inc.; HAL Technologies, Inc.; ITIS S.A. R.L. (France); ImageLinks, Inc.; Manatee Investment Corporation; Maritime Communication Services, Inc.; Medacoustics, Inc. (54%); Question d'Image S.A.S. (France); VFC Capital, Inc.; Wallaby Network Services, Inc.; Worldwide Electronics, Inc.

PRINCIPAL COMPETITORS

General Dynamics Corporation; Lucent Technologies Inc.; Motorola Inc.

FURTHER READING

Haber, Carol, "Harris' Lanier Spin-Off Set," *Electronic News,* July 12, 1999, p. 36.

"Harris Completes Exigent Offer," *Satellite News,* May 21, 2001.

"Harris Corp. Completes Acquisition of Leitch Technology," *Sound & Video Contractor,* October 26, 2005.

"Harris Is Selling Most of Its Chip Business," *New York Times,* June 3, 1999, p. C2.

"Harris Sells Business to Intersil," *Wall Street Journal,* August 17, 1999.

"Harris to Acquire Leitch Technology," *Broadcast Engineering,* September 6, 2005.

"Harris to Sell Unit, Spin Off Subsidiary and Eliminate Jobs," *Wall Street Journal,* April 14, 1999.

"Harris to Spin Off Chip Biz," *Electronic News,* June 7, 1999.

"Leitch CEO Says U.S. Buyer Will Speed Journey to China," *Hamilton Spectator,* September 2, 2005.

Hays plc

141 Moorgate
London, EC2M 6TX
United Kingdom
Telephone: (20) 7628-9999
Fax: (20) 7222-8243
Web site: http://www.hays-plc.com

Public Company
Incorporated: 1965 as Farmhouse Securities
Employees: 9,394
Sales: £1.64 billion ($3 billion) (2005)
Stock Exchanges: London
Ticker Symbol: HAS
NAIC: 541612 Human Resources and Executive Search
Consulting Services; 56131 Employment Placement
Agencies

■ ■ ■

Hays plc provides specialist recruitment and human resource (HR) Services, offering temporary and permanent staffing to customers across the globe. The company has 220 offices in the United Kingdom, as well as locations in Holland, Belgium, France, Germany, Switzerland, Austria, Czech Republic, Poland, Spain, Portugal, and South Africa. Hays operates as the largest specialist recruitment firm in Australia and New Zealand and is focused on penetrating the Canadian market as well. The company serves clients across a wide range of industries; some of its customers include Vodaphone, PricewaterhouseCoopers, KPMG, Deutsche Bank, and Bank of New York. During the 1990s chairman Ronnie

Frost took Hays on an acquisition campaign both to strengthen its core areas in its United Kingdom base and to insert the company into the European market. After his retirement in 2001, the company underwent a strategic review and opted to sell off assets unrelated to its core personnel operations.

ORIGINS

Although Frost would become the chief architect of Hays plc's growth, the company had been in the distribution business for nearly 125 years before coming under Frost's sway. The Hays business had begun in 1867, operating wharf facilities on the Thames in London, where it received dairy products shipped from New Zealand and other British colonies. Hays would gradually grow into a prominent cold storage provider, especially for dairy products. The company also would extend its services to distribution, while extending its London properties to include many prime Thames-side locations, including the eponymous Hays Wharf. By the late 1970s, Hays would come under control of the Kuwaiti Investment Office, acting as a holding company. In the late 1980s, however, Hays would be taken over by Ronnie Frost, who then took Hays public in 1989.

Ronnie Frost had had his own history with the Kuwaiti Investment Office. Frost started his own company, called Farmhouse Securities, in 1965. The company's original area of business was as a poultry wholesaler. Speaking of the period with the *Financial Times*, Frost would say: "Wonderful training. You'd approach someone, and in those days it could have been John Sainsbury himself or just a market trader. You'd

COMPANY PERSPECTIVES

The strategy Hays has adopted is based on seven operational objectives: to focus on the development of specialist professional recruitment services; to achieve accelerated international expansion primarily through organic growth, as well as carefully selected acquisitions; to maintain balanced growth in our share of the specialist permanent and temporary job markets; to increase our share of the public sector recruitment market; to enhance our range of HR services; to maintain high margins based on a tight yet flexible cost base and increased operational efficiencies; and to further develop the high brand recognition of Hays internationally.

have to adjust immediately." Frost's ability to "adjust" would become one of the principal assets of Farmhouse Securities, as was his dedication: it was not uncommon for Frost to put in 18-hour workdays. In the late 1960s and early 1970s the ambitious Frost extended the company into the distribution sphere, with an emphasis on cold storage facilities for its poultry and other products.

In the 1970s Frost would take Farmhouse Securities on a massive expansion program, opening or acquiring cold storage and other facilities throughout the United Kingdom. By the late 1970s Farmhouse Securities had built up a network of facilities capable of providing products to more than two-thirds of the United Kingdom. The company also built a fleet of trucks—one of the country's largest—to serve its storage facilities and its customers.

Farmhouse Securities' expansion would leave the company vulnerable to changes in the economic climate. After nearly three decades of strong growth since World War II, the British economy, along with much of the West, collapsed in the 1970s. Spurred by the Arab Oil Embargo and the oil-producing countries' sudden decision to raise world oil prices, the recession would strike particularly hard in the United Kingdom. Farmhouse Securities' finances, given its huge fleet of trucks, came under attack both from the rising oil prices and the drop in distribution activity. Despite its efforts to surmount its fragility in the new economic climate, Farmhouse Securities quickly found itself struggling to survive.

By the end of the 1970s Farmhouse Securities was on the verge of declaring bankruptcy. Frost, however, was not about giving up, telling the *Financial Times:* "There was too much blood and time invested in this business to let it go, but it was scary. We'd got to the stage of banks stopping cheques." Frost hung on into the new decade. But by 1981 it was too late. In that year Frost sold Farmhouse Securities to the Kuwaiti Investment Office. Frost would remain in charge of the company he had founded, however.

1990-2000: EXPANSION

Giving up control of Farmhouse Securities had enabled the company to survive its financial problems as the British economy began to recover in the 1980s. Frost had had no intention of relinquishing permanent control of Farmhouse Securities: even as he sold the company, Frost made plans to buy back not only Farmhouse Securities, but the Hays wharf and distribution business as well.

Regaining control of the company proved more difficult than expected. It was not until 1987—the day after the October stock market crash—that the Kuwaiti Investment Office finally agreed to sell Frost back his business. For pounds 257 million, Frost regained control not only of the Farmhouse Securities businesses, but the Hays Distribution companies as well, which provided the name for the new company, Hays Plc. Joining the company's ranks was also a personnel and recruitment arm, which had been founded in 1969 and added to the Hays group in 1986. Another Hays business was its Document Exchange Service, later known as Hays DX, which had started up in 1975, offering business-to-business, overnight, and other specialty mail and delivery services. Hays DX would later build a strong focus on such sectors as the banking and accounting industries.

Frost set about imposing Hays as one of the United Kingdom's premier logistics and business services groups. To fund the company's proposed expansion, Frost led Hays to a public listing in 1989. The public offering would get off to a rocky start, however. Coming on the same day as the resignation of Britain's chancellor of the exchequer, Nigel Lawson, the Hays stock float would be forced to cut its initial price by some 15 percent. This proved to be only a temporary setback. In the 1990s Hays would become the darling of the London Stock Exchange, posting some of the decade's strongest performances.

Hays' growth would come primarily from the company's own internal expansion, as the company captured a stronger share of its market and expanded into new markets. Unwilling to compete with larger

KEY DATES

1867: The Hays business begins operating wharf facilities on the Thames in London.

1965: Ronnie Frost establishes Farmhouse Securities.

1981: Frost sells Farmhouse Securities to the Kuwaiti Investment Office.

1987: The Kuwaiti Investment Office agrees to sell Frost back his business; Frost regains control of the Farmhouse Securities businesses and the Hays Distribution companies; the company changes its name to Hays plc.

1989: Hays goes public.

2001: Frost retires.

2002: New CEO Colin Matthews launches a strategic review of the company.

2003: Hays begins to sell assets unrelated to its personnel business.

2004: The company's logistics division is sold; DX Services plc is spun off.

firms, the company shrewdly sought out niche opportunities in which to focus its energy, capturing leading shares of such segments as the chemicals transportation and logistics segment. The company also avoided direct exposure in the retail distribution market, which was undergoing a cutthroat shakeout in the 1990s, leading to more and more meager margins as the United Kingdom slipped into the extended recession of the first part of the decade. While parts of Hays' business inevitably suffered from the recession and the resulting drop in demand for its distribution services, the company's three-prong approach enabled it to achieve some stability. The difficult economic climate, for example, would prove a boon to Hays' personnel services division, as companies looked more and more for temporary personnel, rather than hiring permanent employees. At the same time, Hays began to look for new markets, extending the company's delivery services into more general postal services, such as sorting and other services for the British post office. Another niche of interest to the company was computer-based records management and data storage, a segment the company would come to dominate after the acquisition of Rockall Scotia Resources in 1994.

Increasing competition in other sectors would bring opportunity to Hays. When British supermarkets began installing gasoline pumps, the country's traditional service stations, including Shell and British Petroleum, found their business under extreme pressure. In response, these companies began developing onsite grocery and convenience services. Hays seized the opportunity to propose its logistics services—coordinating an extremely complex provisions operation combining goods from various segments, from foods to clothing to other products, into one service. The initiative paid off: Hays was awarded contracts from Shell, followed by British Petroleum, in 1996.

Hays had already become adept at such complex logistics operations through its association with Carrefour, the French hypermarket giant. Where the company had remained focused on the United Kingdom markets, in the 1990s the company recognized the need to expand its services onto the European continent. France would provide the company's initial entry, as Hays began making small acquisitions of companies in its three primary sectors. Germany and the Benelux countries would soon follow.

Hays continued to target internal growth, while preparing an extensive series of so-called "bolt-on" acquisitions to boost its presence in specific markets, and especially in building its continental presence. Most of these acquisitions were on a relatively modest scale. In January 1999, for example, the company announced the purchase of France Partner, one of that country's top express parcel delivery services, for £19.5 million. This acquisition, however, followed on that of Colirail, in December 1998 for £40 million, and Delta Medical Express Group, acquired for £2.2 million in 1998, boosting the company to a 20 percent market share in the next-day parcel sector in France.

These acquisitions also complemented the strong moves that the company had made in building out its logistics network, with acquisitions including FDS in 1997 and Fril in 1994, strengthening the company's presence in France and the Benelux countries, as well as the takeover of Mordhorst, in 1993, which provided Hays with its German market foothold. The acquisition of Sodibelco in April 1998 brought the company's logistics operations into Italy. In the late 1990s Hays also began spreading its personnel and recruitment wings, with acquisitions including France's Sitinfo in October 1998, itself following on the June 1998 purchases of Alpha TT, Quasar, and Arec, three French specialist recruitment agencies.

By 1999 Hays had established a firm position in each of its specialty areas across much of Western Europe, with near-future plans to expand into Spain, as well as to build a presence in the Eastern European market as well. While Ronnie Frost remained the guiding force of the company's growth, Hays would receive credit for building a strong management team, including retaining most of the executive staff of its acquisitions. This team was expected to continue to build on Hays' status as a world-leading business services group.

CHANGES IN THE NEW MILLENNIUM

By the start of the new millennium, Hays stood as a conglomerate of sorts, with a large group of holdings—thanks to Frost's acquisition spree during the 1990s. Global economies were fickle during this time period however, and Hays found itself in a precarious situation as profits began to falter.

Frost retired in 2001, leaving Bob Lawson at the helm as chairman. Colin Matthews was brought in as CEO in 2002. Under his direction, the company launched a strategic review of its operations which took place from November 2002 to February 2003. Upon completion of the review, Hays announced a major restructuring that would leave the company focusing solely on its personnel business. Matthews gave insight into the rationale behind the strategy telling the *Financial Times*, "The linkages and synergies of the four divisions are not strong enough and not valuable enough to justify keeping a multi-business group together." Furthermore, the company's 2003 annual report explained its decision to keep its personnel business, which was responsible for nearly 60 percent of total profits. According to the report, the personnel division was "well-placed to take advantage of major, very attractive opportunities which deserve the focused and undivided attention of the entire Company."

As such, Hays set plans in motion to jettison its entire Commercial division for £225.5 million. Four transactions were part of that disposal including the sale of its Information Management Services unit to Mountain Europe Ltd. in a £200 deal. The three other sales divvied up Hays' Business Outsourcing operations. In addition, its Logistics Division was sold to Platinum Equity Holdings LLC for $175 million. The final step in the company's transformation came in November 2004, when the company spun off its mail business, DX Services plc.

Matthews, uninterested in heading up a personnel business, left the company to pursue other options. Denis Waxman was named his replacement in July 2004. In the short-term, Hays' restructuring appeared to have paid off. The company reported record profits in fiscal 2005 with net income climbing to $244.3 million, an increase of 103.9 percent over the previous year. During 2005, the company experienced a 19 percent increase in recruitment consultants and opened 27 new offices. Overall, the company had 326 offices in 16 countries.

As Hays prepared to finish out the first decade of the new millennium, the company stood as a provider of specialist recruitment and HR services for permanent and temporary staff. Its clients could be found across many industries including financial services, sales and marketing, and education. While the long-term success of Hays' restructuring remained to be seen, company management was optimistic the company was on the right path for growth in the years to come.

M.L. Cohen
Updated, Christina M. Stansell

PRINCIPAL SUBSIDIARIES

Hays Holdings Ltd.; Hays Overseas Holdings Ltd.; Hays Commercial Services Ltd.; Hays Personnel Services (Holdings) Ltd.; Hays Holdings BV (Netherlands); Hays Specialist Recruitment Ltd.; Hays Personnel Services (Australia) Pty Ltd. (Australia); Hays Travail Temporaire SASU (France); Hays IT SASU (France); Hays Personnel Services (Canada) Inc. (Canada); Hays Personnel Services BV (Netherlands); Hays AG (Germany); Hays (Schweiz) AG (Switzerland); Hays Osterreich GmbH (Austria); Hays Czech s.r.o (Czech Republic); Hays Personnel Services (Poland) Sp.zo.o (Poland); Hays Personnel Services Espana SA (Spain); Hays Personnel Espana Temporal SA (Spain); Hays Overseas (Portugal) SGPS LDA (Portugal); Hays Specialist Recruitment (Ireland) Ltd.; Hays NV (Belgium); Hays Personnel Services (Sweden) AB (Sweden).

PRINCIPAL COMPETITORS

Adecco S.A.; Manpower Inc.; Vedior N.V.

FURTHER READING

Ahmad, Sameena, "Acquisitive Hays Set for Next Pounds 100m Buy," *Independent*, August 21, 1997, p. 18.

Cope, Nigel, "Hays Delivering the Goods in France," *Independent*, January 6, 1999, p. 17.

Felsted, Andrea, "Hays Chief Plans to Break Up Group," *Financial Times*, March 5, 2003.

Gresser, Charis, "The Thrill of Making Money for Others," *Financial Times*, September 24, 1997.

Grimond, Magnus, "The Three Facets of Hays," *Independent*, September 17, 1997, p. 26.

"Hays Profits Fall, Expects New Chief Executive Soon," *Financial News*, September 10, 2002.

"Hays Shrugs Off the Threat of Recession," *Independent*, September 15, 1998, p. 23.

Jameson, Angela, "Frost's Empire Unravels," *Times*, March 5, 2003.

"Platinum Equity LLC: Logistics Business Is Acquired from Hays for $175.3 Million," *Wall Street Journal*, November 28, 2003.

Potter, Ben, "New Ideas Help Frost Chill the Opposition," *Daily Telegraph*, September 15, 1998.

Richard, Phillips, "Hays Delivers the Goods," *Independent*, December 15, 1996, p. B6.

"Return of the Milk Train," *Dairy Industries International*, November 1, 1997, p. 33.

Stevenson, Tom, "A Bargain To Be Made in Hays While It's Marked Down," *Independent*, March 4, 1997, p. 16.

Tringham, Melanie, "Hays' Sights on Euro Expansion," *Daily Telegraph*, March 5, 1998.

Warner, Jeremy, "New Man at Hays," *Independent*, September 10, 2003, p. 19.

O» HEXAGON

Hexagon AB

———•———

Cylindervägen 12
Box 1112 SE-131
26 Nacka Strand,
Sweden
Telephone: (46) 8 601 26 20
Fax: (46) 8 601 26 21
Web site: http://www.hexagon.se

Public Company
Incorporated: 1975 as Eken Industri & Handel AB
Employees: 6,000
Sales: SEK 8.26 billion ($1.24 billion) (2004)
Stock Exchanges: Stockholm SWX Swiss
Ticker Symbol: HEXA B
NAIC: 326220 Rubber and Plastics Hoses and Belting
Manufacturing; 326291 Rubber Product Manu-
facturing for Mechanical Use; 333910 Pump and
Compressor Manufacturing; 333995 Fluid Power
Cylinder and Actuator Manufacturing; 334419
Other Electronic Component Manufacturing;
334513 Instruments and Related Products Manu-
facturing for Measuring, Displaying, and Control-
ling Industrial Process Variables; 334519 Other
Measuring and Controlling Device Manufacturing;
339991 Gasket, Packing, and Sealing Device
Manufacturing; 551112 Offices of Other Holding
Companies

■ ■ ■

Hexagon AB is a global technology group. It aims to
achieve earnings per share growth of at least 15 percent

a year in market-leading businesses. Innovation and efficiency are the other pillars of its success. One of the
group's main focuses is metrology, or measuring
technology; it has acquired the venerable Brown &
Sharpe machine tool business. It owns other, engineering-
related businesses and holdings in advanced polymers.

ORIGINS

Hexagon AB is not related to a Swedish conglomerate of
the same name that existed in the 1970s and 1980s.
Hexagon AB instead traces its origins to the founding of
Eken Industri och Handel AB, which was registered on
September 25, 1975. Eken Industri merged with its parent company, Investment AB Eken, in May 1987. The
group then had annual turnover of more than SEK 400
million.

Hexagon Aktiebolag was formed in 1992. It was led
by industrialist Torbjörn Ek. Soon after its launch,
Hexagon AB bought a 49.9 percent voting interest (and
19 percent equity interest) in Eken Industri & Handel
AB from the Sparta savings bank. Hexagon soon raised
its voting shares to a 50.1 majority.

At the time of its acquisition by Hexagon, Eken Industri had four divisions: communications equipment,
which made antennas for mobile phones and radios;
industrial automation; building and interior design; and
vehicles, which included Bilmo of Lund, Sweden's largest agent for Volkswagen automobiles.

When it bought into Eken, Hexagon had controlling interests in three other companies, including Bruces
Mekaniska Verkstad AB, a maker of ships' hulls; Diana

COMPANY PERSPECTIVES

It is our firm belief that no financial organisation can afford to be an institution. Therefore Hexagon's ultimate strategic objective is to make money for its owners. Hexagon is a listed company. Being a listed company means that your share price will be affected by, not only your own financial performance, but also by the general trend in the capital market. We believe that the best guarantee to secure and enrich our shareholders is to have a consistent and high growth of Hexagon's earnings per share. Our most important strategic objective is to achieve an earnings per share growth of at least 15 per cent per annum. This objective should always guide our actions.

Control; and a conference center. These three together had revenues of about SEK 150 million a year.

Eken Industri bought Bruces Shipyard, Diana Control, and Dacke Hydraulik from Hexagon in August 1993 for about SEK 50 million. It also paid SEK 4 million for the Hexagon name, and was officially renamed Hexagon AB on October 28, 1993.

Hexagon AB's estimated annual sales of SEK 1.4 billion in 1994 nearly doubled within a couple of years. It was a busy acquirer, but also sold off about ten businesses from 1993 to 1997. In April 1994 Hexagon bought Gislaved Gummi AB. Gislaved produced rubber components and was a global market leader in plate heat exchanger gaskets. It had annual sales of SEK 175 million and employed 275 people. A few months later, Hexagon acquired Johnson Metall Group from Outokumpu Copper Oy.

Acquisitions for 1996 included those of SwePart AB, which added to Hexagon's Niche Manufacturing business area, and refrigeration specialist AKA Industriprodukter AB, part of Industrial Components and Systems, which also included Dacke Hydraulik and flow technology company Gustaf Fagerberg Holding. AKA had revenues of about SEK 770 million a year. The third business area was Industrial Food Technology, consisting of Norfoods (which was made up of R Lundberg and the newly acquired LG Fredriksson International). Hexagon divested the Bruces shipyard in January 1997, while selling off most of its majority stake in Svedbergs.

Part of Hexagon's stated focus was on wholly owned subsidiaries that complemented other units. Its subsidiaries traded mostly within the Nordic countries, though some industrial products were sold as far as Germany, the United States, and Russia.

NEW FOCUS FOR 2000 AND BEYOND

In 1998, Melker Schörling acquired the controlling interest in Hexagon from Torbjörn Ek and became the group's new chairman. A new management team was installed in 2000 as the group set out to refocus on its core strengths. The new standard was earnings per share growth of at least 15 percent a year. The Norfoods division was sold off to a private equity fund (Segulah II) and a new business area was created for wireless companies, including Moteco AB. AKA's SEK 314 million refrigerator business had been sold in 1999, as was a fire door company Robust Staldorrar RSD AB.

Toward the end of 2000, Hexagon began a major acquisition, buying the metrology, or measuring technology, business of Brown & Sharpe Manufacturing Co. for about $170 million. The unit had annual sales of $321 million, and represented most of Brown & Sharpe's revenues. Brown & Sharpe dated back to 1833 and was a Rhode Island machine tools institution. Its employment had peaked at 11,000 during World War I. At the time of the sale, it was technically in default on debts of $77 million after losing $43 million in 1999. For its part, Hexagon was thriving, with sales exceeding SEK 5 billion in 2000. Included in the Brown & Sharpe acquisitions was DEA S.p.A., a leading Italian metrology company that dated back to 1963.

There was more dealmaking in 2001. Early in the year, Hexagon sold AKA Industriprodukter and Gustaf Fagerberg to Indutrade AB, and its JMBC unit underwent a management buyout. It bought Polarteknik PMC Oy AB, a tiny Finnish producer of pumps and valves. Engineering and Automation business areas were established, followed by the creation of Hexagon Metrology a few months later. Hexagon ended the year by selling off its Wireless business area to Finland's Perlos Corporation. Wireless then had 185 employees in Sweden, Asia, and the United States and had annual revenues of nearly SEK 100 million.

Brown & Sharpe's software unit, Xygent Inc., was acquired in 2002. Hexagon also bought out a supplier of software used by Brown & Sharpe's machinery called Wilcox and Associates Inc. Hexagon was shopping for other metrology businesses as well, such as the contact measurement unit of Newport Corporation.

Other notable acquisitions in 2002 included the Rissa, Norway plant of hydraulic cylinders producer Cylinderservice A/S, and Italy's MIRAI S.R.L., a small

KEY DATES

1975: Eken Industri & Handel AB is launched.
1992: Hexagon development group acquires control of Eken Industri and Handel AB.
1993: Eken is renamed Hexagon AB.
1994: Hexagon buys rubber components manufacturer Gislaved Gummi AB.
1998: Melker Schörling acquires controlling interest in Hexagon from Torbjörn Ek.
2000: Hexagon refocuses on market-leading businesses, and begins the acquisition of the Brown & Sharpe metrology business.
2001: The Wireless business area is divested.
2002: Hexagon buys Brown & Sharpe's software unit.
2003: A new Polymers business area is formed from Gislaved Rubber Group.
2004: The acquisition of Belgium's Thona Group makes the Polymers unit a world leader; the Romer metrology businesses are acquired.
2005: Automation is divested; Leica Geosystems is acquired.

company that made software for measuring large sheet metal parts.

In April 2003 the Polymers business area was formed from Gislaved Rubber Group (once part of Engineering), which had bought German rubber compounding company GPD Technology GmbH the previous summer. Product lines included heat exchanger gaskets, extrusions, and rubber and plastics wheels. It had operations in Sri Lanka (Elastomeric Piliyandala) making lower cost bulk products. Sweden's Stellana AB was another part of Polymers. The May 2004 acquisition of the Thona Group of Belgium made the new group a global leader in the polymer compounds market. Thona, which had been established in 1991, brought with it plants in the Czech Republic and North America. Hexagon acquired the U.S.-based polyurethane wheel business of Trostel SEG Inc. in 2005

The Measurement Technologies unit was augmented in February 2004 by the acquisition of Sheffield Automation L.L.C.'s coordinate measurement machines business, which was based in Wisconsin and had an estimated $17 million in annual sales. The metrology business of Korea ErFa Systems Eng. Co. was added the next month, and Romer S.A. of France and Romer Inc. of the United States followed in the summer of 2004.

The next year, the company's Italian measuring technology companies were renamed Hexagon Metrology.

Sales were SEK 8.26 billion in 2004. Hexagon sold off its Automation business area in July 2005. Segulah Nordic II AB was the buyer. The group bought Leica Geosystems Holdings S.A. in October 2005, besting a $1 billion offer from U.S. technology group Danaher Corporation. Hexagon subsequently began listing its shares on the SWX Swiss Exchange (they were already traded in Stockholm).

Frederick C. Ingram

PRINCIPAL SUBSIDIARIES

Brown & Sharpe Precizika (Lithuania); Hexagon Automation AB; Hexagon Foervaltning AB; Hexagon Holdings Inc. (United States); Hexagon Metrology AB; Hexagon Polymers AB; Johnson Industries AB; Johnson Metall AB; Kramsten Food And Drink Suppliers AB; Megufo AB; Outokumpu Nordic Brass AB; PMC Technology A/S (Denmark); Polarteknik PMC (Finland); Roeomned AB; Swepart AB; Swepart Transmission AB; Tecla AB.

PRINCIPAL DIVISIONS

Engineering; Measurement Technologies; Polymers.

PRINCIPAL COMPETITORS

Carl Zeiss IMT Corporation; Mitutoyo America Corporation; Nikon Instruments Inc.; Tomkins PLC.

FURTHER READING

"Atle Takes Over Refrigerator Company," *Nordic Business Report*, March 15, 1999.

Dusharme, Dirk, "Emerging Metrology Technologies," *Quality Digest*, June 2003.

"Eken to Buy Hexagon Units, Change Name," *Dagens Industri*, August 12, 1993, p. 20.

"Gislaved Sold to Hexagon," *European Rubber Journal*, April 17, 1994, p. 2.

"Hexagon AB Acquires Italian Sheet Metal Applications Developer MIRAI Srl," *Nordic Business Report*, October 4, 2002.

"Hexagon AB Sells Fire Door Company," *Nordic Business Report*, May 31, 1999.

"Hexagon Acquires Finnish Engineering Firm," *Nordic Business Report*, November 15, 2001.

"Hexagon Acquires 49.9% Voting Stake in Eken," *Svenska Dagbladet*, December 15, 1992, p. 1.

"Hexagon Acquires Wilcox and Associates," *Nordic Business Report,* September 13, 2001.

"Hexagon Acquires Xygent to Sell Its Measuring Technology," *Nordic Business Report,* August 20, 2002.

"Hexagon Automation Acquires Hydraulic Cylinders Manufacturing Plant in Norway," *Nordic Business Report,* September 26, 2002.

"Hexagon Seeks Institutional Backers," *Svenska Dagbladet,* June 13, 192, p. 7.

"Hexagon Still Looking for Acquisitions; Major Deal in Nano Sector Possible," *AFX International Focus,* October 10, 2005.

"Incentive Sells AKA Industriprodukter," *Reuters News,* May 6, 1996.

"Investment AB Eken of Sweden Is to Merge Its Operations with Those of Its Subsidiary Eken Industri AB," *Svenska Dagbladet,* May 6, 1987, p. 1.

"Outokumpu Sells Johnson Metall Group to Hexagon," *Reuters News,* September 30, 1994.

"Perlos Acquires Swedish Mobile Phone Antennas Maker Moteco," *Nordic Business Report,* December 20, 2001.

Stape, Andrea L., "Parent of North Kingstown, R.I., Toolmaker Buys Wisconsin Manufacturer," *Providence Journal Bulletin* (Rhode Island), February 28, 2004.

———, "Rhode Island-Based Software Unit of Former Manufacturing Firm Is Sold," *Providence Journal Bulletin* (Rhode Island), August 21, 2002.

"Swedish Hexagon Buys Metrology Operations from Korea ErFa Systems," *Swedish News Digest,* March 9, 2004.

Tate, Pamela, "Brown & Sharpe to Sell Metrology Unit for $160M," *Dow Jones News Service,* November 17, 2000.

Vallejo, Maria P., "Newport Completes Sale of U.S. Metrology Assets," *Dow Jones News Service,* June 3, 2002.

White, Liz, "Hexagon Buys Italian Wheel Maker, Expands," *European Rubber Journal,* October 1, 2004, p. 2.

———, "Hexagon Buys Thona, Takes European Top Spot," *European Rubber Journal,* May 1, 2004, p. 4.

———, "Hexagon Forms Polymer Unit, Aims for Growth," *European Rubber Journal,* June 1, 2003, p. 5.

———, "Hexagon Polymers Has Major Plans for Growth: Acquisition of GFD Adds to Hexagon's Sales; Further Expansion and Investments Are Likely," *European Rubber Journal,* October 2003, p. 2.

Wyss, Bob, "Rhode Island Industrial Tools Giant Sells Assets to Swedish Company," *Providence Journal* (Rhode Island), November 18, 2000.

Hoffman Corporation

---

805 S.W. Broadway, Suite 2100
Portland, Oregon 97205
U.S.A.
Telephone: (503) 221-8811
Fax: (503) 221-8934
Web site: http://www.hoffmancorp.com

Private Company
Incorporated: 1954
Employees: 1,460
Operating Revenues: $1.38 billion (2005 est.)
NAIC: 236210 Industrial Building Construction; 236220 Commercial and Institutional Building Construction; 237990 Other Heavy and Civil Engineering Construction; 238210 Electrical Contractors; 238220 Plumbing, Heating, and Air-Conditioning Contractors; 541611 Administrative Management and General Management Consulting Services

■ ■ ■

One of the largest general contractors and construction managers in the United States, Hoffman Corporation, which does business as Hoffman Construction Company, has built some of the most well-known modern structures in Portland, Oregon, and Seattle, Washington. The company has in-house expertise in mechanical, electrical, structural, and architectural engineering. Hoffman is a privately held company, with all corporate stock owned by employees.

ORIGINS IN 1921

Lee Hawley (L. H.) Hoffman established Hoffman & Rasmussen, a construction company, in 1921. L. H.'s father, the first Lee Hoffman, had come west in 1870 to help build covered bridges on the Willamette River that runs through Portland, Oregon. He had built a successful career in construction, married, and had two children, a daughter, Margery, in 1888, and a son, L. H., in 1884. After Hoffman's untimely death in 1895, the family moved east to Boston.

L. H. Hoffman attended Harvard College where he earned a degree in architecture in 1906. Two years later, he joined a successful Portland-based architectural firm, where he discovered his true calling lay in contract management. After working as the firm's general inspector, he eventually left the firm. During World War I, Hoffman served as a land agent for the Warren Spruce Company, logging, hauling, and manufacturing "spruce clears" for airplane manufacture.

Hoffman & Rasmussen completed several apartment buildings, after which Hoffman went on to work as a sole proprietor. His company played a key role in Portland's building boom in the 1920s, as the city transformed itself from a riverbank town and shopping port to a modern metropolis with high-rise buildings, garages, theaters, and elegant retail stores. By 1927, Hoffman's company had more than 400 employees and a payroll of $30,000 a month. During this decade, the company built a steady succession of small projects, such as dance halls, service stations, grain storage facilities, and terminals. It also built Portland's then-tallest building, the Terminal Sales Building, in 1926, and such

COMPANY PERSPECTIVES

Hoffman Construction Company has extensive experience in a wide variety of specialties. We thrive on challenges that call for innovative solutions, and we believe the key to our success lies in the extra measure of creativity we bring to the art of building.

notable Portland landmarks as the Heathman Hotel, the Public Service Building, and the Portland Theater in 1927.

Hoffman & Rasmussen had 32 contracts in 1929. However, the Great Depression slowed investment in construction nationwide. Contracts numbered 30 in 1930, 13 in 1931, and ten in 1932. In order to remain successful, Hoffman moved his company in a new direction in the 1930s. While the firm's first decade had concentrated on private sector apartments, small factories, theaters, and high-rise buildings, the company now embarked on a series of cultural projects, such as the Portland Art Museum and the library of Willamette University in Salem, Oregon. It also undertook public projects for federal, state, and county governments, including courthouses and post offices and highway-related construction. This work took the company outside of Portland and earned it a reputation in the Northwest for constructing quality facilities.

During World War II, the company refocused its efforts again, working on several defense projects, including warehouses, barracks, and hospitals for the military, and civilian housing and urban facilities surrounding federal installations. The company also built facilities for the production of raw materials for manufacturing airplanes. From 1942 to about 1952, Hoffman worked on the Hanford Nuclear Reservation, part of the Department of Defense's Manhattan project, building shops, offices, schools, theaters, and houses in the new town of Richmond, Washington. All together, Hoffman carried out $49 million in wartime construction for the federal government, representing nine joint ventures and three solo projects.

POSTWAR ACTIVITIES

With the war over, L. H. Hoffman's company resumed commercial construction as the American economy made the shift back from war supplies. The company also provided support for the Northwest's growing wood products industry, taking on new clients and constructing or enlarging new facilities for repeat customers.

Throughout the 1940s, clients represented a veritable who's who of important landmarks and players in Portland: Meier & Frank, Crown Mills, Irving Dock, the Portland Art Museum, Pacific Power & Light, Sears Roebuck and Company, the National Biscuit Company, and the *Oregonian*.

During the 1950s, Hoffman continued to work in commercial construction, building schools, department stores, and other office buildings, sometimes making use of the precast, tilt-up concrete panel construction the company had introduced to the Pacific Northwest in 1949. This building method entailed pouring concrete walls in forms that lay on top of an already poured concrete floor. Once the concrete had cured, special lift equipment raised the panel to position, and crews locked it in with welded steel dowels. However, the paper and pulp industry came to represent Hoffman's bread and butter business during the 1950s. The changing policies of the U.S. Forest Service created a thriving national publishing industry, and the mounting demand for pulp and paper products drove the region's pulp processors to upgrade and expand their plants. New projects in pulp, paper, and sawmill facilities ranged from small jobs, to massive, complex installations. The company also continued to work for the federal government at the Hanford Nuclear Works in Washington state as the Cold War drove a regular program of military preparedness.

The company itself underwent significant organizational changes beginning in the mid-1950s. In 1954, L. H. Hoffman, turned over his sole proprietorship to his sons, Eric and Burns. A year later, Hoffman Construction Company became an Oregon corporation owned by the Hoffman sons.

EXPANSION: 1965-89

Burns left the company in 1965 to pursue his own business and investments, at which time, Eric bought out his brother's interest. In 1967, Eric hired Cecil W. Drinkward, an engineer and graduate of the California Institute of Technology and former employee of Del E. Webb Company, to become general manager of Hoffman's construction operations. Also, in 1967, Eric Hoffman devised an employee stock ownership plan whereby key company officials could purchase shares, which they sold back to the company upon retirement or severance.

During the late 1960s, Hoffman and Drinkward hired new management to expand the company's operations, and increased its number of estimators and superintendents. They also moved the company to embrace new technology. The paper and pulp industry had once again kept Hoffman Construction

KEY DATES

1921: L. H. Hoffman establishes Hoffman & Rasmussen.

1955: L. H. Hoffman retires; Burns Hoffman becomes president of Hoffman Construction Company.

1959: L. H. Hoffman dies.

1965: Eric Hoffman becomes sole proprietor of the company.

1968: The company initiates employee ownership.

1967: Cecil W. Drinkward joins the company as vice-president and general manager.

1975: Eric Hoffman becomes chairman, and Drinkward president of the company.

1985: Wayne Drinkward joins the company.

1992: Wayne Drinkward becomes president.

2000: The company moves its headquarters to the Fox Tower in downtown Portland.

Company with contracts for retrofits, reconstruction, and new buildings during the first half of the 1960s. During the second half of the decade, as the Pacific Northwest stirred with economic vitality, and towns and cities grew, Hoffman Construction Company focused on the need for new commercial construction. Defense and federal contracts also continued into the 1960s, and HUICO, a division of the company, began to manufacture pipe for nuclear reactors.

Eric Hoffman became chairman of Hoffman Construction Company in 1975 and Drinkward its president. Throughout the 1970s, the two men established Hoffman's reputation for handling new and challenging contracts. A succession of large, industrial projects demonstrated the company's ability to handle buildings of extreme complexity and size, such as a submarine base for the government and the Northwest's largest cement plant. In the 1970s, Hoffman also became a primary builder of nuclear power plants in the Northwest. The company entered the oil industry during the oil boom of the late 1970s, when it began to provide oil field "service modules," along with schools and office buildings in Alaska. The company marked its entry into the high-tech industry in 1978 when it constructed a silicon wafer plant in north Portland for a German company.

The 1970s and 1980s also saw a return to commercial construction for Hoffman Construction Company with a focus on high-rise office buildings. In 1970, the company built the new Georgia-Pacific Building in Portland and moved its headquarters to occupy an entire floor of the building. There it remained until 1983, when it moved into its own new building, the Hoffman Columbia Plaza. Although the construction industry as a whole came upon hard times during the early 1980s, with unemployment in the industry averaging 20 percent, Hoffman's expertise put it in high demand in the Pacific Northwest.

By the end of the 1980s, Hoffman had completed several more important Portland buildings (the Justice Center and the Portland Center for the Performing Arts, among them) and its office buildings had established its presence along the eastern seaboard in the state of New York and in Washington, D.C. Hoffman also continued its involvement with the oil industry, and, by the early 1990s, the company had extended its reach north to the Arctic Circle, west to the Aleutian Islands, and south to the Gulf of New Mexico. It also expanded geographically with water purification facilities in California and Alaska in 1989.

BOOM AND BUST: 1990-2000

Rising markets pushed construction industry revenues to new heights during the first half of the 1990s. In 1994, a year of economic recovery for the United States, construction contracts nationwide increased 15 percent in volume for commercial buildings, 53 percent for government buildings, 27 percent for apartments, and six percent for educational buildings. "The Northwest," according to Hoffman's vice-president for development and marketing, Bart Eberwein, in a 1995 *Engineering News-Record* article, was "enjoying its day in the sun."

Certainly, the Hoffman Construction Company was flourishing. The favorable business climate encouraged businesses to expand their manufacturing capabilities; they invested in new structures and upgraded facilities to meet the needs of the Northwest's growing population. This, plus the increasing number of firms relocating to the Northwest, created a wave of work that made Hoffman the 13th largest general builder in the nation in 1994 with revenue of $539 million, up from 42nd the year before. By 1996, Hoffman was the second largest with revenues of $660 million. Wayne Drinkward replaced Cecil W. Drinkward, his father in 1992, as president of Hoffman, and throughout the 1990s, the company undertook a series of major projects that reshaped the Portland skyline, including the Portland Building and the Oregon Convention Center. It also undertook a $104 million expansion of the terminal at Portland International Airport that it completed in 2003 that included reconstruction of the 20-year old concourse and built a $6.4 million cargo facility for Delta airlines. Hoffman constructed a series of buildings for Intel in Oregon, New Mexico, and Arizona, as well as a number of facilities for other major high tech manufacturers who rushed to construct new computer chip and related plants to meet demand. The company also maintained its public sector contracts for prison facilities, educational buildings, and water treatment plants.

By 1997, however, the Northwest's building boom of the mid-1990s had begun to drop off as the Asian crisis led to a slowdown throughout the high tech industry. Still, a healthy Portland economy kept local contractors busy. In fact, finding skilled labor proved more of a challenge for them than finding work. With the "city of bridges'" healthy business environment and rising rents, office buildings and suburban housing starts were on the increase—along with cultural projects. Hoffman Construction Company took part in the construction of Portland's new light rail in 1997. In 1998, it began work on Doernbecher Children's Hospital, part of the Oregon Health Sciences University's medical complex. In 1997, Hoffman was second among builders in Washington, Oregon, and Alaska, with $535 million in total revenue and about 350 salaried and 500 hourly employees.

With these projects, Hoffman consolidated its reputation in the construction industry for its willingness to tackle almost anything. In building the Fox Tower skyscraper, beginning in 1999 in downtown Portland, Hoffman employed a "jump form" construction system to create the building's reinforced concrete elevator core. This system, which it had earlier perfected in working on the city's light rail system, entailed casting the base of the tower from a rectilinear mold into which workers poured a liquid concrete mix. Hoffman also undertook the city's deepest excavation ever in building the tower's parking garage—60 feet, or to within inches of Portland's water table. After finishing the Fox Tower in 2000, Hoffman moved its headquarters into the building's 21st floor.

The Experience Music Project (EMP), an undulating, metal-clad structure at the base of the Space Needle in Seattle, Washington, represented a second innovative project for Hoffman in 1999. Hoffman brought on several local collaborators for the project, which was designed entirely with three-dimensional computer models rather than two dimensional plans and elevations: Angle Detailing Inc. for the detailed construction documents; Columbia Wire and Iron Works for the structural steel; and Benson Industries, Inc. to design and build the building's glass systems. "We've done gunite, metal panels and curved beams," said the project manager in a 1999 *Oregonian* article, adding "But we've

never done it like they are being done in this recipe. We are applying technology from the manufacturing industry to construction."

Such construction challenges were paralleled by accounting challenges in 1999 when Hoffman garnered headlines for a state auditor's report detailing $4 million in questionable payments received while working on the Snake River Correctional Institution in eastern Oregon. The company protested that it was within its contract rights and that it had completed the project on time and within budget. However, it returned a sum of money to its client to lay the issue to rest.

2000 AND BEYOND

As America's economic expansion began to slow around the turn of the century, general builders surprised everyone by continuing to shatter revenue records with double digit growth. Hoffman ranked 21st with its revenue of $826 million in 2000. It employed 275 full-time and 1,000 part-time employees. When the need for new microchip manufacturing plants brought about a resurgence in high-tech markets from 1999 to 2001, Hoffman became the nation's second fastest growing firm among top general builders.

However, the years 2001 to 2003 were dismal ones for the Northwest construction industry and challenging for Hoffman. The general and commercial building market stalled during the early 2000s as the economy floundered—falling 31 percent from 2000-2003. Hoffman's yearly revenue topped $1 billion in 2001, then fell to $486 million in 2003. But by 2002, revenue had increased again to $842.5 million, and Hoffman, the largest general contractor in the Pacific Northwest, was back on a growth track, taking advantage of the shift to a health care building market. "Part of this is that the baby boomers are aging. They are demanding single rooms in lodge-like settings, and they have the money and the medical coverage to get it," explained Bart Eberwein, Hoffman's vice-president of development and marketing in a 2003 *Engineering News-Record* article. Another area of growth that Hoffman exploited was the need for housing in Portland's downtown as people began a reverse commute to work in its suburbs.

In fact, Hoffman continued to focus on region rather than a type of construction. "You can be a niche player, but that's a risk," said Drinkward in a 2005 *Oregonian* article. He added: "We seek to be wide-ranging." The company's unofficial motto at the time was "Semper Gumby: Always be flexible." Hoffman also had a policy of never abandoning its core, longer-term clients, even when that meant passing up work, and, as a result, when the technology building boom ended, the company had other work to turn to.

In the early 2000s, the company continued its focus on public buildings with the construction of Seattle's Central Library and Justice Center and the city's new City Hall. The library was composed of five platforms, each positioned off center, and encased by a lattice work of glass and aluminum. In 2005, it partnered with Andersen Construction Company to build Biomedical Research Building and new Patient Care Facility for Oregon Health Sciences University. And, as always, Hoffman kept its eye out for the next construction trend. As Drinkward put it in the 2005 *Oregonian*: "We're nomads in a desert, always looking for what's coming next."

Carrie Rothburd

PRINCIPAL COMPETITORS

Bechtel Group Inc.; Black & Veatch Holding Company; Fluor Corporation; Hensel Phelps Construction Company; McCarthy Building Companies Inc.; Foster Wheeler Ltd.; Skanska USA Building Inc.; Turner Corporation.

FURTHER READING

Bacon, Sheila, "Northwest Construction Names Top 50 Contractors in Pacific Northwest," *Northwest Construction*, August 1998, p. 11.

Beckham, Stephen Dow, *Hoffman Construction Company: 75 Years of Building*, Portland: Hoffman Corporation, 1995.

Brinckman, Jonathan, "Contractor Keeps Catching Wave," *Oregonian*, January 20, 2005, p. D1.

Gragg, Randy, "Museum Design Tests Hoffman's Learning Curve," *Oregonian*, April 11, 1999, p. C1.

———, "Out of the Foxhole," *Oregonian*, March 1, 1999, p. C1.

Grogan, Tim, "Builders Flourish With Recovery," *Engineering News-Record*, May 22, 1995, p.70.

Tulacz, Gary J., "Health Care Remains in Good Health But Other Market Sectors Hurting," *Engineering News-Record*, May 19, 2003, p. 71.

Hunting plc

3 Cockspur Street
London, SW1Y 5BQ
United Kingdom
Telephone: (44) 20 7321-0123
Fax: (44) 20 7839-2072
Web site: http://www.hunting.plc.uk

Public Company
Incorporated: 1874
Employees: 2,188
Sales: £1.25 billion ($2.41 billion) (2004)
Stock Exchanges: London
Ticker Symbol: HTG
NAIC: 422710 Petroleum Bulk Stations & Terminals; 333319 Other Commercial and Service Industry Machinery Manufacturing; 213111 Drilling Oil and Gas Wells; 213112 Support Activities for Oil and Gas Field Exploration

■ ■ ■

Hunting plc is one of the world's leading providers of specialist services to the oil and gas industry. The London-based company is a leading supplier of tubular goods, particularly for the North Sea and Gulf of Mexico offshore oil and gas exploration markets, and is the world's top supplier of oil platform accessories. Hunting is the world's leading—and oldest—oil and gas tanker broker. The company, through subsidiary Gibson Energy Ltd., is also involved in oil and gas marketing and distribution, moving more than 90 billion barrels of oil and gas per year, and operating more than 260 miles of pipeline, 27 terminals, and storage facilities with a capacity of some two million barrels. These operations, which generate nearly 70 percent of group sales, are focused in large part on the Canadian market. Hunting is also Canada's second largest retailer of propane gas, with a capacity of more than 200 million liters per year. Hunting has long held direct interests in the oil and gas exploration and drilling markets, with production focused primarily in the southern United States and in the Gulf of Mexico. Another Hunting division produces drill rods for fiber optics and other communications applications. Into the mid-2000s, Hunting successfully completed a streamlining effort, which saw it shed most of its diversified operations in order to focus more tightly on the energy services market. Nonetheless, the company maintains a strong international presence, with operations in some 100 countries. Listed on the London Stock Exchange, Hunting is controlled by the founding Hunting family, which owns nearly 30 percent of the group's stock. The family is represented by Chairman Richard H. Hunting. Day-to-day operations are overseen by Chief Executive Dennis L. Proctor. In 2004, Hunting produced revenues of more than £1.25 billion ($2.4 billion).

OIL TRANSPORT PIONEER IN THE 19TH CENTURY

The Hunting family was one of the pioneers of the international petroleum trade, becoming one of the first in the world to recognize the future importance of petroleum-based fuels, and particularly the need to provide specialized transportation for crude and refined oil products. The Hunting family's interest in the ship-

COMPANY PERSPECTIVES

The Hunting community is committed to the protection of the environment no matter where in the world we operate. We aim to use renewable resources wherever possible and develop manufacturing processes and procedures such that any impact on the environment, if any, is reduced to a practicable minimum. We take the view that sustainable development is in the interests of all our stakeholders and include environmental issues in our planning and decision-making. Policy is developed at a corporate level and encourages each operating unit to: Develop and implement their own procedures whilst conducting regular reviews to ensure that they are maintained and refined; Reduce waste, emissions and promote the use of recycled materials; Pay special regard to the environmental issues and requirements of the communities and locations in which we work and live; Be involved in and understand the particular environmental issues relating to the industry in which we operate; Promote employee awareness of their own responsibilities and encourage participation in voluntary environmental projects.

ping industry itself dated to 1874, when Charles Hunting founded his own shipping firm in England. Hunting's son, Charles Samuel Hunting, is credited with steering the family company into the oil business. The younger Hunting spent a good deal of time traveling about the world in order to research the nascent oil industry. Hunting's interests led him to pursue various investments, including exploring for oil in Russia, establishing London's first oil refinery. Hunting's interest soon turned to the newly developing oil market in the Gulf of Mexico. These interests led the Hunting family to invest in a new, specialized shipping vessel, and in the 1890s, the Hunting company became one of the first in the world to feature dedicated oil tankers in its fleet.

Into the early part of the 20th century, Hunting, later joined by sons Percy and Lindsay, built up one of the world's largest independently operated fleets of oil tankers. The outbreak of World War I cut short the family-owned company's expansion, however. By the end of the war, most of the company's fleet had been destroyed. Into the 1920s, Hunting was forced to rebuild, now under the leadership of Percy Hunting.

During that period, the company entered the tanker brokering business as well, acquiring Gibsons. That operation, founded around the start of the 20th century, was initially meant to provide fixing and handling services to Hunting's own fleet. Before long, however, Hunting Gibsons emerged as a world-leading broker for the oil and gas markets, and also helped establish Hunting as a major player in the energy services market.

Through the 1930s, Hunting explored new areas of operations. The aviation sector appeared to be a natural extension for the company, and by the end of the decade Hunting had established itself as an internationally known name in aircraft manufacture. The company specialized in building small, wooden-frame aircraft, and developed a number of its own aircraft designs, such as the Proctor, and the BAC 1-11, which became one of the top-selling British aircraft internationally. The company's aircraft manufacturing operations played a major role in the British military effort during World War II. In addition to production of its own designs, Hunting also produced a number of third-party designs, such as the Mosquito and the Oxfords. By the end of the war, the company had boosted its aircraft division, acquiring Percival Aircraft Ltd. in 1944. That purchase also gave the company a small Canadian subsidiary. In the meantime, Hunting also had launched its own aviation operation, notably providing aerial survey services.

POSTWAR DIVERSIFICATION

Hunting recognized a new opportunity in the immediate postwar years, that of offering air transportation services. As such, the company became one of the first independent British companies to offer civilian passenger transport in the second half of the 1940s. Hunting Air Transport quickly built up a fleet of aircraft, including eight Viking aircraft, and became one of the United Kingdom's major domestic carriers by the early 1950s, flying nearly 60,000 passengers per year. The company also added international flights, notably between London and South, Central, and East Africa. Into the 1950s, Hunting also began offering direct flights between the United Kingdom and destinations on the European continent. As an offshoot, the company became a ticketing agent. In 1947 and 1948, for example, the company worked with the Canadian government to arrange flights for some 8,000 people emigrating to Canada in the aftermath of World War II. The company formally launched a dedicated ticketing subsidiary in 1952.

By then, too, Hunting had decided to convert its aircraft production from wood-frame construction to new all-metal designs, including company-developed Prince aircraft for civilian transport. That design also

KEY DATES

1874: Charles Hunting establishes a shipping business in England.
1944: Percival Aircraft manufacturing operations are acquired.
1952: The company launches Hunting Geophysics Ltd., pioneering the aerial geophysical prospecting market.
1957: The company diversifies into heating and air conditioning engineering.
1962: After further diversification, such as in plastics manufacturing, the company launches Hunting Light Industries.
1967: The company begins providing services to the North Sea offshore oil industry.
1989: The Hunting family merges its three publicly listed holdings into a single publicly listed entity, Hunting PLC.
1999: Hunting exits the aviation market.
2001: Hunting exits the defense market and completes the disposal of its diversified operations to become a focused energy services group; the company acquires Thread Tech Energy Systems, and Columbia Fuels, both in Canada, as part of an acquisition drive to boost energy services operations.
2002: Roforge in France, which supplies valves to global energy industries, is acquired.
2005: The company acquires Cromar Ltd. based in Aberdeen, with subsidiaries in Houston and Singapore, which provides services and equipment to the energy market.

was adapted for use in military applications, notably for the Royal Air Force at home, and for a number of foreign air forces. The Prince also was redeveloped as the Sea Prince for the Royal Navy. Concurrent with the growth of its aircraft manufacturing operation, Hunting built up an aircraft maintenance arm, under the Field Aircraft Services name. That company also added subsidiaries in Canada, South Africa, and Rhodesia. At first focused on Hunting's own air transport operations, Field soon began providing services to other airlines, such as the British European Airways, as well as a contract to overhaul the United States Air Force's European-based Dakota fleet.

Meanwhile, Hunting had continued building its operations in the oil industry. In 1951, the company

expanded into the Canadian oil marketing and distribution market, establishing Gibson Petroleum Marketing. That company grew into one of Canada's largest distributors of oil and gas, operating pipelines, terminals, and storage facilities. Gibson Energy also established itself as one of the country's top retailers of propane gas. Elsewhere, Hunting's oil and gas exploration efforts had paid off with the launch of production of crude oil in Texas and Arkansas. The company also found a way to combine its two primary markets of energy services and aviation, more or less creating a new field of geophysical prospecting. That business was based on the company's earlier aerial survey operations, which into the 1950s extended throughout the British Commonwealth, and included subsidiaries in London, East Africa, Canada, Pakistan, South Africa, and Rhodesia, as well as partnerships in Australia and New Zealand. With a fleet of more than 38 aircraft, Hunting emerged as a leading provider of aerial services. In the early 1950s, the company's Canadian operations pioneered the use of aircraft in geophysical prospecting. Hunting recognized the importance of this field, particularly given the global population explosion into the second half of the century, and the need to develop new resources to support this population. As such, Hunting rolled out its geophysical prospecting operations onto an international scale, with the creation of a dedicated subsidiary, Hunting Geophysics, in 1953.

By the end of the 1950s, Hunting also had begun to look beyond its core businesses for growth. In 1957, for example, the company decided to extend its engineering expertise into the growing field of heating and ventilation, forming a new subsidiary Hunting Mhoglas. By the early 1960s, the company had expanded into plastics manufacturing as well, and in 1962 the company created a new subsidiary, Hunting Light Industries, to contain its various diversified engineering and plastics businesses. Other operations grouped under Hunting Light Industries included the Field Aircraft Services group, including its African subsidiaries. The Hunting group itself was by then controlled by Pat Hunting, son of Percy Hunting.

Hunting increasingly sought outside capital to fuel its expansion, giving rise to a fairly complex organization—by the end of the 1960s, the Hunting family's interests were represented by three publicly listed companies, each of which also maintained significant shareholdings in the others. During the 1960s, the company also began retailing petroleum products, especially in Canada, where it became one of the market leaders. This was especially true in the retail distribution of propane gas; by the end of the century, Hunting claimed the number two spot in the Canadian market for this segment.

RESTRUCTURED AND STREAMLINED FOR THE NEW CENTURY

Hunting added a new service component in the 1960s when it began providing drilling equipment and support services to the North Sea offshore oil industry. That operation was launched as a joint venture, Hunting Barnard Oilfield Services, in 1967, controlled at 60 percent by Hunting. This business, which later came under full ownership by Hunting, became a significant part of Hunting's operations into the 2000s.

Into the 1980s, the Hunting group of businesses included the three public companies, Hunting Gibson, Hunting Associated Industries, and Hunting Petroleum Services. Under the leadership of Clive Hunting, the company began to streamline its rather complex ownership structure. In 1985, for example, Hunting Gibson acquired the Hunting Group, which had remained the Hunting family's private investment vehicle for its controlling stakes in the three publicly listed companies. By 1989, Hunting had completed its reorganization, merging the three publicly listed companies under a single publicly listed entity, Hunting plc. Following the restructuring, the Hunting family's control of the company was reduced to just 30 percent. At the same time, the family stepped down from direct oversight of the company's operations, instead taking up the chairman's position, first under Clive Hunting, and then, into the 2000s, under Richard Hunting.

Hunting's exposure to the defense and aviation industries left the company vulnerable in the early 1990s. The collapse of the Soviet empire and the end of the Cold War caused a dropoff in defense spending around the world. The outbreak of war in the Persian Gulf also led to a downturn in the aviation industry. Pressure on these operations continued throughout the decade, and by the late 1990s Hunting had decided to abandon the aviation business, selling off its aviation holdings by 1999.

Hunting's reorganization continued into the first half of the 2000s, which saw the company exit most of its defense operations in 2001 and the disposal of most of its other diversified businesses, such as operations in automobile parts manufacturing. In this way, the company transformed itself from a diversified "mini-conglomerate" into a company dedicated to the energy services market. As such, the company launched a series of acquisitions into the mid-2000s. In 1998, for example, the company acquired Landell Industries, which expanded Hunting's position in the Gulf of Mexico market.

In 2001, Hunting acquired two Canadian oil services companies, Thread Tech Energy Systems and Columbia Fuels. The former provided oilfield tubulars and connections, while the latter focused on propane equipment supply and services, in large part on Vancouver Island. Other acquisitions followed, including 2002's purchase of Roforge, in France, which manufactured steel valves for the global energy, refining, and petrochemical industries. In 2005, the company added operations in Aberdeen, Houston, and Singapore through its purchase of Cromar Ltd. The addition of Cromar expanded Hunting's energy services profile, adding new areas such as a wireline pressure control, perforating tools, and other specialized equipment. Hunting continued to build on its heritage as one of the world's oldest and leading providers of services to the international energy industry.

M. L. Cohen

PRINCIPAL SUBSIDIARIES

Aero Sekur S.p.A. (Italy); Canwest Propane Ltd. (Canada); E. A. Gibson Shipbrokers Limited (England & Hong Kong); Gibson Crude Oil Purchasing Co. Ltd. (Canada); Gibson Energy Ltd. (Canada); Hunting Airtrust Tubulars Pte Limited (China and Singapore; 50%); Hunting Energy France S.A.; Hunting Energy Services (International) Ltd.; Hunting Energy Services Holdings Inc. (United States); Hunting Oilfield Services (International) Pte Ltd. (Singapore); Hunting Oilfield Services (UK) Ltd.; Hunting Performance Inc. (United States); Hunting Pipeline Services LLC (United States); Hunting Specialised Products Limited; INTERPEC SAS (France); Larco SAS (France); Moose Jaw Asphalt Inc. (Canada); Roforge SAS (France); Tenkay Resources Inc. (United States).

PRINCIPAL COMPETITORS

Baker Hughes UK Ltd.; Kvaerner E and C plc; Canadian Superior Energy Inc.; M. W. Kellogg Ltd.; Paladin Resources plc; Expro International Group plc; Saipem (UK) Ltd.; Halcrow Group Ltd.; SLP Engineering.

FURTHER READING

"Hunting Buys Two Canadian Firms," *Daily Deal,* December 6, 2001.

"Hunting Plc Combines Three US Entities As Hunting Energy Services LP," *Petroleum Finance Week,* February 11, 2002.

"Hunting Plc," *Oil and Gas Journal,* March 4, 2002, p. 91.

The Source
for Critical Information and Insight™

IHS Inc.

---

15 Inverness Way East
Englewood, Colorado 80112
U.S.A.
Telephone: (303) 790-0600
Toll Free: (800) 525-7052
Fax: (303) 754-3940
Web site: http://www.ihs.com

Public Company
Incorporated: 1994
Employees: 2,300
Sales: $476.1 million (2005)
Stock Exchanges: New York
Ticker Symbol: IHS
NAIC: 541512 Computer Systems Design Services;
  511140 Database and Directory Publishers; 511210
  Software Publishers; 551112 Offices of Other
  Holding Companies

■ ■ ■

IHS Inc. is a global supplier of technical information, decision support tools, and related services to several industries. Originally using microfilm to allow compact storage of technical catalogs that once took up reams of paper, IHS was early to switch to electronic delivery and has embraced the Internet since the mid-1990s. The company has expanded its product line from aerospace offerings to regulatory information and the defense, automotive, construction, electronics, and energy industries. Most of its revenues are based on subscriptions and the company boasts very high renewal rates.

IHS is a New York Stock Exchange publicly traded company.

ORIGINS

IHS Inc. traces its origins back to the late 1950s when it was launched by Richard O'Brien, a product editor for one of Rogers Publishing Company's trade magazines. Readers were complaining of the difficulty of getting up-to-date product information from vendors, so O'Brien led an effort to compile and index product catalogs for dissemination on the compact, and relatively inexpensive, medium of microfilm. This work was carried out by the Technical Services Division established by Rogers in 1959.

The division was spun off as Information Handling Services (IHS) in 1961 as Cahners acquired Rogers. Early users included Martin-Marietta and Convair Astronautics. IHS soon was producing a Military Specifications File for government contractors. It eventually became known as Information Handling Services Inc. (IHS). The company's early business would be supplying microfilm catalogs of aerospace engineering product information. The company's first product was called the Vendor Specs Microfilm File, or VSMF. IHS eventually was owned by international holding company TBG Inc., which was itself controlled by the Thyssen-Bornemisza family of Thyssen AG fame.

Edward M. "Ted" Lee led the company in the 1970s. He was credited with growing its business while developing a reputation as a good employer. Under his leadership, revenues rose to $32 million in 1977. The company got a new president in 1981, Michael J.

COMPANY PERSPECTIVES

For nearly 50 years, IHS has helped customers harness the power of information to improve their business results. This is the essence of IHS today, and it is what makes us unique compared with all of our competitors. While much has changed over that period, this is the common denominator that unifies our organization— the promise to provide our customers with the technical information, tools, and operational and advisory services necessary to help them make critical business decisions, maximize their core business processes and improve productivity. And we will continue expanding our offerings further to include knowledge-based solutions and industry insight that provide strategic benefit to our customers around the world.

Timbers, who formerly had led a government procurement agency and marketing research consultancy.

The space needed to store vast technical product catalogs that once took up reams would be shrunk even more as new electronic formats were developed. Responding to demand from its engineer customers, who were enthusiastic early personal computer users, IHS began producing CD-ROMs in 1985. IHS was investing $10 million over a three-year period to convert to the new technology, according to *Business Week*. This was a colossal task that required scanning more than ten million printed pages.

The company dominated the standards and regulatory publishing field with sales of $70 million a year in the mid-1980s. By 1988, the company Information Handling Services had revenues of $120 million; the larger IHS Group employed 1,100 people, more than half of them at its Colorado headquarters. IHS was making 13 million frames of microfilm products a year, making it the largest commercial producer in the world.

At the time of its 30th anniversary, IHS, which exported to more than 80 countries, was building a new $5 million, 64,000-square-foot headquarters building in Englewood, Colorado. A holding company, IHS Group, was established in 1999 to oversee new subsidiaries.

ACQUISITIVE DECADE: 1990-2000

IHS was a voracious acquirer in the 1990s. The decade started with the purchase of the Haystack product line, which was bought from Ziff-Davis Technical Informa-

tion Company. Haystack's defense parts database complemented IHS's existing MasterNET CD-ROMs. Eighteen months later, in September 1991, IHS sold Predicasts Inc., a Cleveland-based supplier of business periodical databases, to Ziff Communications.

IHS Group revenues exceeded $191 million in 1991. Information Handling Services Inc. accounted for about 75 percent of the total. The group then had 1,600 employees.

Information Handling Services Inc. expanded in the southern hemisphere by acquiring Australia's Hinton Information Services Pty. Ltd. in 1993. Hinton was based in Sydney and specialized in engineering and medical information. Among a handful of other acquisitions in 1993, IHS bought Newton, Massachusetts-based Cahners Technical Information Service (CTIS) from Reed Publishing (USA) Inc. CTIS produced Computer Aided Product Selection (CAPS) databases for electrical engineers. IHS was developing its CAD capabilities to make it easier for product designers to retrieve and incorporate graphical component information through its new CAPSCAD product.

Edwards Publishing Company, which specialized in publishing electronics connectors catalogs, was acquired toward the end of 1994. Another purchase, Global Info Centre Hong Kong Ltd., brought IHS into Southeast Asia and China. By this time, international sales were accounting for more than 30 percent of IHS Group revenues.

ONLINE IN 1995

IHS bought Portland's Creative Multimedia Inc. for $30 million in 1995. Creative made multimedia products such as CD-ROMs. The real focus of IHS's future, however, would be online development.

The company took its products onto the Internet in 1995. The web allowed the company to incorporate changes into its databases as they were reported and streamlined the delivery of information to customers. IHS was using search technology developed by CADIS, Inc. of Boulder, Colorado. IHS Group sales were about $257 million in 1995.

IHS Group stepped into the oil and gas information industry with the 1996 acquisition of Petroconsultants S.A. Petroconsultants was based in Geneva, Switzerland and had annual revenues of $40 million and 250 employees. It lacked CD-ROM and Internet products when acquired. IHS sold off hospital software supplier Health Care System during the year, while buying South African trade and reference press The Communications Group and U.S. government-oriented electronic database publisher RBP Associates.

KEY DATES

1959: Rogers Publishing Company forms a unit to supply microfilm catalogs of aerospace engineering product information.
1961: Technical Services Division is spun off as Information Handling Services (IHS).
1976: The company builds a 133,000-square-foot headquarters in Englewood, Colorado.
1977: Revenues are $32 million.
1985: Sales are $70 million; the company begins to produce CD-ROMs.
1988: IHS makes three million feet of microfilm.
1989: The IHS Group holding company is formed.
1990: A new world headquarters opens in Colorado.
1991: Revenues exceed $191 million.
1994: IHS Inc. is incorporated in Delaware.
1995: Online versions of catalogs are made available; group revenues are about $257 million.
1997: Several databases are combined into an online Engineering Resource Center for the IHS Specs & Standards service.
1998: Microfilm production ends.
2005: IHS goes public on the New York Stock Exchange.

The company's microfilm production was finally shut down in 1998. By this time, it was accounting for just 5 percent of revenues, which totaled $415 million.

NEW STRUCTURE, NEW VENTURES FOR THE NEW MILLENNIUM

In 1999, IHS was expanding its product line to include regulatory information. IHS expanded into another new market by acquiring CenBASE/Materials Information Service from CenTOR Software Corporation. At the end of the year, IHS sold off its handful of trade magazine titles to PennWell of Tulsa, Oklahoma. In November 2000, the company sold West Group its environmental and human resources businesses while its financial division was acquired by Wolters Kluwer a couple of months later.

The company formed a joint venture in 2000 to publish standards for the British Standards Institution. IHS had relationships with more than 200 standards bodies for engineering alone.

Robert R. Carpenter, a technology services industry veteran, became IHS Group CEO in February 2001. One of his priorities for the company was expanding online offerings. In November 2001, the company launched a worldwide hosting service. It was assisting the U.S. Air Force and Navy in bringing their maintenance manuals onto the Internet. Group revenues were $400 million in 2001, half from outside the United States. IHS had 60,000 end-users in more than 90 countries.

The company continued to expand its scope through alliances. In 2003, it became the official English language distributor for Russia's Gosstandart standards organization. It also was teaming with Inventory Locator Service, L.L.C. in an integrated supply chain management service. IHS spent more than $70 million on other acquisitions in 2004, including two parts information specialists, Houston's Intermat Inc., and Virginia Beach's USA Information Systems Inc. In September, IHS acquired Cambridge Energy Research Associates (CREA) for $31 million. Noted economics author Daniel Yergin, who had founded CREA, remained with the firm as chairman.

PUBLIC IN 2005

IHS Inc., the Delaware corporation formed in 1994, underwent an initial public offering (IPO) on the New York Stock Exchange on November 11, 2005 (it had originally been scheduled for May). By this time, energy-related products were accounting for about half of sales, and the stock was billed as a play on the booming oil and gas market. The offering valued the company at

Several of the company's databases were combined into the web-based Engineering Resource Center in 1997. IHS claimed the world's largest collection of commercial standards, regulatory standards, and electronic components catalogs.

The group was still adding to its holdings in 1997. It bought the United Kingdom's ESDU International PLC, an engineering design guide publisher founded in 1940. It also added Mexico's Documenta, S.A. de C.V. By this time, IHS was active in 90 countries. Other deals included the trade of Creative Multimedia and other consideration for Dataware Technologies Inc.'s services business, and the purchase of Medical Data International.

IHS bought online sourcing service Industry.net in late 1997. It had once been part of bankrupt Nets Inc. and had an estimated 450,000 users. Another end of the year acquisition was that of Houston-based energy publisher Petroleum Information/Dwights L.L.C., whose origins dated back to the 1960s. This gave IHS Group a total of 3,150 employees.

nearly $1 billion; it did not raise funds for the company, which already had plenty of cash on its books, but allowed leading shareholder TBG Holdings to liquidate part of its holdings. TBG retained 62 percent of equity and 88 percent of voting rights after the IPO.

Revenues were $476 million in 2005. Its flagship VSMF product had expanded to three million pages of listings from more than 25,000 manufacturers. The 2005 acquisition of the United Kingdom's American Technical Publishers Ltd. extended IHS's reach in Europe and Africa.

Frederick C. Ingram

PRINCIPAL DIVISIONS

Aerospace; Defense; Automotive; Construction; Electronics; Energy.

PRINCIPAL COMPETITORS

The McGraw-Hill Companies; Reed Elsevier Group; Thomson Corporation.

FURTHER READING

Amole, Tustin, "Edward M. Lee, Former IHS President, 'Idea Man,'" *Rocky Mountain News* (Denver), September 7, 1997, p. 10B.

Atchison, Sandra D., "For Microfilm, the Writing Is on the Wall—With Customers Demanding Electronic Data, A Top Information Supplier Switches to Compact Disks," *Business Week*, March 10, 1986, p. 118B.

"ATP Acquisition Broadens IHS's Footprint in Europe, Asia and Middle East," *Electronic Information Report*, April 11, 2005.

Chakrabarty, Gargi, "Energy Company IHS Going Public; It Looks to Capitalize on Market, Raise Up to $300 Million," *Rocky Mountain News* (Denver), February 8, 2005, p. 7B.

"Company Interview: Robert R. Carpenter, IHS Group," *Wall Street Transcript*, January 14, 2002.

"Dataware to Sell Services Operations for $25.2 Million," *Dow Jones Online News*, September 26, 1997.

Goering, Richard, "Parts Information Is Going On-Line—Calling 555-DATA," *Electronic Engineering Times*, July 26, 1993, p. 1.

Greim, Lisa, "Information Firm Plays for Big Stakes; Low Profile, High-Tech IHS Group Seeks Place Among Major Companies," *Rocky Mountain News* (Denver), September 8, 1997, p. 6B.

"How Was IHS Started?," *IHS Informant*, July 2003.

"IHS Acquires CenBASE/Materials Information Service," *Worldwide Databases*, April 1, 1999.

"IHS Acquires Petroconsultants; Launches New Expansion Strategy," *Electronic Information Report*, October 25, 1996.

"IHS Acquires USAInfo, Intermat in Back-to-Back Deals," *Electronic Information Report*, September 27, 2004.

"IHS Completes Sale of Publishing Group Assets," *Business Publisher*, December 24, 1999, p. 6.

"IHS Group Thinks Vertically for Strategic Partnerships in 2001," *Electronic Information Report*, February 9, 2001.

"IHS Group to Be Provider of British Standards," *Online Newsletter*, March 1, 2000.

"IHS Group Unveils Corporate Internet Strategy," *Worldwide Databases*, June 1, 1996.

"IHS Introduced the IHS Engineering Resource Center," *Information Today*, June 1, 1997, p. 51.

"IHS Microfilm Products Give Way to Electronic Information Services," *Information Intelligence Online Newsletter*, January 1, 1999, p. 3.

"IHS on Acquisition Spree," *Electronic Information Report*, November 18, 1994.

"Information Handling Services Acquires Haystack from Ziff-Davis," *IDP Report*, March 23, 1990, p. 8.

Kokmen, Leyla, "Local Database Publisher Acquires Texas Firm," *Denver Post*, December 30, 1997, p. C1.

Manning, Jeff, "Colorado Firm Buys Creative Multimedia," *Portland Oregonian*, June 8, 1995, p. E1.

"Medical Data International Sold to Information Handling Services Group," *Business Publisher*, November 17, 1997.

Milstead, David, "IHS Stock Up 7% in Debut on NYSE; Metro Publisher of Tech Info Sells 14.5 Million Shares," *Rocky Mountain News* (Denver), November 12, 2005, p. 3C.

Richardson, Glen, "Information Baron," *Denver Business*, December 1, 1989, p. 8.

Smith, Kerri S., "Pet Pup Unwelcome at Work; Woman Training Dog to Assist Disabled Could Lose Her Job," *Rocky Mountain News* (Denver), August 27, 1996, p. 2B.

Trommer, Diane, "IHS Acquires Industry.net—Co. to Revamp Site, Which Has Stagnated Since Nets Inc. Failure," *Electronic Buyers' News*, November 17, 1997, p. 72.

"West Group Acquires Regulatory, Compliance Products," *Information Today*, January 1, 2001, p. 62.

IMAX Corporation

2525 Speakman Drive
Sheridan Science and Technology Park
Mississauga, Ontario L5K 1B1
Canada
Telephone: (905) 403-6500
Fax: (905) 403-6450
Web site: http://www.imax.com

Public Company
Incorporated: 1967 as IMAX Systems
Employees: 363
Sales: $136 million (2004)
Stock Exchanges: NASDAQ
Ticker Symbol: IMAX
NAIC: 51211 Motion Picture & Video Production;
42141 Photographic Equipment & Supplies
Wholesalers; 512131 Motion Picture Theaters,
Except Drive-in; 71399 All Other Amusement &
Recreation Industries; 33431 Audio & Video
Equipment Manufacturing; 333315 Photographic
and Photocopying Equipment Manufacturing;
325992 Photographic Film, Paper, Plate, and
Chemical Manufacturing

■ ■ ■

IMAX Corporation, founded in 1967 and headquartered
in Mississauga, Canada, is the pioneer and leader of
giant-screen, large-format film entertainment. Using its
proprietary technology, the company projects movies on
screens that are up to eight stories high and 120 feet
wide in theaters owned by museums, science centers,
and commercial operators. In 2002, the company
launched IMAX DMR, which allows any feature film to
be digitally re-mastered to fit an IMAX screen. IMAX
DMR releases include *Apollo 13, Star Wars Episode II:
Attack of the Clones, The Matrix Reloaded, The Matrix
Revolutions, Harry Potter and the Prisoner of Azkaban,*
and *SpiderMan 2.* In 2004, *Polar Express* became the
first Hollywood movie to be released in IMAX 3-D. The
movie became the company's highest and fastest grossing digitally re-mastered release. In 2006, there were
250 IMAX theatres in 36 countries across the globe.

YOUNG FILMMAKERS: 1965-67

Founded in 1967 by a group of five filmmakers and
inventors who wanted to show off the beauty of the
medium, IMAX Systems, as it was known then, has
since consistently delivered the world's premiere
cinematic experiences on huge screens. Independent
filmmaker Graeme Ferguson had attended Galt Collegiate Institute in Galt, Ontario, Canada, where he met
Robert Kerr and Bill Shaw, and the three men founded
a student newspaper together. Ferguson went on to the
University of Toronto, where he began making films.
One summer, he was selected to be an intern at the
National Film Board of Canada (NFB), and he went on
to become an independent filmmaker, eventually working in New York. In 1965, Ferguson was asked by the
Canadian Expo Corporation to do a film for Expo '67
in Montreal, but it had to be produced by a Canadian
company. Kerr was at the time serving as mayor of Galt
and still managing the printing company he had sold.
Ferguson approached him about setting up a film

production company. Kerr agreed, and they produced the film *Polar Life* for Expo '67.

Meanwhile, film producer Roman Kroitor had also been a summer intern at NFB. He began working there full-time after finishing college. In 1965 he suggested the board form a committee to produce a multiple-image, experimental film for the 1967 Expo. Kroitor's concept was selected, and he produced *Labyrinth*.

Expo '67 proved to be the birthplace of big-screen movie production. Other forerunners in big-screen production were in attendance there, including Colin Low, Kroitor's codirector on *Labyrinth*; Christopher Chapman; Francis Thomson; and Alexander Hammid, all of whom Ferguson would turn to as IMAX Corporation developed.

A NEW COMPANY: 1967

In 1967 Fuji Bank of Japan asked Kroitor to produce a film for Osaka, Japan's Expo '70, with partial financing provided by Fuji. Kroitor turned to Ferguson and Kerr to help him do it. Multiscreen Corporation was created, with Ferguson as the president. In order to showcase the new film, the company would have to create new technology for it, including a new camera to shoot images on a film frame ten times larger than the normal 35mm format, new equipment to project those larger frame images onto a six-story-high screen, and other accoutrements such as new lenses, sound equipment, lighting, and seating arrangements.

Norwegian-born inventor Jan Jacobson, located in Copenhagen, Denmark, was able, in less than three months, to design a new camera to use 65 mm film horizontally. But the projector proved to be a tougher issue to handle. The company acquired a patent for a Rolling Loop projector from Ronald Jones, a machine shop owner in Brisbane, Australia, but it needed to be adapted to handle the larger size film. The partners turned to old friend Bill Kerr. Kerr had gone to work for Ford Motor Company for a few years as an engineer, eventually moving on to CCM, a sporting goods and bicycle manufacturing company. Kerr and Jones worked together via airmail across two continents to develop the projector. Meanwhile, Kroitor moved to Japan, along with Canadian director Donald Brittain and cameraman Georges Dufaux, to work with Asuka Productions to develop the movie they would show. Despite drawbacks, cash flow problems, and bouts of frustration, the projector and film were finished, and *Tiger Child* played on the big screen at Expo '70, while the audience was carried through the theater continuously on a large rotating platform, each observer viewing the endless film from a different starting point.

In 1971, Ontario Place, a government-sponsored theme park in Toronto, included Cinesphere, a theater showcasing new technology. Ontario Place bought the Expo '70 projector, which was brought back from Japan, refined a bit, and installed in the spring of 1971. That first IMAX projector was still running at Ontario Place at the end of the 20th century. The first film shown there, *North of Superior*, was produced by the company, which quickly gained a reputation for its projectors and sound systems, as well as for showing educational films created by institutions such as The Kennedy Space Center and Grand Canyon National Park. Over the next decade, the company would not only change its name several times, but change leadership and ownership as well, nevertheless while building more IMAX theaters and creating more movies for the medium.

COMPETITION GROWS AND RAISES TECHNICAL STANDARDS

In 1983, Douglas Trumbull, special effects wizard (*2001: A Space Odyssey*; *Close Encounters of the Third Kind*; *Star Trek: The Motion Picture*) and director (*Brainstorm*), and Robert Brock, restaurant and hotel mogul (Brock Hotels, Park Inns International Inc.), founded Showscan Film Corporation, an IMAX competitor. Showscan revolutionized the industry, releasing a new cinematographic technique in February 1984 that offered a three-dimensional picture without viewers having to wear the infamous blue-and-red glasses. Showscan began showing films at 60 frames per second, rather than the normal 24 frames per second. The company built four prototype theaters, including one in Dallas, connected with Brock's Showbiz Pizza Place restaurant outlets, and began showing a movie called *New Magic*. In August 1990, the company changed its name to Showscan Corporation. Meanwhile, in 1986, Iwerks Entertainment Inc. sprang up in California, reincorporating in Delaware in October 1993 under the same name. A year later, Iwerks acquired Omni Films International Inc. for approximately $19.17 million.

KEY DATES

1967: A group of five filmmakers and inventors establish IMAX Systems.

1970: The company's large-screen projector debuts.

1990: The company unveils its new 3-D technology, IMAX Solido.

1994: WGIM Acquisition Corporation acquires IMAX; the company goes public.

1997: IMAX is awarded the only Oscar Award given for Scientific and Technical Achievement by the Academy of Motion Picture Arts and Sciences.

2002: IMAX DMR, digitally re-mastering technology, is launched.

2003: The IMAX MPX format enables multiplex operators to install lower-cost IMAX theaters in existing locations.

2004: *Polar Express* becomes the first Hollywood film to be released in IMAX 3D.

At Expo '90, also held in Osaka, Japan, IMAX unveiled its new 3-D technology, IMAX Solido, which gave new life to a medium plagued with terrible 3-D renditions. The film shown there, the first of many to be produced eventually by the company, was *Echoes of the Sun*, a mostly computer-generated picture coproduced with Japanese company Fujitsu, and shown on a wraparound screen and viewed with battery-powered goggles. The first 3-D IMAX theater was built in Vancouver that year.

NEW OWNERS: 1994

In August 1994, competitor Showscan, with which Douglas Trumbull was associated, changed its name to Showscan Entertainment Inc. to reflect its more comprehensive focus. That year, WGIM Acquisition Corporation (made up of investment group Wasserstein Perella & Company, owned by Bruce Wasserstein and Joseph Perella, both formerly of First Boston; Cheviot Capital Advisors, led by Bradley J. Wechsler and Richard L. Gelfond; and some private investors, including Douglas Trumbull), bought out IMAX's five original owners and The Trumbull Company Inc. for approximately $100 million. Later that year, IMAX went public, selling its stock for $13.50 per share.

With the acquisition of Trumbull, IMAX also acquired Trumbull subsidiary Ridefilm Theaters, a motion simulator company known for its creation of rides based on movies. Douglas Trumbull was the creative mastermind behind the design of IMAX Ridefilm, described by the company as "the most immersive, dynamic and realistic simulation product available." The 18-person modular system featured 180-degree, spherically-curved screens; proprietary orthogonal-motion base technology; high-speed, high-resolution projector technology; and six-track DTS sound. The attraction remained unparalleled by the end of the century, leaving IMAX as the industry leader over competitors such as Iwerks and Showscan, with more than 20 ride locations throughout the world, including the United States, China, France, Japan, Korea, the United Kingdom, Thailand, Norway, Canada, Brazil, Argentina, and the Philippines. Entertainment produced on the rides included features such as Asteroid Adventure; Crashendo; Dolphins—The Ride; Fun House Express; In Search of the Obelisk; and ReBoot: The Ride and ReBoot: Journey into Chaos, based on the computer-animated television program of the same name.

Using IMAX HD Dome and motion simulation, the most advanced motion picture and special effects technology, IMAX Simulator Rides revolutionized the attractions industry. In 1997 the company built its first motion simulator theater ride in Thailand, at Major Cineplex's entertainment complex on Sukhumvit Road, near the city of Ekamai. By this time, the company already featured simulator rides in Germany, at Caesar's Palace in Las Vegas, and at Universal Studios in both Los Angeles and Orlando, showing such features as *Race for Atlantis, Asteroid Adventure*, and *Back to the Future—The Ride*. Meanwhile, in July 1997, Showscan Entertainment acquired 15 percent of Reality Cinema Pty. Ltd. in Darling Harbour, Sydney, Australia.

Also in 1997, in order to allow more than one theater to open per year, the company hired Toronto-based Young & Wright Design Architects to design a prototype theater which could be duplicated across the country, a move many other companies were preparing as well. Additionally that year, the company received the only Oscar Award given for Scientific and Technical Achievement by the Academy of Motion Picture Arts and Sciences. Total IMAX revenue for 1997 reached $158.5 million.

In January 1998, despite the Asian economic crisis, interest in the entertainment industry in that region of the world was increasing. Early in the year, IMAX Corporation entered into an agreement to build a 600-seat IMAX 3D theater in Bangkok, Thailand (the first in that country). The theater was to be operated by Cinema Plus Ltd., IMAX's Australian licensee, and Major Cineplex Company Ltd., a 40-year-old company operating in the areas of entertainment, retail, and real estate, with 75 screens in Thailand.

That March, the company revolutionized three-dimensional cinema again with a new prototype theater, the IMAX 3D SR, located at the Arizona Mills shopping mall in Tempe, Arizona. It was the first of 12 3D screens to be built by the joint venture between IMAX Theater Holdings Inc. of Canada and Ogden Film & Theater Inc. of New York. The addition of the $7 million, 59-X-82-foot screen and 22,000-square-foot theater made the greater Phoenix area the only marketplace supporting two IMAX theaters; the other, which featured a regular IMAX screen, was located in Scottsdale, Arizona, another suburb of Phoenix. Two additional 3D screens opened that year in Nyack, New York, and Miami, Florida, marking another milestone for the company: this was the first time it had featured multiple screen openings in one year. The new technology offered both two-dimensional, regular movie format, and three-dimensional features requiring the use of a headset and cordless ski-goggle type headsets containing liquid-crystal lenses which worked in sync with the projector lenses.

As of early 1999 there were more than 180 permanent IMAX theaters in 25 countries, with a backlog of more than 75 theater systems scheduled to open in 15 new countries during the next few years. Over 500 million people had seen an IMAX presentation since the medium premiered in 1970, and the company had forged strategic alliances and relationships with some of the most prominent corporations in the world, including The Walt Disney Company, Famous Players Inc. (a subsidiary of Viacom Inc.), and Loews Cineplex Corporation, to name a few. The agreement with Famous Players included building IMAX 3D theaters in ten of Famous Players' new and existing theaters in Canada. For fiscal 1998, total revenue climbed again, reaching $190.4 million, with a net income of $1.8 million.

At the beginning of 1999, the company estimated that more than 65 million people worldwide would attend an IMAX theater during the calendar year, and with more theaters opening around the world, the company moved into the 21st century with the potential to continue dominating its niche markets, especially since it had signed a deal with Disney subsidiary Buena Vista Pictures for the exclusive giant-screen release of Fantasia 2000, a remake of the classic animated feature.

IMAX IN THE NEW MILLENNIUM

IMAX faced challenges in 2000 brought on by a slowing North American entertainment market. When the company issued profit warnings in its third quarter, share price fell by 70 percent. Overall, approximately 12 of its customers went bankrupt that year, leaving IMAX with nearly $100 million in debts. The company launched a cost cutting program and began to develop new technologies that would fuel its future growth.

In 2000, the company sold its first commercial digital DLP Cinema Projector used in a multiplex to Japan's T-Joy Co. Ltd. This project displayed digital images from satellite or DVD, versus a 35 millimeter film reel. Two years later, the company launched IMAX DMR, which allowed feature films to be digitally remastered into the IMAX format. The first film released in the new format was *Apollo 13: The IMAX Experience*. Co-chairman and co-CEO Richard Gelfond shed some light on the company's DMR strategy in a December 2005 *USA Today* interview claiming, "We were aware that in order to really grow our business, we needed to penetrate the commercial market. It was just too expensive to make original films, and we didn't want to be in the business of making bets on which films were going to be winners and which were going to be losers. So we developed the technology that enabled us to take the best of Hollywood's films in a year, typically about five or six or seven, and turn them into IMAX films."

Another important new development in IMAX's offerings was IMAX MPX. The MPX format enabled multiplex operators to install IMAX theaters in existing locations at a lower cost than building a new theater from the ground up. The company's first MPX contract was with Jack Loeks Theatres in 2003. That same year, *The Matrix Revolutions: The IMAX Experience* made its debut. Its release marked the first time that a movie simultaneously hit screens in both regular and IMAX formats.

The company signed a lucrative deal with National Amusements in 2004 that called for the opening of 18 IMAX MPX theaters over the next several years. At the same time, *The Polar Express* became the first movie to be released in IMAX 3-D. It quickly became the company fastest and highest grossing digitally remastered IMAX release. By March 2006, IMAX's version of the movie had grossed over $60 million.

In January 2005, IMAX expanded its reach in China by teaming up with Lark International Multimedia to install six MPX theater systems. It signed a deal with Racemic International Group to install three theater systems in Chile and Venezuela. The company was also focused on growth in Russia, Poland, and India. Later that year, AMC Entertainment Inc. announced it would install five MPX theater systems in its largest megaplexes in the United States.

With revenues and profits on the rise, IMAX appeared to be on track for growth in the years to come, especially in international markets. While management remained optimistic about the company's future prospects, IMAX's success hinged on consumer demand for its larger-than-life movies. Gelfond summed up his take on IMAX movie-goer's experience in the aforementioned interview— "It's like first class in the airlines or it's like Starbucks, where a certain segment of the population will pay a premium price for a premium experience. I think it gives consumers something they couldn't get in the home ... a really special movie experience."

Daryl F. Mallett
Updated, Christina M. Stansell

PRINCIPAL SUBSIDIARIES

David Keighley Productions 70MM Inc.; IMAX II U.S.A. Inc.; IMAX Chicago Theatre LLC; IMAX Indianapolis LLC; IMAX Japan Inc.; IMAX Minnesota Holding Co.; IMAX (Netherlands) B.V.; IMAX Rhode Island Limited Partnership; IMAX Sandde Animation Inc.; IMAX Scribe Inc.; IMAX Space Ltd.; IMAX Theatre Holding Co.; IMAX Theatre Holdings (OEI) Inc.; IMAX Theatre Management Company; IMAX Theatre Services Ltd.; IMAX U.S.A. Inc.; Miami Theatre LLC; Parker Pictures Ltd.; Nyack Theatre LLC New York; Ridefilm Corporation; Sacramento Theatre LLC; Sonics Associates, Inc.; Starboard Theatres Ltd.; Tantus Films Ltd.; Wire Frame Films Ltd.; RPM Pictures Ltd.; Tantus II Films Ltd.; Big Engine Films Inc.; Taurus-Littrow Productions Inc.; 3D Sea II Ltd.

PRINCIPAL COMPETITORS

Regal Entertainment Group; SimEx-Iwerks Inc.; Tix Corporation.

FURTHER READING

Booth, Cathy, " IMAX Gets Bigger (by Getting Smaller): The Megamovie Company Is Downsizing into Lesser Burgs," *Time*, June 29, 1998, p. 48.

Carrns, Ann, "Atlanta on Short List for Ridefilm Site," *Atlanta Business Chronicle*, October 6, 1995, p. 5A.

Creno, Glen, "New Arizona IMAX Theater Goes After Mall Crowd," *Knight-Ridder/Tribune Business News*, July 22, 1996.

Dries, Mike, "On Track to 500 Screens, Marcus Theaters Teams with IMAX," *Business Journal-Milwaukee*, May 1, 1998, p. 5.

Elmer-DeWitt, Philip, "Grab Your Goggles, 3-D is Back! Eye-Popping Realism Gives New Life to an Old Craze," *Time*, April 16, 1990, p. 77.

Graves, Jacqueline M., "These Movies Are Going to Be Big, Really Big," *Fortune*, June 12, 1995, p. 24.

Howard, Bob, "San Bernardino, Calif., Officials to Set Policy on Big-Screen Theaters," *Knight-Ridder/Tribune Business News*, May 21, 1996.

Insana, Ron, " IMAX Chief Sees a Big Future in Big Screens," *USA Today*, December 5, 2005, p. B4.

Johnson, Ted, and Diane Goldner, "Bigscreens Make Mainstream Breakout Bid," *Variety*, January 27, 1997, p. 5.

Keating, Peter, Jim Frederick, Susan Scherreik, and Penelope Wang, "Word on the Street," *Money*, February 1999, p. 65.

La Franco, Robert, "The Biggest Show on Earth: Siegfried & Roy Grab IMAX Riches by Their Tigers' 3-D Tails," *Forbes*, September 21, 1998, p. 228.

Lieberman, David, " IMAX Supersizes its Plans for Future Flicks," *USA Today*, December 17, 2002, p. B3.

McCollum, Brian, "Myrtle Beach, S.C., Theater Builder Signs Big-Screen Deal with IMAX," *Knight-Ridder/Tribune Business News*, July 7, 1995.

Messinger, Rob, "Large-Screen Cinema Battle Takes Shape in Ontario, Calif.," *Knight-Ridder/Tribune Business News*, April 30, 1996.

Netherton, Martha, *Business Journal—Serving Phoenix & the Valley of the Sun*, November 21, 1997, p. 1.

O'Brien, Tim, "Joint Venture Strengthens IMAX's European Presence," *Amusement Business*, February 13, 1995, p. 26.

Olson, Eric J., "Giant Screens Poised for Big Impact," *Variety*, January 4, 1999, p. 9.

Perkins, Tara, "Despite Digital Onslaught, IMAX Lives Large," *The Canadian Press*, February 18, 2006, p. C7.

Ray, Susan, "Giant-Screen Theaters Riding Wave of Increased Interest, Sales," *Amusement Business*, September 12, 1994, p. 22.

——, " IMAX, Trumbull Co. Joining Forces," *Amusement Business*, January 17, 1994, p. 26.

——, "Leisure Technology: Location Based Entertainment Leads the High-Tech Charge," *Amusement Business*, September 12, 1994, p. 17.

Russell, John, "Cinemark Considers 24-Screen Theater in Akron, Ohio," *Knight-Ridder/Tribune Business News*, November 4, 1998.

——, " IMAX Expands Its Large-Format Movies into Commercial Theater Complexes," *Knight-Ridder/Tribune Business News*, January 6, 1999.

Serino, Joseph, "'Signature Entertainment' Gaining Ground in Urban Development Field," *Amusement Business*, July 8, 1996, p. 26.

Smith, Elliot Blair, "California's Edwards Theaters Circuit Has Big Plans for IMAX," *Knight-Ridder/Tribune Business News*, July 8, 1997.

Tillson, Tamsen, " IMAX Beefs up Network with Eye on Hollywood," *Variety*, February 23, 1998, p. 30.

Turner, Dan, "Iwerks Sues Competitor over Unfair Practices," *Los Angeles Business Journal*, March 4, 1996, p. 10.

Turnis, Jane, "Cinemark Plans Megaplex, IMAX Theater in Colorado Springs, Colo.," *Knight-Ridder/Tribune Business News*, February 22, 1999.

Waal, Peter, "The Plot Quickens," *Canadian Business*, June 26, 1998, p. 52.

Wadley, Jared, "San Bernardino County, Calif., May Get Giant-Screen Theater," *Knight-Ridder/Tribune Business News*, February 21, 1996.

Whitelaw, Kevin, "At the Movies: 3-D Comes to the Giant Screen," *U.S. News & World Report*, September 16, 1996, p. 68.

Zoltak, James, "Cinema Plus Deal to Give IMAX Corp. Presence in Australia, New Zealand," *Amusement Business*, January 15, 1996, p. 22.

———, " IMAX Lands Five Theater Orders for Hammons Projects," *Amusement Business*, July 24, 1995, p. 34.

IMG

1360 East 9th Street, Suite 100
Cleveland, Ohio 44114
U.S.A.
Telephone: (216) 522-1200
Fax: (216) 522-1145
Web site: http://www.imgworld.com

Wholly Owned Subsidiary of Forstmann Little & Co.
Founded: 1960 as International Management Group
Employees: 2,100
Sales: $1 billion (2004)
NAIC: 711320 Promoters of Performance Arts, Sports, and Similar Events without Facilities

■ ■ ■

IMG, once known as International Management Group, is the world's leading sports and lifestyle management and marketing company, representing more than 1,000 clients. The firm is best known for the roster of sports stars it represents, including Vince Carter, Jeff Gordon, Jaromir Jagr, Derek Jeter, Peyton Manning, Maria Sharapova, Michael Schumacher, Annika Sorenstam, Venus Williams, and Tiger Woods. IMG also represents coaches such as Denny Green and Steve Mariucci; sportscasters like Bob Costas and John Madden; and models (sometime actresses), including Tyra Banks, Elizabeth Hurley, Kate Moss, and Liv Tyler. Moreover, IMG represents the interests of such organizations as the Grammys, The Nobel Foundation, the Royal and Ancient Golf Club of St. Andrews, the USGA, the U.S. Olympic Committee, Wembley National Stadium, and

Wimbledon. IMG divides its business into two segments: IMG Sports and Entertainment, and IMG Media. The cornerstone of the latter is subsidiary TWI, which serves as IMG's television, radio and new media arm. It is the world's largest independent producer and distributor of sports programming, covering more than 240 sports in 200 countries. IMG also acts as a literary agent and is involved in golf course design. IMG has been a pioneer in many ways, credited with the introduction of the corporate tent at major sports events and the commonplace practice of paying athletes appearance fees that are sometimes greater than first place prize money. In addition to its Cleveland, Ohio, headquarters, IMG maintains 70 offices in 30 countries.

ORIGINS

IMG was founded by Mark Hume McCormack, who was born in Chicago in 1930, the son of a farm journal publisher. At the age of six he suffered a skull fracture in an automobile accident, preventing him from pursing contact sports. Instead he found an outlet for his competitive drive by taking up golf, taught to him by his father. McCormack was an accomplished enough golfer to win the Chicago prep title and play number one at the College of William and Mary, as well as qualify for the British and U.S. amateur championships and the U.S. Open. It was during his collegiate days in a match with Wake Forest that McCormack played against Arnold Palmer. It would be the start of a friendship that would prove pivotal in both of their careers. After graduating from William & Mary in 1951, McCormack earned a degree from Yale Law school, and then following a stint in the Army as a law instructor he took a position with the Cleveland-based law firm of Arter, Hadden, Wykoff and Van Duzer.

Although McCormack decided against making competitive golf his career, he did not lose his love for the game. In addition to his duties at Arter & Hadden, he began to book exhibition matches for professional golfers. Some of them soon began asking him to review their endorsement contracts, including Palmer who was emerging as a star on the professional tour. McCormack told London's *Observer* in a 1999 interview, "I started out giving tax advice to golfers, filling in forms, sending off returns — freeing their time up so they could play more golf." In 1960 he experienced something of an epiphany, which he described to *Daily News Record* in 1985: "It occurred to me that if a company had a recognizable name which could be put on a new product, that product could have instant recognition. Usually, you have to spend hundreds of thousands of dollars to educate the public to new products, but if you have a famous name associated with it, it gives you a head start." Fortunately for McCormack he had a friend with a famous name, his college golfing nemesis Arnold Palmer. McCormack convinced Palmer to become his first client, the deal formalized with nothing more than a handshake, and International Management Group was born.

In the year before signing with McCormack, Palmer had earned $60,000. Two years later that amount would increase to $500,000, but this would just be a down payment on the hundreds of millions of dollars Palmer would earn even after he ceased to be a competitive golfer. From the start, McCormack proved savvy about how to leverage a personality's franchise. "We never let our licenses advertise Palmer's wins, although they wanted to," McCormack told *Daily News Record*. "We knew that one day he wouldn't be winning any more, and we didn't want him to lose his impact." Palmer's success with McCormack caught the attention of other top golfers. Later in 1960 Gary Player signed on as a client, and then in 1961 amateur star Jack Nicklaus approached McCormack during a tournament and asked to have a word after the completion of the round. This meeting led to further talks and in December 1961

Nicklaus turned professional, with McCormack acting as his representative, and launched his stellar pro tour career in 1962.

The "Big Three"— Palmer, Player, and Nicklaus — dominated golf for the next decade, and with McCormack landing endorsement deals for them, they soon earned more money off the course than on. Moreover, their increased stature raised golf's profile with the general public and made professional golf popular, especially on television, and it became an even more lucrative occupation.

INTERNATIONAL EXPANSION: 1960-99

McCormack's ambitions, however extended far beyond the Big Three and golf. A visionary, he was already thinking in global terms. Early on he signed endorsement deals in Japan and England, and although the amount of business did not justify it, he began opening international offices. In 1964 IMG opened an office in Asia, followed two years later by a London office. In 1967 the firm signed Tony Jacklin, England's best golfer, which established a strategy of signing a country's top athlete and then leveraging that connection to win bigger future prizes. In the case of England, the Jacklin connection led to IMG a few years later signing the Royal and Ancient Golf Club of St. Andrews as a long-term client. This game plan was applied to sports other than golf as well. In 1968 IMG signed French skier Jean-Claude Killy after winning three gold medals in the Winter Olympics. Although his competitive skiing came to an end, Killy enjoyed a highly successful career as an IMG client. Some 20 years later it was Killy who convinced the Albertville Olympic Committee to use IMG to handle its marketing for the 1992 Winter Games. In 1968 IMG signed Australian tennis star Rod Laver, a move that not only provided the firm with a foothold in a new sport but also led to IMG representing the Australian Open, Wimbledon, and the U.S. Open — three of tennis's four Grand Slam events. IMG also advanced on other fronts during the 1960s. In 1964 it staged its first golf event, the World Matchplay Championship, and two years later opened a Los Angeles office and founded TWI, which would produce a number of made-for-television golfing and sporting events. In 1967 IMG Literary and IMG Broadcasting were founded, the latter the result of signing top sportscaster Chris Schenkel. A year later IMG Football was launched, its first client Minnesota Viking's quarterback Fran Tarkington. In 1969 IMG signed its first baseball player, Brooks Robinson; its first motorsports client, Jackie Stewart, launching IM Motorsports; and its first model, Jean Shrimpton.

KEY DATES

1960: Mark McCormack launches company by signing Arnold Palmer.
1966: TWI is founded.
1971: Royal & Ancient Golf Club of St. Andrews becomes a client.
1978: A relationship with Nobel Foundation established.
1983: IMG Artists is launched.
1986: "Stars on Ice" begins.
1996: Tiger Woods signs as client.
2003: McCormack dies.
2004: Forstmann Little & Co. acquires IMG.

In 1970 IMG lost a major client in Nicklaus, who according to *Sport Illustrated,* was reportedly frustrated at playing "second fiddle" to Palmer at IMG. "To have held on to Nicklaus, I couldn't have expanded the company," McCormack explained to the magazine. "I'd have had to personally watch over him. Instead, I was creating IMG. I'd have won the battle and lost the war." Instead McCormack continued to pursue his plan of global conquest in the sports representation field. In 1970 IMG signed its first basketball player, John Havlicek. A year later it added Brazilian soccer superstar Pele as a client. Also in 1971 an Australian office was opened and IMG Consulting was established. In the early 1970s IMG became involved in client-designed golf courses, with an Arnold Palmer-designed course opening in Japan in 1973. IMG's revenues reached $25 million in 1975, but McCormack was far from content. In the second half of the decade IMG opened an office in Canada in 1977 and Brazil in 1979. The firm also signed its first woman golfer, Nancy Lopez, which led to a heavy involvement in women's golf. IMG made additional strides in its tennis business, signing both Chris Evert and Martina Navratilova as clients, and in 1979 the firm staged its first event in China, a tennis exhibition match between Jimmy Conners and Bjorn Borg. Far afield from sports, IMG established its relationship with the Nobel Foundation in 1978.

The early 1980s saw IMG bring televised National Football League games to Great Britain and a number of other entertainment firsts. In 1983 it staged the first Skins Game, a made-for-television golf format that would become an annual event. Also in 1983 IMG first became involved with the Olympics. It was IMG that led to the games being spread over three weekends for the benefit of television ratings, starting with the Winter

Games in Calgary in 1988. IMG produced its first ice show in 1986, the "Scott Hamilton America Tour," which led to the perennially popular "Stars on Ice" tour. IMG continued to build its tennis profile during the 1980s, acquiring Nick Bollettieri Tennis Academy in 1987, which provided it access to rising talent and set the stage for the creation of a Men's Tennis division in 1988, when Andre Agassi, James Courier, and Pete Sampras were signed. IMG also bolstered its roster of baseball clients, which only numbered ten, by acquiring Reich, Landman and Berry in 1987. Within three years IMG would be representing 75 baseball players. In addition, IMG built up its basketball and football divisions in the late 1980s and became involved in cricket, representing the interests of West Indies Cricket Board. On the non-sports front, the firm founded IMG Artists in 1983 (with violinist Itzhak Perlman becoming the centerpiece), acquired Laraine Ashton in 1987 to start IMG Models, and in 1989 began representing Oxford University for licensing.

IMG continued to grow in the United States while also expanding its international reach and growth beyond sports. The firm bought its first CART car race in 1991, and became involved with the Rugby World Cup in 1992. In that same year IMG signed a 12-year deal with USA Volleyball to take advantage of the sport's Olympic popularity but according to *Brandweek,* "IMG's efforts to build the same fizzled when volleyball's marketing rights became entangled in a dispute with the Atlanta Olympic marketing group."

In 1994 IMG formed a soccer division, and then in 1996 it began to represent stadiums and arenas. It was also in the 1990s that IMG became a sports team owner, acquiring a club in the Chinese Basketball Association in 1995 and purchasing a first division French soccer team, Racing Club de Strasbourg, in 1997. The firm considered golf, McCormack's first love, to be a market that was essentially "fully valued," however. McCormack told *Brandweek* in March 1996 that golf was "peaking a little bit. I don't see it growing at the same levels. The worst thing to get into in golf today is the sponsorship of a PGA [Tour event]. It costs so much and you only get a week out of it." But that would all change later in 1996 when Tiger Woods turned professional and took the game to even greater heights. Woods had been a golfing prodigy since childhood and IMG began courting his family when Woods was just 13, currying favor by hiring his father as a junior golf scout, bringing much appreciated income to the household. That would end when Woods enrolled at Stanford University to make sure there was no violation with the National Collegiate Athletic Association (NCAA). It was no surprise that when Woods decided to become a professional after his sophomore year in college that he would sign with IMG. Other notable developments in the 1990s included the signing of the Rock and Roll Hall of Fame as a client in 1993; the establishment of the TWI Interactive division in 1996; the addition of the Kennedy Space Center as a client in 1997; and the creation of a private equity fund to invest in the sports industry, formed with Chase Capital Partners in 1998.

NEW CENTURY, NEW OWNERSHIP

The terrorist attacks on the United States on September 11, 2001, along with a depressed economy, hurt IMG's business, as many companies cut back on sponsorships. Over the course of the next 18 months IMG eliminated some 400 positions, roughly 17 percent of its staff. The firm also spun off Elevation Motorsports, a subsidiary that owned the Grand Prix of Cleveland, and unloaded Racing Club de Strasbourg. After experiencing a difficult 2002, IMG hoped to rebound in 2003, but in January the 72-year-old McCormack suffered a heart attack during dermatology surgery. He would linger in a coma for four months before dying on May 16, 2003. McCormack was replaced by long-time lieutenants Bob Kain and Alastair Johnston, who took over as co-chief executive officers. Their tenure would be short-lived, however. There was talk of McCormack's family selling a portion of the company to fund expansion, or even taking IMG public. Shortly after McCormack's death, however Theodore (Ted) Forstmann of private equity firm Forstmann Little & Co. began courting the family. Forstmann was long-time friends with McCormack (they served together on the board of directors of Gulfstream Aerospace Corporation) and his second wife, and the two men had discussed becoming partners. In October 2004 he succeeded in convincing the family he was the man to carry on what McCormack had begun and Forstmann Little completed a purchase of IMG for a reported $700 million to $750 million.

Forstmann became a hands-on manager, taking over as IMG's CEO. He then tried to balance his pledge of preserving McCormack's legacy with the application of sound business practices. Kain and Johnston were eased aside and in 2005 George Pyne, former chief operating officer of NASCAR, was installed as president. According to *Forbes,* Forstmann also got rid of some of the "ex-jocks and sports-fan lawyers" that held prominent posi-

tions and "stocked the IMG board with titans of business." Overall, he cut IMG's work force by 10 percent to 2,100. However, Forstmann was becoming involved in a far different world than the buying and selling of companies which had garnered him a personal fortune of more than $700 million and made him famous during the leveraged buyout heyday of the 1980s. "Forstmann has entered the service business," wrote *Forbes* in 2005, "where competitors plot to steal managers and their clients, and keeping pampered personalities in check is critical. ... To keep his managers content, Forstmann has done something that even the beloved McCormack never did. He has given or sold equity in the firm to some 80 IMG executives. So if he does flip this baby, cutting costs and selling IMG at a profit, they, too, will get rich."

Ed Dinger

PRINCIPAL COMPETITORS

Advantage International LLC; Live Nation, Inc.; William Morris Agency, Inc.

FURTHER READING

Brady, Diane, "IMG: Show me The Bottom Line," *Business Week,* July 12, 2004, p. 82.

Doward, Jamie, "It's a Fair Way of Making Money," *Observer* (London), June 13, 1999, p. 5.

Keeton, Ann, "McCormack Scores Big," *Daily News Record,* November 11, 1985, p. 25.

Mortland, Shannon, "IMG Charts Leaner Future," *Crain's Cleveland Business,* June 2, 2003, p. 1.

Pulley, Brett, "The Barbarian at the First Tee," *Forbes,* July 4, 2005, p. 122.

Schmuckler, Eric, "Still the One," *Brandweek,* March 11, 1996, p. 28.

Spander, Art, "New Man at the Helm of IMG," *Daily Telegraph* (London), October 5, 2004.

Strange, Curtis, "The Most Powerful Man in Sports," *Sports Illustrated,* May 21, 1990, p. 98.

Sweeney, James F., " The Care and Feeding of Tiger," *Cleveland Plain dealer,* March 30, 1997, p. 10.

Vinella, Susan, and Corwin A. Thomas, "The Grandmaster of the Sports Deal," *Cleveland Plain Dealer,* April 22, 2001, p. 1A.

Indel, Inc.

10 Indel Avenue
Rancocas, New Jersey 08073-0157
U.S.A.
Telephone: (609) 267-9000
Toll Free: (800) 257-9527
Fax: (609) 267-5705
Web site: http://www.indelinc.com

Private Company
Founded: 1954 as Inductotherm
Sales: $800 million (2005 est.)
NAIC: 333994 Industrial Process Furnace and Oven
Manufacturing

■ ■ ■

Indel, Inc. is a private company based in Rancocas, New Jersey, located in the outskirts of Philadelphia. It is the parent company of more than 65 engineering and technology companies split between two business groups: the Inductotherm Group and the Diversified Technology Group. About 40 of the Indel subsidiaries are to be found in the Inductotherm Group, manufacturing and servicing induction-heating equipment—furnaces that melt metal by electric current. Some of the subsidiaries also make equipment to melt other materials. The Diversified Technology Group is composed of more than 25 companies divided among six divisions: Metal Products & Components, including metal fabrication and magnetic stampings; Electrical Components and systems engineering, which offers capacitors, high-voltage power systems, and electric sensing and safety devices;

Electronics, such as graphic display systems, temperature and electronic controls, pay phone electronics, and electronic coin mechanisms and scanners; Engineered Products, including steam generators and ultrasonic welding equipment; Network Communications, including products such as fiber-optic data communication and voice & data switching systems; and Plastic Products, manufacturing injection blow molding machinery and structural foam funeral products such as caskets, graveliners, and vaults.

POSTWAR ORIGINS

Indel was cofounded and headed for almost all of its history by Henry M. Rowan. He was born in 1923, the son of a doctor who would lose his wealth when the stock market crashed in 1929, an event that ushered in the decade-long Great Depression. To make matters worse, his parents divorced in that tumultuous year. His mother would singlehandedly raise Rowan and his three siblings, embodying the lessons of thrift and self-reliance she impressed upon them by returning to college to earn an advanced degree in botany and zoology. When he was just nine years of age Rowan went into business, raising chickens and selling the eggs. His mother was his only customer, and she proved a hard-nosed one, refusing to pay anything more than the best wholesale price. She was also his banker, lending Rowan the money he needed to operate his business—a role he would play with the many companies he acquired later in life.

Molded to be driven and hardworking, Rowan enrolled in a dual-degree program at Williams College in Massachusetts, and gained acceptance to the Massachusetts Institute of Technology. His studies, however, were interrupted by a stint in the Army Air Corp. He completed his training to be a bomber pilot just as the war came to a close, and then returned to MIT to complete his bachelor's of science degree in electrical engineering in 1947. He then took a position at Trenton, New Jersey-based Ajax Electrothermic Corporation, a pioneer in the development of induction-melting furnaces, relying on electromagnetic fields. Rowan was a salesman who also serviced the equipment he sold, with the latter task more to his liking. Despite his frustrations with the way Ajax was run, he learned about the foundry owners he would one day be selling to when he launched his own company. One of those owners was a man named Paul Foley, an ex-Navy commander who had started up Harcast Investment Casting Company in Glenolden, Pennsylvania, a company that made complex parts using wax patterns. Rowan impressed Foley when Rowan, paying a sales call, asked a salesman from a rival company who had just completed his pitch for a new melt unit to stay for his presentation. In that way, he said, the other rep could offer counter arguments. But Rowan's analysis of what Harcast needed and how the Ajax equipment he recommended would ideally serve the intended purpose was so convincing that there was no counter argument to be made. Rowan got the business and came to know Foley better during the installation of the melt unit and training he provided.

Rowan left Ajax in 1952 to take a job as an engineer and plant manager with Marine Manufacturing & Supply, a New Brunswick hardware and deck machinery manufacturer for ships. One day in 1953 Foley telephoned Rowan to see if he could make an induction furnace for Harcast. Rowan agreed to tackle the assignment in his spare time, using the garage of his house as a workshop and the backyard for a bonfire to heat the necessary copper. The result was a first-class furnace and an offer from Foley to go into business with him making more induction-melting furnaces for the foundry market. Rowan declined, electing to keep his steady job, but a shipbuilding boom that had driven the business of Marine Manufacturing & Supply collapsed. Foley's proposal now looked more inviting.

In 1954 Rowan and Foley launched a company called Inductotherm with a $10,000 investment. To come up with his share of the seed money, the 31-year-old Rowan sold his home in Trenton and moved his family into a rental house in Pennsylvania. Inductotherm set up operations in a vacant little office at Harcast and had one young employee, Jess Cartlidge, who was paid 75 cents an hour as a mechanic. Rowan had hired Cartlidge originally when he was just 13 to help him build the house he sold to fund Inductotherm, paying him pocket change to pull nails from board and carry cinder blocks. Cartlidge became a virtual member of the Rowan family and would one day become president of Inductotherm Japan. But at the moment such a thought would have seemed pure fantasy, given that they sat idle for three or four months before receiving their first order: a $50,000 contract from General Electric for a control panel to a vacuum furnace. Another job soon followed, a $25,000 contract from the U.S. Mint in Philadelphia for an induction-melting furnace. At the end of the first year Inductotherm realized a profit of $500.

With Inductotherm on its feet, Rowan was eager to expand the business. As orders came in the company outgrew its space and in 1955 moved to a larger facility in Delanco, New Jersey, the site of a former hosiery mill. Foley, who continued to run Harcast, could not devote enough attention to Inductotherm and soon sold his interest to Rowan for $52,500, payable in installments. Rowan then began to build a management team to help him expand Inductotherm, men who would still play key roles 30 years later: Roy T. Ruble, Jack Agnew, Thomas H. Pippitt, and Bob Sundeen. Business was so strong that in 1961 Inductotherm was able to move out of the ex-hosiery plant, buy a 90-acre farm in Rancocas, and build a new plant. Not only did the site offer ample room for future expansion, it was ideally located some 15 miles northeast of Philadelphia with direct access to the New Jersey Turnpike and later to Interstate 295, which connected the New Jersey and Pennsylvania Turnpikes. The campus eventually would grow to 250 acres.

AN INDUSTRY LEADER: 1960-90

During this early period, Inductotherm built a healthy business supplying furnaces used in the manufacture of jet engines. In 1963 the Consarc subsidiary was established to design and build super-pure vacuum-melt furnaces used to produce the superalloys needed in jet engines. As people became concerned

KEY DATES

1954: Inductotherm is founded by Henry Rowan and Paul Foley
1961: The company moves to the Rancocas campus.
1963: Consarc is formed.
1968: The first solid-state power supply is developed for an induction furnace.
1992: Henry Rowan donates $100 million to Glassboro State College.
2002: Inductotherm Group is formed.

about pollution in the 1960s, the company benefited because induction furnaces produced a small fraction of the emissions common in fuel-fired furnaces. Moreover, Inductotherm introduced innovations that revolutionized the technology. Small induction furnaces had been powered by motor generators or banks of transformers, but in 1968 Inductotherm introduced the world's first solid-state power supply for induction melting, making possible the building and operation of much larger furnaces.

Having established Inductotherm as an industry leader, Rowan fueled further growth in the 1960s and 1970s through scores of acquisitions. According to a 1983 company profile published in the *Philadelphia Inquirer*, "It bought up small companies in related fields. It expanded overseas, setting up operations in Australia, Brazil, Britain, Canada, Japan, and Mexico." The Mexico operation, despite being the best in the country, was unable to overcome the devaluation of the peso and had to be shut. Otherwise, Inductotherm enjoyed immense success during its first 25 years of operation. It was not until the recession of the early 1980s that Inductotherm did not enjoy a profitable month. The furnace business was hard hit, depressing sales and earnings, and forcing the company to cut its workforce by nearly 400 jobs to 2,600.

Although an engineer by training, Rowan proved to be a solid businessman. He permitted subsidiaries a great deal of autonomy but expected results. In many ways he acted like their banker instead of their owner. The parent company lent money to the subsidiaries, as much as 5 percent over prime, and charged for every service provided. In effect, he was treating his managers in a way similar to the way his mother treated him when he was raising chickens and selling her eggs. One of those managers, James F. Rinard, president of Vantage Products Corp., told the *Inquirer*, "He breathes on me hard and I get mad at him, but I don't stay mad. He

can be very generous. He's almost a father image. … His dog is the only one that doesn't jump when he talks to him."

Other than the extended interview he gave to the *Inquirer*, Rowan generally avoided the press and tried to keep Inductotherm out of the newspapers. That would become impossible in the 1990s when his need for a new challenge and innate generosity garnered him a great deal of publicity, whether he wanted it or not. In 1989 a local college, Glassboro State College, approached Rowan about making a donation to the school's $16.8 million library fund. Little known outside of its area, Glassboro was founded in 1923, a small state-funded school with few sources of private money, mostly known for its teaching programs. Its only claim to fame came in 1967 when President Lyndon Johnson and Soviet Premier Aleksei Kosygin met on the campus for two days of talk. Money in the school endowment fund totaled no more than $500,000. Rowan offered $1,500 for the library project, thus establishing a relationship with the school.

1990-2000: NEW DIRECTIONS

According to *Business News New Jersey*, "As the 1990s began, Rowan was nearing retirement, which he dreaded and his business no longer provided the challenge it once did." He was approached by Glassboro's chief fund raiser, Phil Tumminia, who told Rowan that if he upped his contribution to the school to $10 million Glassboro would name the new library after him. However, Rowan was not interested, nor did he care to have the new business school named after him for $30 million. "Finally during a visit in the summer of 1991, Rowan asked Tumminia what the college would do with $100 million. The stunned Tumminia returned to his car and using a car phone called Herman James, the college president, who was working at home. James told him to get right back to Rowan and tell him they would name the college after him if he gave that much." It took several months to work out the details, and in the meantime MIT came calling, asking graduates to contribute to a $700 million program. Nevertheless, Rowan decided to give his money to Glassboro, where he believed $100 million could have a significant impact. As part of the agreement, the college agreed to establish an engineering school and set up a scholarship program for children of Inductotherm employees. Rowan's donation was announced to the world on July 3, 1992, and as the largest single donation to a public college ever made, and the second largest ever in the United States (private Emory University received a $105 million gift in 1979) it became national news. The donation was not without controversy, however. Some Glassboro alumni criticized the school for selling its name, and some portrayed Rowan as an egotist. Nevertheless, Glassboro changed its name to Rowan University and later opened the engineering school dear to its benefactor's heart.

Rowan may not have been as challenged in running Inductotherm as he once had been, but he did not retire. He continued to guide the family of companies he had accumulated over the years. He also indulged his love of flying (for years he had visited customers in a single-engine airplane), as the company invested in a Learjet and built a runway on the Rancocas campus. But even this luxury he made into a money-making investment, as he explained to Newark's *Star-Ledger* in 1996: "We call a plant superintendent, the guy we're trying to sell a furnace to, and invite him to visit our plant, and he'll say, 'Yeah, gee, maybe I'll do it.' And then you tell him, 'We'll pick you up in a Learjet at your airport at 7:30 in the morning, and take you to Alabama to see a similar unit, and then we'll take you to Pittsburgh to see another unit similar to yours. ... and then we'll fly you to our plant in New Jersey. We'll get there about noon and have lunch, meet the engineering group, and we'll get you home by dinner time.' The superintendent would tell the vice president and right on up the line executives would express interest in making the trip. 'Pretty soon you've got the whole team,' Rowan said. 'We've had about a 99 percent success rate on that type of selling. We've had some 200 such trips in the six years we've had the Lear.'"

As the U.S. economy boomed in the 1990s, Inductotherm prospered. In 1997 revenues totaled about $780 million, a 15 percent increase over the prior year. Problems with the Asian economy and declines in the stock market held back growth somewhat in the late 1990s, but Inductotherm entered the new century in strong shape. The company retained its entrepreneurial spirit, continuing to look for new opportunities. For example, in 2001 it launched Inductotherm Automation, Inc. in Canonsburg, Pennsylvania to act as an automation control systems integrator and solutions provider. Rowan also reorganized his family of subsidiaries, creating the Inductotherm Group and Diversified Technology Group in 2002. He then created Indel, Inc., to serve as the parent company and management service company of the subsidiaries. Despite his 80-plus years, he did not indicate that he ever planned to retire.

Ed Dinger

PRINCIPAL SUBSIDIARIES

Astronics Corporation; SPX Corporation; Thermadyne Holdings Corporation.

FURTHER READING

"A $100 Million Investment," *Business News New Jersey*, December 13, 1995, p. 4.

Barr, Stephen, "Top of the Heap: The Fifty Wealthiest New Jerseyans," *Business News New Jersey*, December 1991, p. 27.

Binzen, Peter, "Determination—A Long, Quiet Climb to an Industry's Leadership," *Philadelphia Inquirer*, July 24, 1983, p. D1.

Dailey, Michele, "Henry Rowan: The Value of a Man," *Rowan Magazine*, Spring 1997, p. 10.

Elliott, Jack, "Golfer, Jersey Executive Testify Aviation Makes World Go 'Round,'" *Star-Ledger* (Newark, N.J.), December 1, 1996, p. 48.

"Inductotherm Industries Forms the Inductotherm Group," *Industrial Heating*, May 2002, p. 16.

Rowan, Henry M., *The Fire Within*, Norwalk, Conn.: Penton Publishing, 1995.

Thomas, Myra A., "Basking in the Glow of Innovation," *Business News New Jersey*, February 16, 1998, p. 4.

Julius Blüthner
Pianofortefabric GmbH

— ■ —

Dechwitzer St. 12 04463
Grossposna,
Germany
Telephone: (49) 34297-7513
Fax: (49) 34297-75150
Web site: http://www.bluethner.de

Private Company
Founded: 1853
NAIC: 339992 Musical Instrument Manufacturing

■ ■ ■

Julius Blüthner Pianofortefabrik GmbH is a family-owned and -operated maker of Blüthner and Haessler grand and upright pianos, considered some of the best models in the world. Based in Grossposna, Germany, the company has a rich heritage dating back to the mid-1800s, but during the second half of the 20th century it was taken over by the East German government. Only since the fall of Communism and the reunification of Germany has the business returned to the ownership of the Blüthner-Haessler family and the company has been able to regain its international prominence. The company offers six models in its line of grand pianos, including full concert grands. The Supreme Edition line offers seven models with more styling than the grands, featuring design elements such as rich carvings and gold leaf. Blüthner also produces five upright piano models, including the Franz Schubert with its more ornate case. All models are available in eight to ten finishes.

PIANO ORIGINS DATING TO 16TH CENTURY

The piano grew out of the harpsichord in the early 1700s; its development was credited to Bartolomeo Cristofori of Italy. It would not be until the middle of the century, however, before the piano gained in popularity and began to supplant the harpsichord as the primary keyboard instrument. The upright piano was created by an Austrian named Johann Schmidt around 1780, and 20 years later Englishman Thomas Loud greatly improved the upright by arranging the strings in a diagonal pattern. In the 1800s most of the great piano makers, including Baldwin and Steinway & Sons, launched their lines. Julius Ferdinand Blüthner was among their number.

Blüthner was born in Falkenhain, Germany, in 1824. He learned the craft of piano making and then broadened his knowledge by drifting from one craftsman to another until November 1853 when he set up shop in Leipzig, Saxony, with three journeymen helpers. In the first year he built ten pianos; the first was sold to a professor at Leipzig University. Blüthner quickly established a reputation for his decorative cases, including distinctive veneers and the use of mother of pearl and gold leaf.

Like other craftsmen, Blüthner marketed his pianos by showing them at fairs and exhibitions where awards were given for the best instruments. In 1865 he took his initial first place prize, awarded at a nearby fair in Merseburg. He quickly graduated from local fairs to international competitions, where his pianos garnered their share of medals and ribbons, including first place

Julius Blüthner Pianofortefabric GmbH

COMPANY PERSPECTIVES

Blüthner instruments can sing, certainly the best you can say about a piano.

recognitions at Paris in 1867, Vienna in 1873, Philadelphia in 1876, Amsterdam in 1883, Antwerp in 1894, and Leipzig in 1897. Benefiting from the acclaim, Blüthner became the official supplier of pianos to a number of European royal courts, including the King of Saxony, the German Kaiser, Queen Victoria of England, the Danish king, the Russian Tsar, and the Turkish Sultan.

Early on, Blüthner sought to tap into foreign markets, at a time when other piano makers were content to do business in their home countries, where they were protected by customs barriers. In 1876 he established his first foreign outpost in London. Others would follow, as Blüthner developed an international distribution network. His instruments would become especially popular in South America, Australia, the Philippines, India, and Bangkok. Increased demand for his pianos led to the enlargement of his Leipzig factory in 1876. He also sought to improve productivity by introducing high technology of the day: a central steam engine that used a series of leather belts to drive the plant's different machines. In 1888 he opened a sawmill outside of Leipzig to produce the different types of boards needed to make his instruments. An expansion of the assembly plant followed in 1890. As a result of these efforts at marketing, distribution, and increased production, Blüthner by 1885 was the largest piano manufacturer in Europe, and by 1897 was producing about 3,000 pianos a year, employing some 700 people.

SECOND GENERATION ASSUMES CONTROL IN 1910

Blüthner groomed his three sons—Robert, Max, and Bruno—in different areas of the business in order to carry on the family business after his departure. Robert studied law and would handle business affairs, while both Max and Bruno focused on the production side. Max headed production, and Bruno focused on the piano-making craft itself. Bruno also was dispatched to Boston in the United States where he learned modern production techniques at Chickering & Sons, one of the most respected piano manufacturers in the world, credited with the first use of a cast iron frame in a concert grand. Upon his return to Leipzig, Bruno was put in

charge of construction and continued the family's tradition for innovation in piano design. All three sons were ready to take over the running of the business when Julius Blüthner passed away in April 1910.

Although Blüthner was surpassed as the largest European piano maker in 1905, it continued to prosper in the new century. The company was little impacted by World War I, the depression that hit Germany in the years immediately after the war, or the economic difficulties that ensued after the U.S. stock crash of 1929. Blüthner grand pianos were used by concert artists around the world, and the company continued to build on its reputation for innovation.

In 1932 a son-in-law, Rudolph Blüthner-Haessler, joined the company and took charge. It was during the 1930s that Blüthner was commissioned to build a lightweight piano that could be used aboard the airship Hindenburg. The company's technicians managed to cut the weight by casting the frame from a special aluminum alloy. Blüthner then received untold publicity when the baby grand, covered in pigskin, was used in a piano concerto held on the Hindenburg's first Atlantic crossing, broadcast live around the world by more than 60 radio stations. On May 6, 1937, the great airship erupted into flames as it was landing in Lakehurst, New Jersey. There would be no further need for more of these lightweight pianos, as the disaster doomed the commercial viability of airships.

Blüthner suffered its own disaster several years later as World War II consumed Europe and led to vast destruction. To aid Nazi Germany's war effort, Blüthner was forced to cease the production of pianos. Instead, it assembled ammunition boxes at its factory located in the heart of Leipzig, close to a number of high-value military targets such as aircraft factories and a "buzz bomb" plant. In one bombing raid conducted by the British in December 1943 the Blüthner facility, including all of its equipment, was completely destroyed by fire.

After the war came to an end in 1945, Blüthner-Haessler was urged to return to making pianos. Hence, a new operation was established in the company's sawmill and in 1948 the first piano was produced and ready for sale. Unfortunately for Blüthner, Leipzig was located in the eastern portion of Germany and fell under the control of the Soviet Union. A Communist regime was installed and private companies like Blüthner had to contend with increasing interference from the government. Nevertheless, Blüthner was able to ramp up piano production and regain its place as a world-class maker of pianos; soon demand for new Blüthner pianos far exceeded the company's ability to produce them. "In the fifties," according to *Director,* "as pressures on private

KEY DATES

1853: Julius Blüthner launches the company in Leipzig.
1910: Blüthner dies and the business is taken over by his sons.
1943: The factory is destroyed by a bombing raid.
1948: Piano production resumes in the former company sawmill.
1972: The East German government assumes ownership.
1990: The Blüthner-Haessler family buys back the company.

industry grew, the family considered moving the business to West Germany. The idea was rejected because of the difficulty of persuading large numbers of skilled workers to go with them." Blüthner-Haessler was convinced that Communism would soon fail and the company stayed put. Instead, East Germany closed its borders to the West and when he died in 1966 the company he brought back to life was steadily being taken over by the state, which had taken a stake in the 1950s and built upon it year by year.

Blüthner-Haessler was succeeded by his son, Ingbert Blüthner-Haessler, the great-grandson of Julius Blüthner. Not yet 30 years of age, he had learned the craft of piano making as an apprentice, spending a year of his apprenticeship in England at Welmar Pianos, whose ties to Blüthner dated to 1876 when Welmar's parent company began importing Blüthner pianos. Business was strong enough (in some cases customers had to wait a year for delivery) to warrant the building of a new plant, which opened in 1970 and greatly increased production capacity. The polishing and spraying departments, in particular, could now take advantage of new methods to speed up production times.

The government took complete control of Blüthner in 1972, but according to *Director*, "Nationalization brought no great changes except that Julius Blüthner Pianofortefabric became VEB Blüthner Pianos." Blüthner-Haessler, who stayed on to run the business, noted, "The extent to which a private owner had been able to operate as an entrepreneur in the planned economy was very limited. Wages, prices of materials and selling prices were fixed. You were only a production manager." The government also added a harpsichord factory to the operation. These were all disturbing developments for Blüthner-Haessler, who recalled, "After we were

nationalized, the thought that I would be the last Blüthner connected with the firm oppressed me. And that seemed inevitable, because my sons were not Communist party members, they were opposition-minded."

1990 AND BEYOND: RETURN TO FAMILY OWNERSHIP

Rudolph Blüthner-Haessler's prediction about the Communist government finally came to pass in the late 1980s. The Berlin Wall, the symbol of Communism, was pulled down and East and West Germany began the process of reunification and the privatization of government-owned businesses like Blüthner. Ingbert Blüthner-Haessler quickly took steps to reacquire the family business, achieving restitution in September 1990. It was a process not without difficulty, however. "He took back the firm under the terms of the Modrow law," *Director* reported, "and so was able to leave behind old debts, but now feels he should have waited. ... 'Lawyers here didn't really know what they were doing. Those who waited, and reprivatized under solid laws and legal knowledge, were better advised.'" To reclaim the Blüthner name, the company had to retire the original company from the trading register in order to rename VEB, which was technically a different entity. A notice was placed in the newspapers announcing Julius Blüthner Pianofortefabric was in "liquidation," leading many to believe that Blüthner would no longer produce pianos, a misunderstanding that would cause problems for the next couple of years.

In the early years after the Blüthner-Haessler family reclaimed control, the company hoped to merely reestablish a foothold in the market. Under Communist control Blüthner had sold about half of its pianos to hard-currency countries, overall a plus, but an economic downturn in the early 1990s made selling to these markets difficult. In 1991 Blüthner generated sales of about DM 5 million and did about the same amount in 1992. The company had to trim its workforce, which was cut from 140 to 80, and for a time there was some consideration given to adding income by making furniture or wood items for the construction field. Blüthner had to raise prices on its instruments, but because wages paid in the former East Germany still lagged behind the West, Blüthner was able to scrape by. Another point of difference between Blüthner and many of its rivals, in particular Steinway and Bechstein, was that because of its isolation for the past half century it did not follow the trend of a harder, metallic sound. Rather, it offered what was described as a warm, more romantic tone. "I think you can see a turn back to pianos of the traditional character among music-lovers," Blüthner-Haessler told *Director* in 1992, "and in any event, I hope the fact that I offer an alternative will give me a market niche."

Blüthner-Haessler was helped in rebuilding the company by his two sons, Knut and Christian. A trained engineer, Knut took up the craft of piano making, working in all areas of production before earning his diploma as a master piano maker in 1999. He would play a key role in the development of a lower-priced piano that avoided using cheap material or shortcuts in construction, or even the borrowing of someone else's design. According to *Music Trades*, Knut Blüthner-Haessler "approached the project from the ground up. The end result is a completely redesigned piano and a totally new production process. The Haessler piano features a continuous bent inner and outer rim that provides a strong foundation for better tone and precise string placement."

Also joining his father, after completing his studies in medicine and economics, was Dr. Christian Blüthner-Haessler. He would oversee sales and finance. By the mid-1990s Blüthner had gained its feet. In 1996 the company opened a new factory in the Leipzig suburb of Stormthal to meet the rising demand, and a year later opened a new exhibition hall where its pianos could be displayed and small concerts held. The new line of less expensive grands and uprights was used to pry open the U.S. market, and as Blüthner progressed in the 2000s, it firmly reestablished itself as one of the top five piano makers in the world—along with Bosendorfer, Bechstein, Baldwin, and Steinway. Blüthner had made 150,000 pianos in its history, and in all likelihood it would produce many thousands more in the years to come.

Ed Dinger

PRINCIPAL SUBSIDIARIES

Blüthner Piano Centre Ltd.; Blüthner Pianos (U.S.A.); Blüthner Pianos (Russia).

PRINCIPAL COMPETITORS

Baldwin Piano, Inc.; L. Bösendorfer Klavierfabrik GmbH; Steinway Musical Instruments, Inc.

FURTHER READING

"Blüthner Piano Bids for U.S. Market," *Music Trades,* February 1999, p. 192.

"Investment Potential Is Music to the Ears," *Africa News Service,* August 7, 2002.

"Making the Sound of Music," *Economist,* June 5, 2003.

Protzman, Ferdinand, "Keeping in Step in a Free Market," *New York Times,* October 15, 1991, p. D1.

Purkiss, Alan, "The Prodigals Come in from the Cold," *Director,* September 1992, p. 54.

Kawai Musical Instruments Manufacturing Co., Ltd.

---

200 Terajima-cho
Hamamatsu, Shizuoka, 430-8665
Japan
Telephone: (81) 053 457 1213
Fax: (81) 053 457 1305
Web site: http://www.kawai.co.jp

Public Company
Founded: 1927 as Kawai Musical Instruments Research
    Institute
Employees: 2,780
Sales: $639.9 million (2005)
Stock Exchanges: Tokyo
Ticker Symbol: KWMS F
NAIC: 339992 Musical Instrument Manufacturing

■ ■ ■

Kawai Musical Instruments Manufacturing Co., Ltd. is second only to Yamaha Corporation in global sales of musical instruments. The Japanese company's core business is the manufacture and marketing of pianos, ranging from less expensive upright and grand pianos to the Shigeru Kawai handcrafted concert grand, one of the most expensive pianos on the market, priced around $65,000. Kawai also makes electronic pianos, electronic organs, synthesizers, guitars, percussion instruments, sells scores and records, offers tuning and repair services, and runs a music school. In addition, the company operates gymnastic schools and sells computers and peripheral devices, sporting goods, leisure-related goods, environmental cleaning supplies, and wood fabricating and metal fabricating devices. Kawai is a public company, listed on the Tokyo Stock Exchange.

ORIGINS

Kawai Musical Instrument Manufacturing Co. was founded by Koichi Kawai. The son of a wagon maker, born in Hamamatsu, Japan, in 1886, Koichi displayed an inventive spirit in his early years. As a youngster he made his own pedal-driven cart and caught the attention of a neighbor, a watchmaker by training who was forced to repair medical equipment to make a living and by chance was enlisted to repair a U.S. reed organ. In 1889 the neighbor launched his own organ manufacturing company, but as the upright piano began to supplant the reed organ in the marketplace, he turned his attention to the development of his own piano using imported parts. It was during this struggle to build a piano that he spied 12-year-old Koichi Kawai riding his pedal contraption. The neighbor's name was Torakusu Yamaha, remembered today as one of the pioneers of the piano industry. He took Kawai under his wing, making him his apprentice, and during the initial decades of the 1900s Kawai played a key role in the research and development efforts of Yamaha's Nippon Gakki Co., which resulted in pianos that won numerous international awards.

Yamaha died in 1917, new management took over, and the company prospered through 1921. Nippon Gakki then experienced a string of setbacks over the next five years: the rising value of the yen that made its products less competitive internationally, a fire and earthquake that damaged or destroyed company facilities, and a crippling labor strike. By 1927 Nippon Gakki was on the verge of ruin, a new president was installed, and the company was reorganized. In that same year, Koichi Kawai decided to strike out on his own and along with seven colleagues left Nippon Gakki to form the Kawai Musical Instrument Research Laboratory in Hamamatsu to design his own piano.

Koichi Kawai soon produced a breakthrough, becoming the first Japanese piano maker to design and build a piano action. Prior to then, Japanese piano makers had to import piano actions from the United States or Germany. By making his own action, Kawai would be able to competitively price his pianos. A year after building the action, Kawai began producing upright pianos. Eighteen months later, he completed his first grand piano. In 1929 the company changed its name to Kawai Musical Instruments Manufacturing Co. Its corporate structure was expanded to partnership status in 1935, and the company took the name of Kawai Musical Instruments Manufacturing, Ltd. In 1930 the company also began to produce reed organs.

PIANO PRODUCTION RESUMES AFTER WORLD WAR II

Japan's economy went on a war footing in 1937 as Japan invaded China, a conflict that began the country's involvement in what would escalate into World War II. Until the end of the war in 1945, Kawai factories produced aircraft parts instead of pianos and organs. With much of Japan's infrastructure devastated, it wasn't until 1948 that Kawai could resume the production of pianos and organs. Within a few years the company was thriving once again, turning out more than 1,500 pianos per year and employing 500 people. The company was incorporated in Japan in May 1951 and took its present name. Kawai built his first concert grand piano in 1952, and his efforts in the field were recognized a year later when he was awarded the Blue Ribbon Medal of Honor from the Emperor, the first person in the piano industry to be recognized. Two years later, in October 1955, Koichi Kawai passed away at the age of 70.

Kawai's 33-year-old son, Shigeru Kawai, took charge of the company his father had founded and transformed

it into a contemporary enterprise, combining his father's handcraftsmanship with modern manufacturing techniques. He established the Arai lumber processing plant in 1957 to supply materials to a new piano assembly plant, which opened four years later and featured a truly modern production line for the first time in company history. While increasing production capacity, Shigeru Kawai took steps to build demand for the company's output. In 1956 he launched the company's music education program, establishing a chain of Kawai Music schools, and to staff them with qualified teachers he began the Kawai Academy of Music. The company developed a door-to-door sales program to push piano lessons and generate piano sales, and within a few years some 2,000 sales representatives combed the country and more than 300,000 Japanese were enrolled in Kawai music schools. To make sure that the pianos the company sold would be used and enjoyed by its customers, Kawai also founded the Kawai Piano Technical Center, which trained technicians to tune and service pianos. In 1959 Kawai became involved in the direct retailing of pianos by opening its own stores, which in addition to selling pianos also serviced them.

Kawai introduced its first electronic organ to the market in 1960. Kawai became a public company in 1961, its stock listed on the Tokyo Stock Exchange. With the company now well established in its home market, Shigeru Kawai set his sights overseas, in particular the United States. In May 1963 Kawai America Corp. was launched. More foreign subsidiaries would soon follow in Australia and Asia. In 1975 Kawai Canada was established, followed a year later by Kawai Deutschland GmbH, located in West Germany. In 1979 Kawai Europe GMbH was formed, also based in West Germany in Dusseldorf. Along the way, Kawai introduced a number of innovations and key products. In 1968 the company introduced its ABS Styran action flanges, replacing some wooden parts in the piano action with longer-lasting, stronger plastic parts that better resisted warping, shrinking, and swelling caused by moisture. Kawai unveiled a transparent grand piano in 1971, and a year later introduced its KG-series of midrange priced grand pianos. A top-end line of hand-built grands, the GS-series, was introduced in 1979.

Kawai began the 1980s with the opening of a new $50 million 300,000-square-foot facility, the Ryuyo Grand Piano Factory & Research Center, capable of turning out more than 60 grand pianos per day. It was here a year later that the company began to build its EX Concert Grands. In 1984 Kawai began the assembly of pianos in Los Angeles on a limited basis, and as the yen rose in value the company elected to build a full-scale plant in Lincolnton, North Carolina, in 1988, which operated under a new subsidiary, Kawai America

KEY DATES

1927: Company founded as Kawai Musical Instruments Research Institute by Koichi Kawai.
1929: Name is changed to Kawai Musical Instruments Manufacturing Company.
1948: Production is resumed after World War II.
1955: Shigeru Kawai succeeds father after Koichi Kawai's death.
1963: Kawai America established.
1979: Kawai Europe launched.
1985: The first digital piano is offered.
1989: Third generation assumes presidency.
1995: RX-series of grand pianos launched.
2002: Shigeru Kawai EX Concert Grand unveiled.

Manufacturing Inc. On the technical side, Kawai in 1981 introduced the EX Concert Grand, which would serve as an opportunity for Kawai to launch innovations, such as carbon "Black Jacks" (a part of the piano action) in 1983. Also of note, Kawai unveiled its first digital piano in 1985. Furthermore, it was during the 1980s that Kawai started several new subsidiaries. In 1980 Kawai Precision Metal Co., Ltd. was formed to bring even more of the piano making process in house. A pair of units was launched in 1985: Kawai Distribution Service Co., Ltd. and Kawai Business Software Co., Ltd., which provided the company with some diversification. Then, in 1989, it formed Japan Leisure Development Co., Ltd. to become involved in leisure and sporting goods.

NEW LEADERSHIP: 1990-2000

A third generation took over the presidency in 1989 when Hirotaka Kawai succeeded his father, who now assumed the chairmanship of the company. Like his father and grandfather, Hirotaka was eager to modernize the piano building process. Under his leadership, Kawai moved into the 1990s by investing tens of millions of dollars to introduce robotics. He also oversaw the launch of manufacturing operations in Malaysia, forming Kawai Asia Manufacturing Sdn. Bhd. in 1991. The Kawai America Manufacturing subsidiary also established Kawai Finishing Inc. in November 1995, and subsequently acquired Continental Finishing Inc., based in Greer, South Carolina, which began producing polyester-coated piano parts under the Kawai Finishing name.

Kawai joined forces with Steinway & Sons in 1991, agreeing to manufacture a new, mid-priced piano line

under the Boston Piano label, in the $8,000 to $15,000 price range, designed by Steinway engineers. The pianos would also be sold through Steinway's global network of dealers. For Steinway the Boston line helped it to better compete in the midprice range, now crowded with Japanese and Korean imports. The contract helped Kawai to broaden its manufacturing base and make use of excess production capacity.

Kawai also added to its own product lines in the 1990s. It introduced the GM-series in 1992 with the GM1, which added a new low price point to Kawai's grand piano offerings. The GM pianos were smaller than the other grands, but offered much of the same styling and quality of its larger counterparts. Nevertheless, the baby grands were an entry level line for Kawai's grand piano lineup. On the other end of the scale, Kawai launched its RX-series of grand pianos in 1995. The 5'10" piano offered the best of Kawai technology and was geared for use at home as well as school, church, and teaching studios. In the upright category, Kawai, along with Yamaha, introduced its "silent" piano in 1993 in Japan, offering an option that made the piano only audible through headphones. It was marketed to people concerned about disturbing their family or neighbors—a major problem given the population density of Japan. According to the *Wall Street Journal,* Kawai and Yamaha once "benefited from a generation of baby boomers longing to be rock stars or the next classical sensation. Today, most silent-piano customers are these formerly rebellious noisemakers, looking to buy a quiet instrument for their children."

With the new century Kawai looked to compete with the most prestigious piano companies in the world at the upper reaches of the market. In 2000 it introduced the Shigeru Kawai limited production series of grand pianos, named after its chairman, offering a number of handcrafted features. Moreover, owners received a visit from one of the company's "Master Piano Artisans," who would apply concert-level voicing, regulation, and tuning to the instruments. But after years of establishing itself in the marketplace on the basis of value, Kawai faced a difficult challenge in changing the perception of the brand. The company persevered, however. It added to its initial three models with the Shigeru Kawai Classic Noblesse in 2001, followed a year later by the Shigeru Kawai EX Concert Grand, which the company promoted by providing it to the Rachmaninoff International Piano Competition, where it was used for all levels of competition. Also of note in the early years of the 2000s, Kawai established the Shigeru Kawai Foundation, its mission to "perpetuate music education and acknowledge significant contributions to the musical arts." The first artists to be honored were Broadway star John Raitt and Elmer Bernstein, an Oscar-winning composer of more than 200 film scores.

Kawai and its rivals had to contend with a slip in demand for pianos in Japan in the 2000s, forcing the company to launch a restructuring effort that was scheduled to be completed by early 2007. The plan called for the phaseout of the Maisaka upright piano plant, with production transferred to an Indonesian facility established in 2001. The company also planned to close its upright piano manufacturing plant in North Carolina. Kawai hoped to make up for lost business at home by focusing more attention on the rapidly growing Chinese market. In 2004 Kawai began to build a piano parts plant in China and by 2007 hoped to have a complete piano plant in operation.

Ed Dinger

PRINCIPAL SUBSIDIARIES

Kawai America Corporation; Kawai Deutschland GmbH; Kawai Europe GmbH; Kawai Asia Manufacturing Sdn. Bhd.; Kawai Finishing Inc.; MIDI Music Center Inc.; Kawai Australia Pty. Ltd.

PRINCIPAL COMPETITORS

Kimball International, Inc.; Yamaha Corporation; Steinway Musical Instruments, Inc.

FURTHER READING

"Individuals Who Made a Difference," *Music Trades,* Annual 1991, p. 202.

"Kawai Brings New Price Points to Grand Piano Market," *Music Trades,* March 1992, p. 168.

"Kawai Celebrates 10 Years of U.S. Piano Production," *Music Trades,* November 1998, p. 106.

"Kawai Musical Instruments Manufacturing Co. Sees 7 Billion Yen Net Loss," *Kyodo News International,* March 30, 2004.

"Kawai Restructures Manufacturing," *Music Trades,* June 2004, p. 42.

"Kawai Unveils Premium Pianos, Honors Bernstein & Raitt," *Music Trades,* March 2000, p. 137.

Sapsford, Jathon, "These Pianos Are Perfectly Tuned for Fans of the Sounds of Silence," *Wall Street Journal,* August 25, 1994, p. B1.

"Steinway to Distribute Kawai-Built Piano," *Music Trades,* April 1991, p. 104.

Klasky Csupo, Inc.

6353 Sunset Boulevard
Hollywood, California 90028
U.S.A.
Telephone: (323) 468-2600
Fax: (323) 468-2675
Web site: http://www.klaskycsupo.com

Private Company
Incorporated: 1982
Employees: 300 (2005 est.)
Sales: $30 million (2005 est.)
NAIC: 512110 Motion Picture and Video Production;
512191 Teleproduction and Other Postproduction
Services; 512199 Other Motion Picture and Video
Industries; 512220 Integrated Record Production/
Distribution

■ ■ ■

Klasky Csupo, Inc. is one of Hollywood's leading
independent animation studios. The firm's work includes
television programs like *Rugrats* and *The Wild Thornberrys* and their spinoff feature films, as well as commercials,
animated title sequences, and music videos. Klasky
Csupo also operates a publishing division and two record
companies, Tone Casualties and Casual Tonalities, which
feature electronic, ambient, and experimental music.
The privately held firm is owned by founders and co-
chairpersons Gabor Csupo and Arlene Klasky.

ORIGINS

Klasky Csupo was founded in 1982 by the husband-
and-wife team of Arlene Klasky and Gabor Csupo
(pronounced Chew-po). Born in Hungary in 1952,
Csupo had studied both music and animation before
escaping his Communist homeland in 1975 by way of
Yugoslavia. After spending time in a German refugee
camp he settled in Sweden, where in 1979 he met
graphic designer Klasky, who was there on vacation.
They fell in love, and after he moved to join her in
California, they were married.

Csupo initially found work animating episodes of
Scooby-Doo for Hanna-Barbera, but after being laid off,
he, Klasky, and two partners decided to start an
animation/graphic design firm in the couple's spare
bedroom. They soon began working on commercials,
title sequences, and other projects, and in 1987 the busy
company moved to larger quarters.

In 1988 the firm animated a series of one-minute
shorts for *The Tracy Ullman Show* called "The Simpsons."
Though created by Matt Groening, many key design
elements were the work of Klasky Csupo, including the
characters' yellow skin tones and mother Marge's blue
hair. The shorts were a hit, and, after a one-hour musical special for HBO, the program began running in
December of 1989 on the Fox network as a half-hour
situation comedy.

RUGRATS DEBUTS IN 1991

In 1989 the firm also began work on a new series called
Rugrats for the Nickelodeon cable network, which

KEY DATES

1982: Klasky Csupo founded in Los Angeles.
1988: Firm wins assignment to animate *The Simpsons*.
1991: *Rugrats* debuts on Nickelodeon.
1994: Adult cartoon Duckman bought by USA Network; record company formed.
1995: Commercial production unit launched.
1996: Three-year "first look" agreement signed with MTV Networks.
1998: *The Rugrats Movie* tops $100 million at U.S. box office; *Wild Thornberrys* debuts on Nickelodeon.
1999: Move to new five-story headquarters building.
2000: Second Rugrats film, *Rugrats in Paris*, released.
2002: Broadcast Design unit formed; Wild Thornberrys feature film released.
2003: *All Grown Up* begins airing on Nickelodeon; *Rugrats Go Wild* film released.
2005: *Rugrats: Tales from the Crib* DVD series debuts.

---

had recently committed $40 million to producing original animation for children. Co-created with Paul Germain, it debuted in 1991 and quickly became a Saturday morning hit. Based on a simple premise ("If babies could talk, what would they say?"), *Rugrats* featured an infant's view of the world, rendered in a distinctive two-dimensional, Eastern European animation style. Big-headed, bald, diapered Tommy Pickles; nervous, orange-haired Chuckie; and twins Phil and Lil got into mischief or were tormented by three-year-old Angelica while their oblivious parents and grandfather went about their own business. The look of the show and its characters was largely the work of Csupo, while Klasky took charge of their story lines. *Rugrats* also featured a distinctive keyboard-based music score courtesy of former Devo front man Mark Mothersbaugh, whose work had come to the attention of Csupo via an experimental solo album.

Klasky Csupo's other work of this period included music videos for Luther Vandross and the Beastie Boys, title sequences for shows like *21 Jump Street* and *In Living Color,* and numerous short segments for *Sesame Street.* The growing company moved to a new, larger space in Hollywood in 1990.

In 1991 Klasky Csupo began using computers to color its cartoons, after scanning black and white line drawings into data files. The company did not generate each animation cell, but rather produced a series of key images for its Korean subcontractors. Those firms then hand-drew and inked up to 23,000 separate pictures that were shot sequentially to yield 22 minutes of action.

In 1992 the studio spent $400,000 of its own funds to produce a 16-minute animated pilot film called *Duckman, Private Dick, Family Man,* which was based on cartoonist Everett Peck's edgy comic about a cigar-smoking, foulmouthed duck. Despite the familiar voice of Seinfeld actor Jason Alexander, the adult-themed show was initially turned down by the networks. The year also saw the loss of Simpsons animation work, which was shifted to a company called Film Roman. In 1993, a new Klasky Csupo series debuted on Nickelodeon. *AAAHH!! Real Monsters!* followed the adventures of a group of young monsters who were learning to scare humans. The year also saw production of "Recycle Rex," a ten-minute educational film for Disney, and a pair of half-hour specials that featured comedian Lily Tomlin's Edith Ann character for ABC.

DUCKMAN DEBUTS ON USA IN 1994

March of 1994 saw the USA Network primetime debut of *Duckman,* which was lauded by critics and began a two-season run. As with *Rugrats,* the studio had turned to a subversive popular musician for the soundtrack, Csupo's longtime inspiration and friend Frank Zappa. Though Zappa had died of cancer in December of 1993, his music was adapted for the series' first season, and his son Dweezil was asked to voice one of the characters.

The popularity of *Rugrats* reached critical mass in 1994 when reruns began appearing on Nickelodeon weeknights at 7:30, in addition to Saturday mornings. The show had already been recognized with two daytime Emmy awards, and it became the network's signature program, as well as inspiring a flood of spinoff products. Nickelodeon was running only the 65 episodes it had already commissioned, however, and, except for primetime specials, no new episodes would be made by Klasky Csupo for several years.

In November 1994 former Will Vinton Entertainment head Terry Thoren was named president and CEO of the studio, with Klasky and Csupo taking the roles of co-chairpersons. His goal was to expand the firm's activities into feature films, video games, and other new media projects. By now the company had assembled a large staff of animators, which ranged from recent film school graduates to Eastern European émigrés.

The year 1994 also saw Gabor Csupo found a record label called Tone Casualties to issue recordings of ambient and experimental music, including some of his own work. Two years later a more commercial sublabel, Casual Tonalities, was added as well.

In 1995 a new children's cartoon called *Santo Bugito* debuted on CBS, which had financed it with ITV and Nickelodeon UK. The program about cartoon bugs living on the Mexican/U.S. border was the first to be owned by Klasky Csupo, bringing potentially lucrative licensing rights, but it was cancelled after just 13 episodes.

KLASKY CSUPO COMMERCIALS FOUNDED IN 1995

Klasky Csupo now employed 200 and had annual revenues estimated at more than $21 million, of which 10 percent or more came from commercials. In 1995 a separate unit, Klasky Csupo Commercials, was formed to take on more of this work. The company was producing ads for agencies that represented such major firms as MCI and Oscar Mayer.

In 1996 the studio signed a three-year "first look" agreement with Viacom unit MTV Networks, whose holdings included Nickelodeon, MTV, HBO, UPN, and Comedy Central. A feature film version of Rugrats was now on the drawing board, which would be released by Viacom division Paramount Pictures. The firm's contract was later extended to five years, with movie development and production made exclusive as well.

In early 1997 Csupo and Klasky divorced, though they continued to work together. At this time the Hungarian animator was opening an art gallery/performance space/restaurant called Lumpy Gravy with his soon-to-be second wife, but it lost money and was closed after two years. In that same year the firm invested several million dollars in new computer equipment so that it could create high-definition animation suitable for conversion to 35-millimeter motion picture film, as it geared up to complete the *Rugrats* feature. During the year production of new *Rugrats* episodes started up again, but *Duckman* and *AAAHH!! Real Monsters!* were cancelled.

In 1998 a new Klasky Csupo series called *The Wild Thornberrys* debuted on Nickelodeon. It followed the story of children whose parents hosted a nature-themed TV show and traveled around the world, with 12-year old Eliza able to communicate with animals. The show became a hit, and it would be produced for a number of seasons.

THE RUGRATS MOVIE TOPS $100 MILLION IN 1998

On November 20, 1998 *The Rugrats Movie* debuted around the United States. Opening weekend ticket sales for the $25 million film were an impressive $27.3 million, and it went on to top $100 million in the United States and Canada, becoming the first non-Disney animated feature to reach this mark.

Other projects at this time included the first of several 40-minute cartoons starring McDonald's clown Ronald McDonald that were sold on videotape at the restaurant chain, and *Stressed Eric,* a downbeat adult show produced for the BBC. Despite critical accolades, only six episodes were produced by Klasky Csupo and American networks expressed little interest in the series. The company also changed the name of its animation unit to the phonetically accurate Class-Key Chew-Po Commercials during 1998.

In August of 1999 a new Nickelodeon show called *Rocket Power* was introduced. Aimed at preteens, it involved a group of surfers and skateboarders growing up in Southern California, and proved a hit with its intended audience. The year also saw the firm move to a five-story building on Sunset Boulevard in Hollywood, which featured Cooltoons, a store that sold its products.

In November 2000 Klasky Csupo's second film, *Rugrats in Paris,* was released, and the $30 million feature went on to take in $76.5 million at the box office in North America. The fall of 2000 also saw the debut of *As Told by Ginger,* a new series produced for Nickelodeon about a teenage girl dealing with the pitfalls of life in junior high school. It proved popular with teens as well as critics, and received an Emmy nomination.

In 2001 Rugrats celebrated its tenth year on television, and the show was honored with a star on the Hollywood Walk of Fame. It was now seen weekly by 27 million viewers, making it the top children's program in both the cable and broadcast arenas. It had been translated into 30 languages for broadcast in 75 countries, and its popularity was a key factor in making Nickelodeon the number one cable network in the United States, with one-third more viewers than nearest competitor TBS, and more than double the total of the Disney Channel.

KA-CHEW!, GLOBAL TANTRUM FORMED IN 2001

In 2001 Klasky Csupo also formed a new live-action commercial division to focus on the youth and young adult markets, Ka-Chew!, as well as Global Tantrum, a new adult film unit that would produce either animated or live-action features. The latter had been created in part to give the firm's artists additional creative outlets, with the first announced project a film based on the writings of underground L.A. poet Charles Bukowski.

In the fall of 2002 Klasky Csupo had three of the ten most popular Saturday children's programs on television, and two of the ten most popular weekday ones. Merchandise sales and other tie-ins to the company's creative properties like *Rugrats* and *The Wild Thornberrys* had accounted for $3.7 billion in sales since the start of 1997, but the firm's cut was small compared with Nickelodeon's.

In September 2002 a story about Klasky Csupo's alleged dissatisfaction with Viacom appeared in *Forbes*. The firm's contract, under which it was paid $450,000 per 22-minute episode, was about to expire, and it was reportedly seeking a larger share of the profits its work brought via syndication through the media giant's various outlets. The article also reported that the company had hired auditors to examine Paramount's books, as it was disputing the share of profits it had received from the two Rugrats movies. The first look contract with MTV Networks limited its ability to perform work for other networks as well, and a recent order of just 20 new cartoon episodes (down from 76 several years earlier) had forced the company to lay off 75 of its staff of 350 animators. However, two weeks after the story was published Csupo told *Variety* that there was no bad blood between the firms.

In late December of 2002 *The Wild Thornberrys Movie* was released, though its business did not approach that of the Rugrats films and it earned just under $40 million in North America. Also in 2002 Klasky Csupo Broadcast Design unit was formed to create animated graphics like the opening segment of MTV's *The Osbournes*. It would later be merged with the firm's commercials unit to operate under the Ka-Chew! banner.

In the summer of 2003 a combined Rugrats/ Thornberrys film, *Rugrats Go Wild*, was released. It, too, peaked at $40 million in ticket sales, despite the presence of celebrity guest voices and the gimmick of "scratch and sniff" cards given away at Burger King and Blockbuster outlets. The firm's recently announced plans to build a ten-story building adjacent to its studio and to hire 750 more employees to work on features were subsequently put on hold.

ALL GROWN UP BEGINS RUN IN 2003

In 2003 a new series, *All Grown Up*, began airing on Nickelodeon. Based on a 2001 Rugrats two-part special called "All Growed Up," it continued the Rugrats' story

with teenaged versions of the same characters, making its debut as the *Rugrats* series itself was officially declared at end. The company's TV animation business was now hurting, in large part due to the success of its long-term employer. Nickelodeon's biggest current hit, *SpongeBob SquarePants,* had come from its own in-house animation studio, and that unit was churning out many of the network's series in place of independent firms like Klasky Csupo.

In 2005 the irrepressible Rugrats appeared once again with a new series of special shows, *Tales from the Crib,* which would feature reworked versions of classic fairy tales. The first, *Snow White,* was aired on Nickelodeon in September and was simultaneously offered for sale on a Paramount DVD, which included two episodes of a Rugrats spinoff called *Pre-School Daze* that had never been used. The year also saw CEO Terry Thoren leave to form a new company of his own, Vibrant Animation. During his 11-year tenure at Klasky Csupo, the firm had produced more than 610 episodes of TV animation, 4 feature films, 14 television pilots, 600 commercials, and 66 music CDs, with another 175 TV and movie projects put into development.

In early 2006 Gabor Csupo took on an outside project for Walt Disney Pictures, directing a live-action film called *The Bridge to Terabithia.* It was based on the Newbery Award-winning book by Katherine Paterson about two children who created an imaginary world.

Nearly a quarter century after its founding, Klasky Csupo, Inc. had established itself as one of the leading independent animation firms in Hollywood, with a string of successful television programs, feature films, commercials, and other work to its credit. The vagaries of television broadcasting had reduced its presence on Saturday mornings, but the firm still had many projects in the pipeline, including animated films for adults.

Frank Uhle

PRINCIPAL SUBSIDIARIES

Ka-Chew!; Tonal Casualties; Klasky Csupo Publishing; Global Tantrum.

PRINCIPAL COMPETITORS

Nickelodeon Animation Studios; The Walt Disney Studios; Sony Pictures Animation; DreamWorks Animation SKG, Inc.; Blue Sky Studios, Inc.

FURTHER READING

Byrnes, Nanette, "The Rugrats' Real Mom and Dad," *Business Week*, October 16, 1995, p. 143.

Cheplic, Matt, "Baby Talk: Making Music-and Mayhem-for Rugrats," *Millimeter*, November 30, 1997.

De Laveaga, Allison, "Color Crew Tunes Up 'The Simpsons' with Mac Palette," *MacWeek*, December 10, 1991, p. 22.

Hall, Lee, "Surf's Up on Nickelodeon," *Electronic Media*, August 16, 1999, p. 32.

Jones, Malcolm, Jr., and Corie Brown, "Chuckie, Phil, Lil—You're Wanted on the Set!," *Newsweek*, November 23, 1998.

Keveney, Bill, "Nickelodeon Comes of Age," *USA Today*, January 12, 2001, p. 1E.

Kit, Zorianna, "Csupo Making 'Monkeys' Out of Comic Book," *Hollywood Reporter*, September 25, 2003, p. 1.

"Klasky Csupo at 20: Animation Powerhouse Spreads Wings As It Grows Up," *Variety*, September 30, 2002, p. A1.

"Klasky Csupo Celebrates 15 Years of Animation Innovation," *Variety*, May 19, 1997, p. A1.

Kuklenski, Valerie, "Growing Pains," *Los Angeles Daily News*, July 21, 2001, p. L3.

Littleton, Cynthia, "Global Tantrum Launches with Bukowski Ani," *Hollywood Reporter*, August 20, 2001, p. 1.

Marlowe, Chris, "Klasky Csupo Bows Tantrum," *Hollywood Reporter*, April 27, 2004.

McNary, Dave, "'Rugrats' Franchise Could Pose Credible Challenge to Disney," *Los Angeles Daily News*, March 23, 1999, p. B1.

Parisi, Paula, "'Duckman' in USA Net's Blind," *Hollywood Reporter*, July 16, 1993, p. 3.

———, "MTV to Unleash 'Monsters'," *Hollywood Reporter*, January 25, 1994, p. 8.

Sharkey, Betsy, "Drawing Powers," *MediaWeek*, April 16, 1996.

Susman, Gary, "Animation Upstart Does It with Style," *Irish Times*, February 11, 2003, p. 14.

Walley, Wayne, "When East Meets West—Animators' Backgrounds Add New Perspective," *Electronic Media*, May 2, 1994.

Williams, Elisa, "Attack of the Rugrats," *Forbes*, September 16, 2002, p. 44.

Lufkin Industries, Inc.

——— ▪ ———

601 South Raguet
Lufkin, Texas 75904
U.S.A.
Telephone: (936) 634-2211
Fax: (936) 637-5272
Web site: http://www.lufkin.com

Public Company
Incorporated: 1902
Employees: 2,300
Sales: $492.2 million (2005)
Stock Exchanges: NASDAQ
Ticker Symbol: LUFK
NAIC: 333911 Pump and Pumping Equipment Manufacturing

■ ■ ■

Based in Lufkin, Texas, Lufkin Industries, Inc., is a public company best known for its counterbalanced pumping unit, the "pumpjack," used in oil fields around the world. The pump's bobbing hammerhead-shaped counterweight has fascinated filmmakers over the years and achieved almost iconic status. All told, Lufkin's Oil Field Division accounts for more than 60 percent of all sales. The division also refurbishes and sells used pumping units and offers installation, field service, and machine shop repair. In addition, Lufkin maintains a Power Transmission Division, which manufactures and services enclosed gear drives for industrial applications such as pumping, power generation, mining, steel and aluminum mills, rubber mills, sugar milling, and cement

mills. Lufkin also operates a Trailer Division, manufacturing and servicing highway freight-hauling trailers.

LUFKIN, TEXAS: 19TH CENTURY TIMBER TOWN

Lufkin Industries was founded in the East Texas town of Lufkin, which itself was founded in 1882 as a stop on the Texas Railway that ran from Houston to Shreveport, Louisiana. It was named after Abraham P. Lufkin, a prominent Galveston merchant, politician, and friend of the railroad's president. As a railroad stop, the town quickly became a commercial center, and lumber became its main trade. Three men came to dominate the business: German immigrant Joseph H. Kurth, Sr.; Sam Weiner, of German Jewish ancestry and raised in Mississippi; and Georgia-born Simon Wood Henderson, Sr. In 1890 they joined forces to form Angelina County Lumber Company, which ran a score of Texas sawmills. The railroad was key, because the mills could no longer rely solely on a local supply of lumber, and had to have materials shipped in. But there developed a need for a local source of parts to repair the sawmills and locomotives. Mills might be forced to shut down for several days before parts and equipment arrived from cities hundreds of miles away.

Frank Kavanaugh, Sr., and his son, Frank Kavanaugh, Jr., operated a small foundry and machine shop in Rusk, Texas, and recognized that the Lufkin sawmills offered a better opportunity for business. In 1901 they decided to move their operation to Lufkin and wrote to Kurth to enlist his help in organizing the venture. Together they would line up investors and customers, and in February 1902, the Kavanaughs, Kurth, Henderson, and Sam Weiner's brother, Eli Weiner, signed the company charter to create the Lufkin Foundry and Machine Shop, capitalized with $30,000. In a subsequent board of director's meeting, Kurth was named the company's first president, with the elder Kavanaugh named vice-president. With 30 years of experience in the foundry and machine field, he also was named the company's first general manager. Within a matter of months, the company was doing business in three frame buildings, offering repair services, a foundry department, blacksmith department, bronze and brass castings, mill supplies, and the buying and selling of used machinery.

A key hire for Lufkin in the early years was Walter Charles "W.C." Trout, who replaced Wiener as secretary in 1905. The 31-year-old Trout, Canadian born, came to the company from Milwaukee's Allis-Chalmers Company, where he designed and sold sawmills. In his mid-20s he came to the conclusion that he wanted to live and work in the South, convinced that conditions were better suited there for workers. According to his ideals, workers should be able to own their own homes, maintain their own gardens, and actively participate in their communities. In the South, he believed, the lower cost of living afforded such an opportunity, and when he was 31 he decided that Lufkin, Texas, was the place where his vision could be fulfilled. For Lufkin Foundry and Machine Company, the arrival of Trout was a godsend. Along with his father, he held a number of patents on sawmill equipment and he was a talented manager as well. In 1906 he succeeded Kavanaugh as general manager of the company, and because of the patents he brought, the company graduated from the repair of locomotives and sawmill equipment to the manufacture of sawmill equipment. By 1910 the company was generating more than $210,000 in sales. It continued to prosper with sawmill equipment over the

next decade, but in the 1920s the sawmill business declined while a new opportunity presented itself.

OIL INDUSTRY FOCUS

Cattle had been king in Texas in the 1800s, but in 1901 the state began a transformation with the discovery of oil at Spindletop. The following year saw another discovery in Saratoga, followed by Sour Lake in 1903, and Humble in 1905. Lufkin began servicing this rising industry in 1918 when it first offered refinery equipment. Then, in the 1920s the company directed even more of its focus on the industry. In 1923 it worked with W.H. Taylor of Gulf Production Company to develop the Lufkin-Taylor rotary drill, Lufkin's first oil field product line. It was followed by a new swivel, traveling and crown blocks, drilling draw works, pipeline fittings, and flanged fittings, as well as pressure-screwed end fittings for refineries.

To drum up oil business Trout made the rounds of the North Texas oil fields, where he listened to oilmen voice their frustrations with the standard pumping rigs, which had not changed much since the discovery of oil in Pennsylvania in the 1880s. These rigs relied on a wooden walking beam and sucker rods, powered by a slow-speed gas or oil engine, which turned a shaft by way of a pulley and flat belt. The spring afforded by the belt and the walking beam were intended to keep the sucker rods from breaking. But rain caused the belts to slip off, and the wooden walking beam was balanced with anything heavy at hand and was quite susceptible to breaking. It was obvious that a better rig was needed.

In 1923 Trout had lunch with the president of Humble Oil and Refining Company and future Texas governor, Ross Sterling, who told him about an experiment conducted by some Humble employees, who had rigged up the worm-geared differential from a tractor to a crank and a motor and pumped a shallow well for 18 months. Sterling challenged Trout to develop a worm-geared apparatus for a pumping rig, one that would be direct-drive, thus eliminating the need for a belt. Trout set to work and soon Lufkin developed the industry's first enclosed, geared oil-well pumping unit, which was set up on a Humble well and went into operation in the winter of 1923. Although the pumping unit was superior to the old rigs, it was not able to stand up to large amounts of water, which cracked shafts and damaged gears. The Lufkin unit appeared to be a costly failure, but Trout refused to give up and invested even more money in its development.

In 1925 Trout met with W.L. Todd, general manager of Simms Oil Company, who liked the geared unit but urged Trout to incorporate a counterbalancing mechanism. Out of this discussion Trout made sketches of a pumping unit with a counterbalanced crank. Back at the shop his people began working to turn his sketches into a viable machine, and in September 1925 a unit was put into a Humble well for a trial. With some adjustments the unit was perfectly balanced between the up and down strokes. It was the answer for which oilmen had been looking, but because of its odd appearance, the rig took some time to catch on.

It was not until the fall of 1926, when the Seminole, Oklahoma, oil field came in that it became widely accepted. It would soon become a standard unit around the world. A Lufkin unit also would hold the distinction of receiving the only stateside damage during World War II. In 1942 a Japanese submarine attempted to destroy the Ellwood oil field along California's coast, firing a pair of torpedoes. They only managed to damage a pumpjack and provide Lufkin with a unique souvenir.

When Kurth died in 1930, Trout succeeded him as Lufkin's president. He took over a company that was faring better than most during the early years of the Great Depression, precipitated by the 1929 stock market crash. Nevertheless, sales fell from $2.1 million in 1929 to $1.5 million in 1930, and less than $450,000 in 1931. The company was forced to shut down its plant in 1932 as it sold off inventory. Fortunately Lufkin had no debt and by 1934 was ready to expand again, opening a sales office in Dallas. The company also tried to diversify by acquiring the struggling Williams Gin Company, which now became the Lufkin Gin Company. When the bottom fell out of the price of cotton, however, the need for cotton gins evaporated and the business was soon shut down. Lufkin enjoyed better success with the 1939 acquisition of Martin Wagon and

Trailer Company, which like Lufkin began in the early 1900s serving the lumber industry. In addition to log wagons, Martin had made its mark with a pair of inventions: the Martin derailer and rerailer and Martin Grip hooks. The company went bankrupt in 1936, was reorganized, and attempted a comeback with the development of a dump trailer. Although the facilities and equipment were outdated, Trout believed that there was an opportunity in the truck industry and he pushed through the purchase of Martin.

Lufkin would soon find a military market for its trailer division with the advent of World War II in the 1940s. In fact, by 1943, about 85 percent of the company's business was war related. The company manufactured gears for Sherman tanks and landing crafts, three-pound cast iron practice bombs dropped by Navy aviators, and carriages for 155-millimeter Howitzers. In addition to truck trailers, the new trailer division manufactured gasoline transports and mobile laundry units.

POSTWAR EXPANSION

Following the war, Lufkin reached a milestone when Trout, whose health was failing, stepped down in 1947. He was succeeded by his son, Walter W. Trout. The company overcame a brief downturn in business, then enjoyed a long run of growth. By 1950 Lufkin tallied sales of nearly $13.7 million from its three divisions: Machinery, Trailer, and Mill Supplies. Lufkin pumpjacks were in use around the world, but the air tanks they used were built by a Houston company. In the 1950s, Lufkin invested in the necessary equipment and began producing its own tanks. The trailer division, in the meantime, benefited from the rise of the trucking industry, the growth of which was spurred by a massive government investment in highway construction. Lufkin began producing all-steel, stainless steel, and aluminum vans and semi-trailers. The Mill Supplies Division began looking to commercial gears for growth. What began after World War II grew in the early 1950s when Lufkin entered the marine gear field. Later in the decade the company expanded it gear-making facilities and offered a complete line of industrial gears, used in paper mills, sugar mills, rubber mills, pipeline pump stations, and chemical plants, as well as on ships and dredges. Also of note during the postwar years, Lufkin employees established a union in 1949 and two years later went on strike for 100 days. In 1954 the company instituted its first pension plan.

The early 1960s was a difficult period for the company. Not only was business in a slump, due in large part to a price war between pumping unit manufacturers, but Lufkin also had to contend with a

February 1961 fire that destroyed its main office. The company overcame these problems and by 1965 sales topped $41 million, of which a record $25 million came from the Machinery Division. Business was so strong, despite another long strike in 1966, that in 1967 Lufkin launched the largest capital expansion program in its history by constructing a new Trailer Division manufacturing facility at a cost of $6 million. The main plant was operational in 1969. Also in 1967 Walter Trout turned over the presidency to R.L. Poland and became Lufkin's first chairman of the board, a post he would hold only until his death in July 1971. Poland had joined the company as a mechanical engineer after serving a four-year stint in the Army during World War II.

In 1970 the company changed its name to Lufkin Industries, Inc., a reflection of successful diversification over the years. The company had become known as Lufkin Foundry, a name that had proven to be increasingly confusing to customers for trailers and precision gears. But Lufkin's main money maker continued to be the Machine Division, which was only one of two major companies now offering oil field pumping units. In 1974, when Lufkin sales first reached the $100 million mark and the company celebrated its 50th year in the pumping unit business, 70 percent of that amount came from the Machinery Division that manufactured the famous pumpjacks. Business continued to boom in the second half of the 1970s. In 1980 sales approached $274 million, of which the Machinery Division contributed 88 percent. It was also in the late 1970s that Lufkin completed its first acquisition since Martin Wagon in 1939, the $1.5 million purchase of Little Rock, Arkansas-based Midwest Casting Corporation in 1977. It mostly produced counterweights and auxiliary weights.

1980 AND BEYOND

Lufkin continued to expand in the early 1980s, adding a major extension to its machine shop in 1980, followed by a new $7.5 million gear manufacturing complex in 1981, which allowed the company for the first time to separate its pumping unit manufacturing operation from its industrial gear manufacturing. Construction of a $20 million large-castings foundry began in 1982. Company sales reached $364 million in 1981, but momentum would stall later in the decade due to a downturn in the oil field industry and years would pass before Lufkin again enjoyed sales at these levels.

By the 1990s the oil field equipment segment as well as the company's power transmission products were profitable, but the highway trailer business was struggling. Management elected to exit the trailer business in 1991 but by early 1994 it gave up on its efforts

to find a buyer and elected to retain the unit. In the meantime, the oil services industry suffered another slump, resulting in a 1993 restructuring effort that included staff reductions. In 1994 Lufkin sold its industrial supplies unit and one of its manufacturing facilities. Lufkin began to rebound in the second half of the 1990s. Sales reached $226 million in 1996 and improved to $287.6 million in 1997, when the company also posted net income of $14.8 million, the highest level since 1985. The year 1997 also saw Lufkin completing a pair of acquisitions that increased Lufkin's oil field service offerings: Fannie Lee Mitchell of Texas, Inc. and Nabla Corporation. Despite a slight downturn in business, three more acquisitions followed in 1998: Lone Star Machine Shop Inc., a Texas company supporting the oil and gas industries; French company COMELOR, maker of industrial gears; and Delta-X Corporation, a Houston supplier of oil-well automation technology.

Business continued to slide in 1999, when sales dipped to $242.5 million and the company posted a $1.3 million loss, but rebounded in 2000 and 2001, as revenues improved to $278.9 and net income totaled $19.5 million in 2001. The energy field was volatile, however, leading to a significant drop in business in 2002. Although sales fell to $228.7 million, Lufkin was still able to squeeze out a profit of $8.5 million. Business bounced back in 2003, and then record oil prices and an improved domestic economy in 2004 resulted in Lufkin's enjoying a bountiful year, with sales soaring to more than $356 million. The trend continued in 2005 when sales increased to $492.2 million and net income totaled $44.5 million.

Ed Dinger

PRINCIPAL SUBSIDIARIES

Lufkin Industries Canada, Ltd.; Lufkin France, EURL; Lufkin Argentina, S.A.; Lufkin Middle East.

PRINCIPAL COMPETITORS

Great Dane L.P.; Utility Trailer Manufacturing Co.; Weatherford International.

FURTHER READING

Bowman, Bob, "Inventing the Oilfield Pumping Unit," *Texas Escapes*, January 18-24, 2004.

Jackson, Elaine, *From Sawdust to Oil*, Houston: Gulf Publishing Company, 1982.

"Lufkin Industries Ends Effort to Find Buyer for Trailer Division," *Dow Jones News Service,* January 10, 1994.

Wilson, Nancy Croom, "Legacy to Lufkin," *Cox News Service,* December 11, 2005.

Magma Design
Automation Inc.

5460 Bayfront Plaza
Santa Clara, California 95054-3600
U.S.A.
Telephone: (408) 565-7500
Fax: (408) 565-7501
Web site: http://www.magma-da.com

Public Company
Incorporated: 1997
Employees: 624
Sales: $145.9 million (2005)
Stock Exchanges: NASDAQ
Ticker Symbol: LAVA
NAIC: 511210 Software Publishers

■ ■ ■

Based in Santa Clara, California, Magma Design Automation Inc. develops software that computer chip designers use to produce complex integrated circuits (ICs). ICs are interconnected layers of semiconductors—electronic components etched onto thin silicon chips that direct the passage of electrical current. They are used in computers, as well as a variety of electronic devices. Magma's electronic design automation (EDA) products, which improve chip performance and help manufacturers to get new chips onto the market faster, include Blast Create, Blast Plan, Blast Fusion, and Blast Noise. These applications are used by a number of leading firms within the technology and electronics industries, including Broadcom, NEC Electronics, Texas Instruments, and Toshiba. In addition to its California

headquarters, Magma has a number of other U.S. locations, including sites in Los Angeles, San Diego, and Orange County, California; Boston; Austin and Dallas, Texas; Durham, North Carolina; and Newcastle, Washington. Internationally, Magma maintains locations in the United Kingdom, Taiwan, The Netherlands, Korea, Japan, Israel, India, Germany, France, China, and Canada.

A SUBMICRON START: 1997-2000

Magma was founded by entrepreneur Rajeev Madhavan and three other EDA industry players: Lukas van Ginneken, Hamid Savoj, and Karen Vahtra. With Madhavan at the helm as CEO, the company raised $115 million in venture capital, which was in ample supply at the height of the dot-com craze.

After training at Bell Northern Research in Canada, Madhavan worked for Cadence Design Systems, performing due diligence reviews of companies that Cadence wanted to acquire. While performing this work, Madhavan was inspired to start his own firm. His entrepreneurial run began in 1992, when he played a role in starting LogicVision Inc., a firm that made chip testing tools. Two years later Madhavan started the EDA firm Ambit Design Systems Inc., which was eventually sold to Cadence for $260 million in cash.

Madhavan's next venture, Magma, was established in response to a pressing industry challenge. During the mid-to-late 1990s, computer chip designs were growing smaller (below 0.13 microns), and chip designers sought ways to fit more circuitry onto individual chips in order to expand their functionality. Existing chip design

---

COMPANY PERSPECTIVES

Magma's mission is to create and deliver the best EDA software products and solutions, encompassing IC design from concept to completion, enabling our customers' commercial success.

methods were increasingly ineffective, however, leading designers to engage in lengthy trial-and-error design processes that caused delays in getting new chips to market. According to the company, Magma was founded in April 1997 with a goal of "combining logic design and physical design into a single system to better address emerging deep submicron design challenges."

Cisco Systems Vice-President Andreas "Andy" Bechtolsheim provided the initial funding to start Magma, which established headquarters in Cupertino, California. This capital was immediately used to develop a product that stood out from the offerings of other industry players. As Magma President and Chief Operating Officer Roy Jewell explained in a November 29, 2005 interview with Chris Hall of DigiTimes.com: "What Rajeev did from Day 1 was establish a world-class R&D team, and our idea was to develop a system, built from the ground up, for IC designs that would incorporate processors at 0.13-micron and below. That meant that, in addition to active circuit components, the system looked at interconnects as an active part of the design and one that also had to be optimized."

In the same interview, Jewell shed some light on the company's strategy for acquiring customers, commenting: "We didn't try to take a shotgun approach in penetrating the market; rather, we tried to select some bigger customers that were right at the sweet spot of our technology. We would have some success with a customer and then build out a much broader business as a result of those successes. We were asked to tackle their hardest designs, the ones that were in trouble, and we went in and solved those problems and got those designs to market. From that success came bigger opportunities for engagement with those customers." Magma's first product, a physical design system called Blast Fusion, hit the market in April 1999—two years after the company was founded. In June the technology giant Intel made an undisclosed investment in Magma, and the firms began working to optimize Magma's products for computer workstations that used Intel's processors. Two months later the company formed Magma KK in Shin-Yokohama, Japan, to serve a growing customer base in

that country. Magma ended 1999 by gaining its largest customer to date, Fujitsu Microelectronics Inc., which reported great success in reducing design times with Blast Fusion.

While Magma's competitors were all working on the development of similar solutions, Madhavan insisted that his company's offering was superior because it was developed from scratch and was not a combination of existing tools. The company ended its 1999 fiscal year with a net loss of $9.27 million on sales of $226,000.

By 2000 Madhavan had raised approximately $54 million in investment capital and established Magma as a major EDA industry player. During its fiscal year the company recorded a net loss of $33.5 million on sales of $1.45 million. At this time, Magma charged approximately $1 million for a three-year Blast Fusion license. In addition to Fujitsu, the company counted such tech heavyweights as Texas Instruments, Sun Microsystems, and AMD as clients. The company added Japan's NEC IC Microcomputer Systems Ltd. to its client roster in June, signing a multiyear agreement to use Blast Fusion in the development of NEC's next-generation microprocessor cores.

Several other important developments also took place at Magma in June 2000. In addition to unveiling its Blast Chip and Blast Noise products, the company announced that it would merge with Moscape Inc., a technology firm that also focused on the issues chip developers faced when designing smaller ICs. According to the company, Moscape's technology eventually formed "the foundation for Magma's comprehensive design, analysis and implementation solutions." The merger was completed in November, at which time Magma announced that it had secured another $28 million in funding. Together, the two companies had raised a total of $91 million in funding.

LEGAL CHALLENGES: 2001 TO PRESENT

By 2001 the $35 billion semiconductor industry was in a downturn. From one standpoint this was a positive factor for Magma and other EDA firms, because during such times semiconductor companies focus on getting new products onto the market quickly to spark sales. With a net loss of $42.3 million on sales of $11.8 million in 2001, Magma needed this added momentum.

In May Magma announced its plans to become a publicly traded company. The company hoped that its initial public offering (IPO) would generate $55 million. Some observers speculated that the company's decision to go public came from investor pressure to raise cash. It also was in May 2001 that Magma gave Chief Operat-

KEY DATES

■

1997: Magma Design Automation is founded by Rajeev Madhavan and several other EDA industry players.

2001: The company completes its IPO, raising $63 million.

2005: Magma is ranked second on Forbes's list of the fastest-growing technology companies.

ing Officer Roy E. Jewell the added title of president. Jewell had joined the company two months before and possessed 12 years of EDA experience.

Although Magma faced stiff competition from big industry players such as Synopsys, Avanti, and Cadence, the company continued to make progress. After the June 2001 release of its Blast Plan design planning product, in October Magma announced that Toshiba America Electronics Components Inc. planned to deploy its software in Toshiba worldwide design centers. In addition, Magma inked a multiyear, multimillion-dollar deal to provide its design software to Broadcom Corp.

In November 2001 the press detailed a breach of contract lawsuit that San Mateo, California-based Prolific Inc. had filed against Magma. Prolific alleged that Magma had failed to pay $3.2 million in royalties for software that Prolific developed for use in Magma's Blast Fusion product. According to the November 19, 2001, issue of *Electronic News,* in addition to the $3.2 million Prolific sought additional compensation for "'willful, fraudulent, [and] oppressive' behavior, including Magma's allegedly false representations regarding 'the reliability, stability and customer base of Magma software.'"

Its legal entanglement aside, Magma ended 2001 on a high note. The company's November 20, 2001 IPO was a tremendous success, raising $63 million. Magma's shares, which were expected to be in the $9 to $11 range, went as high as $20 on the day of the IPO, closing at $18.

In March 2002, Magma ended its fiscal year on improved financial footing, reporting a net loss of $8.6 million on revenues of $46.4 million. In May of 2002 the editors of *Red Herring* magazine named the company to The Red Herring 100, an annual ranking that, according to a *Business Wire* release, "recognizes the top 50 public and the top 50 private companies whose services, business models, products and quality of management define business innovation."

Magma's legal situation with Prolific continued to escalate in mid-2002. After Magma filed a countersuit against Prolific in January over claims that Prolific's software did not work and that the company did not meet certain engineering obligations, Prolific filed an amended complaint in May, suing Rajeev Madhavan and ten other Magma board members and financial stakeholders for $100 million over charges that included breach of contract, libel, and defamation.

According to *Electronic News,* Prolific and other parties alleged "that Magma prevented the release of the Prolific software while it worked on its own route to the same end, which it called 'super cells,' and also maneuvered for Prolific competitor Cadabra, instead of Prolific, to be acquired for 20 million shares by Numerical Technologies." In the same article, Magma COO Roy Jewell described the lawsuit as "frivolous and an abuse of the legal system."

Other developments in 2002 included the opening of several new facilities, including sites in Taiwan and Korea. Magma ended the year by announcing the availability of its Blast Fusion APX, which offered a number of improvements over the previous version Blast Fusion.

New product introductions continued in 2003, including Blast Create and Blast Rail. That year, Magma went on an acquisition spree, acquiring Aplus Design Technologies in July, followed by Random Logic Corp. and Silicon Metrics in October. The latter acquisition led to the formation of Magma's Silicon Correlation Division. It also was in October of 2003 that Magma underwent a physical expansion by moving to a 130,000-square-foot facility in Santa Clara, California.

Internationally, in 2003 Magma announced plans to open sales and support offices in the Chinese cities of Beijing, Shanghai, and Shenzhen. In addition, the company indicated that it would invest $6.5 million over the following three years in India. In particular, Magma's plans included the establishment of an Indian research and development facility to serve that country's growing EDA market.

Magma's acquisition activity continued in 2004. In April the company completed its acquisition of Mojave Inc. in a cash and stock deal worth approximately $25 million. The acquisition allowed Magma to release a new IC design product called Quartz DRC. Performance milestones could make the deal worth as much as $115 million to Mojave shareholders through 2009.

Magma's revenues reached $113.7 million in 2004, up from $75.1 million the previous year. The company's net income also increased, from $3.1 million to $11.5 million. A number of new product introductions were made in 2004, including Quartz Formal and Blast Power.

That year, Magma inked a deal with the Chinese Academy of Science to establish a nanotechnology integrated circuit design lab.

Magma garnered recognition from Deloitte Technology in 2004 when the company ranked seventh on Deloitte's list of North America's fastest growing technology firms. Outside recognition continued into 2005. In addition to ranking first on *Electronic Business*'s list of "Best Small Electronics Companies" for the third consecutive year, Magma was listed second by *Forbes* on that publication's list of the fastest-growing technology companies.

Another legal entanglement came in September 2004 when Magma's competitor, Synopsys, sued Magma for patent infringement. Synopsys claimed that the patents in question were Synopsys property because Magma Chief Scientist Dr. Lukas van Ginneken, who was named as an inventor on the patents, conceived the inventions while working for Synopsys. Magma denied any wrongdoing in a December 5, 2005 *Business Wire* news release, claiming that Synopsys put the "inventions into the public domain well before Magma applied for its patents." Magma further asserted that "at least some of the patents' inventions were conceived by employees at Magma, giving Magma an ownership interest in the patents."

By mid-2005 the Synopsys situation had resulted in investors filing a class action lawsuit against Magma, claiming that company insiders concealed the risk the lawsuit presented to investors and, instead of admitting to it, sold 4.4 million shares of Magma stock while it was "artificially inflated," reaping profits of nearly $82.4 million.

In December 2005 the U.S. District Court for the District of Northern California announced that, instead of proceeding with a scheduled hearing, the court would rule on the patent case based on written records provided by each company. As of early 2006, the outcome of Magma's legal situation remained to be seen.

In 2005 Magma's revenue ($145.9 million) increased 28 percent over the previous year. As a whole, the EDA industry was growing at a rate of about 2.8 percent, based on Gartner Dataquest figures. In the aforementioned DigiTimes.com interview with Chris Hall, Magma President and COO Roy Jewell commented on his company's position during the mid-2000s, stating: "Today our customers are mainly in the wireless and consumer spaces, and that means our products have had to evolve. Our tools are still being applied to the most aggressive designs, but that aggressiveness is not simply defined by pure performance. Rather, that aggressiveness is defined by power optimiza-

tion, by being able to support a number of different functionalities on the same chip."

Paul R. Greenland

PRINCIPAL COMPETITORS

Synplicity; Synopsys, Inc.; SILVACO; Mentor Graphics; Intrinsix; Cadence Design Systems; Applied Wave Research; Ansoft; Agilent EEsof.

FURTHER READING

"A Scorching IPO for Magma," *Business Week,* December 3, 2001.

Hall, Chris, "The EDA Volcano: Q&A with Magma Design Automation," DigiTimes.com, November 29, 2005.

"Investor Notice: Murray, Frank & Sailer LLP Has Filed a Shareholder Class Action Against Magma Design Automation, Inc. – LAVA," *PrimeZone Media Network,* June 16, 2005.

"Magma and Chinese Academy of Science to Set Up Nanotechnology Lab," *China Business News,* February 5, 2004.

"Magma Completes Acquisition of Mojave," *Business Wire,* April 29, 2004.

"Magma Completes Merger with Moscape and Raises $28 Million in Funding," *Business Wire,* November 6, 2000.

"Magma Design Automation and Moscape Inc. Agree to Merge; Agreement Emphasizes Importance of Electrical Integrity Solutions for Complex Deep Sub-micron Design," *Business Wire,* June 5, 2000.

"Magma Design Automation Inc. to Invest US$6.5 MLN in India," *AsiaPulse News,* August 29, 2003.

"Magma IPO Raises $63M," *Electronic News,* November 26, 2001.

"Magma Makes van Ginneken Deposition Public; Includes Synopsys Threats to Sue van Ginneken for $200 Million," *Business Wire,* May 6, 2005.

"Magma Named to the Red Herring 100; Recognized by Red Herring Editors for Innovation and Business Strategy," *Business Wire,* May 13, 2002.

"Magma Ramps Up Sales and Support to Serve Japanese Semiconductor Industry; Magma KK Established with Support from SC Hightech," *Business Wire,* December 13, 1999.

"Magma Receives Intel Investment," *Semiconductor Industry & Business Survey,* June 1, 1999.

"Magma Reports Record Revenue and Pro Forma Profits for Fourth Quarter of Fiscal Year 2002," *Business Wire,* April 24, 2002.

"Magma Signs Broadcom to Multimillion-Dollar, Multi-Year Agreement for Deployment of Magma Software," *Business Wire,* October 31, 2001.

"Magma Strikes Deal for Mojave," *Daily Deal,* February 25, 2004.

"Magma to Speak at 'IC Design Forum' in Shanghai; Opening Direct Offices in China," *Business Wire,* August 29, 2003.

"Milberg Weiss Announces the Filing of a Class Action Suit Against Magma Design Automation Inc. and Certain of Its Officers and Directors on Behalf of Investors," *Business Wire,* June 14, 2005.

Morrison, Gale, "Magma Case Shows EDA's Nasty Side: As Allegations Grow, So Does the List of Players," *Electronic News,* May 20, 2002.

———, "Magma Hauls in Fujitsu," *Electronic News,* November 15, 1999.

———, "Magma Wins NEC Japan," *Electronic News,* June 19, 2000.

———, "Prolific Blasts Pre-IPO Magma: Company Is Cagey About Suit Specifics But Says It Wants More Than the $3 Million in Lawsuit," *Electronic News,* November 19, 2001.

"Motions in Magma-Synopsys Patent Case to Be Determined Without Oral Argument; Court Ruling Acknowledges

Magma As Owner of Record, Synopsys Might Demonstrate Co-Ownership," *Business Wire,* December 5, 2005.

Much, Marilyn, "Exec Has Designs on a Bigger Market Share," *Investor's Business Daily,* October 24, 2003.

Musero, Frank, "Magma Hopes to Melt Market Adage," *IPO Reporter,* May 28, 2001.

"Roy Jewell Promoted to President of Magma; Elected to the Magma Board of Directors," *Business Wire,* May 30, 2001.

Santarini, Michael, "Magma's IPO Plunge Seen As Test for EDA Firms," *Electronic Engineering Times,* May 21, 2001.

———, "Prolific Files $3.2M Suit Against Magma," *Electronic Engineering Times,* November 12, 2001.

"Synopsys Accused of Antitrust Violations in Magma Court Filing," *Business Wire,* October 19, 2005.

Takahashi, Dean, "How Hot Is Magma," *Electronic Business,* June 2000.

"Toshiba to Deploy Magma Software in Worldwide Design Centers; Effectiveness of Blast Fusion Validated on Three Toshiba Deep Submicron Designs," *Business Wire,* October 25, 2001.

Magyar Telekom Rt

Krisztina krt 55
Budapest,
Hungary
Telephone: (36) 06 1 457 4000
Fax: (36) 06 1 458 7176
Web site: http://www.matav.hu

Public Company
Incorporated: 1991
Employees: 13,724
Sales: EUR 2.5 billion ($3.05 billion) (2004)
Stock Exchanges: Budapest New York
Ticker Symbol: MTAV.B MTA.N
NAIC: 517110 Wired Telecommunications Carriers; 238210 Electrical Contractors; 423690 Other Electronic Parts and Equipment Merchant Wholesalers; 517212 Cellular and Other Wireless Telecommunications; 518111 Internet Service Providers

∎∎∎

Magyar Telekom Rt is Hungary's leading telecommunications provider. The former Hungarian state telecom monopoly has transformed itself into a modern, competitive company providing a full range of fixed-line residential and commercial and mobile telephone services, Internet access, including ADSL-based broadband services, and cable television services. Known as Matav until it changed its name in 2005, Magyar Telekom has also completed a re-branding of its services, adopting the brand of its majority shareholder,

Deutsche Telekom. Magyar's T-Mobile Hungary subsidiary provides GSM and 3G mobile telephony services to more than four million customers in Hungary, and its part of the T-Mobile Group, one of the world's largest mobile telephone service providers. The company's T-Com division provides wireline services including the T-Online internet service, wireless internet services, and T-Kabel, the second-largest cable television provider in Hungary. Magyar Telekom's corporate services are developed under its T-Systems unit, which includes telecommunications, IT infrastructure and outsourcing services. In addition to its domestic operations, Magyar Telekom has also been building its own international portfolio, through the acquisitions of Telekom Montenegro, MakTel, based in Macedonia, and Orbitel, a leading wireline and Internet service provider in Bulgaria. In February 2006, the company entered Romania, launching an entirely new service, Eufonika. Magyar Telekom is listed on the Budapest and New York stock exchanges; Deutsche Telekom owns more than 59 percent of the company's shares. Magyar Telekom is led by chairman of the board Elek Staub and posted revenues of EUR 2.5 billion ($3 billion) in 2005.

AUSTRIA-HUNGARY PTT BEGINNINGS IN THE 19TH CENTURY

Magyar Telekom, formerly known as Matav, inherited one of Central Europe's worst-performing telecommunications networks when it was privatized in the early 1990s. Yet Hungary had played a role in the beginnings of the international telecommunications industry in the late 1800s. Indeed, the technology behind the first telephone exchanges was developed by Hungar-

COMPANY PERSPECTIVES

We have reached a major milestone not only in the life of our company but also of domestic telecommunications since Hungary's largest re-branding ever started on May 6, 2005. The Magyar Telekom Group members T-Com, T-Online, T-Mobile, T-Systems and T-Kábel joined their skills to enable you to use the possibilities of communications in a more convenient and simpler way. With the re-branding a unique group of companies was created on the domestic telecommunications market: the T-brand represents the complete telecommunications portfolio. Today there is no telecommunications service in Hungary that this Group cannot provide.

ian inventor and Thomas Edison associate Tivadar Puskás. After installing the first telephone networks in London and Brussels in 1876, Puskás returned to Edison's laboratory in Menlo Park to develop his idea for a telephone exchange, which he completed, but did not patent, in 1877. In 1879, Puskás, joined by brother Ferenc, returned to Hungary with the exclusive rights to install telephone exchanges throughout the Austria-Hungary empire. The brothers at first sought investors in order to build a telephone network in Budapest; unable to find financial backing, the Puskás invested their own funds in the network. By 1881, the Budapest exchange was operational, becoming only the fourth telephone exchange in the world. Puskás later went on to install the first telephone network in Madrid, among other activities.

In 1887, the Austria-Hungarian government began exerting its control over the empire's growing telephone networks. As elsewhere in Europe, telephone and telegraph operations were then placed under the auspices of the post office, forming the empire's PTT. Further legislation passed in 1888 took the next step further, granting the PTT the monopoly over all of the empire's telephone, telegraph and post office operations, including the installation and operation of all telephone networks destined for public use. Development of the empire's telephone network continued under the PTT. In 1890, the capital cities of Vienna and Budapest had been connected by the first trunk line. By the middle of that decade, most of the major cities in the Austria-Hungarian empire had been connected to the telephone network. Nonetheless, penetration of telephone usage lagged far behind most of the empire's European counterparts.

With the breakup of the empire and Hungary's independence at the end of World War I, the new Hungarian Post Office was forced to rebuild its telephone, telegraph and postal networks. During the 1920s, the Hungarian Post installed a new 250-watt radio-telephone tower outside of Budapest and became the country's major radio broadcaster as well.

Following World War II, the Post Office was once again forced to rebuild the country's telephone infrastructure. Radio broadcasting resumed soon after, and in the 1950s, the Post Office became responsible for the country's television broadcasting as well. During the 1960s, the telephone network began adopting new telecommunications technologies. Yet investment in the expansion of the country's telephone network remained minimal, in part because of the Soviet-dominated government's desire to maintain control of the flow of communications both within the country and internationally. The Hungarian telephone network continued to lag behind the rest of Europe, and even most of its Central and Eastern European counterparts. Into the early 1990s, a ten-year waiting list for receiving one's telephone connection was not uncommon. Even as late as 1994, national fixed-line penetration rates had barely passed 15 percent.

The first signs of change appeared in the late 1970s. In 1977, the post office inaugurated the country's first satellite telecommunications capacity. The beginning of economic reforms, designed to liberalize the market and introduce foreign investment in the country, led to the creation of a new, independent authority, the Hungarian Post Centre, in 1983. This proved the first step toward the liberalization and privatization of the country's telecommunications market.

In 1989, the new Hungarian government broke up the Hungarian Post, splitting it into three separate companies. This division was formalized in 1991 when the three former post companies were reincorporated as independent companies. The Post's telecommunications operations then became known as Matav Magyar Tavkozlesi Rt (Matav Hungarian Telecommunications Company).

PRIVATIZATION IN 1994

Matav began to prepare for its privatization. In 1993, the government passed a new Telecommunications Act, which effectively ended the company's telecommunications monopoly. The new legislation also permitted the company to open its shareholding to

KEY DATES

1881: The first telephone exchange in Hungary is installed.

1888: Austria-Hungarian government establishes a state-owned monopoly over public telecommunications under PTT.

1915: Telephone operations are brought under control of the Hungarian Post Office.

1990: Post office operations are split into three component parts of broadcasting, postal services, and telecommunications.

1991: Matav Magyar Tavkozlesi Rt is formally incorporated.

1993: Magyarcom consortium (Deutsche Telekom and Ameritech) acquires 30 percent of Matav.

1995: Magyarcom acquires majority control of Matav.

1997: Matav goes public with a listing on Budapest and New York stock exchanges.

2000: Deutsche Telekom buys out SBC, becoming Matav's majority shareholder.

2001: Matav acquires 100 percent control of mobile telephone provider Westel; acquires local telephone provider Emitel; acquires Makedonski Telekomunikacii (MakTel).

2004: Company's mobile telephone operations are re-branded as T-Mobile Hungary.

2005: Company extends T brand across all services and changes its name to Magyar Telekom.

outside investors. By the end of 1993, the Hungarian government had agreed to sell more than 30 percent of Matav to Magyarcom, a consortium composed of Deutsche Telekom and Ameritech (later SBC), for $875 million. As part of the purchase, Matav received a national concession to operate fixed line telephone services, as well as the continued control over the country's long-distance and international market.

In 1994, Matav's monopoly was officially ended, when the government sold off five regional concessions, establishing as many local telecommunications companies. Matav nonetheless retained control of the country's largest concession, covering more than 70 percent of Hungary's population. During this period, the company invested massively in upgrading and expanding its telephone network. By the end of the decade, Matav had eliminated its waiting list and had

largely surpassed its Central European counterparts in terms of market penetration.

The next phase in Matav's privatization came in 1995, when the Magyarcom consortium paid the Hungarian government a further $850 million to raise its stake to more than 67 percent. The total value of the Matav privatization placed it as the largest in Central Europe to that date. Matav in the meantime benefited from Deutsche Telekom's industry-leading technology, allowing Matav to develop a modern telecommunications infrastructure on par with the rest of Europe. By the beginning of the 2000s, Matav had spent more than $1.7 billion upgrading and expanding its infrastructure, boosting national fixed-line penetration past 40 percent, and as high as 53 percent in the Budapest market.

The company also expanded into other services, buying up a 51 percent stake in mobile telephone services provider Westel, the market leader with a 53 percent share at the beginning of the 2000s. Matav also operated its own internet services provider, Axelero, which remained the country's leading ISP into the 2000s.

The Hungarian government completed the privatization of Matav in 1997, when the company listed its shares on the New York and Budapest stock exchanges. The simultaneous offering, which also represented the first listing by a Central European company on the New York Stock Exchange, reduced the government's holding to just 5 percent. In 1999, the Hungarian government sold off this stake as well, retaining only a so-called "golden share" of the company, retaining veto control over major corporate decisions. Magyarcom's holding was then reduced to just over 59.5 percent.

RE-BRANDING: 2000 AND BEYOND

In 2000, Deutsche Telekom bought out SBC's share of Matav, paying $2.2 billion to take the majority control of the Hungarian telecom leader. Soon after, Matav took over full control of Westel, and began rolling out a new mobile network based on the GSM standard.

The full liberalization of Hungary's telecommunications market was completed in 2001. While Matav retained a majority share of the market through the middle of the decade, the company began exploring further growth on the international market. This led Matav to Macedonia in 2001, where it acquired the majority stake in that country's former telecom monopoly, Makedonski Telekomunikacii, otherwise known as MakTel. The company also increased its Hungarian position that year, buying up local provider Emitel, which served the South Alfold region.

Matav restructured its operations at the beginning of 2002, establishing four primary business divisions:

residential, business, internet and mobile. The company also began rolling out ADSL-based broadband services in the early 2000s and by 2003 had signed up its 100,000th subscriber. Matav's entry into broadband was supported once again by Deutsche Telekom's expertise. Deutsche Telekom's support for Matav went beyond providing technological expertise, however, as the German telecommunications giant also helped Matav develop its financial and accounting operations.

The close relationship with its parent company became still more apparent in 2004, when Matav re-launched the Westel mobile telephone service under the internationally recognized T-Mobile brand. In that year, also, Matav paid EUR 68 million for one of Hungary's three 3G mobile licenses.

The success of the T-Mobile re-branding led Matav to complete a more thorough re-branding in 2005. By May of that year, the company had shed its name—which for many retained negative associations as the former telephone monopoly—and adopted the new name of Magyar Telekom. The T brand was then extended across the group's range of services, including T-kabel, its cable television wing, and T-system, which provided IT services to the business market. Following the re-branding, Magyar Telekom merged with its fixed-line operations with its T-Mobile Hungary subsidiary, in order to achieve operating efficiencies.

Magyar Telekom continued to scout out further international expansion opportunities. The company won its bid for 75 percent of former state-owned monopoly Telekom Montenegro at the beginning of 2005. In November of that year, the group won its bid to acquired Orbitel, based in Bulgaria, one of that country's leading fixed-line and mobile contenders. Returning to Hungary at the end of 2005, the company boosted its IT services component through the purchase of Dataplex Kft. Backed by the mighty Deutsche Telekom, Magyar Telekom turned toward the second half of the 2000s as one of the Central European region's most dynamic telecommunications players.

M.L. Cohen

PRINCIPAL SUBSIDIARIES

BCN Rendszerház; Cardnet; Emitel; EPT; Integris Rendszerház; InvesTel; MakTel (Makedonski Telekomunikacii) (Macedonia); Telekom Montenegro (Telekom Crne Gore); T-Kábel; T-Mobile Magyarország; T-Online.

PRINCIPAL COMPETITORS

Vodafone plc; Siemens AG; France Telecom S.A.; Telefon 2000 Sp zoo; Telekomunikacja Polska S.A; Telekom Austria AG; Pannon GSM Rt.

FURTHER READING

Handford, Richard, "Eastern European Incumbents Could Broaden Horizons After EU Accession," *Telecom Markets*, July 29, 2003, p. 8.

"Hungary—Free Airtime for New Matav Subscribers," *Tarifica Alert*, March 22, 2005.

"Hungary's Matav Reaches Target of 200,000 ADSL Clients," *Internet Business News*, December 20, 2004.

Kester, Eddy, "Matav Hopes That New Year Will Bring a Buzz to Business," *Financial Times*, January 3, 2001, p. 26.

———, "Reforms May Open Up the Competition," *Financial Times*, May 27, 2003, p. 4.

"Matav Announces New Moniker," *TelecomWeb News Digest*, January 24, 2005.

"Matav Puts Final Seal on Telekom Montenegro Purchase," *Europe Intelligence Wire*, March 29, 2005.

"Matav Ready for Competition," *EuroInvest*, June 2001, p. 41.

Matav Seeks New Growth Areas," *Telecoms Deal Report*, September 1, 2000.

Mooney, Elizabeth V., "Hungary's Matav Expects Penetration to Peak at 75%," *RCR Wireless News*, March 3, 2003, p. 7.

Parks, Sarah, "Europe's Rising Star: Hungary Opens Its Telecom Market Just as Its Economy Experiences Strong Growth," *America's Network*, February 1, 2002, p. 23.

Ritman, Alex, "Pink T by the Danube," *Global Telecoms Business*, March-April 2005, p. 10.

Smyth, Robert, "Matav Rebranding Seen as Positive Move," *Budapest Business Journal*, January 31, 2005.

MARVEL

Marvel Entertainment, Inc.

417 Fifth Avenue, 11th Floor
New York, New York 10016
U.S.A.
Telephone: (212) 576-4000
Fax: (212) 576-8517
Web site: http://www.marvel.com

Public Company
Incorporated: 1939 as Timely Publications; 1988 as Toy
    Biz Inc.
Employees: 630
Sales: $390.5 million (2005)
Stock Exchanges: New York
Ticker Symbol: MVL
NAIC: 53311 Lessors of Nonfinancial Intangible Assets
    (except Copyrighted Works); 51113 Book Publishers

■ ■ ■

With over 5,000 proprietary characters in its arsenal, Marvel Entertainment, Inc., is one of the world's leading character-based entertainment companies. Marvel is involved in the creation of feature films, DVD/home videos, video games, and television shows. Its characters are also licensed for use in apparel, toys, collectibles, and snack foods. In addition, Marvel's comic book operations command nearly 50 percent of the comic book market. Falling sales and profits forced Marvel to file for Chapter 11 bankruptcy protection in 1996. Toy Biz Inc. acquired the company in 1998 and adopted the Marvel Enterprises name. The company's name was changed to Marvel Entertainment in 2005.

TOY BIZ'S CANADIAN ROOTS

The history of Toy Biz can be traced to Chantex Inc., a Canadian company created in the late 19th century. Sol Zuckerman, the founder's grandson, inherited the business in 1961, when it was earning $160,000 in sales. The restless 21-year-old maintained the family firm as a core interest, bringing its sales to nearly $4.5 million by 1980. In the meantime, he devoted more of his concentration to the acquisition and operation of several Montreal nightclubs and toyed with the idea of running for public office. Zuckerman's tony discotheques were frequented by celebrities, and he earned a reputation as a fast-talking, fast-moving wheeler-dealer. Zuckerman beat a hasty retreat from the disco scene in 1980, however, after witnessing the assassination of a colleague by letter bomb. In the 1980s, he revisited the infants' and children's goods business that had bored him in years past.

Zuckerman transformed himself into one of Canada's highest-flying merger and acquisition artists during the ensuing decade, and his family business emerged as one of the country's fastest-growing enterprises. In 1980, he merged Chantex Inc. with Earl Takefman's Randim Marketing, Inc., a manufacturer and wholesaler of school supplies, to form Charan Industries Inc. By the time Charan went public in 1984 its annual revenues had multiplied fivefold from 1980, to $20 million. The firm's Charan Toy Co., Inc. subsidiary emerged as a leading toy company with a particular emphasis on licensing. In 1985, it held the Canadian rights to nine of the top ten toys in the North American market, including the immensely popular Cabbage Patch Kids name and logo.

COMPANY PERSPECTIVES

It is our intention to continue to protect and nurture the growth of the value of the Marvel brand around the globe. This brand provides a powerful point of differentiation in the eyes of the consumer, and therefore an important and overarching competitive edge for our company and our partners. We are firmly committed to building upon this key advantage in the years to come.

Charan employed what analyst Ira Katzin of Prudential-Bache Securities Canada Ltd. (Toronto) called "a very novel approach" to consumer goods branding, an approach that would be carried on when Charan Toy was reborn as Toy Biz. The company was among the first to implement its brands—both licensed and proprietary—very broadly, applying the venerable Cooper hockey equipment brand (acquired in the mid-1980s) to Charan's existing childrenswear line, for example. This strategy would become commonplace throughout the consumer goods and entertainment industries and form a cornerstone of Toy Biz's success in the 1990s.

PERLMUTTER ACQUISITION REINVIGORATES TOY BIZ

Zuckerman did not see the benefits of these strategies, however, for he sold the toy business in the late 1980s. Charan soon re-emerged as an American-owned company, Toy Biz. In 1990, Toy Biz was acquired by independent investor Isaac Perlmutter, who installed himself as chairman and brought in Joseph Ahern as chief executive officer. Cost controls, innovative licensing agreements, and fresh toy-designing talent allowed the new management team to ride a rising tide of interest in classic comic book characters during the decade.

Trained as an accountant, Ahern had previously worked to bring toymaker Coleco Industries Inc. out of bankruptcy. Ahern's bottom-line focus was reflected in Toy Biz's low overhead. The company owned no real property, instead leasing a modest headquarters in New York City and an Arizona warehouse. It also limited costs by outsourcing most manufacturing to China and concentrating most of its sales efforts on mass merchandisers. This low overhead structure gave Toy Biz a remarkably low employee-to-sales ratio, generating nearly $2 million in annual revenues for each employee in the mid-1990s.

Low overhead was just one factor in Toy Biz's equation for success. As it had been in the 1980s, licensing continued to be an important element of the company's strategy. This time, however, Toy Biz forged a singular agreement with Marvel Entertainment Group, best known for its well-established cast of comic book characters. Instead of signing the short-term (one- to five-year) license typical of the industry—an agreement it had previously utilized—in 1990 Toy Biz exchanged 46 percent of its equity for an "exclusive, perpetual, royalty-free license" to Marvel's characters. Toy Biz focused its earliest efforts on just a few of the series' more than 3,500 characters, especially emphasizing Spider-Man and the Uncanny X-Men.

This strategic alliance was mutually beneficial. For Toy Biz, it eliminated royalties that would otherwise have cost the company anywhere from 6 to 12 percent of its sales of Marvel character toys. Marvel's top-ranked comic books and animated television shows amounted to free advertising for the action figures and other playthings marketed by Toy Biz. Harry De Mott II, an analyst with CS First Boston, told *Forbes'* Suzanne Oliver that "The cartoons are like a half-hour infomercial for Toy Biz products." And Marvel's stake in Toy Biz gave it much higher returns than it would have made from mere royalties.

Toy designer Avi Arad was yet another element of Toy Biz's success. Over the course of his 20-year career, Arad had a hand in the creation of over 160 toys for such major manufacturers as Mattel Inc., Hasbro, Inc., Tyco Toys, Inc., Nintendo, and Sega. Upon joining Toy Biz on a part-time basis in 1993, Arad received a 10 percent stake in the company in addition to his salary. His 22-person product development staff accounted for about 20 percent of Toy Biz's total employment. As executive producer of animated television programs for Marvel and the creator of toys for Toy Biz, he personally represented the intersection of Marvel and Toy Biz's interests. Arad could, for example, coordinate the launch of characters on television screens and toy store shelves. He specialized in action figures and earned a reputation for combining materials in unique ways. Arad's creativity wasn't limited to cartoons and action figures; his resume included Baby Bubbles and Roller Blade Baby.

CONTINUED SUCCESS FOR TOY BIZ

The combination of strict cost controls, an advantageous licensing agreement, and top talent helped Toy Biz achieve the industry's fattest profit margins. Its 24 percent margin topped giant Mattel's profit ratio by over one-fifth in 1995. Furthermore, the Toy Biz/Marvel confederation opened the door to a myriad of other

KEY DATES

1939: The first issue of Marvel Comics is printed.
1941: Marvel introduces Captain America.
1961: The Fantastic Four make their debut.
1986: Marvel is sold to New World Pictures.
1988: New World sells Marvel to the Andrews Group, Inc.; Toy Biz Inc. incorporates in the United States.
1990: Isaac Perlmutter buys Toy Biz; company exchanges 46 percent of its equity for an "exclusive, perpetual, royalty-free license" to Marvel's characters.
1991: Marvel goes public.
1996: Marvel files for Chapter 11 bankruptcy protection.
1998: Toy Biz acquires Marvel and adopts the Marvel Enterprises name.
2005: Company changes its name to Marvel Entertainment.

synergistic business opportunities. Marvel Entertainment was just one segment of Ronald O. Perelman's diverse empire, a group that had been launched in 1978 with a $1.9 million bank loan and had by the early 1990s grown to include Revlon Inc., Coleman Worldwide Corporation, Consolidated Cigar Corporation, New World Communications Group, and First Nationwide Bank, among others. Perelman, who was appointed board chairman of Toy Biz in 1995, sought to expand cooperation among his business interests. Toy Biz soon held licenses of a more typical short-term nature for other brands in the Perelman family. The toy company designed and distributed Revlon fashion dolls and Coleman toy camping equipment, for example.

Toy Biz also licensed brands from companies outside the Marvel/Perelman universe. Its Hercules and Zena Warrior Princess action figures were based on the MCA/Universal television series shown on many New World television stations. Licensing agreements with Gerber and NASCAR expanded the company's toy-marketing realm to educational playthings for toddlers and racing-related cars, action figures, and computer games. These powerful trademarks commanded higher retail prices than generic toys, and held sway over quality- and brand-conscious parents as much as children. Popular proprietary Toy Biz toys included Baby Tumbles Surprise, Baby So Real, Wild and Wacky Painter, and Battle Builders.

Toy Biz boasted an impressive arsenal of growth strategies for the years leading up to the turn of the 21st century. At the core of its great potential was the largely-untapped cast of Marvel comic book characters. Noting that the company had started by promoting Marvel's best-known characters, Ahern boasted that "We have only picked the low-hanging fruit." As the marketing cache of these personalities inevitably waned, Toy Biz looked forward to mining the potential of Captain America, the Fantastic Four, the Incredible Hulk, Ghost Rider, and literally thousands more characters. Early in 1996 the company launched its Classic Heroes candy division, which marketed candy/toy combinations featuring Marvel characters.

Toy Biz also hoped to benefit from the creation of Marvel Films, a production company expected to be launched in 1997. Led by Avi Arad, this new venture would produce both live action and animated films based on Marvel characters, adding yet another head to the Hydra-like entertainment company. Its first project was expected to feature the Incredible Hulk character.

Toy Biz entered what was expected to be the toy industry's second-fastest growing segment, electronic learning aids (ELA), in 1996. The toy company signed a licensing agreement with Apple Computer that year to produce a line of electronic and soft toys with the Apple name and logo. Toy Biz hoped to benefit from Apple's strong presence in educational computers, and Apple hoped that an association with play would cement its position in the hearts and minds of young consumers and future computer buyers. In addition, Toy Biz augmented its position in the industry through the 1995 acquisition of two toy companies, Spectra Star, Inc. and Quest Aerospace Education, Inc. Spectra Star specialized in kites and yo-yos, while Quest made small model rockets. Toy Biz expected acquisitions such as these to fuel continued growth in the late 1990s.

In spite of all these positive factors, continued prosperity was not a foregone conclusion. The toy industry was very competitive, and Toy Biz was a relatively small player in a world dominated by giants like Mattel, Hasbro, and Tyco. Like all its competitors, Toy Biz was subject to the vagaries of consumer tastes. Corporate executives realized that the leading products and characters of 1996 could be the big losers of 1997. But these general concerns paled in comparison with the issues raised by Ronald Perelman's 1996 bid for full control of Toy Biz. This apparently logical move appeared less prudent in light of Marvel Entertainment's financial difficulties mid-decade. Following a loss on the third quarter of 1996, Marvel slashed one-third of its comic book workforce and sought to restructure over $1 billion in debt. Marvel ended up filing for Chapter 11 bankruptcy protection that year.

HISTORY OF MARVEL

Marvel was founded in the late 1930s by Martin Goodman, a New York publisher of pulp magazines. In 1939, Goodman was convinced by a sales manager for Funnies, Inc., a collection of artists and writers who produced complete comic book packages to be printed and distributed by publishers, that comic books would be a good investment. Funnies, Inc., provided Goodman with material featuring a superhero character, the Sub-Mariner, who was part man and part fish. The title of this experimental venture would eventually become the banner of a pulp empire: Marvel Comics.

In addition to the Sub-Mariner, the first issue of Marvel Comics also featured the Human Torch. Priced at ten cents, it was published in October 1939 and reprinted the following month. Providing colorful, action-packed escapism at the Depression-era price of ten cents an issue, Marvel comic books were an instant success.

Both the Torch and the Sub-Mariner exhibited traits that many Marvel heroes would come to share. They were both flawed protagonists and angry young men. Unlike other comic heroes such as Superman, they were rebels rather than upstanding role models for the youth of America. The Torch and the Sub-Mariner spoke in slang and exhibited adolescent traits, making flip comments while they wreaked havoc.

With the success of his first issues, Goodman became his own one-man staff and formed a new company, Timely Publications. He began publishing two new lines of comics, Daring Mystery Comics, and Mystic Comics, searching endlessly for marketable superheroes who would sell comics issue after issue. In addition, as a result of Goodman's concern about the threat posed by Hitler's Germany, Timely Publications' characters began to combat the Nazis even before the United States formally entered the war. In February 1940, for instance, the Sub-Mariner took on a Nazi U-Boat.

THE RISE OF CAPTAIN AMERICA IN 1941

In March 1941, Marvel pushed this concept one step further, introducing Captain America to fight the Nazis. With the arrival of this character, Timely's comic books sky-rocketed in popularity, as the first number sold nearly one million copies. Flush with this success, the company inaugurated four new titles in 1941. With the actual U.S. entry into the war that Timely's heroes had been

fighting for over a year, much of the company's staff joined the military. Despite the general shortage of manpower, and a later shortage of paper, the comics business boomed during the war.

Around this time, Timely branched out from superheroes to humor, adding Comedy Comics, Joker Comics, and Krazy Komics. In addition, the company produced a number of lines featuring funny animals, which appealed to younger children more than the violent superheroes comics. With this success, Timely expanded its staff and moved its offices to the Empire State Building.

In 1943, the company expanded its audience further when it discovered that teenage girls would purchase comic books directed to them. *Miss America* featured a female superhero in its first issue, but turned to teen beauty tips in its second, attaining lasting popularity along with *Patsy Walker*, a serial about dating and dances.

In the wake of the war, the superhero franchise weakened, and the comic book industry as a whole went into a slump. In an effort to revive sales, Timely tried crime comics, cowboy comics, romance titles, and finally, cowboy romance. The old superheroes, the Torch, the Sub-Mariner, and Captain America, were "retired" by 1950.

Despite the death of the old heroes, Timely's operations overall were still going strong. In 1950, the company was producing 82 separate titles—written and drawn by a "bullpen" of company talent—each month. At this time, with the outbreak of the Korean War, Timely also began to produce a new generation of war comics. Created by actual veterans, these issues portrayed war in a new way, showing the pain and misery experienced by the average soldier.

SURVIVING CHALLENGES IN THE 1950S

Early in the 1950s, Goodman decided to increase his profits by setting up his own national distribution system, which he called the Atlas News Company. To raise money for this expensive venture, he cut back on office overhead, and switched his staff of writers and artists to freelance status. By the end of 1951, Timely had been converted to Atlas Publishing, and a black and white globe logo was appearing on the front of the company's comic books. In addition to war comics, Atlas published a large number of horror issues, with titles like *Adventures into Weird Worlds*. In the mid-1950s, the comic book industry came under attack from groups that saw it as a pernicious influence in society. In 1954, the U.S. Senate formed a Subcommittee to Investigate Juvenile Delinquency, which heard testimony in April of that year that comic books were causing violence in society. In a brief spasm of hysteria, customers boycotted stores, comic books were publicly burned, sales plummeted, and a number of comic book producers went out of business. Atlas saw its revenues shrink drastically, and the company moved from its offices in the Empire State Building to smaller quarters at 655 Madison Avenue.

The comic book publishers who survived this crisis, including Atlas, formed the Comics Magazine Association of America in 1955. Immediately, the association set up a censorship board, the Comics Code Authority, whose seal of approval on the front of a comic book guaranteed inoffensiveness (and, many readers believed, blandness). After attaining an all-time high in popularity in the early 1950s, sales of comic books began to drop precipitously.

By 1957, with little product to distribute, Atlas' distribution operations had become a drain on income, and they were shut down. Goodman turned instead to American News Company, another distributor, to place his products in stores and newsstands. With the overall depression in the industry, however, this company soon failed as well, and Goodman was left with no means of distributing his comic books. In desperation, he made a deal with arch-rival D.C. Comics, which agreed to distribute just eight of Goodman's titles a month.

NEW CHARACTERS BRING SUCCESS IN THE 1960S

The company limped along on this basis for three years, until late 1961, when a new idea for a comic book series won widespread popularity and returned the company to financial health. In November, 1961, Goodman's top writer and artist produced *The Fantastic Four*, which featured a superhero group and concentrated more on the complex personalities of the characters and less on the machinations of plot. Featuring The Thing, Mr. Fantastic, Human Torch, and Invisible Girl, *The Fantastic Four* was an immediate hit, and fan mail began to pour in.

The debut of *The Fantastic Four* was followed by the introduction of the *Incredible Hulk* and *Spider-Man*, in short order. By 1962, Goodman's company was once again thriving, as baby boomers discovered a new generation of comics heroes. Although the word "Marvel" was not yet appearing on comic books, the company's work bore a small "MC" insignia, and was conceptually linked by the idea that the "Marvel universe" contained all the superheroes, who knew each other and interacted.

In May 1963, Goodman's comic books began bear-

ing the words "Marvel Comics Group" on the cover of its issues in a vertical box, surrounding the head of the superhero in question. Marvel had been the name on the first series of comics the company published, and it now became the focus of the company's promotional efforts.

Throughout the mid-1960s, Marvel continued to introduce new characters, such as the Avengers, the X-Men—and Daredevil, a blind attorney—among others. To capitalize on the popularity of its large stable of superheroes, the company began to merchandise products that featured their images, such as T-shirts, board games, and model kits. In 1966, a half-hour television show called *The Marvel Super Heroes* was syndicated to stations around the country. The following year, Saturday morning cartoons featuring The Fantastic Four and Spider-Man were introduced on the ABC television network.

By 1968, Marvel was selling 50 million comic books a year. With this strong performance, the company was able to revise its distribution arrangement with D.C. Comics, which had limited production of its own comics, to put out as many different titles as demand warranted. With his valuable franchise established, Goodman sold his businesses in the fall of 1968 to the Perfect Film and Chemical Corporation, which soon changed its name to the Cadence Industries Corporation. Within the structure of Cadence, Goodman's properties were grouped together under one name, Magazine Management.

By 1969, it had become clear that the most recent boom in the comics industry was over. Marvel began to shed titles as sales weakened. In an effort to increase its flexibility, Marvel ended its distribution agreement with D.C. Comics and signed with the Curtis Circulation Company, a large magazine wholesaler, which allowed the publisher greater independence.

FINANCIAL HARDSHIPS BEGIN 1970

Marvel experienced a period of instability in the early 1970s, as the company's old guard of editors and corporate executives retired and their replacements came and went. In an effort to shuck off the outdated Comics Code restrictions, Marvel published three anti-drug theme *Spider-Man* issues that had been suggested by the U.S. Department of Health, Education, and Welfare. When the Comics Code board rejected the issues because rules forbade any mention of drugs at all, Marvel published the comics without the Comics Code seal of approval. This move eventually led to a loosening of restrictions—and was important because comics had begun to lose ground to television and other media.

With fewer prohibitions on subject matter, Marvel began to feature such previously forbidden characters as vampires and werewolves as heroes and villains. The company also began an affirmative action push, including more black characters and more strong female figures. In an effort to make a place for more artistic efforts, Marvel also began to offer black-and-white comics magazines, which were pitched to an older audience than its color comics.

In May 1975, Marvel published *Giant-Size X-Men*, a special large-format issue that re-introduced the characters which would become the company's most popular franchise. Featuring characters from around the world, the X-Men were designed to be marketed in foreign as well as domestic markets.

Despite the success of this new line, however, Marvel had lost $2 million by the middle of 1975. The company was in bad financial shape. Although Marvel's sales remained strong, its profits had dropped. The comics industry's traditional retail outlets, small community stores, were being replaced by big chain grocery stores which did not carry comics. The number of distribution outlets was shrinking. In addition, paper prices had risen, cutting into earnings. In response to this financial crisis, Cadence installed a new company president, who pared the number of titles produced, firmed up publishing schedules, and reorganized sales and distribution. Throughout the late 1970s, Marvel cut back on expenses and new publications in an effort to remain profitable.

Among Marvel's bright spots during this time was the 1977 hit television series *The Incredible Hulk*. This suggested that fertile ground for Marvel's future growth might lie in spin-offs from the company's core comics business. In the late 1970s, a number of television shows featuring Marvel characters were created, and Marvel also licensed characters and stories from other sources for its own comics. These moves were motivated as much by desperation as they were by expansionism, because by 1979 the market for comic books had shrunk to an all-time low.

In the early 1980s, Marvel reorganized its somewhat chaotic corporate structure in an effort to recover from this slump, and began to increase its staff and its output. The company had a steady hit with the X-Men franchise, and was also starting to benefit from a change in the way comics were distributed. In the past, comics had been sold on newsstands with a lot of other publications; but with the rise in comic book collecting, stores devoted exclusively to sales of comic books began to open. Between 1981 and 1982, this direct sales market came to account for half of Marvel's sales. Noting this increase, Marvel began to produce special issues to be sold in this market. In addition, the company continued to publish graphic novels, which provided longer and more sophisticated tales of featured heroes.

In 1985, Marvel also moved to include younger children in its market when it produced Star Comics, which featured humor, talking animals, and child characters. These comics were sold to children in mall bookstores, a new outlet for comic book distribution. By the mid-1980s, Marvel was starting to see its circulation rebound, reaching 7.2 million a month by the end of 1984. Sales were driven by the network of 3,000 comics specialty shops that had sprung up. By the end of 1985, Marvel's revenues had reached $100 million, driven in part by licensing agreements for products featuring its characters.

CHANGES IN OWNERSHIP: 1986-90

This success attracted the attention of members of the financial industry. In 1986, Marvel was sold to New World Pictures, a movie company that wanted the publisher's stable of characters and animation studio, for $46 million. This move touched off a series of corporate transformations for the company. In November, 1988, New World announced that a series of losses had caused it to sell Marvel to the Andrews Group, Inc., for $82.5 million. The Andrews Group was a subsidiary of a holding company called the McAndrews & Forbes Group, which was owned largely by investor Ronald Perelman.

In June 1991, in an effort to raise $48 million, Marvel announced that it would sell stock to the public for the first time. With this money, the company planned to pay off bank debts and increase publishing, distribution, and licensing operations. As a publicly held company, Marvel also began to step up its marketing activities and diversified into a number of different fields related to its publishing empire.

In September 1992, Marvel purchased the Fleer Corporation, a trading card company, for $265 million. In the spring of 1993, Marvel also invested $7 million to buy 46 percent of Toy Biz, Inc., a New York-based toy manufacturer. The company then hired a top toy designer to make successful action hero toys out of familiar Marvel figures. These characters demonstrated booming popularity in the early 1990s.

By late 1993, Marvel was publishing nearly twice as many titles as it had in 1989. The company's revenues had increased steadily during that time, as distribution expanded to new venues, like record stores and drug stores, and overseas markets opened up. In addition, the company stepped up its efforts to sell space in comic books for advertising, and kicked off a licensing campaign to extend its market into Europe, Africa, and the Middle East. Marvel also signed a number of movie deals to support this effort.

In 1993, Marvel declared its ambition to be among the world's top five licensors and set plans in motion to grow its business through acquisition. With a stable of popular characters, and the potential to invent more when the need arose, Marvel appeared to have successfully made the transition from children's publisher to marketing monolith. In 1995, it acquired trading card company SkyBox International. Marvel's success proved short-lived however, and by the mid-1990s sales and profits had come to a screeching halt and the company was drowning in debt from its purchases over the past several years. Marvel was forced to file for Chapter 11 bankruptcy protection in 1996.

THE TOY BIZ ACQUISITION IN 1998

After Marvel declared bankruptcy, a very heated and public battle for the company ensued. In a deal that seemed to benefit himself, Perelman offered to buy Marvel. Shareholders balked at the 85 cents per share offer, claiming it severely undervalued the company. In 1997, Perelman lost control of the company after the bankruptcy courts gave to the nod to bondholders, allowing them to foreclose on 80 percent of company stock. Bondholders gained control of Marvel's board, ousted Perelman, and elected Carl Icahn to head up the new board. Marvel then unsuccessfully sued Perelman, its banks, and major Toy Biz shareholders, claiming mismanagement had led to its demise.

In December 1997, bankruptcy courts appointed a trustee to oversee Marvel. Icahn was unsuccessful in his attempts to restructure the company and eventually agreed to a reorganization plan in which Marvel would be acquired by Toy Biz. Icahn received stock in the new company as well as a $3.5 million cash payment. Marvel emerged from bankruptcy in October 1998 and Toy Biz changed its name to Marvel Enterprises Inc.

Under the leadership of chairman Morton Handel, Marvel Enterprises prepared to enter the new millennium. It sold its Fleer-SkyBox trading business and its Panini sticker manufacturing unit. It also settled a long-standing dispute with several movie studios and eventually agreed to allow Sony Pictures Entertainment to develop the *Spider-Man* movie franchise. As part of that deal, Marvel formed a merchandise agreement with Sony Pictures Consumer Products. *Spider-Man*, released in 2002, raked in over $100 million in just three days after its release. *Spider-Man 2* came out two years later and secured $180 million after just five days in theaters. Spider-Man's original creator, Stan Lee, sued Marvel for

10 percent of the profits related to the *Spider-Man* franchise. Courts ruled in his favor in 2005.

The company adopted the Marvel Entertainment moniker in 2005 as part of its strategy to focus on developing movies, television shows, and video games based on its burgeoning character library. During that year, Marvel landed several licensing deals with publishers to promote the Captain America, Fantastic Four, Incredible Hulk, Iron Man, The Avengers, and X-Men characters. It also secured rights to be the licensee for the recently released *Curious George* movie as well as the television series. Marvel formed partnerships with several gaming systems including Xbox, Nintendo, and Playstation to develop character-based accessories.

On the entertainment front, *The Fantastic Four* movie was released in July 2005. Marvel also formed a multi-picture alliance with Lions Gate's Family Home Entertainment division to develop and produce animated DVD features based on Marvel characters. The company forged an alliance with Antefilms Distribution of France to produce an animated series based on the Fantastic Four. The series was scheduled to launch in 2006.

Isaac Perlmutter, Toy Biz's former chairman, was named Marvel CEO in 2005. The company he now headed was vastly different from the Toy Biz operation he bought in 1990. With an arsenal of 5,000 characters and a highly recognized brand, Marvel Entertainment would no doubt be entertaining a wide range of consumers, moviegoers, gamers, and comic book fans for years to come.

Elizabeth Rourke
Updated, Christina M. Stansell

PRINCIPAL SUBSIDIARIES

Marvel Characters, Inc.; Marvel Entertainment Group Inc.; Marvel Sales Corp.; MRV, Inc.; Spider-Man Merchandising LP (50%); Compania de Juguetes Mexicanos, S.A. de C.V. (Mexico); Marvel Enterprises International Ltd. (United Kingdom); Toy Biz International Ltd. (Hong Kong; 99%); Marvel Toys Ltd. (Hong Kong); Marvel Enterprises Japan K.K. (Japan).

PRINCIPAL COMPETITORS

DC Comics Inc.; Hasbro Inc.; Mattel Inc.

FURTHER READING

"A Marriage of Corporate Celebrities," *Mergers & Acquisitions*, September, 1992.

Anderson, Richard W., "BIFF! POW! Comic Books Make a Comeback," *Business Week*, September 2, 1985.

Benezra, Karen, "Marvel Wants to Be a Movie Mogul," *MEDIAWEEK*, July 8, 1996, p. 4.

Bryant, Adam, "Pow! The Punches that Left Marvel Reeling," *New York Times*, May 24, 1998.

Burke, Dan, "Hitting His Stride," *Canadian Business*, September 1987, pp. 32-43.

Chiang, Christopher, "The X-Men," *Forbes*, April 26, 1993, pp. 18-19.

Cuff, Daniel F., "Publisher Expects Sale to Aid Marvel Comics," *New York Times*, November 28, 1986.

Daniels, Les, *Marvel: Five Fabulous Decades of the World's Greatest Comics*, New York: Harry N. Abrams, Inc., 1991.

Dwek, Robert, "Marvel Takes License with Spider-Man," *Marketing*, August 19, 1993.

Fitzgerald, Kate, "Beleaguered Apple Finds Friend in Toyland," *Advertising Age*, February 12, 1996, p. 39.

Henry, Gordon M., "Bang! Pow! Zap! Heroes are Back," *Time*, October 6, 1986.

Kanner, Bernice, "Comics Relief," *New York*, October 25, 1993.

Liebeck, Laura, "Licensed, Novelty Ideas Abound as Candy Manufacturers Toy with Combo Introductions," *Discount Store News*, March 18, 1996, p. 3F.

Lippman, John, "Perelman's Andrews Group Restructures Bid for Toy Biz Amid Trouble at Marvel," *Wall Street Journal*, November 21, 1996, p. 7B.

"Marvel Enterprises Seeks Chief Executive," *Wall Street Journal*, October 18, 1998, p. B13.

"Marvel Plan to Merge with Toy Biz Passes Muster with Icahn," *Wall Street Journal*, July 31, 1998.

McKay, Shone, "Charan Industries," *Canadian Business*, July 1986, pp. 58-59.

Oliver, Suzanne, "A Marvelous Annuity," *Forbes*, November 4, 1996, pp. 178-179.

"Parlaying Strengths in the Toy Field," *Mergers & Acquisitions*, July-August 1993, p. 51.

Ransom, Diana, "Licensing Deals are Marvel-ous," *Knight Ridder Tribune Business News*, June 23, 2005.

Rosenberg, Robert J., "Marvel's Misery," *BusinessWeek*, May 6, 2002.

Ryan, Ken, "Toy Biz Lands 'Apple for Kids,'" *HFN: The Weekly Newspaper for the Home Furnishings Network*, February 19, 1996, p. 92.

Sandler, Linda, "Heard on the Street: Marvel Investors Find the Perils in Perelman's Superhero Plan," *Wall Street Journal*, November 18, 1996, p. 1C.

Schonfeld, Erick, "Spider-Man Spins Gold for Billionaire Perelman," *Fortune*, March 4, 1996, p. 207.

Spiro, Leah Nathans, "The Operator: An Inside Look at Ron Perelman's $5 Billion Empire," *Business Week*, August 21, 1995, pp. 54-60.

White, Erin, "Spider-Man Tries New Web Tricks," *Wall Street Journal*, May 9, 2000.

Wilensky, Dawn, "Toys Have 'License' to Thrill," *Discount Store News*, February 5, 1996, pp. 27-28.

Morrison & Foerster LLP

---

425 Market Street
San Francisco, California 94105-2482
U.S.A.
Telephone: (415) 268-7000
Fax: (415) 268-7522
Web site: http://www.mofo.com

Private Company
Founded: 1883 as O'Brien & Morrison
Employees: 1,002
Sales: $169 million (2004)
NAIC: 541110 Offices of Lawyers

■ ■ ■

Based in San Francisco, Morrison & Foerster LLP, is the largest law firm in California and the 16th largest in the United States. It maintains 12 offices in the United States, including Los Angeles, New York, Palo Alto, and Washington, D.C., as well as international offices in Beijing, Brussels, Hong Kong, London, Shanghai, Singapore, and Tokyo. All told, the firm employs more than 1,000 attorneys. Morrison & Foerster's intellectual property practice is especially strong. With 300 attorneys it is one of the largest in the world, providing a complete range of services involving patent, trademark, and copyright matters. Another strong suit is the firm's corporate practice, which employs attorneys involved in areas such as mergers and acquisitions, and securities offerings, catering to companies at all stages of their development, from start-ups to well-established multinational companies. Clients include notable corporations such as Apple, Hershey Foods Corporation, JPMorgan Chase & Co., Nextel Communications, Oracle Corporation, Thomson, Toshiba Corporation, VISA U.S.A. Inc., and Yahoo! Inc. Morrison & Foerster is known as a progressive, socially conscious firm and is involved in a great deal of pro bono work, including high-profile death penalty cases. It is also one of the top-ranked law firms in terms of the ethnic diversity of its workforce. Moreover, it has been named to numerous lists as one of the best places to work.

HERITAGE DATING TO 19TH CENTURY

Although Morrison & Foerster did not begin its rise to prominence until the late 1960s, its origins date to the 19th century. The man behind the Morrison name was Alexander Francis Morrison. Born in Weymouth, Massachusetts, in 1856, Morrison was raised in San Francisco from the age of eight. He graduated from the University of California in 1878, and then earned a law degree from Hastings College of the Law in 1881. Morrison began his law career in San Francisco in 1881, joining the firm of Cope & Boyd. Two years later he and a colleague, Thomas V. O'Brien, struck out on their own, establishing the firm of O'Brien & Morrison. The man who supplied the second half of the Morrison & Foerster name, Constantine E.A. Foerster, joined the firm in 1890. In 1892 he and Morrison dissolved what was then known as O'Brien, Morrison & Daingerfield and opened a new law firm, Morrison & Foerster, a name that would become Morrison, Foerster & Cope in 1897 when Walter B. Core became a partner. A year later Foerster died and his name was dropped. It would return decades later after his son, Roland C. Foerster, joined the firm.

In 1921 Morrison undertook a goodwill trip to Asia at the behest of the Chamber of Commerce, contracted pneumonia, and died in Singapore. Although the firm was subsequently dissolved and reorganized, Morrison's name was retained. He also was remembered in the community through the philanthropic work performed by his widow, May Treat Morrison, an accomplished painter and teacher in her own right. Through the bequests she made, helped in part by her husband's former law firm, Morrison's name would be associated with libraries, a visiting lecture series, scholarships, and a planetarium.

PERMANENT NAME CHANGE IN 1975

The firm became known as Morrison, Foerster, Holloway, Clinton & Clark in 1961, and then in 1975 permanently adopted the Morrison & Foerster name. At this point the firm began to expand beyond the Bay Area and to grow into one of the country's leading law firms. The first major step was the opening of its first office (aside from an office to serve a client in San Diego in the early 1950s), established in Los Angeles in November 1974 to service a major client, Crocker National Bank. According to Amy Singer, writing for the *American Lawyer* in a 1990 article, "Associate James DeMeules nailed up a plaque with the firm's name ... to the door of an office inside the Crocker Bank building." Crocker recently had acquired the statewide branch network of another bank and asked that its law firm provide lawyers in southern California. After working out of the bank for three months, DeMeules set up shop across the street with enough space for a dozen lawyers. Although the office landed work from a handful of other clients, it was clearly there to service Crocker and had little aspirations beyond that.

Maintaining a second office proved problematic for Morrison & Foerster. According to the *American Lawyer*, "The early years were marked by frustrations and petty squabbles. Recruiting was difficult, and the L.A. lawyers generally lacked credibility with San Francisco." Moreover, Morrison & Foerster was not well known in

Los Angeles, and recruits were not convinced that the firm had a true commitment to southern California. The Los Angeles office, as a result, had difficulties building a core group of competent and dedicated attorneys, hindered in part by a feeling of being second class members of the firm. "The office's lack of independence was obvious," wrote Singer. "Until 1980 all recruits—associates as well as partners—had to fly to San Francisco for interviews, and snippy comments and jokes indicated to L.A. lawyers how some of their northern cohorts felt. ... It didn't help that for several years the firm's L.A. associates were paid below the going rates in the city, because Morrison didn't offer associates year-end bonuses and profit sharing, as many top L.A. firms did." When salaries were adjusted in Los Angeles, however, the upper range of associate salaries approached that of junior partner rates in San Francisco, which became another source of friction between the two cities.

As Morrison & Foerster worked to improve relations in Los Angeles, it opened more offices. In 1979 the firm added operations in Denver and Washington, D.C. A year later, Morrison & Foerster went international, opening a London office. Also in 1980 the firm added a Saudi Arabia office through acquisition, but it proved to be a misstep. The head of the practice wanted to use the resources of the home office to expand significantly, but San Francisco was more interested in keeping the office small, with its function to generate business for the U.S. offices. After two years the office closed. Next, Morrison & Foerster opened an office in Hong Kong in 1983.

A 1983 Price Waterhouse report revealed that Morrison & Foerster's net income per partner had slipped well below the median of rival San Francisco law firms. According to the *National Law Journal*, "In 1984, the century-old firm was rocking. Plagued with an in-house debate over profitability, there were a number of disturbing defections that undercut morale. And there were some grumblings from partners in the Los Angeles office that they weren't adequately represented in the firm's governing body." The firm's chairman, Marshall L. Small, turned over the reins to a younger partner, Carl A. Leonard, who streamlined the policy committee, bringing in new members. Leonard also made it a priority to integrate the Los Angeles office, adding a Los Angeles partner to the firm's seven-member points committee that voted on partner compensation as well as the non-lawyer partnership review committee. Moreover, Morrison & Foerster began dispatching some of its San Francisco attorneys to Los Angeles to beef up some of the practice groups. Leonard also tackled the issue of diversity. In 1978 the firm named its first woman partner, but it was still lacking in terms of ethnic representation. That would begin to change in the 1980s under Le-

KEY DATES

1883: Alexander Francis Morrison and Thomas V. O'Brien form San Francisco law firm O'Brien and Morrison.
1890: Constantine E.A. Foerster joins the firm.
1989: Foerster dies; the firm is renamed Morrison & Cope.
1921: Morrison dies during a Far East trip.
1961: The firm becomes Morrison, Foerster, Holloway, Clinton & Clark.
1974: The Los Angeles office is opened.
1975: The name is shortened to Morrison & Foerster.
1980: London becomes the first international branch.
1987: The New York office opens.
1998: The Beijing office opens.
2000: The northern Virginia office opens.
2001: The firm strengthens its position in Latin America by forging an alliance with the 22-lawyer Buenos Aires, Argentina-based firm of Alvarez Prado, Cabanellas & Kelly.

onard's watch and ultimately become a strong suit.

In the second half of the 1980s Morrison & Foerster continued to grow at a rapid clip. It moved into the outlying Bay Area, opening successful offices in Walnut Creek in 1984 and Palo Alto in 1985. Another office, established in Woodland Hills, home to a number of San Fernando Valley high-technology companies, lasted less than two years, however. In 1987 Morrison & Foerster established a beachhead in New York City by acquiring the 22-attorney firm of Parker Auspitz Neesemann & Delhanty. In that same year, Morrison & Foerster took advantage of a change in Japanese law allowing American lawyers to practice there and became one of the first U.S. firms to open an office Tokyo. It primarily served inbound investors and the interests of Crocker National Bank in Hong Kong.

Morrison & Foerster continued to expand in the early 1990s, opening offices in Sacramento and Brussels in 1991, the former city important because it was the capital of California and the latter important because it would function as a capital for a united Europe. But by now a number of California firms had begun to recognize that with the California economy faltering it was a time for retrenchment. While Morrison & Foerster was hanging its shingle in new locales, the firm was, in the words

of the *Recorder*, "... scaling back expansion plans, reconfiguring compensation schemes and raising partnership standards. Others had to lay off associates." Morrison & Foerster benefited from a major sex discrimination case it was handling for State Farm Insurance Cos., which generated fees of $61 million for the firm in 1990 and 1991. After State Farm settled in early 1992 there was no work to take its place. Moreover, Japan, which had been supplying an abundance of work, also was struggling. It proved to be a difficult year as revenues fell by 8 percent to $200 million and profits dipped 30 percent to $235,000 per partner, "near the bottom of the nation's biggest firms," according to the *Recorder*.

RENEWED EXPANSION: 1995 AND BEYOND

To weather the recession, Morrison & Foerster was forced to institute some cost-saving measures, but as the economy picked up in the mid-1990s prosperity returned and the firm was able to resume its expansion strategy, albeit without Leonard, who quit the firm in 1994 to work as a consultant. Morrison & Foerster opened an office in Singapore in 1997, followed by a branch in Beijing in 1998 to further flesh out its Asia practice. It became one of just a handful of U.S. law firms licensed to practice in the People's Republic of China. In the United States the firm also opened an office in San Diego in 1999 to serve the biotech, Internet, telecommunications, and other high-tech industries in the area. During the second half of the 1990s, the firm enjoyed a great deal of success in its corporate practice, involved in a number of initial public offerings in the high-technology sector, in particular new media concerns in both California's Silicon Valley and Silicon Alley of New York City's Lower Manhattan.

With the collapse of the high-tech sector in the early 2000s, Morrison & Foerster had to look for new business from new sources. It also continued to open new offices. The firm established a new office in northern Virginia, located in McLean, to serve clients in the technology, life sciences, and financial services industries in the key Washington, D.C. market. Practices included Intellectual Property, Government Contracts, Litigation, Labor, and Corporate Finance. In 2001, Morrison & Foerster opened an office in Century City to supplement the Los Angeles branch and focus on the needs of the worldwide entertainment industry. Also in 2001, Morrison & Foerster strengthened its toehold in Latin America by forging an alliance with the 22-lawyer Buenos Aires, Argentina-based firm of Alvarez Prado, Cabanellas & Kelly.

After nearly 100 years of operating as a San Francisco law firm, Morrison & Foerster, in little more than a generation, transformed itself into a worldwide player. In keeping with this new role, the firm's chairman, Keith Wetmore, relocated to the New York office in 2006. Not only did the move reflect the firm's commitment to the increasingly important New York office, which now included 150 attorneys, but as the financial capital of the world New York was the logical place from which to monitor Morrison & Foerster's global responsibilities and aspirations.

Ed Dinger

PRINCIPAL COMPETITORS

Orrick, Herrington and Sutcliffe L.L.P.; Pillsbury Winthrop Shaw Pittman LLP; Reed Smith LLP.

FURTHER READING

"Alexander F. Morrison: The Lawyer and Citizen," *California Law Review,* March 1927, p. 185.

Cooper, Cynthia L., and Rita Henley Jensen, "MoFo Gains with Pain and Glory," *National Law Journal,* January 15, 1990, p. 1.

Garrity, Brian, "A S.F. Law Firm Takes Wing with Tech IPO Clients," *Investment Dealers' Digest,* December 14, 1998, p. 12.

"In 50 Years on the Job, MoFo's Small Has Seen It All," *Recorder,* November 22, 2004.

Orenstein, Susan, "Culture & Cash: Morrison & Foerster Struggles to Keep Its Balance in the Wake of Plunging Profits," *Recorder,* August 2, 1993, p. 1.

Rauber, Chris, "Morrison & Foerster Tries Capital Strategy for Growth," *San Francisco Business Times,* January 4, 1991, p. 8.

Singer, Amy, "Sixteen Years Later MoFo's L.A. Office Is for Real," *American Lawyer,* July/August 1990, p. 66.

mothercare

Mothercare plc

—■—

Cherry Tree Road
Watford, Hertfordshire WD24 6SH
United Kingdom
Telephone: (44) 1 923 241 000
Fax: (44) 1 923 240 944
Web site: http://www.mothercare.com

Public Company
Incorporated: 1972
Employees: 5,149
Sales: $859.9 million (2005)
Stock Exchanges: London
Ticker Symbol: MTC
NAIC: 448130 Children's and Infants' Clothing Stores

■ ■ ■

Mothercare plc is a retailer that sells maternity clothing, apparel for babies and young children, home and travel products, and toys. As of 2005, the company had 231 stores in the United Kingdom and 220 franchise locations in Europe, the Middle East, and Asia. In 1986, Mothercare became the second major component of the Storehouse plc retail group along with Bhs (formerly British Home Stores). Plagued by weak sales and falling profits, Storehouse sold Bhs in 2000, dissolved its holding company structure, and adopted the Mothercare plc name.

CREATION AND DEVELOPMENT

Mothercare founder Selim Zilkha was born and educated in the United States and served in the U.S. armed forces during World War II. Descended from an affluent banking family, Zilkha began to seek alternate business interests in Britain during the late 1950s. After touring France's Prenatal shops, he sought to import the concept of a one-stop maternity and infant store to Great Britain. Moving quickly, Zilkha assembled a group of investors to acquire the ten-store Lewis and Burrows nursery furniture chain. Zilkha converted a section of one of these stores to a "mother-to-be-and-baby department" and hired several buyers to choose merchandise. The experiment, which lost £180,000 over a two-year period, was later characterized as "a complete fiasco."

Zilkha sold the chain in 1960 but did not give up on the concept. Before the year was out, he acquired the 50-store W. J. Harris chain, which sold very traditional baby carriages and nursery furniture. He shuttered half the stores, changed the chain's name to Mothercare, and revamped its merchandise to offer "everything for the mother-to-be and her baby under five." This one-stop concept included modestly priced maternity apparel, infant and children's wear, furniture, strollers, and even baby food. Zilkha also hired Prenatal's M. Mazard as an adviser but was still unable to mirror the French chain's success.

In 1963, the frustrated banker-turned-retailer invited an acquaintance, Barney Goodman, to join him in the business. The move proved a catalyst for success. The partners split the corporate responsibilities with special concentration on personnel, merchandising and distribution. Their "systems-based" management scheme included the adoption of a computerized ordering and distribution system as early as 1964. This highly efficient centralized purchasing program helped give

Mothercare more purchasing power than the independent boutiques that constituted most of its competition. These controls in turn allowed the budding chain to offer its goods at lower prices while maintaining high profit margins.

After going public in 1972, Mothercare enjoyed several years of growth and prosperity. Barty Phillips, author of *Conran and the Habitat Story*, characterized the company as "one of the very few British firms who have had the courage to go into Europe and the determination to make it work." International expansion started in 1968, when Mothercare launched its first location in Denmark. Over the course of the next nine years, it established operations in Switzerland, Norway, Germany, Austria, Holland, and Belgium. Mothercare acquired an American maternity apparel chain in 1976 and converted it to the British format the following year. The chain expanded from 139 stores to 417 by 1981, and pre-tax profits multiplied from £3 million in 1972 to £22.3 million in the fiscal year ended March 1980.

1981 MERGER WITH HABITAT

The magic began to wear off in the early 1980s, however: pre-tax profits slid nearly 19 percent to £18.1 million in fiscal 1981. Several factors induced the decline. Although the American operation had expanded to nearly 200 stores by the early 1980s, it had yet to achieve consistent profitability. At the same time, Mothercare allowed its image to erode. Instead of going upmarket, the chain tried to compete on price with bargain outlets like Woolworth's, Boots and Littlewoods. Stores and merchandise were characterized as "dull" and "clinical." Gary Warnaby, writing for the International Journal of Retail & Distribution Management in 1993, also noted that "Selim Zilkha seemed to have lost interest in the company."

Whatever the causes, in 1981 Zilkha and Goodman sold their 423-store Mothercare chain to Habitat plc, a 52-unit home furnishings chain founded by Terence Conran. The leveraged buy out cost tiny Habitat £50 million ($239 million). Barney Goodman, who had moved to the United States to launch operations there, returned to Great Britain to help smooth the transition.

Although Habitat was only one-third the size of Mothercare, it had cultivated a much more upscale image. Both chains had originated in the early 1960s. Habitat's moderately-priced, own-design furniture was a British decorating phenomenon—Conran was even knighted "for services to British design and industry." The charismatic designer hoped to imbue Mothercare with Habitat's cachet while maintaining its much-heralded back-office strengths. Habitat, in turn, would use Mothercare's established operations in 10 countries as jumping-off points for its own internationalization. Over the ensuing 18 months, Conran undertook a gradual, subtle revamp of the Mothercare stores and merchandise that culminated in a mid-1983 relaunch featuring a new catalog and gala fashion show. Habitat/Mothercare's first year together appeared a success; profits of £19 million seemed to bode well for the coming decade.

Mothercare was the first in a series of acquisitions that expanded Habitat from a strictly British chain with about £67.2 million in annual revenues to an international retail empire with over £1 billion by 1986. Habitat/Mothercare plc capped its growth spurt with the 1986 acquisition of British Home Stores, a troubled 130-unit department store chain. Conran hoped that he could do for British Home Stores what he had done for Mothercare: infuse the "dowdy" chain with Habitat's marketing and design savvy.

A new holding company, Storehouse plc, was formed with Conran as chairman and CEO. Mothercare was one of seven chains in the group, which boasted more than six million square feet of selling space. Over the next three years, Storehouse attempted to reposition British Home Stores, but a serious retail downturn in the late 1980s thwarted the turnaround. By mid-1987, the conglomeration appeared to have failed so miserably that even Conran flirted with breaking up the retail group. The October 1987 stock market crash and two takeover attempts brought an end to Conran's career at Storehouse in 1988. Group pre-tax profits plunged from about £130 million in 1987 to £11.3 million in 1989.

Mothercare struggled unsuccessfully to regain its former glory during this turbulent period. A 1988 attempt to adopt barcode scanning backfired and resulted in what Marketing magazine's Suzanne Bidlake called "a stock replenishment and customer service fiasco." Competitors took advantage of the corporate confusion: by 1992, Britain's Adams chain had grown to within 14 stores of Mothercare's 254 domestic units, and department stores like Woolworth's, C&A, and Marks & Spencer expanded their maternity and children's offerings as well as their market shares. While the Storehouse subsidiary maintained dominant stakes in the British

KEY DATES

1960: Selim Zilkha acquires the 50-store W. J. Harris chain, which is later renamed Mothercare.

1963: Zilkha invites Barney Goodman to join the business.

1968: International expansion begins; Mothercare launches its first location in Denmark.

1972: Mothercare goes public.

1976: The company acquires an American maternity apparel chain.

1981: Zilkha and Goodman sell the Mothercare chain to Habitat plc.

1986: Habitat/Mothercare plc acquires British Home Stores (Bhs); Storehouse plc is formed to act as a holding company.

2000: Bhs is sold; the company is renamed Mothercare.

maternity wear and nursery equipment markets, it fell to third in infants' and children's wear by the end of 1992.

At the end of the 1980s, Storehouse executives decided to limit their efforts to Mothercare UK and British Home Stores (subsequently renamed Bhs). Having spun off most of its smaller chains including Habitat, Storehouse sold Mothercare Stores, Inc., the U.S. arm of its maternity chain, to American investment company Bain Capital Inc. in 1991. The £7.5 million ($13.5 million) loss on the transaction contributed significantly to Mothercare's £3.9 million pre-tax loss on the fiscal year ended March 28, 1992.

ATTEMPTING TO TURN AROUND: 1990-2000

Backed by an economic upswing, Mothercare's turnaround proceeded gradually under the direction of a succession of CEOs over the ensuing years. Derek Lovelock replaced exiting chief Peter James in 1990. Lovelock emphasized international growth (excluding the United States) via franchising. In 1992, he hired marketing specialist Patricia Manning away from competitor Woolworth's in an effort to boost Mothercare's market share. Marketing strategies in the early 1990s included cross-brand promotions and point-of-sale displays.

Lovelock led the subsidiary until mid-year, when American Ann Iverson was hired away from Bonwit Teller. Iverson stepped up the pace of the reorganization,

leading the first full-scale revamp of Mothercare's store concept in nearly 20 years. The new store layout featured a park-like setting complete with lampposts and talking trees. Many locations were enlarged, and the variety of products was scaled back. In 1993, Iverson told WWD's James Fallon that "In trying to offer everything, we offered too much." By the end of 1995, 127 of Mothercare's stores had been converted to the new format. A new advertising campaign featuring television, print, and outdoor media helped promote the changes.

Iverson's cost-cutting efforts, which included a reduction of middle management, began to bear fruit in the mid-1990s. In a press release summarizing the first six months of fiscal 1995 (ended October 14, 1995), Storehouse chairman Ian Hay Davidson called Mothercare's performance "particularly pleasing." Same store sales had increased 2 percent annually, and pre-tax profits nearly doubled. The company expected to achieve a net of £17 million on the year, nearing its 1980 record of £22 million. In an apparent show of confidence, Storehouse announced its plan to acquire Boots Company plc's Children's World for £62.5 million ($95.8 million).

Although the chain had, in the words of Verdict Research's Hilary Monk, "lost a lot of credibility" over the course of its decade-long decline, a Mothercare executive asserted that "No one has such a strong brand name in kids as we do." It remained to be seen whether that trademark would regain its market dominance in the latter half of the 1990s.

During the mid-to-late 1990s, Mothercare remained an anchor in Storehouse's holdings. At the time, Storehouse ranked among the United Kingdom's top ten retail holding companies. The firm's 142 company-owned and 51 franchised Bhs department stores sold apparel, housewares, and giftware under the Bhs, Universal, and The One and Only trademarks. The 263 company-owned and 109 franchised Mothercare stores constituted Britain's largest retailer of clothing and housewares for mothers and their young children. The chains had international franchisees throughout Europe, the Middle East, and Asia.

At this time, Storehouse and its subsidiaries fell victim to weak market conditions in the retail industry, which were especially harsh in the children's clothing market. Problems resurfaced in the late 1990s for Mothercare as sales remained flat. As such, Storehouse launched a restructuring plan for the chain and began to shutter some of its smaller stores.

NEW DIRECTIONS IN EARLY 2000

Big changes were on the horizon for the company in the first year of the new millennium. Storehouse sold the Bhs chain to retail entrepreneur Philip Green in a Euro 325.7 million deal. At that time, the company decided to dissolve its holding company structure and adopt the Mothercare plc name. Chris Martin, a Storehouse executive, was named CEO of the revamped company. Under his leadership, the firm embarked on a new strategy to restore Mothercare's brand image and return the children's clothing retailer into a profitable entity.

Shoring up Mothercare's bottom line however, proved to be a daunting task. Intense competition, issues related to inadequate store stock and product availability, and poor customer service kept shoppers at bay. Martin resigned in 2002 along with chairman Alan Smith. The company posted large losses during the fiscal year of $54.8 million.

Under the leadership of new CEO Ben Gordon and chairman Ian Peacock, Mothercare slowly began to rebuild the company. As part of its turnaround strategy, the company refurbished its UK stores, began buying directly from suppliers, and constructed a national distribution center. The company also focused heavily on its international operations, which by 2005 nearly outnumbered its domestic locations. With costs in the United Kingdom on the rise, Mothercare anticipated increased global expansion in the years to come. The company signed a franchise agreement for 40 stores in India and also opened its first location in Jordan in early 2006. By now, there were 84 stores in the Middle East including in the Kingdom of Saudi Arabia, United Arab Emirates, Oman, Qatar, Bahrain, and Lebanon.

Mothercare's efforts began to pay off. The company returned to profitability in fiscal 2004, securing a net income of $57 million. Sales climbed to $858.9 million the following year. While Mothercare appeared to have overcome significant challenges, it had yet to prove that its turnaround would produce long-term results. Nevertheless, the company's management team remained optimistic and was confident Mothercare was on the right path to success in the years to come.

April Dougal Gasbarre
Updated, Christina M. Stansell

PRINCIPAL DIVISIONS

Mothercare International; Mothercare Direct; U.K. Stores.

PRINCIPAL COMPETITORS

Debenhams plc; Marks & Spencer Group p.l.c.; NEXT plc.

FURTHER READING

Bidlake, Suzanne, "City Jitters Persist in Wake of Storehouse Loss," *Marketing*, June 8, 1989, p. 13.
——, "Mothercare in Global Push," *Marketing*, February 8, 1990, p. 1
——, "Rebirth for Mothercare?" *Marketing*, March 5, 1992, p. 2.
"Companies: Storehouse Names New CEO in Step Toward Revival," *Wall Street Journal Europe*, May 26, 2000.
Fallon, James, "Bain Capital Acquires Mothercare for $11M," *WWD*, March 20, 1991, p. 12.
——, "The Nurturing of Mothercare: A Fun Conception," *WWD*, February 16, 1993, p. 12.
Ferry, Jeffrey, "Broken by the Bottom Line," *Forbes*, November 1989, p. 180.
"Homing in on Mums," *Marketing*, March 15, 1990, p. 13.
Kleinman, Mark, "Mothercare Faces Up to its Failure," *Marketing*, August 29, 2002, p. 13.
Lebow, Joan, "Conran's Sibling Targets Moms and Kids," *Crain's New York Business*, November 17, 1986, p. 6.
"Mothercare Opens Store in Jordan," *Knight Ridder Tribune Business News*, January 27, 2006.
"Mothercare Relies on Overseas Stores to Boost Profits," *Estates Gazette Interactive*, November 17, 2005.
Phillips, Barty, *Conran and the Habitat Story*, London: Weidenfeld and Nicolson, 1984, pp. 108-116.
Robins, Gary, "Downsizing Trims Cost at Mothercare," *Stores*, October 1991, p. 28.
Robinson, Jeffrey, "A Touch of Class; It's Paid Off for Habitat-Mothercare," *Barron's*, December 3, 1984, pp. 68-69.
Smith, Geoffrey N., "Another Try," *Forbes*, August 11, 1986, p. 112.
"Storehouse PLC' Born of UK Retailers' Merger," *Daily News Record*, January 8, 1986, p. 17.
"Storehouse Dives into the Red," *Northern Echo*, May 26, 2000, p. 17.
"Time to Rebuild Mothercare," *Marketing*, June 11, 1998, p. 13.
Warnaby, Gary, "Storehouse," *International Journal of Retail & Distribution Management*, May-June 1993, pp. 27-34.
Whelan, Sean, "Battered Storehouse Tightens Up Its Act," *Marketing*, December 8, 1988, pp. 13-16.

Moy Park Ltd.

———————■———————

Food Park
39 Seagoe Industrial Area
Craigavon,
United Kingdom
Telephone: +44 028 3835 2233
Fax: +44 028 3833 9390
Web site: http://www.moypark.com

Wholly Owned Subsidiary of OSI Group L.L.C.
Incorporated: 1961
Employees: 7,000
Sales: £600 million ($1.02 billion) (2004)
NAIC: 112320 Broilers and Other Meat-Type Chicken
    Production; 311615 Poultry Processing; 424430
    Dairy Products (Except Dried or Canned) Merchant
    Wholesalers

■■■

Moy Park Ltd. is one of Europe's leading suppliers of poultry, and the largest food processing company in Northern Ireland. The company, with headquarters in Craigavon, operates as a vertically integrated producer, with its own parent/hatchery facilities, as well as primary and value-added processing plants in Northern Ireland, England, and France. The company's chickens are supplied by a network of more than 450 farmers and, since its acquisition of GW Padley Poultry in 2004, its own poultry farm holdings. The company also conducts its own research and development both in new food preparations and in new packaging techniques and technologies. Moy Park employs more than 7,000 people

and processes more than two million birds per week. In addition to whole and parted frozen and fresh chickens, the company produces its own line of poultry-based readymade and prepared foods under its own brand and under third-party and private label brands. Moy Park is a subsidiary of Chicago-based OSI Group LLC. The company is led by managing director Trevor Campbell. Following the Padley acquisition, Moy Park's sales are estimated to reach more than £600 million ($1.02 billion).

FARMING BUSINESS ORIGINS IN 1943

Moy Park originated as a small farming business in Moygashel, in Northern Ireland, in 1943. Through the 1950s, the farm branched out into several areas, including growing potatoes and producing milk and eggs. The appearance of the first supermarkets during this period provided an opportunity for the company to extend its business into a new area, that of the processing of frozen chickens.

Moygashel initially reserved its production for the local market. The company expanded in 1960 when it became the managing member of the Ulster Farmers Cooperative, which operated a processing facility in Moira. This expansion, coupled with the rise of the supermarket channel and the growing demand for frozen and prepared chicken products, led the company to establish a new subsidiary dedicated to its chicken production and processing operations. The new subsidiary, Moy Park Ltd., was formed in 1961.

COMPANY PERSPECTIVES

Welcome to Moy Park Limited. Based at Craigavon, Northern Ireland, and with further sites in Northern Ireland, England and France, Moy Park supplies own label and customer branded chicken products to leading retail and foodservice customers across Europe. Moy Park are Quality Food Winners, gaining a Q Award at the annual Quality Food and Drink Awards as well as being a Gold Medal winner in 'The Grocer' magazine's prestigious Gold Awards. Moy Park has a positive impact on the local community as recognised through Business in The Community's PerCent standard.

Into the 1960s, the fast-growing supermarket groups in the United Kingdom had begun seeking producers capable of handling the large volumes their sales networks required. Moy Park, which took over the Moira processing facility, was able to meet this challenge, and by 1963 the company had begun shipping its poultry products in Great Britain proper. The continued growth of the supermarket sector encouraged Moy Park to invest in its own expansion. In 1966, the company stepped up its production by some 400 percent by opening a new factory in Moira.

The need for further investment in order to keep up with the fast-changing pace of the new large-scale distribution market led Moygashel to seek a larger partner. In 1968, the company agreed to be acquired by rising conglomerate Courtaulds. In this way, Moy Park was assured of continued capital for its expansion. By 1972, the company's production had increased more than ten times over its production levels just a decade earlier. Moy Park also made its first investments in developing vertically integrated operations, building a hatchery during the 1960s. The company added a second hatchery specifically for its broiler stock in 1973.

INDEPENDENCE: 1980-2000

Until the mid-1970s, the company's business remained wholly focused on the production of whole frozen chicken. Yet the growing dominance of the supermarket sector also stimulated demand for value-added chicken products. With a new generation of processing equipment and machinery, the automated production of fresh, parted chicken allowed Moy Park, among other poultry producers, to expand its product line. The company

expanded its Moira facilities to include fresh chicken and chicken parts processing into the middle of the decade. Yet the company's most significant launch into the emerging prepared foods market came in 1975, with the opening of a new state-of-the-art processing facility in Coolhill in 1975. The opening of this facility was further significant for the company, as it was the first in Northern Ireland to be granted an export license for the European market. That license set the stage for Moy Park's development into one of the region's leading poultry suppliers.

England remained the company's largest market, and Moy Park moved to increase its presence there. In 1980, the company acquired its first factory in England, through the purchase of Kew House Farm. Soon after, the company found a new managing director in Trefor Campbell, who had joined Moygashel in 1960 before working for Moy Park. Appointed in 1983, Campbell soon found himself leading a management buyout (MBO) of Moy Park, after Courtaulds began streamlining its operations in the early 1980s. The MBO was completed in 1984, and Moy Park became an independent company for the first time.

Moy Park now launched a new growth phase, backed by a move into a new and expanded headquarters and production facility in Craigavon soon after the buyout. Over the next several years, Moy Park made a series of investments in expanding its new production facilities. This expansion was made in large part to support the company's entry into new product areas—the production of prepared meals and convenience foods. Moy Park built up its own research and development operations in order to create new food recipes and production technologies. By the end of the 1980s, the company had launched a number of prepared foods lines, including widely popular chicken burgers, as well as marinated chicken products, and prepared recipes, such as Chicken Tikka flavored parts, stuffed chickens, and, in 1991, the company's Self-Basting Chicken. The company's continued expansion of its production capacity led to a full-scale refurbishing of the Craigavon site that year.

EUROPEAN LEADER IN 2000

Moy Park retained its strong growth momentum into the 1990s. The company took its first step beyond the United Kingdom in 1991 when it formed a poultry production joint venture with Bourgoin, then France's leading poultry producer. As part of that joint venture, held at 70 percent by Moy Park, the company opened a production site at Hénin-Beaumont, in the Pas-de-Calais area, and began producing processed chicken products for the French market.

Into the mid-1990s, Moy Park's expansion continued. The company formed a new chicken processing

KEY DATES

1943: Moygashel is founded as a small farming business.

1960: The business acquires Ulster Farmers Cooperative and its processing facility in Moira.

1961: Moy Park is incorporated as a poultry products subsidiary.

1963: The company begins supplying the U.K. supermarket sector.

1966: Courtaulds acquires Moygashel and begins expansion of Moy Park's production.

1973: Moy Park opens a second broiler chicken stock breeding hatchery.

1980: Kew House Farm in England is acquired.

1984: MBO is led by managing director Trefor Campbell, who acquires Moy Park from Courtaulds; Moy Park moves to a new headquarters and production facility in Craigavon.

1991: Moy Park forms a joint venture with Bourgoin of France.

1994: The Ferne Foods joint venture is formed in England.

1996: OSI acquires Moy Park.

1997: A second plant is acquired in Marquise, France.

1998: The company acquires full control of the joint venture in France.

1999: A new production plant is opened in Dungannon.

2000: The company acquires full control of the Ferne Foods joint venture.

2004: GW Padley Poultrey and Dove Valley are acquired.

2005: The company announces a £40 million investment program.

joint venture with England's Ferne Foods in 1994. Moy Park also expanded its vertically integrated operations, building a new parent stock hatchery in Carn, which also became the site for a new cold-storage facility. The company also moved its sales and marketing operations closer to its primary customers, the British supermarket sector, opening a new office in Crewe.

By the mid-1990s, however, Moy Park found itself under pressure from an increasingly globalized poultry industry, especially with the ambitious growth of Brazil as one of the world's major chicken producers. Moy Park was forced to look for a larger partner, and in 1996 the company agreed to be acquired by OSI Group, a leading meat, poultry, and foods group based in Chicago, Illinois.

The backing of OSI enabled Moy Park to continue investing in its expansion. A major step forward came with the launch of construction of a £13 million production facility at Dungannon in 1996. Completed in 1999, the new factory boasted a processing capacity of more than 500,000 chickens per week, boosting the group's total processing capacity to more than one million.

Moy Park also stepped up its presence in France in the second half of the 1990s. The company acquired a second processing facility, formerly operated as Cuisine de Licques, in Marquise, near Dunkirk, in 1997. The following year, it bought out its joint venture partner Bourgoin (which soon after went bankrupt). Moy Park, too, was feeling the pinch of a difficult economic market, and by 1999, the company had slipped into losses.

Backed by OSI, however, Moy Park continued investing in expansion. In 2000, for example, the company earmarked some £14 million to expand its three facilities in Moira, Dungannon, and Craigavon in order to step up production of value-added products, such as breaded and roasted chicken and processed fresh chicken. Also in 2000, Moy Park acquired full control of the Ferne Foods joint venture. To *Farming Life,* Trefor Campbell described the group's investment program as "part of an ongoing strategy to maintain our overall competitiveness as a high service level and low cost producer for key customers. This is essential because we are operating in an intensely competitive marketplace and have to contend with the continuing difficulty of high Sterling rates. The winners in our markets will be those who can match a competitive strategy with the right investment decisions and a well-trained, motivated team."

The company drive to boost its value-added product range included an interest in developing new packaging and preparation methods. In 1999, for example, the company introduced a new microwaveable chicken. The packaging for the new product featured built-in browning devices and fat absorbing pads, and boasted the ability to cook a whole chicken in just 27 minutes. Another Moy Park innovation was debuted in 2003, with the launch of a microwaveable tub containing flavored chicken wings and strips.

By the mid-2000s, Moy Park's difficulties were behind the company and it looked forward to further expansion. The company took a major step in 2004, when OSI acquired two British poultry companies. The first, GW Padley Poultry, was one of the United Kingdom's largest producers, with its own chicken farms, as well as processing plants in Grantham, Wisbech, Anwick, and Bury St. Edmunds. The addition of Padley helped to double Moy Park's total production capacity, boosting sales to more than £600 million ($1.02 billion). Soon after, OSI added a second U.K. poultry acquisition, that of Dove Valley, based in Ashbourne, which primarily supplied whole chicken and chicken portions, but also had begun to market its own cooked chicken products. Both acquisitions were placed as subsidiaries under Moy Park.

The acquisitions helped secure Moy Park's position among the leaders in the European poultry market, while also transforming the company into Northern Ireland's largest processed foods group. Moy Park showed no signs of slowing down, and in 2005 the company announced that it was launching a new, £40 million investment program in order to expand its production capacity.

M. L. Cohen

PRINCIPAL SUBSIDIARIES

MPP Holdings Ltd.

PRINCIPAL COMPETITORS

Grampian Country Food Group Ltd.; Glon Sanders; COOAGRI; AIA Agricola Italiana Alimentare; Nutreco Espana S.A.; Cooperatie Cehave Landbouwbelang U.A.; Sovereign Food Investments Ltd.; Astral Foods Ltd.; VIVATIS Holding AG; Rainbow Chicken Ltd.; Eggbert Eggs Proprietary Ltd.; Sanders Ouest S.A.S.

FURTHER READING

"Chicago Giants Feather the Nest," *Grocer,* May 15, 2004, p. 61.

"Good News for the British Chicken Business," *Belfast Telegraph,* May 10, 2004.

"Innovation on the Menu," *Belfast Telegraph,* April 21, 2004.

"Microwave Pecking Order Takes in Chicken," *Packaging Magazine,* December 2, 1999, p. 13.

"Microwaveable Chicken Introduced by Moy Park," *Grocer,* October 16, 1999, p. 21.

"Moy Park Ready for Demands of Future," *News Letter,* January 5, 2002, p. 34.

Sutton, Neil, "Ruffling Feathers," *Grocer,* October 9, 2004, p. 46.

"Uncertainty Looms Over Dark Meat Imports," *Farmers Guardian,* June 24, 2005, p. 18.

NACCO Industries, Inc.

5875 Landerbrook Drive, Suite 300
Cleveland, Ohio 44124-4017
U.S.A.
Telephone: (440) 449-9600
Fax: (440) 449-9607
Web site: http://www.nacco.com

Public Company
Incorporated: 1925 as North American Coal Corporation
Employees: 11,600
Sales: $2.78 billion (2004)
Stock Exchanges: New York
Ticker Symbol: NC
NAIC: 551112 Offices of Other Holding Companies

■ ■ ■

NACCO Industries, Inc., is a holding company whose subsidiaries are involved in lift trucks, housewares, and mining. Its three major businesses are NACCO Materials Handling Group (NMHG), Hamilton Beach/Proctor-Silex Inc., and North American Coal Corporation. NMHG controls nearly 13 percent of the global market for lift trucks sold under the Hyster and Yale brand names. Hamilton Beach/Proctor-Silex manufactures housewares products that can be found in discount department stores, warehouse clubs, and mass merchants. Its Kitchen Collection subsidiary operates as the leading specialty retailer of kitchen products with 188 stores found in factory outlet malls across the United States. NACCO's original business, North American

Coal, is the largest miner of lignite coal in the United States and one of the top ten largest coal producers.

EARLY HISTORY

NACCO's story is very much the story of its founder, Frank E. Taplin, who founded the North American Coal Corporation in 1925. A native of Cleveland, Ohio, which today is still the headquarters of NACCO Industries, Taplin was born in 1875 with obvious entrepreneurial talents. When he was only seventeen he became an office boy, then salesman, for the Standard Oil Company in Cleveland. He went on from there to become a salesman for the Pittsburgh Coal Company, and finally, at age 25, he became the sales manager of the Youghiogheny and Ohio Coal Company. Coal was king in the United States at the turn of the century. Virtually all of the country's energy needs were met by it. Not surprisingly for an enterprising young American who had started his career in an oil company, Taplin would turn his energies to the coal industry, and especially to establishing a coal business of his own.

His sales experience paid off: in 1913 he bought the Cleveland and Western Coal Company, an imposing name for a small business that as yet only sold rather than manufactured coal. With war breaking out in Europe, however, business boomed in the United States, and soon Taplin's firm was in a position to expand its business and enter coal mining on its own. With the U.S. in the war by 1917, the demand for coal was high and the time ripe for Cleveland and Western to acquire three mines, to be followed by others. Postwar recession and a national coal miners' strike in 1919 did not make a serious dent in the company's fortunes. In 1925, with

COMPANY PERSPECTIVES

NACCO's overall strategy is to increase shareholder value by implementing initiatives designed to achieve long-term profit growth. NACCO's long-term perspective is reflected in four guiding principles: secure highly professional management teams; build industry-leading market positions; create sustainable competitive advantage positions; and attain industry-leading operational effectiveness and efficiencies.

the incorporation of the Powhatan Mining Company, operator of Ohio's largest mechanized deep mine, the Cleveland and Western Coal Company changed its name to the North American Coal Corporation, or NACCO.

As long as Frank Taplin was president and chairman of the privately owned company, NACCO expanded, despite labor and legal disputes that troubled the company during its early years. More ominous than these problems was the steady decline in the use of coal as an energy source, even though the country's vast coal reserves were second in the world only to the Soviet Union's.

The company's steady growth continued under Taplin's leadership even during the hard-hit 1930s. Although the company suffered financial losses during the Depression, Taplin was in the forefront in the fight to extend NRA codes to the coal industry that would raise coal miners' wages and reduce their hours of work. Unfortunately, his death in 1938 left NACCO rudderless as well as mired in legal disputes.

POSTWAR SURVIVAL

The outbreak of World War II signaled an end to the Depression and started the upswing of many private fortunes, but NACCO's circumstances were still grim. By 1942, however, a new president had taken the helm: the energetic, able Henry G. Schmidt, who left his engineering position at Goodyear Tire and Rubber Company to guide NACCO back to prosperity during the war years, and to postwar expansion thereafter.

At the end of the war, the future of coal seemed locked into permanent decline. Not only did imported oil become the main American energy source, but so did natural gas, initially abundant but finite in the long run. Significant demand for coal in the postwar years, however, came from utility companies, which were

expanding at a dizzying rate to meet Americans' increasing electricity needs. In 1946, only 10 percent of NACCO's coal was used by utility companies; by the late 1950s, this figure rose to over 50 percent. The rest of the coal demand came from the steel, cement, and chemical industries. In the postwar period, NACCO mirrored the tendency of other large mining companies toward increasing consolidation and expansion. This occurred in part because of the few large corporations, primarily giant industries and utility companies, which constituted the company's major customers.

By 1952 NACCO consisted of four large coal-mining subsidiaries that engaged in underground mining. Since the late 1930s, however, bituminous coal extracted from underground mines was giving way increasingly to lignite coal extracted from strip mines. Extraction from strip mining was not only more efficient but also more economical and far less dangerous than deep coal mining. As a result, NACCO acquired its first lignite field in North Dakota in 1957. Indian Head Mine, which contained the richest lignite coal deposits in North America, would be NACCO's most productive mine for decades to come. Five years after the acquisition of Indian Head Mine and other mining properties in North Dakota as well as in West Virginia, NACCO became the ninth-largest coal producer in the United States, with 70 percent of its coal purchased by utility companies.

Throughout the 1960s, NACCO expanded its coal production and business opportunities with utility companies in New York, Pennsylvania, and Ohio, as well as with the United Power Association in the Great Plains states. In this agreement, NACCO would provide one million tons of coal annually to the power company from its Indian Head Mine. In 1972 NACCO committed itself to provide the Michigan Wisconsin Pipeline Company with billions of tons of coal from its North Dakota reserves, which would be turned into liquified gas. Turning coal into gas for use as a liquid fuel was done successfully by the petroleum-starved Germans in World War II; with natural gas levels in the United States reaching a plateau in the early 1970s, gasified coal seemed to have a promising future. In anticipation, NACCO pledged to build the first major coal gasification plant in the nation, to be completed in 1981. With lignite coal mining playing an increasingly important role, NACCO turned its North Dakota and Texas operations in 1974 into a separate operation, the Western Division. In the early 1970s, NACCO's Western Division acquired the Falkirk Mining Company and Coteau Properties Company in North Dakota as wholly owned subsidiaries.

KEY DATES

1913: Frank E. Taplin buys the Cleveland and Western Coal Company.

1925: Western Coal changes its name to North American Coal Corporation (NACCO).

1957: NACCO acquires its first lignite field in North Dakota.

1986: NACCO adopts a holding company structure and is renamed NACCO Industries, Inc.

1988: The Kitchen Collection Inc. and WearEver-ProctorSilex Inc. are acquired.

1989: Hyster Company is purchased; WearEver is sold.

1990: Proctor-Silex merges with Hamilton Beach Inc.

1995: NACCO Materials Handling Group acquires the Italian warehouse equipment maker DECA.

1996: Italy's ORMIC is purchased.

2000: North American Coal acquires an interest in two lignite mining companies and a stake in 640 million tons of undeveloped lignite coal reserves.

HOLDING COMPANY STRUCTURE LEADS TO DIVERSIFICATION

While profits could not have seemed better in the late 1970s, despite the passage of strict federal mine safety laws as well as frequent strikes and walkouts by the United Mine Workers, doubts were growing as to whether NACCO could remain profitable in the future. The replacement of coal with nuclear power, and the certainty of stricter environmental legislation that could raise costs even further, made the future of coal seem dim. By then, Henry Schmidt had long since retired, and a new team of managers, headed by Chairman Otes Bennett, Jr. and President/CEO Ward Smith, were at the helm to oversee a drastic alteration of their company.

In May 1986 the alteration was complete: the company would no longer be a coal-mining company with its entire profit derived from the manufacture and sale of coal, but instead would become a holding company. Renamed NACCO Industries, Inc., the new structure enabled the company to diversify. The North American Coal Corporation became a wholly owned subsidiary; although it was the oldest component of NACCO Industries, it would within a few years cease to be the biggest or most important (in 1990 it generated

only 23 percent of NACCO's operating profit). The second subsidiary became the newly acquired Yale Materials Handling Corporation, a top-of-the-line forklift truck manufacturer with factories in the United States, Great Britain, and Japan (a joint venture with Sumitomo Heavy Industries, Ltd.).

Market analysts had expected NACCO to diversify into energy-related businesses and, surprised by the dissimilarity of its subsidiaries, forecasted negative consequences. Instead, by 1990 the Journal of Corporate Finance reported that NACCO Industries had become "one of the top performers" on the New York Stock Exchange. No doubt part of the reason for its success was the company's emphasis on decentralization, with each subsidiary operating on its own, with only target-setting and incentives from above.

Only a few years after restructuring, NACCO's coal-mining subsidiary sold off its bituminous coal-mining operations in the East, and concentrated instead on the mining of billions of tons of lignite, surface-mined coal in North Dakota and Texas. Through its long-term contracts with utility companies, the North American Coal Corporation proved to be recession resistant, generating a modest but important cash flow for the holding company's other business ventures. By 1990 the coal company, consisting of its own wholly owned subsidiaries Falkirk Mining Company, Coteau Properties, Sabine Mining Company, and the newest, Red River Mining Company, trimmed its staff by 30 percent and decentralized its operations to its individual mines. With full or partial interest in most of the 37 billion tons of North Dakota's coal reserves, the North American Coal Corporation was the tenth-largest coal-mining firm in the United States, despite trimming off its bituminous operations.

GROWTH THROUGH ACQUISITION

NACCO Industries continued to diversify beyond these two subsidiaries. In 1989 and 1990, the holding company acquired the market leader in forklift truck manufacturing, the Hyster Company, as well as Proctor-Silex, a leader in the manufacture of home electrical appliances. In 1990 NACCO's managers announced the combination of Hyster and Yale to form a wholly owned subsidiary, Hyster-Yale Materials Handling, Inc., which became the biggest industrial lift truck manufacturer in North America (under separate brand names) and a serious competitor on the world market. Hyster-Yale became NACCO's biggest subsidiary, generating 67 percent of operating profit in 1990. The move was hailed on Wall Street as a sign of increased efficiency and long-term profitability. The downside of the merger of the two top-of-the-line lift truck companies was its vulnerability to the vicissitudes of the market: in 1991, profits of the subsidiary fell 14 percent from the previous year, due to 1990's recession.

The year 1990 also saw bold moves on the part of NACCO in the merger of Proctor-Silex, manufacturer of heat-generating electrical appliances such as toasters and coffee makers, with Hamilton Beach, maker of kitchen items such as blenders, mixers, and food processors. NACCO's third subsidiary, Hamilton Beach/Proctor-Silex, became the leader in small kitchen appliances in the United States and, unlike Hyster-Yale, remained very profitable throughout the recession.

NACCO's fourth subsidiary, The Kitchen Collection, acquired in 1988, was a chain of 72 stores (with more planned in the 1990s) located throughout the United States. The Kitchen Collection sold primarily factory-outlet Hamilton Beach/Proctor-Silex appliances and other kitchen items. Though small, The Kitchen Collection expanded continuously and proved to be recession resistant. Together, housewares (Hamilton Beach/Proctor-Silex and The Kitchen Collection) generated 10 percent of NACCO's profit in 1991.

With three subsidiaries acquired in the space of one-and-a-half years, NACCO Industries planned to concentrate on development rather than further business acquisitions. From a venerable coal company to a vibrant and dynamic holding company with dissimilar businesses and global interests (in which coal mining held only a backseat), NACCO became a new company. President and CEO Alfred M. Rankin, Jr., together with Chairman of the Board Ward Smith, acted as the strategists and target setters of the decentralized corporation. Their goal continued to be turning NACCO Industries subsidiaries into the top market leaders in their respective enterprises and globalizing the company. While the 1990s recession dampened profits and resulted in many job layoffs, the worldwide recovery of the market offset these losses. The North American Coal Corporation planned to mine billions of tons of bituminous coal outside of Anchorage, Alaska, for the Japanese market; Hyster-Yale had important interests in Great Britain, Germany (Jungheinrich), and Japan (Sumitomo Heavy Industries), with growing interests in other Far Eastern countries. Cost-cutting and incentive measures had resulted in NACCO becoming an aggressive new competitor on the global market.

1995 AND BEYOND

During the mid-1990s, NACCO began to expand and strengthen its geographic reach. In 1995, NACCO Materials Handling Group acquired DECA, an Italian

warehouse equipment manufacturer. A similar company, ORMIC, was purchased the following year to secure the company's foothold in the Italian market. Operations in this business segment were bolstered further with the 1999 purchase of Van Eijle BV, a Dutch importer/exporter of forklift trucks. That same year, the company opened a warehouse in Shanghai, China.

On the housewares front, NACCO acquired the remaining 20 percent of Hamilton Beach/Proctor-Silex from Glen Dimplex. In 1997, production began at a Hamilton Beach/Proctor-Silex plant in Mexico. Two years later, this subsidiary landed a contract to provide a line of General Electric Co. branded appliances to Wal-Mart Stores.

NACCO and its three major business units—NACCO Materials Handling Group, NACCO Housewares Group, and North American Coal—faced challenges at it entered the new millennium. Conditions began to weaken in NACCO's key markets, which forced the company to adopt a restructuring plan in order to strengthen each of its business units. As part of this plan, NACCO announced a sweeping cost reduction program. A plant in Danville, Illinois, closed and a facility in Mexico was shuttered as NACCO Housewares shifted the majority of its production to China.

Another component in NACCO's strategy was to make key acquisitions in order to shore up long-term profits. As such, North American Coal acquired Phillips Coal Company's 75 percent stake in Mississippi Lignite Mining Company, its 50 percent interest in Red River Mining Company, and its stake in 640 million tons of undeveloped lignite coal reserves in 2000. NACCO's Kitchen Collection subsidiary launched the Gadgets and More retail stores the following year.

Overall, the company posted a $36 million loss in 2001 mainly due to charges related to its restructuring and downsizing initiatives. The company's management team, led by CEO Rankin Jr., was confident the restructuring efforts would pay off in the long run. Rankin Jr. was quoted in a May 2002 *Wall Street Journal*, claiming, "We have a very good cost structure in place and are in position to benefit as markets for our products improve." Sure enough, the company returned to profitability in 2002 and posted a net income of $42.4 million. Profit climbed even higher in 2003, reaching $52.8 million.

Costs for material products like steel and petroleum skyrocketed in 2004. Weak sales in the retail housewares sector coupled with unfavorable currency exchange rates in Europe forced profits to fall by 9.3 percent that year. Thanks to its restructuring and cost reduction efforts over the past several years, NACCO and its subsidiaries met these challenges head on. In fact, the company appeared to be well positioned for success in the years to come.

Sina Dubovoj
Updated, Christina M. Stansell

PRINCIPAL SUBSIDIARIES

Altoona Services, Inc.; Bellaire Corporation; The Coteau Properties Company; The Falkirk Mining Company; Grupo HB/PS, S.A. de C.V.; Hamilton Beach/Proctor-Silex, Inc.; Hamilton Beach/Proctor-Silex de Mexico, S.A. de C.V.; Housewares Holding Company; HB-PS Holding Company, Inc.; Hyster-Yale Materials Handling, Inc.; The Kitchen Collection, Inc.; Mississippi Lignite Mining Company; NACCO Materials Handling Group, Inc.; NACCO Materials Handling Group, Ltd.; NACCO Materials Handling, B.V.; NACCO Materials Handling, S.p.A.; NACCO Materials Handling Ltd.; NMH Holding, B.V.; NMHG Australia Holding Pty Ltd.; NMHG Distribution B.V.; NMHG Financial Services, Inc.; NMHG Holding Co.; NMHG Mexico S.A. de C.V.; NMHG Oregon, Inc.; The North American Coal Corporation; North American Coal Royalty Company; Oxbow Property Company LLC; Powhatan Corporation; Proctor-Silex Canada, Inc.; Red Hills Property Company LLC; Red River Mining Company; The Sabine Mining Company; Sumitomo-NACCO Materials Handling Group, Ltd. (Japan; 50%).

PRINCIPAL COMPETITORS

Arch Coal Inc.; CLARK Material Handling Company; Salton Inc.

FURTHER READING

Gerdel, Thomas, "NACCO's Approach May Raise Profile," *Plain Dealer*, November 28, 2004.

"NACCO Adds to Lignite Holdings With Phillips Coal Acquisition," *Coal Week*, October 16, 2000.

"NACCO Materials Buys Italian Warehouse Equipment Business," *Portland Oregonian*, August 1, 1996.

Oihus, Colleen, *A History of Coal Mining in North Dakota, 1873-1982*, Bismarck, 1983.

Luxenberg, Stan, "Unearthing Profits from Cleaner Coal: Strikes and Surpluses Have Stung the Mining Companies," *New York Times*, December 17, 1989.

Lappen, Alyssa A., "A Chip Off the Old Block (NACCO President A. M. Rankin)," *Forbes*, April 16, 1990.

"Forging a Synergistic Portfolio from a Diverse Combination," *Journal of Corporate Finance*, Summer 1990.

Levkovich, Tobias M., "NACCO Industries," Smith Barney, October 3, 1990.

"NACCO Industries, Inc.," *Wall Street Journal*, March 18, 1992.

"NACCO Industries, Inc.," *Business Journal-Portland*, July 13, 1992.

"Research Bulletin, NACCO Industries," Donaldson, Lufkin & Jenrette, August 19, 1992.

Winter, Ralph E., "NACCO Benefits From Cuts, Restructuring," *Wall Street Journal*, May 15, 2002.

———, "NACCO Says Net in '99 to Trail High '98 Level," *Wall Street Journal*, May 17, 1999.

———, "NACCO Says Power Woes May Help It, But Down the Road," *Dow Jones Newswires*, May 9, 2001.

New England Business Service, Inc.

500 Main Street
Groton, Massachusetts 01471
U.S.A.
Telephone: (978) 448-6111
Fax: (978) 449-3419
Web site: http://www.nebs.com

Wholly Owned Subsidiary of Deluxe Corporation
Incorporated: 1952
Employees: 4,356
Sales: $551.2 million (2003)
NAIC: 323116 Manifold Business Forms Printing

■ ■ ■

New England Business Service, Inc. (NEBS) is a leading supplier of office products and business services in North America. The company's product line includes business forms, checks and banking supplies, labels, envelopes, business stationery, cards, and calendars, and a wide range of office equipment and other supplies. NEBS also provides promotional printing, logo design, and payroll services. NEBS was acquired by Deluxe Corporation in 2004 and operates as part of Deluxe's Small Business Services group.

CATALOG SALES REACH MORE CUSTOMERS: 1952–70

NEBS had its start in 1952, when Al Anderson, a forms salesman based in Cleveland, Ohio, became aware of the lack of customized forms in the small quantity and reasonable price range that would make them accessible to the average small business. Instead, small retailers, beauty salons and barber shops, electricians and plumbers, and other small service businesses often used their rubber stamps on generic carboned forms. Anderson decided to fill this business niche. Because of the scattered nature of the small business market, he decided that direct-mail marketing would be the most efficient and least costly way to build his company. Moving to Townsend, Massachusetts, he assembled a selection of business forms manufactured by a variety of outside printing companies, put together a brochure, and mailed it. He focused his sales efforts on smaller companies with 20 or fewer employees, that is, customers for whom buying custom-printed business forms was usually unrealistic because of the large print-runs per form required from most printed form suppliers. The idea was a success; orders came pouring in and by 1955 Anderson had moved NEBS out of his backyard barn into real office space. He also hired Jay R. Rhoads, Jr., to help handle the business side of his growing forms business. By 1968 NEBS was posting $3.5 million in net sales. The 90,000 active customers for its products were serviced by 163 full- and part-time employees.

PRINTING CAPABILITIES PROVIDE KEY TO EXPANSION: 1970–80

In 1970 Anderson retired, leaving CEO Rhoads to expand NEBS's marketplace. Working closely with his brother, Richard H. Rhoads, now company president and director, Rhoads planned for an ambitious expan-

COMPANY PERSPECTIVES

◆

SBS leverages the expertise gained over more than a half century as a business-to-business market leader to accomplish its value proposition of letting customers buy when, where, and how they want, from experts who know their business, understand their needs, and simplify their office operations.

sion of the company. Realizing that the average customer purchased only a limited quantity of any one form during a given year, NEBS concentrated on the efficient management of large volumes of small orders. The company could soon pride itself on a six-day forms turnaround schedule. Because of its ability to respond quickly to customers depending on it for the forms they used in their day-to-day operations, reorders quickly reached a rate of more than 70 percent of sales volume.

A crucial element of any major growth, Rhoads realized, was ending NEBS's reliance on outside vendors to provide its base forms. With printing capabilities of its own, the company would be able to capture wholesaler profits as well as the retail markup it currently earned. By 1973, with 315 employees and net sales of $11 million, NEBS expanded its customer base to 258,000, thereby reaching the point where it could absorb the overhead of its first large-run high-speed printing press. With the addition of the press, NEBS expanded its Townsend office and warehouse facilities, upgraded its computer system, and began expanding its product line.

Over the next few years Rhoads also would set up printing plants in Peterborough, New Hampshire, and Maryville, Missouri, to better serve NEBS customers on a regional level. In addition, through the 1976 establishment of office and production facilities for NEBS Business Forms, Ltd., in Midland, Ontario, the company expanded its sales territory into the English-speaking regions of Canada (bilingual forms would be marketed beginning in 1985). This expanded sales territory, growing far outside the New England region to encompass both the United States and Canada, was aided by the introduction of a toll-free 800 number for phone sales. By 1981, 40 percent of the orders for NEBS products were received by phone.

In October 1977 NEBS went public with an offering of 50,000 shares of common stock; the company would be listed on the NASDAQ beginning in December 1980. With sales now passing $30 million

and a customer base that included more than 411,000 small businesses in both the United States and Canada, 1977 would be a banner year for the company. However, it was only the beginning of a major growth spurt. As its customer base grew by 41 percent to 700,000 very small business firms by 1981, net sales followed suit, reaching $79 million by the end of fiscal 1981. Although the inflationary national economy had impacted these sales figures, NEBS's actual growth could be measured by the 1,300 employees now promoting and producing its products. Company estimates, which put "real" growth in 1981 at 9.7 percent, reflected the company's corporate restructuring activities and capital expenditures in anticipation of further expansion. The NEBS Forms Division, which accounted for the largest percentage of both sales and profit, had become an independent operating entity in 1980. Corporate offices, in search of more space, were relocated to Groton, and plans were implemented for the construction of a manufacturing plant in Flagstaff, Arizona, to better service customers in the Western states. In 1981, NEBS also made a three-for-two split of its common stock to encourage additional investment in the company.

CHANGES AND NEW MARKETS: 1980–90

As the company progressed through the sluggish 1980s, its project development program remained its primary focus. Alerted early on to the possible proliferation of computers in small businesses, NEBS began serving the needs of those firms investing in first-generation computer technology. Custom-printed continuous forms, perforated into pages and lined by "pin" holes for use with dot matrix printers, became a top seller for NEBS, which offered small companies competitive prices and fast service. In addition, the 1984 acquisition of the Santa Clara, California-based Devoke Company allowed NEBS to offer its customers special-purpose computer furniture as well.

The market for computer-related products would begin to level off in mid-decade, a lull after the storm of PC installations in the small business market. This slowdown caused NEBS to divest itself of its Devoke subsidiary by the end of the decade. In addition, the company worked to restructure and adjust its product mix in an effort to battle the increasingly stagnant office supply market that characterized the late 1980s. In 1986, for instance, after a year of relatively flat earnings, NEBS implemented several programs to make its order entry and production processes more efficient. An automated order entry system was initialized, thereby decreasing the turnaround time for customer orders. Combining this with other restructuring and cost-containment measures

KEY DATES

1952: Al Anderson establishes NEBS.
1973: The company opens its first printing plant.
1977: The company goes public.
1988: NEBS opens an overseas division in the United Kingdom.
1997: The company buys Chiswick Trading.
1998: McBee Systems, Inc. is acquired.
2003: NEBS purchases Safeguard Business Systems Inc.
2004: Deluxe Corpporation acquires NEBS.

and a 7 percent reduction in staff, the company was able to report another banner year, increasing earnings by 30 percent to $16.89 million.

In addition to expanding its product line, the company continued to expand its market. Its Canadian subsidiary entered the French-speaking Quebec market in 1985, offering a line of bilingual forms modeled on the traditional NEBS line. In 1988 NEBS opened an overseas division, entering the office forms market in the United Kingdom as NEBS Business Stationery. Headquartered in Chester, England, this division marketed a complete selection of forms and other office products throughout Great Britain and Northern Ireland. Domestically, DFS Business Forms, a network of independent dealers, was implemented as a means to further increase visibility and market share among very small businesses.

Small retail operations proved to be an especially lucrative niche for NEBS, which provided everything from bags, tags, and signage to preprinted sales slips, company check systems, and labels. Products also were made available on recycled paper. Another cause for optimism was the continuous increase in government-imposed regulations of small business enterprises in both the United States and Canada. An increasing bureaucracy would generate increasing numbers of forms, some of which NEBS could provide. As accounting software systems began to be adopted by small firms, NEBS created and marketed compatible forms under its NEBS Computer Forms division. Checks, invoices, statements, and purchase orders were designed for compatibility with software vendors such as Quicken, Peachtree Accounting, Open Systems, and DacEasy. Estimating its potential customer base at approximately five million small businesses in 1980, NEBS would see its share of that base grow to almost 25 percent by the end of the decade.

PERSONAL COMPUTERS POSING A THREAT TO THE FUTURE

Ironically, the computer technology that had sparked NEBS's expansion in the early 1980s was threatening to undermine it by the 1990s. The proliferation of desktop publishing software, color laser printers, and "designer" papers allowed even simple home-office businesses to produce sophisticated letterheads, forms, business cards, and labels on a PC, bypassing the need for the custom printing services that NEBS provided.

In response, the company began to enter the software market in the 1990s. In addition to continuing to offer forms compatible with the major accounting software packages then on the market, NEBS developed Form Filling, a software package designed to eliminate tedious setup of computer-generated forms. Form Filling was competitively priced and marketed along with a broad range of forms that included payroll check systems with detailed stubs, all of which were available as laser or dot-matrix forms.

Early in the decade, NEBS acquired SYCOM, Inc., a Madison, Wisconsin-based marketer of custom business forms to professional offices. Marketed both by mail and phone, SYCOM forms provided the company with a specialized product geared for accountants, attorneys, dentists, and other professionals in the healthcare field. In January 1993 it also would acquire rights to the One-Write Plus software developed by MECA Software, Inc. Through this acquisition the company gained both a distributor network and a skilled sales and service staff for the popular, easy-to-use general ledger software package. One-Write Plus would be managed through NEBS Software, Inc.

Fluctuations in the nationwide small business economy, which had boomed during the 1980s, would tend downward in the early 1990s. During 1991 alone a Dun & Bradstreet report showed that small business failures had reached 43 percent, and the number of new small firms opened during the year rose only 3 percent from 1990. In 1990 NEBS reported net income of $20.6 million; only two years later it would see that figure shrink to $15.47 million. By 1993 net income reached a record low: $14.2 million on sales of $237.1 million to more than one million small businesses.

In an attempt to combat lackluster sales and dropping earnings, NEBS developed a new product line, aggressively pursued its custom forms market, and reorganized its distribution network. Although the market for manual forms had begun to contract, due in part to both the adoption of computerized accounting systems and the proliferation of technologically enhanced electronic point-of-sale equipment, management also recognized the need to more actively promote these forms, which they viewed as a "point of entry" into the NEBS product line. The DFS Business Forms dealer base, expanded to include the growing number of office supply "superstores," renewed their efforts to market NEBS software to computer peripherals retailers. The company also began a telemarketing program, combining catalog mailings with customer contact by phone. In 1993 the company's 2,217 employees were able to serve the needs of more than 1.2 million small business customers, with a 48-hour turnaround time between order receipt and shipment.

MORE COLORFUL PALETTE REVITALIZING LACKLUSTER SALES IN THE 1995

NEBS achieved banner success in 1995, with sales for the company's domestic operations alone reaching $241.8 million. Net income for 1995, which had begun a slow rebound from its 1993 low, reached $16.3 million on total sales of $263.7 million. Part of the reason for the turnaround was a cost-reduction program implemented by the company that resulted in the layoff of 100 employees. In addition, the company decided to close its SYCOM subsidiary, integrating that company's operations into their NEBS counterparts.

Much of the credit for the company's financial turnaround also was given to the introduction of "Company Colors" forms and stationery. Responding to customer demand for more image-conscious printed products without the expense of custom printing, NEBS created desktop papers, as well as coordinating letterhead, business cards, and forms, all using a palette of the five most popular two-toned color combinations. This program would be modified into NEBS Colors in 1996. Another factor contributing to overall growth in 1995 was the introduction of the Page Magic desktop software package, along with a line of coordinating paper products. In addition, many of NEBS's most popular manual forms were redesigned to achieve a more contemporary look.

During 1995 the company also formed an alliance with Kinko's, Inc., a successful photocopy center with more than 750 branches located throughout the United States. In an effort to generate new forms business for the company, NEBS placed custom printing consultants into 22 selected Kinko's copy center locations, where they could help customers design custom business forms, brochures, and other stationery items. These orders could be immediately sent to company printing plants for quick production and delivery. Unfortunately, the partnership did not produce the desired results and the company closed these custom-printing desks in September 1996.

LOOKING TO THE FUTURE OF SMALL BUSINESSES

From its beginnings as a producer of preprinted business forms, NEBS continually transformed itself to meet future challenges. Rededicating itself as "The Small Business Resource" in 1996, the company released several CD-ROM products designed to help entrepreneurs plan, structure, and finance their fledgling business operations. Increased resources were channeled into the expansion of mailing lists and development of Success Reference Guides, an enlarged catalog and small business resource system that includes the company's complete product line. Reengineering was begun on NEBSnet, a computer graphics workstation that enhanced retail customer orders. The company furthered its future focus by introducing www.nebs.com, a web site organized around business advice and product promotion.

During fiscal 1996 NEBS continued its efforts to adapt to a changing small business climate. Meanwhile, the December 1995 retirement of CEO Richard H. Rhoads ended a combined 25 years of leadership by the Rhoads brothers. Under the new leadership of incoming CEO and President Robert J. Murray, the company effected a new organizational structure and rededicated itself to the direct marketing of forms and related office products for small businesses. Such refocusing efforts included directing NEBS resources toward software distribution rather than more costly software development. Selling its One-Write Plus software to Peachtree Software Inc. in early 1996, NEBS retained distribution rights and an exclusive marketing agreement for One-Write Plus-compatible forms.

The company's organizational restructuring would prove costly in the short run. By the close of its fiscal year in June 1996, NEBS reported net income of $11.929 million; further setbacks were suffered after the company was ordered to pay a pre-tax charge of $5.2 million after closing its satellite sales desks in Kinko's retail copy centers. But the establishment of a Business Management group to engage in strategic policy and product development and an increased level of operating efficiency boded well for the future. By 1996 the company had a working relationship with more than 25,000 retail dealers, representing only 10 percent of the total private label business forms reseller's market. NEBS's decision to grow retail outlets through its DFS units marked this market as the focus of future growth for the company.

During this time period, NEBS continued to be aware that its overall performance was directly related to the health of the small business community, both in the United States and elsewhere. And that community was ever changing. The ubiquitous PC streamlined accounting methods, while shifting consumables caused NEBS to refine its product mix continuously. The increasing sophistication with which small business owners planned their promotional strategies—through creativity, professionalism, and the development of a striking and unique image—directed the company's efforts in promoting its forms business. Continuing to market its products to the ten million small businesses and more than 20 million in-home offices throughout the United States, Canada, and the United Kingdom, NEBS increasingly focused its marketing efforts on retail, although the direct mail of repeat orders continued to be the company's primary area of profitability. With almost five decades of experience within this expanding market, NEBS remained uniquely qualified to profit from the long-term trend toward increased small business ownership.

A NEW OWNER IN THE NEW MILLENNIUM

During the late 1990s, NEBS diversified its holdings through a series of acquisitions. The purchase of Chiswick Trading and its industrial packaging products line in 1997 was expected to bolster sales by $45 million. NEBS also purchased U.K.-based Standard Forms Ltd., McBee Systems Inc., and RapidForms. In 1997, profits increased by 56 percent over the previous year. Two years later, the company partnered with WebNow.com in a venture to offer its customers web site design and web hosting.

The company's strategy to add new customers, increase its product line, and branch out into new business areas continued in the early years of the new millennium. In 2000, NEBS added promotional apparel manufacturer Premium Wear Inc. to its arsenal in a $38 million deal. The company also purchased a stake in Advantage Payroll Services. By increasing its interest in the company over the next several years, NEBS was able to add payroll services to its burgeoning array of business services. Safeguard Business Systems Inc., a company that sold business products to more than 600,000 small businesses in North America, was purchased in 2003 for more than $70 million in cash.

In order to cut costs and shore up profits, NEBS made a series of restructuring moves during this time period. It combined the operations of McBee Systems and RapidForms to create the Integrated Marketing Services Group division. It also consolidated its offices in Canada, closed a plant in Virginia, and cut approximately 45 jobs. By this time, NEBS had caught

the eye of Deluxe Corp., a check printer and marketer. Deluxe had left the catalog industry in 1998 to diversify into electronic payment services. Its expansion efforts had failed to pan out, and it was looking to gain a foothold in the catalog sector of the business market once again. Sure enough, Deluxe made a play for NEBS and acquired the company in June 2004 for approximately $745 million in cash and assumption of nearly $160 million in debt.

For NEBS, Deluxe served as an anchor for long-term growth. At the same time, Deluxe hoped to capitalize on NEBS's product line and its large customer base. Overall, Deluxe was able to serve an additional three million customers as a result of the union. Deluxe chairman and CEO Lawrence Mosner commented on the purchase in a July 2004 *Catalog Age* article, claiming, "There are 23 million small businesses in the U.S. The combined Deluxe/NEBS business serves almost 25% of that number, plus there's tremendous opportunity for growth."

After completion of the deal, NEBS was positioned as the cornerstone in Deluxe's Small Business Services (SBS) group. Deluxe sold NEBS's operations in the United Kingdom and France and also set plans in motion to sell the PremiumWear subsidiary. Overall, SBS supplied more than six million small business customers with a wide variety of office products and services. While long-term success of the NEBS/Deluxe union remained to be seen, NEBS appeared to be well positioned for future growth.

Pamela L. Shelton
Updated, Christina M. Stansell

PRINCIPAL SUBSIDIARIES

Chiswick, Inc.; McBee Systems, Inc.; NEBS Business Products Ltd. (Canada); NEBS Payroll Service Ltd. (Canada); PremiumWear, Inc.; Rapidforms, Inc.; Russell & Miller, Inc.; Safeguard Business Systems, Inc.; Safeguard Business Systems Ltd. (Canada); VeriPack.com, Inc.

PRINCIPAL COMPETITORS

John H. Harland Company; Office Depot Inc.; Staples Inc.

FURTHER READING

Del Franco, Mark, and Paul Miller, "Deluxe Returns to Catalogs with NEBS Acquisition," *Catalog Age*, July 2004, p. 7.

Dowling, Melissa, "NEBS Acquires Chiswick Trading," *Catalog Age,* June 1997, p. 7.

Miller, Paul, "NEBS to Trim Down," *Catalog Age,* November 2000, p. 6.

"NEBS Acquires Safeguard Business Systems," *Business Forms, Labels & Systems,* July 20, 2003, p. 8.

"New England Business Services to Buy Premium Wear Inc. for 0.81 Times Revenue," *Weekly Corporate Growth Report,* June 12, 2000.

Oberndorf, Shannon, "NEBS Back on Track," *Catalog Age,* February 1998, p. 9.

New Flyer Industries Inc.

—————— ■ ——————

711 Kernaghan Avenue
Winnipeg, Manitoba R2C 3T4
Canada
Telephone: (204) 224-1251
Fax: (204) 224-4214
Web site: http://www.newflyer.com

Public Company
Incorporated: 1930 as Western Auto and Truck Body
   Works
Employees: 1831
Sales: CAD $614.1 million ($526.88 million) (2005)
Stock Exchanges: Toronto
Ticker Symbol: UFL.UN
NAIC: 336100 Motor Vehicle Manufacturing

■ ■ ■

New Flyer Industries Inc. is the largest bus manufacturer in North America. The publicly traded Canadian company produces buses used by urban transit operations as well as Bus Rapid Transit (BRT) systems. New Flyer also offers shuttles used in such places as airports, car rental facilities, universities, and park and ride operations. Over the years New Flyer has been responsible for a number of bus innovations, including the introduction of low-floor technology to the North American market, articulated buses, advanced electronics, and buses capable of using alternative fuels. In addition to its headquarters and manufacturing plant located in Winnipeg, Manitoba, New Flyer operates plants in St. Cloud and Crookston, Minnesota.

ORIGINS DATE TO 1930

New Flyer was founded in 1930 in Winnipeg by John Coval as Western Auto and Truck Body Works. Coval and his five employees built both truck and bus bodies. It wasn't until 1937 that the company began manufacturing complete buses. The first three buses, capable of carrying 32 passengers, were sold to the Grey Goose Bus Lines, Ltd. In 1941 the company displayed its innovative spirit by introducing the first front-engine intercity bus, the 28-passenger "Western Flyer." In 1943 the company introduced what it called the "Bruck," a combination truck and bus. Essentially, the last rows of the bus were replaced by a storage compartment accessible from the outside by a rear door. World War II intervened and Western focused on producing truck bodies for the military until the war ended in 1945, at which point it introduced a 32-passenger Western Flyer. It was also in 1945 that Western Auto and Truck Body Works took the name of its signature product, becoming Western Flyer Coach Ltd.

During the postwar years, Western Flyer eased out of the truck body business to focus all of its attention on bus manufacturing, especially custom-built highway coaches. In 1946 Western Flyer produced a pair of sightseeing buses for Salt Lake City, Utah, believed to be the first time a Canadian bus maker had made a sale in the United States. The company introduced 40-passenger buses in 1949: the C-40, intended for city use, and the T-40, intended for transit companies. The vehicles also found a military market, as the Canadian Department of National Defense and the United States Air Force bought more than 350 of them over the next 20 years.

A major development in the 1950s was the introduction of the "Canuck" model in 1953, Western Flyer's first rear-engine bus. It could accommodate 33 passengers. Two years later the company unveiled its first two-level coach ("deck-and-a-half"), the T36-40 2L, which featured transparent roof panels. During the 1950s, the company also introduced new Canuck models: in 1955, the Canuck P-37, a newly styled and more technically advanced bus, capable of carrying 37 passengers; and in 1958, the P-41 Canuck, a diesel-powered bus that could accommodate 41 passengers.

Western Flyer continued to grow in the early 1960s. To meet demand, it opened a new plant in Winnipeg, which was also a preliminary step for the company's move into transit bus manufacturing. In the meantime, the company introduced the Canuck 500 in 1964, and the Canuck 600, a stretched version of the 500, in 1967. In that same year, Western Flyer introduced the D700, the company's first transit bus. The intercity market was by now dominated by General Motors, forcing Western Flyer and other small companies out of the market. In 1968 the last Canuck 600 rolled off the company's assembly line, and instead of coaches the company began to concentrate on transit city buses. In addition to the D700, Western Flyer also tried to serve this market with the introduction of an electric trolley coach, the 700E, a bus that was powered by overhead trolley power lines but relied on tires rather than tracks. The vehicles were then sold to the Toronto Transit Commission as part of a 150-bus and trolley bus order in 1968.

GOVERNMENT INTERVENTION SAVES COMPANY IN 1971

Despite the change in focus, Western Flyer struggled financially. It was bought by Detroit businessman Thomas J. Ault in 1970 but just a year later required Canadian government intervention to stay business. In 1971 the Manitoba Development Corporation, an entity owned by the Manitoba government, acquired a 74-percent interest in the company, which was subsequently renamed Flyer Industries Ltd. In 1971 the company generated just $3 million in sales, leading to a loss of $500,000. During the rest of the decade, Flyer concentrated on the development and selling of large heavy duty transit buses. The Series 800, available as a diesel bus or trolley coach, was introduced in 1973. The major customer for this model was the San Francisco Municipal Railway.

Flyer fared no better under a new name, however. According to the *Globe and Mail*, Flyer "became a Government money pit as the province attempted to maintain the much-needed jobs. Intermittent layoffs and complaints from buyers tarnished the company's image. Stuck with a public relations liability, the Government looked for a buyer." Over the course of 15 years of government assistance Flyer lost about CAD $75 million and became saddled with debt. In 1986 the Manitoba government found a buyer in Dutch businessman Jan den Oudsten, whose family owned the Den Oudsten Busworks, the Netherland's largest city-bus maker. The tenth child among 14 siblings and an engineer by training, Den Oudsten, who was in his early 50s, had spent his life in the bus business and was a dominant figure in his family's concern. "At the time," Den Oudsten told the *Winnipeg Free Press*, "people in Holland was saying I was crazy to come to North America." Den Oudsten paid just CAD $1 million for Flyer, which he promptly renamed New Flyer Industries in 1986. Moreover, the government also agreed to cover CAD $56 million in debts and warranty obligations. For his part, Den Oudsten was required to operate the Winnipeg plant until 1991, after which he was free to close the plant or move.

Although Den Oudsten Bus Works held no stake in New Flyer, which was owned separately by Jan den Oudsten, it did provide much needed help. New Flyer workers were flown to Holland for five months to study how work was done at Den Oudsten Busworks, where a modified version of Japanese manufacturing technique was in place. Essentially, workers were given more responsibility and were less burdened by management supervision. Not only did the workforce begin to change its attitude, it would also be influenced by the new owner, who became a familiar sight on the shop floor and demonstrated his dedication to turning around the company. On a production level, New Flyer made other changes. The design of its buses was altered; for example, aluminum was replaced with easier to assemble glass-fibre outer panels. As a result, production time was cut, providing New Flyer with a competitive edge in price that helped it win public tender contacts. Den Oudsten also cut costs by eliminating layers of management and by trimming the number of office workers. The ranks in these area were thinned from 110 to 60. The plant employment of 70 soon rose, however, as an increase in business led to the callback of more than 200 workers over the next year and a half. To be close to a major

```
┌─────────────────────────────────────────────────┐
│                                                   │
│              KEY DATES                            │
│                  ■                                │
│  ─────────────────────────────────────────────   │
│                                                   │
│   1930:  Western Auto and Truck Body Works is     │
│          founded.                                 │
│   1941:  The company introduces the "Western      │
│          Flyer" bus.                              │
│   1945:  The company's name is changed to Western │
│          Flyer Coach Ltd.                         │
│   1971:  The government of Manitoba acquires      │
│          control and renames it Flyer Industries  │
│          Ltd.                                     │
│   1986:  Jan Den Oudsten acquires the company and │
│          renames it New Flyer Industries Inc.     │
│   2002:  KPS Special Situations Fund acquires the │
│          company.                                 │
│   2004:  The company is sold to Harvest Partners  │
│          Inc.                                     │
│   2005:  New Flyer Industries Inc. is taken       │
│          public.                                  │
│                                                   │
└─────────────────────────────────────────────────┘
```

customer, the company also opened an assembly plant in Union City, California, near Oakland. After it proved not to be an efficient operation, nor conveniently located for shipping to new customers, that plant was moved in 1990 to Grand Forks, North Dakota.

After the sale to Den Oudsten, New Flyer soon began establishing itself as a technology leader. In 1988 the company introduced low-floor technology, pioneered by its Dutch cousin company, to North America. These buses rode lower to the ground, making them easier to enter and exit than buses with a standard height floor. This was especially helpful for seniors, people with disabilities, and parents traveling with small children, groups that comprised a large share of bus ridership. A prototype was ready in 1988 and was used to land a major contract with the Port Authority of New York and New Jersey. The first of these buses were delivered in 1989. New Flyer, again with the help of Den Oudsten Bus Works, also began work on articulated buses, which were essentially a pair of buses hinged together in order to negotiate turns. The first 60-foot articulated bus was delivery to San Mateo County in California in 1990. Two years later articulated trolley buses were introduced into the San Francisco Railway system.

PERIOD OF INNOVATION: 1990–2000

A number of innovations followed in the 1990s, due in large measure to the company's ability to secure a three-year, $15 million loan from a U.S. bank, Congress Financial (with the help of the provincial government), after being turned down by Canadian banks. In 1993

New Flyer became the first bus manufacturer to implement programmable logic controlled (PLG) multiplexing on all of its bus models. It also began investing in alternative fuels. In 1994 it offered the first compressed natural gas-powered buses in North America and worked with Ballard Power Systems to develop the world's first hydrogen fuel cell-powered bus (self-contained fuel cells used hydrogen to produce electricity chemically while producing water as a byproduct). These did not prove to be commercial successes, however. In 1998 the company fared better with the introduction of the first diesel-electric hybrid bus, first delivered to California's Orange County. The wheels were driven by an electric motor while the diesel engine, only half the size of a conventional bus engine, kept the batteries fully charged. As a result, fuel consumption was cut by about 40 percent and the buses created less pollution. During the 1990s, New Flyer also refined some of its technologies, culminating in the 1999 introduction of the Invero, a premium, low-floor bus featuring stylish bodywork, using composite materials and modular construction, and advanced electronic controls. It was lighter than other buses, easier to maintain, and less costly to operate. It was also easier to drive and offered other driver amenities, including a better layout of the instrument panel, easy-to-read and clearly marked gauges, better mirror locations, ergonomic foot pedals, and a highly adjustable seat to alleviate driver fatigue. Passengers were catered to by an improved air conditioning system, large seat-level windows that were easy to open and close, and easy to reach driver-alert pull cords.

Also of note during the 1990s was the expansion of the Winnipeg plant to meet demand for New Flyer buses. The North Dakota final assembly plant was also moved to Crookston, Minnesota, in 1996. Then, in 1999, the facility was expanded and a third plant was opened in St. Cloud, Minnesota. The extra capacity was needed to take on major contracts signed in the late 1990s with Seattle and Los Angeles that pushed the company's backlog of work above the CAD $1 billion mark.

New Flyer entered the new century with great expectations but soon experienced growing pains. In February 2001 the company furloughed a quarter of its workforce in the Winnipeg plant, about 440 people, because, according to management, it was making bodies faster than the assembly plants could use them. All but 100 workers were recalled two months later, but in November 2001, 500 workers were laid off, leading to concern about the health of the company. Rumors also began to circulate about New Flyer being sold or a new partner being brought in. Some of the company's problems could be tied to the terrorist attacks of September 11, 2001 and the United States' subsequent military action in Afghanistan and Iraq. Local American governments, which were New Flyer's primary customers and were dependent on federal transportation grants, grew cautious about committing to new bus purchases, fearful that federal money would be diverted to support the newly launched war on terror.

The rumors proved accurate, and in early 2002 majority control of New Flyer was purchased by New York-based KPS Special Situations Fund for CAD $40 million. KPS then provided a $44 million investment to help grow the business. Jan den Oudsten retained a minority stake in New Flyer but gave up his job as CEO. In his place KPS installed John Marinucci, who had headed a rail car manufacturing company in Hamilton, Ontario. He took over a company suffering from severe cash flow problems. Because of its financial uncertainty, customers were increasingly reluctant to commit to long-term contracts. "Our problems were not so much a result of the market dwindling or any cyclicality of the market," Marinucci told the press in his first media interview after taking over in April 2002. He wasted little time proving his point by implementing a turnaround plan developed with KPS. By the summer of 2003, workers were being recalled, and in October of that year New Flyer added CAD $425 million worth of orders from Seattle and Vancouver to complete a quick return to health.

In December 2003 KPS took steps to realize a major profit on its investment. A preliminary deal was arranged to sell the company to New York private equity firms Harvest Partners Inc. and Lightyear Capital LLC, which beat out a dozen other suitors. The deal was completed in March 2004 and according to *Financial Post*, KPS "walked away with about 7.5 times its initial investment, or about $300 million. As it was a private deal, neither side provided an exact purchase price."

Harvest indicated that it planned to hold onto New Flyer for about five years. But in August 2005 the new owners cashed in some of their interest when New Flyer engineered an initial public offering of stock, resulting in gross proceeds of CAD $200 million.

Ed Dinger

PRINCIPAL DIVISIONS

Manufacturing; Service; Parts.

PRINCIPAL COMPETITORS

Gillig Corporation; North American Bus Industries, Inc.; Orion Bus Industries.

FURTHER READING

Cash, Martin, "$425 in Orders Revs Up Bus Firm," *Winnipeg Free Press*, October 25, 2003, p. A1.

———, "Bus Firm Founder Receives Honour," *Winnipeg Free Press*, October 16, 2003, p. C10.

———, "Flyer Moving in 'Right Direction,'" *Winnipeg Free Press*, August 13, 2003, p. B9.

———, "New Flyer CEO Eyes Rebound For Bus Maker," *Winnipeg Free Press*, September 16, 2002, p. B4.

———, "New Flyer Lays off 500," *Winnipeg Free Press*, November 22, 2003, p. b4.

———, "N.Y. Equity Firms Buying Rejuvenated Transit Bus Maker," *Winnipeg Free Press*, December 16, 2003, p. C7.

———, "Return on Sale of New Flyer 1,000 Per Cent," *Winnipeg Free Press*, December 17, 2003, p. C8.

———, "Straight Talk at New Flyer," *Winnipeg Free Press*, September 14, 2003, p. B4.

Dabrowski, Wotjek, "How Management's Pitch Set Wheels Turning: Bus Maker New Flyer," *Financial Post*, May 25, 2004, p. E6.

Douglas, John, "Flyer Firm Unbankable in Canada," *Winnipeg Free Press*, September 23, 1994.

Fallding, Helen, "New Flyer Gets a New Lease on Life," *Winnipeg Free Press*, March 19, 2002, p. A5.

Gage, Ritchie, "New Flyer Industries Workers Go Dutch To Develop A Feel for the Profit Motive," *The Globe and Mail*, January 16, 1988, p. B5.

MacFadyen, Kenneth, "KPS Drops Off Bus Co.," *Buyouts*, January 5, 2004.

McNell, Murray, "City Bus Maker Predicts Bright Days Ahead," *Winnipeg Free Press*, November 16, 2005, p. B9.

New York Community Bancorp, Inc.

<hr>

615 Merrick Avenue
Westbury, New York 11590
U.S.A.
Telephone: (516) 683-4100
Fax: (516) 683-4424
Web site: http://www.mynycb.com

Public Company
Incorporated: 1993 as Queens County Bancorp, Inc.
Employees: 2,029
Sales: $1.13 billion (2004)
Stock Exchanges: New York
Ticker Symbol: NYB
NAIC: 522319 Mortgage and Nonmortgage Loan Brokers

■ ■ ■

Listed on the New York Stock Exchange, New York Community Bancorp, Inc. (NYCB) is a holding company for New York Commercial Bank and New York Community Bank. The latter, formerly known as Long Island Commercial Bank, serves small and medium-sized businesses and consumers in Long Island and Brooklyn, while the former is one of the five largest thrifts in the United States, boasting some 140 branch offices and assets of more than $26 billion. New York Community Bank has been cobbled together by the acquisition of several New York metropolitan-area community banks, the names of which the thrift continues to use as a way to connect with local residents. They include Queens County Savings Bank, serving the borough of Queens with 34 branches; Roslyn Savings Banks, whose 60 locations serve residents of New York's Nassau and Suffolk Counties; Richmond County Savings Bank, a Staten Island thrift with 23 branches; Roosevelt Savings Bank, maintaining nine branches in Brooklyn; CFS Bank, with single branches in Manhattan and the Bronx and four branches in Westchester County; First Savings Bank of New Jersey, operating four branches in Bayonne, New Jersey; and Ironbound Bank, operating four branches in New Jersey's Essex and Union Counties. In addition, NYCB launched New York Community Bank in 2005 by opening a branch under that name in The Bronx. NYCB mostly focuses on multifamily residential mortgages, which accounts for about 80 percent of all loans, but it also offers to consumers checking, savings, investment, and insurance products as well as online banking; and checking, cash management, lending, property management, and other services to business customers.

ORIGINS DATING TO 19TH CENTURY

NYCB considers Queens County Savings Bank as its founding institution. It was chartered by the state of New York in April 1859, becoming the first bank in Queens, the residents of which were grateful they no longer had to venture into Manhattan to take care of their banking needs. It remained a community bank, focused on the borough of Queens, and it was not until the early 1990s that Queens County Savings, under the leadership of NYCB's chief executive officer, Joseph R. Ficalora, began its transformation.

Ficalora was born and raised in Queens. He first

came to work for Queens County Savings in 1965 at the age of 18. He began taking night classes at Queensboro Community College and went to work as a part-time teller, considering a job at the bank as a better option than the drugstore and grocery store where he had been employed previously. He did not intend to devote his life to banking. Rather, Ficalora considered becoming a psychiatrist. In 1968 he joined the military, serving one year in Vietnam and three years as an occupational service psychiatric specialist, an experience that soured him on a career in psychology. He returned to work at Queens County Savings in the early 1970s and decided that he preferred to serve people through community banking. He earned degrees from Pace University and the American Institute of Banking and began to work his way up through the bank's management ranks, becoming president and chief operating officer in 1989. Four years later he was named chief executive officer.

Ficalora quickly convinced the board of directors that the bank should make a public offering of stock, not only to grow the business but also to increase shareholder value. In July 1993 Queens County Bancorp, Inc. was incorporated and Ficalora was named president and chief executive officer. The corporation then acquired all of the capital stock of Queens County Savings Banks and subsequently made an initial public offering of stock. The shares began trading on the NASDAQ. Ficalora took an early stab at expansion through acquisition, but his attempt to add Bayside Federal Savings was thwarted by North Fork Bancorp, which made a higher bid. Five years later North Fork outbid him again in picking up Jamaica Savings Bank. Despite these disappointments, Ficalora was not desperate enough to overpay for a property, preferring to bide his time and grow Queens County internally, taking advantage of the consolidation that was taking place in New York City's banking industry. According to *Business Week* in a 2004 profile of Ficalora, "One by one, rivals such as Chemical Bank, Manufacturers Hanover, and Dime Savings were swallowed up by even bigger banks. Their names disappeared and branches closed. Disgruntled customers flocked to Ficalora's bank." Along the way, he also fended off a takeover bid from Emigrant Savings Bank, which according to press accounts was looking to make itself more attractive to big bank suitors.

NEW CENTURY BRINGING FIRST MAJOR ACQUISITION

By the end of the 1990s Queens County operated 14 branches. Although it was doing well as a multifamily apartment lender in the metropolitan area, it lacked a sufficient amount of low-cost deposits to help it fund additional loans. As a result, it had to borrow from the Federal Home Loan Bank, a far more expensive approach to doing business because the interest rates were 5 to 6 percent, rather than the 2 to 3 percent of checking accounts. This situation was the catalyst for Ficalora's first acquisition, which came in 2000 when Queens County acquired Haven Bancorp for a reported $196 million in stock. Haven was the holding company for CFS Bank, founded in 1889 as Columbia Building & Loan Association. In the 1930s it became Columbia Savings and Loan, and after receiving a federal charter in 1938 became Columbia Federal Savings Bank. It adopted the CFS Bank name in 1997, which it applied to the 62 supermarket branches it opened—but unfortunately at too rapid a pace. Earnings suffered and Haven's board members urged a sale of CFS. Queens County and CFS were a perfect fit, as the former gained the low-cost deposits it needed to expand its loan portfolio and CFS gained the financial security it needed. Following the completion of the deal, Queens County changed its name to reflect its geographic expansion, becoming New York Community Bancorp, Inc.

In 2001 NYCB elected to sell seven of the CFS supermarket branches located in northern New Jersey and southern Connecticut that were outside of its core market. The rest of the year was dominated by further expansion, as NYCB completed the acquisition of Staten Island-based Richmond County Financial Corporation in an all-stock deal valued at $802 million, a steep price but one that Ficalora believed was warranted in order to achieve a much needed increase in size. Like NYCB, Richmond traced its history to the 19th century, with its founding in 1886. It was also a fast-growing thrift, bringing with it other banking brands. In addition to Richmond County Savings Bank, NYCB added First Savings Bank of New Jersey, founded in 1889, and of more recent origin, Ironbound Bank, founded in 1988 in the Ironbound section of Newark, New Jersey. NYCB also picked up South Jersey Bank, the eight branches of

KEY DATES

1859: Queens County Savings Bank is chartered.
1993: Queens County Bancorp is incorporated.
2000: Haven Bancorp is acquired and the name is changed to New York Community Bancorp.
2001: Richmond County Financial Corporation is acquired.
2003: Roslyn Savings Bank is acquired.
2005: Long Island Financial Corporation is acquired; the name is changed to New York Commercial Bank.

which it would sell off in 2003. All told, Richmond brought with it 33 branches in Staten Island, Brooklyn, and New Jersey and increased NYCB's assets from $4.7 billion to $8.7 billion, and deposits from $3.2 billion to $5.6 billion—essentially doubling NYCB's size and making it one of the United States top 15 thrifts. There were other tangible benefits as well. NYCB achieved a strong presence in a rapidly growing Staten Island, attractive because of its high percentage of upper-middle-class families; gained a larger footprint in the New York metropolitan area and added Richmond's seasoned management team, which could help NYCB fill in the market with additional branches; and received a 47 percent interest in well-respected investment adviser Peter B. Cannell & Co., which had $650 million in assets under management. NYCB subsequently acquired a 100 percent stake in the firm. As a result, Ficalora told *US Banker,* "We can provide an array of products and financial services equal to any megabank."

NYCB's growth in the early 2000s was impressive. Total assets increased from $4.7 billion in 2000 to more than $11.3 billion in 2002, and net income during this period soared from less than $25 million to nearly $230 million. After digesting the Richmond acquisition in 2002, NYCB was ready in 2003 to expand even further.

In October 2003 NYCB completed the acquisition of Nassau County's Roslyn Savings Bank in a stock transaction valued at $1.58 billion. Roslyn was another venerable institution in the area, established in 1876. Ficalora was in Europe on business when bidding began on the Long Island thrift in June 2003. He hurried home and in a matter of days he and his team put together a winning offer, which was not the highest bid but Roslyn believed represented the best possibility for improving shareholder value. Ficalora also was helped to some extent by longstanding ties between the two banks.

Back in the 1960s Queens County Savings and Roslyn teamed up with Richmond County Savings and Roosevelt Savings Bank to form a consortium called CompuThrift, which provided technology assistance to the member banks. After CompuThrift shut down in the late 1980s, the banks became clients of The BISYS Group Inc. and continued to work together on technology issues. Roslyn then acquired Roosevelt in 1999 and two years later NYCB acquired Richmond. It was fitting in a way that the four banks would be brought together when NYCB acquired Roslyn.

The advantages of NYCB and Roslyn joining forces were manifold. According to *Crain's New York Business,* the thrifts were "different in just the right places. New York Community excels at generating loans, while Roslyn is strong in deposit gathering. Moreover, the two have different strengths within commercial lending. Roslyn does extremely well at construction lending. ... New York Community is strong in making real estate loans to owners of rent-controlled buildings, a highly stable and dependable niche." According to *American Banker,* "Roslyn's hidden jewel is a portfolio of mortgage-backed securities that, when liquidated, could give New York Community cash flow to boost its real estate lending."

The Roslyn deal moved NYCB into a new level of prominence. Previously the eleventh largest holder of deposits in the New York region, it now only trailed J.P. Morgan Chase & Co. and Citigroup Inc. Moreover, with assets of more than $23.4 billion by the end of 2003, NYCB was now one the country's 50 largest banks.

Ficalora remained committed to pursuing a community banking approach, relying on long-term customer loyalty to familiar names. In early 2004 NYCB applied the Roslyn name to 30 CFS supermarket-based branches and a pair of Queens County branches in Nassau and Suffolk counties. It also revived the Roosevelt Savings name, which Roslyn had retired after acquiring the thrift, and used it on Brooklyn operations. Roosevelt's connection to the borough dated to 1895 when it was founded as Eastern District Savings Bank. It assumed the Roosevelt name in 1920 as a way to honor Theodore Roosevelt, former governor of New York and the 26th President of the United States.

UP FOR SALE IN 2004

NYCB's spectacular growth made Ficalora something of a cult hero in some investment circles, but his reputation would be tarnished somewhat in 2004 when NYCB stumbled. It raised $400 million in a secondary stock offering in order to acquire GreenPoint Finance Corp., only to see Ficalora's old nemesis, North

Fork, take the prize. In order to make use of the cash, Ficalora invested it along with short-term borrowings to buy $2.6 billion in securities. However, when interest rates increased, NYCB was exposed to significant losses. According to *American Banker,* "The leverage shocked investors when it was revealed in April." With a sudden loss in investor confidence, the price of its stock plummeted, and NYCB hired Bear Stearns Cos., Citigroup Inc., and Sandler O'Neill & Partners LP to consider strategic options, essentially putting itself up for sale. Although there was interest from a number of quarters, no bids were tempting enough for the bank to give up its independence. Instead, NYCB sold off investment securities to pay down debt, wrote off losses, and restructure its balance sheet. It was bitter medicine to swallow, but NYCB was soon ready to resume its growth. Now, however, it was looking at commercial lending, a move intended to offset declining profits in retail lending.

In 2005 NYCB used $69.8 million in stock to acquire commercial bank Long Island Financial Corp., founded in 1989 by former New York State Assembly speaker Perry B. Duryea, Jr. The firm became available after loan defaults caused net income in 2003 to drop by nearly 50 percent. Long Island Financial had $539.7 million in assets and operated 12 branches in Suffolk, Nassau, and Brooklyn. NYCB then renamed it New York Commercial Bank to form the foundation for a commercial banking unit. To bolster its push into commercial lending, NYCB agreed in October 2005 to pay $400 million for Atlantic Bank of New York, owned by the National Bank of Greece. In the deal that was still pending in 2006, New York Commercial Bank would add five branches in Queens and Manhattan, one in Brooklyn, four in Westchester County, and two on Long Island. Also of note, in 2005 NYCB launched a new banking brand, New York Community Bank, opening its first branch in the Co-Op City section of the Bronx.

Ed Dinger

PRINCIPAL DIVISIONS

New York Commercial Bank; New York Community Bank.

PRINCIPAL COMPETITORS

Astoria Financial Corporation; HSBC USA Inc.; JPMorgan Chase & Co.

FURTHER READING

Der Hovanesian, Mara, "Hometown Banker in the Big City," *Business Week,* March 29, 2004, p. 96.

Fredrickson, Tom, "Roslyn Deposits to Fuel NY Community Lending," *Crain's New York Business,* July 14, 2003, p. 3.

Harrigan, Susan, "New York Community Bancorp to Buy Long Island Financial," *Newsday,* August 3, 2005.

"Local Touch in Big Town," *US Banker,* May 2001, p. 61.

Moyer, Liz, "No Buyer, More Investor Angst for N.Y. Community," *American Banker,* June 18, 2004, p. 20.

Padgett, Tania, "CEO of New York Community Bancorp Is Well-Versed in Acquisitions," *Newsday,* July 3, 2004.

———, "New York Community Bancorp Agrees to Buy Roslyn Bancorp," *Newsday,* June 28, 2003.

Rieker, Matthias, "What Next N.Y. Community?," *American Banker,* July 6, 2004, p. 1.

Sikora, Martin, "NYCB Grows Choosey After a Buying Spurt," *Mergers & Acquisition: The Dealmaker's Journal,* January 1, 2004.

Solnik, Claude, "King of Queens," *Long Island Business News,* January 11, 2002, p. 5A.

Wipperfurth, Heike, "Expansion Leaves Thrift Hungry for More," *Crain's New York Business,* November 5, 2001, p. 10.

Neways, Inc.

---■---

2089 West Neways Drive
Springville, Utah 84663
U.S.A.
Telephone: (801) 418-2000
Fax: (801) 418-2195
Web site: http://www.neways.com

Private Company
Incorporated: 1992
Employees: 600
Sales: $400 (2005 est.)
NAIC: 325411 Medicinal and Botanical Manufacturing

■ ■ ■

Neways, Inc. is a multilevel marketing company that develops, produces, and distributes personal care products, cosmetics, and nutritional supplements that are free of the toxic ingredients the company says are to be found in everyday products. Critics, on the other hand, say Neways distorts scientific research and engages in scare tactics to promote its products as healthy alternatives. The privately held company has created a distribution network that spans 23 countries. In addition to its Springfield, Utah headquarters, Neways (through subsidiary Neways International) maintains offices in 11 other countries, including Australia, Canada, Germany, Israel, Japan, Malaysia, Mexico, New Zealand, Russia, Singapore, and the United Kingdom.

ORIGINS

Neways was founded by Thomas E. Mower and his wife, Leslie D. Mower. According to company information, Mower was a research scientist. In the 1970s he and his wife launched a commercial chemical company called Nubrite. Leslie Mowers's background, as she told *Utah Business,* was more less academic: "[Mower] put herself through beauty school and nursing school. ... At 18, she began working with the Salt Lake City Police Department on their narcotics squad." In an interview she gave to *Icon* magazine, Mower said she "trained as a nurse, later as a secretary and then spent two years in make-up artistry." Nubrite, according to *Icon,* "used harsh chemicals in more than 400 different industrial products, including engine degreasers, which they sold to airports, garages and convalescent centers. Each product was governed by OSHA (Occupational Safety Health Hazard) and inspectors would come in to check if the people mixing the chemicals were wearing gloves, goggles and protective clothing."

After running Nubrite for a dozen years, the Mowers came to a crossroads in their business careers when Tom Mower asked his wife why she needed such a wide assortment of cosmetics and other skin care products. According to *Icon,* "they looked at the ingredients on the back of the product labels and were shocked to see the same ingredients in Dee's beauty products that OSHA had told them not to get on their employees' skin." This was the event that led the couple to begin researching the ingredients found in personal care products. Company material maintains that Tom Mower came to realize that many of these ingredients "were ineffective and very out of date in relationship to the technological breakthroughs and discoveries that had been made in biochemistry. In addition, many of the ingredients were now found to be potentially harmful to the skin, to many of the internal organs, and to the general health of people using them." According to *Icon,* "Tom and Dee started making toxin-free products slowly from home, until in 1987 they realized they needed a proper office and manufacturing plant and Dee asked her father for a loan to pay for their expansion."

The Mowers, who were no longer involved with Nubrite and had been using their kitchen table and a shed behind their Fairview, Utah, home, now set up shop in Salem, Utah, to develop their own line of personal care products, sold under the Neways label. To market them, the Mowers chose to pursue a multilevel marketing program, combining direct marketing and franchising, best known for its use by Amway Corporation. Individuals were recruited as independent contractors on a franchise basis to sell the Neways products and also to recruit new franchisees. They then received commissions on the products they sold as well as from the sales of the franchisees they brought into the network. Explaining why the Mowers chose multilevel marketing, company literature maintained, "Conventional advertising is expensive and really doesn't tell anything about the products being sold other than to enhance name recognition and support illusionary cosmetic benefits. Neways felt that word of mouth is the best form of advertising." More so, "By avoiding the outrageous sales and advertising costs that almost all other cosmetic companies bear, Neways was able to pay for the expensive ingredients necessary to give the products the performance people were looking for."

Starting out with hair care and skin products, Neways quickly moved beyond the United States, spreading its network of independent contractors to Canada. "And once NAFTA (the North American Free Trade Agreement) went into effect, pushing Canada into recession," Tom Mower told *Success* in a 1998 article, "we thought it only natural to expand overseas." According to *Success,* Neways' first stop was Australia, "which, by virtue of its being English-speaking, allowed the company to transfer its marketing, packaging, and promotional strategies seamlessly. Once established down under, Mower expanded the company's operations into New Zealand and Malaysia, two countries with ties to Australia."

SWIFT GROWTH: 1990-2000

In 1992 the Mowers incorporated Neways, ushering in a number of developments in the 1990s. Also in 1992 the company introduced a line of nutritional products, added distributors in the United Kingdom, and began developing a line of cosmetics, which were unveiled in 1994, sold under the Leslie DeeAnn label. In that same year, the company established itself in Russia, which in turn opened up Eastern Europe. As the business grew, Neways's manufacturing and distribution facility was hard pressed to keep pace, and in 1997 the company completed a major expansion of its Salem operation. It also introduced in 1997 one of its best-selling products, a nutritional supplement called Maximol Solutions. Neways then entered Japan in 1998 followed by the Philippines and Israel. According to what Tom Mower told the press, Neways did about $170 million in worldwide sales in 1997 and $300 million in 1998.

If Mower's numbers were accurate, Neways was indeed a major success story, but the company's rise did not occur without a measure of controversy. In 1993 the company was forced by the Food and Drug Administration to recall a weight-loss product called "Quickly" because it contained potentially dangerous amounts of furosemide, a powerful diuretic that required a doctor's prescription and should only be taken under medical supervision. Neways was also accused of misrepresenting scientific research to scare consumers away from common products and steer them to Neways's "safer" products.

In 1993 the company supported its claim in a products usage brochure that sodium lauryl sulfate (SLS) and sodium laureth sulfate (SLES), found in shampoos and soaps, had toxic properties and could present dangerous side effects by citing research conducted by Dr. Keith Green, Regents Professor of Ophthalmology at the Medical College of Georgia. According to syndicated columnist and author Paula Begoun, Neways

1987: Thomas and Leslie Dee Ann Mower begin selling Neways products.
1992: The company is incorporated.
1994: Neways enters Russia.
1998: Neways enters Japan.
2003: Neways pleads guilty to selling a product containing prescription human growth hormone.
2005: Thomas and Dee Ann Mower and former corporate counsel are convicted by a federal jury on tax evasion changes.

reported, "A study from the Medical College of Georgia indicates that SLS is a systemic, and can penetrate and be retained in the eye, brain, heart, liver, etc., with potentially harmful long-term effects. It could retard healing and cause cataracts in adults, and can keep children's eyes from developing properly." Begoun interviewed Green, who insisted that his work was completely misquoted: "There is no part of my study that indicated any [eye] development or cataract problems from SLS or SLES and the body does not retain those ingredients at all. We did not even look at the issue of children, so that conclusion is completely false because it never existed. The Neways people took my research completely out of context and probably never read the study at all." Moreover, Green told Begoun, "The statement like 'SLS is a systemic' has no meaning. No ingredient can be a systemic unless you drink the stuff and that's not what we did with it. Another incredible comment was that my study was 'clinical,' meaning I tested the substance on people, [but] these were strictly animal tests. Furthermore, the eyes showed no irritation with the 10-dilution substance used! If anything, the animal studies indicated no risk of irritation whatsoever!" Green also said he dropped this line of research and maintained that no follow-up studies on SLS and SLES were conducted by researchers "because the findings were so insignificant."

In the summer of 1993 Dr. Green contacted Neways about its misleading characterization of his research and in September of that year Tom Mower sent a letter to all Neways distributors admitting that its brochure's assertions about Green's research were "either partially or wholly incorrect. We wish to issue a public apology to Dr. Green for the mistakes made in mixing information from different sources which was attributed to him. In the future, please do not refer to Dr. Green and his

studies." The matter did not end there, however. References to Green's work continued to appear in Neways's literature and audio tapes, prompting legal counsel, Andrew Newton for the Medical College of Georgia, in 1997 to threaten legal action if the company did not cease citing Green's study. In November 1997 Neways once again sent a letter to distributors telling them to stop distributing company literature using the misinformation and to refrain from using it on their independent web sites. Nevertheless, in 1998 Newton once again contacted Neways, writing, "At first, I was willing to give you the benefit of the doubt that these were the lingering effects of your previous publications, for which you might not necessarily be responsible. However, I was quite alarmed when I visited your web site today (August 26, 1998), and found the exact same false and libelous reference to the Medical College of Georgia. ... This must stop."

According to Neways's critics, the flap with Dr. Green was not an isolated incident. A competitor in the natural products field, Melaleuca, Inc., issued a white paper, "Are Your Personal Care Products Safe?," in which it contended that Neways spread rumors about the dangers of common ingredients: "It is easy to understand why they stick to their story—even when authorities like their own 'experts' and respected organizations like the American Cancer Society and the Cosmetic, Toiletry, and Fragrance Association say they are wrong," opined the paper's authors. "They have gained thousands of customers because of their tactics. It has worked for them."

LEGAL CHALLENGES IN 2000

Although such criticism could be dismissed as the sour grapes of a jealous rival, there was no disputing the legal difficulties Neways and its founders faced in the new century. In 1999 the company began distributing an oral spray called BioGevity, which it claimed could improve sexual performance, lower cholesterol, decrease wrinkle appearance, help reduce body fat, and provide other rejuvenating benefits. FDA investigators discovered, however, that BioGevity contained human growth hormone (HGH), illegal without a doctor's prescription and when misused by adults could lead to cardiovascular disease, nervous disorders, and the enlargement and distortion of facial features. The company sold about 100,000 bottles of BioGevity by April 2000 before pulling the product. Neways was subsequently charged by the government and settled the matter in October 2003 by agreeing to pay a $500,000 criminal fine and forfeiting $1.25 million in profits it realized from the sale of BioGevity from March 1999 to April 2000. A spokesperson for Neways acknowledged the company's mistake in selling a product containing HGH, adding, "We relied on advice from vendors who told us there was no problem."

In the meantime, Neways founders, who divorced in 2000 yet continued to run the company together, became caught up in their own legal problems. In December 2001 Tom Mower and Leslie Mower both were charged with one count of conspiracy and six counts of tax evasion. The indictment alleged that they failed to report $3 million in commission income on their personal joint tax returns for 1992 through 1997 and that they used the unreported income to buy assets such as 1,400 acres of land. Moreover, the indictment alleged that they used false names and Social Security numbers to conceal the income, falsified corporate books and records, used a fraudulent loan document to conceal commission income from Australia, and also placed themselves in an advantageous position at the top of Neways's marketing structure in the United States, Australia, and Malaysia. The Mowers pleaded innocent. In April 2003, a federal grand jury indicted former Neways attorney, James Thompson, charging him with conspiracy and obstructing an IRS investigation. A second conspiracy charge also was lodged against the Mowers, who were accused of working with Thompson to conceal another $1 million in Neways sales.

By this point the Mowers had given up their corporate posts, and in June 2002 Michael Cunningham was named Neways's chief executive officer. Cunningham had been with the company for ten years and had headed the Australian office, Neways's most profitable market. The company continued to prosper despite the legal difficulties facing its founders. In April 2003 Neways opened a new corporate headquarters in Springville, Utah, and the Mowers stood together at the podium for the ceremony. While Cunningham portrayed the occasion as a "kind of a crossroads" for Neways, maintaining that the company had "gone from an entrepreneurial company to stretching our legs and growing and becoming a worldwide operation," he could not escape questions about the charges facing the Mowers. "It's not an issue that we're going to discuss and it has nothing to do with this company," Cunningham told the press. "It's a personal issue with Tom and Dee and it should be left there ... we wish them the best."

Distancing the Mowers from Neways was difficult given that some of the hidden funds were supposedly used to fund the building of a Salem warehouse. They couple also continued to travel around the world promoting Neways, and their son, Thomas Mower, Jr., served as Neways's president. In March 2005 the Mowers were convicted by a federal jury of income tax evasion and conspiracy, and Thompson also was found guilty of conspiracy and corruptly impeding the due administration of tax laws. Sentencing was scheduled for June 2005, but was delayed as the Mowers sought to have a U.S. district judge reverse the conviction and grant a new trial. Their motions were denied in August 2005 and, barring a successful appeal, they still faced the prospect of serving time in prison.

Ed Dinger

PRINCIPAL SUBSIDIARIES

Neways International.

PRINCIPAL COMPETITORS

Avon Products, Inc.; Forever Living Products International, Inc.; GNC Corporation.

FURTHER READING

Begoun, Paula, "Sodium Lauryl Sulfate & Sodium Laureth Sulfate," www.cosmeticscop.com.

Carricaburu, Lisa, "Springville, Utah-Based Supplement Maker Pleads Guilty in Hormone Case," *Salt Lake Tribune,* October 7, 2003.

Christopher, Elisha, "Executive Living: Leslie Deeann Mower," *Utah Business,* March 2002, p. 39.

Dethman, Leigh, "No New Trial for Neways Founders," *Deseret Morning News,* August 20, 2005.

Fattah, Geoffrey, "Pop, Fanfare Greet Opening of Neways," *Deseret Morning News,* April 29, 2003, p. B1.

Lynch, Colum, "Earth Shakers," *Success,* December 1998, p. 86.

Manson, Pamela, "Multi-Level Marketing Executives Convicted of Tax Evasion Charges," *Salt Lake Tribune,* March 19, 2005.

"Mower Power: Leslie DeeAnn Mower," www.canceractive.com.

Welling, Angie, "2 Images of Neways Founders Depicted," *Deseret Morning News,* March 8, 2005.

Nippon Meat Packers, Inc.

6-14, Minami-Honmachi 3-chome
Chuo-ku
Osaka, 541-0054
Japan
Telephone: (06) 282-3031
Fax: (06) 282-1056
Web site: http://www.nipponham.co.jp

Public Company
Incorporated: 1949
Employees: 2,589
Sales: Yen 934.6 billion ($8.7 billion) (2005)
Stock Exchanges: Tokyo
Ticker Symbol: 2282
NAIC: 311611 Animal (Except Poultry) Slaughtering;
    115114 Postharvest Crop Activities

■ ■ ■

Nippon Meat Packers, Inc., is Japan's leading meat processing company. Through its group of over 120 subsidiaries, the international company sells beef, pork, and chicken, as well as processed and cooked foods. A mislabeling scandal in 2002 tarnished Nippon Meat Packers' image and led to a major drop in profits. Since that time, the company has worked to restore consumer confidence and shore up sales and profits.

EARLY HISTORY

In March, 1942, just a few months after the bombing of Pearl Harbor, president and founder of Nippon Meat Packers, Yoshinori Okoso, started in the meat business by establishing the Tokushima Meat Processing Factory in Tokushima. After seven years of producing hams and sausages, Okoso founded the Tokushima Ham Company, the forerunner to Nippon Meat Packers.

Supplies of genuine pork were scarce during World War II and on into the 1950s. As a result, the company often used rabbit and fish meat for their hams and sausages. Despite the hardships of short supply, the company's growth remained steady through the 1950s, marked in 1956 by the construction of the company's Osaka plant.

Pork shortages persisted into the 1960s, when mutton was used as a pork substitute. The company continued to grow, and by 1960, it began offering shares on the Osaka stock exchange. Two years later, the company appeared on the second section of the stock exchange in Tokyo, and in 1967, the company was promoted to the first sections of both the Tokyo and Osaka exchanges.

Growth in the 1960s came through the founding of new companies and links with existing ones. In 1963, the year the company adopted its present name, Nippon Meat Packers, the Torise Ham Company became an affiliate. Five years later, the company founded Nippon Broilers Company, a production and breeding facility for pigs and broiler chickens. The company has since set up similar facilities such as the Japan Farm, Kyushu Farm, Shiretoko Farm, and Tohoku Farm. In 1969, Nippon Meat Packers entered into business with Swift & Company, of the United States, one of the largest meat producers in the world at that time. The association lead to the sale of Swift brand hams and sausages in the Japanese market.

COMPANY PERSPECTIVES

We will share the pleasure of good food and the enjoyment of good health with people throughout the world. We will value the gift of life and not compromise on quality; we will take the best possible care in offering food that is a joy to eat. We will pioneer the discovery of new eating possibilities to contribute to making life enjoyable and healthy.

Also in 1969, Nippon Meat Packers established one of its most important product-development tools, the Housewives Directors Group. The group gathered opinions and complaints from women regarding the taste, price, packaging, and advertisement of Nippon Meat Packers' products. The organization helped the company produce big sellers such as Bun-ta-ta sausages, Winny skinless wieners, and Swift Loaf.

DIVERSIFICATION BEGINS IN 1970

The early 1970s were a time of diversification for Nippon Meat Packers. In 1970, the company founded a school known as the Nippon Meat Academy. In 1973, the company entered the food service business with the founding of its John Bull restaurant which it opened as a way of collecting product information and introducing new recipes. It soon opened other restaurants including Berni Inn, a combined pub and steak house; Yashiro, a *shabu shabu* restaurant; and Schau Essen Haus, a German-style pub.

Besides branching into restaurants, the company entered professional sports with the founding of the Nippon-Ham Fighters baseball club. Investment in the baseball team proved a successful advertising vehicle for both the company and the ham industry in Japan.

In the later 1970s, Nippon Meat Packers began taking global interests. In 1976, the company issued 7.5 million Continental Depositary Receipts on the stock exchange in Luxembourg. The following year, in 1977, the company founded Day-Lee Meats, in Los Angeles. Since then, Nippon Meat Packers has set up affiliates in Australia, Singapore, England, and Canada.

The 1980s were marked by continued growth and the introduction of several successful lines of meat. In 1981, the company introduced thin-sliced ham. Only half a millimeter thick, the product became one of the company's biggest sellers in the ham market and even won the Nihon Keizai Shimbun's (Japan's business newspaper) award for "Superior Product of the Year" in 1982. Growth in production and development continued in 1986, with a new production plant at Shizuoka and a new research center in the Ibaraki plant. The facilities improved the company's technology and processing capabilities. Also in 1986, Nippon Meat Packers introduced its highly successful raw ham products known as Schau Schinken.

Nippon Meat Packers' production extended into western Japan in 1987, with the establishment of the Hyogo Polka plant.

The company continued to grow both by adding processing facilities and introducing new food lines. In 1988 alone, the company introduced three new products: the Essen Burg, Mini Polka, and Lemon Chicken.

Introducing new meats and meat products to the Japanese diet made Nippon Meat packers one of the country's top food producers in the 1990s and put Nippon Meat Packers in a strong position to grow with the meat industry in Japan. The company held its leading industry position into the early years of the new millennium.

OVERCOMING SCANDAL IN THE NEW MILLENNIUM

While Nippon Meat Packers remained dedicated to expanding its business at the start of the new century, it was forced to deal with a major scandal. In 2001, the Japanese meat industry was hit hard by an outbreak of Bovine Spongiform Encephalopathy (BSE), or mad cow disease. The disease infected Japanese cattle and sales of beef fell dramatically. As such, the government launched a plan to help those in the industry by offering a beef buyback program. In 2002, Japan's Ministry of Agriculture, Forestry, and Fisheries uncovered evidence that Nippon Meat Packers had mislabeled imported beef as domestic in order to receive the benefits of the buyback program.

As part of the investigation, the company's beef was pulled from store shelves and chairman and founder Okoso was forced to resign—he died at age 90 in April 2005. The company also set up a Quality Assurance Division, a Corporate Ethics Committee, and a Safety & Testing Office. Overall, profits fell by 75 percent in 2002.

The company spent much of the latter half of 2002 and 2003 rebuilding consumer confidence. Management worked to shore up sales and profits and continued to make strategic moves to bolster its business. The company acquired frozen seafood processor Hoko Fishing to strengthen is processed foods division.

KEY DATES

1942: Yoshinori Okoso establishes the Tokushima Meat Processing Factory.
1949: Okoso establishes Tokushima Ham Company, the forerunner to Nippon Meat Packers.
1956: A plant opens in Osaka.
1960: The company goes public.
1963: The company adopts the Nippon Meat Packers name.
1969: Nippon Meat Packers enters into business with U.S.-based Swift & Company.
1986: A line of popular raw ham products known as Schau Schinken is launched.
2002: The company admits to mislabeling imported beef as domestic in order to receive benefits of a government buyback program.
2005: Founder Okoso dies.

In December 2003 Japan implemented a ban on U.S. beef imports after a cow in the United States was found with BSE. At the same time, the price of poultry increased as a result of outbreaks of avian flu in Asia. With bans on chickens from Thailand, China, and the United States, Nippon Meat Packers stood well positioned to benefit from its international importing operations in Australia as well as from its partnerships in Brazil.

Net sales increased during 2004 and 2005 along with net income. Eyeing its global operations as crucial to future growth, Nippon Meat Packers established an International Business Affairs Department in February 2005. The company also restructured domestic production operations and opted to shutter its Osaka Kita and Wakayama plants in 2006. While it appeared as though Nippon Meat Packers had successfully overcome the mislabeling scandal, the company remained dedicating to restoring its tarnished image. With a longstanding history as Japan's leading meat processor, the company would no doubt continue supplying consumers with meat, processed foods including sausages, and dairy products in the years to come.

Updated, Christina M. Stansell

PRINCIPAL SUBSIDIARIES

Nippon White Farm Co. Ltd.; Nippon Swine Farm Co. Ltd.; Texas Farm LLC; Oakey Holdings Pty. Ltd.; Nippon Food Packers Inc.; Nippon Pure Food Inc.; Oakey Abattoir Pty. Ltd.; Thomas Borthwick & Sons (Australia) Pty. Ltd.; Shizuoka-Nippon Ham Co. Ltd.; Nagasaki-Nippon Ham Co. Ltd.; Nippon Ham Shokuhin Co. Ltd.; Nippon Ham Sozai Co. Ltd.; Thai Nippon Foods Ltd.; Tohoku-Nippon Ham Co. Ltd.; Minami-Nippon Ham Co. Ltd.; Japan Food Corporation; Nippon Meat Packers Australia Pty. Ltd.; Day-Lee Foods Inc.; Higashi Nippon Food Co. Ltd.; Kanto Nippon Food Co. Ltd.; Naka Nippon Food Co. Ltd.; Nishi Nippon Food Co. Ltd.; Nippon Ham Hokubu Choku-Han Co. Ltd.; Nippon Ham Tobu Choku-Han Co. Ltd.; Nippon Ham Chubu Choku-Han Co. Ltd.; Nippon Ham Kinki Choku-Han Co. Ltd.; Nippon Ham Seibu Choku-Han Co. Ltd.; Nippon Logistics Group Inc.; Marine Foods Co. Ltd.; Nippon Luna Co. Ltd.; HOKO Co. Ltd.; Hokkaido Nippon Ham Fighters Co. Ltd.; Osaka Football Club Co., Ltd.

PRINCIPAL COMPETITORS

Itoham Foods Inc.; Maruha Group Inc.; Tyson Fresh Meats Inc.

FURTHER READING

"Fading Effect of Scandal Helps Nippon Meat Packers Inc. Post Sharp Profit Gain," *Knight Ridder Tribune Business News,* May 18, 2004.

"Heads Roll at Nippon Meat Packers," *Nikkei Weekly,* August 26, 2002.

"Japan Minister Hails Nippon Meat Chm.'s Resignation," *Jiji Press English News Service,* August 27, 2002.

"Japan Police Raid Nippon Meat Packers' Affiliates Over Illegal Pig Vaccination," *Knight Ridder Tribune Business News,* July 20, 2004.

"Nippon Meat Expects Loss for Year," *Dow Jones Newswires,* September 23, 2002.

"Nippon Meat Packers' Profit Hurt by Beef Scandal," *Jiji Press English News Service,* May 20, 2003.

"Nippon Meat Packers Working to Regain Public Trust," *Nikkei Report,* November 19, 2002.

"Nippon Meat's Biz Suspension to Continue into Sept.," *Jiji Press English News Service,* August 26, 2002.

"Police Raid Nippon Meat Packers in Beef Scandal," *Jiji Press English News Service,* October 1, 2002.

"Yoshinori Okoso, Nippon Meat Packers Founder, Dies at 90," *Knight Ridder Tribune Business News,* April 28, 2005.

The North Face, Inc.

2013 Farallon Drive
San Leandro, California 94577
U.S.A.
Telephone: (510) 618-3500
Fax: (510) 618-3531
Web site: http://www.thenorthface.com

Wholly Owned Subsidiary of VF Corporation
Incorporated: 1994 as The North Face, Inc.
Employees: 859
Sales: $238 million (2005 est.)
NAIC: 448190 Other Clothing Stores; 315999 Other
   Apparel Accessories and Other Apparel Manu-
   facturing

■ ■ ■

The North Face, Inc., is a manufacturer and distributor of high-grade equipment and apparel used in mountaineering, skiing, and backpacking. While the reputation of North Face was built on outfitting expeditions, the company's growth in the 1990s came through the introduction of high-tech apparel in upscale retail stores. With Summit Shops, North Face established its use of a "store within a store" concept. In 2006, there were approximately 100 Summit Shops located within retail shops in the U.S. There were also ten North Face retail stores scattered across California, Colorado, Illinois, Massachusetts, New York, Oregon, Virginia, and Washington. Overall, North Face products could be found in over 3,500 locations across the globe. The

company fell on hard times in the late 1990s and was eventually purchased by VF Corporation in 2000.

THE EARLY YEARS: 1965–73

According to the 1996 company prospectus, the name North Face originated with the company's founders and comes from the fact that the north face of a mountain in the northern hemisphere is usually the most formidable and challenging for mountain climbers. North Face was founded in 1965 by outdoor enthusiasts retailing premium-grade backpacking and climbing equipment. North Face began to wholesale and manufacture backpacking equipment in 1968. The business continued to grow and expand. In the early 1970s North Face added outerwear to its product line.

INNOVATION IN PRODUCT DESIGN: 1975–90

Innovative product design and consistent development and introduction of new products have always been North Face's greatest strengths. In 1975 North Face introduced a benchmark in the outdoor equipment industry with its geodesic dome tent. This design became the standard for lightweight, high-performance tents used in high-altitude and polar expeditions. The geodesic dome also became very popular for general backpacking and camping as well. The same year North Face also introduced another original, sleeping bags incorporating shingled construction of synthetic insulation. Like the dome tent, these sleeping bags have become the industry standard.

   In the early 1980s the company launched its "extreme skiwear" line. Another addition to the North

Face product line came in 1988, when the Expedition System was introduced. A complete line of severe cold weather clothing consisting of integrated components, the Expedition System was designed to be used together in various combinations. According to the company, there was wide use of this clothing system by world-class mountain climbers. By the late 1980s North Face was the only manufacturer and distributor in the United States of a comprehensive line of premium-grade, high-performance equipment and apparel used in mountaineering, skiing, and backpacking.

SHAKY GROUND FOR NORTH FACE

While the reputation of North Face products has remained sound, internal decision-making was occasionally questioned. During the growth phase of the 1980s, the company attempted to manufacture all of its own products. This led to problems of obsolete materials, large amounts of capital invested in an inventory of finished goods, and late delivery of high-demand products. However, these were not the only detriments to the financial health of North Face. In the late 1980s, North Face opened outlet stores to sell lower-priced products in an effort to dispose of obsolete materials. The product reputation of North Face was based on a high-end, or expensive, association with the inherent product quality. The lower-priced products confused or missed the intended consumers and did not help the company's overall image. Also, these outlets were not well received by North Face's wholesale customers and were eventually closed. All of these business activities had a negative effect on North Face's finances and launched the company into the next phase of its history.

In May 1988, Odyssey Holdings, Inc. (OHI) acquired the company, known at that time as North Face Corporation. OHI owned about 30 companies in the outdoor and brand-name apparel industry and was at that time headed by William N. Simon, who soon became president of North Face.

In January 1993, a new executive staff was recruited to make needed changes in North Face's operations. Among those newly recruited was Marsden S. Cason, who was at that time the president of North Face and a director and executive officer of OHI. Some of the significant changes initiated by the new management team included hiring experienced executives and operating managers, establishing a focus on sales and gross margin, expanding contracted sources of goods and materials, closing discount outlets, and discontinuing unprofitable product lines. Eventually, as a result of these initiatives, the company would realize a significant increase in sales and profits. However, in 1993 the parent company, OHI, filed for protection under Chapter 11 of the U.S. Bankruptcy Code.

A DRAMATIC TURNAROUND BEGINNING IN 1994

North Face continued to operate at a loss until 1994, when the strategic changes mentioned began to take a positive effect; 1994 was a year of significant transitions for North Face. On June 7 the company was purchased at public auction for $62 million by a group consisting of J.H. Whitney & Co., Cason, and William S. McFarlane. On June 8, 1994, TNF Holdings changed its name to The North Face, Inc. Also in June 1994 Cason was appointed CEO of North Face.

INTO THE NEW MILLENNIUM: OPPORTUNITIES, THREATS, AND A LOOK TO THE FUTURE

One of the inherent weaknesses of being in a focused, niche industry, according to experts, is attempting to sustain growth in a field with a limited number of customers. This is what necessitated the introduction of Summit Shops selling Tekware as North Face attempted during the 1990s to obtain a share of the leisure apparel industry. Such a shift represented a major departure from traditional North Face territories. North Face's success in this new venture depended, in part, upon the buyers of casual wear, a market that can be fickle. For North Face, entering this market could be seen by industry observers as either a weakness or an opportunity. In addition, another possible weakness that presented itself was overdependence on contracted vendors to supply the majority of the company's manufactured goods.

The largest area of opportunity that North Face was involved in was the expansion into the casual apparel industry with the introduction of "Summit Shops." Another area of opportunity for North Face was the possibility of future government contracts for tent sales, given the company's longtime association as a supplier to the U.S. Marines Corps. Finally, further development and introduction of new and innovative designs of

KEY DATES

1965: North Face is established.

1968: The company begins to wholesale and manufacture backpacking equipment.

1975: North Face introduces a benchmark in the outdoor equipment industry with its geodesic dome tent.

1988: Odyssey Holdings, Inc. (OHI) acquires North Face.

1993: OHI files for bankruptcy.

1994: The company is purchased at public auction for $62 million by a group consisting of J.H. Whitney & Co., Marsden Cason, and William S. McFarlane; company name is changed to The North Face Inc.

1996: The North Face goes public; the Tekware line is launched.

1999: Plans to take the company private fail; accounting irregularities force the company to restate its earnings from the past two years.

2000: VF Corporation acquires The North Face.

products in the future seemed to be a likely avenue for North Face to gain or retain market share.

Nonetheless, North Face faced very real threats to its future growth. While the company remained subject to the same kinds of business threats that any business faced, such as major shifts in consumer tastes and preferences, its most prevalent threat was competition. Archrival Patagonia, for example, had historically carried a very similar product line. And there always loomed the threat of new competition because of relatively low barriers to entry and the possibility of a breakthrough in product design.

While North Face had weathered some rough and challenging times, the company seemed by the mid-1990s to be on firm footing and ready to begin another new phase. North Face recommended itself as a company poised for future growth by building on its strengths: brand-name recognition, product reputation and differentiation, innovative product design and diversity, aggressive entry into the casual wear market, and, as attested to by company profits and increases in the value of the company's stock, the decisive and able senior-level management that would continue to drive North Face's climb to success.

NEW OWNERSHIP

Shortly after going public in 1996, North Face began to face a series of problems that nearly led to its demise. Rumors began to spread that in certain instances, the company shipped products ahead of schedule and often over-shipped products to stores in order to record the sale. In 1998, James Fifield took over as CEO. He moved company headquarters to Carbondale, Colorado, which was near his home in Aspen. Overall, the move cost approximately $5 million. At the same time, Fifield and Leonard Green & Partners—a leveraged-buyout firm—announced plans to take North Face private at $17 a share. Shareholders balked at the offer claiming it undervalued the company.

It was at this time that North Face announced that it was considering restating its results from 1997 and 1998 due to accounting irregularities. Share price fell from over $27 per share to $13 per share after the announcement and trading of its stock was halted for nearly a month. The company released its new figures which revealed that 1998 sales had been overstated by six percent, or $16 million, and earnings had been inflated by 42 percent. Sales and earnings had also been overstated in 1997. Slowly but surely, shareholders began to file class action lawsuits claiming the company had inflated its results in order to boost its share price.

Plans to take the company private failed and Fifield resigned his post in 1999. Company headquarters returned to California in 2000. By this time, North Face's financial condition had deteriorated significantly due to distribution problems and costs related to the failed buyout and the moving of company headquarters. VF Corporation, one of the world's largest apparel companies, swooped in just days after North Face announced that it was facing a Chapter 11 bankruptcy protection filing. VF bought North Face for $24.5 million in August 2000.

Under the wing of VF, which recorded $5.6 billion in sales in 2000, North Face received an instant cash infusion. The sale benefited VF as well. The North Face brand gave it a stronger foothold in the outdoor apparel segment. In fact, North Face quickly became the cornerstone in VF's Outdoor Apparel and Equipment Coalition. This division included North Face, JanSport, and Eastpack. In 2004, Vans, Kipling, and the Napapijri brands were added to this coalition.

By 2005, North Face's financial problems were a thing of the past and demand for its products was strong. VF's outdoor apparel unit was experiencing significant year-over-year profit growth: 34 percent in 2003; and 61 percent in 2004. With the support of one of the largest apparel companies in the world, The North Face appeared to be well positioned for future growth. Indeed, the North Face logo would no doubt remain on the backs of outdoor enthusiasts for years to come.

Karen Leslie Boyd
Updated, Christina M. Stansell

PRINCIPAL COMPETITORS

K2 Inc.; L.L. Bean Inc.; Patagonia.

FURTHER READING

Cohen, Bud, "Management Teams Buys North Face for $59M," *Daily News Record*, June 2, 1994, p. 11.

Coleman, Calmetta, "North Face CEO Quits After His Plan to Take Company Private Falls Apart," *Wall Street Journal*, September 2, 1999, p. B5.

Coleman, Calmetta, and Robert Berner, "North Face Loses Footing, Takes Tumble," *Wall Street Journal*, March 12, 1999, p. B15.

Cunningham, Thomas, and Arnold J. Karr, "VF to Buy North Face," *Women's Wear Daily*, April 10, 2000.

Heisler, Eric, "VF Realigns After Several Acquisitions," *Greensboro News & Record*, October 18, 2000, p. B8.

Henderson, Barry, "North Face: Peaking Out?," *Barron's*, March 9, 1998.

Lubove, Seth, "Katmandu Comes to Neiman Marcus," *Forbes*, October 21, 1996, p. 42.

Maycumber, S. Gray, "Performing on a Broader Stage; Performance Fibers and Fabrics Moving into Mainstream Apparel," *Daily News Record*, September 16, 1996, p. 4.

Morris, Kathleen, "Egg All Over North Face," *Business Week*, June 21, 1999.

"North Face Inc. (New Securities Issues)," *Wall Street Journal*, July 2, 1996, p. C18(E).

"The North Face, Inc. Upgrades Sales Force," *PR Newswire*, November 27, 1996, p. 1127SFW017.

"North Face IPO Is a Hit on First Day," *WWD*, July 3, 1996, p. 10.

"North Face Posts 62.4% Net Rise, Plans Secondary Offering," *WWD*, October 30, 1996, p. 14.

"North Face Sold for $25 Million," *Denver Post*, April 8, 2000.

Oring, Sheryl, "$200M Bankruptcy Snags Local Retailers; North Face, Sierra Designs Hit," *San Francisco Business Times*, January 29, 1993, p. 1.

"Outerwear Firm North Face Plans to Raise $30M in IPO; Expects to Use Proceeds to Cut Debt," *Daily News Record*, June 21, 1996, p. 22.

Scott, Mary, "North Face Dismisses 7 of 10 Reps," *STN*, November 1994, p. 3.

Socha, Miles, "The North Face (Plans to Open 25 In-Store Shops)," *Daily News Record*, May 29, 1996, p. 3.

White, Constance C. R. "North Face's Tekware," *New York Times*, April 16, 1996, p. B14.

NSS Enterprises, Inc.

3115 Frenchmens Road
Toledo, Ohio 43607
U.S.A.
Telephone: (419) 531-2121
Fax: (419) 531-3761
Web site: http://www.nss.com

Private Company
Founded: 1911
Employees: 280
Sales: $41.5 million (2005)
NAIC: 333319 Other Commercial and Service Industry
    Machinery

■ ■ ■

NSS Enterprises, Inc. is a privately-owned, Toledo, Ohio-based manufacturer of floor care products for commercial, industrial, and institutional applications. The company's full range of equipment includes carpet vacuums, sweepers, carpet extractors, wet/dry vacuums, floor machines, burnishers, and pressure washers. Prices range from under $500 to more than $15,000. NSS also sells heavy-duty tools and accessories for use with its equipment. Major customers includes the United States government; the Big Three automakers, which use the equipment for their showrooms and repair facilities; hospitals; casinos, resorts, and hotels; factories; schools; airlines; and big box retailers. NSS equipment can be purchased in 60 countries around the world. In the United States, the company has more than 400 distributors and service centers.

NSS GROWS OUT OF 19TH CENTURY CARPET CLEANING TECHNOLOGY

NSS first made its mark with the vacuum cleaner. The forefather of all vacuum cleaners was an 1869 non-electric device called the "Whirlwind," which created suction using a hand crank. Several years later a brush roll was added to improve performance, but even then, the device still relied on a cumbersome hand crank. The next major development came in 1901 when British engineer Herbert C. Booth created a gas-powered, wagon-mounted vacuum cleaner; it was parked outside a home to be cleaned and long hoses were drawn through the windows to power the sweeper attachments. The first "portable" vacuum cleaner, which weighed a mere 92 pounds, was introduced in 1905. Two years later a more user-friendly model was invented by a Canton, Ohio, janitor named James Spangler, whose creativity was prompted by a persistent cough caused by the dust thrown up from the carpet sweeper he used. He built his own vacuum cleaner using an old fan motor mounted on a soap box fixed to a broom handle, and for a dust collector he relied on a pillow case. He received a patent on the design in 1908 and began producing commercial versions, which weighed in at 40 pounds. One of his first customers was a cousin who was married to a saddlemaker and leather merchant named William H. Hoover. With the emergence of automobiles reducing the market for saddles, Hoover was looking for a new endeavor. He liked Spangler's invention, took a stake in his cousin's Electric Suction Sweeper Company, became president, eventually acquired control, and in 1922 renamed it the Hoover Company.

COMPANY PERSPECTIVES

We are creating new momentum, and a new direction. And we believe that our new position statement best describes that direction: More Than Meets The Floor.

Another man fascinated with the commercial potential of vacuum motor technology was Julius Bevington, an executive at Bissell Manufacturing Company, which produced components for the Ford Motor Company. In 1911 he convinced his boss, Fred Bissell, to diversify by producing vacuum motors that could be used for a wide range of industrial uses. Although NSS traces its origins to this 1911 date, it would be the 1920s before Bevington took a partner, Edward Rosenberg, and bought Bissell's vacuum motor unit. Using their initials, they called the company B&R Manufacturing Co., although Bissell's owner, Fred Bissell, retained an interest in the company. B&R would later change its name to National Super Suction Company, reflective of the high-powered industrial vacuum cleaners the company manufactured. A further name change resulted in the company becoming known as the National Super Service Co. The main product was the Super Cleaner, a heavy duty vacuum cleaner used in buildings, furnaces, and heating plants.

In 1940 National Super Service introduced the first model in its highly successful "Pig" canister vacuum cleaner. It represented a major step in the development of the heavy-duty vacuum cleaner. With the motor housed in a cast-aluminum alloy body, it was a extremely durable machine. In addition, its longevity was maintained by the inclusion of a "scrap trap" that preventing large objects from being pulled through the fan. The Pig was also very effective in cleaning high, out-of-the way areas, like ceilings, skylights, and vents. According to the company, the Pigs were so hearty that in 1995 a 50-year-old unit was still being used in an Indianapolis movie theater, where it was put to the test every day sucking up popcorn, candy, and other stray items that littered the aisles.

WORLD WAR II INTERRUPTS GROWTH

World War II disrupted the affairs of National Super Service, which was doing a roaring business in 1941. However, with the United States' entry into the conflict, the company was denied key raw materials, which were now diverted to the war effort. The company had built up a supply of vacuum cleaners that lasted through 1942, but for the rest of the war, it was lucky to scrounge up renewal parts for the thousands of Super Cleaners that were in use at the time. The company's production capacity was now utilized to produce commutators, which were used in aircraft and tank engines. As the war was entering the final several months, Fred Bisell, in September 1944, finally sold his stake in National Super Service to Bevington and Rosenberg.

After the war, Bevington's son, John F. Bevington, joined the company after graduating from John Carroll University. He first went to work in the office and later turned his attention to sales, which gave him the opportunity to become intimately familiar with the distributors of National Super Service. He also became well connected in the industry, serving as the company's representative at trade shows and conventions. John Bevington would become a founding member and board member of both the International Sanitary Supply Association and the American Association of Cleaning Equipment Manufacturers.

John Bevington eventually bought out his father and Rosenberg, but not before the first generation of ownership was involved in yet another technological breakthrough. In 1947 National Super Service introduced the first wet/dry vacuum. Until that time, vacuuming water was a highly dangerous task, one that could easily lead to the electrocution of the operator. National Super Service solved this problem by way of an internal by-pass motor that not only protected the operator but also extended the life of the motor. This design breakthrough would lay the foundation for later heavy-duty models, the NSS Colt and BP-Ranger.

Under John Bevington's leadership, National Super Service continued to be an industry leader in technology innovations. In 1972 the company developed a cold-water extractor. Hot water extraction was used to deep-clean synthetic rugs by laying down a solution of water and detergent in a pressurized mist that loosened the dirt in the carpet's fabrics. The dirt and water was then vacuumed out of the carpet, but the process required a great deal of water and even the highest quality hot water extractors were only able to remove 70 percent to 90 percent of the moisture. As a result, carpets were often damaged, experiencing shrinkage as well as the fading and running of colors. Cold (or warm) water extraction, on the other hand, did not encounter these side effects. Furthermore, National Super Service's engineers greatly improved the ability of the machine to pull water out of carpets by stacking vacuum motors to dramatically increase power.

KEY DATES

1911: The company is founded as part of the Bissell Manufacturing Company.
1940: The "pig" canister vacuum is introduced.
1947: National Super Service develops the first wet vacuum.
1972: The company introduces the cold water extractor.
1984: National Super Service begins building vacuum cleaner bodies with rotomolded polyethylene.
1999: John Bevington retires and sells the business to his son, Mark.
2004: The company becomes NSS Enterprises, Inc.

TECHNOLGOICAL ADVANCES IN THE MODERN ERA

The 1970s saw other advances for National Super Service. In 1976 it introduced a propane-powered buffing machine, the first full-line manufacturer to do so. The buffer was capable of extremely high speeds to produce a shine that became known as the "wet look," which became the standard finish of the industry. A year later National Super Service solidified its industry lead in this area by offering the first high-speed, corded electric buffer. This development launched an industry race to develop new floor pads and chemicals to give floors the highly desirable wet look. National Super Service also set another industry standard in 1984 when it became the first floor care equipment company to make machine bodies out of rotomolded polyethylene, a lightweight yet durable material. Ultimately, all large burnishers, sweepers, and scrubbers would rely on it.

Perhaps the greatest advance for National Super Service in the last 15 years of the century was not in research and development but in a modification of its business model. Instead of merely selling equipment and accessories, it sought to become a resource and service company, one that sold complete solutions. National Super Service was also uniquely positioned in the United States because it remained privately owned and unlike its large competitors had not been gobbled up by foreign companies. The sales force had longstanding ties with retailers and paid regular visits to make sure they understood their customers' needs. The company also took the time to make inroads with companies and distributors that might have been dissatisfied with their current supplier. Given that National Super Service was involved in what amounted to a non-growth industry, luring away the customers of the competition was an imperative to increasing market share. It the early 1990s, National Super Service developed a six-part direct mail program that targeted top-level managers at select companies. They received an introductory letter, followed in one-week intervals by four mailers that included premiums to get attention, and finally a call-for-action follow-up letter that asked prospects to set aside 30 minutes to speak with a regional manager.

In its marketing effort National Super Service emphasized that the way it serviced its accounts was far superior to that of the competition. This customer service approach evolved into the Total-Logistics Control (TLC) program, which permitted distributors and corporate clients to customize their relationship with National Super Service, allowing them to pay for what they actually needed. The menu of programs and services the company offered as a solutions provider was long and varied. It included onsite installations, operator training, program manual development, facility surveys and workloading, central service dispatch and repairs, planned maintenance programs, rental and loaner machines, order tracking, and follow-up audits.

In a 2003 article, *Chain Store Age* offered an example of how the company was able to help a major retailer with training. According to vice president Tom Dyszkiewicz, "The company was experiencing difficulty with in-house cleaning staff due to turnover and their national scope of operations." To address this problem, National Super Service was hired to conduct 70 workshops to train the retailer's employees after closing hours. A maintenance schedule was also developed so that employees and their supervisors knew what needed to be done on a daily, weekly, and monthly basis. The benefits of the program included a better trained work force, less machine downtime because of proper usage, and, most important of all, cleaner floors.

National Super Service also launched the NSS Institute, which conducted three-day seminars several times a year. Sales managers, equipment specialists, product managers, and sales representatives were taught how to best sell NSS equipment, learning inside tips and tricks of the trade. Service managers, equipment specialists, service technicians, and product managers were taught how to repair NSS equipment, as well as how to perform preventive maintenance.

In 1999 John Bevington retired as president and chief executive officer of National Super Service and sold the business to his son, Mark Bevington. In July 2004 the elder Bevington died at the age of 79 from complications of strokes. The company he devoted his life to was now in the hands of a third generation, providing the kind of continuity that could not be matched elsewhere in the floor care equipment industry. The company changed its name to NSS Enterprises, Inc., but remained steadfast in its approach to doing business, emphasizing a strong research and development program and a devotion to customer service. In the early 2000s the commitment to product development was evident with the introduction of the Ultra Maxx, the floor care equipment industry's first 27-inch walk-behind battery-powered burnisher. Another example of the company's commitment to new products was the 2006 introduction of the battery-powered Colt 800 PB Wet/Dry Vacuum, designed to be used where electrical outlets were not available or impractical, such as cleaning up food or liquid spills in an occupied area. There was every reason to believe that more innovative products were to come and that NSS was positioned to enjoy many more years of success as it approached its 100th anniversary.

Ed Dinger

PRINCIPAL DIVISIONS

Manufacturing; Sales; Support Services; Strategic Accounts; Marketing.

PRINCIPAL COMPETITORS

AB Electrolux; The Hoover Company; Shop-Vac Corporation.

FURTHER READING

"John F. Bevington, 1925-2004," *Blade (Toledo, Ohio).* July 2, 2004.

Mark, Amanda, "Vacuuming Our Way into the Future," *Cleaning Maintenance Management,* October 2004.

Nolan, Paul, "Direct Mail Campaign Polishes Image of Floor Maintenance Manufacturer," *Potentials in Marketing,* October 1991, p. 38.

"NSS," *Chain Store Age,* March 2003, p. 17A.

"NSS Takes the Cord Out of the Vacuuming Equation," *ICS Cleaning Specialist,* January 2006, p. 64.

OBAYASHI

Obayashi Corporation

Shinagawa Intercity Tower B
2-15-2 Konan, Minato-Ku
Tokyo, 108-8502
Japan
Telephone: (81) 35 769 1111
Fax: (81) 35 769 1910
Web site: http://www.obayashi.co.jp

Public Company
Incorporated: 1892
Employees: 13,533
Sales: ¥140.46 billion ($13.06 billion) (2005)
Stock Exchanges: Tokyo
Ticker Symbol: 1802
NAIC: 236220 Commercial and Institutional Building
   Construction; 541330 Engineering Services; 561110
   Office Administrative Services

■ ■ ■

Obayashi Corporation is one of Japan's leading construction groups, and is also a leading player on the global construction market, with subsidiaries in the United States, Thailand, Taiwan, China, Indonesia, and elsewhere. Obayashi provides a full range of general contractor services in both the public works and private building sectors, including home building. The company also develops its own range of technologies, and has played a leading role in the development of earthquake-resistant construction techniques. In 2005, for example, the company introduced new technology designed the reduce the impact of vertical earthquakes on building

structures by as much as 75 percent. The company is also a leading developer of tunnel building technologies, and is also a major road-builder and bridge-builder. Other company operations include urban planning and architectural services; real estate and property development; environmental and waste services; the manufacture, sale, and leasing of construction machinery and equipment; the manufacture and distribution of construction and building materials, as well as fittings, furniture, and other wood products; building and facility management, maintenance, and security services; and insurance, financing, and related services, among others. Obayashi is quoted on the Tokyo Stock Exchange. The founding Obayashi family remains active in the company's management. In 2005, Obayashi's revenues topped ¥140 billion ($13 billion).

OSAKA ORIGINS IN THE 19TH CENTURY

Obayashi traced its origins to the 1890s, when Yoshigoro Obayashi won a contract to build a paper mill in Abe, Osaka. The project, one of the largest in Osaka at the time, established Obayashi as an important name in the regional construction market, and led to the founding of the Obayashi Corporation in 1892. Within a decade, Obayashi had begun to develop national ambitions, and at the beginning of the 20th century, the company entered the Tokyo market, opening its office in that city in 1902. The outbreak of war with Russia in 1905 provided the company with a new series of contracts, including an order for 100 barracks and ten field hospitals, which the company completed in just three weeks.

COMPANY PERSPECTIVES

Corporate Stance: Our primary raison d'etre is to improve global standards of living while contributing to the advancement of society and development of the world. In order to do this, we must: 1. Refine our creativity and perceptions; then call on the accumulated technology and wisdom of the company to add new value to the concept of space. 2. Expand our individuality; yet respect human frailties. 3. Stay in harmony with nature; blend in with local societies; and put our hearts into creating a more vibrant, richer culture. Management Stance: First, empathize with your customers. Second, strive to be ahead of the times, to discover and develop new demands. Third, become a vigorous, powerful group. Fourth, make a contribution to society.

The company emerged as one of the country's leading construction groups in 1911, when it completed Tokyo Station, at the time the largest steel-frame building in Japan. Over the next decades, Obayashi, led by Obayashi's son Yoshiro Obayashi, continued to establish its reputation, building landmarks such as the Sumitomo Building in Osaka and the Merchant Marine Building in Kobe, Japan. When the Kanto Earthquake leveled much of Tokyo in 1923, Obayashi played a prominent role in rebuilding the city. The company later played a prominent role in supporting Japan's military effort during the war with China, and then during World War II. This led Toshiro Obayashi to turn over the company to his son-in-law in 1946, who then changed his name to Obayashi. Toshiro Obayashi remained at the company's head until his death in the early 2000s.

Toshiro Obayashi led the rebuilding of the company into the 1950s, when it once again began winning contracts for large-scale projects, such as an extension to the Tokyo Railroad Station, and also completed its first hydro-electric dam, the Nukabira Dam. During the 1950s, as well, Obayashi added its first overseas projects. In 1956, for example, the Singapore government tapped Obayashi to complete a major land reclamation project. That project, which ultimately involved transporting more than eight square miles of land, was finally completed in 1984. In 1964, the company entered the Thailand market, opening its first overseas subsidiary. Back at home, Obayashi built the Hotel Empire, considered the first true high-rise building in Japan. In the 1960s, Obayashi also added road-building to its list of projects.

BECOMING A TECHNOLOGY PIONEER IN 1960

Into the 1960s, Obayashi not only regained its position as one of Japan's leading construction groups, the company also established itself as a major construction technologies developer. In 1961, for example, the company developed its own Wet Screen technology for building concrete walls, based on a method originally developed in France. The company's activities in the road-building sector led to an extension into tunneling, and the company once again displayed its engineering strength with the introduction of its first company-developed tunneling technologies. In 1970, the company also introduced a new lightweight roofing design. The completion of the company's Obayashi Main Office in Osaka functioned as something of a showcase for the group's engineering capabilities, boasting an energy-efficient design and also claiming the distinction of being one of Japan's tallest skyscrapers.

Other major contracts in the 1970s included the construction of both the U.S. and U.S.S.R. embassy buildings in Tokyo. The company also began opening new subsidiaries in the Southeast Asian region through the 1970s. The company also entered the U.S. market, partnering with Oakland, California's James E. Roberts in the mid-1970s. By 1978, Obayashi had acquired a 50 percent stake in Roberts, then full control in 1983. By then, the company had secured its first major U.S. contract, with a bid to build a sewer system for the city of San Francisco, starting in 1979. The company added another major project in 1985 when it completed the Toyota automobile plant in Kentucky. The following year, Obayashi joined the U.S. Civil Engineering Society, placing it in position to build its operations in the country. By 1989, Obayashi had confirmed its interest in the U.S. market, when it acquired E.W. Howell, a major contractor in the midwestern and northern regions of the United States. By then, the company also had completed its first project in mainland China, the renovation of the Shanghai International Airport, starting in 1984.

Obayashi's tunneling expertise in the meantime had made it a major player in that sector in Japan and elsewhere. During the 1980s, for example, the company completed a number of important tunneling projects, including the Seikan Tunnel linking Honshu and northern Hokkaido. The company's bridge-building project of the time also included participation in the

KEY DATES

1892: Yoshigoro Obayashi founds a construction company in order to build a paper mill in Osaka.

1902: The company opens an office in Tokyo.

1911: Tokyo Station, then the largest steel structure in Japan, is completed.

1916: Yoshiro Obayashi takes over as head of the company.

1946: Son-in-law Toshiro Obayashi becomes head of the company, remaining as chairman and CEO until his death in the early 2000s.

1956: Obayashi builds its first hydroelectric dam and emerges as a major player in the Japanese civil engineering sector; the company begins a land reclamation project in Singapore (completed in 1984).

1961: The company develops Wet Screen technology for building concrete walls.

1964: The company opens an office in Thailand.

1978: The company acquires 50 percent of James E. Roberts in San Francisco.

1984: The company wins a contract to renovate Shanghai International Airport in China.

1989: E.W. Howell in the United States is acquired; a subsidiary is formed in The Netherlands.

1991: A subsidiary is established in Germany.

1995: The company builds the Maghna Gunmti Bridge in Bangladesh.

1999: The company builds Stadium Australia for the 2000 Olympic Games.

2002: The company completes Kobe Wing Stadium, the Rappongi Hills Gate Tower, and the NHK Osaka Broadcasting Station and Osaka Museum of History complex.

2003: A subsidiary is formed in order to diversify into energy services market in Japan.

2005: John S. Clark Company in North Carolina is acquired.

North and South Bisan-Seto Bridges. In this way, the company helped complete the linking of Japan's main islands.

The company entered the European market in the 1990s, completing the Nissan Europe headquarters building in Amsterdam in 1991. In that year, the company formed a joint venture with Fluor Daniels of the United States to build a new passenger terminal for the Kansai International Airport. Meanwhile, Obayashi continued to seek new business sectors, such as the building of golf courses, while also developing new reactor containment structures for nuclear power stations. In another technology extension, Obayashi developed a method of cutting reinforced concrete using lasers.

Other Obayashi innovations of the period included the Intellipack air-conditioning system; a cold concrete manufacturing method using liquefied chlorine; a computer-based system for predicting the behavior of cracking in concrete walls; a vertical waste-removal conveyor system for tunneling projects; and carbon fiber-reinforced plastic. The company contributed to the development of underground building structures with the launch of a new "super-rib" construction method, as well as adapting its wet screen concrete techniques for underground construction projects.

INTERNATIONAL CONSTRUCTION GIANT IN THE 21ST CENTURY

During the 1990s, the company expanded its operations onto an international scale as well, completing major projects throughout the Southeast Asian region. The company added a subsidiary in Taiwan in 1991, then entered the German market with a technology exchange agreement with that country's Ed. Zubrin. The company then formed its own German subsidiary, Obayashi Projektbau. By the mid-1990s, the company operated subsidiaries in more than 15 international markets. In England, meanwhile, the company built the Bracken House building in London in 1991.

The group's major overseas civil engineering projects included Bangladesh's Maghna Gunmti Bridge, finished in 1995; two segments of Los Angeles' Metro Rail project; Boston's Central Artery Tunnel, completed in 1996; the Esplanade Bridge, in Singapore, which was completed in 1997; a new land reclamation project in Singapore, at Changi East, the first phase of which was completed in 1997; and the M2 Motorway in New South Wales, Australia, also completed in 1997.

At the same time, Obayashi completed a number of landmark buildings worldwide, such as the BCD Tower in Jakarta, Indonesia, in 1993; the Kewalram Office Building in Kuala Lumpur, Malaysia, in 1994; the SCB building in Bangkok and the Toyota Gateway Plant, also in Thailand, both completed in 1995; the Kitano New York and the Beverly Hills Hotel, also in 1995; the Dalian Senmao Building in Dalian, China, in 1996; a factory for Sanyo Home Appliances in Vietnam in 1997. Toward the end of the decade, the company also became a major contractor for the 2000 Olympic Games in Sydney, winning the contract to build the Stadium Australia, completed in 1999.

In Japan, the company remained a leading player in both civil engineering and architectural sectors, completing projects such as the Maiko Tunnel in Hyogo Prefecture in 1997. In that year, as well, the company completed the massive Tokyo Wan Aqua-Line in Chiba Prefecture. Like many of the company's large-scale projects, the Aqua-Line was carried out as part of a joint venture, in this case with partners Trans-Tokyo Bay Highway Corporation and architects Nikken Sekkei. The company then joined in the construction of the Tokyo Electric Power Co. Thermal Power Station in Chiba City, completed in 1998. Among the company's major architectural projects of the time were the Kikkosan Rinnoji Daigomado Temple in Tochigi Prefecture, completed in 1998; the Suntory Takasago factory in Hyogo Prefecture in 1999; and the Festivalgate amusement and entertainment complex in Osaka in 1997.

Obayashi entered the 2000s strongly, winning contracts to build two segments of Taiwan's high-speed railway, and a contract to build the Namba New Central Area, on the former site of the Osaka baseball stadium, as well as its bid to build a 380,000-square-meter office building as part of the Roppongi 6-Chrome project in Tokyo (one of Japan's largest office building projects). In 2001, Obayashi began construction of a desalinization plant for the Fukuoka Water Supply Authority, which, with a capacity of more than 50,000 cubic meters of fresh water daily, became Japan's largest. The company also continued its tradition of developing innovative building technologies, such as a new system to prevent groundwater contamination, and a new base isolation system offering shock resistance for lightweight buildings.

Into the mid-decade, Obayashi completed a number of other major projects in Japan, such as the Kobe Wing Stadium, the Rappongi Hills Gate Tower, and the NHK Osaka Broadcasting Station and Osaka Museum of History complex. The company also completed a segment of the Singapore Mass Rapid Transport system, and two other Singapore structures, China Square Central and Gallop Green, as well as the Hsin Yi Star Building in Taiwan. By then, Takeo Obayashi had taken over as chairman and CEO of the company, following the death of his father, Toshiro Obayashi.

A slowdown in the Japanese construction market, and in the international construction and civil engineering markets in general, encouraged Obayashi to continue to develop its diversified operations into the mid-2000s. As such, the company launched a new energy services division, winning a contract with the city of Ikeda and the Osaka Prefecture to introduce energy conservation methods at their joint government offices. In support of that effort, the company launched a new energy services subsidiary, Esco, in 2003. The company also stepped up its efforts to boost its operations in the private construction sector in order to reduce its reliance on public works projects. Meanwhile, the company continued to secure a number of major overseas contracts, such as one to build six bridges in Vietnam, as well as a tunnel beneath the Saigon River, in 2004.

Obayashi expanded its U.S. interests again at the end of 2005, when it announced its acquisition of John S. Clark Company, based in North Carolina. That company, which focused on the southeastern region, helped boost Obayashi's presence in the U.S. retail construction market, as well as its position in multi-family construction. With more than ¥140 billion ($13 billion) in revenues at the end of 2005, Obayashi remained a major global construction group into the new century.

M. L. Cohen

PRINCIPAL SUBSIDIARIES

E.W. Howell Co., Inc. (United States); James E. Roberts-Obayashi Corporation (United States); Obayashi (Shanghai) Construction Co., Ltd; Obayashi Construction, Inc. (United States); Obayashi Finance International (Netherlands) B.V.; Obayashi USA, LLC; Oc Real Estate Management LLC (United States); Pt. Jaya Obayashi (Indonesia); Taiwan Obayashi Corporation; Thai Obayashi Corporation Ltd.

PRINCIPAL COMPETITORS

Sumitomo Corporation; Taisei Corporation; Shimizu Corporation; Mitsui Fudosan Company Ltd.; Takenaka Corporation; Haseko Corporation; Nishimatsu Construction Company Ltd.; Kumagai Gumi Company Ltd.

FURTHER READING

"Japan's Obayashi Builds Six Bridges in Central, Central Highlands," *Vietnam News Briefs*, February 20, 2004.

"Japan's Obayashi Unveils New Earthquake Technology," *Asia Pulse*, January 31, 2005.

"Obayashi Shield Tunneler Speeds Underpass Work," *Asia Pulse*, January 31, 2005.

"Obayashi to Build River Tunnel," *Saigon Times Magazine*, December 25, 2004.

Olin

Olin Corporation

——— ■ ———

190 Carondelet Plaza, Suite 1530
Clayton, Missouri 63105-3443
U.S.A.
Telephone: (314) 480-1400
Fax: (314) 862-7406
Web site: http://www.olin.com

Public Company
Incorporated: 1892 as Western Powder Company
Employees: 5,800
Sales: $1.997 billion (2004)
Stock Exchanges: New York
Ticker Symbol: OLN
NAIC: 325181 Alkalies and Chlorine; 325998 All Other Miscellaneous Chemical Product Manufacturing; 331421 Copper (Except Wire) Rolling, Drawing, and Extruding; 331492 Secondary Smelting, Refining, and Alloying of Nonferrous Metals (Except Copper and Aluminum); 332993 Ammunition (Except Small Arms) Manufacturing; 334419 Other Electronic Component Manufacturing

■ ■ ■

Olin Corporation, based in Clayton, Missouri, is involved in three business lines: chlor alkali products, brass, and Winchester Ammunition. Olin is one of the largest producers of chlorine and caustic soda, the former used in swimming pool and spa sanitizers and the production of polyvinyl chlorides plastics (PVS), the latter a basic ingredient in household and institutional cleaning products, and the fabric and pulp and paper industries. Olin Brass produces copper and copper alloy strip used to mint coins and found in a wide variety of automotive, housing, electronics, and ammunition products. Olin's Winchester Ammunition unit is an offspring of the legendary arms manufacturer, Winchester Repeating Arms Company. Olin sold the firearms business in 1981 and now only produces ammunition under the Winchester name. Olin is a public company listed on the New York Stock Exchange.

1892 ORIGINS

Olin Industries was founded in 1892 as the Western Powder Company by a former baseball player named Franklin Olin. The Du Pont family and their Gunpowder Trust acquired 49 percent of Olin's company in 1909, and they nearly replaced Olin, who scrambled for the remaining 51 percent and retained control.

Western's first acquisition after the incident, Winchester Arms, was a defensive move against Du Pont, which might have purchased the company to deprive Western of a customer for its gunpowder. The Winchester plants, famous for "the guns that won the West," acquitted themselves admirably during the two world wars; for example, they put an important new gun, the M1 Carbine, into production in just 13 days. Besides the gunpowder and munitions factories, Western Powder also operated a brass works at that time.

When Franklin Olin retired, he kept most of the Western Powder Company's stock for himself and divided the rest between his two sons, Spencer and John. They consolidated Western's properties and renamed the enterprise Olin Industries. Soon Olin Industries began to diversify into paper, fuel, petrochemicals, cel-

COMPANY PERSPECTIVES

■

Olin is committed to long-term growth and prosperity for all those connected with us. Customers must grow and prosper from the superior value of products, services and solutions that we offer, or they will go elsewhere. Customers are essential to our long-term prosperity. Good employees will commit to Olin if they grow professionally, personally and financially. For us to be successful in the competitive environment in which we operate, Olin must attract, develop and hold the best people. Stockholders expect a superior total return on their investment in Olin over the long term. The commitment and support of our stockholders is essential for us to renew Olin through continued investment. Communities want Olin to act responsibly and to contribute to social and economic prosperity. Therefore, for Olin to be able to operate and prosper, we must be a good neighbor. Over time, none of those connected with us can be advantaged at the expense of the others. All must prosper or none will prosper.

lophane, and lumber. The company was managed by John and Spencer Olin along with Bill Hanes. All three were in their sixties, and the lack of a suitable candidate to succeed John, who was president, was the major concern of a company that was otherwise in excellent shape.

The lack of a logical successor was an important factor in John Olin's proposal to Tom Nicholls, the 44-year-old president of Mathieson Chemical Company, which manufactured ammonia and caustic soda, to merge their companies. Starting in 1947 Nicholls, with the help of his friend John Leppart, had transformed Mathieson, a small regional chemical company that concentrated on a few commodity chemicals, into a company with $366 million in sales—a 600 percent increase over Mathieson's performance before Nicholls took over. This dramatic turnaround was accomplished by a diversification into less cyclical products and the acquisition of companies with strong marketing organizations.

John Olin and Tom Nicholls were friends; in fact, they often went hunting together. The idea of a merger was first broached in 1951, but discarded because a satisfactory division of power did not seem possible. Nicholls headed a company almost equal to Olin in size, and neither he nor John Olin wanted to be subordinate

to the other. Nevertheless, a merger remained tempting because it would further Olin's new expansion into chemicals and bring Mathieson closer to consumers. The companies had previously cooperated on a rocket fuels venture which proved they could work together.

During the initial discussions of a merger between the two corporations, Mathieson purchased Squibb, a well known manufacturer of pharmaceuticals that was only slightly smaller than itself. In 1953, while on a hunting trip, Olin finally convinced Nicholls that a merger was possible. Within a matter of days Bill Hanes had arrived at a satisfactory division of power. The new Olin-Mathieson would be run by a triumvirate of John Olin, Nicholls, and Hanes. Olin would be chairman, Nicholls president, and Hanes head of finance.

MAJOR 1953 MERGER
TRANSFORMS COMPANY

The press offered its congratulations in 1953 when the agreement took place. Many analysts remarked on the compatibility of the Olin and Mathieson operations and the apparent dovetailing of their strategic directions. Mathieson was moving from basic chemicals to consumer goods while Olin, a manufacturer of consumer goods, was moving into basic chemicals. The only indication of trouble came from inside the company. Said an Olin-Mathieson executive soon after the merger, "We'll have to keep Tommy (Nicholls) from expanding for the present; this is a time to digest."

However, the desire to diversify triumphed over prudence. Within 18 months of its incorporation the Olin Mathieson Chemical Company had purchased three new businesses: Marquardt Aircraft, Blockson Chemical, and the Brown Paper Mill Company. This last purchase alone cost $90 million. By 1958 Olin Mathieson was producing one of the widest assortments of products of any company in the United States, yet its strategy was not proving successful. Sales for that year were a disappointing $20 million, although Bill Hanes had said in 1956 that sales would soon be hitting $1 billion. The causes of Olin Mathieson's poor performance were manifold.

The August 1958 issue of *Fortune* magazine accused the company of allowing itself to be constantly sidetracked. Indeed, Olin Mathieson seemed to lack direction. Part of the problem lay in its strategy of diversification and part in the structure of the new company itself. Fortune called the management of Olin Mathieson "a loose confederation of tribal chieftains." This charge was borne out by a 1958 meeting where the 36 research chiefs met for the first time and two of them discovered that they had been doing identical research on a fuel additive.

The lack of communication and poor diversification strategy led to the 1957 purchase of an aluminum plant. The aluminum industry was an expensive one to enter and the purchase of the aluminum works put Olin Mathieson into debt. In addition, the timing of the purchase could not have been worse, as a soft market was imminent. The business community was surprised at the poor planning of the aluminum operation because Olin Mathieson had not secured a source of bauxite, a principal ingredient in aluminum manufacture and one that was frequently in short supply. For the next two decades Olin Mathieson would find its fortunes rising and falling with the profitability of aluminum.

Nicholls was soon promoted to the board, John Olin became chairman of the executive committee, and Stan Osborne became president. Osborne was a feisty but accessible administrator. He was also a Spanish history buff; in fact, he was engaged in writing a book on that very subject when he was promoted. Determined to avoid the corporate equivalent of the sinking of the Spanish Armada, he began to dispose of unprofitable and incompatible product lines and assure a supply of bauxite. Osborne undertook cost control measures, including a $20,000 cut in his own salary. The business press praised his damage control.

After the two bad years of 1957 and 1958 when sales declined, the balance sheet began to improve. In 1959 profits increased 17 percent over the previous year, but that rate of growth did not continue. Although Osborne's cost-cutting measures kept the company from disaster, he was clearly frustrated by the company's slow progress. He resigned in 1963 for a career in banking.

Throughout the 1960s Olin Mathieson continued to be plagued by the same problems that had come to light in 1958. In 1967 the new president, a man named Grand, initiated a program not unlike Osborne's recovery plan. Unprofitable divisions were ordered to show an 8 percent yearly increase in profits. This was not an unattainable figure for most of the divisions. Even Squibb, which was responsible for a quarter of the company's sales, was producing a mediocre 5 percent return on assets. In 1967 Grand planned a program of expansion into recreation, housing, lumber, and chemicals. In 1969 the company adopted the name Olin Corporation.

In what was developing into a disheartening pattern, Olin celebrated the new decade with a decline in profits. A prolonged strike by American autoworkers decreased the market for aluminum. Furthermore, new environmental regulations were expensive. Two plants, one manufacturing DDT and the other soda ash, had to be shut down because they could not meet environmental protection standards. These closings resulted in a $26 million loss. The timing of Olin's new housing venture recalled its venture into aluminum, since the market went into a downslide soon after Olin entered it. Sporting goods, sold through the Winchester division, became one of the company's priorities. Olin ski equipment was marketed and sold successfully.

SUDDEN DEATH CHANGES MANAGEMENT RANKS IN 1971

Grand died suddenly in 1971. In 1974 the next president of Olin, James Towey, was able to boast an 80 percent jump in earnings, largely due to the sale of the aluminum operations and polyester film factories which had been depressing earnings. The aluminum works had earned $19 million over a ten-year period and had lost $32 million. The chemicals division, always a company mainstay, performed well, and the agricultural products division prospered. Brass and paper, steady sources of income, held their ground. In 1975 the company continued to sell unprofitable product lines, such as a parka business it had bought a few years before.

In the late 1970s housing and Winchester Arms took on the role of the ill-fated aluminum works in suppressing profits. Winchester's operating profits plunged 37 percent in one year, despite the quality of its guns and their name recognition. Olin elected to focus its attention on ammunition and in 1981 divested the firearms portion of Winchester.

Forbes once referred to Olin as the world's longest-running garage sale. Indeed, the company had a habit of buying unprofitable businesses and then selling them within a few years, often at a loss. In 1985 the profitable but slow-growing paper division was sold, along with the last of the home-building concerns. The company's divestment caused shareholders' equity to drop by 25 percent, although its shares went up three points.

To reinvigorate the company, Olin looked to metal and chemical products, especially chemicals used by the electronics industry. This began with the expansion in electronics and aerospace during 1980. In 1985 Olin acquired Rockcor Inc., which produced rockets, gas generators, and data systems for battlefield intelligence, as well as devices to measure the strength of underground nuclear tests. In 1985 Olin lost twice as much money as it made the previous year.

The leaders of the company, John Johnstone, Jr., and chairman John Henske, cut back programs that cost the company a $330 million pretax charge in 1985, including car and boat flares, cellophane, skis, cigarette paper, and photographic chemicals. By the late 1980s these changes resulted in Olin achieving record earnings, but a recession in the early part of the 1990s wiped out any gains. In 1991 Johnstone announced another round of streamlining, divesting several under-performing chemical lines and its European sporting ammunition business. All told, Olin sold or closed down 18 non-strategic businesses and product lines that were failing to live up to expectations.

1990 AND BEYOND

Olin elected to focus on three core businesses: metals, chemicals and defense, and sporting ammunition. In 1992 the company established a new aliphatic diisocyanate (ADI) unit in Lake Charles, Louisiana, which prepared it for a major push into the area of performance urethanes, used in coatings for products on cars and appliances. The investment built on Olin's $450-million per year position in the urethane-based toluene diisocyanate (TDI) market. In order to expand its supply operations to the microelectronics industry, Olin built a new 211,000-square-foot plant in Mesa, Arizona, to produce a chemical used in the production of semiconductors. Strategic investments made over several years, combined with reductions in salaried personnel and other operating costs, enabled Olin to increase earnings as the economy strengthened. In early 1994 Olin acquired GenCorp's Aerojet medium caliber ammunition business, making Olin one of only two U.S. producers of medium caliber ammunition. Also during that year, the Brass, Electronic Materials, and Winchester divisions earned record operating profits, while Chlor-Alkali Products, biocides, pool chemicals, Ordnance, and Aerospace showed significant improvements. Under the leadership of Johnstone as chairman and CEO and Donald W. Griffin as president and COO, Olin posted record sales of $2.7 billion and earnings of $91 million, an important increase from 1993 sales of $2.4 billion

and earnings of $40 million before a $132 million after tax-charge to income, which resulted in a net loss of $92 million that year.

With most of the cutbacks completed, Johnston stepped down as CEO, turning over the reins to Griffin, but Olin still remained a collection of incongruous assets, a company that had difficulty generating much excitement on Wall Street. More pruning ensued. In 1996 the TDI and ADI isocyanates business was sold to Arco Chemical for $565 million in cash, and the Ordnance and Aerospace divisions were spun off to shareholders as Primex Technologies. A few smaller non-strategic assets were also divested over the next two years, but the most significant step taken occurred in early 1999 when Olin spun off its specialty chemical business as a separate publicly traded company called Arch Chemicals, Inc., with every Olin stockholder receiving one share of Arch Chemical for every two shares of Olin stock held.

Arch took with it nearly $900 million in annual sales, leaving Olin with about $1.4 billion in business, but one more narrowly focused. Olin's first year without its specialty chemical business proved difficult, however, as sales from continuing operations dipped to $1.3 billion and earnings per share fell from $.79 to $.36. The company rebounded in 2000, as sales totaled $2.5 billion and earnings per share jumped to $1.80.

The company then grew its core businesses through the $49 million acquisitions of Monarch Brass & Copper Corp. in June 2001. Later in the year Griffin turned over the president and CEO positions to 51-year-old Joseph D. Rupp, although Griffin stayed on as chairman. The company then added Chase Industries Inc. in 2002, paying $176 million in stock. Chase, based in Montpelier, Ohio, produced brass rods for plumbing fixtures, heating and air conditioning products, industrial valves, and was especially strong in the housing and construction industries.

With the U.S. economy struggling, Olin had to weather difficult conditions in the early 2000s, prompting some cost-cutting measures. In early 2004 the company decided to move its headquarters from Connecticut to its East Alton, Illinois, facility, home of Winchester Ammunition, a switch that along with a cut in corporate staff saved about $6 million a year. The company also moved 150 jobs from a Winchester Rimfire production line in East Alton to a more efficient plant in Oxford, Mississippi. Olin's national headquarters would stay in East Alton for just a short period, as the company moved its corporate offices to an office tower in Clayton, Missouri, close to St. Louis. In the meantime, business was booming for Olin. A surge in demand for chlorine drove business in 2004, and then in 2005 the global metals markets experienced its own rally, due primarily to the need to feed China's fast-growing economy. As a result, Olin's brass division prospered and the company's balance sheet was flush. Sales approached $2 billion in 2004 and improved to $2.4 billion in 2005, while net income increased from $.80 per share to $1.86 per share.

Updated, Beth Watson Highman
Updated, Ed Dinger

PRINCIPAL SUBSIDIARIES

A.J. Oster Caribe, Inc.; A.J. Oster Foils, Inc.; A.J. Oster West, Inc.; Bridgeport Brass Corporation; Chase Industries Inc.; Monarch Brass & Copper Corp.; Olin Chlor Alkali Products; Winchester Ammunition.

PRINCIPAL COMPETITORS

Alliant Techsystems Inc.; Blount International, Inc.; Ryerson, Inc., Inc.

FURTHER READING

Burrough, D. J., "Olin Building $30 Million Mesa Plant," *Business Journal*, October 28, 1994, p. 1.

Caney, Derek J., "Olin's Plans $132M Corporate Restructuring, Job Cutbacks," *American Metal Market*, December 20, 1993, p. 8.

Chang, Joseph, "Olin Is Coming Under Pressure to Pick Up restructuring Pace," *Chemical Market Reporter*, April 20, 1998, p. 1.

Elliott, Alan R., "Manufacturer Turns In Record Results, Thanks To High Copper Prices," *Investor's Business Daily*, May 2, 2005, p. A08.

Highlights in the History of Olin Corporation, Stamford, Conn.: Olin Corporation, 1992, 21 p.

Hunter, David, "Olin Adds Value with Performance Urethanes Unit," *Chemical Week*, May 20, 1992, p. 8.

Lubove, Seth, "No More Adventurism," *Forbes*, December 7, 1992, p. 122.

"Norwalk, Conn.-Based Metals Firm To Cut Jobs," *Waterbury Republican-American* (Connecticut), June 27, 2001.

"Olin Draws Black Ink in 1st Qtr. with Earnings of $23.6 Million," *American Metal Market*, April 27, 1992, p. 6.

"Shhh! Olin Plans New Brass Mill but Don't Tell Anyone," *St. Louis Business Journal*, April 5, 1993, p. 4.

"St. Louis-Based Olin Has New National Headquarters at The Plaza In Clayton," *Daily Record* (St. Louis), April 15, 2005.

Thomas, Jr., Robert M., "Spencer Truman Olin, Executive for Olin Corporation, Dies at 96," *New York Times*, April 17, 1995, p. B9.

Westervelt, Robert, "Olin: Change For The Better," *Chemical Week*, February 7, 1996, p. 26.

OM Group, Inc.

127 Public Square
1500 Key Tower
Cleveland, Ohio 44114-1221
U.S.A.
Telephone: (216) 781-0083
Fax: (216) 781-1502
Web site: http://www.omgi.com

Public Company
Incorporated: 1991
Employees: 1,400
Sales: $1.3 billion (2004)
Stock Exchanges: New York
Ticker Symbol: OMG
NAIC: 331492 Secondary Smelting, Refining, and Alloying of Nonferrous Metal; 325998 All Other Miscellaneous Chemical Product and Preparation Manufacturing; 325118 All Other Basic Inorganic Chemical Manufacturing

∎ ∎ ∎

Created through the 1991 merger of America's Mooney Chemicals, Inc., Finland's Kokkola Chemicals Oy, and France's Vasset, S.A., OM Group, Inc. is one of the world's largest vertically integrated producers and marketers of metal-based specialty chemicals made mostly from cobalt and nickel. These chemicals are used in the production of more than 625 items used in a variety of industries including aerospace, hard metal

tools, appliance, rubber, automotive, ceramics, paints and ink, catalysts, electronics, petrochemicals, stainless steel, magnetic media, and rechargeable battery chemicals. OM serves approximately 1,700 customers in 50 countries and has manufacturing facilities in Africa, Asia-Pacific, Canada, Europe, and the United States. OM faced challenges in the early years of the new millennium due to a slowdown in cobalt sales. When the company reported an unexpected $71 million third-quarter loss in 2002, shareholders filed class action lawsuits and an investigation into the company's accounting practices was launched. In response to the hardships, OM restructured operations and sold off assets to pay down debt.

POSTWAR FOUNDATION AND DEVELOPMENT

Predecessor Mooney Chemical Co. was founded in 1946 in Cleveland, Ohio, by namesake James B. Mooney and a partner, Carl A. Reusser. The firm manufactured carboxylates (metal soaps) from a variety of metals, with an emphasis on cobalt. Isolated by Swedish chemist Georg Brandt in 1730 or 1742, cobalt ore was long used by potters and glassmakers to give their wares a rich blue color. The metal's name is German in origin; copper miners who discovered this vexing substance mixed in with their target material cursed it as "Kobold," the "devil's imp." Later research showed that cobalt (like lead) was useful as a drier in paint, printing inks, and petroleum. Cobalt, nickel, lead, and other metal "soaps" were sold by Mooney Chemical under the "Organ-o-Metal Chemicals" brand. Leading paint companies headquartered in Cleveland became Mooney Chemical's most important customers.

The African country of Zaire (specifically its Shaba province) became the world's leading cobalt producer in the 1920s and continued to occupy that position throughout the 20th century, producing about one-third of the world's output in the late 1980s. The vast majority of cobalt ore is found in the presence of copper and nickel ores. The cobalt is separated from the other ores during the smelting process, when it is concentrated in the slag layer. A variety of processes can then be used to extract the cobalt from the slag.

By forging strong ties with copper and nickel miners in Zaire and Zambia, James B. Mooney was able to obtain cobalt-laden slag direct from the source. The personal contacts and high level of vertical integration developed during Mooney Chemicals' early years would become key contributors to the company's success in the decades to come. Strong business relationships helped Mooney maintain its supply of cobalt despite the countries' political and economic vacillations. In 1994, James P. Mooney asserted, "When [cobalt] supplies are limited, we're at the head of the line." Vertical integration helped Mooney Chemicals maintain some of the highest levels of productivity in the cobalt specialty-chemicals industry. In the mid-1990s, for example, OM Group's sales per employee were more than double the industry average, at $850,000 compared with less than $300,000.

Cobalt markets were limited in large part to paint and petroleum manufacturers in the 1940s and 1950s, but intractable strikes at Canadian nickel mines helped boost awareness and use of cobalt as a nickel substitute in the late 1960s. Although cobalt was more expensive than nickel, it was harder and more heat resistant. "Superalloys" (combinations of metals that had properties well-suited for particular applications) developed in the 1960s and 1970s further expanded the markets for cobalt to include aerospace, magnets, catalysts, and electronics.

FAMILY SUCCESSION AND CORPORATE REORGANIZATION: 1970-90

Seventh of the founder's 14 children, James P. Mooney emerged as the one with the interest and intelligence needed to run the family business. Having been immersed in the cobalt trade from childhood (he dined with African mining executives as a teenager, for example), the younger Mooney joined the company in 1971 at the age of 23. Just four years later, he advanced from a sales position to join three of his brothers at the company's top executive offices. That is when the patriarch, who had been diagnosed with Lou Gehrig's disease, retired and moved to Florida.

Because of a corporate aversion to debt, acquisitions were infrequent. Nevertheless, Mooney expanded its product line through the purchases of a Mobil Oil Co. subsidiary in Pennsylvania, Chicago's Lauder Chemical, and Cleveland's Harshaw Chemical in the 1960s, 1970s, and 1980s. By 1984, the niche company's 40 employees generated about $2 million in annual sales.

After about 45 years of family ownership, many in the Mooney clan were ready to divest their stakes in the business. Unwilling to relinquish his birthright, President James Mooney sought out a sympathetic acquirer. He found it in Finnish mining powerhouse Outokumpu Oy, which was then looking for a way to spin off its peripheral cobalt operations. In 1991, Mooney Chemicals, Inc., was acquired for about $50 million and merged with Outokumpu's Kokkola Chemicals Oy (in Finland) and Vasset, S.A. (in France). Renamed Outokumpu Metals Group, the reformed company operated as a subsidiary of the Finnish giant until 1993, when the parent company spun off its 96 percent share to the public as OM Group. James Mooney continued to own about 4 percent of the "new" firm and serve as its chief executive officer.

The merger dramatically expanded Mooney's geographic reach as well as its product line. OM Group emerged as the self-proclaimed "world's first company to manufacture a complete line of cobalt and nickel powders and inorganic salts." New products targeted customers in the steel, magnet, and battery industries. Foreign sales increased from 10 percent of annual revenues pre-merger to slightly more than 50 percent by the end of 1993.

INCREASING CAPACITY: 1990-99

OM Group looked forward to reaping the benefits of increased capacity, a strategic partnership, and acquisitions in the mid- to late 1990s. In 1994, the company invested $19.7 million in a physical plant,

KEY DATES

1946: Mooney Chemical Co. is established in Cleveland, Ohio.

1991: Mooney Chemicals, Kokkola Chemicals, and Vasset merge to form Outokumpu Metals Group.

1993: The company goes public under the OM Group moniker.

1995: OM enters the chemical recycling industry through the acquisition of Hecla Mining Co.'s Apex mining division in Utah.

2001: Degussa Metals Catalyst Cerdec AG (dmc2) is acquired.

2002: The company posts a $71 million third-quarter loss; shareholders file class action lawsuits against OM Group.

2003: The Precious Metals Group, including dmc2, is sold.

2005: Mooney resigns; OM settles the class action lawsuits.

Although OM's array of products had increased to more than 350 items for more than a dozen industries by the mid-1990s, more than two-thirds of those chemicals were still derived from the company's core metal, cobalt. An estimated one-fifth of OM's revenues continued to be derived from paint ingredients and another fifth was generated by petroleum refining catalysts. The remaining 60 percent of sales was distributed among the plastics, ceramics, rubber, glass, and adhesives industries.

After nearly a quarter-century with the company, James Mooney set up an orderly plan of succession with the promotion of North American operations head Eugene Bak to the dual offices of president and chief operating officer in 1995. Despite all of the changes endured by the company and the industry, this realigned management team faced many of the same challenges and enjoyed several enduring corporate strengths nurtured throughout OM's history. Potential pitfalls included high capital expenses; ongoing turbulence in the cobalt market due in part to upheaval in supplier countries like Zaire; and currency fluctuations, especially against the Finnish markka. OM Group faced these hazards armed with high levels of vertical integration and productivity, a conservative balance sheet, and a zeal for innovation.

OVERCOMING CHALLENGES IN THE NEW MILLENNIUM

OM entered the new millennium intent on remaining a leading force in the industry. This strategy was demonstrated in 2001 when the company made a play for Degussa Metals Catalysts Cerdec AG (dmc2), a precious metals and metals management concern. The $1.08 billion deal was finalized in the fall of that year and significantly expanded OM's operations.

Unfortunately, the synergies expected from the union failed to materialize and OM was left with a growing debt load. At the same time, sales of cobalt were faltering due to lack of demand from the aerospace industry; according to the company, this industry generally consumed nearly 40 percent of the world's cobalt production. Nevertheless, company management remained optimistic and continued to forecast positive results. When the company reported an unexpected $71 million third-quarter loss in 2002, however, shareholders took immediate action. OM stock fell from a high of more than $70 per share to just $4 per share after the announcement and class action lawsuits were filed accusing company officials of issuing misleading statements in order to boost OM's stock price. A November 2002 *Crain's Cleveland Business* article published chief financial officer Thomas Miklich's response to the crisis: "I think

increasing its capacity to produce specialty chemicals vital to the manufacture of rechargeable nickel-hydride and lithium-ion batteries for the growing array of portable electronic cellular phones, laptop computers, and cordless tools. The mid-1995 creation of D&O Inc., a Japan-based joint venture between OM and Dainippon Ink & Chemicals Inc., was a key component of this strategy. OM hoped that its cooperative enterprise would capture 15 percent of the $470 million Japanese market for cobalt-nickel inorganic compounds by the dawn of the 21st century.

OM Group also boosted its capacity to manufacture polyvinyl chloride (PVC) heat-stabilizers. These specialty chemicals composed of barium and calcium zinc were an environmentally correct additive used to help PVC plastics retain their color and strength during manufacturing. These highly specialized substances ended up in mundane household items such as shower curtains, garden hoses, and toys. In the fall of 1995, OM entered the chemical recycling industry through the acquisition of Hecla Mining Co.'s Apex mining division in Utah. Born of the 1976 Resource Conservation & Recovery Act, companies like Apex recycle used electroplating solutions and chemical and petroleum catalysts and extract the valuable cobalt, nickel, and other metals. These materials can then be reused in (and resold to) the oil refining and electroplating industries.

where we misled ourselves is the fact of what—of really how bad the economy—how long the aerospace industry would stay down and, you know, there's really not any other explanation than we just, you know, probably had some rose-colored glasses on."

After the third-quarter announcement, OM launched a sweeping restructuring effort that included the sell-off of noncore assets, cost-cutting measures, and layoffs. Overall, the company expected to shore up nearly $100 million to pay down debt. In July 2003, OM completed the sale of its Precious Metals Group, which included dmc2, for approximately $814 million. It sold its copper powders business, SCM Metal Products Inc., in April of that year.

As part of an internal investigation into its inventory accounting practices, OM announced that it would restate its financial statements from 1999 to 2003. The company pointed the finger at accounting irregularities—improperly recorded inventory adjustments—caused by former employees. As a result of the investigation, OM delayed filing its 2003 financial results until March 2005.

CEO James Mooney resigned in January 2005. Joseph Scaminace, a Sherwin-Williams executive, was named his replacement later that year. During the remainder of 2005 and into 2006, OM worked to finalize its restructuring efforts. The company settled the shareholder class action lawsuits in June 2005. With its problems seemingly behind it, OM's management team was confident the company was well positioned for growth in the years to come.

April Dougal Gasbarre
Updated, Christina M. Stansell

PRINCIPAL SUBSIDIARIES

Fidelity Chemical Products Malaysia Sdn. Bhd. (Malaysia); OM Holdings, Inc.; OMG Americas, Inc.; OMG Asia-Pacific Co., Ltd. (Taiwan); OMG Belleville, Limited (Canada); OMG Europe GmbH (Germany); OMG Fidelity, Inc.; OMG Finland Oy (Finland); OMG Harjavalta Chemicals Holding B.V. (Netherlands); OMG Harjavalta Nickel Oy (Finland); OMG Japan, Inc. (Japan); OMG Jett, Inc.; OMG Kokkola Chemicals Holding B.V. (Netherlands); OMG Kokkola Chemicals Oy (Finland); OMG Chemicals Pte. Ltd. (Singapore); OMG Thailand Co., Ltd. (Thailand); OMG Vasset, S.A. (France); Harko C.V. (Netherlands); Groupement Pour Le Traitement Du teril De Lubumbashi (55%); Societe De Traitement du Terril De Lubumbashi (55%); OMG Cawse Pty. Ltd. (Australia); OMG U.K. Ltd. (United Kingdom); OMG KG Holdings, Inc.

PRINCIPAL COMPETITORS

Engelhard Corporation; Inco Limited; Johnson Matthey Public Limited Company.

FURTHER READING

Chapman, Peter, "Metal Chemical Recycling Grows," *Chemical Marketing Reporter,* December 25, 1995, pp. 7, 22.

Chynoweth, Emma, "Mooney Merges with Outokumpu," *Chemical Week,* October 2, 1991, p. 14.

Coeyman, Marjorie, "OMG's Chemistry Turns Cobalt to Gold," *Chemical Week,* January 19, 1994, pp. 60-61.

Cohn, Lynne M., "Eugene Bak Appointed OM Group President, Chief Operating Officer," *American Metal Market,* July 25, 1994, p. 5.

———, "Life-Long Interests Focused on Metals," *American Metal Market,* May 12, 1994, p. 6.

Croghan, Lore, "OM Group: Watch the Earnings," *Financial World,* May 9, 1995, p. 24.

Dodosh, Mark, "OM in Rough Waters," *Crain's Cleveland Business,* November 18, 2002, p. 3.

Ember, Lois R., "Many Forces Shaping Strategic Minerals Policy," *Chemical & Engineering News,* May 11, 1981, pp. 20-25.

Fine, Daniel I., "The Growing Anxiety Over Cobalt Supplies," *Business Week,* April 16, 1979, pp. 51, 54.

Furukawa, Tsukasa, "Dainippon, OM Group Form Alliance," *American Metal Market,* June 8, 1995, p. 5.

"Metal Chemical Recycling Grows," *Chemical Marketing Reporter,* December 25, 1995, pp. 7, 22.

Mooney, Barbara, "Overcoming Cobalt Blues," *Crain's Cleveland Business,* January 24, 1994, p. 2.

"OM Group Agrees to Buy Degussa Unit in $1.08 Billion Deal," *Wall Street Journal,* April 24, 2001.

"Outokumpu Prepares to Sell Cleveland-Based OM Group," *American Metal Market,* April 7, 1993, p. 5.

Plishner, Emily S., "OM Group to Go Public," *Chemical Week,* April 14, 1993, p. 13.

Robinson, Simon, "Scaminace Heads for OM Group As New CEO," *European Chemical News,* June 6, 2005, p. 10.

Sherman, Joseph V., "No Cobalt Blues," *Barron's,* May 11, 1970, pp. 11, 17.

Taub, Stephen, "OM Group Blames Past Employees for Accounting Problems," *CFO.com,* August 4, 2004, p. 1.

Walsh, Kerri, "Mooney Steps Down from OMG," *Chemical Week,* January 19, 2005, p. 9.

———, "OM Group to Restate Earnings," *Chemical Week,* March 24, 2004, p. 9.

Yerak, Becky, "Expansion, New Products Help OM Meet Goals," *Plain Dealer,* May 16, 1995, p. 12C.

———, "Mooney Chemicals Merges," *Plain Dealer,* October 3, 1991, p. 2E.

Ore-Ida Foods Inc.

357 6th Avenue
Pittsburgh, Pennsylvania 15222
U.S.A.
Telephone: (412) 237-5700
Fax: (412) 237-3584
Web site: http://www.oreida.com

Wholly Owned Subsidiary of Heinz U.S. Consumer Products
Incorporated: 1951 as Oregon Frozen Foods Company
Sales: $1.9 billion (Heinz U.S. Consumer Products 2004)
NAIC: 311411 Frozen Fruit, Juice, and Vegetable Manufacturing

■ ■ ■

Best known for its Tater Tots, Ore-Ida Foods Inc. is the leading retail brand of frozen potato products in the United States. There are many varieties of Ore-Ida products found in grocery stores across the country, including its new Extra Crispy line, seasoned potatoes, hash browns, home-style fries, roasted potatoes, and onion rings. Ore-Ida is part of Heinz U.S. Consumer Products division, which is a subsidiary of H. J. Heinz Company.

EARLY HISTORY

The company was founded in the early 1920s by F. Nephi and Golden T. Grigg, brothers in a small town in eastern Oregon who were peddling fresh sweet corn in their early teens. Going door-to-door in a horse-drawn wagon, they learned that people wanted sweet corn fresh from the field, as corn loses its sugar and moisture content quickly. The brothers discovered that by picking the corn around midnight—a cool and dewy hour—they caught the kernels at their peak of freshness. At first they tended their own small plot of produce, but before long they had to buy vegetables from others. They began shipping corn by railroad to other cities, packing their sweet corn in crushed ice to keep it fresh on its way to kitchens up to 600 miles away. Customers as far away as Portland, Salt Lake City, and Butte, Montana, were loyal to the Griggs' sweet corn.

By 1942 growing demand forced the brothers to modernize their packing methods. Corn that had been pre-cooled in ice water was packed into crates, and then more ice was loaded on top as the corn traveled in trucks and railroad cars to its destination. In 1943 a new quick-freeze factory was built in their town of Ontario, Oregon, by the Bridgford Company of California. Beginning in 1947 the brothers began sending much of their sweet corn to the factory. Within a year, they were shipping their fresh frozen sweet corn as far away as Washington, D.C., and Los Angeles. Production and sales tripled. They expanded their sweet corn acreage to 2,000 for the 1949 season.

Problems were brewing at the Bridgford plant, however, which evidently had been designed without consideration of the area's climate and agricultural conditions—or even its employees—the plant had no heat, parking lots, or lunchroom. The plant closed down in September 1948 and was in bankruptcy court by early 1950. Realizing that frozen foods were the wave of the future, the Grigg brothers—whose operation became the Oregon Frozen Foods Company in 1951—set their sights on purchasing the bankrupt plant. When the foreclosure sale was held in 1952 the Griggs were prepared with money they had raised by mortgaging their homes and property, but the bidding drove the plant's price up to nearly twice what they had expected. The Griggs had inspired much confidence over the years, though, and soon other investors were flocking to join the venture. One man even sold his farm to help secure the plant.

After the purchase, the Griggs realized that their processing season would have to expand to justify the expense of the plant. They initially tried small amounts of seasonal fruits and vegetables, but they needed more volume. In eastern Oregon and southwestern Idaho there was one big money crop that seemed to vie with the brother's sweet corn: potatoes. So in 1952, Ore-Ida Potato Products Incorporated was created as another operating company, leasing the plant for use when the season's corn processing was done.

THE BIRTH OF TATER TOTS IN 1953

Oregon Frozen Foods still had hurdles ahead. Having mortgaged everything they owned, the Griggs had to make the round of banks to secure operating capital. It soon became clear that not everyone shared their vision. Many lenders balked at the idea of frozen potatoes. Wouldn't the potatoes turn black? Frozen food wouldn't sell. What folks wanted was fresh. The young company ended up using raw potatoes as collateral for the loans it needed. With the loans in place, about 100 employees began running the potatoes through a carrot peeler. The company's first French fried potato was processed in 1952. The following year, Tater Tots were born.

Part of the genius of Tater Tots was the fact that it made a byproduct into a top-selling product. Nephi Grigg took the potato slivers left over from shaving potatoes into French fries—which ordinarily were sold for a pittance and used for livestock feed—ground them together, added flour and spices, and pushed the mix through holes cut into plywood. Then he cooked the results in hot oil. The brothers were so enthusiastic

about the future of frozen foods that they traveled to woo potential customers themselves, with briefcases filled with samples of their products in dry ice.

The company's main business was soon the processing and sale of frozen potato products. From 1951 to 1960 the company expanded dramatically. It was producing about 300,000 pounds of saleable potatoes a day, which requires twice that amount in raw potatoes, creating a serious storage problem. Plants processing potatoes could only run from August through April until long-haul storage was born in the 1960s, after which the company could receive shipments from California throughout the year to keep the potato processing running year-round. In 1960, with the company's products selling throughout the United States and into parts of Canada, a second factory was built in Burley, Idaho, to meet production demands. The new $3 million plant produced 500,000 pounds of potatoes a day.

Until this point, Ore-Ida had been a web of small companies, many run by friends and family of the Grigg brothers. In 1961 these entities were merged, becoming Ore-Ida Foods Inc., and the company went public, raising almost $2.5 million. With the fresh funds, another facility was purchased in Burley; later another plant was built in Greenville, Michigan.

In 1962 Ore-Ida began processing and marketing French fried onion rings and fresh frozen chopped onions, made from sweet Spanish onions. These, and fresh frozen corn, quickly became high-volume items. Although depressed potato prices and other factors generated a net operating loss for the six-month period that ended in April, sales were still increasing and a new onion processing addition was completed to meet the demand for French fried onion rings. Sales grew from more than $24 million in 1963 to nearly $31 million in 1964, and the company's plants were transforming one million pounds of raw produce into packaged products every day. Between 1964 and 1965 the company doubled its capacity again, and the Griggs brothers, who found the sudden growth dizzying, decided to sell.

BECOMING A DIVISION OF H. J. HEINZ IN 1965

Ore-Ida was purchased by H. J. Heinz Company, which also was going through growing pains in 1965 as it evaluated its potential for becoming a giant in the frozen food industry, which appeared to be poised for explosive growth. Ore-Ida provided a perfect opportunity for Heinz to diversify and to expand its position in frozen foods. In a stock swap worth about $27 million, Ore-Ida became a division of Heinz, under the name Ore-Ida Foods Inc.

KEY DATES

1951: The Oregon Frozen Foods Company is incorporated.

1952: The Grigg brothers and a group of investors buy the quick-freeze Bridgford plant; Ore-Ida Potato Products Incorporated is created.

1953: The company introduces Tater Tots.

1960: A second factory is built in Burley, Idaho, to meet production demands.

1961: The company goes public as Ore-Ida Foods Inc.

1965: Ore-Ida is purchased by H. J. Heinz Company.

1980: The company acquires Gagliardi Brothers, which produces a regional line of Steak-umm products.

1994: Ore-Ida sells its Steak-umm line.

1997: Heinz sells its Ore-Ida foodservice operations but keeps the retail brand.

2003: Ore-Ida becomes part of Heinz's newly created U.S. Consumer Products division.

Not long after the acquisition, Ore-Ida began losing money, which was a shock to everyone familiar with the company. When Heinz dispatched a team to investigate, they discovered a system of mismanagement that included contracting from farms in which company executives had a stake at inflated prices. Despite Heinz's reputation for having a hands-off policy with subsidiaries, it axed virtually all of Ore-Ida's senior management in a single bloody Monday in August 1967.

Nephi Grigg, who had been the company's president since 1951 and had served on the Heinz board of directors since the merger, left Ore-Ida in 1969 to pursue other interests. Grigg went on to spend much time in the service of his Mormon faith, serving as a bishop, a Stake High Council member, and a mission president. Robert K. Pedersen became president and CEO of Ore-Ida. Pedersen invested in new products, new facilities, new packaging, and extensive market research. The company gained market share, moving from a roughly 20 to 50 percent share of the frozen potato business between 1971 and 1982, and plants continued to be built, expanded, and upgraded. In 1975 Ore-Ida unveiled its first national network television campaign, which marked the first time any frozen potato brand had appeared on television.

EXPANSION THROUGH ACQUISITION: 1970–96

In 1977 Paul Corddry became president. That year, Ore-Ida purchased Baltino Foods, an Ohio-based company that manufactured frozen and refrigerated pizza products, and changed its name to Massilon. Corddry continued the company's efforts to build brand recognition; in 1978 alone, $15 million was spent for ads on television and in women's magazines.

Heinz acquired Foodways National, Inc., that same year and made Foodways a subsidiary of Ore-Ida. Operating two factories in Connecticut and New York, Foodways produced Weight Watchers frozen entrees. At the time, Foodways was considered "the Listerine of frozen dinners," as Corddry put it, featuring "lousy food, medicinal-looking packaging." Ore-Ida spent more than a year repackaging and improving the product line before developing new products. Competition between Weight Watchers and Lean Cuisine helped build the category, and Foodways eventually overtook Lean Cuisine to bring a steady stream of profits to Ore-Ida.

In 1980 Ore-Ida purchased Gagliardi Brothers, which produced a regional line of Steak-umm products. Although sales of Ore-Ida's frozen potato product line did not increase, profits doubled between 1982 and 1987, in large part because of Foodways' success. In 1987 Foodways' momentum dropped, and a huge potato crop depressed prices—in fact, the crop was so huge that supermarkets were giving away free bags of potatoes. Ore-Ida recovered in the following years, though, with market share going from 44 percent back up to 50 percent between 1988 and 1991.

Meanwhile, the company continued to expand its product line, both through acquisition and in-house product development. Bavarian Specialty Foods was purchased by Heinz and added to Ore-Ida's family in 1989, as was Celestial Farms in 1990. The following year Heinz formed Weight Watchers Food Company, which included Foodways. Ore-Ida also developed new lines of twice-baked potatoes, microwave potatoes, and battered fries.

In 1991 Heinz also acquired JL Foods, a major supplier of frozen foods to the foodservice industry. Three of JL's six subsidiaries—Delicious Foods, Oregon Farms, and Chef Francisco—were integrated into Ore-Ida. At the same time, 1991 was another rough year for the company, as economic recession combined with another boom crop. Ore-Ida lost three to four share points and profits sagged. Between 1992 and 1993 Ore-Ida closed plants, consolidated operations, and sold interests.

Ore-Ida became the number one seller of frozen appetizers overnight through Heinz's $90 million acquisition of Moore's and Domani brands from Clorox's Food Service Products Division. In 1994 Ore-Ida sold its Steak-umm business in order to expand its production of pasta and sandwich lines. Microwaveable mashed potatoes were introduced, as were Fast Fries, the first retail oven-baked product to replicate the taste and texture of fast-food restaurant French fries. In 1995 Nephi Grigg died. The Tater Tots he invented some 40 years earlier still sold like mad.

1997 AND BEYOND

During the late 1990s and into the new millennium, Heinz underwent several restructuring efforts that affected Ore-Ida. During 1997 Heinz began selling off some of its domestic operations in order to expand into new international markets. As such, it sold its Ore-Ida foodservice operations to McCain Foods, the world's largest manufacturer of French fries. The Ore-Ida retail brand was not part of the sale. During the following year, Heinz combined Ore-Ida with its Weight Watchers Gourmet Food Company subsidiary to form the Heinz Frozen Food Company. Ore-Ida became part of Heinz's newly created U.S. Consumer Products division in 2003.

Tater Tot celebrated its 50th anniversary in 2004. The company marked the occasion by launching its sixth variety of the Tot—Extra Crispy. Extra Crispy golden crinkles, Ore-Ida Extra Crispy Easy Fries (a microwaveable product), and Ore-Ida Fast Food Fries also hit store shelves. An Ore-Ida brand manager commented on the new products in a February 2005 *Frozen Food Age* article, claiming, "The Extra Crispy product line was developed to address what consumers told us was still the number-one need in the frozen retail potato category—a crispier, more golden brown French fry." The company used television advertising for the first time in nearly ten years to promote its new Extra Crispy items.

While the new line bolstered company sales and market share almost immediately, not all of Ore-Ida's new product launches were a success. In 2002 the company introduced Funky Fries, which came in a variety of offbeat colors and flavors, including blue, chocolate, and cinnamon and sugar. The novelty item failed to be a hit with shoppers and was discontinued the following year.

During this time period, many food manufacturers scrambled to keep pace with the low-carb diet craze brought on by the popularity of the Atkins and South Beach diets. Ore-Ida stood in an enviable position due to the fact that most of its consumers were under the age of 12. In fact, 80 percent of Ore-Ida consumption was in households with children and by 2006, Ore-Ida had a 53.2 percent share of the $850.6 million frozen potato market. With successful new products, a strong brand name, and the backing of one of the world's largest food manufacturers, Ore-Ida potatoes would no doubt be found on dinner plates for years to come.

Carol I. Keeley
Updated, Christina M. Stansell

PRINCIPAL COMPETITORS

ConAgra Foods Inc.; JR Simplot Company; McCain Foods Limited.

FURTHER READING

"Extra Crispy Fries at Home," *Food Processing*, November 1, 2005.

Foa Dienstag, Eleanor, *In Good Company: 125 Years at the Heinz Table*, Warner Books, 1994.

"Heinz Grows Crispy and Smart," *Frozen Food Age*, February 1, 2005, p. 26.

"H. J. Heinz Agrees to Buy Ore-Ida for $30 Million," *Wall Street Journal*, May 21, 1965, p. 5.

Howard, Theresa, "Baked Fries Pack a Punch," *USA Today*, September 27, 2004.

"It's Not Too Hard to Sell Ore-Ida Easy Fries," *Brandweek*, September 19, 2005.

Lindeman, Teresa, "Heinz Acts to Make Ore-Ida a Little More All-Righta," *Pittsburgh Post-Gazette*, May 2, 2004.

———, "Heinz Takes Aim at Drooping Potatoes," *Pittsburgh Post-Gazette*, October 4, 2003.

"The Ore-Ida Story," *Sunday Argus Observer*, June 5, 1983, Sec. E.

Reyes, Sonia, "Heinz Making Noise for Ore-Ida French Fries," *Brandweek*, May 3, 2004.

Thayer, Warren, "Ore-Ida, Weight Watchers Wed," *Frozen Food Age*, December 1998.

O'Reilly Automotive, Inc.

———— ■ ————

233 South Patterson
Springfield, Missouri 65802
U.S.A.
Telephone: (417) 829-5727
Toll Free: (800) 755-6759
Fax: (417) 874-7163
Web site: http://www.oreillyauto.com

Public Company
Incorporated: 1957 as Springfield Supply and Motor
 Parts, Inc.
Employees: 17,410
Sales: $2.05 billion (2005)
Stock Exchanges: NASDAQ
Ticker Symbol: ORLY
NAIC: 421120 Motor Vehicle Supplies and New Parts
 Wholesalers; 441310 Automotive Parts and Acces-
 sories Stores

■ ■ ■

O'Reilly Automotive, Inc., sells a variety of new and re-
manufactured auto parts, accessories, equipment, and
supplies to both "do-it-yourself" (DIY) customers and
professional car mechanics and service technicians. A
portion of its business consists of selling parts wholesale
to independent auto parts stores. A family firm, O'Reilly
serves customers in mainly smaller communities in the
Midwest and the South. The company has grown
enormously since going public in 1993, reaching 1,470
stores by the end of 2005. Business typically follows an
annual cycle, peaking as the extremes of summer

and winter inflict seasonal fatigue and accidents on
automobiles.

EARLY ORIGINS

O'Reilly Automotive was founded by the descendants of
Michael Byrne O'Reilly, an Irishman who fled the terrible potato famine in 1849. He came to St. Louis,
earned a law degree, and worked as a title examiner.

His son was the first in the family to work in the
auto parts industry. Charles Francis O'Reilly began in
1914 as a traveling salesman for Fred Campbell Auto
Supply in St. Louis. In 1927 Charles's request for a
transfer to the Springfield, Missouri, area was granted.
By 1932, in the depth of the Great Depression, Charles
was a manager of Link Motor Supply and his son Charles
H. "Chub" O'Reilly had worked two years for Link.
The father and son provided the crucial leadership to
make Link the main auto parts store in the Springfield
region.

In 1957 Link planned to retire Charles F. O'Reilly,
age 72, and reassign his son Chub O'Reilly to Kansas
City as part of a corporate reorganization in which Link
was bought by Meyers Motor Supply in Joplin, Missouri.
In a phone interview, Chub O'Reilly said he did not
want to live in Kansas City because it was "too big"
with all its "hustle and bustle" and heavy traffic. In addition, he did not want to uproot his family and be
separated from those he loved.

Hence, the father and son broke away from Link
and formed their own company. They founded O'Reilly

Automotive in 1957 with 12 employees, some of whom owned stock in the new firm. (The company was originally incorporated as Springfield Supply and Motor Parts, Inc., in August 1957 but renamed O'Reilly Automotive, Inc., a couple of months later.) Charles F. O'Reilly was the first president, and Charles H. O'Reilly was the vice-president. In Springfield they rented their first building at 403 Sherman, an old structure they extensively remodeled. With the help of some excellent salesmen who also left Link, sales at O'Reilly reached $700,000 in 1958, the company's first full year in business.

When it began operations, O'Reilly Automotive faced the challenge of persuading major brand auto parts companies to sell them parts. Link Motor Supply Company tried to stop the manufacturers from selling to O'Reilly, but the O'Reilly founders gained the cooperation they needed because of their many years of working closely with the manufacturers' sales representatives. Early in its history, then, O'Reilly was able to sell A.C. Delco batteries and other brand name products.

In 1957 O'Reilly Automotive sold almost all its items wholesale to various garages and industrial customers who employed professional mechanics or installers. Gradually, however, they sold more parts retail to individuals who wanted to fix up their own cars.

ACCELERATING GROWTH: 1960–90

In October 1960 O'Reilly started Ozark Automotive Distributors to buy parts directly from manufacturers and then distribute those parts to O'Reilly and to independent automotive jobbers in the Springfield area. The following year O'Reilly Automotive's and Ozark's combined sales reached $1.3 million.

At first O'Reilly Automotive grew slowly. For example, its initial branch store in Springfield was not opened until July 1965. Ten years later, in 1975, O'Reilly's annual sales reached $7 million, and the company built a new 52,000-square-foot warehouse at 223 South Patterson in Springfield to serve its nine stores, all located in southwest Missouri. Chub O'Reilly said building the company's first warehouse was a "tremendous change." Later the firm increased the capacity of the Springfield distribution center to 297,000 square feet and built other distribution centers in Kansas City, Missouri (93,183 square feet) and Oklahoma City (122,800 square feet). By 1980 all four of Chub O'Reilly's children (Charles, Lawrence, and David O'Reilly and Rosalie O'Reilly Wooten) had become leaders in the growing family business.

In the early 1980s modest expansion occurred. In February 1983 O'Reilly opened its first store outside of Missouri in Berryville, Arkansas, a small town close to the southern Missouri border and thus close to the other O'Reilly stores. The Berryville store, the firm's 38th store, was gained as part of a seven-store acquisition of a parts company based in Harrison, Arkansas.

In 1986 the company decided for the first time to start stores in cities with more than 100,000 people. In August 1986 O'Reilly opened its first store in the Kansas City, Missouri metropolitan area. Eventually O'Reilly operated stores in other cities, such as Omaha, Oklahoma City, Tulsa, Des Moines, Wichita, and Kansas City, Kansas, but the firm continued its basic strategy of locating most of its stores in smaller communities.

PUBLIC IN 1993

O'Reilly became a public corporation in April 1993 with the initial public offering of its stock. The following year the company began to remodel stores to conform to a standardized design featuring better lighting, increased parking, higher ceilings, and separate counters for professional installers.

In 1997 O'Reilly added ten new stores in both Nebraska and Oklahoma, eight in Kansas, seven in Iowa (the first in that state), four in Missouri, and one in Arkansas, for a company record high of 259 stores. As of December 31, 1997, O'Reilly owned 131 of those stores, leased 69 from others, and leased 59 stores from O'Reilly family real estate investment partnerships. With 1997 product sales of $316.4 million, up 22.1 percent from 1996, and 1997 net income of $23.1 million, an increase from 1996 net income of $19 million, O'Reilly proclaimed in its annual report that 1997 was "Our best year ever." Other statistics supported that conclusion, for the firm's total assets ($247.6 million) and

KEY DATES

1957: The company is incorporated in Missouri as Springfield Supply and Motor Parts, Inc. (soon renamed O'Reilly Automotive, Inc.).

1958: Sales are $700,000 in the company's first full year.

1960: O'Reilly forms Ozark Automotive Distributors.

1965: O'Reilly opens its first branch store in Springfield.

1975: The company has nine stores and builds its first warehouse; sales reach $7 million.

1983: An acquisition expands the chain into Arkansas.

1993: O'Reilly goes public.

1998: The acquisition of Houston-based Hi-Lo Automotive, Inc. brings O'Reilly nearly 200 new stores at a cost of $48 million.

2001: Total sales are about $1 billion.

2003: The 1,000th store is opened.

2005: Sales reach $2 billion.

stockholders' equity ($182 million) reached record levels. Also in 1997, O'Reilly conducted a two-for-one split of its common stock. At the end of 1997 O'Reilly employed 3,945 nonunionized individuals at its parts stores, distribution centers, and headquarters, but a major expansion was imminent.

In January 1998 the firm spent $47.8 million, or $4.35 per common share, to complete the acquisition of the Houston-based public company called Hi-Lo Automotive, Inc. (NYSE: HLO), which had sales of about $238 million for the year ending on December 31, 1997. The merger came after Hi-Lo ended its announced merger with Discount Auto Parts, Inc. Donaldson, Lufkin & Jenrette Securities Corporation advised O'Reilly on this merger, and NationsBank provided the financing. The St. Louis law firm of Gallop Johnson & Neuman, L.C. gave O'Reilly legal counsel on this and other concerns.

The purchase of Hi-Lo furnished O'Reilly with 189 new stores in California, Texas, and Louisiana. Hi-Lo's properties also included a 375,000-square-foot distribution center in Houston. As soon as the deal was complete, O'Reilly began converting Hi-Lo stores to the new owner's systems and strategies. Chub O'Reilly said that this was a major challenge, in part because the company had to replace Hi-Lo's older computers with

new IBM computers. With good advance planning, however, this conversion took place rapidly as about 200 Team O'Reilly members left headquarters to supervise the changes at the Hi-Lo stores.

In April 1998 O'Reilly sold its seven Hi-Lo California stores to a competitor, Auto Parts Wholesale, doing business as Carquest of California. "The sale of these stores will allow us to concentrate our efforts on Hi/Lo's core business in Texas and Louisiana," stated President and Chief Operating Officer Larry O'Reilly in an April 30 press release.

The Hi-Lo acquisition, by far the largest in O'Reilly's history, propelled the company into the ranks of the nation's top ten auto parts chains. At the end of the first quarter ending March 31, 1998, O'Reilly operated 460 stores in nine states: Arkansas (17), Illinois (1), Iowa (10), Kansas (46), Missouri (111), Nebraska (11), Oklahoma (78), Louisiana (17), and Texas (169). The company planned in 1998 to add another 38 stores, as well as its fifth distribution center in Des Moines, Iowa, a warehouse with 160,000 square feet. O'Reilly estimated that its 1998 sales would exceed $615 million. O'Reilly also planned to open 80 new stores in 1999.

O'Reilly's competitors in the do-it-yourself market included chains such as Pep Boys, AutoZone, Parts America (formerly called Western Auto), independent stores, car dealerships, and large discount stores (like K-Mart) that carried auto parts. Competing in the professional installer market were car dealers, AutoZone, independent stores, and national warehouse distributors and associations, such as Carquest, Parts Plus, and the National Automotive Parts Association (NAPA).

O'Reilly felt in 1998 that it was prepared to expand and thus help consolidate what it called in its 1997 10-K SEC Report a "still highly fragmented" industry. The ability of chains like O'Reilly and its major competitors to engage in efficient purchasing, inventory, and advertising because of economies of scale gave them a major advantage over small independent parts dealers. The chains also could spend more money on training their store personnel, a necessity as cars became more and more complex with the use of microcomputers and other high-tech electronics. The days of the simple "grease-monkey" were long gone.

O'Reilly's inventory management and distribution system was a good example of a modern high-tech operation. Each O'Reilly store was linked by computer to a distribution center. Bar codes enabled the company to record automatically when a part was sold and then order a replacement part from a distribution center. O'Reilly had an inventory of more than 105,000 SKUs (stock keeping units), so the necessity of such a computerized system was obvious.

Like other firms, O'Reilly worked to make sure its computer systems were prepared to deal with the "millennium bug" and thus be able to recognize the year 2000. The firm's management expected the Y2K project to be "substantially complete by early 1999," according to its 1997 annual report.

To keep its customers happy, O'Reilly started its "Right Part, Right Price, Right Now" policy, which gave customers a 5 percent discount on the retail price if one of the company's 15,000 most commonly requested items was not available immediately. Items usually were available from another store or a warehouse within 24 hours. According to O'Reilly annual reports, "The Company believes that its principal strengths are its ability to provide both the DIY and Professional Installers same day or overnight availability to more than 105,000 SKUs."

O'Reilly served its professional installer customers by using vans or small trucks to deliver parts and supplies, granting trade credit to qualified individuals, employing sales representatives specializing in the professional installer market, and conducting seminars on technical, safety, and business issues. The firm also published Tech Talk three times a year, Tools & Equipment twice a year, and the Finisher's Choice (paint and body catalog) quarterly for its professional installer market.

The company relied on purchasing parts and supplies from about 350 vendors, including name brand companies such as A.C. Delco, Gates Rubber, Prestone, Quaker State, STP, Armor All, and Turtle Wax. Most products were covered by manufacturers' warranties, but O'Reilly also provided warranties on some products. O'Reilly sold some of its own private label parts as well.

For several years O'Reilly has sponsored race cars as part of its advertising program. At state fairs, smaller local races, and major shows, O'Reilly has promoted its name and image on stock cars and high-powered race cars. For example, in June 1998 the 27th annual O'Reilly Spring Nationals were held at the Tulsa International Raceway. On its web site, O'Reilly listed the dates of more than 100 events between June and November 1998 at which the company was sponsoring contestants, including some truck and tractor pulls and bike racing competitions.

O'Reilly remained a family firm. Its officers included Chub O'Reilly, chairman emeritus; Charlie O'Reilly, board chairman; David O'Reilly, president and chief executive officer; Larry O'Reilly, president and chief operating officer; Rosalie O'Reilly Wooten, executive vice-president; and Ted Wise, executive vice-president.

The auto parts industry recognized the leadership of

O'Reilly officers. The Automotive Warehouse Distribution Association honored David O'Reilly and the *Automotive Aftermarket* magazine presented both David and Larry O'Reilly with Retailers of the Year awards. Such recognition was based in part on the fact that O'Reilly Automotive consistently had increased its annual sales and net income from 1989 through 1997. Based on that financial performance and the major acquisition of Hi-Lo in 1998, O'Reilly Automotive seemed well prepared to continue its role as a major auto parts supplier in its chosen markets.

NEW LEADERSHIP, NEW GOALS FOR THE NEW MILLENNIUM

The position of company president was held by someone from the O'Reilly family until 1999, when Greg Henslee and Ted Wise were selected to share the office. (Henslee, with the company since 1989, succeeded David O'Reilly as CEO in 2004, while Wise, who had joined in 1970, would become chief operating officer.) *Investor's Business Daily* later commented on their careful efforts to perpetuate the company's culture. "If team members are happy and pleased with the company they're working for, they'll treat customers the way they want to be treated," said Henslee.

By the end of 2000, O'Reilly had 672 stores. Sales were about $900 million. O'Reilly had started another vehicle for growth, an online parts ordering alliance with General Parts Inc. and other investors.

Much of the company's growth was coming through shrewd acquisitions. O'Reilly built up its Texas holdings with the purchase of a handful of small companies, including Gateway Auto and Hinajosa Automotive. It added the 14-store KarPro Auto Parts chain in 2000. KarPro, based in Little Rock, had sales of about $25 million a year.

In 2001, Mid-State Automotive Distributors, owned by a publicly traded British company, was acquired for $19.5 million and the assumption of debts worth $26.5 million. The deal extended O'Reilly's reach east of the Mississippi. O'Reilly was the fifth largest consumer auto parts chain in the country. The aftermarket parts industry was thriving in the slow lane economy, as people tried to keep older cars on the road longer.

O'Reilly opened its one thousandth store, in Chattanooga, in January 2003. The company had gone from 145 stores when it went public less than ten years earlier. O'Reilly was preparing for a push into the Southeast by opening a distribution center in Mobile, Alabama. Sales exceeded $1.5 billion in 2003.

Although O'Reilly had a relatively long tradition in an established industry, the business was being managed like a state-of-the-art enterprise, observed many commentators in the business and trade press. The company was a practitioner of the new art of demand management, using sophisticated software to handle products from thousands of vendors. This freed up $66 million in a few years, according to *KMWorld*, while shifting more of inventory from the stores to the ten distribution centers. Net income of $140 million for 2004, when revenues were $1.7 billion, was ten times the figure for 1995. The company became ever more profitable as it increased in scale; net income per share was on a steady climb from $0.41 in 1995 to $1.87 in 2004.

O'Reilly bought W.E. Lahr Co. and its Midwest Auto Parts unit for $61 million in June 2005. Its founder, Bill Lahr, had died the previous year; he had reportedly admired O'Reilly's business practices. Midwest had 71 stores in five states, 700 employees, and sales of about $100 million a year.

Most of O'Reilly's new stores were being added in the Southeast; a 358,000-square-foot distribution center was opened in the Atlanta area in February 2005. By this time, the company had 30 stores in the area, but the new center had the capacity to supply another 230. O'Reilly had set a goal of reaching $2 billion in sales by 2005, according to *Investor's Business Daily*. It made its goal, doubling revenues in just four years. O'Reilly had 1,470 stores at the end of 2005 and planned to add up to 175 in 2006.

David M. Walden
Updated, Frederick C. Ingram

PRINCIPAL SUBSIDIARIES

Ozark Automotive Distributors, Inc.; Greene County Realty Co.; O'Reilly II Aviation, Inc.; Ozark Services, Inc.; Hi-Lo Investment Company; Hi-Lo Management Company.

PRINCIPAL COMPETITORS

AutoZone, Inc.; Advance Auto Parts; CSK Auto Corporation; The Pep Boys-Manny, Moe and Jack, Inc.; Wal-Mart Stores, Inc.

FURTHER READING

Adams, Tony, "O'Reilly Automotive Enters Columbus, Ga., Auto Parts Market," *Columbus Ledger-Enquirer* (Georgia), January 20, 2005.

"CEO Interview: David O'Reilly; O'Reilly Automotive," *Wall Street Transcript*, April 14, 2003.

DePass, Dee, "Missouri Company to Buy Midwest Auto Parts," *Star Tribune* (Minneapolis), May 10, 2005, p. 2D.

Ewing, Terzah, "Highly Effective Management Team," *Forbes*, October 23, 1995, pp. 312ff.

Gallanis, Peter J., "O'Reilly Driving Force Behind Parts Network," *DSN Retailing Today*, September 4, 2000, p. 4.

Gentry, Connie Robbins, "Cruise Control: O'Reilly Automotive, Inc. and AutoZone, Inc. Drive the Automotive-Parts Market," *Chain Store Age*, November 2004, pp. 50f.

Gray, Tom, "O'Reilly Automotive Inc./Springfield, Missouri; Bad Weather, Economy Equal Good News Here," *Investor's Business Daily*, February 6, 2001, p. A12.

Halverson, Richard, "O'Reilly's Family Strategy Counters Auto Megachains," *Discount Store News*, November 4, 1996, pp. 23f.

Howell, Debbie, "O'Reilly Automotive Opens 1,000th Store," *DSN Retailing Today*, February 24, 2003, pp. 5f.

Jennings, Jason, *Think Big Act Small: How America's Best Performing Companies Keep the Start-up Spirit Alive*, New York: Portfolio, 2005.

Lamont, Judith, "O'Reilly Auto Parts Meets Demand for All Seasons," *KMWorld*, October 2002, p. 6.

Much, Marilyn, "Two Heads Better Than One; Solid Teamwork; O'Reilly Automotive's Greg Henslee and Ted Wise Lead Together," *Investor's Business Daily*, September 9, 2005, p. A3.

"O'Reilly 40th Year: 1957–1997," *Aftermarket Business*, December 1, 1997, pp. 19–31.

"O'Reilly Moves East with Mid-State Acquisition," *Aftermarket Business*, September 2001, p. 16.

Wirebach, John, "Is O'Reilly the Sharpest Auto Chain in the Country?," *Aftermarket Business*, October 2001, p. 11.

Woods, Walter, "Two Auto Companies to Open Distribution Centers in Atlanta Metro Area," *Atlanta Journal-Constitution*, December 11, 2004.

Orszagos Takarekpenztar es Kereskedelmi Bank Rt. (OTP Bank)

H-1051
Nádor u. 16
Budapest,
Hungary
Telephone: (36) 06 1 473 5000
Fax: (36) 06 1 312 6858
Web site: http://www.otpbank.hu

Public Company
Incorporated: 1949
Employees: 7,777
Total Assets: EUR 19.7 billion ($24 billion) (2005)
Stock Exchanges: Budapest
Ticker Symbol: OTP
NAIC: 522110 Commercial Banking

■ ■ ■

Orszagos Takarekpenztar es Kereskedelmi Bank Rt., or OTP Bank, is Hungary's leading commercial bank and one of the fastest-growing players in the Central European banking market. The former state-controlled saving bank monopoly has successfully navigated privatization and the liberalization of the Hungarian banking sector to retain its leading market shares. The company claims 29 percent of the retail deposit market, and 40 percent of the country's credit market, as well as a 36 percent share of retail foreign currency deposts, and 49.7 percent and 35.3 percent of the housing loan and consumer credit markets. The company's Hungarian network includes nearly 440 branches and 1,500 ATMs, as well as telephone, Internet, and mobile banking

services. Altogether the bank serves more than 3.5 million customers in Hungary. OTP has also launched an effort to become a major bank in the Central European region. The company operates subsidiaries Romania, Slovakia, Croatia, and Bulgaria—where its subsidiary, DSK Bank, has become market leader. OTP is actively seeking expansion in other regional markets, including Serbia and Ukraine. The company submitted a bid to buy Ukraine's Ukrsotsbank in February 2006. Unlike many of its regional counterparts, OTP has built its position without the backing of a major financial partner, in part because the Hungarian government retains a "golden share" in the company, restricting foreign shareholdings and placing ownership limits on the bank. The chairman, CEO, and architect of OTP's growth since its privatization in the mid-1990s is Sandor Csanyi. OTP is listed on the Budapest Stock Exchange and had total assets in excess of EUR 19.5 billion ($24 billion) in 2005.

ORIGINS

The elections of 1947 brought Hungary's Stalinist-oriented Communist Party to control, placing the country under the dominance of the Soviet Union. The nationalization of the country's assets quickly followed, as the state took over its industries, including the banking industry. In 1949, the Hungarian government established a new bank, Orszagos Takarekpenztar Bank, or the National Saving Bank, in 1949, which then became the monopoly for all savings deposits in the country. The bank also became the sole source of housing loans in Hungary.

Over the next several decades, OTP's mandate expanded to include real estate transactions and services

COMPANY PERSPECTIVES

■

The Bank's strategy In order to maintain development and steady growth and hence shareholders' confidence the Bank Group has prepared for future challenges. In the heart of its business strategy for 2005–2009 lies the maximization of shareholder value by achieving an outstanding consolidated financial performance in European terms. OTP Bank Group's vision is to become a determining financial provider in the region while retaining the market leadership in Hungary. The strategic aim of the Bank is to achieve/retain market leadership or a dominant position in all segments of financial services in Hungary and to become a major player in the markets of its subsidiaries.

such as foreign currency deposits and exchange and municipal banking services. OTP also became responsible for operating the state lottery during the years of Communist Party control. Despite the expansion of its mandate, OTP remained limited by the Communist-styled separation of banking functions, which restricted the bank from industrial and commercial lending and from conducting foreign trade operations.

OTP established a branch network reaching throughout most of the country, opening nearly 400 offices nationwide. Yet services were kept to a minimum: checking accounts were unheard of, automated teller machines were non-existent, and computer technology was lacking. As was typical of most Soviet-bloc industries and government-owned businesses, OTP grew into a bloated, overly bureaucratic organization, with nearly 17,000 employees, inefficient operations, and no commitment to operating at a profit.

Yet Hungary became the first of the Soviet-bloc countries to begin the process of liberalization that ultimately resulted in the collapse of communist domination. In the late 1970s, the Hungarian government began authorizing trade with and investment from Western sources, and as such the National Bank of Hungary established a number of joint-venture banks, such as the Central-European International Bank, set up in 1979, and joint ventures with Citibank and Raiffeisen in the 1980s. The National Bank then shed its commercial banking functions, transforming itself into a Western-style central bank.

These moves allowed Hungary to become the

region's most dynamic market, introducing modern banking techniques, practices and services, and, importantly, allowing the country to develop a new generation of highly educated and trained bankers. Among this generation was Sandor Csanyi, who completed a Ph.D. in Economics at the University of Budapest in 1983. Csanyi joined the civil service and quickly rose to prominence in the Finance and Agricultural ministries. In 1989, however, as Hungary emerged from Soviet dominance, Csanyi left to join the K&H Bank (the Commercial and Credit Bank), a spinoff of the National Bank, and served as deputy CEO at K&H until 1992.

In that year, Csanyi was appointed chairman and CEO of OTP bank, charged with modernizing its operations and preparing the bank for privatization or sale to a foreign investor. Csanyi's political clout and economic prowess helped him push through a sweeping restructuring of OTP. By the end of 1994, OTP had reduced its number of managers from more than 200 to just 65. At the same time, Csanyi replaced much of the bank's existing management with a new, hand-picked team, drawing from the vast talent pool that was by then available in the country. OTP also cut through its rank and file, slashing more than 8,000 jobs by the end of the decade. Continuing in its cost-cutting efforts, OTP began centralizing its back-office operations, rolling out an information technology infrastructure throughout its branches. Meanwhile, the bank developed its own computer technology, and launched the country's first true checking account system. Coupled with the bank's strong branch network presence, OTP not only retained its dominance in the savings market, but also captured a leading share of other consumer and retail banking areas. The bank's commitment to technology also allowed it to secure contracts with the national government and many of the country's municipal governments, providing electronic salary payments and direct bill-paying services. By the end of the decade, OTP had also added such innovations as debit cards, mobile telephone banking services, and Internet banking services.

OTP's commitment to introducing new technology and services enabled the company to weather the flood of foreign competition that occurred as the banking sector was liberalized in the early 1990s. OTP's own privatization was slated for the mid-1990s. A number of members of the Hungarian government, including the country's finance minister, at first favored seeking foreign buyers for the bank; the move would likely have raised more immediate capital than a public offering. Yet Csanyi, backed by his political connections and economic clout, convinced the government to maintain OTP as a Hungarian-owned institution.

As such, OTP was placed on the Budapest stock exchange. As part of the privatization, the Hungarian government drafted rules limiting individual foreign shareholders in the bank to just 5 percent of its stock. Domestic shareholders were limited to a maximum 10 percent stake. By the end of the decade, the bank's privatization had been completed and nearly all of OTP's shares had been placed on the Budapest exchange; the government held onto a so-called "golden share," however, giving it veto rights over certain policy decisions and any potential merger or de-merger operations.

REGIONAL PLAYER IN THE NEW CENTURY

OTP remained focused on the retail banking sector into the early 2000s, while also building up a new commercial and corporate wing. Meanwhile, the wave of foreign-owned financial institutions entering the country competed especially for the country's corporate and industrial sector. In this way, OTP was able to maintain clear dominance over the country's retail sector into the new century. Into the early 2000s, OTP attempted to gain more control over the Hungarian banking sector, when it launched a takeover effort for the country's number two retail bank, Postabank. Under private

ownership, that formerly state-owned bank had run aground in the late 1990s, requiring a bail-out from the Hungarian government. Yet OTP's bid was rejected, amid opposition that the acquisition would give the bank too much control over the country's retail banking market.

Finding its growth limited at home, OTP targeted international expansion. The bank's expertise as a former state-owned bank negotiating a liberalized market also gave it an edge over its competitors as it developed the strategy for its next growth phase. By the early 2000s, most of the countries in the Central European had successfully completed their own transition to free-market economies, including the liberalization and privatization of their state-controlled banking assets. OTP became determined to transform itself into a major player in the retail banking sector in Central Europe.

OTP at first targeted Romania, negotiating to acquire that country's leading bank, Banca Comerciala Romania. However, amid ethnic tensions between the country's Romanian and ethnic Hungarian populations, the government of Romania decided to postpone the bank's sale.

Instead, OTP moved into Slovakia, buying up that country's IRB Bank in 2002 for EUR 12 million. OTB renamed its new subsidiary as OTP Banka Slovensko, restructured and modernized its operations, and transformed it into the country's fastest-growing bank, with particular success in the mortgage lending market. Building on that success, OTP next targeted Bulgaria, buying up that country's DSK Bank for EUR 311 million. DSK, then Bulgaria's second-largest bank in total assets, was also that country's leading retail bank. Under OTP, DSK launched a range of new and improved products and services, including new credit cards, long-term deposits, and electronic services. The bank also began opening new branches, with 320 branches in operation by the end of 2004, and more than 350 branches by the beginning of 2006.

OTP finally succeeded in entering Romania, when it acquired RoBank, a corporate banking specialist. While the organization was a relatively minor player, with a market share of just 1 percent, the purchase gave OTP a foothold in that country, ahead of the future privatization of the country's state-owned banks. Under OTP, RoBank changed its name to OTP Banka Romania and launched its own retail banking operation, and began preparations to offer other financial services, such as insurance and leading products. The bank then began opening a new branches, targeting a future total of 100 branches or more.

OTP's next stop on its regional expansion path came in March 2005, when the bank acquired Croatian Nova Banka. That bank operated its own 90-branch network, primarily on Croatia's coast, and counted more than 500,000 customers.

By the beginning of 2006, OTP was prepared to further its expansion in the region. In February of that year, the bank targeted two new countries for expansion, launching bids for Serbia's Splitska Banka, and Ukraine's Ukrsotsbank. While the company was facing heavy competition for the latter bank, notably from Italy's Banca Intesa, both offers confirmed Csanyi's ambition to develop OTP into one of the major banking players in the Central European region.

M. L. Cohen

PRINCIPAL SUBSIDIARIES

DSK Bank EAD (Bulgaria); Hungarian International Finance Ltd.; Merkantil Bank Ltd.; Merkantil Car Ltd.; OTP Bank Romania S.A. (Romania); OTP Banka Hrvatska (Croatia); OTP Banka Slovensko, a.s. (Slovakia); OTP Building Society Ltd.; OTP Factoring Ltd.; OTP Fund Management Ltd.; OTP Garancia Insurance Ltd.; OTP Mortgage Bank Ltd.; OTP Pension Fund Ltd.; OTP Real Estate Ltd.; OTP Travel Ltd.

PRINCIPAL COMPETITORS

ING Bank (Magyarorszag) Rt.; Kereskedelmi es Hitelbank Rt.; Magyar Kuelkereskedelmi Bank Rt.; CIB Koezep-Europai Nemzetkoezi Bank Rt.; Erste Bank Hungary Rt.; Raiffeisen Bank Zrt.; HVB Bank Hungary Rt.; Magyar Fejlesztesi Bank Rt.; Budapest Bank Rt.; Postbank and Savings Bank Corp; Citibank Zrt.; Deutsche Bank Rt.

FURTHER READING

"Boom Time for CEE Banking," *The Banker*, October 1, 2005.

Buerkle, Tom, "Hungary Banker," *Institutional Investor International Edition*, December 2004, p. 20.

Condon, Christopher, "Budapest's Power Banker," *Business Week*, March 24, 2003, p. 35.

"Hungary's OTP will Keep Ukraine on Acquisition Map," *portfolio.hu*, February 15, 2006.

Jones, Colin, "OTP Leads the Way," *The Banker*, July 2002, p. 70.

——, "First Glimpses of Consolidation," *The Banker*, January 2001, p. 82.

"OTP Bank at Profit Record and in New Countries," *Euromoney*, July 2005, p. 121.

"OTP Bank: Going from Strength to Strength," *Euromoney*, January 2005, p. 63.

"OTP Bank: Playing a Meaningful Regional Role," *Euromony*, October 2004, p. 79.

"OTP Success May Kick-Start Sales," *Privatisation International*, August 1995, p. 13.

"OTP to Expand in Romania," *Bucharest Daily News*, February 14, 2006.

"A Success Story of Central and Eastern Europe," *Euromoney*, January 2006, p. 149.

The Pampered Chef Ltd.

One Pampered Chef Lane
Addison, Illinois 60101-5630
U.S.A.
Telephone: (630) 261-8900
Toll Free: (800) 266-5562
Fax: (630) 261-8522
Web site: http://www.pamperedchef.com

Private Company
Incorporated: 1983 as The Pampered Chef, Ltd.
Employees: 1,000
Sales: $1 billion (2006 est.)
NAIC: 332214 Kitchen Utensil, Pot, and Pan
Manufacturing; 454390 Other Direct Selling
Establishments

∎∎∎

The Pampered Chef Ltd. is a leading supplier of kitchen-related products. It is one of America's top direct-selling organizations, and has international offices in Canada, the United Kingdom, and Germany. By the time of its silver anniversary, the operation had grown from a one-woman show in a suburban Chicago kitchen to a staff of more than 950 in four facilities with sales approaching $1 billion. The Pampered Chef's army of more than 70,000 "Independent Kitchen Consultants" sells a line of about 200 professional-quality kitchen items featuring utensils and unglazed stoneware cook vessels. The stunning growth of "The Kitchen Store That Comes to Your Door" mirrored two important trends of the 1980s and 1990s: the proliferation of home-based businesses

and "nesting." Berkshire Hathaway acquired the company in 2002.

FOUNDED IN 1980

The Pampered Chef was founded in 1980 by Doris Christopher, who like many women in her generation sought to balance a vital professional career with a fulfilling home life. Having interrupted her career as a home economics teacher with the University of Illinois Cooperative Extension Service to raise her two daughters from birth to school age in the late 1970s, the 35-year-old Christopher found herself at a crossroads. As she described it in an April 1996 interview for the *Chicago Tribune*, Christopher began to seek "a part-time job that would allow me to be a mom too." Quickly narrowing her focus to self-employment opportunities that capitalized on her interests and experience in the kitchen, she investigated catering and retail sales of cooking utensils. However, she eliminated both these options because catering demanded long, odd hours, and retailing required a high capital investment. Husband Jay urged her to launch a party-plan, direct-selling operation à la Tupperware, but Doris balked, recalling in a November 1996 *Success* piece, "I thought home parties were a waste of time, that perhaps the products were overpriced."

With the continuing support of her spouse, who reminded her that her business could be set up in any way she wished, Christopher began to realize that her cooking and teaching expertise was perfectly suited to the demonstration techniques often used in direct selling, and that there was an untapped market for professional-quality, multi-use kitchen gadgets. Armed

COMPANY PERSPECTIVES

We are committed to providing opportunities for individuals to develop their God-given talents and skills to their fullest potential for the benefit of themselves, their families, our customers and the company.

We are dedicated to enhancing the quality of family life by providing quality kitchen products, supported by service and information for our Consultants and customers.

with this core concept and a $3,000 cash-out from a life insurance policy, the mom-turned-entrepreneur bought a dozen each of about 70 kitchen gadgets from Chicago's wholesale Merchandise Mart. The Pampered Chef would not require one more dime of additional financing over the course of its first decade-and-a-half in business, funding all its growth from cash flow.

Christopher set her home-selling events apart from their predecessors by calling them "kitchen shows" and naming her sales representatives "kitchen consultants." She scheduled her first kitchen show for October 1980, avoiding what she called the "silly games" that characterized other home-selling parties and opting instead for an entertaining evening of cooking demonstrations, eating the fruits of the demo, and some low-pressure selling. That first night's recipe was leavened with trepidation: Christopher later recalled that "during the entire drive to my first show, I vowed that I would never, ever do this again. My stomach was in knots. Of course, on the drive home, I knew differently."

EXPONENTIAL GROWTH: 1980–95

This modest beginning belied the phenomenal growth to come. She brought in a friend as a part-time sales representative in May 1981, and had recruited a total of 12 kitchen consultants by the end of the year. Sales passed $200,000 by 1983, and more than doubled in 1984. Warehousing of the burgeoning business's products outgrew the Christopher family's household basement that year, when TPC's headquarters were moved to a 2,500-square-foot building. By 1987, the business generated by the company's more than 200 sales representatives demanded a full-time purchasing, warehousing, and distribution staff. Husband Jay quit his job as a marketing executive that year to join his wife's company as executive vice-president of operations.

By the end of the decade, TPC boasted 700 kitchen consultants. Coverage in nationally circulated magazines in the early 1990s brought another wave of consultants on board, and by 1993 the company had sales representatives in all 50 states.

Although direct, demonstrative selling proved a powerful marketing method for TPC, its sourcing of unique and useful kitchen tools was also vitally important. In 1995 Christopher told *Inc.* magazine's Robert A. Mamis: "People I knew didn't like to cook, because it wasn't easy for them. Part of me said, 'Maybe I can never convert them.' But another part said, 'They're using knives that aren't sharp and forks with missing tines. If they had the right tools, it would be fun.'" But finding the right tools was not easy for the average cook; they were expensive rarities in retail stores, and even if a budding chef found them, she'd likely have an even harder time figuring out how to use and care for them properly.

Christopher sought to fill this market void with a line of high-quality, multipurpose wares. She assembled an array of about 150 products ranging from peelers and juicers to bakeware and cookware, about one-third of which were exclusive to TPC. Although TPC often had a hand in the development and refinement of the products it carried—making them more ergonomic or combining several functions in a single tool, for example—it did not manufacture them. Many were emblazoned with their makers' names and marks, then packaged in TPC boxes with the marketer's use-and-care information. Believing that the origin of the utensils was far less important to her customers than knowing how to use them, Christopher created an in-house test kitchen to develop simple yet innovative recipes and menus that used TPC products. Although many of the company's gadgets had more than one use—the "Bar-B-Boss," for example, incorporated a bottle-opener, fork, and knife in one grill tool—TPC's creatively written recipes often required more than one TPC tool. Something as simple as a tray of crudités could call for three separate TPC tools: a v-shaped cutter, lemon zester, and "garnisher" (a wavy cutter). A plan for a whole meal might specify more than a dozen different products. When compiled in a company cookbook and used in kitchen shows, these recipes became powerful selling tools.

Years of trial and error resulted in fairly simple pricing and commission plans. Christopher arrived at an individual item's retail price by multiplying its wholesale cost by two. An initial investment of $100 bought a new kitchen consultant a set of about two dozen kitchen gadgets to use in demonstrations. As new utensils were introduced (two or three times each year), sales reps were required to purchase samples for demonstration

KEY DATES

1980: Doris and Jay Christopher launch The Pampered Chef from their basement; sales total about $6,700.

1981: The company has lined up a dozen Independent Kitchen Consultants.

1982: Sales are $100,000.

1983: The company is incorporated.

1984: TPC's headquarters are moved to a 2,500-square-foot building.

1987: Sales reach $1 million.

1990: Sales reach $10 million; TPC has 700 kitchen consultants

1991: The "Round-Up from the Heart" drive is launched to raise money for Second Harvest food banks.

1996: A Canadian unit is launched.

1998: Sales are $500 million.

2000: The Help Whip Cancer campaign is started.

2001: Sales pass $700 million.

2002: Berkshire Hathaway acquires the company.

2003: Sheila O'Connell Cooper succeeds company founder Doris Christopher as CEO.

purposes. Christopher kept all new introductions—even obvious dogs—on the line for at least one year.

Following recipes written with TPC tools in mind, kitchen consultants guided kitchen show attendees in the use and care of the equipment. The consultants—99 percent of them women—started out earning a 20 percent commission on gross sales and earned an extra 2 percent after exceeding $15,000 in sales. The chief executive who had started out seeking a part-time job did not expect her recruits to commit to a 40-hour (or more) week; instead, she required a meager $200 bimonthly sales quota. On top of commissions, incentives for prolific sellers included all-expenses-paid family vacations to Disney World. TPC literature emphasized that a career in direct sales "is considered by many to be a ground-floor opportunity with no glass ceiling."

LATE DECADE DEVELOPMENT

That assertion was perhaps best exemplified by Doris Christopher herself, for what started out as a part-time job had turned into the chief executiveship of a multimillion-dollar nationwide venture by the mid-1990s. Although the founder has commented only half-jokingly that she might not have launched TPC had she

known what she was getting into, the effort made her a millionaire many times over. When growth began to spiral out of the entrepreneur's control, she was compelled to hire outsiders with expertise in the management of large, growing businesses.

The Pampered Chef also earned Christopher national recognition. In 1992 the School of Human Resources and Family Studies Home Economics Alumni Association at her alma mater, the University of Illinois, recognized her with an Award of Merit. Ernst & Young, Inc., and Merrill Lynch named her a regional National Entrepreneur of the Year in 1994, and *Inc.* gave her a tongue-in-cheek MBA—a "Master of Bootstrapping Administration"—in 1995.

TPC's charitable activities were in keeping with the company's food orientation. Launched in 1991, its "Round-Up from the Heart" promotion set aside $1 for every kitchen show hosted by its representatives between September 1 and December 31 of each year, and encouraged customers to round their orders up to the nearest dollar. The firm donated these extra funds—a total of more than $1.3 million in its first five years—to Second Harvest food banks across the country.

Americans were spending increasing amounts of their free time, not to mention disposable income, on entertaining at home in the late 1980s and early 1990s. Kitchens were recognized as the "heart and hearth" of the household. Many categories of consumer goods—including cookware—were buoyed by this strong and ongoing trend known as "nesting" or "cocooning." Given retail analysts' predictions that this homeward movement would continue for decades, The Pampered Chef appeared poised to build on its success. Christopher revealed that she expected the privately owned company to generate $300 million in revenues in 1996. Furthermore, the businesswoman predicted that "a billion dollars isn't far in our future." By the end of 1997, The Pampered Chef had more than 38,000 sales representatives and 600 staffers at its headquarters.

NEW OWNERSHIP IN THE NEW CENTURY

The philanthropic activities of the company and its founders continued. They gave $15 million to Concordia University, a Lutheran-sponsored school where Jay Christopher's father had worked as legal counsel, in 1999. Four years later, they gave a similar award to fund a new library at Jay Christopher's alma mater, Valparaiso University in Indiana. In 2000, a gift from the Christophers helped launch the Family Resiliency Program at the University of Illinois.

Doris Christopher published a book celebrating family mealtimes called *Come to the Table: A Celebration of Family Life* in 1999. "Isn't it worth the investment of effort and time to summon your family to the table?," she asks, echoing the mission of The Pampered Chef.

By the time of The Pampered Chef's 20th anniversary in 2000, annual sales were more than $600 million. It had around 1,000 corporate employees and about 60,000 reps calling on 12 million customers. The firm's international reach extended beyond North America to Germany and the United Kingdom. In 2000, The Pampered Chef launched its "Help Whip Cancer" promotion to raise funds for the American Cancer Society through the sale of items such as specially made measuring spoons and bag clips.

The Pampered Chef had grown into three buildings with more than 800,000 square feet of space, and was expanding still further with the construction of a new 780,000-square-foot headquarters and distribution center (it officially opened in October 2002). According to the *Chicago Daily Herald*, Christopher wept with joy at the dedication of her firm's new headquarters building in October 2002. "The building," she said, "is much more than a testament to how far we've come. It is a statement of our firm belief in the incredible future we have ahead of us."

Incentives helped keep the company in the Chicago area village of Addison. The local chamber of commerce named Doris Christopher its business person of the year in 2001. Sales were $740 million in 2001. By this time the company had 1,100 corporate employees.

Berkshire Hathaway Inc., the holding company led by legendary Omaha investor Warren Buffet, acquired The Pampered Chef in the fall of 2002. (The purchase price was not disclosed.) The Pampered Chef's financials were strong as ever. While growing revenues 232 percent between 1995 and 2001, noted *Fortune Small Business*, the company still had not managed to pick any debts beyond the original $3,000 used to launch the business.

Although Buffet was known for leaving acquired companies in the hands of existing management, Doris Christopher soon turned the CEO job over to Sheila O'Connell Cooper, a transition that had already been under way. A former executive with Mary Kay Corp. before joining Pampered Chef in 2000 as president and chief operating officer, O'Connell Cooper had launched BeautiControl Inc. and sold it to Tupperware Corp. before joining The Pampered Chef. Marla C. Gottschalk, formerly an executive with Kraft Foods, Inc., took the roles of president and chief operating officer in November 2003.

O'Connell Cooper told *ChicagoBusiness.com* part of her mission was to reach new users, including men. The sales force, which then numbered 71,000 reps, had been composed almost entirely of women. The company also was aiming to sell more to minorities. The product line already had begun to expand beyond chef's tools.

Doris Christopher published another book in 2005, *The Pampered Chef®: The Story of One of America's Most Beloved Companies.* "If you chase the money, you'll never get it. But if you chase after your dream to serve others, the money will follow you," she wrote. With sales approaching $1 billion, The Pampered Chef was a colossal success that flew in the face of the career woman myth, according to a profile of Doris Christopher in the *Chicago Sun-Times.* "Most women were not that woman," noted Christopher.

April Dougal Gasbarre
Updated, Frederick C. Ingram

PRINCIPAL COMPETITORS

Bed Bath & Beyond; Tupperware Brands Corporation; Williams-Sonoma, Inc.; WKI Holding Company, Inc.

FURTHER READING

Browning-Bias, Kristen, "Table Means All to Chef Founder; Book Celebration of Family Life," *Denver Post*, March 7, 2001, p. F3.

Christopher, Doris, *Come to the Table*, New York: Warner Books, 1999.

———, *The Pampered Chef®; The Story of One of America's Most Beloved Companies*, New York: Currency, 2005.

Cooper, Cord, "IBD's 10 Secrets to Success: Take Action; Breathe Life into Dreams," *Investor's Business Daily*, July 6, 2005, p. A4.

Daily, Patricia Wallace, "Pampered Chef Founder Named Addison Business Person of the Year," *Chicago Daily Herald*, January 28, 2001, p. 10.

Fitzpatrick, Michele L., "Recipe for Success," *Chicago Tribune*, April 14, 1996, Sec. 17, pp. 1, 7.

Grondin, Kathryn, "Pampered Chef Now Calls Addison Home," *Chicago Daily Herald*, October 19, 2002, p. 3.

Hau, Caroline, "Party Profits," *U.S. News & World Report*, October 20, 2003.

Heckel, Jodi, "Head of Addison, Ill.-Based Pampered Chef Says Family Still Comes First," *News-Gazette* (Champaign-Urbana, Ill.), August 11, 2003.

Kaiser, Rob, "Warren Buffet Buys Addison, Ill.-Based Pampered Chef Kitchen Goods Company," *Chicago Tribune*, September 27, 2002.

Littman, Margaret, "Pampered Chef Hits on Recipe for Growth: Family-Friendly Firm Rides Wave of Direct Sales," *Crain's Chicago Business*, December 8, 1997, p. 7.

Mamis, Robert A., "Master of Bootstrapping Administration," *Inc.,* August 1995, pp. 40-43.

Mawhorr, S. A., "Few Changes Expected After Pampered Chef Sale," *Chicago Daily Herald,* September 25, 2002, p. 1.

———, "Pampered Chef Owners Give $15 Million to Concordia," *Chicago Daily Herald,* November 12, 1999, p. 6.

The Pampered Chef, Ltd., "The Pampered Chef, Ltd. Celebrates 20th Anniversary; Company Founder and President Savors the Company's Sweet Success," Addison, Ill.: The Pampered Chef, Ltd., October 12, 2000.

———, "The Pampered Chef, Ltd. Raises $750,000 in the Fight to 'Help Whip Cancer,'" Addison, Ill.: The Pampered Chef, Ltd., August 15, 2001.

"The Pampered Chef Story," *Food, Family & Friends: Quick & Easy Recipes for Everyday Occasions,* New York: Time-Life Custom Publishing, 1995, pp. 5-9.

Piccininni, Ann, "Home Parties: Mixing Selling with Socializing—There's Also a Future in Management," *Chicago Tribune,* July 26, 1992, p. 18SW.

Pickett, Debra, "Sunday Lunch with ... The Pampered Chef Creator; 'I Remember Thinking About California and Wondering If People There Cooked,'" *Chicago Sun-Times,* September 4, 2005, p. 26.

Quigley, Kelly, "Pampered Chef Names New CEO," *ChicagoBusiness.com,* January 21, 2003.

Rodkin, Dennis, "Up the Down Economy," *Chicago,* May 1992, pp. 85-91.

Roha, Ronaleen R., "Want to Buy a Potato Peeler? Wanna Sell a Bunch of 'Em?," *Kiplinger's Personal Finance Magazine,* March 1, 1997, p. 101.

Sanchez, Robert, "Perks Kept Pampered Chef Home in Addison," *Chicago Daily Herald,* December 6, 2000, p. 7.

Spragins, Ellyn, "Building a Company Warren Buffet Would Buy," *Fortune Small Business,* February 1, 2003, p. 51.

Warshaw, Michael, "Home-Based $300 Million," *Success,* November 1996, p. 23.

Pearl Musical Instrument Company

10-2-1 Yachiyodai-Nishu Yachiyo
Chiba, 276-0034
Japan
Telephone: (81) 047 484-9111
Fax: (81) 047 482-5797
Web site: http://www.pearldrum.com

Private Company
Founded: 1946
Employees: NA
Sales: NA
NAIC: 339992 Musical Instrument Manufacturing

■ ■ ■

Pearl Musical Instrument Company, based in Yachiyo, Japan, is a global manufacturer and exporter best known for its drum kits used by popular rock, country, and jazz musicians. The company also produces drums and equipment used by marching bands and pipe and drum units. Pearl serves the concert market, offering drums under its own name and a variety of instruments, parts, and accessories under the Adams Concert label, including timpani, marimbas, xylophones, bell and glockenspiels, chimes, and vibraphones. The Pearl Percussion label offers such instruments as congas, bongos, djembes, timbales, cowbells, as well as stands and replacement heads. Also found under the Pearl Percussion label are a wide variety of "effects" items for hand use or additions to drum sets, including tambourines, the liso shaker, ganziero, maracas, metal

guiro, new clave blocks, a variety of bells, and the charrasquita. In addition the company sells jackets, shirts, t-shirts, and hats promoting the Pearl logo. A private company, with little published financial information available, Pearl exports to more than 60 companies. It maintains a United States subsidiary, Pearl Corporation, in Nashville.

POSTWAR ORIGINS

Pearl rose from the ashes of World War II, and was founded in Tokyo in 1946 by Katsumi Yanagisawa. With just two employees working out of a 300-square-foot shed, he began making music stands. The United States' occupation forces had brought their culture to the country, engendering a love of baseball and jazz in Japan. Love for the latter, as well as an increasing emphasis on music education in the schools, fueled demand for music stands and instruments. Because there were virtually no drums being produced domestically, despite a high demand for them, Yanagisawa expanded beyond his successful music stand business in 1950 and began producing handmade snare drums and bass drums, which he copied from American designs. He also redesigned his music stands to accommodate cymbals. He now called his company Pearl Industry, Ltd., which he soon changed to Pearl Musical Instrument Company. He enjoyed immediate success in the percussion field, and by 1953 he was producing complete drum sets, as well as cymbals, marching drums, Latin percussion instruments, and timpani. In 1957 Yanagisawa was joined by his eldest son, Mitsou, an engineer, who played a major role in the creation of an export division. Pearl now began to export its products through agents and trading companies.

The rise of rock and roll in the United States in the 1950s, a phenomenon that swept the world, led to the creation of small rock bands anchored by drum sets. To grab a share of this immense market, Pearl opened a new 15,000-square-foot factory in Chiba, Japan. In that same year the company began exporting to the U.S. market under the label of original equipment manufacturers. All told, Pearl drums were sold under more than 30 names, including Apollo, Crest, Revere, Lyra, Roxy, Coronet, and Majestic. The inexpensive kits were responsible for attracting a large number of young customers who wanted to take up the drums and join rock bands.

In 1965 Mitsuo Yanagisawa succeeded his father as Pearl's chief executive officer and chairman. The company now turned away from producing low-profit, inexpensive drum sets for others, electing instead to grow the Pearl brand. His long-range plan was to produce instruments that could rival the quality of market leaders Ludwig, Slingerland, and Gretsch. He also sought to improve productivity by installing the latest machinery in the Chiba factory. In addition he assembled a global sales and service network, which was then able to support the 1966 launch of the "President Series," Pearl's first professional-level drum kits, which were developed with the help of jazz artists Art Blakey and J.C. Heard (who was also signed as an endorser). With the President drums Pearl became the first Japanese drum brand to crack the U.S. and United Kingdom markets. Private label manufacturing was now a thing of the past and to keep up with rising demand, Pearl opened a second factory in Chiba in 1968. It was also in 1968 that the company expanded beyond percussion instruments, introducing a line of flutes that ranged from student models to professional instruments fashioned out of gold and silver.

WESTERN INROADS: 1970–80

The 1970s offered Pearl an opportunity to make inroads in Western countries, which were thrown into recession by the 1973 Middle East oil crisis. Pearl, as well as other Japanese drum makers Tama and Yamaha, increased their research and development efforts to improve quality, especially in their professional drum sets. In 1972 Pearl introduced fiberglass and wood fiberglass shells, the start of a number of innovations Pearl brought to the industry. A year later Pearl introduced transparent drums featuring acrylic plastic seamless shells. Then, in 1978, the company introduced its Vari-Pitch Cannons, and in 1979 began selling its Syncussion electric drum system. Because of a general economic boom for Japan during the early 1970s, production costs in the country soared. As a result, a sister company was established in Taiwan and much of Pearl's manufacturing was transferred there starting in 1973. Over the years, another four Taiwanese factories were added, and the original Chiba facility would be dedicated to the production of products for the Japanese market.

Although Pearl was proving to be a force for innovation in the drum field, it had an easier time achieving success in the budget category. In 1984 the company introduced its Export Series drum set, which provided beginning drummers with everything they needed in one package. It would become one of the best-selling drum sets in the world. For the professional market Pearl introduced a number of products during the 1980s. One was the CZX Custom Series, one of the most expensive kits on the market. Handcrafted in Japan, it featured shells made entirely of maple, including an outside veneer of costly Italian Birdseye maple, one of the rarest woods on earth. Not actually maple but a phenomenon that occurs within several kinds of timber, Birdseye maple offered a distinctive pattern and was scratch resistant once finished. Also in the 1980s Pearl unveiled its Custom Class snare drums, which used steam-bent maple shells to produce a smooth, distinctive sound. The Championship FFX free-floating marching snare drum was introduced, featuring a free-floating lug design allowing the shells to better vibrate and produce a richer tone that projected farther than drums using a nonfloating design. The FFX also employed an aluminum edge ring and robust die cast hoops, capable of handling the tremendous tension needed for the Kevlar heads that were being used by drum corps. In addition, Pearl introduced a pair of Championship marching drum carriers, including a tight-fitting fiberglass vest. The 1980s also saw the introduction of the P-950 Super Pro Chain Drive pedal for the bass drum, which featured double chains for reliability and was easily removed, a boon for professionals who repeatedly set up and broke down their equipment.

For many years Pearl drums were distributed in the United States through a pair of distributors, Heater

KEY DATES

1946: Company founded in Tokyo by Katsumi Yanagisawa to make music stands.
1950: Yanagisawa begins making drums for domestic market.
1965: Mitsou Yanagisawa succeeds father as CEO and chairman.
1966: Pearl offers first professional drum set, the President Series.
1973: Taiwanese operations begin.
1989: U.S. subsidiary opens headquarters in Nashville, Tennessee.
1993: Afro Percussion acquired.
1997: Pearl enters drum corps market.
2000: Ready-Set-Go entry level drum set introduced.

Music and Chicago Musical Instrument company. Norland Music bought the two companies, and, in 1979, Pearl bought the drum division and renamed it Pearl International. In 1989 the subsidiary purchased land close to the airport in Nashville, Tennessee, to build a new warehouse and office complex, which opened in 1990 and also served as Pearl's U.S. headquarters. Also in 1990, Pearl International changed its name to Pearl Corporation.

According to *Music Trades* in a 2002 profile of the company, "In the '80s and early-'90s, Pearl drew plenty of pop star power from endorsing drummers in band such as KISS, Motley Crue, Bon Jovi, and The Red Hot Chili Peppers." But along the way, opined *Music Trades,* the company "made a couple of miscalculations in the way it has presented its wares." David Howe, Pearl's vice-president of sales and marketing, told the publication, "When the super-band era was over, we decided that maybe it wasn't important to focus so much on endorsers in our marketing, and we stopped using them as much in ads and catalogs." Pearl President Andy Ito added, "A drum is a round piece of wood. You have to put a personality with it, and endorsers are the best vehicle for doing that, making it cool or traditional or whatever. Some of our competitors were better at attaching a personality to their product." Pearl also neglected to continue to build its brand. "For a short period we overlooked the effect of consumers seeing the same drum logo every time they turned on MTV," Howe explained. "There's a lot of value in that. So we made a complete turnaround; everything we do now has an artist in it."

HAND PERCUSSIONS: 1990-2000

Another problem Pearl encountered involved its entry into hand percussion instruments after the 1993 acquisition of Afro Percussion, a company that was already well established in Europe. Pearl tried to market the products globally but quickly realized how difficult it was to gain entry into stores. Moreover, Pearl underestimated the need for product innovation in the hand percussion field. It was only after the company made a greater commitment to the category and began to distinguish itself from the competition, especially with the introduction of new accessory items, that it finally began to establish itself in hand percussions. Even in its core business, drum kits, Pearl had to overcome obstacles. In 1991 it launched its entry-level Forum Series drum sets but enjoyed only limited success. Realizing the kits were priced too high for the beginners' market, Pearl began making changes to bring the value in line with the price. After cutting some corners, Pearl upgraded the kit with better mounts and shells and eventually offered a set that became an industry standard for beginners.

Other developments in the 1990s included the introduction of the B-513 P 3x13 brass piccolo and the M-513P 3X13 maple piccolo snare drums, which would become the top-selling drums in the company's history. Pearl also introduced its Masters Series, a high-end drum set, the innovative PowerShifter Bass Drum Pedal, and in 1997 Pearl entered the pipe band market with the introduction of its first line of snare drums in this category. It was not a highly profitable niche, but the pipe band business played an important role in adding synergy to the company's product development efforts. Pearl also introduced the industry's first magnesium carrier for the drum corps market, the Symphonic snare drum, and became the exclusive worldwide distributor of Adams timpani and mallet instruments.

Also of importance in the company's growth during the 1990s was the creation of a proprietary sales force in 1992 to sell and service all Pearl Percussion products in the United States, a task previously handled by Gibson U.S.A. Because Pearl had grown so quickly in the previous decade, the Gibson sales representatives were unable to devote enough attention to the Pearl lines and provide the level of dealer service Pearl desired. Once the Gibson distribution agreement was terminated, Pearl was then able to institute tighter rules regarding dealer advertised prices, prohibiting them from advertising prices in excess of 35 percent to 40 percent off suggested list price, depending on the item. "We got tired of seeing the Pearl product footballed around in advertising," Bob Morrison, Pearl Corporation's director of marketing, told the press. By curbing this practice, Pearl was able to better protect the value of its brand.

Pearl continued to unveil new product lines and repacked others in the new century. After working with dealer focus groups, the company introduced the Ready-Set-Go drum kit in 2000, which packaged the Forum drum set with cymbals, a seat, sticks, and a video for young beginners at a price point parents found attractive. The company also upgraded its perennially popular Export line with the 2000 addition of its Integrated Suspension System, which allowed the tom shells to resonate fully and create a richer sound. The ready-to-play set was also reinvigorated with the addition of two new colors: "Mirror Chrome" and "Charcoal Metallic." For the higher end of the market, Pearl introduced the Masterworks Series, a made-to-order series that customers could customize by choosing a variety of woods and shell thicknesses. Also of note in the 2000s, Pearl incorporated a state-of-the-art warehouse management system in its Nashville location to combine accounting, credit, order entry, and warehouse functions, allowing the company to closely monitor productivity and inventory levels. In this way, Pearl was able to keep overhead costs in check, an important component in the company's efforts to maintain a balance between price and value. Offering the right amount of quality for the dollar had been a key factor in Pearl's rise to the top ranks of the drum industry and promised to remain just as important in the years to come.

Ed Dinger

PRINCIPAL SUBSIDIARIES

Pearl Corporation (United States); Pearl Music Europe B.V. (Holland); Pearl Musical Instrument Co. of Taiwan; Pearl (UK) Ltd.

PRINCIPAL COMPETITORS

Drum Workshop, Inc.; Gibson Guitar Corporation; Yamaha Corporation.

FURTHER READING

"Pearl Announces All-New Sales Force," *Music Trades,* August 1992, p. 80.

"Pearl Completes Move to New Nashville Facility," *Music Trades,* January 1991, p. 34.

"Pearl Export Raises the Standard with I.S.S.," *Music Trades,* July 2000, p. 194.

"Pearl Reigns in Dealer Discount Advertising," *Music Trades,* March 1993, p. 48.

"Why Pearl is Percussion?," *Music Trades,* February 1, 2002, p. 146.

Pentax Corporation

2-36-9 Maeno-cho
Itabashi-ku
Tokyo,
Japan
Telephone: (81) 03 3960 5151
Fax: (81) 03 3960 2063
Web site: http://www.pentax.co.jp

Public Company
Incorporated: 1919 as Asahi Kogaku Goshi Kaisha (Asahi
    Optical Joint Stock Co.)
Employees: 5,490
Sales: ¥133.56 trillion ($1.2 billion) (2005)
Stock Exchanges: Tokyo
Ticker Symbol: 7750
NAIC: 333315 Photographic and Photocopying Equip-
    ment Manufacturing; 423410 Photographic Equip-
    ment and Supplies Merchant Wholesalers; 423460
    Ophthalmic Goods Merchant Wholesalers; 541512
    Computer Systems Design Services

■ ■ ■

Pentax Corporation is one of the world's best-known
names in the camera industry, and has long served as a
photographic equipment pioneer. The company
continues to produce cameras and other photographic
equipment, including its *ist D Digital SLR cameras,
the Optio-series of digital compact cameras, the MZ
range of autofocus SLR film cameras, and the ESPOP-
series of compact film cameras. Pentax also produces
interchangeable camera lenses and lens adapters, as well

as other accessories, and a variety of other optical-related
products, including binoculars and telescopes; medical
equipment, including endoscopes and fiberscopes; and
medical fine ceramics products, including its Apaceram
artificial bones and artificial dental roots. In addition,
Pentax has developed a number of software and
information technology operations, including text-to-
speech and related applications. Pentax also continues to
produce its original product, optical lenses, through a
joint venture with Seiko formed by a merger in 2003.
Like many of the former Japanese film camera giants,
including Nikkon and Minolta, Pentax has been hit
hard by the switch to digital cameras at the start of the
new century; the massive consumer shift to the digital
format, together with the onrush of new competitors
and Pentax's own late entry into the digital market
caused a severe drop in the company's revenues at the
beginning of the decade. Seeking a larger partner, in late
2005 the company signed a production agreement with
Samsung; the first Pentax-designed, Samsung-produced
digital camera debuted in January 2006. Pentax is listed
on the Tokyo Stock Exchange, and is led by President,
CEO, and Chairman Fumio Urano. In 2005, the
company posted sales of ¥133.56 trillion ($1.2 billion).

LENS MANUFACTURER IN 1919

Pentax originated as a small manufacturer of eyeglass
lenses, Asahi Kogaku Goshi Kaisha (Asahi Optical Joint
Stock Co.), founded by Kumao Kajiwara, in Toshima, a
suburb of Tokyo, in 1919. Asahi quickly established a
reputation for the quality of its lenses, due in part to the
company's adoption of polishing techniques more commonly used for microscopes and telescopes. Asahi

extended his operations into other lens categories, such as film projection lenses, starting in 1923. By the early 1930s, Asahi had begun to produce camera lenses as well, including for future Japanese photographic equipment leaders Minolta, starting in 1932, and then Konica in 1933. In support of this, the company built a new factory outside of Tokyo in 1934.

Into the 1930s, Asahi's production turned more and more toward the production of camera lenses on the one hand, and production of optical equipment, such as periscopes and gunsights and the like, for the Japanese military. The installation of a military government in 1937, however, placed Asahi's operations under government supervision, and production was wholly turned over to producing optical equipment for the military.

By then, Kajiwara had died, and the company's leadership was taken over by a relative, Saburo Matsumoto, who also had worked for Asahi for several years

before starting a career as a printer. Matsumoto had developed an interest in photography—and even owned one of the first German-made single-lens reflex cameras—and had begun to plan Asahi's expansion from the production of camera lenses to the cameras themselves. With Asahi's production placed under military supervision, however, Matsumoto was forced to seek a new outlet for his plans. In 1938, Matsumoto bought a small factory in Tokyo, and renamed it as Asahi Optical Co. Ltd. There, Matsumoto resumed production of camera lenses.

Soon after, however, the new factory's production was turned over to support the country's military effort as well. During the war, the Japanese government discouraged the development of a consumer photography market. Nonetheless, Asahi remained in the photography business, producing aerial photography and related photographic equipment for the military. In this way, the company was able to develop its lens production and polishing technologies during the war.

By the end of the war, the Asahi factories had been destroyed and much of the company's workforce had been killed. In order to pay off the company's debt, and with little hope of recovering the money owed to it by the disbanded military government, Matsumoto sold off the remains of the company's equipment and inventory, freeing himself of debt.

Asahi managed to resume operations by the summer of 1946, when the company received its first orders for supplying binocular lenses for the U.S. occupying force. Before long, the company began to pick up new lens supply and polishing contracts from the country's camera makers.

Matsumoto, however, now became determined to transform Asahi from a mere parts supplier to a full-fledged consumer products manufacturer. Asahi's first product was a telescope, produced in the spring of 1948 specifically for a total eclipse of the sun visible from northern Japan that year. The company's telescope featured a tube made of cardboard, as well as the company's high-quality lenses. The success of the telescope, which was meant as a temporary product only, led the company to look for something more permanent. Matsumoto quickly settled on the production of binoculars, a small but promising market in Japan at the time. By the end of the year, Asahi had launched its highly popular "Jupiter" compact binoculars, which became a huge consumer hit not only in Japan but overseas as well. The success of the Jupiter was credited, in large part, to the company's commitment to high quality. As part of the design of the Jupiter, the company had helped develop a new lens coating technique, in

KEY DATES

1919: Kumao Kajiwara founds Asahi Kogaku Goshi Kaisha (Asahi Optical Joint Stock Co.) to produce eyeglass lenses.

1923: Production of lenses for film projectors begins.

1932: Production of camera lenses begins.

1937: The military government forces the company to convert production for military purposes.

1938: Under the leadership of Saburo Matsumoto, the company acquires a small factory, renamed as Asahi Optical Co., in order to continue to produce camera lenses.

1946: With the factories destroyed, Asahi relaunches production of lenses for the Occupation forces.

1948: Asahi Optical launches its first consumer product, a telescope for viewing the solar eclipse in northern Japan; the company then launches its first full-fledged consumer product, the Jupiter binoculars.

1949: Development of the first SLR camera begins.

1951: The first Asahiflex camera is released.

1957: The new "Pentax" SLR camera, featuring a pentaprism, is launched.

1962: The company opens its first European sales subsidiary in Belgium.

1971: Asahi Optical is listed on the Tokyo Stock Exchange.

1973: The company opens its first foreign manufacturing plant in Hong Kong.

1975: A manufacturing plant in Taiwan is opened.

1976: The company establishes its first U.S. sales and distribution subsidiary.

1982: Further expansion is under way in Europe, with subsidiaries in Switzerland, Sweden, and The Netherlands.

1983: The company launches its first medical ceramics product, the Apaceram artificial tooth root.

1986: The first compact zoom camera is launched.

1990: The company establishes a manufacturing plant in the Philippines, and begins licensed manufacturing in China.

1994: A manufacturing plant in Vietnam is opened.

1999: Camera sales drop as competitors introduce the new digital camera format.

2001: Fumio Urano becomes CEO and chairman and leads the company on a strategic review.

2002: The company changes its name to Pentax and begins developing its own digital camera technology.

2003: The successful Optio digital camera line is launched.

---

conjunction with Nagoya University, which produced a sharper and more durable lens.

PHOTOGRAPHIC PIONEER BY 1951

Matsumoto now turned his attention to developing Asahi's first camera. For this, Matsumoto was determined to develop the company's own technology, rather than imitate the industry-leading German camera designs of the time. Matsumoto gathered a small design team and set out to create a new single-lens reflex (SLR) camera that would work with the 35mm film standard. With no SLR cameras from which to work, Asahi's research and development team was forced to invent the camera from scratch. Nonetheless, by the end of 1949, the company had succeeded in creating a working prototype.

By 1951, Asahi had succeeded in developing a finished product, dubbed the Asahiflex. The company at first attempted to market its camera to store directly, but met with refusal from storeowners to carry the camera. The company continued to make improvements to the Asahiflex's design, and in 1952 reached a distribution agreement with Hattori Tokeiten (the future Seiko Corporation). The camera, the first of its kind in Japan, proved a huge hit, and before long the company stepped up its production from 200 units per month to more than 500 per month.

Asahi continued to make improvements to the Asahiflex, such as adding a pre-set aperture ring in 1953. This ring gave the photographer greater ease while focusing. By 1954, the company had launched the next generation of Asahiflex cameras. In the meantime, the company began developed of a new camera design, the world's first SLR camera to incorporate a pentaprism. This camera was launched in 1957 as the Pentax, and it thrust Asahi onto the world camera stage.

The success of the Pentax was immediate, and by the mid-1960s the company had sold more than one million SLR cameras. By then the company had added a new innovation, the Spotmatic, which took exposure measurements through the camera lens. The Spotmatic helped further boost Pentax sales, which topped two million units sold by the beginning of the 1970s.

INTERNATIONAL PRODUCTION: 1980–2000

By then, Asahi had opened its first distribution subsidiary in Europe, in Belgium, in 1962. The company opened a new factory in Tochigi in 1968, and by 1971 had gone public with a listing on the Tokyo Stock Exchange. Two years later, Asahi opened its first foreign manufacturing plant, in Hong Kong. This was followed by the opening of a factory in Taiwan in 1975, and sales and distribution subsidiaries in the United States (1976) and Canada (1978).

By then, too, Asahi had begun to diversify its operations, entering the computer market with the launch of its Photoplotter automatic drafting system in 1973. Into the 1980s, the company's diversified interests expanded to encompass the field of medical ceramics, notably with the 1983 début of its Apaceram artificial tooth root. In 1985, the company added another medical product, Apatite, an artificial bone filler.

Asahi's international development continued as well, with new subsidiaries established in France in 1981, and Switzerland, Sweden, and The Netherlands in 1982. The company also expanded its eyeglass lens sales, with the launch of Pentax Vision Inc. in the United States.

In the meantime, Asahi remained a leading innovator in the camera market. Among the company's successes were the launch of the world's first compact zoom-lens camera in 1986, and the first autofocus SLR to feature built-in autoflash in 1987. In that year, as well, the company adapted its camera technology to the medical market, launching production of a its first electronic endoscope.

Toward the end of the decade, the company began to shift more of its production outside of Japan. The company reached a licensing agreement in Gansu Optical Instruments Industrial in China, which began producing Pentax-branded compact autofocus cameras for the Chinese market. That year, Asahi set up its own production facility in the Philippines Mactan Export Processing Zone, where it began producing its lower-priced camera range. The company continued opening new production facilities through the 1990s, adding a plant for the manufacture of eyeglass lenses in the Philippines in 1992, and a new optical device facility in Vietnam in 1994.

GOING DIGITAL IN THE NEW CENTURY

Throughout the 1990s, Asahi continued to turn out new Pentax camera models, including 1997's 645N, the world's first medium-format autofocus SLR. Yet the company's commitment to film cameras, a policy held to by the founding Matsumoto family still in control of the company's direction, was to cost it dearly into the new century. The arrival of the first digital cameras caught the company off guard; by the beginning of the 2000s, the company's camera sales had dropped in half.

Fumio Urano, the company's top design engineer, was brought in to lead the company in 2001, becoming company president, CEO, and chairman. Urano led the company on a strategic turnaround, not only embracing the new digital format, but becoming determined to become a technology leader. As part of that review, Asahi changed its name to the more well-known Pentax name.

The company quickly held true on its promise. In 2003, for example, the company launched its Optio line of extremely compact digital cameras. By 2004, the company had introduced its latest innovation, the *ist DS line of single-reflex digital cameras, which became the smallest and lightest cameras on the market to allow interchangeable lenses. The company also launched a new low-priced digital camera line that year. The new models helped restore the company to profitability.

Yet the rise of a raft of new competitors, including low-priced competitors from China, but also such unlikely camera producers as printer manufacturers Hewlett Packard and Epson, and appliance manufacturers such as Panasonic, continued to place Pentax under pressure. In response, Pentax sought further extensions to its diversified operations. In 2004, for example, the company acquired Microline Inc., based in the United States, which allowed it to enter the market for laparoscopic instruments. In late 2005, the company began exporting its video endoscopy systems to the global market, and in January 2006, the company acquired Voiceware Co., a producer of text-to-speech software technologies.

Pentax also sought to protect its corporate position. In 2005, the company adopted a "poison pill" defense in order to protect itself from a potential hostile takeover attempt. Later in that year, the company aligned itself with Korea's Samsung Corporation, in order to take advantage of that group's massive marketing and distribution capabilities. Under that agreement, Samsung launched its own digital camera, based on Pentax's *ist D format, in January 2006. In this way, the Pentax name appeared certain to remain an industry pacesetter into the twenty-first century.

M. L. Cohen

PRINCIPAL SUBSIDIARIES

Pentax (SCHWEIZ) AG (Switzerland); Pentax (Shanghai) Corporation; Pentax Benelux B.V. (Netherlands); Pentax Canada Inc.; Pentax of America Inc.; Pentax Cebu Philippines Corporation; Pentax Europe GmbH (Germany); Pentax Europe N.V. (Belgium); Pentax France S.A.; Pentax Fukushima Co., Ltd.; Pentax Hong Kong Ltd.; Pentax Imaging Company (United States); Pentax Industrial Instruments Co., Ltd.; Pentax Medical Company (United States); Pentax Optotech Co., Ltd.; Pentax Scandinavia AB; Pentax Service, Co., Ltd.; Pentax Tohoku Co., Ltd.; Pentax U.K. Ltd.; Pentax VN Co., Ltd. (Vietnam).

PRINCIPAL COMPETITORS

Tomoegawa Paper Company Ltd.; Canon Inc.; Fuji Photo Film Company Ltd.; Sony USA Inc.; Ricoh Company Ltd.; Xerox Corporation; Eastman Kodak Co.; Konica Minolta Holdings Inc.; Olympus Corporation; Nikon Corporation; Agfa-Gevaert Group; SAGEM S.A.; Oce N.V.; 3M Deutschland GmbH.

FURTHER READING

"Asahi Optical to Change Name to Pentax," *Japan Weekly Monitor*, May 27, 2002.

"Camera Makers Turn Focus to Biotech," *Asahi Shimbun*, June 25, 2005.

"Japan's Pentax to Start European Sales of Artificial Bones," *Jiji Press*, June 28, 2004.

Jonkman, Peter, "A New Vision on the History of the Asahiflex," *Spotmatic Magazine*, January 2001.

"Lens Firms Seiko and Pentax Are to Merge," *Optician*, August 15, 2003, p. 1.

"New Subsidiary at Pentax," *GEO: connexion*, September 2004, p. 8.

"Pentax Acquires U.S. Surgical Device Maker," *Jiji Press*, December 15, 2004.

"Pentax Consolidation," *Photo Trade News*, May 2004, p. 8.

"Pentax Plays Digital Catch-Up with Passion," *Rocky Mountain News*, October 11, 2004, p. 5B.

"Pentax, Samsung Unit in Digital Camera Tie-up," *PC Magazine Online*, October 12, 2005.

"Pentax, Seino Get Shareholders' Go-Ahead for 'Poison Pill,'" *Jiji Press*, June 24, 2005.

"Pentax Swings Back to Black on Solid Sales, Cost Cuts," *Japan Weekly*, May 30, 2003.

"Pentax to Slash 300 Jobs," *Jiji Press*, May 24, 2005.

Poppen, Julie, and Greg Scoblete, "Samsung Announces First d-SLR Release," *TWICE*, January 30, 2006.

White, Derek J., "A Brief History of the Asahi Optical Corporation, *Spotmatic Magazine*, April 2002.

PerkinElmer, Inc.

—■—

45 William Street
Wellesley, Massachusetts 02481-4078
U.S.A.
Telephone: (781) 237-5100
Fax: (781) 237-9386
Web site: http://www.perkinelmer.com

Public Company
Incorporated: 1939
Employees: 10,000
Sales: $1.47 billion (2005)
Stock Exchanges: New York
Ticker Symbol: PKI
NAIC: 334516 Analytical Laboratory Instrument Manufacturing

■ ■ ■

PerkinElmer Inc. is a leading provider of analytical instruments used in the health sciences and industrial sciences markets. With operations in more than 125 countries, the company provides tools and instrumentation for drug discovery, genetic screening, and environmental and chemical analysis. It also offers technology solutions for biomedical imaging. A key contributor to the development of optical tools such as the infrared spectrometer, the spectrophotometer, and laser retroreflectors, the company is also known for its work on NASA's Hubble Space Telescope, an ambitious and ultimately unsuccessful project that has nevertheless provided scientists with some valuable information through space photography. The company has experienced several major organizational overhauls since the 1980s and announced plans to sell its fluid sciences division in 2005.

EARLY HISTORY

PerkinElmer Inc. traces its roots to the early 1930s when a common fascination with astronomy brought together an otherwise unlikely duo: Charles W. Elmer, the head of a firm of court reporters who was already not far from retirement age, and Richard Perkin, a young investment banker who had left Pratt Institute in Brooklyn, New York, after a year of studying chemical engineering to try a Wall Street career. The two met when Perkin dropped in on an astronomy lecture Elmer delivered at the Brooklyn Institute of Arts & Sciences. They soon became friends and also recognized a common interest in turning their hobby into a business opportunity in precision optics. Deciding to set up shop in New York City, Perkin raised $15,000 in start-up capital from his relatives, and Elmer was able to contribute $5,000. They ordered equipment from Europe, and on April 19, 1937, they formed Perkin-Elmer as a partnership.

Perkin and Elmer started their optical design and consulting business in a small Manhattan office, but within a year they were producing optical components in Jersey City, New Jersey. On December 13, 1939, they incorporated. The company moved to Connecticut's Fairfield County in 1941—initially to Glenbrook outside Stamford, later to Norwalk, and then to Wilton.

The onset of World War II made clear the importance of an American source for precision instru-

COMPANY PERSPECTIVES

PerkinElmer, Inc. is focused in the following businesses—Life and Analytical Sciences, Optoelectronics and Fluid Sciences. Combining operational excellence and technology expertise with an intimate understanding of its customers' needs, PerkinElmer provides products and services in health sciences and industrial sciences markets that require innovation, precision and reliability.

ments, and Perkin-Elmer was able to operate at a profit from the start. In 1942, it became the first optical instrument maker to win a Navy "E" (for Excellence). The principal wartime products were instruments and components used in airplane range finders, bombsights, and reconnaissance systems. The company also was able, however, to arrange for research that extended its optical know-how into a brand new field, coming out with its initial infrared spectrometer in 1944. Germany also had done work in infrared spectroscopy, but had put it aside to concentrate on more urgent military needs, enabling Perkin-Elmer to build a substantial lead. The production of a spectrometer, which uses infrared rays for quick and accurate analysis of chemical compounds, was the start of a whole array of analytical instruments, such as gas chromatographs (which Perkin-Elmer introduced in 1955 as its second major analytical group) and atomic absorption spectrophotometers, collectively ushering in a new era in analytical laboratory operations. The equipment was used both for research and for production control, as well as several other activities, including crime investigations.

POSTWAR GROWTH

After the war the company was chosen to design and build the 33-inch Baker Schmidt telescope, which Harvard University installed in 1950 at an observatory in South Africa. As part of its defense work, in 1955, it built a Transverse Panoramic Camera, the 12- by 14-foot frames of which could take precise horizon-to-horizon aerial reconnaissance pictures from 40,000 feet, a major achievement in those presatellite days. From the early, unmanned satellite launchings on, Perkin-Elmer instruments were used regularly in spacecraft. Furthermore, the company remained a leading supplier of missile guidance equipment to the military.

During the 1950s Perkin-Elmer also moved energetically into foreign markets. It set up a manu-

facturing affiliate in West Germany in 1954 and in Britain in 1957, while sales units were established in several more countries. In 1960 a Japanese production unit, Hitachi Perkin-Elmer, was established, with Hitachi Ltd. holding a 51 percent interest. Cofounder Elmer died at age 83 in 1954. A year later the company sold its first stock to the public and began trading over the counter. On December 13, 1960—21 years to the day since Perkin-Elmer incorporated—Dick Perkin bought the first 100 shares for $47.50 a share at the traditional New York Stock Exchange ceremonies as Perkin-Elmer was listed with the ticker symbol PKN. Perkin-Elmer's stock underwent four 2-for-1 stock splits through the 1990s. While PKN tended to be quite a volatile stock, prices were generally well above that early level.

Perkin served as president and chairperson until June 1961, when he brought in Robert E. Lewis, who had been president of Argus Camera and Sylvania Electric, to take over as president and chief executive. Perkin remained chairperson, concentrating on long-range plans and overseas development, until his death at age 62 in 1969.

Perkin-Elmer came early to the laser era in 1961. In fact, the whole concept was so new that the unit handling the development was called the Optical "Maser" Department, because when Dr. Theodore Maiman first came out with the beams at Hughes Aircraft in 1960, their name was derived from Microwave Amplification by Stimulated Emission of Radiation. Since light waves, shorter and with higher frequency than microwaves, can be concentrated into narrower beams and operate at higher speed, the technology quickly centered on the optical maser version, that is, light beams. It was not long before "l" for light replaced the "m" and the term became laser. Most of Perkin-Elmer's laser work in the 1960s was in defense and space applications. One triumph came in 1969 when the Apollo 11 astronauts, their helmet visors protected by a Perkin-Elmer coating, deployed Perkin-Elmer laser retroreflectors on the moon's surface; shooting beams from earth at these reflectors later permitted extremely accurate distance measurements.

DIVERSIFICATION: 1970–85

During the 1960s, the company made some acquisitions supplementing internal expansion of its instrument line. Then, in the 1970s, in line with a trend in American corporate culture, Perkin-Elmer undertook a number of ambitious diversification moves. The foundation was laid for what Perkin-Elmer calls its material sciences business with the acquisition in September 1971 of METCO Inc. of Westbury, New York, the leading supplier of plasma and flame spray

KEY DATES

1937: Charles W. Elmer and Richard Perkin form Perkin-Elmer as an optical design and consulting business.

1939: The company incorporates.

1942: Perkin-Elmer becomes the first optical instrument maker to win a Navy "E" (for Excellence).

1944: The company launches its initial infrared spectrometer.

1955: A Transverse Panoramic Camera is developed.

1960: Perkin-Elmer lists on the New York Stock Exchange.

1971: METCO Inc. is acquired.

1977: Perkin-Elmer receives a contract to develop the Hubble Space Telescope for NASA.

1993: Applied Biosystems is purchased.

1995: Tony L. White is named president, chairman, and CEO; the company begins restructuring into two distinct groups: Analytical Instruments and Applied Biosystems.

1999: The Analytical Instruments division is sold to EG&G Inc.; EG&G changes its name to PerkinElmer Inc.

2005: PerkinElmer plans to sell its fluid sciences division.

material and equipment. (After acquiring the corporation, Perkin-Elmer opted to lowercase the name to "Metco.") The Metco thermal spraying process applied a metal or ceramic coating to improve a part's wear, corrosion rate, or heat resistance. The improved surface provided by such spraying can permit the use of less expensive materials in all sorts of machinery and engine components.

Also during this time, Perkin-Elmer sought to take advantage of the transistor boom by entering the semiconductor equipment business. In 1973 it introduced the Micralign projection mask aligner, designed to facilitate the production of semiconductors. The company entered yet another popular field the following year, acquiring Interdata, Inc., active in superminicomputers.

While building up its presence in these new areas, Perkin-Elmer also continued to enhance its analytical instrumentation and optical lines. Among major optical assignments, Perkin-Elmer received in 1977 the prime contract to develop the Hubble Space Telescope for NASA. This particular project proved to be a mixed blessing. After the $1.5 billion telescope was finally launched into space in 1990, it was discovered that the Hubble could not achieve its full mission because of some design and manufacturing flaws. Even so, it has been able to send back, as the *New York Times* put it, "valuable pictures of the near and far heavens."

In the instrumentation area, Perkin-Elmer began to introduce increasingly computerized equipment. For instance, in 1975 it brought out an infrared spectrometer controlled by a microprocessor; a decade later, the company offered augmented automation by use of robotics. Meanwhile, in 1977 Perkin-Elmer had further broadened its product base through the acquisition of Physical Electronics Industries, which specialized in surface science analytical instruments used to examine the chemical composition and bonding of the first few atomic layers of a surface. Later, the company began to explore biotechnology instrumentation.

RESTRUCTURING IN 1987

Up until the mid-1980s, Perkin-Elmer's growth formula had resulted in generally rising sales to a record $1.3 billion in the July 1985 fiscal year, compared with only around $300 million by the mid-1970s and less than $50 million in 1963. Profits, while more volatile, also had grown strongly from around $2 million in 1963. Profits peaked at $82.6 million, however, in fiscal year 1981. By the latter part of the 1980s, Perkin-Elmer determined that massive diversification no longer paid off. Again like so many other corporations, it entered a series of divestitures and restructurings.

Even as it proudly celebrated the 50th anniversary of Perkin-Elmer's start as a partnership, management bluntly told stockholders in the 1987 annual report that in this "watershed year ... we faced the realities of a significantly changed marketplace. We recognized that markets for high technology goods ... have become much more competitive." The message was accompanied by a $95 million restructuring charge, which left the company $18 million in the red for the July 1987 year, its first recorded loss.

This first stage of restructuring consisted mainly of dropping unprofitable product lines, consolidating plants, and streamlining sales and service operations, as well as scaling back their workforce by 6 percent. The company maintained its six basic business lines: analytical instruments, semiconductor equipment, optical systems, materials and surface technology, minicomputers, and the German manufacturing unit called Bodenseewerk Geraetetechnik (BGT), which specialized in missile and other avionic systems for the United States as well as the German government.

Fiscal 1988 brought the anticipated rebound, with profits of $72 million. By the end of the year an agreement had been reached to withdraw from the computer business. Back in 1985, Perkin-Elmer had put its computer business into a new subsidiary called Concurrent Computer Corporation and had sold an 18 percent stake to the public. The company arranged to sell its remaining 82 percent interest to Massachusetts Computer Corporation. The sale was completed early in fiscal 1989, with Perkin-Elmer realizing a moderate profit on the transaction.

As fiscal 1989 progressed, management decided on a far more drastic restructuring, dropping three more major business segments and leaving a company centered on just two basic fields: analytical instruments and material sciences. As a measure of the magnitude of these steps, the historically recalculated revenues from "continuing operations" for fiscal 1987 came to only $600 million or less than half the record $1.3 billion that all of the then-operating units had actually brought in. For fiscal 1989, both sales and profits from continuing operations showed healthy gains over the two preceding years, but an $82 million write-down of the businesses being dropped resulted in a net loss of $24 million.

Most of the actual divestitures took place between November 1989 and May 1990. BGT in Germany was sold to the Diehl Group. The Hughes Aircraft subsidiary of General Motors acquired most of the Government Systems (formerly called Optical Systems) operations, though some parts of this business were sold separately, in several instances to companies set up by former Perkin-Elmer subsidiary managers. Most of the semiconductor equipment operation was placed in a unit then acquired by Silicon Valley Group, while another portion went to a company formed by unit management. In three of the divestitures, Perkin-Elmer, at least temporarily, took a minority stake to facilitate the deal. While these dispositions had required a write-down of book value, the sales generated net cash inflow of nearly a quarter of a billion dollars. Perkin-Elmer used it to buy back some ten million common shares, more than 20 percent of the total outstanding.

CONTINUED REFOCUSING OF THE COMPANY THROUGH 1995

The more narrowly focused Perkin-Elmer boosted sales and turned a $44 million profit in fiscal 1990, but the next year, with problems aggravated by worldwide weak economies, the Persian Gulf war, and other international turmoil, events proved that the company was not yet in the clear. Gaynor N. Kelley, who had started at Perkin-Elmer in 1950, became president in 1985, and added

the titles of chairperson and CEO in October 1990, cited the "excellent potential" of the company's two remaining businesses, but told stockholders in the fiscal 1991 annual report that "our management team concluded that additional changes were necessary to achieve that potential." He added: "This was a sobering realization because our company had already experienced tremendous upheaval." Another $53 million was set aside for necessary restructuring, this time pushing fiscal 1991 results $15.6 million into the red.

Kelley had started on his task almost as soon as he was placed in full charge. In December 1990, he issued a call to action, noting that while the company was intent on "preserving the things we do that work well, and changing those things that do not," it needed to recognize that customers are increasingly "solution-oriented rather than technology-oriented." He solicited help from teams of employees from all sectors of the company to implement his goals and develop new products that customers would want.

Whereas the United States was Perkin-Elmer's single largest market, it accounted for less than 50 percent of total company business; most of the foreign volume came from Europe. Kelley began formulating steps to attract more Pacific business, but his basic principle was that the company's products generally have a worldwide rather than localized market. Consequently, he instituted a switch from operating by geographical units to organizing around the product on a worldwide basis. The entire global instrument business was divided into three major groups: life sciences, organic sciences, and inorganic sciences. At the same time, management of the materials sciences operation was overhauled. The July 1992 year saw recovery with revenues at a post-divestiture high of $911 million and profits of $59 million. In *Forbes*, Reed Abelson ventured that Perkin-Elmer "seems finally on the right track."

Perkin-Elmer's contraction of its business lines did not mean abandonment of an aggressive search for new opportunities within its chosen fields. A prime example was the company's growing interest in biotechnology instrumentation. In 1986 Perkin formed a joint venture with biotech specialist Cetus Corporation. Utilizing the polymerase chain reaction (PCR) technique developed by Cetus, the venture produced DNA instrumentation products that could amplify DNA from tiny samples. In December 1991 Cetus was acquired by Chiron Corporation after selling its PCR technology to major drug producer Hoffmann-La Roche. As a result the Perkin-Cetus venture was replaced by a long-term agreement with Hoffmann. In early 1993 Perkin acquired Applied Biosystems, an expert in DNA sequencing and synthesizing systems, which could become the base for Perkin-Elmer's total biosystems effort. It is in such ways that Perkin-Elmer counted on invigorating its business without straying from its instrument orientation.

CHANGE: 1995 AND BEYOND

During the mid-1990s, Perkin-Elmer failed to shore up profits due to slow growth and expensive restructuring charges. By 1995, shareholders were dissatisfied with Perkin-Elmer's direction and demanded the company take action to increase shareholder value. Kelley stepped down that year and was replaced by Tony L. White. Under his leadership, Perkin-Elmer's operations were divided into two major divisions: Analytical Instruments and Applied Biosystems.

Over the next several years, the company made several acquisitions to bolster its holdings. Tropix Inc., a drug candidate screener, was added to its arsenal in 1996. It also purchased GenScope and genetic analyst firm PerSeptive Biosystems. After this purchase, the company teamed with Celera Genomics to map the humane genome.

In 1999, the structure of Perkin-Elmer changed dramatically. PE Corporation was formed as a holding company to oversee the operations of Applied Biosystems and its newly created unit, Celera. PE Corporation eventually adopted the Applera corporate moniker.

Meanwhile, the Analytical Instruments division, including the Perkin-Elmer name, was sold to EG&G Inc. EG&G had been established in 1947 by MIT professor Harold E. Edgerton and several former students and had been involved in a wide variety of activities including nuclear weapons management for the government. The company had been faltering in recent years and brought in Gregory L. Summe in 1998 to turn around the business. Summe cut jobs, sold off businesses, and spearheaded the Perkin-Elmer deal in 1999. In July, EG&G adopted the PerkinElmer Inc. name. Shortly thereafter, it sold the EG&G Technical Services business to the Carlyle Group investment firm.

When the dust settled on the reorganization, Perkin-Elmer stood as a company focused on life sciences, fluid sciences, optical-electronics, and analytical instruments. By 2002, nearly 80 percent of what was the old EG&G had been sold. Two years later, the company integrated its life science and analytical instruments businesses. Together, the new unit accounted for 65 percent of revenues in 2003.

Over the next several years, the company disposed of noncore assets and strengthened its major divisions by making key purchases and strategic partnerships. Perkin-Elmer increased its stake in Bragg Photonics Inc., a high-speed fiber optics communications component manufacturer. It also formed a licensing agreement with Incyte Genomics Inc. to develop DNA research capabilities. Acquisitions over the next several years included drug discovery tool manufacturer NEN Life Sciences Inc., Packard BioScience Co., and Elcos AG.

In 2005, PerkinElmer set plans in motion to jettison its fluid sciences business unit. Once completed, the company would strictly cater to the healthcare and life sciences markets. Under Summe's leadership, Perkin-Elmer had transformed itself into a leader in those markets—and this transformation appeared to be paying off. In 2004, revenue increased by 10 percent over the previous year. With sales and profits on the rise, Perkin-Elmer appeared to be well positioned for growth in the years to come.

Henry Hecht
Updated, Christina M. Stansell

PRINCIPAL COMPETITORS

Agilent Technologies Inc.; Thermo Electron Corporation; Waters Corporation.

FURTHER READING

Abelson, Reed, "Getting Its Act Together," *Forbes,* August 31, 1992.

Ackerman, Jerry, "Renamed Wellesley, Mass.-Based PerkinElmer Inc. Turns Focus to Biotech Field," *Knight Ridder Tribune Business News,* August 6, 2000.

Kirchofer, Tom, "PerkinElmer Re-Emerging from Transformation," *Boston Herald,* April 8, 2002.

"The March of Science on Both Coasts," *Investor's Reader,* December 18, 1963.

"Perkin-Elmer Picks a Head," *Investor's Reader,* May 10, 1961.

"Perkin-Elmer—Prospects After a Year of New Management," *Instrument Business Outlook,* September 30, 1996.

"PerkinElmer: Refocused and on the Move," *Instrument Business Outlook,* June 15, 2004.

"PerkinElmer's Challenging Changes," *Instrument Business Outlook,* November 15, 2000.

Reisch, Marc S., "PerkinElmer Hones Life Science Plan," *Chemical & Engineering News,* December 5, 2005, p. 38.

"Richard Scott Perkin," *Investor's Reader,* April 25, 1962.

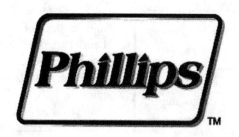

Phillips International, Inc.

1 Massachusetts Avenue N.W., Suite 610
Washington, D.C. 20001
U.S.A.
Telephone: (202) 842-2002
Fax: (202) 216-9188
Web site: http://www.phillips.com

Private Company
Incorporated: 1974 as Phillips Publishing Company
Sales: $245 million (2005 est.)
NAIC: 511210 Software Publishers; 516110 Internet Publishing and Broadcasting

■ ■ ■

Phillips International, Inc., provides investment information to subscribers through newsletters, fax and email services, and web sites. The company's Phillips Investment Resources division offers investment advice from a range of financial editors, who publish their own respective newsletters and provide their services through web sites or e-mail services to customers.

ORIGINS

In January 1974 Tom Phillips began Phillips Publishing in the converted garage of his home in Chevy Chase, Maryland, with three employees, two newsletters, and $1,000. Prior to his foray into the publishing business, Phillips had earned a B.A. in political science from Dartmouth College and an M.A. in journalism from The American University. He then gained experience in the publishing world after being employed at two large

national advertising agencies and a Washington, D.C., publishing firm. With this experience behind him, Phillips launched his business with a contrarian view in mind. Instead of focusing on mass media, he ran in the opposite direction, realizing that the public was being overwhelmed with information but starved for knowledge and advice. As a result, he founded the company as an independent newsletter business that could provide subscribers with actionable information or advice. His newsletter venture became an immediate success, earning nearly $300,000 in sales in the first year, beginning an unbroken record of sales increases for each succeeding year.

GROWTH, EXPANSION, AND REORGANIZATION: 1990–2000

In subsequent years, Phillips greatly expanded the newsletter business by focusing on fast growing markets where there was a need for insight and analysis. In July 1991, the company formed Phillips Publishing International, Inc., as a holding company. In the same year, the company acquired Hart Publications, Inc., a leading publisher in the global oil and gas industry. In 1992, the original Phillips Publishing was reorganized into two subsidiaries, including Phillips Publishing, Inc., which focused on improving subscribers' health and financial wealth, and Phillips Business Information, Inc., which provided market-focused analysis and advice for business-to-business customers. The following year, in September 1993, Phillips formed Eagle Publishing, Inc., as a separate subsidiary to publish public policy periodicals with a conservative, free enterprise focus and to oversee the Conservative Book Club. In December

1993, Eagle Publishing acquired Regnery Gateway, a publisher of conservative books. Regnery president Alfred Regnery agreed to the acquisition to spur the firm's growth. He saw synergistic opportunities in the deal, including having Phillips's newsletter and magazine writers and editors produce books for the book division, and promoting titles through Eagle's conservative weekly newspaper, Human Events. Phillips's resources were also seen to help reduce Regnery's dependence on the trade market for survival. As part of the acquisitions agreement, Al Regnery joined Phillips to continue to direct the book division, which was to be known as Regnery Publishing Inc.

In March 1996, Phillips Publishing announced a ten-year deal with Fabian Investment Resources of Huntington Beach, California, requiring Phillips to provide marketing and direct mail assistance and Fabian to contribute investment opinions and new products to the joint venture. Under the agreement, each would own an unspecified amount in Fabian Investment Resources. Phillips Publishing, which earned $186 million in 1995 sales, had become something of a star maker with more than 1 million subscribers through its investment, health, and business-to-business publications. Phillips's other investment titles included The *Independent Advisor* for Vanguard investors, Mark Skousen's *Forecasts & Strategies*, Richard Young's *Intelligence Report*, John Dessauer's *Investor's World*, and the celebrated *The Garzarelli Outlook*. In May 1996, a family dispute among descendants of the Gulf Publishing Company founder Ray Lofton Dudley led one faction of the family to buy out the other side's interest, fending off a hostile take over bid by Phillips Publishing International. Members of the Dudley side of the family agreed to sell their stake in the company to Gulf Publishing for an estimated $3.6 million. The move ended Phillips's attempt to augment its ten oil and gas periodicals with the rival 80-year-old company.

In 1997, Elaine Garzarelli, one of Wall Street's star market strategists, began feuding with Phillips Publishing, the publisher of her investment newsletter and a slew of mutual fund reports. Phillips said that the *Garzarelli Outlook* had lost about 30,000 subscribers from its peak of approximately 82,000 in late 1996, a claim that Garzarelli disputed. Garzarelli said her newsletter had only lost 15,000 subscribers and that Phillips shared blame for the decline by hyping her sell signal in its direct-mail advertisements. Nonetheless, whatever the precise number of lost subscribers, it was clear that Garzarelli's newsletter was bleeding customers primarily due to her ill-timed bet in 1996 that the market was nearing a correction. As press reports indicated that the future of *Garzarelli Outlook* was doomed, Phillips Publishing signed controversial stock picker and mutual fund manager Louis Navellier to write the Navellier Blue Chip Growth Letter under its company banner. Navallier had made news when the board of trustees of one of the mutual funds he managed accused him of providing incomplete information about the ownership of his investment company and tried unsuccessfully to oust him. The Garzarelli-Phillips feud, however, came at a difficult time for the newsletter business after the Security and Exchange Commission (SEC) began to take a closer look at the booming industry, especially the growth of mutual fund newsletters that were tailored to the small investor. According to a 1985 Supreme Court free speech ruling, the SEC could only indirectly regulate financial newsletters. But the Court's decision still permitted the agency to monitor the business. As result, the SEC had taken action against several newsletters for making misleading claims and failing to disclose conflicts of interest concerning newsletter writers who also had investment businesses. As a major player in the mutual fund newsletter business, Phillips also came under SEC scrutiny, but the company claimed that it held itself to the highest ethical standards.

At the end of 1997, Phillips Publishing International agreed to provide access to its 70 high profile business and financial news sources through InfoMation Publishing Corporation's web-based Echo service, which operated to monitor and deliver new and focused news and information to businesses. Echo innovative system worked by continually updating information and reducing the growing problem of information overload by delivering only crucial data. By utilizing this system, Phillips joined other Echo partners, such as the Financial Times Corporate Alert data feed, NewsAlert, Quote.com, and Telecommunications Reports International.

In March 1998, founder and president Tom Phillips made what he termed as an intensely personal decision by retaining Goldman Sachs & Co. to find a buyer for

KEY DATES

1974: Company is founded by Thomas L. Phillips.
1992: Company reorganizes into two separate subsidiaries—Phillips Publishing, Inc. and Phillips Business Information, Inc.—under the Phillips Publishing International, Inc., umbrella.
1993: Company launches Eagle Publishing, Inc.
1999: Company changes name to Phillips International, Inc.
2000: VS&A Communications Partners II LP acquires Phillips Business Information.
2004: Company sells Phillips Health division to two New York-based investment firms.

the firm, which had 1997 sales of $307 million, up from $261 million the previous year. Phillips said he planned to hold onto one of the company's four subsidiaries, Eagle Publishing, Inc., publisher of conservative public policy publications that he intended to run as a personally owned company. The other three subsidiaries included Phillips Publishing Inc., a leading provider of health and investment periodicals; Phillips Business Information, a producer of newsletters, magazines, conferences, seminars, CD ROMS, online services and directories for businesses; and Hart Publications, Inc, the leading publisher of energy related magazines, newsletters, directories, and information products to the global energy industry. In order for Phillips Publishing International to reach sales of $500 million and beyond and become a major Fortune 500 company, Phillips believed it needed to be bought out by a major corporation with the capital to take it to the next level. Nonetheless, after six months of exploring future directions for the company, he announced in September that the company would stay independent. At the time, Phillips Publishing International had offices across the United States and the United Kingdom with 1,200 employees and more than 100 magazines, newsletters, directories, and other products serving both the business and consumer markets. The company also ran a rapidly growing vitamin and nutritional supplement subsidiary. In making the decision, Tom Phillips said that remaining private would allow the firm to chart its own destiny by building a stronger, more profitable business, enabling it to go public in the future and gain access to capital markets. To position itself for an Initial Public Offering (IPO), in October 1998 the company combined its three business-to-business

subsidiaries—Phillips Business Information, Inc., Knowledge Industry Publications, Inc., and Hart Publications, Inc.—into an expanded market-focused Phillips Business Information, Inc. The move to combine the three subsidiaries formed a publishing powerhouse with more than $100 million in annual sales.

RESTRUCTURING: 2000 AND BEYOND

On July 1, 1999, after more than six months of planning, Eagle Publishing Inc. separated from Phillips to become an independent company with Jeffery J. Carneal remaining as president. Eagle founder, chairman, and majority owner Tom Phillips continued in his role as chairman of both Phillips Publishing International and Eagle. Since the firm's founding in 1993, Eagle had become a multi-faceted publisher of trade books, consumer book clubs, a conservative weekly newspaper, newsletters, and list management. The company's product lines included Regnery Publishing, Human Events, Evans-Novak Political Report, Conservative Book Club, Christian Book Club, and Movie and Entertainment Book Club. Both Carneal and Tom Phillips believed the separation was the best way for both firms to pursue their respective marketplaces. However, some observers noted that when the effort to sell Phillips Publishing International failed to win any suitors, the company decided to dump risky ventures and aggressive growth strategies to maximize profits for an initial public offering by 2001.

In August 1999, the firm continued its reorganization by changing its name to Phillips International Inc. Founder Tom Phillips said the name change reflected the company's 25-year evolution from strictly a print publisher to a major diversified corporation offering a wide variety of products and services to consumers and businesses. The company's major subsidiaries at the time included Phillips Publishing Inc., publisher of consumer newsletter and other products; Doctors Preferred Inc., a provider of vitamins and nutritional supplements; and Phillips Business Information Inc., which offered products and services to business-to-business customers. In October 1999, however, Phillips Publishing Inc., the consumer division, split into two parts, including Phillips Health and Phillips Investment Resources to enhance service to customers.

On March 30, 2000, after months of negotiations, Phillips signed a contract to sell its health information publishing and nutritional products business to Your Health Inc., a privately held company based in New York. Although the terms of the agreement were not disclosed, the deal provided that Your Health Inc. deposit $10 million into an escrow account within three days.

When the deposit was not made on time, Your Health agreed to make a non-refundable $2 million payment directly to Phillips and put $8 million into the escrow account the next day. Although Phillips received $1.5 million, the $8 million was never deposited. On April 13, company Chairman Tom Phillips terminated the agreement, citing breach of contract by Your Health Inc., and filed a federal lawsuit seeking $500,000 that was promised but never delivered by Your Health Inc. The Phillips' suit also sought judicial confirmation that the breech of contract severed all obligations to provide any of its proprietary intellectual property to Your Health Inc. After terminating the deal, Tom Phillips said that the Phillips Health Group was no longer up for sale and would continue to grow as part of Phillips International.

In October 2000, however, the company signed a definitive agreement to sell Phillips Business Information, Inc. to VS&A Communications Partners II LP, the private equity affiliate of New York-based media merchant bank Veronis Suhler. The subsidiary's major magazines and newsletters included Via Satellite, Communications Technology, Rotor & Wing, and Defense Daily. Moreover, Hart Publications, a division of Phillips Business Information and a specialist in publishing for the global energy industry, was sold to Chemical Week Associates, a portfolio company of VS&A Communications Partners II LP. After spinning off these assets in deal worth about $100 million, Phillips International planned to continue its consumer investment and health publishing businesses, which were anticipated to generate more than $250 million in revenue in 2000 and which had more than 1.5 million subscribers to its consumer newsletters and online services. In the same month that it sold its business-to-business media division, Phillips International bolstered its investment services by acquiring Louis Navellier's *MPT Review*, then rated by the *Hubert Financial Digest* as the number one investment advisory service.

In August 2004, Phillips International signed an agreement to sell most of the assets of its Phillips Health division to two New York-based private equity investment firms, ACI Capital Co. and American Securities Capital Partners LLC. The Phillips Health division with annual revenues of approximately $180 million provided health and wellness newsletters to subscribers from specialists in alternative medicine. Also included in the deal was the division's Doctors Preferred unit, a direct-marketer of branded nutritional supplements.

After selling off most of its divisions, Phillips International became primarily a publisher of investment information through newsletters, e-mail services, and web sites. Its one remaining division consisted of Phillips Investment Resources, which provided investment advice from a range of financial editors, who each issued their own newsletter, as well as web site or e-mail services to subscribers.

Bruce P. Montgomery

PRINCIPAL DIVISIONS

Phillips Investment Resources.

PRINCIPAL COMPETITORS

Bankrate Inc.; The Kiplinger Washington Editors, Inc.

FURTHER READING

Bruno, Michael P., "Phillips International to Join Strategy.com," *Newbytes*, February 1, 2000.

"De Marco, Donna, "Potomac, Md.-Based Publisher Sells Media Division to New York Merchant Bank," *Knight-Ridder/Tribune Business News*, October 5, 2000.

"Eagle Publishing, Inc. Becomes an Independent Company," *PR Newswire*, June 30, 1999.

Gasparino, Charles, "Fund Track: Garzarelli Feuds with Publisher Over Newsletter," *Wall Street Journal*, July 29, 1997.

"Phillips International, Inc. Terminates Contract to Sell its Health Group to Your Health Inc.," *PR Newswire*, April 17, 2000.

"Phillips Publishing International Inc. Retains Goldman, Sachs & Co. to Explore New Directions for Future Growth," *Business Wire*, March 10, 1998.

"Phillips Publishing International, Inc. Unifies Business-To-Business Units to Create $100 Million Market-Focused Publisher," *PR Newswire*, October 2, 1998.

"Phillips Publishing International, Inc. Will Remain Independent," *PR Newswire*, September 10, 1998.

Pybus, Kenneth R., "Gulf Publishing Takes Over," *Houston Business Journal*, May 10, 1996.

Swibel, Matthew, "Proceeds from Phillips Deal Could Channel Growth," *Washington Business Journal*, April 14, 2000.

Taylor, Cathy, "Cathy Taylor Column," *Orange County Register*, April 1, 1996.

"Your Health Inc. to Acquire Health Division of Phillips International, Inc.," *Business Wire*, April 4, 2000.

PKF

Accountants & business advisers

PKF International

——■——

Farringdon Place
20 Farringdon Road
London, EC1M 3AP
United Kingdom
Telephone: (44) 20 7065 0000
Fax: (44) 20 7065 0650
Web site: http://www.pkf.com

International Association
Incorporated: 1969
Employees: 13,500
Sales: $1.2 billion (2005)
NAIC: 541211 Offices of Certified Public Accountants; 541213 Tax Preparation; 541214 Payroll Services; 541219 Other Accounting Services; 541611 Administrative Management and General Management Consulting Services

■ ■ ■

PKF International is a worldwide network of accounting and professional advisors. The group promises local knowledge and personalized service backed by international resources and quality standards. PKF is made up of about 380 member firms operating in more than 100 countries. Together, its constituent firms, which are legally independent, make PKF International a global leader in business advisory services. Rather than compete with the Big Four for clients among the multinationals, PKF focuses on serving mid-size companies and has developed specialties in areas such as the hospitality, healthcare, and sports industries.

FORMING THE ASSOCIATION IN 1969

PKF International was formed in 1969 as an association of four member firms in the United Kingdom, Canada, the United States, and Australia. Worldwide fees were about $15 million. The group would be known as the Pannell Kerr Forster International Association until January 2000, when it adopted the name PKF International (it also had used the name Pannell Kerr Forster Worldwide).

Over the next three decades, PKF would grow from four member firms to more than 380 from countries all over the world. In 1987, PKF signed up Fiduciaire Expertise Conseils (FEC) as its representative in France. It was replaced seven years later, however, after failing to take the brand beyond Paris, its sole base of operations. An eight-member group trading as PKF France was formed in 1994 to replace FEC. The new group was led by Janny Marque & Associés.

PKF ranked as the world's tenth largest accounting business in 1991, with 272 offices and 8,000 employees. It was restructuring due to consolidation in the industry.

U.K. ORIGINS

The U.K. member of the original quartet was then known as Pannell, Fitzpatrick & Co., a name it adopted in 1967. It traced its origins back to August 1869, when accountant William Henry Pannell set up W.H. Pannell & Co. in London after a seven-year apprenticeship with Hart, Brothers & Co. Pannell took on his articled clerk, William Hardy, as a partner in 1885. One of the firm's

COMPANY PERSPECTIVES

Our member firms are independent, local, "home grown" organizations and proud of it. They choose to belong to PKF International, to be subject to the standards this requires, and to prove they are worthy of the standard. And they enjoy the relationships and opportunities that international association brings. However they are truly local, and understand the real meaning of doing business in their country. When you want to establish your business in their country, they are the ones who can make sure you get off on the right foot, in a fashion that will be welcomed. We operate in a global marketplace that when successful, recognizes diversity. Through your local PKF firm you can achieve the best of both—a true understanding of the unique local culture, matched with a global perspective and organization.

early clients, African Lakes Corporation Limited, would still be with the firm more than 100 years later.

In 1942, Pannell & Co. was combined with Crewdson, Youatt & Howard and Lewis, Hardy & Co. to form Pannell, Crewdson & Hardy. In 1948, the firm opened its first overseas office in Belize. It was merged yet again, with Fitzpatrick, Graham & Co., in 1963. Pannell Fitzpatrick & Co. took the name Pannell Kerr Forster in September 1980. This practice was followed at the same time by Harris Kerr Forster & Company in the United States. In 2000, the firms adopted the styling "PKF International."

Pannell Kerr Forster in the United Kingdom was quick to follow the top tier accounting firms in publishing annual financial reports in the mid-1990s. The firm announced plans to merge with Robson Rhodes in 1999 amid a trend for consolidation among Britain's mid-tier accounting firms. The Robson deal was called off, however, due to differences in the firms' approaches to international business, reported the *Financial Times*. While PKF members were all essentially mid-tier companies, Robson's RSM International network was seeking to compete with top-tier firms for multinational clients. PKF instead was focusing on niche markets such as healthcare.

The U.K. firm exceeded £100 million ($145 million) in fee income for the first time in 2001, noted the *International Accounting Bulletin*. It was ranked eighth in the country with about 30 offices, but still considered a mid-tier firm, a description that suited its representatives. Corporate finance was the fastest growing part of its business. Assurance and advisory work accounted for about 40 percent of the total, followed by consultancy. It was developing specialties in consulting for several industries, including hospitality, sports, professional services, healthcare, construction, e-commerce, and the public sector.

In 2005 the U.K. firm became PKF (UK) LLP, a limited liability partnership. This happened in spite of an increase in regulatory burdens for LLPs. PKF UK had 1,500 employees in 27 offices in 2005.

U.S. ORIGINS

The U.S. member of the original four to form the association was Harris, Kerr, Forster & Co. It dated back to 1911, when Scottish immigrant Errol Kerr set up Harris, Allan & Co. in New York City with his London-based partner, William Harris. The firm's original quarters were in Madison Avenue's famous Ritz-Carlton Hotel, which was just opening and was Kerr's first U.S. client. This was the beginning of the firm's longstanding specialty in hotels. Harris Allan eventually became Harris, Kerr & Cook, and merged with W.J. Forster & Co. to form Harris, Kerr, Forster & Co. in 1933. William J. Forster had started his namesake firm in New York in 1923.

Pannell Kerr Forster Consulting was spun off in a late 1991 restructuring. It would be based in San Francisco, while the audit, tax, and general business accounting operation remained based in New York City. PKF Consulting started off with 125 employees and offices in nine U.S. cities. Its CEO Patrick Quek told the *San Francisco Business Times* the consulting business had revenues of up to $15 million. There were other PKF consulting operations elsewhere in the world, mostly in Commonwealth countries. The U.S. consulting business was known for a hotel industry survey it had been publishing since 1936.

At the time of the consulting spinoff in 1991, several PKF accounting offices were closed, including the one in Denver, which had opened in 1962. It had been Denver's tenth largest accounting firm, with 35 employees. The U.S. accounting operations still had 11 offices and 400 employees, a spokesperson told the *Practical Accountant*. PKF also sold its healthcare-related business in New Jersey, New York, and Philadelphia to Ernst & Young.

A fast-growing U.S. member had been added, Houston's Pannell Kerr Forster of Texas, P.C. The increasing complexity of filing returns following the tax reform of the mid-1980s prompted a wave of consolida-

KEY DATES

1869: The W.H. Pannell accounting firm is established in London.

1911: The precursor to Harris, Kerr & Co. is formed in New York City.

1969: Accounting firms in the United Kingdom, Canada, United States, and Australia join to form the Pannell Kerr Forster International Association.

1980: The U.K. and U.S. firms are renamed "Pannell Kerr Forster."

1991: The U.S. operations are restructured; PKF Consulting is spun off.

2000: The association becomes known as PKF International.

2003: PKF International nearly doubles operations with the addition of Polaris North America.

tion, and PKF Texas added some smaller firms in the Dallas area.

The U.S. firm was enjoying several years of double-digit growth around the turn of the millennium and was quickly developing a client list among local technology companies in addition to its traditional hospitality business. An official told the *Practical Accountant* that it and other mid-tier firms had been helped by the exit of scandalized accounting giant Arthur Anderson from the Houston market, while reform measures such as Sarbanes-Oxley resulted in the remaining Big Four farming out more projects to smaller firms. PFK Texas had revenues of $9 million in 2002.

AUSTRALIAN AND CANADIAN ORIGINS

Australia was represented by Wilson, Bishop, Bowes & Craig among the original four members of the association. In the 1960s, PKF's Australian member, then G.T. Hartigan & Company, had developed a thriving audit business, notably for Mirror Newspapers, which later evolved into Rupert Murdoch's News Corporation. By 1987, the Australian Pannell Kerr Forster had gross fee income of AUD 25 million. It had become one of the first Western accounting firms to open offices in China, an official told *Business Review Weekly*.

PKF's Melbourne office merged with that of rival Nelson Wheeler in 1988, helping to push PKF's Australian revenues beyond AUD 50 million a year. It

then had more than 700 employees in the country, including about 80 partners.

In 2001 a proposed merger between the Australian member of PKF and Investor Group was canceled. PKF Australia Limited was nevertheless becoming a leading mid-tier accounting firm in its home market. It was beginning to be thought of as an alternative to Australia's "Big Four," according to the *Australian Financial Review*. PKF's Sydney office merged with that of the Rowlands firm in July 2003 as PKF Australia looked to add on smaller offices in the country, an official told *Business Review Weekly*.

Campbell, Sharp, Nash & Field was the original Canadian member of the association. In 1991, Pannell Kerr MacGillivray, then PKF Worldwide's representative in Canada, merged with Grant Thornton International's Doane Raymond to form Doane Raymond Pannell. Pannell Kerr MacGillivray's consulting arm was spun off at the same time. The newly merged firm, Canada's sixth largest accounting practice, retained its affiliation with Grant Thornton while becoming a "correspondent" of PKF Worldwide.

PKF INTERNATIONAL IN 2000 AND BEYOND

PKF International had revenues of $766 million in 1999. It had operations in about 100 countries. The group got a big boost when Polaris North America joined the organization in January 2003.

PKF International streamlined its structure and management in 2005. It was grouped into four regions, which each elected representatives for the International Board of Directors. The regions were divided into Africa; the Americas; Asia Pacific (including India); and Europe/Middle East (including North Africa). PKF then had more than 380 member firms operating in 119 countries. Annual revenues were about $1.2 billion.

Frederick C. Ingram

PRINCIPAL DIVISIONS

Africa; Americas; Asia Pacific; Europe/Middle East.

PRINCIPAL COMPETITORS

BDO International; Deloitte Touche Tohmatsu; Ernst & Young; Grant Thornton International; KPMG; PricewaterhouseCoopers.

FURTHER READING

"Accountancy Firms Join Hands," *Accountancy,* March 6, 1991, p. 12.

"Australia's Investor Group Scraps US$25 Mln Merger with PKF," *Asia Pulse,* June 25, 2001.

Boreham, Tim, "The Audit Choice: Big Firms Do Think Small," *Business Review Weekly,* February 16, 1990, p. 109.

"Businesses Leasing on Large Scale; Firms Take Offices in Midtown and Downtown Areas of Manhattan," *New York Times,* February 22, 1933, p. C38.

Dobbie, Mike, "Pannell Specialises in Getting On with It," *Business Review Weekly* (Australia), April 10, 1987, p. 127.

Dunstan, Barrie, "Merger Creates Accounting Giant," *Australian Financial Review,* January 18, 1988, p. 20.

"Ernst & Young Gets Pannell Kerr Health Unit," *Philadelphia Business Journal,* December 16, 1991, p. 4.

"Errol Kerr, Long in Accounting, 73," *New York Times,* April 19, 1951, p. 31.

Gillette, Bill, "PKF Aims to Expand Services, Number of Offices," *Hotel & Motel Management,* September 16, 1996, pp. 3f.

"Growth Despite Soft Economy," *Practical Accountant,* April 2003, pp. 34f.

Kelly, Jim, "Accounting Firms Urged to Reform; Growing Pressure to Use Single System for Reporting Financial Results," *Financial Times* (London), December 23, 1996, p. 6.

———, "Pannell Kerr and Robson Rhodes to Merge," *Financial Times,* March 9, 1999, p. 28.

———, "PKF and Robson Scrap Merger," *Financial Times* (London), April 26, 1999, p. 24.

Lynch, Damien, "PKF Claims Edge Over Mid-Tier Rivals," *Australian Financial Review,* February 4, 2005.

———, "PKF Ready to Help Blow the Whistle," *Australian Financial Review,* August 13, 2004, p. 58.

"Medium-Sized Firms—PKF Posts Improved Fee Income Figures," *Accountancy,* December 6, 1999, p. 7.

Meyerowitz, Stephen A., "Marketing the Professions," *New York Times,* November 24, 1985, p. F19.

"A New Beginning," *International Accounting Bulletin,* December 23, 1999, p. 6.

"Pannell Fitzpatrick & Co.; Harris Kerr Forster & Company," *The Times* (London), September 1, 1980, p. 24.

"Pannell Kerr Forster Replaces French Firm," *European Accountant,* December 1994, p. 4.

"PKF and Robsons' Merger Is Off," *Accountancy,* May 5, 1999, p. 5.

"PKF Enjoys Steady Growth," *International Accounting Bulletin,* November 30, 2000, p. 4.

"PKF's Fee Income Exceeds £100m," *International Accounting Bulletin,* November 15, 2001, p. 2.

Preston, Darrell, "Tannery Accounting Firm Succumbs to Merger Trend," *Dallas Business Journal,* November 6, 1989, pp. 1f.

Rauber, Chris, "Pannell Kerr's Split Opens Slot for Hotel Adviser," *San Francisco Business Times,* December 13, 1991, p. 12.

Smith, Gerd, "Pannell Kerr Closes Up Shop; Ex-Employees Open New Firm," *Denver Business Journal,* January 31, 1992, p. 4.

Stevens, Michael G., "Practice Innovators," *Practical Accountant,* September 2001, pp. 24ff.

Strauss, Marina, "Two Major Accounting Firms Merge; 11 Partners Eschew Mega-Deal, Get 'Back to Basics' and Form Regional Practice," *Globe and Mail* (Canada), January 22, 1991, p. B8.

Thomas, Tony, "Why PKF Joined Investor," *Charter* (Australia), May 31, 2001, pp. 28-32.

"UK Accountancy Firms That Are Thinking of Becoming Limited Liability Partnerships (LLPs) Could Be in for Some Expensive Surprises," *International Accounting Bulletin,* October 16, 2001, p. 9.

Walters, Kath, "Rowlands Joins PKF," *Business Review Weekly* (Australia), July 10, 2003, p. 72.

Pride International, Inc.

———■———

5847 San Felipe, Suite 3300
Houston, Texas 77057
U.S.A.
Telephone: (713) 789-1400
Fax: (713) 789-1430
Web site: http://www.prde.com

Public Company
Incorporated: 1966 as Pride Oilwell Service Company
Employees: 13,700
Sales: $1.71 billion (2004)
Stock Exchanges: New York
Ticker Symbol: PDE
NAIC: 213111 Drilling Oil and Gas Wells; 213112 Support Activities for Oil and Gas Operations

■ ■ ■

As one of the world's largest drilling contractors, Pride International, Inc., provides contract drilling, maintenance, workover, and engineering services to oil and gas companies worldwide, operating both offshore and on land in more than 50 countries and marine provinces. Pride also designs specialized drilling equipment and provides project management. Headquartered in Houston, Texas, the company has more than 13,000 employees representing 50 nationalities and has offices in Africa, Asia, Europe, and South America. Pride operates in the world's most active exploration and production areas, with a market presence in West Africa, South America, the Gulf of Mexico, the Mediterranean, Middle East and Southeast Asia. The company's global fleet of 288 rigs comprises a marine fleet of 61 rigs that include ultra-deepwater drill ships, deepwater semisubmersibles, jackup rigs, tender-assisted barges and platform rigs, which operate in West and South Africa, the Gulf of Mexico, the Mediterranean, the Middle East, India and Southeast Asia, and the North Sea. Pride also operates 227 land drilling and work-over rigs in South America, North Africa, the Middle East, Chad, and Kazakhstan. The company is organized under five operating segments: Eastern Hemisphere, which covers off shore and land drilling activities in Europe, Africa, the Middle East, Southeast Asia, Russia and the Commonwealth of Independent States; Western Hemisphere, which includes off shore drilling activities in Latin America; U.S. Gulf of Mexico, which comprises the U.S. offshore platform and jackup rig fleets; Latin America Land; and E&P Services.

BEGINNINGS

Pride International dates to 1966 when it was founded in Alice, Texas, as the Pride Oilwell Service Company with six workover rigs. In 1978, the company was acquired by Dekalb Corporation and operated as wholly-owned subsidiary until August 1988, when Pride Petroleum Services, Inc. (another subsidiary of Dekalb) became the surviving corporation of a merger on June 24, 1988, with Pride Oilwell Service Company. As a result of these events in 1988, Pride emerged as an independent public company trading on the NASDAQ and soon began a series of acquisitions to grow the business.

In 1989, Pride expended approximately $4 million in cash and/or Pride common stock to make several acquisitions, including the operations and facilities of El Campo, Texas, and Lovington, New Mexico, districts of Alliance Well Services, Inc. and the fixed assets of Mack Chase, Inc., including 17 well serving rigs. The company also acquired 12 well-servicing rigs from Eagle Creek Mining and Drilling of Tact, California, and took part in the new market of Horizontal Drilling by providing rigs to horizontally re-drill wells.

1990–2000: ACQUISITIONS AND EXPANSION OVERSEAS

In 1990, Pride's aggressive business expansion comprised the acquisitions of the fixed assets of Ranger Well Service, Inc. and East Texas Packer Sales and Service, Inc, including 12 rigs in East Texas. Nine oilfield companies, including 83 rigs, were also acquired, bringing Pride's total number of well-servicing rigs to 409 and its total of all U.S.-based well serving rigs to seven percent. Pride increased its operations in West Texas with the purchase of Snyder Well Servicing and C.R.C Source Services, as well as its South Texas and South Central Texas activities with the acquisition of Reading & Moore Well Service, OK Well Service, South Texas Swabbing, and two rigs from Pacer Atlas. In December 1990, the company also bought Valley Hyperclean, a California oilfield services firm that specialized in well bore cleaning and production enhancement.

In 1991, the company formed Pride International, Inc. as wholly owned subsidiary after executives from Kuwait Petroleum Company requested urgent assistance to help restore that country's oil fields following the Persian Gulf War. To begin the restoration work, Pride

deployed seven swabbing rigs and crews to Kuwait in the last week of April. In May, the company acquired ten well-servicing rigs as well as support equipment and an operating location in Liberty, Texas. It further ventured into the international arena when Quintana Trading Company, a subsidiary of Quintana Petroleum Company of Houston, Texas, selected Pride to work on their POVH field workover project in Tyumen Province in Russia. By the end of 1991, with the acquisition of 17 more well-servicing rigs in December, Pride's domestic fleet of rigs totaled 437 operating in 29 locations.

As a result of the Quintana deal, in 1992, Pride International shipped one rig to Russia as part of the joint U.S./Russian project in Western Siberia, later augmented in 1993 by two additional rigs and other heavy support equipment. The international subsidiary also leased two Pride rigs and support equipment to a Venezuelan firm, expanding its global reach into South America. Venturing further into South America, in 1993 Pride bought a controlling interest in an Argentine drilling and well-servicing company with a fleet of 23 rigs. The company also purchased a 100 percent interest in a Venezuelan drilling and well-servicing company with 12 well-servicing and three drilling rigs. Pride acquired the Bos~nos Aires firm from Western Atlas International, renaming it Pride Petrotech Sampic. The acquisition of Perforaciones Western CA (renamed Pride International C.A.), an established contractor in Venezuela, came with the option to purchase an affiliated Columbian firm.

In 1994, Pride International continued to expand operations in Argentina by acquiring a local competitor with four rigs and by sending 17 additional rigs to the country, increasing the Argentine rig fleet from 23 to 43 rigs. In addition, as Pride more than doubled in size, it also began marine operations in Venezuela, building two state-of-the-art drilling/workover barge rigs and contracting them to a subsidiary of the Venezuela national oil company. In March 1994, Pride acquired X-Pert Enterprises, Inc. of Hobbs, New Mexico, a provider of lease maintenance service with 35 rigs. Pride also expanded its existing fluids hauling business with the acquisition of an oilfield trucking fleet in East Texas. In June, 1994, Pride's acquisition of the largest fleet of platform workover rigs in the U.S. Gulf of Mexico gave it a fleet of 22 rigs comprising 45 percent of the regional market.

Pride's rapid pace of growth and acquisitions continued throughout the remainder of the 1990s. In March 1995, the company acquired a 35-rig competitor in New Mexico, and in October, Pride International purchased Marlin Columbia Drilling Company, Inc. from the Royal Dutch/Shell group of companies.

KEY DATES

1966: Company is formed in Alice, Texas, as Pride Oilwell Service Company.

1978: Dekalb Corporation acquires Pride, operating it as a subsidiary.

1988: Pride emerges as an independent public company trading on the NASDAQ.

1993: Pride acquires two well servicing and drilling operations in Argentina and Venezuela.

1996: Pride acquires Latin American companies Quitral-Co S.A.I.C. and Ingeser S.A.

1997: Pride Petroleum Services is renamed Pride International, Inc., and is listed on the New York Stock Exchange; company sells its U.S. land-based well-servicing operation.

1998: Pride completes acquisition of the Amethyst I, a semisubmersible drilling rig.

2003: Pride begins operations in Kazakhstan with the first of two land rigs and delivers and installs the first of the deepwater rigs off the shore of Angola.

Quitral-Co S.A.I.C., a major competitor in Latin America, was acquired in April 1996, adding 110 land rigs and making Pride the largest rig contractor south of the U.S. border. In October 1996, the company tripled the size of its operations with the acquisition of Ingeser S.A., becoming the largest contractor in Columbia with a fleet of 19 intermediate depth rigs. When Pride sold its U.S. land-based well-servicing operations in February 1997, it completed its transition from a being domestic land well services company to one of the world's largest onshore and offshore drilling contractors. Operating under the name, Pride International, Inc., in March 1997, the firm acquired Forasol-Foramer, a French based drilling company with marine and land-based operations worldwide. Pride added 13 mat-supported jackup rigs acquired from Noble Drilling Corporation in May 1997, expanded its mobile off-shore drilling units with the acquisition of Piranha, a tender-assisted rig, and the Pride Pennsylvania, a 300-foot water depth independent-leg cantilever jackup rig. In a joint ownership venture with Sonangol, the state-owned oil company of Angola, Pride began construction of the Pride Africa, one of two ultra-deepwater drill ships with the capability of working in water depths of up to 10,000 feet. The drilling ship was being built initially for drilling development wells in the huge Girrasol and Dalia fields off the coast

of Angola. After being listed on the New York Stock Exchange, Pride issued 2,865,000 shares of common stock at an initial price to the public of $35 per share.

During 1998, Pride acquired a 60 percent controlling interest in the assets of Bolivia's formerly state-owned oil company, including 13 drilling and workover rigs, oilfield trucks, and related drilling equipment. Pride also signed an agreement through its subsidiary, Foramer S.A., with Elf Exploration Angola, for the construction and operation of a second new ultra-deepwater drill ship to operate off the coast of Angola. In October 1998, Pride completed the $85 million purchase of the M.S.V. *Amethyst* (renamed *Pride South America*), a self-propelled semisubmersible drilling rig that could work in water depths of up to 4,000 feet. The rig was equipped to provide offshore drilling, deep well intervention, and maintenance and pipeline construction services. With the aim of further developing its deepwater fleet, Pride began participating in joint ventures to build, own, and operate six enhanced Amethyst-class semisubmersible rigs, which were to operate off the coast of Brazil under charter and service contracts with Petrobus Brasilia S.A.

In March 1999, Ray H. Tolson retired from his position as chairman of the board and chief executive officer, a post he held since 1975. Paul A. Bragg, Pride's president and chief operating officer since 1997, succeeded Tolson as CEO. He was additionally elected to fill the vacancy on the board of directors left by Tolson's retirement. In April 2000, Pride formed its Exploration and Production Services division after the acquisition of Servicios Especiales San Antonio S.A. from Perez Companc S.A. for $78 million and the assumption of $17 in debt. It also signed a contract to provide drilling and related services for exploration and development in the central African country of Chad. To pursue the project, the company ordered three new mobile drilling rigs and two high-performance workover rigs for work in Central Africa.

In January 2001, Pride was able to resolve long-standing difficulties concerning its deepwater rig contracts with the Brazilian state oil company. As a minority owner in the Amethyst project to deliver four rigs to Petrobras, Pride experienced three years of difficulties due to repeated delays and other problems, threatening the viability of the business deal. After months of talks between Pride and Petrobras, the Houston based company crafted a two-part deal. First, Pride agreed to a new five-year charter and service contracts enabling Petrobras to operate two of the four rigs. Second, Pride offered to acquire complete ownership of the two rigs, formerly known as the *Amethyst 6* and the *Amethyst 7*.

2000 AND BEYOND: CONTINUED EXPANSION AND RESTRUCTURING

In May 2001, in a merger agreement that surprised Wall Street, Pride International, Inc. ended up being the buyer instead of the seller, purchasing rival Marine Drilling Companies in a $2 billion deal. The total value of the merger estimated at $6.2 billion fell to $4.2 billion within 24 hours after Pride's stock price collapsed 15.7 percent. The steep decline in share price came as the market soured on news that Pride would not be bought out by a larger firm. The combined company kept the Pride International, Inc., name and continued to trade on the New York Stock Exchange. The merger formed one of the world's largest offshore drilling operators with an offshore fleet of 77 rigs, including 2 drill ships, 11 semisubmersibles rigs, 35 jackup rigs, and 29 tender-assist barge and platform rigs. With this large global fleet, Pride was in a better position to compete for global projects. The merger further allowed the company to dedicate more cash flow to reduce its debts. In 2001, Pride also expanded its deepwater fleet with the completion of two deepwater semisubmersibles, the *Pride Carlos Walter* and the *Pride Brazil,* as well as obtained projects to construct and operate four deepwater platform drilling rigs, including the *Kizomba* (Angola), *Holstein* (Gulf of Mexico), *Thunderhorse* (Gulf of Mexico), and *Mad Dog* (Gulf of Mexico). Despite the rapid expansion of its global fleet of rigs, Pride International reported a loss for 2002 of $8.2 million, down from 2001 earnings of $127.2 million. The company attributed the earnings decline to weak conditions in the U.S. Gulf of Mexico jackup market, as well as to declining results for its international land exploration and production services operations due to decreased activity in Argentina and Venezuela.

In May 2003, Pride was awarded six new contracts by a unit of Mexican state oil company, Pemex, increasing its contract backlog by $220 million. In November, the *Kizomba* began operations for Esso Exploration Angola, a subsidiary of ExxonMobil Corporation, under a contract that was due to expire in 2008. Pride also began operations of two large land rigs in Kazakhstan on an artificial island in the northeast Caspian Sea. During the fourth quarter of 2003, Pride signed a ten-year contract extension for the drill ships, *Pride Angola* and *Pride Africa,* which would keep the rigs in continuous operation through 2010 at estimated earnings of $610 million. In 2005, the company announced plans to sell its 227 land rigs, or 25 percent of its total fleet, to become an all-marine rig supplier because of their lower rate of return than the offshore assets. The immediate priority of the company, which had a market capitalization of $3.3 billion, was to reduce its debt to a capital ratio to 30 percent from 38 percent. In June 2005, Pride International announced a change of leadership to carry out the company's new direction with the board of directors electing Louis A. Raspino to serve as the new president and chief executive officer, replacing Paul A. Bragg. Raspino had been serving as executive vice-president and chief financial officer since joining Pride in 2003. With global demand for oil and gas supplies skyrocketing with the rapid economic expansions of India and China, Pride International appeared to be well positioned to earn markedly better profits than it did in the 1990s.

Bruce P. Montgomery

PRINCIPAL SUBSIDIARIES

Amethyst Financial Company, Ltd. (British Virgin Islands); Andre-Maritime Ltd. (Bahamas); Basafojagu (HS) Inc. (Liberia); Bigem Holdings N.V. (Netherlands Antilles); Caland Boren B.V. (Netherlands); Criwey Corporation (Argentina); Davana Finance S.A. (Panama); Dundee Corporation (Liberia); Forafels Inc. (Panama); Foral S.A. (France); Gisor UK Ltd.; Martin Columbia Drilling (British Virgin Islands); Petrodrill Corporation Ltd. (Bahamas); Pride Offshore, Inc.

PRINCIPAL COMPETITORS

Nabors Industries Ltd.; Saipem S.p.A.; Transocean Inc.

FURTHER READING

Akani, Fred, "Pride Building Drillship for Angolan Prospects," *Offshore,* November 1997.

"Drilling Co. Looking to Sell Assets," *Corporate Financing Week,* May 30, 2005.

Eisen, Peter, "Pride International's Venture with YPFB Signals Effort to Diversify in Latin America," *Oil Daily,* May 26, 1998.

"Merging Contractors Pursuing Drilling Rig Contracts on a Package Basis," *Offshore,* September 2001.

"Pride Announces Acquisition of Dynamically Positioned Semisubmersible Rig," *PR Newswire,* April 7, 1998.

"Pride Finalizes Joint Venture with Sonangol for Dynamically Positioned Drill Ship," *PR Newswire,* January 26, 1998.

"Pride International to Sell 4 Rigs for $25.5 Million," *America's Intelligence Wire,* June 27, 2005.

"Pride-Marine Drilling Combination Would Create a Solid Jackup Competitor," *Petroleum Finance Week,* May 28, 2001.

"Pride, Marine Drilling Merge in $2 Billion Deal," *Oil Daily,* May 25, 2001.

"Pride South Pacific Commences Work in West Africa," *PR Newswire*, December 5, 2002.

"Pride Wins Praise for Resolving Rig Disputes with Petrobras," *Oil Daily*, January 30, 2001.

"Russian Group Touring U.S. Oil Operations," *Oil and Gas Journal*, December 16, 1991.

Spencer, Starr, "Pride Envisions Selling Land Fleet, Focusing on Offshore," *Platt's Oilgram News*, March 7, 2005.

San Diego Padres Baseball Club L.P.

9449 Friars Road
San Diego, California 92108
U.S.A.
Telephone: (619) 881-6500
Fax: (619) 497-5339
Web site: http://www.padres.com

Private Company
Incorporated: 1968
Sales: $106 million (2005 est.)
NAIC: 711211 Sports Teams and Clubs

■ ■ ■

The San Diego Padres Baseball Club L.P., headed by software millionaire John Moores, owns the San Diego Padres of the National League of Major League Baseball. Since its start as an expansion team, no major league team has had a worse winning percentage. A perennial last place club, the Padres have won just two National League championships and never achieved a World Championship during its history. The team has also been a consistent money loser, due in some part to the unique geography of its market. With desert to the east, the Pacific Ocean to the west, Los Angeles to the north with its highly popular Dodgers and American League Angels, the Padres have been forced to look to the south to Mexico to win new fans and generate the revenues necessary to make it competitive—and one day, perhaps, profitable. A positive development for the club was the 2004 opening of a $450 million state-of-the art baseball park, Petco Park. The project was fraught with delays and in order to get the facility built, the Padres agreed to become participants in real estate development projects surrounding Petco.

EARLY 20TH-CENTURY ORIGINS

The first professional San Diego baseball team to don the Padres name was the Pacific Coast League franchise that moved to the city from Los Angeles, where it had played as the Hollywood Stars. A last place team in 1935, the Stars suffered from poor attendance, and their financial condition worsened when their landlord at Wrigley Field, another PCL team, the Los Angeles Angels, decided to double the rent. Instead the Stars owner took his club south, signing a deal with the City of San Diego in January 1936. The team went from being Stars to Padres but remained also-rans. About the only thing noteworthy about the Padres in its early years was the presence of a 17-year-old player named Ted Williams, who in December 1937 was sold to the Boston Red Sox and begin a hall-of-fame career.

San Diego, at the time, was far removed from Major League Baseball. The PCL had roots older than the American League, and on the West Coast around the turn of the century it was considered to be of major league caliber. That would all change when the established National League and upstart American League settled a war between themselves by signing the "National Agreement" and formed Major League Baseball. In effect, they declared every league but their own to be the minors, the players of which they were free to "draft" — or steal, from the perspective of leagues like the PCL. Eventually everyone was bullied into sign-

KEY DATES

1936: Pacific Coast League's San Diego Padres begin play.
1955: C. Arnholt Smith buys Padres.
1968: Smith wins National League expansion franchise for San Diego.
1969: San Diego Padres begin play in National League.
1973: Ray Kroc acquires Padres.
1983: Kroc dies and ownership passes to wife.
1990: Tom Werner-led group acquires team.
1995: John Moores buys Padres.
2004: Petco Park opens.

ing on, but as a result the western part of the United States was denied major league baseball because. Until the 1950s there were no major league teams west of St. Louis, but that changed when the Boston Braves moved to Milwaukee in 1953 and enjoyed a tremendous surge in attendance. With the advent of reliable air travel, the travel restrictions that had prevented coast-to-coast major league baseball evaporated and club began to look to fast-growing West Coast cities to relocated their franchises. In the most significant moves, the Brooklyn Dodgers claimed Los Angeles and the New York Giants moved to San Francisco.

NEW OWNERSHIP IN 1955

While Major League baseball was moving west, the San Diego Padres were changing ownership. In 1955 the club was sold to Jim Lane, president of Westgate-California Tuna Packing, but he was really just a front for a wheeler-dealer named C. Arnholt Smith, the man who would one day bring Major League baseball to San Diego. Smith's life was a rags to riches to prison story. Born in Walla Walla, Washington, in 1899, Smith moved to San Diego as a child, where he dropped out of high school to work in a grocery store and later became a bank messenger. In 1933 he managed to scrape enough money together to acquire a controlling interest in the United States National Bank, and around it he would build a financial empire that would include Westgate, a conglomerate that at its height controlled 60 companies worth $2 billion, including a shipyard, real estate developments and Yellow Cab franchises. His wealth also brought him into the sphere of politicians, in particular Richard Nixon. In 1946 he supported Nixon's election to Congress, and 22 years later was a major fundraiser of Nixon in his bid for the presidency and so

close a confidant that he watched the 1968 election results on television with Nixon in his New York suite.

When Smith wasn't hobnobbing with politicians, building his business empire, or promoting his beloved San Diego, he was trying to become a Major League baseball owner. In 1960 the National League and American League agreed to expand, each adding two teams. Smith tried to land the franchise slated for Los Angeles, which would become the Angels, but lost out to Cowboy crooner Gene Autry. Several years later, however, baseball was ready to expand further. With the help of former Dodger general manager Buzzie Bavasi, he succeeded in winning one of the four expansion teams slated to begin play in 1969. Part of San Diego's appeal was that it already had a large stadium. Local sports editor Jack Murphy had led the campaign for a new stadium to house the San Diego Chargers American League football team. The 50,000-seat facility opened in 1967 as San Diego Stadium and was available for the Padres when they began play in 1969. After Murphy died in 1980, the stadium would become known as Jack Murphy Stadium. In 1997 Qualcomm would buy the naming rights.

The Padres were not as popular with local baseball fans as Smith and Bavasi had hoped, however. Perhaps some of that disinterest was caused by the team's brown and tan uniforms, which Smith insisted were colors he liked and not an attempt to emulate the look of a real padre. Years later when Steve Garvey signed as a free agent and first tried on the uniform, he commented, "I look like a taco." A more likely reason for poor attendance was the club's dismal play. The established major league teams were only willing to part with older players and marginal talent in stocking the expansion teams, and so it was no surprise that the Padres and the other new National League team, the Montreal Expos, finished with 52 wins and 110 losses in 1969. Whatever the reasons, Padres' attendance was little more than 500,000, the worst in both leagues and a far cry from the million mark the club needed to reach to break even.

During each of the first five years of its existence, the San Diego Padres won the fewest games in the National League and drew the fewest fans in all the majors. The team's futility, however, would soon be overshadowed by the cloud of scandal that enveloped the team's owner. Once named Mr. San Diego by a grateful community, C. Arnholt Smith saw his financial empire crumble in 1973. In reality it was a house of cards, with Westgate-California propped up by United States National Bank. Smith's shady dealings came to light when the bank, saddled with an outstanding debt of $400 million, failed in 1973. At the time, it was the largest bank failure in the history of the United States. Smith soon faced charges of grand theft, fraud, and income tax evasion. He was eventually convicted of income tax fraud, grand theft, and embezzlement, and sentenced in 1979. After five years of legal maneuvering he managed to have his sentence reduced to one year because he was not expected to live much longer. And so at the age of 85 he was sent to a Federal honor farm where he served about seven months, spending the time mostly tending roses. Once again Smith's accounting proved elusive: He did not die until June 1996 at the age of 97.

As Smith's difficulties were unfolding in 1973 he attempted to cut his losses with the Padres by selling the team for $12 million to a buyer who planned to move the franchise to Washington, D.C. Although the city of San Diego threatened to sue, the deal appeared so certain to go through that in December 1973 team files and equipment were packed, new Washington uniforms were made, and even baseball cards of Padre players in their new Washington Stars' uniform were printed. At the eleventh hour Ray Kroc, the man behind the McDonald's fast food chain, stepped in to buy the club and keep it in San Diego.

Kroc inherited an inept baseball team, but he was not a man to blithely accept failure. At his first home game as owner, Kroc, frustrated by the Padres poor play, seized the public address microphone and exclaimed "I've never seen such stupid ball playing in my life." The players were angered by the outburst, Major League baseball insisted that Kroc apologize, but the fans loved the candor of the new owner, who was committed to give them a better entertainment product. That product did not, however, include more wins, as the team again finished last in its division, but it did feature novelty. The day of Kroc's outburst was also the debut of a new mascot, the KGB Chicken, later known as the San Diego chicken, and eventually just The Chicken. He was highly entertaining and the forefather to scores of mascots that cropped up in professional sports over the years to come. In 1974, for the first time, the San Diego Padres drew more than one million in attendance.

Under Kroc's ownership, the Padres added better players and finally rose above last place, and in 1978 posted its first winning record. However, the team returned to the bottom of the standings in 1980 and 1981 before once again gaining respectability. The Padres were on the verge of success when Kroc died in January 1984. His wife Joan became owner of the Padres. Later that year, the team won the National League West and defeated the Chicago Cubs for the National League pennant before losing to the Detroit Tigers in the World Series. Nearly two million fans came to Jack Murphy

Stadium to watch the Padres that year, and another 2.2 million came out the following season, but the Padres were once again descending into mediocrity. In 1987 they returned to last place.

In the late 1980s the Padres improved, finishing second in the National League West in 1989, and Joan Kroc decided now was the time to sell the team. There was no shortage of suitors, including Sid and Jenny Craig, owner of Jenny Craig Weight Loss Centers; an investment group head by former player Steve Garvey; and Los Angeles Lakers owner Jerry Buss. The successful bidder in April 1990 was a group of 15 investors headed by Tom Werner, a television producer of such popular television situation comedies as *The Crosby Show* and *Roseanne*.

New ownership took over at a difficult time for baseball. Player salaries were escalating rapidly, and it was becoming increasingly difficult for small- and medium-sized market teams like the Padres to compete against the likes of the New York Yankees, New York Mets, and Los Angeles Dodgers, which received far more money in their radio and television contracts. San Diego tried to generate extra revenue by selling 50 home games on Cox Cable as a pay-per-view, but the team was limited in its choices given its location, surrounded by desert, water, and Dodger fans. The team began looking to Mexico for a much-needed source of revenues, but fans of the team south of border found it difficult to take in a game. Tickets were too expensive for the market, there were delays at the border, and group transportation was not available. The Padres would not make significant inroads into the Hispanic market until a new ownership team took charge.

1994 BRINGS ANOTHER OWNERSHIP CHANGE

The Werner group did not have the deep pockets necessary to subsidize the perennial money-losing Padres. In the summer of 1993 the club conducted what many called a fire sale, unloading all of its stars, with the exception of hometown hero Tony Gwynn. When it was over the Padres had slashed its payroll to $10.3 million, the lowest in the majors. The Padres also finished once again in last place, 43 games behind first place Atlanta. In December 1994 a group headed by Larry Lucchino and John Moores, the former supplying the baseball savvy and the latter the cash. bought the Padres. Moores was worth an estimated $400 million, a fortune he derived from BMC Software, which he founded in Houston in 1980. He would need that largesse to keep the Padres in business. In his first year as owner, the team lost $17 million, but a large portion of that money was the result of free agent spending, which at least gave the Padre's longsuffering fans some hope. They were soon given something even more tangible when in 1996 the team surprised everyone by eclipsing the Dodgers on the last day of the season to win the National League West title. They were soon dispatched by the St. Louis Cardinals in the playoffs, however.

In tandem with improvement on the field, the Padres made strides at the gate, especially with Hispanic fans. The team hired a director of Hispanic Marketing and began addressing the problems Mexicans faced in attending Padres' games. In conjunction with Mexican Beer company Tecate, the Padres created the "Domingos Padres Con Tecata" program, which provided Mexican fans with a ticket and bus transportation to Sunday home games at a cost that was less than the regular price of a ticket. Moreover, the buses passed through the border at a special bus lane, eliminating the delays that had previously troubled fans. As a result of this program and better play on the field, the Padres saw their attendance double from 1.1 million in 1995 to 2.2 million in 1996.

But even two million in attendance was not sufficient to prevent the Padres from continuing to lose money. What the team needed in order to survive in San Diego were the revenue streams that came with a new ballpark. Moores publicly expressed that view in 1996 and a year later Mayor Susan Golding's task force charged with looking into the matter agreed with him. The city and the ball club now began to work together to develop a new baseball-only ballpark in downtown. In 1998 San Diego voters approved the creation of a 26-block redevelopment area to build a $400 million ballpark. It certainly didn't hurt that the Padres enjoyed their finest season, winning 98 regular season games, then beating the Houston Astros and Atlanta Braves before falling to the New York Yankees in the World Series. Nevertheless, the club still lost around $7 million, providing a further rationale for a new ballpark.

Construction on the new facility was begun in 1999 but soon halted because the city had not completed an environmental study. It would be just one of a number of delays caused by lawsuits. In order to see the project to completion the Padres, along the way, would have to invest more money in the redevelopment of the area, but finally in 2004 the Padres new home, called Petco

Park (the result of a $60 million naming fee paid by the San Diego-based Petco pet supply company) opened. In addition the Padres and Cox Cable joined forces to launch a new digital cable channel devoted exclusively to the Padres.

In its inaugural season at Petco, the Padres sold 20,000 season tickets, far better than the previous high of 12,800 in 1983. It was also continuing to succeed at courting Hispanic fans. Moreover, the Padres were fielding a playoff-caliber team. For the first time in its history, it appeared the team had a chance to become a profitable franchise.

Ed Dinger

PRINCIPAL COMPETITORS

Angels Baseball LP; Los Angeles Dodgers Inc.; San Francisco Baseball Associates LP.

FURTHER READING
Donoho, Ron, "Can A Nice Guy Finish First?," *Sales & Marketing Management,* November 1996, p. 20.

Poucher, Julie, "Padres Look South to Help Market Team," *San Diego Business Journal,* March 29, 2004, p. 14.

Hobbs, Bill, "Baseball Proving Popular with Mexican Population," *Amusement Business,* July 21, 1997, p. 37.

Hock, Sandy, "Oh, Doctor — Padres Need New Revenue as Player Salaries Climb," *San Diego Business Journal,* March 18, 1991, p. 1.

"New Ballpark, New Padres?," *Business Week Online,* March 31, 2004.

Noble, Holcomb B., "C. Arnholt Smith, 97, Banker and Padres Chief Before a Fall," *New York Times,* June 11, 1996, p. B12.

Swank, Bill, *Baseball in San Diego: From the Padres to Petco.* Charleston, S.C.: Arcadia, 2004, 128 p.

Thorn, John et al, *Total Baseball,* Kingston, NY: Total Sports, 1999, 2,538 p.

Van Housen, Caty, "The Profits Keep On Fadin' As Padres Keep On Tradin'," *San Diego Business Journal,* July 5, 1993, p. 1.

Ward, Denise T., "Cox Inks 10-Year Padres Deal," *San Diego Business Journal,* April 9, 2001, p. 1.

SAS Institute Inc.

SAS Campus Drive
Cary, North Carolina 27513
U.S.A.
Telephone: (919) 677-8000
Toll Free: (800) 727-0025
Fax: (919) 677-4444
Web site: http://www.sas.com

Private Company
Incorporated: 1976 as SAS Institute, Inc.
Employees: 9,528
Sales: $1.53 billion (2004)
NAIC: 511210 Software Publishers

■ ■ ■

Privately held SAS Institute Inc. (the name is pronounced like "sass") is one of the largest independent software companies in the world. (It is not related to the Scandinavian airline SAS.) The company leases, rather than sells, its statistical analysis software, which is installed in more than 40,000 businesses, universities, and government agencies worldwide. The Institute's flagship product is an integrated system for enterprise-wise information delivery providing organizations with tools to access, manage, analyze, and present their data within an applications development environment. SAS has worked to make it easier for non-technical professionals to use. Headquartered in Cary, North Carolina, near the Research Triangle Park, about half of the company's employees are based overseas. By remaining privately held through the tech bubble and bust, SAS was able to retain its unique, college-like culture, while maintaining research and development spending.

COLLEGIATE ORIGINS

SAS Institute was founded and incorporated in 1976 by North Carolina State University professor, Dr. James Goodnight and John Sall. The two academics had developed a statistical analysis software package for their own research use that had become popular with faculty at N.C. State and a number of other universities throughout the South. "Eventually, our fledgling operation grew too big to run out of our offices at State, and they invited us to leave," Goodnight told *Business Leader* magazine, adding "So, we moved across Hillsborough Street, and that's how it all started."

Over the next 18 years, Goodnight's and Sall's single software package, dubbed "Statistical Analysis System," grew into a modular information delivery system used by 98 percent of the Fortune 100 companies. In 1994, the company could boast over three million users in 120 countries, 12 U.S. regional offices, subsidiaries in 29 nations, and distributors in 20 others, and over 3,000 employees worldwide. In 1993, the company recorded sales revenues of $420.3 million, which marked a 15 percent increase over the year before. The figure also established the company's 17th consecutive year of double-digit growth in revenue.

These figures represent financial success that any company would envy. Most members of the SAS "family" attributed the Institute's success to a single philosophy: listen carefully to your customers and give them exactly what they want. "Here at SAS, we do software development by users for users," Vice-President of North American Sales and Marketing Barrett R. Joyner told *Business Leader*. He explained, "While we certainly need to be profitable in order to stay in business, our primary focus isn't making money; it's solving problems. We want to provide our users—business people, researchers, scientists—with advanced technology that will enable them to access, manage, analyze, and present their data effectively so that they can make sound business decisions."

This approach was obvious in the company's flagship software product, the SAS System for Information Delivery, which could be used in almost every computing environment, from the laptop computer to the data center. The system was an integrated suite of software products that provided users with a wide range of capabilities that they could set up in whatever combination they required. At the heart of the SAS System was a single software package called "Base SAS," which provided data management, analysis, and report writing. The rest of the system comprised more than 20 modular software packages that linked with the base software. These packages enabled users to add specialized functions, such as spreadsheets, graphics, quality improvement, project management, cooperative processing, applications development, and more, depending on the needs of their company.

Another component behind SAS's financial success was its commitment to research and development investments. In 1993, SAS Institute heralded its eighth consecutive year of leading the software industry in the percentage of revenue devoted to research and development. That year, the company reinvested a record-setting $143 million, or 34 percent of revenue, to improving its array of products. On average, the top 100 revenue-generating software companies reinvested

less than 20 percent of revenue in research and development (R&D). SAS Institute's management team said that its commitment ensured that the company would continually provide its customers with software that exploits the latest technology. To support its massive R&D effort, the Institute built a five-story research and development building, with a virtual data center in each of its 1,100 offices.

SAS Institute's researchers had some unconventional methods for problem-solving. With roots based in Goodnight's and Sall's former campus offices, most of the researchers at the Institute took a "technological garage" approach to their work. Their style was similar to two entrepreneurs in their garage who start out with a crazy idea and end up with a product that earns millions of dollars. The Institute's management team encouraged its developers to follow up on all promising ideas, even if they seemed to have no immediate practical applications. The company conducted usability studies to determine the value of each piece of research. Many such projects—which may have never been initiated in other companies—ended up becoming real money-earners. The Institute's leadership firmly believed that this type of strategy encouraged developers to start projects even though they may not lead to end products and fostered the creativity and freedom that could lead to tremendous product innovation.

SAS Institute's marketing group also had its own distinct business philosophy. Rarely did the group resort to such marketing standbys as market penetration studies or competitive analysis. Instead, the company's marketing team preferred to rely on the SAS customers themselves via users groups. Since SAS Institute's inception, the direction of its research and development was largely driven by Institute customers, who were encouraged to express their opinions about the company's software products and services through formal and informal channels. To keep up with changing demands, SAS sponsored a network of more than 200 local, regional, national, international, in-house, and special-interest users groups. In 1993, the Institute experimented with the most extensive usability test ever performed on software. Preparing for major enhancements to the menu-driven interface to the SAS System—SAS/ASSIST software—marketing, training, and software development staff teamed up to conduct a three-phased study. They invited computer users of various experience levels to put the new version of SAS/ASSIST software through its paces and provide feedback. The company's annual SASware Ballot, a survey distributed to all SAS users, also provided a way for users to provide feedback to the Institute's management and influence development efforts, from general issues to specific enhancements.

KEY DATES

1976: SAS Institute is founded by academics associated with North Carolina State University.
1978: SAS has 600 customers.
1980: European headquarters are established.
1982: Subsidiary is launched in Australia.
1983: On-site health care center established at the Cary, N.C., complex.
1985: Subsidiaries are launched in Japan and Hong Kong.
1994: SAS has more than three million users and 3,000 employees worldwide; revenues exceed $400 million.
1997: A subsidiary is established in India.
1999: Sales exceed $1 billion.
2000: Fortune ranks company as America's second best place to work.

In addition, SAS Institute held frequent users group conferences to provide a forum for Institute developers to meet directly with SAS System users. This free-flowing exchange of ideas led to software enhancements and new services that addressed the real computing issues that organizations faced. For example, in 1992, SAS introduced a series of Information Delivery Strategy conferences for information systems executives. These conferences gave the participants the chance to see the software operating in simulated vertical market settings and to voice their opinions to members of the Institute's marketing and development staffs.

As Joyner told *Business Leader:* "We're not a marketing-driven company. Throughout the 1980s, when a lot of other software companies were mesmerized by market share, we focused on talking face-to-face with users and meeting their needs. The competition saw us as a bunch of naive yokels who just fell off the turnip truck. In the last couple of years, though, many of our competitors have realized the value of being customer-driven." The ultimate measurement of the company's responsiveness was that the overwhelming majority of SAS software sites were renewing their annual software licenses year after year. According to the company's 1993 annual report, 95 percent of Fortune 500 companies that licensed SAS software that year elected to renew their licenses.

SAS Institute also made a concerted effort to develop close relationships with other firms in the field. The company believed that this strategy helped them to bring cutting-edge products to market rapidly. SAS Institute, for example, was one of the early participants in Microsoft Windows NT development and one of the first vendors to work with Digital Equipment Corporation on their ALPHA AXP project for RISC-based processors. In 1991, SAS struck a formal business partnership with Intel, one of the world's leading computer chip manufacturers. The agreement allowed for technology exchanges between the Institute and Intel and ensured that the two companies would forge a strong alliance between future generations of SAS software and Intel chips. In 1993, SAS Institute completed the development of an internal compiler that exploited the groundbreaking "Pentium" processor.

The business relationship with Microsoft Corporation was sealed in 1989 to give SAS access to Microsoft's operating system development information. The result of this deal was the delivery of releases of the SAS System for Windows and Windows NT in 1993. The relationship between the two companies became even stronger when SAS representatives sat on Microsoft's Independent Software Vendor Advisory Council. In addition to these two major agreements, SAS also had close working relationships with database companies, including Oracle, Sybase, Informix, and Ingres to ensure that its customers had easy access to the data they needed regardless of the manufacturer.

SAS Institute also stood firmly by its commitment to quality. Although "quality assurance" became one of the buzzwords of the early 1990s, SAS Institute had a long-standing reputation for producing software products that were reliable and high quality. "Quality is part of the culture here," Lynne Fountain, manager of public affairs, told *Business Leader.* She added, "Everyone who works here is really proud to be a part of SAS, and it shows in everything we do—from the quality of our products to the attractiveness of our campus and the gourmet food in our cafeteria."

SAS Institute also differentiated itself by its sales strategy. Its sales employees did not earn commission because the company wanted them to concentrate on finding the best way to solve customers' problems. Instead of "selling" its products the way its customers did, SAS licensed the base SAS software and modules on an annual basis. Prices varied according to the platform the customer decided to use. At the end of the licensing period, a customer could add or drop components to accommodate changing business requirements or decline to renew at all.

From the time it was founded in 1976, SAS Institute displayed a commitment to its work force, as well as to its customers. Like most high-technology firms of the late 20th century, SAS Institute understood that its continued success lay in its ability to attract and retain high-quality, intelligent, competent employees. As a result, the Institute made sure that its workers enjoyed bright, airy, well-equipped office buildings and could use an on-site recreation and fitness center along with an on-site health care center. The Institute also offered its employees two on-site Montessori child care centers and the "Generation to Generation" program, which helped employees cope with the needs of aging relatives. These types of employee amenities helped SAS to earn a place on the list of "100 Best Companies for Working Mothers" by *Working Mother* magazine for several consecutive years. Most important, however, they helped SAS Institute maintain an average annual turnover rate of a mere three percent when the national industry average was 22 percent.

SAS Institute's business strategy for the future was to continue to exploit a variety of new technologies to meet its customers' needs. A good example of this was SAS Executive Information Systems (EIS). This software package was introduced in 1992 on an experimental basis as part of a SAS System upgrade. This new module made highly complex data very "user friendly." With it, developers could make corporate data accessible to even the most computer-illiterate executives among the customer base. According to Goodnight, who served not only as president, but also as director of research and development, "SAS/EIS is one of the most important products in our history. It provides our customers with the tools to deliver information to anyone in their organization quickly and efficiently, allowing them to make better, more informed business decisions."

SAS/EIS software and other new SAS products incorporated cutting-edge technologies and applications, such as object-oriented programming technology, which allowed objects built for one application to be reused in others. This technology dramatically increased the efficiency and productivity of software development. SAS was also breaking new research ground in such areas as imaging, geographic information systems, and online user documentation. The company was hard at work developing several new products for niche markets. In 1992, for example, SAS introduced its first vertical market product for the pharmaceutical and biotechnology industries.

EXPANDING THROUGH 1999

Several new offices were opened across the United States in the mid-1990s. SAS also established subsidiaries in several foreign countries, from Brazil to Russia. A subsidiary was established in India in 1997. By the late 1990s, the company had 5,000 worldwide employees

and more than 30,000 customer sites. Sales passed $1 billion in 1999.

Expansion continued at home. In 1999, SAS added its 22nd building to the complex in Cary, North Carolina. Amenities such as the health and fitness center had been upgraded. The recreation center got a ten-lane swimming pool in 1999.

The organization maintained its reputation as a veritable case study in profits through pampering. However, the *Wall Street Journal* questioned whether the lavish perks couple with relatively modest salaries didn't make SAS a "bastion of smothering paternalism." At any rate, the policies helped keep turnover quite low, and working hours reasonable, in a industry with fierce competition for time and talent.

In 2000, *Fortune* ranked SAS as America's second best place to work. By this time, 90 percent of the Fortune 500 used SAS software. However, noted Dow Jones, the company's name was much less familiar than some of its publicly-traded competitors. The company's logo and corporate identity were updated in time for its silver anniversary in 2001. This included a new tag line, "The Power to Know."

Goodnight owned two-thirds of the company, his co-founder John Sall the other third. (The two were also partners in other ventures, including a the defunct Midway Airlines Corporation.) With an estimated valuation of more than $20 billion, SAS was considered the world's largest privately owned software company. The company was preparing an initial public offering (IPO) of up to one-fifth of its stock. However, this was scrapped. SAS had no shortage of cash, and regulatory burdens were becoming tougher than ever. In addition, officials explained to *The News & Observer*, the company's long-term perspective (investing a quarter percent of revenue in R&D) would not have been appreciated at that time by analysts focused on quarterly numbers.

INDEPENDENT THROUGH TECH BOOM AND BUST

After two dozen years of double digit growth, sales were flat in 2001 at $1.1 billion. The company was nevertheless surviving relatively well as the tech bubble burst. In hindsight, the decision to drop the planned IPO seemed brilliant, as it allowed SAS to avoid the cost-cutting that followed the boom, observers told *USA Today*.

SAS was one of the few software companies to add workers in the ensuing economic slowdown. By the end of 2003 it about 10,000 employees, half of them in the United States and 80 percent of these at the Cary campus. SAS was expanding internationally and also taking advantage of lower development costs overseas. It site in Pune, India, was relatively tiny, with less than a half dozen employees, but growing fast. According to *Workforce Management,* most of SAS's turnover was involuntary. *Industry Week* reported the company was receiving 200 applications for every job.

Heightened interest in security and financial fraud following the terrorist attacks on September 11, 2001, was opening up new markets. The company's software was also being used to help medical researchers sift through mountains of patient information. Sales-generating business intelligence applications were a good seller in slow times; forecasting tools were particularly in demand. Part of SAS's growth was coming by acquisitions. The company bought six smaller companies between 2000 and 2003.

A GROUNDBREAKING RELEASE IN 2004

As the economy edged into a recovery, SAS was producing advertising aimed at convincing more high-level executives that the company was more than a good place to work. One of SAS's main objectives was making its sophisticated products easier for non-technical personnel to use. The company rolled out its SAS9 software in March 2004. Billed as the most significant release in SAS's history, it was said to revolutionize the business intelligence industry by allowing more users access to data. The software was also made multithreaded to take advantage of a new generation of processors. By mid-2005, half of SAS's 42,000 customers had installed SAS9.

Wendy Johnson Bilas
Updated, Frederick C. Ingram

PRINCIPAL COMPETITORS

Business Objects S.A.; Cognos Inc.; Hyperion Solutions Corporation; Oracle Corporation.

FURTHER READING

Belsie, Laurent, "Work's Next Leap Forward," *Christian Science Monitor,* November 18, 2002, p. 14.

Conlin, Michelle, and Kathy Moore, "Dr. Goodnight's Company Town," *Business Week,* June 19, 2000, p. 192.

Dyrness, Christina, "At SAS, Good News and Bad," *News & Observer* (Raleigh), March 11, 2003, p. D1.

———, "Fight Could Help SAS," *News & Observer* (Raleigh), June 10, 2003, p. D1.

———, "Making It Easier to Use," *News & Observer* (Raleigh), January 3, 2003, p. D1.

———, "No Life of Riley as SAS Works on Its Latest," *News & Observer* (Raleigh), April 15, 2003, p. D1.

———, "Plays Well with Numbers," *News & Observer* (Raleigh), May 7, 2003, p. F6.

———, "Software Optimism," *News & Observer* (Raleigh), January 19, 2003, p. E3.

Feder, Barnaby J., "SAS Institute Patient with Stock Offering," *New York Times,* October 2, 2000, p. C4.

Fisher, Jean P., "SAS Grant Helps Research Into HIV," *News & Observer* (Raleigh), January 15, 2003, p. F1.

Hansen, Fay, "The Turnover Myth: Part 1 of 2," *Workforce Management,* June 1, 2005, p. 34.

Holt, Nancy D., "Workspaces: A Look at Where People Work," *Wall Street Journal,* November 5, 2003, p. B8.

Jackson, Joab, "Intelligence Apps Look to Future," *Government Computer News,* July 25, 2005, p. 24.

Lloyd, Mary Ellen, "SAS Adds Marketing on Slow Road to Software Giant's IPO," *Dow Jones News Service,* December 27, 2000.

McClenahen, John S., "Dr. Goodnight's Good Days: For the CEO of SAS, Success Is Partly a Product of 'Management by Loitering'," *Industry Week,* December 2004, pp. 43ff.

Maney, Kevin, "SAS Workers Won When Greed Lost; Tech CEO Bucked Pressure to Go Public, Preserving Homey Culture," *USA Today,* April 22, 2004, p. B1.

O'Reilly, Charles, and Jeffrey Pfeffer, *Hidden Value: How Great Companies Achieve Extraordinary Results with Ordinary People,* Cambridge, Mass.: Harvard Business School Press, 2000.

Parker, Vicki Lee, "Luxury Hotel Project Moves to SAS," *News & Observer* (Raleigh), April 23, 2004, p. D1.

———, "SAS Buys Mass. Company," *News & Observer* (Raleigh), October 9, 2003, p. D1.

———, "SAS Grows in India; Its Hiring Slows in Cary," *News & Observer* (Raleigh), November 11, 2003, p. D1.

———, "SAS on a Quest to Enhance Image," *News & Observer* (Raleigh), August 29, 2003, p. D1.

———, "SAS Releases New Version of Its Flagship Software," *News & Observer* (Raleigh), March 31, 2004, p. D1.

Romani, Jane Hairston, "SAS Institute: 21st Century Technology ... Today," *Business Leader,* December 1993.

Schellhardt, Timothy D., "An Idyllic Workplace Under a Tycoon's Thumb," *Wall Street Journal,* November 23, 1998, p. B1.

The SCO Group Inc.

355 South 520 West, Suite 100
Lindon, Utah 84042-1911
U.S.A.
Telephone: (801) 765-4999
Fax: (801) 765-1313
Web site: http://www.thescogroup.com

Public Company
Incorporated: 1993
Employees: 166
Sales: $36 million (2005)
Stock Exchanges: NASDAQ
Ticker Symbol: SCOX
NAIC: 511210 Software Publishers

■ ■ ■

Based in Lindon, Utah, The SCO Group Inc. owns the UNIX operating system. Operating systems are software applications that control a computer's basic operations and hardware. UNIX was originally developed in 1969 by researchers at AT&T, including Dennis Ritchie and Ken Thompson. UNIX, which allows computer systems to be accessed by more than one person at a time, played a key role in the development of the Internet.

In addition to serving as the exclusive licensor to UNIX-based system software providers, SCO also markets software for different computer systems, including those that are embedded, distributed, and network-based. The company's products include SCO Open-Server, a computing platform for small and medium-sized firms, as well as the UNIXWare operating system for large enterprise applications.

SCO's customers include thousands of resellers and developers across the globe who serve a variety of industries, ranging from manufacturing and finance to retail and healthcare. SCO provides localized support, education, and professional services through its SCO Global Services unit.

A FAMILY AFFAIR: 1979–89

SCO's roots stretch back to 1979 when Chicago native Larry Michels and his son, Doug, established a UNIX consulting firm called the Santa Cruz Operation. According to *Nation's Business*, after graduating from the University of Illinois, the elder Michels relocated to southern California during the early 1950s to work as an electrical engineer in the defense industry. Larry Michels later established a credit card verification firm, which he sold in 1969 to TRW. After a ten-year stint with TRW, Michels worked as a management consultant and moved to Santa Cruz, California, where his son was studying computer science at the University of California.

The oldest of four children, Doug Michels had found weekend employment with his father during high school. While he vowed to never work for his father again, Doug shared Larry's entrepreneurial spirit and started a computer consulting company while he was a college student. Ultimately, Larry and Doug's consulting work began to mesh. Larry, who focused on the strategic and organizational aspect of consulting projects, started to rely on Doug to provide input on technology issues.

COMPANY PERSPECTIVES

As the owner of the UNIX operating system, The SCO Group (SCO) has established itself as a leading provider of innovative UNIX solutions. Millions of customers in more than 82 countries depend on SCO for the Power of UNIX.

In time, they decided to merge their businesses, in order to share overhead. Larry Michels served as president and CEO of the new firm, while Doug became SCO's lead strategist and assumed the title of vice-president.

SCO achieved pioneer status in 1983 when the company unveiled its SCO XENIX System V for Intel 8086 and 8088 processor-based personal computers, giving small businesses access to an affordable "business-critical computing system." The following year, SCO developed a two-tier channel for distributing general purpose operating systems, working with application developers, computer manufacturers, distributors, and resellers across the globe.

SCO experienced difficult times during the mid-1980s, namely in the area of cash flow. Although the company remained a private enterprise, it began accepting outside investors, including rival Microsoft, which acquired a 20 percent ownership stake. This support allowed the firm to continue growing. In 1986 SCO established headquarters in Europe after acquiring a division of United Kingdom-based Logica Ltd.

The IBM PC effectively opened personal computing to the masses, as many manufacturers began to manufacture IBM-compatible computers. UNIX, which had been created to run on powerful minicomputers, had more to offer than the somewhat limited MS-DOS operating system used by IBM-compatible PCs. As PCs became more powerful, they eventually had the capacity to run UNIX operating systems. It was this development that set the stage for SCO's initial success. Under a license from AT&T, SCO began marketing UNIX-based operating systems for PCs.

Several important developments took place in 1987. That year, SCO unveiled SCO XENIX 386, which it describes as the "the first 32-bit operating system (and first UNIX System) for Intel 386 processor-based systems." A related development was SCO's "386 Summit"—a gathering of software developers and hardware manufacturers that focused on 32-bit business computing with Intel computer hardware.

By 1989 the small consulting firm that father and son had founded to share overhead had evolved into a sizable and successful enterprise, with sales of approximately $100 million and 900 employees. The company achieved great success with its niche focus on UNIX for PCs, as opposed to larger mainframe and minicomputers. Beyond the operating system itself, SCO offered support services that made UNIX palatable to new users, and attempted to make the system more user-friendly.

In the July 1989 issue of *Personal Computing,* David Fiedler, editor of the UNIX newsletter *Unique,* commented: "Anyone can go to AT&T, get a license, recompile some code, and sell a Unix product. But SCO goes way beyond that. They add the necessary connections, the telephone support, the extra value. And to a large extent, that's what people are buying, not just the disk and the manual."

SCO ended the 1980s by unveiling two new products. These included SCO UNIX System V/386. With an eye on making UNIX more appealing to business users on higher-end PC workstations, the company also introduced the first 32-bit graphical user interface for UNIX, called SCO Open Desktop.

RAPID CHANGE: 1990–2002

The success that SCO found during the late 1990s continued into the early 1990s. Despite an economic recession, the company's sales increased 30 percent in 1991, reaching $135 million. While this was encouraging, SCO's growth presented some unique problems and challenges at the leadership level. In particular, these problems were related to the father-son element and Doug and Larry's management style. At times, investors and employees had a difficult time discerning who was in charge, and Doug was not always given the respect that was commensurate with his position.

Larry Michels provided insight on this situation in the April 1990 issue of *Inc.,* explaining: "My son, Doug, and I built this company together, to indulge ourselves in doing what we do, dabbling in high-tech management issues. And we really do manage it together. He's the number-two person, but it's hard at times to see if he's CEO, chairman of the board, or executive vice-president. The roles shift as we move through daily business. Employees sometimes try to deal with us separately, as if we're not equals." In order to resolve these issues, SCO eventually hired James E. Braeher, an executive consultant from Monterey, California, who worked with the company's management team to improve communications.

The early 1990s were marked by a flurry of important developments at SCO. With the acquisition of a firm called HCR, the company established SCO Canada in 1990. Several product introductions followed, including a family of operating system products marketed under the SCO OpenServer name in 1992.

According to *Software Magazine*, in January 1993 Larry Michels stepped down as SCO's president and CEO. His resignation followed lawsuits and allegations from California state agencies that he sexually harassed several SCO employees. SCO board member Jim Harris immediately replaced Michels. Harris eventually was succeeded by Lars Turndal, an executive who had joined SCO in 1988.

SCO acquired British software company IXI Ltd. several months later. IXI maintained operations in Cambridge, United Kingdom, and functioned as SCO's development center. Finally, in tandem with its strategy to sell large, mission-critical computer systems to large corporations, SCO became a public company in 1993 and was listed on the NASDAQ.

SCO acquired another British company called Visionware in 1994, and the company formed an office in Leeds, United Kingdom. A major development took place the following year when SCO acquired Novell's UNIX business. The deal included the UNIX System V source code, which Novell had obtained from AT&T, as well as the UNIXWare 2 operating system, and made SCO the supplier of the source code used by virtually all UNIX vendors. Source code is the human-readable programming language in which a computer application is written.

In 1995 SCO reorganized into decentralized business units in order to be more responsive to customers. SCO Chairman and CEO Lars Turndal retired in July of that year. Retaining his status as chairman, he stayed with the company in a consulting capacity and was suc-

ceeded by SCO President and Chief Operating Officer Alok Mohan, who had led the company's reorganization efforts earlier in the year.

SCO's sales increased to approximately $200 million in 1996. By this time the company licensed UNIX to hundreds of technology companies. In addition to smaller firms, SCO's client base included the likes of IBM, Fujitsu, Hewlett Packard, NCR, and Digital Equipment Corp. The company proceeded to release a number of new products in 1997, including its UNIXWare 7 operating system.

In mid-1998 Novell gave up its partial ownership stake in SCO, selling the 6.1 million shares of SCO stock it had obtained in 1995 as part of the UNIXWare sale. With support from Intel, that same year IBM and SCO teamed up for Project Monterey. According to SCO, the project aimed "to develop a high-volume enterprise UNIX system," resulting in one product line for "entry-level servers to large enterprise environments." SCO ended the 1990s with cofounder Doug Michels serving as president and CEO.

By the new millennium SCO had been contending with strong competition from Linux—a free, "open-source" operating system based on UNIX. With open source software, developers and programmers are able to make changes to a program's source code as they wish; it is not controlled by any one organization. This competition came to a head in August of 2000, when Orem, Utah-based Caldera Systems Inc., a Linux vendor, announced that it planned to acquire SCO's Server Software and Professional Services Divisions, becoming Caldera International.

Established as Caldera Inc. in 1994 by Ray Noorda and Ransom Love, Caldera had just completed its initial public offering and gained a listing on the NASDAQ. The $120 million cash and stock deal, which was completed in 2001, created the largest UNIX reseller channel in the world. Although it resulted in the combination of Linux with UNIXWare and OpenServer, the result was not a completely open source product. In the August 7, 2000 issue of *Inter@ctive Week*, Ransom Love indicated that customers would receive restricted, and not completely open, licenses. "Business users would like someone to have ownership so someone also has responsibility for maintenance and support," he explained.

After the Caldera deal, SCO was left with Tarantella, a UNIX-based application service provider (ASP) product that allowed users to access a variety of applications remotely, via a browser. With Doug Michels at the helm, the company changed its name to Tarantella Inc. Michels stepped down as the company's CEO in December 2003, and Tarantella was eventually purchased by Sun Microsystems in 2005 for $25 million.

Caldera carried on with the technology that had been the core of SCO's business, releasing Open UNIX 8 in 2001. That year, the company established operations in Japan called Caldera K.K. with assistance from Hitachi and Fujitsu. In 2002 Caldera returned to its roots by completing a stock repurchase and changing its name to The SCO Group (SCO), with Darl McBride serving as CEO.

INTELLECTUAL PROPERTY
BATTLES: 2003 AND BEYOND

In 2003 SCO became involved in a flurry of litigation. The company sued IBM over what it called "tortuous interference, unfair competition, and breach of contract," and claimed that IBM was illegally using UNIX source code in the Linux operating systems it used to run IBM servers.

SCO's lawsuit was a source of controversy within the technology industry. Some observers criticized SCO's motivations, arguing that the basis of the litigation was inaccurate. Others claimed that it would slow down the open source software movement, while some supported SCO's right to sue. In any case, IBM and Linux vendor Red Hat reacted by filing their own lawsuits against SCO. In addition, IBM alleged that SCO had violated a number of its copyrights. SCO also filed a "slander of title" suit against Novell in 2003. Amidst this activity, SCO's distribution of Linux was halted. The company began concentrating on UNIX development and formed its SCOsource Division to enforce its intellectual property rights.

In 2004 SCO announced that its once struggling UNIX division was profitable again. The company continued to face substantial legal bills, however, in the wake of additional litigation, including intellectual property suits it filed against AutoZone and Daimler-Chrysler for alleged software agreement violations. According to an August 9, 2005 *IDG News Service* article, SCO's legal fees were expected to total nearly $40 million by January 2006. After this time, the company's legal fees would be capped as part of an agreement between SCO and its attorneys.

In the same *IDG News Service* article, SCO CEO Darl McBride said that most of his company's employees were focused on technology, and not the firm's legal battles. He remarked that the same held true for most of SCO's customers, explaining that they had been supportive. Other observers were critical, however, of the legal activity and its effects, labeling it as selfish and arguing that it had ruined the SCO organization.

In 2005 SCO continued to introduce new products,

including its Me Inc. Mobile Services mobile computing platform. It had been a difficult year financially, however; SCO reported a loss of $10.7 million. The company's sales, which totaled $36 million, were down almost 16 percent from the previous year. In addition, its employee base had declined more than 33 percent, to 200.

As SCO moved forward into 2006, McBride was optimistic about his company's prospects, and that SCO's UNIX business was profitable again. Whatever the outcome, the company's pending lawsuits would clearly have a major impact on the next chapter of its history.

Paul R. Greenland

PRINCIPAL DIVISIONS

UNIX; SCOsource.

PRINCIPAL COMPETITORS

International Business Machines Corporation; Novell, Inc.; Red Hat, Inc.; DaimlerChrysler Corporation.

FURTHER READING

Babcock, Charles, "Caldera Acquires SCO's Unix Divisions," *Inter@ctive Week,* August 7, 2000.

Barrier, M., "How a California Software Firm Is Trying to Open Up the Personal Computer's Future," *Nation's Business,* March 1992.

Connor, Dominic, "SCO Is Right to Go After Linux Users," *Computer Weekly,* October 14, 2003.

Conrath, Chris, "Deconstructing SCO," *Computerworld,* September 8, 2000.

Deckmyn, Dominique, "SCO's CEO Says Unix Sell-Off Is 'Right Deal,'" *Computerworld,* August 14, 2000.

Foley, John, "Can SCO Run Unix?," *InformationWeek,* March 25, 1996.

Leach, Norvin, "SCO Acquires British Software Maker IXI," *PC Week,* March 8, 1993.

MacMillan, Michael, "Passing the Torch," *Computing Canada,* August 18, 2000.

Martins, China, "SCO Chief Swears Company Would Survive Legal Fallout," *IDG News Service,* February 5, 2006.

Mateyaschuk, Jennifer, "Novell to Sell Stakes in Corel and SCO," *InformationWeek,* July 6, 1998.

"Michels Quits As Tarantella CEO," *Linux Gram,* December 15, 2003.

Moody, Glyn, "Facts and Effects of Caldera/SCO vs. IBM," April 8, 2003.

"News in Brief," *Software Magazine,* January 15, 1993.

O'Malley, Christopher, "Bringing Unix to PCs: Doug Michels, Santa Cruz Operation Inc.," *Personal Computing,* July 1989.

Panettieri, Joseph C., "Turndal to Retire As SCO's Chief," *InformationWeek,* June 12, 1995.

Pavlicek, Russell C., "Revisionist History," *InfoWorld,* March 24, 2003.

Robinson, Robin, "SCO Welcomes Linux Competition; Company Says Linux No Threat to Revenues from Direct Copy Sales or Reseller Network," *Computerworld,* March 6, 2000.

Shriane, Brendan, "Lawsuit Threatens Future of Open-Source Software," *Wenatchee Business Journal,* October 2003.

Wojahn, Ellen, "Fathers and Sons," *Inc.,* April 1990.

Sequana Capital

———■———

25, Avenue Franklin D. Roosevelt
Paris 75008
France
Telephone: (33) 1 56 88 78 00
Fax: (33) 1 56 88 78 77
Web site: http://www.sequanacapital.fr

Public Company
Incorporated: 1848
Employees: 53,600
Sales: $5.8 billion (2004)
Stock Exchanges: Paris
Ticker Symbol: VOR
NAIC: 551112 Offices of Other Holding Companies

■ ■ ■

Sequana Capital, formerly known as Worms et Cie, has a longstanding history of being one of the most illustrious names in French financial history. The company avoided a hostile takeover attempt in 1997 by agreeing to be acquired by Someal, an investment partnership controlled by longtime Worms et Cie ally, the Agnelli family of Italy, via its Ifil investment vehicle. During the early years of the new millennium, the company restructured its holdings and its major assets now include: Arjo Wiggins, a leading paper manufacturer; Antalis, a paper and visual communication media distributor; fund management company Permal Group; and Société Générale de Surveillance (SGS), an inspection, verification, testing, and certification company. The company adopted its current moniker in 2005.

COAL BEGINNING IN THE 19TH CENTURY

The acquisition of Worms et Cie by Someal marked the end of more than 150 years of active Worms family leadership in the company that bears its name. Although the family would come to represent the new French financial "nobility" in the 20th century, Worms et Cie had decidedly common origins. Born in 1801, Hypolite Worms, a wholesaler and shipping agent, opened an office in Paris in 1841. The end of the French monarchy, reestablished on the heels of the French revolution, was once again in the air, falling before the brief civil war of 1848. In that same year, Worms, together with a number of associates, the families of whom would remain shareholders in the company until the end of the 20th century, began importing English coal to France.

Worms and his associates reorganized the company, forming Worms et Cie, a limited partnership that remained in place until the mid-1990s. Among the features of this partnership was a pyramid-like structure of a small number of directors. For much of the company's history, these directors were also among the company's capitalists. As Worms et Cie diversified over the decades, individual directors typically became responsible for a particular branch of the company's development. For much of the company's history, however, a member of the Worms family provided the company's leadership.

The end of the 1848 civil war led to the creation—and brief existence—of the Second Republic. One of the preoccupations of the new civil government was the rising rate of unemployment, particularly in the Parisian

COMPANY PERSPECTIVES

■

Although it has changed its name, the company still has the same mission: to create value for its shareholders through pro-active management of its investment portfolio and to seek out new growth opportunities. Sequana Capital intends to maintain a constant dialogue with the management teams of its investee companies in order to optimize their operating performances, adapt their resources to their needs and market circumstances and implement appropriate measures so as to accompany their growth, while respecting their individual corporate culture.

region, as the provincial population began a shift to the city center. The government created "national workshops" (*ateliers nationaux*) with the goal of providing work for the country's unemployed. While this policy had the effect of attracting still more of the population to the capital city—and further exacerbating the unemployment problem—the availability of a cheap and abundant labor force and the rise in industrial activity came at the right time for Worms et Cie and its coal import business. Worms et Cie prospered, and continued to see its fortunes—and financial influence—rise, even after the foundering of the Second Republic and the rise to power of Emperor Napoleon III in the formation of the Second Empire in 1852. Under Napoleon, the industrialization of France took on a new pace, fueling the demand for coal—and the growth of Worms et Cie. France's increasingly international interests, in parallel with Napoleon III's belligerence, led Worms et Cie to develop a new direction: that of shipping operations. Launched in 1856, the shipping wing of Worms et Cie soon became its principal activity and led the company to expand its operations on an international level.

The company's first foreign office was opened in Port Säid, Egypt, in 1869. The company's operations soon spread throughout northern Africa, especially among France's zone of colonial influence. By then Hypolite Worms was preparing to pass on the company's leadership to the next generation, his nephew Henri Goudchaux. Under Goudchaux, Worms et Cie's shipping empire took on an even greater influence, even as Napoleon III's empire collapsed, replaced by the more durable Third Republic.

While coal-burning steam engines had provided the backbone of the Industrial Revolution, the end of the 19th century saw the emergence of a new type of engine requiring a new type of fuel source: petroleum. Worms et Cie adapted to the new market, expanding its trade activities to include the sale of petroleum, at first for Marcus Samuel & Co., beginning in 1892 and, starting in 1986, Shell of the Netherlands, with principal ports at Egypt, Marseilles, and the Sudan.

20TH-CENTURY INDUSTRIAL FINANCIERS

In the early years of the 20th century, a new Worms name joined the company's group of directors: Hypolite Worms, born in 1889 and named for his grandfather, who had died in 1877. While Henri Goudchaux's interest had focused on expanding Worms et Cie's shipping activities, the younger Hypolite Worms was interested in bringing Worms et Cie beyond merchant activities and into the industrial and financial realms. A first step toward becoming one of France's leading industrial concerns was the company's move into shipbuilding. Encouraged by the French government, preoccupied with fighting World War I, Worms et Cie opened its shipyard near Le Havre in 1916, supplying merchant and other ships. Worms et Cie itself made use of its shipyards, building up a fleet of oceangoing vessels that led the company to create the Nouvelle Compagnie Havraise Pénninsulaire (NCHP), in 1934, launching the company in long-haul shipping.

Meanwhile, Hypolite Worms had brought the company's growing influence to bear on the financial market in the postwar era. In 1928, Worms formed its Services Bancaires (banking services), which evolved into the Banque Worms in the 1960s. In the 1930s, Worms et Cie quickly became a prominent source of investment capital in France's industrial landscape, including financing the creation of the national airline, Air France. On the industrial front, Worms et Cie opened a new subsidiary, Société Française de Transports Pétroliers, dedicated to oceangoing petroleum transportation.

Worms et Cie, which maintained close ties with England, continued operations through World War II, angering the Vichy French authorities; yet the refusal to interrupt its activities also brought the company into difficulties with the French justice system, eager to purge the country of its collaborationist taint, in the postwar years. The company was not, however, convicted of collaborationist activities, and the charges against it were dropped.

In the meantime, Hypolite Worms extended the company's financial activities into the insurance industry, taking shares in companies La Préservatrice and La Foncière in 1949. Both companies were nearly as old as Worms et Cie. La Préservatrice had been founded in

KEY DATES

∎

1841: Hypolite Worms, a wholesaler and shipping agent, opens an office in Paris.

1848: The company incorporates.

1856: Worms et Cie expands into shipping.

1916: The company opens its shipyard near Le Havre.

1928: Services Bancaires (banking services) is formed.

1949: Worms et Cie buys shares in two insurance companies, La Préservatrice and La Foncière.

1966: The company closes its shipyard.

1968: Real estate subsidiary Unibail is created.

1989: Préservatrice Foncière Assurances merges with GPA Assurances to form insurance subsidiary Athena.

1996: Worms et Cie reorganizes as a public shareholding company.

1997: Worms et Cie is acquired by investment group Someal; the company shifts its focus to its industrial investments, including Saint Louis and Arjo Wiggins.

2005: The company changes its name to Sequana Capital.

1861 in Brussels, before becoming a French corporation in 1877, building up a network of 450 branch offices by the end of the century. La Foncière was founded in 1877, developing fire, transport, and life insurance activities, and worldwide operations by the dawn of the 20th century. Under Worms et Cie's control, the two companies established the basis for the later formation of Athena Assurances, formed in 1989.

EVOLVING IN THE POSTWAR ERA

Worms et Cie's financial activities took on a greater importance for the company in the postwar years, as France's economy boomed with the postwar reconstruction effort. In the 1950s, Worms et Cie began offering complete financing for the construction of factories located outside of France. Worms et Cie's banking wing took on a new dimension with the establishment of the Banque Worms in the mid-1960s, which led to the company's move into real estate leasing with the creation of a new subsidiary, Unibail, in 1968. While the company built its financial activities, it began to slow its industrial operations, closing its shipyard in 1966, and ending its Worms shipping line in 1968. The rest of the

company's maritime activities were brought under the umbrella group Compagnie Navale Worms in the early 1970s.

At the start of the 1970s, Worms et Cie took over Pechelbronn, a holding company that took on the role of an important investment vehicle for the firm, and was renamed as Worms et Cie during a company reorganization in 1991. The 1970s proved a quiet time for the company; while continuing its maritime activity, the company's banking arm, and in particular Banque Worms, had become its central activity. The company's industrial activity consisted chiefly of a series of investments, gaining shares in Saint Louis and Arjomari Prioux, but also in such names as Lancel and Dior, and in General Biscuit and Presses de la Cité. However, Worms et Cie's leadership was aging, and the company, which had grown to be identified with establishment France, was seen as slipping toward decline.

The nationalization of the Banque Worms by the French government provided something of a wake-up call for the company. Deprived of its central business, Worms et Cie recognized a need for a new generation of management—and the reappearance of a Worms at the company's helm. Nicholas Clive Worms, born in 1942 and the sole male heir to the family fortune, had joined the family firm in 1970, but was not elevated to a director's position until the early 1980s. Worms quickly surrounded himself with an able group of directors, notably Jean-Phillipe Thierry, leading the insurance wing, while turning his personal attention to the company's industrial investments.

Under Nicholas Worms, the company moved toward a dual focus on insurance and industrial investments. After the loss of Banque Worms—which had its main branch in the company's traditional headquarters—Worms et Cie quickly regrouped its financial activities into Banque Demachy, which became Demachy Worms et Cie at the end of the decade. Worms et Cie also maintained parts of its maritime operations through the 1990s—in 1986, Worms et Cie took over the former Elf subsidiary Compagnie Nationale de Navigation, which became the new name for the company's ship-fittings operations. In the same period, Worms et Cie interrupted its shipping operations, selling off the Nouvelle Compagnie Havraise Péninsulaire. The company did not rebuild its shipping activity until the mid-1990s, taking over the management of Total's petroleum transport fleet. This became something of a Worms et Cie specialty, especially with the partnership agreement reached with Compagnie Maritime Belge in 1995.

By the 1990s, however, the company's insurance arm, Athena, had taken on the central role. Formed in

1989 with the merger of Worms et Cie's Préservatrice Foncière Assurances, with GPA Assurances (former Groupe des Populaires d'Assurances, and including Proxima, CGS, and Athena Banque), Athena reached FRF 18 billion in revenues by the mid-1990s. At the same time, Worms et Cie focused its industrial investments on two vehicles: the group Saint Louis, one of France's leading sugar producers and distributors, and the Arjo Wiggins Appleton paper manufacturing group. In each of these, Worms et Cie built controlling shareholder positions.

After nearly 150 years as a limited partnership, Worms et Cie, which by the 1990s counted nearly 100 partners among the heirs of the founding families, as well as investors among Italy's Agnelli family, and others, reorganized as a public shareholding company in 1996. The change exposed the company to a hostile takeover threat by François Pinault. One of France's most successful entrepreneurs, Pinault had already built the distribution empire Pinault-Printemps-Redoute, grouping the famed department stores with the country's leading catalog sales firm, as well as other retail activities, including the FNAC chain of book, music, computer, and stereo stores. Pinault, however, also was president of Artemis, a fast-growing name in the country's financial-insurance circles. Pinault saw an opening to add Athena to the Artemis portfolio, and rapidly built up a shareholding position in Worms et Cie.

Pinault struck in September 1997 with an offer of FRF 410 per share in cash, valuing Worms et Cie at some FRF 28 billion. Worms et Cie scrambled to shield itself from the hostile takeover attempt. By the beginning of October 1997, the company had found its white knights. Two of the Worms et Cie's major shareholders and longtime investment allies—the insurance group AGF and the Agnelli family holding vehicle Ifil—responded to Pinault's cash offer with a stock and cash offer worth FRF 465 per share. This offer, which raised Worms et Cie's valuation to FRF 32 billion, took a two-pronged approach. The Athena insurance subsidiary was acquired by AGF, as part of its bid to strengthen its share of the French insurance market. Worms et Cie instead regrouped around its industrial investments, principally its control of Saint Louis and Arjo Wiggins, with a new owner: Someal, a holding company composed of the Worms family (28.2 percent), Ifil (56.5 percent), and AGF (15.3 percent).

The deal was accepted in December 1997, placing Worms et Cie out of reach of Pinault. But the deal also meant the end of active Worms family management in the firm, as Nicholas Clive Worms stepped aside to a board position, with leadership taken by Dominique Auburtin. In addition to the firm's former industrial and maritime holdings, the new ownership took on certain Ifil holdings, including its positions in the hotel and travel group Accor and the Agnelli family's shares in Danone. With its focus on industrial investments, the "new" Worms et Cie was poised to continue its legacy as a pillar of French economic history.

CHANGES IN THE NEW MILLENNIUM

Additional changes were on the horizon for Worms et Cie as it entered the new millennium. Before adopting its new name in 2005, the company made several strategic moves in regard to its holdings. As part of a restructuring plan to reduce debt and shore up profits, the company sold assets and realigned its businesses. In 2000, the company acquired the 60 percent of Arjo Wiggins Appleton it did not already own in a deal worth approximately $2 billion. The following year, it sold its U.S. Appleton Papers Inc. subsidiary to employees and expected to raise nearly $1 billion in the process. Subsidiaries Carbonless Europe and Antalis were created at this time. Carbonless Europe eventually was folded into Arjo Wiggins's operations in 2003. Worms et Cie also exited the sugar business by selling its stake in Financiere Franklin Roosevelt, the parent company of Saint Louis Sucre, in 2001.

By 2005, Worms et Cie's business focus had changed dramatically. Its major assets included: Arjo Wiggins, a leading paper manufacturer; Antalis, a paper and visual communication media distributor; fund management company Permal Group; and Société Générale de Surveillance (SGS), an inspection, verification, testing, and certification company. The company sold a majority interest in the Swiss Permal Group to Legg Mason Inc. in late 2005 while retaining a minority stake in the firm.

The company changed its articles of association and corporate governance system to become a société anonyme with a Board of Directors in 2005. At the same time, it laid the Worms et Cie name to rest and officially adopted the Sequana Capital moniker—Sequana is the Latin word for the river Seine. In a May 2005 press release, company officials explained that the new name was chosen "to better reflect its vocation, profile, and ambitions. The choice of a neutral name like 'Sequana' avoids any risk of confusion with its investee companies and the addition of the word 'Capital' clarifies its true business activity. The new name therefore more fairly reflects the investment strategy pursued by the Group for several years."

Only time would tell if the company's actions over the past several years would pay off in the long run.

While revenue had increased each year from 2002 to 2004—rising from $4.6 billion to $5.8 billion—net income was fluctuating due to restructuring charges and challenging economic conditions, especially in the paper sector. In fact, the company posted an $87.3 million loss in 2004. Company management, however, was optimistic that Sequana Capital was on the right path for growth in the years to come.

M. L. Cohen
Updated, Christina M. Stansell

PRINCIPAL SUBSIDIARIES

Arjo Wiggins S.A.S.; Antalis; Permal Group; Société Générale de Surveillance (23.8%).

PRINCIPAL COMPETITORS

International Paper Company; Matussière et Forest S.A.; Stora Enso Oyj.

FURTHER READING

Abescat, Bruno, "Le retour des Worms," *Nouvel Observateur,* May 29, 1987, p. 45.

Almi, Jannick, "Worms et Cie: la contre-attaque des AGF," *La Vie Française,* October 11, 1997, p. 14.

"AWA Gets Worms As Full Owner," *PIMA's North American Papermaker,* July 1, 2000.

Bertier, Etienne, "Les Volte-Face de MM. Worms," *L'Expansion,* April 1, 1988, p. 201.

Chaperon, Isabelle, "Worms & Cie: une mutation conduite á pas comptés," *Les Echos,* September 22, 1997, p. 27.

Chevrillon, Hedwige, and Yannick Le Bourdonnec, "Worms, le retour aux valeurs familiales," *L'Expansion,* July 17, 1993, p. 118.

Denis, Anne, and Pascalle Santi, "Worms et Cie: l'avenir d'Athena au centre de la strategie," *Les Echos,* February 25, 1997, p. 17.

"France's Worms Sees More Restructuring in 2002," *Dow Jones International News,* June 3, 2002.

"Legg Mason Inc.—Completes Acquisition of Permal," *Market News Publishing,* November 3, 2005.

"Le nouveau Worms & Cie affiche une stratégie centrée sur l'industrie," *Les Echos,* September 5, 1998, p. 22.

"Name Change for Worms & Cie," *Les Echos,* May 4, 2005.

Scott, Andy, "Poor Results Lead to Arjo Restructure," *Print Week,* October 2, 2003.

"Worms & Cie to Sell Appleton to Employees," *Printing World,* October 8, 2001, p. 27.

Showtime Networks, Inc.

1633 Broadway
New York, New York 10019
U.S.A.
Telephone: (212) 708-1600
Fax: (212) 708-1217
Web site: http://www.sho.com

Wholly Owned Subsidiary of CBS Corporation
Incorporated: 1976
Employees: 650
Sales: $906 million (2005)
NAIC: 515120 Television Broadcasting; 515210 Cable
and Other Subscription Programming; 512110 Motion Picture and Video Production; 512191 Teleproduction and Other Postproduction Services

∎ ∎ ∎

Showtime Networks, Inc., owns and operates subscription-based cable television networks Showtime, The Movie Channel, and FLIX, along with related multiplexed digital networks like Showtime Extreme, Showtime Women, and Showtime HD. The company also offers pay-per-view sports events and concerts; operates and co-owns the Sundance Channel; and has a joint venture with Zone Vision to run an advertising-supported network in Turkey. The firm's signature network, which features a mix of recent hit movies and original programming like *The L Word* and *Fat Actress,* is the number three U.S. subscription cable channel after HBO and Starz.

BEGINNINGS

The origins of Showtime Networks, Inc. (SNI) date to 1976, when Viacom, Inc. (once a part of CBS, but spun off in 1971 because of antitrust concerns) created a new subscription-based cable television network in the mold of market leader Home Box Office (HBO). On July 1, 1976 Showtime began airing on several cable systems that Viacom owned in northern California, charging a monthly subscription fee of $9.95 ($2 more than HBO typically cost). Showtime was launched nationally in 1978, and by the end of 1981 its subscriber base had grown to 2.8 million, a third the total of HBO. That year saw the network post its first profit.

In 1982 Showtime began shooting new episodes of *The Paper Chase,* a critically acclaimed drama about law students that had run on CBS for just one season starting in 1978. Its creator and principal stars would be involved with the Showtime version, which eventually was produced for three more seasons. The network budgeted $500,000 per episode to shoot the program on the 20th Century Fox lot, making it the first original cable series made at a major studio. Other original shows also were being produced at this time, including a comedy series called *Bizarre,* but the network's bread and butter continued to be recent Hollywood hits.

In September 1983 the firm merged with The Movie Channel (TMC) in a joint venture between Viacom International, Warner Communications, and the American Express Company, which would own 50 percent, 40.5 percent, and 9.5 percent, respectively. TMC was a pay-cable service that had about half as many subscribers as Showtime. December saw the

---

KEY DATES

1976: Viacom, Inc. creates a subscription-based cable network called Showtime.
1978: Showtime is made available nationally.
1983: The company merges with The Movie Channel (TMC).
1992: The new lower cost FLIX movie channel is launched; a lawsuit with Time Warner is settled; a new production unit is formed.
1996: The Sundance Channel is launched in partnership with Robert Redford.
2000: The gay-themed *Queer as Folk* series debuts and proves a hit.
2003: New programmer Robert Greenblatt boosts production of original series.
2006: SNI becomes part of CBS, Inc. with the breakup of Viacom into two units.

---

company sign a five-year, $500 million deal that gave it exclusive rights to air films from Paramount Pictures, and buy a small pay-cable service called Spotlight for an estimated $40 million. Showtime had 4.8 million subscribers and TMC had 2.6 million.

In 1986 Showtime began running *It's Gary Shandling's Show,* a sitcom starring stand-up comic Shandling. The creative half-hour sitcom won critical raves and was later shown on the new Fox broadcast network after episodes had been seen on Showtime. That year also saw the firm begin airing boxing matches as pay-per-view events, and later forming a partnership with legendary boxing promoter Don King for a regular series of bouts featuring top boxers like Mike Tyson and Evander Holyfield. By 1988, SNI had revenues of $420 million, though it posted a loss of $13.3 million for the year.

In 1989 Showtime parent Viacom sued HBO owner Time, Inc., and several cable TV units it also owned, alleging that antitrust violations had kept Showtime from having a fair competitive advantage and asking for a total of $2.4 billion in damages. By this time the company's pay-per-view unit Showtime Event Television was airing boxing matches as well as concerts by acts like the teen-pop group New Kids on the Block, who viewers could catch "live" on TV for a fee of about $20. Sister network TMC continued to focus exclusively on theatrical films. Also in 1989 Viacom entered into talks with cable system operator TCI, who would buy half of the firm for $225 million. The negotiations dragged on,

and were finally abandoned as TCI began preparing its own Showtime-like services called Encore and Starz.

While the total number of pay-cable subscribers had increased each year in the late 1970s and early 1980s, the middle of the latter decade saw a slowdown as home videocassette players and rental tapes made access to recent hit movies, long the cornerstone of channels like HBO and Showtime, not only cheaper and more convenient for viewers, but more timely, as the tapes were available up to six months before titles appeared on TV. Cable service providers also were raising their rates more and more often while many additional basic cable channels (such as commercial-free American Movie Classics) were being launched, making the $10 monthly fee for HBO or Showtime seem like a luxury.

Concerned about these trends, in 1990 the firm proposed a new fee structure to cable operators that would reduce the rates paid by subscribers as a way to increase subscription levels over time, though it required that the cable system pay Showtime a small fee for all subscribers. Some companies agreed to the proposal, while others did not. The company also appointed one-time HBO marketing executive Matthew Blank president and chief operating officer of SNI during the year, with Tony Cox remaining chairman and CEO.

In 1992 a new network called FLIX was launched, which was a lower-cost subscription channel that carried movies from the 1960s through the 1990s, including many that had already premiered on Showtime. August of that year saw a settlement reached in the firm's suit against Time Warner, Inc., which would result in wider distribution of SNI offerings on Time's cable systems, joint marketing campaigns by SNI and HBO, new cooperation between Time units and SNI sister firm MTV Networks, the transfer of Viacom's Milwaukee, Wisconsin, cable system to Time Warner, and a cash payment from Time to Viacom of $95 million.

FORMATION OF SHOWTIME ENTERTAINMENT GROUP IN 1992

The year 1992 also saw SNI form a new unit called Showtime Entertainment Group to produce up to 20 original movies per year for the network, along with some of its continuing series like *Fallen Angels,* which would be directed by famous actors like Tom Cruise, Tom Hanks, and Sigourney Weaver. Other projects included remakes of 1950s American International drive-in titles like *Rock All Night* and *Dragstrip Girl,* directed by the likes of Quentin Tarantino and John Milius and made in partnership with Spelling Films International and CBS/Fox Video. The latter would also be released theatrically overseas.

The firm's first joint ad campaign with HBO debuted in early 1993. The multimillion dollar effort, which was the most ever spent to promote cable broadcasting, included television and radio ads, print, direct mail, and more. The year also saw SNI pursue a new strategy of releasing films it had produced to U.S. theaters to give them added cachet. Titles handled this way included Drew Barrymore-starring *Guncrazy* and documentary *Hearts of Darkness,* about the production of Francis Ford Coppola's *Apocalypse Now.*

The year 1993 also saw formation of a new business development unit to seek brand extensions and other new products, and the signing of an exclusive seven-year deal with MGM that covered as many as 150 theatrical releases for a total possible value of up to $1 billion. Other pacts had been made with New Line, TriStar, Orion, and Castle Rock during this period, and Viacom's merger with Paramount Pictures would give SNI exclusive use of that studio's titles beginning in 1998.

In late 1994 and 1995 the firm began preparations to launch several digital multiplex channels, which included a Spanish-language version of Showtime and other thematically programmed film channels. These were run on digital cable systems that had hundreds of channels, and gave subscribers to Showtime additional choices at any given viewing time.

In early 1995 Tony Cox departed SNI and the firm let 45 staffers go as it restructured to become a unit of Blockbuster Entertainment, which Viacom had recently purchased. Also in 1995 the company began tripling production of original movies to more than 40 per year under new president of programming Jerry Offsay, with a total budget of approximately $150 million. Theatrical runs would be sought for as many as possible, as would video sales through Blockbuster.

LAUNCH OF THE SUNDANCE CHANNEL IN 1996

In February 1996 SNI and actor/director Robert Redford launched a new subscription-based cable channel, which would feature independent and foreign films, called the Sundance Channel after Redford's annual festival in Utah. A stake was subsequently sold to Poly-Gram Filmed Entertainment. In March SNI bought 12 percent of new studio Phoenix Pictures, whose output would be aired exclusively by the firm's networks. For 1996 the company had revenues of $669.7 million.

In 1998 SNI's new in-house ad agency launched a $40 million campaign to re-brand the Showtime channel under the tagline, "No Limits." In May of that year the network acquired the controversial French-produced film *Lolita,* which had been rejected by all of the Hol-lywood studios because of its subject matter, a middle-aged man's sexual obsession with an underage girl. The Samuel Goldwyn Company subsequently agreed to distribute it to theaters.

In 1999 the firm invested several million dollars in the new digital television recorder manufacturer TiVo Inc., and also began making plans for more digital channels, including a high-definition (HD) one, which used the new video format that had been created to replace the lower-resolution standard that dated to the 1940s. SNI was now in third place behind both HBO and Encore's Starz channel, but its profit margins were up thanks to the growth of satellite dish subscribers and the increasing amount of low-budget original programming it ran, including soft-core pornographic series *Beverly Hills Bordello* and a $14 million miniseries about the Bonanno crime family. SNI took in an estimated $800 million in 1999, with a profit of $136 million. The network was now running 35 to 40 original movies and six to seven series per year, mostly shot in Canada where costs were lower and the government offered substantial subsidies. By the end of 1999 the firm's subscription total was up 65 percent from just five years earlier.

In 2000 SNI doubled its boxing events to a twice-monthly schedule, most of which aired on Showtime. The network also had strong pay-per-view boxing and wrestling franchises going, and aired other special pay events like a concert by rock band Kiss.

INTRODUCTION OF *QUEER AS FOLK* IN LATE 2000

In December Showtime debuted a new Americanized version of the hit British series *Queer as Folk,* about the lives of seven gay men and women living in Pittsburgh. It was launched with a major ad campaign in both straight and gay media, and the show proved a major success. The firm had also begun broadcasting ad-supported channels in Spain and Turkey as joint ventures with other companies, and had invested in Replay TV, which made a TiVo-like device.

In 2001 SNI made further changes to its multiplex channels, adding Showtime Next, for 12- to 17-year-old viewers, Showtime Women, and Showtime Familyzone, as well as renaming several others. *Queer as Folk* was the top-rated program on the network, and its success led to the creation of a number of licensed products, including calendars, posters, coffee mugs, and more.

In 2003 Showtime introduced *Penn & Teller: Bullshit!,* in which the edgy magic/comedy duo exposed frauds in a variety of areas including science, health, and spiritualism. In the spring the firm laid off 10 percent of its workforce, a move attributed to the U.S. economic slowdown.

Summer of 2003 saw the producer of HBO's hit *Six Feet Under,* Robert Greenblatt, hired as SNI's president of entertainment. He immediately decided to cut production of TV movies to just 12 per year, while increasing the number of original series. HBO had been extremely successful in recent years with series like *The Sopranos* and *Sex and the City,* while Showtime's once-vaunted slate of original TV movies had left little lasting impression. In November 2003 Showtime aired the controversial miniseries *The Reagans* after recently acquired Viacom sister unit CBS had decided not to broadcast it.

The network's lineup of gay-themed shows was bolstered in January 2004 when a new series called *The L Word* premiered. The show, about a group of lesbians, was promoted heavily, and proved an even bigger hit than *Queer as Folk.* SNI had started a range of marketing techniques, including sponsoring gay pride events around the United States, to reach the gay and lesbian community.

The fall of 2004 saw the firm begin rolling out its most ambitious schedule of original series to date. *Huff,* the first show produced with Robert Greenblatt's input, starred Hank Azaria as a burned-out psychologist. At $2 million per episode it was SNI's most expensive series ever, but despite a major marketing campaign its ratings did not meet expectations. During 2005 other new series were added, including *Weeds,* about a suburban mom who sold marijuana, and *Fat Actress,* a reality/comedy show about the efforts of former *Cheers* star Kirstie Alley to lose weight.

Although Showtime had less than half of HBO's 27 million subscribers, and was even further behind the potential audience of the broadcast networks, it was trying to increase viewership by offering programs via Showtime on Demand (which allowed subscribers instant playback of requested shows) and DVD sets of its hit series. For the March 7, 2005 premiere of *Fat Actress,* Showtime offered a free Internet stream of the show to entice new viewers, while now offering them premiums like a $25 gift certificate for Apple products, two Xbox video games, or a year's worth of Haagen Dazs ice cream. In the fall the network also introduced *Barbershop,* a black-cast comedy series based on the hit MGM movies, and *The Cell,* about an undercover agent infiltrating a small group of U.S.-based terrorists.

Viacom's 2000 merger with CBS had begun coming unraveled, and when the two firms decided to split up, several units were reassigned, including SNI, which on January 1, 2006 became part of CBS Corp. That company's other holdings included the CBS and UPN broadcast networks and other television, radio, advertising, theme park, and publishing companies. As the merger was being finalized, SNI laid off about 10 percent of its staff of 700.

In early 2006 SNI added Showtime Interactive to its growing online offerings, which allowed subscribers to watch hundreds of hours of programs as well as unseen footage, all at DVD-like quality for $1.99 per show. In late 2005 the firm had begun offering audio podcasts (programs downloadable from the Internet) of specially created content, and in February 2006 several of its series were added to Apple's iTunes online store for purchasers to view on the video iPod.

Thirty years after its founding, Showtime Networks, Inc. had grown to operate several cable networks and a pay-per-view service, and was beginning to offer its content as downloadable files over the Internet. Although the company earned steady annual profits, it was continuing to seek ways to emerge from the shadow of larger rival HBO.

Frank Uhle

PRINCIPAL SUBSIDIARIES

The Movie Channel; FLIX; SET (Showtime Event Television) Pay Per View.

PRINCIPAL COMPETITORS

Home Box Office, Inc.; Starz Entertainment Group L.L.C.; Turner Broadcasting System, Inc.; NBC Universal, Inc.; Fox Entertainment Group, Inc.; The Walt Disney Company.

FURTHER READING

Barnes, Brooks, "Showtime Tries Harder," *Wall Street Journal,* August 27, 2004, p. W7.

Battaglio, Stephen, "Showtime to Make 40 New Films a Year," *Hollywood Reporter,* October 5, 1994, p. 1.

Boyle, Joseph R., "Pay TV: Between a Rock and a Hard Place?," *Multichannel News,* May 21, 1990, p. 5.

Carter, Bill, "Redford and Showtime Plan New Cable Movie Channel," *New York Times,* January 18, 1995, p. 5.

Flamm, Matthew, "It's Showtime! Network Scores with Edgy Hits," *Crain's New York Business,* July 12, 2004, p. 4.

Haley, Kathy, "Making a Business of Pushing TV's Boundaries," *Multichannel News,* July 23, 2001, p. 3A.

Hettrick, Scott, "Blank in for Cox at Showtime," *Hollywood Reporter,* February 21, 1995, p. 1.

Higgins, John M., "Showtime: FTC Says 'Yes,' TCI 'No,'" *Multichannel News,* December 17, 1990, p. 1.

——, "Showtime Suffering in Cable Growth," *Multichannel News,* August 5, 1996, p. 42.

Hogan, Monica, "Showtime Makes Pitch to Gays, Lesbians," *Multichannel News,* October 30, 2000, p. 10.

Hornaday, Ann, "Channel Executive Seeks to Build Showtime's Slate of Original Fare," *New York Times,* August 29, 1994, p. 6.

Kafka, Peter, "Win, Place, Showtime," *Forbes,* August 9, 1999, p. 52.

McAvoy, Kim, "Showtime," *Broadcasting & Cable,* October 11, 1999, p. 54.

Mitchell, Kim, "Showtime Will Stay Course on Original Shows," *Multichannel News,* December 6, 1993, p. 30.

Moss, Linda, "Showtime Flexes Plex; Adds Eight Feeds," *Multichannel News,* August 11, 1997, p. 8.

Nibley, Marybeth, "Viacom Sues Time, Says HBO, Other Time Cable Units Break Antitrust," *Associated Press,* May 9, 1989.

Reynolds, Mike, "Who's Laughing Now? (Showtime Networks)," *Cable World,* December 13, 1999, p. 62.

Rifkin, Glenn, "Showtime's Shock Therapy," *Forbes,* February 28, 1994, p. 82.

Romano, Allison, "Leading the Charge: How Bob Greenblatt Plans to Turn Showtime into a Prime Time Powerhouse," *Broadcasting & Cable,* November 1, 2004, p. 16.

Schlosser, Jon, "Showtime Fights for Screen Time," *Broadcasting & Cable,* April 14, 1997, p. 58.

Stilson, Janet, "Flix: Showtime's Latest Fix for Premium Category," *Multichannel News,* April 13, 1992, p. 3.

Voorhees, John, "Showtime's Original Programming Outshines Its Cable Competition," *Seattle Times,* November 25, 1985, p. D8.

Wallenstein, Andrew, "Showtime Goal Is 'To Get Attention and Be Bold,'" *Hollywood Reporter,* March 4, 2005.

———, "Showtime Work Force Cut By 10%: Rival HBO Also Trims Jobs," *Hollywood Reporter,* May 6, 2003, p. 4.

Skyy Spirits LLC

1 Beach Street, Suite 300
San Francisco, California 94133
U.S.A.
Telephone: (415) 315-8000
Fax: (415) 315-8001
Web site: http://www.campari.com

Wholly Owned Subsidiary of Davide Campari-Milano S.p.A.
Founded: 1988
Employees: 80
Sales: $74 million (2004 est.)
NAIC: 312140 Distilleries

■ ■ ■

A subsidiary of the Italian beverage company Davide Campari-Milano SpA, Skyy Spirits LLC produces America's second-highest selling super-premium vodka. Skyy Vodka is known for its thorough distillation and filtering process, which the company claims removes most of the impurities it says are responsible for the symptoms of a morning-after hangover. In addition to its original vodka, the San Francisco-based company offers Skyy90, created specifically for use in martinis; flavored vodkas that include Skyy Melon, Skyy Berry, Skyy Vanilla, Skyy Citrus, and Skyy Orange; and Skyy Cosmo Mix, used to make Skyy Citrus Cosmopolitans. Skyy also distributes Cutty Black whisky and Miller's London Dry Gin.

ORIGINS OF SKYY VODKA

Skyy Vodka was created by Brooklyn-born millionaire and maverick inventor Maurice Kanbar. A mechanical engineer by training, he would hold more than 36 successful patents on a wide variety of products. The foundation of his fortune, when he was still in his early 20s, came from the 1960s invention of the D-Fuzz-It Sweater Comb, used to remove "pills" of fabric that form on sweaters. Other Kanbar inventions included the Safetyglide hypodermic needle protector cap and a cryogenic cataract remover. In the early 1970s he also launched the first East Coast multi-screen movie theatre: the Quad Cinema in New York City's Greenwich Village. It was in 1988 that Kanbar was inspired to create Skyy Vodka after suffering from a headache caused by after-dinner cocktails. He talked about his hangover with a physician friend, who told him that the symptoms might have been caused by congeners, natural toxins that are produced during the distillation process in making spirits. Kanbar told the *Toronto Star* in a 2001 interview, "I said to myself, 'If someone would create a dependably pure vodka that wouldn't give me a headache, I would drink it.'" Sensing a business opportunity, he began conducting research on congeners and the distillation process.

According to Eban Shapiro writing for the *Wall Street Journal*, "The search for a bender without consequences dates back to the ancient Greeks, who believed that wearing amethyst, also known as the Drunkard's Stone, protected them from alcohol's ill effects. Even 'The Dialogues of Plato' contains a discussion of 'how can we drink with least injury to ourselves.' But the Golden Age of Hangover Research came in the 1960s." It was during this period that one study found that just one out of 30 test subjects who got drunk on vodka reported a severe hangover, compared to a third of the subjects who drank bourbon and suffered from severe hangovers. Because vodka contained one of the lowest congener contents of all alcoholic beverages, Kanbar reasoned that congeners were the primary contributor to the severity of a hangover. He decided to use vodka as a starting point for a hangover-free liquor, then try to make it as congener-free as possible.

Kanbar began searching for a distiller to work with on his idea for a purer vodka. "They thought I was nuts," he told the *Toronto Star,* adding "I finally found a distillery to distill it four times. They said they would do it if I paid for it beforehand." Following distillation, Kanbar had his vodka subjected to a three-step filtration process to remove odor-forming compounds. After patenting the process Kanbar tried to sell it and move on to other projects, but once again he was met with skepticism. "There were already strong vodka brands around," he told *Beverage Industry* in a 2000 profile. He explained: "Nobody felt it was a real proposition—that people really cared about impurities in their vodka."

Kanbar decided to invest his own money and market the vodka himself. In 1992, working out of his San Francisco apartment, he began selling the vodka in a clear stock bottle, essentially going door to door to bars and restaurants. It was while gazing out of his apartment at the beautiful sky above San Francisco that he hit upon the brand name "Sky," because it connoted purity and balance, like the vodka he had produced. A second "y" was added to the name to help it stand out and for trademark purposes. He then began using a cobalt blue bottle, which referenced the name and was also more stylish than the clear glass bottles used to contain competing vodkas.

SKYY VODKA INTRODUCED IN 1993

With all the pieces in place, Skyy Vodka was introduced in 1993 and rolled out nationwide a year later. It enjoyed

exceptional success in large part because of timing: the economy was on an upswing and younger people were rediscovering the cocktail, eschewing the spritzers and wine coolers of the 1980s. In 1994 Kanbar attended the 1994 Wine and Spirits Wholesalers convention in New Orleans, at a time when Skyy had a presence in only a handful of states through commissioned brokers. He approached some national distributors about carrying Skyy Vodka but they asked to wait until the convention was over before meeting with him. In the meantime, regional wholesalers who had heard about Skyy Vodka's success in California approached Kanbar and sought to represent the brand in their markets. By the time the national companies got back to him, Kanbar had cobbled together his own plan for national distribution. In 1994, the company had sold an impressive 190,000 cases of Skyy Vodka and was poised to enjoy even stronger growth.

By that point, Kanbar had reached his limit as an executive, preferring to create enterprises and then turn them over to someone with more management skills. He recruited his 27-year-old nephew, David Kanbar, owner of a small New York mortgage business, who sold his company and moved to San Francisco, where Skyy was still just a three-man operation working out of his uncle's apartment. They soon decided that they needed the services of someone experienced in the liquor business. Two executives did not pan out but the third did. He was Anthony Foglio, the chief operating officer and president of IDV North American, the spirits division of Grand Metropolitan plc. Foglio brought along his right hand man, Keith Greggor, and together they were instrumental in taking Skyy Vodka to the next level. Sales grew to 375,000 cases in 1995 and 585,000 cases in 1996.

Another important element in the brand's success was its marketing, which was put in the hands of people who were part of the target demographic. "A lot of these larger spirits companies are full of old farts," Skyy's director of marketing Dan DeDalt told *Marketing News* in 1995. "It's different at Skyy. We go into the hip bars because we know what's happening. We know what entertainment to get involved with because we know what's cool with our own group." To appeal this age group, Skyy Vodka advertising took an increasingly edgy tone. For example, one print ad featured a young man in a red leather chair straddled by a red-headed dominatrix. On a side table was a bottle of Skyy and a pair of empty martini glasses. According to Erika Brown writing about Skyy in *Forbes* in 1998, "Maurice grouses

KEY DATES

1988: Maurice Kanbar decides to create a "hangover-free" vodka.
1993: Skyy Vodka is introduced.
1994: Skyy Vodka is distributed across the United States.
1998: Skyy Cinema campaign is launched.
2000: Skyy Citrus is introduced.
2002: The Campari Group acquires controlling interest in the company.
2004: Skyy begins distributing Cutty Black whisky.
2005: Skyy90 is introduced.

that he doesn't 'get' the ad campaign, but is willing to let Foglio take charge."

A PASSION FOR FILM HELPS BUILD THE BRAND

One of Kanbar's many interests was film. He gave generously to New York University's New York School of Film, which was ultimately renamed the Maurice Kanbar Institute of Film and Television. In 1998 Skyy found a way to incorporate the medium of film into its branding efforts, with the launch of the Skyy Cinema campaign. The company sponsored 30 independent film festivals and premieres, including the surprise hit of summer 1999, *The Blair Witch Project*. It also developed a series of short independent films that focused on a "cocktail moment." Moreover, a wordless print ad campaign displayed Skyy Vodka in film noir-like settings that encouraged viewers to imagine their own scenarios. Over the next five years approximately 50 such vignettes would be presented, some of which included celebrities like Ben Stiller, and others of which stirred public controversy. According to Skyy, the campaign was instrumental in raising brand awareness 200 percent. The Skyy Cinema campaign continued in 2003 with new print ads that featured actors Tave Dies, Heather Graham, John Leguizamo, Kyle MacLachlan, and Gretchen Mol. These ran in such magazines as *Maxim, Cosmopolitan*, and *Stuff*. In addition, Skyy began commissioning original content short films for viewing on its Web site, and established the Skyy Vodka Short Film Project, a contest in which entrants submitted a five-minute tape explaining why they wanted to be filmmakers. The three finalists would then be given a chance to shoot a short film in New York City, each relying on the same script, with a 72-hour time limit.

NEW CENTURY BRINGS NEW FLAVORS

At the start of the 2000s, Skyy Vodka sales approached the one million case mark with no signs of tapering off. Skyy took its first step in expanding the product line in 2000 with the introduction of Skyy Citrus, combining vodka with the essences of lemon, lime orange, tangerine, and grapefruit. Interviewed by *Beverage Industry* in June 2000, Kanbar said, "It took years to develop because we wanted to create a complex flavor, one you couldn't achieve by simply squeezing a lemon into your vodka on the rocks." Skyy Vodka passed Russia's Stolichnaya brand of vodka, becoming the second largest super-premium vodka brand in America, trailing only Sweden's Absolut. Skyy's success had already caught the attention of Italy's Campari Group, which bought an 8.9 percent interest in 1998 as part of a cross-marketing alliance: Compari would distribute Skyy Vodka in more than 100 markets outside of the United States. In early 2002, Campari acquired a controlling stake in a $207.5 million deal by purchasing another 50 percent from Kanbar, allowing the latter to concentrate on his other inventions and providing plenty of cash for his philanthropic projects. The change in ownership also improved Skyy's ability to grow as an international brand, while presenting Campari with a greater opportunity to expand in the United States.

Under Campari control, Skyy picked up the pace in filling out its portfolio. In 2002 it began selling Skyy Cosmo Mix, which contained a blend of cranberry, lime, and orange liqueur flavoring that could be blended with Skyy Citrus to produce a cosmopolitan cocktail. The pink drink had become popular due to exposure on television shows like *Sex in the City*. As a result it had become one of the most frequently ordered cocktails in lounges and restaurants across the country. The company became involved in a new category of 5 percent malt beverages, engendered by the popularity of Smirnoff Ice and quickly joined by the likes of Bacardi Silver, Captain Morgan Gold, and Sauza Diablo. Skyy entered the fray by creating a joint venture with Miller Brewing company, resulting in the introduction of Skyy Blue. In 2003 Skyy rolled out new flavored vodkas: Skyy Spiced, a blend of natural spice flavors including cinnamon, nutmeg and clove, which the company touted as a good mix with cola; Skyy Berry, a blend of all natural raspberry, blueberry, and blackberry flavors, good for mixing with lemon-lime soda; and Skyy Vanilla, a blend of Madagascar vanilla bean with a hint of amaretto, which was suggested as the basis for a Skyy Vanilla Martini. Along with the introduction of the new flavored vodkas, Skyy made changes to its packaging. Added to the signature cobalt blue bottle were such touches as a new cap, a sleeker neck design, and color differentiated logos, including a silver Skyy logo for the original Skyy Vodka and color-coded logos for each of the flavors. In January 2004 Skyy added another flavor, Skyy Melon, combining honeydew, cantaloupe, and watermelon flavoring, suited for creating a variety of fruit cocktails. Later in the year the company unveiled Skyy Orange, a mix of Brazilian and Blood Orange.

Skyy Spirits also began picking up the distribution of outside brands, courtesy of its corporate parent. In 2004 it began bottling and selling Cutty Black whisky under a license with the United Kingdom's Berry Bros. and Rudd, LTD., after the new 100-proof whisky performed well in test marketing. Skyy added the U.S. distribution rights to Miller's London Dry Gin in 2005. Skyy sales reached 1.9 million cases in 2004, which represented a 72 percent increase since 2000. The company was poised to continue the trend in the coming years, as it continued to build up its portfolio. In 2005 it introduced a 90 proof vodka, Skyy90, an upscale spirit retailing around $35 for a 750ml bottle. It was produced at a new state-of-the art distillery that housed a proprietary finishing stage able to eliminate all water and by-products from the fermentation process. By this point, Skyy had established its identity in the marketplace based on style and prestige, and it was no longer marketed as the cure for the common hangover.

Ed Dinger

PRINCIPAL COMPETITORS

Allied Domecq plc; Brown-Forman Corporation; V&S Vin & Sprit AB.

FURTHER READING

Brown, Erika, "Will Uncle Maurice Let Go?," *Forbes*, September 7, 1998, p. 92.

Bruss, Jill, "Compari Takes to the Skyy," *Beverage Industry*, January 2002, p. 8.

————, "Skyy Vodka," *Beverage Industry*, October 2000, p. 48.

Gordon, Daphne, "Curing Fuzzy Heads and Fuzzy Sweaters," *Toronto Star*, February 18, 2001, p. EN06.

Hamilton, William L., "Pie-in-the-Sky Spirits," *New York Times*, March 30, 2003, p. 9.

Hein, Kenneth, "Skyy Sets the Stage in Sultry Cinematic Scenes," *Brandweek*, June 17, 2002, p. 8.

Hochstein, Mort, "Nation's Restaurant News," February 13, 1995, p. 45.

Howard, Theresa, "Marketers of the Next Generation: Teresa Zepeda," *Brandweek*, November 8, 1999, p. 38.

"Maurice Kanbar," *Beverage Industry*, June 2000, p. 78.

Shapiro, Eben, "Marketing: 'Hangover-free' Vodka Makes Some Queasy," *Wall Street Journal*, October 31, 1994, p. B1.

Sinton, Peter, "Campari Takes Bigger Slice of Skyy," *San Francisco Chronicle*, December 14, 2001, p. B1.

The Stabler Companies Inc.

635 Lucknow Road
Harrisburg, Pennsylvania 17110
U.S.A.
Telephone: (717) 234-3106
Fax: (717) 236-1281
Web site: http://www.stablercompaniesinc.com

Private Company
Incorporated: 1955
Sales: $200 million (2004 est.)
NAIC: 212321 Construction Sand and Gravel Mining;
233110 Land Subdivision and Land Development;
234110 Highway and Street Construction

■ ■ ■

The Stabler Companies Inc. is a privately-owned collection of subsidiaries primarily involved in transportation-related products and services and real estate development. The anchor of the company is Eastern Industries, Inc., which builds and repairs roads and provides quarry aggregates used in the making of concrete. Eastern also owns Work Area Protection Corporation, a Chicago-area maker and distributor of cones, drums, barricade lights, vests, "stop/slow" paddles, message boards, and other safety products. In a similar vein, Protection Services Inc. offers traffic control products and services, including signs, barriers, cones, and electronic message boards. Precision Solar Controls, based in Garland, Texas, manufacturers solar-powered highway message systems and traffic lights. Stabler's ASTI Transportation Systems subsidiary is involved in a wide variety of high-

technology transportation products, including traffic congestion detectors, over-height vehicle detectors, flooded roadway detectors, speed limit systems, roadside cameras to help monitor and improve traffic flow, and alarm systems to alert construction workers when a vehicle has violated a safety zone. Stabler Land Company is a real estate development subsidiary, whose primary interest is the Stabler Center, a planned corporate and residential community located in Pennsylvania's Lehigh Valley, strategically located near New York City, Philadelphia, and Washington, D.C. Finally, Stabler Companies also owns the Center Valley Club, a tournament-caliber golf course that is part of the Stabler Center. The company also operates DBS Trans Inc., which provides helicopter service for the affiliated companies, and SCI Products Inc., holder of patents on several of the Stabler's products and operator of a sales force for Work Area Protection and Precision Solar Controls.

INFLUENCE OF THE GREAT DEPRESSION

The man behind the Stabler name was Donald Billman Stabler, born in Williamsport, Pennsylvania, in 1908. He learned the value of hard work from his father, George William Stabler, who had been raised on a Pennsylvania farm, cobbled together an education by attending a Williamsport business school, and then became a circulation director of *Grit*, a weekly newspaper popular with rural America. The younger Stabler was able to attend Lehigh University, a well-regarded engineering school, and earn a bachelor's degree in civil engineering in 1930. He then took a job with a Pittsburgh contractor, Dravo Corporation, but due to the Great Depression that was precipitated by the stock market crash of 1929, he was laid off after just six months. His father then managed to pay for Stabler to return to Lehigh and earn a master's degree in 1932. He now found work with a Harrisburg contractor. Although the pay was meager, just $15 a week, the work was challenging. "It was the best training I've ever had in my life," he told the Allentown *Morning Call* in a 1989 interview. In 1940 Stabler was ready to strike out on his own, and with $1,300 in savings he laid the foundation for the Stabler Companies by starting Stabler Construction Company in Harrisburg. He already had a contract in hand, having made a successful $40,000 bid on a road work contract in Huntingdon County. He also operated a sole proprietorship, Donald D. Stabler Contractor. The early years were a struggle, however, and to make ends meet he also served as superintendent of public works at Fort Indiantown Gap, a facility that would soon be humming with activity as the United States entered World War II. Stabler attempted to enlist in the military but was rejected because of poor eyesight.

POSTWAR BOOM

Following the war and a brief recession, the U.S. economy roared to life and the federal and state governments made a vast commitment to a highway building program, deemed an important component of national defense given the potential need to moved troops and materials from coast to coast. As a result, Stabler received a bounty of road building contracts. The year 1955 was a watershed for Stabler's business and his family. He merged Donald B. Stabler Contractor and Stabler Construction Company to form Stabler Companies, and in that same year began to diversify. He added to Stabler Companies by forming Protection Services to produce construction safety products and acquired State Aggregate, a sand and gravel company that operated quarries in northeastern Pennsylvania. But it was also in 1955 that his daughter, Beverly Anne, turned 16 and received a driver's license. On a family trip late in the

year, Stabler and his second wife, Dorothy Louis Stabler, were driving in one car while his daughter followed in a second car. She was struck by a drunk driver, was severely injured, and was for many years confined to The Woods School, a institution in Bucks County, Pennsylvania, devoted to the developmentally retarded and people with the kind of head injuries Beverly received. The incident sparked the philanthropy that would become a hallmark of Stabler's life. He and his wife launched the Donald B. and Dorothy L. Stabler Foundation to support central Pennsylvania colleges and hospitals. He also became a generous supporter of Lehigh University, not only contributing money for building programs and establishing scholarships but also by devoting his time. He served as a member of the board of trustees for more than 30 years, and during his two-year term as head of the school's alumni association, he traveled almost 20,000 miles to visit 30 alumni clubs, the most any president ever completed.

EASTERN INDUSTRIES: KEY 1976 ACQUISITION

Despite his personal tragedy and increasing volunteer work, Stabler continued to grow his business empire. The next addition of note came in 1965 when he launched DBS Transit Company. It initially supplied trucks to Stabler's construction and materials companies, but later it would provide helicopter service to the subsidiaries. The most significant acquisition in the history of the Stabler Companies occurred in 1976 when Eastern Industries, Inc., was purchased, along with subsidiaries Elco Paving and Elco Hausman Construction, which provided blacktop, sewer grading, and concrete construction services in the Lehigh Valley. The business started out in 1941 as Eastern Lime Corporation and provided limestone to cement companies as well as agricultural limestone and crushed stone for ready-mix concrete and highway construction. Eastern added its first quarry in 1957 and a year later became involved in the blacktopping business when it acquired Harlem Blacktop, Inc. The company entered the block and masonry industry in 1961, and in 1965 the collection of business began operating under the Eastern Industries name. Over the next decade it added further materials, equipment rental, and construction assets until in March 1976 Stabler's Protection Services bought 98 percent of its stock. The year was also noteworthy because Stabler, now in his late 60s, underwent successful open heart surgery.

Despite his age, Stabler looked to new challenges in the 1980s, moving beyond the construction field he knew so well to real estate development. In 1983 he formed Stabler Development Company to own and lease

KEY DATES

1950: Donald Stabler forms Stabler Construction Company.
1955: Stabler Companies is incorporated.
1965: DBS Transit Company is launched.
1976: Eastern Industries is acquired.
1984: Stabler Land Company is formed.
1986: Work Area Protection Corporation is acquired.
1992: The Center Valley Club opens.
1997: Donald Stabler dies at age 89.
2003: SCI Products Inc. Is formed.

his real estate interests, primarily the quarries that supplied aggregate for construction purposes. A year later he launched Stabler Land Company to develop 1,700 acres of Lehigh Valley property. About 1,600 of those acres were acquired in 1984 from Gulf & Western Natural Resources Group, the land part of New Jersey Zinc Company and available after the mining operations were shut down in 1983. Knowing that Interstate 78, which would provide a direct link to the New York metropolitan area, was likely to be built, Stabler believed that the Lehigh Valley was set to enjoy the benefits of its proximity to major Eastern Seaboard cities and envisioned building a major technology research center, similar to Princeton's prestigious Forrestal Center, home to such major research facilities as the Plasma Physics Laboratory. "I have always like the Valley," Stabler told the *Morning Call* in 1995, adding, "When this opportunity came along, it was sort of the fruition of an inward dream I really didn't realize was there. It just sort of developed as my thinking went along." What would one day became the Stabler Center became his "baby," as he once describe it, and the preoccupation for the rest of his life.

Going from vision to realization, however, required a great deal of patience and resolve. First Stabler had to secure permission to build by winning over area residents concerned how such a massive development would affect the rural character of the community. An example of Stabler's commitment to the project and salesmanship occurred in January 1985 when he faced some 200 hostile residents at an area high school. With his only aid a chalkboard, he made his pitch. "Stabler turned his 5-foot 5-inch frame to the blackboard and began scribbling in big letters," according to the *Morning Call.* "The development's assessment, he said, would be at least $168 million. The township supervisors and school

district officials at the meeting perked up. That meant at least $10 million in real estate taxes." He further wrote, "Add 50 percent to your township budget. Triple your school district budget." Furthermore, he argued that development was coming to the area whether he did it or not, whether the residents liked it not. He offered them quality development from someone with a concern for the local environment. "We don't want any trash development. We want something to be proud of. We're not big city slickers. We're just like you guys." According to the newspaper account, "The crowd grew silent. Stabler put on his raincoat and, followed by his architect, slowly marched out of the auditorium, leaving behind the message on the blackboard. ... Several months later, Stabler's plans for an office park were approved."

The township approvals he needed were all in place by 1987, but Stabler soon faced another major obstacle: a real estate crash that caused a slump in the corporate real estate market. However, because his business was diversified, he was able to wait out conditions. In the meantime, Stabler did not neglect his core businesses. In 1986 Eastern acquired Work Area Protection Corporation, the largest maker of traffic cones in the United States, followed in 1990 with the addition of Precision Solar Controls Inc., a major supplier of solar-power message systems, LED traffic lights, and monitoring systems.

Stabler's vision for the development of the Lehigh Valley began to take shape in the 1990s, but progress proved elusive. Stabler had always predicted that the project would take 20 to 25 years to be completed, and was aware he would not be alive to see his dream fulfilled. What he did witness were essentially minor achievements. The Center Valley Club and its upscale 18-hole public golf course opened in June 1992, and later in the decade it would host a pair of PGA Nike golf tournaments. In the meantime plans for a three-story office building fell through and only a handful of companies located facilities in the massive site. In 1994 an ALDI Foods distribution center opened on a 66-acre lot, followed by offices of a law firm and AD computers, a payroll processing company. In 1995 SPJ Properties of Parsippany, New Jersey, was hired to lure research and technology-oriented companies and other major businesses, but nothing materialized from these efforts.

STABLER DIES IN 1997

On December 30, 1997, a week after he turned 89 years old, Donald Stabler died at his Bal Harbour, Florida, winter home. Eight years younger, his widow inherited most of his fortune, although a great deal of that was already earmarked for the charities the couple had supported for so many years. She would live until February 2005 when she passed away in Florida at the age of 90. Before he died, Stabler groomed his successor, Cyril C. Dunmire, Jr., who was president of Protection Services and then in 1995 became president and chief operating officer of Stabler Companies. Upon Stabler's death, he became chairman of the board. The Stabler Companies carried on without its founder, the individual subsidiaries continuing to pursue their own agendas, while complimentary businesses were added. In 1999 ASTI Transportation Systems, a developer of intelligent transportation systems based in New Castle, Delaware, was brought into the fold. Stabler Companies then formed SCI Products to hold a number of patents and provide a sales force to represent the products of Work Area Protection and Precision Solar Controls.

Although movement had been slow, Donald Stabler's pet development project began to finally take shape following his death, albeit it required some deviation from his original plan for Stabler Center. In 2000 Liberty Properties Trust broke ground on a $10 million, 70,000-square-foot office building that when it was opened was immediately occupied. In March 2001 plans were announced to build a 225-room hotel at the entrance of Center Valley Golf Course, but difficult economic condition forced that project to be put on hold. A similar situation occurred with Optimum Corporation, a Florida Internet company, which in July 2001 agreed to build a $3 million, 25,000 square-foot research and development. Several months later, due to a severe slump in the telecommunications industry, the project was shelved. A minor accomplish in 2002 was the opening of the Allentown Business School at Stabler Center. Also, about 100 homes were built in a residential district that could accommodate ten times that number.

Part of the reason for slow progress at Stabler Center was a desire to stick as close as possible to Donald Stabler's vision. Officials at Stabler Land Development had been extremely selective about tenants over the years, because the company was privately owned and did not have debt to service. This factor, along with difficulties in gaining subdivision permits, prevented Stabler Center from taking advantage of the Internet-boom of the late 1990s, which in many ways turned out to be a blessing in disguise. To help spur development, local officials, desperate for tax revenues, made changes to township zoning ordinances, which would allow for the development of smaller office buildings at Stabler Center, as well as a taller conference center, restaurants, and boutiques. The zoning changes had the desired effect and within two years Stabler Center, in the words of the *Morning Call*, emerged as "one of the region's hottest development sites." Olympus America agreed to move its headquarters there from Long Island; plans for a 427,000-square-foot upscale mall were announced; D&B Corporation was also looking to build a 167,000-square-foot building to replace its Bethlehem, Pennsylvania, offices; and in December 2005 Sierra Management Company broke ground on the first of a three-building, campus-style complex, with one of the unit devoted to medical tenants. Sierra owned land in the Stabler Center on which it planned to build the long-proposed executive conference center, Saucon Creek Resort. Plans were also in the works for a 372-home "active adult" community. While many of these projects were not what Donald Stabler had in mind when he bought the old New Jersey Zinc property a generation earlier, there was still plenty of land available should a major technology research tenant materialize.

Ed Dinger

PRINCIPAL SUBSIDIARIES

Eastern Industries, Inc.; Precision Solar Controls; Protection Services Inc.; Stabler Land Company; Work Area Protection; ASTI Transportation Systems, Inc.; DBS Transit Inc.; Stabler Development Company; SCI Products Inc.

PRINCIPAL COMPETITORS

Ashland Paving and Construction, Inc.; J.F. Shea Company, Inc.; Trafficmaster plc.

FURTHER READING

Blumenau, Kurt, "Ground Is Broken at Stabler On Another Office Building," *Morning Call* (Allentown, Pa.), December 9, 2005, p. D1.

Fricker, Dan, "Stabler Will Leave Giant Economic Monument," *Morning Call* (Allentown, Pa.), February 26, 1989, p. B4.

Higham, Scott J., "Stabler Dreams A Slick Mix For Upper Saucon," *Morning Call* (Allentown, Pa.), February 22, 1987, p. B4.

McDermott, Joe, "Stabler Center Focus May Shift," *Morning Call* (Allentown, Pa.), August 7, 2003, p. A1.

———, "Stabler Center Taking Steps Toward Fulfillment," *Morning Call* (Allentown, Pa.), August 20, 1995, p. 1.

"Whatever Became of … Plans For A Conference Center Near the Center Valley Club?," *Morning Call* (Allentown, Pa.), July 25, 2004, p. B3.

STERLING CHEMICALS

Sterling Chemicals, Inc.

---

333 Clay Street, Suite 3600
Houston, Texas 77002-4109
U.S.A.
Telephone: (713) 650-3700
Fax: (713) 654-9551
Web site: http://www.sterlingchemicals.com

Public Company
Incorporated: 1986
Employees: 336
Sales: $851.7 million (2004)
Stock Exchanges: OTC
Ticker Symbol: SCHI
NAIC: 325110 Petrochemical Manufacturing; 325188
   All Other Basic Inorganic Chemical Manufacturing;
   325199 All Other Basic Organic Chemical
   Manufacturing

■ ■ ■

Sterling Chemicals, Inc., is a petrochemical manufacturer focused on styrene, acetic acid, and plasticizers. Most of the company's customers use Sterling Chemicals' products to manufacture other chemicals and products used to produce packaging and plastic items, adhesives, and coatings. High raw material costs and a slowdown in Sterling Chemicals' key markets wreaked havoc on the company's bottom line in the early years of the new millennium. Burdened with a massive debt load, the company was forced to file for Chapter 11 bankruptcy protection in 2001. Sterling Chemicals emerged the fol-

lowing year thanks to an equity infusion by Resurgence Asset Management LLC.

EARLY HISTORY

Sterling Chemicals, Inc., was founded in 1986 to acquire and operate Monsanto Co.'s petrochemical plant in Texas City, Texas. The purchase was completed on August 1, 1986. The cost, $213 million, was financed in part by a syndicate of banks led by Chase Manhattan Bank, which provided a public offering of $120 million of subordinate notes and $140 million in credit.

The Texas City facility was on a 250-acre site on Galveston Bay, about 45 miles from downtown Houston, where Sterling Chemicals established its corporate headquarters. Production from the plant consisted of acrylonitrile, styrene monomer, lactic acid, acetic acid, tertiary butylamine, and plasticizers. These chemicals, through intermediate products, became integral elements in finished goods such as synthetic fibers, coatings and adhesives, plastics, and synthetic rubbers used in many household and industrial applications.

Sterling Chemicals was founded on the premise that there was a "window of opportunity" for the chemicals produced at the Texas City complex because of rising demand and no new manufacturing capacity in the offing. Gordon A. Cain, leader of Sterling Group Inc., the investor group that founded the chemical company and chairman of Sterling Chemicals' board, was a retired chemical industry executive who acquired several chemical complexes from major companies during the recessionary period of the early 1980s. He owned 10.8 percent of the stock at the end of 1994; J. Virgil Wag-

COMPANY PERSPECTIVES

Our objectives are to be a premier producer of petrochemicals, to maintain a strong market position, to achieve first quartile cost performance in all of our major products and to provide superior customer service.

goner, president and chief executive officer of the company from its inception, owned 8.2 percent.

"As long as oil was selling for $30 a barrel," Cain told a *Houston Post* reporter, "there was a trend to build plants like this in Saudi Arabia." But, he continued, as a result of lower oil prices, which even fell below $10 a barrel in 1986, "There's no incentive to build competing plants in that part of the world." Cain also foresaw that the new venture would benefit from the lower cost of petroleum feedstocks (because of the lower price of crude oil) that served as Sterling Chemicals' raw material and from a weakening dollar, which would make the company's products more competitive in the world chemical markets.

Contributing to Sterling Chemicals' low costs was a small corporate staff with minimum layers of management and a cooperative workforce. Company officials established an employee stock ownership plan and later, a profit-sharing plan, in order to gain greater productivity from a highly unionized labor force with strict work rules and a long history of adversarial relations with management. About 12 percent of the common stock was held by employees in 1988. The company was contributing, in 1990, 60 cents for every dollar employees put into the stock-option program.

The new company had an anchor client in Monsanto, which was paying Sterling Chemicals a fee and a share of the profits to convert its petroleum feedstocks. The Texas City facility was the only one in the United States producing synthetic lactic acid, a preservative, and tertiary butylamine, used significantly by Monsanto in rubber production. Within a year of Sterling Chemicals' founding, the prices of its two main products—styrene monomer and acrylonitrile—had risen. For its first fiscal year (ended September 30, 1987), the company reported revenues of $413.2 million and net income of $47.4 million. The long-term debt of $187.3 million had been reduced to $116 million. Total common stockholders' equity had increased from $5.1 million to $52.4 million. Results were so good in Sterling Chemicals' initial year

that its board approved a voluntary distribution to its employees that came out to be about $2,500 each.

SUCCESS LEADS TO EXPANSION IN 1988

Fiscal 1988 was a year of spectacular success for Sterling Chemicals. The company reported revenues of nearly $699 million and a whopping net income of $213.1 million. Long-term debt dropped to $86.3 million, while stockholders' equity rose to $90.6 million. Sterling Chemicals ranked first for the year among all *Fortune* 500 companies in return on assets and second in return on sales. The company attributed its outstanding performance to a favorable supply/demand situation, availability of raw materials at reasonable costs, the relatively weak dollar, lack of easily substitutable materials, and a healthy world economy. Shortly before October 1988 Sterling Chemicals became a publicly traded company, with its stock listed on the New York Stock Exchange. Stockholders sold 12.65 million shares (more than 20 percent of the stock outstanding) at $16 a share in the initial public offering.

A program of expansion also was under way. BP Chemicals America Inc., a U.S. subsidiary of British Petroleum Co., was working with Sterling Chemicals to increase its acrylonitrile capacity by 55 percent and its acetic acid capacity by a minimum of 100 million pounds a year. A sodium cyanide facility also was being constructed at the Texas City site, by E.I. du Pont de Nemours and Co. Sterling Chemicals reported that much of its production was committed through long-term contracts with companies like BP Chemicals and Du Pont enabling it to lower working-capital requirements for raw materials and inventories and to lower its overhead by dispensing with the need for a sales force and many other staffers. A company executive told *Barron's* that its selling and administrative costs were only one-quarter those of most competitors. In 1990 the company had an entire corporate staff of only 22 and a marketing department of only six.

Revenues fell to $580.8 million in fiscal 1989, and net income to $103.9 million. During the year available supplies of styrene monomer (Sterling Chemicals' major product) and acrylonitrile increased while demand weakened, resulting in price declines from what had been unprecedented levels. The dollar strengthened appreciably, reducing demand for Sterling Chemicals' product line overseas. There was a general slowdown in the housing and automobile industries, and fashion changes resulted in decreased demands for acrylic fibers. Sterling Chemicals' income-to-sales ratio of 18 percent remained enviable, and its stock reached a record high,

KEY DATES

1986: Sterling Chemicals, Inc. is established to acquire and operate Monsanto Co.'s petrochemical plant in Texas City, Texas.

1988: The company goes public.

1992: The pulp-chemical division of Albright & Wilson is purchased.

1996: A leveraged buyout group buys the company and renames it Sterling Chemicals Holding.

2001: The company files for Chapter 11 bankruptcy protection.

2002: The company emerges from bankruptcy and changes its name back to Sterling Chemicals, Inc.

2005: Sterling Chemicals exits the acrylonitrile market.

exceeding $18 a share. The company was entering a downward spiral, however, that would not end until 1994.

SETBACKS BEGIN IN 1990

During fiscal 1990 Sterling Chemicals' revenues fell to $506 million and its net income to $59.1 million. A severe freeze along the Texas Gulf Coast in December 1989 resulted in a two-week shutdown of the company's production and some degree of impairment for up to two months. The Iraqi invasion of Kuwait in August 1990 disrupted the styrene market as prices for raw materials escalated rapidly. The worldwide market for acrylonitrile continued to be affected adversely by the weakening in the East Asian market for synthetic fiber, particularly acrylic fiber. Sterling Chemicals, however, announced completion of three projects: the modernization of its styrene monomer plant, an increase in the capacity of the acrylonitrile plant, and expansion of the acetic acid facility. By August 1990 Sterling Chemicals had spent about $150 million to upgrade its production facilities.

During fiscal 1991 revenues rose to $542.7 million, but net income dropped to $36.8 million. Management cited oversupply in the petrochemical industry, including the opening of new styrene plants in the Far East, and declining demand as the reasons for lower profitability. A cogeneration project was under construction as a joint venture with a subsidiary of Union Carbide Industrial Gases, Inc., in order to provide added supplies of steam and electricity. This facility was completed in 1992.

Sterling Chemicals suffered a loss of $5.9 million in fiscal 1992, with its revenues plummeting to a five-year low of $430.5 million. Management cited worldwide oversupply of styrene monomer and a shutdown of acrylonitrile production for routine maintenance. It also reported that a profit would have been earned except for a one-time charge for prior years recognizing liability for post-retirement benefits.

In August 1992 Sterling Chemicals purchased the pulp-chemical division of Albright & Wilson, a division of Tenneco Canada, Inc., for about $302 million. The acquisition included four Canadian facilities for the production of sodium chlorate, used in the bleaching of pulp for the manufacture of paper. It also included ERCO Systems Group, which was licensing and constructing large-scale generators to convert the sodium chlorate into chlorine dioxide as an environmentally preferred alternative to elemental chlorine in pulp bleaching. In making this purchase Sterling Chemicals raised its long-term debt from $72.6 million to $300.2 million.

Sterling Chemicals increased its fiscal 1993 revenues to $518.8 million because of $119.3 million from the newly acquired pulp-chemical business. The company suffered its second consecutive annual loss, ending $5.4 million in the red. Its stock sank to a record low of $3.50 a share during the year. Management noted that, with three styrene monomer plants being constructed in East Asia and one in Europe, supply for the chemical seemed likely to exceed demand for several more years. It also said demand for acrylonitrile from export customers had weakened. The pulp-chemicals business was profitable despite lower demand than forecast, attributed to the recessionary North American economy.

MARKET IMPROVEMENT MID-DECADE

The fortunes of Sterling Chemicals turned around in 1994. Revenues increased to a solid $700.8 million, and net income was $19.1 million. The company said that demand for its petrochemical products, including styrene monomer, had grown significantly during the year, primarily because of a healthier world economy. Sterling Chemicals' pulp-chemical plants were operating near full capacity at the end of the fiscal year. Eight ERCO Systems generators started up in 1994, and several more were under construction in China.

Sterling Chemicals' pride in its impressive environmental and safety record was shaken in May

1994, when an ammonia leak in one of its Texas City plants sent nearly 1,400 people to a local hospital for treatment. Eight of them were hospitalized. Officials determined that the leak was caused by a worker mistakenly turning a valve that controlled hot water flow to an ammonia vaporizer.

In the best performance by Sterling Chemicals since it became a public company, revenues reached a record $1.03 billion in fiscal 1995, and net income came to more than $150 million. Strong worldwide demand and market growth from global economic expansion benefited sales of both styrene monomer and acrylonitrile. High North American demand led to record production and sales volume of chlorine dioxide, derived from sodium chlorate. Royalty revenues from installed generator technology also grew. During the fiscal year the company's major customers were British Petroleum and its subsidiaries, accounting for 16.5 percent of revenues, and Mitsubishi International Corp., accounting for 12.6 percent. Revenue from exports came to nearly 52 percent of the total, with Asia accounting for 64 percent and Europe for 36 percent.

During the fiscal year Sterling Chemicals reduced its long-term debt by $89 million, to $103.6 million. The company obtained a $275 million bank credit facility, and the pulp-chemicals unit received a separate $60 million credit facility. Most of this new financing was earmarked for a three-year, $200 million capital-spending program. Under construction at Texas City in 1995, in conjunction with BP Chemicals, was an expansion of acetic acid capacity and a world-scale unit for the production of methanol. About half the methanol would be used as a raw material for the production of acetic acid, with the rest available to BP. A partial-oxidation unit by Praxair, Inc. would refurbish Sterling Chemicals' existing synthesis gas reformer, freeing it for methanol production. This unit also would convert natural gas into carbon monoxide and hydrogen for use in the production of acetic acid and plasticizers.

Also under construction in 1995 was Sterling Chemicals' first sodium chlorate plant in the United States. The 110,000-ton-per-year facility in Valdosta, Georgia, would be the company's second largest for this purpose and would increase its capacity to produce this chemical by 30 percent. Production was scheduled to begin in December 1996.

Sterling Chemicals announced on January 29, 1996, that it had entered discussions with a number of third parties with respect to the possible sale of the company in a single transaction or a series of related transactions. Shares of the stock immediately rose 35 percent, from $9.25 to $12.50 a share. Employees and directors owned about 30 percent of the stock in 1995.

At the end of fiscal 1995 Sterling Chemicals' 290-acre facility in Texas City included one of the world's largest units for the production of styrene monomer, with an annual capacity of more than 1.5 billion pounds. This unit accounted for more than one-third of the company's total chemical production capacity and for about 11 percent of total domestic capacity of this chemical. Derivatives of styrene monomer, a raw material, were being used in the production of foam products such as ice chests, residential sheathing, egg cartons, insulation, and protective packagings; housings for computers, telephones, videocassettes, small home appliances, and automotive parts; and for tableware, luggage, packing, toys, textile products, and synthetic rubber products.

Sterling Chemicals' annual production capacity of acrylonitrile was in excess of 700 million pounds. It was the second largest domestic producer of the chemical, with about 31 percent of total domestic capacity. Produced using ammonia, air, and propylene as raw materials, it was being used in synthetic fibers for apparel, rugs, and blankets; in polymer products for casings for ice chests, hard luggage, calculators, telephone handsets, and computers; in automotive parts; and for synthetic rubber products.

Sterling Chemicals' share of domestic capacity for acetic acid production came to 13 percent and was scheduled to reach nearly 800 million pounds annually with the completion of the expansion of the unit. Produced using methanol and carbon monoxide as raw materials, its largest use was in the production of vinyl acetate. BP Chemicals was marketing the unit's production. The company's plasticizer capacity was about 280 million pounds a year. Its plasticizers were being used in producing flexible vinyl plastics for consumer products and building materials. BASF Corp. was marketing Sterling Chemicals' plasticizers.

Sterling Chemicals was the only domestic producer of synthetic lactic acid, with an annual capacity of 19 million pounds. It was being used as a preservative for food products, for the manufacture of acrylic enamel, for silk finishing, and in intravenous solutions. The company was also the only U.S. producer of tertiary butylamine, and one of only three worldwide, with an annual capacity of 21 million pounds. This chemical was being used for silicone caulk, in tires and hoses, and as a chemical intermediate. It was being purchased and resold by Flexsys, a joint venture of Monsanto and Akzo Nobel N.V. The company's annual capacity of sodium cyanide was 100 million pounds. It was being used for electroplating and to enhance the recovery of precious metals. The unit was operated by Sterling Chemicals but owned by Du Pont, which marketed its output.

Sterling Chemicals' revenues from pulp chemicals came to $143.95 million, or 14 percent of the company total, in fiscal 1995. Its net income came to $9.7 million, or 6.4 percent, of the company total. Sterling Pulp Chemicals, Ltd. was the second largest supplier of sodium chlorate to the North American pulp and paper industry, with about 20 percent of the market. It had headquarters in Toronto and held four manufacturing plants: at Buckingham, Quebec; Grand Prairie, Alberta; Thunder Bay, Ontario; and Vancouver, British Columbia. These plants had a combined capacity of about 350,000 tons. The Georgia facility under construction would increase capacity by more than 30 percent. The Buckingham facility also was producing small amounts of sodium chlorite, using sodium chlorate as a raw material. Sodium chlorite was being used as an antimicrobial agent in water treatment, as a disinfectant for fresh produce, for treatment of industrial waste water, and for oil field microbe control. Sterling Pulp Chemicals' ERCO Systems Group was licensing, designing, and overseeing construction of large-scale generators at pulp mill sites. These generators were converting sodium chlorate to chlorine dioxide for the bleaching of kraft pulp. ERCO had supplied about two-thirds of the generators in use worldwide.

OVERCOMING CHALLENGES: 1996 AND BEYOND

During 1996, the company announced that it was seeking alternatives—including a possible sale of the firm—to enhance shareholder value. Sure enough, Sterling Group Inc. and several other investors made a $668.4 million play for the company later that year. The leveraged buyout group completed the deal and changed the name of the company to Sterling Chemicals Holding.

The remainder of the 1990s proved difficult for Sterling Chemicals. While it attempted to strengthen its core business through the purchase of the acrylic fibers business of Cytec Industries, it faced challenges when a fire forced the shutdown of its Texas City petrochemical facility. Operations at its Texas City methanol plant also were shuttered due to low foreign prices of natural gas.

The company brought in Shell Chemical executive Peter De Leeuw in 1998, who was charged with the task of shoring up profits and sales. De Leeuw set several plans in motion to grow the company without incurring additional debt. As such, Sterling Chemicals opted to form joint ventures and strategic partnerships to take advantage of growth opportunities in foreign markets. For example, the company teamed up with BP Chemicals to create Anexco, an acrylonitrile marketing joint venture in Asia.

Despite its attempts to control costs, Sterling Chemicals found itself in a precarious financial situation at the start of the new millennium. Losses in fiscal 1999 had been significant and forced the company to lay off employees. High raw material and energy costs, as well as faltering petrochemical demand, left the company struggling under a $1 billion debt load. Unable to make its interest payments, Sterling Chemicals had no choice but to declare Chapter 11 bankruptcy protection in July 2001. The company's foreign subsidiaries were not included in the filing.

By the time the company emerged from Chapter 11 in December 2002, private investment firm Resurgence Asset Management LLC had made a $60 million equity investment in Sterling Chemicals, giving it an 87 percent stake in the company. As part of its reorganization, the company reverted back to its Sterling Chemicals, Inc. moniker. Restructuring efforts also included the sale of its pulp chemicals business to Superior Propane Inc. for $375 million in cash.

Company management was confident that the reorganization put Sterling Chemicals on track for future growth. Co-CEO David Elkins assured investors in a company press release claiming, "We are very pleased with the outcome of our restructuring process. Our new capital structure is designed to support the company over the long-term, including during recurring cyclical downturns in the market for our petrochemicals products. We believe the steps we have taken to strengthen our balance sheet and improve liquidity have put Sterling on solid footing for the future."

Resurgence took Sterling Chemicals public once again in 2003. Two years later, the company announced that it would shutter its unprofitable acrylonitrile and derivative businesses. By this time, Sterling Chemicals was focused on its core petrochemical products—styrene, acetic acid, and plasticizers. By controlling costs and capitalizing on positive cyclical periods in its key markets, the company believed that it was well positioned to overcome any challenges that may come its way.

Robert Halasz
Updated, Christina M. Stansell

PRINCIPAL SUBSIDIARIES

Sterling Chemicals Energy Inc.

PRINCIPAL COMPETITORS

Chevron Phillips Chemical Company LLC; Lyondell Chemical Company; Solutia Inc.

FURTHER READING

Brammer, Rhonda, "Sterling Value?," *Barron's,* October 9, 1995, p. 17.

Byrne, Harlan S., "Sterling Chemicals Inc.," *Barron's,* March 13, 1989, pp. 45-46.

Clouser, Gary, "Sterling Chemicals Reports Fiscal 2002 Loss of $35.9-Mil," *Platts International Petrochemical Report,* December 20, 2002.

———, "US' Sterling to Split Pulp, Petrochemicals Businesses," *Platts International Petrochemical Report,* May 17, 2002.

Fletcher, Sam, "Oil Slump Helps Monsanto Sale," *Houston Post,* August 20, 1986, p. 1E.

———, "Sterling Chemicals Able to Beat Highs and Lows of Price Extremes," *Houston Post,* August 6, 1990, p. 4C.

Holman, Kelly, "Sterling Chemicals Goes Bankrupt," *Daily Deal,* July 18, 2001.

Johnson, Don, "US' Sterling Chemicals to Exit Acrylonitrile, Derivative Markets," *Platts International Petrochemical Report,* September 23, 2005.

"Sterling Chemicals Agrees to Be Bought by Investment Group for $668.4 Million," *Wall Street Journal,* April 26, 1996, p. A4.

"Sterling Sells Pulp Business," *Chemical Market Reporter,* January 6, 2003.

Towasser, Nicholas, "Sterling's Reorg Plan Confirmed by U.S. Bankruptcy Court," *Platts International Petrochemical Report,* November 29, 2002.

Wruck, Karen Hopper, and Michael C. Jensen, "Science, Specific Knowledge, and Total Quality Management," *Journal of Accounting & Economics,* 18 (1994), pp. 247-87.

stewart

Stewart Information Services Corporation

---■---

1980 Post Oak Boulevard, Suite 800
Houston, Texas 77056
U.S.A.
Telephone: (713) 625-8100
Toll Free: (800) 729-1900
Fax: (713) 552-9523
Web site: http://www.stewart.com

Public Company
Incorporated: 1908 as Stewart Title Guaranty Company
Employees: 8,961
Operating Revenues: $2.18 billion (2005)
Stock Exchanges: New York
Ticker Symbol: STC
NAIC: 524127 Direct Title Insurance Carriers

■ ■ ■

Headquartered in Houston, Texas, Stewart Information Services Corporation provides title insurance and related services through more than 8,000 offices and agencies in the United States and abroad. Through Stewart Title, National Title, and other subsidiaries, the company writes title insurance policies. Stewart Information Services also provides mortgage origination process services, including credit reports, property valuations, property information reports, and tax services, in addition to offering post-closing lender services and automated county clerk land records. The company's real estate information division comprises Stewart Transaction Solutions, which offers an Internet-based transaction management platform under the name SureClose. Stewart's REIData subsidiary provides electronic transaction services. The company offers its various title insurance and information services to a broad variety of customers, such as government entities, real estate developers, and mortgage lenders. Its international operations are located in more than a dozen countries, including Australia, Canada, Costa Rica, the Dominican Republic, Mexico, Poland, Turkey, and the United Kingdom.

ORIGINS

The origins of Stewart Information Services Corporation can be traced to 1893 in Galveston, Texas, after Mac Stewart, a young Galveston lawyer, bought the Gulf City Abstract Company and renamed it Stewart Law & Land Title Office. He operated the business of issuing abstracts until 1905, when he and his brother, Minor Stewart, offered the first title insurance in Texas by providing indemnity against loss due to title claims. In 1897, W. C. Morris, an Arkansas orphan who grew up to become a significant player in the company's future, joined the firm as a stenographer and later married into the Stewart family. In 1900, the great Galveston hurricane together with the discovery of oil in Beaumont in 1901 greatly accelerated the growth of the fledgling firm by creating an urgent need for accurate land documentation in Texas. Chartered in 1908, the Stewart Title Guaranty Company became the first title insurance underwriter in the state, and it soon began opening offices in Dallas, Houston, San Antonio, El Paso, and other cities under the leadership of W.C. Morris. In 1956, the company expanded beyond Texas, opening an office in New Mexico. By 1960, the company had operations in Arizona, California, Florida, and Louisiana under the leadership of Stewart Morris, Sr., who became president of Stewart Title when both his father and cousin died in 1950. At the same time, his brother Carloss Morris took over Stewart Guaranty. The company hit another milestone in 1965, when it established its first affiliation with a computerized title operation in Los Angeles. Two years later in 1967, Stewart assisted in forming another computerized title plant in Houston.

EXPANSION IN U.S. AND
OVERSEAS BEGINS IN 1970

In 1970, Stewart Information Services Corporation was formed as a holding company, presaging future expansion into the broader field of real estate information. One year after the company went public in 1972, the firm built a new corporate office in Houston, a sign of Stewart's growing prosperity. In 1975, brothers Carloss Morris and Stewart Morris, Sr., who led the company's expansion after their father's death in 1950, assumed control of management with plans for greater expansion in the title insurance and real estate industry. The brothers subsequently invested $2.4 million in 1977 to develop computer services for the title industry in order to chart operations and real estate information. By 1981, Stewart Information Services Corporation was issuing policies through more than 1,000 offices in 38 states. Six years later in 1987, it was issuing polices through more than 2,000 U.S. offices as its Stewart affiliate, Landata Geo Services, the company's software research and development arm, was winning international contracts in the Caribbean, Egypt, Morocco, and Guatemala for geographic information systems and aerial photography. Landata Systems soon became the nation's largest provider of software for the title industry. When Stewart, Jr., struck a deal with Microsoft Chairman Bill Gates to adapt its system to Windows, it catapulted the firm well ahead of its competition.

Stewart entered the 1990s with 2,700 offices issuing polices throughout all 50 states. The company's expanding business included searching, examining, closing, and insuring titles to homes and other properties. Stewart's customers encompassed home buyers and sellers, attorneys, builders, developers, lenders, and real estate brokers. Stewart Information also sold computer-related services and information to the real estate industry from its database systems. Its Landata Systems was producing digitized map systems and other information for U.S. and foreign governments and private entities.

The company formed Stewart Information International in 1992 to coordinate its various global enterprises. The international subsidiary was listed on the New York Stock Exchange in 1994, becoming the first stock quoted on the New York Exchange on the first trading day of 1995. The international subsidiary also provided some groundbreaking services to former Soviet republics and other emerging nations. In Moldavia, the company issued 53,000 deed certificates to peasants who worked the land that was previously owned by the Soviet government or communist communes. The firm also introduced a registry of mortgages on movable property in Hungary so that people could obtain credit from foreign banks to buy needed farm equipment.

By 1998, the firm was offering title insurance and other real estate information products and services through 150 subsidiaries and more than 3,800 U.S. offices and several foreign countries. The company had pioneered the use of computers in the industry, transforming a centuries-old system of hand-written land records into a fully automated system of electronic information storage and retrieval. In June 1998, with the acquisition of First Arkansas Title Corporation of Pine Bluff, Stewart Information announced that its subsidiary title insurers had begun offering services through more than 4,000 offices worldwide. As one of the country's leading title insurance companies, Stewart Information intended to make further acquisitions to spur growth and profitability. It also continued to invest heavily in technology to improve automated services to its numerous clients. With its electronic commerce tool, SureClose, clients could order via its network or the Internet a range of services, including flood determination, valuations and closing document preparation, as well as traditional title and closing services. The SureClose system worked by routing orders through Stewart's National Order Center and directing them to the appropriate agent within its national and international network. The company was on a profitable run by the end of 1998 with year-end record revenues approaching $1 billion. The company attributed these results to low interest rates, strong job growth, robust housing sales, and a wave of refinancings, all of which enabled it to

KEY DATES

1893: Company founded as Stewart Law & Land Title Office.
1908: Stewart Title Guaranty Company is chartered and becomes first title insurance underwriter in Texas.
1950: Stewart Morris, Sr., become president of Stewart Title and brother Carloss Morris takes over management of Stewart Guaranty.
1970: Stewart Information Services Corporation is formed as a holding company.
1972: Company goes public.
1992: Stewart Information International is formed.
1999: Malcolm S. Morris and Stewart Morris, Jr., are elected as co-CEOs.
2002: Company opens new subsidiary in Mexico, becoming first licensed title insurance underwriter approved by the Mexican government.
2003: Company expands into Asia with purchase of majority stake in Escrow A&K in Seoul, Republic of Korea.
2005: Stewart Title Ltd. opens office in London, England.

open new offices, make new acquisitions, and compete in all domestic U.S. real estate markets.

In 1999, new leadership assumed control of Stewart Information Services Corporation when Malcolm S. Morris and Stewart Morris, Jr., sons of Carloss and Stewart, Sr., respectively, were elected co-CEOs. Malcolm was also elected chairman of the board of directors, while Stewart was elected to the additional position of president of the company. After resigning their posts, Carloss Morris and Stewart Morris were elected advisory directors. Having worked in every department of the company since they were very young, both Malcolm and Stewart, Jr., stepped up in 1991 to assume management of the company's core businesses. As Malcolm managed the underwriting subsidiaries, Stewart, Jr., had pioneered the technology end of the business since 1975. The company prospered throughout the 1990s, making *Fortune* Magazine's list of the 100 fastest growing companies in 1998 and 1999.

2000 AND BEYOND

In May 2000, Stewart Information announced that its title insurers were offering products through more than 5,000 offices in the U.S. and abroad. The company passed the 5,000 mark with the acquisition of Security Lake Title Guaranty, Inc. of Moses Lake, Washington. Stewart Information's strategy continued to call for the pursuit of acquisition and expansion opportunities that would strengthen its presence as the premiere national title and real estate information services provider.

For the year 2000, Stewart Information reported revenues of $935 million, a 12.7 percent decrease from 1999. The company attributed the results to softening market conditions from a slowing economy and expenditures to expand the company. Although the company had made sizeable cuts in staff in existing operations, its staffing numbers nevertheless remained flat because of new acquisitions and growth in the commercial and technology areas. Stewart had especially tried to position itself for growth in the higher-profit commercial lines of the business. To this end, the company expanded offices and personnel in its National Title Services unit, which served the national commercial and residential markets. The company anticipated better results ahead with new investments in e-commerce to expand its connectivity and productivity with clients.

In January 2001, Stewart International, the wholly owned subsidiary of Stewart Information Services opened a new office in the Dominican Republic to provide title guaranty, escrow, and closing services for buyers and sellers of residential and commercial property throughout the country. The company also announced plans in July to make a public offering of 2.5 million shares of its common stock. The company intended to use the proceeds of the offering for acquiring new companies or assets complimentary to its own business, as well for working capital and paying off debt.

In January 2002, Stewart Information Services opened a new subsidiary in Mexico City, becoming the first licensed title insurance underwriter approved by the government of Mexico. By bringing its international efforts to Mexico, the company aimed to create a network of representatives across the country to facilitate the title investigation process. Stewart Information believed that having title insurance available for Mexican property would serve to move more foreign capital into the country. At the same time, Landata Group Inc., another Stewart subsidiary, announced the formation of a new operating subsidiary, Ultima Corporation, to develop and deliver the industry standard for title plant software through technological innovation, product integration, and information distribution via the Internet. Landata Group also joined with IBM to modernize public land records for the Romanian government. In April 2002, moreover, the company's subsidiary, Landata Research,

Inc., changed its name to Stewart Business Information to better inform customers of its Stewart affiliation.

In January 2003, Landata Group merged two operating entities to form Stewart Geo Technologies, an international provider of geospatial solutions, including mapping services, geographic information systems (GIS) application development, GIS consulting, and Internet data integration and publication. Stewart Geo Technologies also acquired the assets of GlobeXplorer Inc., a provider of satellite images and aerial photography via the Internet. Stewart Geo Technologies subsequently set up GlobeXplorer as an operating subsidiary, which then acquired Citipix aerial imagery from Eastman Kodak Company. The acquisition of Citipix imagery allowed GlobeXplorer to continue to meet customer requirements for new imagery. Stewart Information Services expanded into Asia in September with the purchase of a majority stake in Escrow A&K, located in Seoul, Republic of Korea. The company was subsequently renamed Stewart Korea Ltd, which would provide escrow services, title searches, and reinsurance to enhance investment opportunities. In October, the company formed a new corporation, Stewart REI Data Inc. to provide comprehensive information solutions to title agents, lenders, real estate agents, and brokers, federal, state and local governments, and other markets. By year's end, Stewart Information Service's revenues rose to a record $2.24 billion. The company also hit records for profits, earnings per share, title orders, and book value per share.

Stewart Title Guaranty Co. announced the formation of a wholly owned subsidiary, Stewart Realty Solutions, in January 2004. The new subsidiary aimed to develop and market a bundle of information services, technology applications, title insurance and closing services, and Internet-based real estate transaction management solutions for U.S. realty firms.

During this time, Stewart International opened a new office in Istanbul, Turkey, offering escrow, title guaranty and closing services to foreign buyers and lenders in Turkey. The company also issued its first commercial title guaranty in Slovakia. The title guaranty covered a portfolio of office buildings in Bratislava with an estimated value of 90 million euros or $120 million dollars. This transaction represented a general move on the part of the company to pursue opportunities in the emerging economies of Central and Eastern Europe, especially after the acceptance of these countries into the European Union.

In April 2005, Stewart Mortgage Information began offering a suite of origination and post-closing products and services to assist mortgage brokers making the transition to becoming mortgage bankers. In November of that year, Stewart Title Ltd., the European title insurance unit of Stewart Title Guaranty Company, expanded into London, England. The new office was established to oversee Stewart Title Ltd.'s U.K. operations and business in Spain, Czech Republic, Poland, Slovakia, Slovenia, Turkey, Romania, and Australia.

Bruce P. Montgomery

PRINCIPAL SUBSIDIARIES

Stewart Title Company; Stewart Title Guaranty Company; Stewart Mortgage Information; Stewart REI Data Inc.; Landata Group Inc.; Landata Systems Inc.; GlobeXplorer LLC; InterCity Companies; Asset Preservation Inc.; Stewart Water Information; Stewart Information International Inc.

PRINCIPAL COMPETITORS

Fidelity National Financial Inc.; The First American Corporation; LandAmerica Financial Group Inc.

FURTHER READING

"Arkansas Title Insurance Company has Joined the Stewart Information Services Corporations Family of Insurers," *PR Newswire*, January 20, 1998.

"Easy Win for Stewart," *Arkansas Business*, April 15, 2002.

Finkelstein, Brad, "Intercounty's Failure Spurs Lawsuit," *National Mortgage News*," October 9, 2000.

"Landata Research, Inc. Announces Name Change to Stewart Business Information," *PR Newswire*, April 2, 2002.

"Recent Acquisitions Puts Stewart at 4,000 Mark," *PR Newswire*, June 24, 1998.

Sinnock, Bonnie, "Stewart Information Services Brings its International Efforts to Mexico," *National Mortgage News*, January 7, 2002.

"Stewart Announces All Time Record Revenues and Earnings," *PR Newswire*, February 11, 1999.

"Stewart Celebrates Growth to 5,000 Offices," *PR Newswire*, May 18, 2000.

"Stewart Does Title Policy in Slovakia," *National Mortgage News*, September 20, 2004.

"Stewart Information Services Corp.," *Houston Business Journal*, August 15, 1988.

Stewart Information Services Corporation Management Changes,"*PR Newswire*, January 31, 2000.

"Stewart Information Services Corporation Reports Earnings," *PR Newswire*, February 13, 1998.

Walden, George, "Federal Lawsuit Examines Stewart Title's Practices," *Arkansas Business*, November 19, 2001.

Stimson Lumber Company Inc.

---

520 S.W. Yamhill Street, Suite 700
Portland, Oregon 97204
U.S.A.
Telephone: (503) 222-1676
Toll Free: (800) 445-9758
Fax: (503) 242-1588
Web site: http://www.stimsonlumber.com

Private Company
Incorporated: 1923
Employees: 2,000
Sales: $245 million (2004 est.)
NAIC: 321210 Veneer, Plywood, and Engineered Wood Product Manufacturing; 113100 Timber Tract Operations; 113210 Forest Nurseries and Gathering of Forest Products; 321113 Sawmills

■ ■ ■

Stimson Lumber Company Inc. is one of the oldest forest products companies in the United States. With about 500,000 acres of timberland in the western states, the company has manufacturing operations at 14 locations in Idaho, Montana, Oregon, and Washington. Products include dimension lumber, boards, posts, plywood, hardboard paneling, siding, and decking made from fir, pine, and cedar. Stimson Lumber Company is a participant in the American Forest Products and Paper Association's Sustainable Forestry Initiative program.

STAKING A CLAIM IN TIMBER IN THE 19TH CENTURY

In 1850, Thomas Douglas (T. D.) Stimson and a business partner staked a 40-acre logging claim in Michigan and began a successful logging business there together. After the two parted ways several years later, Stimson continued to acquire timberlands on his own, to establish lumber camps, and to sell logs to mills in Muskegon, Michigan. He left his business to pursue a career in mining when oil was discovered across the border in Canada, and by 1864, he had lost everything he had.

A determined man, Stimson returned to logging in the second half of the 1860s, and by 1871 he had acquired enough acreage in northern Michigan to establish his own mills, which he equipped with modern steam-powered machinery. In 1873, Stimson incorporated the company as Stimson Clark Manufacturing Company. By the early 1880s, Stimson's business was the third largest mill operation in Muskegon, Michigan. In 1885, he moved to Chicago, leaving management of the business to his sons. However, the increasingly poor quality of timber and worker unrest in the Midwest led him to travel westward again in search of timberland for further growth. In 1888, he set out with his sons, sailing up the Columbia River to Portland and on to the Puget Sound. They explored the backwoods for weeks, impressed by the quality of the timber and the density of tree growth. By November, the men had arrived in Seattle, a saltwater port that assured a continuous market for lumber.

COMPANY PERSPECTIVES

■

One of the most valuable assets of Stimson Lumber Company is its forestlands. The primary purpose of these lands is to provide high quality harvestable timber on an economical basis through sustainable forestry practices. Sustainable forestry means managing our forests to meet the needs of the present without compromising the ability of future generations to meet their own needs. This is done by practicing a land stewardship which integrates the growing, nurturing, and harvesting of trees for useful wood products with the conservation of soil, air and water quality and fish and wildlife habitat.

Stimson decided to move his business to the Pacific Northwest and sent two of his sons, Willard Horace and Charles Douglas, ahead to acquire timberlands there in 1889. Willard purchased acreage in Snohomish County, on Hood Canal, in the area around Tillamook, Oregon, and in California. Charles bought a sawmill in Ballard, Washington. In January 1890, the Stimson Mill Company incorporated in Ballard and within a month was processing lumber, laths, and shingles. Within a few years, the Stimson Mill Company was on its way to becoming the largest and most modern mill in the Seattle area. In 1892, when demand for lumber slowed, Charles looked south to California to sell the company's excess capacity.

Willard Horace took over the business after his father died in 1898, the year in which Charles Willard, Stimson's grandson, also joined Stimson Lumber, and soon showed his acumen for tough negotiating. By 1912, Charles Willard led the company in the sale of the Ballard mill and moved Stimson Mill Company's operations to Hood Canal to log surrounding timberlands. In 1923, he purchased one of the oldest mills in Seattle, the Brace-Hergert Mill. The mill became known as the Stimson Lumber Company; it employed more than 200 men and produced about 50 million feet of fir lumber annually.

SURVIVING SETBACKS IN THE FIRST HALF OF THE 20TH CENTURY

However, by 1929, the area around Hood Canal had been cleared of quality timber, and the company faced its second move—this time to the Tillamook Region of western Oregon to make use of 25,000 acres of old growth forest that T. D. Stimson had purchased. During the period from 1929 to 1981, the company reinvested in timberland holdings and diversified its product line. Harold Miller, Charles' son-in-law, led the Stimson Lumber Company in building a state-of-the-art sawmill in Forest Grove and in remaining viable in an increasingly competitive market.

Throughout the Great Depression, Stimson Lumber never shut its mills or laid off workers. Even the fires in western Oregon during the 1930s and 1940s, the "Tillamook Burn," did not halt its growth, and in the mid-1940s, the company began making hardboard or "sandalwood" out of its burned, cracked, and stained green wood through its Stimson Forest Fiber Products subsidiary. Hardboard is a product similar to particleboard, used for paneling and floors.

By the late 1940s and early 1950s, resource shortages led to more acquisitions again—of related businesses as well as tracts of timberland. Stimson Lumber bought up parcels ranging in size from a few to 1,000 acres in Columbia, Clatsop, and Yamhill counties in Oregon and in Clark County in Washington. A 10,000-acre purchase of redwood timberland in Del Norte County, California in the 1950s led to the establishment of Miller Redwood Company as a subsidiary.

In 1962, the company extended its reach yet further when it purchased Northwest Petrochemical Company in Anacortes, Washington, a company that manufactured phenol, a chemical used in processing hardboard. Northwest Petrochemical later supplied the phenol used in Stimson Lumber Company's plywood plant in Merlin, Oregon, which it purchased in 1976. In the mid-1960s, Miller waged a hearty battle against the Johnson administration to keep the company's redwood holdings out of a proposed national park with the support of then-governor Ronald Reagan. In the end, those in charge shifted the park boundaries, and Miller ceded only a few thousand acres.

MODERN CONCERNS: 1980-2000

The 1980s were a decade of growing shortages of raw materials for the lumber products industry, stemming in part from the export of logs to Far East. The company continued on its path of acquisitions. In 1980, Miller led the company's largest purchase to date—almost 28,000 acres in the Grand Ronde region in western Oregon—leaving it with total holdings of almost 70,000 acres. After Miller died in 1981, company leadership passed to Darrell Schroeder, an employee who had been with the company since 1946. Under Schroeder, the company continued to expand steadily,

KEY DATES

◾

1890: The Stimson Mill Company is formed.

1898: Stimson dies; William Horace Stimson takes charge of the company; Charles Willard Stimson joins the company.

1912: The company moves its operations to Hood Canal.

1923: The company purchases the Brace-Hergert Mill, which becomes known as the Stimson Lumber Company.

1929: Harold Miller leads the company in a move to the area around Tillamook, Oregon.

1962: Stimson Lumber Company purchases Northwest Petrochemical Company.

1981: Harold Miller dies; Darrell Schroeder takes over leadership of the company.

1991: Dan Dutton succeeds Schroeder as head of Stimson Lumber Company.

1994: Stimson buys Champion International Corporation's manufacturing facilities at Bonner and Libby, Montana

2000: Andrew Miller becomes company president; Stimson Lumber buys Idaho Forest Industries.

building a dimension mill in Forest Grove and acquiring a heavy timber mill in Clatskanie and a cutting mill in Oregon City. However, despite its acquisitions, Stimson felt the pressure of shortages, and, in 1988, shut down the second shift at its Clatskanie mill.

In 1990, the spotted owl came under the protection of the Endangered Species Act, and tensions between environmentalists and those in the lumber business really began to heat up. The owl's endangered species status put thousands of acres of federal land in western Oregon off limits to harvest and led to inflated timber prices. At the same time, fewer housing starts resulted in a sagging lumber and plywood market. The timber industry as a whole embarked on a roller coaster ride; while prices rebounded briefly at the start of 1993, they soon after tumbled rapidly. As a result, there were 36 mill closures in the Pacific Northwest in 1992, and 27 in 1993. After Dan Dutton succeeded Schroeder as head of Stimson Lumber Company in 1991, the company, which employed about 2,000 in five states, closed an old-growth-dependent sawmill in Oregon City.

Stimson also made the decision to increase its land base as a means of assuring a stable supply of logs for its sawmills, and, by 1993, had increased its timberland holdings from about 80,000 acres to about 120,000. In addition, the company improved its mills and invested more in thinning and fertilizer as a means of growing more timber in a relatively short period of time. As a result, by 1993, only 36 million board feet of Stimson's raw materials came from public lands under contract for logging, down two-thirds from 1989. In 1996, it purchased another 107,000 acres from Plum Creek in northeast Washington and north Idaho in the Colville National Forest.

The company also pursued an active course of manufacturing acquisitions. In 1994, it bought Champion International Corporation's manufacturing facilities at Bonner and Libby, Montana—three lumber mills and two plywood operations, including one of the world's largest plywood mills. The 1996 Plum Creek purchase added another mill in Colville, Washington. By the end of the 1990s, Stimson owned a mill at Clatskanie, Oregon, two sawmills and a hardboard plant at Forest Grove, Oregon, a plywood plant and stud mill in Bonner, Montana, a plywood plant at Libby, Montana, and about 290,000 acres in four northwestern states and northern California. It employed about close to 2,000 people.

2000 AND BEYOND

In 2000, Stimson Lumber bought Idaho Forest Industries of Coeur d'Alene, bulking up its acreage by another 90,000 and gaining three mills in an area where it already operated five mills. Crown Pacific sold all of its Montana land to Stimson—16,500 in northwest Montana—bringing Stimson's holdings to more than 400,000 acres. That same year, at the request of Home Depot, Stimson's largest customer, all of its forestlands and its log procurement program underwent a rigorous independent third-party review for compliance with the sustainable forestry initiative program standards. "We have a heartfelt view of the land," Andrew Miller, who became company president in 2000, asserted in a 2000 *Spokesman-Review* article of that year. He added, "Timberland is a multi-generational investment. Some of the property we're logging for the third time."

However, the company went head-to-head with environmentalists when it sued for road access to the land in Idaho it had purchased from Plum Creek, which was surrounded by the LeClerc grizzly bear management area in the Selkirk Mountains of the Colville National Forest. According to the Alaska Native Lands Conservation Act and Forest Service regulations, the agency must provide roads to private lands within National Forest boundaries. The Plum Creek land, according to environmentalists, was within area was critical to recovery of grizzly bears, caribou, lynx, and bull trout.

The U.S. Forest Service decided to allow the company to build or reopen almost three miles of road in the Colville National Forest in 2001. Stimson insisted it would mitigate the impacts of its logging on wildlife by limiting the size of cuttings and cutting only at certain times of year. The non-profit Defenders of Wildlife petitioned the Fish and Wildlife Service to designate the area critical habitat, while the Sierra Club sued the Forest Service and the U.S. Fish and Wildlife Service in federal court.

In a more positive exchange also that year, Stimson sold nearly 25,000 acres of redwood land in California to Save-the-Redwoods League, its Mill Creek property, containing 125 acres of old growth redwood, home to several endangered species of fish. Andrew Miller in *San Jose Mercury News* in 2001 said of the sale, "The trend going forward in California for resource businesses is only getting more challenging and negative. Oregon and Washington have less bureaucracy and fewer costly citizen lawsuits." Elsewhere in the *San Francisco Chronicle* that year, Miller called the land an "ecological crown jewel" because it connected "the national park with the state park, both beautiful old-growth parks, and connects the Pacific Ocean with the U.S. Forest Service land."

Meanwhile domestic lumber prices were falling in the face of competition from Canadian woods suppliers. In 2002, they fell yet further fell after the 2002 implementation of a 27 percent softwood duty on Canada. The tariff, intended to limit Canadian imports led companies from north of the border to beat the penalty by maximizing production. When their American rivals did the same, lumber prices hit record lows. By 2003, slumping lumber prices led to the closure of five mills in the Pacific Northwest. Stimson closed its mill in Libby, Montana, which had been losing $500,000 a month.

At the end of 2005, the company closed its Atlas mill in Coeur d'Alene, putting 120 people out of work. This mill had manufactured cedar and pine boards for siding, fencing, decking, and trim, but customers' preference for vinyl siding and composite decking made it obsolete. However, there were purchases as well: In 2004, Stimson bought a small remanufacturing mill in Hauser, Idaho, adding to its three sawmills in North Idaho. It also began work on 4,000 feet of road in the Kaniksu National Forest in Northeast Washington to gain access to additional parcels of its land in the South Fork Mountain Roadless area.

Carrie Rothburd

PRINCIPAL COMPETITORS

Georgia-Pacific Corporation; International Paper Company; Weyerhauser Company.

FURTHER READING

Drumheller, Susan, "Idaho Forest Service Must Consider Lumber Company's Plan," *Spokesman-Review*, February 8, 2001.

"Exporting Logs Not a Panacea," *Oregonian*, February 9, 1988.

"Forest Owners See Fairer Future in Measure 37," *Oregonian*, December 22, 2004.

Greenwood, John, "Tariffs Backfiring on U.S. Industry: Higher Production Depresses Prices," *National Post's Financial Post & FP Investing*, July 2, 2003, p. FP6.

"Growing Its Own," *Oregonian*, April 25, 1993.

Hagengruber, James, "Lumber Company Gets Approval to Build Forest Access Road Near Idaho Border," *Spokesman-Review*, March 24, 2004.

Kay, Jane, "Smith River Forest Deal fits Del Norte's Redwood Parks," *San Francisco Chronicle*, June 29, 2001, p. A8.

Kramer, Becky, "Portland, Oregon-Based Lumber Firm Turns to Idaho to Increase Its Timberland," *Spokesman-Review*, November 19, 2000.

Olsen, Ken, "Analysis of Washington Logging Roads Must Examine Impact on Grizzlies," *Spokesman-Review*, June 26, 1998.

Reese, April, "Endangered Species: Woodland Caribou At Risk From Timber Access Request, Enviros Say," *Greenwire*, March 7, 2001.

Rogers, Paul, "Deal Struck to Preserve 25,000 Acres of California Redwoods," *San Jose Mercury News*, June 28, 2001.

Ross, John R., and Margaret Byrd Adams, *The Builder's Spirit: The History of Stimson Lumber Company*, Portland: John Ross and Associates, 1983.

Villamina, Molly, "Enviros Petition for Caribou Critical Habitat Designation," *Land Letter*, December 19, 2002.

Sunburst Shutters Corporation

3999 Ponderosa Way
Las Vegas, Nevada 89119
U.S.A.
Telephone: (702) 870-4488
Toll Free: (888) 765-9966
Fax: (702) 870-6070
Web site: http://www.sunburstshutters.com

Private Company
Incorporated: 1979
Employees: 640
NAIC: 326122 Plastics Pipe and Pipe Fitting Manufacturing

∎ ∎ ∎

Sunburst Shutters Corporation has 35 retail stores and has licensed more than 75 companies in North America to sell its proprietary "Polywood" shutters. In addition, the company's Polywood shutters and other shutter products are sold through some Home Depot, Expo Design Center, and Lowe's locations nationwide.

1979-90: A HOBBY IN WOODWORKING BECOMES A NATIONWIDE BUSINESS

Ron Swapp founded Sunburst Shutters and Design Studio in 1979 in Phoenix, Arizona. Swapp, then a pharmaceutical sales representative, had been building plantation shutters on his own as a sideline for several years. Believing that the intense sun and climate in Phoenix made it a market rife with opportunity for

shutter sales, Swapp left his sales job and devoted himself to his fledgling business full-time. In 1982, he shortened the name of his company to Sunburst Shutters and hired shop personnel.

Swapp's interest in plantation shutters began when he and his wife decided that they wanted to put plantation shutters in their windows. Plantation shutters are a window treatment made originally of wood. The louvers in the shutter panels open and close—in the case of Sunburst shutters, on a tilt rod. The shutter panels attach securely to a frame around the window, and may be pushed to the side of the window in accordion-like folds. After shopping around and not finding anything that he liked, Swapp ordered the components needed to construct shutters from a company in California and built a set himself. Family, friends, and neighbors saw Swapp's shutters and wanted some of their own, and so, for a while, Swapp built plantation shutters as a hobby in his garage. "None of his first handful of customers paid him more than what it cost him," according to his nephew and future partner, Dix Jarman in a 2004 *Las Vegas Review-Journal* article. "It wasn't a business idea, because he wasn't marking them up at all. My uncle was just doing favors."

In 1987, Swapp hired Dix Jarman to open a branch of Sunburst Shutters in Las Vegas, Nevada. Jarman had just completed Brigham Young University with a degree in business. According to Jarman, who recalled how the partnership began in a *Las Vegas Review-Journal* article in 2004, "I graduated from college in 1987 with a business degree, and he [Swapp] and I were joking around on a family vacation at the beach when he asked me what I was planning to do. He said, 'We should get together

COMPANY PERSPECTIVES

■

Our mission is to bring beautiful, quality shutters into
the homes of our customers that will add value to
their home and last a lifetime.

and put this shutter thing on the map,' so in 1988 we
formed a partnership and I opened an office ... in Las
Vegas."

Las Vegas offered a great market for shutters. "The
town was just starting to kick in," Jarman, who opened
the store with his wife, remembered: "We looked at our
budget and had a goal for 1988, our first year. We
thought $100,000 in sales would cover our hard costs.
Instead we did just over $1 million, and that's when we
knew we really had something." Jarman later opened the
company's Hawaii store.

1990: THE INTRODUCTION OF POLYWOOD AND EXPANSION OVERSEAS

The company grew steadily. In 1990, Jarman moved the
headquarters to Las Vegas. By the early 1990s, with
stores now overseas, Swapp and Jarman began to search
for a wood-alternative to improve their product. Up to
this time, Sunburst's shutters had both mortise and
tenon and dowel joints for durability and were
constructed entirely of furniture-grade, kiln-dried and
water-sealed basswood, but wood would often warp,
chip, crack, or peel. Swapp and Jarman believed that
there was a material better suited for the fabrication of
custom shutters than wood. With the help of some
European companies, they developed a synthetic called
Polywood, an engineered wood substitute that was
stronger than wood, and wouldn't warp, chip, fade,
crack, or peel. Polywood was also waterproof, fire-
resistant, and termite-proof. It insulated up to 70 percent
more efficiently than wood and 1,600 percent more
than aluminum mini-blinds. And although the material
itself cost twice as much as wood, the savings in labor in
building the shutters rendered the final product less
expensive than wood shutters.

With Polywood, the company greatly improved its
manufacturing efficiencies. According to Jarman, "Polywood allowed [Sunburst] to manufacture a quality shutter with much less equipment and fewer problems than
you get with real wood, like one piece is straight but
another isn't; one piece has a knot, another doesn't.
[B]ecause Polywood is man-made, every piece is perfect."

These efficiencies Sunburst allowed Sunburst to open
branch stores in a variety of locations including Southern
California; Dallas and Houston, Texas; and Orlando and
Tampa, Florida.

Within a short time, Sunburst Shutters opened
stores in all the big shutter markets. The first year of
their introduction, Polywood shutters represented more
than $6 million of Sunburst Shutters' revenues, and by
1994, Polywood shutters were the fastest growing shutter brand in the country. In 1995, Polywood shutters accounted for more than 80 percent of all of Sunburst
Shutters' sales.

In 1998, more than $50 million in Polywood shut-
ters were sold in the United States, Canada, Australia,
and Saudi Arabia. By 2003, with new stores opening
regularly, the company had 25 outlets nationwide. By
the end of 2004, with 28 stores, more than six million
shutters sold, and Sunburst products sold in national
home improvement chains, the company was growing at
a rate of 20 percent or more each year.

As part of the company's 25th anniversary celebration, it gave away free shutters to customers across the
nation, "Polywood has been to Sunburst Shutters what
the Model T was to Ford," announced Dix Jarman,
then-chief executive, in an October 1, 2004, company
press release. He continued, "The company now has 10
times as many stores after introducing Polywood to the
window covering market, and more than 75 percent of
our historical revenue is from Polywood shutters, even
though we've only offered Polywood for 13 years."
Sunburst Shutters did about $70 million per year in
sales nationwide in addition to another $30-plus million
in wholesale markets where the company didn't install
its shutters directly. There were 40 employees in Las
Vegas and more than 640 nationwide.

2004–05: THE CHOICE OF ENVIRONMENTALISTS AND CHILDREN'S ADVOCATES

Another boon to business occurred in 2004 when the
United States Consumer Product Safety Commission
and the Window Covering Safety Council jointly
declared October to be National Window Covering
Safety Month. According to figures issued by these
groups a year later, about 359 infants and children had
accidentally strangled to death in window cords from
1981 to 1995, or one every two weeks on average. While
mini-blind companies used the month to remind
consumers to repair or replace corded window coverings
purchased before 2001, Sunburst Shutters promoted its
cordless alternative to blinds. "Shutters open and close
without cords and they cannot be rolled up and down

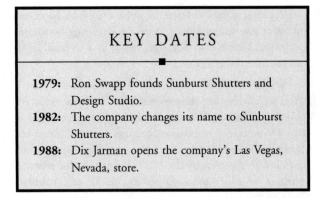

KEY DATES

1979: Ron Swapp founds Sunburst Shutters and Design Studio.
1982: The company changes its name to Sunburst Shutters.
1988: Dix Jarman opens the company's Las Vegas, Nevada, store.

like mini-blinds. These two features significantly reduce any hazard to children," Jarman explained in a 2004 company press release.

In December 2004, Sunburst introduced another product, its Ultra Clear version of the Polywood shutter, which aimed to target more modern tastes. In the Ultra Clear model, a concealed mechanism for controlling the shutters' louvers replaced the tilt rod. However, it was Sunburst's classic wood shutters that were chosen late in 2004 for use in an installment of television's "Extreme Makeover: Home Edition." The show's designers selected Sunburst Shutters to provide the window treatments on one of the show's projects, which was filmed in New Orleans in 2005.

Also in 2005, the company took part in national Earth Day. "In making a real wood shutter, more than 50 percent of a tree is wasted before it even gets to your window," explained Dix Jarman in a press release; however, "the Polywood shutter is made from a recyclable wood substitute and a byproduct of natural gas, not a petroleum-based product." It achieved two environmentally sound goals: reducing the amount of energy used in a home and lessening the manufacturer's impact on natural resources.

Parents as well as environmentalists approved of Sunburst Shutters' products. In 2005, Parents for Window Blind Safety (PWBS), an organization dedicated to educating the public about the hazards that corded window coverings present to children, awarded Sunburst Shutters its Safety Seal of Approval after rigorously testing its products. Sunburst was the first shutter company to receive this award. Following the recognition, PWBS and Sunburst Shutters teamed up to donate more than $4,500 worth of shutters to Kiddie Kare, a daycare center in Phoenix, Arizona. Sunburst Shutters also installed $6,000 worth of shutters in a Nashville daycare facility.

By late 2005, Polywood shutters had become the top selling shutter brand in the world, although the company had never penetrated deeply into the commercial market, except in Las Vegas, Nevada. Swapp, withdrawn from active management of the company, continued to oversee ongoing product development and the development of growth strategies. At the mid-decade point, Swapp and others at Sunburst Shutters strategized how to expand into the commercial market nationwide, confident that they would be able to do so.

Carrie Rothburd

PRINCIPAL COMPETITORS

Overhead Door Corporation; Saunders Brothers.

FURTHER READING

Jones, Chris, "Nevadan At Work," *Las Vegas Review-Journal,* December 5, 2004.

The Susan G. Komen
Breast Cancer Foundation

5005 LBJ Freeway, Suite 250
Dallas, Texas 75244
U.S.A.
Telephone: (972) 855-1600
Toll Free: (800) 462-9273
Fax: (972) 855-1605
Web site: http://www.komen.org

Nonprofit Organization
Incorporated: 1982
Employees: 169Revenues: $209.34 million (2005)
NAIC: 81331 Social Advocacy Organizations

■ ■ ■

The Susan G. Komen Breast Cancer Foundation is a leading advocacy group in the fight against breast cancer. The Komen Foundation is one of the nation's largest private funders of cutting-edge research, which has led to scientific breakthroughs such as the discovery of the BRCA-1 gene. The Komen Foundation promotes awareness of breast cancer in the United States and abroad. Komen is a textbook study in cause-related marketing. Marketers of consumer goods ranging from yogurt to cars have launched special promotions to support the Foundation. More than half the group's donations come from the well-known Komen Race for the Cure Series. More than a simple fundraiser, the Series is an educational vehicle to get people active and involved in the cause. Participants are invited to wear pink back signs in honor and memory of loved ones who have fought breast cancer, while survivors are encouraged to celebrate their survival by wearing pink caps and T-shirts. The Komen Foundation also supports public education, screening, treatment, and advocacy.

FORMED IN 1982

The Susan G. Komen Breast Cancer Foundation was started by Nancy Brinker in honor of her sister who had died of the illness. A former model and homecoming queen, Susan Goodman Komen passed away on August 4, 1980 after fighting breast cancer for three years. She was just 36 years old. Her sister, Nancy Brinker, had promised her she would do something to help other women with the disease. Susan had apparently died after poorly considered treatment options, and patient education would be a key part of the Komen Foundation's mission. The group was launched in Texas in 1982 by Brinker.

Brinker was not the first advocate for breast cancer patients. First Lady Betty Ford had prompted a surge in mammograms in 1974 after she told the country she had breast cancer, helping to open a dialogue about the disease. At the time, there was a taboo about discussing breasts in public. Ford became an enthusiastic early supporter of the Komen Foundation.

Brinker was perhaps ideally qualified for her role as advocate. She relates in her book *Winning the Race* that at age six she had helped her sister stage a neighborhood variety show to raise money for the Polio Association. She was married to Norman Brinker, an entrepreneur who had launched the national restaurant chains Steak & Ale and Chili's Inc. In addition, notes *PR Week*, Brinker had picked up some marketing sense from her former boss, Neiman Marcus founder Stanley Marcus. Brinker was ranked one of the 20th century's most important women by *Ladies Home Journal*.

The Komen Foundation was started with just $200 and a shoebox full of names. One of the earliest fundraising events was a polo tournament that raised $30,000 to benefit Houston's M.D. Anderson Hospital. By the end of 1983, the Foundation had raised $150,000, according to *Winning the Race*. Brinker later told *Business Week* the local oil boom had helped the Foundation's early fundraising efforts.

In 1983, Brinker decided to hold a 5K road race, tapping into the popularity of jogging to get people involved. The first Komen Race for the Cure was held on October 2, 1983 in Dallas and drew 800 people. Though the Race started as a simple community involvement experience and annual mammogram reminder, it later evolved into the Komen Foundation's signature event. Peoria, Illinois, hometown to the Goodman sisters, held its first Race for the Cure in 1985, when 1,250 women participated. Nineteen years later, in 2004, it drew 30,000 people, or one-fifth the town's population, according to the *Chicago Sun-Times*. Peoria was also home to one of the first branches of the Komen Foundation's Affiliate Network.

In 1984, Brinker herself was diagnosed with breast cancer, adding "survivor" to her many roles. Her diagnosis did not appear to slow her down. "She is one of the most outstanding and effective women I know," Ross Perot told *The Dallas Morning News*, which published a detailed profile of Brinker in December 1987. By this time, the Komen Foundation had raised more than $4 million and had 400 volunteers.

While cause-related marketing had been practiced by the March of Dimes and other charities, the Komen Foundation took the concept to new levels. Early attempts to place mammogram reminder tags with new bras were repulsed by marketers unwilling to associate their products with the disease. However, Brinker recalled in a memoir, changing demographics were on her side. Women's participation in the job market was increasing, bringing them new importance as consumers. Companies eventually warmed to the cause as a way to connect with female buyers.

Nearby Baylor University Medical Center joined the Komen Foundation on a number of projects including a toll-free information line. By 1990, the two were developing a $12 million cancer hospital and research center in partnership with the University of Texas Southwestern Medical Center.

ADVANCING THE CAUSE: 1990–2000

Komen Race for the Cure events were held in nine cities in 1990. *Runner's World* published a profile of the series in its July 1991 issue. The Foundation had assets of $3 million by this time, and the group was raising more than $1 million a year. There were four prongs to its mission. Besides raising money for breast cancer research and promoting greater awareness of the disease, it also funded screenings and treatments for low-income women. By the mid-1990s, the Komen Foundation had funded more than 170 grants. The Race for the Cure Series, which had spread to four dozen cities, was the chief funding source. Susan Braun, a veteran of Bristol-Myers Squibb, became the Foundation's CEO in 1996, and more professional staff were hired.

Federal government spending on breast cancer research was also growing, quadrupling to $400 million in four years, noted the *Houston Chronicle*. Komen's advocacy efforts went beyond calls for more federal spending. It successfully lobbied for passage of quality standards for mammograms. The Mammography Quality Standards Act became law in 1992. In earlier years, the group had successfully pushed for state legislation requiring insurance companies to pay for mammograms for women over 35.

The retail sector also stepped up its involvement during the 1990s. Manufacturers of women's clothing and household items were incorporating more of the color pink in their collections as they rolled out lingerie and other items to raise money and promote breast cancer awareness. In 1996, Lee Jeans began sponsoring another big fundraiser, Lee National Denim Day, in which employees at participating companies donated five dollars in exchange to wear blue jeans to work. The raised for local education and screening. The affiliates were sponsoring outreach programs to make screening and education accessible to underserved populations, including African-American and Hispanic communities. In 2004, nearly 1.5 million people took part in the Komen Race for the Cure, which brought in $97 million from the United States and abroad. By this time, noted *Business Week,* the Komen Foundation had raised a total of $630 million. Of this, $180 million was invested in research grants.

More than three million people visited the website, komen.org, in 2004, while the National Toll-Free Breast Care Helpline fielded 61,000 calls and 1,600 e-mails. In the fiscal year ended March 31, 2005, the Foundation and its affiliates had total revenues of more than $200 million. Three-quarters of that figure was spent on research, public health education, screening, and treatment services.

The cause continued to gain momentum, enlisting support from a variety of corporate partners and sponsors. Quilted Northern, New Balance, and Pier 1 all continued successful programs promoted during National Breast Cancer Awareness Month. A number of other special products tagged to donations were unveiled by makers of home goods, cosmetics, and a wide range of other products, including pink M&Ms candies. General Mills was extending the popular Yoplait mail-in lid program to its Country Hearth bread; Yoplait was also sponsoring its second annual Champions program to acknowledge leaders in the fight against breast cancer. In 2005 Nancy Brinker was honored with the esteemed Mary Woodard Lasker Award for Public Service in recognition for her unflagging efforts to eradicate breast cancer. By late 2005, the Komen Foundation and its affiliates had raised over $750 million to fund research, education, screening, and treatment for breast cancer.

Frederick C. Ingram

KEY DATES

1982: Susan G. Komen Breast Cancer Foundation established.
1983: First Komen Race for the Cure 5K race held in Dallas, Texas, with 800 participants.
1990: Pink ribbons are distributed at the very first Komen National Race for the Cure in Washington, D.C., as a way to recognize breast cancer survivors.
1997: Yoplait launches Save Lids to Save Lives.
2000: First international Race for the Cure held in Rome.
2004: Race for the Cure raises nearly $100 million.

---

program, launched in the mid-1990s, brought in $1.5 million its first year. Yoplait USA, Inc. began its highly visible Save Lids to Save Lives campaign in 1997. The company, whose marketing was geared toward women, made a donation based on the number of specially printed pink lids mailed in by consumers.

By the end of the 1990s, scores of consumer brands, such as American Express and Ford Motor Company, had cause-related marketing tied to breast cancer. One survey reported that such promotions reached one-quarter of American women in 1998. Major retail chains such as Nordstrom's were providing funds and hosting events such as talks by survivors in their stores. J.C. Penney Co. was a national sponsor of the Komen Race for the Cure.

Yoplait became the national presenting sponsor of the Komen Race for the Cure Series in 2001. By this time, the Komen Foundation had more than 40,000 volunteers and 1.3 million participated in the Race for the Cure. (The first international Race had been held in Rome in May 2000; it drew 5,600 participants.)

20TH ANNIVERSARY IN 2002

At the time of its 20th anniversary in 2002, the Komen Foundation had raised more than $400 million and awarded more than $68 million in research grants. Corporate partners included American Airlines, BMW, Hallmark, Johnson & Johnson, the Kellogg Company, and Pier 1. The Komen Race for the Cure had grown to about 100 events worldwide. The U.S. government's annual spending on breast cancer research, treatment, screening, and education had increased to $766 million.

The Komen Foundation had more than 100 affiliates, which retained up to 75 percent of the funds they

FURTHER READING

Arnst, Catherine, "Nancy G. Brinker: Promise Keeper; The Crusader's Race for the Cure Has Been Key to Funding Advances in Breast Cancer Research," *Business Week,* October 17, 2005, p. 24.

Barker, Leslie, "Breast Cancer: A Sister's Story" (review of *The Race Is Run One Step at a Time*), *Dallas Morning News,* August 11, 1990, p. 1C.

"Breast Cancer Awareness Stamp Slated for June," *Stamps,* March 30, 1996, p. 1.

"Breast Cancer: Komen Foundation Earns Praise for Its Work," *Dallas Morning News,* October 17, 1992, p. 30A.

Brinker, Nancy G., "Breast Cancer's Complexities," *Boston Globe,* Op-Ed Sec., April 27, 1999, p. A15.

————, "Progress against a Killer," *Dallas Morning News*, October 31, 1993, p. 6J.

Brinker, Nancy G., and Catherine McEvily Harris, *The Race Is Run One Step at a Time: My Personal Struggle and Every Woman's Guide to Taking Charge of Breast Cancer*, New York: Simon & Schuster, 1990, 1995.

Brinker, Nancy G., and Chriss Anne Winston, *Winning the Race: Taking Charge of Breast Cancer; My Personal Story and Every Woman's Guide to Wellness*, Irving, TX: Tapestry Press, 2001.

"Campaign: Yoplait Ups Role in Cancer Battle with 'Champions' Push," *PR Week* (U.S.), September 20, 2004, p. 19.

"Cause-Related Buzz: Giving Cancer the Boot," *Footwear News*, October 24, 2005, p. 19.

Feldman, Claudia, "Then & Now: 1991; Nancy Brinker," *Houston Chronicle*, Texas Magazine, July 10, 1994, p. 13.

"General Mills Extends Donation Programs," *Promo (Online Exclusive)*, October 13, 2005.

Green, Sherri Deatherage, "Komen Uses Business Savvy in Breast-Cancer Fight," *PR Week* (U.S.), October 6, 2003, p. 12.

Jennings, Diane, "A Dinner of Truffles and Flourishes," *Dallas Morning News*, November 4, 1984, p. 3E.

Kalson, Sally, "A Cancer Survivor Mobilizes," *Pittsburgh Post-Gazette*, March 6, 1994, p. F1.

Klemesrud, Judy, "Nancy G. Brinker Discusses Her Efforts on Behalf of Breast Cancer Research," *New York Times Abstracts*, August 5, 1985, p. 5.

Kowalchik, Claire, "Race for the Cure," *Runner's World*, July 1991, pp. 52ff.

Malone, Scott, "Going Casual, Saving Lives," *WWD*, December 12, 2000, p. 11.

Meinert, Dori, "Brinker No Longer Ambassador to Hungary," *State Journal-Register*, July 18, 2003, p. 41.

————, "Ex-Peorian Expected to Get Ambassadorship—Bush to Nominate Nancy Brinker to Position in Hungary," *Peoria Journal Star*, May 25, 2001, p. A1.

Ontiveros, Sue, "Suzy's Race," *Chicago Sun-Times*, Lifestyles Sec., October 1, 2004, p. 62.

"Passage of Mammography Quality Standards Reauthorization Act of 2004 Lauded," *Women's Health Weekly*, November 11, 2004, p. 39.

Peppard, Alan, "Breast Cancer Group Gets Financial Boost," *Dallas Morning News*, October 30, 1987, p. 31A.

Perry, Linda, "Foundation Enlists Hospitals in Mission of Prevention," *Modern Healthcare*, September 3, 1990, p. 36.

Poe, Alysia, "Two Voices, One Goal: The Stars of *Desperate Housewives*, Marcia Cross and James Denton, Have Each Found a Way to Help Out in the Battle Against Breast Cancer," *In Style*, October 2005, p. 367.

Primeau, Marty, "Nancy Brinker: She Understand the Movers and Shakers of Dallas. And When It Comes to the Susan G. Komen Foundation, They Understand She Means Business," *Dallas Morning News*, December 20, 1987, p. 1E.

Seckler, Valerie, Sharon Edelson, and David Moin, "Retailers: In the Front Lines," *WWD*, October 6, 1997, pp. S2f.

Secondo, Carrie, "Leading the Race for a Cure," *Mason Spirit*, Winter 2001.

"Suppliers Figure Big in Combating Cancer," *Chain Drug Review*, October 24, 2005, pp. 30f.

Thompson, Susan H., "The Power of Pink Ribbons," *Tampa Tribune*, Baylife Sec., October 22, 1999, p. 1.

TEAC®

TEAC Corporation

—■—

3-7-3 Naka-cho
Musashino-shi
Tokyo, 180-8550
Japan
Telephone: (81) 422 52 5000
Fax: (81) 422 55 8959
Web site: http://www.teac.co.jp

Public Company
Incorporated: 1953 as Tokyo Television Acoustic
    Company
Employees: 6,719
Sales: $961 million (2005)
Stock Exchanges: Tokyo
Ticker Symbol: 6803
NAIC: 334310 Audio and Video Equipment
    Manufacturing; 334111 Electronic Computer
    Manufacturing; 334112 Computer Storage Device
    Manufacturing; 334419 Other Electronic Compo-
    nent Manufacturing

■ ■ ■

TEAC Corporation is one of the world's top names in
audio and visual recording equipment, and a leading
producer to data storage equipment and related products.
The company's operations are divided into three primary
categories. Under Peripheral Equipment, TEAC produces
computer peripheral devices, including optical (CD,
DVD) drives and magnetic drives, and related calibra-
tion media, including compact discs, DVDs, cassettes,
diskettes, and the like. The company's Professional Audio

Products division produces a wide range of audio
products for both the professional recording and
consumer markets. In addition to the range of TEAC-
branded consumer products, the company is a leading
producer of professional recording equipment under the
Tascam and TEAC names. TEAC's third division is its
Information Products division, which produces equipment and systems for in-flight entertainment systems,
data storage and measurement products, including
recorders for the aviation industry, call monitoring
systems and video surveillance equipment, and medical
and industrial filing systems. TEAC operates subsidiaries
in more than 13 countries, including the United States,
United Kingdom, Germany, Australia, Malaysia, Singapore, Mexico, Indonesia, Taiwan, China and Italy. At
the end of 2005, the company had also entered negotiations for a possible manufacturing partnership with
Japanese rival Pioneer Corporation. The company is
listed on the Tokyo Stock Exchange, and posted revenues
of more than $960 million in 2005. Yoshiaki Sakai leads
the company as president, CEO and chairman of the
board.

JAPANESE AUDIO TAPE PIONEER IN 1953

Katsuma Tani began his professional career as an aviation and aeronautics engineer. In the aftermath of World
War II, however, Tani's interests turned toward the
developments in recording technology. In 1953,
Tani founded a new company, the Tokyo Television
Acoustic Company in order to develop new magnetic
recording technologies for the audiovisual industry. The
company's launched its first product, a reel-to-reel tape

COMPANY PERSPECTIVES

Since its inception in 1953, the guiding principle of TEAC Corporation has been to enrich our society through our innovative audio products and increase the productivity of our customers through our computer peripheral products by producing filling the demand for high quality recording products. Over the past fifty years, TEAC has been committed to the creation, production and introduction of many innovative products incorporating our advanced research, design and production technologies. By maintaining TEAC's corporate culture, "respect creativity and honesty," we will continue to demonstrate our ability to contribute to the enjoyment and productivity of our millions of customers worldwide. We would like to thank you very much the continuous support you have extended to us.

machine that year. In 1956, Tani, joined by his brother, formed a second company dedicated to the development of audio products, called Tokyo Electro Acoustic Company. In 1964, the two companies were merged into a new company, TEAC, which also became the company's primary brand name.

By the mid-1960s, TEAC had already established itself as a world leader in audio tape technologies. The company also recognized an opportunity for adapting its expertise in magnetic tape to the rapidly evolving computer industry. Before the end of the decade, TEAC had already developed its first tape-based data storage products. That category was to remain a company mainstay into the next century, becoming the major source of group revenues.

The Tani brothers continued seeking new expansion opportunities for its magnetic tape expertise. The booming international music industry in the 1960s, which also a rapid evolution of recording techniques and technologies, provided the company with its next avenue for growth. Toward the end of the decade, the Tani brothers, together with one of TEAC's senior engineers, decided to launch a new research and development unit, called TEAC Audio Systems Corporation, or TASC. That subsidiary was charged with designing a new range of products built on the company's recording technologies and designed for use by professional musicians and recording studios. By the beginning of the 1970s, Tasc had developed the first in a line line of TEAC-branded

recorders and mixers. These included the revolutionary 3300 series, which provided simultaneous recording and playback of up to four tracks.

From the start, the Tasc unit targeted the market in the United States, which had already established itself as the center of the international music scene. In 1971, TEAC created a new subsidiary, TASC America, or Tascam. The subsidiary's name was quickly adopted as the brand name for the group's professional recording equipment, and the first Tascam-branded products debuted in 1973. While Tascam produced equipment for the recording industry, its primary target was to develop products for use by musicians in a home studio environment. The relatively low-priced Tascam equipment represented a new revolution in recording—and subsequently in the musical industry itself. As the barrier to high quality recording was lowered, a new generation of 'independent' musicians and labels appeared, challenging the grip on the international music market by the small number of large-scale players.

RECORDING REVOLUTION: 1970-80

Tascam's breakthrough product arrived in 1976, with the launch of the Series 80-8, a highly durable, easy to calibrate" eight-track reel-to-reel recorder. Priced at $3,500—about one-third the cost of its nearest competitor—the 80-8 received strong reviews and support from such bodies as the Recording Industry Artists of America (RIAA). The 80-8 quickly made its mark on the professional music industry, serving as the recording base for such hit groups of the period as Boston and Kansas.

The company's next major innovation came in 1979, when the company launched a new concept in home recording equipment: the Portastudio. Featuring a built-in mixer, the Portastudio distinguished itself as the world's first recorder that provided the ability to record up to four tracks simultaneously on standard cassette tape. The Portastudio was also priced to come within reach of the home recording enthusiast. The Portastudio's portability also made it a popular product among professional musicians as well. Over the next decades, the company sold more than one million Portastudios worldwide.

During the 1970s, TEAC itself had continued to grow strongly. The company achieved strong success on the international market, backed by the development of a network of subsidiaries, particularly in Germany, the United Kingdom, France, Belgium, Australia and elsewhere. In the United States, the company's subsidiary, TEAC Corporation of America (TCA), had helped establish TEAC as one of the fastest-growing home audio

KEY DATES

1953: Katsuma Tani founds Tokyo Television Acoustic Company and releases first product, a reel-to-reel tape recorder.

1956: Tokyo Electronic Audio Corporation is launched.

1964: Company adopts TEAC name.

1971: After creating research unit TASC (TEAC Audio Systems Corporation), TEAC launches Tasc America, or Tascam, in order to produce recording equipment for the music industry.

1973: TEAC America takes over Tascam, which becomes TEAC's international recording equipment brand.

1978: TEAC debuts world's first 5.25" floppy drive.

1979: Tascam Portastudio debuts.

1983: TEAC launches 3.5" diskette drive.

1989: A high-capacity, small-format data drive is launched.

1994: A 4X speed CD-ROM drive is introduced.

1995: Tascam launches its first mini-disk-based recorder player.

1998: Tascam debuts its first hard-disk based digital recording system.

2001: Tascam acquires NemeSys and its Gigasampler and Gigastudio software.

2005: Tascam enters talks with Pioneer to develop optical drives.

DATA STORAGE LEADER IN THE NEW CENTURY

The rapid adoption of computer technology by the corporate market in the 1980s brought an increased demand for TEAC's specialty in tape-based data storage products. The company met the demand by launching new generations of higher-capacity, smaller-format storage products. In 1989, for example, the company introduced a 600 megabyte cassette-based drive, more than tripling the size of the largest drives that had been available. At the same time, the company introduced a line of small-format SCSI-II hard drives, which especially targeted the growing market for portable computers. The rise of the home computer market, and the growth of a small-scale networking market led TEAC to launch a line of data storage products for the retail market in 1990. This line included the company's new high-speed TurboTape backup drives, which boasted the ability to back up as much as 100 megabytes in just 15 minutes.

TEAC also emerged as an important supplier of data storage and other systems for the aviation industry. As such the company's video cassette recording units were adopted by the United States Air Force for its F-16 fighter and other aircraft. TEAC's VCRs were also adapted for use in NASA's space shuttle program. The company's expertise in video recording technology also allowed it to establish itself a major brand name in the home VCR market as well.

TEAC continued to build its hard drive technology through the 1990s, releasing such innovative products as a docking bay, capable of holding two removable, cassette-cased hard-drives, in 1993. The company was also helping to drive development of CD-ROM drives, releasing its 4X-speed drive in 1994. By then, however, the company, facing intense price pressure as the electronics manufacturing market shifted further toward Taiwan, and then to mainland China, saw its profits drop sharply. The company also faced mounting pressure as the industry momentum shifted from tape-based backup systems to highly popular cassette systems, such as Iomega's hugely successful Zip Drive. By 1995, the company had begun to post losses, which reached nearly $69 million in 1993, and nearly $44 million in 1994. TEAC fought back, launching its own high-capacity, high-speed data systems, such as it HiFD large-capacity IDE drive released in 1998.

The company's Tascam unit had also begun to adapt to the times, as new digital recording technologies were rapidly making tape-based recording, at least on the home and small-scale studio level, obsolete. The company debuted its first mini-disk-based recorder player in 1995. Two years later, the company launched a new generation of the Portastudio, which provided the

brands. In 1973, TCA absorbed Tascam, and the Tascam brand name was transferred under the control of the parent company in Japan. This marked the international rollout of the Tascam line.

TEAC had meanwhile continued to develop its interest in data storage. The development of the first mini computers at the end of the 1970s provided a new product category for the company, which became the world's first producer of 5.25-inch floppy disc drives. In 1983, the company also became one of the first to begin producing the new 3.5-inch disk drives, which rapidly became the standard in the new personal computer market. TEAC's rollout of its 3.5-inch drive quickly met with controversy, however, after the company, along with Sony and Mitsubishi, were charged with patent infringement. TEAC reached an out-of-court settlement which included a lump sum payment and an agreement to pay royalties on further sales of its 3.5-inch disk drives.

capability of recording and mixing up to eight tracks to mini-disk. The following year, Tascam released its own hard-disk based digital recording system, which was rapidly becoming the industry standard.

TEAC, through Tascam, quickly proved itself a driving force in the digital recording market, launching the US-428 audio and MIDI computer interface in 2000. The following year, the company launched the SX-1 Digital Production Environment, a recording workstation combining hard disk recording, MIDI and audio sequencing and editing, digital mixing and even the ability record to CD. That year, the company also expanded its operations to include a software wing, with the acquisition of Nemesys Music Technologies. Based in Austin, that company had developed the ground-breaking Gigastudio and Gigasampler line.

TEAC had in the meantime continued to expand its international manufacturing network, in part to support its strong entry into the new DVD drive segment. During the 1990s and into the 2000s, the company shifted a growing share of its production to the Southeast Asian region. In support of this, the company added subsidiaries in Malaysia, Indonesia, Singapore, Taiwan and in mainland China. Not all of the group's international subsidiaries were performing well, however. In 2005, for example, the company was forced to rescue its failing Australia operations, taking full control of the joint venture in order to shield it from bankruptcy.

TEAC's own sales dipped somewhat into the mid-2000s. The company nonetheless continued to drive forward. At the end of 2004, the company released a new USB-based television tuner for personal and desktop computers. The company also began eyeing external growth as well, and in December 2005, the company announced that it had entered talks to join with struggling Japanese rival Pioneer in the development of new optical drives. After more than 50 years, TEAC remained a leader in recording the world's data.

M.L. Cohen

PRINCIPAL SUBSIDIARIES

Dongguan Dongfa TEAC Audio Co. Ltd.; Fuji Yoshida TEAC Corporation; Mts Corporation; P.T. TEAC Electronics Indonesia; Selepas; Taiwan TEAC Corporation; Tascam Corporation (United States); TEAC America, Inc.; TEAC Audio (China) Co., Ltd.; TEAC Australia Pty., Ltd.; TEAC Canada Ltd.; TEAC Electronics Sdn. Bhd. (Malaysia); TEAC Esoteric Company; TEAC Europe GmbH; TEAC Instruments Corporation; TEAC Italiana SpA; TEAC Mexico, S.A. de C.V.; TEAC Shanghai Ltd.; TEAC Singapore Pte Ltd.; TEAC Sse Ltd. (United Kingdom); TEAC System Create Corporation; TEAC UK Ltd.

PRINCIPAL COMPETITORS

Thomson Multimedia Inc.; Hitachi Ltd.; Matsushita Electric Industrial Co. Ltd.; Sony Corporation; Samsung Electronics Company Ltd.; NEC Corporation; Fujitsu Ltd.; Toshiba CorpSharp Corporation; LG Electronics Inc.; Philips Electronics North America Corporation; Pioneer Corporation; Alps Electric Company Ltd.

FURTHER READING

"TEAC America Launches Online Store," *PR Newswire*, November 28, 2004.

"TEAC Debuts 16x DVD," *CD Computing News*, October 1, 2004.

"Troubled TEAC Gets Extension," *Australasian Business Intelligence*, June 22, 2005.

Technip

Tour Technip 6-8
Allée de l'Arche 92400
Courbevoie,
France
Telephone: (33) 1 4778-2121
Fax: (33) 1 4778-3340
Web site: http://www.technip.com

Public Company
Incorporated: 1958 as Compagnie Française d'Etudes et de Construction Technip
Employees: 20,000
Sales: FRF 5.14 billion ($6.35 billion) (2004)
Stock Exchanges: New York Euronext Paris
Ticker Symbol: TKP
NAIC: 213112 Support Activities for Oil and Gas Operations; 236210 Industrial Building Construction; 237120 Oil and Gas Pipeline and Related Structures Construction; 237990 Other Heavy and Civil Engineering Construction; 333132 Oil and Gas Field Machinery and Equipment Manufacturing

■ ■ ■

Technip is a leading global engineering firm with a focus on the energy industry. Its main line of business is constructing turnkey oil production and refining facilities. Although oil and natural gas projects account for most of its business, the company also works on a wide range of industrial plants. An experienced firm, the company has completed more than 2,000 projects in more than 115 countries. About 20 percent of its 20,000-strong workforce is based in France. It has major foreign offices in Italy, Germany, the United Kingdom, Norway, Finland, The Netherlands, the United States, Brazil, Abu-Dhabi, China, India, Malaysia, and Australia. Africa and the Middle East account for about half of revenues. The company maintains a fleet of more than a dozen vessels to service offshore projects.

ORIGINS

Technip was established in 1958 by IFP, Institut Français du Pétrole, as Compagnie Française d'Etudes et de Construction Technip. Tasked with engineering refineries and petrochemical plants in France and its territories, Technip was building a liquefied natural gas (LNG) facility in Algeria in 1962. A second such plant followed ten years later.

Technip was involved with Eastern European markets well before the fall of the Iron Curtain. It was building chemical plants and refineries in Bulgaria by 1972. Technip's New York engineering office, which was working on some projects in the U.S.S.R., was scaled back in the late 1970s due to a lack of U.S. sales.

In the early 1980s, Technip was busy building projects such as an LNG plant in Iraq and a chemical factory in Saudi Arabia. Export sales were FRF 2.6 billion in 1981, according to *Les Echos.* Another source, however, had total turnover at FRF 2.7 billion in 1982. The number of employees at the company reached 3,500 in 1983.

1984 CRISIS

The company underwent restructuring and rounds of layoffs in the mid-1980s. Technip lost FRF 1.42 billion ($148 million) in 1984, when it had about 2,750 employees. They were on strike in January 1985 to protest job cuts. Company president Pierre-Marie Valentin told *Platt's Petrochemical Report* that the problems were due to Technip's high costs and relatively narrow range of process services. He added that the French engineering sector was in need of consolidation. Technip was able to take over competitor Creusot-Loire Entreprises (CLE), the project engineering unit of Creusot Loire S.A., during the industry downturn. CLE also was making layoffs, cutting its 1,100-strong workforce by a third.

Petro-Canada, which had been using Technip for consulting and repair work, invested in the company during its mid-1980s crisis. The French government soon stepped in, however. The oil company Société National Elf Aquitaine ended up with about one-third of shares. IFP retained a similar holding. The remainder was held by the TOTAL oil company, Gaz de France, and some French banks, which had written off loans worth FRF 428 million in the restructuring.

Technip was soon in the black again. Turnover reached FRF 7 billion in 1986, with a net profit of FRF 30 million. Hydrocarbons and bulk chemical work accounted for half of the group's business. By the end of the decade, Technip had joined the Soviet Union in an engineering joint venture and was building a number of plants in China. It also established a branch office in Abu Dhabi that would over the course of a couple of decades develop a considerable design capacity. By 1990 Technip counted more than 1,000 contract awards in 85 countries. Sales exceeded FRF 7 billion ($1 billion) in the early 1990s and the company was profitable. It had 5,400 employees, more than half of them overseas. According to Reuters, international work was soon accounting for 92 percent of turnover. In 1993 Technip expanded into different types of plant construction through the purchase of Speichim, which specialized in the phosphate and agrochemical segments.

PUBLIC IN 1994

Technip underwent a public stock offering in France in 1994 in an offering that valued the firm as a whole at about FRF 4 billion (roughly $750 million). Elf, Total, Gaz de France, and IFP each eventually reduced their holdings to 12 percent. The company's shares listed on the New York Stock Exchange in 2001.

Technip's Asian business was dampened by the financial crisis in the region in the late 1990s, but overall the company was able to make progress. It acquired the oil and environmental businesses of Mannesmann Demag in 1999.

A MAJOR MERGER AFTER 2000

Sales were a little shy of FRF 3 billion in 2000. In April, Technip acquired an initial 29.7 percent investment in Coflexip, an offshore construction specialist.

In October 2001, Technip acquired a majority (98.36 percent) holding in Coflexip as well as a controlling interest in ISIS, a holding company that formerly had been owned by the national oil institute IFP. The group was subsequently known as Technip-Coflexip for a couple of years. Coflexip had itself made a major acquisition in January 2001, buying Aker Maritime's Deepwater Division.

Coflexip was merged with Technip in July 2003, when the group name went back to simply Technip. The company's corporate identity was updated, and three Paris offices employing 2,700 people consolidated into one tower in the business center La Défence. During the year, Technip Germany launched a joint venture with a unit of Russia's Lukoil.

KEY DATES

1958: Technip is formed by a state-owned oil institute.
1984: Rival Creusot-Loire Entreprises is acquired during an industry downturn.
1994: The company goes public in Paris.
2001: Shares trade on the New York Stock Exchange; the Coflexip offshore oil rig venture is acquired; the company is renamed Technip-Coflexip.
2003: The company is renamed Technip as it absorbs Coflexip; the Paris offices are consolidated at La Défence.
2005: Technip launches the $4 billion Qatargas II joint venture.

With net sales of FRF 5.1 billion in 2004, the company was counted among the top five full-service engineering and construction firms for the hydrocarbon/petrochemical industry, which accounted for 95 percent of revenues.

Technip specialized in lump sum turnkey (LSTK) projects for major oil companies and governments in emerging markets, a business that was proving less attractive to U.S. companies. Technip continued to be heavily involved in the Middle East. Qatargas II, a colossal $4 billion LNG joint venture with Japan's Chiyoda Corporation, was launched toward the end of 2004. An executive told *Middle East Economic Digest* that the company had traditionally lost out to low-cost Japanese companies in the Gulf's LNG business. After acquiring Coflexip, Technip pushed into Egypt's offshore market, while it withdrew from Iraq, where it once had a thriving presence, due to security and political issues.

Business Week Online observed that Technip was poised to profit from high oil prices due to renewed interest in oil production and development. At the same time, it avoided the more risky exploration side of the business. The company also was studying opportunities outside the energy sector, in fields such as fertilizers and life sciences. It was putting its Speichim treatment technology to use in ethanol and biodiesel plants.

Frederick C. Ingram

PRINCIPAL SUBSIDIARIES

CITEX (99.97%); COFRI (99.99%); Engineering Re (Switzerland); Eurobatch (99.76%); PT Technip Indonesia (60%); S.C.I. CB3 Defense; Seal Engineering (99.76%); SNPE Ingénierie Defense (99.96%); Technip Americas (United States); Technip C.I.S. (Russia; 70%); Technip Eurocash (60%); Technip Far East (Malaysia); Technip France (77.61%); Technip Germany; Technip Holding Benelux B.V. (Netherlands); Technip Iberia (Spain; 99.99%); Technip International AG (Switzerland; 99.84%); Technip Italy (95.30%); Technip Nouvelle-Calédonie (New Caledonia); Technip Offshore International; Technip Overseas (Panama); Technip Portugal (77.08%); Technip Tianchen (China; 60%); Technip TPS (99.94%); TPG UK (90%); TPL—Tecnologie Progetti Lavori (Italy; 95%); TTIL SNC (60%).

PRINCIPAL DIVISIONS

Offshore SURF (Subsea Umbilicals, Risers, Flowlines); Offshore Facilities; Onshore/Downstream Industries.

PRINCIPAL COMPETITORS

Saipem S.p.A.; Stolt Offshore M. S. Limited.

FURTHER READING

Alperowicz, Natasha, "Contractors Seek New Work Overseas," *Chemical Week* (French Chemicals, An Industry Review), May 5, 1993, p. S9.

Beckman, Jeremy, "French Offshore Contractors Start Year with Major Contracts," *Offshore*, May 2004, p. 110.

———, "Technip-Coflexip Merger Creates Fifth-Ranked Upstream Contractor," *Offshore*, May 2002, p. 81.

"Engineering for Growth: Paris-Based Engineering Contractor Technip Is Expanding Its Middle East Portfolio with a Raft of Major New Projects," *MEED Middle East Economic Digest*, October 24, 2003, pp. 49f.

"France's Technip Unveils Bourse Listing Plans," *Reuters News*, October 5, 1994.

Housego, David, "Price for Technip Rescue Likely to Be Further Job Cuts," *Globe and Mail* (Canada), June 10, 1985.

Kelly, Andrew, "Technip CEO Urges Oil Firms to Cut Contractors Some Slack," *Oil Daily*, October 13, 2004.

"*Les Echos* Has Published a List of French Companies That Exported Over FFr 1bn in 1981," *Les Echos*, September 15, 1982.

"Société Technip Receives $236 Million Iraqi Contract," *Wall Street Journal*, March 12, 1980.

"Technip Engineers Several New Deals," *Chemical Market Reporter*, October 25, 2004, p. 10.

"Technip, Isis and Coflexip to Combine Forces," *Alexander's Gas & Oil Connections*, July 31, 2001.

"Technip Needs New Shareholders," *Informations Chimie Hebdo*, January 14, 1987, p. 7.

"Technip of France Planning to Take Over Unit of Financially Troubled Creusot-Loire S.A.," *Wall Street Journal,* February 1, 1984.

"Technip on the Road to Recovery," *Chimie Actualitiés,* July 7, 1987, p. 3.

"Technip Retrenches," *Chemical Week,* April 19, 1978, p. 68.

"Technip Takes Steps to Restructure with Threat of Further Job Losses," *Platt's Petrochemical Report,* July 4, 1985, p. 6.

"Technip to Set Up a Joint Subsidiary in the USSR," *Chimie Actualitiés,* January 13, 1989, p. 6.

Wahlgren, Eric, "Technip: Slick Play on the Oil Boom," *Business Week Online,* June 1, 2004.

Tektronix, Inc.

14200 S.K. Karl Braun Drive
Beaverton, Oregon 97077
U.S.A.
Telephone: (503) 627-7111
Fax: (503) 627-2406
Web site: http://www.tek.com

Public Company
Incorporated: 1946 as Tekrad, Inc.
Employees: 3,834
Sales: $1.03 billion (2005)
Stock Exchanges: New York
Ticker Symbol: TEK
NAIC: 334515 Instrument Manufacturing for Measuring and Testing Electricity and Electrical Signals

■ ■ ■

Tektronix, Inc., founded in 1946, is the world's second largest supplier of electronic testing and measuring devices. The company develops, manufactures, and markets oscilloscopes—instruments used to measure and display electrical signals—as well as logic analyzers, signal sources, spectrum analyzers, and communication and video test equipment. Tektronix serves many industries, including computing, communications, semiconductors, education, government, military, aerospace, research, automotive, and consumer electronics. The company spent the majority of the 1990s restructuring and eventually split itself into two major divisions in 1999. Xerox bought its printer operations, leaving it focused on its testing and measuring devices. Tektronix made its largest acquisition to date in 2004 when it purchased Inet Technologies Inc.

EARLY HISTORY

Tektronix was founded by three U.S. Coast Guard veterans and an electronics expert from the U.S. Army Signal Corps. Portland native Melvin Jack Murdock spent World War II as a Coast Guardsman, maintaining radio equipment for the Navy and planning for a career once the war ended. By 1945, he had convinced two friends, Glenn Leland and Miles Tippery, that the three of them should start their own business, although none had an idea exactly what that business should be. They also decided to bring in Charles Howard Vollum, a graduate of Portland's Reed University with a degree in physics who had operated a radio repair business in the back room of an appliance store Murdock had owned before the war. Vollum was then designing radar sighting devices for the Signal Corps.

In December 1945 the four servicemen met in Portland to draft articles of incorporation for a broadly defined company that would manufacture, sell, install, repair, "and otherwise handle and dispose of" electronic equipment. They called their company Tekrad, which was incorporated on January 2, 1946. Vollum was president and Murdock vice-president. The name was changed to Tektronix, Inc., a month later when they learned about a California company that had registered a similar name, Techrad.

Although Tektronix was still without a specific product or purpose, Vollum decided to build an oscil-

COMPANY PERSPECTIVES

Our strategy is to focus our efforts on selecting product categories with the communications test and general purpose categories where Tektronix either has a market leadership position or where we believe Tektronix can grow to a market leadership position. We are focused on long term growth from three perspectives—growing market share in core product categories where Tektronix already has a strong market position, expanding the addressable market for core categories, and leveraging existing strengths into adjacent products categories.

loscope from spare electronics parts being stockpiled by his partners from postwar government surplus sales. At the time, the Du Mont Company was the leading manufacturer of oscilloscopes, which were indispensable to the rapidly growing electronics industry. Vollum, who had built his first oscilloscope while in college, believed he could design one that was better and would sell for less than half what Du Mont charged. Vollum later told *Forbes* that Du Mont "wanted to fool around with big-time television. They were complacent about their scope."

Vollum completed his oscilloscope in the spring of 1946. It was far more accurate than anything then on the market. Unfortunately, it also was so large that it covered Vollum's entire workbench. He immediately began working on a more compact model, and Murdock brought in another buddy from the Coast Guard, a machinist named Milt Bave, to help with the design. The redesign took 12 months, but in May 1947 Tektronix sold the first "portable" oscilloscope to the University of Oregon Medical School. The model 511, which became known as the Vollumscope, weighed 50 pounds.

In 1947 Tektronix had sales of $27,000. The next year, sales increased almost tenfold, to $257,000, and the customer list included most of the major electronics research firms in the United States, including Hewlett-Packard, Philco Radio Corporation, RCA Laboratories Division, Westinghouse Electric Company, and AT&T Bell Laboratories. In 1948 Tektronix also sold its first oscilloscope overseas, to the L. M. Ericcson Telephone Company of Sweden. By 1950, Tektronix was manufacturing its seventh generation of oscilloscopes, the model 517. Orders were backlogged six months to a year, and annual sales had exceeded $1 million.

TEK CULTURE LEADING TO SUCCESS: 1950–70

By the early 1950s, Murdock was already beginning to lose interest in managing Tektronix. He took up flying and started an aircraft sales company on the side. Vollum, however, continued to be a driving force within the company. Under his direction, Tektronix began manufacturing its own cathode-ray tubes when it could not get the quality Vollum wanted for his oscilloscopes. Vollum also conceived the idea of a basic oscilloscope that could be adapted with "plug-in" devices, rather than special oscilloscopes for different applications. The plug-in oscilloscopes, introduced in 1954, were an instant success. By 1955, the 530 Series accounted for half the oscilloscopes sold by Tektronix. In 1956 Tektronix passed Du Mont for leadership in the market. Riding the crest of solid-state electronics, Tektronix's revenues grew an astonishing 4,000 percent in the 1950s, to $43 million in sales in 1960.

It was also during the 1950s that "Tek culture" began to take shape. Even before the company was founded, Murdock had insisted that future employees would be treated with respect, everyone would be on a first-name basis, and there would be no perks for executives. Murdock even talked about the ideal size for a company to maintain a casual, family atmosphere—no more than a few dozen people. Although Tektronix paid lower wages than other manufacturers in the Portland area, the company provided medical coverage, profit sharing, and other benefits. There were few unbreakable rules, and engineers were encouraged to pursue their individual interests. Tek culture was praised by management consultants, and Tektronix was cited in the book *The 100 Best Companies to Work for in America*. Tek culture was later blamed, however, for some of the company's inability to adjust to competitive changes in the 1980s.

As Tektronix was getting ready to enter the 1960s, which included work on a new 300-acre headquarters campus in Beaverton, Oregon, Vollum convinced the board of directors to appoint Bob Davis as executive vice-president. As vice-president for manufacturing from 1954 until 1958, Davis had begun to bring some order to the rapidly growing, unstructured Tektronix organization. Restructuring was a necessity, but Vollum had neither the experience nor the inclination to give the business of management the attention it needed. Davis would report to Vollum, but he would have sole responsibility for the day-to-day operation of the company. Initially the appointment of the energetic Davis was greeted as a positive step. But inevitably, "the

KEY DATES

◾

1946: Melvin Jack Murdock, Glenn Leland, Miles Tippery, and Howard Vollum establish Tektronix.

1947: Tektronix sells the first "portable" oscilloscope to the University of Oregon Medical School.

1956: The company assumes the leading position in the oscilloscope market.

1963: Tektronix goes public.

1974: The company diversifies with the purchase of Grass Valley Group.

1990: Jerome Meyer takes over as CEO.

1999: Tektronix splits itself into two major divisions; Xerox Corp. buys its printer division in a $950 million deal.

2004: Inet Technologies Inc. is acquired.

old scope warriors," as Marshall M. Lee called longtime employees in his book *Winning with People: The First 40 Years of Tektronix,* came to resent the changes.

Despite significant growth under Davis and the formation of the company's first foreign subsidiaries, by 1962, Vollum was persuaded to re-assume control. At the time, Tektronix's future seemed secure. The company went public in 1963, and was listed on the New York Stock Exchange in 1964. The company continued to bring out more advanced testing equipment, and by 1969, Tektronix controlled 75 percent of the world's market for oscilloscopes. Sales had reached $148 million, and Vollum told *Forbes*: "[There] is an ever-expanding market [for oscilloscopes]. Wherever electronics go, the oscilloscope goes."

Despite its stellar performance and Vollum's optimism, however, in the late 1960s Tektronix was not a favorite among financial experts. There were growing indications that Tektronix's dependence on basically one product was a dangerous strategy, especially with the growth of computers with internal testing programs that no longer required oscilloscopes. Equally troubling was that Tektronix had little marketing experience, since its principal product, the oscilloscope, had practically sold itself for 25 years by being better and cheaper than the competition. Many analysts felt that an early attempt to diversify into programmable calculators had failed because of a lack of market savvy. There was also the lingering need to bring the entire, free-flowing Tektronix organization under better control.

OVERCOMING CHALLENGES: 1970–90

Earnings fell for the first time in fiscal 1971, by a devastating 34.7 percent. Early in the year employees took unpaid time off to avoid layoffs, but it did not help. That autumn, Tektronix announced the first layoffs in its fast-paced history. Adding to the pain that year was the death of Murdock, who drowned when his seaplane flipped during takeoff on the Columbia River. Murdock had not been active in daily management of the company for many years, but he had stayed on as chairman of the board and was generally regarded as the person who gave Tektronix its strategic vision. Less than two weeks after Murdock's death, Vollum suffered a heart attack. Vollum recovered, but he resigned as president in 1972.

At the same time, Tektronix was beginning to have some success with graphic display terminals, which would become the company's second largest revenue producer. In 1964 Tektronix developed a way to retain an image on a cathode ray tube (CRT) for up to 15 minutes, instead of the split second that images normally lasted before they needed to be regenerated. This was a tremendous advance for oscilloscopes, and for several years Tektronix used its discovery only in its own products. However, the new technology was also valuable for displaying maps, charts, and other graphics on computer terminals, and in 1969 the company decided to sell CRT terminals for other applications.

Unfortunately, the first terminals, introduced in 1970, were over-engineered and costly. Earl Wantland, then executive vice-president who would later succeed Vollum as president, organized an Information Display Group to concentrate on redesigning the terminals to reduce the final cost. For perhaps the first time since Vollum built his 511 oscilloscope, Tektronix was designing a product for a competitive market, rather than creating the most sophisticated gadget with the blind faith that engineers somewhere would buy it. When the terminals reappeared a year later, the price had been cut by 60 percent, from $10,000 to $4,000.

From a marketing perspective, the timing was also better, with the emergence of computer-aided design in several industries being a perfect fit for the new graphics terminals. By 1975, Tektronix controlled 50 percent of the market, and the $50 million a year in terminal sales represented about 15 percent of the company's total business. Tektronix had rebounded from a dismal start to the 1970s by joining the *Fortune* 500 in 1975. It had $336.6 million in sales, which placed it 457th on the list of the largest industrial companies in the United States.

Tektronix also took a successful step into diversification in 1974 when it acquired the Grass Valley Group, a California company that made electronic systems to provide special effects for television. By 1978, *Forbes* was able to report that Tektronix "has finally begun to alter its image as a one-product company whose basic technology, the cathode ray tube, was about to be obsoleted by the digital revolution." Although the bulk of its business still centered on oscilloscopes, Tektronix was then selling more than 700 products customized to various market segments, including government, education, broadcast television, and computer industries, in addition to the electronics and electrical equipment markets.

Once again, the future looked bright for Tektronix. The company passed the $1 billion mark in sales in 1981, and then, once again, the marketplace, and this time, the advance of technology, caught the engineering-driven company off guard. Tektronix was slow to switch from making analog test equipment to digital equipment. And when it made the switch, Tektronix found that low-cost Japanese competitors had beaten it to the portable oscilloscope marketplace. The company also was three years late entering the market for color display terminals, which slashed its share of the market for graphics terminals in half, from a high of 51 percent in 1979 to 26 percent in 1983.

Between 1979 and 1984 earnings fell more than 40 percent. The company suffered through more layoffs, and several top executives and engineers left to form competitors such as Mentor Graphics, Graphics Systems Software, and Northwest Instruments. In 1984 *Business Week* reported: "Now Tek must come from behind again, in what is likely to be the most critical recoup in its 38-year history," as the company belatedly entered the market for computer-aided engineering (CAE) workstations. It was a marketplace battle that Tektronix would eventually lose.

In 1982 competitors had begun offering fully integrated CAE workstations, which threatened the market for Tektronix's stand-alone graphics terminals and electronic testing equipment. Heretofore, Tektronix had been content to be a supplier to the computer industry and reportedly had passed on several opportunities to purchase small computer manufacturers, including an upstart Digital Equipment Corporation. In fact, Tektronix engineers had designed a technical workstation in the 1970s, but the company never brought it to market. Then in 1984 Tektronix attempted to counter the attack on its core businesses by forming a systems development division. Charles Humble, then a columnist for the *Portland Oregonian,* wrote of Tektronix's 1984 annual report: "It is about a company that is torn between restructuring and testing the waters of the future, and a company that can't give up the security of past successes."

Early in 1985 Tektronix acquired CAE Systems Inc. In April of that year it introduced its first CAE workstation. The product line, however, was short-lived. Four months later, the company announced that instead of producing workstations, it would develop software for other manufacturers. That, too, faltered. In 1988 Tektronix sold its CAE operations for $5 million to Mentor Graphics. Estimates of Tektronix's losses in the abortive effort to enter the CAE market ranged from $150 million to $225 million.

Despite annual revenues that had almost doubled in ten years to $1.4 billion, Tektronix also reported its first-ever loss of $16.7 million for fiscal 1988. David Friedley, a marketing-oriented Tektronix division manager, succeeded Wantland as president in November 1987. He later told *Forbes,* "The first thing we did was stop the bleeding." In addition to getting out of unprofitable business, Friedley eliminated 2,500 jobs at Tektronix over the next two years.

Business Week later reported that Friedley "cut through ... bureaucracy like a logger through the nearby Oregon timber." But it was not enough. Tektronix returned to modest profitability in 1989, due to stringent cost-cutting and a new line of color printers. But its financial troubles were far from over. By early 1990, the company was again posting losses, and there were rumors that Friedley would be fired, especially since Tektronix stock had fallen in value from $31 a share in 1987 to a 14-year low of $12.75 a share. A financial analyst for Prudential-Bache Securities, Inc., told *Business Week* that meetings with Tektronix "were like watching the grass grow." The anticipated shake-up came in March 1990, with the company headed toward a $92.5 million loss (in large part due to restructuring) for the fiscal year. Robert Lundeen, a former Dow Chemical Co. executive and Tektronix's chairman of the board, and William Walker, another board member, ousted Friedley and took over operational control of the company.

Citing the need to reverse the financial losses, Lundeen told Portland's *Business Journal,* "I don't think management realized how urgent it was that we get there quickly." Lundeen told *Forbes,* "I'd like the new Tektronix style to be more cosmopolitan," and he complained, "We're still doing things the Beaverton way." Lundeen initiated another 1,300 layoffs. In a blow to its corporate image, Tektronix also transferred more than 1,200 workers from Vancouver, Washington, to Oregon, leaving vacant a 488,000-square-foot manufacturing facility in Jack Murdock Park, an industrial center named for the company's cofounder.

For years, Tektronix had been the largest employer in Oregon, with a high of more than 24,000 employees in 1981, but by the end of 1991, the company had a workforce of about 12,000.

REGROUPING IN 1990

Lundeen ran Tektronix as interim president for six months, until October 1990 when the company hired Jerome J. Meyer, a former senior executive with Sperry Univac and Honeywell, Inc. Meyer took over a company with stagnant sales, a lack of market focus, and badly in need of restructuring. Tektronix rebounded from a dismal 1990 to post a modest $45 million profit in 1991. Meyer was rewarded by being named chairman of the board as well as president. But when Meyer reported on the results of his first full year at Tektronix, for fiscal 1992, the company was again in a slump. Sales had hit a nine-year low, with earnings of about $27 million.

Just prior to Meyer joining the company, Tektronix's market value was falling from about $1.3 billion in 1987 to less than $400 million in 1990, and the company was seen by many analysts as a potential takeover target. In September 1990 the board of directors adopted an antitakeover "poison pill," which entitled existing shareholders to purchase stock at half price if an investor acquired more than 20 percent of the company's stock. At the time, Jean Vollum, the widow of cofounder Howard Vollum, who had died in 1986, was the largest single shareholder with about 8.1 percent of the outstanding shares.

In 1992 a group headed by George Soros began buying Tektronix stock. By the fall of 1992, the Soros Group owned about 13.9 percent of the company, and was demanding three seats on the board of directors. In November three new members were added to the board of directors, including Tektronix's president, Delbert W. Yocam. At that time, the Soros Group agreed not to acquire more than 14.9 percent of the company. That agreement was to run through March 15, 1994.

P. C. Chatterjee, a New York financier who represented the Soros Group in dealings with Tektronix, also was openly critical of Meyer, including his decision to move corporate headquarters from the Beaverton campus to Wilsonville, Oregon. In what was viewed by many as another move to satisfy the Soros Group, Tektronix had brought in Yocam, a former Apple Computer executive, to assume the duties of president just days before the 1992 annual meeting. Meyer remained chief executive officer and chairman of the board.

According to a company spokesperson, Yocam's role was to execute strategies shaped by Meyer and to align Tektronix's product portfolio with growth markets. In one of his first moves, Yocam reorganized Tektronix into five business divisions: test and measurement products, television products, television production/distribution products and systems (the Grass Valley Group being responsible for this), graphics printing and imaging products, and network displays and display products. Essentially, each division was structured as its own independent business with full profit and loss responsibility. The idea behind this move was to enable divisions to make timely decisions relative to customer issues, and to put more emphasis on developing new products to meet the customers' needs. In addition, support groups would be better equipped to provide world-class service.

In 1992 and 1993 Tektronix continued to strengthen its management team, recruiting aggressive individuals with proven track records from successful, fast-growing companies. Carl Neun, formerly senior vice-president of administration and CFO of Conner Peripherals, joined Tektronix as vice-president and CFO. John Karalis, vice-president of corporate development, was previously general counsel with Apple Computer and the Sperry Corporation. Daniel Terpack, formerly general manager with Hewlett-Packard, became vice-president of test and measurement. Deborah Coleman, vice-president of materials operations, held several vice-president positions with Apple Computer before joining Tektronix.

In the fourth quarter of fiscal year 1993, Tektronix took a pretax charge of $150 million for a restructuring that was to accelerate the strategic changes Meyer had mapped out in 1990. As a result, the company reported a net loss for the year of $55 million ($1.83 per share). Without the restructuring charges, net earnings for fiscal year 1993 were $39 million, or $1.30 per share, up 29 percent from 1992. New sales were up for the first time in four years, $1.302 billion compared with $1.297 billion in 1992. The restructuring was viewed by Tektronix management as an investment in the future and was expected to speed up improvements in profitability and allow the company to focus its resources on growth. Under the restructuring, Tektronix planned to exit nonstrategic businesses, consolidate facilities, discontinue older products, and cut employment by 8 percent (about 800 jobs) through attrition and layoffs.

Also in 1993 Tektronix reduced administrative costs by $30 million, received a $31 million dividend from Sony/Tektronix, its joint venture company in Japan, and refinanced its debt structure. Regarded by some as long overdue decisions, the latest actions taken by Tektronix resulted in renewed belief by some analysts that the company was moving in the right direction. Even in the sluggish economy of the early 1990s, the company's performance showed improvement. By 1996, Tektronix appeared to be back on solid footing. At this time, the company focused on its video and networking businesses in an attempt to broaden its revenue stream.

2000 AND BEYOND

Tektronix found itself in a precarious situation as it prepared to enter the new millennium. In 1998, the company voluntarily recalled 60,000 of its oscilloscopes after it was discovered that incorrect use of the product could cause the ground connection to fail, which in turn could cause serious injury or death. To make matters worse, the Asian economic crisis was wreaking havoc on the company's bottom line. With its video and network business struggling and losses mounting, the company found itself in restructuring mode once again.

Along with cutting more than 1,000 jobs, Tektronix set plans in motion to sell its network displays division to Network Computing Devices Inc. in 1998. In June 1999, the company made a bold move when it announced that it would split itself into two major divisions—a unit focused on color printers and another on its test and measurement equipment. In September, Xerox Corp. bought the company's printer division in a $950 million deal.

Tektronix's efforts appeared to pay off as sales and profits began to rise. Rick Wills took over as CEO in 2000 and was named chairman the next year. Under his leadership, the company made several key acquisitions to bolster its core business. Over the next several years, the firm purchased Bluetooth wireless testing devices from Motorola and Adherent Systems, a video test product manufacturer based in the United Kingdom.

The company set its sights on Inet Technologies Inc., a network communications software manufacturer, in 2004. The $495 million purchase—completed in September—was the largest in Tektronix's history and strengthened its foothold in the growing communications field. An October 2004 *Oregonian* article explained the impetus behind the deal: "By selling Tektronix equipment used to set up and repair networks, along with the Inet software used to monitor them, Tek expects to expand its customer base and do more to mine revenue from new communications technologies such as next-generation wireless phones and phone calls over the Internet." Sure enough, Tektronix gained access to large customers, including AT&T Corp., British Telecom, and Deutsche Telecom after the Inet purchase. Overall, the company's recent acquisitions coupled with resurgence in the high-tech industry left it on solid ground. Sales climbed to $920.6 million in 2004 while net income skyrocketed to $118.2 million. During 2005,

the company continued to reap the benefits of the Inet deal when a slowdown in demand for the company's test and measurement equipment threatened to weaken sales and profits. Demand for Inet's products and services remained strong, however, and pushed the company's sales past the $1 billion mark. Although the company remained subject to the fickle tendencies of the high-tech industry, Textronix appeared to be positioned for growth in the years to come.

Dean Boyer
Updated, Christina M. Stansell

PRINCIPAL SUBSIDIARIES

Tektronix Network Systems Pty. Ltd. (Australia); Tektronix GmbH (Austria); Tektronix N.V. Belgium; Tektronix Industria e Comercio Ltda. (Brazil); Inet Technologies Brazil Ltda.; Tektronix Canada Inc.; Tektronix Electronics (China) Co., Ltd.; Tektronix (China) Co., Ltd.; Tektronix Oy (Finland); Inet Technologies France S.A.R.L.; Tektronix S.A. (France); Tektronix Berlin GmbH & Co. KG (Germany); Tektronix Berlin Verwaltungs GmbH (Germany); Tektronix GmbH (Germany); Tektronix Network Systems GmbH (Germany); Tektronix Hong Kong Limited; Tektronix Engineering Development (India) Private Limited; Tektronix (India) Private Limited; Tektronix Padova S.p.A. (Italy); Tektronix S.p.A. (Italy); Inet Technologies Japan KK; Tektronix Japan Ltd.; Inet Global Korea Limited Company; Tektronix Korea, Ltd.; Tektronix, S.A. de C.V. (Mexico); Inet Technologies Netherlands B.V.; Tektronix Distribution Europe B.V. (The Netherlands); Tektronix Holland B.V. (Netherlands); Inet Worldwide Telecommunications Ptd. Ltd. (Singapore); Tektronix Southeast Asia Pte. Ltd. (Singapore); Tektronix Espanola, S.A. (Spain); Tektronix AB (Sweden); Tektronix International GmbH (Switzerland); Tektronix International Sales GmbH (Switzerland); Tektronix Taiwan, Ltd.; Tayvin 160 Ltd. (United Kingdom); Tektronix Cambridge Ltd. (United Kingdom); Tektronix Europe Ltd. (United Kingdom); Tektronix Network Systems Ltd. (United Kingdom); Tektronix U.K. Ltd.; Tektronix U.K. Holdings Ltd.; Tektronix U K Development Centre Ltd.; Maxtek Components Corporation; Inet Technologies International, Inc.; Tektronix Texas LLC; Tektronix Analysis Software, Inc.; Tektronix Asia, Ltd.; Tektronix Development Company; Tektronix Export, Inc.; Tektronix Federal Systems, Inc.; Tektronix International, Inc.

PRINCIPAL COMPETITORS

Agilent Technologies Inc.; Anritsu Corporation; Rohde & Schwarz GmbH & Co. KG.

FURTHER READING

Benner, Susan, "Life in the Silicon Rain Forest," *Inc.,* June 1984. pp. 112-21.

Brandt, Richard, "Textronix (sic) Atten-hut!," *Business Week,* April 18, 1988, p. 33.

Conner, Margery S., "Good Engineering Decisions Are Key to Improving U.S.'s Competitive Stance," *EDN,* October 1, 1987, pp. 73-80.

Hill, Gail Kinsey, "Tektronix Inc.: Will the Cuts Be the Last?," *Business Journal* (Portland, Ore.), June 4, 1990, p. 2.

Hoj, Robert D., "Turning Around 'a Battleship in a Bathtub,'" *Business Week,* May 7, 1990, p. 122.

"How to Be Big Though Small," *Forbes,* May 15, 1974, p. 115.

Humble, Charles, "Annual Report from Tektronix Inc. Takes on Defensive Tone," *Portland Oregonian,* August 26, 1984, p. E1.

King, Harriet, "'High Powered' President for Tektronix," *New York Times,* September 11, 1992.

LaPolla, Stephanie, "New Tektronix Chief Outlines Strategy," *PC Week,* October 26, 1992, p. 163.

Lee, Marshall M., *Winning with People: The First 40 Years of Tektronix,* Beaverton, Ore: Tektronix, Inc., 1986.

Manning, Jeff, "Does Soros Group Want to Take Over Tek?," *Business Journal* (Portland, Ore.), August 17, 1992, p. 1.

———, "Golf Junkets May Handicap Tek's Meyer," *Business Journal* (Portland, Ore.), October 5, 1992, p. 1.

———, "Managers Forced to Make Further Cuts at Troubled Tek," *Business Journal* (Portland, Ore.), February 12, 1990, p. 3.

———, "Shake-up Follows Ouster of Tektronix's Friedley," *Business Journal* (Portland, Ore.), April 30, 1990, p. 1.

———, "Soros, Tek Reach Accord After Nasty Board Control Battle," *Business Journal* (Portland, Ore.), November 16, 1992, p. 1.

———, "Tek Gives Soros Advance Cold Shoulder," *Business Journal* (Portland, Ore.), August 24, 1992, p. 1.

———, "Tek Fills Spot with Former Apple Exec," *Business Journal* (Portland, Ore.), September 14, 1992, p. 1.

———, "Tek Heads into Annual Meeting with Intrigue on Agenda," *Business Journal* (Portland, Ore.), September 21, 1992, p. 4.

———, "Tek Officials Deny Plan Is a Response to Takeover Threat," *Business Journal* (Portland, Ore.), September 3, 1990, p. 2.

———, "Tek's Workstation Line to Close If Buyer Not Found in 60 Days," *Business Journal* (Portland, Ore.), October 15, 1990, p. 1.

———, "Tektronix Scopes Out Corporate Reworking," *Business Journal* (Portland, Ore.), March 25, 1991.

Montgomery, Leland, "The Agony of Jerry Meyer," *Financial World,* December 8, 1992, pp. 24-25.

Olmos, Robert, "Tek Adds 'Job-Sharing' to Its List of Worker Benefits," *Portland Oregonian,* January 29, 1978, p. A17.

Painter, John, Jr., "Success of Tektronix, Oregon's Largest Employer, Surprises Founder," *Portland Oregonian,* April 6, 1975, p. A30.

Pitta, Julie, "Can Dinosaurs Adapt?," *Forbes,* March 4, 1991, p. 122.

Pratt, Gerry, "Time-Off Experiment Bolsters Tektronix," *Portland Oregonian,* April 23, 1971.

"President for Tektronix Hired from Honeywell," *New York Times,* October 25, 1990.

Rivera, Dylan, "Slipping Tek Profits Reflect Slowdown," *Oregonian,* September 16, 2005, p. B1.

Rogoway, Mike, "Tek Betting on Telecom Rise," *Oregonian,* October 14, 2004, p. C1.

———, "Tektronix Turns the Corner," *Oregonian,* June 28, 2004, p. C1.

"Selective Success," *Forbes,* June 15, 1969, p. 50.

"Shedding a One-Product Image," *Business Week,* February 16, 1976, pp. 91-92.

Sorensen, Donald J., "Ex-Tektronix Employees Form Own High-Tech Firms," *Portland Oregonian,* March 8, 1982, p. D7.

———, "Fred Meyer, Tektronix Join Elite Billion-Dollar Sales Firms," *Portland Oregonian,* January 6, 1980, p. C7.

"Tektronix Cofounder City's '1st Citizen,'" *Portland Oregonian,* February 2, 1974.

"Tektronix Joins Nation's 'Top 500,'" *Portland Oregonian,* May 13, 1976, p. B7.

"Tektronix Recalls Oscilloscopes," *Computer Dealer News,* July 6, 1998, p. 6.

"Tektronix's Push to Get Back on the Fast-Growth Track," *Business Week,* September 17, 1984, pp. 108-10.

"Tektronix: Where One Product Isn't Enough," *Business Week,* August 4, 1973, pp. 65-66.

Tripp, Julie, "John Gray to Replace Vollum As Tektronix Chairman," *Portland Oregonian,* February 3, 1984.

Wiegner, Kathleen K., "Life in The Fast Lane," *Forbes,* April 3, 1978, p. 57.

———, "'Manufacturing Was an Afterthought,'" *Forbes,* January 27, 1986, pp. 34-35.

———, "Nice Guys Finish Last," *Forbes,* June 26, 1989.

Woog, Adam, *Sezless Oysters and Self-Tipping Hats: 100 Years of Invention in the Pacific Northwest,* Seattle, Wash.: Sasquatch Books, 1991, pp. 209-11.

Yim, Su-Jin, "Tektronix's Bold Move: Divide and Survive," *Oregonian,* June 27, 1999, p. E1.

———, "Xerox, Tek Pair Up," *Oregonian,* September 27, 1999, p. B1.

TenneT

TenneT B.V.

P.O. Box 718
Arnhem,
Netherlands
Telephone: (31) 026 373 11 11
Fax: (31) 026 373 11 12
Web site: http://www.tennet.org

State-Owned Company
Incorporated: 2001
Employees: 328
Sales: EUR 416 million ($500 million) (2004)
NAIC: 221122 Electric Power Distribution

■ ■ ■

TenneT B.V., the Transmission System Operator (TSO) formed in 1998 as part of the liberalization of The Netherlands' electricity sector, oversees the country's high-voltage power grid, providing interconnection services among the country's electricity producers and regional power grid operators, as well as connections to the European power grid network. TenneT operates 380 kV and 220 kV grids on a national scale and, since its acquisition of regional grid operator Transportnet Zuid-Holland in 2003, the 150 kV grid in South Holland. The company is responsible for guaranteeing the security and continuity of The Netherlands' power supply, as well as providing connections to the power grid to customers (primarily energy producers and distributors). TenneT is also responsible for maintaining and expanding the country's high-voltage grid infrastructure. TenneT also works in partnership with other European

TSOs. The company is part of the Belpex consortium, formed in 2005 in partnership with Belgian TSO Elia, French counterpart RTE, and the APX and Powernext power exchanges. In January 2006, Belpex received authorization to apply for a license to operate the power exchange in Belgium. TenneT also has formed an interconnector partnership with Norway's Statnett to lay a 600 MW subsea power cable between Norway and The Netherlands. That cable is expected to be operational by 2007. TenneT is controlled by The Netherlands' government. In 2004, the company posted revenues of EUR 416 million ($500 million).

ORIGINS IN LIBERALIZING THE DUTCH ENERGY MARKET

In most of Europe, electrical power generation was brought under direct government oversight, if not outright control, by the early 20th century. The importance of electrical power to the development of industry and modern domestic infrastructure encouraged governments to place strict controls and regulation on its generation and transmission, and for the most part the operation of the power grids became the responsibility of the national government. In The Netherlands, however, provincial and regional governments long retained a strong counterbalance to the national government. The national government first attempted to take control of the country's growing electrical generation and transmission market in 1921, establishing a government-owned national electric utility. This effort, as well as a number of others in the years leading to World War II, failed in the face of resistance from regional and local governments, which were

COMPANY PERSPECTIVES

Mission: TenneT is the independent and impartial market facilitator in the liberalised energy market. With its high-grade transmission grid and customised services it markets and develops a comprehensive range of transmission and system services as well as supplying services aimed at boosting the market mechanism and encouraging the development of a sustainable energy supply system. All these services are made available to the market on the basis of impartiality.

Vision: TenneT is keen to take its development as a reputable TSO in the Dutch and Northwestern European market to an even higher level so as to strengthen its market position, as this would enable TenneT to be of optimum service to Dutch society, to its shareholder and to its own staff, both now and in times to come.

unwilling to relinquish control of their electrical power operations.

The need to rebuild the country's electrical infrastructure, as well as the high investment costs required to modernize the country's power distribution network, offered a new opportunity to create a central body operating on a national scale. In 1949, the country's major electrical power producers joined together to form the Samenwerkende Elektriciteitsproductiebedrijven, or SEP. This body provided representation and coordination for the country's electrical power producers. SEP's first task was to establish a national power grid, and it was granted control of the country's high-voltage power grid. SEP also took charge of the national distribution of electrical power, acting as an exchange through which excess capacity and capacity shortfalls could be balanced among the Dutch provinces. In this way, the SEP helped guarantee the continuity of electrical power and the security of the Dutch electrical infrastructure, providing a backbone for the country's industrial expansion.

With electrical power generation and distribution handled by dozens of companies throughout the country, The Netherlands' electricity market remained highly innovative. The smaller companies were hampered in their ability to invest in expanding their infrastructure. Following the formation of the SEP, the Dutch government launched a new effort to streamline the industry, with the ultimate goal of creating a single, nationally

operating and state-run electricity body as found elsewhere in Europe. Into the 1970s, the government had succeeded in narrowing the field to just four regional companies, EZH in the southwest, UNA in the northwest, EPZ in the southeast, and EPON in the northeast. By the end of the decade, however, the government's efforts to streamline the industry to a single company had failed.

The 1980s marked a turning point for the European electrical power market, as new European Union directives called for the deregulation and liberalization of national markets, including the ending of government-owned monopolies and the creation of a true cross-border electrical market. Toward that end, the Dutch electrical power market took its own steps toward liberalization: In a compromise agreement made with the government in 1988, the four electric utilities agreed to divide their operations into their power generation and power distribution components. This separation was only partially carried out, however, and into the 1990s, The Netherlands continued to lack a truly competitive electricity market. The liberalization of the European electrical market, launched in the 1990s, saw the rise of a number of large-scale, internationally operating companies. In order to remain competitive on this new international market, the Dutch electrical power groups began to push for further liberalization of the Dutch market. As part of that process, however, the Dutch government insisted that it be given control of the country's high-voltage grid and infrastructure. By 1998, agreement had been reached with the electrical power producers on the transfer of the high-voltage grid to government oversight, which led to the passage of the New Electricity Act and the formation of TenneT in 1998. TenneT was then placed under the oversight of the Ministry of Economic Affairs; nonetheless, SEP retained ownership of TenneT.

NATIONAL GRID OPERATOR IN 2001

Negotiations continued between the Dutch government and SEP, leading to the passage of new legislation, the OEPS Act (for Electricity Production Sector Transition Act), in 2001. This legislation stipulated that the SEP be dissolved, transferring ownership of TenneT to the Dutch government. The act also obliged the government to purchase TenneT from its previous owners. TenneT now became an autonomously operating company, and was permitted to raise capital on the free market.

With responsibility for the country's 380 kV and 220 kV power grid, TenneT also was granted authority to conduct an auction for cross-border imported power,

KEY DATES

1949: SEP (Samenwerkende Elektriciteitsproductie-bedrijven) is created by Dutch electricity producers to install and oversee a national high-voltage grid.

1998: As part of legislation liberalizing the Dutch electricity market, SEP transfers oversight of the high-voltage grid to the Dutch government, which forms TenneT.

2001: The Dutch government buys TenneT and SEP is dissolved; TenneT launches subsidiaries TSO Auction, Groencertificatiebeheer, Elined, and Nlink; a stake in Powernext is acquired; the APX power exchange is acquired.

2002: Elined sets up the Relined joint venture with ProRail to link fiber optic networks.

2003: Subsidiary EnerQ is founded; Groencertificatiebeheer changes its name to CertiQ; Transportnet Zuid-Holland is acquired as part of effort to establish full control of the national power grid.

2004: The company acquires EnergieKreuze, an online auction serving the power and gas markets in Belgium and The Netherlands; UKPX, the largest energy exchange in the United Kingdom, is acquired.

2005: A joint venture is formed with Norway's Statnett to construct a subsea interconnector cable between the two companies; the Belpex joint venture is formed with Powernext and Elia.

2006: Belpex receives permission to apply for a license to operate a power exchange in Belgium.

notably from Germany and Belgium. In January 2001, TenneT created a new subsidiary, TSO Auction. That company acted as an auctioneer for the country's five cross-border interconnection points between Germany and Belgium, working with its TSO counterparts in Germany (E.ON Netz and TWE Net) and Belgium (Elia) to establish the free flow of energy allotments among the three countries.

Continuing its international objectives, TenneT founded another subsidiary, Nlink, which began negotiating to create an interconnection between The Netherlands and the United Kingdom. By May 2001, TenneT also had acquired stakes in the Amsterdam Power Exchange (APX) seen as an important complement to its TSO Auction operations. At the end of 2001, TenneT joined with France's RTE and Elia to acquire control of the Powernext Power Exchange in Paris.

The Dutch government's efforts to encourage the development and use of renewable energy sources gave TenneT a new area of operation. In May 2001, the Ministry of Economic Affairs issued a decree requiring TenneT to implement a "Green Certificate" system, awarding certificates—and tax exemptions—to producers of renewable energy. In July 2001, the company launched a new subsidiary, Groencertificatiebeheer, to govern the distribution of the certificates.

TenneT explored other areas of expansion as well. In 2001, the company formed another subsidiary, Elined, in order to exploit the extra capacity of the fiber optic network that had been deployed across its high-voltage grid. That subsidiary also became responsible for leasing space on its high-voltage pylons for telecommunications and radio transmission antennas. TenneT then began negotiations with Dutch rail track management company, Railinfrabeheer, to link their fiber optic networks. These talks led to the creation of a joint venture called Relined in 2002.

INTERNATIONAL REACH IN THE NEW CENTURY

Nlink's efforts to create an interconnection with the United Kingdom paid off in 2002, with the formation of a joint venture company, BritNed, with a subsidiary of British TSO Transco. BritNed began plans to launch construction of the interconnector, which was expected to be operational as early as 2007. In 2002, as well, TenneT expanded into the United Kingdom through APX's acquisition of its British counterpart APX UK.

New Dutch legislation passed in 2003 providing subsidies for the companies meeting environmental quality standards added a further extension to TenneT's range of operations. In response, the company added a new subsidiary, EnerQ, to oversee these operations. The legislation also expanded the role of Groencertifcatiebeheer, adding oversight to more than 2,000 combined heat and power producers. As a result, that subsidiary changed its name, to CertiQ.

Into the mid-2000s, TenneT launched an effort to take full control of The Netherlands' high-voltage (50 kV and more) power grid. The company made an important step toward that goal with the acquisition in

2003 of Transportnet Zuid-Holland (TZH) for EUR 249 million. That purchase added TZH's 680 kilometers of high-voltage connections, including nearly 550 kilometers of a 150 kV lines and some 180 kilometers of 380 kV lines.

TenneT expanded its power auction operations in 2004 with the acquisition of EnergieKreuze, an online auction that served as an exchange for long-term power and gas contracts between The Netherlands and Belgium. Also that year, APX joined with partners Huberator and Endex to form a new joint venture gas exchange in Belgium. The company also acquired a second British power exchange, UKPX, then the largest in the United Kingdom. The acquisition was then merged with APX, taking on the name of APX Power Ltd.

In July 2005, TenneT expanded its exchange operations again, joining with Elia and Powernext of France to form the Belpex power exchange. By January 2006, the joint venture had been given permission to apply for a license to operate in Belgium. In the meantime, TenneT had continued to seek opportunities to expand its international interconnector business. This led the company to form a partnership with Norway's Statnett in 2005. That partnership quickly received the go-ahead to construct a 600 MW subsea cable linking The Netherlands and Norway. Completion of the project was expected for 2007. TenneT had established itself as a major partner in the creation of a Europeanwide energy market in the new century.

M. L. Cohen

PRINCIPAL SUBSIDIARIES

CertiQ; Elined; EnerQ; Groencertificatiebeheer; TenneT Holding B.V.; TenneT TSO B.V.; TenneT Zuid-Holland; TSO Auction.

PRINCIPAL COMPETITORS

Electricite de France; RWE AG; ENI S.p.A.; E.ON AG; ENEL S.p.A.; National Grid Transco plc; Tractebel S.A.; Endesa S.A.

FURTHER READING

"Dutch Power Links," *World Gas Intelligence,* January 21, 2004, p. 4.

"Dutch Utilities Oppose Government's Network Spin-Off Plan," *World Gas Intelligence,* April 7, 2004, p. 7.

"Nordic-Dutch Interconnector to Go Ahead," *Utility Week,* January 14, 2005, p. 10.

"TenneT Buys EnergieKreuze," *Gas Connections,* June 24, 2004, p. 5.

"TenneT Takes Over Transportnet Zuid-Holland," *Utility Week,* June 27, 2003, p. 14.

TIFFANY & CO.

Tiffany & Co.

—■—

727 Fifth Avenue
New York, New York 10022
U.S.A.
Telephone: (212) 755-8000
Fax: (212) 230-6633
Web site: http://www.tiffany.com

Public Company
Incorporated: 1868
Employees: 7,341
Sales: $2.2 billion (2005)
Stock Exchanges: New York
Ticker Symbol: TIF
NAIC: 334518 Watch, Clock, and Part Manufacturing;
    339911 Jewelry (except Costume) Manufacturing;
    44831 Jewelry Stores

■ ■ ■

Founded in 1837, Tiffany & Co. has long been renowned for its luxury goods, especially jewelry, and has sought to market itself as an arbiter of taste and style. Tiffany designs, manufactures, and sells jewelry, watches, and crystal glassware. It also sells other timepieces, sterling silverware, china, stationery, fragrances, and accessories. Many of these products are sold under the Tiffany name, at Tiffany stores throughout the world as well as through direct-mail, corporate merchandising, and the Tiffany Web site. The company branched out in the early years of the new millennium, opening retail locations under the Temple St. Clair and Iridesse monikers. It also acquired a major-ity stake in Little Switzerland, a duty-free specialty retailer found the Caribbean, Alaska, and Florida.

EARLY HISTORY

In 1837 Charles Lewis Tiffany and John F. Young opened Tiffany & Young, with $1,000 in backing from Tiffany's father. Located on Broadway opposite Manhattan's City Hall Park, this store sold stationery and a variety of "fancy goods," including costume jewelry. Unlike other stores of the time, Tiffany featured plainly marked prices that were strictly adhered to, sparing the customer the usual practice of haggling with the proprietor. Tiffany also departed from the norm by insisting on cash payment rather than extending credit or accepting barter.

In 1841 Tiffany and Young took on another partner, J. L. Ellis, and the store became Tiffany, Young & Ellis. By 1845 the store was successful enough to discontinue paste (costume jewelry) and begin selling real jewelry, as well as the city's most complete line of stationery. Silverware was added in 1847. In addition to these main items, Tiffany's also sold watches and clocks, a variety of ornaments and bronzes, perfumes, preparations for the skin and hair, dinner sets, cuspidors, moccasins, belts, and numerous other sundries, including Chinese bric-a-brac and horse and dog whips.

The new partner's capital enabled Young to go to Paris as a buyer, and he later established a branch store there. When the French monarchy was overthrown in 1848, Young purchased some of the crown jewels and also a bejeweled corset reputed to belong to Marie Antoinette. A shrewd publicist, Tiffany was quick to exploit this coup. He teamed up with P. T. Barnum, to their mutual profit, on a number of ventures and presented a gem-studded miniature silver-filigree horse and carriage as a wedding present to Tom Thumb and his bride. He introduced sterling silver to the United States in 1852, a year after contracting John C. Moore to produce silverware exclusively for the company. In 1853 he bought out his partners, and the firm became Tiffany & Co.

During the Civil War, the company was an emporium for military supplies, producing swords and importing rifles and ammunition. During the Gilded Age that followed, its main problem was finding enough jewelry to satisfy overwhelming customer demand. By then it also had established dominance in the American silverware market. In 1868 a London branch store was added and Tiffany & Co. was incorporated, with its proprietor as president and treasurer. Also in that year, Moore's workshop became part of the firm. The store, which had been inching uptown with the city itself, moved into a newly constructed, company-owned building adjoining Union Square in 1870.

Tiffany's prestige reached a new level when the company won the gold medal for jewelry and grand prize for silverware at the Paris Exposition in 1878. Soon it was serving as a jeweler, goldsmith, and silversmith to most of the crowned heads of Europe. Its real clientele, however, came from the burgeoning ranks of America's wealthy, many with far more cash than taste. Tiffany accommodated them all, no matter how ostentatious or whimsical their desires. The height (or depth) of vulgarity was reached when Diamond Jim Brady ordered, and Tiffany duly produced, a solid gold chamber pot for Lillian Russell, with an eye peering up in the center of the bottom. It was estimated in 1887

that Tiffany's vaults held $40 million in precious stones. Among these was the largest flawless and perfectly colored canary diamond ever mined. This 128.5-carat "Tiffany Diamond," still held by the New York store, has been valued by the company at $22 million.

In 1894 a factory was established in New Jersey in Forest Hill, which was later annexed by Newark, for the manufacture of silverware, stationery, and leather goods. Charles Tiffany died in 1902, leaving an estate estimated at $35 million. He was the only Tiffany to run the company. Louis Comfort Tiffany, his eldest son to survive childhood, was an accomplished artist who sometimes made jewelry for Tiffany but was best known for his Art Nouveau stained glass windows and lamps. In 1905 the store had moved into quarters at Fifth Avenue and 37th Street designed by Stanford White in the form of a Venetian palazzo, and two years later John C. Moore, great-grandson of the silversmith, became president.

Tiffany's sales volume rose from $7 million in 1914 to $17.7 million in 1919. This figure was seldom if ever matched during the 1920s, but profits remained high and dividends rose steadily. A share of stock bought in 1913 for $600 was worth the same in 1929, but split five-for-one in 1920 and also earned close to $10,000 in dividends over that period.

OVERCOMING THE DEPRESSION

Even the rich cut back on luxury goods after the 1929 stock market crash. Tiffany's sales fell 45 percent to $8.4 million in 1930, dropped another 37 percent to $5.4 million in 1931, and yet another 45 percent to a rock bottom $2.9 million in 1932, when the federal government imposed an additional 10 percent on the excise tax for jewelry. There were staff layoffs in 1933, 1934, 1935, 1938, and 1939. The company lost about $1 million a year throughout the decade, but, dipping into its capital reserve, never stopped paying a dividend, although it fell to $5 a share in 1940. In that year $3.6 million had to be taken from the reserve just to stay in business, and the London store was closed.

Also in 1940, Tiffany moved uptown for the sixth and last time, to the southeast corner of Fifth Avenue and 57th Street, where it put up a $2.5 million Art Deco seven-story building. It was the first completely air-conditioned building in New York. Louis de B. Moore succeeded his father as president in that year. During World War II the Newark factory (which made surgical instruments during World War I) was chiefly given over to military production. It made precision parts for anti-aircraft guns (which it made again during the Korean War) and fitting blocks for airplanes.

KEY DATES

1837: Charles Lewis Tiffany and John F. Young open Tiffany & Young.
1841: Tiffany and Young take on another partner, J. L. Ellis, and the store becomes Tiffany, Young & Ellis.
1853: Tiffany buys out his partners and the firm becomes Tiffany & Co.
1940: The company moves to its Fifth Avenue location.
1955: To prevent Bulova Watch Co. from taking control, Tiffany heirs and close associates sell Hoving Corp. 51 percent of Tiffany stock.
1961: Hoving and a group of investors gain control of Tiffany.
1978: Tiffany & Co. is sold to Avon Products Inc.
1984: Avon agrees to sell Tiffany to an investor group led by its chairman, William R. Chaney.
1987: Tiffany goes public.
2001: The company buys a 45 percent stake in duty-free retailer Little Switzerland.
2004: The Iridesse retail concept is launched.

Tiffany's fortunes revived somewhat in this period, but in 1949 earnings came to only $19,368. Net profits were a mere $14,787 in 1952, when the Paris store was closed, and $24,906 in 1953. The company's $7 million in 1955 sales was no more than it had taken in during 1914. Conservative management and outdated styles were blamed by restive shareholders. One of these was Harry Maidman, a realtor attracted mainly by Tiffany's long-term lease to the land under its prime-location building. He quietly bought up at least 30 percent of the stock. Denied a seat on the board of directors, Maidman sold his shares in 1955 to the Bulova Watch Co. To prevent Bulova from taking control, Tiffany heirs and close associates sold Hoving Corp., owner of neighboring Bonwit Teller, 51 percent of the stock for $3.8 million.

Walter Hoving, who soon became chairman and chief executive officer of Tiffany, had to report to the General Shoe Corp. (later Genesco, Inc.), which took a majority share of his own company in 1956. He did not win firm control of the store until 1961, when he assembled a group of investors that bought out Genesco and Bulova. Nevertheless, Hoving immediately put his stamp on Tiffany by conducting the first bargain sale in

the firm's history to clear out merchandise he considered gaudy or vulgar. He dropped diamond rings for men for that reason and discontinued leather goods, antiques, silver plate, brass, and pewter as not worthy of Tiffany's attention.

1960-70: FOCUSING ON "AESTHETICS"

Hoving recruited a galaxy of stars to create a new standard of quality for Tiffany's products. Jean Schlumberger was hired to design its finest and most expensive jewelry. Henry Platt expanded the jewelry workshop's staff from eight to sixty, and later enlisted Elsa Peretti, Angela Cummings, and Paloma Picasso to create jewelry exclusively for Tiffany. Van Day Treux, the new design director, revived vermeil (gold-plated sterling silver) and old patterns of silver flatware and commissioned new china. Gene Moore, put to work dressing the store's windows, spent nearly 40 years creating striking and often provocative displays.

"Aesthetics," Hoving pronounced, "if properly understood, will almost always increase sales." To broaden the base of its clientele, the store added high-quality but lower-priced goods such as silver key rings for $3.50. By the early 1960s a third of the store's patrons were living 100 miles or more away. One of the firm's many longtime sales clerks said, "It's gotten so there are customers here whose names I don't even know." A San Francisco store was added in 1963, and branches in Chicago, Houston, Beverly Hills, and Atlanta soon followed.

The balance sheet reflected Tiffany's turnaround. Annual sales reached $21.9 million in fiscal year 1966 (ending January 31, 1967). Net profits rose every year, from $173,612 in 1955 to $1.7 million in 1966. That year about 65 percent of Tiffany's volume came from jewelry, 18 percent from silver, 14 percent from china and glassware, and the remaining 3 percent from stationery (engraved, not printed) and specialty items. The company made all its diamond jewelry and a small part of its gold jewelry in the Fifth Avenue store itself. Virtually all of it was designed by the staff. Nearly all of its sterling silver (carried by 150 franchised dealers as well as Tiffany stores) also was staff-designed, and 85 percent was being manufactured in the Newark plant. China and glassware were being made to company specifications. Tiffany's catalog (free until 1972) was the first major catalog entirely in color.

NEW OWNERSHIP: 1970-89

Business continued to grow in the 1970s. Sales increased from $23 million in 1970 to $35.2 million in

1974. Net income passed the $1 million mark in 1972 and reached $2.1 million the following year. In November 1978 Tiffany & Co. was sold to Avon Products Inc., the world's leading manufacturer and distributor of cosmetics and costume jewelry, for about $104 million in stock. Tiffany's sales had reached $60.2 million and net profits about $4 million in the previous fiscal year. Hoving remained chairman and chief executive officer until the end of 1980, when he retired.

Avon spent $53 million (raising some of it by selling some of its inventory of uncut diamonds) to open Tiffany stores in Dallas and Kansas City, expand its direct mail orders, introduce Tiffany credit cards, and streamline and computerize its back-office operations. But its ratio of operating profits to revenue fell from 17.6 percent to 6.5 percent between 1979 and 1983, mainly because it tried to compete with department stores in selling low-margin watches, china, and glassware. A 1984 Newsweek article noted that the Fifth Avenue store had stocked so many inexpensive items that it began looking like Macy's during a white sale, and that customers had complained about declining quality and service. In August 1984 Avon agreed to sell Tiffany to an investor group led by its chairman, William R. Chaney, for $135.5 million in cash. The company had earned only $984,000 in 1983 on sales of $124.2 million.

Under its new management Tiffany & Co. shifted direction again. It sought to reassure the affluent but socially insecure patron that Tiffany's taste remained "safe." The firm also cut costs by closing the Newark plant and its Kansas City store, cutting staff, and embarking on a program to wholesale its jewelry and silverware and the line of leather products that had been restored under Avon's management. Tiffany lost $5.1 million in 1984 and $2.6 million in 1985, mainly because of heavy interest costs on borrowing to pay off Avon, but in 1986 it earned $6.7 million on net sales of $182.5 million, despite paying out $9.1 million for interest on its debt. During 1987 it earned $16.8 million on net sales of $230.5 million.

Tiffany went public again in 1987, raising about $103.5 million by selling 4.5 million shares of common stock. About $43 million of this sum was earmarked to retire nearly all of the company's outstanding debt. The new public company no longer owned the Fifth Avenue building nor the land beneath it, which it had purchased for $2.8 million in 1963. (The air rights over the building had been sold in 1979 to Donald Trump, owner of neighboring Trump Tower, for $5 million.)

"Tiffany," a fragrance, was introduced in 1987 at $220 an ounce and marketed by department stores across the country. Wool and silk scarves were introduced the same year, shortly after neckties had been added, and the company's line of handbags, evening purses, wallets, and briefcases expanded. A London store was reintroduced in 1986 and stores in Munich and Zurich opened in 1987 and 1988, respectively. Emphasizing its glitter in 1988, Tiffany displayed, in five of its stores, a collection of 22 individual pieces of jewelry made in its own workshop and valued at more than $10 million. All but one piece sold. Paradoxically, perhaps, but profitably, Tiffany's emphasis on luxury drew in the masses; as many as 25,000 people visited the store on a Saturday during the holiday season.

1990 AND BEYOND

Tiffany's catalog mailings reached 15 million in 1994. These publications were seen as a powerful sales and image tools for the stores as well as a source of profit in themselves. The company's direct-marketing effort also included business-to-business sales, which included a corporate gift catalog each year. Corporate customers purchased Tiffany products for business gift giving, employee service and achievement recognition awards, customer incentives, and other purposes.

The Far East played an important role in Tiffany's resurgence. Mitsukoshi Ltd., the "Bloomingdale's of Japan," which began stocking Tiffany items in its department stores and smaller shops in 1972, accounted for $26.5 million of Tiffany's $290 million in sales in 1988. Mitsukoshi bought 10 percent of Tiffany's stock in 1989 to increase its earlier 3 percent stake; it eventually sold its stake in 1999. Tiffany opened two stores in Hong Kong during 1988 and 1989, a third in Taiwan in 1990, and a fourth in Singapore in 1991.

Tiffany suffered a serious setback in 1992 when sales to Mitsukoshi fell 35 percent, from an estimated $113 million in 1991. Hurt by a recession, Japanese consumers had cut back spending, catching the retailer with more inventory than it needed. In 1993 Tiffany assumed direct responsibility for sales, merchandising, and marketing at Mitsukoshi's 29 Tiffany boutiques, taking a $32.7 million after-tax charge to buy them and run them on its own. This restructuring was largely responsible for a $10.2 million loss in 1993 despite sales of $566.5 million, a 16 percent gain. In spite of the setback, Tiffany ranked sixth out of 28 public specialty retailers in return on equity from 1989 to 1993, averaging an annual 18.8 percent over this period.

Also in 1992 the company, affected by curbed spending during the 1990–91 recession in the United States, again began to emphasize mass merchandising. A new information campaign stressed that the average Tiffany purchase was under $200 and that diamond engagement rings started at only $850. It sent "How to Buy a Diamond" brochures to 40,000 people who called a toll-free number. To keep the company from losing its cachet, however, it continued to maintain its high-style image through books on Tiffany objects and in-store table setting displays. Avoiding calling Tiffany a luxury-goods firm, Chaney described it as "a design-led business offering quality products at competitive prices."

During fiscal 1994 Tiffany's net sales rose to $682.8 million, of which U.S. retail accounted for 45 percent, international retail 41 percent (up from 32 percent two years earlier), and direct marketing 14 percent. (Despite this breakdown, "retail" also included wholesale sales.) Net income rebounded to $29.3 million. Long-term debt was $101.5 million at the end of 1994. In mid-1995 Tiffany was leasing 18 retail stores in the United States and was completing two more, in Short Hills, New Jersey, and Chevy Chase, Maryland. Another 11 were abroad. Tiffany was also operating Faraone stores in Milan and Florence, many boutiques in Japanese stores, and one in Taiwan. Other parties operated four Tiffany boutiques in South Korea and one each in the Philippines, Abu Dhabi, Taiwan, Hong Kong, Hawaii, and Guam. Four Faraone boutiques were in Japanese department stores.

Of merchandise offered for sale by Tiffany in fiscal 1994, 26 percent was produced by the company itself. Finished jewelry was produced in Tiffany's own workshop and also purchased from more than 100 manufacturers. The company acquired Howard H. Sweet & Son, Inc., a manufacturer of gold and silver jewelry and chains in fiscal 1989, and McTeigue & Co., a manufacturer of gold jewelry, in fiscal 1990. Cut and polished diamonds were being purchased from a number of sources. Diamond jewelry accounted for about 22 percent of Tiffany's net sales in fiscal 1994.

A single manufacturer produced Tiffany's silver flatware patterns from Tiffany's proprietary dies by use of its traditional manufacturing techniques. Likewise, engraved stationery was being purchased from a single manufacturer. A Paris workshop decorating hand-painted tableware was acquired in fiscal 1991. In the same year Tiffany established a watch assembly, engineering, and testing operation in Lussy-sur-Morges, Switzerland. The following year the company acquired Judel Glassware Co., Inc., producer of crystal glassware in Salem, West Virginia. A distribution facility was being leased in Parsippany, New Jersey, and additional warehouse space in adjacent Pine Brook, New Jersey.

During the late 1990s, Tiffany focused on boosting its profits by offering fine diamond jewelry. Realizing that its vertically integrated structure bode well for profits, the company purchased a 14.9 percent stake in Aber Resources in 1999. The Canadian firm owned part of the Diavik Diamond Project, a Canadian mine that began producing gem-quality diamonds in 2002. The company sold its stake in Aber in 2004 after it secured a diamond supply contract that extended into 2013.

Tiffany entered the new millennium on solid ground. Overall, the company's earnings had risen at 24 percent compound annual growth rate from 1996 to 2001. To keep its momentum, Tiffany launched an aggressive growth strategy. By increasing its store count, Tiffany hoped to cash in on middle-income shoppers. An April 2002 *Forbes* article described the scene at a suburban Tiffany store. "Shoppers clutching Gap and Benneton bags clogged the aisles and elbowed one another to get to the store's self-service corner, where boxes of sterling-silver key rings, pendants and charm bracelets, many priced under $100, were stacked and prepackaged in Tiffany's trademark robin's-egg blue. For customers needing service, staffers roved the sales floor passing out beepers." Analysts warned that this strategy could possibly tarnish the prestigious brand. Nevertheless, Tiffany's management anticipated that offering and promoting lower-priced merchandise would lure new customers and spark growth at its retail locations.

The company moved into the Caribbean market in 2001 when it acquired a 45 percent stake in Little Switzerland, a duty-free retailer based in the U.S. Virgin Islands. It increased its stake to 98 percent the following year. During 2003, Tiffany launched a new retail concept under the name Temple St. Clair. Two stores, one in California and one in New Jersey, were opened that year and sold trendy jewelry ranging from $500 to $35,000 per piece. In 2004, the company launched another retail concept, this time focusing on pearls. Named Iridesse, the new stores carried merchandise ranging from $50 to $50,000.

In 2004, the company opened ten stores and boutiques: four in the U.S., three in Japan, one in Taipei, one in Shanghai, and one in London. It also launched several new jewelry lines including Atlas, Voile, and Rose. That year, sales increased to $2.2 billion while net income climbed to $304.3 million. In early 2006, the company ended its stockholder rights plan, more commonly known as a poison pill plan that prevented hostile takeovers. The action prompted speculation that the company could possibly go up for sale in the near future.

Robert Halasz
Updated, Christina M. Stansell

PRINCIPAL SUBSIDIARIES

Tiffany and Company; Laurelton Diamonds Inc.; East Pond Holdings Inc.; Tiffany & Co. International.

PRINCIPAL COMPETITORS

Bulgari S.p.A.; LVMH Moet Hennessy Louis Vuitton SA; Compagnie Financiere Richemont SA.

FURTHER READING

Byrne, Harlan S., "Sparkling Scheme?," *Barron's*, July 26, 1999, p. 16.

Carpenter, Charles H., *Tiffany Silver*, New York: Dodd, Mead, 1978.

Gallagher, Leigh, "All-You-Can-Eat Breakfast at Tiffany's," *Forbes*, April 15, 2002.

Green, Barbara, "Tiffany Backs Temple St. Clair in New Retail Jewelry Venture," *National Jeweler*, August 16, 2003, p. 4.

Francke, Linda Bird, "That Tiffany Touch," *New York*, December 22, 1980, pp. 23-26, 28.

Frazier, Mya, "Tiffany Things Outside Blue Box to Peddle Pearls," *Advertising Age*, May 23, 2005, p. 12.

Haden-Guest, Anthony, "Tiffany's Big Gamble," *New York*, October 15, 1984, pp. 36, 38-41, 43.

Lacossitt, Henry, "Treasure House on Fifth Avenue," *Saturday Evening Post*, January 24, 1953, pp. 30, 102, 104, 106; and January 31, 1953, pp. 30, 100, 109-110.

Palmer, Kimberly, "Tiffany & Co. Branches Out Under Alias," *Wall Street Journal*, July 23, 2003, p. B1.

Pouschine, Tatiana, "Tiffany: Act II," *Forbes*, November 11, 1991, pp. 70-73.

Prial, Frank J., "The Tiffany Touch," *Wall Street Journal*, December 24, 1968, pp. 1, 8.

Purtell, Joseph, *The Tiffany Touch*, New York: Random House, 1971.

Slom, Stanley H., "The Connoisseur: Walter Hoving Makes His Impeccable Taste a Tiffany Trademark," *Wall Street Journal*, October 27, 1975, pp. 1, 17.

Sparks, Debra, "Attention Tiffany Shoppers," *Financial World*, July 19, 1994, pp. 32-35.

"Tiffany's Off on a Spree," *Business Week*, October 6, 1962, pp. 54-55.

Trachtenberg, Jeffrey A., "Cocktails at Tiffany," *Forbes*, February 6, 1989, pp. 128, 130.

Wayne, Leslie, "At Tiffany, A Troubled Transition," *New York Times*, October 16, 1983, Sec. 3, pp. 1, 30.

Young, Vicki M., "Tiffany & Co. Stirs Talk by Ending Poison Pill," *WWD*, January 23, 2006, p. 16.

Zinn, Laura, and Uchida, Hiromi, "Who Said Diamonds Are Forever?," *Business Week*, November 2, 1992, pp. 128-29.

Trane

One Centennial Avenue
Piscataway, New Jersey 08855-6820
U.S.A.
Telephone: (732) 980-6000
Fax: (732) 980-3340
Web site: http://www.trane.com

Business Segment of American Standard Companies Inc.
Incorporated: 1913 as The Trane Company
Employees: 27,100
Sales: $6.02 billion (2005)
NAIC: 333415 Air-Conditioning and Warm Air Heating Equipment and Commercial and Industrial Refrigeration Equipment Manufacturing; 334512 Automatic Environmental Control Manufacturing for Residential, Commercial, and Appliance Use

■ ■ ■

Trane is a leading global manufacturer of commercial and residential heating, ventilation, and air conditioning systems and comprises the Air Conditioning Systems and Services Segment of its parent, American Standard Companies Inc., accounting for nearly 60 percent of American Standard's revenues in 2005.

WISCONSIN ORIGINS

The Trane story begins with James Trane, who emigrated from Norway to La Crosse, Wisconsin, in 1864. After working in the plumbing trade, Trane opened his own store in 1885. According to company lore, he was a stickler for quality and good service from the beginning.

Trane was also a product innovator. Trane Vapor Heating, a new kind of low-pressure steam heat, was introduced in 1913. Around this time, Trane brought his son, Reuben, into the business, which was incorporated as The Trane Company. Within a couple of years, they had dropped the plumbing business to concentrate on heating products.

Reuben Trane had studied mechanical engineering at the University of Wisconsin in Madison, and he is credited with coming up with the idea for the convector radiator in 1925. The device circulated hot water or steam through a coil, rather than the heavy cast-iron used in radiators of the day. Reuben Trane also started the company's training program for engineering graduates.

1930–50: A NEW INDUSTRY

The Trane Company became a pioneer in the new field of air conditioning (though credit for the industry's birth goes to competitor Carrier). The Trane Unit Cooler, introduced in 1931, blew air over coils containing well water. While midwestern movie theaters were famous early users of Trane products, the general economy and home starts were at a standstill during this time due to the Great Depression. Nevertheless, notes the company, Trane survived and was able to develop a number of innovations that would be used in commercial heating and cooling applications for decades to come. One of these was the first hermetic centrifugal refrigeration machine, called the Turbovac.

The Allied war effort made use of Trane's ingenuity during World War II. The company's heating and cooling technology was used in industries ranging from armament production to food dehydration. Trane outfitted thousands of naval vessels and produced a critical component for fighting aircraft called the intercooler. This lightweight and efficient new heat exchanger allowed Allied piston engine performance to match that of the Germans.

POSTWAR EXPANSION

Following the war, Trane benefited from the domestic building boom. The company expanded vertically, making its own reciprocating compressors since 1950.

Until the mid-1950s, Trane's business was focused on applied air conditioning systems, which were custom designed and assembled on site. In the latter half of the decade, the company found success in unitary air conditioners, which were delivered to the customer mostly assembled.

At the time, Trane did not make window units, but the residential market for central heating and air conditioning units would take off at the end of the 1950s. Until then, most of the home HVAC market in the United States was dominated by subsidiaries of industrial giants such as Borg-Warner, Chrysler, General Electric (GE), General Motors, and Westinghouse. According to *Forbes,* of the three remaining major independents, Trane was a distant second to Carrier Corporation (annual sales $250 million) but was growing. Its sales of $81.6 million for 1958 were up 237 percent in ten years. The U.S. air conditioning industry as a whole was valued at $3 billion and had scarcely begun to be penetrated. Only 7 percent of homes built in 1959 included air conditioning. Central heating and air then cost an average of $1,500.

The 1960s were a period of global expansion. In 1958, Trane had acquired a minority stake in CEMAT

of Epinal, France; it was later renamed Société Trane. Trane built new plants after acquiring a controlling stake in 1964. The company also added plants in the United States, in Lexington, Kentucky, in 1963 and in Rushville, Indiana, in 1972. Trane's production and research and development (R&D) facilities in La Crosse, Wisconsin, were also expanded. Trane began manufacturing in Great Britain in 1971 at a site in Colchester.

Most of Trane's business was in large industrial and commercial units. The company thrived in the booming construction market of the 1960s. Sales reached $253 million in 1970. One-fifth of this was in exports, mostly for industrial applications. Trane was reaching new heights in other ways: a version of the company's intercooler was used on the Apollo 15's lunar rover in 1971.

ENERGY CONSCIOUS: 1970-80

Trane was led through most of the 1970s by Thomas Hancock, who became CEO in 1966. He was succeeded in 1978 by William G. Roth.

In a period of high energy costs, commercial customers often chose to install new, more efficient equipment, noted *Barron's.* Such capital outlays were easier to sell if they could pay for themselves in three years. Trane provided economic analysis of potential savings through its TRACE computer program, introduced in 1973. Sales reached $427 million in 1975; net income was $15 million. Trane spent heavily on research and capital improvements in the last half of the decade, preparing a slew of energy-conscious products for the residential and commercial markets. By 1979, sales were up to $658 million, and the company's $250 million backlog had grown to $355 million.

A couple of acquisitions during the 1970s broadened the company's offerings. Arctic Traveler Corporation, a maker of truck refrigerators, was acquired in 1970. It soon expanded into cooling devices for buses and trains. Trane bought controls company Sentinel Electronics Corporation in 1978. In the same year, it also added Charlotte-based compressor remanufacturer ServiceFirst.

MERGERS AND ACQUISITIONS: 1980-90

Though the commercial construction market was cooling, Trane's plants were running at near capacity as the company entered the 1980s. In a foreshadowing of the acquisitive decade, in 1979 the company had bought back a $14 million block of shares from Tyco Laboratories, Inc., a notorious takeover artist. At this time, Trane was maintaining a slight lead in the large commercial air conditioner market.

KEY DATES

1885: James Trane opens plumbing store in La Crosse, Wisconsin.

1913: Trane Vapor Heating is invented; The Trane Company is incorporated.

1925: Reuben Trane develops the convector radiator.

1931: Trane introduces its first air conditioner.

1938: The Turbovac hermetic centrifugal refrigeration machine is introduced.

1958: Success of unitary air conditioners prompts construction of a new Trane plant in Tennessee; global expansion begins.

1970: Sales exceed $250 million.

1978: Controls manufacturer Sentinel Electronics Corporation and the ServiceFirst compressor rebuilder are acquired.

1982: General Electric's central air conditioning unit is acquired in $135 million deal.

1984: Trane is acquired by American Standard.

1995: Company joins Chinese manufacturing joint ventures.

2006: CleanEffectsT central air cleaning technology is launched.

Trane underwent a couple of major deals in short proximity in the environment of a rapidly consolidating industry. In 1982, the company acquired GE's central air conditioning department in a deal worth $135 million (the window unit business was not included). With $325 million in annual sales, GE's central units were a leader in the residential and light industrial market, an area where Trane's marketing and distribution lagged. GE was getting out of air conditioners since it did not have a commercial offering to help weather the highly cyclical residential market, according to *Business Week.* While the deal was strategically shrewd, it was risky because of the debt it involved. The GE unit brought with it three plants in Tyler, Texas; Trenton, New Jersey; and Fort Smith, Arkansas, as well as access to a network of 5,500 GE dealers.

Trane was itself acquired by American Standard Inc. on February 24, 1984. The moved saved Trane from a hostile takeover from IC Industries, Inc. and others who had been circling the company for years. American Standard was a familiar name in the plumbing business; it also had a unit that produced truck brakes. According to *Business Week,* American Standard had unsuccessfully tried to enter the air conditioner market in the 1960s.

Meanwhile, Trane continued to roll out new products. The Model CVHE CenTraVac®, which was evolved from the company's Turbovac, was a three-stage centrifugal water chiller introduced in 1981. The efficient new design became an industry standard. It was updated with the Series R® CenTraVac® in 1987, which was supplied by a new plant in Pueblo, Colorado.

Trane launched or acquired a number of overseas plants in the late 1980s and early 1990s. Locations included Malaysia, Taiwan and Egypt. The company had opened domestic sites in Louisiana and Georgia and bought Texas heat pump business Command-Aire. Trane was also upgrading its information systems.

CHALLENGES: 1990-99

Trane had a new CEO as it entered the 1990s, American Standard veteran Tom Smith. He described the challenges facing the company to *Air Conditioning, Heating & Refrigeration News:* "The change in our industry is substantial—in environmental issues, consumer demands, energy needs, ad infinitum. Responding to the rate of change will drive us into the next century." Sales were nearly $2 billion in 1990 in spite of a subdued market.

In 1995, Aire Systems, a Fort Smith, Arkansas producer of custom air handlers, was acquired. This was followed three years later by the purchase of Rockingham, North Carolina's Industrial Sheet Metal and Mechanical Corp., which made customized industrial HVAC systems.

Trane began offering a temporary cooling service in 1996. Called ChillerSource, it allowed businesses to maintain operations if their regular air conditioning failed or if they needed additional cooling for industrial processes.

SHIFTING PRODUCTION IN 2000 AND BEYOND

The early years of the millennium saw layoffs in several states and strikes at the Fort Smith, Arkansas, and Lexington, Kentucky, plants over rising employee healthcare contributions. Slow sales were one reason for the cutbacks, however the company was also standardizing the production of its coils at a location near Columbia, South Carolina. Trane was soon opening facilities in North and South Carolina, while shifting some production to Mexico and China.

Overseas markets were expected to be a source of growth, including China, where Trane had annual sales of $100 million. In 2001, Trane joined Daikin of Osaka, Japan, in what was billed as the world's largest air conditioner manufacturing alliance. *Japan Consumer Electronics Scan* reported the aim was to stave off new low-cost competitors from China and South Korea.

In 2004, Trane consolidated its three Chinese factories into one site in Taicang in the Jiangsu province. The company also had 26 service centers in China. The fast growth there—sales rose more than 30 percent in 2003—was coming from newly affluent consumers, a government willing to upgrade public buildings, and foreigners investing in new properties, an executive told *Air Conditioning, Heating & Refrigeration News.*

Trane was seeing a renewed interest in absorption chillers, a cooling technology that ran on natural gas or steam. Trane had been offering the technology since the 1950s; it had been popular in the late 1980s when gas was cheap. Large institutions were again studying them as electric rates hit new highs. Absorption chillers could use excess heat from other industrial processes. An official told *Contract Business* that China was Trane's largest market for them at the time.

Following great consumer demand for air cleaning products, in 2006 Trane rolled out its Clean EffectsT line. This used technology similar to ionic air cleaners but was incorporated into the central heating and cooling system. It was billed as the most effective way for circulating clean air throughout a home.

Frederick C. Ingram

PRINCIPAL DIVISIONS

Commercial Systems; Residential Systems.

PRINCIPAL COMPETITORS

Carrier Corporation; Johnson Controls, Inc.

FURTHER READING

Brim, Risa, "Lexington, Ky., Heating Systems Plant Workers End Strike, Accept Contract," *Knight Ridder/Tribune Business News*, March 24, 2001.

———, "Air-Conditioning Systems Maker to Lay Off 200 Workers in Lexington, Ky.," *Lexington Herald-Leader*, December 6, 2002.

"Daikin, Trane Create Biggest Air Conditioner Alliance," *Japan Consumer Electronics Scan*, November 26, 2001.

"Forecast: Fair and Cooler," *Forbes*, October 15, 1959, p. 32.

Gertzen, Jason, "About 350 Trane Workers in La Crosse, Wis., to Lose Their Jobs," *Milwaukee Journal Sentinel*, October 30, 2003.

"Hot Spell at Trane: Grabbing a Bigger Share of Commercial Air Conditioning," *Barron's*, February 25, 1980, pp. 41, 48.

Klump, Edward, "Strike Ends at Heating and Cooling Unit Maker in Fort Smith, Ark.," *Arkansas Democrat-Gazette*, April 14, 2002.

Metz, Robert, "Trane's Deal for G.E. Unit," *New York Times*, October 14, 1982, p. D10.

Miller, Mike, "A Visit with Trane's President: Tom Smith," *Air Conditioning, Heating & Refrigeration News*, August 19, 1991, pp. 26ff.

Norton, John, "Air Conditioning Maker American Standard's Chief Foresees Continued Growth," *Pueblo Chieftain*, May 22, 2002.

"Ohio DSO Hosts IAQ Rollout," *Air Conditioning, Heating &Refrigeration News*, January 23, 2006, p. 22.

"Operations at Trane Heat Up as Orders Rise," *Barron's*, November 21, 1977, pp. 37-38.

Powell, Peter, "Trane Factory Targets Growing China Market," *Air Conditioning, Heating & Refrigeration News*, September 6, 2004, p. 10.

Radding, Alan, "The Trane Co. Combines Old, New for Tech Overhaul," *InfoWorld*, December 5, 1994, p. 76.

Stakes, Valerie, "Absorption Chillers: Here to Stay," *Contracting Business*, January 2005, pp. 65ff.

"Too Hot? Too Cold? Trane Loves It," *Financial World*, February 21, 1973, pp. 24, 27.

"Trane Has Finally Found a Refuge," *Business Week*, December 19, 1983, p. 33.

"Why Trane Expanded Its Cooling Capacity," *Business Week*, July 26, 1982, p. 25.

Trek Bicycle Corporation

801 West Madison Street
Waterloo, Wisconsin 53594
U.S.A.
Telephone: (920) 478-2191
Fax: (920) 478-2774
Web site: http://www.trekbikes.com

Private Company
Incorporated: 1976
Employees: 1,500
Sales: $600 million (2005 est.)
NAIC: 336991 Motorcycle, Bicycle, and Parts Manufacturing

■ ■ ■

Trek Bicycle Corporation is the largest U.S. manufacturer of bicycles sold by specialty retailers. Distributors in more than 65 countries sell Trek's mountain, road, children's, recumbent, police, and BMX bikes. As a sponsor of racing teams and athletes, Trek had the good fortune of signing Lance Armstrong in 1997. Armstrong became the first American to win the Tour de France in 1999 while riding on an American team and on an American-made bike. The bike he was riding, Trek's OCLV Carbon 5200, quickly became one of the most popular road bikes in history. Trek and Armstrong experienced marked success in the early years of the new millennium—by 2005 Armstrong had won seven consecutive Tour de France races.

EARLY HISTORY

Trek was established in 1976, at the peak of the 1970s bicycle boom. Its founders were Dick Burke, president of Milwaukee-based appliance and electronics distributor Roth Co., and Bevill Hogg, the proprietor of a chain of bike stores, one of which was located in nearby Madison. With financial backing from Roth's parent company, the Brookfield, Wisconsin-based Intrepid Corporation, Burke and Hogg launched Trek in an old warehouse in Waterloo, Wisconsin, located halfway between Milwaukee and Madison. With a workforce of about five, the company began making high-quality, lightweight steel bicycle frames by hand. From the outset, Trek committed itself to selling bicycles primarily through specialty bicycle stores, rather than through general retail outlets. This decision helped the company to maintain its image as a supplier of equipment for serious bicycling enthusiasts. Trek quickly became a favorite brand among that connoisseur market, and independent bicycle shops have remained Trek's most important outlet.

Competing primarily against European and Japanese manufacturers, Trek began to have an impact quickly, gaining industry attention both for the quality of its bikes and for being an American company. Trek bicycles were especially popular in the Midwest, the company's own backyard. By 1978, however, Trek was distributing to both coasts, as well as to other bicycling hotspots, such as Colorado. After only three years in business, the company's annual sales had grown to $750,000.

By 1980, Trek had outgrown its original plant. The company moved to a new facility in Waterloo, and there

COMPANY PERSPECTIVES

We are a dynamic, innovative company that will compete in global markets and strive for excellence in every aspect of our business. The foundation for our commitment will be to: provide our customers with timely delivery of quality products and services at competitive values; create and maintain a positive environment for our customers and employees; and to reward our employees and stockholders for the company's performance. To achieve this mission, we will endeavor to: timely design, engineer, manufacture and/or market world class products with satisfactory financial potential in which we are or can be an industry leader; encourage proactive change, create major innovation, and accept risk and failure as building components for ultimate success; and commit the necessary financial and qualified human resources to support the strategic and tactical growth plans of the company.

it began mass-producing bicycles. Sales were so brisk that Trek also contracted a Taiwanese firm to produce some of the company's bikes. Among bicycling enthusiasts, Trek was quickly gaining a reputation as a producer of the very highest caliber of bicycles available, and its sales reflected that reputation. During the early 1980s, sales virtually doubled each year.

THE AGE OF MOUNTAIN BIKES

In 1983 Trek became a fairly early entrant into the mountain bike market, with the introduction of its 850 model. Developed in California in the late 1970s, mountain bikes featured more comfortable seats, fatter tires, and more gears than the ten-speed road bikes that dominated the market at the time. Fueled in large part by the surging popularity of mountain bikes, Trek sold more than 45,000 bikes in 1984. The company also launched its Trek Components Group that year.

During the 1980s, Trek was one of the very few American companies that stood in the way of an all-out takeover of bicycle manufacturing by Taiwanese factories. Although even Trek continued to import some of its bikes from Taiwan, the company found that it was able to offset the somewhat higher costs associated with manufacturing in America by saving on ocean shipping and cutting out other middlemen. Even labor costs proved to be a relatively minor problem, since making

bikes was seen by young employees, many of them avid bicycling hobbyists themselves, as a fairly glamorous job, and those employees, therefore, were willing to work for rather modest wages. As Trek expanded its facilities over the next several years, it was able to rely less and less on imports.

After a conflict with cofounder Burke, Hogg left Trek in 1985 to start his own bicycle company in California. In spite of the changes, Trek continued to grow at an impressive rate. In 1985 the company introduced its first aluminum road bike, Model 2000. Its first carbon composite road bike, Model 2500, hit the market the following year. By 1986 sales had soared to $16 million, and surging demand led to the addition of 75,000 square feet to the company's Waterloo manufacturing facility.

A NEW PHILOSOPHY FOR 1990

Ten years of startling growth did not come without problems, however. As Burke explained in a 1996 *Capital Times* (Madison, Wisconsin) interview, "In all fairness, Bevill [Hogg, company cofounder] was more of a dreamer than a manager." Although sales remained solid, Trek began to experience difficulties in a number of areas. Unsold inventory began to pile up, and as a result the company was losing money. With morale nearing rock bottom, Burke decided to take over the day-to-day management of the company. He instituted a "back to basics" approach, emphasizing sensible business practices and quality service. His new mission statement had four components: "Produce a quality product at a competitive price, deliver it on time in a positive environment."

Burke's new approach began to pay off quickly. Improved efficiency and marketing, combined with Trek's ongoing reputation for turning out quality products, breathed new life into the company's sagging bottom line. Sales doubled in each of the next three years. In 1987 Trek successfully introduced a new line of mountain bikes, and their popularity helped the company sell a total of about 100,000 bicycles in 1988.

Trek continued to find innovative ways to make money during the last years of the 1980s. In 1988 the company introduced a line of bicycling apparel. The following year, Trek entered the stationary bicycle market with Trek Fitness bikes. In 1989 the Jazz line of children's bicycles were introduced, and the company opened subsidiaries in Great Britain and Germany. Within five years, international sales accounted for about 35 percent of the company's business. By 1990 mountain bikes made up nearly half the bicycles sold in the United States, and Trek was prepared to claim a strong share of those sales. The company sold 350,000 bikes altogether that year. Trek's sales grew to about $175 million for fis-

---

KEY DATES

■

1976: Dick Burke and Bevill Hogg establish Trek.
1983: Trek enters the mountain bike market.
1985: The company introduces its first aluminum road bike, Model 2000; Hogg leaves Trek.
1992: Trek develops the Optimum Compaction Low Void (OCLV) carbon fiber lamination process.
1993: Gary Fisher Mountain Bike Company is acquired.
1997: Trek signs Lance Armstrong.
1999: Lance Armstrong wins his first Tour de France.
2003: Trek Travel is launched; Villiger is acquired.
2005: Armstrong wins his seventh consecutive Tour de France.

---

cal 1991, and the company had about 700 employees by that time.

THE HIGH-TECH DECADE

During the first part of the 1990s, Trek remained at the technological forefront among bicycle manufacturers. Throughout the 1980s, the company had succeeded in developing advanced materials that enabled it to maximize the lightness and strength of its bicycle frames. These breakthroughs led to the 1992 development of the Optimum Compaction Low Void (OCLV) carbon fiber lamination process. Using the OCLV process, Trek was able to make the lightest production frames in the world, weighing in at a mere 2.44 pounds. Trek's first OCLV carbon road bike, Model 5500, was introduced in 1992, and its first OCLV carbon mountain bikes, Models 9800 and 9900, were unveiled a year later.

Meanwhile, another expansion project took place at Trek's Waterloo plant, which now measured 140,000 square feet. During the early 1990s, the bicycle industry in the United States experienced a bit of a sales slump. To compensate, Trek looked to boost its sales in other areas. The company continued to emphasize international growth during this period. Sales in Japan, for example, grew by about 40 percent per year from 1991 through 1993. Trek also concentrated more on sales in Europe, where it was gaining a solid reputation among bicycle buyers who had long thought of American bikes as heavy, clunky monsters built for kids.

In addition, the company began to focus more on the sale of bicycling accessories. Beginning in 1992, Trek

assembled helmets out of parts purchased from other companies at a new plant in Oconomowoc, Wisconsin. By 1993 the plant was making helmets at a rate of about half a million a year, double its total from 1992. Trek also launched a small line of tandem bikes in 1992. Although a relatively small market, the tandem bikes proved popular among family fitness buffs.

In 1993 Trek acquired the Gary Fisher Mountain Bike Company, the company founded by and named for the originator of the mountain bike. Gary Fisher's sales increased tenfold in its first year as part of the growing Trek empire, from $2 million to $20 million. Altogether, company sales reached $230 million for 1993, a $20 million increase from the previous year. That modest increase was impressive considering that it came during a period so difficult for bike makers that it saw longtime industry giant Schwinn sink into bankruptcy. Having passed competitors Specialized and Cannondale, Trek was now the clear market leader in specialty bike shop sales. By this time, exports generated $80 million of Trek's sales, and the company maintained seven overseas distribution operations—one in Japan and the other six in Europe.

Trek passed the $250 million mark in sales in 1994. By that time, the company was manufacturing 65 different models in its Wisconsin plants, including road bike, mountain bike, hybrid, and tandem styles. Trek expanded its children's bicycle business that year with the introduction of a line called Trek Kids. A number of major developments took place at Trek in 1995. That year, the company opened a new state-of-the-art manufacturing facility in Whitewater, Wisconsin. The Whitewater plant, capable of producing 3,000 bicycles a day, dwarfed the company's other factories.

ACQUISITIONS MID-DECADE

Trek also bought out two smaller niche-market competitors in 1995: Bontrager Bicycles, based in Santa Cruz, California, and Klein Bicycles of Chehalis, Washington. Those companies' plants remained in operation after the purchases. On top of those additions, Trek signed a ten-year licensing deal with bicycle-racing superstar Greg LeMond to use his name on a line of road bikes. In addition, the company introduced a new line of mountain bikes featuring an innovative Y-shaped frame. Trek's Y-frame received an "Outstanding Design and Engineering Award" from *Popular Mechanics* magazine, and the U.S. Secret Service even bought a few Y-frame bikes for patrolling the grounds of the White House.

Mostly on the continuing strength of mountain bike sales, Trek's revenue grew to $327 million in 1995, a jump of nearly 19 percent. In early 1996, the company announced plans to add another 45,000 square feet to its Oconomowoc distribution center. It also announced its intention to build a distribution center in Atlanta to go with its existing centers in New Jersey and southern California. Around the same time, Trek revealed that it was joining forces with Volkswagen of America to form a professional mountain bike team. The Trek/Volkswagen alliance went further yet, with the introduction of the Volkswagen Jetta Trek, a car that comes equipped with a mountain bike and rack.

In 1996, Trek also began planning a retail "super-store" on the west side of Madison, Wisconsin. The announcement did not sit particularly well with the specialty retailers already selling Trek bikes in the area. Although the company had dabbled in retail operations before (Trek had another retail store already operating in Madison, and flirted briefly with part ownership of a chain of stores in northern California), Burke insisted that it was not about to plunge into retail as a major part of its operation. The company eventually withdrew from the retail market in 1999, leaving the sale of its bikes in the hands of independent distributors and specialty retailers.

Meanwhile, Trek continued to beat out much of the competition in terms of quality and service, as it sought to solidify its position at the front of the high-end bicycle pack. Its ability to thrive during a period in which the bicycle industry as a whole was more or less stagnant suggested that Trek was poised to maintain its dominant position.

TREKKING INTO 1997 AND BEYOND

Indeed, Trek's popularity skyrocketed in the late 1990s due in part to the signing of soon-to-be record breaker Lance Armstrong. Armstrong joined Trek and the U.S. Postal Team in 1997 shortly after he was diagnosed with cancer. Two years later, Armstrong became the first American riding an American-made bike to win the Tour de France. The Trek OCLV Carbon 5200 he was riding quickly became one of the fastest-selling bikes in the United States. Armstrong's athleticism would eventually go down in history; he won his seventh consecutive Tour in 2005.

During this time period, the company remained steadfast to its goal of providing superior products and service. In 1998 the company established its Advanced Concept Group (ACG). ACG's focus was to test new material applications and suspension technology. In 1999, Trek became the official licensee for Nike cycling products. One year later, the company launched a new line of bicycles and accessories designed specifically for women. By this time, Trek's parent, Intrepid, had sold off its other businesses and adopted the Trek name.

Trek entered the new millennium under the leadership of Burke's son, John. The company continued to expand its offerings and move into new markets. Trek's Project One program, which allowed customers to design and build their own bike, debuted in 2001. Through Project One, customers could design a one-of-a-kind bike by selecting everything from the bike frame to colors and wheels. After finishing the design online, customers could take their order to a Trek dealer and then have their customized bike delivered to the store in approximately six weeks.

The company also launched new bike designs, most often after Armstrong won the Tour de France riding a new product. Armstrong rode the new Madone SL in 2004 and the bike became available to biking enthusiasts shortly thereafter. Two new bike designs, the TTX time trial bike and the Madone SSLx made with OCLV Carbon Boron, were used by Armstrong during the 2005 racing season and made available to the public in 2006. The company completed construction on its 43,000-square-foot addition to its Waterloo factory early that year. The new space was created to house a larger OCLV carbon plant and engineering and research and development departments.

Along with bolstering its product line, Trek focused on strengthening its international business at this time. As part of this strategy, Trek added Swiss bicycle company Villiger to its arsenal in 2003 as well as Diamant, the oldest bike company in Germany. Trek Travel also was created that year to offer bicycling vacations in locations across the globe. The company moved into the Chinese market in 2005 when it opened two stores in Beijing and signed deals with 20 Chinese distributors.

Trek appeared to be poised for future growth. The company had become a favorite among biking enthusiasts thanks in large part to Armstrong's star quality. Trek bikes could be found across the globe and were used by children, novices, ardent fans, and professionals. Even residents at 1600 Pennsylvania Avenue were known to ride Trek products. In fact, when asked in 2005 what type of bike he rode, President Bush responded, "I'm not supposed to endorse products, but it's called a Trek."

Robert R. Jacobson
Updated, Christina M. Stansell

PRINCIPAL COMPETITORS

Cannondale Bicycle Corporation; Pacific Cycle Inc.; Specialized Bicycle Components Inc.

FURTHER READING

Adams, Caralee J., "Trek's Leap into Lighter Bikes," *Wall Street Journal*, February 22, 1999.

Barrett, Rick, "A Bicycle Built for You," *Milwaukee Journal Sentinel*, August 28, 2005.

Cooper, Chris, "Marketing Nirvana Is to Be a President's Preferred Brand," *Wall Street Journal*, April 18, 2005, B1.

Crenshaw, John, "Trek Hits the Deutsche Mark," *Bicycle Retailer*, August 15, 2005.

Fauber, John, "Riding a Profitable Cycle," *Milwaukee Journal*, September 15, 1991.

———, "Riding Up in a Down Market," *Milwaukee Journal*, October 24, 1993.

Gribble, Roger A., "Trek Builds Worldwide Reputation," *Wisconsin State Journal*, February 14, 1993.

Hajewski, Doris, "Trek Starts Selling Bicycles in China," *Milwaukee Journal Sentinel*, October 12, 2005.

Holley, Paul, "Trek Bicycle Plans Addition in Oconomowoc," *Business Journal of Milwaukee*, February 3, 1996, p. 4.

Ivey, Mike, "Trek Cycles to the Top" (Madison, Wis.), *Capital Times*, March 29, 1996, p. C1.

Schubert, John, "Trek Is Going Strong," *Bicycling*, March 1984, p. 137.

Stein, Jason, "Trek Service: From Worst to the Best," *Wisconsin State Journal*, February 23, 2003, p. C1.

"Trek Buys Villiger Bike Assets," *Wisconsin State Journal*, December 11, 2002, p. C10.

Tucows Inc.

■

96 Mowat Avenue
Toronto, Ontario M6K 3M1
Canada
Telephone: (416) 535-0123
Fax: (416) 531-5584
Web site: http://www.tucowsinc.com

Public Company
Incorporated: 1993
Employees: 170
Sales: $44.7 million (2004)
Stock Exchanges: American Toronto
Ticker Symbol: TCX TC
NAIC: 518210 Data Processing, Hosting, and Related
Services

■ ■ ■

Headquartered in Toronto, Ontario, and with offices in Flint, Michigan, and Starkville, Mississippi, Tucows Inc. is a leading provider of Internet services and download libraries. The company serves a worldwide distribution network of approximately 6,000 Internet service providers (ISPs), Web hosting companies, and related firms. Tucows' customers use its services to develop solutions for an estimated 40 million end users around the world, including individual consumers, small and medium-sized enterprises (SMEs), and large organizations. Tucows is an accredited registrar with the Internet Corporation for Assigned Names and Numbers (ICANN), the nonprofit organization that manages the Internet's domain name (unique names that identify Web sites) system. As the world's largest domain registration wholesaler, with some 4.7 million names under management, the majority of Tucows' earnings comes from domain name registration services, as well as the provision of digital certificates (electronic documents that authenticate individuals and Web sites), blogging software, spam and virus protection, hosted e-mail services, tools for creating Web sites, and a billing system called Platypus. In keeping with its reputation as the "original software download site," Tucows.com hosts more than 40,000 software titles that its experts have tested, rated, and reviewed. Through 1,000 partner sites worldwide, individuals are able to download these software titles quickly.

INTERNET PIONEER: 1993–98

The Ultimate Collection of Winsock Software (TU-COWS) was established in 1993 by Scott Swedorski, a library worker in Flint, Michigan. Inspired by the public's growing interest in the World Wide Web, Swedorski began offering software downloads for the Windows 3.1, Windows 95, and Macintosh operating systems on his personal Web site. He quickly gained pioneer status as a provider of "shareware" and "freeware"—applications that users can use at little or no charge. Having a little fun with the name TUCOWS, Swedorski began evaluating software according to a "five-cow" rating system. His software collection swiftly evolved from an acronym into a fledgling enterprise. The company's first office was about the size of a bedroom, filled with consumer-grade computer hardware.

As an article in the December 2000 issue of *Boardwatch Magazine* explained, "Swedorski originally developed the Tucows site to teach local teachers and librarians how to use the Internet. The initial site had tutorials and software about getting on and using the Net. As more software became available and use of the Internet grew, word of mouth and thousands of personal e-mails helped the site become more well-known outside its home in Flint."

In what seemed to be the blink of an eye, Tucows became so popular that a worldwide network of ISPs began "mirroring" (maintaining copies of) its software collection in order to minimize bandwidth costs and allow local users to download large files more easily and quickly. The first mirror site, a South African ISP called LIA, went online in 1996, and by 1997 some 100 mirror sites offered Tucows' content.

In 1995 Tucows was acquired by Toronto-based Internet Direct, a Canadian ISP and the second Tucows mirror site. The acquisition gave Internet Direct access to Tucows' vast content library and customer base and provided much-needed resources for Tucows' initial growth and expansion.

A NEW DOMAIN: 1999–2003

In 1999 Steinmetz Technology Holding Inter-national acquired Tucows from Internet Direct, although the latter firm retained a majority ownership stake. At this time Elliot Noss was named president and CEO, and the company's name changed to Tucows Inc. In April of that year, an agreement between the U.S. Department of Commerce and ICANN ended the monopoly on domain name registration, which had been held by Network Solutions Inc. of Herndon, Virginia. Tucows received accreditation from ICANN to serve as a domain name registrar and began registering domains for $13 each,

well below the initial industry price point of about $70.

In addition to consumer-direct domain name sales through its Domain Direct Service, Tucows began wholesaling domain name registrations in January 2000 when it launched the Open Shared Registration System (OpenSRS). According to Tucows, OpenSRS is the technical infrastructure through which ISPs can "offer, brand and manage the delivery of domain names, digital certificates, web publishing, email and other services to their customers." After starting with .com, .net, and .org domains, others followed including .uk, .ca, .info, .biz, .name, .us, .cn, and .de.

The OpenSRS system became Tucows' cash cow; in 2000 it produced ten times the revenue generated by the entire enterprise in 1999. This prosperity furthered the company's growth. By late 2000 Tucows' employees worked from a converted warehouse that offered all the amenities young tech workers could want, including basketball, foosball, massages, and free lunch on Friday.

Tucows ended 2000 with 220 employees and sales of $28 million, up from $4 million the previous year. In the December 2000 issue of *Boardwatch Magazine*, Swedorski commented on the role his company had played to date in forming the Internet: "It is so exciting to see what the Internet has become," he said. "It is just awesome that, by creating the first mirroring system and one of the first software archives, I have actually played a part in its development."

On the service front, in April 2001 Tucows announced that it would begin registering multilingual domain names, allowing customers throughout the world to obtain domains in their native alphabets. With some 70 languages available, Tucows offered about three times as many languages as other registrars. In May 2001 Tucows launched Liberty Registry Management Services (LibertyRMS), which offered so-called "generic top-level" Web site domains like .info. Tucows later sold LibertyRMS to a company named Afilias.

A major development occurred on August 28 when Tucows merged with Philadelphia-based Infonautics Inc., a financially struggling, publicly traded Internet information services provider that operated a subscription-based article database called Electric Library, a free online encyclopedia called Encyclopedia.com, and other services. The all-stock deal allowed Tucows to become a publicly traded company without an initial public offering. Tucows' shareholders gained an 80 percent ownership stake in Infonautics, and the merged companies—with an estimated market value of $41 million—adopted the name Tucows Inc.

Despite a difficult economic climate that wreaked havoc on the technology sector, Tucows ended 2001 on

KEY DATES

1993: The Ultimate Collection of Winsock Software (TUCOWS) is established in 1993 by Scott Swedorski.

1999: Tucows receives accreditation from the Internet Corporation for Assigned Names and Numbers (ICANN) to serve as a domain name registrar.

2004: The company celebrates ten years of operations, registers its fourth millionth domain name, and has a customer base of 6,000 resellers.

a high note when SnapNames rated the company as the fastest-growing domain name registrar of the year, netting 620,012 new domain names in the .com, .net, and .org categories.

By mid-2002 Tucows had some 3.7 million domain names under management. In terms of market share, the company was second only to VeriSign, Inc. Tucows also offered customers the ability to download approximately 30,000 different software titles. The company's offerings expanded when it began selling digital certificates, as well as an array of other digital security products and services, from GeoTrust Inc. to its base of 5,000 resellers. In the July 15, 2002 issue of *Market News Publishing*, GeoTrust CEO Neal Creighton said, "GeoTrust's partnership with Tucows and the subsequent exposure of our services to its broad reseller network will offer many small and medium-sized businesses powerful, fast and cost-effective security without the burden of additional infrastructure expenses, administration, and management."

In August of 2002 Tucows sold its Encyclopedia.com and eLibrary reference sites to Alacritude LLC, a Chicago-based firm established by Hoovers.com cofounder Patrick Spain, for $1.5 million. Subscriptions to these offerings, which were not core services for Tucows, had been declining. Alacritude planned to use the sites as the nucleus of an affordable online information retrieval service for individual consumers.

It also was in August of 2002 that Tucows introduced OpenHRS, a platform similar to its OpenSRS that domain name resellers and registrars could use for registering domains. By offering an outsourced solution, resellers could avoid the cost of building their own registration systems.

Tucows' lineup of wholesale services continued to grow in 2003. Early in the year, the company began offering e-mail services to its customer base. The company ended the year by unveiling Managed DNS, a service that resellers could use to offer more reliable domain name services.

MOO-VING FORWARD: 2004 AND BEYOND

The mid-2000s were marked by a flurry of activity at Tucows. In 2004 the company celebrated ten years of operations. In addition to reaching that milestone, Tucows also registered its fourth millionth domain name. The company's base of resellers had grown to 6,000, and it offered some 40,000 downloadable software titles. Commenting on his company's accomplishments in a March 10, 2004 *PR Newswire* release, Tucows President and CEO Elliot Noss said, "From the beginning, our focus has been to develop a strong, sustainable relationship with webhosting companies and ISPs that service small and medium-sized businesses. In an industry known for its high customer churn, and, given the particularly challenging environment the Internet industry faced over the last three years, it is notable that Tucows has achieved both longevity and continued growth."

By the mid-2000s "blogging" had become a popular activity among Web users. Short for Web log, blogs are one-to-many, Web-based journals on virtually every conceivable topic. In order to support the growth of this technology, Tucows acquired BlogRolling.com—a Web log tracking service that tracked more than 500,000 Web log links—in February of 2004. Three months later the company unveiled Blogware, a wholesale blogging service for Web hosting providers and ISPs. According to Tucows, this wholesale service—which its customers had been beta testing since 2003—was the first of its kind.

Tucows acquired Boardtown Corporation in April 2004, which resulted in the introduction of the Platypus Billing System for ISPs two months later. The company also released its wholesale Email Defense Service, which allowed resellers to provide protection against "spam," or unwanted e-mail messages, as well as Tucows Website Builder.

Tucows was originally conceived as a software download service. Ten years later many of the services that consumers used were Web-based, including sites devoted to travel services, coupons, mortgage loans, photo hosting, and more. In tandem with this, Tucows launched its online services library in mid-2004, giving customers access to service listings, complete with familiar "five-cow" ratings prepared by Tucows' editors.

Tucows ended 2004 by adding a mobile phone content library in conjunction with Mediaplazza. The service offered users access to games, wallpaper, and ring tones for mobile devices.

Tucows finished 2004 on solid footing. Net revenues reached $44.7 million, up 20 percent from the previous year. This strong performance continued in 2005. The company's fiscal third quarter, which ended September 30, marked its sixteenth consecutive quarter of positive cash flow from operations, and its thirteenth consecutive quarter of profitability. Another milestone that quarter was the firm's listing on both the American Stock Exchange and the Toronto Stock Exchange. "As we move forward, we are firmly focused on growing the contribution from services like blogware and messaging to both revenue and gross margin," Noss explained in a November 8, 2005 news release. "At the same time, we are continuing to pursue growth in our core domain business."

Following this strategy, in December 2005 Tucows announced an $8 million deal with San Francisco-based Critical Path Inc.—a provider of messaging solutions for mobile, broadband, and fixed-line service providers. The agreement resulted in Tucows' acquisition of Critical Path's customer base, as well as its hosted messaging communications infrastructure, and gave Tucows a leadership position in the area of hosted e-mail services for ISPs and Web hosting companies.

Heading into the second half of the 2000s, many small and medium-sized businesses still had yet to develop Web sites. For this reason, the market for selling Internet services to this target group remained strong. Based on its track record of serving firms of this size, Tucows appeared to be poised for continued growth.

Paul R. Greenland

PRINCIPAL COMPETITORS

Network Solutions; Register.com; Verio; VeriSign, Inc.

FURTHER READING

"American Stock Exchange Lists Common Stock of Tucows Incorporated," *PR Newswire*, August 19, 2005.

Dillich, Sandra, "Tucows Undercuts Competition," *Computer Dealer News*, December 3, 1999.

Erickson, Todd Judd, Charmaine D'Silva, and Scott Swedorski, "A Barnyard Success Story," *Boardwatch Magazine*, December 2000.

Hane, Paula J., "Tucows Sells Two Former Infonautics Services," *Information Today*, October 2002.

"Hoover's Co-Founder Launches New Venture," *The Simba Report on Directory Publishing*, October 2002.

"Infonautics Merges," *Philadelphia Business Journal*, March 30, 2001.

Kanaley, Reid, "Tucows to Buy Troubled Pennsylvania Dot-Com Infonautics," *The Philadelphia Inquirer*, March 29, 2001.

Sands, Kathleen, "Bovine Bliss," *NetGuide*, January 1997.

"Tucows Acquires BlogRolling.com; Tucows Extends Capabilities of New Blogware Service; Acquires Popular BlogRolling.com Weblog Tracking Service," *PR Newswire*, Feb 27, 2004.

"Tucows Announces World's Largest Global Channel to Offer Multilingual Domain Name Registration in 70 Languages," *123 Jump*, April 27, 2001.

"Tucows Breaks through 4 Million Domain Names under Management Mark; Leading Wholesaler of Internet Services Also Celebrating 10 Year Anniversary," *PR Newswire*, March 10, 2004.

"Tucows Gains Market Share: Named Fastest-Growing Registrar in Net New Domain Name Registrations; Industry Report Names Tucows Top Net Gainer in .com, .net and .org in 2001," *PR Newswire*, January 23, 2002.

"TUCOWS INC.—Partners with GeoTrust to Provide Enhanced Internet Security Solutions," *Market News Publishing*, July 15, 2002.

"TUCOWS INC.—Sees Strengthened Domain Name Market," *Market News Publishing*, May 1, 2002.

"Tucows Introduces Hosted Registrar Service," *WHIR News*, August 14, 2002.

"Tucows Launches New Mobile Phone Content Library," *PR Newswire*, December 15, 2004.

"Tucows Launches Online Services Library," *Worldwide Videotex Update*, May 2004.

Tupperware Brands
Corporation

—■—

14901 South Orange Blossom Trail
Orlando, Florida 32837
U.S.A.
Telephone: (407) 826-5050
Toll Free: (800) 366-3800
Fax: (407) 826-8268
Web site: http://www.tupperware.com

Public Company
Incorporated: 1946 as Earl S. Tupper Company
Employees: 5,900
Sales: $1.28 billion (2004)
Stock Exchanges: New York
Ticker Symbol: TUP
NAIC: 422130 Sanitary Food Containers Wholesaling;
    326199 Kitchen Utensils, Plastics, Manufacturing

■ ■ ■

Tupperware Brands Corporation, whose well-known Tupperware parties have spread to more than 100 countries, is one of the largest direct sellers in the world. Relying on independent consultants rather than employees for sales in most markets, the company generates more than $1 billion in revenues a year. Although plastic food storage containers have been Tupperware's mainstay for decades, in the 1990s the company expanded into kitchen tools, small appliances, and baby and toddler products. In 2000, beauty products became a new avenue for growth. Though Tupperware is known as an icon of postwar American life, U.S. sales declined steadily in the 1980s and 1990s at the same time international sales expanded, with the result that more than 85 percent of company revenues were coming from international business by the mid-1990s. Headquartered in Florida, the company has just one domestic manufacturing facility, in Hemingway, South Carolina. The company identifies itself with its direct marketing channel. Its sales force, after the acquisition of Sara Lee's direct-sales cosmetics business in 2005, numbered about two million independent representatives worldwide.

COMPANY ORIGINS

Company founder Earl Tupper was an early plastics pioneer and ambitious entrepreneur. An early tree surgery venture failed in 1936. The self-educated young inventor then found work at Doyle Works, a subcontractor for DuPont Co. By 1938 Tupper was ready to strike out on his own and devote himself to research in plastics. That year he started his own company, Earl S. Tupper Co., leaving DuPont with only his experience and a discarded piece of polyethylene, remains from the oil refining process that no one had yet manipulated into a practical form. Tupper's fledgling company kept afloat by making plastic parts for gas masks in World War II, although Tupper continued to pursue his research with polyethylene. Tupper modified his own refining process, searching for more useful and appealing forms of plastic.

By 1942 Tupper had developed a plastic that was both durable and safe for food storage. The lightweight, flexible, and unbreakable material was also clear, odorless, and nontoxic. Tupper dubbed the new material Poly-T, and he further refined the product over the next

COMPANY PERSPECTIVES

Tupperware is one of the most trusted names in housewares. We offer the highest quality products, with the finest design features to meet your special needs. Whether it's getting a good, hot meal on the table at the end of a busy day, toting a nutritious lunch to work, or taking time to learn a new baking secret with your children — Tupperware makes it all possible.

few years. In 1946 he founded a new company, Tupperware, and began manufacturing food storage and serving containers with Poly-T. The containers were enhanced the following year with the unique Tupperware seal, an innovation that consumers would find useful well into the future. Tupper had gotten the idea for the airtight seal from a paint can lid.

Although Tupper quickly found department and hardware stores to carry his product, customers were harder to come by. Consumers were unfamiliar with the benefits of the new material and did not know how to operate the seal. Sales finally took off in the late 1940s when a few direct sellers of Stanley Home Products added Tupperware to their demonstrations. The products flourished with the direct selling approach because salespeople could explain the benefits of the plastic and personally demonstrate the seal to consumers. In addition, Stanley Home Products salespeople did not sell door to door, but rather sold their products at home parties. This method was particularly suited to Tupperware sales because homemakers felt they were getting advice from other homemakers who actually used the products.

EXPANSION: 1950–70

The most successful early direct seller of Tupperware was Brownie Wise, a Detroit secretary and single mother. Tupper hired her in 1951 to create a direct selling system for his company. Within a few months Tupper had established the subsidiary Tupperware Home Parties, Inc. and had abandoned selling his products through retail stores. Wise's home party system used a sales force of independent consultants who earned a flat percentage of the goods they sold and won incentives in the form of bonuses and products. Wise, together with Gary McDonald, another Stanley veteran, created the Tupperware Jubilee, an annual sales convention that became famous and provided a format for the conventions of numerous direct-selling companies.

Sales skyrocketed, multiplying 25 times within three years. By the late 1950s Tupperware had become a household name. With almost no advertising, Tupperware had created phenomenal brand awareness. The company's rapid success can be attributed to its recruitment of almost 9,000 independent consultants by 1954, most of them women, and their enthusiastic spread of Tupperware parties.

Tupperware home parties provided an easy entree into the workforce for women. Able to schedule the parties around their home and family responsibilities, women could earn extra cash and get together with friends and neighbors at the same time. In addition, the home party plan provided a milieu in which women were trusted as salespeople, unlike door-to-door sales, where women were not accepted at the time.

In 1958 Wise resigned from her vice-president position and Tupper sold the company to Rexall Drug. Despite the change in management the company continued to thrive. Throughout the 1960s and 1970s sales and earnings doubled every five years. The company had grown not only in the United States but also had entered and thrived in several foreign countries. Tupperware's first venture outside the United States was to Canada in 1958. Tupperware parties were soon being thrown in Latin America, Western Europe, and Japan. International sales became a significant source of revenue for Tupperware in the 1970s, and Rexall Drug, which had become Dart Industries, had changed the subsidiary's name to Tupperware International.

SLIPPING SALES IN 1983

Sales exceeded the half billion dollar mark in 1976. Four years later Dart Industries and Kraft Inc. merged, and the newly formed company looked to subsidiary Tupperware International to fuel its growth. Tupperware's growth slowed in the early 1980s, however, and by 1983 the subsidiary had cut 7 percent from its sales and lost 15 percent from its earnings. Several factors contributed to the slip in sales and earnings. Competition had increased from Rubbermaid Inc., Eagle Affiliates, and other retail companies. In addition, an economic recovery had allowed many part-time sales people to find full-time work elsewhere, and the movement of women into the workforce had dried up the company's source for part-time labor and limited the time many women had to attend parties. The company exacerbated the labor problem, however, by not enticing people with higher commissions and by lowering the quality of their bonus prizes.

KEY DATES

1942: Earl Tupper develops plastic material suitable for food storage.

1946: Earl S. Tupper Company established.

1947: The lid of a paint can inspires design for the airtight Tupperware seal; revenues reach $5 million.

1951: Tupperware drops retail sales altogether in favor of home party approach.

1954: Brownie Wise, head of nearly 9,000 independent sales consultants, becomes first female to make cover of *Business Week*.

1958: Rexall Drug buys company from Tupper.

1976: Sales exceed $500 million.

1996: Tupperware spun off from Premark International (formerly Rexall and Dart International).

2000: BeautiControl direct-selling cosmetics business acquired.

2005: Company renamed Tupperware Brands Corporation; acquires Sara Lee's beauty supply business.

Sales continued to fall, slipping 6 percent in 1984, from $827 million to $777 million. Even worse, earnings plummeted 27 percent, to $139 million. The following year was no better; sales dropped to $762 million and earnings declined to a mere $96 million. Tupperware finally took action, bringing in a new management team in 1985. K. Douglas Martin took over as president of Tupperware USA, and Dart and Kraft moved William L. Jackson from the company's Duracell battery division to the chairmanship of Tupperware. Having made significant improvements in the Duracell division, Jackson was expected to help turn Tupperware around.

Jackson immediately made several changes. To bolster slipping party attendance, he loosened the rules governing parties and allowed adaptations to the parties that would appeal to working women, such as shorter parties and parties thrown at the workplace. In addition, Jackson worked to improve Tupperware's training of its salespeople and eliminated any bonuses and sales incentives that appeared ineffective. Over the next couple of years Jackson instituted further changes. The company introduced its first catalog, which was sent out only in response to requests made to its toll-free number. In addition, national print and television advertising was

stepped up to help counteract competition from Rubbermaid and other retail product lines. To improve the company's delivery speed, Tupperware built several new warehouses and a large distribution center.

New products in the mid-1980s helped boost both sales and company morale. In 1985 Tupperware introduced Ultra 21, a line of cookware to which market research had shown consumers would respond favorably. The company's new microwave cookware did very well and by 1987 had shown significant growth. Other products, including the company's traditional storage containers, struggled merely to maintain their sales figures.

UNEVEN RECOVERY IN 1986

In 1986 Dart and Kraft reversed their ill-fated merger. Dart renamed itself Premark International Inc., and former Kraft president Warren Batts took over as chair and chief executive officer. Tupperware apparently responded well to the change. Although the subsidiary posted a $58 million loss in 1986, its profits rose 48 percent in 1987.

Progress at Tupperware was uneven over the next several years. Sales in the United States continued to decline, although international business grew steadily. As a result, the proportion of U.S. to international sales gradually shifted until international sales accounted for more than half the company's revenues in 1992. That year, Tupperware's operations in the United States reported a loss of $22 million. In another management shift, Rick Goings, executive at direct sales leader Avon, took over as president of Tupperware in 1992.

In an effort to halt the decline in U.S. earnings, Tupperware cut costs and stepped up its sales force recruiting efforts. In addition, the company moved into direct mail, for the first time sending out unsolicited catalogs in 1992. Sales representatives provided names and addresses and paid Tupperware 65 cents for each catalog sent to one of their customers. Catalog customers then bought directly from their sales representatives. The company saw the catalog as yet another way to entice busy working women back into the Tupperware fold.

In 1993 the company was again enjoying profits in the United States, with earnings that year at $12.5 million. Sales also continued to grow internationally, helping improve the company's image on Wall Street. Shares of Premark International rose from $48 at the beginning of 1993 to $88 at the end of the year, due in large part to Tupperware's recovery.

Overall sales continued to improve in the mid-1990s, in part fueled by massive product introductions. Tupperware brought out approximately 100 new products between 1994 and 1996, including entire new product lines and specialty items catering to particular needs internationally, such as Kimono Keepers in Japan. As had been the case for the 1980s, international sales growth outstripped that in the United States. Sales in the Far East and Latin America boomed, while sales in the United States improved slowly. As a result, by 1996, Tupperware relied on international business for 85 percent of its revenues and 95 percent of its profits.

INDEPENDENCE IN 1996

Tupperware's finances continued to improve. By 1996 sales had reached 1.4 billion with earnings of $235 million. Premark International's food equipment and decorative product businesses were not faring quite as well: $2.2 billion in sales resulted in $168 million in earnings. Premark shares were trading well below competitors as a result, and management felt Tupperware was being held back by the company's other businesses. Consequently, in May 1996, Premark International spun off Tupperware, making it an independent public company. Premark shareholders received one share of Tupperware stock for each Premark share they held.

Wall Street responded positively to the spinoff; Tupperware shares began trading at $42 and soon rose to $55. Certain analysts sang the company's praises, including David Boczar, who told Financial World, "There is a perception of higher quality with Tupperware as well as the multifunctionality of the products, and also the nature of the distribution." He felt that the long-term prospects for the newly independent company were good.

The steady improvement in sales and earnings in the mid-1990s faltered in 1997. Revenues declined from a high of $1.37 billion in 1996 to $1.23 billion in 1997. Earnings plummeted 53 percent, from $175 million in 1996 to $82 million in 1997. Several factors had contributed to the decline. Domestically, a change in the company's sales plan led to a loss in its vital sales force. Quite a few sales representatives left Tupperware when the company raised the level of sales needed to qualify for a company minivan. Tupperware later renewed its recruiting efforts by offering subcompact company cars to sales representatives.

Internationally, the Asian economic crisis significantly affected Tupperware's performance, which relied on Japan alone for 12 percent of its sales in 1996. In addition, a third party vendor delayed Tupperware's delivery of products to its Japanese sales representatives, causing a major customer service problem. Although sales in the Far East continued to decline as the economic

crisis there deepened, Tupperware hoped its expansion into India, Russia, and China in 1997 would offset the loss in sales.

In 1997 Tupperware experienced further discord with some of its U.S. consultants when it began enforcing a company policy prohibiting the sale of Tupperware online. The company's crackdown included cutting off from their distributors consultants who refused to shut down their web sites. Consultants with web sites resented the intrusion into how they ran their businesses, for as independent franchise owners, Tupperware consultants are not employees. By early 1998, however, only six web sites remained in operation from a high of almost 100 in 1996. Lawrie Hall, director of external affairs at Tupperware, explained the policy to *Fortune*: "We believe that the product-demonstration and customer services that our consultants offer face to face can't be adequately provided in an Internet environment." The following year, in a complete about-face from that position, Tupperware announced plans to sell merchandise over its own corporate web site.

Sales and earnings fell further in 1998. Revenues declined to $1.1 billion, a 21 percent decline since the company was divested from Premark two years earlier. Net income fell to $69 million, the company's lowest profits since its loss in 1992. Further erosion of the company's independent sales force in the United States was responsible in part for the decline in domestic sales. Internationally, slipping sales in Latin America and Japan posed the greatest threat to overall growth.

In the late 1990s Tupperware pursued several strategies to combat persistent declines in sales in the United States. Diversifying its distribution channels was one strategy. Tupperware had plans for selling over the Internet, through television infomercials, and at shopping mall kiosks. Diversifying its product line was another. Throughout the middle to late 1990s, Tupperware had been expanding into new product areas, including kitchen tools, small kitchen appliances, and children's products. Tupperware introduced a new sales technique in April 1998 with the "Demo in a Box." Consultants could purchase these boxes that come completely outfitted with recipes, apron, invitation inserts, video and audio training tapes, etc. Internationally, Tupperware continued to move into new geographic areas and to expand its independent sales force.

Although some analysts saw hope in the company's move into more traditional retail venues, overall confidence on Wall Street was low, as evidenced by the 63 percent decline in the company's stock price between 1997 and 1999. However, new products were being introduced each month along with hostess incentives to keep interest high for customers to host and attend frequent parties, and customer loyalty remained strong.

NEW PRODUCTS FOR THE NEW MILLENNIUM

Tupperware entered a new market in late 2000 with the purchase of BeautiControl Inc., a Dallas-based direct-sales marketer of cosmetics and nutritional products. The price was about $60 million. With fewer women staying home to raise families, domestic arts were less in vogue; however there was strong interest in beauty products through the direct sales channel.

In 2002, Tupperware tried mass retail distribution for well-known brand via Target department stores (and, to a lesser extent, Kroger grocery stores). However, this was cancelled after eight months because the success of the venture cut into home-based sales.

Tupperware was facing competition from the top and bottom ends of its traditional market. Cheap, disposable plastic containers from GladWare and Ziploc were available at supermarkets, where they were likely more of a challenge for down-market rival Rubbermaid Newell Inc. Company insiders derided Rubbermaid products as being for garbage more than for food, and perceived their true competition to be more from the likes of upscale retailer Williams-Sonoma. However, another direct sales force was storming through affluent U.S. suburbs: that of The Pampered Chef, Ltd., which focused on kitchen utensils and cookware.

By this time, only a fifth of Tupperware's sales were coming from North America. Half of overall revenues ($1.3 billion in 2004) were coming from Europe. The company was looking for growth in Latin America, particularly in cosmetics.

There were layoffs in 2003 and 2005. Tupperware's only U.S. facility was a plant in Hemingway, South Carolina, which also served as a distribution center. While the company had established a factory in Japan to suit the local market, it shut down a product development center there in 2003, leaving design operations in Florida and Belgium. Tupperware operated several other plants around the world, including one in China, where products were distributed entirely through small retail outlets until a ban on direct sales was lifted. Tupperware was aiming to outsource about half of its products.

In the United States, the Tupperware party was being embraced by a new generation of time-strapped, sophisticated females looking for fun social outings. The *New York Times* described the ritual as a "book club meeting without the book." In Manhattan, at least, the guests were being plied with cocktails rather than tea as the timing of the event was shifted from late afternoon to evening.

Unfortunately, the original concept was running into difficulties on the other side of the Atlantic. In 2003 the company shut down its direct sales operations in Great Britain, where it had had 1,700 consultants, while keeping other distribution options open.

The product range had continued to evolve. Top new products included breathable containers for storing vegetables and accordion-like, collapsible containers. Tupperware was also expanding its range of kitchen items with products such as cookware and dishes.

BRAND NEW NAME IN 2005

Reflecting its identity as a "multibrand, multicategory direct-sales company," in December 2005 the company was renamed Tupperware Brands Corporation. At the same time, the beauty side of the business was enhanced with the purchase of Sara Lee's direct-sale, beauty supply line for around $560 million. After this acquisition, beauty products, where were expected to be a key source of future growth, accounted for more than one-third of Tupperware's total sales. All of Sara Lee's 900,000 cosmetics sales representatives at the time were operating outside the United States.

Susan Windisch Brown
Updated, Frederick C. Ingram

PRINCIPAL DIVISIONS

Europe; Asia Pacific; Latin America; North America; BeautiControl North America.

PRINCIPAL COMPETITORS

Avon Products Inc.; Mary Kay Inc.; Newell Rubbermaid Inc.; The Pampered Chef, Ltd.; Williams-Sonoma, Inc.

FURTHER READING

Badenhausen, Kurt, "Tupperware: No Party Pooper," *Financial World*, July/August 1997, pp. 20-22.

———, "Tupperware: Party On," *Financial World*, September 16, 1996, p. 24.

Boyd, Christopher, "Tupperware Exits Target Partnership in Change of Strategy to Support Agents," *Knight Ridder/Tribune Business News*, June 18, 2003.

"CEO Interview: Rick Goings, Tupperware Corporation," *Wall Street Transcript Digest*, October 7, 2002.

Chediak, Mark, "Tupperware Brand Reflects 'Multibrand, Multicategory Direct-Sales Company," *Orlando Sentinel*, December 6, 2005.

Clarke, Alison J., *Tupperware: The Promise of Plastic in 1950s America*, Smithsonian Books, 2001.

Daily, Jo Ellen, and Mark N. Vamos, "How Tupperware Hopes to Liven Up the Party," *Business Week*, February 25, 1985, pp. 108-09.

DeRosa, Angie, "Tupperware to Outsource Half Its Line," *Plastics News*, April 26, 2004, p. 1.

Foderaro, Lisa W., "Tupperware Parties for the Cosmo Set," *New York Times*, February 1, 2003, p. B1.

Fusaro, Roberta, "Tupperware to Sell on the Web," *Computerworld*, February 8, 1999, p. 8.

Galvin, Andrew, "Contain Yourself," *Orange County Register (California)*, November 21, 2002.

Hannon, Kerry, "Party Animal," *Forbes*, November 16, 1987, pp. 262-70.

Kapner, Suzanne, "It's Official: British Society Outlasts Tupperware Parties," *New York Times*, January 24, 2003, p. W1.

Kinkead, Gwen, "Tupperware's Party Times Are Over," *Fortune*, February 20, 1984, pp. 113-20.

Marcial, Gene G., "Get Ready for a Tupperware Party," *Business Week*, May 9, 1994, p. 80.

Mink, Michael, "Entrepreneur Earl Tupper—Self-Educated Inventor Cleaned Up in the Kitchen," *Investor's Business Daily*, July 14, 2000, p. A3.

Rees, Jenny, "The Party's Over for Tupperware's Out-of-Date Girly Nights In," *Western Mail* (Cardiff, Wales), January 24, 2003, p. 3.

Spiegel, Peter, "Party On," *Forbes*, May 3, 1999, p. 76.

"Tupperware Rolls Out Catalog Nationwide," *Catalog Age*, November 1992, p. 27.

Sun, Nina Ying, "Tupperware Taking Unconventional Road; Firm Diversifying Its Product Range," *Plastics News*, November 14, 2005, p. 8.

"Tupperware Leaps Into Cosmetic Sales," *Mergers & Acquisitions Journal*, November 2000, p. 16.

Warner, Melanie, "Can Tupperware Keep a Lid on the Web?," *Fortune*, January 12, 1998, p. 144.

Weiner, Steve, "Waif Makes Good," *Forbes*, November 14, 1988, pp. 76, 80.

Wessel, Harry, "Tupperware Turning to Tupperwear?," *Orlando Sentinel*, August 11, 2005.

U.S. Home Corporation

—————■—————

10707 Clay Road
Houston, Texas 77041
U.S.A.
Telephone: (713) 877-2311
Fax: (713) 877-2392
Web site: http://www.lennar.com

Wholly Owned Subsidiary of Lennar Corporation
Incorporated: 1959 as U.S. Home and Development
    Corporation
Employees: 2,026
Sales: $2.14 billion (2005)
NAIC: 23321 Single Family Housing Construction

■ ■ ■

U.S. Home Corporation constructs new homes in 15 states across the country. As part of Lennar Corporation, which acquired U.S. Home in 2000, the company is situated in the upper echelon of homebuilders in the nation. U.S. Home caters to first time buyers, move-up, pre-retirement, and retirement clientele. The company builds in some of the fastest growing areas in the country including Arizona, California, Colorado, Florida, Georgia, Maryland, Michigan, Missouri, Nevada, New Jersey, North Carolina, Ohio, Pennsylvania, Virginia, and Washington, D.C.

ORIGINS AND EARLY YEARS

The company was founded by Robert H. Winnerman in his home state of New Jersey and was incorporated in New Jersey as Accurate Construction Co. on April 27, 1954. The company became U.S. Home Corporation by merger on September 1, 1959. Headquartered at Perth Amboy, New Jersey, during its first decade the start-up company's projects were primarily confined to that state.

Then in 1969 Winnerman began to carry out his expansion plans after acquiring the necessary capital through a public stock offering. In February of 1969 U.S. Home offered 315,000 common shares and $4 million convertible debentures and that June joined the American Stock exchange. Winnerman attracted investors by proposing to develop a nationwide home-building company, in what was then a geographically divided market, which was to succeed with economies of scale.

The initial acquisition by U.S. Home was the acquisition of Imperial Homes and Rutenberg Homes owned by Charles and Arthur Rutenberg. Arthur Rutenberg became president of U.S. Homes and Charles became chair of the executive and finance committees of the board. U.S. Home began acquiring one home builder after another and many building suppliers, such as lumber and concrete companies as well. Winnerman offered stock in U.S. Home to builders in exchange for turning over their company ownership to him. By 1972, there were 23 companies under U.S. Home's control, and it had become the nation's largest home builder, a position it would hold through the mid-1980s.

Although Winnerman's argument, that economies of scale would make it more profitable than its competitors, did not prove entirely true, the company succeeded nevertheless by being in the right place at the right time. U.S. Home's national expansion strategy coincided with

COMPANY PERSPECTIVES

With a pre-owned home, it may be difficult to tell the quality of components that are behind the walls or the level of maintenance that occurred to the home over the years by the previous owner. With a new home, you can find out exactly what materials were used in the home and watch the construction of your home occur—giving you a higher level of comfort for the overall quality of your home.

a significant growth in the housing market. Housing starts in 1971 were the greatest in 20 years, with levels surpassing for the first time those of the post-World War II boom.

That year shareholders voted to shorten the company's name from U.S. Home and Development Corporation to U.S. Home Corporation. Five new directors were elected, and the number of common shares was increased from 5 to 15 million. In the early 1970s U.S. Home began to diversify by providing rental units, apartments, and some commercial developments.

One of the disadvantages of growing by acquisition was that the entrepreneurs who were bought out tended to still want to make their own decisions and did not fit well into the corporate mold. The consequence was a high rate of turnover of chief executives, which would consistently plague U.S. Home. The first of these executive changes involved Arthur Rutenberg, who had been 50 percent owner of Florida-based Imperial Homes Corporation and Rutenberg Homes, that state's largest "scattered lot" builder. These two companies had been U.S. Home's first major acquisition in 1969. Arthur Rutenberg subsequently became the president of U.S. Home for a short period, while Winnerman remained as chair. When Arthur resigned, Charles became president. Eventually, however, a power struggle developed between Charles and Winnerman, and in 1973 Winnerman was forced to resign, his shares in the company bought out. Under Charles Rutenberg's chairmanship headquarters were moved from New Jersey to Clearwater, Florida.

In 1972 Rutenberg decided to purchase 3H Building Corporation of Chicago, which, unfortunately, proved a bad buy. It lost $200,000 on sales in its first five months under U.S. Home ownership. As a result the new subsidiary was considerably cut down. Losses of 3H contributed to U.S. Home's deficit of $2.98 million for 1974, not only the company's first annual loss, but also the first quarterly downturn the company had

sustained since going public. At the same time, there were other factors that contributed to this sudden decline from profits of $12.8 million in 1973. Most significant was the U.S. government's freeze on subsidized housing. This adversely effected U.S. Home's Communities Division, which built subsidized housing in New Jersey and Pennsylvania. Other concurrent problems included a slowdown in sales due to higher interest rates. Industry experts said U.S. Home should have secured more borrowing money ahead of time to forestall the ill effects of interest rate increases. Meanwhile, contributing to lower demand for new homes was the 1973 energy crisis, which prompted consumers to reconsider the commuting expenses of moving to new homes in the suburbs. To top it all off, prices of lumber and other building materials had jumped that year.

In 1977, Rutenberg left the company, having brought in Ben Harrison to serve as president. Harrison resigned in a policy dispute and was replaced as president by Guy Odom, who proceeded to double the size of the company. After Charles Rutenberg's resignation, Guy Odom also replaced him as chief executive officer. In February 1979 the company moved its headquarters from Florida to Houston, Texas. Here again the company was well positioned to take advantage of the local housing boom, a consequence of the growth in the Texas oil industry. Soon it gained 20 percent of the Houston area market and earned nearly a third of its revenues locally, as the 1981-82 housing recession did not effect this city.

U.S. Home's strategy was to acquire land, develop its own lots, and build on speculation. U.S. Home's aggressive building policy worked well during the 1970s when a high rate of inflation encouraged property purchases as investments. The large purchases of land and its development into subdivided lots, however, made the selling of undeveloped land the main source of U.S. Home's profits for a time after 1980.

OVERCOMING CHALLENGES BEGINNING IN 1983

By the mid-1980s U.S. Home abandoned its strategy of trying to be in every major U.S. market and shifted to emphasizing profits. Instead of piling up debt, it sought to diversify in less capital-intensive ways. Earlier in the 1980s, it had begun seeking partners for joint-ventures in its successful retirement communities, of which it had six by 1981, primarily in Texas and Florida. In 1983 it joined the ranks of builders who were giving home buyers a special kind of mortgage insurance, which paid principal, interest, tax, and hazard insurance payments for as long as 12 months after the buyer loses his

KEY DATES

1954: Robert H. Winnerman establishes Accurate Construction Co.

1959: U.S. Home and Development Corporation is formed through a merger.

1969: The company goes public.

1971: The company adopts the U.S. Home Corporation moniker.

1972: By now, U.S. Home is the nation's largest home builder.

1983: U.S. Home enters the manufactured housing market by acquiring Brigadier Industries Corporation and Interstate Homes.

1985: Sales decline to $922 million, bringing the company down to second place among the nation's builders.

1991: The company files for Chapter 11 bankruptcy protection.

1993: U.S. Home emerges from bankruptcy.

2000: Lennar Corporation purchases U.S. Home, doubling the size of Lennar.

or her job. Around this time U.S. Home was the first homebuilder to use mortgage-backed bonds for financing.

In early 1983 U.S. Home went into the manufactured housing business when it acquired two firms: Brigadier Industries Corp., a manufacturer of mobile homes, for stock valued at $25.5 million, and Interstate Homes, a maker of modular homes. U.S. Home's revenues had topped the $1 billion mark for the first time in 1980. In 1983 sales peaked at $1.152 billion. This was also the year U.S. Home reached its peak in number of homes built—14,028 nationwide.

Odom had initially hoped that the mobile home business would increase marginal profits. However, the ventures ended up losing money, partially due to U.S. Home's initial lack of management experience in this field. His idea was to establish a network of dealers selling U.S. Homes mobile products exclusively. But the dealers preferred the traditional method of handling a broad line of mobile homes supplied by several manufacturers. The mobile home division reported increasing operating losses of $5 million in 1983, $9.7 million in 1984, and $15 million in 1985.

Business overall soured in 1984 when Odom erroneously predicted that interest rates would decline in the election year. While other builders held back, U.S. Home continued to build beyond sale orders. As interest rates went up slightly, new orders dropped by 30 percent in May. By August that year U.S. Home was stuck with 1,700 completed but unsold homes.

At the same time the company was dealt an especially severe blow in its own backyard, the Houston market. The national housing recession eventually came to affect Houston, and the recovery there lagged behind. More significantly, the Texas oil boom of the 1970s was over, as the price of oil fell and the industry declined. U.S. Home meanwhile had become too dependent on the Houston market, which had accounted for 40 percent of the company's total construction in 1982 with 4,975 new homes. Yet its hold on the Houston metropolitan area had been slipping as other large homebuilders began to enter the increasingly competitive Houston market. The rental sector also emerged as tough competition as a consequence of a 1981 municipal housing law that indirectly encouraged the building of rental units.

During the period between 1983 and 1985 the company had to resort to selling more than 3,000 of its slow moving inventory of homes to the syndicator, Equity Programs Investment Corporation (EPIC). The latter in turn rented out the houses, lowering the value of the neighborhoods, which prompted some home-owning neighbors to sue U.S. Home. This particularly hurt U.S. Home's reputation, since it relied heavily on customer referrals. It sold 2,286 houses at discounts to EPIC in 1984 for a loss of $1.5 million, contributing to a net loss for 1984 of $43.9 million on total sales of $1.1 billion. Another 250 of U.S. Home's projects had to be auctioned off. The company also implemented a program of offering home sales to rental tenants for interest rates 1 percent below the going market rate and accepting the last 12 months rent as part of the purchase price.

Following losses in two straight quarters and indications of a large deficit for the year, Odom resigned in 1984. He turned over his posts of chair and chief executive officer to George Matters, who had been president since 1980. Robert Strudler then became president.

Matters proceeded to cut costs and reduced overhead by about $70 million in 1985. Losses were reduced to $9 million, although sales also declined to $922 million, bringing the company down to second place among the nation's builders. To cut losses the company trimmed operations in several states. It closed operations in markets where business was weak and cut housing and land inventories in all of its markets. It began to withdraw from Amarillo, Texas; Birmingham, Alabama; Oklahoma City and Tulsa, Oklahoma; and Seattle.

Chicago operations were reduced substantially. Consolidation eliminated 14 building divisions.

Matters failed, however, to go far enough to cut costs where it was most needed: in the mobile homes division and in the depressed Houston market. Twenty-three of U.S. Home's active subdivisions in Houston were losing money that year. Financial troubles contributed to another executive shakeup. Matters resigned as CEO, replaced by Robert Strudler. Isaac Heimbinder, who had been chief financial officer, took over Strudler's post as president. Matters had been criticized for failing to respond quickly enough to declining housing demand. Strudler and Heimbinder in turn proceeded to cut U.S. Home's Texas operations in half, reducing the number of subdivisions in which it was operating from 70 to 34. They also finally sold off the failing mobile home business.

The company immediately posted two consecutive profitable quarters and its stock went up at the end of 1986. In 1988, however, U.S. Homes ended a year profitably—for the first time since 1983—with a net income of $5 million on sales of $735 million. This reflected further progress in reducing general, administrative, and selling costs. The company continued to improve its cash flow in 1989, although profits and sales had declined even further to $1.24 million and $675.56 respectively, bringing it down to ninth place in the nation's industry. U.S. Home continued to streamline operations, deploying assets in strong markets in California, Florida, and Denver, while closing them in Albuquerque, Atlanta, and Charlotte and reducing them in Phoenix and Tucson.

CONTINUED PROBLEMS AND BANKRUPTCY: 1990–95

Then in 1990 the housing industry entered a recession again, with the lowest level of housing starts since the early 1980s. By early 1991 home values were depressed as much as 30 percent in some areas. Other factors hurting the industry at this time included regulations affecting building suppliers of lumber and cement. Local zoning laws and building codes made housing more expensive as well. U.S. Home based its strategy, in facing these unfavorable conditions, on geographic diversity, low overhead, and low inventories, so as to better withstand the inevitable cycles of the housing industry. The company achieved the lowest number of completed unsold units in 15 years.

The national housing slump and a shortage of credit prompted U.S. Home to take an $82.2 million write-off in the fourth quarter of 1990. This comprised provisions for discontinued operations, provisions relating to the disposition of excess land and housing inventories in markets where the company had reduced its operations, and litigation costs. It closed the year with an unprecedented $101.6 million loss. U.S. Home's difficulty in restructuring its debt was also representative of an overall lack of credit for the housing industry, although new house sales picked up again in early 1991.

By spring 1991 U.S Home had been unsuccessful for nearly a year in trying to get a group of 17 banks to restructure its $156 million debt, which had been renewed annually since 1973. In April it filed in a New York court for Chapter 11 bankruptcy protection from creditors. Its objective was to reorganize. At the same time U.S. Home secured $72 million of debtor-in-position financing from General Electric Capital Corporation, using its unsecured projects as capital. The company was thus able to continue business as usual.

Despite remaining under bankruptcy protection, U.S. Home managed to increase sales for 1992 to $689.9 million up from $485.3. It completed 5,015 homes, up 39 percent from the previous year, which was the most it had built since 1989. Although the net loss for the year was still high at $21.35 million, this reflected reorganization charges of $50.7 million, and the company had an operating profit of $30 million.

In March 1993 U.S. Home submitted its reorganization plan, offering $165 million in new debt plus stock to settle $297 million in unsecured claims. The plan went into effect, and the company came out of bankruptcy that June upon the selling of $200 million in 10-year high-yield bonds. At the same time it gained additional working capital from another four-year loan from the GE Capital Corporation. The company also named six new directors to its 11-member board. When U.S. Home emerged from Chapter 11, all senior creditors were paid in full and shareholder value was significantly increased from shareholder value at the inception of the bankruptcy. The issuance of public debt simultaneously with the emergence from Chapter 11 was an unprecedented event. The company was able to accomplish this because of its excellent operating performance while in Chapter 11. In 1992 the company earned in excess of $29 million on a 39 percent increase in homes delivered. In 1993 the company's performance continued to improve—operating earnings for the first six months exceeded $17 million.

In mid-1993 U.S. Home was active in 26 metropolitan areas in Florida, California, Arizona, Maryland, Minnesota, New Jersey, Texas, Nevada, Virginia, and Colorado. Project sizes ranged from 50 to 1,000 units, and the company was ranked the fourth-largest home builder in the country.

SUCCESS: 1996 AND BEYOND

As U.S. Home entered the latter half of the 1990s, it appeared to have overcome its financial problems of the past. In 1996, U.S. Home put a poison pill, or shareholder's rights plan, in effect to help prevent any hostile takeover attempts. Two years later, the company partnered with the Mexican home building firm GIG Desarolladores Inmobilarios S.A. de C.V. to build homes in Texas and Arizona. The partnership also gave U.S. Home an opportunity to move into the Mexican market in the future. The company posted record earnings in 1999.

Changes were on the horizon for U.S. Home as the company ushered in a new century. In February 2000, Lennar Corporation made a $476 million play for the company. The deal came at a time when the homebuilding industry was experiencing a wave of merger activity. When the dust settled, Lennar, Centex, and Pulte Homes were left standing as the three largest companies in the U.S. homebuilding sector.

For U.S. Home, the union with Lennar made sense. Together, the company would have a strong hold over 11 states. Six of those had the fastest growing populations in the U.S. including Texas, Florida, California, Colorado, Arizona, and Nevada. Lennar was particularly interested in U.S. Home's growing business in Colorado. Overall, sales in those six states would represent nearly 91 percent of business for the combined company. Robert Strudler, U.S. Home's chairman and co-CEO at the time, supported the union in a February 2000 *Houston Business Journal* article claiming, "We believe the combination of Lennar and U.S. Home will create a bigger, stronger and faster-paced organization."

Meanwhile, U.S. Home was subject to an investigation led by Florida's attorney general. Customers had made numerous complaints against the company, claiming it was not responsive to home buyers' complaints and failed to deliver on the promises it published in its marketing materials—the company claimed it was a zero-defect company with 100 percent customer satisfaction and provided a one-year warranty for the home. Overall, Florida's fast growing new home construction market came under scrutiny as local investigations revealed that homes were being built at breakneck speed with a major shortage of skilled workers. In fact, the *Orlando Sentinel* and a local news channel led the first statistically valid assessment of the quality of new home construction in Florida. The investigation uncovered thousands of problems, which in the end averaged out to 7.5 per new home.

Despite the bad press related to quality issues, U.S. Home forged ahead with its growth plans. In 2001, the company partnered with the California Energy Com-

mission to develop the largest solar residential project in the U.S. The Bickford Ranch community, a 1,942-acre master-planned community in western Placer County, remained in the developmental stages in 2006. U.S. Homes also bought Don Galloway Homes and Sunstar Homes in 2001. The company continued to invest in new developments including the Williamsburg Colonial Heritage golf course community in Virginia.

During 2005, U.S. Home appeared to on solid ground as its parent posted record profits. While analysts believed the U.S. housing market was headed for a slowdown, mortgage rates remained at historically low levels. With the backing of one of the nation's largest homebuilders, U.S. Home stood well positioned to handle any obstacles that may come its way.

Heather Behn Hedden
Updated, Christina M. Stansell

PRINCIPAL COMPETITORS

Centex Homes; KB Home; Pulte Homes Inc.

FURTHER READING

Cronan, Carl, "Lennar, U.S. Home a Good Fit," *The Business Journal*, February 25, 2000.

Davis, Jo Ellen, "U.S. Home Pays a Big Price for a Turnaround," *Business Week*, November 25, 1985, pp. 114-18.

Donahue, Gerry, "U.S. Home Corporation (Gearing Up for Recovery)," *Builder*, May 1992, p. 217.

Greer, Jim, "U.S. Home Gets New Address in Acquisition by Florida Firm," *Houston Business Journal*, February 25, 2000.

Guido, Daniel Walker, "Costly Mistakes," *Builder*, September 2000.

Haggman, Matthew, "Lennar Boasts Record Annual Profit," *Knight Ridder Tribune Business News*, December 15, 2005.

Klempin, Raymond, "A Surprising Shakeup at U.S. Home," *Houston Business Journal*, May 26, 1986, p. 1.

Lerner, Michele, "Williamsburg Gains Idyllic Golf Community," *Washington Times*, October 3, 2003, F35.

"News of Realty: Acquisition Plan," *New York Times*, April 22, 1969, p. 74.

O'Neal, Michael and Robert Block, "A Sudden Departure from U.S. Home," *Business Week*, May 26, 1986, pp. 45-46.

"One-Thousand Home Community Will Use Solar Power," *Environmental Design and Construction*, September/October 2001.

Sidden, Jennifer Boyd, "U.S. Home to Acquire Local Home Builder," *Business Journal*, December 7, 2001.

Somoza, Kelly F., "U.S. Home Corp. Announces Financial Results," *Business Wire*, February 9, 1989.

Tracy, Dan, "Good Enough Means Shoddy Work on Most Homes Built in Orlando, Fla. Area," *Knight Ridder Tribune Business News*, November 2, 2003.

"U.S. Home: A Cozy Investment?," *Business Week*, March 30, 1987, p. 74.

"U.S. Home Corp.: Chapter 11 Protection Ends as Reorganization Proceeds," *Wall Street Journal*, June 22, 1993, P. B4.

"U.S. Home Files Plan of Reorganization, Posts 4th-Period Loss," *Wall Street Journal*, March 4, 1993, p. B5.

"U.S. Home Gets Ruling on Loan," *Wall Street Journal*, May 16, 1991, p. B12.

"U.S. Home's Big Mistake," *Business Week*, January 12, 1974, pp. 44-45.

"U.S. Home's Financial Roof Is Leaking," *Business Week*, September 17, 1984, pp. 118-121.

UNITRIN

Unitrin Inc.

One East Wacker Drive
Chicago, Illinois 60601
U.S.A.
Telephone: (312) 661-4600
Fax: (312) 494-6995
Web site: http://www.unitrin.com

Public Company
Incorporated: 1990
Employees: 8,400
Operating Revenues: $3.04 billion (2004)
Stock Exchanges: New York
Ticker Symbol: UTR
NAIC: 524113 Direct Life Insurance Carriers; 524114 Direct Health and Medical Insurance Carriers; 524126 Direct Property and Casualty Insurance Carriers

∎ ∎ ∎

Although Chicago-based Unitrin Inc. has only existed as a stand-alone company since 1990 when it was spun off from conglomerate Teledyne Inc., the firm has become a leader in the insurance industry with over $9 billion in assets, six million policies in force, and $2.5 billion in annual premium revenues. The company provides property and casualty insurance, life and health insurance, and consumer financial services to individuals, families, and small businesses. Unitrin's Property & Casualty Insurance Group, which includes Kemper Auto and Home, Unitrin Specialty, and Unitrin Business Insurance, accounts for 75 percent of the company's an-

nual insurance premiums. Unitrin's Fireside Bank specializes in automobile loans and has 28 branches in California.

TELEDYNE GIVES BIRTH TO UNITRIN IN 1990

Unitrin was founded as a subsidiary of Teledyne Inc. Best known for the Water Pik dental aid and ubiquitous Shower Massage, Teledyne began business in 1960 as a semiconductor manufacturer. Before the decade was over, Teledyne began acquiring undervalued companies of various sizes; pursuing this strategy aggressively into the 1970s and 1980s, Teledyne became one the most successful and recognized corporations in the United States under the leadership of legendary entrepreneur Henry E. Singleton.

By the late 1980s Singleton began to break up his extensive and increasingly unwieldy empire. In 1986 he spun off the Argonaut Group Inc., a worker's compensation insurance provider, with great success: Argonaut's original $20 per share stock appreciated 240 percent by 1990. Shortly before Unitrin's slated debut, Teledyne (with $4.6 billion in revenue for 1989) treated stockholders to a five-for-one stock split in March 1990. Believing Unitrin could duplicate Argonaut's good fortune, Singleton (who remained chairman of both new ventures) spun Unitrin off to shareholders in April 1990 at $31.25 per share, trading on NASDAQ. Beginning its independent corporate life as a holding company for several insurance carriers, Unitrin divided its business into three major categories: life and health insurance; property and casualty insurance; and consumer finance, which covered a variety of services including automobile and industrial loans.

UNITRIN'S INSURANCE DIVISIONS

Unitrin's life and health division comprised three large wholly owned subsidiaries: United Insurance Company of America, rated A+ by A. M. Best; Union National Life Insurance Company, also rated A+ by Best; and the Pyramid Life Insurance Company, rated A- by Best. In addition to its high industry ratings, Unitrin differentiated itself from a slew of health and life insurance carriers (which numbered about 1,800 in the United States by 1995) not by offering an unusual mix of products, but instead by providing typical policies with an unusual method of marketing these products. Life insurance policies were offered in standard increments of up to $250,000 for individuals and groups (such as employees of large companies and credit unions) in permanent and term policies; health insurance was sold to both individuals and groups on either a limited-benefit or major medical coverage basis with a maximum risk of $500,000 in any one calendar year.

Yet what drew many customers to Unitrin's insurance packages was the old-fashioned concept of selling services door-to-door with some 4,000 sales representatives (out of a total of 5,300 in the division), who visited middle- and lower-income suburban and rural communities. As a convenience, agents then returned monthly to pick up premium payments, omitting postal services and delays. Although there were two-and-a-half dozen competitors in the "home service" market, Unitrin carved out a comfortable niche in 26 states and the District of Columbia, and within five years this segment generated almost 80 percent of the life and health insurance division's premiums.

Unitrin's second major insurance segment in property and casualty policies covered automobiles and motorcycles, homes, watercraft, and commercial businesses from fire, theft, and other property damage. Worker's compensation policies were also available to small and medium-sized companies. The property/

casualty division worked through five subsidiaries: Financial Indemnity Company, rated A+ by Best; the Milwaukee Insurance Companies (including Alpha Property & Casualty, Milwaukee Guardian, and Milwaukee Safeguard Insurance companies—all part of a 1995 merger), rated A-; Trinity Universal Insurance Company, rated A++; Union National Fire Insurance Company, rated A; and United Casualty Insurance Company of America, rated A+ by Best, with 1,700 divisional employees and approximately 15,000 independent agents across the nation. Premium sales were concentrated in the South (predominantly Louisiana, with 6 percent of the division's sales), Midwest (especially Illinois, Minnesota, and Wisconsin for a combined total of 19 percent), Texas (32 percent), and California (12 percent of premiums). Geographic hazards included hurricanes in the South (generally worse in the fall), windstorms, tornadoes, and flooding in the Midwest (in the spring), and fires in the West. Much like the weather, profitability in the casualty and property insurance companies tended to be cyclical and easily driven by pricing competition and a flooded marketplace.

Unitrin's consumer finance division, which conducted business through the Fireside Thrift Company, located in Newark, California, was chiefly involved in financing used automobiles from dealerships. Fireside also sold consumers personal loans using automobiles as collateral, and offered timely service and flexible terms to win clients over its competition. Fireside's activities were financed by thrift investment certificates (ranging from 31 days to five years), money market accounts, and IRAs, products routinely offered by banks, savings and loans, and other industrial loan providers.

Following its earlier success while still part of Teledyne, Inc., Unitrin posted sales of $1 billion from premiums and consumer finance loans in its first independent year. Total revenue was over $1.25 billion for 1991, with net income of $136 million. The following year, premiums and consumer finance services increased to $1.1 billion and total revenues to $1.36 billion, but net income fell to $123 million due to a one-time accounting charge of $40 million.

By 1993 the life and health insurance segment generated about half of Unitrin's revenues ($688 million), property and casualty brought in $570.8 million, and consumer finance $81.3 million. The following year (1994) consumer finance performed better than its siblings, climbing more than 12 percent to $91.4 million, while property/casualty was up 10 percent to $575.6 million, and the life/health division fell to $667.6 million due to a lower sales volume, except in individual traditional life insurance, which increased in volume.

KEY DATES

1990: Teledyne Inc. spins off Unitrin.
1991: Total revenue surpasses $1.25 billion.
1994: The company fends off a takeover attempt by American General Corporation.
1995: Unitrin's wholly owned subsidiary, Dallas-based Trinity Universal Insurance Company, merges with the Milwaukee Insurance Group, Inc.
1998: Reliable Life Insurance Company and Reserve National Insurance Company are acquired.
2002: The personal lines property and casualty insurance business of Kemper Insurance Companies is purchased.

Operating profits dropped for property/casualty, falling from 1993's $76 million to $65.5 million, but the other two segments saw healthy increases: consumer finance rose from 1993's $25.8 million to $31 million, and life/health reached $68.7 million from 1993's $54.5 million—all this despite a serious threat to the company's well-being by a hostile takeover attempt.

FIGHTING OFF AN UNWANTED SUITOR IN 1994

Unitrin spent the second part of 1994 fending off a $2.6 billion takeover bid by American General Corporation, an insurance carrier headquartered in Houston, whose business was very similar to its own. Though American General said it originally broached the subject of a merger to Unitrin's management in January 1994, the aggressor went public with its intentions in early June. Hoping to swallow Unitrin's home service business, American General was also attracted to Unitrin's $1.4 billion in excess capital and undervalued assets (major shares in Litton Industries Inc., Curtiss-Wright Corporation, and Western Atlas Inc.) which were listed on Unitrin's books at cost rather than stock value. If the takeover succeeded, American General stood to gain combined assets of $50 billion with a customer base over eight million.

On June 26, 1994, Unitrin unequivocally rejected the $50.38 per share offer and adopted a poison pill defense. Despite American General's hints of sweetening the offer or paying with stock instead of cash (for shareholder tax purposes), Unitrin remained steadfast and initiated a stock buyback plan of ten million shares, or 19 percent of its stock (51.8 million shares outstand-

ing), to placate frustrated shareholders and increase the board's controlling interest. American General then took Unitrin to court and argued that such a repurchase plan would prove harmful to shareholders of both companies, as Unitrin's board could effectively block any acquisition regardless of shareholders' best interests. A Delaware Chancery Court judge agreed and issued a restraining order against Unitrin's proposed stock buyback until September 27, 1994. Having gained the advantage and still hoping Unitrin's board would reconsider, American General extended its merger offer from October through November 30, then again to February 7, 1995. Unitrin continued to resist, and on December 13 the Delaware Supreme Court overturned the lower court's injunction, freeing Unitrin to repurchase its stock. As the tumultuous 1994 ended, Unitrin's total revenues climbed to $1.37 billion, just slightly over the previous year's $1.36 billion. Yet the big news was in net income: 1993's figure of $95 million was surpassed by $148 million for 1994.

As Unitrin entered its fifth year of independence, the company continued buying back its stock to keep American General and other rumored suitors at bay. Unitrin's maneuvers paid off: American General's takeover bid quietly expired on February 7, 1995, and was not renewed. During the time Unitrin was facing off against American General, former parent Teledyne Inc. underwent a similar battle with WHX Corporation, run by Ron LaBow, previously of junk bond haven Drexel Burnham Lambert. That two of Henry Singleton's companies were waging a fierce battle for survival struck many Wall Streeters as the ultimate irony. Many analysts believed that it was only a matter of time before Singleton's other spin-off, the Argonaut Group Inc., became a takeover target.

The remainder of 1995 brought several highs for Unitrin, including an agreement between subsidiary Financial Indemnity Company and Allstate of California to market Unitrin automobile insurance policies throughout the state. In a move Unitrin's management found "too good a business fit to pass up," Unitrin's wholly owned subsidiary, Dallas-based Trinity Universal Insurance Company, merged with the Milwaukee Insurance Group, Inc. ($186 million in 1994 for net premiums written), for $92.6 million in cash. Milwaukee Insurance, rated B++ at the time of acquisition due to some recent financial difficulties, nicely complemented Trinity's property and casualty operations (the only state in which the two companies were in direct competition was Illinois) and was a holding company of Milwaukee Mutual Insurance Company, a venerable family-owned business founded in 1917 to fill the needs of new auto owners and drivers.

By the end of 1995, Unitrin had bought back 8.7 million of its shares for $416 million, raising the total number of repurchased shares from August 1994 to 13.5 million or $661 million, in hopes of preventing future hostile takeover attempts. Year-end total revenues were $1.45 billion ($649.7 million from the life and health division, $631.5 million from property/casualty, and $106.5 million from consumer finance). With over five million policies in force across the United States, $5 billion in assets, and a growing number of consumer finance clients (100,000 in 1995), Unitrin had proved its mettle to both the insurance industry and the enclaves of Wall Street.

1995 AND BEYOND

During the latter half of the 1990s, Unitrin worked to strengthen its holdings. It added Union Automobile Indemnity Co. to its arsenal in January 1997. Reliable Life Insurance Co. was purchased the following year. At the time, Reliable controlled nearly 38 percent of the home service life insurance market in Missouri. Unitrin also bought Oklahoma City-based Reserve National Insurance Company in 1998. The deal gave the company a stronger foothold in a growing segment of the health insurance market that provided limited benefit accident and health insurance products to customers in rural areas. Unitrin's Property and Casualty Group increased its presence in Texas and the Pacific Northwest in 1999 through its acquisition of Valley Group Inc.

Unitrin entered the new millennium on solid ground. By 2001, the company had over $7 billion in assets and revenues exceeding $2.5 billion. In 2002, the company made a play for the personal lines property and casualty insurance business of Kemper Insurance Companies. The division, called Individual and Family Group (IFG), added yet another facet to its personal lines that were sold through independent agents. When asked in a March 2005 Best's Review interview about the strategy behind the deal, Richard Vie, Unitrin's chairman and CEO, explained, "First, it's a great national brand name with a very strong, old and established following among their independent agents. They'd been reasonable profitable, and they were concentrated in the part of the country where Unitrin wasn't. They were primarily in the East, and Unitrin's property/casualty group was primarily west of the Mississippi." Vie went on to comment, "It had a good geographic fit with Unitrin's Multi-Lines ground and its flagship brand, Trinity Universal."

In 2004, the company combined its Multi Lines insurance segment into the Kemper Auto and Home division. As a result of the restructuring, the company created Unitrin Business Insurance (UBI) in January 2005 to oversee its commercial lines business.

Overall, the company's bottom line benefit from its recent growth strategy. In 2003, revenues climbed 28 percent over the previous year while net income grew to $123.6 million. Unitrin's stock price grew by 50 percent during the year. The company's Fireside Bank division, responsible for its subprime auto loan business, recorded profits of $41 million on revenues of $196 million, making it Unitrin's most profitable segment at the time.

Even as its Auto and Home unit was kept on its toes during the unprecedented spout of hurricanes in 2004 and 2005, Unitrin fared well. In fact, net income nearly doubled in 2004 to $240.2 million. Unitrin's good fortunes continued in 2005 when both net income and revenues rose. With a solid strategy in place, Unitrin appeared to be on track for additional success in the years to come.

Taryn Benbow-Pfalzgraf
Updated, Christina M. Stansell

PRINCIPAL COMPETITORS

American International Group Inc.; Nationwide Mutual Insurance Company; State Farm Mutual Automobile Insurance Company.

FURTHER READING

"American General Gains against Unitrin Buyback," Wall Street Journal, October 14, 1994, p. A4.

Bell, Allison, "Unitrin Seals Deal for Reliable," *National Underwriter Life & Health Financial Services*, June 1, 1998.

Buckler, Arthur, and Leslie Scism, "Unitrin Counters American General on Takeover Bid," *Wall Street Journal*, August 5, 1994, pp. A2, A10.

"Divorce Singleton Style," *Forbes*, June 25, 1990, p. 142.

"Judge Temporarily Blocks Unitrin from Buying Back 19% of Stock," *Wall Street Journal*, August 29, 1994, p. B6.

Lazo, Shirley A., "Unitrin Increases Its Quarterly by 25%," *Barron's*, February 6, 1995, p. 37.

Mullins, Robert, "In Unitrin Deal, Milwaukee Insurance Chose Partner Carefully," *Business Journal*, July 15, 1995, pp. 2A, 3A.

Murphy, H. Lee, "As Market Plateaus, Unitrin Sitting Pretty," *Crain's Chicago Business*, April 5, 2004.

Rees, David, "Events Swirling around Teledyne Intrigue Analysts," *Los Angeles Business Journal*, March 26, 1990, p. 9.

Roush, Chris S., "Unitrin Agrees to Acquire Kemper's Personal Lines Business for at Least $45M," *SNL Insurance Daily Proprietary Articles*, April 15, 2002.

Scism, Leslie, "American General Corp. Seeks to Buy Life Insurance Unit of American Brands," *Wall Street Journal,* November 29, 1994, p. A3.

Scism, Leslie, and Arthur Buckler, "American General Makes Bid for Insurer," *Wall Street Journal,* August 4, 1994, p. A3.

———, "Unitrin Clears Buyback of 19% of Stock; American General Files to Raise Its Stake," *Wall Street Journal,* August 15, 1994, pp. A2, A6.

Scism, Leslie, and Greg Steinmetz, "Famed Conglomerate Builder Singleton Plays a Key Role in Battle for Unitrin," *Wall Street Journal,* August 9, 1994, p. A3.

Sloan, Allan, "Teledyne's Henry Singleton Finds Takeover Shoe on the Other Foot," *Washington Post,* January 24, 1995, p. D3.

"Unitrin Completes Acquisition of Reserve National," *Business Wire,* September 30, 1998.

"Unitrin Completes Acquisition of Valley Group Inc.," *Business Wire,* June 17, 1999.

Veverka, Mark, and Leslie Gornstein, "How Insurer Plans to Battle for Its Life," *Crain's Chicago Business,* August 8, 1994, pp. 4, 45.

"Way to Grow," *Best's Review,* March 1, 2005.

Verizon Communications Inc.

---

140 West Street
New York, New York 10036
U.S.A.
Telephone: (212) 395-2121
Toll Free: (800) 621-9900
Fax: (212) 869-3265
Web site: http://www.verizon.com

Public Company
Incorporated: 2000
Employees: 210,000
Sales: $75.1 billion (2005)
Stock Exchanges: New York
Ticker Symbol: VZ
NAIC: 513310 Wired Telecommunications Carriers;
513322 Cellular and Other Wireless Tele-
communications

■ ■ ■

Verizon Communications Inc., formed in June 2000 with the merger of Bell Atlantic and GTE, is a leading provider of communications services. The company's business is split into four main operating segments. Domestic Telecom provides wireline and telecom-munications services including broadband. Verizon Wireless is the second-largest wireless provider in the U.S. with over 51 million customers across the United States. Verizon's Information Services unit is involved in directory publishing and electronic commerce services. The company's International arm provides wireline and wireless operations in the Americas and Europe. Accord-

ing to the company, its network connects more than 1.5 billion telephone calls each day. Verizon acquired rival MCI Inc. in an $8.5 billion deal in 2006.

A HISTORY OF BELL ATLANTIC

In January 1982, the U.S. Department of Justice ended a 13-year antitrust suit against the world's largest corporation, the American Telephone and Telegraph Company (AT&T). Pursuant to a consent decree, AT&T maintained its manufacturing and research facilities, as well as its long-distance operations. On January 1, 1984, AT&T divested itself of 22 local operating companies, which were divided among seven regional holding companies (RHCs).

Thus Bell Atlantic was formed from AT&T. The new company served the northern Atlantic states and oversaw seven telephone subsidiaries. AT&T as a competitor proved an immediate and ever-present chal-lenge for Bell Atlantic. In February 1984 the company announced the formation of Bell Atlanticom Systems, a systems and equipment subsidiary to market traditional, cordless, and decorator telephones; wiring components; and home security and healthcare systems. Bell Atlantic Mobile Systems took off early from the starting gate: in March 1984 the company introduced Alex, a cellular telephone service to commence a month later in the Washington, D.C., and Baltimore, Maryland, markets. Bell Atlantic Mobile Systems invested $15.1 million in the fledgling cellular service.

In April 1984 Bell Atlantic went to court over the Federal Communications Commission's (FCC) delay in charging tariffs for customers accessing the local network. Delaying implementation of the access fee not only violated the consent decree, Bell Atlantic charged, but it also caused Bell Atlantic and its sibling RHCs to cover some of AT&T's service costs in the interim. To make matters worse, because Bell Atlantic was the lowest-cost provider of all the RHCs, it was losing the most money. (The FCC system was one of allocation, with access-fee funds collected first, then distributed to RHCs based on the company's cost.) Bell Atlantic planned to succeed in spite of the access fee tangle and subsequently allotted more than half of its construction budget for improvement of the network. Bell Atlantic became the first RHC to employ the use of digital termination systems, a microwave technology for local electronic message distribution. The company experimented with a local area data transport system, and planned to install 50,000 miles of optical fiber within a year.

Bell Atlantic made several major acquisitions in its first year of operation, including Telecommunications Specialists, Inc. (TSI), a Houston-based interconnect firm; New Jersey's Tri-Continental Leasing Corporation (Tri-Con), a computer and telecommunications equipment provider; and MAI's Sorbus Inc. division, the second-largest U.S. computer service firm.

With the most aggressive diversification of all the RHCs, Bell Atlantic planned to be a full-service company in the increasingly related merging telecommunications and computer sectors. As a struggle for large customers was inevitable, and because the larger customers could potentially set up their own information systems, the company decided to target medium-sized customers. Bell Atlantic offered this customer base everything from information services equipment and data processing to computer maintenance.

Of all the unregulated businesses Bell Atlantic was just entering, competition threatened to be even stiffer in the private branch exchange (PBX) market. By early 1985 IBM and Digital Equipment were offering maintenance for their mainframe users, a large portion of Bell Atlantic's recently acquired Sorbus customer base. Eighteen months after divestiture, Bell Atlantic, along with its sibling RHCs and other companies, real-

ized that convergence of telephone hardware and computer data processing was a huge business. Over the next several years the RHCs repeatedly petitioned the Department of Justice for business waivers to become more competitive in not only the national but international telecommunications market.

By the end of 1985 Bell Atlantic earnings were $1.1 billion on revenues of $9.1 billion. Rated against its competitors, Bell Atlantic was the only RHC close to turning a profit on its unregulated businesses, worth $600 million in revenues. While profits remained strong in Bell Atlantic's local phone service, its Yellow Pages directory publishing division, due to a disagreement, began to compete with Reuben H. Donnelly Corporation, its previous publisher.

In the meantime, the long-distance market moved uncomfortably close to the RHC's local turf. AT&T and other carriers began competing to carry toll calls in local areas. While this would seem to benefit the residential consumer, it did not; outside competitors cutting into RHC profits merely threatened the very profit margin that helped subsidize the cost of local service. Ending its second year in operation, Bell Atlantic's chairman and CEO, Thomas Bolger, described the restrictions on RHCs as "the most significant problem in the telecommunications industry" in Telephone Engineer & Management's mid-December 1985 issue and he requested the Justice Department come to a decision before the scheduled January 1, 1987 date. If the purpose of the breakup was to promote maximum competition in the industry, the RHCs reasoned that they, the most likely competitors of industry leaders AT&T and IBM, should not be prohibited from fully competing.

In July 1987 Bell Atlantic announced a restructuring plan, combining operations of basic telephone service and unregulated businesses. The plan also called for all staff of separate Bell Atlantic telephone companies to report to their respective presidents.

The tables turned rather quickly for Bell Atlantic. In January 1988 the company found itself, along with BellSouth, accused of misconduct in bidding attempts to win government contracts. Senator John Glenn of Ohio led the accusations that the two RHCs had been given confidential price information by a General Services Administration chief. Bell Atlantic disputed the charges entirely, claiming that the senator's report was inaccurate.

Bell Atlantic implemented another reorganization in 1989 by trimming its management staff less 1,700 employees through voluntary retirement and other

KEY DATES

2000: Verizon Communications is formed by the merger of Bell Atlantic and GTE. The company purchases OnePoint Communications Corporation, and is renamed Verizon Avenue.

2001: Verizon earns federal approval to offer long distance service in Connecticut and Pennsylvania: Verizon Wireless joins forces with Lucent Technologies. Verizon Avenue offers high-speed Internet access service nationwide.

2006: Verizon completes its $8.5 billion purchase of MCI Inc.

incentive plans. During this time, Bell Atlantic invested $2.3 billion in network services to upgrade telephone facilities.

To compete in mobile communications, the company marketed an extremely lightweight cellular telephone; at the same time, Bell Atlantic Paging's customer base grew, with a 16 percent increase. In partnership with GTE, Bell Atlantic Yellow Pages increased its customer base through a new subsidiary, the Chesapeake Directory Sales Company. Bell Atlantic Systems Integration was formed in 1989 to research and explore marketing capabilities in voice and data communications, as well as in artificial intelligence.

Perhaps the biggest opportunity for Bell Atlantic came at year-end 1989, when it stepped up activity in the international arena. Economic changes in the Soviet Union and Eastern Europe opened up entirely new possibilities in global telecommunications. Slowly exploring opportunities abroad since divestiture, Bell Atlantic was, by 1989, assisting in the installation of telephone software systems for the Dutch national telephone company, PTT Telecom, B.V., as well as for the national telephone company in Spain. A Bell Atlantic German subsidiary was awarded a contract to install microcomputers and related equipment at U.S. Army locations in Germany, Belgium, and the United Kingdom. With consultants located in Austria, France, Italy, and Switzerland, Bell Atlantic planned a European headquarters, Bell Atlantic Europe, S.A., to be located in Brussels, Belgium.

In the United States, however, Bell Atlantic kept running into challenges. In April 1990, the company's Chesapeake and Potomac Telephone Company was charged with fraud and barred from seeking federal contracts. Bell Atlantic fought back, citing a double standard in that the U.S. Department of Treasury allowed AT&T to win contracts without necessarily having all the required equipment immediately available, while it had barred the Chesapeake and Potomac Telephone Company from doing so. Undaunted by its squabbles with the government, Bell Atlantic had created the world's largest independent computer maintenance organization by 1990, able to service some 500 brands of computers. With the January 1990 purchase of Control Data Corporation's third-party maintenance business, Bell Atlantic sealed its position as the leader in maintenance of both IBM and Digital Equipment Corporation systems.

In the early and mid-1990s Bell Atlantic's international division thrived. In 1990 alone the corporation made several significant ventures, which included teaming up with the Korean Telecommunications Authority in a variety of research, marketing, and information exchanges; joining U.S. West to modernize Czechoslovak telecommunications; and partnering with Ameritech and two New Zealand companies to acquire the Telecom Corporation of New Zealand.

In 1992 Bell Atlantic acquired Metro Mobile, the second-largest independent cellular radio telecommunications provider in the United States. This particular transaction gave Bell Atlantic the most extensive cellular phone coverage on the East Coast, while a joint venture with NYNEX and GTE to combine their respective cellular networks into one huge national service made news from coast to coast.

The year 1995 proved pivotal for Bell Atlantic's future. A long-awaited ruling in the federal courts gave the company a sweet victory; a federal judge finally ruled in favor of the Baby Bells to offer long-distance services. Bell Atlantic wasted little time, becoming the first Baby Bell to jump into the long-distance market by recruiting customers in Florida, Illinois, North and South Carolina, and Texas in early 1996. Another major development in 1996 was the announcement that Bell Atlantic and NYNEX would merge and become the nation's second-largest telephone company. Though the official announcement came as a surprise to few (rumors had been swirling for months), the deal was at once controversial and ironic—once-struggling Baby Bells were beginning to rival their old parent company. Soon after news of the merger was made public, a new operating unit called Bell Atlantic Internet Solutions debuted, giving customers in Washington, D.C., Philadelphia, and New Jersey a wide range of both business and residential Internet-based products and services.

Bell Atlantic's merger with NYNEX was completed in early 1997. The new company's assets serviced 25 percent of the overall U.S. market in 13 states and accounted for about 140 billion minutes of long-distance traffic; the region not only held one-third of the Fortune 500's headquarters, but the U.S. government's nerve center as well. South of the border, Bell Atlantic continued its varied international coups, this time investing another $50 million in its Mexican venture to gain controlling interest in Grupo Iusacell, of which it had previously owned 42 percent.

By early 1998 the new Bell Atlantic had 39.7 million domestic access lines, 5.4 million domestic wireless customers, 6.3 million global wireless customers, and services in 21 countries worldwide. The company was also the world's largest publisher of both print and electronic directories, with over 80 million distributed annually. After a rocky road as Bell Atlantic's local markets were forced open to competitors, the company was taking advantage of new opportunities in the $20 billion long-distance market and the $8 billion video market, and was continuing to expand globally.

A HISTORY OF GTE

In March 1990, the largest merger in the history of the telecommunications industry united two former U.S. competitors, GTE Corporation and Contel Corporation, under the GTE name. With a market value of $28 billion, the merged company became a telecommunications powerhouse. Designed to take advantage of the two companies' complementary businesses, the merger strengthened GTE's assets in two of its three major areas of operations: telephone service and telecommunications products.

GTE's heritage can be traced to 1918, when three Wisconsin public utility accountants pooled $33,500 to purchase the Richland Center Telephone Company, serving 1,466 telephones in the dairy belt of southern Wisconsin. From the outset, John F. O'Connell, Sigurd L. Odegard, and John A. Pratt worked under the guiding principle that better telephone service could be rendered to small communities if a number of exchanges were operated under one managing body.

The first two decades of operation involved numerous acquisitions and growth. By 1935 the company resurfaced as General Telephone Corporation, operating 12 newly consolidated companies. John Winn, a 26-year veteran of the Bell System, was named president. In 1936 General Telephone created a new subsidiary, General Telephone Directory Company, to publish directories for the parent's entire service area.

In 1940 LaCroix was elected General Telephone's first chairman, and Harold Bozell, a former banker for Associated Telephone Utilities, was named president. Like other businesses, the telephone industry was under government restrictions during World War II, and General Telephone was called upon to increase services at military bases and war-production factories.

Following the war, General Telephone reactivated an acquisitions program that had been dormant for more than a decade and purchased 118,000 telephone lines between 1946 and 1950. In 1950 General Telephone purchased its first telephone equipment manufacturing subsidiary, Leich Electric Company, along with the related Leich Sales Corporation.

In 1959 General Telephone and Sylvania Electric Products merged, and the parent's name was changed to General Telephone & Electronics Corporation (GT&E). The merger gave Sylvania, a leader in such industries as lighting, television and radio, and chemistry and metallurgy, the needed capital to expand. For General Telephone, the merger meant the added benefit of Sylvania's extensive research and development capabilities in the field of electronics. Other acquisitions in the late 1950s included Peninsular Telephone Company in Florida, with 300,000 lines, and Lenkurt Electric Company, Inc., a leading producer of microwave and data transmissions system.

The middle of the century saw more deals and acquisitions for GT&E, as well as some dangerous controversy. In March 1970 GT&E's New York City headquarters was bombed by a radical antiwar group in protest of the company's participation in defense work. In December of that year the GT&E board agreed to move the company's headquarters to Stamford, Connecticut.

After initially proposing to build separate satellite systems, GT&E and its telecommunications rival, American Telephone and Telegraph Company, announced in 1974 joint venture plans for the construction and operation of seven earth-based stations interconnected by two satellites. That same year Sylvania acquired name and distribution rights for Philco television and stereo products. GT&E International expanded its activities during the same period, acquiring television manufacturers in Canada and Israel and a telephone manufacturer in Germany.

In 1976, the company reorganized along five global product lines: communications, lighting, consumer electronics, precision materials, and electrical equipment. GT&E International was phased out during the reorganization, and GTE Products Corporation was formed to encompass both domestic and foreign manufacturing and marketing operations. At the same time, GTE Communications Products was formed to oversee operations of Automatic Electric, Lenkurt, Sylvania, and GTE Information Systems.

Another reorganization followed in 1979. GT&E Products Group was eliminated as an organizational unit and GTE Electrical Products, consisting of lighting, precision materials, and electrical equipment was formed. Vanderslice also revitalized the GT&E Telephone Operating Group in order to develop competitive strategies for anticipated regulatory changes in the telecommunications industry. GT&E sold its consumer electronics businesses, including the accompanying brand names of Philco and Sylvania in 1980, after watching revenues from television and radio operations decrease precipitously with the success of foreign manufacturers. Following AT&T's 1982 announcement that it would divest 22 telephone operating companies, GT&E made a number of organizational and consolidation moves.

In 1982 the company adopted the name GTE Corporation and formed GTE Mobilnet Inc. to handle the company's entrance into the new cellular telephone business. In 1983 GTE sold its electrical equipment, brokerage information services, and cable television equipment businesses.

GTE became the third-largest long-distance telephone company in 1983 through the acquisition of Southern Pacific Communications Company. At the same time, Southern Pacific Satellite Company was acquired, and the two firms were renamed GTE Sprint Communications Corporation and GTE Spacenet Corporation, respectively. Through an agreement with the Department of Justice, GTE conceded to keep Sprint Communications separate from its other telephone companies and limit other GTE telephone subsidiaries in certain markets.

In 1984 GTE formalized its decision to concentrate on three core businesses: telecommunications, lighting, and precision metals. That same year, the company's first satellite was launched, and GTE's cellular telephone service went into operation, and GTE's earnings exceeded $1 billion for the first time.

Beginning in 1986 GTE spun off several operations to form joint ventures. In 1986 GTE Sprint and United Telecommunication's long-distance subsidiary, U.S. Telecom, agreed to merge and form US Sprint Communications Company, with each parent retaining a 50 percent interest in the new firm. That same year, GTE transferred its international transmission, overseas central office switching, and business systems operations to a joint venture with Siemens AG of Germany, which took 80 percent ownership of the new firm. The following year, GTE transferred its business systems operations in the United States to a new joint venture, Fujitsu GTE Business Systems, Inc., formed with Fujitsu Ltd., which

retained 80 percent ownership. In 1987, the company organized its telephone companies around a single national organization headquartered in the Dallas, Texas, area.

In 1988, GTE divested its consumer communications products unit as part of a telecommunications strategy to place increasing emphasis on the services sector. The following year GTE sold the majority of its interest in US Sprint to United Telecommunications and its interest in Fujitsu GTE Business Systems to Fujitsu.

In 1989 GTE and AT&T formed the joint venture company AG Communication Systems Corporation, designed to bring advanced digital technology to GTE's switching systems. GTE retained 51 percent control over the joint venture, with AT&T pledging to take complete control of the new firm in 15 years.

With an increasing emphasis on telecommunications, in 1989 GTE launched a program to become the first cellular provider offering nationwide service, and introduced the nation's first rural service area providing cellular service on the Hawaiian island of Kauai. The following year GTE acquired the Providence Journal Company's cellular properties in five southern states for $710 million and became the second-largest cellular-service provider in the United States.

In 1990 GTE reorganized its activities around three business groups: telecommunications products and services, telephone operations, and electrical products. That same year, GTE and Contel Corporation announced merger plans that would strengthen GTE's telecommunications and telephone sectors. Following action or review by more than 20 governmental bodies, in March 1991 the merger of GTE and Contel was approved.

GTE Corporation ranked as the world's third-largest publicly owned telecommunications company in 1996. With over 20 million telephone access lines in 40 states, the communications conglomerate was America's leading provider of local telephone services. The $6.6 billion acquisition of Contel Corporation in 1990 nearly doubled GTE's Mobilnet cellular operations, making it the second-largest provider of cellular telephone services in the United States, with over two million customers. GTE's strategy for the mid- to late-1990s focused on technological enhancement of wireline and wireless systems, expansion of data services, global expansion, and diversification into video services.

In 1990 Contel completed the biggest acquisition in its history, a $1.3 billion purchase of McCaw Cellular Communications, Inc.'s controlling interests in 13 cellular markets, added more than six million potential customers and doubled Contel's cellular potential population market (known in the industry as POPs). While important, that move was eclipsed by the merger with GTE announced later that same year. Through that transition, the two former competitors were expected to integrate telephone and mobile-cellular operations and capitalize on business unit similarities in the field of satellite communications as well as in communications systems and services targeting government entities.

Over half of Contel's $6.6 billion purchase price, $3.9 billion, was assumed debt. In 1992, in order to reduce that obligation, the company sold its North American Lighting business to a Siemens affiliate for over $1 billion, shaved off local exchange properties in Idaho, Tennessee, Utah, and West Virginia to generate another $1 billion, divested its interest in Sprint in 1992, and sold its GTE Spacenet satellite operations to General Electric in 1994.

The long-heralded telecommunications bill, expected to go into effect in 1996, promised to encourage competition among local phone providers, long-distance services, and cable television companies. Many leading telecoms prepared for the new competitive realities by aligning themselves with entertainment and information providers. GTE, on the other hand, continued to focus on its core operations, seeking to make them as efficient as possible. In 1992 a sweeping reorganization effort was launched that was characterized by *Telephony* magazine as "easily one of the nation's largest re-engineering processes."

Among other goals, GTE planned to double revenues and slash costs by $1 billion per year by focusing on five key areas of operation: technological enhancement of wireline and wireless systems, expansion of data services, global expansion, and diversification into video services. GTE hoped to cross-sell its large base of wireline customers on wireless, data and video services by launching Tele-Go, a user-friendly service that combined cordless and cellular phone features. The company bought broadband spectrum cellular licenses in Atlanta, Seattle, Cincinnati and Denver, and formed a joint venture with SBC Communications to enhance its cellular capabilities in Texas. In 1995 the company undertook a 15-state test of videoconferencing services, as well as a video dialtone (VDT) experiment that proposed to offer cable television programming to 900,000 homes by 1997. GTE also formed a video programming and interservices joint venture with Ameritech Corporation, BellSouth Corporation, SBC Communications, and The Walt Disney Company in the fall of 1995. Foreign efforts included affiliations with phone companies in Argentina, Mexico, Germany, Japan, Canada, the Dominican Republic, Venezuela, and China. The early 1990s reorganization included a 37.5 percent

work force reduction, from 177,500 in 1991 to 111,000 by 1994. The fivefold strategy had begun to bear fruit by the mid-1990s. While the communication conglomerate's sales remained rather flat, at about $19.8 billion, from 1992 through 1994, its net income increased by 43.7 percent, from $1.74 billion to a record $2.5 billion during the same period.

By 1996 GTE Corporation ranked as the world's third-largest publicly owned telecommunications company. With over 20 million telephone access lines in 40 states, the communications conglomerate was America's leading provider of local telephone services. The $6.6 billion acquisition of Contel Corporation in 1990 nearly doubled GTE's Mobilnet cellular operations, making it the second-largest provider of cellular telephone services in the United States, with over two million customers.

THE TELECOMMUNICATIONS ACT OF 1996

The year 1996 would be as pivotal as 1984 in the telecommunications industry. The Telecommunications Act was designed to meet the needs of communications for the new century. By this time communications had invaded all aspects of life: wireless, television, computer, the Internet, commerce, education, and research. Until then the communications industry had consisted of telephone service. Broadcast, electricity, and computing had their own industries.

The new law eradicated these boundaries. The Telecommunications Act allowed for any company to compete in any industry. Electric companies could provide Internet access if they wanted. Cable bills could be consolidated with phone bills. The heart of the Telecommunications Act was to allow more competition among communications providers. This also meant that different companies could offer different parts of a phone service, and consumers could choose which company they wanted to pay for each part (for "local" versus "long" distance).

The concept was not new; what was new was the advent of advanced equipment and technology that allowed such industries to meld. The Telecommunications Act not only allowed companies to interconnect—it required it.

Because of the available technology and the freedom to offer more services, phone companies began massive restructuring and acquisitions. Four of seven Regional Bell operating companies disappeared shortly after the Telecommunications Act was passed; in addition to these, Bell Atlantic joined the buying frenzy by purchasing NYNEX, Vodafone AirTouch, and GTE. This new conglomerate formed Verizon Communications and Verizon Wireless in April 2000.

VERIZON COMMUNICATIONS FORMS

Verizon, whose name is a combination of the Latin word *veritas* and the word "horizon," combined consumer and business services into one massive $58 billion deal. The wireless division got underway first; the Verizon moniker and logos appeared soon after. The re-branding and melding of the two companies was a formidable task; when the merger was first announced in July 1998 Bell Atlantic operated in 13 Mid-Atlantic states and encompassed local telephone service, video, Internet, and wireless divisions. GTE had wireless, Internet, video, local telephone, and long-distance service in 28 (mostly western) states.

By July 2000, the merger had been approved by the FCC and Verizon was on its way to establishing a complete communications business. However, the company faced several problems from the start: an 18-day strike left the company with 280,000 repair requests to handle; plans to sell DSL Internet connection services were delayed; the company was not allowed to offer long distance in 12 of 13 of its home states; and an initial public offering of Verizon Wireless was postponed several times due to lack of investor interest. In addition, profits for the year fell below expectations, and the initial forecast for 2001 was reduced a third.

More trouble came for Verizon at the end of the year when it pulled out of a merger with NorthPoint, a DSL business. The $800 million deal was to commence at the start of 2001, but Verizon discontinued it at the last minute, citing NorthPoint's weakening financial position. Verizon had hoped to expand its out-of-region service and compete with cable companies for Internet service. In December NorthPoint sued Verizon for $1 billion in damages. NorthPoint accepted Verizon's $175 million settlement offer in 2002.

Despite these obstacles, the company remained optimistic. The company was especially proud of its 28 million customers, 63 million phone lines, and coverage in 67 of the country's biggest cities. With telecom service regulations lifted, Verizon set out to offer complete packages of services. The wireless side of the company was optimistic as well; Verizon Wireless planned to spend more than $3 billion to upgrade its network. They also struck a deal with Nortel Networks to supply equipment over a two-year period.

Verizon's visions for 2001 focused on international expansion. While they already had some links to Toronto, Hong Kong, and Tokyo, the company wanted to expand into major cities in Europe, Asia, and Latin America. They would also offer their Internet services (under the Genuity brand name). New York would be the connecting state while the company waited for approval to add other regions. The company planned a five-year, $1 billion expansion.

In March 2001, Verizon Wireless joined forces with Lucent Technologies in a $5 billion deal to offer the next generation of high-speed Internet services and wireless technology. With Sprint on their heels, the two companies planned to work on advancements in high-speed mobile Internet services. Verizon Wireless had 27.5 million voice and data customers. The deal would double Verizon's existing voice capacity.

After a little more than a year, Verizon was operating in 40 different countries, had 27.5 million customers, and $65 billion in annual revenue. Further expansion, advanced Internet technologies, and broader service was on the agenda for the immediate future.

THE 2005 MCI DEAL

Before Verizon made its play for MCI in 2005, the company spent time divesting certain assets in order to trim debt. Under the leadership of CEO Ivan Seidenberg, Verizon sold its stakes in several wireless operators including Cable and Wireless, STET Hellas, Eurotel Praha, Grupo Iusacell, and CTI Holdings. It also jettisoned its interest in Telecom New Zealand, and many of its access lines in Alabama, Kentucky, and Missouri.

By early 2004, Verizon was well positioned at the top of the telecommunications heap. It was facing staunch competition however, from the likes of cable companies that were expanding into voice services. According to a 2004 *Fortune* article, cable companies had collectively spent $75 billion in recent years to upgrade their systems to offer customers voice, high-speed Internet, and cable. As such, Verizon teamed up with DirecTV to offer customers digital broadcast satellite services along with voice and Internet services.

In a move designed to strengthen its position in the rapidly changing industry, Verizon offered $6.3 billion to acquire MCI Inc. in February 2005. MCI was a global communications provider with revenues exceeding $20 billion. MCI and WorldCom Inc. had joined together in 1997 in what was the largest merger in U.S. corporate history at the time. The $37 billion union eventually ended in disaster. WorldCom declared bankruptcy in 2002 during a highly publicized accounting scandal. MCI emerged from Chapter 11 protection in April 2004.

Shortly after Verizon made its offer for MCI, competitor Qwest Communications International Inc.

came in with an offer of its own. A hotly contested bidding war ensued but in the end, MCI accepted Verizon's $8.5 billion bid—which was less than Qwest's $9.74 billion offer—because of the company's stronger financial position and its long-term prospects. The FCC approved the deal in October and Verizon completed the purchase in January 2006.

When the dust settled on the MCI deal, Verizon stood as a leading communications services provider and Verizon Wireless held the number two position behind Cingular Wireless. While Verizon anticipated the addition of MCI would leave it better positioned to succeed in the ever-changing telecommunications industry, its competitors continued to grow even larger. SBC Communications teamed up with AT&T Corporation in 2005 to create the largest telecommunications company in United States. Then in early 2006, AT&T set plans in motion to acquire BellSouth Corporation in a $67 billion deal. If completed, the union would bring together a large portion of the former AT&T monopoly that had been broken up in 1984. With its chief rival growing even larger, many analysts speculated that Verizon may choose to adopt a growth-through-acquisition strategy.

Meanwhile, Verizon management remained optimistic about the company's future and planned to expand further into next-generation broadband services, divest its directories business, and attempt to purchase the shares of Verizon Wireless it didn't already own. Seidenberg was quoted in a 2006 *Wall Street Journal* article claiming, "Our strategy is to be a customer-focused leader in consumer broadband and video, as well as business and government services, in both the landline and wireless environments. We believe that our superior networks are the basis for innovation and competitive advantage in communications."

Updated, Kerri DeVault
Updated, Christina M. Stansell

PRINCIPAL SUBSIDIARIES

Verizon California Inc.; Verizon Delaware Inc.; Verizon Florida Inc.; Verizon Hawaii Inc.; Verizon Maryland Inc.; Verizon New England Inc.; Verizon New Jersey Inc.; Verizon New York Inc.; Verizon North Inc.; Verizon Northwest Inc.; Verizon Pennsylvania Inc.; Verizon South Inc.; GTE Southwest Incorporated; Verizon Virginia Inc.; Verizon Washington, DC Inc.; Verizon West Virginia Inc.; Cellco Partnership; Verizon Capital Corporation; Verizon Global Funding Corporation; Verizon Information Services Inc.; Verizon International Holdings Ltd.

PRINCIPAL COMPETITORS

AT&T Inc.; Sprint Nextel Corporation; Qwest Communications International Inc.; BellSouth Corporation.

FURTHER READING

"Bad Connection?," *Business Week*, August 28, 2000, p. 56.

Barrett, Paul M., "Legal Beat: Justices Question Congress' Ban on Phone Concerns Offering Cable," *Wall Street Journal*, December 7, 1995, p. B10.

Belson, Ken, "Huge Phone Deal Seeks to Thwart Smaller Rivals," *New York Times*, March 6, 2006.

———, "MCI Shareholders Vote for Sale to Verizon," *New York Times*, October 7, 2005.

———, "Verizon Loses Some Edge Atop the Bells," *New York Times*, December 28, 2005.

Bernier, Paula, "AT&T, GI Win Round 1 of GTE's Video Rollout," *Telephony*, March 13, 1995, p. 6.

Bradbury, Steven, and Kelion Kasler, "Verizon Communications: The Merger of Bell Atlantic and GTE," *Coporate Finance*, November 2000, pp. 47-48.

Byrne, Harlan S., "Sleepy No More," *Barron's*, January 16, 1995, p. 15.

Cauley, Leslie, "Bell Atlantic and NYNEX Discuss Merger to Form Second-Biggest Phone Firm," *Wall Street Journal*, December 18, 1995, p. A3.

———, "Bell Atlantic and NYNEX Merger Talks Highlight Roles of Smith and Seidenberg," *Wall Street Journal*, December 19, 1995, p. A3.

———, "Technology & Telecommunications: Baby Bells Square Off Against AT&T on Calling Cards, U.S. West Agreement," *Wall Street Journal*, October 27, 1995, p. B3.

Creswell, Julie, "Ivan Seidenberg, CEO of Verizon, Vows to Overpower the Cable Guys by Plowing Billions Into a '90s-Style Broadband Buildout," *Fortune*, May 31, 2004.

"The Foreign Invasion: New Zealand Discovered the Benefits of Letting Global Companies Be a Part of Reform," *Wall Street Journal*, October 2, 1995, p. R16.

Gold, Howard, "Tom Bolger's OneStopShop," *Forbes*, March 25, 1985.

Gold, Jacqueline S., "GTE: Poor Connection," *Financial World*, October 26, 1993, p. 19.

Greene, Tim, "Those Baby Bells Are Growing up Fast," *Network World Fusion*, November 20, 2000.

Grice, Corey, "Digital Darwinism," *CNET News.com*, February 1, 2001.

———, "Verizon Who?," *CNET News.com*, April 3, 2000.

"GTE's New Twist on Cellular," *Electronics*, April 25, 1994, p. 1.

Heskitt, Ben, "Nortel Nabs $500 Million Deal with Verizon," *CNET News.com*, April 12, 2000.

Jones, Jennifer, "Verizon's Top Lawyer Blasts FCC," *InfoWorld*, August 22, 2000.

King, Carol, "Lucent, Verizon Bet $5 Billion on 3G," *InternetNews*, March 19, 2001.

Klebnikov, Paul, "TechnoSkeptic," *Forbes*, February 26, 1996, p. 42.

Lannon, Larry, "Bell Atlantic's Bolger Demands His Freedom," *Telephony*, July 14, 1986.

Lavin, Douglas, "European Phone Giants Challenge Italy," *Wall Street Journal*, November 16, 1995, p. A14.

"Lucent, Verizon in Major Wireless Deal," *Reuters*, March 19, 2001.

Martin, Michael, "Verizon Expands International Telecom Horizons," *Network World*, February 12, 2001, p. 10.

———, "Verizon Leaves NorthPoint at the Altar," *Network World*, December 4, 2000, p. 98.

Mason, Charles, "RHC Barred Federal Contracts," *Telephony*, April 16, 1990.

———, "Sculpting a New Industry Structure," *Telephony*, April 19, 1993, p. 88.

McCarthy, Thomas E., *The History of GTE: The Evolution of One of America's Great Corporations*, Stamford, Conn., GTE Corporation, 1990.

Meeks, Fleming, "'Fail' Is Not a Four-Letter Word," *Forbes*, April 30, 1990.

Mikolas, Mark, "What Makes Charles Run," *TE&M*, April 1, 1987.

Naik, Gautam, "Technology & Telecommunications: Bells Venture Likely to Place Cellular Order," *Wall Street Journal*, November 10, 1995, p. B2.

Naraine, Ryan, "Verizon Slams 'Broadband Bill,'" *Internet.com*, May 23, 2001.

Neighly, Patrick, "Verizon Wireless Announces First Boss," *America's Network*, May 15, 2000, p. 8.

Ryan, Vincent, "Download: Only the Beginning," *Telephony*, June 26, 2000.

Stone, Martin, "NorthPoint's $1B Suit against Verizon Proceeds," *Washington Post*, February 16, 2001.

Tell, Lawrence J., "Footloose and Fancy Free," *Barron's*, November 12, 1984.

"Verizon and NorthPoint Merge DSL Businesses," *America's Network*, September 2000, pp. 32-33.

"Verizon Faces Lawsuit," *Utility Business*, January 2001, p. 12.

"Verizon, Lucent Enter 3-Year, $5B Partnership," *Capital Distict Business Review*, March 19, 2001.

Waters, Richard, "Verizon Plans $1bn Expansion," *Financial Times FT.com*, February 6, 2001.

Weber, Tony, "Verizon Stumbles out of the Blocks," *Telephony*, August 14, 2000, p. 28.

Welti, Patty, "Dream Job for GTE, IBM," *America's Network*, January 1, 1996, p. 18.

Woolley, Scot, "The New Ma Bell," *Forbes*, April 16, 2001, pp. 68-71.

Young, Shawn, "Verizon Closes its MCI Purchase," *Wall Street Journal*, January 7, 2006.

Vicunha Têxtil S.A.

Av. Sargento Herminio 2965
Fortaleza, Ceará 60350-502
Brazil
Telephone: (55) 85 499-1000
Fax: (55) 11 2187-2399
Web site: http://www.vicunha.com.br

Public Company
Incorporated: 1949 as Têxtil Elizabeth S.A.
Employees: 12,645
Sales: BRL 1.57 billion ($535.84 million) (2004)
Stock Exchanges: São Paulo
Ticker Symbol: VINE3; VINE5; VINE6
NAIC: 313111 Yarn Spinning Mills; 313210 Broadwoven Fabric Mills; 313241 Weft Knit Mills

■ ■ ■

Vicunha Têxtil S.A. is, in terms of annual sales level, the largest Brazilian enterprise in the textiles and clothing sector. Vertically integrated, Vicunha is engaged in spinning, weaving, and knitting textile fibers, dyeing and printing fabrics, and making garments. Its products consist of filaments, yarns, denim fabrics and twills, natural- and synthetic-fiber knitted fabrics, synthetic woven fabrics, and ready-made articles of clothing. Each one of these areas constitutes a business unit. Vicunha has offices or subsidiaries in the United States, Europe, China, Argentina, and Colombia and exports its products to 80 countries.

TEXTILE INDUSTRY GIANT: 1946–88

Vicunha's origins go back to 1946, when Sam Rabinovich founded a small weaving plant in São Roque, São Paulo. Two years later, Fiação e Tecelagem Campo Belo S.A. came on stream. This facility is credited with introducing natural and artificial and synthetic-fiber blends into Brazil and contributing in a decisive way to numerous advancements in fabric-dyeing processes. In 1949 Mendel and Eliezer Steinbruch, who were related by marriage to Rabinovich, began running the São Roque weaving mill, which had 27 looms and was named Têxtil Elizabeth S.A. Under the Elizabeth trademark, this company gained prominence in the production of circular-knit and flat-woven fabrics—especially those in nylon. Campo Belo provided Elizabeth with yarn.

The Rabinovich and Steinbruch families joined forces in 1966 to build their first joint enterprise, the Brasibel textile company, which began operating with leased machinery and facilities. Like Têxtil Elizabeth, Brasibel produced 100 percent woven polyester-filament fabrics. The following year the owners acquired what, at the time, was the largest worsted mill in South America, Lanifício Varam, which also was known for its traditional woolen yarns. The name of this business was changed to Vicunha in 1969 because one of its worsted brands used the wool of this highly prized Andean animal.

The next step in the growth of what was now called the Vicunha group came in 1970, when the Rabinovich and Steinbruch families joined with two groups in the

COMPANY PERSPECTIVES

With the aim of constantly improving and innovating in its production methods, Vicunha Têxtil consistently invests in technology and training its professional staff to ensure its modern industrial facilities' continued effectiveness. All this dedication is reflected in the company's competitiveness, in the quality of products which it manufactures and its progressive expansion into international markets.

state of Ceará, the Otoch and Baquit families, to found Fiação Nordeste do Brasil S.A. Finobrasa in the city of Fortaleza. The significant increase in production capacity allowed the Vicunha group to increase its share of the domestic market and begin to compete aggressively abroad. Another partnership, in 1972, this time with the Renner group of the state of Rio Grande do Sul, resulted in the creation of Têxtil RV Ltda., a clothing firm. In 1974 Vicunha acquired the Textília and TBT weaving mills.

The Vicunha group acquired Fibra S.A., the national leader in synthetic and artificial yarns for the textile industry, from an Italian group in 1982. This addition, which included the company's plant in Americana, São Paulo, broadened the group's production of artificial and synthetic fibers. By 1988 Fibra was responsible for one-third of Vicunha's annual revenue. Vicunha, in 1984, acquired the Renner group's interest in Lee S.A., the principal Brazilian subsidiary of the U.S. jeans manufacturer Lee Apparel Co., Inc. During the same year, Vicunha expanded its activities in northeastern Brazil by establishing Vicunha Nordeste S.A. It founded, in 1988, Elizabeth Nordeste S.A., a spinning mill, subsequently adding a knitting facility. During this period Vicunha also purchased a securities dealer that it named Fibrasa and founded a bank it named Banco Fibra S.A.

FACING FOREIGN COMPETITION BEGINNING IN 1990

The revenues of the Vicunha group came $700 million in 1988 and $1.2 billion the following year. By 1990 the group was a complex of 26 companies employing 26,000 people and producing everything in the textile sector. But in legal terms, it did not exist at all. Some of the companies, like Campo Belo S.A., belonged entirely to the Rabinovich family; others, like Elizabeth S.A., belonged entirely to the Steinbruch family. Still others,

such as Fibra, the group's biggest enterprise, and Tecil S.A. Comércio de Tecidos, a fabrics retail chain with 18 units, were owned jointly. Jacks Rabinovich, who succeeded his father, collaborated closely with Mendel Steinbruch in group matters. They formed a formidable team, with the former, an engineer, concentrating on production, and the latter, a born salesman, on commerce. What they had in common was a determination to avoid borrowing money and instead to plow their profits back into the various enterprises of the group. Benjamin Steinbruch, Mendel's eldest son, was his heir apparent and director-superintendent for the group's joint holdings. Fibra and Elizabeth were registering annual earnings of 40 percent or higher on revenues, and Elizabeth was honored by the business magazine *Exame* in 1990 as company of the year.

The early 1990s were a period of crisis for the Brazilian economy, and even more so for the textile sector. Because of newly adopted free-trade policies, cheap textiles from the Far East were now entering Brazil and undercutting domestic manufacturers like Vicunha, which saw its revenues fall to $1.1 billion in 1991 and its profit to practically zero. As an alternative to laying off employees, the company reduced working hours in its 37 plants. It looked for new retail outlets for its clothing and found one in the DB Brinquedos chain, which began carrying its Lee Kids jeans. Vicunha also opened ten stores in shopping centers. But revenues were no higher in 1992, although the company founded its first international branch, Brastex S.A., in Buenos Aires.

Faced with stagnation in their core line of business, the Vicunha partners cast an eye on the enterprises being privatized by the Brazilian government in the early 1990s. In 1993 they landed one of the biggest—Companhia Siderúrgica Nacional (CSN), Brazil's largest steelmaker. Vicunha paid $160 million for 9.1 percent of CSN, with the major part of the purchase financed by the government development bank BNDES. Soon after, Vicunha became CSN's major shareholder. This proved to be an extremely lucrative investment for Vicunha and also brought to national prominence Benjamin Steinbruch, who succeeded his father as Rabinovich's partner on Mendel's death in 1994 and a year later was able to make himself president of CSN. The partners also invested Vicunha's money in four CSN-related companies: an electricity distributor and three railways, and even in a cellular telephone company. Steinbruch's boldest step came in 1997, when he and other investors secured a controlling interest in newly privatized Companhia Vale do Rio Doce (CVRD), the world's largest producer and exporter of iron ore. Control over the combination of CVRD's iron ore and CSN's

KEY DATES

1946: Sam Rabinovich opens a small weaving plant in the state of São Paulo.

1948: The creation of Campo Belo S.A. introduces a variety of textile-fiber blends to Brazil.

1949: The weaving mill, run by two Steinbruch brothers, becomes Têxtil Elizabeth S.A.

1966: The Steinbruch and Rabinovich families open their first joint enterprise, Brasibel.

1967: Acquisition of a large worsted mill leads to what becomes known as the Vicunha group.

1970: Vicunha takes a half-share in Finobrasa, adding to the group's productive capacity.

1982: Vicunha purchases Fibra S.A., the national leader in yarns for the textile industry.

1989: The group, consisting of 26 companies, reaches annual revenue of $1.2 billion.

1993: Vicunha invests in CSN, Brazil's largest steelmaker, and soon is the leading shareholder.

1994: Vicunha forms a joint venture to make nylon with DuPont do Brasil Ltda.

1996: Vicunha fields four of Brazil's eight largest textile firms but loses money in textiles.

2001: All of the group's textile operations are folded into a new company, Vicunha Têxtil S.A.

2003: Sale of two units enables Vicunha to make its first profit in a decade from textile operations.

2004: Vicunha accounts for about 40 percent of Brazil's production of blue denim for jeans.

steel and related power and transport facilities made Steinbruch for a time the most powerful businessman in Brazil and, in 1998, boosted the net worth of the Vicunha group to BRL 3 billion (about $2.5 billion).

The Vicunha group was not doing nearly as well in textiles. Nevertheless, it continued to hold a powerful presence in this sector, fielding four of the eight largest Brazilian textile firms in terms of revenue. The biggest, Vicunha Nordeste, was the second largest textile enterprise in Brazil. Its three factories produced blue denim and employed 5,800 employees. Fibra ranked sixth among textile firms. Fibra DuPont Sudamerica S.A., a joint venture with Du Pont do Brasil Ltda. organized in 1994 to manufacture nylon and merging two Fibra plants in Brazil with a DuPont plant in Argentina, ranked seventh, and Elizabeth was eighth. In addition, Vicunha acquired, in 1996, the controlling interest in Hering Têxtil do Nordeste, a knitted

undershirt manufacturer—the largest in Brazil—owned by rival textile firm Companhia Hering.

Yet, in terms of combined annual revenue, Vicunha's textile holdings remained stagnant—even though it had spent nearly $1 billion modernizing its plant and equipment during the last ten years. Its fabrics and clothing were still losing ground to the cheaper goods of its Asian competitors. Accordingly, the company was shifting its operations based in the state of São Paulo to northeastern and west-central Brazil, where labor was cheaper. One new Vicunha operation in the northeast was Fibrasil. A 150,000-square-meter plant was opened about ten miles from Recife, Pernambuco.

The economic problems that resulted in the devaluation of the Brazilian unit of currency, the real, in early 1999 raised the Vicunha group's debt, which was in large part dollar-denominated, to BRL 1 billion (about $500 million). Steinbruch retained his command of CSN only by selling Vicunha's participation in CVRD. Meanwhile, under his younger brother, Ricardo, Vicunha's textile area was being reorganized, with concentration on the cotton segment and the further movement of facilities to the northeast, where costs were lower. The intention was to integrate all factors of production vertically: fibers, fabrics, and clothing. By 1999 Vicunha accounted for 6 percent of world production of fabric for blue jeans and was expected to earn $150 million that year, after losing money since 1994. Nevertheless, this did not come to pass.

RETRENCHING AND REFOCUSING: 2001–04

All the textile enterprises were united in 2001 into Vicunha Têxtil S.A., with ownership divided equally between the Steinbruch and Rabinovich families. Ricardo Steinbruch became chairman of the board, while Pedro Felipe Borges III, vice-president of Vicunha Nordeste—the parent company's only profitable unit—was appointed president. Before the year had ended, six of the 21 remaining factories had been closed and 3,000 employees had been dismissed. In 2002 the production of blue jeans fabric and synthetic knitwear, the company's areas of greatest volume and profitability, were chosen to be its strategic focus. Accordingly, Vicunha stopped selling filaments and fibers to others, and the division remained in business only to supply Vicunha itself. The company's efforts to make and sell a range of clothing within Brazil were abandoned; this division was confined to the manufacture of basic goods such as T-shirts for export. More than 1,200 additional workers were let go. With most of its debt of BRL 450 million (about $150 million) coming due in 2003, Vicunha sold its half-interest in the Fibra DuPont joint venture in early 2003 and its sewing threads division to a Scottish company, Coats Corrente. Reversing nearly a decade of red ink, Vicunha earned a net profit in 2003 and 2004.

With these changes Vicunha retained four divisions, but the textile division concentrated on producing blue denim. The yarn division turned to synthetic knitwear. The fibers and clothing divisions remained the same. The challenge was to work coordinated and to end the fiefdoms of the past. This was an admittedly slow process, given the sprawling corporate culture of the firm. A company executive told Cristiane Mano of *Exame,* "We are in an atypical situation, in which the system of each unit speaks a different language"—or what Mano called "a technological Tower of Babel, with a dozen distinct systems." One important step was to combine the two logistics areas—in São Paulo and the Northeast—in Fortaleza. Three factories that were practically neighbors in Itatiba, São Paulo, were combined into one.

Vicunha had 13 factories in five Brazilian states in 2004. The company accounted for about 40 percent of Brazil's production of blue denim that year. Its clients in this field included Calvin Klein, Diesel, DKNY, Gap, Guess, Levi's Docker's, Liz Claiborne, and Tommy Hilfiger. Synthetic fiber production was aimed at bettering the company's position in markets such as activewear and industrial fabrics. Its garments, all in cotton, were being sent overseas for private labels. The company also was selling the polymers, methanol, and sodium sulfide and sulfate byproducts that resulted from its fiber and

yarn treatment processing. Textília S.A., a holding company for the Steinbruch and Rabinovich families, had the controlling interest in Vicunha Têxtil.

Robert Halasz

PRINCIPAL SUBSIDIARIES

Finobrasa Agroindustrial S.A.; Maracanaú Comércio e Representação Ltda.; Nova Marajo S.A.; Vanini Nordeste S.A.; Vicunha S.A.; Vicunha Europe S.A.R.L. (Switzerland); Vicunha Overseas, Inc. (U.K.).

PRINCIPAL COMPETITORS

Companhia Hering; Coteminas S.A.; Grendene S.A.; Santista Têxtil S.A.; São Paulo Alpargatas S.A.

FURTHER READING

"Amarrota, desbota e perde o vinco," *Exame,* January 8, 1992, pp. 40-41.

Bernhoeft, Gustavo, "Do Outro Lado," *Exame,* September 8, 1999, pp. 54-56, 58.

"Fibra-DuPont to Build 10,000-Metric-Ton Nylon Plant," *Daily News Record/DNR,* August 8, 1995, p. 11.

"The Iron Chancellor," *Economist,* January 17, 1998, p. 63.

Mano, Cristiane, "Hora de tirar o atraso," *Exame,* March 12, 2003, pp. 42-44, 46.

Nogueira, Paulo, "Quem vai para o trono é uma aliança singular," *Exame,* September 5, 1990, pp. 44-52.

Vassallo, Cláudia, "Por que a Vicunha está na CSN e na Vale," *Exame,* June 4, 1997, pp. 12-14.

Vergilli, Rodney, "Os teares continuam a pleno vapor," *Exame Melhores e Majores 1997,* pp. 206, 208.

Walsworth Publishing Company, Inc.

■

306 North Kansas Avenue
Marceline, Missouri 64658-2105
U.S.A.
Telephone: (660) 376-3543
Toll Free: (800) 369-2646
Fax: (660) 258-7798
Web site: http://www.walsworthyearbooks.com

Private Company
Founded: 1937
Employees: 1,500 (est.)
Sales: $100 million (2005 est.)
NAIC: 511130 Book Publishers

■ ■ ■

Walsworth Publishing Company, Inc. is a family owned and operated publishing company located in Marceline, Missouri, best known as the hometown of Walt Disney. Walsworth's main focus is the publishing of more than 5,000 high school yearbooks each year. Not only does the company print the yearbooks, it provides a complete range of services to help high school students produce professional quality work. On the production side, Walsworth educates students through desktop publishing seminars and offers online tools to help yearbook editors design pages and create covers. Walsworth also helps students finance their books through advertising programs. Telephone, fax, and e-mail support is available for assistance in all aspects of the yearbook program. In addition, Walsworth maintains a commercial book division, which publishes textbooks, cookbooks, travel guides, and encyclopedias. It especially caters to the needs of university publishers and technical and scientific publishers. Despite its relatively small size, Walsworth has made an ongoing commitment to investing in state-of-the art printing technology. It is one of only a handful of publishers with a full line of in-house printing capabilities, including prepress capabilities, printing, binding, and special finishes such as foil stamping, embossing, and debossing. As a result, Walsworth is contracted by larger publishers to do trade work. The company maintains its headquarters and finishing plant in Marceline, handles sales and marketing out of its Kansas City, Missouri, office, and runs regional offices throughout the United States. Furthermore, Walsworth owns Walsworth Yearbook Ltd. in Edinburgh, Scotland, and Virginia Beach, Virginia-based The Donning Company Publishers, a specialty publisher of limited-edition commemorative biographies and histories of businesses, schools, and communities.

COMPANY'S FOUNDING IN 1937

Walsworth was founded in Marceline in 1937 by three brothers: Don, Ed, and Bill Walsworth. Originally known as Walsworth Brothers, the company was an adjunct to a local theater endeavor. Don's wife, Joy, was in charge of mounting the plays, while he put together the programs, sold the advertising, and printed the show bills. In the beginning the programs were crude publications, composed on a borrowed typewriter and reproduced on a mimeograph machine. The brothers drummed up more business by producing show bills

---

COMPANY PERSPECTIVES

Walsworth has prospered into the technology leader in the yearbook industry as part of our goals of providing customers with the best possible service while helping them produce yearbooks of superior quality.

---

and selling ads for theaters in surrounding states. They also ventured beyond programs by printing cookbooks collected by their relatives.

Walsworth expanded further after World War II came to an end in 1945. Its salesmen continued to sell show bill advertising, but the company also began printing books for veteran organizations and produced other memorial volumes to commemorate people's military service, as well as church cookbooks. In 1947 Walsworth began producing high school yearbooks, a field for which it was highly suited. At the time, yearbook publishers produced the books free of charge for students, with the profits coming from the sale of local advertising. It was, in fact, the sale of ads in all of its books that was the key revenue stream.

The company changed its name to Walsworth Publishing Company, Inc. in 1956. A year later, one of the founders' sons, Don Walsworth, came to work for the family business. He would become the key to Walsworth's rise to prominence. From his early childhood he knew he wanted to be involved in the printing field. In elementary school he helped produce show bills by shaking up scores of gallon jugs of chemicals and developer needed in the paper film photographic process in use at the time. "Man, did I hate doing that," he told *Printing Impressions* in a 2003 profile. "But once I got into high school, I worked on making plates and became pretty efficient at that." He became an education major at the University of Missouri-Columbia, where he also played on the varsity basketball team before breaking an arm during his sophomore year. In addition, he traveled to Pittsburgh, Pennsylvania, to take printing courses at Carnegie Tech. It was also during his sophomore year that his parents died. By the time Don Walsworth joined his uncles to help run the family business after he graduated from college in 1957, yearbooks were unquestionably the main product, but Walsworth remained more of an advertising company than a publisher. The yearbook business was very much a seasonal affair. In the spring, as the yearbooks were produced, the company was a whirl of activity, but production was slow the rest of the year, forcing regular

layoffs. As a result, it was difficult to retain an experienced workforce necessary to grow the business, and all too often valuable equipment stood idle. Walsworth attempted to rectify these problems by convincing a number of schools to take delivery of their yearbooks in the fall rather than the spring. The company had two busy seasons, which helped to even out production, but spring time, as school came to the close for the year, remained the preferred time for yearbooks. In the 1960s Walsworth began to focus more on commercial printing to achieve balance. Walsworth also shifted its focus away from ad sales and began concentrating on the production of the yearbooks, which it now sold to the schools instead of giving them away.

SECOND GENERATION TAKING CHARGE IN 1967

Don Walsworth assumed the presidency of the company in 1967. He took over a small business that was not even a breakeven affair. According to *St. Louis Business Journal*, Walsworth's liabilities exceeded its assets. However, that would change under Don Walsworth's leadership. In 1970 the company added a commercial printing department and had the production capabilities needed to take on specialty publications like church directories and history books, as well as the reprinting of books. Walsworth launched its commercial book division in 1974 in order to produce high-quality, four-color books, such as community history volumes, military books, and other general trade publications. But just as important as the investment in new printing equipment was the creation of a new force of sales representatives (or reps). In this way, yearbook reps could concentrate on schools and their specific needs, while the new reps, more knowledgeable about the printing needs of commercial customers, could concentrate on their area of expertise.

Walsworth continued to grow its capability over the next decade. Company headquarters expanded in downtown Marceline, and the company opened a large finishing plant in the town and a prepress facility in nearby Brookfield. Walsworth's yearbook sales and marketing office also was opened in Kansas City during this period. In the meantime, another generation of the Walsworth family became involved in the business. In 1982, after graduating from the University of Missouri, Ed Walsworth joined his father. He started out as a commercial book sales representative, but soon graduated to management posts, eventually becoming executive vice-president overseeing manufacturing and plant management personnel. In addition, he launched Quality Binding L.L.C. in 1988, serving as its president and chief executive officer until it was sold in 2002.

KEY DATES

1937: Don, Ed, and Bill Walsworth form Walsworth Brothers to produce theater programs.
1947: The company begins producing yearbooks.
1957: The name is changed to Walsworth Publishing Company, Inc.
1967: Second generation Don O. Walsworth assumes the presidency.
1974: Commercial Book Division is formed.
1990: A major expansion effort is launched.
1999: The company begins a large investment in new equipment and technologies.

Walsworth acquired The Donning Company Publishers in 1985 and launched another expansion effort in 1990, but given the rise of new high technology introduced in the publishing field the company was essentially forced to make ongoing investments to stay current. "If you don't stay on the cutting edge, I'm afraid you'll get lost in the shuffle," Don Walsworth told *Printing Impressions*. "We have great people here analyzing it constantly. A couple of our employees concentrate solely on new products, methods, new techniques and material. They travel the country and the world to do that, and that's how we stay abreast of the market."

In the late 1990s Walsworth began to automate its prepress workflow by implementing the Adobe PDF software. The company encouraged schools to submit all of their copy as PDF files and within a short time had completely transitioned to the new process. As a result, composition that once took weeks to do was now complete in a matter of days. Lead times were shortened and Walsworth was able to turn around projects much quicker than before. According to the company, it operated the largest computerized prepress production center in a single location in the United States.

Walsworth also embraced the Internet, using it to provide technical support as well as to serve as a storehouse for design suggestions, graphics, easy-to-use templates, and articles written for novice editors. Don Walsworth told *Printing Impressions* that one of the key factors in the company's success was simplicity. "We try to make it as easy as possible for customers to perform whatever they have to do, be it commercial printing or yearbooks." He added, "We're not selling printing per se; we're selling security." The company's new capabilities also allowed it to use Marceline as a remote production site for Walsworth Yearbook Limited, established in

Edinburgh, Scotland, in 2000. PDF files were created in Scotland, then transmitted to Marceline, where the books were printed, bound, and then shipped to Scotland for delivery.

NEW CENTURY BRINGS MAJOR INVESTMENTS

Starting in the late 1990s and through 2004, Walsworth invested more than $30 million on new technology, new presses, new bindery equipment, and plant expansions. For example, in the early 2000s Walsworth added a new four-color digital HP/Indigo press, plastic coiling equipment, a hi-die punchee, roll sheeter, and a U.V. coater. Much of the specialized equipment allowed Walsworth to pursue new sources of business. The company enjoyed particular success in the children's niche market, landing substantial business from the likes of Leap Frog and CRC Press. The new equipment also helped Walsworth to win more business from technical and scientific publishers and contract work from the major publishers like Houghton Mifflin. While yearbook publishing remained the company's chief business, a willingness to invest in new technologies and equipment played a significant role in the growth of the commercial book division. Don Walsworth summarized the company's approach for *Printing Impressions* in 2003: "We've been innovative in various technologies. We've been pioneers in many different areas: page pagination, complete pagination, eight-up film, computer-to-plate and now computer-to-press. We've been innovators, not followers. We maintain an entrepreneurial atmosphere here. We're somewhat of a risk taker, but we want the rewards, too."

Don Walsworth was 69 years old when he spoke to *Printing Impressions* after the publication named him as one of its 2003 inductees to the RIT Printing Industry Hall of Fame. He received less welcome publicity in 2003 when he was named a curator at the University of Missouri and received scrutiny because his company did printing work for the university, which to some represented a conflict of interest. According to public records Walsworth received less than $280,000 in business with the school between 1997 and 2003, a small fraction of the company's revenues, which totaled in the neighborhood of $100 million a year. Some of that work included the programs and media guide produced for the university's athletic teams. Don Walsworth maintained that he was not directly involved in the bids his company made to win university business and had nothing to hide. Nevertheless, the issue continued to prove nettlesome. In October 2005 the University of Missouri curators approved a new conflict-of-interest policy to prevent curators from making money in connection to the university until they had been out of office for two years. An exemption was carved out for Don Walsworth, however, stirring up further controversy. He did not lack defenders, who pointed out that the amount of free printing his company performed for the university—pocket sports schedules, season ticket brochures, and posters—far exceeded Walsworth's for-profit work for the school.

Despite his age, Walsworth was very much involved at the University of Missouri, especially with his beloved basketball team, and remained in charge of the family printing business. His son Ed left in 2002 to start a new company, Walsworth Solutions, to provide schools with online software applications to serve their printing needs. Another son, Don Walsworth, Jr., stepped in to support Walsworth Publishing. The younger Walsworth, a Stanford University graduate in economics, had shared his father's passion for golf and spent 15 years as a professional golfer, competing around the world, before turning his attention to the family business. As president, he was in all likelihood his father's heir apparent.

Ed Dinger

PRINCIPAL SUBSIDIARIES

The Donning Company Publishers; Walsworth Yearbook Ltd. (Scotland).

PRINCIPAL COMPETITORS

American Achievement Corporation; Jostens, Inc.; Lifetouch Inc.

FURTHER READING

Cagle, Erik, "Selling Peace of Mind," *Printing Impressions,* September 2003, p. 30.

Carlisle, Nate, "New University of Missouri Curator Downplays Firm's Ties to College," *Columbia Daily Tribune,* January 17, 2003.

Friedman, Leah, "Walsworth Leads Family Publishing Co. Back into Profits," *St. Louis Business Journal,* June 28, 2004.

O'Connor, John, "High School Yearbooks Becoming High-Tech," *State Journal-Register* (Springfield, Ill.), July 1, 1996.

Zagier, Alan Scher, "Marceline Publisher Bypasses Curators' Conflict of Interest Rules," *Associated Press,* October 7, 2005.

Wawa Inc.

———— ■ ————

260 Baltimore Pike
Wawa, Pennsylvania 19063
U.S.A.
Telephone: (610) 358-8000
Fax: (610) 358-8878
Web site: http://www.wawa.com

Private Company
Incorporated: 1968
Employees: 13,000
Sales: $2.8 billion (2003)
NAIC: 311511 Fluid Milk Manufacturing; 447110 Gasoline Stations with Convenience Stores

■ ■ ■

With 550 outlets in 2006, Wawa Inc. is one of the largest privately held convenience store chains in the United States. These 24-hour-a-day stores are located for the most part in suburban areas of Delaware, Maryland, New Jersey, Pennsylvania, and Virginia. Wawa convenience stores sell coffee, built-to-order hoagies, hot breakfast sandwiches, salads, fresh fruits, and produce. The company also owns a dairy that supplies its stores with fresh milk, and Wawa brand juices and teas.

TEXTILE AND DAIRYING ORIGINS

Wawa's origins go back to 1803, when the Millville Manufacturing Co. was founded. This enterprise operated textile mills in several states, including major plants in southern New Jersey. In the late 19th century Millville owner George Wood became interested in dairy farm-

ing, and he imported cows from Guernsey in the Channel Islands of the United Kingdom. A Philadelphia resident, Wood had bought a summer home for his family in Wawa, a suburb west of Media, in 1890, and he established a small plant there in 1902 to process his dairy products. (Wawa is the word for goose in the native American Lenni Lenape language, and a goose appears on the corporate logo.) Pasteurization was unknown then, but using strict sanitary methods, Wood produced a raw milk, Certified Wawa Milk, that was recommended as safe by many Philadelphia doctors.

By the 1960s Millville Manufacturing had ceased operations, and consumers were buying milk from supermarkets rather than relying on Wawa Dairy Farms for home delivery. Deciding to counter the supermarket trend, Grahame Wood, Jr., grandson of George Wood, opened the first Wawa Food Market in Folsom, Pennsylvania in 1964.

Featuring brand-name milk, butter, and ice cream from the dairy, it was an immediate success. Two more stores were added by the end of the first year of operation. The 1968 edition of Dun and Bradstreet's *Million Dollar Directory* listed Wawa Dairy Farms as having 250 employees and $9 million in annual sales. In that year Wawa Dairy Farms and Wawa Food Markets merged into the Millville Manufacturing Co., whose principal assets consisted of real estate in southern New Jersey, to form Wawa Inc.

With the added resources of Millville's real estate, Wawa's number of stores reached 40 by the end of 1968 and 80 by the end of 1970. Some of these were operat-

COMPANY PERSPECTIVES

Just like a majestic flock of Canada Geese flying synchronously in "V" formation, we employ the principles of teamwork, group consensus and encouragement in our company. We think it's the only way to fly. And because of this philosophy, we've been able to accomplish feats that others would consider impossible. That's why, in our market area, our customers tell us that we define what a convenience store should be.

ing around-the-clock by the late 1970s. By the end of the decade sales had reached $140 million a year, and the number of employees had grown to 2,200. Grahame Wood was chairman and chief executive officer, and Richard D. Wood, Jr., a cousin, was president.

In 1977 Wawa began testing a paperless cash-access system at 12 Pennsylvania stores. Customers who presented a Provident National Bank card to a Wawa clerk and entered their personal security number on a separate keyboard could withdraw up to $25 a day from their bank accounts. ATM services were developed in later years, and all Wawa stores had ATMs by 1995.

CONVENIENCE WITH A WHOLESOME IMAGE

Traditionally the best-selling convenience store items have been gasoline, beer, and cigarettes. Only a very few Wawa stores sold gasoline at this time, however, and none sold beer (as much a reflection of local zoning prohibition as corporate philosophy), lottery tickets, or sex-oriented magazines. Even cigarettes were restricted to displays behind smoked glass. Instead Wawa specialized in high-quality perishables, including lunchtime sandwiches, and became the first convenience store operator to offer fresh, prepackaged entrees.

The typical convenience store customer was seen as a young blue-collar male, but Wawa found it could do well among working women as well by keeping its stores neat and clean and by carrying a much greater selection than most of its rivals. These goods included produce— absent from most convenience stores—and a large selection of delicatessen items. In 1985 the company began test-marketing Lite Bite salads, its first product directly targeted to working women. These salads were made in the stores themselves and prepared from Wawa's own produce. Wawa reported sales of about $360 million in

1986 and was opening some 50 locations a year in the late 1980s. Sales per store, which averaged $11,000 a week in 1979, had jumped to $20,000 a decade later.

Wawa's stores, which averaged 3,000 square feet, contained—in contrast to most of its competitors—no aisle or countertop displays. "The conventional merchandising wisdom in a convenience store is to get the customer to buy something she didn't really walk in to buy," Frederic Schroeder, Wawa's vice-president for marketing, told a *Chain Store Age Executive* reporter in 1987. "But our No. 1 aim is to get the customer in and out quickly. Architecturally, we made the checkout area remote from the sandwich/deli area. This is more labor-intensive, but we feel it makes it much more comfortable for the consumers to shop our stores. We also removed the beverage area from the deli, also to make it easier for customers to get in and out of our stores." In terms of Wawa's merchandise mix, Schroeder went on to say, "We started putting much more emphasis on poultry in our deli area, and on offering lower-sodium foods and foods with a lower fat content. We also continue to promote our produce heavily, and we've added more single-serve fruit juices. ... Our studies show that in our stores we have over 85 percent of what is available in the average supermarket, and approximately 70 percent of this is selling for comparable prices."

In order to stimulate slow dinnertime business, Wawa tested in 50 stores during 1989–90 a Fresh Buffet line of chilled entrees, priced from $2.99 to $3.99. Working in partnership with Key Fresh, a division of Keystone Frozen Foods, Wawa offered customers these items in a special refrigerated case, set at very precise temperatures. Shelf life from day of manufacture was approximately 10 to 14 days, which translated to about seven days at store level if delivered promptly. A freshness indicator showed how long a package had been in the case. The first six items were chicken Mexican, chicken Oriental, chicken Mornay, beef teriyaki, and two types of lasagna. Wawa found that the buyers tended to be women and customers with higher incomes than typical convenience store patrons. This line was dropped, however, in favor of promoting the more profitable sale of hoagie sandwiches and cigarettes.

By the end of 1990 the Wawa chain had grown to about 485 stores in Connecticut, New Jersey, Pennsylvania, Maryland, and Delaware. This period was, however, a difficult one for Wawa. According to Ralph Wood, company profits declined from about 1987 to mid-1991, and the number of customers actually fell in 1989 and 1990. Better management was one reason credited for the subsequent turnaround: the turnover of store managers dropped from 30 percent in 1987 to less than 10 percent in 1991.

KEY DATES

1803: Millville Manufacturing Co. is established.
1902: George Wood opens a milk plant in Wawa, Pennsylvania.
1964: Grahame Wood, Jr., opens the first Wawa Food Market in Folsom, Pennsylvania.
1968: Wawa Dairy Farms and Wawa Food Markets merge with the Millville Manufacturing Co. to form Wawa Inc.
1977: Wawa begins testing a paperless cash-access system at 12 Pennsylvania stores.
1985: The company begins test-marketing Lite Bite salads, its first product directly targeted to working women.
1994: Wawa celebrates its 30th anniversary as a convenience store enterprise; as part of its promotional blitz the company gives away one 1960's Mustang a day for 30 days.
2005: Howard Stoeckel becomes the first nonfamily CEO.

In 1991 prepared foods (as opposed to packaged items) were accounting for 25 percent of Wawa's sales, with the average gross margin per location, after spoilage, 55 percent. The biggest sales and profit category was deli, mostly sliced meats and cheeses and including local favorites such as hoagie sandwiches. Wawa also was selling a line of low-sodium deli meats and cheeses. Women accounted for about 40 percent of the chain's customers. Wawa's deli facilities were making more than 50,000 sandwiches a day in 1992, when it had the hoagie declared the official sandwich of Philadelphia through a promotion that secured 30,000 signatures to support the designation. On Hoagie Day—May 6, 1992—the company celebrated by building a 500-foot-long sandwich. Wawa stores were making 174,000 hoagies each week for their customers. Two years later, the company celebrated its 30th anniversary as a convenience store enterprise with a promotional blitz. Because its start-up coincided with Ford Motor Company's introduction of the wildly popular Mustang, Wawa gave away one 1960s Mustang a day for 30 days.

Wawa began a program of eliminating ozone-layer-depleting chlorofluorocarbons (CFCs) in 1988. Wawa-owned refrigerated units like walk-in coolers and deli/dairy cases in its stores were being slowly replaced or converted, with completion of the project scheduled for 1996. The company was installing scanning in all of its

stores by the end of 1995 and had installed personal computers and software from Park City Group at each of its locations.

In the early 1990s Wawa's expansion slowed to some 20 store openings a year. Instead the company emphasized remodeling at $300,000 per store. Although store size stayed about the same, sometimes the company had to buy the lot next door to increase parking for the growing number of customers, who brought the weekly sales level per store to $35,000 in July 1994. To gauge its customer service, Wawa had what it called its 155-second rule, denoting the average time a customer was in a convenience store. All operations in a Wawa store were geared to get the customer in and out during that time. To meet this standard, the company was working on better ordering systems for the deli sections, speeding up the checkout process, and possibly using telephone and fax ordering to spread out preparation time. It also recognized the need to add more counter space for customers.

An Associated Press survey of Wawa's stores in 1996 found yuppie favorites like kiwis, mineral water, pasta salad, cappuccino, and yogurt available along with the predictable cookies and candy bars in its stores. Some of the larger ones had installed espresso bars where customers could order their coffee with frothy, steamed milk or one of 20 kinds of Italian syrup. Wawa offered its own special coffee blend, which had become its leading ready-to-serve around-the-clock product. The company also was developing an English muffin-based line of breakfast sandwiches. In order to compete better with fast-food outlets as well as supermarket chains, Taco Bell burritos and Pizza Hut personal-pan pizzas had been added to the deli counters, and a downtown Philadelphia food court that opened in 1994 offered fast food only in a choice of Taco Bell, Pizza Hut, or two Wawa house formats—Hoagie Time or Coffee Time.

Wawa's plans as of 1994 called for 1,000 stores by the year 2000, spending $5 million to $6 million per year over a six-year period. To meet its stores' growing demand for milk and juice, the company also was expanding its dairy and warehouse operations. The land behind the dairy would be used for a new refrigerated warehouse, and additional storage silos also were planned. The remodeled dairy, doubled in capacity, would offer the latest in state-of-the-art computerized processing, new equipment for solution recovery, and recycling of solvents. "We also want to make our dairy more visitor friendly," Richard Wood told a reporter. "When everything is finished, we hope to offer tours to schoolchildren."

At least ten more Wawa stores were expected to be selling gasoline by the year 2000, on properties larger than its current superstores, which averaged about 5,000 square feet. The company felt that getting into the gas business was necessary to compete with oil company convenience store chains like Sun Co. Inc.'s A-Plus. Wawa had gas pumps in about 30 outlets during the 1970s but dismantled them in all but two outlets by the early 1980s because profits were too low.

MARKING SUCCESS IN 1997 AND BEYOND

While less ambitious then originally planned, Wawa's growth strategy was paying off. Indeed, sales surpassed the $1 billion mark in 1997. The company exited the oversaturated Connecticut market during this time period to focus on expansion in Virginia. While Wawa opened new stores, the company remained dedicated to providing convenience to its customers. In 1997 the company promoted its no-surcharge policy on its ATM machines.

Wawa also continued to add gasoline pumps at its stores. In fact, by 2000 nearly 45 Wawa stores were offering gasoline to customers. Just four years later, that number had grown to 142 locations as every new store the company opened had gasoline pumps. Each new store cost about $4 million to build and was on as much land as an average drugstore.

During the early years of the new millennium, Wawa focused on ushering customers in and out of its stores as quickly as possible. For example, the company's popular coffee section was set up in stations that allowed customers to pour coffee in one section and get cream and sugar in another section. By offering its coffee in strategically placed stations, Wawa customers could serve themselves efficiently without getting in the way of one another.

Howard Stoeckel, who joined Wawa in 1987, became the first nonfamily CEO in early 2005. Under his leadership, Wawa continued to keep pace with customer demands. In partnership with Chase Bank USA, Wawa launched its Visa Rewards credit card with contactless technology in late 2005. An October 2005 *Philadelphia Inquirer* article explained the benefits of contactless technology reporting, "A shopper simply holds her card within two inches of a radio-frequency reader to pay for purchases at the register. The reader flashes green almost instantly and beeps to signal that the charge was made." Wawa installed new state-of-the-art scanners that enabled customers to use their Chase blink card, MasterCard PayPass, or American Express Expresspay.

Wawa had more than 500 stores in its arsenal and was known throughout the industry for its high level of customer service and solid brand image. As such, Wawa was in an enviable position in the highly competitive convenience store market. Each year, the company served more than 300 million customers and sold more than 125 million cups of coffee, 35 million hoagies, and more than 92 million quarts of its own dairy products, juices, and teas. Stoeckel commented on the company's simple, yet lasting commitment to its customers at the 2004 National Association of Convenience Stores conference. "Why do we exist?," he asked the audience. His response: "To simplify our customers' lives."

Robert Halasz
Updated, Christina M. Stansell

PRINCIPAL COMPETITORS

7-Eleven Inc.; Green Valley Acquisition Co.; Sheetz Inc.

FURTHER READING

Belden, Tom, "Philadelphia Area's Wawa Dairy Operation Celebrates 100th Anniversary," *Philadelphia Inquirer,* August 5, 2002.

Brooke, Bob, "Wawa Wants to Double the Number of Its Stores," *Philadelphia Business Journal,* September 30, 1994, pp. 3-4.

Brubaker, Harold, "Paying in a Blink," *Philadelphia Inquirer,* October 27, 2005.

Dowdell, Stephen, "Convenience Chain Sets Rollout of Chilled Entree," *Supermarket News,* December 3, 1990, pp. 1, 42.

Embrey, Alison, "The Wawa Way," *Convenience Store News,* December 13, 2004.

Hussey, Anita, "C-Store Competition: Fighting for the Foodservice Dollar," *Progressive Grocer,* February 1991, pp. 130-32.

Pamplin, Claire, "Wawa Hits 40," *Convenience Store News,* April 12, 2004.

"Waiting for a Wawa," *Evansville Courier,* June 30, 1996, pp. E1-E2.

Wallace, David, "Fattening Up on Value, Sandwiches," *Philadelphia Business Journal,* October 7, 1991, p. 11.

"Wawa Inc.," *Convenience Store News,* August 3, 1998.

"Wawa No Longer a Family Affair," *Convenience Store News,* December 13, 2004.

"Wawa Sets Sites on Female Market Segment," *Chain Store Age Executive,* July 1987, pp. 18, 20, 22.

*Transforming Energy
into Solutions*

Weg S.A.

Avenida Prefeito Waldemar Grubba, 3300
89256-900 Jaraguá do Sul, Santa Catarina
Brazil
Telephone: (55) 47 3372-4000
Fax: (55) 47 3372-4010
Web site: http://www.weg.com.br

Public Company
Founded: 1961 as Electromotores Weg
Employees: 13,503
Sales: BRL 2.2 billion ($750.85 million) (2004)
Stock Exchanges: São Paulo
Ticker Symbol: ELMJ3, ELMJ4
NAICs: 325510 Paint and Coating Manufacturing;
333999 All Other General Purpose Machinery
Manufacturing; 335311 Power, Distribution, and
Specialty Transformer Manufacturing; 335312 Motor and Generator Manufacturing; 551112 Offices
of Other Holding Companies

■ ■ ■

Weg S.A. is the leading Latin American manufacturer of electric motors. A holding company, it is also engaged, through subsidiaries, in the manufacture, sale, and export of alternators, generators, ring motors, industrial electrical components, automation systems, programmable controls, electrical panels, and paints and varnishes. Of its 10 industrial plants, five are in Brazil, two in Argentina, and one each in Mexico, Portugal, and China. The company also has subsidiaries for marketing and distribution in 14 countries in Europe, the Americas, Australia, and Japan. Through subsidiaries, branch offices, and sales representatives, the company is present in over 100 countries on five continents.

ELECTRIC MOTORS AND MORE: 1961-89

The name Weg derives from the initials of the first names of its founders: Werner Ricardo Voigt, Eggon João da Silva, and Geraldo Werninghaus. They founded the enterprise in 1961, with da Silva, who was a bank administrator, its president and majority shareholder. Voight an electronic technician, became industrial director; Werninghaus a mechanical technician, was director-superintendent. They began production in Jaraguá do Sul, Santa Catarina, turning out 146 electric motors that year. Output reached 4,085 pieces in 1962. Weg began selling abroad for the first time in 1970, when it began exporting to neighboring Uruguay.

By 1981, when Weg's production of electrical motors had reached almost 1 million single-phase and three-phase units a year, it was the leading manufacturer of these motors in Latin America. Nevertheless, the company had already decided on a program of diversification to avoid dependency on any one line of business. Its first measures in this regard did not stray far from the original purpose. Weg Máquinas was founded in 1980 to produce continuous-current motors, generators, alternators, and other electric components. Weg Acionamentos was established the same year to produce industrial systems and converters in what proved to be a short-lived and ill-fated joint venture with the Swedish company ASEA AB (later part of ABB Ltd.). Soon after, Weg Transformadores was created to administer the acquisition of a small transformer factory. In 1984 Weg traveled far afield, acquiring Penha Pescados, a shrimp-fishing operation with six ships. At about the same time the parent company purchased Michigan Tintas, a paint manufacturer that became Weg Química and expanded to also turn out varnishes, resins, tar, and turpentine. This entailed the creation of Weg Florestal for the exploitation of raw material from the pine species *Pinnus elliott*. Some five million trees had been planted by mid-1985. In this period Weg also engaged in grinding soybeans for oil and meal and in fish farming.

Motors for industrial use or in home appliances accounted for 80 percent of Weg's revenue of 164 billion cruzeiros (about $115 million) in 1984, when all but two of the seven company units—Acionamentos and Transformadores—were profitable. The following year Weg Acionamentos entered information technology, developing software for use in automating industrial processes.

By this time Weg was the principal business enterprise in Jaraguá do Sul, a city of perhaps 50,000 inhabitants. In order to avoid a flood of migrants to the city seeking work, the company hired people who were born there. Weg had, in its methodical way, implemented a German system for training workers that broke down each task, from the simplest to the most complex, establishing standards for quality and time spent to completion. Subjected to rigid discipline during a three-year regimen of 4,000 to 5,000 hours, the trainees emerged as either maintenance mechanics, wood modelmakers, ironworkers, or electricians, if not designated for the electronics sector, in which case they received even more training. Only the most capable youths were chosen for this program. "One of the requirements is that these youths be sons of workers," Euclides Emmendoerfer, director of industrial relations for the firm, explained to the Brazilian business magazine *Exame* in 1985, "because we want professionals dedicated to the company and not simply to use Weg as a trampoline leading to the university." The best of these graduates and higher-level hires were eligible for a further eight-month executive-track leadership course. During the late 1980s Weg worked hard to raise its export level. In 1989, for example, it introduced an electric motor developed specifically for the market in Canada, where the government had adopted a program of reducing energy consumption. By this time the North American market was the largest individual one for the company's motors. Taiwan was another important export market for the firm, which in that year sold its products in 54 countries. Also that year, da Silva became chairman of Weg, yielding the presidency to Décio da Silva, his son. One of the junior da Silva's first tasks was dealing with a labor strike, the second in Weg's history.

SEEKING OPPORTUNITY ABROAD IN 1993

The severe recession of the early 1990s threw Weg into the red, and in 1991 it lost money—$25 million—for the first and only time. One result was a greater emphasis on the core business of producing and selling motors instead of engaging in diversification. By 1993, the business had regained its stride. Weg Electric Motors Corporation, in the United States, and Weg Europe S.A., in Belgium, had been established to drum up business, guarantee delivery, and provide technical support abroad. Cost control, beyond a 15 percent cut in employment, yielded savings such as a 14 percent drop in the company's own electricity consumption through means as simple as lowering the height of lamps. The following year Weg established subsidiaries in Argentina and Japan and purchased 15 percent of the common stock of Perdigão S.A. Comércio e Indústria, Brazil's second-largest meat and poultry processor. (Nildemar Secches, Perdigão's chief executive, became Weg's chairman of the board in 2004.)

Weg was one of three companies that won an award for quality control in 1997. It was striving to raise its productivity by at least 10 percent a year. By 1998 Weg was fifth in the world in motor production, trailing only the German firm Siemens AG, the Swiss-based company ABB Ltd., Emerson of the United States, and Toshiba Corporation of Japan. The company had almost doubled its annual revenue in the five previous years. About one-fifth of the 1997 total of $532 million came from exports. Some 600 employees were studying foreign languages with the encouragement (and stipends) offered by Weg, and 150 of the firm's employees were working abroad. Weg's profit-sharing plan provided for the distribution of up to one-eighth of its net profits to the employees.

The devaluation of Brazil's currency in early 1999 made exports cheaper and favored a strategy of globalization for Weg. The goal for 1999 was $139 million in export revenue. Another result was higher prices

KEY DATES

1961: The company is founded by three residents of Santa Catarina state.

1970: The company first exports its products, to Uruguay.

1980: Weg begins producing electrical components other than motors.

1981: Weg is South America's leading producer of electrical motors.

1984: The company begins making paints, varnishes, resins, tars, and turpentine.

1985: Weg Acionamentos S.A. begins developing software for automating industrial processes.

1989: Weg's products are sold in 54 countries.

1991: In the midst of a recession, Weg loses money for the first and only time.

1998: Weg has almost doubled its annual revenue in five years.

2002: The company has acquired factories in Argentina, Mexico, and Portugal since 2000.

2005: Weg purchases a manufacturing plant in China to make electric motors.

internally, and to combat the risk of prices spiraling out of control, the company immediately began negotiating with its suppliers and searching for ways to keep prices stable. Some higher costs were inevitable; for example aluminum or copper, necessary raw materials, were quoted in dollars, which now became more expensive. On the other hand, Weg also became more competitive domestically since imported motors, pumps, and other machines became more expensive. Weg was planning to open, late in 1999, a new plant in the Jaraguá complex that would augment its production of motors for home appliances such as vacuum cleaners and washing machines. Weg was also about to open a new factory for transformers and to increase its production of generators and high-tension motors.

A TRUE INTERNATIONAL ENTERPRISE: 2000–05

Weg initiated a new international expansion in 2000, when it bought an Argentine factory. Next, it began to produce engines in Mexico, and in 2002 it acquired a factory in Portugal. The following year it established subsidiaries in Colombia and Chile. In 2004 Weg opened the largest industrial electric-motor manufacturing plant in the world. This new 9.5-million-square-foot facility

was located next to the company's existing Jaraguá plant. Here, as in the other Brazilian manufacturing facilities, Weg controlled all production steps, from the foundry works and stamping to enameling and packaging. Weg also claimed the world's largest cast-iron-frame motors, eight units of which were being used in a Chilean copper mine.

In 2004 Weg was a company with annual net sales of BRL 2.2 billion ($750.85 million, in terms of the average currency rate during that year). Exports accounted for about 40 percent of the total. The company produced 10.42 million electric motors. Weg held 70 percent of the domestic market in electric motors and was exporting them to 80 countries. Electric motors accounted for 56 percent of sales, with three-phase motors, which were principally capital goods, representing 35 percent, and single-phase motors, chiefly used in durable consumer goods, 21 percent. High-tension motors and generators accounted for 12 percent of sales; automated equipment, 12 percent; transformers, 7 percent; paints and varnishes, 7 percent; and motor controls systems, 6 percent. The company continued to focus on industrial solutions within Brazil, with systems of industrial automation, construction of substations, and furnishing of equipment and services in order to install hydroelectric, thermoelectric, and wind-generation systems. It was in the process of establishing a plant in São Bernardo do Campo, São Paulo, for the production of high-voltage motors and generators.

The company bought a factory in China in 2005, becoming only the fifth Brazilian enterprise to do so. With Chinese wages about 30 percent lower than those in Brazil, this new factory was seen as a low-cost means of supplying the Brazilian market as well as a base for selling Weg's products in the Far East. However, negotiations were lengthy and required immersion in the local culture, understanding of its nuances in communications, and general confidence-building. "The Orientals never say anything in a direct form," Weg's Asian-division director told Flávio Costa for *Exame.* He continued, "Much time passes before accepting or rejecting a proposal."

Although a public corporation, Weg remained, in 2005, closely held, with family members of the founders holding almost all the common shares. Two of the founders had retired, and the third, Werninghaus, had died, but Décio da Silva, Eggon's only son, remained executive president, and three children of the founders were on the six-member board. The corporate culture, as described once again in an *Exame* article, this time in 1998, was one of "Prussian" order, efficiency, and precision that perhaps belied popular conceptions of Brazil. The 12 children of the founders were enrolled in the 1970s in a program that included courses, foreign languages, general culture, and travel, supervised by Gerd Edgar Baumer, vice-chairman of the board. Family members who wanted to work for Weg were required to follow the same steps as other employees in order to prove their competence. Da Silva himself had passed through a rigorous apprenticeship in every operation of the business and had tained experience working for other enterprises in Germany and Italy.

Robert Halasz

PRINCIPAL SUBSIDIARIES

Weg Australia Pty, Ltd. (Australia); Weg Electric Motors Corporation (United States); Weg Equipamientos Eléctricos S.A. (Argentina); Weg Euro Indústria Eléctrica S.A. (Portugal); Weg Europe S.A. (Belgium); Weg Exportadora S.A.; Weg Indústrias S.A.; Weg México, S.A. de C.V. (Mexico); Weg Nantong Electric Motors Manufacturing (China).

PRINCIPAL DIVISIONS

Automation; Chemicals; Controls; Machines; Motors; Transformers.

PRINCIPAL COMPETITORS

ABB Ltd.; Emerson; Empresa Brasileira de Compressores S.A.; Siemens AG; Toshiba Corporation.

FURTHER READING

Caetano, José Roberto, "Ganhar ou Ganhar," *Exame,* February 10, 1999, pp. 53-54.

———, "Pequena espaçosa," *Exame,* July 5, 1998, pp. 50-52, 54.

Costa, Flávio, "Como falar mandarim," *Exame,* February 16, 2005, 72-73.

Janssen-Decker, Renata S., "WEG—a Global Company," *Pit & Quarry,* September 2004, p. 76.

Mautone, Silvana, "Prontos para herdar," *Exame,* September 28, 2005, pp. 98-99.

"O groupo Weg aposta firme na automaçao," *Exame,* July 8, 1985, pp. 65-67.

"Troca de óleo," *Exame,* September 29, 1993, p. 63.

"Weg Claims Andes Record," *Power Engineer,* December/January 2003/04, p. 7.

Weleda AG

Stollenrain 11
CH-4144 Arlesheim,
Switzerland
Telephone: (41) 61 7052-121
Fax: (49) 61 7052-310
Web site: http://www.weleda.ch

Private Company
Incorporated: 1922 as Internationale Laboratorien und
    Klinisch-Therapeutisches Institut Arlesheim A.G.
Employees: 1,343
Sales: CHF 249.3 million ($295 million) (2005)
NAIC: 325620 Toilet Preparation Manufacturing;
    325412 Pharmaceutical Preparation Manufacturing;
    325411 Medicinal and Botanical Manufacturing;
    325611 Soap and Other Detergent Manufacturing

■ ■ ■

Weleda AG is a globally active manufacturer of natural cosmetics, nutritional supplements and over-the-counter (OTC) drugs with a strong foothold in Germany, Switzerland, and France. Cosmetics generate roughly two-thirds of Weleda's revenues. The lion's share of pharmaceutical sales stems from the cancer remedy "Iscador," which is distributed in the United States as a homeopathic prescription drug under the name "Iscar." In addition to headquarters in Arlesheim, Switzerland, where the company owns a large pharmacy, the Weleda group consists of more than 15 subsidiaries, mainly in Western Europe, and North and South America. The two most important ones are located in Schwäbisch

Gmünd, Germany, and Huningue, France. All body care products and most of the OTC drugs are manufactured in Switzerland, Germany, and France, using more than 400 organic ingredients from 30 countries. In its core European markets Weleda products are mainly distributed through pharmacies and drugstores. In large Japanese cities the company runs specialty stores under its own brand name. The Swiss General Anthroposophical Society and the association Clinical-Therapeutical Institute are major shareholders of the company, pointing back to Weleda's origins in the 1920s.

APPLYING ANTHROPOSOPHY TO MEDICINE IN 1922

Weleda owes its existence to Rudolf Steiner, an Austrian philosopher, and his partner Ida Wegman, a Dutch physician. Steiner, a convinced theosophist with a Ph.D. in philosophy from Vienna's Ecole Polytechnique, created a spiritually infused philosophy—which he called anthroposophy—that centered on human development. At the core of his theory was to view humans as an indivisible whole consisting of the physical body, the conscious mind, and the spiritually connected soul. Anthroposophical medicine was a logical extension of Steiner's ideas. Not only the physical, but also the mental and spiritual components, including the social context of a patient, had to be taken into account in order to make true healing possible. Since humans and their evolution were deeply rooted in living nature, pure natural remedies were needed to successfully treat disease.

While Steiner developed the theoretical foundation for this revolutionary concept of medicine at his School

COMPANY PERSPECTIVES

■

The forces of our body, soul, and spirit are intrinsically connected, and they are closely related to the processes that occur in nature. Based on this insight, Weleda has developed the purest body care formulations and holistic, homeopathic and anthroposophic medicines, containing wholesome active ingredients since 1921—in harmony with nature and the human being. *Pure Ingredients:* Weleda skin care products are formulated naturally, without the use of synthetic fragrances, colors or preservatives. We do not test our products or ingredients on animals, and our formulations are free of genetically modified organisms. *Pure Cultivation:* We use only the purest materials—grown biodynamically, organically and naturally—in our own gardens in Europe and though our unique partnerships with farmers throughout the world. These sources ensure the highest quality products and help to maintain the delicate balance of nature. *Pure Harvesting:* Biodynamic and organic gardens are similar to one another in that they both work to enhance the soil and cultivate plants that are free of synthetic fertilizers and pesticides. Biodynamic cultivation, however, goes a step further. Homeopathic preparations are used to enhance the vitality of the plants. Each plant is harvested by hand at its peak, according to the season, time of day, and position of the planets in the universe. *Pure Processing:* After harvesting, we process and combine raw materials according to holistic criteria, with slow and careful hand processing, so that we can maintain the vital essences of the plants as much as possible. *Pure Cooperation:* Weleda participates in cultivation projects to support the sustainable development and recovery of the living organisms of the earth. These projects offer ecological, economical and social benefits to our cultivation partners. Ultimately, the Weleda customer reaps these benefits through the high quality formulations that result.

of Spiritual Science in Dornach near Basel in Switzerland, Wegman began to apply it in her own medical practice at the Institute of Clinical Medicine in neighboring Arlesheim. Together they developed the fundamental principles of anthroposophical medicine and a growing list of natural remedies based on these

principles. A medicine, for example, had to stem from a plant, animal, or mineral with a special evolutionary affinity to the sick organ or organ system. Specific anthroposophical methods for the generation of medicines included, for example, the "vegetabilization" of metals and metallic minerals by using metals as "fertilizers," and the "Rh-Method" of making plant-based solutions more durable without using alcohol through a series of movements and exposures to light, heat, or cold. In addition to medical uses Steiner suggested formulas for nutritional supplements and for use in cosmetics.

Two corporate structures had been created in 1920 as organizational frameworks for realizing anthroposophical ideas and for generating revenues to support its institutions, including Steiner's School of Spiritual Science and a free Waldorf school in Stuttgart, Germany. The first one, Futurum Konzern AG, was based in Arlesheim and included Wegman's clinic and a chemical-pharmaceutical laboratory. The second one, Der Kommende Tag AG, which means "the coming day," was located in Stuttgart and consisted of a clinic and laboratory similar to those in Arlesheim. In addition, there was a fabrication operation for producing medicines and a sales department, which had been created to satisfy the growing demand by the clinics in Arlesheim and Stuttgart for anthroposophical medicines. In the early 1920s, a time of increasing economic volatility, social stagnation, and political radicalization, Futurum Konzern and Der Kommende Tag increasingly struggled with financial difficulties. To save the adjunct clinics and pharmaceutical operations, Steiner and Wegman pushed the idea of spinning these operations off as independent ventures. In April 1922 the newly formed Internationale Laboratorien und Klinisch-Therapeutisches Institut Arlesheim AG, consisting of Futurum's clinic and laboratory, commenced business and was officially registered in November. By that time the Arlesheim laboratories' list included 295 medical drugs and combination preparations. After Wegman's clinic was separated from the company in mid-1924, the latter was renamed Internationale Laboratorien Arlesheim AG. Later that year Internationale Laboratorien acquired a pharmaceutical production in Schwäbisch Gmünd, Germany, as well as the laboratory, pharmaceutical production, and sales offices in Stuttgart from Der Kommende Tag. The new German subsidiary, with 12 employees, manufactured plant-based formulas for medical, nutritional and cosmetic use in large amounts.

Right from the beginning Steiner envisioned the International Laboratories operating on a global scale. It soon became evident, however, that the company name was already being used by other firms in the United States and England. Steiner suggested "Weleda" instead—a general name in the Celtic tradition for wise

KEY DATES

1922: Internationale Laboratorien und Klinisch-Therapeutisches Institut Arlesheim AG is officially registered.

1923: Large-scale manufacture of natural remedies and cosmetic preparations commences.

1924: "Weleda" is registered as a trademark in Switzerland and Germany.

1941: Weleda's forced closure is prevented despite a ban on anthroposophical enterprises by the Nazi government.

1956: The company's first medical herb farm opens in Germany.

1964: Supplemental cancer remedy "Iscador" is approved by health insurers.

1976: The official German Book of Homeopathic Medications contains considerable input from Weleda.

1992: Weleda is present in 30 countries around the world.

1998: The company launches the GLS Weleda Fund to attract private investors.

1999: Weleda's first U.S. catalogue is mailed to more than 5,000 households.

2001: Weleda is Germany's third largest manufacturer of baby care cosmetics.

women with a deep understanding of nature, and in particular the name of a famous ancient Germanic priestess and healer. In 1924 "Weleda" was registered as a trademark in Switzerland and Germany. In addition to the existing one in France, two foreign subsidiaries—now bearing the Weleda name—were established in the United Kingdom and The Netherlands. Rudolf Steiner's death in 1925 was a huge loss for the anthroposophical medicine movement in general and Weleda in particular. His vast legacy also included the company's logo, an upright staff with a spiral form winding around it, enclosed by two wavy lines, which symbolized integrity, truth and healing, social interaction, and protection. It was first registered as a trademark in March 1923. In 1928 the general assembly of shareholders approved Weleda AG as the new company name.

MODERATE POSTWAR GROWTH

At the beginning of the 1930s the Great Depression crossed the Atlantic and hit continental Europe. Weleda's output went up—yet prices began to fall. But this was only a minor disturbance compared with the following Nazi regime in Germany, which threatened the entire existence of the company. In 1935 the Hitler-led government banned the Anthroposophical Society in Germany. With the onset of World War II in 1939 sales dropped dramatically. Two years later a decree shut down all anthroposophical enterprises. As soon as Weleda's managing director, Fritz Goette, received notice to close down operations in late June 1941, he protested sharply and set the wheels in motion to prevent the end of the company. There were different speculations among journalists and historians about possible reasons for his success: was it influential friends or foul compromises with the Nazis? No one there, however, could protect the company from Allied bombings when the war returned to Germany. In 1944 the Stuttgart-based production was moved to Schwäbisch Gmünd, which was not hit as hard as big German cities were. Weleda survived the devastating war.

As early as 1945 the company resumed operations with about 150 employees. As Germany was rebuilt in record speed in the postwar decade, the company's workforce roughly doubled. In the mid-1950s Weleda's management made a strategic decision. To have total control over critical supplies of raw materials, Weleda began to employ a growing army of organic farmers who cultivated herbs and aromatic plants. The company's first medical herb farm after World War II near Schwäbisch Gmünd opened in 1956. Over the years additional sites were set up in France, England, South America, and New Zealand. At the same time Weleda's network of suppliers gradually expanded. The organic ingredients used in the growing number of Weleda products were shipped to the production sites in Germany, Switzerland, and France from almost all parts of the globe.

1964 APPROVAL OF ISCADOR

The approval of Weleda's mistletoe-based cancer remedy Iscador by several health insurers in 1964 was the catalyst for its wider use in the medical community, especially in Germany. As early as in 1917 Steiner recommended using mistletoe to treat cancer. Following his advice, Wegman together with the Swiss pharmacist A. Hauser developed the first extract in water from the mistletoe plant called Iscar and began treating cancer patients at her practice in Zurich. The Iscar injections worked surprisingly well. Patients reported feeling better and having less pain. Steiner also recommended special procedures for preparing the mistletoe extract, which were explored by a growing number of researchers. In 1935 the Verein für Krebsforschung, the Association for Cancer Research, was founded in Arlesheim to study Iscar (later Iscador) and to improve the methods for preparing mistletoe extracts. To intensify these studies, the Hiscia Institute was set up in Arlesheim in 1949, where a growing staff of physicians and natural scientists optimized the Iscador range. The Hiscia Institute also took on the production of the basic mistletoe tincture, which was then diluted and bottled at Weleda's production facility in Schwäbisch Gmünd. In 1963 a clinic specializing in treating cancer patients with mistletoe extracts and in additional supplementary therapies based on anthroposophical and conventional medicines was added.

Iscador became Weleda's most important pharmaceutical product, accounting for up to two-fifths of the company's medicinal sales. In Germany in particular, Iscador became widely used as a supplemental therapy along with surgery, chemotherapy, and radiotherapy. In the United States the product was introduced as a homeopathic prescription drug under the name Iscar.

ACCELERATED GROWTH BEGINS IN 1990

Throughout the prosperous postwar era and the economic stagnation of the 1970s and 1980s, up until the 1990s, the company grew slowly, but steadily. With some 400 employees until 1990, Weleda had remained a fairly small enterprise. It was in the early 1990s when the combination of two factors accelerated Weleda's growth: a more systematic and strategic approach to marketing and the rising popularity of natural cosmetics.

The company began to focus on a closer direct relationship to its customers, mainly through a full-color customer magazine. Beginning in the mid-1990s the company also began to invite customers to open houses—or more precisely—to "open gardens." At such events visitors were able to inspect Weleda's organic herb gardens and to learn about biodynamic farming and alternative therapies using herbs and plants. Other events included "Parent-Child-Weeks" for promoting Weleda's line of baby care products or "Health Weeks" for people interested in alternative medicine and self-medication.

The late 1990s were the starting point for a series of new product launches to stimulate consumer appetite for Weleda cosmetics and OTC drugs. In 1998 a new "Wild Rose" body care line was first introduced, including body milk and two crèmes. Weleda's line of toothpastes and oral hygiene products was relaunched in the same year. The year 2000 saw the extension of the company's popular baby care line by a facial crème and

body oil and the relaunch of two body oils and a cream bath. The newly introduced nose spray Rhinodoron was an instant success.

The significant investment in systematic marketing paid off. Weleda products received several awards at major trade shows. For example, Weleda Wild Rose Oil received the "Product of the Year" Award at the Biofach trade fair in Frankfurt in 1996. In a 2002 *Reader's Digest* consumer survey, the Weleda brand ranked third in Germany in the skin care product category. By that time Weleda was Germany's third largest manufacturer of baby care products and held a 30 percent market share in the cosmetic oils segment.

While Germany and Switzerland remained Weleda's main markets, the company intensified efforts to expand its distribution networks in the United Kingdom, Spain, Italy, The Netherlands, and Scandinavia. Other important target markets were Japan and the United States. At the same time the ties with distributors abroad were tightened, resulting in a consolidation of most foreign licensees into majority-owned Weleda subsidiaries. By the end of the 1990s Weleda had emerged as a mid-sized global player with an annual turnover of CHF 200 million.

FUTURE CHALLENGES

With natural cosmetics already generating a rising share of Weleda's revenues, the pharmaceutical branch got hit hard by ever-increasing demands from German regulators. In 1993 the Gesundheitsstrukturgesetz, a new law reorganizing the healthcare sector in Germany, raised patient co-payments for medication. Consequently, Weleda's sales of medicines suffered significantly. The same trend occurred in other countries. Most important, the requirements for registering homeopathic medicines increased. To meet the new demands from EU-regulators in Brussels, Weleda had to invest in expensive analytical equipment. Ten extra specialists were hired to prepare dossiers for the international registration of Weleda's medicines. A new German law effective in 2003 prescribed pharmaceutical manufacturers a 6 percent price cut, again reducing the company's sales.

To compensate for the increasing losses generated by Weleda's pharmaceutical branch since the early 1990s, the company straightened its product lines, cutting the number of medicines by 30 percent. Furthermore, the company reorganized internal processes to focus even more on customer demands and to better utilize existing talent. To finance further growth without compromising Weleda's philosophy and principles, the company's management came up with a creative solution for boosting its capital base. In September 1998 Weleda launched a money market fund through GLS-Gemeinschaftsbank, a bank based in Bochum, Germany, that focused on ethical investment. Within two months the bank lined up 550 investors, raising DEM 10 million—at that time roughly $6 million. A second offering in 2005 yielded another EUR 10 million—about $11.85 million.

Convinced that Weleda's medical branch would become profitable again in the mid-term because of a constantly expanding market for alternative medications, the company launched several major investment projects. In Arlesheim a brand new production facility for tinctures and medicines was built, greatly expanding Weleda's processing capacity. The new production line enabled the company to concentrate much of the tincture extraction in Switzerland that had been done previously in various European countries. The new facility also included a visitor center and a new administrative building for Weleda headquarters. Another brand new processing facility and visitor center were built in Schwäbisch Gmünd in addition to a new medical herb farm on 4.5 acres that employed 20 gardeners in 2005.

Although the company was planning to grow moderately, CEO Mathieu van den Hoogenband intended to keep focusing distribution on pharmacies and selected drugstores. A factory sale outlet for 10,000 Weleda visitors in Schwäbisch Gmünd was intended to generate additional revenues. Committed to strict environmental principles, such as keeping all of its products free from genetically modified ingredients, the company enforced its high standards with a number of "farm controllers" who visited Weleda's worldwide suppliers and refused to cooperate with manufacturers that engaged in animal tests. Most important, Weleda was committed to remaining an independent enterprise. The roughly 2,000 German and Dutch investors in the GLS Weleda Fund provided financial backing but had no voting rights. The Swiss General Anthroposophical Society and the Clinical-Therapeutical Institute remained the two major shareholders of the company that assured adherence to Rudolf Steiner's original vision of medicines that enhanced human well-being and self-healing rather than treating symptoms of disease.

Evelyn Hauser

PRINCIPAL SUBSIDIARIES

Weleda AG (Germany); Weleda S.A. (France; 80.5%); Weleda N.V. (Netherlands); Weleda (UK) Ltd. (93.8%); Weleda Italia S.R.L. (Italy); Weleda GmbH & Co. KG (Austria); Weleda Holding AB (Sweden; 95.5%); Weleda Inc. (U.S.A.); Weleda do Brasil (Brazil); Birseck-Pharmacy Arlesheim (Switzerland); Weleda S.A. Madrid (Spain); Weleda S.A. (Chile; 92.2%); Weleda S.A. (Argentina; 99.4%); med. Weleda Moskau (Russia; 75%); Weleda spol. s.r.o. Prag (Czech Republic; 99.3%); Weleda (Australasia) Ltd. (New Zealand; 99.52%); HeartBalance AG (Switzerland; 50%); Weleda Finance AG.

PRINCIPAL COMPETITORS

Yves Rocher S.A.; Beiersdorf AG; Johnson & Johnson; Avon Products, Inc.; ratiopharm GmbH.

FURTHER READING

Aykroyd, Bettina, "Rhythms of Nature and Authenticity," *Soap & Cosmetics,* August 2000, p. 37.

Bässler, Rüdiger, "Im Garten der heilenden Pflanzen ist die Welt in Ordnung," *Stuttgarter Zeitung,* September 27, 2005, p. 6.

Bullion, Constanze von, "Frostcreme für Menschenversuche der Nazis," *Süddeutsche Zeitung,* October 5, 1996.

Kugler, Walter, *Rudolf Steiner und die Gründung der Weleda,* Dornach, Switzerland: Rudolf Steiner Verlag, 1997.

Overstolz, Angelika, *Iscador – Mistelpräparate aus der anthroposophisch erweiterten Krebsbehandlung,* Basel, Switzerland: Verlag für Ganzheitsmedizin, 2005.

Skarka, Christine, "Weleda Deutschland wächst mit den Aufgaben," *Lebensmittel Zeitung,* September 27, 2002, p. 18.

"Weleda gibt seine Heilmittel-Sparte nicht verloren," *Frankfurter Allgemeine Zeitung,* June 10, 2003, p. 21.

WELK MUSIC GROUP

The Welk Group, Inc.

2700 Pennsylvania Avenue
Santa Monica, California 90404
U.S.A.
Telephone: (310) 829-9355
Fax: (310) 315-9306

Private Company
Incorporated: 1955 as Teleklew Productions, Inc.
Employees: 1,350 (est.)
Sales: $45.4 million (2005 est.)
NAIC: 721110 Hotels (Except Casino Hotels) and Motels; 711310 Promoters of Performing Arts, Sports, and Similar Events with Facilities; 531311 Residential Property Managers; 512220 Integrated Record Production/Distribution; 512120 Motion Picture and Video Distribution; 531120 Lessors of Nonresidential Buildings (Except Miniwarehouses)

∎ ∎ ∎

The Welk Group, Inc., owns record companies, resorts, a film studio, and other real estate assets, and also syndicates reruns of *The Lawrence Welk Show* for television. Its divisions include Welk Music Group, which consists of Vanguard, Sugar Hill, and Ranwood Records; Welk Resort Group, which operates a hotel/theater facility in Branson, Missouri, and two resorts in Southern California; marketing firm Klew Media; and Welk Syndication. The company was founded by bandleader Lawrence Welk and is owned and managed by his heirs, including CEO and Chairman Lawrence (Larry) Welk, Jr.

RURAL ORIGINS

The Welk Group traces its beginnings to 1955, when bandleader Lawrence Welk founded a firm called Teleklew Productions, Inc. to produce his ABC television program and manage his business affairs. Born in 1903 near Strasburg, North Dakota, Welk was one of eight children of poor, German-speaking immigrants from the Alsace-Lorraine region between Germany and France. He quit school in the fourth grade to work full-time on the family farm, where in the evening his father taught him to play the pump organ and an old button accordion.

At 13 Welk began playing music at social events in the area, and his father later bought him an expensive professional accordion on the condition that he turn over his earnings from music and remain on the farm until he was 21. At 17 he formed The Biggest Little Band in America with a drummer, and at 21 he began playing around the upper Midwest while starting to learn English, having spoken only German at home. The following year he made his radio debut on WNAX in Yankton, South Dakota, where he began appearing regularly for no pay in exchange for the chance to promote his public appearances.

Welk was a natural entrepreneur, and when not performing he also tried his hand at several small businesses, including a burger stand with an accordion-shaped grill that served "squeezeburgers." Music was his first love, however, and in the late 1920s and early 1930s he toured the country with groups like the six-piece Lawrence Welk and His Hotsy-Totsy Boys, Lawrence Welk and His Honolulu Fruit Gum Orchestra, and

KEY DATES

■

1955: The Lawrence Welk Show debuts on ABC-TV; Teleklew Productions, Inc. formed.

1957: Welk starts music publishing acquisitions with Harry Von Tilzer catalog.

1961: Teleklew moves into new headquarters building in Santa Monica, California.

1964: Acquisition of mobile home park and golf course near San Diego, California.

1970: Welk acquires Jerome Kern song catalog for $3.2 million.

1971: Lawrence Welk Plaza opens with 21-story office, 16-story apartment buildings.

1971: ABC cancels Welk's TV show; successful 11-year syndication run begins.

1979: Welk buys Ranwood Records.

1986: Vanguard Records acquired.

1987: Reruns of Welk's show begin airing on PBS.

1988: Music publishing business sold for $25 million.

1992: Lawrence Welk dies at 89; ownership of firm passes to his family.

1994: Branson theater/hotel complex opens.

1998: Sugar Hill Records acquired.

2004: Welk Group buys movie production facility in L.A. for $10 million.

Lawrence Welk and His Novelty Orchestra, whose music generally consisted of polkas and popular tunes of the day arranged for dancing.

While playing in Pittsburgh in 1938, Welk's ten-piece band became known as The Champagne Music Makers after a radio listener wrote in to say that his music had the bubbly quality of champagne. Capitalizing on the theme, he soon hired a full-time "Champagne Lady" vocalist, recorded tunes like "Bubbles in the Wine" for Vocalion Records and other labels, and later added an onstage bubble-making machine. Welk's growing success also led to appearances in several short films, beginning with Paramount's 1939 "Champagne Music of Lawrence Welk."

THE LAWRENCE WELK SHOW
DEBUTS IN 1955

The mid-to late 1940s saw Welk continue to tour the United States from his adopted home of Chicago, at the same time that many of the big bands of the 1930s were fading away. In 1951 his manager secured an engagement at the Aragon Ballroom near Los Angeles, and he soon decided to settle in the area. Welk also began appearing on television locally via KTLA, and in 1955 he was offered a 13-week summer replacement show on the national ABC network. Though few thought it would generate much interest, the program was a surprise hit and was quickly added to the fall schedule. Major sponsors of the evening Saturday show included the makers of Dodge cars and Geritol, a vitamin and mineral supplement that promised increased vim and vigor. To manage his business affairs and answer his fan mail, Welk founded Teleklew Productions, Inc., whose name combined part of the word "television" with his own name spelled backwards. The bandleader would serve as its chairman and president.

Though critics derided his music as bland and lacking in spontaneity, many Americans (especially those who were older, from a rural background, and with lower income and education levels) were hungry for Welk's brand of clean-cut entertainment with a nostalgic and often patriotic touch, and his German-accented phrases "ah-one an' ah-two" and "wunnerful, wunnerful" soon became part of the vernacular. His hit show and the attendant record albums and personal appearances proved highly lucrative, and in 1956 Welk's gross income reached $3 million. The bandleader's popularity was such that he was asked to play at the inaugural ball of President Dwight D. Eisenhower the following January.

Having grown up in poverty, Welk knew the value of money and kept a tight rein on his finances. Despite his success, he paid all of his musicians union scale, though he did vest them in a profit-sharing plan after ten years' service. None had a contract, and each could be replaced if their ranking on the bandleader's "fever chart" slipped or if they caused controversy, as Champagne Lady Alice Lon did in 1959 by wearing a skirt cut too short to suit Welk. He reasoned that the performers' associations with him brought the potential for lucrative personal appearance and recording contracts, and many did remain a part of "the Welk family" for decades despite the low pay.

In 1957 Teleklew Productions spent a reported $200,000 to buy the Harry Von Tilzer music publishing company of New York. Welk would go on to buy many such firms, assembling a library of copyrights that brought him increasing amounts of royalty income. His own music recordings were also doing well, and he enjoyed a run of several dozen chart-making albums as well as a number one single in 1961 with "Calcutta."

In addition to music publishing, Welk was also beginning to invest in real estate. In 1961 Teleklew Productions moved its offices to the top floor of the newly built six-story Lawrence Welk-Union Bank Building on Wilshire Boulevard in Santa Monica. In 1964 Welk bought a mobile home park for retirees in Escondito, California (near San Diego), which had 104 home sites, a nine-hole golf course, a clubhouse, and a small restaurant. Over the next several years he doubled the number of sites, expanded the restaurant and golf course, and added a hotel. Featured on one of his TV shows in 1965 and mentioned frequently thereafter, it became a tourist attraction in its own right, and its gift shop would do a strong trade in Welk souvenirs and recordings.

The 1960s also saw Welk's music publishing holdings expanded dramatically, with a total of 16 firms acquired by 1970 that held copyrights to 4,600 songs. That year Welk made his largest purchase to date, paying $3.2 million for the catalog of Jerome Kern, which included standards like "Smoke Gets in Your Eyes" and "Ol' Man River."

NEW BUILDINGS, TV SYNDICATION IN 1971

Welk's real estate empire was continuing to grow as well, and 1971 saw the completion of Lawrence Welk Plaza, a joint venture between Teleklew and architects/ engineers Daniel, Mann, Johnson, & Mendenhall. The Santa Monica project consisted of the 16-story Champagne Towers apartment building, which boasted ocean views and a rooftop pool, and a 21-story office tower that would house the headquarters of both General Telephone and Teleklew. In addition to producing the TV show and overseeing Welk's music publishing and real estate operations, the firm also managed his and his band members' personal appearances and operated a marketing unit that sold products like "Lawrence Welk Musical Spoons." Welk himself had recently published the first of several books for Prentice-Hall, an autobiography cowritten with Bernice McGeehan called *Wunnerful, Wunnerful*.

In early 1971 the ABC television network, responding to pressure from advertisers seeking a younger demographic, announced that it would end the 16-year run of *The Lawrence Welk Show* in the fall. Though the program's ratings had declined, it was still frequently among the top 20 each week, and angry fans swamped the network with more than one million telegrams, letters, and phone calls. Buoyed by the support, Welk quickly lined up a group of stations to show the program in syndicated form, and it began to run on more than 180 outlets around North America. This number eventually topped 250, more than had carried it on ABC, and Welk reportedly earned more from its syndication than he had with the network.

In 1979 Welk began a $12 million upgrade to his mobile home park that would boost the number of units to 452, expand the hotel and restaurant, and add stores, a museum of memorabilia, and a new 300-seat dinner theater. Lawrence Welk Country Club Village was the second-most popular tourist attraction in Southern California after Disneyland, drawing more than 40,000 people each month.

Also in 1979 Welk purchased Ranwood Records, a Nashville-based label that had been founded in 1967 by Lawrence Welk, Jr., and Randy Wood. It recorded country, pop, and easy listening artists like Pete Fountain, The Mills Brothers, and Lawrence Welk himself.

In February 1982 Welk's syndicated television program taped its last new show and the 79-year-old bandleader officially retired. His son Lawrence "Larry" Welk, Jr., had already taken control of his business interests by this time.

In 1983 the company formed a joint partnership with Ira Pittleman to launch Heartland Music to sell records via direct marketing. One of Heartland's best-selling artists was a Romanian panflute virtuoso named Gheorghe Zamfir, whose recordings were hawked incessantly on late-night cable TV. During the mid-1980s his albums of sentimental standards (with titles dictated by Heartland) sold 750,000 copies.

In 1984 a new round of expansion was begun at Welk's Escondito property that included several hundred time-share condominiums, a second golf course, another theater, and more shopping. Over the next several years some 15,000 people would pay between $10,000 and $14,000 to own one of the condos for a week per year.

VANGUARD RECORDS ACQUIRED IN 1986

In 1986 Welk purchased the highly respected Vanguard Records, which had been founded in 1950 by brothers Seymour and Maynard Solomon. It was best known for folk music by artists like Pete Seeger and Joan Baez, but had also issued blues, rock, jazz, and classical recordings. Welk would reissue most of its catalog on the new compact disc format, as well as sell some recordings through Heartland Music.

In 1987 *The Lawrence Welk Show* found a new life on public television, where old episodes were aired with new "wraparound" segments featuring original cast members. The program's return was greeted enthusiastically by Welk's fans, and it soon became a regular weekend offering on many stations.

In 1988 Welk's music copyrights were sold to Poly-Gram International Music Publishing for a reported $25 million. The sale included some 27,000 copyrights that had originally been held by 103 different publishing houses. In 1990 the firm also sold Vanguard Records' classical music catalog back to Seymour Solomon, who had founded a new classical label called Omega.

The late 1980s and early 1990s saw the company, now known as the Welk Group, expand its time-share condominium offerings with a 162-unit converted hotel in Palm Springs called Lawrence Welk's Desert Oasis and a 58-unit joint venture in Hawaii called the Maui Schooner. The company's annual revenues were now estimated at $100 million.

In May of 1992 89-year-old Lawrence Welk died of pneumonia. He was survived by his wife of 61 years, Fern, two daughters, and son Larry, who would continue to run a business empire that had reportedly made his father the richest man in Hollywood after Bob Hope.

BRANSON RESORT OPENS IN 1994

In 1993 ground was broken on another new project, the $20 million Welk Resort Center in Branson, Missouri, which had recently become a prime destination for those seeking family-friendly entertainment. The facility would include a 160-room hotel, the 500-seat Stage Door Canteen restaurant, and the 2,300-seat Champagne Theater. Nearly two dozen members of Welk's television family, including accordionist Myron Floren, pianist Jo Ann Castle, and vocalists The Lennon Sisters, began appearing there in two daily shows after it opened in 1994, with outside acts later booked as well. That same year the Northridge earthquake in California caused structural damage to the firm's 16-story Champagne Towers apartment building, which was subsequently closed for repairs and later sold to the Irvine Company.

In 1995 the firm's Welk Music Group unit bought a children's record label, Music for Little People, but two years later it was sold back to founder Leib Ostrow. At the same time a 50 percent stake in Heartland Music was sold to Time-Life, Inc.

In 1998 the Welk Group acquired Sugar Hill Records, a 20-year-old label that was home to bluegrass and country artists like Doc Watson and Ricky Skaggs. After the purchase, label founder Barry Poss would continue to run it from Durham, North Carolina. The Sugar Hill acquisition took place as the firm was also beginning to reinvigorate Vanguard, which had primarily sold back-catalog material since being acquired. Now run by Larry Welk's son Kevin, 29, and with former Columbia Nashville executive Steve Buckingham handling artist development, a number of new performers were signed including Patty Larkin and John Hiatt.

In future years Vanguard would add 1990s hitmakers Blues Traveler and Hootie and the Blowfish, while Sugar Hill found success with contemporary bluegrass group Nickel Creek. Both labels were distributed by sister unit Welk Music Distribution.

In 2001 the firm's resort unit started a four-year, $33 million project to add 200 more time-share condominiums and a 3,500-square-foot recreation center to its Escondito property. Two years later Heartland Music was purchased by Infinity Resources, Inc. In 2004 the company spent $10 million to buy the Barwick film production facility in Los Angeles, whose 5.4-acre lot included four sound stages. Renamed Welk Studios, it was leased to production services company Quixote Studios. Also in 2004 the company formed a partnership with SullivanShows called Welk-Sullivan Productions to manage and promote the firm's Branson resort.

In 2005 the Welk Group submitted a winning $2.5 million bid for 26 acres of coastal property a few miles north of Los Angeles. Before it could be developed, the company would face significant cleanup costs to remove toxic wastes that had accumulated during the site's use as a metal recycling plant. The year 2005 also marked the 50th anniversary of the network debut of *The Lawrence Welk Show*, reruns of which continued to be aired weekly by 277 public stations around the United States to an audience of some 2.5 million viewers.

Over 50 years The Welk Group, Inc. had evolved into a diverse organization that included real estate, music, television, and other interests. CEO Larry Welk, Jr., was following his father's business model of making prudent investments that had the potential for long-term growth, and the firm was solidly positioned for future profitability.

Frank Uhle

PRINCIPAL SUBSIDIARIES

Welk Resort Group; Welk Music Group; Welk Syndication; Welk Studios LP; Klew Media.

PRINCIPAL COMPETITORS

Marriott Vacation Club International; Cendant Corp.; Bluegreen Corp.; Rounder Records; Rebel Records; Red House Records; Herschend Family Entertainment Corp.; Syncor Entertainment, Inc.; Shoji Entertainment, Inc.; Moon River Enterprises, Inc.

FURTHER READING

Bessman, Jim, "WMG at 50," *Billboard*, May 6, 2000, p. 44.
Boldt, Megan, "Ten Years after His Death, the 'King of Champagne Music' Lives On," *Associated Press Newswires*,

November 9, 2002.

Flint, Peter B., "Lawrence Welk, the TV Maestro of Champagne Music, Dies at 89," *The New York Times*, May 19, 1992, p. B8.

Gould, Jack, "TV: Welk, A Surprise Hit," *The New York Times*, February 10, 1956, p. 45.

Hicks, Ron, "The Wunnerful Life of Lawrence Welk," *The Los Angeles Times*, May 30, 1981, p. SD-C1.

Hobbs, Bill, "Airlines and Four Theaters Add to Branson Repertoire," *Amusement Business*, September 27, 1993, p. 34.

Hunter, Nigel, "PolyGram Acquires Welk Catalogs," *Billboard*, October 8, 1988, p. 5.

Johnson, Robert, "Haunting Melodies Make Zamfir a Star of Cable TV Ads—But the Panflutist Loathes Lounge-Lizard Music," *The Wall Street Journal*, August 9, 1989.

Kluge, P.F., "The Then Generation—The Elderly, the Rural, the Sedate Still Love Lawrence Welk's Show," *The Wall Street Journal*, June 15, 1970, p. 1.

Martens, Todd, "'The Welk Name Didn't Mean Anything, To Be Honest,'" *Billboard*, March 19, 2005.

Menconi, David, "Welk Group Buys Sugar Hill Records," *The News & Observer* (Raleigh, NC), October 3, 1998, p. D1.

Millay, Christine, "Welk Resort Undergoing $33 Million Expansion," *The San Diego Union-Tribune*, May 12, 2001, p. N1.

Ramirez, Anthony, "Lawrence Welk Village Is Growing," *The Los Angeles Times*, October 2, 1984, p. SD-C2.

Simross, Lynn, "Lawrence Welk at 75 Still Pleases People," *The Los Angeles Times*, September 11, 1978, p. OC-B1.

Turpin, Dick, "Lawrence Welk Plaza: For Champagne Tastes," *The Los Angeles Times*, April 11, 1971, p. M1.

Underwood, Elaine, "The World of Welk," *Brandweek*, September 16, 1991, p. 12.

"Welk Champagne Music Comes to the Garden," *The New York Times*, June 8, 1979, p. C15.

Welk, Lawrence, and Bernice McGeehan, *Wunnerful, Wunnerful: The Autobiography of Lawrence Welk*. Englewood Cliffs, NJ: Prentice-Hall, 1971.

"Welk Resort Expanding," *The Timeshare Beat*, July 3, 2000.

Whitlock-Espinosa, Margit, "Renovation with Style," *Resort Trades Management Operations*, May/June, 2004.

William Reed Publishing Ltd.

Broadfield Park
Crawley, RH11 9RT
United Kingdom
Telephone: (44) 1293 613 400
Fax: (44) 1293 601 340
Web site: http://www.williamreed.co.uk

Private Company
Incorporated: 1862
Employees: 242
Sales: $45 million (2005 est.)
NAIC: 511120 Periodical Publishers

■ ■ ■

William Reed Publishing Ltd. is one of the United Kingdom's leading private publishers of specialized trade magazines, including its oldest and flagship magazine, *The Grocer.* First published in 1862, *The Grocer* remains the leading magazine targeting the supermarket sector in the United Kingdom and elsewhere, with a circulation of more than 43,000 copies. In addition to that title, William Reed publishes a number of specialist titles, focused on the grocery, retailing, drinks & hospitality, and food manufacturing industries. The company's nearly 20 magazine titles include *Convenience Store, Morning Advertiser, Food Manufacture, British Baker, Forecourt Trader, Multiple Buyer & Retailer,* and *Restaurant Magazine.* William Reed also publishes newsletters and directories, including *Hotel Report, Leisure Report, M&C Report, Morning Advertiser Directory, Restaurant Handbook, The Grocer Directories,* and a

number of annual business guides for the retail, restaurant, travel, gaming, and related industries. William Reed has extended its publishing empire to the Internet, with web sites supporting many of its publications, as well as Internet-specific sites, such as grocerjobs.co.uk, foodmanjobs.co.uk, and careersinfoodanddrink.co.uk. The company also has parlayed its specialist publishing status into one of the United Kingdom's major events operations. Each year, the company hosts a variety of annual events, conferences, exhibitions, and awards, including the Baking Industry Awards, the Bar Awards, the Grocer Gold Awards, International Beer Competition, and the like. William Reed Limited remains a privately owned company led by the Reed family, now in its fifth generation under Charles Reed.

FOUNDING A TRADE PUBLISHER IN THE 19TH CENTURY

Born in 1830, William Reed's early working life included a career as a sugar merchant. A Yorkshire native, Reed developed contacts with many of England's grocers, as well as an insight into issues specific to this sector. In the early 1860s, Reed prepared to marry into the prominent Morgan family. The five Morgan brothers, who originally had established themselves as bankers, but also owned businesses in ironmongering and "sundries," had entered into the publishing business in 1859, with the publications of *The Ironmonger* and *Chemist & Druggist.* Initially intended to support their other businesses, both titles quickly became popular trade magazines and indeed were credited with pioneering the trade journal market in England. Morgan Brothers eventually came to focus on publishing, going public in 1949, and later merging with Grampian and forming the basis of United Business Media. *Chemist & Druggist* itself remained in print into the 21st century.

William Reed decided to capitalize on his knowledge of the grocery sector, and founded a new company, William Reed Publishing, in London. In 1862 Reed launched his own trade title, *The Grocer.* Featuring news items and focusing on issues related to the retail sector, *The Grocer* found ready success among Britain's grocers. By 1863, Reed had begun expanding his scope, adding a supplement, the *Wine Trade Review,* to his magazine. The following year, Reed targeted the brewing industry, with the *Brewers Journal,* and its supplement, *Hop & Malt Trades Review.*

William Reed died in 1920 and was succeeded by his son, Leicester Morgan Reed, a successful lawyer, who continued building on his father's success. In 1927, the company reincorporated as a registered private company, and Reed took up the position of chairman of the board and managing director. The company expanded its title range again in the mid-1930s, when the *Wine and Spirit Trade Review* was published as a separate magazine for the first time in 1935.

The next generation of Reeds took over in 1944, under CW Reed. Serving as managing director and chairman into the early 1980s, CW Reed oversaw the company's expansion. In 1959, the company began publishing its "Grocer buff list," providing a comprehensive listing of manufacturer's suggested retail prices for the supermarket industry. The company added new titles in the 1970s, including *Off License News,*

covering the retail alcoholic beverage trade, in 1970, and acquiring *Cash and Carry News* in 1974. That title was later replaced by a new, more expansive journal, *Independent Retailer and Caterer,* in 1981.

By then, William Reed had begun to explore new business opportunities that allowed the company to capitalize on the success of *The Grocer* and other titles in its list. In the late 1970s, Reed started developing its expertise in the organization of events, notably with the launch of the annual Sales Assistant of the Year Awards, held for the first time in 1979.

DIVERSIFYING PRODUCTS: 1987–99

The success of this event led the company to develop other events, awards, and conferences, such as the Baking Industry Awards, which debuted in 1987 in association with *British Baker* magazine. By then, the company had added another highly successful new title, *Convenience Store,* launched in 1985, which boasted a circulation even higher than Reed's *Grocer* flagship by the end of the century.

In 1990, William Reed, led by Laurence Reed since 1984, added a new Directories division when it acquired the *Food* directory from Britain Buyers Guide. The company added a number of other directory titles, such as the *Grocer Directory of Manufacturers & Suppliers, Morning Advertiser Directory,* and *Retail & Shopping Centre Directory,* through the 1990s.

William Reed also continued to develop its range of events, adding the Grocery Advertising and Marketing Industry Awards in 1994, the International Beer Competition in 1995, the Supermeat Awards in 1999, and the Food Manufacture Excellence Awards in 2001.

During the 1990s, William Reed continued to expand its range of products for the retailing sector, adding titles such as *Forecourt Trader* in 1991, which was expanded with the addition of *Forecourt News* in 1996, and *Value Retailer* in 1995 (renamed as *Multiple Buyer and Retailer* in 1998).

During the late 1990s, William Reed began expanding its media range, notably with the launch of web sites backing a number of its titles. In 1998, the company also launched a new division, the William Reed Knowledge Store, providing a range of database, directory, and other support services to the food and food retailing industry. The following year, the company added a new web site and service, grocerjobs.co.uk. This site was followed by a second jobs search site, foodmanjobs.co.uk, in 2001. The online version of *The*

KEY DATES

1862: William Reed founds a publishing company in London and launches *The Grocer* magazine.

1863: The company launches the *Wine Trade Review* as a supplement to *The Grocer*.

1920: William Reed dies and son Leicester Morgan Reed takes over as head of the company.

1927: William Reed Publishing incorporates as a registered private company.

1935: A separate magazine, *Wine and Spirit Trade Review*, is launched.

1954: William Reed introduces the "Grocer buff list."

1974: *Cash and Carry* magazine is acquired.

1979: The Sales Assistant of the Year Award is launched as the company expands into event organization.

1985: *Convenience Store* magazine is launched.

1987: The Baking Industry Awards are launched in partnership with the *British Baker* magazine.

1990: William Reed acquires the *Food* directory and launches its Directories division.

1994: The company launches the Grocery Advertising and Marketing Industry Awards.

1995: The International Beer Competition is launched.

1999: William Reed launches the Supermeat Awards, as well as the web site, grocerjobs.co.uk.

2000: The company launches GrocerTV; *Morning Advertiser* is acquired.

2002: The company launches grocer.co.uk.

2003: Martin Info is acquired.

2004: The company launches *Scottish Local Retailer* and *MA Scotland*, acquires Food Trade Directories, and establishes a conference division.

2005: The company acquires trade show Foodex Meatex, as well as publication titles *Meat Trades Journal*, *Hotel & Restaurant*, and *Restaurant*.

Grocer went live the following year. By then, William Reed had expanded its *Grocer* franchise to include GrocerTV, a half-hour program presented on the Sky Digital television service.

ACQUISITIONS IN 2000

Into the 2000s, William Reed, which then came under the leadership of the fifth generation of the Reed family, Charles Reed, launched a new expansion drive. Acquisitions became an important feature of the company's growth during this time. In 1999, for example, the company acquired *CTN,* a weekly targeting the confectionery, tobacco, and news agency market, from Quantum Publishing. The company then merged that title into *The Grocer* in order to expand the latter's range of coverage of the retail sector.

In 2000, William Reed acquired the *Morning Advertiser,* which had been in publication since 1794. The company also added *Food Manufacture* magazine that year. In 2003, William Reed acquired Martin Info, then followed that purchase in 2004 with the acquisition of Food Trade Directories. Not all of the group's growth came through acquisitions, however. In 2001, the company launched a new title, *CLASS* magazine. This was followed by the launches of *Scottish Local Retailer* and *MA Scotland* in 2004.

The company also continued to extend its magazine titles into other categories, particularly the organization of awards events. *CLASS* magazine was extended in 2003 with the creation of the Bar Awards. This event was joined that same year by the Grocer Gold Awards. Also in 2003, the company launched a new jobs fair seminar, Careers in Food & Drink Live! The success of the group's events operations led it to create a new division, for its conferences activities, in 2004.

In the mid-2000s, William Reed continued to seek out new expansion opportunities. At the beginning of 2005, the company acquired the license to publish *Pro Wholesaler,* originally launched in 1989 by the Federation of Wholesale Distributors. Soon after, the company expanded its events offering with the purchase of Foodex Meatex, the leading trade show for the U.K. meat industry. In June 2005, the company formed a joint venture with The Restaurant Game, called William Reed Hospitality. That venture combined the magazine titles *Restaurant* and *Hotel & Restaurant,* with events including the Restaurant Live and the World's 50 Best Restaurant Awards. By the end of that year, the company had added several more titles, including *Wine and Spirit International, Drinks International,* and *Wine International,* as well as the awards events International Wine Challenge and International Spirits Challenge, from Wilmington Group. Also in that year, the company acquired *British Baker,* first published in 1885, and *Meat Trades Journal,* which appeared by the early 1890s. As it approached its 150th anniversary, William Reed

Publishing remained a dedicated partner to the United Kingdom's food and food retail industries.

M. L. Cohen

PRINCIPAL SUBSIDIARIES

William Reed Hospitality.

PRINCIPAL COMPETITORS

News Corporation Ltd.; Pearson PLC; Reed Elsevier PLC; United Business Media PLC; Thomson Corporation PLC; Modern Times Group; Wenner Media; Ziff-Davis Inc.

FURTHER READING

"Foodtech Exhibition Acquired by YPL Exhibitions Ltd.," *Food Trade Review,* November 2002, p. 680.

"How to Keep Ahead of the Game," *Grocer,* November 18, 2000, p. 35.

"Plaudits for Wm Reed at Britvic/PPA Awards," *Grocer,* May 4, 2002, p. 16.

"William Reed Acquires Foodex Meatex," *Frozen & Chilled Foods,* March-April 2005, p. 7.

"William Reed Forms Hospitality Arm," *Grocer,* June 25, 2005, p. 14.

"Wm. Reed Helps Career Minded," *Grocer,* June 29, 2002, p. 12.

"Wm. Reed Stable Grows," *Grocer,* September 17, 2005, p. 9.

"Wm. Reed Takes on Publishing of Pro Wholesaler," *Grocer,* January 15, 2005, p. 8.

Index to Companies

Allgemeine Schweizerische Uhrenindustrie, **26** 480

Allhabo AB, **53** 85

Allia S.A., **51** 324

Alliance Amusement Company, **10** 319

Alliance Assurance Company, **III** 369–73; **55** 333

Alliance Atlantis Communications Inc., **39** 11–14

Alliance Capital Management Holding L.P., **22** 189; **63** 26–28

Alliance de Sud, **53** 301

Alliance Entertainment Corp., **17** 12–14 *see also* Source Interlink Companies, Inc.

Alliance Gaming Corp., **15** 539; **24** 36

Alliance International LLC, **73** 283–84

Alliance Manufacturing Co., **13** 397

Alliance Packaging, **13** 443

Alliance Paper Group, **IV** 316

AllianceWare, Inc., **16** 321

Alliant Energy Corp., **39** 261

Alliant Techsystems Inc., **8** 21–23; **30** 34–37 (upd.); **77** 25–31 (upd.)

Allianz AG, **57** 18–24 (upd.); **60** 110; **63** 45, 47

Allianz AG Holding, **III** 183–86; **15** 10–14 (upd.)

Allied Bakeries Limited *see* Greggs PLC.

Allied Chemical *see* General Chemical Corp.

Allied Chemical & Dye Corp., **7** 262; **9** 154; **22** 29

Allied Color Industries, **8** 347

Allied Communications Group, **18** 77; **22** 297

Allied Construction Products, **17** 384

Allied Corporation *see* AlliedSignal Inc.

The Allied Defense Group, Inc., **65** 30–33

Allied Department Stores, **50** 106

Allied Distributing Co., **12** 106

Allied Domecq PLC, **24** 220; **29** 18–20; **52** 416; **54** 229; **59** 256; **71** 69

Allied Drink Distributors Ltd., **68** 99

Allied Dunbar, **I** 427

Allied Engineering Co., **8** 177

Allied Fibers, **19** 275

Allied Food Markets, **II** 662

Allied Gas Company, **6** 529

Allied Grape Growers, **I** 261

Allied Health and Scientific Products Company, **8** 215

Allied Healthcare Products, Inc., **24** 16–19

Allied Holdings, Inc., **24** 411

Allied Irish Banks, plc, **16** 13–15; **43** 7–10 (upd.)

Allied Leisure, **40** 296–98

Allied-Lyons plc, **I** 215–16, 438; **9** 100; **10** 170; **13** 258; **21** 228, 323; **29** 18, 84; **50** 200 *see also* Carlsberg A/S.

Allied Maintenance Corp., **I** 514

Allied Mills, Inc., **10** 249; **13** 186; **43** 121

Allied Pipe & Tube Corporation, **63** 403

Allied Plywood Corporation, **12** 397

Allied Products Corporation, **21** 20–22

Allied Radio, **19** 310

Allied Safety, Inc. *see* W.W. Grainger, Inc.

Allied Shoe Corp., **22** 213

Allied-Signal Corp., **I** 414–16 *see also* AlliedSignal, Inc.

Allied Signal Engines, **9** 12–15

Allied Steel and Conveyors, **18** 493

Allied Stores Corporation, **II** 611–12; **9** 211; **10** 282; **13** 43; **15** 94, 274; **16** 60; **22** 110; **23** 59–60; **25** 249; **31** 192; **37**

Allied Strategies Inc. *see* Sleeman Breweries Ltd.

Allied Structural Steel Company, **10** 44

Allied Supermarkets, Inc., **7** 570; **28** 511

Allied Suppliers, **II** 609; **50** 401

Allied Telephone Company *see* Alltel Corporation.

Allied Towers Merchants Ltd., **II** 649

Allied Van Lines Inc. *see* Allied Worldwide, Inc.

Allied Waste Industries, Inc., **50** 13–16

Allied Worldwide, Inc., **49** 20–23

AlliedSignal Inc., **22** 29–32 (upd.); **29** 408; **31** 154; **37** 158; **50** 234

Allis Chalmers Corporation, **I** 163; **III** 543–44; **9** 17; **11** 104; **13** 16–17, 563; **21** 502–03; **22** 380; **50** 196

Allis-Gleaner Corp. *see* AGCO Corp.

Allison Engine Company, **21** 436

Allison Engineering Company *see* Rolls-Royce Allison.

Allison Gas Turbine Division, **9** 16–19, 417; **10** 537; **11** 473

Allmanna Svenska Elektriska Aktiebolaget *see* ABB Ltd.

Allmänna Telefonaktiebolaget L.M. Ericsson *see* Telefonaktiebolaget L.M. Ericsson.

Allmerica Financial Corporation, **63** 29–31

Allnet, **10** 19

Allo Pro, **III** 633

Allor Leasing Corp., **9** 323

Allou Health & Beauty Care, Inc., **28** 12–14

Alloy & Stainless, Inc., **IV** 228

Alloy, Inc., **55** 13–15

Allparts, Inc., **51** 307

Allserve Inc., **25** 367

Allsport plc., **31** 216, 218

The Allstate Corporation, **10** 50–52; **27** 30–33 (upd.); **29** 397; **49** 332

ALLTEL Corporation, **6** 299–301; **46** 15–19 (upd.); **54** 63, 108

Alltrans Group, **27** 472

Alltrista Corporation, **30** 38–41

Allwaste, Inc., **18** 10–13

Allweiler, **58** 67

Alma Media Group, **52** 51

Almac Electronics Corporation, **10** 113; **50** 42

Almac's Inc., **17** 558–59

Almacenes de Baja y Media, **39** 201, 204

Almaden Vineyards, **13** 134; **34** 89

Almanacksförlaget AB, **51** 328

Almanij NV, **44** 15–18 *see also* Algemeene Maatschappij voor Nijverheidskrediet.

Almay, Inc. *see* Revlon Inc.

Almeida Banking House *see* Banco Bradesco S.A.

Almys, **24** 461

ALNM *see* Ayres, Lewis, Norris & May.

Aloe Vera of America, **17** 187

Aloha Airlines, Incorporated, **9** 271–72; **21** 142; **24** 20–22

ALP *see* Associated London Properties.

Alp Sport Sandals, **22** 173

Alpargatas *see* Sao Paulo Alpargatas S.A.

Alpex, S.A. de C.V., **19** 12

Alpha Airports Group PLC, **77** 32–35

Alpha Beta Co., **II** 605, 625, 653; **17** 559

Alpha Engineering Group, Inc., **16** 259–60

Alpha Healthcare Ltd., **25** 455

Alpha Processor Inc., **41** 349

Alpha Technical Systems, **19** 279

Alphaform, **40** 214–15

Alphanumeric Publication Systems, Inc., **26** 518

Alpharma Inc., **35** 22–26 (upd.)

Alphonse Allard Inc., **II** 652; **51** 303

Alpine Confections, Inc., **71** 22–24

Alpine Electronics, Inc., **13** 30–31

Alpine Gaming *see* Century Casinos, Inc.

Alpine Lace Brands, Inc., **18** 14–16

Alpine Securities Corporation, **22** 5

Alpnet Inc. *see* SDL PLC.

Alpre, **19** 192

Alps Electric Co., Ltd., **II** 5–6; **13** 30; **44** 19–21 (upd.)

Alric Packing, **II** 466

Alrosa Company Ltd., **62** 7–11

Alsco *see* Steiner Corporation.

Alsen-Breitenbury, **III** 702

ALSO Holding AG, **29** 419, 422

Alsons Corp., **III** 571; **20** 362

Alsthom, **II** 12

Alsthom-Atlantique, **9** 9

Alta Dena, **25** 83, 85

Alta Electric Company, **25** 15

ALTA Health Strategies, Inc., **11** 113

Alta Vista Company, **50** 228

Altadis S.A., **72** 6–13 (upd.)

Altamil Corp., **IV** 137

Altana AG, **23** 498

AltaSteel Ltd., **51** 352

AltaVista Company, **43** 11–13

ALTEC International, **21** 107–09

Altenburg & Gooding, **22** 428

Altera Corporation, **18** 17–20; **43** 14–18 (upd.); **47** 384

Alternative Living Services *see* Alterra Healthcare Corporation.

Alternative Tentacles Records, **66** 3–6

Alternative Youth Services, Inc., **29** 399–400

Alterra Healthcare Corporation, **42** 3–5

Altex, **19** 192–93

Althouse Chemical Company, **9** 153

Alticor Inc., **71** 25–30 (upd.)

Altiris, Inc., **65** 34–36

Altman Weil Pensa, **29** 237

AmeriFirst Bank, **11** 258
Amerifirst Federal Savings, **10** 340
AmeriGas Partners, L.P., **12** 498, 500; **56** 36
AMERIGROUP Corporation, 69 23–26
Amerihost Properties, Inc., 30 51–53
AmeriKing Corp., **36** 309
Amerimark Inc., **II** 682
Amerin Corporation *see* Radian Group Inc.
AmeriServe Food Distribution *see* Holberg Industries, Inc.
Amerisex, **64** 198
AmeriSource Health Corporation, 37 9–11 (upd.)
AmerisourceBergen Corporation, 64 22–28 (upd.)
Ameristar Casinos, Inc., 33 39–42; **69** 27–31 (upd.)
AmeriSteel Corp., **59** 202
AmeriSuites, **52** 281
Amerisystems, **8** 328
Ameritech Corporation, V 265–68; **18** 30–34 (upd.)
Ameritech Illinois *see* Illinois Bell Telephone Company.
Ameritrade Holding Corporation, 34 27–30
Ameritrust Corporation, **9** 476
Ameriwood Industries International Corp., 17 15–17; **59** 164
Amerock Corporation, 13 41; **53** 37–40
Ameron International Corporation, 67 24–26
Amerop Sugar Corporation, **60** 96
Amersham PLC, 50 21–25; **63** 166
Ames Department Stores, Inc., 9 20–22; **30** 54–57 (upd.)
Ametek Inc., **9** 23–25; **12** 88; **38** 169
N.V. Amev, III 199–202
AMEX *see* American Stock Exchange.
Amey Plc, 47 23–25; **49** 320
AMF *see* American Machinery and Foundry, Inc.
AMF Bowling, Inc., 19 312; **23** 450; **40** 30–33
Amfac Inc., I 417–18, 566; **10** 42; **23** 320
Amfac/JMB Hawaii L.L.C., 24 32–35 (upd.)
AMFM Inc., **35** 221, 245, 248; **37** 104; **41** 384
Amgen, Inc., 10 78–81; **30** 58–61 (upd.)
Amherst Coal Co., **7** 309
AMI *see* Advanced Metallurgy, Inc.
AMI Metals, Inc. *see* Reliance Steel & Aluminum Company.
AMICAS, Inc., 69 32–34
Amiga Corporation, **7** 96
Aminoil, Inc. *see* American Independent Oil Co.
Amisys Managed Care Information Systems, **16** 94
Amitron S.A., **10** 113; **50** 43
Amity Leather Products Company *see* AR Accessories Group, Inc.
AMK Corporation, **7** 85; **21** 111

Amko Service Company, **74** 363
Amkor Technology, Inc., 69 35–37
AMLI Realty Company, **33** 418, 420
Amling Co., **25** 89
Ammirati Puris Lintas, **14** 316; **22** 294
Amnesty International, 50 26–29
Amoco Corporation, IV 368–71; **14** 21–25 (upd.) *see also* BP p.l.c.
AMOR 14 Corporation, **64** 95
Amorim Investimentos e Participaço, **48** 117, 119
Amorim Revestimentos, **48** 118
Amoskeag Company, 8 32–33; **9** 213–14, 217; **31** 199
Amot Controls Corporation, **15** 404; **50** 394
AMP, Inc., II 7–8; **14** 26–28 (upd.)
Ampacet Corporation, 67 27–29
Ampad Holding Corporation *see* American Pad & Paper Company.
AMPAL *see* American-Palestine Trading Corp.
AMPCO Auto Parks, Inc. *see* American Building Maintenance Industries, Inc.; ABM Industries Incorporated.
Ampeg Company, **48** 353
AMPEP, **III** 625
Ampersand Ventures, **73** 227–28
Ampex Corporation, 17 18–20
Amphenol Corporation, 40 34–37
Ampol Petroleum Ltd., **III** 729; **27** 473
Ampro, **25** 504–05
AMR *see* American Medical Response, Inc.
AMR Combs Inc., **36** 190
AMR Corporation, 28 22–26 (upd.); **52** 21–26 (upd.)
AMR Information Services, **9** 95
Amram's Distributing Limited, **12** 425
AMRE, **III** 211
AMREP Corporation, 21 35–37; **24** 78
Amro *see* Amsterdam-Rotterdam Bank N.V.
Amrop International Australasia, **34** 249
AMS *see* Advanced Marketing Services, Inc.
Amsbra Limited, **62** 48
Amscan Holdings, Inc., 61 24–26
Amsco International, **29** 450
Amserve Ltd., **48** 23
AmSouth Bancorporation, 12 15–17; **48** 15–18 (upd.)
Amstar Corp., **14** 18
Amstar Sugar Corporation, **7** 466–67; **26** 122
Amsted Industries Incorporated, 7 29–31; **66** 27
Amsterdam-Rotterdam Bank N.V., II 185–86
Amstrad plc, III 112–14; **48** 19–23 (upd.)
AmSurg Corporation, 48 24–27
AMT *see* American Machine and Tool Co., Inc.; American Materials & Technologies Corporation.
Amtech *see* American Building Maintenance Industries, Inc.; ABM Industries Incorporated.

Amtech Systems Corporation, **11** 65; **27** 405
Amtel, Inc., **8** 545; **10** 136
Amtorg, **13** 365
Amtrak *see* The National Railroad Passenger Corporation.
Amtran, Inc., 34 31–33
AmTrans *see* American Transport Lines.
Amurol Confections Company, **58** 378
Amvac Chemical Corporation, **47** 20
Amvent Inc., **25** 120
AMVESCAP PLC, 65 43–45
Amway Corporation, III 11–14; **13** 36–39 (upd.); **30** 62–66 (upd.) *see also* Alticor Inc.
Amy's Kitchen Inc., 76 26–28
Amylin Pharmaceuticals, Inc., 67 30–32
ANA *see* All Nippon Airways Co., Ltd.
Anacomp, Inc., **11** 19
Anaconda Aluminum, **11** 38
Anaconda Co., **7** 261–63
Anaconda-Jurden Associates, **8** 415
Anadarko Petroleum Corporation, 10 82–84; **52** 27–30 (upd.); **65** 316–17
Anadex, Inc., **18** 435–36
Anaheim Angels Baseball Club, Inc., 53 41–44
Anaheim Imaging, **19** 336
Analex Corporation, 74 20–22
Analog Devices, Inc., 10 85–87; **18** 20; **19** 67; **38** 54; **43** 17, 311; **47** 384
Analogic Corporation, 23 13–16
Analysts International Corporation, 36 40–42
Analytic Sciences Corporation, 10 88–90; **13** 417
Analytical Nursing Management Corporation (ANMC) *see* Amedisys, Inc.
Analytical Science Laboratories Inc., **58** 134
Analytical Surveys, Inc., 33 43–45
Analytico Food BV *see* Eurofins Scientific S.A.
Anam Group, 21 239; **23** 17–19
Anarad, Inc., **18** 515
Anaren Microwave, Inc., 33 46–48
Anchor Bancorp, Inc., 10 91–93
Anchor Brake Shoe, **18** 5
Anchor Brewing Company, 47 26–28
Anchor Corporation, **12** 525
Anchor Gaming, 24 36–39; **41** 216
Anchor Hocking Glassware, 13 40–42; **14** 483; **26** 353; **49** 253; **53** 39
Anchor Motor Freight, Inc., **12** 309–10
Anchor National Financial Services, Inc., **11** 482
Anchor National Life Insurance Company, **11** 482
Andenne Bricolage BVBA, **68** 64
Anders Wilhelmsen & Co., **22** 471
Andersen, 68 23–27 (upd.)
Andersen Consulting *see* Accenture Ltd
Andersen Corporation, 9 344; **10** 94–95; **11** 305; **22** 346; **39** 324
Andersen Worldwide, 29 25–28 (upd.); **57** 165
Anderson Animal Hospital, Inc., **58** 354

Arkansas Louisiana Gas Company *see* Arkla, Inc.
Arkia, **23** 184, 186–87
Arkla, Inc., V 550–51; **11** 441
Arla Foods amba, 48 35–38
Arlington Securities plc, **24** 84, 87–89
Arlon, Inc., **28** 42, 45
Armani *see* Giorgio Armani S.p.A.
Armaris, **75** 126
Armaturindistri, **III** 569
Armco Inc., IV 28–30 *see also* AK Steel.
Armement Sapmer Distribution, **60** 149
Armin Corporation *see* Tyco International Ltd.
Armor All Products Corp., 16 42–44
Armor Elevator, **11** 5
Armor Holdings, Inc., 27 49–51
Armour *see* Tommy Armour Golf Co.
Armour & Company, **8** 144; **12** 198; **13** 21, 506; **23** 173; **55** 365
Armour-Dial, **8** 144; **23** 173–74
Armour Food Co., **12** 370; **13** 270
Armstrong Air Conditioning Inc. *see* Lennox International Inc.
Armstrong Tire Co., **15** 355

Armstrong World Industries, Inc., III 422–24; **22** 46–50 (upd.)
Armtek, **7** 297
Army and Air Force Exchange Service, 39 27–29
Army Cooperative Fire Insurance Company, **10** 541
Army Ordnance, **19** 430
Army Signal Corps Laboratories, **10** 96
Arnold & Porter, 35 42–44
Arnold Clark Automobiles Ltd., 60 39–41
Arnold Communications, **25** 381
Arnold Electric Company, **17** 213
Arnold Industries Inc., **35** 297
Arnold, Schwinn & Company *see* Schwinn Cycle and Fitness L.P.
Arnold Thomas Co., **9** 411
Arnoldo Mondadori Editore S.p.A., IV 585–88; **19** 17–21 (upd.); **54** 17–23 (upd.)
Arnott's Ltd., 66 10–12
Aro Corp., **III** 527; **14** 477, 508; **15** 225
Aromat Corporation, **III** 710; **7** 303
Aromatic Industries, **18** 69
ArQule, Inc., 68 31–34
Arrendadora del Norte, S.A. de C.V., **51** 150
Arriva PLC, 69 42–44
Arrosto Coffee Company, **25** 263
Arrow Air Holdings Corporation, 55 28–30
Arrow Electronics, Inc., 10 112–14; **50** 41–44 (upd.)
Arrow Freight Corporation, **58** 23
Arrow Furniture Co., **21** 32
Arrow Pacific Plastics, **48** 334
Arrow Shirt Co., **24** 384
Arrowhead Mills Inc., **27** 197–98; **43** 218–19
Arsam Investment Co., **26** 261
Arsynco, Inc., **38** 4
The Art Institute of Chicago, 29 36–38

Art Van Furniture, Inc., 28 31–33
Artal Luxembourg SA, **40** 51; **33** 446, 449; **73** 379
Artal NV,
Artear S.A. *see* Grupo Clarín S.A.
Artec, **12** 297
Artech Digital Entertainments, Inc., **15** 133
Artek Systems Corporation, **13** 194
Artémis Group, **27** 513
Artes Grafica Rioplatense S.A., **67** 202
Artesian Manufacturing and Bottling Company, **9** 177
Artesian Resources Corporation, **45** 277
Artesyn Solutions Inc., **48** 369
Artesyn Technologies Inc., 46 35–38 (upd.)
Artex Enterprises, **7** 256; **25** 167, 253
ArthroCare Corporation, 73 31–33
Arthur Andersen & Company, Société Coopérative, 10 115–17 *see also* Andersen.
Arthur D. Little, Inc., 35 45–48
Arthur H. Fulton, Inc., **42** 363
Arthur J. Gallagher & Co., 73 34–36
Arthur Murray International, Inc., 32 60–62
Arthur Rank Organisation, **25** 328
Arthur Young & Company *see* Ernst & Young.
Artigiancassa SpA, **72** 21
Artisan Entertainment Inc., 32 63–66 (upd.)
Artisan Life Insurance Cooperative, **24** 104
Artisoft, Inc., **18** 143
Artistic Direct, Inc., **37** 108
Artists & Writers Press, Inc., **13** 560
Artists Management Group, **38** 164
ArtMold Products Corporation, **26** 342
Artra Group Inc., **40** 119–20
Arts and Entertainment Network *see* A&E Television Networks.
Arundel Corp., **46** 196
Arval *see* PHH Arval.
Arvin Industries, Inc., 8 37–40 *see also* ArvinMeritor, Inc.
ArvinMeritor, Inc., 54 24–28 (upd.)
A/S Air Baltic Corporation, 71 35–37
AS Estonian Air, 71 38–40
ASA Holdings, **47** 30
Asahi Breweries, Ltd., I 220–21; **20** 28–30 (upd.); **52** 31–34 (upd.)
Asahi Chemical Industry Co., **I** 221
Asahi Corporation, **16** 84; **40** 93
Asahi Denka Kogyo KK, 64 33–35
Asahi Glass Company, Ltd., III 666–68; **11** 234–35; **48** 39–42 (upd.)
Asahi Komag Co., Ltd., **11** 234
Asahi Kyoei Co., **I** 221
Asahi Medix Co., Ltd., **36** 420
Asahi National Broadcasting Company, Ltd., 9 29–31
Asahi Real Estate Facilities Co., Ltd. *see* Seino Transportation Company, Ltd.
Asahi Shimbun, **9** 29–30
Asanté Technologies, Inc., 20 31–33

ASARCO Incorporated, IV 31–34; **40** 220–22, 411
ASB Agency, Inc., **10** 92
ASB Air, **47** 286–87
Asbury Associates Inc., **22** 354–55
Asbury Automotive Group Inc., 26 501; **60** 42–44
Asbury Carbons, Inc., 68 35–37
ASC, Inc., 55 31–34
ASCAP *see* The American Society of Composers, Authors and Publishers.
Ascend Communications, Inc., 24 47–51; **34** 258
Ascension Health, **61** 206
Ascential Software Corporation, 59 54–57
ASCO Healthcare, Inc., **18** 195–97
Asco Products, Inc., **22** 413
Ascom AG, 9 32–34; **15** 125
Ascotts, **19** 122
ASCP *see* American Securities Capital Partners.
ASD, **IV** 228
ASD Specialty Healthcare, Inc., **64** 27
ASDA Group Ltd., II 611–12; **28** 34–36 (upd.); **64** 36–38 (upd.)
ASEA AB *see* ABB Ltd.
Aseam Credit Sdn Bhd, **72** 217
Asepak Corp., **16** 339
A.B. Asesores Bursatiles, **III** 197–98; **15** 18
ASF *see* American Steel Foundries.
ASG *see* Allen Systems Group, Inc.
Asgrow Florida Company, **13** 503
Asgrow Seed Co., **29** 435; **41** 306
Ash Company, **10** 271
Ash Resources Ltd., **31** 398–99
Ashanti Goldfields Company Limited, 43 37–40
Ashbourne PLC, **25** 455
Ashdown *see* Repco Corporation Ltd.
Ashland Inc., 19 22–25; **50** 45–50 (upd.)
Ashland Oil, Inc., IV 372–74 *see also* Marathon.
Ashley Furniture Industries, Inc., 35 49–51
Ashtead Group plc, 34 41–43
Ashton-Tate Corporation, **9** 81–82; **10** 504–05
Ashworth, Inc., 26 25–28
ASIA & PACIFIC Business Description Paid-in Capital Voting Rights, **68** 30
Asia Oil Co., Ltd., **IV** 404, 476; **53** 115
Asia Pacific Breweries Limited, 59 58–60
Asia Pulp & Paper, **38** 227
Asia Shuang He Sheng Five Star Beer Co., Ltd., **49** 418
Asia Television, **IV** 718; **38** 320
Asia Terminals Ltd., **IV** 718; **38** 319
AsiaInfo Holdings, Inc., 43 41–44
Asiamerica Equities Ltd. *see* Mercer International.
Asian Football Confederation, **27** 150
Asiana Airlines, Inc., 24 400; **46** 39–42
ASICS Corporation, 24 404; **57** 52–55
ASK Group, Inc., 9 35–37

Chesapeake Paperboard Company, **44** 66

Chesapeake Utilities Corporation, 56 60–62

Cheshire Building Society, 74 84–87

Chesebrough-Pond's USA, Inc., 8 105–07

Chessington World of Adventures, **55** 378

Chester Engineers, **10** 412

Cheung Kong (Holdings) Limited, IV 693–95; 18 252; **20 131–34 (upd.); 23** 278, 280; **49** 199 *see also* Hutchison Whampoa Ltd.

Chevignon, **44** 296

Chevrolet, **9** 17; **19** 221, 223; **21** 153; **26** 500

Chevron U.K. Ltd., **15** 352

ChevronTexaco Corporation, IV 385–87;19 82–85 (upd.); 47 70–76 (upd.), 343; **63** 104, 113

Chevy Chase Savings Bank, **13** 439

Chevy's, Inc., **33** 140

Chevy's Mexican Restaurants, **27** 226

ChexSystems, **22** 181

Cheyenne Software, Inc., 12 60–62

CHF *see* Chase, Harris, Forbes.

Chi-Chi's Inc., 13 151–53; 51 70–73 (upd.)

CHI Construction Company, **58** 84

Chi Mei Optoelectronics Corporation, 75 93–95

Chiasso Inc., 53 98–100

Chiat/Day Inc. Advertising, 9 438; **11 49–52** *see also* TBWA/Chiat/Day.

Chiba Gas Co. Ltd., **55** 375

Chiba Mitsukoshi Ltd., **56** 242

Chibu Electric Power Company, Incorporated, V 571–73

Chic by H.I.S, Inc., 20 135–37; 54 403

Chicago and North Western Holdings Corporation, 6 376–78

Chicago and Southern Airlines Inc. *see* Delta Air Lines, Inc.

Chicago Bears Football Club, Inc., 33 95–97

Chicago Blackhawk Hockey Team, Inc. *see* Wirtz Corporation.

Chicago Board of Trade, 41 84–87

Chicago Bridge & Iron Company, **7** 74–77

Chicago Cutlery, **16** 234

Chicago Faucet Company, **49** 161, 163

Chicago Flexible Shaft Company, **9** 484

Chicago Heater Company, Inc., **8** 135

Chicago Magnet Wire Corp., **13** 397

Chicago Medical Equipment Co., **31** 255

Chicago Mercantile Exchange Holdings Inc., 75 96–99

Chicago Motor Club, **10** 126

Chicago Musical Instrument Company, **16** 238

Chicago National League Ball Club, Inc., 66 52–55

Chicago O'Hare Leather Concessions Joint Venture Inc., **58** 369

Chicago Pacific Corp., **III** 573; **12** 251; **22** 349; **23** 244; **34** 432

Chicago Pizza & Brewery, Inc., 44 85–88

Chicago Pneumatic Tool Co., **III** 427, 452; **7** 480; **26** 41; **28** 40

Chicago Rawhide Manufacturing Company, **8** 462–63

Chicago Rollerskate, **15** 395

Chicago Screw Co., **12** 344

Chicago Shipbuilding Company, **18** 318

Chicago Sun-Times, Inc., **62** 188

Chicago Times, **11** 251

Chicago Title and Trust Co., **10** 43–45

Chicago Title Corp., **54** 107

Chicago Tribune *see* Tribune Company.

Chichibu Concrete Industry Co. Ltd., **60** 301

Chick-fil-A Inc., 23 115–18

Chicken of the Sea International, 24 114–16 (upd.)

Chico's FAS, Inc., 45 97–99; 60 348

Chicobel S.A. Belgique *see* Leroux S.A.S.

Chief Auto Parts, **II** 661; **32** 416

Chieftain Development Company, Ltd., **16** 11

Child World Inc., **13** 166; **18** 524; **76** 108

Childers Products Co., **21** 108

Children's Book-of-the-Month Club, **13** 105

Children's Comprehensive Services, Inc., 42 70–72

Children's Discovery Centers of America *see* Knowledge Learning Corporation.

Children's Hospitals and Clinics, Inc., 54 64–67

The Children's Place Retail Stores, Inc., 37 80–82

Children's Record Guild, **13** 105

Children's Television Workshop, **12** 495; **13** 560; **35** 75

Children's World Learning Centers, **II** 608; **13** 48

Children's World Ltd. *see* The Boots Company PLC.

ChildrenFirst, Inc., 59 117–20

Childtime Learning Centers, Inc., 34 103–06 *see also* Learning Care Group, Inc.

Chiles Offshore Corporation, 9 111–13; 57 126; **59** 322

Chili's Grill & Bar *see* Brinker International, Inc.

Chilton Corp., **25** 239; **27** 361

Chilton Publications *see* Cahners Business Information.

Chilton Vending Co. *see* American Coin Merchandising, Inc.

Chimney Rock Winery, **48** 392

China Airlines, 34 107–10; 39 33–34

China Coast, **10** 322, 324; **16** 156, 158

China.com Corp., **49** 422

China Communications System Company, Inc. (Chinacom), **18** 34

China Development Corporation, **16** 4

China Eastern Airlines Co. Ltd., 31 102–04; 46 10

China International Capital Corp., **16** 377

China International Trade and Investment Corporation *see* CITIC Pacific Ltd.

China Life Insurance Company Limited, 65 103–05

China Merchants International Holdings Co., Ltd., 52 79–82

China National Aviation Company Ltd., **18** 115; **21** 140; **66** 192

China National Cereals, Oils and Foodstuffs Import and Export Corporation (COFCO), 76 89–91

China National Heavy Duty Truck Corporation, **21** 274

China National Machinery Import and Export Corporation, **8** 279

China National Offshore Oil Corporation, **71** 383

China National Petroleum Corporation, 46 86–89

China Netcom Group Corporation (Hong Kong) Limited, 73 80–83

China OceanShipping Company, **50** 187

China Resources (Shenyang) Snowflake Brewery Co., **21** 320

China Southern Airlines Company Ltd., 31 102; **33 98–100; 46** 10

China Telecom, 50 128–32

China Unicom, **47** 320–21

chinadotcom Corporation *see* CDC Corporation.

Chinese Electronics Import and Export Corp., **I** 535

Chinese Metallurgical Import and Export Corp., **IV** 61

Chinese Petroleum Corporation, IV 388–90, 493, 519; **31 105–108 (upd.)**

The Chinet Company, **30** 397

Chipcom, **16** 392

Chipotle Mexican Grill, Inc., 63 280, 284–85; **67 107–10,** 268

Chippewa Shoe, **19** 232

CHIPS and Technologies, Inc., 6 217; **9 114–17**

Chiquita Brands International, Inc., 7 84–86; 21 110–13 (upd.); 38 197; **60** 268

ChiRex, **38** 380

Chiro Tool Manufacturing Corp., **III** 629

Chiron Corporation, 7 427; **10** 213–14; **36 117–20 (upd.); 45** 94

Chisholm Coal Company, **51** 352

Chisholm-Mingo Group, Inc., 41 88–90

Chitaka Foods International, **24** 365

Chittenden & Eastman Company, 58 61–64

Chiyoda Fire and Marine, **III** 404

Chock Full o'Nuts Corp., 17 97–100; 20 53

Chocoladefabriken Lindt & Sprüngli AG, 27 102–05; 30 220

Choice Hotels International Inc., 14 105–07; 26 460

ChoiceCare Corporation, **24** 231

ChoicePoint Inc., 31 358; **65 106–08**

Chorion PLC, **75** 389–90

Chorus Line Corporation, 30 121–23

Chouinard Equipment *see* Lost Arrow Inc.

Chovet Engineering S.A. *see* SNC-Lavalin Group Inc.

Chr. Hansen Group A/S, 70 54–57

Consolidated TVX Mining Corporation,
61 290
Consolidated Tyre Services Ltd., IV 241
Consolidated Vultee, II 32
Consolidation Coal Co., 8 154, 346–47
Consolidation Services, 44 10, 13
Consorcio G Grupo Dina, S.A. de C.V.,
36 131–33
Consorcio Siderurgica Amazonia Ltd. *see*
Siderar S.A.I.C.
Consortium, 34 373
Consortium de Realisation, 35 329
Consortium De Realization SAS, 23 392
Consoweld Corporation, 8 124
Constar International Inc., 8 562; 13
190; 32 125; 64 85–88
Constellation Brands, Inc., 68 95–100
(upd.)
Constellation Energy Corporation, 24 29
Constellation Enterprises Inc., 25 46
Constinsouza, 25 174
Constitution Insurance Company, 51 143
Construcciones Aeronáuticas SA, 7 9; 12
190; 24 88 *see also* European
Aeronautic Defence and Space
Company EADS N.V.
Construction Developers Inc., 68 114
Construction DJL Inc., 23 332–33
Constructora CAMSA, C.A., 56 383
Constructora y Administradora Uno S.A.,
72 269
Construtora Norberto Odebrecht S.A. *see*
Odebrecht S.A.
Consul GmbH, 51 58
Consul Restaurant Corp., 13 152
Consumer Access Limited, 24 95
Consumer Products Company, 30 39
Consumer Value Stores *see* CVS
Corporation.
Consumer's Gas Co., I 264
ConsumerNet, 49 422
Consumers Cooperative Association *see*
Farmland Industries, Inc.
Consumers Distributing Co. Ltd., II 649,
652–53
Consumers Electric Light and Power, 6
582
The Consumers Gas Company Ltd., 6
476–79; 43 154 *see also* Enbridge Inc.
Consumers Mutual Gas Light Company
see Baltimore Gas and Electric
Company.
Consumers Power Co., 14 133–36
Consumers Public Power District, 29 352
Consumers Union, 26 97–99
Consumers Water Company, 14
137–39; 39 329
Contact Software International Inc., 10
509
Container Corporation of America, V
147; 8 476; 26 446
The Container Store, 36 134–36
Container Transport International, III 344
Contaminant Recovery Systems, Inc., 18
162
CONTAQ Microsystems Inc., 48 127
Conte S.A., 12 262
Contech, 10 493

Contel Corporation, V 296–98; 13 212;
14 259; 15 192; 43 447
Contempo Associates, 14 105; 25 307
Contempo Casuals, Inc. *see* The Wet Seal,
Inc.
Contemporary Books, 22 522
Content Technologies Inc., 42 24–25
Contex Graphics Systems Inc., 24 428
Conti-Carriers & Terminals Inc., 22 167
Contico International, L.L.C., 51 190
ContiCommodity Services, Inc., 10
250–51
ContiGroup Companies, Inc., 43
119–22 (upd.)
Continental AG, V 240–43, 250–51,
256; 8 212–14; 9 248; 15 355; 19
508; 56 67–72 (upd.)
Continental Airlines, Inc., I 96–98; 21
140–43 (upd.); 52 89–94 (upd.)
Continental American Life Insurance
Company, 7 102
Continental Baking Co., 7 320–21; 12
276; 13 427; 27 309–10; 38 252
Continental Bank Corporation, II
261–63, 285, 289, 348; 47 231 *see also*
Bank of America.
Continental Bio-Clinical Laboratories, 26
391
Continental Cablevision, Inc., 7 98–100
Continental Can Co., Inc., 10 130; 13
255; 15 127–30; 24 428; 26 117, 449;
32 125; 49 293–94
Continental-Caoutchouc und
Gutta-Percha Compagnie *see*
Continental AG.
Continental Carbon Co., 36 146–48
Continental Care Group, 10 252–53
Continental Casualty Co., III 228–32; 16
204
Continental Cities Corp., III 344
Continental Corporation, III 239–44,
273; 10 561; 12 318; 15 30; 38 142
Continental Design, 58 194
Continental Divide Insurance Co., III
214
Continental Electronics Corporation, 18
513–14
Continental Emsco, 24 305
Continental Equipment Company, 13 225
Continental Express, 11 299
Continental Fiber Drum, 8 476
Continental Gas & Electric Corporation,
6 511
Continental General Tire Corp., 23
140–42
Continental Grain Company, 10
249–51; 13 185–87 (upd.); 30 353,
355; 40 87 *see also* ContiGroup
Companies, Inc.
Continental Group Co., I 599–600
Continental Hair Products, Inc. *see* Conair
Corp.
Continental Health Affiliates, 17 307
Continental Homes Inc., 26 291; 58 84
Continental Illinois Corp. *see* Continental
Bank Corporation.
Continental Investment Corporation, 9
507; 12 463; 22 541; 33 407

Continental Medical Systems, Inc., 10
252–54
Continental Milling Company, 10 250
Continental Modules, Inc., 45 328
Continental Motors Corp., 10 521–22
Continental Mutual Savings Bank, 17 529
Continental Oil Co. *see* ConocoPhillips.
Continental Packaging Inc., 13 255
Continental Plastic Containers, Inc., 25
512
Continental Reinsurance, 11 533
Continental Research Corporation, 22
541
Continental Restaurant Systems, 12 510
Continental Risk Services, III 243
Continental Scale Works, 14 229–30
Continental Telephone Company *see* GTE
Corporation.
Continental Wood Preservers, Inc., 12
397
ContinueCare Corporation, 25 41
Continuum Electro-Optics, Inc. *see* Excel
Technology, Inc.
Continuum Health Partners, Inc., 60
97–99
Contran Corporation, 19 467
Contrans Acquisitions, Inc., 14 38
Contred Ltd., 20 263
Control Data Corporation, III 126–28
Control Data Systems, Inc., 10 255–57
Control Systemation, Inc. *see* Excel
Technology, Inc.
Controladora Comercial Mexicana, S.A.
de C.V., 36 137–39
Controladora PROSA, 18 516, 518
Controlled Materials and Equipment
Transportation, 29 354
Controlonics Corporation, 13 195
Controls Company of America, 9 67
Controlware GmbH, 22 53
Convair, 9 18, 498; 13 357
Convenient Food Mart Inc., 7 114; 25
125
Convergent Technologies, 11 519
Converse Inc., 9 133–36; 31 134–38
(upd.), 211
Convotherm Ltd. *see* Enodis plc.
Conway Computer Group, 18 370
Conwest Exploration Company Ltd., 16
10, 12; 43 3
Conycon *see* Construcciones y Contratas.
Conzinc Riotinto of Australia *see* CRA
Limited.
Cook Bates Inc., 40 347–48
Cook Data Services, Inc., 9 73
Cook Standard Tool Co., 13 369
Cooke Engineering Company, 13 194
Cooker Restaurant Corporation, 20
159–61; 51 82–85 (upd.)
Cooking and Crafts Club, 13 106
Cookson Group plc, III 679–82; 44
115–20 (upd.)
CoolBrands International Inc., 35
119–22
Coolidge Mutual Savings Bank, 17 529
CoolSavings, Inc., 77 120–124
Coop Schweiz Genossenschaftsverband,
48 114–16

Dürrkopp Adler AG, **62** 132
Dutch Boy, **II** 649; **10** 434–35
Dutch Crude Oil Company *see* Nederlandse Aardolie Maatschappij.
Dutch State Mines *see* DSM N.V.
Dutchland Farms, **25** 124
Duttons Ltd., **24** 267
Duty Free International, Inc., **11** 80–82
  see also World Duty Free Americas, Inc.
Duval Corp., **7** 280; **25** 461
DVI, Inc., **51** 107–09
DVM Pharmaceuticals Inc., **55** 233
DVT Corporation *see* Cognex Corporation.
DWG Corporation *see* Triarc Companies, Inc.
Dyas B.V., **55** 347
Dyckerhoff AG, **35** 151–54
Dycom Industries, Inc., **57** 118–20
Dyersburg Corporation, **21** 192–95
Dyke and Dryden, Ltd., **31** 417
Dylex Limited, **29** 162–65
Dymed Corporation *see* Palomar Medical Technologies, Inc.
DYMO *see* Esselte Worldwide.
Dynaction S.A., **67** 146–48
Dynalectric Co., **45** 146
DynaMark, Inc., **18** 168, 170, 516, 518
Dynamem Corporation, **22** 409
Dynamic Capital Corp., **16** 80
Dynamic Controls, **11** 202
Dynamic Foods, **53** 148
Dynamic Health Products Inc., **62** 296
Dynamic Homes, **61** 125–27
Dynamic Microprocessor Associated Inc., **10** 508
Dynamics Corporation of America, **39** 106
Dynamit Nobel AG, **III** 692–95; **16** 364; **18** 559
Dynamix, **15** 455
Dynapar, **7** 116–17
Dynaplast, **40** 214–15
Dynascan AK, **14** 118
Dynasty Footwear, Ltd., **18** 88
Dynatech Corporation, **13** 194–96
Dynatron/Bondo Corporation, **8** 456
DynCorp, **45** 145–47
Dynea, **68** 125–27
Dynegy Inc., **47** 70; **49** 119–22 (upd.)
Dyno Industrier AS, **13** 555
Dyson Group PLC, **71** 132–34
Dystrybucja, **41** 340

E

E&B Company, **9** 72
E&B Marine, Inc., **17** 542–43
E. & J. Gallo Winery, **I** 242–44; **7** 154–56 (upd.); **28** 109–11 (upd.)
E&M Laboratories, **18** 514
E & S Retail Ltd. *see* Powerhouse.
E! Entertainment Television Inc., **17** 148–50
E-Mex Home Funding Ltd. *see* Cheshire Building Society.
E-mu Systems, Inc., **57** 78–79
E-Pet Services, **74** 234
E-Stamp Corporation, **34** 474

E-Systems, Inc., **9** 182–85
E*Trade Financial Corporation, **20** 206–08; **60** 114–17 (upd.)
E-II Holdings Inc. *see* Astrum International Corp.
E-Z Haul, **24** 409
E-Z Serve Corporation, **17** 169–71
E A Rosengrens AB, **53** 158
E.B. Badger Co., **11** 413
E.B. Eddy Forest Products, **II** 631
E.C. Snodgrass Company, **14** 112
E.C. Steed, **13** 103
E. de Trey & Sons, **10** 270–71
E.F. Hutton Group, **II** 399, 450–51; **8** 139; **9** 469; **10** 63
E.F. Hutton LBO, **24** 148
E.H. Bindley & Company, **9** 67
E.I. du Pont de Nemours and Company, **I** 328–30; **8** 151–54 (upd.); **26** 123–27 (upd.); **73** 128–33 (upd.)
E.J. Brach & Sons *see* Brach and Brock Confections, Inc.
E.J. Longyear Company *see* Boart Longyear Company.
E. Katz Special Advertising Agency *see* Katz Communications, Inc.
E.M. Warburg Pincus & Co., **7** 305; **13** 176; **16** 319; **25** 313; **29** 262
E. Missel GmbH, **20** 363
E.On AG, **50** 165–73 (upd.); **51** 217; **59** 391; **62** 14
E.piphany, Inc., **49** 123–25
E.R.R. Enterprises, **44** 227
E. Rabinowe & Co., Inc., **13** 367
E. Rosen Co., **53** 303–04
E.S. International Holding S.A. *see* Banco Espírito Santo e Comercial de Lisboa S.A.
E.V. Williams Inc. *see* The Branch Group, Inc.
E.W. Howell Co., Inc., **72** 94–96 *see also* Obayashi Corporation
The E.W. Scripps Company, **IV** 606–09; **7** 157–59 (upd.); **28** 122–26 (upd.); **66** 85–89 (upd.)
E. Witte Verwaltungsgesellschaft GmbH, **73** 326
EADS N.V. *see* European Aeronautic Defence and Space Company EADS N.V.
EADS SOCATA, **54** 91–94
Eagel One Industries, **50** 49
Eagle Airways Ltd., **23** 161
Eagle Credit Corp., **10** 248
Eagle Distributing Co., **37** 351
Eagle Family Foods, Inc., **22** 95
Eagle Floor Care, Inc., **13** 501; **33** 392
Eagle Gaming, L.P., **16** 263; **43** 226; **75** 341
Eagle Global Logistics *see* EGL, Inc.
Eagle Hardware & Garden, Inc., **16** 186–89
Eagle Industries Inc., **8** 230; **22** 282; **25** 536
Eagle Managed Care Corp., **19** 354, 357; **63** 334

Eagle-Picher Industries, Inc., **8** 155–58; **23** 179–83 (upd.)
Eagle Plastics, **19** 414
Eagle Sentry Inc., **32** 373
Eagle Thrifty Drug, **14** 397
Eagle Trading, **55** 24
Eagle Travel Ltd., **IV** 241
Earl Scheib, Inc., **32** 158–61
Early American Insurance Co., **22** 230
Early Learning Centre, **39** 240, 242
Earth Resources Company, **17** 320
Earth Wise, Inc., **16** 90
Earth's Best, Inc., **21** 56; **36** 256
The Earthgrains Company, **36** 161–65; **54** 326
EarthLink, Inc., **33** 92; **36** 166–68; **38** 269
EAS *see* Engineered Air Systems, Inc.; Executive Aircraft Services.
Easco Hand Tools, Inc., **7** 117
Easi-Set Industries, Inc., **56** 332
Eason Oil Company, **6** 578; **11** 198
East African External Communications Limited, **25** 100
East African Gold Mines Limited, **61** 293
East Hartford Trust Co., **13** 467
East Japan Railway Company, **V** 448–50; **66** 90–94 (upd.)
The East New York Savings Bank, **11** 108–09
East Tennessee Steel Supply Inc. *see* Siskin Steel & Supply Company.
East-West Airlines, **27** 475
East-West Federal Bank, **16** 484
East West Motor Express, Inc., **39** 377
Easter Enterprises *see* Nash Finch Company.
Easter Seals, Inc., **58** 105–07
Easterday Supply Company, **25** 15
Eastern Air Group Co., **31** 102
Eastern Airlines, **I** 66, 78, 90, 98–99, 101–03, 116, 118, 123–25; **6**, 104–05; **8** 416; **9** 17–18, 80; **11** 268, 427; **12** 191, 487; **21** 142, 143; **23** 483; **26** 339, 439
Eastern Australia Airlines Pty Ltd., **24** 396; **68** 306
Eastern Aviation Group, **23** 408
Eastern Carolina Bottling Company, **10** 223
The Eastern Company, **48** 140–43
Eastern Electricity, **13** 485
Eastern Enterprises, **6** 486–88
Eastern Industries, Inc. *see* Stabler Companies Inc.
Eastern Kansas Utilities, **6** 511
Eastern Machine Screw Products Co., **13** 7
Eastern Market Beef Processing Corp., **20** 120
Eastern Pine Sales Corporation, **13** 249
Eastern Platinum Ltd. *see* Lonmin plc.
Eastern Shore Natural Gas Company, **56** 62
Eastern Software Distributors, Inc., **16** 125
Eastern States Farmers Exchange, **7** 17

Glass Glover Plc, **52** 419

Glasstite, Inc., **33** 360–61

GlasTec, **II** 420

Glastron *see* Genmar Holdings, Inc.

Glatfelter Wood Pulp Company, **8** 413

Glaxo Holdings plc, I 639–41; 9 263–65 (upd.)

GlaxoSmithKline plc, 46 201–08 (upd.)

Gleason Corporation, 24 184–87

Glemby Co. Inc., **70** 262

Glen & Co, **I** 453

Glen Alden Corp., **15** 247

Glen Dimplex, 78 123–127

Glen-Gery Corporation, **14** 249

Glencairn Ltd., **25** 418

Glencore International AG, **52** 71, 73; **73** 391–92

The Glenlyte Group, **29** 469

Glenlyte Thomas Group LLC, **29** 466

Glenmoor Partners, **70** 34–35

Glenn Advertising Agency, **25** 90

Glenn Pleass Holdings Pty. Ltd., **21** 339

GLF-Eastern States Association, **7** 17

Glico *see* Ezaki Glico Company Ltd.

The Glidden Company, I 353; 8 222–24; 21 545

Glimcher Co., **26** 262

Glitsch International, Inc. *see* Foster Wheeler Corp.

Global Access, **31** 469

Global Apparel Sourcing Ltd., **22** 223

Global Berry Farms LLC, 62 154–56

Global BMC (Mauritius) Holdings Ltd., **62** 55

Global Card Holdings Inc., **68** 45

Global Communications of New York, Inc., **45** 261

Global Crossing Ltd., 32 216–19

Global Engineering Company, **9** 266

Global Health Care Partners, **42** 68

Global Hyatt Corporation, 75 159–63 (upd.)

Global Imaging Systems, Inc., 73 163–65

Global Industries, Ltd., 37 168–72

Global Information Solutions, **34** 257

Global Interactive Communications Corporation, **28** 242

Global Marine Inc., 9 266–67; 11 87

Global Motorsport Group, Inc. *see* Custom Chrome, Inc.

Global One, **52** 108

Global Outdoors, Inc., 49 173–76

Global Petroleum Albania S.A./Elda Petroleum Sh.P.K., **64** 177

Global Power Equipment Group Inc., 52 137–39

Global Switch International Ltd., **67** 104–05

Global TeleSystems, Inc. *see* Global Crossing Ltd.

Global Vacations Group *see* Classic Vacation Group, Inc.

Global Van Lines *see* Allied Worldwide, Inc.

GlobalCom Telecommunications, Inc., **24** 122

GlobaLex, **28** 141

Globalia, **53** 301

GlobalSantaFe Corporation, 48 187–92 (upd.)

Globalstar Telecommunications Limited, **54** 233

GLOBALT, Inc., **52** 339

Globe Business Furniture, **39** 207

Globe Feather & Down, **19** 304

Globe Newspaper Co., **7** 15

Globe Pequot Press, **36** 339, 341

Globe Steel Abrasive Co., **17** 371

Globe Telegraph and Trust Company, **25** 99

Globelle Corp., 43 368

Globenet, **57** 67, 69

Globetrotter Communications, **7** 199

Globo, **18** 211

Globus *see* Migros-Genossenschafts-Bund.

Glock Ges.m.b.H., 42 154–56

Gloria Jean's Gourmet Coffees, **20** 83

La Gloria Oil and Gas Company, **7** 102

Glosser Brothers, **13** 394

Glotel plc, 53 149–51

Gloucester Cold Storage and Warehouse Company, **13** 243

Glow-Tec International Company Ltd., **65** 343

Glowlite Corporation, **48** 359

Gluek Brewing Company, 75 164–66

Glycomed Inc., **13** 241; **47** 222

Glyn, Mills and Co., **12** 422

GM *see* General Motors Corporation.

GM Hughes Electronics Corporation, II 32–36; 10 325 *see also* Hughes Electronics Corporation.

GMARA, **II** 608

GMR Properties, **21** 257

GNB International Battery Group, **10** 445

GNC *see* General Nutrition Companies, Inc.

GND Holdings Corp., **7** 204; **28** 164

GNMA *see* Government National Mortgage Association.

Gnôme & Rhône, **46** 369

The Go-Ahead Group Plc, 28 155–57

GO/DAN Industries, Inc. *see* TransPro, Inc.

Go Fly Ltd., **39** 128

Go-Gro Industries, Ltd., **43** 99

Go Sport *see* Groupe Go Sport S.A.

Go-Video, Inc. *see* Sensory Science Corporation.

Goal Systems International Inc., **10** 394

goClick *see* Marchex, Inc.

Godfather's Pizza Incorporated, 25 179–81

Godfrey Co., **II** 625

Godfrey L. Cabot, Inc., **8** 77

Godiva Chocolatier, Inc., 64 154–57

Godsell, **10** 277

Godtfred Kristiansen, **13** 310–11

Goelitz Confectionery Company *see* Herman Goelitz, Inc.; Jelly Belly Candy Company.

GOFAMCLO, Inc., **64** 160

Goggin Truck Line, **57** 277

GoGo Tours, Inc., **56** 203–04

Göhner AG, **6** 491

Gokey Company, **10** 216; **28** 339

Gol Linhas Aéreas Inteligentes S.A., 73 166–68

Gold Bond Stamp Company *see* Carlson Companies, Inc.

Gold Corporation, **71** 3–4

Gold Exploration and Mining Co. Limited Partnership, **13** 503

Gold Fields Ltd., IV 94–97; 62 157–64 (upd.)

Gold Kist Inc., 7 432; 17 207–09; 26 166–68

Gold Lance Inc., **19** 451–52

Gold Lion, **20** 263

Gold Prospectors' Association of America, **49** 173

Gold Star Chili, Inc., **62** 325–26

Gold'n Plump Poultry, 54 136–38

Gold's Gym International, Inc., 71 165–68

Goldblatt's Department Stores, **15** 240–42

Golden Bear International, **33** 103; **42** 433; **45** 300; **68** 245

Golden Belt Manufacturing Co., 16 241–43

Golden Books Family Entertainment, Inc., 28 158–61

Golden Circle Financial Services, **15** 328

Golden Corral Corporation, 10 331–33; 66 143–46 (upd.)

Golden Enterprises, Inc., 26 163–65

Golden Gate Airlines, **25** 421

Golden Gates Disposal & Recycling Co., **60** 224

Golden Grain Macaroni Co., **II** 560; **12** 411; **30** 219; **34** 366

Golden Krust Caribbean Bakery, Inc., 68 177–79

Golden Moores Finance Company, **48** 286

Golden Nugget, Inc. *see* Mirage Resorts, Incorporated.

Golden Ocean Group, **45** 164

Golden Partners, **10** 333

Golden Peanut Company, **17** 207

Golden Poultry Company, **26** 168

Golden Press, Inc., **13** 559–61

Golden Road Motor Inn, Inc. *see* Monarch Casino & Resort, Inc.

Golden Sea Produce, **10** 439

Golden Skillet, **10** 373

Golden State Foods Corporation, 32 220–22

Golden State Newsprint Co. Inc., **IV** 296; **19** 226; **23** 225

Golden State Vintners, Inc., 33 172–74

Golden Telecom, Inc., 59 208–11

Golden West Financial Corporation, 47 159–61

Golden West Homes, **15** 328

Golden West Publishing Corp., **38** 307–08

Golden Youth, **17** 227

Goldenberg Group, Inc., **12** 396

Goldfield Corp., **12** 198

Goldfine's Inc., **16** 36

Industrial Services Group, Inc., **56** 161
Industrial Services of America, Inc., 46
  247–49
Industrial Shows of America, **27** 362
Industrial Tectonics Corp., **18** 276
Industrial Tires Limited, **65** 91
Industrial Trade & Consumer Shows Inc.
  see Maclean Hunter Publishing Limited.
Industrial Trust Co. of Wilmington, **25**
  540
Industrial Trust Company, **9** 228
Industrias Bachoco, S.A. de C.V., 39
  228–31
Industrias del Atlantico SA, **47** 291
Indústrias Klabin de Papel e Celulose S.A.
  see Klabin S.A.
Industrias Nacobre, **21** 259
Industrias Negromex, **23** 170
Industrias Penoles, S.A. de C.V., 22
  284–86
Industrias Resistol S.A., **23** 170–71
Industrie Natuzzi S.p.A., 18 256–58
Industrie Zignago Santa Margherita
  S.p.A., 67 210–12, 246, 248
Les Industries Ling, **13** 443
Industriförvaltnings AB Kinnevik, **26**
  331–33; **36** 335
AB Industrivärden, **32** 397
Induyco *see* Industrias y Confecciones,
  S.A.
Indy Lighting, **30** 266
Indy Racing League, **37** 74
Inelco Peripheriques, **10** 459
Inespo, **16** 322
Inet Technologies Inc. *see* Tektronix Inc.
Inexco Oil Co., **7** 282
Infineon Technologies AG, 50 269–73
Infinity Broadcasting Corporation, 11
  190–92; 48 214–17 (upd.)
Infinity Enterprises, Inc., **44** 4
Infinity Partners, **36** 160
INFLEX, S.A., **8** 247
Inflight Sales Group Limited, **11** 82; **29**
  511
InfoAsia, **28** 241
Infocom, **32** 8
InfoCure Corporation *see* AMICAS, Inc.
Infogrames Entertainment S.A., 35
  227–30
Infonet Services Corporation *see*
  Belgacom.
Infoplan, **14** 36
Informa Group plc, 58 188–91
Informatics General Corporation, **11** 468;
  25 86
Information Access Company, 17
  252–55
Information and Communication Group,
  14 555
Information Associates Inc., **11** 78
Information Builders, Inc., 14 16; **22**
  291–93
Information Consulting Group, **9** 345
Information, Dissemination and Retrieval
  Inc., **IV** 670
Information Holdings Inc., 47 183–86
Information International *see* Autologic
  Information International, Inc.

Information Management Reporting
  Services *see* Hyperion Software
  Corporation.
Information Management Science
  Associates, Inc., **13** 174
Information Please LLC, **26** 216
Information Resources, Inc., 10 358–60
Information Spectrum Inc., **57** 34
Informix Corporation, 10 361–64, 505;
  30 243–46 (upd.)
Infoseek Corporation, **27** 517; **30** 490
InfoSoft International, Inc. *see* Inso
  Corporation.
Infostrada S.p.A., **38** 300
Infosys Technologies Ltd., 38 240–43
Infotech Enterprises, Ltd., **33** 45
Infotechnology Inc., **25** 507–08
Infotel, Inc., **52** 342
Inframetrics, Inc., **69** 171
Infun, S.A., **23** 269
ING Australia Limited, **52** 35, 39
ING, B.V., **14** 45, 47; **69** 246, 248
Ing. C. Olivetti & C., S.p.A., III
  144–46 *see also* Olivetti S.p.A
ING Groep N.V., **63** 15
Ingalls Quinn and Johnson, **9** 135
Ingalls Shipbuilding, Inc., 12 28,
  271–73; 36 78–79; **41** 42
Ingear, **10** 216
Ingefico, S.A., **52** 301
Ingenico—Compagnie Industrielle et
  Financière d'Ingénierie, 46 250–52
Ingenious Designs Inc., **47** 420
Ingersoll-Rand Company, III 473,
  525–27; 10 262; **13** 27, 523; **15** 187,
  223–26 (upd.); 22 542; **33** 168; **34**
  46; **55 218–22 (upd.)**
Ingka Holding B.V. *see* IKEA
  International A/S.
Ingleby Enterprises Inc. *see* Caribiner
  International, Inc.
Inglenook Vineyards, **13** 134; **34** 89
Ingles Markets, Inc., 20 305–08
Inglis Ltd. *see* Whirlpool Corporation.
Ingram Book Group, **30** 70
Ingram Industries, Inc., 11 193–95; 49
  217–20 (upd.) *see also* Ingram Micro
  Inc.
Ingram Micro Inc., 24 29; **52 178–81**
AB Ingredients, **II** 466
Ingredients Technology Corp., **9** 154
Ingres Corporation, **9** 36–37; **25** 87
Ingwerson and Co., **II** 356
INH *see* Instituto Nacional de
  Hidrocarboros.
Inha Works Ltd., **33** 164
INI *see* Instituto Nacional de Industria.
Initial Electronics, **64** 198
Initial Security, 64 196–98
Initial Towel Supply *see* Rentokil Initial
  Plc.
Inktomi Corporation, 41 98; **45 200–04**
Inland Container Corporation, 8
  267–69
Inland Motors Corporation, **18** 291
Inland Paperboard and Packaging, Inc., **31**
  438
Inland Pollution Control, **9** 110

Inland Steel Industries, Inc., IV 113–16;
  19 216–20 (upd.)
Inland Valley, **23** 321
Inmac, Inc., **16** 373
Inmobiliaria e Inversiones Aconcagua S.A.,
  71 143
Inmos Ltd., **11** 307; **29** 323
Inmotel Inversiones, **71** 338
InnCOGEN Limited, **35** 480
The Inner-Tec Group, **64** 198
InnerCity Foods Joint Venture Company,
  16 97
Inno-BM, **26** 158, 161
Inno-France *see* Societe des Grandes
  Entreprises de Distribution,
  Inno-France.
Innova International Corporation, **26** 333
Innovacom, **25** 96
Innovation, **26** 158
Innovative Marketing Systems *see*
  Bloomberg L.P.
Innovative Pork Concepts, **7** 82
Innovative Products & Peripherals
  Corporation, **14** 379
Innovative Software Inc., **10** 362
Innovative Sports Systems, Inc., **15** 396
Innovative Valve Technologies Inc., **33**
  167
Innovex Ltd. *see* Quintiles Transnational
  Corporation.
Inovoject do Brasil Ltda., **72** 108
Inpaco, **16** 340
Inpacsa, **19** 226
Inprise/Borland Corporation, **33** 115; **76**
  123–24
Input/Output, Inc., 73 184–87
INS *see* International News Service.
Insa, **55** 189
Insalaco Markets Inc., **13** 394
Inserra Supermarkets, 25 234–36
Insight Enterprises, Inc., 18 259–61
Insight Marques SARL IMS SA, **48** 224
Insignia Financial Group, Inc. *see* CB
  Richard Ellis Group, Inc.
Insilco Corporation, 16 281–83
Insley Manufacturing Co., **8** 545
Inso Corporation, 26 215–19; 36 273
Inspiration Resources Corporation, **12**
  260; **13** 502–03
Inspirations PLC, **22** 129
Insta-Care Holdings Inc., **16** 59
Insta-Care Pharmacy Services, **9** 186
Instant Auto Insurance, **33** 3, 5
Instant Interiors Corporation, **26** 102
Instapak Corporation, **14** 429
Instinet Corporation, 34 225–27; 48
  227–28
Institute de Development Industriel, **19**
  87
Institute for Professional Development, **24**
  40
Institute for Scientific Information, **8** 525,
  528
Institution Food House *see* Alex Lee Inc.
Institutional Financing Services, **23** 491
Instituto Bancario San Paolo di Torino, **50**
  407

M

Messner, Vetere, Berger, Carey, Schmetterer, **13** 204
Mesta Machine Co., **22** 415
Mestek, Inc., 10 411–13
Met Food Corp. *see* White Rose Food Corp.
Met-Mex Penoles *see* Industrias Penoles, S.A. de C.V.
META Group, Inc., **37** 147
Metaframe Corp., **25** 312
Metal Box plc, I 604–06 *see also* Novar plc.
Metal-Cal *see* Avery Dennison Corporation.
Metal Casting Technology, Inc., **23** 267, 269
Metal Office Furniture Company, **7** 493
AB Metal Pty Ltd, **62** 331
Metalcorp Ltd, **62** 331
Metales y Contactos, **29** 461–62
Metaleurop S.A., 21 368–71
MetalExchange, **26** 530
Metall Mining Corp., **27** 456
Metallgesellschaft AG, IV 139–42; 16 361–66 (upd.)
MetalOptics Inc., **19** 212
Metalúrgica Gerdau *see* Gerdau S.A.
Metalurgica Mexicana Penoles, S.A. *see* Industrias Penoles, S.A. de C.V.
Metaphase Technology, Inc., **10** 257
Metatec International, Inc., 47 245–48
Metcalf & Eddy Companies, Inc., **6** 441; **32** 52
Metcash Trading Ltd., 58 226–28
Meteor Film Productions, **23** 391
Meteor Industries Inc., 33 295–97
Methane Development Corporation, **6** 457
Methanex Corporation, 12 365; 19 155–56; 40 316–19
Methode Electronics, Inc., 13 344–46
MetLife *see* Metropolitan Life Insurance Company.
MetMor Financial, Inc., **III** 293; **52** 239–40
Meto AG, **39** 79
MetPath, Inc., **III** 684; **26** 390
Metra Corporation *see* Wärtsilä Corporation.
Metra Steel, **19** 381
Metragaz, **69** 191
Metrastock Ltd., **34** 5
Metric Constructors, Inc., **16** 286
Metric Systems Corporation, **18** 513; **44** 420
Metris Companies Inc., 56 224–27
Metro AG, 23 311; 50 335–39
Metro Distributors Inc., **14** 545
Metro-Goldwyn-Mayer Inc., 25 326–30 (upd.)
Metro Holding AG, **38** 266
Métro Inc., 77 271–275
Metro Information Services, Inc., 36 332–34
Metro International SA, **36** 335
Metro-Mark Integrated Systems Inc., **11** 469

Metro-North Commuter Railroad Company, **35** 292
Metro Pacific, **18** 180, 182
Metro-Richelieu Inc., **II** 653
Metro Southwest Construction *see* CRSS Inc.
Metro Support Services, Inc., **48** 171
Metrocall, Inc., 18 77; 39 25; 41 265–68
Metrol Security Services, Inc., **32** 373
Metroland Printing, Publishing and Distributing Ltd., **29** 471
Metromail Corp., **IV** 661; **18** 170; **38** 370
Metromedia Companies, 7 91, 335–37; 14 298–300
Metromedia Company, 61 210–14 (upd.)
Metronic AG, **64** 226
Metroplex, LLC, **51** 206
Métropole Télévision S.A., 76 272–74 (upd.)
Metropolis Intercom, **67** 137–38
Metropolitan Baseball Club Inc., 39 272–75
Metropolitan Broadcasting Corporation, **7** 335
Metropolitan Clothing Co., **19** 362
Metropolitan Distributors, **9** 283
Metropolitan Edison Company, **27** 182
Metropolitan Financial Corporation, 12 165; 13 347–49
Metropolitan Furniture Leasing, **14** 4
Metropolitan Life Insurance Company, III 290–94; 52 235–41 (upd.)
The Metropolitan Museum of Art, 55 267–70
Metropolitan Opera Association, Inc., 40 320–23
Metropolitan Reference Laboratories Inc., **26** 391
Metropolitan Tobacco Co., **15** 138
Metropolitan Transportation Authority, 35 290–92
MetroRed, **57** 67, 69
Metrostar Management, **59** 199
METSA, Inc., **15** 363
Metsä-Serla Oy, IV 314–16 *see also* M-real Oyj.
Metsec plc, **57** 402
Metso Corporation, 30 321–25 (upd.)
Mettler-Toledo International Inc., 30 326–28
Mettler United States Inc., **9** 441
Metwest, **26** 391
Metz Baking Company, **36** 164
Metzdorf Advertising Agency, **30** 80
Metzeler Kautschuk, **15** 354
Mexican Metal Co. *see* Industrias Penoles, S.A. de C.V.
Mexican Restaurants, Inc., 41 269–71
Meyer Brothers Drug Company, **16** 212
Meyer Corporation, **27** 288
Meyerland Company, **19** 366
Meyers Motor Supply, **26** 347
Meyers Parking, **18** 104
The Meyne Company, **55** 74
Meyr Melnhof Karton AG, **41** 325–27

M4 Data (Holdings) Ltd., **62** 293
M40 Trains Ltd., **51** 173
MFS Communications Company, Inc., 11 301–03; 14 253; 27 301, 307
MG&E *see* Madison Gas & Electric.
MG Holdings *see* Mayflower Group Inc.
MG Ltd., **IV** 141
MGD Graphics Systems *see* Goss Holdings, Inc.
MGIC Investment Corp., 45 320; 52 242–44
MGM *see* McKesson General Medical.
MGM Grand Inc., 17 316–19
MGM Mirage *see* Mirage Resorts, Incorporated.
MGM Studios, **50** 125
MGM/UA Communications Company, II 146–50 *see also* Metro-Goldwyn-Mayer Inc.
MGN *see* Mirror Group Newspapers Ltd.
MGT Services Inc. *see* The Midland Company.
MH Alshaya Group, **28** 96
MH Media Monitoring Limited, **26** 270
MHI Group, Inc., **13** 356; **16** 344
MHS Holding Corp., **26** 101
MHT *see* Manufacturers Hanover Trust Co.
MI *see* Masco Corporation.
MI S.A., **66** 244
Mi-Tech Steel Inc., **63** 359–60
Miami Computer Supply Corporation *see* MCSi, Inc.
Miami Power Corporation *see* Cincinnati Gas & Electric Company.
Miami Subs Corp., **29** 342, 344
Micamold Electronics Manufacturing Corporation, **10** 319
Mich-Wis *see* Michigan Wisconsin Pipe Line.
Michael Anthony Jewelers, Inc., 24 334–36
Michael Baker Corporation, 14 333–35; 51 245–48 (upd.)
MICHAEL Business Systems Plc, **10** 257
Michael C. Fina Co., Inc., 52 245–47
Michael Foods, Inc., 25 331–34
Michael Joseph, **IV** 659
Michael Page International plc, 45 272–74; 52 317–18
Michael's Fair-Mart Food Stores, Inc., **19** 479
Michaels Stores, Inc., 17 320–22; 71 226–30 (upd.)
MichCon *see* MCN Corporation.
Michelin *see* Compagnie Générale des Établissements Michelin.
Michie Co., **33** 264–65
Michigan Automotive Compressor, Inc., **III** 638–39
Michigan Automotive Research Corporation, **23** 183
Michigan Bell Telephone Co., 14 336–38; 18 30
Michigan Carpet Sweeper Company, **9** 70
Michigan Consolidated Gas Company *see* MCN Corporation.

Miller Brewing Company, **I** 269–70; **12** 337–39 (**upd.**) *see also* SABMiller plc.

Miller Companies, **17** 182

Miller Container Corporation, **8** 102

Miller Exploration Company *see* Edge Petroleum Corporation.

Miller Freeman, Inc., **IV** 687; **27** 362; **28** 501, 504

Miller Group Ltd., **22** 282

Miller Industries, Inc., 26 293–95

Miller, Mason and Dickenson, **III** 204–05

Miller-Meteor Company *see* Accubuilt, Inc.

Miller, Morris & Brooker (Holdings) Ltd. *see* Gibbs and Dandy plc.

Miller Plant Farms, Inc., **51** 61

Miller Publishing Group, LLC, 57 242–44

Miller, Tabak, Hirsch & Co., **13** 394; **28** 164

Millet, **39** 250

Millet's Leisure *see* Sears plc.

Millicom, **11** 547; **18** 254

Milliken & Co., V 366–68; **17** 327–30 (**upd.**); **29** 246

Milliken, Tomlinson Co., **II** 682

Milliman USA, 66 223–26

Millipore Corporation, 25 339–43

Mills Clothing, Inc. *see* The Buckle, Inc.

The Mills Corporation, 77 280–283

Millway Foods, **25** 85

Milne & Craighead, **48** 113

Milne Fruit Products, Inc., **25** 366

Milnot Company, 46 289–91; **51** 47

Milpark Drilling Fluids, Inc., **63** 306

Milsco Manufacturing Co., **23** 299, 300

Milton Bradley Company, 21 372–75

Milton Light & Power Company, **12** 45

Milton Roy Co., **8** 135

Milupa S.A., **37** 341

Milwaukee Brewers Baseball Club, 37 247–49

Milwaukee Cheese Co. Inc., **25** 517

Milwaukee Electric Railway and Light Company, **6** 601–02, 604–05

Milwaukee Electric Tool, **28** 40

MIM Holdings, **73** 392

Mimi's Cafés *see* SWH Corporation.

Minatome, **IV** 560

Mindpearl, **48** 381

Mindport, **31** 329

Mindset Corp., **42** 424–25

Mindspring Enterprises, Inc., **36** 168

Mine Safety Appliances Company, 31 333–35

The Miner Group International, 22 356–58

Minera Loma Blanca S.A., **56** 127

Mineral Point Public Service Company, **6** 604

Minerales y Metales, S.A. *see* Industrias Penoles, S.A. de C.V.

Minerals & Metals Trading Corporation of India Ltd., IV 143–44

Minerals and Resources Corporation Limited *see* Minorco.

Minerals Technologies Inc., 11 310–12; **52** 248–51 (**upd.**)

Minerec Corporation, **9** 363

Minerva SA, **72** 289

Minerve, **6** 208

Minet Group, **III** 357; **22** 494–95

MiniScribe, Inc., **10** 404

Minitel, **21** 233

Minivator Ltd., **11** 486

Minneapolis Children's Medical Center, **54** 65

Minneapolis-Honeywell Regulator Co., **8** 21; **22** 427

Minneapolis Steel and Machinery Company, **21** 502

Minnehoma Insurance Company, **58** 260

Minnesota Brewing Company *see* MBC Holding Company.

Minnesota Linseed Oil Co., **8** 552

Minnesota Mining & Manufacturing Company, I 499–501; **8** 369–71 (**upd.**); **26 296–99** (**upd.**) *see also* 3M Company.

Minnesota Paints, **8** 552–53

Minnesota Power & Light Company, 11 313–16

Minnesota Power, Inc., 34 286–91 (**upd.**)

Minnesota Sugar Company, **11** 13

Minnetonka Corp., **III** 25; **22** 122–23

Minntech Corporation, 22 359–61

Minn-Dak Farmers Cooperative, **32** 29

Minolta Co., Ltd., III 574–76; **18** 93, 186, **339–42** (**upd.**); **43 281–85** (**upd.**)

Minorco, **IV** 97; **16** 28, 293

Minstar Inc., **11** 397; **15** 49; **45** 174

Minton China, **38** 401

The Minute Maid Company, 28 271–74, 473; **32** 116

Minuteman International Inc., 46 292–95

Minyard Food Stores, Inc., 33 304–07

Mippon Paper, **21** 546; **50** 58

Miquel y Costas Miquel S.A., 68 256–58

Miracle Food Mart, **16** 247, 249–50

Miracle-Gro Products, Inc., **22** 474

Miraflores Designs Inc., **18** 216

Mirage Resorts, Incorporated, 6 209–12; **28 275–79** (**upd.**)

Miraglia Inc., **57** 139

Miramax Film Corporation, 64 282–85

Mirant, **39** 54, 57

MIRAX Corporation *see* JSP Corporation.

Mircali Asset Management, **III** 340

Mircor Inc., **12** 413

Mirror Group Newspapers plc, 7 341–43; **23 348–51** (**upd.**); **49** 408; **61** 130

Misceramic Tile, Inc., **14** 42

Misr Airwork *see* AirEgypt.

Misr Bank of Cairo, **27** 132

Misrair *see* AirEgypt.

Miss Erika, Inc., **27** 346, 348

Miss Selfridge *see* Sears plc.

Misset Publishers, **IV** 611

Mission Group *see* SCEcorp.

Mission Jewelers, **30** 408

Mission Valley Fabrics, **57** 285

Mississippi Chemical Corporation, 8 183; **27** 316; **39 280–83**

Mississippi Gas Company, **6** 577

Mississippi Power Company, **38** 446–47

Mississippi River Corporation, **10** 44

Mississippi River Recycling, **31** 47, 49

Mississippi Valley Title Insurance Company, **58** 259–60

Missoula Bancshares, Inc., **35** 198–99

Missouri Book Co., **10** 136

Missouri Fur Company, **25** 220

Missouri Gaming Company, **21** 39

Missouri Gas & Electric Service Company, **6** 593

Missouri Pacific Railroad, **10** 43–44

Missouri Public Service Company *see* UtiliCorp United Inc.

Missouri Utilities Company, **6** 580

Mist Assist, Inc. *see* Ballard Medical Products.

Mistik Beverages, **18** 71

Misys PLC, 45 279–81; **46 296–99**

Mitchel & King Skates Ltd., **17** 244

Mitchell Energy and Development Corporation, 7 344–46; **61** 75

Mitchell Home Savings and Loan, **13** 347

Mitchell International, **8** 526

Mitchells & Butlers PLC, 59 296–99

MiTek Industries Inc., **IV** 259

MiTek Wood Products, **IV** 305

Mitel Corporation, 15 131–32; **18** 343–46

MitNer Group, **7** 377

MITRE Corporation, 26 300–02

Mitre Sport U.K., **17** 204–05

MITROPA AG, 37 250–53

Mitsubishi Aircraft Co., **9** 349; **11** 164

Mitsubishi Bank, Ltd., II 321–22 *see also* Bank of Tokyo-Mitsubishi Ltd.

Mitsubishi Chemical Corporation, I 363–64; **56 236–38** (**upd.**)

Mitsubishi Corporation, I 502–04; **12** 340–43 (**upd.**)

Mitsubishi Electric Corporation, II 57–59; **44 283–87** (**upd.**)

Mitsubishi Estate Company, Limited, IV 713–14; **61 215–18** (**upd.**)

Mitsubishi Foods, **24** 114

Mitsubishi Group, **7** 377; **21** 390

Mitsubishi Heavy Industries, Ltd., III 577–79; **7 347–50** (**upd.**); **40 324–28** (**upd.**)

Mitsubishi International Corp., **16** 462

Mitsubishi Kasei Corp., **14** 535

Mitsubishi Kasei Vinyl Company, **49** 5

Mitsubishi Materials Corporation, III 712–13; **38** 463

Mitsubishi Motors Corporation, 9 349–51; **23 352–55** (**upd.**); **57** 245–49 (**upd.**)

Mitsubishi Oil Co., Ltd., IV 460–62

Mitsubishi Rayon Co. Ltd., V 369–71

Mitsubishi Shipbuilding Co. Ltd., **9** 349

Mitsubishi Trust & Banking Corporation, II 323–24

Mitsui & Co., Ltd., I 505–08; **28** 280–85 (**upd.**)

National Rifle Association of America, **37** 265–68

National Rubber Machinery Corporation, **8** 298

National Sanitary Supply Co., **16** 386–87

National Satellite Paging, **18** 348

National School Studios, **7** 255; **25** 252

National Science Foundation, **9** 266

National Sea Products Ltd., **14** 339–41

National Security Containers LLC, **58** 238

National Semiconductor Corporation, **II** 63–65; **6** 261–63; **26** 327–30 (upd.); **69** 267–71 (upd.)

National Service Industries, Inc., **11** 336–38; **54** 251–55 (upd.)

National Shoe Products Corp., **16** 17

National Slicing Machine Company, **19** 359

National-Southwire Aluminum Company, **11** 38; **12** 353

National Stamping & Electric Works, **12** 159

National Standard Co., **IV** 137; **13** 369–71

National Starch and Chemical Company, **32** 256–57; **49** 268–70

National Steel and Shipbuilding Company, **7** 356

National Steel Corporation, **IV** 163, 236–37, 572; **V** 152–53; **8** 346, 479–80; **12** 352–54; **26** 527–29 *see also* FoxMeyer Health Corporation.

National Student Marketing Corporation, **10** 385–86

National System Company, **9** 41; **11** 469

National Tea, **II** 631–32

National Technical Laboratories, **14** 52

National TechTeam, Inc., **41** 280–83

National Telecommunications of Austin, **8** 311

National Telephone and Telegraph Corporation *see* British Columbia Telephone Company.

National Telephone Co., **7** 332, 508

National Thoroughbred Racing Association, **58** 244–47

National Trading Manufacturing, Inc., **22** 213

National Transcommunications Ltd. *see* NTL Inc.

National Union Electric Corporation, **12** 159

National Utilities & Industries Corporation, **9** 363

National Westminster Bank PLC, **II** 333–35; **13** 206

National Wine & Spirits, Inc., **49** 271–74

Nationale-Nederlanden N.V., **III** 308–11; **50** 11

Nationar, **9** 174

NationsBank Corporation, **10** 425–27 *see also* Bank of America Corporation

NationsRent, **28** 388

Nationwide Cellular Service, Inc., **27** 305

Nationwide Credit, **11** 112

Nationwide Group, **25** 155

Nationwide Income Tax Service, **9** 326

Nationwide Logistics Corp., **14** 504

Nationwide Mutual Insurance Co., **26** 488

NATIOVIE, **II** 234

Native Plants, **III** 43

NATM Buying Corporation, **10** 9, 468

Natomas Company, **7** 309; **11** 271

Natref *see* National Petroleum Refiners of South Africa.

Natrol, Inc., **49** 275–78

Natronag, **IV** 325

NatSteel Electronics Ltd., **48** 369

NatTeknik, **26** 333

Natudryl Manufacturing Company, **10** 271

Natura Cosméticos S.A., **75** 268–71

Natural Alternatives International, Inc., **49** 279–82

Natural Gas Clearinghouse *see* NGC Corporation.

Natural Gas Corp., **19** 155

Natural Gas Pipeline Company, **6** 530, 543; **7** 344–45

Natural Gas Service of Arizona, **19** 411

Natural Ovens Bakery, Inc., **72** 234–36

Natural Selection Foods, **54** 256–58

Natural Wonders Inc., **14** 342–44

NaturaLife International, **26** 470

Naturalizer *see* Brown Shoe Company, Inc.

The Nature Company, **10** 215–16; **14** 343; **26** 439; **27** 429; **28** 306

The Nature Conservancy, **26** 323; **28** 305–07, 422

Nature's Sunshine Products, Inc., **15** 317–19; **26** 470; **27** 353; **33** 145

Nature's Way Products Inc., **26** 315

Naturin GmbH *see* Viscofan S.A.

Naturipe Berry Growers, **62** 154

Natuzzi Group *see* Industrie Natuzzi S.p.A.

NatWest Bancorp, **38** 393

NatWest Bank *see* National Westminster Bank PLC.

Naugles, **7** 506

Nautica Enterprises, Inc., **18** 357–60; **44** 302–06 (upd.)

Nautilus International, Inc., **13** 532; **25** 40; **30** 161

Navaho Freight Line, **16** 41

Navajo LTL, Inc., **57** 277

Navajo Refining Company, **12** 240

Navajo Shippers, Inc., **42** 364

Navan Resources, **38** 231

Navarre Corporation, **22** 536; **24** 348–51

Navigant International, Inc., **47** 263–66

Navigation Mixte, **III** 348

Navire Cargo Gear, **27** 269

Navisant, Inc., **49** 424

Navistar International Corporation, **I** 180–82; **10** 428–30 (upd.) *see also* International Harvester Co.

NAVTEQ Corporation, **69** 272–75

Navy Exchange Service Command, **31** 342–45

Navy Federal Credit Union, **33** 315–17

Naxon Utilities Corp., **19** 359

Naylor, Hutchinson, Vickers & Company *see* Vickers PLC.

NBC *see* National Broadcasting Company, Inc.

NBC Bankshares, Inc., **21** 524

NBC/Computer Services Corporation, **15** 163

NBD Bancorp, Inc., **11** 339–41 *see also* Bank One Corporation.

NBGS International, Inc., **73** 231–33

NBSC Corporation *see* National Bank of South Carolina.

NBTY, Inc., **31** 346–48

NCA Corporation, **9** 36, 57, 171

NCB *see* National City Bank of New York.

NCC Industries, Inc., **59** 267

NCC L.P., **15** 139

NCH Corporation, **8** 385–87

nChip, **38** 187–88

NCL Holdings *see* Genting Bhd.

NCNB Corporation, **II** 336–37; **12** 519; **26** 453

NCO Group, Inc., **42** 258–60

NCR Corporation, **III** 150–53; **6** 264–68 (upd.); **30** 336–41 (upd.)

NCS *see* Norstan, Inc.

NCS Healthcare Inc., **67** 262

NCTI (Noise Cancellation Technologies Inc.), **19** 483–84

nCube Corp., **14** 15; **22** 293

ND Marston, **III** 593

NDB *see* National Discount Brokers Group, Inc.

NDL *see* Norddeutscher Lloyd.

NE Chemcat Corporation, **72** 118

NEA *see* Newspaper Enterprise Association.

Nearly Me, **25** 313

Neatherlin Homes Inc., **22** 547

Nebraska Bell Company, **14** 311

Nebraska Book Company, Inc., **65** 257–59

Nebraska Cellular Telephone Company, **14** 312

Nebraska Furniture Mart, **III** 214–15; **18** 60–61, 63

Nebraska Light & Power Company, **6** 580

Nebraska Power Company, **25** 89

Nebraska Public Power District, **29** 351–54

NEBS *see* New England Business Services, Inc.

NEC Corporation, **II** 66–68; **21** 388–91 (upd.); **57** 261–67 (upd.)

Neckermann Versand AG *see* Karstadt AG.

Nedcor, **61** 270–71

Nederland Line *see* Stoomvaart Maatschappij Nederland.

Nederlander Organization, **24** 439

Nederlands Talen Institut, **13** 544

Nederlandsche Electriciteits Maatschappij *see* N.E.M.

Nederlandsche Handel Maatschappij, **26** 242

Nederlandsche Heidenmaatschappij *see* Arcadis NV.

Ocular Sciences, Inc., 65 273–75
Oculinum, Inc., **10** 48
Odakyu Electric Railway Co., Ltd., V
487–89; 68 278–81 **(upd.)**
Odd Job Trading Corp., **29** 311–12
Odda Smelteverk A/S, **25** 82
Odebrecht S.A., 73 242–44
Odeco Drilling, Inc., **7** 362–64; **11** 522;
12 318; **32** 338, 340
Odegard Outdoor Advertising, L.L.C., **27**
280
Odetics Inc., 14 357–59
Odhams Press Ltd., **IV** 259, 666–67; **7**
244, 342; **17** 397–98
ODL, Inc., 55 290–92
ODM, **26** 490
ODME *see* Toolex International N.V.
Odwalla, Inc., 31 349–51
Odyssey Holdings, Inc., **18** 376
Odyssey Partners Group, **II** 679; **V** 135;
12 55; **13** 94; **17** 137; **28** 218
Odyssey Press, **13** 560
Odyssey Publications Inc., **48** 99
Odyssey Re Group, **57** 136–37
OEA *see* Autoliv, Inc.
OEC Medical Systems, Inc., 27 354–56
Oelwerken Julius Schindler GmbH, **7** 141
OEN Connectors, **19** 166
OENEO S.A., 74 212–15 **(upd.)**
Oetker Gruppe, **75** 332, 344
Ofek Securities and Investments Ltd., **60**
50
Off Wall Street Consulting Group, **42**
313
Office Depot, Inc., 8 404–05; **23**
363–65 **(upd.); 65** 276–80 **(upd.)**
Office Electronics, Inc., **65** 371
Office Mart Holdings Corporation, **10**
498
Office Systems Inc., **15** 407
The Office Works, Inc., **13** 277; **25** 500
OfficeMax Inc., 15 329–31; **43** 291–95
(upd.)
OfficeTiger, LLC, 75 294–96
Official Airline Guides, Inc., **IV** 643; **7**
312, 343; **17** 399
Officine Alfieri Maserati S.p.A., 11 104;
13 28, 376–78
Offset Gerhard Kaiser GmbH, **IV** 325
The Offshore Company, **6** 577; **37** 243
Offshore Food Services Inc., **I** 514
Offshore Logistics, Inc., 37 287–89
Offshore Transportation Corporation, **11**
523
O'Gara Company, **57** 219
Ogden Corporation, I 512–14; **6**
151–53 *see also* Covanta Energy
Corporation.
Ogden Food Products, **7** 430
Ogden Gas Co., **6** 568
Ogden Ground Services, **39** 240, 242
Ogilvy & Mather Worldwide, **22** 200; **71**
158–59
Ogilvy Group Inc., I 25–27, 31, 37,
244; **9** 180 *see also* WPP Group.
Oglebay Norton Company, 17 355–58
Oglethorpe Power Corporation, 6
537–38

Oh la la!, **14** 107
Ohbayashi Corporation, I 586–87
The Ohio Art Company, 14 360–62; **59**
317–20 **(upd.)**
Ohio Ball Bearing *see* Bearings Inc.
Ohio Barge Lines, Inc., **11** 194
Ohio Bell Telephone Company, 14
363–65; **18** 30
Ohio Boxboard Company, **12** 376
Ohio Brass Co., **II** 2
Ohio Casualty Corp., 11 369–70
Ohio Coatings Company, **58** 363
Ohio Crankshaft Co. *see* Park-Ohio
Industries Inc.
Ohio Edison Company, V 676–78
Ohio Farmers Insurance Company *see*
Westfield Group.
Ohio Mattress Co., **12** 438–39
Ohio Pizza Enterprises, Inc., **7** 152
Ohio-Sealy Mattress Mfg. Co., **12** 438–39
Ohio Valley Electric Corporation, **6** 517
Ohio Ware Basket Company, **12** 319
Ohlmeyer Communications, **I** 275; **26**
305
OHM Corp., **17** 553
Ohmeda *see* BOC Group plc.
Ohmite Manufacturing Co., **13** 397
OIAG *see* Osterreichische Industrieholding
AG.
Oil and Natural Gas Commission, IV
483–84
Oil and Solvent Process Company, **9** 109
Oil-Dri Corporation of America, 20
396–99
Oil Drilling, Incorporated, **7** 344
Oil Dynamics Inc., **43** 178
Oil Equipment Manufacturing Company,
16 8
Oil Shale Corp., **7** 537
Oil States International, Inc., 77
314–317
Oilfield Industrial Lines Inc., **I** 477
The Oilgear Company, 74 216–18
Oilinvest *see* National Oil Corporation.
Oji Paper Co., Ltd., IV 320–22; **57**
272–75 **(upd.)**
Ojibway Press, **57** 13
OJSC Wimm-Bill-Dann Foods, 48
436–39
OK Turbines, Inc., **22** 311
Okay, **68** 143
O'Keefe Marketing, **23** 102
Oki Electric Industry Company,
Limited, II 72–74; **15** 125; **21** 390
Okidata, **9** 57; **18** 435
Oklahoma Airmotive, **8** 349
Oklahoma Entertainment, Inc., **9** 74
Oklahoma Gas and Electric Company,
6 539–40; **7** 409–11
Oklahoma Publishing Company, **11**
152–53; **30** 84
Okuma Holdings Inc., 74 219–21
Okura & Co., Ltd., IV 167–68
Olan Mills, Inc., 62 254–56
Oland & Sons Limited, **25** 281
Olathe Manufacturing, **26** 494
OLC *see* Orient Leasing Co., Ltd.
Old America Stores, Inc., 17 359–61

Old Chicago *see* Rock Bottom
Restaurants, Inc.
Old Colony Envelope Co., **32** 345–46
Old Country Buffet Restaurant Co.
(OCB) *see* Buffets, Inc.
Old Dominion Freight Line, Inc., 57
276–79
Old Dominion Power Company, **6** 513,
515
Old El Paso, **14** 212; **24** 140–41
Old Harbor Candles, **18** 68
Old Kent Financial Corp., 11 371–72
Old Mutual PLC, IV 535; **61** 270–72
Old National Bancorp, 14 529; **15**
332–34
Old Navy, Inc., 70 210–12
Old 97 Company, **60** 287
Old Orchard Brands, LLC, 73 245–47
Old Quaker Paint Company, **13** 471
Old Republic International
Corporation, 11 373–75; **58** 258–61
(upd.)
Old Spaghetti Factory International
Inc., 24 364–66
Old Stone Trust Company, **13** 468
Old Town Canoe Company, 74 222–24
Oldach Window Corp., **19** 446
Oldcastle, Inc., **60** 77; **64** 98
Oldover Corp., **23** 225
Ole's Innovative Sports *see* Rollerblade,
Inc.
Olean Tile Co., **22** 170
Oleochim, **IV** 498–99
OLEX *see* Deutsche BP Aktiengesellschaft.
Olex Cables Ltd., **10** 445
Olin Corporation, I 379–81; **13** 379–81
(upd.); 78 270–274 **(upd.)**
Olinkraft, Inc., **11** 420; **16** 376
Olive Garden Italian Restaurants, **10** 322,
324; **16** 156–58; **19** 258; **35** 83
Oliver Rubber Company, **19** 454, 456
Olivetti S.p.A., 34 316–20 **(upd.); 38**
300; **63** 379
Olivine Industries, Inc., **II** 508; **11** 172;
36 255
Olmstead Products Co., **23** 82
OLN *see* Outdoor Life Network.
Olsten Corporation, 6 41–43; **29**
362–65 **(upd.); 49** 265 *see also* Adecco
S.A.
Olympia & York Developments Ltd., IV
720–21; **6** 478; **8** 327; **9** 390–92
(upd.); 30 108
Olympia Arenas, Inc., **7** 278–79; **24** 294
Olympia Brewing, **11** 50
Olympia Entertainment, **37** 207
Olympiaki, **III** 401
Olympic Courier Systems, Inc., **24** 126
Olympic Fastening Systems, **III** 722
Olympic Insurance Co., **26** 486
Olympic Packaging, **13** 443
Olympic Property Group LLC *see* Pope
Resources LP.
Olympic Resource Management LLC *see*
Pope Resources LP.
Olympus Communications L.P., **17** 7
Olympus Optical Company, Ltd., **15** 483
Olympus Partners, **65** 258

Olympus Sport *see* Sears plc.

Olympus Symbol, Inc., **15** 483

OM Group, Inc., 17 362–64; **78**
275–278 (upd.)

Omaha Public Power District, **29** 353

Omaha Steaks International Inc., 62
257–59

Omega Gas Company, **8** 349

Omega Group *see* MasterBrand Cabinets,
Inc.

Omega Protein Corporation, **25** 546

OmegaTech Inc. *see* Martek Biosciences
Corporation.

O'Melveny & Myers, 37 290–93

OMI Corporation, **IV** 34; **9** 111–12; **22**
275; **59** 321–23

Omnes, **17** 419

Omni ApS, **56** 338

Omni Construction Company, Inc., **8**
112–13

Omni Hotels Corp., 12 367–69

Omni-Pac, **12** 377

Omni Services, Inc., **51** 76

Omnibus Corporation, **9** 283

Omnicad Corporation, **48** 75

Omnicare, Inc., 13 49 307–10

Omnicom Group Inc., I 28–32; **22**
394–99 (upd.); **77** 318–325 (upd.)

Omnipoint Communications Inc., **18** 77

OmniSource Corporation, 14 366–67

OmniTech Consulting Group, **51** 99

Omnitel Pronto Italia SpA, **38** 300

OMNOVA Solutions Inc., 59 324–26

Omron Corporation, 28 331–35 (upd.);
53 46

Omron Tateisi Electronics Company, II
75–77

ÖMV Aktiengesellschaft, IV 485–87

On Assignment, Inc., 20 400–02

On Command Video Corp., **23** 135

On Cue, **9** 360

On-Line Systems *see* Sierra On-Line Inc.

Onan Corporation, **8** 72

Onbancorp Inc., **11** 110

Once Upon A Child, Inc., **18** 207–8

Ondulato Imolese, **IV** 296; **19** 226

1-800-FLOWERS, Inc., 26 344–46; **28**
137

1-800-GOT-JUNK? LLC, 74 225–27

1-800-Mattress *see* Dial-A-Mattress
Operating Corporation.

180s, L.L.C., 64 299–301

One For All, **39** 405

One Price Clothing Stores, Inc., 20
403–05

17187 Yukon Inc., **74** 234

One Stop Trade Building Centre Ltd. *see*
Gibbs and Dandy plc.

O'Neal, Jones & Feldman Inc., **11** 142

OneBeacon Insurance Group LLC, **48**
431

Oneida Bank & Trust Company, **9** 229

Oneida County Creameries Co., **7** 202

Oneida Gas Company, **9** 554

Oneida Ltd., 7 406–08; **31** 352–55
(upd.)

ONEOK Inc., 7 409–12

Onex Corporation, 16 395–97; **65**
281–85 (upd.)

OneZero Media, Inc., **31** 240

Ong First Pte Ltd., **76** 372, 374

Onion, Inc., 69 282–84

Onitsuka Co., Ltd., **57** 52

Online Financial Communication
Systems, **11** 112

Only One Dollar, Inc. *see* Dollar Tree
Stores, Inc.

Onoda Cement Co., Ltd., III 717–19 *see
also* Taiheiyo Cement Corporation.

Onomichi, **25** 469

OnResponse.com, Inc., **49** 433

Onsale Inc., **31** 177

Onstead Foods, **21** 501

OnTarget Inc., **38** 432

Ontario Hydro Services Company, 6
541–42; 9 461; **32** 368–71 (upd.)

Ontario Power Generation, **49** 65, 67

Ontario Teachers' Pension Plan, 61
273–75

OnTrack Data International, **57** 219

OnTrak Systems Inc., **31** 301

Onyx Acceptance Corporation, 59
327–29

Onyx Software Corporation, 53 252–55

O'okiep Copper Company, Ltd., **7**
385–86

Opel AG *see* Adam Opel AG.

Open *see* Groupe Open.

Open Board of Brokers, **9** 369

Open Cellular Systems, Inc., **41** 225–26

Open Market, Inc., **22** 522

OpenTV, Inc., **31** 330–31

OPENWAY SAS, **74** 143

Operadora de Bolsa Serfin *see* Grupo
Financiero Serfin, S.A.

Operation Smile, Inc., 75 297–99

Operon Technologies Inc., **39** 335

Opinion Research Corporation, 46
318–22

Opp and Micolas Mills, **15** 247–48

Oppenheimer *see* Ernest Oppenheimer
and Sons.

Oppenheimer & Co., Inc., **17** 137; **21**
235; **22** 405; **25** 450; **61** 50

The Oppenheimer Group, 76 295–98

Oppenheimer Wolff & Donnelly LLP,
71 262–64

Opryland USA, **11** 152–53; **25** 403; **36**
229

Opsware Inc., 49 311–14

Optel S.A., **17** 331; **71** 211

OPTi Computer, **9** 116

Opti-Ray, Inc., **12** 215

Optical Corporation *see* Excel Technology,
Inc.

Optical Radiation Corporation, **27** 57

Optilink Corporation, **12** 137

Optima Pharmacy Services, **17** 177

Option Care Inc., 48 307–10

Optische Werke G. Rodenstock, 44
319–23

OptiSystems Solutions Ltd., **55** 67

Opto-Electronics Corp., **15** 483

Optus Communications, **25** 102

Optus Vision, **17** 150

Opus Group, 34 321–23

Oracle Corporation, 6 272–74; **24**
367–71 (upd.); **67** 282–87 (upd.)

Orange *see* Wanadoo S.A.

Orange and Rockland Utilities, Inc., **45**
116, 120

Orange Glo International, 53 256–59

Orange Julius of America, **10** 371, 373;
39 232, 235

Orange Line Bus Company, **6** 604

Orange PLC, **24** 89; **38** 300

Orange Shipbuilding Company, Inc., **58**
70

OraSure Technologies, Inc., 75 300–03

Orb Books *see* Tom Doherty Associates
Inc.

Orb Estates, **54** 366, 368

ORBIS Corporation, **59** 289

Orbis Entertainment Co., **20** 6

Orbis Graphic Arts *see* Anaheim Imaging.

Orbital Engine Corporation Ltd., **17** 24

Orbital Sciences Corporation, 22
400–03

Orbitz, Inc., 61 276–78

Orbotech Ltd., 75 304–06

Orchard Supply Hardware Stores
Corporation, 17 365–67

Orchid Biosciences Inc., **57** 309, 311

Orcofi, **III** 48

OrderTrust LLP, **26** 440

Ore-Ida Foods Inc., 13 382–83; **78**
279–282 (upd.)

Orebehoved Fanerfabrik, **25** 464

Oregon Ale and Beer Company, **18** 72;
50 112

Oregon Chai, Inc., 49 315–17

Oregon Coin Company, **74** 14

Oregon Craft & Floral Supply, **17** 322

Oregon Cutting Systems, **26** 119

Oregon Dental Service Health Plan,
Inc., 51 276–78

Oregon Freeze Dry, Inc., 74 228–30

Oregon Metallurgical Corporation, 20
406–08

Oregon Pacific and Eastern Railway, **13**
100

Oregon Steel Mills, Inc., 14 368–70; **19**
380

O'Reilly Automotive, Inc., 26 347–49;
78 283–287 (upd.)

Orenda Aerospace, **48** 274

The Organic and Natural Food Company,
74 384

Organic Valley (Coulee Region Organic
Produce Pool), 53 260–62

Organización Soriana, S.A. de C.V., 35
320–22

Organizacion Techint, **66** 293–95

Organon, **63** 141

ORI *see* Old Republic International
Corporation.

Orico Life Insurance Co., **48** 328

Oriel Foods, **II** 609

Orient, **21** 122

Orient Express Hotels Inc., **29** 429–30

Orient Leasing *see* Orix Corporation.

Orient Overseas, **18** 254

Oriental Brewery Co., Ltd., **21** 320

Oxirane Chemical Corporation, **64** 35
OXO International, **16** 234
Oxycal Laboratories Inc., **46** 466
OxyChem, **11** 160
Oxygen Business Solutions Pty Limited *see*
Carter Holt Harvey Ltd.
Oxygen Media Inc., **28** 175; **51** 220
Ozark Automotive Distributors, **26**
347–48
Ozark Utility Company, **6** 593; **50** 38
OZM *see* OneZero Media, Inc.

P

P&C Foods Inc., 8 409–11
P&C Groep N.V., **46** 344
P & F Industries, Inc., 45 327–29
P&F Technologies Ltd., **26** 363
P&G *see* Procter & Gamble Company.
P&L Coal Holdings Corporation, **45** 333
P & M Manufacturing Company, **8** 386
P & O *see* Peninsular & Oriental Steam
Navigation Company.
P.A. Bergner & Company, **9** 142; **15**
87–88
P.A. Geier Company *see* Royal Appliance
Manufacturing Company.
P.A.J.W. Corporation, **9** 111–12
P.A. Rentrop-Hubbert & Wagner
Fahrzeugausstattungen GmbH, **III** 582
P.C. Richard & Son Corp., 23 372–74
P.D. Associated Collieries Ltd., **31** 369
P.D. Kadi International, **I** 580
P.E.C. Israel Economic Corporation, **24**
429
P.F. Chang's China Bistro, Inc., 37
297–99
P.G. Realty, **III** 340
P.H. Glatfelter Company, 8 412–14; 30
349–52 (upd.)
P.Ink Press, **24** 430
P.R. Mallory, **9** 179
P.S.L. Food Market, Inc., **22** 549
P.T. Asurasi Tokio Marine Indonesia, **64**
280
P.T. Bridgeport Perkasa Machine Tools, **17**
54
P.T. Darya-Varia Laboratoria, **18** 180
P.T. Gaya Motor, **23** 290
P.T. GOLD Martindo, **70** 235
P.T. Indomobil Suzuki International, **59**
393, 397
P.T. Samick Indonesia, **56** 300
P.T. Satomo Indovyl Polymer, **70** 329
P.T. Unitex, **53** 344
P.V. Doyle Hotels Ltd., **64** 217
P.W. Huntington & Company, **11** 180
P.W.J. Surridge & Sons, Ltd., **43** 132
Paaco Automotive Group, **64** 20
Pabst Brewing Company, **I** 255; **10** 99;
18 502; **50** 114; **74** 146
Pac-Am Food Concepts, **10** 178; **38** 102
Pac-Fab, Inc., **18** 161
PAC Insurance Services, **12** 175; **27** 258
PACCAR Inc., I 185–86; 26 354–56
(upd.)
PacDun *see* Pacific Dunlop.
The Pace Consultants, Inc. *see* Jacobs
Engineering Group Inc.

PACE Entertainment Corp., **36** 423–24
Pace Express Pty. Ltd., **13** 20
Pace Foods Ltd. *see* Campbell Soup
Company.
Pace Management Service Corp., **21** 91
PACE Membership Warehouse, Inc. *see*
Kmart Corporation.
Pace Pharmaceuticals, **16** 439
Pacemaker Plastics, Inc., **7** 296
Pacer International, Inc., 54 274–76
Pacer Technology, 40 347–49
Pacer Tool and Mold, **17** 310
Pacific Advantage, **43** 253
Pacific Air Freight, Incorporated *see*
Airborne Freight Corp.
Pacific Air Transport, **9** 416
Pacific and European Telegraph Company,
25 99
Pacific Bell *see* SBC Communications.
Pacific Car & Foundry Company *see*
PACCAR Inc.
Pacific Coast Feather Company, 67 209,
294–96
Pacific Communication Sciences, **11** 57
Pacific Destination Services, **62** 276
Pacific Dunlop Limited, 10 444–46 *see*
also Ansell Ltd.
Pacific Electric Light Company, **6** 565; **50**
365
Pacific Enterprises, V 682–84; 12 477
see also Sempra Energy.
Pacific Finance Corp., **9** 536; **13** 529; **26**
486
Pacific Forest Products Ltd., **59** 162
Pacific Fur Company, **25** 220
Pacific Gamble Robinson, **9** 39
Pacific Gas and Electric Company, V
685–87 *see also* PG&E Corporation.
Pacific Glass Corp., **48** 42
Pacific Guardian Life Insurance Co., **III**
289
Pacific Home Furnishings, **14** 436
Pacific Indemnity Corp., **III** 220; **14** 108,
110; **16** 204
Pacific Integrated Healthcare, **53** 7
Pacific Lighting Corp. *see* Sempra Energy.
Pacific Linens, **13** 81–82
Pacific Link Communication, **18** 180
Pacific Lumber Company, **III** 254; **8**
348–50
Pacific Magazines and Printing, **7** 392
Pacific Mail Steamship Company *see* APL
Limited.
Pacific Media K.K., **18** 101
Pacific Monolithics Inc., **11** 520
Pacific National Insurance Co. *see* TIG
Holdings, Inc.
Pacific Natural Gas Corp., **9** 102
Pacific Northwest Laboratories, **10** 139
Pacific Northwest Pipeline Corporation, **9**
102–104, 540; **12** 144
Pacific Northwest Power Company, **6** 597
Pacific Petroleums Ltd., **9** 102
Pacific Plastics, Inc., **48** 334
Pacific Power & Light Company *see*
PacifiCorp.
Pacific Pride Bakeries, **19** 192
Pacific Publications, **72** 283–84

Pacific Recycling Co. Inc., **IV** 296; **19**
226; **23** 225
Pacific Resources Inc., **IV** 47; **22** 107
Pacific Sentinel Gold Corp., **27** 456
Pacific/Southern Wine & Spirits, **48** 392
Pacific Stock Exchange, **48** 226
Pacific Sunwear of California, Inc., 28
343–45; 47 425
Pacific Telecom, Inc., 6 325–28
Pacific Telesis Group, V 318–20 *see also*
SBC Communications.
Pacific Teletronics, Inc., **7** 15
Pacific Towboat *see* Puget Sound Tug and
Barge Company.
Pacific Trail Inc., **17** 462; **29** 293, 295–96
Pacific Western Extruded Plastics
Company *see* PW Eagle Inc.
Pacific Wine Co., **18** 71; **50** 112
PacifiCare Health Systems, Inc., 11
378–80
PacifiCorp, Inc., V 688–90; 7 376–78;
26 357–60 (upd.); 27 327, 483, 485;
32 372; **49** 363, 366
Package Products Company, Inc., **12** 150
Packaged Ice, Inc., **21** 338; **26** 449
Packaging Corporation of America, 12
376–78; 51 282–85 (upd.)
Packard Bell Electronics, Inc., 10 564;
11 413; **13 387–89**, 483; **21** 391; **23**
471; **57** 263
Packard Motor Co., **8** 74; **9** 17
Packerland Packing Company, **7** 199, 201
Pacolet Manufacturing Company, **17** 327
Pact, **50** 175
PacTel *see* Pacific Telesis Group.
Paddock Publications, Inc., 53 263–65
PAFS *see* Pacific Alaska Fuel Services.
Page, Bacon & Co., **12** 533
Page Boy Inc., **9** 320
Page Plus NV *see* Punch International
N.V.
PageAhead Software, **15** 492
Pageland Coca-Cola Bottling Works, **10**
222
PageMart Wireless, Inc., **18** 164, 166
Paging Network Inc., 11 381–83
Pagnossin S.p.A., 73 248–50
Pagoda Trading Company, Inc. *see* Brown
Shoe Company, Inc.
Paid Prescriptions, **9** 346
Paige Publications, **18** 66
PaineWebber Group Inc., II 444–46; 22
404–07 (upd.)
Painter Carpet Mills, **13** 169
PairGain Technologies, **36** 299
Paisley Products, **32** 255
La Paix, **III** 273
Pak-a-Sak, **II** 661
Pak Mail Centers, **18** 316
Pak Sak Industries, **17** 310; **24** 160
Pakhoed Holding, N.V., **9** 532; **26** 420;
41 339–40
Pakistan International Airlines
Corporation, 46 323–26
Pakkasakku Oy, **IV** 471
Paknet, **11** 548
Pakway Container Corporation, **8** 268
PAL *see* Philippine Airlines, Inc.

Qantas Airways Ltd., **6** 109–13; **24** 396–401 (upd.); **68** 301–07 (upd.)
Qantas Airways Limited,
Qatar General Petroleum Corporation, **IV** 524–26
Qiagen N.V., **39** 333–35
Qingdao Haier Refrigerator Co., Ltd., **65** 167, 169
Qintex Australia Ltd., **II** 150; **25** 329
QLT Inc., **71** 291–94
QMS Ltd., **43** 284
QO Chemicals, Inc., **14** 217
QSC Audio Products, Inc., **56** 291–93
QSP, Inc. *see* The Reader's Digest Association, Inc.
Qtera Corporation, **36** 352
Quad/Graphics, Inc., **19** 333–36
Quad Pharmaceuticals, Inc. *see* Par Pharmaceuticals Inc.
Quail Oil Tools, **28** 347–48
Quaker Alloy, **39** 31–32
Quaker Fabric Corp., **19** 337–39
Quaker Foods North America, **73** 268–73 (upd.)
Quaker Oats Company, **II** 558–60; **12** 409–12 (upd.); **34** 363–67 (upd.)
Quaker State Corporation, **7** 443–45; **21** 419–22 (upd.) *see also* Pennzoil-Quaker State Company.
QUALCOMM Incorporated, **20** 438–41; **47** 317–21 (upd.)
Qualcore, S. de R.L. de C.V., **51** 116
Qualipac, **55** 309
QualiTROL Corporation, **7** 116–17
Quality Assurance International, **72** 255
Quality Aviation Services, Inc., **53** 132
Quality Bakers of America, **12** 170
Quality Chekd Dairies, Inc., **48** 337–39
Quality Courts Motels, Inc. *see* Choice Hotels International, Inc.
Quality Dining, Inc., **18** 437–40; **63** 80
Quality Food Centers, Inc., **17** 386–88
Quality Inns International *see* Choice Hotels International, Inc.
Quality Markets, Inc., **13** 393
Quality Oil Co., **II** 624–25
Quality Paperback Book Club (QPB), **13** 105–07
Quality Products, Inc., **18** 162
Qualix S.A., **67** 347–48
Quanex Corporation, **13** 422–24; **62** 286–89 (upd.)
Quanta Computer Inc., **47** 322–24
Quanta Display Inc., **75** 306
Quanta Systems Corp., **51** 81
Quanterra Alpha L.P., **63** 347
Quantex Microsystems Inc., **24** 31
Quantronix Corporation *see* Excel Technology Inc.
Quantum Chemical Corporation, **8** 439–41; **11** 441; **30** 231, 441
Quantum Computer Services, Inc. *see* America Online, Inc.
Quantum Corporation, **10** 458–59; **62** 290–93 (upd.)
Quantum Health Resources, **29** 364
Quantum Marketing International, Inc., **27** 336

Quantum Offshore Contractors, **25** 104
Quantum Overseas N.V., **7** 360
Quantum Restaurant Group, Inc., **30** 330
Quarex Industries, Inc. *see* Western Beef, Inc.
Quark, Inc., **36** 375–79
Quarrie Corporation, **12** 554
Quebec Credit Union League, **48** 290
Quebéc Hydro-Electric Commission *see* Hydro-Quebéc.
Quebecor Inc., **12** 412–14; **19** 333; **26** 44; **29** 471; **47** 325–28 (upd.)
Queen City Broadcasting, **42** 162
Queens Isetan Co., Ltd. *see* Isetan Company Limited.
Queensborough Holdings PLC, **38** 103
Queensland Alumina, **IV** 59
Queensland and Northern Territories Air Service *see* Qantas Airways Limited.
Queensland Mines Ltd., **III** 729
Quelle Group, **V** 165–67 *see also* Karstadt Quelle AG.
Quesarias Ibéricas, **23** 219
Quest Aerospace Education, Inc., **18** 521
Quest Diagnostics Inc., **26** 390–92
Quest Education Corporation, **42** 212
Quest Pharmacies Inc., **25** 504–05
Questa Oil and Gas Co., **63** 408
Questar Corporation, **6** 568–70; **26** 386–89 (upd.)
Questor Management Co. LLC, **55** 31
Questor Partners, **26** 185
The Quick & Reilly Group, Inc., **18** 552; **20** 442–44; **26** 65
Quick Pak Inc., **53** 236
Quicken.com *see* Intuit Inc.
Quickie Designs, **11** 202, 487–88
The Quigley Corporation, **62** 294–97
Quik Stop Markets, Inc., **12** 112
Quiksilver, Inc., **18** 441–43; **27** 329
QuikTrip Corporation, **36** 380–83
Quill Corporation, **28** 375–77; **55** 354
Quillery, **27** 138
Quilmes Industrial (QUINSA) S.A., **57** 74, 76–77; **67** 315–17
Quilter Sound Company *see* QSC Audio Products, Inc.
Quimica Geral do Nordeste S.A., **68** 81
Química y Farmacia, S.A. de C.V., **59** 332
Quimicos Industriales Penoles *see* Industrias Penoles, S.A. de C.V.
Quincy Family Steak House, **II** 679; **10** 331; **19** 287; **27** 17, 19
Quiñenco S.A., **69** 56–57; **70** 61–62
Quintana Roo, Inc., **17** 243, 245; **25** 42
Quintel Communications, Inc., **61** 375
Quintex Australia Limited, **25** 329
Quintiles Transnational Corporation, **21** 423–25; **68** 308–12 (upd.)
Quintron, Inc., **11** 475
Quintus Computer Systems, **6** 248
Quixote Corporation, **15** 378–80
Quixtar Inc. *see* Alticor Inc.
Quixx Corporation, **6** 580
The Quizno's Corporation, **32** 444; **42** 295–98
Quoddy Products Inc., **17** 389, 390

Quotron Systems, Inc., **IV** 670; **9** 49, 125; **30** 127; **47** 37
Quovadx Inc., **70** 243–46
QVC Inc., **9** 428–29; **10** 175; **12** 315; **18** 132; **20** 75; **24** 120, 123; **58** 284–87 (upd.); **67** 206
Qwest Communications International, Inc., **37** 312–17
QwikSilver II, Inc., **37** 119

R

R&B Falcon Corp. *see* Transocean Sedco Forex Inc.
R&B, Inc., **51** 305–07
R & B Manufacturing Co., **III** 569; **20** 361
R&D Systems, Inc., **52** 347
R&O Software-Technik GmbH, **27** 492
R&S Home and Auto, **56** 352
R&S Technology Inc., **48** 410
R. and W. Hawaii Wholesale, Inc., **22** 15
R-Anell Custom Homes Inc., **41** 19
R-B *see* Arby's, Inc.
R-Byte, **12** 162
R-C Holding Inc. *see* Air & Water Technologies Corporation.
R.B. Pamplin Corp., **45** 350–52
R.C. Bigelow, Inc., **49** 334–36
R.C. Willey Home Furnishings, **72** 291–93
R. Cubed Composites Inc., **I** 387
R.E. Funsten Co., **7** 429
R.G. Barry Corp., **17** 389–91; **44** 364–67 (upd.)
R.G. Dun-Bradstreet Corp. *see* The Dun & Bradstreet Corp.
R. Griggs Group Limited, **23** 399–402; **31** 413–14
R.H. Donnelley Corporation, **61** 81–83
R.H. Macy & Co., Inc., **V** 168–70; **8** 442–45 (upd.); **30** 379–83 (upd.)
R.H. Stengel & Company, **13** 479
R.J. Reynolds, **I** 261, 363; **II** 544; **7** 130, 132, 267, 365, 367; **9** 533; **13** 490; **14** 78; **15** 72–73; **16** 242; **21** 315; **27** 125; **29** 195; **32** 344 *see also* RJR Nabisco.
R.J. Reynolds Tobacco Holdings, Inc., **30** 384–87 (upd.)
R.J. Tower Corporation *see* Tower Automotive, Inc.
R.K. Brown, **14** 112
R.L. Crain Limited, **15** 473
R.L. Manning Company, **9** 363–64
R.L. Polk & Co., **10** 460–62
R-O Realty, Inc., **43** 314
R.P.M., Inc., **25** 228
R.P. Scherer Corporation, **I** 678–80
R.R. Bowker Co., **17** 398; **23** 440
R.R. Donnelley & Sons Company, **IV** 660–62; **38** 368–71 (upd.)
R.S.R. Corporation, **31** 48
R.S. Stokvis Company, **13** 499
R. Scott Associates, **11** 57
R-T Investors LC, **42** 323–24
R. Twining & Co., **61** 395
R.W. Beck, **29** 353
R.W. Harmon & Sons, Inc., **6** 410

Service Merchandise Company, Inc., V 190–92; 6 287; 9 400; 19 395–99 (upd.)

Service Products Buildings, Inc. *see* Turner Construction Company.

Service Q. General Service Co., I 109

The ServiceMaster Company, 6 44–46; 23 428–31 (upd.); 68 338–42 (upd.)

Services Maritimes des Messageries Impériales *see* Compagnie des Messageries Maritimes.

ServiceWare, Inc., 25 118

Servicios de Corte y Confeccion, S.A. de C.V., 64 142

Servicios Financieros Quadrum S.A., 14 156; 76 129

Servisair Plc, 49 320

Servisco, II 608

ServiStar Coast to Coast Corporation *see* TruServ Corporation.

ServoChem A.B., I 387

Servomation Corporation, 7 472–73

Servomation Wilbur *see* Service America Corp.

Servoplan, S.A., 8 272

SES Staffing Solutions, 27 21

Sesame Street Book Club, 13 560

Sesamee Mexicana, 48 142

Sessler Inc., 19 381

Setagaya Industry Co., Ltd., 48 295

SETCAR, 14 458

Seton Scholl *see* SSL International plc.

Seven Arts Limited, 25 328

7-Eleven, Inc., 32 414–18 (upd.); 36 358

Seven-Eleven Japan Co. *see* Ito-Yokado Co., Ltd.

Seven Generation, Inc., 41 177

Seven Hills Paperboard, LLC, 59 350

Seven Network Limited, 25 329

Seven-Up Co., 18 418

SevenOne Media, 54 297

Sevenson Environmental Services, Inc., 42 344–46

Seventh Generation, Inc., 73 294–96

Seventh Street Corporation, 60 130

Severn Trent PLC, 12 441–43; 38 425–29 (upd.)

Severonickel Combine, 48 300

Seversky Aircraft Corporation, 9 205

Severstal Joint Stock Company, 65 309–12

Sewell Plastics, Inc., 10 222

Sextant In-Flight Systems, LLC, 30 74

Seymour Electric Light Co., 13 182

Seymour International Press Distributor Ltd., IV 619

Seymour Press, IV 619

Seymour Trust Co., 13 467

SF Bio, 52 51

SF Recycling & Disposal, Inc., 60 224

SFI Group plc, 51 334–36

SFIC Holdings (Cayman) Inc., 38 422

SFIM Industries, 37 348

SFNGR *see* Nouvelles Galeries Réunies.

SFS Bancorp Inc., 41 212

SFX Broadcasting Inc., 24 107

SFX Entertainment, Inc., 36 422–25

SG Cowen Securities Corporation, 75 186–87

SG Racing, Inc., 64 346

SGC *see* Supermarkets General Corporation.

SGE *see* Vinci.

SGI, 29 438–41 (upd.)

SGL Carbon Group, 40 83; 46 14

SGLG, Inc., 13 367

SGS-Thomson Microelectronics, 54 269–70

Shakespeare Company, 22 481–84

Shakey's Pizza, 16 447

Shaklee Corporation, 12 444–46; 39 361–64 (upd.)

Shalco Systems, 13 7

Shampaine Industries, Inc., 37 399

Shamrock Advisors, Inc., 8 305

Shamrock Broadcasting Inc., 24 107

Shamrock Capital L.P., 7 81–82

Shamrock Holdings, 9 75; 11 556; 25 268

Shamrock Oil & Gas Co., 7 308

Shan-Chih Business Association, 23 469

Shana Corporation, 62 142

Shandong Nichirei Foods Company Ltd. *see* Nichirei Corporation.

Shandwick International, 47 97

Shanggong Co. Ltd., 65 134

Shanghai Asia Pacific Co., 59 59

Shanghai Autobacs Paian Auto Service Co., 76 38

Shanghai Baosteel Group Corporation, 71 327–30

Shanghai Crown Maling Packaging Co. Ltd., 13 190

Shanghai Dajiang, 62 63

Shanghai General Bearing Co., Ltd., 45 170

Shanghai International Finance Company Limited, 15 433

Shanghai Kyocera Electronics Co., Ltd., 21 331

Shanghai Petrochemical Co., Ltd., 18 483–85; 21 83; 45 50

Shanghai Shesuo UNF Medical Diagnostic Reagents Co., 61 229

Shanghai Tobacco, 49 150, 153

Shangri-La Asia Ltd., 71 331–33

Shanks Group plc, 45 384–87

Shannon Aerospace Ltd., 36 426–28

Shannon Group, Inc., 18 318, 320; 59 274, 277

Shansby Group, 27 197; 43 218; 64 265

Shanshin Engineering Company Ltd., 60 236

Share Drug plc, 24 269

Shared Financial Systems, Inc., 10 501

Shared Medical Systems Corporation, 14 432–34

Shared Technologies Inc., 12 71

Shared Use Network Systems, Inc., 8 311

ShareWave Inc., 48 92

Shari Lewis Enterprises, Inc., 28 160

Sharmoon, 63 151

Sharon Steel Corp., 7 360–61; 8 536; 13 158, 249; 47 234

Sharp Corporation, II 95–96; 12 447–49 (upd.); 40 391–95 (upd.)

Sharp Water, Inc., 56 62

The Sharper Image Corporation, 10 486–88; 23 210; 26 439; 27 429; 62 321–24 (upd.)

Sharples Separator Company, 64 17

Shasta Beverages *see* National Beverage Corp.

Shato Holdings, Ltd., 60 357

Shaw Communications Inc., 26 274; 35 69

The Shaw Group, Inc., 50 427–30; 64 372

Shaw Industries, Inc., 9 465–67; 40 396–99 (upd.)

Shaw's Supermarkets, Inc., II 658–59; 23 169; 56 315–18

Shawell Precast Products, 14 248

Shea Homes *see* J.F. Shea Co., Inc.

Sheaffer Group, 23 54, 57

Shearer's Foods, Inc., 72 323–25

Shearman & Sterling, 32 419–22

Shearson Hammill & Company, 22 405–06

Shearson Lehman Brothers Holdings Inc., II 450–52; 9 468–70 (upd.)

Shedd Aquarium Society, 73 297–99

Shedd's Food Products Company, 9 318

Sheffield Exploration Company, 28 470

Sheffield Forgemasters Group Ltd., 39 32

Sheffield Silver Company, 67 322–23

Shekou Container Terminal, 16 481; 38 345

Shelby Insurance Company, 10 44–45

Shelby Steel Processing Co., 51 238

Shelby Williams Industries, Inc., 14 435–37

Shelco, 22 146

Sheldahl Inc., 23 432–35

Shelf Life Inc. *see* King Kullen Grocery Co., Inc.

Shell *see* Royal Dutch/Shell Group; Shell Oil Company; Shell Transport and Trading Company p.l.c.

Shell Canada Limited, 32 45

Shell Chemical Corporation, IV 531–32, 540; 8 415; 24 151

Shell Forestry, 21 546; 50 58

Shell France, 12 153

Shell Oil Company, IV 540–41; 14 438–40 (upd.); 41 356–60 (upd.)

Shell Transport and Trading Company p.l.c., IV 530–32 *see also* Royal Dutch Petroleum Company; Royal Dutch/Shell.

Shell Western E & P, 7 323

Sheller-Globe Corporation, I 201–02

Shells Seafood Restaurants, Inc., 43 370–72

Shelly Brothers, Inc., 15 65

Shenzhen Namtek Co., Ltd., 61 232–33

Shepherd Hardware Products Ltd., 16 357

Shepherd Neame Limited, 30 414–16

Shepherd Plating and Finishing Company, 13 233

Shepler Equipment Co., 9 512

Signode Industries, **III** 519; **22** 282

Sika Finanz AG, **28** 195

Sikes Corporation, **III** 612

Sikorsky Aircraft Corporation, 24
440–43

SIL&P *see* Southern Illinois Light &
Power Company.

SILA *see* Swedish Intercontinental Airlines.

Silband Sports Corp., **33** 102

Silenka B.V., **III** 733; **22** 436

Silex *see* Hamilton Beach/Proctor-Silex
Inc.

Silgan Holdings Inc., **26** 59

Silhouette Brands, Inc., 55 348–50

Silicon Beach Software, **10** 35

Silicon Compiler Systems, **11** 285

Silicon Energy Corporation, **64** 205

Silicon Engineering, **18** 20; **43** 17

Silicon Graphics Inc., 9 471–73 *see also*
SGI.

Silicon Light Machines Corporation, **48**
128

Silicon Magnetic Systems, **48** 128

Silicon Microstructures, Inc., **14** 183

Siliconware Precision Industries Ltd., 73
300–02

Silit, **60** 364

Silk-Epil S.A., **51** 58

Silkies, **55** 196

Silknet Software Inc., **51** 181

Silo Electronics, **16** 73, 75

Silo Holdings, **9** 65; **23** 52

Silo Inc., **V** 50; **10** 306, 468; **19** 123; **49**
112

Silver Burdett Co., **IV** 672, 675; **7** 528;
19 405

Silver Cinemas Inc., **71** 256

Silver City Airways *see* British World
Airlines Ltd.

Silver City Casino *see* Circus Circus
Enterprises, Inc.

Silver Dollar City Corporation *see*
Herschend Family Entertainment
Corporation.

Silver Dollar Mining Company, **20** 149

Silver Dolphin, **34** 3, 5

Silver Furniture Co., Inc., **15** 102, 104

Silver King Communications, **25** 213

Silver Screen Partners, **II** 174

Silverado Banking, **9** 199

Silverado Partners Acquisition Corp., **22**
80

Silverline, Inc., **16** 33

Silvermans Menswear, Inc., **24** 26

SilverPlatter Information Inc., 23
440–43

Silvershoe Partners, **17** 245

Silverstar Ltd. S.p.A., **10** 113; **50** 42

Silverstein Properties, Inc., 47 358–60;
48 320

Simco S.A., 37 357–59

Sime Darby Berhad, 14 448–50; **36**
433–36 (upd.)

Simeira Comercio e Industria Ltda., **22**
320

SIMEL S.A., **14** 27

Simer Pump Company, **19** 360

SIMEST, **24** 311

Simi Winery, Inc., **34** 89

Simicon Co., **26** 153

Simkins Industries, Inc., **8** 174–75

Simmons Company, 34 407; **47 361–64**

Simon & Schuster Inc., IV 671–72; **19**
403–05 (upd.)

Simon de Wit, **II** 641

Simon DeBartolo Group Inc., **26** 146; **27**
401; **57** 234

Simon Engineering, **11** 510

Simon Marketing, Inc., **19** 112, 114

Simon Property Group, Inc., 27
399–402

Simon Transportation Services Inc., 27
403–06

Simons Inc., **26** 412

Simple Shoes, Inc., **22** 173

Simplex Industries, Inc., **16** 296

Simplex Technologies Inc., 21 460–63

Simplex Wire and Cable Co. *see* Tyco
International Ltd.

Simplicity Manufacturing, Inc., 64
353–56

Simplicity Pattern Company, **I** 447; **8**
349; **23** 98; **29** 134

Simpson Investment Company, 17
438–41

Simpson Marketing, **12** 553

Simpson Thacher & Bartlett, 27 327; **39**
365–68

Simpson Timber Company *see* PW Eagle
Inc.

Simpsons *see* Hudson's Bay Company.

SIMS Deltec, Inc. *see* Deltec, Inc.

Sims Telephone Company, **14** 258

Simsmetal USA Corporation, **19** 380

SimuFlite, **II** 10

Simul International Inc. *see* Benesse
Corporation.

Simula, Inc., 41 368–70

Simulaids, Inc., **62** 18

SINA Corporation, 69 324–27

Sinai Kosher Foods, **14** 537

Sinclair Broadcast Group, Inc., 25
417–19; 47 120

Sinclair Paint Company, **12** 219

Sinfor Holding, **48** 402

Sing Tao Holdings Ltd., **29** 470–71

Singapore Airlines Ltd., 6 117–18; **12**
192; **20** 313; **24** 399; **26** 115; **27** 26,
407–09 (upd.), 464, 466; **38** 26

Singapore Alpine Electronics Asia Pte.
Ltd., **13** 31

Singapore Candle Company, **12** 393

Singapore Petroleum Co., **IV** 452

Singapore Shinei Sangyo Pte Ltd., **48** 369

Singapore Technologies Engineering Ltd.,
61 43

Singapore Telecom, **18** 348

Singer & Friedlander Group plc, 41
371–73

Singer Company, **9** 232; **11** 150; **13**
521–22; **19** 211; **22** 4; **26** 3; **29** 190
see also Bicoastal Corp.

The Singer Company N.V., 30 417–20
(upd.)

Singer Hardware & Supply Co., **9** 542

Singer Sewing Machine Co., **12** 46

Singer Supermarkets, **25** 235

The Singing Machine Company, Inc.,
60 277–80

Singular Software, **9** 80

Sinister Games, **41** 409

Sinkers Inc., **21** 68

Sino Life Insurance Co., **64** 280

Sinochem *see* China National Chemicals
Import and Export Corp.

Sinopec *see* China National Petroleum
Corporation.

Sintel, S.A., **19** 256

Sioux City Gas and Electric Company, **6**
523–24

Sioux City Newspapers, **64** 237

SIP *see* Società Italiana per L'Esercizio
delle Telecommunicazioni p.A.

Siporex, S.A., **31** 253

Sir Speedy, Inc., 16 448–50; **33** 231

SIRCOMA, **10** 375

SIREM, **23** 95

The Sirena Apparel Group Inc., **25** 245

Sirius Satellite Radio, Inc., 69 328–31

Sirloin Stockade, **10** 331

Sirrine *see* CRSS Inc.

Sirte Oil Company *see* Natinal Oil
Corporation.

Sirti S.p.A., 76 326–28

Siskin Steel & Supply Company, 70
294–96

Sistema JSFC, 73 303–05

Sisters Chicken & Biscuits, **8** 564

Sisters of Bon Secours USA *see* Bon
Secours Health System, Inc.

SIT-Siemens *see* Italtel.

SITA Telecommunications Holdings *see*
Equant N.V.

Sitca Corporation, **16** 297

Sithe Energies, Inc., **24** 327

Sitintel, **49** 383

Sitmar Cruises, **22** 445

Six Continents PLC, **54** 315; **59** 298

Six Flags, Inc., 17 442–44; **54 333–40**
(upd.)

Six Industries, Inc., **26** 433

61 Going to the Game!, **14** 293

Sixt AG, 39 369–72

Sizeler Property Investors Inc., **49** 27

Sizzler International Inc. *see* Worldwide
Restaurant Concepts, Inc.

SJB Equities, Inc., **30** 53

SJW Corporation, 70 297–99

The SK Equity Fund, L.P., **23** 177

Skånska Ättiksfabriken A.B. *see* Perstorp
AB.

Skadden, Arps, Slate, Meagher & Flom,
10 126–27; **18 486–88; 27** 325, 327

Skaggs-Albertson's Properties, **II** 604

Skaggs Companies, **22** 37

Skaggs Drug Centers, Inc., **II** 602–04; **7**
20; **27** 291; **30** 25–27; **65** 22

Skagit Nuclear Power Plant, **6** 566

Skalli Group, 67 349–51

Skandia America Reinsurance Corp., **57**
135–36

Skandia Insurance Company, Ltd., 50
431–34

Tanox, Inc., **77** 429–432
Tantalum Mining Corporation, **29** 81
TAP—Air Portugal Transportes Aéreos Portugueses S.A., 46 396–99 (upd.)
Tapemark Company Inc., 64 373–75
Tapiola Insurance, **IV** 316
Tapis-St. Maclou, **37** 22
Tappan *see* White Consolidated Industries Inc.
Tara Foods, **II** 645
Target Corporation, 10 515–17; 27 451–54 (upd.); 61 352–56 (upd.)
Target Marketing and Promotions, Inc., **55** 15
Target Marketing Systems Inc., **64** 237
Target Rock Corporation, **35** 134–36
Tarkett Sommer AG, 25 462–64
Tarmac America, **64** 379–80
Tarmac plc, III 751–54; 14 250; 28 447–51 (upd.); 36 21
Taro Pharmaceutical Industries Ltd., 65 335–37
TAROM S.A., 64 376–78
Tarragon Oil and Gas Ltd. *see* Unocal Corporation.
Tarragon Realty Investors, Inc., 45 399–402
Tarrant Apparel Group, 62 351–53
Tarsa, **63** 151
TASC *see* Analytical Sciences Corp.
Tascam *see* TEAC Corporation
Taser International, Inc., 62 354–57
Tasman Pulp and Paper Co. Ltd. *see* Fletcher Challenge Ltd.
Tastee Freeze, **39** 234
Tasty Baking Company, 14 485–87; 35 412–16 (upd.)
Tasukara Company Ltd., **62** 170
TAT European Airlines, **14** 70, 73; **24** 400
Tata Airlines *see* Air-India Limited.
Tata Enterprises, **III** 43
Tata Industries, **20** 313; **21** 74
Tata Iron & Steel Co. Ltd., IV 217–19; 44 411–15 (upd.)
Tata Tea Ltd., 76 339–41
Tate & Lyle PLC, II 580–83; 7 466–67; 13 102; 42 367–72 (upd.)
Tatham Corporation, **21** 169, 171
Tatham/RSCG, **13** 204
Tati SA, 25 465–67
Tatneft *see* OAO Tatneft.
Tattered Cover Book Store, 43 406–09
Tatung Co., 23 469–71
Taubman Centers, Inc., 75 364–66
Taurus Exploration, **21** 208
Taurus Programming Services, **10** 196
TaurusHolding GmbH & Co. KG, 46 400–03
Tax Management, Inc., **23** 92
Taylor & Francis Group plc, 44 416–19
Taylor Aircraft Corporation, **44** 307
Taylor Corporation, 36 465–67; 37 108
Taylor Guitars, 48 386–89
Taylor Made Golf Co., 23 270, 472–74; 33 7
Taylor Material Handling, **13** 499
Taylor Medical, **14** 388

Taylor Nelson Sofres plc, 34 428–30; 37 144
Taylor Petroleum, Inc., **17** 170
Taylor Publishing Company, 12 471–73; 36 468–71 (upd.)
Taylor Woodrow plc, I 590–91; 13 206; 38 450–53 (upd.)
Tayto Ltd., **22** 515
Tazo Tea Company, **50** 450
TB Wood's Corporation, 56 355–58
TBC Corp., **20** 63
TBS *see* Turner Broadcasting System, Inc.
TBWA/Chiat/Day, 6 47–49; 43 410–14 (upd.) *see also* Omnicom Group Inc.
TC Advertising *see* Treasure Chest Advertising, Inc.
TC Debica, **20** 264
TCA *see* Air Canada.
TCBC *see* Todays Computers Business Centers.
TCBY Enterprises Inc., 17 474–76
TCF *see* Tokyo City Finance.
TCF Financial Corporation, 47 399–402
TCH Corporation, **12** 477
TCI *see* Tele-Communications, Inc.
TCI Communications, **29** 39
TCI Inc., **33** 92–93
TCI International Inc., **43** 48
TCJC *see* Charisma Brands LLC
TCM Investments, Inc., **49** 159
TCO *see* Taubman Centers, Inc.
TCPL *see* TransCanada PipeLines Ltd.
TCS Management Group, Inc., **22** 53
TCW Capital, **19** 414–15; **76** 330
TD Bank *see* The Toronto-Dominion Bank.
TD Brasil, Ltda., **74** 338
TDC A/S, 63 371–74
TDK Corporation, II 109–11; 17 477–79 (upd.); 49 390–94 (upd.)
TDL Group Ltd., 46 404–06
TDL Infomedia Ltd., **47** 347
TDS *see* Telephone and Data Systems, Inc.
TEAC Corporation, 78 377–380
Teachers Insurance and Annuity Association-College Retirement Equities Fund, III 379–82; 45 403–07 (upd.)
Teachers Service Organization, Inc., **8** 9–10
Team America, **9** 435
Team Penske *see* Penske Corporation.
Team Rental Group *see* Budget Group, Inc.
Teams, Inc., **37** 247
Teamsters Central States Pension Fund, **19** 378
Teamsters Union, **13** 19
TearDrop Golf Company, 32 445–48
Tech Data Corporation, 10 518–19; 74 335–38 (upd.)
Tech/Ops Landauer, Inc. *see* Landauer, Inc.
Tech Pacific International, **18** 180; **39** 201, 203

Tech-Sym Corporation, 18 513–15; 44 420–23 (upd.)
Tech Textiles, USA, **15** 247–48
Techalloy Co., **IV** 228
Techgistics, **49** 403
Techint Group, **63** 385
Technair Packaging Laboratories, **18** 216
TECHNE Corporation, 52 345–48
Technical Ceramics Laboratories, Inc., **13** 141
Technical Coatings Co., **13** 85; **38** 96–97
Technical Materials, Inc., **14** 81
Technical Olympic USA, Inc., 75 367–69
Technicare, **11** 200
Technicolor Inc., **28** 246
Technicon Instruments Corporation, **III** 56; **11** 333–34; **22** 75
Technifax, **8** 483
Technip, 78 381–384
Techniques d'Avant-Garde *see* TAG Heuer International SA.
Technisch Bureau Visser, **16** 421
Technitrol, Inc., 29 459–62
Technology Management Group, Inc., **18** 112
Technology Resources International Ltd., **18** 76
Technology Venture Investors, **11** 490; **14** 263
Technophone Ltd., **17** 354
Techserviceavia, CJSC, **68** 204
Techsource Services, Inc., **60** 185
TechTeam Europe, Ltd., **41** 281
Techtronic Industries Company Ltd., 73 331–34
Teck Corporation, 9 282; 27 455–58
Tecnacril Ltda, **51** 6
Tecnamotor S.p.A. *see* Tecumseh Products Company.
Tecneco, **IV** 422
Tecnipapel-Sociedade de Transformaçao e Distribuiçao de Papel, Lda, **60** 156
Tecnipublicaciones, **14** 555
Tecnost S.p.A., **34** 319
TECO Energy, Inc., 6 582–84
Tecom Industries, Inc., **18** 513–14
Tecomar S.A., **50** 209
Tecsa, **55** 182
Tecstar Inc. *see* Starcraft Corporation.
Tectrix Fitness Equipment, Inc., **49** 108
Tecumseh Products Company, 8 514–16; 71 351–55 (upd.)
Ted Bates, Inc., **10** 69; **16** 71–72; **50** 537
Teddy's Shoe Store *see* Morse Shoe Inc.
Tee Vee Toons, Inc., 57 357–60
Teekay Shipping Corporation, 25 468–71
Teepak International, **55** 123
Tees and Hartlepool, **31** 367, 369
Tefal *see* Groupe SEB.
TEFSA, **17** 182
TEIC *see* B.V. Tabak Export & Import Compagnie.
Teijin Limited, V 380–82; 61 357–61 (upd.)
Teikoku Jinken *see* Teijin Limited.
Teikoku Oil Co., Ltd., **63** 312

Universal Studios Florida, **14** 399
Universal Studios, Inc., 33 429–33
Universal Tea Co., Inc., **50** 449
Universal Telephone, **9** 106
Universal Textured Yarns, **12** 501
Universe Tankships, **59** 198
UNIVERSELLE Engineering U.N.I. GmbH, **60** 194
University HealthSystem Consortium, **53** 346
University of Phoenix, **24** 40
Univisa, **24** 516
Univision Communications Inc., 18 213; **24** 515–18; **41** 150–52; **54** 72–73, 158
Unix System Laboratories Inc., **25** 20–21; **38** 418
UNM *see* United News & Media plc.
Uno-e Bank, **48** 51
Uno Restaurant Holdings Corporation, 18 538–40; **70** 334–37 **(upd.)**
Uno-Ven, **IV** 571; **24** 522
Unocal Corporation, IV 569–71; **24** 519–23 **(upd.); 71** 378–84 **(upd.)**
Unova Manufacturing Technologies Inc., **72** 69, 71
UNR Industries, Inc. *see* ROHN Industries, Inc.
Unterberg Harris, **25** 433
UNUM Corp., 13 538–40
UnumProvident Corporation, 52 376–83 **(upd.)**
Uny Co., Ltd., V 209–10; **49** 425–28 **(upd.)**
UO Fenwick, Inc., **74** 370
UOB *see* United Overseas Bank Ltd.
UPC *see* United Pan-Europe Communications NV.
UOD Inc. *see* Urban Outfitters, Inc.
UPI *see* United Press International.
Upjohn Company, I 707–09; **8** 547–49 **(upd.)** *see also* Pharmacia & Upjohn Inc.
UPM-Kymmene Corporation, 19 461–65; **50** 505–11 **(upd.)**
UPN *see* United Paramount Network.
Upper Deck Company, LLC, **34** 448; **37** 295
Upper Peninsula Power Co., **53** 369
UPS *see* United Parcel Service, Inc.
UPS Aviation Technologies, Inc., **60** 137
UPSHOT, **27** 195
Urban Outfitters, Inc., 14 524–26; **74** 367–70 **(upd.)**
Urbaser SA, **55** 182
Urbium PLC, 75 389–91
URS Corporation, 45 420–23
URSI *see* United Road Services, Inc.
Urwick Orr, **II** 609
US *see also* U.S.
US Airways Group, Inc., I 131–32; **6** 131–32 **(upd.); 28** 506–09 **(upd.); 52** 24–25, **384–88 (upd.)**
US Industrial Chemicals, Inc., **8** 440
US Industries Inc., **30** 231
US Monolithics, **54** 407
US 1 Industries, **27** 404
US Order, Inc., **10** 560, 562

US Repeating Arms Co., **58** 147
US Sprint Communications Company *see* Sprint Communications Company, L.P.
US Telecom, **9** 478–79
US West Communications Services, Inc. *see* Regional Bell Operating Companies.
USA Cafes, **14** 331
USA Floral Products Inc., **27** 126
USA Interactive, Inc., 47 418–22 **(upd.); 58** 117, 120
USA Networks Inc., **25** 330, 411; **33** 432; **37** 381, 383–84; **43** 422
USA Security Systems, Inc., **27** 21
USA Truck, Inc., 42 410–13
USAA, 10 541–43; **62** 385–88 **(upd.)**
USANA, Inc., 27 353; **29** 491–93
USCC *see* United States Cellular Corporation.
USCP-WESCO Inc., **II** 682
Usego AG., **48** 63
USF&G Corporation, III 395–98 *see also* The St. Paul Companies.
USFL *see* United States Football League.
USFreightways Corporation, **27** 475; **49** 402
USG Corporation, III 762–64; **26** 507–10 **(upd.)**
USH *see* United Scientific Holdings.
Usinas Siderúrgicas de Minas Gerais S.A., 77 454–457
Usinger's Famous Sausage *see* Fred Usinger Inc.
Usinor SA, 42 414–17 **(upd.)**
Usinor Sacilor, IV 226–28
USLD Communications Corp. *see* Billing Concepts Corp.
USM, **10** 44
USO *see* United Service Organizations.
Usource LLC, **37** 406
USPS *see* United States Postal Service.
USSC *see* United States Surgical Corporation.
USSI *see* U.S. Software Inc.
UST Inc., 9 533–35; **42** 79; **50** 512–17 **(upd.)**
UST Wilderness Management Corporation, **33** 399
Usutu Pulp Company, **49** 353
USV Pharmaceutical Corporation, **11** 333
USWeb/CKS *see* marchFIRST, Inc.
USX Corporation, IV 572–74; **7** 193–94, **549–52 (upd.)** *see also* United States Steel Corporation.
UT Starcom, **44** 426
Utag, **11** 510
Utah Construction & Mining Co., **14** 296
Utah Federal Savings Bank, **17** 530
Utah Gas and Coke Company, **6** 568
Utah Medical Products, Inc., 36 496–99
Utah Mines Ltd., **IV** 47; **22** 107
Utah Power and Light Company, 9 536; **12** 266; **27** 483–86 *see also* PacifiCorp.
UTI Energy, Inc. *see* Patterson-UTI Energy, Inc.
Utilicom, **6** 572
Utilicorp United Inc., 6 592–94 *see also* Aquilla, Inc.

UtiliTech Solutions, **37** 88
Utility Constructors Incorporated, **6** 527
Utility Engineering Corporation, **6** 580
Utility Fuels, **7** 377
Utility Line Construction Service, Inc., **59** 65
Utility Service Affiliates, Inc., **45** 277
Utility Services, Inc., **42** 249, 253
Utility Supply Co. *see* United Stationers Inc.
Utopian Leisure Group, **75** 385
UTStarcom, Inc., 77 458–461
UTV *see* Ulster Television PLC.
Utz Quality Foods, Inc., 72 358–60
UUNET, 38 468–72
UV Industries, Inc., **7** 360; **9** 440
Uwajimaya, Inc., 60 312–14

V

V.L. Churchill Group, **10** 493
VA Linux Systems, **45** 363
VA TECH ELIN EBG GmbH, 49 429–31
VA Technologie AG, **57** 402
Vacheron Constantin, **27** 487, 489
Vaco, **38** 200, 202
Vaculator Division *see* Lancer Corporation.
Vacuum Metallurgical Company, **11** 234
Vacuum Oil Co. *see* Mobil Corporation.
Vadoise Vie, **III** 273
VAE AG, **57** 402
VAE Nortrak Cheyenne Inc., **53** 352
Vail Associates, Inc., 11 543–46; **31** 65, 67
Vail Resorts, Inc., 43 435–39 **(upd.)**
Vaillant GmbH, 44 436–39
Val Corp., **24** 149
Val-Pak Direct Marketing Systems, Inc., **22** 162
Val Royal LaSalle, **II** 652
Valassis Communications, Inc., 8 550–51; **37** 407–10 **(upd.); 76** 364–67 **(upd.)**
ValCom Inc. *see* InaCom Corporation.
Valdi Foods Inc., **II** 663–64
Vale do Rio Doce Navegacao SA—Docenave, **43** 112
Vale Harmon Enterprises, Ltd., **25** 204
Vale Power Company, **12** 265
Valenciana de Cementos, **59** 112
Valentine & Company, **8** 552–53
Valentino, **67** 246, 248
Valeo, 23 492–94; **66** 350–53 **(upd.)**
Valero Energy Corporation, 7 553–55; **71** 385–90 **(upd.)**
Valhi, Inc., 10 435–36; **19** 466–68
Valid Logic Systems Inc., **11** 46, 284; **48** 77
Vality Technology Inc., **59** 56
Vallen Corporation, 45 424–26
Valley Bank of Helena, **35** 197, 199
Valley Bank of Maryland, **46** 25
Valley Bank of Nevada, **19** 378
Valley Crest Tree Company, **31** 182–83
Valley Deli Inc., **24** 243
Valley Fashions Corp., **16** 535
Valley Federal of California, **11** 163

VWR United Company, **9** 531
Vycor Corporation, **25** 349
Vyvx, **31** 469

W

W&A Manufacturing Co., LLC, **26** 530
W&F Fish Products, **13** 103
W & J Sloane Home Furnishings Group, **35** 129
W + K *see* Wieden + Kennedy.
W de Argentina–Inversiones S.L., **63** 377
W.A. Krueger Co., **19** 333–35
W.A. Whitney Company, 53 353–56
W. Atlee Burpee & Co., 11 198; **27** 505–08
W.B Doner & Co., 10 420; **12** 208; **28** 138; **56** 369–72
W.B. Saunders Co., **IV** 623–24
W.C. Bradley Co., 18 516; **69** 363–65
W.C.G. Sports Industries Ltd. *see* Canstar Sports Inc.
W.C. Smith & Company Limited, **14** 339
W. Duke Sons & Company, **27** 128
W.E. Andrews Co., Inc., **25** 182
W.E. Dillon Company, Ltd., **21** 499
W.F. Kaiser, **60** 364
W.F. Linton Company, **9** 373
W.G. Yates & Sons Construction Company *see* The Yates Companies, Inc.
W.H. Brady Co., 16 518–21*see also* Brady Corporation.
W.H. Gunlocke Chair Co. *see* Gunlocke Company.
W.H. Smith & Son (Alacra) Ltd., **15** 473
W H Smith Group PLC, V 211–13
W Jordan (Cereals) Ltd., 74 382–84
W.L. Gore & Associates, Inc., 14 538–40; **26** 417; **60** 321–24 (upd.)
W.M. Bassett Furniture Co. *see* Bassett Furniture Industries, Inc.
W.O. Daley & Company, **10** 387
W.P. Carey & Co. LLC, 49 446–48
W.R. Bean & Son, **19** 335
W.R. Berkley Corporation, 15 525–27; **74** 385–88 (upd.)
W.R. Breen Company, **11** 486
W.R. Case & Sons Cutlery Company *see* Zippo Manufacturing Company.
W.R. Grace & Company, I 547–50; **50** 78, 522–29 (upd.)
W. Rosenlew, **IV** 350
W.S. Barstow & Company, **6** 575
W.T. Grant Co., **16** 487
W.T. Rawleigh, **17** 105
W.W. Grainger, Inc., V 214–15; **26** 537–39 (upd.); **68** 392–95 (upd.)
W.W. Kimball Company, **12** 296; **18** 44
W.W. Norton & Company, Inc., 28 518–20
Waban Inc., V 198; **13** 547–49; **19** 449 *see also* HomeBase, Inc.
Wabash National Corp., 13 550–52
Wabash Valley Power Association, **6** 556
Wabtec Corporation, 40 451–54
Wachbrit Insurance Agency, **21** 96
Wachovia Bank of Georgia, N.A., 16 521–23

Wachovia Bank of South Carolina, N.A., 16 524–26
Wachovia Corporation, 12 516–20; **46** 442–49 (upd.)
Wachtell, Lipton, Rosen & Katz, 47 435–38
The Wackenhut Corporation, 13 124–25; **14** 541–43; **28** 255; **41** 80; **63** 423–26 (upd.)
Wacker-Chemie GmbH, 35 454–58
Wacker Oil Inc., **11** 441
Waco Aircraft Company, **27** 98
Wacoal Corp., 25 520–24
Waddell & Reed, Inc., 22 540–43; **33** 405, 407
Wade Smith, **28** 27, 30
Wadsworth Inc., **8** 526
WaferTech, **18** 20; **43** 17; **47** 385
Waffle House Inc., 14 544–45; **60** 325–27 (upd.)
Wagenseller & Durst, **25** 249
Waggener Edstrom, 42 424–26
The Wagner & Brown Investment Group, **9** 248
Wagner Castings Company, **16** 474–75
Wagner Litho Machinery Co., **13** 369–70
Wagner Spray Tech, **18** 555
Wagonlit Travel, **22** 128; **55** 90
Wagons-Lits, **27** 11; **29** 443; **37** 250–52
Waha Oil Company *see* Natinal Oil Corporation.
AB Wahlbecks, **25** 464
Waitaki International Biosciences Co., **17** 288
Waitrose Ltd. *see* John Lewis Partnership plc.
Wakefern Food Corporation, 33 434–37
Wako Shoji Co. Ltd. *see* Wacoal Corp.
Wal-Mart de Mexico, S.A. de C.V., 35 459–61 (upd.)
Wal-Mart Stores, Inc., V 216–17; **8** 555–57 (upd.); **26** 522–26 (upd.); **63** 427–32 (upd.)
Walbridge Aldinger Co., 38 480–82
Walbro Corporation, 13 553–55
Walchenseewerk AG, **23** 44
Waldbaum, Inc., 19 479–81
Walden Book Company Inc., 17 522–24
Waldorf Corporation, **59** 350
Wales & Company, **14** 257
Walgreen Co., V 218–20; **20** 511–13 (upd.); **65** 352–56 (upd.)
Walk Haydel & Associates, Inc., **25** 130
Walk Softly, Inc., **25** 118
Walker & Lee, **10** 340
Walker Dickson Group Limited, **26** 363
Walker Digital, **57** 296–98
Walker Interactive Systems, **11** 78; **25** 86
Walker Manufacturing Company, 19 482–84
Walkers Snack Foods Ltd., 70 350–52
Walkins Manufacturing Corp., **III** 571; **20** 362
Walkup's Merchant Express Inc., **27** 473
Wall Drug Store, Inc., 40 455–57
Wall Street Deli, Inc., 33 438–41

Wallace & Tiernan Group, **11** 361; **52** 374
The Wallace Berrie Company *see* Applause Inc.
Wallace Computer Services, Inc., 36 507–10
Wallace International Silversmiths, **14** 482–83
Wallbergs Fabriks A.B., **8** 14
Wallin & Nordstrom *see* Nordstrom, Inc.
Wallis *see* Sears plc.
Wallis Arnold Enterprises, Inc., **21** 483
Wallis Tractor Company, **21** 502
Walnut Capital Partners, **62** 46–47
Walrus, Inc., **18** 446
Walsin-Lihwa, **13** 141
Walsworth Publishing Company, Inc., 78 445–448
The Walt Disney Company, II 172–74; **6** 174–77 (upd.); **30** 487–91 (upd.); **63** 433–38 (upd.)
Walter Bau, **27** 136, 138
Walter E. Heller, **17** 324
Walter Herzog GmbH, **16** 514
Walter Industries, Inc., III 765–67; **22** 544–47 (upd.); **72** 368–73 (upd.)
Walter Kidde & Co., **73** 208
Walter Wilson, **49** 18
Walter Wright Mammoet, **26** 280
Walton Manufacturing, **11** 486
Walton Monroe Mills, Inc., 8 558–60
Wanadoo S.A., 75 400–02
Wang Global, **39** 176–78
Wang Laboratories, Inc., III 168–70; **6** 284–87 (upd.)
WAP, **26** 420
Waples-Platter Co., **II** 625
Warbasse-Cogeneration Technologies Partnership, **35** 479
Warburg Pincus, **9** 524; **14** 42; **24** 373; **61** 403; **73** 138
Warburg USB, **38** 291
Warburtons Bakery Cafe, Inc., **18** 37
Ward's Communications, **22** 441
Wards *see* Circuit City Stores, Inc.
Waremart *see* WinCo Foods.
WARF *see* Wisconsin Alumni Research Foundation.
Waring and LaRosa, **12** 167
The Warnaco Group Inc., 12 521–23; **46** 450–54 (upd.) *see also* Authentic Fitness Corp.
Warner & Swasey Co., **8** 545
Warner Communications Inc., II 175–77 *see also* AOL Time Warner Inc.
Warner Cosmetics, **III** 48; **8** 129
Warner Electric, **58** 67
Warner-Lambert Co., I 710–12; **10** 549–52 (upd.)
Warner Roadshow Film Distributors Greece SA, **58** 359
Warners' Stellian Inc., 67 384–87
Warrantech Corporation, 53 357–59
Warrell Corporation, 68 396–98
Warren Apparel Group Ltd., **39** 257
Warren Bancorp Inc., **55** 52
Warren Bank, **13** 464
Warren Frozen Foods, Inc., **61** 174

Weirton Steel Corporation, IV 236–38; 7 447, 598; 8 346, 450; 10 31–32; 12 352, 354; 26 407, 527–30 (upd.)

Weis Markets, Inc., 15 531–33

The Weitz Company, Inc., 42 431–34

Welbilt Corp., 19 492–94; 27 159

Welborn Transport Co., 39 64, 65

Welch Engineering Ltd. *see* Swales & Associates, Inc.

Welch's, 25 366

Welco Feed Manufacturing Company, 60 316

Welcome Wagon International Inc., 16 146

Weldless Steel Company, 8 530

Weleda AG, 78 457–461

The Welk Group, Inc., 78 462–466

Wella AG, III 68–70; 48 420–23 (upd.)

Welland Pipe Ltd., 51 352

Wellborn Paint Manufacturing Company, 56 98

Wellby Super Drug Stores, 12 220

WellChoice, Inc., 67 388–91 (upd.)

Wellcome Foundation Ltd., I 713–15 *see also* GlaxoSmithKline plc.

Weller Electric Corp., II 16

Wellington Management Company, 14 530–31; 23 226

Wellington Sears Co., 15 247–48

Wellman, Inc., 8 561–62; 21 193; 52 408–11 (upd.); 64 86

Wellmark, Inc., 10 89

Wellness Co., Ltd., IV 716

WellPath Community Health Plans, Inc., 59 140

WellPoint Health Networks Inc., 25 525–29

Wellrose Limited, 53 333

Wells Aircraft, 12 112

Wells Fargo & Company, II 380–84; 12 533–37 (upd.); 38 483–92 (upd.) *see also* American Express Company.

Wells Fargo HSBC Trade Bank, 26 203

Wells-Gardner Electronics Corporation, 43 458–61

Wells Rich Greene BDDP, 6 50–52

Wells' Dairy, Inc., 36 511–13

Wellspring Associates L.L.C., 16 338

Wellspring Resources LLC, 42 429

Welsh Associated Collieries Ltd., 31 369

Welsh, Carson, Anderson & Stowe, 65 128–30; 71 117–19

Welsh Water *see* Hyder plc.

Wendel Investissement, 57 381

Wendy's International, Inc., 8 563–65; 23 504–07 (upd.); 47 439–44 (upd.)

Wenger S.A., 21 515; 74 375–77

Wenmac Corp., 51 368

Wenner Media, Inc., 32 506–09

Werco, Inc., 54 7

Werkhof GmbH, 13 491; 62 336

Werknet, 16 420; 43 308

Werner Baldessarini Design GmbH, 48 209

Werner Die & Stamping, 69 38

Werner Enterprises, Inc., 26 531–33

Werner International, III 344; 14 225

Wertheim Schroder & Company, 17 443

Weru Aktiengesellschaft, 18 558–61; 49 295

Wesco Financial Corp., III 213, 215; 18 62; 42 32–34

Wesco Food Co., II 644

Wescot Decisison Systems, 6 25

Weseley Software Development Corp. *see* RedPrairie Corporation.

Wesley Jessen VisionCare Inc., 65 274

Wesley's Quaker Maid, Inc. *see* Farmer Jack Supermarkets

Wesper Co., 26 4

Wesray and Management, 17 213

Wesray Capital Corporation, 13 41; 17 443; 47 363

Wesray Corporation, 22 55

Wesray Holdings Corp., 13 255

Wesray Transportation, Inc., 14 38

Wessanen *see* Koninklijke Wessanen nv.

Wessanen USA, 29 480

Wesson/Peter Pan Foods Co., 17 241

West Australia Land Holdings, Limited, 10 169

West Bend Co., 14 546–48

West Coast Entertainment Corporation, 29 502–04

West Coast Grocery Co., II 670; 18 506; 50 456

West Coast Machinery, 13 385

West Coast Power Company, 12 265

West Coast Restaurant Enterprises, 25 390

West Coast Savings and Loan, 10 339

West Company, 53 298

West Corporation, 42 435–37

West End Family Pharmacy, Inc., 15 523

West Fraser Timber Co. Ltd., 17 538–40

West Georgia Coca-Cola Bottlers, Inc., 13 163

West Group, 34 438, 502–06 (upd.)

West Harrison Gas & Electric Company *see* Cincinnati Gas & Electric Company.

West Los Angeles Veterinary Medical Group, Inc., 58 355

West Lynn Creamery, Inc., 26 450

West Marine, Inc., 17 541–43; 37 398

West Missouri Power Company *see* UtiliCorp United Inc.; Aquilla, Inc.

West Newton Savings Bank, 13 468

West Newton Telephone Company, 14 258

West One Bancorp, 11 552–55; 36 491

West Penn Electric *see* Allegheny Power System, Inc.

West Penn Power Company, 38 38–40

West Pharmaceutical Services, Inc., 42 438–41

West Point-Pepperell, Inc., 8 566–69 *see also* WestPoint Stevens Inc.; JPS Textile Group, Inc.

West Publishing Co., 7 579–81 *see also* The West Group.

West Side Printing Co., 13 559

West Shore Pipe Line Company, 70 35

West TeleServices Corporation *see* West Corporation.

West Texas LPG Pipeline Limited Partnership, 70 35

West Texas Utilities Company, 6 580

West Union Corporation, 22 517

West Virginia Bearings, Inc., 13 78

West Virginia Pulp and Paper Co. *see* Westvaco Corporation.

Westaff Inc., 33 454–57

WestAir Holding Inc., 11 300; 25 423; 32 336

Westamerica Bancorporation, 17 544–47

Westar Energy, Inc., 57 404–07 (upd.)

Westbrae Natural, Inc., 27 197–98; 43 218

Westburne Group of Companies, 9 364

Westchester County Savings & Loan, 9 173

Westchester Specialty Group, Inc., 26 546

Westclox Seth Thomas, 16 483

WestCoast Hospitality Corporation, 59 410–13

Westcon Group, Inc., 67 392–94

Westcor Realty, 57 235

Westcorp Financial Services *see* WFS Financial Inc.

Westcott Communications Inc., 22 442

Westdeutsche Landesbank Girozentrale, II 385–87; 33 395; 46 458–61 (upd.); 47 83

Westec Corporation *see* Tech-Sym Corporation.

Westell Technologies, Inc., 57 408–10

Westerbeke Corporation, 60 332–34

Western Aerospace Ltd., 14 564

Western Air Express, 9 17

Western Air Lines, I 98, 100, 106; 21 142; 25 421–23

Western Areas Ltd., 61 292

Western Atlas Inc., 12 538–40

Western Australian Specialty Alloys Proprietary Ltd., 14 564

Western Auto, 19 223; 57 11

Western Auto Supply Co., 8 56; 11 392

Western Automatic Machine Screw Co., 12 344

Western Bank, 17 530

Western Beef, Inc., 22 548–50

Western Bingo, 16 471

Western Company of North America, 15 534–36

Western Crude, 11 27

Western Data Products, Inc., 19 110

Western Digital Corp., 25 530–32

Western Edison, 6 601

Western Electric Co., II 57, 66, 88, 101, 112; 7 288; 11 500–01; 12 136; 13 57; 49 346

Western Electric Manufacturing Company, 54 139

Western Empire Construction *see* CRSS Inc.

Western Equities, Inc. *see* Tech-Sym Corporation.

Western Family Foods, 47 457; 53 21

Western Federal Savings & Loan, 9 199

Western Fire Equipment Co., 9 420

Western Forest Products Ltd., 59 161

Wimpey International Ltd., **13** 206

Win-Chance Foods, **II** 508; **36** 255

Win Schuler Foods, **25** 517

Winbond Electronics Corporation, 74 389–91

Wincanton plc, 52 418–20

Winchell's Donut Houses Operating Company, L.P., 60 356–59

WinCo Foods Inc., 60 360–63

Wincor Nixdorf Holding GmbH, 69 370–73 (upd.)

Wind River Systems, Inc., 37 419–22

Windmere Corporation, 16 537–39 *see also* Applica Incorporated.

Windmere-Durable Holdings, Inc., **30** 404

WindowVisions, Inc., **29** 288

Windsong Exports, **52** 429

Windsor Forestry Tools, Inc., **48** 59

Windsor Manufacturing Company, **13** 6

Windsor Trust Co., **13** 467

Windstar Sail Cruises *see* Carnival Corporation.

Windsurfing International, **23** 55

Windswept Environmental Group, Inc., 62 389–92

Windward Capital Partners, **28** 152, 154

The Wine Group, Inc., 39 419–21

Wine World, Inc., **22** 78, 80

Winegard Company, 56 384–87

Winfire, Inc., **37** 194

Wingate Partners, **14** 521, 523

Winget Ltd. *see* Seddon Group Ltd.

Wings & Wheels, **13** 19

Wings Luggage, Inc., **10** 181

WingspanBank.com, **38** 270

Winkelman Stores, Inc., **8** 425–26

Winlet Fashions, **22** 223

Winmark Corporation, 74 392–95

Winn-Dixie Stores, Inc., II 683–84; 21 528–30 (upd.); 59 423–27 (upd.)

Winnebago Industries Inc., 7 589–91; 22 207; 27 509–12 (upd.)

Winners Apparel Ltd. *see* The TJX Companies, Inc.

Winning International, **21** 403

WinsLoew Furniture, Inc., 21 531–33 *see also* Brown Jordan International Inc.

Winston & Strawn, 35 470–73

Winston Furniture Company, Inc., **21** 531–33

Winston Group, **10** 333

Winter Hill Frozen Foods and Services, **55** 82

WinterBrook Corp., **26** 326

Winterflood Securities Limited, **39** 89, 91

Wintershall AG, **IV** 485; **38** 408

Winterthur Group, III 402–04; 68 402–05 (upd.)

Winthrop Lawrence Corporation, **25** 541

Winton Engines, **10** 273

Winyah Concrete & Block, **50** 49

Wipro Limited, 43 465–68

Wire and Cable Specialties Corporation, **17** 276

Wire and Plastic Products PLC *see* WPP Group PLC.

Wireless Hong Kong *see* Hong Kong Telecommunications Ltd.

Wireless LLC, **18** 77

Wireless Management Company, **11** 12

Wiretel, **76** 326–27

Wiron Prefabricados Modulares, S.A., **65** 363

Wirtz Corporation, 72 374–76

Wisconsin Alumni Research Foundation, 65 365–68

Wisconsin Bell, Inc., 14 551–53; 18 30

Wisconsin Central Transportation Corporation, 24 533–36

Wisconsin Dairies, 7 592–93

Wisconsin Energy Corporation, 6 601–03, 605; 54 417–21 (upd.)

Wisconsin Gas Company, **17** 22–23

Wisconsin Power and Light, **22** 13; **39** 260

Wisconsin Public Service Corporation, 6 604–06; **9 553–54** *see also* WPS Resources Corporation.

Wisconsin Steel, **10** 430; **17** 158–59

Wisconsin Tissue Mills Inc., **8** 103

Wisconsin Toy Company *see* Value Merchants Inc.

Wisconsin Wire and Steel, **17** 310; **24** 160

Wise Foods, Inc., **22** 95

Wise Solutions, Inc. *see* Altiris, Inc.

Wiser's De Luxe Whiskey, **14** 141

Wispark Corporation, **6** 601, 603

Wisser Service Holdings AG, **18** 105

Wistron Corporation *see* Acer Incorporated.

Wisvest Corporation, **6** 601, 603

WiSys Technology Foundation, **65** 367

Witco Corporation, I 404–06; 16 540–43 (upd.)

Wite-Out Products, Inc., **23** 56–57

Witech Corporation, **6** 601, 603

Withington Company *see* Sparton Corporation.

Wittgensteiner Kliniken Gruppe, **56** 141

Wittington Investments Ltd., **13** 51

The Wiz *see* Cablevision Electronic Instruments, Inc.

Wizards of the Coast Inc., 24 537–40; 43 229, 233

WizardWorks Group, Inc., **31** 238–39

WL Ross & Co., **67** 125

WLIW-TV *see* Educational Broadcasting Corporation.

WLR Foods, Inc., 14 516; 21 534–36; 50 494

Wm. B. Reily & Company Inc., 58 372–74

WM Investment Company, **34** 512

Wm. Morrison Supermarkets PLC, 38 496–98

Wm. Underwood Company, **40** 53

Wm. Wrigley Jr. Company, 7 594–97; 58 375–79 (upd.)

WMC, Limited, 43 469–72

WMF *see* Württembergische Metallwarenfabrik AG (WMF).

WMS Industries, Inc., 15 537–39; 53 363–66 (upd.)

WMX Technologies Inc., 17 551–54

Wolf Furniture Enterprises, **14** 236

Wolfe & Associates, **25** 434

Wolfe Industries, Inc., **22** 255

Wolff Printing Co., **13** 559

Wolfgang Puck Worldwide, Inc., 26 534–36; 70 364–67 (upd.)

Wolohan Lumber Co., **19** 503–05

Wolseley plc, 64 409–12

Wolters Kluwer NV, IV 611; **14 554–56; 31** 389, 394; **33 458–61 (upd.)**

The Wolverhampton & Dudley Breweries, PLC, 57 411–14

Wolverine Equities Company, **62** 341

Wolverine Insurance Co., **26** 487

Wolverine Tube Inc., 23 515–17

Wolverine World Wide, Inc., 16 544–47; 59 428–33 (upd.)

Womack Development Company, **11** 257

Womacks Saloon and Gaming Parlor, **53** 91

Womble Carlyle Sandridge & Rice, PLLC, 52 421–24

Women's Specialty Retailing Group *see* Casual Corner Group, Inc.

Women's World, **15** 96

Wometco Coca-Cola Bottling Co., **10** 222

Wometco Coffee Time, **I** 514

Wometco Enterprises, **I** 514

Wonderware Corp., **22** 374

Wong International Holdings, **16** 195

Wood Hall Trust plc, I 592–93; 50 200

Wood-Metal Industries, Inc. *see* Wood-Mode, Inc.

Wood-Mode, Inc., 23 518–20

Wood River Oil and Refining Company, **11** 193

Wood Shovel and Tool Company, **9** 71

Wood, Struthers & Winthrop, Inc., **22** 189

Wood Wyant Inc., **30** 496–98

Woodbridge Winery, **50** 388

Woodbury Co., **19** 380

Woodcock, Hess & Co., **9** 370

Woodcraft Industries Inc., 61 398–400

Woodhill Chemical Sales Company, **8** 333

Woodland Publishing, Inc., **37** 286

Woodlands, **7** 345–46

Woodmen of the World Life Insurance Society, **66** 227–28

Woods Equipment Company, **32** 28

Woodside Petroleum, **63** 440

Woodside Travel Trust, **26** 310

Woodville Appliances, Inc., **9** 121

Woodward-Clyde Group Inc., **45** 421

Woodward Foodservice Ltd. *see* The Big Food Group plc.

Woodward Governor Company, 13 565–68; 49 453–57 (upd.)

Woodworkers Warehouse, **22** 517

Woolco Department Stores *see* Woolworth Corporation.

Woolrich Inc., 62 393–96

The Woolwich plc, 30 492–95; 64 50

Woolworth Corporation, V 224–27; 20 528–32 (upd.) *see also* Kingfisher plc; Venator Group Inc.

Woolworth Holdings *see* Kingfisher plc.

Woolworth's Ltd., **II** 656 *see also* Kingfisher plc.

Wooster Preserving Company, **11** 211

Worcester Gas Light Co., **14** 124

Worcester Wire Works, **13** 369

Word, Inc., **14** 499; **38** 456

Word Publishing, **71** 401

WordPerfect Corporation, **10** 556–59 *see also* Corel Corporation.

WordStar International, **15** 149; **43** 151 *see also* The Learning Company Inc.

Work Wear Corp., **II** 607; **16** 229

Workflow Management, Inc., **65** 369–72

Working Assets Funding Service, **43** 473–76

Working Title Films, **23** 389

Workman Publishing Company, Inc., **70** 368–71

Workscape Inc., **42** 430

World Acceptance Corporation, **57** 415–18

World Airways, **10** 560–62; **28** 404

World Bank Group, **33** 462–65

World Book Group *see* Scott Fetzer Company.

World Book, Inc., **12** 554–56

World Championship Wrestling (WCW), **32** 516

World Color Press Inc., **12** 557–59; **19** 333; **21** 61

World Commerce Corporation, **25** 461

World Communications, Inc., **11** 184

World Duty Free Americas, Inc., **29** 509–12 (upd.)

World Duty Free plc, **33** 59

World Film Studio, **24** 437

World Flight Crew Services, **10** 560

World Foot Locker, **14** 293

World Fuel Services Corporation, **47** 449–51

World Gift Company, **9** 330

World International Holdings Limited, **12** 368

World Machinery Company, **45** 170–71

World Minerals Inc., **60** 16

World Online, **48** 398–39

World Poker Tour, LLC, **51** 205, 207

World Publications, LLC, **8** 423; **65** 373–75

World Savings and Loan, **19** 412; **47** 159–60

World Service Life Insurance Company, **27** 47

World Trade Corporation *see* International Business Machines Corporation.

World Trans, Inc., **33** 105

World Wrestling Federation Entertainment, Inc., **32** 514–17

World Yacht Enterprises, **22** 438

The World's Biggest Bookstore, **58** 185

World's Finest Chocolate Inc., **39** 422–24

WorldCom, Inc. *see* MCI WorldCom, Inc.

WorldCorp, Inc., **10** 560–62

WorldGames, **10** 560

The WorldMark Club, **33** 409

Worldmark of Wisconsin Inc. *see* Brady Corporation /idx>

Worlds of Fun, **22** 130

Worlds of Wonder, Inc., **25** 381; **26** 548

Worldview Systems Corporation, **26** 428; **46** 434

WorldWay Corporation, **16** 41

Worldwide Fiber Inc., **46** 267

Worldwide Insurance Co., **48** 9

Worldwide Logistics, **17** 505

Worldwide Restaurant Concepts, Inc., **47** 452–55

Worldwide Semiconductor Manufacturing Co., **47** 386

Worldwide Underwriters Insurance Co., **III** 218–19

Wormald International Ltd., **13** 245, 247; **63** 403

Worms et Cie, **27** 513–15 *see also* Sequana Capital.

Worth Corp., **27** 274

Worthen Banking Corporation, **15** 60

Worthington Foods, Inc., **14** 557–59

Worthington Industries, Inc., **7** 598–600; **21** 537–40 (upd.)

Woven Belting Co., **8** 13

WP Spinnaker Holdings, Inc. *see* Spinnaker Exploration Company.

WPL Holdings, **6** 604–06

WPM *see* Wall Paper Manufacturers.

WPP Group plc, **6** 53–54; **22** 201, 296; **23** 480; **48** 440–42 (upd.); **66** 157, 160, 378 *see also* Ogilvy Group Inc.

WPS Resources Corporation, **53** 367–70 (upd.)

Wrafton Laboratories Ltd., **59** 332

Wrather Corporation, **18** 354

Wrenn Furniture Company, **10** 184

WRG *see* Wells Rich Greene BDDP.

Wright & Company Realtors, **21** 257

Wright Aeronautical, **9** 16

Wright Company, **9** 416

Wright Group, **22** 519, 522

Wright Manufacturing Company, **8** 407

Wright Medical Group, Inc., **61** 401–05

Wright Plastic Products, **17** 310; **24** 160

Wrightson Limited, **19** 155

WS Atkins Plc, **45** 445–47

WSGC Holdings, Inc., **24** 530

WSI *see* Weather Services International.

WSI Corporation, **10** 88–89

WSM Inc., **11** 152

WSMC *see* Worldwide Semiconductor Manufacturing Co.

WSMP, Inc., **29** 202

WTD Industries, Inc., **20** 533–36

Wurlitzer Co., **17** 468; **18** 45

Württembergische Metallwarenfabrik AG (WMF), **60** 364–69

WVPP *see* Westvaco Corporation.

WVT Communications *see* Warwick Valley Telephone Company.

WWG Industries, Inc., **22** 352–53

WWT, Inc., **58** 371

WWTV, **18** 493

Wyandotte Chemicals Corporation, **18** 49

Wyant Corporation, **30** 496–98

Wycombe Bus Company, **28** 155–56

Wyeth, **50** 535–39 (upd.)

Wyeth-Ayerst Laboratories, **25** 477; **27** 69

Wyle Electronics, **14** 560–62; **19** 311

Wyly Corporation, **11** 468

Wyman-Gordon Company, **14** 563–65

Wymar, **76** 347

Wynkoop Brewing Company, **43** 407

Wynn's International, Inc., **22** 458; **33** 466–70

Wyse Technology, Inc., **10** 362; **15** 540–42

X

X-Acto, **12** 263

X-Chem Oil Field Chemicals, **8** 385

X-Rite, Inc., **48** 443–46

XA Systems Corporation, **10** 244

Xaos Tools, Inc., **10** 119

Xaver Fendt GmbH & Co. KG *see* AGCO Corporation.

XCare.net, Inc. *see* Quovadx Inc.

Xcel Energy Inc., **73** 384–89 (upd.)

Xcor International, **15** 538; **53** 364–65

Xeikon NV, **26** 540–42; **66** 260

Xenell Corporation, **48** 358

Xenia National Bank, **9** 474

Xenotech, **27** 58

Xeron, Inc., **56** 62

Xerox Corporation, **III** 171–73; **6** 288–90 (upd.); **26** 543–47 (upd.); **69** 374–80 (upd.)

Xetra, **59** 151

Xiamen Airlines, **33** 99

Xilinx, Inc., **16** 548–50

Xing Technology Corp., **53** 282

XM Satellite Radio Holdings, Inc., **69** 381–84

XMR, Inc., **42** 361

XP, **27** 474

Xpect First Aid Corp., **51** 76

Xpert Recruitment, Ltd., **26** 240

Xpress Automotive Group, Inc., **24** 339

XR Ventures LLC, **48** 446

XRAL Storage and Terminaling Co., **IV** 411

Xros, Inc., **36** 353

Xstrata PLC, **73** 390–93

XTO Energy Inc., **52** 425–27

XTRA Corp., **18** 67

Xtra Limited New Zealand, **54** 355–57

XTX Corp., **13** 127

Xuzhuo Liebherr Concrete Machinery Co. Ltd., **64** 241

Xynetics, **9** 251

Xytek Corp., **13** 127

Y

Yacimientos Petrolíferos Fiscales Sociedad Anónima *see* Repsol-YPF SA.

Yageo Corporation, **16** 551–53

Yahoo! Inc., **27** 516–19; **70** 372–75 (upd.)

Yakima Products Inc., **76** 120

Yakovlev, **24** 60

Yale and Valor, PLC, **50** 134–35

Yamagata Enterprises, **26** 310

Yamaha Corporation, **III** 656–59; **16** 554–58 (upd.); **40** 461–66 (upd.)

Yamaha Motor Co., Ltd., **59** 393, 397

Yamaha Musical Instruments, **16** 202; **43** 170

Index to Industries

Accounting

Advertising & Other Business Services

Bio-Technology

Chemicals

Conglomerates

The Procter & Gamble Company, 67
(upd.)
PT Astra International Tbk, 56
Pubco Corporation, 17
Pulsar Internacional S.A., 21
R.B. Pamplin Corp., 45
The Rank Organisation Plc, 14 (upd.)
Raymond Ltd., 77
Red Apple Group, Inc., 23
Roll International Corporation, 37
Rubbermaid Incorporated, 20 (upd.)
Samsung Group, I
San Miguel Corporation, 15
Sara Lee Corporation, 15 (upd.); 54
(upd.)
Schindler Holding AG, 29
Sea Containers Ltd., 29
Seaboard Corporation, 36
Sealaska Corporation, 60
Sequa Corporation, 54 (upd.)
Sequana Capital, 78 (upd.)
ServiceMaster Inc., 23 (upd.)
SHV Holdings N.V., 55
Sideco Americana S.A., 67
Sime Darby Berhad, 14; 36 (upd.)
Sistema JSFC, 73
Société du Louvre, 27
Standex International Corporation, 17; 44
(upd.)
Stinnes AG, 23 (upd.)
Sudbury Inc., 16
Sumitomo Corporation, I; 11 (upd.)
Swire Pacific Limited, I; 16 (upd.); 57
(upd.)
Talley Industries, Inc., 16
Tandycrafts, Inc., 31
TaurusHolding GmbH & Co. KG, 46
Teijin Limited, 61 (upd.)
Teledyne, Inc., I; 10 (upd.)
Tenneco Inc., I; 10 (upd.)
Textron Inc., I; 34 (upd.)
Thomas H. Lee Co., 24
Thorn Emi PLC, I
Thorn plc, 24
TI Group plc, 17
Time Warner Inc., IV; 7 (upd.)
Tokyu Corporation, 47 (upd.)
Tomen Corporation, 24 (upd.)
Tomkins plc, 11; 44 (upd.)
Toshiba Corporation, I; 12 (upd.); 40
(upd.)
Tractebel S.A., 20
Transamerica–An AEGON Company, I;
13 (upd.); 41 (upd.)
The Tranzonic Cos., 15
Triarc Companies, Inc., 8
Triple Five Group Ltd., 49
TRW Inc., I; 11 (upd.)
Tyco International Ltd., 63 (upd.)
Unilever, II; 7 (upd.); 32 (upd.)
Unión Fenosa, S.A., 51
United Technologies Corporation, 34
(upd.)
Universal Studios, Inc., 33
Valhi, Inc., 19
Valores Industriales S.A., 19
Veba A.G., I; 15 (upd.)
Vendôme Luxury Group plc, 27

Viacom Inc., 23 (upd.); 67 (upd.)
Virgin Group, 12; 32 (upd.)
Votorantim Participações S.A., 76
W.R. Grace & Company, I; 50
Walter Industries, Inc., 72 (upd.)
The Washington Companies, 33
Watsco Inc., 52
Wheaton Industries, 8
Whitbread PLC, 20 (upd.)
Whitman Corporation, 10 (upd.)
Whittaker Corporation, I
Wirtz Corporation, 72
WorldCorp, Inc., 10
Worms et Cie, 27
Yamaha Corporation, 40 (upd.)

Construction
A. Johnson & Company H.B., I
ABC Supply Co., Inc., 22
Abertis Infraestructuras, S.A., 65
Abrams Industries Inc., 23
Aegek S.A., 64
Alberici Corporation, 76
Amec Spie S.A., 57
AMREP Corporation, 21
Anthony & Sylvan Pools Corporation, 56
Asplundh Tree Expert Co., 59 (upd.)
ASV, Inc., 34; 66 (upd.)
The Auchter Company, 78
The Austin Company, 8
Autoroutes du Sud de la France SA, 55
Balfour Beatty plc, 36 (upd.)
Barratt Developments PLC, I
Barton Malow Company, 51
Bauerly Companies, 61
BE&K, Inc., 73
Beazer Homes USA, Inc., 17
Bechtel Group, Inc., I; 24 (upd.)
Bellway Plc, 45
BFC Construction Corporation, 25
Bilfinger & Berger AG, I; 55 (upd.)
Bird Corporation, 19
Birse Group PLC, 77
Black & Veatch LLP, 22
Boral Limited, 43 (upd.)
Bouygues S.A., I; 24 (upd.)
The Branch Group, Inc., 72
BRISA Auto-estradas de Portugal S.A., 64
Brown & Root, Inc., 13
Bufete Industrial, S.A. de C.V., 34
Building Materials Holding Corporation,
52
Bulley & Andrews, LLC, 55
C.R. Meyer and Sons Company, 74
CalMat Co., 19
Cavco Industries, Inc., 65
Centex Corporation, 8; 29 (upd.)
Chugach Alaska Corporation, 60
Cianbro Corporation, 14
The Clark Construction Group, Inc., 8
Colas S.A., 31
D.R. Horton, Inc., 58
Day & Zimmermann, Inc., 31 (upd.)
Dick Corporation, 64
Dillingham Construction Corporation, I;
44 (upd.)
Dominion Homes, Inc., 19
The Drees Company, Inc., 41

Dycom Industries, Inc., 57
E.W. Howell Co., Inc., 72
Edw. C. Levy Co., 42
Eiffage, 27
Ellerbe Becket, 41
EMCOR Group Inc., 60
Empresas ICA Sociedad Controladora,
S.A. de C.V., 41
Encompass Services Corporation, 33
Engle Homes, Inc., 46
Environmental Industries, Inc., 31
Eurotunnel PLC, 13
Fairclough Construction Group PLC, I
Fleetwood Enterprises, Inc., 22 (upd.)
Fluor Corporation, I; 8 (upd.); 34 (upd.)
Forest City Enterprises, Inc., 52 (upd.)
Fred Weber, Inc., 61
George Wimpey plc, 12; 51 (upd.)
Gilbane, Inc., 34
Granite Construction Incorporated, 61
Granite Rock Company, 26
Great Lakes Dredge & Dock Company,
69
Grupo Dragados SA, 55
Grupo Ferrovial, S.A., 40
H.J. Russell & Company, 66
Habitat for Humanity International, 36
Heery International, Inc., 58
Heijmans N.V., 66
Henry Boot plc, 76
Hensel Phelps Construction Company, 72
Hillsdown Holdings plc, 24 (upd.)
Hochtief AG, 33
Hoffman Corporation 78
Horton Homes, Inc., 25
Hospitality Worldwide Services, Inc., 26
Hovnanian Enterprises, Inc., 29
IHC Caland N.V., 71
J.A. Jones, Inc., 16
J.F. Shea Co., Inc., 55
J.H. Findorff and Son, Inc., 60
Jarvis plc, 39
JLG Industries, Inc., 52
John Brown PLC, I
John Laing plc, I; 51 (upd.)
John W. Danforth Company, 48
Kajima Corporation, I; 51 (upd.)
Kaufman and Broad Home Corporation,
8
KB Home, 45 (upd.)
Kellogg Brown & Root, Inc., 62 (upd.)
Kitchell Corporation, 14
The Koll Company, 8
Komatsu Ltd., 16 (upd.)
Kraus-Anderson, Incorporated, 36
Kumagai Gumi Company, Ltd., I
L'Entreprise Jean Lefebvre, 23
Ledcor Industries Limited, 46
Lennar Corporation, 11
Lincoln Property Company, 8
Lindal Cedar Homes, Inc., 29
Linde A.G., I
MasTec, Inc., 55
Matrix Service Company, 65
McCarthy Building Companies, Inc., 48
Mellon-Stuart Company, I
Michael Baker Corp., 14
Modtech Holdings, Inc., 77

Electrical & Electronics

Financial Services: Banks

Financial Services: Excluding Banks

Zurich Financial Services, 42 (upd.)

Food Products

A. Moksel AG, 59
Agway, Inc., 7
Ajinomoto Co., Inc., II; 28 (upd.)
Alabama Farmers Cooperative, Inc., 63
The Albert Fisher Group plc, 41
Alberto-Culver Company, 8
Aldi Group, 13
Alfred Ritter GmbH & Co. KG, 58
Allen Canning Company, 76
Alpine Confections, Inc., 71
Alpine Lace Brands, Inc., 18
American Crystal Sugar Company, 11; 32
   (upd.)
American Foods Group, 43
American Italian Pasta Company, 27; 76
   (upd.)
American Maize-Products Co., 14
American Pop Corn Company, 59
American Rice, Inc., 33
Amfac/JMB Hawaii L.L.C., 24 (upd.)
Amy's Kitchen Inc., 76
Annie's Homegrown, Inc., 59
Archer-Daniels-Midland Company, 32
   (upd.)
Archway Cookies, Inc., 29
Arcor S.A.I.C., 66
Arla Foods amba, 48
Arnott's Ltd., 66
Associated British Foods plc, II; 13 (upd.);
   41 (upd.)
Associated Milk Producers, Inc., 11; 48
   (upd.)
Atlantic Premium Brands, Ltd., 57
August Storck KG, 66
Aurora Foods Inc., 32
Awrey Bakeries, Inc., 56
B&G Foods, Inc., 40
The B. Manischewitz Company, LLC, 31
Bahlsen GmbH & Co. KG, 44
Balance Bar Company, 32
Baltek Corporation, 34
Bar-S Foods Company, 76
Barilla G. e R. Fratelli S.p.A., 17; 50
   (upd.)
Barry Callebaut AG, 71 (upd.)
Bear Creek Corporation, 38
Beatrice Company, II
Beech-Nut Nutrition Corporation, 21; 51
   (upd.)
Bel/Kaukauna USA, 76
Ben & Jerry's Homemade, Inc., 10; 35
   (upd.)
Berkeley Farms, Inc., 46
Besnier SA, 19
Bestfoods, 22 (upd.)
Bettys & Taylors of Harrogate Ltd., 72
Birds Eye Foods, Inc., 69 (upd.)
Blue Bell Creameries L.P., 30
Blue Diamond Growers, 28
Bob's Red Mill Natural Foods, Inc., 63
Bobs Candies, Inc., 70
Bonduelle SA, 51
Bongrain SA, 25
Booker PLC, 13; 31 (upd.)
Borden, Inc., II; 22 (upd.)

Boyd Coffee Company, 53
Brach and Brock Confections, Inc., 15
Brake Bros plc, 45
Bridgford Foods Corporation, 27
Brigham's Inc., 72
Brioche Pasquier S.A., 58
Brothers Gourmet Coffees, Inc., 20
Broughton Foods Co., 17
Brown & Haley, 23
Bruce Foods Corporation, 39
Bruegger's Corporation, 63
BSN Groupe S.A., II
Bumble Bee Seafoods L.L.C., 64
Bunge Brasil S.A. 78
Bunge Ltd., 62
Burns, Philp & Company Ltd., 63
Bush Boake Allen Inc., 30
Bush Brothers & Company, 45
C.H. Robinson Worldwide, Inc., 40
   (upd.)
Cadbury Schweppes PLC, II; 49 (upd.)
Cagle's, Inc., 20
Cal-Maine Foods, Inc., 69
Calavo Growers, Inc., 47
Calcot Ltd., 33
Campbell Soup Company, II; 7 (upd.); 26
   (upd.); 71 (upd.)
The Campina Group, 78
Campofrío Alimentación S.A, 59
Canada Packers Inc., II
Cargill Inc., 13 (upd.)
Carnation Company, II
The Carriage House Companies, Inc., 55
Carroll's Foods, Inc., 46
Carvel Corporation, 35
Castle & Cooke, Inc., II; 20 (upd.)
Cattleman's, Inc., 20
Celestial Seasonings, Inc., 16
Central Soya Company, Inc., 7
Chelsea Milling Company, 29
Chicken of the Sea International, 24
   (upd.)
China National Cereals, Oils and
   Foodstuffs Import and Export
   Corporation (COFCO), 76
Chiquita Brands International, Inc., 7; 21
   (upd.)
Chock Full o'Nuts Corp., 17
Chocoladefabriken Lindt & Sprüngli AG,
   27
Chr. Hansen Group A/S, 70
CHS Inc., 60
Chupa Chups S.A., 38
Clif Bar Inc., 50
Cloetta Fazer AB, 70
The Clorox Company, 22 (upd.)
Clougherty Packing Company, 72
Coca-Cola Enterprises, Inc., 13
Cold Stone Creamery, 69
Coleman Natural Products, Inc., 68
Community Coffee Co. L.L.C., 53
ConAgra Foods, Inc., II; 12 (upd.); 42
   (upd.)
The Connell Company, 29
ContiGroup Companies, Inc., 43 (upd.)
Continental Grain Company, 10; 13
   (upd.)
CoolBrands International Inc., 35

CPC International Inc., II
Cranswick plc, 40
CSM N.V., 65
Cumberland Packing Corporation, 26
Curtice-Burns Foods, Inc., 7; 21 (upd.)
Czarnikow-Rionda Company, Inc., 32
Dairy Crest Group plc, 32
Dalgety, PLC, II
Danisco A/S, 44
Dannon Co., Inc., 14
Darigold, Inc., 9
Dawn Food Products, Inc., 17
Dean Foods Company, 7; 21 (upd.); 73
   (upd.)
DeKalb Genetics Corporation, 17
Del Monte Foods Company, 7; 23 (upd.)
Di Giorgio Corp., 12
Diageo plc, 24 (upd.)
Diamond of California, 64 (upd.)
Dippin' Dots, Inc., 56
Dole Food Company, Inc., 9; 31 (upd.);
   68 (upd.)
Domino Sugar Corporation, 26
Doskocil Companies, Inc., 12
Dot Foods, Inc., 69
Dreyer's Grand Ice Cream, Inc., 17
The Earthgrains Company, 36
Emge Packing Co., Inc., 11
Empresas Polar SA, 55 (upd.)
Eridania Béghin-Say S.A., 36
ERLY Industries Inc., 17
Eskimo Pie Corporation, 21
Ezaki Glico Company Ltd., 72
Farley's & Sathers Candy Company, Inc.,
   62
Farmland Foods, Inc., 7
Farmland Industries, Inc., 48
Ferrero SpA, 54
Fieldale Farms Corporation, 23
Fleer Corporation, 15
Fleury Michon S.A., 39
Florida Crystals Inc., 35
Flowers Industries, Inc., 12; 35 (upd.)
Fonterra Co-Operative Group Ltd., 58
FoodBrands America, Inc., 23
Foster Poultry Farms, 32
Fred Usinger Inc., 54
Fresh America Corporation, 20
Fresh Foods, Inc., 29
Friesland Coberco Dairy Foods Holding
   N.V., 59
Frito-Lay Company, 32
Frito-Lay North America, 73 (upd.)
Fromageries Bel, 23
Fyffes Plc, 38
Galaxy Nutritional Foods, Inc., 58
Gardenburger, Inc., 33; 76 (upd.)
Geest Plc, 38
General Mills, Inc., II; 10 (upd.); 36
   (upd.)
George A. Hormel and Company, II
George Weston Limited, 36 (upd.)
Gerber Products Company, 7; 21 (upd.)
Ghirardelli Chocolate Company, 30
Givaudan SA, 43
Glaces Thiriet S.A., 76
Glanbia plc, 59
Global Berry Farms LLC, 62

Food Services & Retailers

Health & Personal Care Products

Health Care Services

Information Technology

Insurance

Mitsui Mutual Life Insurance Company, III; 39 (upd.)
Modern Woodmen of America, 66
Munich Re (Münchener Rückversicherungs-Gesellschaft Aktiengesellschaft in München), III; 46 (upd.)
The Mutual Benefit Life Insurance Company, III
The Mutual Life Insurance Company of New York, III
Nationale-Nederlanden N.V., III
New England Mutual Life Insurance Company, III
New York Life Insurance Company, III; 45 (upd.)
Nippon Life Insurance Company, III; 60 (upd.)
Northwestern Mutual Life Insurance Company, III; 45 (upd.)
NYMAGIC, Inc., 41
Ohio Casualty Corp., 11
Old Republic International Corporation, 11; 58 (upd.)
Oregon Dental Service Health Plan, Inc., 51
Palmer & Cay, Inc., 69
Pan-American Life Insurance Company, 48
The Paul Revere Corporation, 12
Pennsylvania Blue Shield, III
The PMI Group, Inc., 49
Preserver Group, Inc., 44
Principal Mutual Life Insurance Company, III
The Progressive Corporation, 11; 29 (upd.)
Provident Life and Accident Insurance Company of America, III
Prudential Corporation PLC, III
The Prudential Insurance Company of America, III; 30 (upd.)
Prudential plc, 48 (upd.)
Radian Group Inc., 42
The Regence Group, 74
Reliance Group Holdings, Inc., III
Riunione Adriatica di Sicurtà SpA, III
Royal & Sun Alliance Insurance Group plc, 55 (upd.)
Royal Insurance Holdings PLC, III
SAFECO Corporaton, III
The St. Paul Companies, Inc., III; 22 (upd.)
SCOR S.A., 20
Skandia Insurance Company, Ltd., 50
StanCorp Financial Group, Inc., 56
The Standard Life Assurance Company, III
State Auto Financial Corporation, 77
State Farm Mutual Automobile Insurance Company, III; 51 (upd.)
State Financial Services Corporation, 51
Stewart Information Services Corporation 78
Sumitomo Life Insurance Company, III; 60 (upd.)
The Sumitomo Marine and Fire Insurance Company, Limited, III

Sun Alliance Group PLC, III
SunAmerica Inc., 11
Svenska Handelsbanken AB, 50 (upd.)
Swiss Reinsurance Company (Schweizerische Rückversicherungs-Gesellschaft), III; 46 (upd.)
Teachers Insurance and Annuity Association-College Retirement Equities Fund, III; 45 (upd.)
Texas Industries, Inc., 8
TIG Holdings, Inc., 26
The Tokio Marine and Fire Insurance Co., Ltd., III
Torchmark Corporation, 9; 33 (upd.)
Transatlantic Holdings, Inc., 11
The Travelers Corporation, III
UICI, 33
Union des Assurances de Pans, III
United National Group, Ltd., 63
Unitrin Inc., 16; 78 (upd.)
UNUM Corp., 13
UnumProvident Corporation, 52 (upd.)
USAA, 10
USF&G Corporation, III
Victoria Group, 44 (upd.)
VICTORIA Holding AG, III
Vision Service Plan Inc., 77
W.R. Berkley Corporation, 15; 74 (upd.)
Washington National Corporation, 12
The Wawanesa Mutual Insurance Company, 68
WellChoice, Inc., 67 (upd.)
Westfield Group, 69
White Mountains Insurance Group, Ltd., 48
Willis Corroon Group plc, 25
Winterthur Group, III; 68 (upd.)
The Yasuda Fire and Marine Insurance Company, Limited, III
The Yasuda Mutual Life Insurance Company, III; 39 (upd.)
Zürich Versicherungs-Gesellschaft, III

Legal Services

Akin, Gump, Strauss, Hauer & Feld, L.L.P., 33
American Bar Association, 35
American Lawyer Media Holdings, Inc., 32
Amnesty International, 50
Andrews Kurth, LLP, 71
Arnold & Porter, 35
Baker & Hostetler LLP, 40
Baker & McKenzie, 10; 42 (upd.)
Baker and Botts, L.L.P., 28
Bingham Dana LLP, 43
Brobeck, Phleger & Harrison, LLP, 31
Cadwalader, Wickersham & Taft, 32
Chadbourne & Parke, 36
Cleary, Gottlieb, Steen & Hamilton, 35
Clifford Chance LLP, 38
Coudert Brothers, 30
Covington & Burling, 40
Cravath, Swaine & Moore, 43
Davis Polk & Wardwell, 36
Debevoise & Plimpton, 39
Dechert, 43

Dewey Ballantine LLP, 48
Dorsey & Whitney LLP, 47
Fenwick & West LLP, 34
Fish & Neave, 54
Foley & Lardner, 28
Fried, Frank, Harris, Shriver & Jacobson, 35
Fulbright & Jaworski L.L.P., 47
Gibson, Dunn & Crutcher LLP, 36
Greenberg Traurig, LLP, 65
Heller, Ehrman, White & McAuliffe, 41
Hildebrandt International, 29
Hogan & Hartson L.L.P., 44
Holland & Knight LLP, 60
Holme Roberts & Owen LLP, 28
Hughes Hubbard & Reed LLP, 44
Hunton & Williams, 35
Jenkens & Gilchrist, P.C., 65
Jones, Day, Reavis & Pogue, 33
Kelley Drye & Warren LLP, 40
King & Spalding, 23
Kirkland & Ellis LLP, 65
Latham & Watkins, 33
LeBoeuf, Lamb, Greene & MacRae, L.L.P., 29
The Legal Aid Society, 48
Mayer, Brown, Rowe & Maw, 47
Milbank, Tweed, Hadley & McCloy, 27
Morgan, Lewis & Bockius LLP, 29
Morrison & Foerster LLP 78
O'Melveny & Myers, 37
Oppenheimer Wolff & Donnelly LLP, 71
Orrick, Herrington and Sutcliffe LLP, 76
Patton Boggs LLP, 71
Paul, Hastings, Janofsky & Walker LLP, 27
Paul, Weiss, Rifkind, Wharton & Garrison, 47
Pepper Hamilton LLP, 43
Perkins Coie LLP, 56
Pillsbury Madison & Sutro LLP, 29
Pre-Paid Legal Services, Inc., 20
Proskauer Rose LLP, 47
Ropes & Gray, 40
Saul Ewing LLP, 74
Shearman & Sterling, 32
Sidley Austin Brown & Wood, 40
Simpson Thacher & Bartlett, 39
Skadden, Arps, Slate, Meagher & Flom, 18
Snell & Wilmer L.L.P., 28
Southern Poverty Law Center, Inc., 74
Stroock & Stroock & Lavan LLP, 40
Sullivan & Cromwell, 26
Vinson & Elkins L.L.P., 30
Wachtell, Lipton, Rosen & Katz, 47
Weil, Gotshal & Manges LLP, 55
White & Case LLP, 35
Williams & Connolly LLP, 47
Wilson Sonsini Goodrich & Rosati, 34
Winston & Strawn, 35
Womble Carlyle Sandridge & Rice, PLLC, 52

Manufacturing

A-dec, Inc., 53
A. Schulman, Inc., 49 (upd.)
A.B.Dick Company, 28

X-Rite, Inc., 48
Xerox Corporation, 69 (upd.)
Yamaha Corporation, III; 16 (upd.)
The York Group, Inc., 50
York International Corp., 13
Young Innovations, Inc., 44
Zebra Technologies Corporation, 53 (upd.)
Zero Corporation, 17
ZiLOG, Inc., 72 (upd.)
Zindart Ltd., 60
Zippo Manufacturing Company, 18; 71 (upd.)
Zodiac S.A., 36
Zygo Corporation, 42

Materials

AK Steel Holding Corporation, 19
American Biltrite Inc., 16
American Colloid Co., 13
American Standard Inc., III
Ameriwood Industries International Corp., 17
Apasco S.A. de C.V., 51
Apogee Enterprises, Inc., 8
Asahi Glass Company, Limited, III
Asbury Carbons, Inc., 68
Bairnco Corporation, 28
Bayou Steel Corporation, 31
Blessings Corp., 19
Blue Circle Industries PLC, III
Bodycote International PLC, 63
Boral Limited, III
British Vita PLC, 9
Brush Engineered Materials Inc., 67
California Steel Industries, Inc., 67
Callanan Industries, Inc., 60
Cameron & Barkley Company, 28
Carborundum Company, 15
Carl-Zeiss-Stiftung, 34 (upd.)
Carlisle Companies Incorporated, 8
Carter Holt Harvey Ltd., 70
Cemex SA de CV, 20
Century Aluminum Company, 52
CertainTeed Corporation, 35
Chargeurs International, 21 (upd.)
Chemfab Corporation, 35
Cimentos de Portugal SGPS S.A. (Cimpor), 76
Cold Spring Granite Company Inc., 16; 67 (upd.)
Columbia Forest Products Inc. 78
Compagnie de Saint-Gobain S.A., III; 16 (upd.)
Cookson Group plc, III; 44 (upd.)
Corning Incorporated, III
CSR Limited, III
Dal-Tile International Inc., 22
The David J. Joseph Company, 14; 76 (upd.)
The Dexter Corporation, 12 (upd.)
Dyckerhoff AG, 35
Dyson Group PLC, 71
ECC Group plc, III
Edw. C. Levy Co., 42
84 Lumber Company, 9; 39 (upd.)
ElkCorp, 52

English China Clays Ltd., 15 (upd.); 40 (upd.)
Envirodyne Industries, Inc., 17
Feldmuhle Nobel A.G., III
Fibreboard Corporation, 16
Florida Rock Industries, Inc., 46
Foamex International Inc., 17
Formica Corporation, 13
GAF Corporation, 22 (upd.)
The Geon Company, 11
Giant Cement Holding, Inc., 23
Gibraltar Steel Corporation, 37
Granite Rock Company, 26
Groupe Sidel S.A., 21
Harbison-Walker Refractories Company, 24
Harrisons & Crosfield plc, III
Heidelberger Zement AG, 31
Hexcel Corporation, 28
Holderbank Financière Glaris Ltd., III
Holnam Inc., 39 (upd.)
Holt and Bugbee Company, 66
Homasote Company, 72
Howmet Corp., 12
Huttig Building Products, Inc., 73
Ibstock Brick Ltd., 14; 37 (upd.)
Imerys S.A., 40 (upd.)
Internacional de Ceramica, S.A. de C.V., 53
International Shipbreaking Ltd. L.L.C., 67
Joseph T. Ryerson & Son, Inc., 15
Lafarge Coppée S.A., III
Lafarge Corporation, 28
Lehigh Portland Cement Company, 23
Manville Corporation, III; 7 (upd.)
Material Sciences Corporation, 63
Matsushita Electric Works, Ltd., III; 7 (upd.)
McJunkin Corporation, 63
Medusa Corporation, 24
Mitsubishi Materials Corporation, III
Nippon Sheet Glass Company, Limited, III
North Pacific Group, Inc., 61
OmniSource Corporation, 14
Onoda Cement Co., Ltd., III
Otor S.A., 77
Owens-Corning Fiberglass Corporation, III
Pilkington plc, III; 34 (upd.)
Pioneer International Limited, III
PPG Industries, Inc., III
Redland plc, III
Rinker Group Ltd., 65
RMC Group p.l.c., III
Rock of Ages Corporation, 37
Royal Group Technologies Limited, 73
The Rugby Group plc, 31
Schuff Steel Company, 26
Sekisui Chemical Co., Ltd., III; 72 (upd.)
Severstal Joint Stock Company, 65
Shaw Industries, 9
The Sherwin-Williams Company, III; 13 (upd.)
The Siam Cement Public Company Limited, 56
SIG plc, 71
Simplex Technologies Inc., 21

Siskin Steel & Supply Company, 70
Solutia Inc., 52
Sommer-Allibert S.A., 19
Southdown, Inc., 14
Spartech Corporation, 19; 76 (upd.)
Ssangyong Cement Industrial Co., Ltd., III; 61 (upd.)
Steel Technologies Inc., 63
Sun Distributors L.P., 12
Symyx Technologies, Inc., 77
Tarmac PLC, III
Tarmac plc, 28 (upd.)
TOTO LTD., III; 28 (upd.)
Toyo Sash Co., Ltd., III
Tuscarora Inc., 29
U.S. Aggregates, Inc., 42
Ube Industries, Ltd., III
United States Steel Corporation, 50 (upd.)
USG Corporation, III; 26 (upd.)
Usinas Siderúrgicas de Minas Gerais S.A., 77
Vicat S.A., 70
voestalpine AG, 57 (upd.)
Vulcan Materials Company, 7; 52 (upd.)
Wacker-Chemie GmbH, 35
Walter Industries, Inc., III
Waxman Industries, Inc., 9
Weber et Broutin France, 66
Wienerberger AG, 70
Wolseley plc, 64
Zoltek Companies, Inc., 37

Mining & Metals

A.M. Castle & Co., 25
Aggregate Industries plc, 36
Agnico-Eagle Mines Limited, 71
Aktiebolaget SKF, 38 (upd.)
Alcan Aluminium Limited, IV; 31 (upd.)
Alcoa Inc., 56 (upd.)
Alleghany Corporation, 10
Allegheny Ludlum Corporation, 8
Alrosa Company Ltd., 62
Altos Hornos de México, S.A. de C.V., 42
Aluminum Company of America, IV; 20 (upd.)
AMAX Inc., IV
AMCOL International Corporation, 59 (upd.)
Amsted Industries Incorporated, 7
Anglo American Corporation of South Africa Limited, IV; 16 (upd.)
Anglo American PLC, 50 (upd.)
Aquarius Platinum Ltd., 63
ARBED S.A., IV, 22 (upd.)
Arch Mineral Corporation, 7
Armco Inc., IV
ASARCO Incorporated, IV
Ashanti Goldfields Company Limited, 43
Atchison Casting Corporation, 39
Barrick Gold Corporation, 34
Battle Mountain Gold Company, 23
Benguet Corporation, 58
Bethlehem Steel Corporation, IV; 7 (upd.); 27 (upd.)
BHP Billiton, 67 (upd.)
Birmingham Steel Corporation, 13; 40 (upd.)
Boart Longyear Company, 26

Zambia Industrial and Mining
Corporation Ltd., IV

Paper & Forestry

Personal Services

Petroleum

Oil States International, Inc., 77
ÖMV Aktiengesellschaft, IV
Oryx Energy Company, 7
Parker Drilling Company, 28
Patina Oil & Gas Corporation, 24
Patterson-UTI Energy, Inc., 55
Pennzoil-Quaker State Company, IV; 20 (upd.); 50 (upd.)
Pertamina, IV; 56 (upd.)
Petro-Canada Limited, IV
Petrobras Energia Participaciones S.A., 72
PetroFina S.A., IV; 26 (upd.)
Petróleo Brasileiro S.A., IV
Petróleos de Portugal S.A., IV
Petróleos de Venezuela S.A., IV; 74 (upd.)
Petróleos del Ecuador, IV
Petróleos Mexicanos, IV; 19 (upd.)
Petroleum Development Oman LLC, IV
Petroliam Nasional Bhd (Petronas), IV; 56 (upd.)
Petron Corporation, 58
Phillips Petroleum Company, IV; 40 (upd.)
Pioneer Natural Resources Company, 59
Pogo Producing Company, 39
Polski Koncern Naftowy ORLEN S.A., 77
Premcor Inc., 37
Pride International Inc. 78
PTT Public Company Ltd., 56
Qatar General Petroleum Corporation, IV
Quaker State Corporation, 7; 21 (upd.)
Range Resources Corporation, 45
Repsol-YPF S.A., IV; 16 (upd.); 40 (upd.)
Resource America, Inc., 42
Rowan Companies, Inc., 43
Royal Dutch/Shell Group, IV; 49 (upd.)
RWE AG, 50 (upd.)
St. Mary Land & Exploration Company, 63
Santa Fe International Corporation, 38
Sasol Limited, IV; 47 (upd.)
Saudi Arabian Oil Company, IV; 17 (upd.); 50 (upd.)
Schlumberger Limited, 17 (upd.); 59 (upd.)
Seagull Energy Corporation, 11
Seitel, Inc., 47
Shanghai Petrochemical Co., Ltd., 18
Shell Oil Company, IV; 14 (upd.); 41 (upd.)
Showa Shell Sekiyu K.K., IV; 59 (upd.)
OAO Siberian Oil Company (Sibneft), 49
Smith International, Inc., 59 (upd.)
Société Nationale Elf Aquitaine, IV; 7 (upd.)
Sonatrach, 65 (upd.)
Spinnaker Exploration Company, 72
Statoil ASA, 61 (upd.)
Suburban Propane Partners, L.P., 30
Sun Company, Inc., IV
Suncor Energy Inc., 54
Sunoco, Inc., 28 (upd.)
Superior Energy Services, Inc., 65
OAO Surgutneftegaz, 48
Swift Energy Company, 63
Talisman Energy Inc., 9; 47 (upd.)
OAO Tatneft, 45
TEPPCO Partners, L.P., 73

Tesoro Petroleum Corporation, 7; 45 (upd.)
Texaco Inc., IV; 14 (upd.); 41 (upd.)
Tidewater Inc., 37 (upd.)
Tom Brown, Inc., 37
Tonen Corporation, IV; 16 (upd.)
TonenGeneral Sekiyu K.K., 54 (upd.)
Tosco Corporation, 7
TOTAL S.A., IV; 24 (upd.)
TransMontaigne Inc., 28
Transocean Sedco Forex Inc., 45
Travel Ports of America, Inc., 17
Triton Energy Corporation, 11
Türkiye Petrolleri Anonim Ortakliği, IV
Ultra Petroleum Corporation, 71
Ultramar Diamond Shamrock Corporation, IV; 31 (upd.)
Union Texas Petroleum Holdings, Inc., 9
Unit Corporation, 63
Universal Compression, Inc., 59
Unocal Corporation, IV; 24 (upd.); 71 (upd.)
USX Corporation, IV; 7 (upd.)
Valero Energy Corporation, 7; 71 (upd.)
Varco International, Inc., 42
Vastar Resources, Inc., 24
Vintage Petroleum, Inc., 42
Wascana Energy Inc., 13
Weatherford International, Inc., 39
Webber Oil Company, 61
Western Atlas Inc., 12
Western Company of North America, 15
Western Gas Resources, Inc., 45
Westport Resources Corporation, 63
The Williams Companies, Inc., IV; 31 (upd.)
World Fuel Services Corporation, 47
XTO Energy Inc., 52
YPF Sociedad Anonima, IV

Publishing & Printing
A.B.Dick Company, 28
A.H. Belo Corporation, 10; 30 (upd.)
AccuWeather, Inc., 73
Advance Publications Inc., IV; 19 (upd.)
Advanced Marketing Services, Inc., 34
Advanstar Communications, Inc., 57
Affiliated Publications, Inc., 7
Agence France-Presse, 34
Agora S.A. Group, 77
American Banknote Corporation, 30
American Girl, Inc., 69
American Greetings Corporation, 7; 22 (upd.)
American Media, Inc., 27
American Printing House for the Blind, 26
American Reprographics Company, 75
Andrews McMeel Universal, 40
The Antioch Company, 40
AOL Time Warner Inc., 57 (upd.)
Arandell Corporation, 37
Archie Comics Publications, Inc., 63
Arnoldo Mondadori Editore S.p.A., IV; 19 (upd.); 54 (upd.)
The Associated Press, 31 (upd.); 73 (upd.)
The Atlantic Group, 23
Axel Springer Verlag AG, IV; 20 (upd.)

Banta Corporation, 12; 32 (upd.)
Bauer Publishing Group, 7
Bayard SA, 49
Berlitz International, Inc., 13
Bernard C. Harris Publishing Company, Inc., 39
Bertelsmann A.G., IV; 15 (upd.); 43 (upd.)
Bibliographisches Institut & F.A. Brockhaus AG, 74
Big Flower Press Holdings, Inc., 21
Blackwell Publishing Ltd. 78
Blue Mountain Arts, Inc., 29
Bobit Publishing Company, 55
Bonnier AB, 52
Book-of-the-Month Club, Inc., 13
Bowne & Co., Inc., 23
Broderbund Software, 13; 29 (upd.)
Brown Printing Company, 26
Burda Holding GmbH. & Co., 23
The Bureau of National Affairs, Inc., 23
Butterick Co., Inc., 23
Cadmus Communications Corporation, 23
Cahners Business Information, 43
Carl Allers Etablissement A/S, 72
CCH Inc., 14
Central Newspapers, Inc., 10
Champion Industries, Inc., 28
Cherry Lane Music Publishing Company, Inc., 62
ChoicePoint Inc., 65
The Christian Science Publishing Society, 55
The Chronicle Publishing Company, Inc., 23
Chrysalis Group plc, 40
CMP Media Inc., 26
Commerce Clearing House, Inc., 7
Concepts Direct, Inc., 39
Condé Nast Publications, Inc., 13; 59 (upd.)
Consolidated Graphics, Inc., 70
Consumers Union, 26
The Copley Press, Inc., 23
Courier Corporation, 41
Cowles Media Company, 23
Cox Enterprises, Inc., IV; 22 (upd.)
Crain Communications, Inc., 12; 35 (upd.)
Current, Inc., 37
Cygnus Business Media, Inc., 56
Dai Nippon Printing Co., Ltd., IV; 57 (upd.)
Daily Mail and General Trust plc, 19
Dawson Holdings PLC, 43
Day Runner, Inc., 14
DC Comics Inc., 25
De La Rue plc, 10; 34 (upd.)
DeLorme Publishing Company, Inc., 53
Deluxe Corporation, 7; 22 (upd.); 73 (upd.)
Dennis Publishing Ltd., 62
Dex Media, Inc., 65
Donruss Playoff L.P., 66
Dorling Kindersley Holdings plc, 20
Dover Publications Inc., 34

SPIEGEL-Verlag Rudolf Augstein GmbH
& Co. KG, 44
Standard Register Co., 15
Tamedia AG, 53
Taylor & Francis Group plc, 44
Taylor Corporation, 36
Taylor Publishing Company, 12; 36 (upd.)
Thomas Nelson, Inc., 14; 38 (upd.)
Thomas Publishing Company, 26
The Thomson Corporation, 8; 34 (upd.);
77 (upd.)
Time Out Group Ltd., 68
The Times Mirror Company, IV; 17
(upd.)
Tom Doherty Associates Inc., 25
Toppan Printing Co., Ltd., IV; 58 (upd.)
The Topps Company, Inc., 34 (upd.)
Torstar Corporation, 29
Trader Classified Media N.V., 57
Tribune Company, IV; 22 (upd.); 63
(upd.)
Trinity Mirror plc, 49 (upd.)
Tyndale House Publishers, Inc., 57
U.S. News and World Report Inc., 30
United Business Media plc, 52 (upd.)
United News & Media plc, IV; 28 (upd.)
United Press International, Inc., 25; 73
(upd.)
Valassis Communications, Inc., 8
Value Line, Inc., 16; 73 (upd.)
Vance Publishing Corporation, 64
Verlagsgruppe Georg von Holtzbrinck
GmbH, 35
Village Voice Media, Inc., 38
VNU N.V., 27
Volt Information Sciences Inc., 26
W.W. Norton & Company, Inc., 28
Wallace Computer Services, Inc., 36
Walsworth Publishing Co. 78
The Washington Post Company, IV; 20
(upd.)
Waverly, Inc., 16
Wegener NV, 53
Wenner Media, Inc., 32
West Group, 7; 34 (upd.)
Western Publishing Group, Inc., 13
WH Smith PLC, V; 42 (upd.)
William Reed Publishing Ltd. 78
Wolters Kluwer NV, 14; 33 (upd.)
Workman Publishing Company, Inc., 70
World Book, Inc., 12
World Color Press Inc., 12
World Publications, LLC, 65
Xeikon NV, 26
Zebra Technologies Corporation, 14
Ziff Davis Media Inc., 12; 36 (upd.); 73
(upd.)
Zondervan Corporation, 24; 71 (upd.)

Real Estate

Alexander's, Inc., 45
Alico, Inc., 63
AMB Property Corporation, 57
Amfac/JMB Hawaii L.L.C., 24 (upd.)
Apartment Investment and Management
Company, 49
Archstone-Smith Trust, 49
Associated Estates Realty Corporation, 25

AvalonBay Communities, Inc., 58
Berkshire Realty Holdings, L.P., 49
Boston Properties, Inc., 22
Bramalea Ltd., 9
British Land Plc, 54
Camden Property Trust, 77
Canary Wharf Group Plc, 30
CapStar Hotel Company, 21
CarrAmerica Realty Corporation, 56
Castle & Cooke, Inc., 20 (upd.)
Catellus Development Corporation, 24
CB Commercial Real Estate Services
Group, Inc., 21
CB Richard Ellis Group, Inc., 70 (upd.)
Chateau Communities, Inc., 37
Chelsfield PLC, 67
Cheung Kong (Holdings) Limited, IV; 20
(upd.)
Clayton Homes Incorporated, 54 (upd.)
Colonial Properties Trust, 65
The Corcoran Group, Inc., 58
CoStar Group, Inc., 73
Cousins Properties Incorporated, 65
Del Webb Corporation, 14
Developers Diversified Realty
Corporation, 69
Duke Realty Corporation, 57
EastGroup Properties, Inc., 67
The Edward J. DeBartolo Corporation, 8
Enterprise Inns plc, 59
Equity Office Properties Trust, 54
Equity Residential, 49
Erickson Retirement Communities, 57
Fairfield Communities, Inc., 36
First Industrial Realty Trust, Inc., 65
Forest City Enterprises, Inc., 16; 52
(upd.)
Gecina SA, 42
General Growth Properties, Inc., 57
Griffin Land & Nurseries, Inc., 43
Grubb & Ellis Company, 21
The Haminerson Property Investment and
Development Corporation plc, IV
Hammerson plc, 40
Harbert Corporation, 14
Helmsley Enterprises, Inc., 39 (upd.)
Henderson Land Development Company
Ltd., 70
Home Properties of New York, Inc., 42
HomeVestors of America, Inc., 77
Hongkong Land Holdings Limited, IV;
47 (upd.)
Hyatt Corporation, 16 (upd.)
ILX Resorts Incorporated, 65
IRSA Inversiones y Representaciones S.A.,
63
J.F. Shea Co., Inc., 55
Jardine Cycle & Carriage Ltd., 73
JMB Realty Corporation, IV
Jones Lang LaSalle Incorporated, 49
JPI, 49
Kaufman and Broad Home Corporation,
8
Kennedy-Wilson, Inc., 60
Kerry Properties Limited, 22
Kimco Realty Corporation, 11
The Koll Company, 8
Land Securities PLC, IV; 49 (upd.)

Lefrak Organization Inc., 26
Lend Lease Corporation Limited, IV; 17
(upd.); 52 (upd.)
Liberty Property Trust, 57
Lincoln Property Company, 8; 54 (upd.)
The Loewen Group Inc., 40 (upd.)
The Macerich Company, 57
Mack-Cali Realty Corporation, 42
Manufactured Home Communities, Inc.,
22
Maui Land & Pineapple Company, Inc.,
29
Maxco Inc., 17
Meditrust, 11
Melvin Simon and Associates, Inc., 8
MEPC plc, IV
Meritage Corporation, 26
The Middleton Doll Company, 53
The Mills Corporation, 77
Mitsubishi Estate Company, Limited, IV;
61 (upd.)
Mitsui Real Estate Development Co.,
Ltd., IV
The Nature Conservancy, 28
New Plan Realty Trust, 11
New World Development Company Ltd.,
IV
Newhall Land and Farming Company, 14
Nexity S.A., 66
NRT Incorporated, 61
Olympia & York Developments Ltd., IV;
9 (upd.)
Park Corp., 22
Parque Arauco S.A., 72
Perini Corporation, 8
Pope Resources LP, 74
Post Properties, Inc., 26
ProLogis, 57
Public Storage, Inc., 52
Railtrack Group PLC, 50
RE/MAX International, Inc., 59
Reading International Inc., 70
Reckson Associates Realty Corp., 47
Regency Centers Corporation, 71
Rockefeller Group International Inc., 58
Rodamco N.V., 26
The Rouse Company, 15; 63 (upd.)
Shubert Organization Inc., 24
The Sierra Club, 28
Silverstein Properties, Inc., 47
Simco S.A., 37
SL Green Realty Corporation, 44
Slough Estates PLC, IV; 50 (upd.)
Sovran Self Storage, Inc., 66
Starrett Corporation, 21
The Staubach Company, 62
Storage USA, Inc., 21
Sumitomo Realty & Development Co.,
Ltd., IV
Sun Communities Inc., 46
Sunterra Corporation, 75
Tanger Factory Outlet Centers, Inc., 49
Tarragon Realty Investors, Inc., 45
Taubman Centers, Inc., 75
Taylor Woodrow plc, 38 (upd.)
Technical Olympic USA, Inc., 75
Tejon Ranch Company, 35
Tishman Speyer Properties, L.P., 47

Retail & Wholesale

Rubber & Tire

Telecommunications

Textiles & Apparel

Tobacco

Utilities

Waste Services

Geographic Index

Takeda Chemical Industries, Ltd., I; 46 (upd.)
TDK Corporation, II; 17 (upd.); 49 (upd.)
TEAC Corporation 78
Teijin Limited, V; 61 (upd.)
Terumo Corporation, 48
Tobu Railway Co Ltd, 6
Toho Co., Ltd., 28
Tohoku Electric Power Company, Inc., V
Tokai Bank, Limited, The, II; 15 (upd.)
Tokio Marine and Fire Insurance Co., Ltd., The, III
Tokyo Electric Power Company, The, 74 (upd.)
Tokyo Electric Power Company, Incorporated, The, V
Tokyo Gas Co., Ltd., V; 55 (upd.)
Tokyu Corporation, V; 47 (upd.)
Tokyu Department Store Co., Ltd., V; 32 (upd.)
Tokyu Land Corporation, IV
Tomen Corporation, IV; 24 (upd.)
Tomy Company Ltd., 65
TonenGeneral Sekiyu K.K., IV; 16 (upd.); 54 (upd.)
Toppan Printing Co., Ltd., IV; 58 (upd.)
Toray Industries, Inc., V; 51 (upd.)
Toshiba Corporation, I; 12 (upd.); 40 (upd.)
Tosoh Corporation, 70
TOTO LTD., III; 28 (upd.)
Toyo Sash Co., Ltd., III
Toyo Seikan Kaisha, Ltd., I
Toyoda Automatic Loom Works, Ltd., III
Toyota Motor Corporation, I; 11 (upd.); 38 (upd.)
Ube Industries, Ltd., III; 38 (upd.)
Unitika Ltd., V; 53 (upd.)
Uny Co., Ltd., V; 49 (upd.)
Victor Company of Japan, Limited, II; 26 (upd.)
Wacoal Corp., 25
Yamaha Corporation, III; 16 (upd.); 40 (upd.)
Yamaichi Securities Company, Limited, II
Yamato Transport Co. Ltd., V; 49 (upd.)
Yamazaki Baking Co., Ltd., 58
Yasuda Fire and Marine Insurance Company, Limited, The, III
Yasuda Mutual Life Insurance Company, The, III; 39 (upd.)
Yasuda Trust and Banking Company, Ltd., The, II; 17 (upd.)
Yokohama Rubber Co., Ltd., The, V; 19 (upd.)

Kuwait
Kuwait Airways Corporation, 68

Kuwait Petroleum Corporation, IV; 55 (upd.)

Latvia
A/S Air Baltic Corporation, 71

Libya
National Oil Corporation, IV; 66 (upd.)

Liechtenstein
Hilti AG, 53

Luxembourg
ARBED S.A., IV; 22 (upd.)
Cargolux Airlines International S.A., 49
Gemplus International S.A., 64
RTL Group SA, 44
Société Luxembourgeoise de Navigation Aérienne S.A., 64
Tenaris SA, 63

Malaysia
Berjaya Group Bhd., 67
Genting Bhd., 65
Malayan Banking Berhad, 72
Malaysian Airlines System Berhad, 6; 29 (upd.)
Perusahaan Otomobil Nasional Bhd., 62
Petroliam Nasional Bhd (Petronas), IV; 56 (upd.)
PPB Group Berhad, 57
Sime Darby Berhad, 14; 36 (upd.)
Telekom Malaysia Bhd, 76
Yeo Hiap Seng Malaysia Bhd., 75

Mauritius
Air Mauritius Ltd., 63

Mexico
Alfa, S.A. de C.V., 19
Altos Hornos de México, S.A. de C.V., 42
Apasco S.A. de C.V., 51
Bufete Industrial, S.A. de C.V., 34
Casa Cuervo, S.A. de C.V., 31
Celanese Mexicana, S.A. de C.V., 54
CEMEX S.A. de C.V., 20; 59 (upd.)
Cifra, S.A. de C.V., 12
Consorcio G Grupo Dina, S.A. de C.V., 36
Controladora Comercial Mexicana, S.A. de C.V., 36
Corporación Internacional de Aviación, S.A. de C.V. (Cintra), 20
Desc, S.A. de C.V., 23
Editorial Televisa, S.A. de C.V., 57
Empresas ICA Sociedad Controladora, S.A. de C.V., 41
Ford Motor Company, S.A. de C.V., 20
Gruma, S.A. de C.V., 31
Grupo Aeropuerto del Sureste, S.A. de C.V., 48
Grupo Carso, S.A. de C.V., 21
Grupo Casa Saba, S.A. de C.V., 39
Grupo Cydsa, S.A. de C.V., 39
Grupo Elektra, S.A. de C.V., 39
Grupo Financiero Banamex S.A., 54

Grupo Financiero Banorte, S.A. de C.V., 51
Grupo Financiero BBVA Bancomer S.A., 54
Grupo Financiero Serfin, S.A., 19
Grupo Gigante, S.A. de C.V., 34
Grupo Herdez, S.A. de C.V., 35
Grupo IMSA, S.A. de C.V., 44
Grupo Industrial Bimbo, 19
Grupo Industrial Durango, S.A. de C.V., 37
Grupo Industrial Saltillo, S.A. de C.V., 54
Grupo Mexico, S.A. de C.V., 40
Grupo Modelo, S.A. de C.V., 29
Grupo Posadas, S.A. de C.V., 57
Grupo Televisa, S.A., 18; 54 (upd.)
Grupo TMM, S.A. de C.V., 50
Grupo Transportación Ferroviaria Mexicana, S.A. de C.V., 47
Hylsamex, S.A. de C.V., 39
Industrias Bachoco, S.A. de C.V., 39
Industrias Penoles, S.A. de C.V., 22
Internacional de Ceramica, S.A. de C.V., 53
Kimberly-Clark de México, S.A. de C.V., 54
Organización Soriana, S.A. de C.V., 35
Petróleos Mexicanos, IV; 19 (upd.)
Pulsar Internacional S.A., 21
Real Turismo, S.A. de C.V., 50
Sanborn Hermanos, S.A., 20
Sears Roebuck de México, S.A. de C.V., 20
Telefonos de Mexico S.A. de C.V., 14; 63 (upd.)
Tubos de Acero de Mexico, S.A. (TAMSA), 41
TV Azteca, S.A. de C.V., 39
Valores Industriales S.A., 19
Vitro Corporativo S.A. de C.V., 34
Wal-Mart de Mexico, S.A. de C.V., 35 (upd.)

Nepal
Royal Nepal Airline Corporation, 41

Netherlands
ABN AMRO Holding, N.V., 50
AEGON N.V., III; 50 (upd.)
Akzo Nobel N.V., 13; 41 (upd.)
Algemene Bank Nederland N.V., II
Amsterdam-Rotterdam Bank N.V., II
Arcadis NV, 26
ASML Holding N.V., 50
Baan Company, 25
Bols Distilleries NV, 74
Buhrmann NV, 41
Campina Group, The 78
CNH Global N.V., 38 (upd.)
CSM N.V., 65
Deli Universal NV, 66
DSM N.V., I; 56 (upd.)
Elsevier N.V., IV
Endemol Entertainment Holding NV, 46
Equant N.V., 52
European Aeronautic Defence and Space Company EADS N.V., 52 (upd.)

DATE DUE

GAYLORD			PRINTED IN U.S.A.